Newsmakers®

ISSN 0899-0417

Newsmakers®

The People Behind Today's Headlines

Laura Avery

Project Editor

2011
Cumulation

Includes Indexes from
1985 through 2011

GALE
CENGAGE Learning™

Detroit • New York • San Francisco • New Haven, Conn • Waterville, Maine • London

Newsmakers 2011, Cumulation

Project Editor: Laura Avery

Editorial Support Services: Emmanuel T. Barrido

Rights Acquisition and Management: Leitha Etheridge-Sims

Imaging: John Watkins

Composition and Electronic Capture: Amy Darga

Manufacturing: Cynde Lentz

For product information and technology assistance, contact us at **Gale Customer Support, 1-800-877-4253.**
For permission to use material from this text or product, submit all requests online at **www.cengage.com/permissions.**
Further permissions questions can be emailed to
permissionrequest@cengage.com

Gale
27500 Drake Rd.
Farmington Hills, MI 48331-3535

ISBN-13: 978-1-4144-4168-9
ISBN-10: 1-4144-4168-1

ISSN 0899-0417

This title is also available as an e-book.
ISBN-13: 978-1-4144-5336-1
ISBN-10: 1-4144-5336-1
Contact your Gale, Cengage Learning sales representative for ordering information.

Printed in the United States of America
1 2 3 4 5 6 7 15 14 13 12 11

Contents

Obituaries

Introduction

Newsmakers provides informative profiles of the world's most interesting people in a crisp, concise, contemporary format. Make *Newsmakers* the first place you look for biographical information on the people making today's headlines.

Important Features

- **Attractive, modern page design** pleases the eye while making it easy to locate the information you need.

- **Coverage of all the newsmakers** you want to know about: people in business, education, technology, law, politics, religion, entertainment, labor, sports, medicine, and other fields.

- **Clearly labeled data sections** allow quick access to vital personal statistics, career information, major awards, and mailing addresses.

- **Informative sidelights essays** include the kind of in-depth analysis you're looking for.

- **Sources for additional information** provide lists of books, magazines, newspapers, and internet sites where you can find out even more about *Newsmakers* listees.

- **Enlightening photographs** are specially selected to further enhance your knowledge of the subject.

- **Separate obituaries section** provides you with concise profiles of recently deceased newsmakers.

- **Publication schedule and price** fit your budget. *Newsmakers* is published in three paperback issues per year, each containing approximately 50 entries, and a hardcover cumulation, containing approximately 200 entries (those from the preceding three paperback issues plus an additional 50 entries), *all at a price you can afford!*

- And much, much more!

Indexes Provide Easy Access

Familiar and indispensable: The *Newsmakers* indexes! You can easily locate entries in a variety of ways through our four versatile, comprehensive indexes. The Nationality, Occupation, and Subject Indexes list names from the current year's *Newsmakers* issues. These are cumulated in the annual hardbound volume to include all names from the entire *Contemporary Newsmakers* and *Newsmakers* series. The Newsmakers Index is cumulated in all issues as well as the hardbound annuals to provide concise coverage of the entire series.

- **Nationality Index**—Names of newsmakers are arranged alphabetically under their respective nationalities.

- **Occupation Index**—Names are listed alphabetically under broad occupational categories.

- **Subject Index**—Includes key subjects, topical issues, company names, products, organizations, etc., that are discussed in *Newsmakers*. Under each subject heading are listed names of newsmakers associated with that topic. So the unique Subject Index provides access to the information in *Newsmakers* even when readers are unable to connect a name with a particular topic. This index also invites browsing, allowing *Newsmakers* users to discover topics they may wish to explore further.

- **Cumulative Newsmakers Index**—Listee names, along with birth and death dates, when available, are arranged alphabetically followed by the year and issue number in which their entries appear.

Available in Electronic Formats

Licensing. *Newsmakers* is available for licensing. The complete database is provided in a fielded format and is deliverable on such media as disk or CD-ROM. For more information, contact Gale's Business Development Group at 1-800-877-4253, or visit our website at http://www.gale.cengage.com/bizdev.

Online. *Newsmakers* is available online as part of the Gale Biographies (GALBIO) database accessible through LexisNexis, P.O. Box 933, Dayton, OH 45401-0933; phone: (937) 865-6800, toll-free: 800-227-4908.

Suggestions Are Appreciated

The editors welcome your comments and suggestions. In fact, many popular *Newsmakers* features were implemented as a result of readers' suggestions. We will continue to shape the series to best meet the needs of the greatest number of users. Send comments or suggestions to:

The Editor
Newsmakers
Gale
27500 Drake Rd.
Farmington Hills, MI 48331-3535

Or, call toll-free at 1-800-877-4253

AC/DC

Rock group

Group formed in 1973 in Sydney, Australia; members include Malcolm Young (born January 6, 1953, in Glasgow, Scotland), guitar; Angus Young (born March 31, 1955, in Glasgow, Scotland), guitar; Bon Scott (born Ronald Belford Scott, July 9, 1946, in Kirriemuir, Scotland; died of alcohol poisoning, February 19, 1980, in London, England), vocals; Brian Johnson (born October 5, 1947, in Newcastle-upon-Tyne, England), vocals; Dave Evans (born July 20, 1953, in Wales), vocals; Phil Rudd (born May 19, 1954, in Melbourne, Australia), drums; Mark Evans (born March 2, 1956, in Melbourne, Australia), bass; Cliff Williams (born December 14, 1949, in Romford, England), bass; Simon Wright (born June 19, 1963, in Alden, England), drums; Chris Slade (born Christopher Rees, October 30, 1946, in Pontypridd, Wales), drums.

Addresses: *Record company*—Columbia Records, 550 Madison Ave., New York, NY 10022. *Web site*—http://www.acdc.com, http://www.acdcrocks.com.

Career

Founded in Sydney, Australia, 1973; original singer Dave Evans replaced by Bon Scott, 1974; released debut album *High Voltage* in Australia, 1975; released *T.N.T.*, 1975; released international version of *High Voltage*, 1976; released *Dirty Deeds Done Dirt Cheap*, 1976; released *Let There Be Rock*, 1977; Cliff Williams replaced Mark Evans on bass, 1977; released *Powerage*, 1978; released live album *If You Want Blood (You've Got It)*, 1978; released *Highway To Hell*, 1979; Brian Johnson replaced Scott as lead vocalist after Scott's death, 1980; released *Back In Black*, 1980; released *For Those About to Rock (We Salute You)*, 1981; released *Flick of the Switch*, 1983; Phil Rudd replaced on drums by Simon Wright, 1983; released compilation album *'74 Jailbreak*, 1984; released *Fly on the Wall*, 1985; released *Who Made Who* soundtrack, 1986; released *Blow Up Your Video*, 1988; released *The Razor's Edge*, 1990; Chris Slade replaced Wright on drums, 1990; released *AC/DC Live*, 1992; Rudd rejoined band, replacing Slade on drums, 1994; released *Ballbreaker*, 1995; released box set *Bonfire*, 1997; released *Stiff Upper Lip*, 2001; released *Black Ice*, 2008; released soundtrack for *Iron Man 2*, 2010.

Awards: Inducted into Australian Recording Industry Association Hall of Fame, 1988; inducted into Rock and Roll Hall of Fame, 2003; ARIA Music Awards for best rock album and highest-selling album, Australian Recording Industry Association, 2009; Grammy Award for best hard rock performance, Recording Academy, for "War Machine," 2010.

Sidelights

AC/DC's wild, deafening hard rock music, built on simple guitar chords and sly, raunchy lyrics, has made them the second-best-selling recording act in history, behind the Beatles. The Australian rockers have sold 200 million records worldwide, including 71 million in the United States. Their most popular album, *Back In Black,* has sold 45 million copies. The band's best-known anthems, including "Highway to Hell" and "You Shook Me All Night Long," set the standard for every hard rock band that came after them, with their playful rudeness and menace, blatant sexuality, and carefree party spirit.

Yet the simple power of AC/DC's music kept critics from respecting them until 30 years after their founding. The band won its first Grammy in 2010, more than three decades after releasing its biggest hits. An AC/DC song from the 2000s sounds a lot like the AC/DC of the 1970s; the band figured out what they were good at early on and stuck to it. "Though AC/DC's songs tend to rely on five or six guitar chords at most, those chords are the very pillars of rock and roll: E, A, D, G, C, and B," explained Anthony Bozza in his book *Why AC/DC Matters.*

Guitarist Malcolm Young founded AC/DC in Sydney, Australia in 1973 with his younger brother, Angus. Ever since, their guitar riffs have formed the band's unshakable core. They took the band's name from two common types of electricity, alternating current and direct current. Depending on which story you believe, the name came from either a vacuum cleaner in their sister Margaret's bedroom or her sewing machine. It proved appropriate, since the Young brothers have taken the power and sheer volume of the electric guitar about as far as it can go. "Their innate electricity is the alternating and direct current of the band," Bozza wrote of the Young brothers in *Why AC/DC Matters*: "Malcolm drives ahead consistently, while his brother alternates wildly."

Margaret Young also helped her brothers create another part of AC/DC's identity. Angus was only 18 when the band formed, and she suggested he wear his school uniform at gigs around Sydney. The contrast between the uniform's disciplined, conformist image and the band's celebration of raunchy misbehavior proved irresistible. Angus' uniform has remained a signature element of the band's stage presence.

Bon Scott, who became AC/DC's lead singer in 1974, spent some of his teenage years in reform school for stealing a car and driving it off a bridge. The Australian Army rejected him as socially maladjusted. The bourbon-guzzling Scott was 28 and a veteran of several rock bands when a mutual friend convinced him to accompany AC/DC on tour as their driver. Though Scott was seven years older than Malcolm and nine years older than Angus, they quickly bonded. Scott's crude sense of humor, his willingness to supply the Youngs with alcohol and marijuana, and his intense performances as a guest vocalist soon convinced the brothers to fire their original lead singer, Dave Evans, and hire him. Performing with younger guys inspired Scott to write the first of the funny, crude lyrics that became a band trademark. "He was the outlaw rock-and-roll front man—and leader—that they desperately needed," Bozza wrote in *Why AC/DC Matters.* "He was something between an older brother and an elder statesman for the Youngs and he took to it with gusto."

Like the Youngs, Scott was born in Scotland and moved to Australia with his family as a boy. But AC/DC's music is full of Australian spirit, Bozza argued in *Why AC/DC Matters.* "Like the pioneers who transformed Australia from a prison colony to a nation, all but one of the essential members of AC/DC were born elsewhere," Bozza wrote. "They were, however, raised there and imbued with the idiosyncratic cultural confluence that makes the island unusual." Australians often absorb both British and American culture and mix those influences with their own nation's rowdy rebellion. "Theirs is a wild-eyed cry of unruly youths from a country founded by convicts," Bozza wrote.

The band released its Australian debut, *High Voltage,* in 1975, followed by *T.N.T.,* also in 1975. In 1976, to introduce AC/DC to the United States and United Kingdom, the band's record company released their international debut, also titled *High Voltage* (confusingly, since it included more songs from *T.N.T.* than from the first album). With its cover art featuring Angus Young sticking his tongue out as he is hit by lightning, *High Voltage* did not impress the critical gatekeepers of the American rock scene. *Rolling Stone* critic Billy Altman dismissed the band as "Australian gross-out champions" (as quoted by Bozza in *Why AC/DC Matters*) and declared that *High Voltage* marked an "all-time low" for hard rock. "AC/DC has nothing to say musically," Altman sneered.

Meanwhile, back home, AC/DC released *Dirty Deeds Done Dirt Cheap* in late 1976. With songs such as "Love At First Feel" and "Problem Child" (an autobiography of sorts for Scott) as well as a title track about hired assassins, the album "served as a call to arms from a group that wanted nothing more than to celebrate the dirtiest, nastiest instincts humans could have," wrote Stephen Thomas Erlewine on the Web site AllMusic. AC/DC began to catch on in the United States in late 1977, when they were chosen to tour with the Canadian rock band Rush and American glam-rockers KISS. The band's albums *Let There Be Rock,* released in the fall of 1977, and *Powerage,* from the spring of 1978, began to sell in the States. Their dramatic, bombastic live shows drew excited audiences. The title of their 1978 live album, *If You Want Blood (You've Got It),* captures the intense spirit of the performances and the relationship between band and audience.

"There are two types of shows," Angus Young told the magazine *Sounds* (as quoted in the book *AC/DC: The Definitive History*). "You can either be like performing seals and just have people sitting there gawking at you. Or you can have an all-in-together thing with the kids and us all having a good time."

AC/DC's next album, *Highway to Hell,* became a worldwide commercial triumph. New producer Robert John "Mutt" Lange helped give the album a more precise and enormous sound than their previous recordings, with Scott's vocals more prominent. Otherwise, AC/DC did not change much, delivering songs packed with more trusty power chords and catchy choruses. "This is the AC/DC you already know and love/hate," declared Dave Lewis in *Sounds* (as quoted in *AC/DC: The Definitive History*), "all thrud-crunch-kerraang-and-whaarrrgh. Music to knock down walls by."

Scott's lyrics showed off his full range of perversities. "This is a veritable rogue's gallery of deviance, from cheerfully clumsy sex talk and drinking anthems to general outlandish behavior," wrote Erlewine on AllMusic. Released in 1979, the album reached the top 20 in the United States and the top ten in Great Britain. It became their first record to sell one million copies.

Highway to Hell was Scott's last album. Years of hard living and extreme partying caught up with him. On February 19, 1980, Scott was found dead in London. He was 33. The coroner listed the official causes of death as "acute alcohol poisoning" and "death by misadventure," according to *AC/DC: The Encyclopaedia.*

It looked like the end for AC/DC. Surely no other singer could match Scott's hair-raising screams or debauched excess. Yet in one of the most astonishing turnarounds in rock history, AC/DC promptly found a replacement singer, Brian Johnson, and recorded a new album, *Back In Black,* that paid tribute to Scott's raucous spirit and proved the equal of any of their previous work.

The band's key members all knew Johnson, lead singer of the British rock band Geordie. Scott himself had shared a concert bill with him in Australia and raved about his talent. Johnson won over the more skeptical Malcolm Young at a London audition with impassioned performances of songs by Ike and Tina Turner and Chuck Berry. Whisked off to the Bahamas to record the new album in April of 1980, Johnson quickly and frantically wrote lyrics to music the Youngs had already created. *Back In Black,* released at the end of July of 1980, made AC/DC into superstars. It immediately topped the British charts and went to number four in the United States. Its longevity is even more impressive: in three decades, it has sold 45 million copies worldwide, 22 million in the United States alone. A single from the album, "You Shook Me All Night Long," became their most popular song, a staple of rock radio for decades following its release.

Their next album's title track, *For Those About To Rock (We Salute You),* reflected all the band's glory and bombast. Again produced by "Mutt" Lange, the album was their first to reach number one in the United States. Rather than trying to mimic their previous album, the band stepped away from its dark intensity, choosing a somewhat lighter feel instead. Some critics consider it a continuation of the band's winning streak, an equal to *Back In Black* and *Highway to Hell,* while others feel it lacks consistency.

After peaking in the early 1980s, AC/DC's commercial and creative success began to decline. Phil Rudd, the drummer, left the band in 1982 and was replaced by Simon Wright. Albums such as 1983's *Flick of the Switch* did not reach the heights of earlier work. The band went without a major hit until "Thunderstruck," released in 1990 from the album *The Razor's Edge.* Yet countless 1980s hard rock acts considered AC/DC a major influence. While many other classic-rock bands, such as the Rolling Stones, experimented with new sounds in the 1980s, trying to stay fresh or relevant, AC/DC made a momentous decision. They would not change.

"People have said we've hung around long enough!" Angus Young told Paul Elliott, a writer for *Kerrang!* (as quoted in *AC/DC: The Definitive History*). "Some bands fade when they try to adapt to what's current. We play rock music. It's a little too late for us to do a ballad. Rock is what we do best. Sometimes I'm asked if I want to play music other than AC/DC. Sure, at home I play a little blues—but after five minutes I'm like, 'Sod this!' and I'm playing hard rock again."

Fans rewarded the band's reliability. In the 1990s, AC/DC attracted large live audiences to their frequent tours. Their 1995 album *Ballbreaker* sold a million copies within six months. The 2001 release *Stiff Upper Lip* also sold well.

In the 2000s, AC/DC at last began to receive critical honors. The generation of music writers who considered the band's work simplistic and repetitive gave way to critics who respected their consistency, longevity, and influence. AC/DC was inducted into the Rock and Roll Hall of Fame in 2003. Their 2008 album *Black Ice* attracted favorable reviews. In 2010, they received their first Grammy award, when their song "War Machine" was named best hard rock performance. That same year, several of their songs appeared in the action film *Iron Man 2*. The band released a best-of compilation named after the movie, again proving their resilience and spreading their overpowering music to even more fans.

Selected discography

High Voltage (Australian version), Albert Productions, 1975.
T.N.T., Albert Productions, 1975.
High Voltage (international version), Epic, 1976.
Dirty Deeds Done Dirt Cheap, Epic, 1976.
Let There Be Rock, Epic, 1977.
Powerage, Epic, 1978.
If You Want Blood (You've Got It) (live), Epic, 1978.
Highway To Hell, Epic, 1979.
Back In Black, Epic, 1980.
For Those About to Rock (We Salute You), Epic, 1981.
Flick of the Switch, Epic, 1983.
'74 Jailbreak (compilation), Epic, 1984.
Fly on the Wall, Epic, 1985.
Who Made Who, Epic, 1986.

Blow Up Your Video, Epic, 1988.
The Razor's Edge, Epic, 1990.
AC/DC Live, Epic, 1992.
Ballbreaker, EastWest, 1995.
Bonfire (box set), EastWest, 1997.
Stiff Upper Lip, EastWest, 2001.
Black Ice, Columbia, 2008.
Iron Man 2 (soundtrack), Columbia, 2010.

Sources

Books

Bozza, Anthony, *Why AC/DC Matters*, William Morrow, 2009.
Dome, Malcolm, and Jerry Ewing, *AC/DC: The Encyclopaedia*, Chrome Dreams, 2008.
Dome, Malcolm, ed., *AC/DC: The Definitive History*, Virgin Books, 2001.

Online

"AC/DC: Biography" AllMusic, http://www.allmusic.com/cg/amg.dll?p=amg&sql=11:kifoxqw5ld0e~T1 (May 24, 2010).
"Angus Young: Biography" AllMusic, http://www.allmusic.com/cg/amg.dll?p=amg&sql=11:kxftxq9gld0e~T1 (May 31, 2010).
"Dirty Deeds Done Dirt Cheap: Overview" AllMusic, http://www.allmusic.com/cg/amg.dll?p=amg&sql=10:hifixq95ld6e (May 24, 2010).
"Highway to Hell" AllMusic, http://www.allmusic.com/cg/amg.dll?p=amg&sql=10:fifixq95ld6e (May 24, 2010).

—Erick Trickey

Jay Adelson

Chief Executive Officer of Digg.com

Born Jay Steven Adelson, September 7, 1970; married; children: three. *Education:* Boston University, B.S., c. 1992.

Addresses: *Home*—Dutchess County, NY. *Office*—Digg, Inc., 135 Mississippi St., 3rd Fl., San Francisco, CA 94107.

Career

Head of network operations, NETCOM On-line Communication Services, 1993-96; co-founder, Digital Equipment Corp., Palo Alto Internet Exchange, 1996, and operations manager, 1996-2003; founder, Equinix, Inc., 1998, and chief technology officer, 1998-2005; chief executive officer, Digg, Inc., 2005—; co-founder, Revision3 Corp., 2005, and board chair, 2005—.

Sidelights

Jay Adelson is the chief executive officer of Digg.com, a content-sharing Web site where users post news items which other users then rank. A high rating can bump a story to the top of Digg's home page in a matter of hours and result in millions of fresh hits to the original source. Digg has been described as the new frontier in media, but it still retains some of the bickering and problems of other online communities. "We allow anyone to submit on a level playing field," Adelson told Noam Cohen in a *New York Times* interview. "We allow the digital democracy to be the fact checkers. There is definitely some risk to that."

PNP/WENN/Newscom

Adelson was born in 1970 and spent his high school years at the private Cranbrook-Kingswood School in Bloomfield Hills, Michigan. At Boston University, he earned degrees in computer science and film and broadcasting, and by 1993 was working as head of network operations at Netcom, an Internet service provider in the San Francisco Bay area. Adelson also founded the Palo Alto Internet Exchange on behalf of the Digital Equipment Corporation, and served as its operations manager from 1996 to 2003.

Adelson made a small fortune in 2000 when a company he co-founded called Equinix became a publicly traded company. He had started it with Al Avery and served as the chief technology officer. Years later, he explained its genesis to *Computerworld* writer Heather Havenstein. "When the Internet became a commercial medium in 1994, all of the Internet had been funded and operated by the government and universities. When it switched over to one operated by telecommunication companies, a very strong hierarchy developed. Tier 1 ISPs, the top five players in the world, would collect a dime on every packet that flowed throughout the Internet." Those carriers, he noted, ran the network access points where data packets were transferred. "Equinix replaced these single, network-owned facilities with Internet business exchanges where anyone could exchange packets with anyone in a neutral playing field," he told Havenstein. "This allowed the dot-coms like Yahoo and Google and others to really exert their might."

Equinix was acquired by a larger company in 2003; Adelson remained with the company through the transition, leaving for another venture in 2005. In 2004, he consulted with Kevin Rose, a tech-savvy Internet-television host, and a few others to launch Digg, Inc. Digg was conceived by Rose as a Web site where users could promote news stories or other Internet pages they liked, and it caught on quickly with the information-technology (IT) crowd when it was launched in late 2004. Adelson has served as Digg's chief executive officer since 2005, and runs the business end while Rose serves as the public face of the company.

Digg was quickly hailed as a fresh new entrant in the so-called "Web 2.0" frontier, referring to the second wave of Internet successes that quickly drew millions of users by providing a platform for users to create and share content on their own; YouTube and Wikipedia are two of the more remarkable digital addresses of the Web 2.0 world. Digg permitted registered users to post a news story they liked; other users then rated it. Hitting the "refresh" button a minute later brought a new ranking of the top stories. The higher a story placed on the home page, the more click-through visits it earned. In some cases, other media sources' Internet servers crashed when one of its stories began receiving hundreds of votes of approval by Digg users. "We filled a void," Adelson theorized about how quickly the site caught on with Web users in an interview with Jefferson Graham for *USA Today*. "In the Digg world, the feedback is instantaneous. There's a euphoria of clicking a button and seeing results in real time."

Digg gained its first rush of free publicity when users promoted a story about technology hackers who gained access to Paris Hilton's phone in February of 2005. A little over two years later, Digg became embroiled in an online battle that crashed its servers temporarily not long after it reached its one-millionth user mark. In May of 2007, Digg users began "digging," or voting approval for a link that contained information about breaking the encryption coding that entertainment industry giants insert into legitimate DVD releases to prevent copies being made. Adelson and Rose, served notice that the information was putting them in danger of violating intellectual property laws, decided to halt the popular story, and users rebelled by reposting and ranking it to the point where all the top-ranked stories at Digg.com's home page were about the encryption key. Adelson and Rose relented, promising users they would no long attempt to censor a story.

Not surprisingly, Digg spawned scores of copycat sites, including Reddit, which was bought by publishing giant Condé Nast in the fall of 2006. Rumors of a Digg sale to another media giant arose periodically, but at the close of 2008 Adelson made a formal announcement that the company was not for sale, and would focus on making acquisitions and generating revenue. There were still rumors that the company would "go public," or making an initial public offering (IPO) of stock. In late 2009 Adelson assured devoted Digg users and media-business analysts that it would not be in the company's near future. "For me to go public, there's probably one absolute necessity, which is I need that capital. I need hundreds of millions of dollars for something" to make an IPO happen, he was quoted as saying by Scott Austin for the *Wall Street Journal* blog Venture Capital Dispatch. "And to be honest, I don't need that capital right now. We've raised enough, we'll be profitable, it's not a problem. I have to go public at some point because I have to give my investors a return, and I want to give my employees something."

Adelson and Rose also founded an Internet protocol television start-up, Revision3, which features video podcasts like Diggnation, a weekly series in which Rose and a co-host discuss the top Digg stories of the week, often from Rose's San Francisco apartment. Adelson divides his time between Digg headquarters in that city and a home in New York's scenic Hudson River Valley area, where his wife and three children also live.

Sources

Books

Marquis Who's Who, Marquis Who's Who, 2009.

Periodicals

Advertising Age, January 8, 2007, p. 26.
Computerworld, May 28, 2007, p. 16.
New York Times, October 13, 2008.
San Francisco Chronicle, September 20, 2009, p. D2.
USA Today, October 24, 2007, p. 3B.

Online

"Digg CEO: Profitability Is Not A Problem Anymore," Venture Capital Dispatch, http://blogs. wsj.com/venturecapital/2009/11/17/digg-ceo-profitability-is-not-a-problem-anymore/ (March 2, 2010).

"Digg: Not for Sale," *BusinessWeek Online,* http://www.businessweek.com/technology/content/dec2008/tc2008121_004686.htm (March 2, 2010).

"Digg This: Deal or No Deal?," *BusinessWeek Online,* http://www.businessweek.com/technology/content/dec2007/tc20071226.tif_842566.htm (March 2, 2010).

—Carol Brennan

Justin Allgaier

Sam Greenwood/Getty Images for NASCAR/Getty Images

Race car driver

Born June 6, 1986, in Riverton, IL; son of Mike (a race car driver and tire distributor) and Dorothy (a tire distributor) Allgaier; married Ashley Hanson, March 4, 2006.

Addresses: *Office*—Penske Racing South, Attn: Justin Allgaier, 200 Penske Way, Mooresville, NC 28115. *Web site*—http://www.justinallgaier.com/.

Career

Began racing quarter-midget cars, 1991; began stock-car racing, 1999; made NASCAR debut, 2005; signed with Roger Penske's Nationwide team, 2008; won his first Nationwide Series race at Bristol Motor Speedway, 2010.

Awards: American Spirit Award, U.S. Air Force, 2005; ARCA Re/Max Series Champion, 2008; Rookie of the Year, Nationwide, 2009; Rookie of the Year, Raybestos, 2009.

Sidelights

Justin Allgaier is a young, up-and-coming race car driver. He made his National Association for Stock Car Auto Racing (NASCAR) debut in 2005 and in 2009 was named the Nationwide Rookie of the Year and the Raybestos Rookie of the Year.

Allgaier, the son of a former race car driver and tire distributors Mike and Dorothy Allgaier, began driving at the age of five in a quarter-midget roadster.

He had seen a quarter-midget car at a friend's house and he begged his dad for one. At first his father refused, but his mother insisted otherwise. Dorothy told Marcia Martinez in the Freeport, Illinois *Journal-Standard,* "I really wanted him and his dad to have a good relationship and I thought if I don't get him into something we were accustomed to, he will never have the relationship with his dad that he needed."

With that, Allgaier began his driving career. Although he was involved in swimming, Boy Scouts, baseball, and basketball, driving was what really grabbed his attention. His father told Martinez, "He started off just mediocre, really. About the third race, it was like the light came on. When he got it figured out, he was competitive about wherever he went." By the time he was 12, Allgaier, nicknamed "Little Gator," was a five-time quarter-midget champion. At 13 he started racing full-bodied stock cars and, by the time he was 14, he became the youngest driver ever to drive in the A Main race of the Chili Bowl.

Allgaier met his future wife, Ashley Hanson, in 2002 at a local school hockey game when they were 15. Hanson had spent a lot of time at the race track watching Allgaier, and had always told her parents that, when she grew up, she would marry him. After meeting at the hockey game the two decided to date, but there was one snag: although he had been driving on the track for years, Allgaier did not yet have a license to drive on the road. The first thing he did when he got his license was to drive to her house, pick her up, and take her to a local race.

Allgaier and Hanson married in 2009 when both were 19. Many of their friends were opposed to the marriage, thinking they were too young. Allgaier told Lee Montgomery in *Scenedaily*, "It's tough being married at a young age, especially in today's society with all the stuff you have going [on] around you. But for me and even her, we went through a lot of stuff that you shouldn't go through at 14, 15, 16 years old and aged very quickly for who we were. Getting married was the next step."

He made his NASCAR debut in 2005 in the Camping World Truck Series, but the following year, he raced ARCA (Automobile Racing Club of America) full-time, appearing in 21 of the 23 events in the series and winning 10th place in the championship.

In 2008, he drove for Allgaier Motorsports, winning six wins in 21 races in the ARCA series and winning the championship. In that same year, he made his debut with Penske Racing in the Nationwide series, driving in four races.

In 2009, Allgaier was named the Nationwide Rookie of the Year and the Raybestos Rookie of the Year. He also won the Re/Max Series Championship in 2009. Allgaier explained to a reporter from *Racer* magazine that transitioning from an ARCA car to a Nationwide vehicle was challenging: "In an ARCA car you have an open motor, so you've got 800-850hp and in a Nationwide car you've got 600-650hp. So it's a lot harder to drive because you have to keep more momentum going in the corners. But these cars also have a shorter wheelbase so they're very twitchy and uneasy. Compared to last year, I'm trying to carry more speed but in a car that's on a razor's edge."

Allgaier won his first NASCAR race, the Scotts Turf Builder 300, at Bristol Motor Speedway in Tennessee, on March 20, 2010. For the rest of the summer he went through 19 races without a win. He returned to Bristol in late August, hoping to win. He told the Sporting News Wire Service, "March to today has felt like five years of not getting into Victory Lane." He modestly added that the win in March may have been a temporary fluke: "We just hit so right that day that it probably elevated us a

little bit more than what we were." In the August race, Allgaier was disappointed when his ride ended in a multiple-car accident; no one was hurt, but he ended the race in 33rd place.

If Allgaier ever were unable to drive, he has two career backup plans. One is that he could work for his father at the family's tire store. Another is graphic design. He started a company called Gator Graffix when he was 12, and designed and printed decals for cars and drivers. He enjoyed creating his own logos, including designing his own helmet.

"I've been extremely blessed," Allgaier told Martinez about his racing career. "Hopefully, all of this is God's plan and this is what he wants me to do. I feel like the way things have happened, there has to be intervention for things to happen the way that they did." In return for what he sees as his blessed life, he is helping others by raising money for an orphanage in Mexico. He told Jeff Gluck on the Web site *SB Nation* that he would rather be known as a great person than a great driver: "You can accomplish every goal in life that you've ever set out for yourself, but if you're not a good person and you don't lead by example, you have nothing."

Sources

Periodicals

Belleville News-Democrat (Belleville, IL), July 31, 2009.
Journal-Standard (Freeport, IL), July 17, 2009.
Racer, December 2009, p. 39.
Sporting News Wire Service, August 20, 2010.
St. Louis Post-Dispatch, July 16, 2010.
Telegraph (Alton, IL), July 15, 2010.

Online

"Interview: Justin Allgaier," *SB Nation,* http://www.sbnation.com/2010/6/30/1544964/justin-allgaier-nascar-racing-2010-penske-verizon-nationwide (August 20, 2010).
Justin Allgaier's Official Web Site, http://www.justinallgaier.com/ (August 28, 2010).
"Kasey Kahne OK after Wild Wreck in Nationwide Race at Bristol," Scene Daily, http://www.scenedaily.com/news/articles/nationwideseries/Kasey_Kahne_OK_after_wild_wreck_in_Nationwide_race_at_Bristol.html (August 28, 2010).
"Penske Racing's Justin Allgaier Focused on Slowing Down in Order to Gain Speed," Scene Daily, http://www.scenedaily.com/news/articles/

nationwideseries/Penske_Racings_Justin_
Allgaier_focused_on_slowing_down_in_order_
to_gain_speed.html (August 20, 2010).

—*Kelly Winters*

Benigno Aquino

AP Images/Craig Ruttle

President of the Philippines

Born Benigno Simeon Cojuangco Aquino III, February 8, 1960, in Manila, Philippines; son of Benigno S. Jr. (a senator and political activist) and Corazon (maiden name, Cojuangco; former President of the Philippines) Aquino. *Education:* Ateneo de Manila University, A.B, 1981.

Addresses: *Home*—Bahay Pangarap, Malacañang Park, Manila, 1000, Philippines. *Office*—Malacañang Palace, Jose P. Laurel St., Manila, 1000, Philippines. *Web site*—http://www.president.gov.ph.

Career

Assistant to the executive director, Philippine Business for Social Progress, 1983-85; assistant retail sales supervisor and assistant promotions manager for Nike, Mondragon Industries Philippines Inc., 1985-86; vice-president, Intra-Strata Assurance Corporation, 1986-92; executive assistant for administration, Central Azucarera de Tarlac, 1993-96, manager for field services, 1996-98; member, House of Representatives of the Philippines, 1998-2007, deputy speaker, 2004-06; secretary general, Liberal Party of the Philippines, 1999-2002 and 2004-06; vice-president, Luzon, 2002-04, vice chairman, 2006—; senator, Senate of the Philippines, 2007-10; president of the Republic of the Philippines, 2010—.

Sidelights

Despite his family background—the only son of martyred political activist Benigno "Ninoy" Aquino Jr. and former President of the Philippines

Corazon Aquino—Benigno S. Aquino III (pronounced "beh-NEEG-no ah-KEE-no") admitted to having little political aspirations beyond serving as a legislator in his home country, the Philippines. After his mother's death in 2009, however, the public called on the senator with a modest legislative record to run for president. Promising to reform corruption in the government and promote economic development, Aquino was elected by a decisive margin and took office in June of 2010. As president, he hoped to root out corruption, revitalize the economy, and maximize opportunities for his countrymen. "We shall defeat the enemy by wielding the tools of justice, social reform, and equitable governance leading to a better life," he claimed in his inaugural address. "With proper governance life will improve for all."

Benigno Simeon Aquino III, better known as "Noynoy" to distinguish him from his father, was born in Manila in 1960. At the time, his father was already politically active as a member of the Liberal Party; in 1967 Ninoy became the youngest person ever elected to the Philippine Senate. He was one of the most vocal opponents of President Ferdinand Marcos, often criticizing his regime for graft and corruption. When the term-limited Marcos declared martial law in 1972 rather than turn over power in the next presidential election, he had the elder

Aquino imprisoned on trumped-up charges. In 1980 Ninoy Aquino suffered a heart attack in prison, and the Marcus government allowed him to seek treatment in the United States. The following year, Noynoy Aquino finished his degree in economics at Ateneo de Manila University then joined his family in exile in Boston. There he aided his parents as a "jack of all trades," as he described it to GMA News. tv: "I was the assistant driver, handyman, gardener, electrician, plumber, [and] dog handler." His father remained an outspoken critic of the Marcos government and was determined to bring democracy back to his country. Hoping to speak to the ailing Marcos about restoring elections, Ninoy Aquino returned to Manila on August 21, 1983, and was immediately shot to death as he exited his plane.

After his father's assassination, Noynoy Aquino returned with his family to the Philippines, where he worked as an executive assistant to the head of a corporate-sponsored nonprofit agency and then as a promotions manager for Nike. In the meantime, public outrage over his father's assassination, coupled with economic troubles and international pressure, led Marcos to finally set the date for new elections. His opposition chose Ninoy's widow, Corazon, as their candidate, and despite her lack of political experience she proved an inspiring speaker. Both sides claimed victory after the 1986 election, but evidence of widespread voter fraud led the military to withdraw their support of Marcos. Corazon Aquino was inaugurated President on February 25, 1986, with Marcos and his wife accepting exile in the United States later that day.

Soon after, Noynoy Aquino settled in as a vice-president in his uncle's insurance company. Politics in the Philippines were less settled; although his mother had been elected by a historic margin, there were still rebels opposed to her presidency. In late August 1987, Aquino heard of a rebel attack and returned home, only to be shot himself. The attack killed three bodyguards and left Aquino with five bullet wounds, but he survived with only minor injuries. After his mother left office in 1992, he took an executive position with another family company, this time a sugar refinery. He left the business to run for the same congressional seat his grandfather, Benigno Q. Aquino, once held. He was elected as congressman from the second district of Tarlac, an agricultural province in the center of Luzon Island, in 1998.

Aquino joined the Liberal Party of his father, making him part of the minority in the Philippine House. During his ten years as a congressman, he used his economics background in introducing bills to benefit Filipino consumers and workers and served on House committees dealing with banking, energy, exports, trade, agriculture, various civil rights issues, and public order and security. He worked to make military fuel procurements transparent and to increase oversight of intelligence financing, and also served as Deputy Speaker of the House from 2004 to 2006. Limited to three terms in the house, Aquino ran for the Senate in 2007. As part of a multi-party coalition in opposition to President Gloria Macapagal Arroyo, Aquino was elected to the Senate, where he worked to raise construction standards in government projects, extend oversight to all government procurements, and check the president's ability to impound congressional budgets. At the time, he had no thought of following his parents into a national leadership role. "I never sought to compete with them because I believe that was a test that was not possible," he told New York Times reporter Norimitsu Onishi. Competing with such iconic figures of democracy "would be a useless venture on my part," he added. "I concentrated on making sure that their sacrifices were not squandered."

Nevertheless, after Corazon Aquino died of cancer in 2009, many of Aquino's countrymen urged him to run in the 2010 presidential elections. After retreating to a convent to consider his options, he announced his candidacy. "I accept the wish of the people," the New York Times's Carlos H. Conde reported him as saying. "I accept the challenge to lead this nation. I want to make democracy work, not just for the rich and well connected, but for everybody." Aquino ran a reformist campaign that promised to bring honesty and efficiency to the government by instituting judicial reforms and investigating outgoing President Arroyo, whose term was tainted by accusations of graft. In an election against eight other candidates—including a self-made billionaire senator, a former movie star, and former President Joseph Estrada—Aquino secured the biggest margin of victory since his mother's election in 1986. He was sworn into office in June of 2010 before a crowd of half a million people, promising in his inaugural speech: "The mandate given to me was one of change. I accept your marching orders to transform our government from one that is self-serving to one that works for the welfare of the nation."

Despite his decisive victory, Aquino faced several challenges as president: his running mate was bested by a rival party candidate for vice president; his Liberal Party had to form a coalition to get a majority in Congress; and former President Arroyo remained in politics as a congresswoman heading the opposition party. The economy of the Philippines was heavily reliant on remittances from emigrants and the budget was in deficit, due in part to corruption consuming an estimated 30 percent of the total. Aquino began his term by creating a truth commission to investigate Arroyo's tenure, appointing a human-rights investigator known for her independence to head the justice department, and firing non-career government officials who had earned their posts through political favors. While critics believed his plan to increase government revenues without raising taxes would fall short of solving the country's budget woes, they praised his appointment of experienced professionals to key financial posts in the government. He also appointed a government negotiator to reopen talks with Islamic separatists in the south of the Philippines.

Aquino came under fire for some of his early actions. In September of 2010, when seven Hong Kong tourists and their guide were killed after being taken hostage by a disgruntled Manila policeman, the president was criticized for not reacting more quickly to the situation. In December of 2010, the Philippine Supreme Court ruled Aquino's Truth Commission to be unconstitutional because it violated an equal protection clause by singling out former President Arroyo. Critics of the ruling point out that the Supreme Court is dominated by appointments made by Arroyo. Aquino also courted controversy by supporting a reproductive health bill that would allow public health facilities to distribute contraceptives, overturning an existing ban in Manila. His stance brought Aquino, a Catholic like 80 percent of his countrymen, criticism from the Church and the possibility of civil disobedience. Despite such criticism, the independence and personal integrity Aquino demonstrated during his early days as president led many observers to believe he could fulfill his promise of bringing political openness and fairness to the Philippines.

Although he came from one of his country's most prominent and privileged families, Aquino believed his role should include helping his less-fortunate countrymen. This was due to his parents' influence, he told *Time International* contributor Ishaan Tharoor: "They made automatic in me the preference to take up the cudgels for those who have less in life, for the powerless," he said. "Why should I veer away from their footprints?" Due to term limits, Aquino was only scheduled to serve one six-year term, but he believed he could make every day count. "My parents sought nothing less, died for nothing less, than democracy and peace. I am blessed by this legacy. I shall carry the torch forward," he noted in his inaugural address. "My hope is that when I leave office, everyone can say that we have traveled far on the right path, and that we are able to bequeath a better future to the next generation."

Sources

Periodicals

Christian Science Monitor, May 11, 2010; June 30, 2010.
Economist, May 15, 2010, p. 43.
Filipino Reporter (New York), October 8-14, 2010, pp. 18, 24.
Financial Times, May 12, 2010, p. 8; June 30, 2010, p. 4.
Guardian, June 30, 2010.
New York Times, August 30, 1987, p. 9; September 10, 2009, p. A18; March 27, 2010, p. A6; May 12, 2010, p. A8; June 10, 2010; July 16, 2010, p. A10; October 11, 2010; December 7, 2010.
Philippine Graphic, April 5-12, 2010.
Time International, April 26, 2010, p. 22.

Online

"Inaugural Address of His Excellency Benigno S. Aquino III, President of the Philippines," Official Gazette of the Office of the President of the Philippines, http://www.gov.ph/2010/06/30/inaugural-address-of-president-benigno-s-aquino-iii-english-translation/ (November 5, 2010).
"Senator Benigno S. Aquino III," Senate of the Philippines, http://www.senate.gov.ph/senators/sen_bio/aquino_noynoy_resume.asp (November 5, 2010).
"The Son Also Rises: Who Is Noynoy Aquino?," GMANews.tv, http://www.gmanews.tv/story/171863/the-son-also-rises-who-is-noynoy-aquino (November 5, 2010).

—*Diane Telgen*

Michael Arrington

Founder of TechCrunch

Born March 13, 1970, in Huntington Beach, CA. *Education:* Claremont McKenna College, B.A., 1992; Stanford Law School, J.D., 1995.

Addresses: *Home*—Seattle, WA. *Office*—The Tech-Crunch Network, 410 Townsend St., San Francisco, CA 94107.

Career

Corporate and securities lawyer, O'Melveny & Myers, mid-1990s; corporate and securities lawyer, Wilson Sonsini Goodrich & Rosati, late 1990s; vice president for business development and general counsel, RealNames, 1999-2000; cofounder, Achex, 2000; chief operations officer, Razorgator, 2002-03; founder and chief executive officer, Zip.ca and Pool.com, c. 2003-04; cofounder, Edgeio, 2005; founder and editor, TechCrunch, 2005—; consultant for information-technology companies.

Sidelights

Michael Arrington is the founder and editor of TechCrunch, a phenomenally successful technology blog. In the space of just five short years since writing his first post on June 11, 2005, Arrington had turned his site a daily must-read for insiders in Silicon Valley. Dealmakers, potential investors, and even business journalists regularly check TechCrunch for the most up-to-date information on the ever-expanding array of gadgetry and the software that runs it in the twenty-first century. "I saw a parade, and I got in front of it," Arrington told Wired.com writer Fred Vogelstein.

Arrington was born in 1970 and grew up in Huntington Beach, California. He majored in economics at Claremont McKenna College, near Los Angeles, and went on to earn a law degree from the prestigious, highly selective Stanford Law School in 1995. For a few years, he worked as a corporate and securities attorney for large law firms in California, helping startups that were funded largely by venture-capital dollars prepare for their initial public offerings, or IPOs. Many young entrepreneurs became millionaires overnight when their Web businesses became publicly traded companies, with Wall Street joining in the frenzy known as the dotcom bubble. Arrington quit his job and joined in, but did so just before the bubble burst and the price of shares for new-technology companies began to crater.

Arrington was initially a vice president for business development and general counsel for RealNames, an idea for a keyword-based Internet-site locator from 1999 to 2000. He then cofounded Achex, an online money-transfer service that could not compete with PayPal, which was cornering that market. Arrington and the other founders sold the remnants of it to a financial-data services company in 2001 for $32 million; by contrast, a year later, eBay bought

PayPal for a stunning $1.5 billion. "I made enough to buy a Porsche," Arrington told Vogelstein about the Achex deal. "Not much more."

Over the next few years, Arrington moved around, either founding or serving as a senior executive for other startups. He was involved with Zip.ca, a Canadian DVD rental service, and Pool.com, a domain-name registry, and was chief operations officer with Razorgator, a ticket-selling and buying service. After saving up some money, he quit working altogether in mid-2004, renting a beachfront condo in the Los Angeles area. "All I did was work out, surf, and watch movies," he said in the Wired.com interview. He was lured back into the game by Keith Teare, a cofounder of RealNames who was trying to launch an online classified-ad aggregator called Edgeio that would compete with Craigslist. Arrington moved to the Palo Alto area in early 2005, renting a house in Atherton.

After so many months of lazing around, Arrington felt like he needed to catch up on what was happening in Silicon Valley—most importantly, which were the most promising new ideas that venture capital firms were funding. He was confounded that there was no single information source for new-technology business, and launched TechCrunch.com from his home in June of 2005. The former attorney and ardent onliner wrote most of the posts himself at first, though he was later able to lure journalists-turned-bloggers and other professionals as contributors. "You know that experiment where the rat hits the lever and the treat comes out? By the third day of writing, I got my first comment from somebody who wasn't my mom," he told Inc. writer Liz Welch. "That's the treat. Then people started subscribing to my RSS feed. Every day, that number would go up—10, 13, 100."

Within a year, Arrington had quit the Edgeio job and was selling ad space on TechCrunch. The blog quickly became a vital source of news and information on what was happening in Silicon Valley, and Arrington became equally famous for the epic parties he threw at his house to promote the site and encourage networking. TechCrunch became a story itself when Arrington's site was the first to break the news that Google was buying YouTube in late 2006. Venture capitalists "and entrepreneurs read Arrington for the same reason they pay attention to any top journalist or columnist," wrote Vogelstein in the Wired.com profile. "He's smart, sourced up, and ahead of the curve."

Arrington is infamously disliked by many people, and has engaged in a few entertaining public feuds with high-profile names like Jason Calcanis, founder of Weblogs, Inc. Others blame Arrington and Tech-Crunch for the failure of their startup, or what some have described as a lack of journalistic ethics. Writing about Arrington's influence in Fortune in 2008, Josh Quittner likened him to the once-feared gossip columnists who could make or break an actor's career, or a influence a film's take at the box office on opening weekend. "A positive mention on Tech-Crunch doesn't necessarily assure a company's success, but it sure helps," Quittner noted. "Tech-Crunch today tops the lists of the most influential—and linked-to—tech blogs, and courting Arrington has become an integral part of the launch cycle."

Still known for the parties that evolved into heady weeklong networking events like the Disrupt conference in San Francisco, Arrington continues to write for TechCrunch and doggedly pursues all the leads that turn up in his inbox every morning in order to make his site the first to deliver a story. On occasion, he'll sit on a story for a day or two, if requested. "Unless I know lots of other journalists are sniffing around, I generally defer to the entrepreneur," he told Inc.'s Welch. "We probably lose half of those stories, but it's the right thing to do. It builds trust. People aren't going to tell you things if they don't trust you."

In September of 2010, Arrington sold TechCrunch to AOL for a reported $25 million. By then, Tech-Crunch headquarters had moved into real office space in downtown San Francisco, and Arrington had moved out of the ragged rental home in Atherton and bought a place in Seattle, where his parents live. He told Welch in the Inc. interview that he was trying to take better care of himself, divulging that during TechCrunch's first few years, "I'd work until I passed out, and wake up eight or nine hours later, which might be 4 p.m. or 3 a.m. Then I'd work again until I passed out. That was my life for four years—it got really bad. I missed a lot of social things. I didn't keep up with friends. I was a mess."

Sources

Periodicals

Business 2.0, September 2006, p. 64.
Fortune, March 31, 2008, p. 42.
Inc., October 2010, p. 124.

Online

"Michael Arrington," CrunchBase.com, http://www.crunchbase.com/person/michael-arrington (November 11, 2010).

"TechCrunch Blogger Michael Arrington Can Generate Buzz ... and Cash," *Wired,* http://www. wired.com/techbiz/people/magazine/15-07/ff_ arrington?currentPage=all (November 2, 2010).

—*Carol Brennan*

Ron Artest

David Sherman/NBAE/Getty Images

Professional basketball player

Born Ronald William Artest, Jr., November 13, 1979, in Long Island City, NY; son of Ronald William, Sr., and Sarah Artest; married Kimisha Hatfield; children: Sade I-Nisha, Ronald William III, Leron, Diamond. *Education:* Attended St. John's University, New York City, NY, 1998-99.

Addresses: *Office*—c/o Los Angeles Lakers, 555 N. Nash St., El Segundo, CA 90245. *Web site*—http://www.ronartest.com/.

Career

Played college basketball at St. John's University, 1997-99; entered National Basketball Association (NBA) draft, 1999; drafted by Chicago Bulls, 1999; played forward for Chicago Bulls, 1999-2002; traded to Indiana Pacers, 2002; played forward for Indiana Pacers, 2002-06; founded and served as chief executive officer, TruWarier Records, Stamford, CT, 2002—; suspended for whole season after altercation with fans during a game in Detroit, 2004-05; traded to Sacramento Kings, 2006; played forward for Sacramento Kings, 2006-08; traded to Houston Rockets, 2008; played for Houston Rockets, 2008-09; signed with the Los Angeles Lakers, 2009. Also founded TruWarier Wear, a clothing line.

Awards: Defensive Player of the Year Award, NBA, 2004; named to Eastern Conference All-Star team, NBA, 2004.

Sidelights

Known as "the Beast" for his ferocious play, National Basketball Association (NBA) star Ron Artest is considered a gifted player with a high basketball IQ and ferocious defensive abilities as well as a sometimes problematic personality. The 6'7" Artest was known for his volatility early his career, culminating in his role in starting an all-out brawl with fans and players in Detroit in 2004. The incident led to Artest being suspended for the rest of the season. Playing for several teams after his return to the league, Artest sometimes struggled with his temper but as he matured he learned to focus his energy on playing basketball to the best of his abilities. One-time Indiana Pacers coach Isaiah Thomas told L. Jon Wertheim of *Sports Illustrated* that "Ron plays with a passion that's uncontrollable. He's in love—in love—with basketball."

Artest was born on November 13, 1979, in Long Island City, New York, the son and one of eight children of Ron Artest, Sr., and his wife, Sarah. He learned to walk at ten months and began playing organized basketball at a local community center when he was ten years old as a way of coping with his parents' divorce. He would also play on the courts near Queensbridge, the housing project where he lived. There, he would take on all challenges and sometimes get into fights over scoring. By 1996, Artest was playing with the Riverside Church Amateur Athletic Union team that went 69-1. Artest played high school basketball at LaSalle Academy as well, where he was a standout forward and considered one of the best prep players in the city. The team won the Catholic High School Association championship in 1997, his senior year.

Because Artest and his girlfriend, Kimisha Hatfield, were going to have a child, Artest signed on to play college ball at the New York-based St. John's University. The Red Storm were going through a rebuilding process under coach Fran Fraschilla, with Artest playing a key role in the school's comeback. During his two years with St. John's under Fraschilla and his successor Mike Jarvis, Artest was sometimes inconsistent but showed flashes of brilliance as a player because of his stand-out defense, skilled shot-making, and hard work. However, his sometimes unpredictable, moody, and take-charge personality came into conflict with his teammates. He told Judy Battista of the *New York Times*, "I try to be a leader, but I'm one of the youngest people on the team. I'm not going to be yelling anymore. It hasn't been working out. Believe me, it hasn't been working out. The way I lead is different. I tell people what's real. I don't think that's the way to do it. I don't know the way to do it."

After leading the Red Storm to the Elite Eight in the National Collegiate Athletic Association basketball tournament in 1999, Artest decided to leave St. John's and enter the NBA draft. He was a first-round draft pick of the Chicago Bulls, then in rebuilding mode after a team-worst won-loss record in 1998-99. Because of his physical play, Artest emerged as a favorite of former Bulls superstar Michael Jordan. Jordan told Chris Ballard of *Sports Illustrated*, "I love Ron Artest. He's got so much intensity and such drive. I wish I could have played against him six years ago." While Artest was emerging as a powerful NBA player, he often played with emotion and displayed a temper that was not always under control. However, Artest was already a solid defender who, after working with a shooting coach during the 2001 off-season, emerged as a strong shooter as well during the 2001-02 season.

In March of 2002, the still-struggling Bulls traded Artest to the Indiana Pacers as part of a seven-player deal. He signed a six-year $42 million deal that October. During the 2002-03 season, Artest played well first as a fill-in for injured shooting guard Reggie Miller than as a starting forward. Be-cause of his physical play and impressive statistics, the Pacers had early season success attributed to Artest and his energy. While he was proving more than adept on the court, many were surprised by his lack of attitude and cockiness off the court. *Sports Illustrated*'s Wertheim wrote that away from the court, "Artest might be the NBA's least imposing player. In a league populated by prima donnas and poseurs, he is free of both pretense and guile. Ask him a question and he'll answer it candidly, making eye contact the entire time…. Yell his name from an arena's upper reaches during pregame warmups and, reflexively, he'll turn and wave or give a thumbs-up."

However, by the end of 2002-03, Artest had been suspended five times by the NBA and once by the Pacers, and was fined $155,000. He also led the league in flagrant fouls, with nine. By the 2003-04 season, Artest seemed to have his temper more under control and he emerged as an even better player. As Jon Krawcyznski of the Associated Press Worldstream wrote in December of 2003, "Calmer and cooler, Artest is getting noticed more this season for his tenacious defensive play and offensive versatility, rather than outlandish outbursts and flagrant fouls." His defense was still unmatched and emerged as a leading scorer on the team. For his outstanding play, Artest was named to the Eastern Conference All-Star team in 2004 and defensive player of the year in the NBA at season's end.

Unfortunately, Artest had not left his hot-headedness behind in the 2004-05 season, though he was averaging 24.6 points and 6.4 rebounds per game. During a game against the Detroit Pistons at the Palace of Auburn Hills in November of 2004, Pistons player Ben Wallace shoved Artest in the neck after a hard foul. Then, a fan in the stands tossed a cup full of beer that hit Artest. Artest reacted by wildly going into the stands after the fan, and an all-out brawl ensued. Because of his outrageous actions, NBA commissioner David Stern suspended Artest without pay for the rest of the season. Artest lost $5 million in salary because of the suspension and was again seen as a problematic player. He had already been suspended for two games by Indiana earlier in the season for asking for a month off due to exhaustion from promoting a rap album by Allure that he was releasing on his label, TruWarier Records, as well as recording his own album. Because of the suspension of Artest and two other Pacers, Indiana went from being a favorite to win the Eastern Conference to perhaps not making the playoffs at all.

After the incident, Artest apologized for his actions. He told Pam Lambert and Kate Klise of *People*, "I just wish the situation hadn't turned out the way it turned out." He added, "You know, you've got fans and 99.9 percent of them are great ... and .1 percent are jerks. There's a lot of negativity in the world. I'm trying to be positive." Despite such regrets, he was charged with misdemeanor assault and battery by Oakland County prosecutors in Michigan.

Artest returned to the Pacers in the summer of 2005 to prepare for the upcoming season by participating in rookie free-agent camp then in summer league games. He vowed to keep his temper under control, telling Cliff Brunt of the Associated Press, "As you get older, you get a bit more wise. Probably next year, you'll see an older guy, an older player. Like everybody else, as they get older, they mature." It was obvious to Pacers coaches that he missed playing the game, who noticed that he kept himself in game shape by working out at the Indianapolis Jewish Community Center. At the beginning of the 2005-06 season, Artest's image seem less tarnished when he announced that he signed a multi-million dollar endorsement deal with k1x-Nation of Hoop, a German-based basketball lifestyle brand.

By December of 2005, however, Artest believed that he could not move past the brawl and suspension while continuing to play in Indiana. He began requesting a trade from the Pacers and the team agreed to accommodate him. He sat while negotiations were ongoing. When Artest's availability was announced, a number of teams expressed interest. He was finally traded to the Sacramento Kings in January of 2006 for Peja Stojakovic. The Kings were struggling when Artest joined them, but they soon improved as Artest got himself into game-playing shape again. Sacramento coach Rick Adelman told David DuPree of *USA Today*, "He's definitely had an impact on the way we defend, because he is a great defender. He gives us a guy who can basically shut down people. He also does things you just can't teach. He has great instinct, and he has great physical ability."

Artest continued to play well for the Kings, though legal troubles still followed him. In July of 2007, the NBA announced that he was suspended for the first seven games of the 2007-08 season because of a misdemeanor domestic violence charge against him from a March 2007 dispute with his wife. Artest remained with Sacramento through the end of the 2008 season, then was traded to the Houston Rockets in the off season. At that time, the Rockets were coached by former Kings coach Adelman, who believed in Artest. Addressing concerns about acquiring Artest, Rockets general manager Daryl Morey told Jon Saraceno of the *USA Today*, "We went into this with eyes wide open. There's risks on a couple of levels with Ron. We gave up some future picks and [developing] Donte Green. And we took some risk on his volatile past. We feel like we can control those [areas].... But he's been a very good [teammate], very competitive and personable with the guys. To win the title, you need to take these calculated risks."

During the 2008-09 season, Artest emerged as a more mellow player for the Rockets, in part because of helpful sessions with a sports psychologist. Ian Thomsen wrote in *Sports Illustrated*, "As his abundant personality quirks have grown more amusing than alarming, Ron Artest has become—of all things—a stabilizing force." Houston struggled early in the season and lost key players to injury but Artest helped move the team forward and into a battle for control of their division by April of 2009. While he had once been a focus of his teams' offenses, the now-mature Artest was a complementary scorer for Houston, averaging about 17.2 points per game through April of 2009. The Rockets reached the Western Conference semifinals, before losing to the eventual NBA champions, the Los Angeles Lakers.

In the 2009 offseason, Artest and Houston did not come to a deal so he signed a five-year, $34-million contract with the Lakers. He continued to see the psychologist to get perspective as he transitioned to his new team and declared that he was willing to play whatever role was necessary to help the defending champions repeat. Early in the 2009-10 season, he struggled a bit on offense while his defense was as strong as ever. After a fall on Christmas night at his home left him with a concussion and away from the team for five games, a case of plantar fasciitis hobbled him in early 2010. Still, of his time in Los Angeles thus far, Artest told the *Daily News of Los Angeles*, "I just focus on the positives. There are so many positives going on.... It's the best situation. I have to take advantage of it and enjoy it."

Away from basketball, Artest was a devoted father and entrepreneur. In addition to his record label, he founded TruWarier Wear, a clothing line. His perspective on life also changed when he visited Africa with the players' union in 2007 as well as when his youngest child was treated for kidney cancer in the fall of 2008. Artest was committed to visiting Africa again, and Rockets teammate Dikembe Mutombo believed it affected him deeply. Mutombo told *Sports Illustrated*'s Thomsen, "He has seen the suffering of the poor, the disease, and he relates it to what is happening to him with his daughter. You don't find that in so many players; that they wake up in the morning and say, 'I am going to Africa and I am going to do more.'"

Selected discography

My World, Lightyear Records, 2006.

Sources

Books

Marquis Who's Who, Marquis Who's Who, 2009.

Periodicals

Associated Press, July 11, 2005; July 21, 2005.
Associated Press State & Local Wire, November 1, 1999; January 4, 2010.
Associated Press Worldstream, December 18, 2003.
Business Wire, November 30, 2005.
Daily News (NY), July 7, 1997, p. 56; April 6, 1999, p. 87; November 22, 2004, p. 3.
Daily News of Los Angeles, October 19, 2009, p. C1; November 3, 2009, p. C1.
New York Times, February 3, 1999, p. D1; December 13, 2005, p. D1; July 15, 2007, p. 6; May 10, 2009, p. SP1.
People, December 6, 2004, p. 103.
Sports Illustrated, February 11, 2002, p. 74; December 16, 2002, p. 110; November 29, 2004, p. 50; October 24, 2005, p. 64; February 6, 2006, p. 50; April 13, 2009, p. 52.
USA Today, December 13, 2004, p. 14C; February 17, 2006, p. 7C; October 28, 2008, p. 4E; October 27, 2009, p. 6C; January 26, 2010, p. 3C.

—A. Petruso

Ben Bailey

Jordan Strauss/WireImage/Getty Images

Comedian and television show host

Born Benjamin Ray Bailey, October 30, 1970, in Bowling Green, KY; son of a bank executive and a college employee; married Laurence; children: one daughter. *Education:* Attended Old Dominion University, c. 1988-92.

Addresses: *Home*—Morris Twp., NJ. *Office*—c/o Discovery Channel, Discovery Communications, One Discovery Pl., Silver Spring, MD 20910. *Web site*—http://www.therealbenbailey.com/.

Career

Stand-up comic in Los Angeles and New York City after 1993; worked as a livery driver and nightclub bouncer; appeared on television comedy series *Late Friday*, NBC, and *Premium Blend*, Comedy Central, 2002; semifinalist, *Star Search*, CBS, 2002. Guest appearances on television include: *Mad TV*, FOX, 2002; *Law & Order: Special Victims Unit*, NBC, 2003; *Hope & Faith*, ABC, 2004; and *30 Rock*, NBC, 2010. Host of television shows, including: *Cash Cab*, Discovery Channel, 2005—; *Cash Cab: After Dark*, Discovery Channel, 2007—; *After the Catch*, Discovery Channel, 2009.

Awards: Daytime Emmy Award for outstanding game show host, Academy of Television Arts & Sciences, for *Cash Cab*, 2010.

Sidelights

Ben Bailey drives the *Cash Cab*, the surprisingly successful game-show hit for cable's Discovery Channel. Launched in 2005, *Cash Cab* has won three consecutive Daytime Emmy Awards, and in 2010 the affable, low-key host and fully licensed New York City taxicab driver took home the Daytime Emmy for Outstanding Game Show Host. Beth Jones, a writer for the *Athens Banner-Herald*, asked Bailey if this unusual dual profession was safe. "Probably not. You can't talk on a cell phone" while driving in the city, he replied, "but you can host a game show."

Bailey was born in 1970 in Bowling Green, Kentucky, as the second of two children in a family that later relocated to Chatham Borough, New Jersey, for his father's job with a major U.S. bank. He left Old Dominion University in Norfolk, Virginia, one semester's worth of credits short of his degree, and moved to Los Angeles in 1993. "I went out there to be an actor," he recalled in an interview with Robert DiGiacomo of the *Press of Atlantic City*, adding that he wound up in a receptionist-type job at The Comedy Store, a highly regarded breaking ground for new talent. "I was in the green room one night.

I gathered a crowd around me when I was telling a story. By the time I was done, I had an audience and I had made them laugh. This [booking agent] came over and said, 'How long have you been doing stand up?' I said, 'I just started.'" The agent offered him a slot on stage a few nights later. "I said no because I was petrified," Bailey admitted to DiGiacomo, but then changed his mind.

After a few years Bailey returned to the New Jersey/New York area and began working the stand-up comedy circuit there. He also worked for a car-hire service for five years, sometimes dropping his limousine passengers at a Broadway theater and then heading over to places like Caroline's or Stand Up New York for a turn at the mike before taking them home. With his imposing physique—the triathlon-competitor Bailey stands six feet, six inches tall—Bailey earned extra income by working a nightclub bouncer.

The dryly witty comic made his television debut in 2002, appearing in a pair of comedy showcases, *Late Friday* and *Premium Blend*, and winning a small part on an episode of *Mad TV*. In 2003, he was a semifinalist on Fox TV's *Star Search*, and went on to land guest roles in *Law & Order: Special Victims Unit* and *Hope & Faith*. In between other stand-up comedy specials and appearances on late-night shows, he won a small part in *Spiderman 2* that did not survive the film editors' final cut. Married by 2004 and still doing stand-up in New York City, Bailey was even quoted in a *New York Times* article in December of that year about a potential labor action by New York City comedians, who were considering petitioning the city to enact minimum-wage laws for performers and hosts at Manhattan comedy clubs. "I could do 30 shows in town and make $800. Or I could work the road and do eight shows and make $2,000," he told the paper's Jesse McKinley. "There's no comparison."

Cash Cab was Bailey's show-business break. A knockoff of an ITV game show launched in Britain in the summer of 2005, the Discovery Channel version presented a similar set-up: unsuspecting passengers enter a seemingly ordinary taxicab, and as the vehicle's secret video cameras show, the driver then flips a switch that turns on special discotheque-style lights on the cab's interior roof and the show's buzzy theme music. The driver then announces "you're in the Cash Cab," and offers the passenger, or passengers, a chance to win money by correctly answering trivia questions.

Bailey had to audition five times for the *Cash Cab* host's job, but his limousine-driving experience gave him a distinct advantage. He did, however, have to pass the rigorous taxi exam which all licensed medallion cab drivers, whose vehicles are permitted to pick up street hails, must pass. "One of the questions on the practice test was 'if you have to go from Broadway and 163rd Street to Yankee Stadium, what bridge do you take?'," Bailey told *Wall Street Journal* writer Joanne Kaufman about the notoriously tough test. "There are eleven bridges between Manhattan and the Bronx alone and 53 tunnels and bridges around Manhattan. I knew I had a lot to learn."

Cash Cab debuted in December of 2005 and, with little promotion, soon gained an avid audience of trivia hounds and game-show enthusiasts. "The addictive series feels like *Candid Camera* in traffic, connecting to everyday life in ways that have been lost by high-stakes 'reality TV,'" declared the *Denver Post*'s Joanne Ostrow. "This isn't about 20-somethings living together in a mansion under the camera's gaze.... On *Cash Cab*, Arkansas tourists headed to a bakery and a couple who speak little English are among those watching the meter."

As ratings climbed for *Cash Cab*, it became more difficult for Bailey to pick up unsuspecting passengers, and some opening segments show him trying to disguise his voice or cover his face as the contestants enter the minivan. The show won three consecutive Daytime Emmy Awards for Outstanding Game/Audience Participation Show, beginning in 2008, and in 2010 Bailey's genial on-screen personality and comic timing garnered the highest-possible industry accolades when he took home the Daytime Emmy for Outstanding Game Show Host. "Initially, the producers wanted me to be mean and ridicule passengers if they got the answer wrong, and I wouldn't do it," he revealed to Kaufman in the *Wall Street Journal* interview. "I didn't want to be mean to strangers."

Bailey also drives the yellow New York City medallion-cab minivan for *Cash Cab: After Dark*, which offers higher payouts for answering more challenging trivia questions. The show was even enshrined in an episode of *30 Rock* in the fall of 2010, when the character played by Tracy Jordan inadvertently hails Bailey's ride as he attempts to get to the hospital for the birth of his child. Bailey had a similar experience when his wife, Laurence, needed to get to the hospital for the birth of their daughter, and he convinced the driver not to get on the perennially congested West Side Highway. "Tenth Avenue," he told the *Wall Street Journal*'s Kaufman, "is the best kept secret on the West Side."

Sources

Athens Banner-Herald (Athens, GA), May 29, 2008.
Daily Post (Liverpool, England), June 23, 2006, p. 2.
Denver Post, April 23, 2006, p. F1.

New York Times, December 22, 2004.
Press of Atlantic City, March 12, 2009, p. 6.
Star-Ledger (Newark, NJ), August 1, 2009, p. M77.
Wall Street Journal, June 26, 2008, p. D7.

—*Carol Brennan*

Sheila Bair

Chairman of the Federal Deposit Insurance Corporation

Born April 3, 1954, in Independence, KS; married to Scott P. Cooper; children: Preston, Colleen. *Education:* University of Kansas, B.A., 1975, J.D., 1978.

Addresses: *Office*—Federal Deposit Insurance Corporation, 550 17th Street NW, Washington, DC 20429.

Career

Bank teller, early 1970s; instructor, University of Arkansas law school, 1978-79; staff, U.S. Department of Health, Education, and Welfare, 1979-81; aide, U.S. Senator Robert Dole, 1981-88; research director, Bob Dole's campaign for president, 1988; lawyer, New York Stock Exchange, c. 1989; ran for Congress in Kansas and lost, 1990; commissioner, Commodities Trading Commission, 1991-95; senior vice-president for government relations, New York Stock Exchange, 1995-2000; assistant Treasury secretary for financial institutions, 2001-02; professor of public policy, University of Massachusetts at Amherst, 2002-06; chairman, Federal Deposit Insurance Corporation, 2006—.

Awards: Author of the Month Awards, *Highlights Magazine for Children,* 2002, 2003, 2004; John F. Kennedy Profile in Courage Award, John F. Kennedy Library Foundation, 2009; Hubert H. Humphrey Civil Rights Award, The Leadership Conference, 2009.

AP Images/Mark Lennihan

Sidelights

Every crisis creates a few heroes after the fact, people who saw the looming dangers others ignored. Though their warnings are usually not heeded in time, their reputation grows when they are proven right. So it is with Sheila Bair, the bank regulator who used the chairmanship of the normally quiet Federal Deposit Insurance Corporation to issue urgent warnings about the dangers of Wall Street investment in subprime loans. In late 2008, when subprime lending caused the American economy to sink into its worst downturn since the Great Depression, supporters of stricter government regulation of finance celebrated Bair's foresight. She received the John F. Kennedy Profile in Courage award, one of the most prestigious honors in government and politics.

Bair was born in 1954 in Kansas and grew up in the small town of Independence. Like her parents, she became a moderate Republican who admired former president Theodore Roosevelt's strict regulation of extremely large businesses. While in college in the early 1970s, Bair worked as a bank teller, an experience that gave her a lifelong respect for the classic, cautious practices of small community banks and their customers. "It was a ritual to come in and make your mortgage payment personally," Bair told Ryan Lizza of the *New Yorker*. "There was a kind of pride in living up to your obligations, and, on the lender side, in making loans that people could understand and afford."

After earning bachelor's and law degrees at the University of Kansas and briefly teaching at a law school in Arkansas, Bair moved to Washington, D.C., in 1979 to work as a government staffer. In 1981, she joined the office of U.S. Sen. Robert Dole of Kansas. She worked for Dole for seven years and served as research director for his failed 1988 campaign for president. After a stint as a lawyer for the New York Stock Exchange, she ran for Congress in 1990 in a Kansas district that included her hometown. But her moderate politics, including support for abortion rights, hurt her campaign, and she narrowly lost in the Republican primary.

In 1991, Dole helped Bair win appointment to a federal commission that regulates parts of the finance industry, the Commodity Futures Trading Commission. There, she proved her foresight by dissenting from a decision requested by the energy company Enron. The commission allowed Enron and other energy companies to conduct certain transactions, known as exchange-traded futures contracts, without regulation by the commission. The decision, which Bair called a dangerous precedent, was one of several deregulatory decisions that made it easier for Enron to engage in the large financial fraud that destroyed the company in 2001.

Bair left the government in 1995 to work at the New York Stock Exchange, but she returned in 2001, when new president George W. Bush named her an assistant treasury secretary in charge of financial institutions. Bair began to take interest in the emergence of subprime mortgages, new loans that did not follow the simple old formula of local banks making loans to local homeowners. Instead, lenders who were not traditional banks were making loans to high-risk borrowers. The loans often included hidden fees and low introductory interest rates that went much higher after a few years. The lenders often did not keep a close eye on the loans, but sold them in bundles to speculators on Wall Street. Bair tried to use her job at the treasury department to curb the lending practices that concerned her. She got the home-loan industry to adopt a code of best practices, but following the code was voluntary.

In 2002, Bair left the treasury department to teach public policy at the University of Massachusetts in Amherst. She also began writing children's stories about the importance of understanding money. Some of her short stories were published in *Highlights Magazine for Children*. She wrote two books for children, published in 2006 and 2008.

After four years in academia, Bair returned to the government in 2006 when Bush appointed her chairman of the Federal Deposit Insurance Corporation, the government company that insures consumers' bank deposits and takes over failing banks. In her new job, Bair looked into subprime lending again and found the practice had gotten riskier. Many lenders were doing very little to confirm the income of the people receiving their loans. They were even charging high penalties to people who tried to pay off their loans early. The FDIC closed a California bank in early 2007 for bad lending, the first government action against a subprime lender. Bair met with mortgage bankers to try to convince them to change their practices. She also wrote to other government bank regulators, asking them to regulate subprime lending more strictly. When they did not respond, she made her concerns public.

At a conference of mortgage lenders in October of 2007, Bair pleaded with lenders to modify the terms of their loans to save more of their borrowers from foreclosure. "Less than one per cent of subprime mortgages that are having problems were being restructured in any meaningful way," she told them (as quoted by Lizza of the *New Yorker*). "We have a huge problem on our hands." She pushed the Bush Administration to create a taxpayer-funded program to modify loans. But other officials balked, believing that the bad loans were too flawed to save. The Treasury Department did announce a plan in December of 2007 based on Bair's ideas, but it was voluntary, and experts predicted it would cover 300,000 or less of the 1.7 million mortgages that were due to reset to higher interest rates.

In October of 2008, investments in bad loans caused several major American financial institutions to fail, triggering a deep recession and a nationwide financial crisis. Bair argued that the government should step in and help modify as many as 1.5 million loans. By then, other federal regulators were coming around to her idea.

Bair found herself in disagreement with Timothy Geither, the head of the Federal Reserve Bank of New York and president-elect Barack Obama's choice for treasury secretary, over how to respond to the financial crisis. Bair and Geithner were among the government financial officials who had a say in the federal bailouts and federally negotiated takeovers of several distressed banking titans, including Citigroup and Wachovia. In general, Bair was often in favor of taking over ailing financial institutions or imposing strict requirements on them in exchange for government aid. Geither was more likely to believe that financial aid alone would allow them to survive the crisis.

Bair spent the next two years in high-level, high-stakes debates about how to regulate large, troubled financial institutions. Impressed with her influence, *Forbes* magazine named her the second most powerful woman in the world in 2009. That year, Obama instituted a controversial mortgage aid program that included many of Bair's ideas.

In early 2010, the FDIC created several new regulations designed to discourage risky behavior by banks. That July, Congress passed a major financial regulation law that included new powers for the FDIC. It allowed Bair's agency to take over and liquidate major financial companies if they are in danger of failure, an expansion of its existing power to close failing banks. In the event of another financial crisis, the FDIC's new role gives the government another option to prevent a giant company from suddenly failing besides bailing it out with tax money. "Shareholders and unsecured creditors should understand that they, not taxpayers, are at risk," Bair warned, according to Sewell Chan of the *New York Times*.

Bair's five-year term as FDIC chairman expires in June of 2011. She declared (according to Bloomberg News) that she would not seek another term, because "new blood and fresh thinking" are important for the agency. She will remain on the FDIC's board of directors through July of 2013.

Selected writings

Children's books

Rock, Brock and the Savings Shock, Albert Whitman and Co., 2006.
Isabel's Car Wash, Albert Whitman and Co., 2008.

Sources

Periodicals

Bloomberg News, November 9, 2010.
New York Times, December 15, 2007, p. C1; August 27, 2008, p. C1; December 11, 2008, p. A1; January 8, 2010, p. B2; October 13, 2010, p. B3.
New Yorker, July 6, 2009.
USA Today, October 3, 2008.

Online

"Board of Directors & Senior Executives," Federal Deposit Insurance Corporation, http://www.fdic.gov/about/learn/board/board.html (November 9, 2010).
"The 100 Most Powerful Women: #2 Sheila Bair," *Forbes*, http://www.forbes.com/lists/2009/11/power-women-09_Sheila-Bair_0R5X.html(November 9, 2010).
"Sheila C. Bair" WhoRunsGov.com, http://www.whorunsgov.com/Profiles/Sheila_C._Bair (November 26, 2010).
"Times Topics: Sheila C. Bair News" *New York Times*, http://topics.nytimes.com/top/reference/timestopics/people/b/sheila_bair/index.html(November 9, 2010).

—*Erick Trickey*

Ban Ki-moon

Chung Sung-Jun/Getty Images

Secretary General of the United Nations

Born June 13, 1944, in Eumseong, South Korea; married Yoo Soon-taek, 1971; children: three. *Education:* Seoul National University, B.S., 1970; Harvard University, M.P.A., 1985.

Addresses: *Office*—United Nations, Office of the Secretary General, Room S-3800, United Nations Plaza, New York, NY, 10017. *Web site*— http:// www.un.org/sg/.

Career

Joined the South Korean foreign service, 1970; worked at Korean embassy in New Delhi, India, 1972-75; permanent observer, Korean Mission to the United Nations, 1978-80; director of the UN Division for South Korea, 1980-83; protocol secretary to the South Korean prime minister, 1985-87; consul general, Korean Embassy to the United States, 1987-90; director general of the North American Affairs bureau, 1990-92; special assistant to the foreign minister, 1992; minister, Korean Embassy to the United States, 1992-95; deputy minister for policy planning affairs, 1995-96; chief of protocol to the South Korean president, 1996; senior adviser for foreign policy and national security to the South Korean president, 1996-98; ambassador to Austria, 1998-2000; vice-minister of foreign affairs and trade, 2000-01; ambassador to the United Nations, 2001-02; ambassador at large of minister of foreign affairs and trade, 2002; adviser to the South Korean president for foreign policy, 2003-04; minister of foreign affairs and trade, 2004-06; Secretary General of the United Nations, 2007—.

Awards: Highest Order of Service Merit, Republic of Korea, 1975, 1986, 2006; Grand-Croix de L'Ordre Nationale, Government of Burkina Faso, 2008; Grand Officier de L'Ordre Nationale, Government of Côte d'Ivoire, 2008.

Sidelights

Ban Ki-moon became the first Asian to head the United Nations (UN) in more than three decades when he ascended to the Secretary Generalship of that body in January of 2007. A lifelong public servant who worked for South Korea's foreign ministry for many years before rising to the UN's top job, the able diplomat won the nickname of the "slippery eel" from the domestic press for his skill at ducking awkward questions. Although some have criticized his mellow approach to his admittedly tough job, others have acknowledged the value of this smooth, meditative style. "It has been my firm belief, sort of my lifestyle and personal philosophy, that sincerity and honesty is the key to everything in diplomacy ... even with people who are involved in conflicts, I have been able to make some personal relationships on the basis of trust, " Ban explained to Warren Hoge of the *New York Times* in 2007.

Ban was born the eldest of the six children of a warehouse owner on June 13, 1944, in Eumseong, South Korea, an area then occupied by Japan. By the time the Korean War erupted in 1950, the warehouse business had gone bankrupt and the family was forced to hide in the mountains. "We were safe ... but we were poor and hungry," Ban recalled to Hoge in another *New York Times* story. "I could see the fighter jets bombing the towns and cities nearby." After the close of hostilities a few years later, the future diplomat became a dedicated student, learning English through diligent practice. His language skills won him a trip to the United States through a Red Cross-sponsored competition. Two life-changing encounters marked this voyage. First, Ban met fellow South Korean high school student Yoo Soon-taek upon his departure; the two married in 1971. Second, the teenager met U.S. president John F. Kennedy as part of his prize, an event that inspired him to pursue diplomacy as a career.

To that end, Ban enrolled at Seoul National University to study international relations, earning his bachelor's degree in 1970. That same year, he qualified to become a diplomat and entered the South Korean foreign service. During his early career, Ban typically pursued postings that allowed him to send money back to his still-struggling family, serving first in Seoul and later in New Delhi, India. In 1975, the rising diplomat began working at UN headquarters in New York City as a permanent observer of the Korean Mission to the international body. Between 1980 and 1983, he directed South Korea's UN Division before filling a variety of diplomatic positions in South Korea, the United States, and Austria over the next 20 years. During a stint in the United States in the mid-1980s, he earned a master's degree in public administration from Harvard University.

An apparent career setback occurred in 2001, however, when Ban—then South Korea's Vice Minister for Foreign Affairs and Trade—caused serious embarrassment for his country. His staff neglected to delete a statement supporting the Anti-Ballistic Missile Treaty from a joint memo to Russia, despite the recent withdrawal of American support for the measure. The mistake led to a public apology from South Korean President Kim Dae Jung and what seemed like certain demotion for Ban. In an effort to avoid being posted on the outskirts of the international community, the diplomat accepted an offer of a post as chief of staff for UN General Assembly president Han Seung Soo. This return to the United Nations, unexpectedly enough, set him on an upward trajectory toward the organization's top job. "Had I been appointed to an ambassadorship somewhere, I simply wouldn't have had this opportunity to be selected secretary general," he admitted to Hoge in the *New York Times*. In time, Ban returned to top-level government work, becoming South Korea's foreign minister in 2004.

In October of 2006, Ban won appointment to succeed two-term incumbent Kofi Annan as the eighth Secretary General of the United Nations, the first time an Asian had held the office since the tenure of Burma's U Thant during the late 1960s and early 1970s. During his acceptance speech, Ban identified several immediate priorities for his administration, including enacting internal reform, improving human rights and health, meeting the threat of terrorism, and slowing negative environmental changes. He was sworn into office on December 14, and formally assumed his new position on January 1 of the following year. In the *New York Times*, Hoge quoted Ban as commenting, "You could say that I am a man on a mission, and my mission could be dubbed 'Operation Restore Trust': trust in the organization, and trust between member states and the Secretariat.... I hope this mission is not 'Mission: Impossible.'"

Despite these good intentions, Ban quickly stirred up controversy on a variety of fronts. Scant days after taking office, the new Secretary General seemingly broke with UN policy against the death penalty by refusing to strongly condemn the execution of former Iraqi Saddam Hussein. Allegations of improper or simply slow appointments to high-ranking organization positions began to circulate, and dissension rumbled over Ban's proposal to divide peacekeeping operations into two units; however, Ban was also lauded for his decision to institute external audits on UN activities after reports of possible bribery in North Korea surfaced, and even critics agreed that the tasks facing him were remarkably challenging ones. Entering office, the Secretary General dealt with ongoing geopolitical challenges such as human rights violations in Darfur, highly strained relations between North and South Korea, rising concerns over Iran's nuclear capabilities, and a long-running war in Iraq.

During 2007, Ban met repeatedly with Sudanese officials to press for an end to the violent crisis in Darfur while managing other issues such as a government crackdown on protests in Myanmar and dealing with climate change. These efforts continued through the following months, even as the United Nations became involved in increasingly tense negotiations regarding the nuclear capabilities of North Korea and Iran. As part of South Korea's foreign ministry, Ban had previous experience dealing with sensitive North Korean relations—and personal feelings about the nation's actions. "There must be some measures taken [about continuing North Korean military and nuclear actions]," David E. Sanger and Thom Shanker of the *New York Times* quoted Ban as saying at a news conference in May of 2010. "The evidence is quite compelling. There is no controversy. Therefore it is the responsibility of the international community to address this issue properly."

Sources

Books

Encyclopedia of World Biography Supplement, vol. 27, Gale, 2007.
Marquis Who's Who, Marquis Who's Who, 2010.

Periodicals

Economist, January 6, 2007, p. 21.

New York Times, October 14, 2006; December 9, 2006, p. A4; December 15, 2006; January 3, 2007; January 12, 2007; January 20, 2007; February 6, 2007, p. A9; March 29, 2007; August 29, 2007; October 6, 2007; November 18, 2007; May 3, 2010; May 24, 2010.
Time, October 16, 2006, p. 63.

Online

"Ban Ki Moon News," *New York Times,* http://topics.nytimes.com/topics/reference/timestopics/people/b/ban_ki_moon/index.html?scp=1&sq=ban%20ki%20moon&st=cse (June 2, 2010).
"Biography of Secretary-General Ban Ki-Moon," United Nations, http://www.un.org/sg/biography.shtml (June 2, 2010).

—*Vanessa E. Vaughn*

Melody Barnes

Brian Kersey/Getty Images

Director of White House Domestic Policy Council

Born Melody C. Barnes, April 29, 1964, in Richmond, VA; daughter of Charles (a military employee) and Mary Frances (a teacher and curriculum administrator) Barnes; married Marland Buckner Jr. (a political consultant), June 13, 2009. *Education:* University of North Carolina—Chapel Hill, B.A., 1986; University of Michigan, J.D., 1989.

Addresses: *Office*—Domestic Policy Council, The White House, 1600 Pennsylvania Ave. NW, Washington, DC 20500.

Career

Admitted to the New York State Bar Association, District of Columbia Bar Association; attorney, Shearman & Sterling, 1989-92; assistant counsel, U.S. House Judiciary Subcommittee on the Constitution, Civil Rights, and Civil Liberties, 1992-94; director of legislative affairs, U.S. Equal Employment Opportunity Commission, 1994-95; chief counsel to Senator Edward M. Kennedy of the Senate Judiciary Committee, 1995-2003; principal, Raben Group, 2003-04, June-October 2008; executive vice president for policy, Center for American Progress, 2004-08; senior domestic policy advisor, Obama for America, June-November 2008; co-director, Agency Review Working Group, Presidential Transition Team, November 2008-January 2009; director, White House Domestic Policy Council, 2009—.

Sidelights

Melody Barnes is a high-ranking White House official who came to the job with the new administration of U.S. President Barack Obama in 2009. An attorney, lobbyist, policymaker, and veteran of Democratic Party politics, she serves as director of Obama's Domestic Policy Council. That office works with the president to create agendas and initiatives on health care, energy, education, and other crucial issues.

Barnes was born in 1964 and grew up in the North Side section of Richmond, Virginia. Her father, Charles, was a civilian employee of the U.S. Army, and her mother was a teacher. The Richmond public schools Barnes attended in her early-elementary years belonged to a system still mired in a long and divisive battle over integration, and the first elementary school she attended was still an all-black school. Her high school was called Jefferson-Huguenot-Wythe and was created from a 1979 plan that merged seven of the city's high schools into three campuses.

After graduating from high school in 1982, Barnes entered the University of North Carolina at Chapel Hill, where she majored in history. Armed with her undergraduate degree, she won a place at the University of Michigan law school, which granted her a juris doctor (JD) in 1989. Like many newly minted Michigan law grads, she had her choice of several plum first-year associate jobs once she passed her bar exam, and chose to work in private practice in Manhattan. Three years later, she entered public service, and found a job in Washington as assistant counsel on the U.S. House Judiciary Subcommittee on the Constitution, Civil Rights, and Civil Liberties in 1992.

Two years later, Barnes was hired by the U.S. Equal Employment Opportunity Commission as its director of legislative affairs. That brought her to the attention of staffers in the office of U.S. Senator Edward M. (Ted) Kennedy, who chose her to serve as chief counsel for the Senate Judiciary Committee he chaired. Barnes held that job for the next eight years, which proved invaluable political training for a future White House job. In 2003, she left that post to become a political consultant with the Raben Group, a Washington lobbying firm. She moved on to a job as executive vice president for policy with the Center for American Progress, a Beltway think tank where for the next four years she drafted policy recommendations. Many of them focused on protecting the reproductive rights of American women and battling conservative policymakers' attempts to dismantle anti-poverty programs.

On the eve of U.S. President George W. Bush's seventh State of the Union address in 2007, Barnes wrote an op-ed piece that appeared on the Web site of the *Washington Post*. In it, she imagined what a "progressive" president might tell Americans in the annual address on his or her administration's efforts to solve various problems, such as the war in Iraq, a reliance on foreign oil, and a faltering economy. "The technologies necessary to dramatically transform our energy future are well within our reach," she imagined a more left-of-center leader might tell the country. "The potential for the United States to pursue a course of innovation that would create good, high-wage jobs has been largely abandoned, leaving our economy dangerously vulnerable to price shocks and upheavals that dampen economic growth and burden middle-class families with unpredictable gas and utility bills."

In June of 2008, Barnes accepted an offer from the Obama for America campaign to serve as a senior domestic policy advisor. This job entailed drafting a cohesive message for the candidate on the campaign trail, and putting in place an outline for new policies should he win the November election. After the momentous victory of election day in November,

Barnes joined the official transition team as co-director of the Agency Review Working Group. Twenty days after Obama's victory at the polls, the president-elect named her director of the Domestic Policy Council in the coming administration in January.

When Barnes first toured what would be her next office space, the hectic pace of the campaign and transition period finally halted for her as she sat in her new chair and realized, "Oh, my God, I'm working for the president of the United States in the West Wing of the White House," she recalled in an interview with *Richmond Times-Dispatch* writer Peter Bacque. Even before the administration took power, Barnes and other advisors were working behind the scenes with members of Congress to win support for Obama's economic stimulus plan, also known as the American Recovery and Reinvestment Act of 2009. After that $787 billion package went into effect, she and other White House staffers turned their focus to securing a new comprehensive health care bill.

In June of 2009, Barnes married Marland Buckner Jr., a political consultant whom she had known for several years. Their story was featured in the "Vows" column of the Sunday *New York Times*. The stress of the 2008 campaign had brought them closer together, she told the paper's Rachel L. Swarns, despite the long hours her job demanded. "He was supportive of me, through all of it," Barnes enthused about her new husband. "He's my friend, my home base, the person I love and trust, respect and admire completely."

Later that year, there was some grumbling about the pickup basketball games that Obama favors to relax with staffers; some pundits wondered if the rough-and-tumble style of play was preventing female associates, lobbyists, and legislators from gaining access to the president in such an informal setting. The president moved to remedy that perception by taking Barnes on a golf outing with another two men. It was a sport she had played for years with her father, she told *New York Times* columnist Maureen Dowd, reporting that she and her boss "gave each other a hard time and psyched each other out. It was all on the line on the 18th hole and I made a clutch putt and now I'm $10 richer."

Sources

Periodicals

New York Times, June 21, 2009; October 28, 2009.
Richmond Times-Dispatch, February 1, 2009.

Online

"Former Kennedy Counsel Will Head Domestic Policy," Politico.com, http://www.politico.com/news/stories/1108/15913.html (March 3, 2010).

"Melody Barnes's Semi-Endorsement Of Gay Marriage Causes Discomfort In White House," Huffington Post, http://www.huffingtonpost.com/2009/11/16/melody-barnes-semi-endors_n_359536.html (March 3, 2010).

"What a Progressive President Might Say," *Washington Post*, http://www.washingtonpost.com/wp-dyn/content/article/2007/01/19/AR20070119.tif01125.html (March 3, 2010).

—*Carol Brennan*

Jeff Beck

AP Images/Matt Sayles

Guitarist

Born Geoffrey Arnold Beck, June 24, 1944, in Wallington, Surrey, England; son of Arnold (an accountant) and Ethel (a chocolate factory worker) Beck; married Sandra Cush (an artist), 2005. *Education:* Attended Wimbledon Art College, London, England.

Addresses: *E-mail*—mail@jeffbeck.com. *Home*—Wadhurst, East Sussex, England. *Management*—Harvey Goldsmith, 13-14 Margaret St., London W1W 8RN, England. *Web site*—http://www.jeffbeck.com.

Career

Professional guitarist and recording artist; member of the Yardbirds, 1965-66; member of the Jeff Beck Group, 1967-69; member of Beck, Bogert & Appice, 1973-74. Performed and recorded as a solo artist, including: *Blow by Blow,* 1975; *Wired,* 1976; *There and Back,* 1980; *Flash,* 1985; *Jeff Beck's Guitar Shop,* 1989; *Frankie's House* (soundtrack), 1992; *Crazy Legs,* 1993; *Who Else!,* 1999; *You Had It Coming,* 2001; *Jeff,* 2003; *Performing This Week ... Live at Ronnie Scott's Jazz Club* (CD/DVD), 2008; *Emotion & Commotion,* 2010. Guest artist on numerous singles and albums, including: Stevie Wonder's *Talking Book,* 1972; Rod Stewart's *Camouflage,* 1984; Tina Turner's *Private Dancer,* 1984; Mick Jagger's *She's the Boss,* 1985 and *Primitive Cool,* 1987; Seal's *Seal,* 1994; Luciano Pavarotti's *Ti Adoro,* 2003; Herbie Hancock's *Imagine Project,* 2010.

Awards: Grammy Award for best rock instrumental performance, National Academy of Recording Arts and Sciences, for "Escape," 1985, (with others) *Jeff Beck's Guitar Shop,* 1989, "Dirty Mind," 2001, "Plan B," 2003, and "A Day in the Life," 2009; BAFTA Award for best original television music, British Academy of Film and Television Arts, for *Frankie's House,* 1992; inducted into Rock and Roll Hall of Fame as member of The Yardbirds, 1992, and as solo artist, 2009; Classic Rock Roll of Honour Award for outstanding contribution, *Classic Rock* Magazine, 2008.

Sidelights

Although guitarist Jeff Beck came to fame in the 1960s playing with the British group The Yardbirds, he never achieved the same commercial success as the group's other lead guitarists, blues-rock star Eric Clapton and heavy metal pioneer Jimmy Page of Led Zeppelin. Yet when his peers have been asked to name the best rock guitarists alive, Beck's name often heads the list. "When he's on, Beck's probably the best there is," Page told Andy Widders-Ellis in *Guitar Player,* while Clapton added: "There's something cool and mean about Becky that beats everyone else." Beck's explorations of the electric guitar's sound led him to record in a variety of genres, often on instrumental-only tracks. While this experimentation sometimes confounded radio programmers and casual listeners, it earned him the admiration of guitarists and critics. As Mikal Gilmore wrote in *Rolling Stone,* during the 1960s and 1970s Beck "was an archetypal figure: a resourceful, iconoclastic guitarist who helped mold and inform many of the rock-related movements ... including psychedelia, heavy metal, art rock, fusion and—yes—punk." In the 2000s Beck enjoyed a resurgence, earning three Grammys for Best Rock Instrumental and induction into the Rock and Roll Hall of Fame as a solo artist.

Beck was born in 1944 in Surrey, England, during the lean years of postwar Britain. Music was an important part of the family's life: his mother and older sister played classical piano, an uncle taught him violin and string bass, and his father collected jazz records. For his parents, "life was tense and music helped them forget about their troubles," the guitarist recalled on his Web site. "I'm sure that made an impression on me." He took piano for two years and sang in a church choir, but it was electric guitar inventor Les Paul's jazz-flavored country that "was the first music that really caught my attention," he recalled to Alan Clayson in *The Yardbirds.* He was also inspired by rockabilly guitarists like Buddy Holly and Cliff Gallup of Gene Vincent and His Blue Caps. He built his own guitar from a cigar box, a picture frame, and household wires. "I used to carry it around without a case so that everyone could see it," Widders-Ellis quoted him as saying. "It was bright yellow with all these wires and knobs; people just freaked out." Throughout the early 1960s Beck played with a series of blues bands, but whenever he fiddled around with his guitar's sound, "everyone would laugh and say, 'Play some proper blues.' There wasn't much room for experimentation," he told Clayson.

In early 1965 Beck got his chance to expand his musical horizons when his friend and fellow guitarist Page recommended him to the Yardbirds. The group was just about to hit the U.S. *Billboard* charts for the first time when lead guitarist Clapton left over musical differences. Beck agreed to replace him. "While Beck's stint with the band lasted only about 18 months, in this period he did more to influence the sound of '60s rock guitar than anyone except Jimi Hendrix," Richie Unterberger noted on the Web site AllMusic. While Clapton found the group's venture into pop a sellout, the critic added, Beck "saw such material as a challenge that offered room for unprecedented experimentation." His first single with the group, "Heart Full of Soul," pioneered the use of sounds from Eastern music, with Beck reproducing the sound of a sitar on his guitar. "Heart Full of Soul" was the first of five singles Beck performed with the Yardbirds—including "Over Under Sideways Down" and "Shapes of Things"—that became

Top 30 hits in America. His experimental sound "was what people wanted," the guitarist told Charles Shaar Murray in the *Independent.* "They didn't want to hear me play definitive blues, they wanted this nutter with this guitar doing these weird noises. And that was all right with me." The Yardbirds' constant touring proved too much for Beck, however, and he left the group during their 1966 American tour. "I was quite messed up," Beck told Clayson. "At 21, I was really on my last legs. I just couldn't handle it."

After hitting the British charts with three forgettable pop singles as a solo artist, Beck decided to get back to his roots with a new band. To form the Jeff Beck Group, he hired drummer Mickey Waller, bassist Ron Wood (who later joined the Rolling Stones), and then-unknown singer Rod Stewart. The group's first album, 1968's *Truth,* featured loud, guitar-solo-heavy versions of blues standards which set the template for later heavy metal bands, similar to what Page would later do with Led Zeppelin. The group embarked on a successful tour of the United States; at a gig in New York, "the audience were standing and cheering," Robert Shelton reported in the *New York Times.* "Beck and his band deal in the blues mostly, but with an urgency and sweep that is hard to resist." Beck often clashed with his bandmates, however, and broke up the group in 1969 before a scheduled appearance at the famous Woodstock Festival. "We were still breaking ground and doing our homework in bars and small venues, and even without the bad vibes in the band, I didn't think we could have pulled it off," he later revealed to Barry Cleveland in *Guitar Player.* "I just didn't think we were big-stage material."

A car accident in late 1969 left Beck sidelined for almost two years, recuperating from a fractured skull. Beck re-formed the Jeff Beck Group with new lineup, including a keyboard player. They recorded two moderately successful albums—the second, self-titled album hit the top 20 of *Billboard*'s album chart in 1972—but the players' musical styles did not gel and Beck disbanded the group. He began touring with former Vanilla Fudge bassist Tim Bogert and drummer Carmine Appice, and the trio's 1973 album *Beck, Bogert & Appice* was a precursor to modern heavy metal. Although it was Beck's best charting-album yet, hitting number 12, he was not happy with the group's musical direction or the quality of their vocals. "I was finished with that style long ago, but if you could zero in on the energy, you got the goods—otherwise, it was a cacophonous, nasty, horrible noise," he later told Clayson. "When we weren't fighting, we were playing trash."

For his next albums, Beck focused on all-instrumental pieces in a jazz-rock fusion style. He worked with George Martin, best-known as the Beatles' producer, for both 1975's *Blow by Blow* and 1976's *Wired*. *Blow by Blow* was Beck's best-selling album yet, with many critics considering it his masterpiece. On *Wired* Beck collaborated with keyboard master Jan Hammer and his band, playing new compositions as well as blues classics. "Many of Beck's older fans claim he's toned down to play this music, but listening closely, you can hear all the fire and imagination that has characterized every phase of his career," John Swenson wrote in *Rolling Stone*. "*Wired* is the realization of a style Beck has been working toward for years, and should finally attract the recognition he deserves." Despite the positive critical response, Beck released only one more studio recording over the next ten years, 1980's *There and Back*.

Beck returned in 1985 with his most pop-oriented album to date. Produced by Niles Rodgers, best known for working with artists like Chic and Madonna, Beck's *Flash* featured his only *Billboard* Hot 100 single, "People Get Ready," with vocals by Stewart. "*Flash* ranks as one of Beck's best ever, a record of awesome guitar prowess and startling commercial daring," David Fricke wrote in *Rolling Stone*. "It is also irrefutable proof that his kind of flash never goes out of fashion." The recording also brought Beck his first Grammy Award for Best Rock Instrumental Performance, for the Hammer composition "Escape." He won a second Grammy (with Terry Bozzio and Tony Hymas) for his 1989 album *Jeff Beck's Guitar Shop*, which returned to a harder-edged sound. "For technique and sheer creativity, Beck's artistry is unmatched since the heyday of Jimi Hendrix," David Hiltbrand wrote in a *People* review. Beck followed up the album with his first U.S. tour in years, performing with the late blues-rock guitarist Stevie Ray Vaughan. As *New York Times* contributor Jon Pareles wrote of the Madison Square Garden stop, Beck "still knows how to make notes sound hard-won—sustained and ethereal, then nasty or tearing—and when he stays with a melody ... it sounds as heartfelt as any vocalist could make it."

Beck spent the 1990s much as he had the previous decade: appearing on other artists' records, touring occasionally—in 1995 he appeared with Latin-rock guitarist Carlos Santana—and making whatever kinds of albums he pleased. In 1992 he worked with keyboardist Jed Leiber to compose his first film soundtrack. Beck used an eclectic mix of musical styles in scoring the television miniseries *Frankie's House*, which was set during the Vietnam War. For his 1993 album *Crazy Legs*, Beck recorded live with the Big Town Playboys to re-create the rockabilly songs of Gene Vincent and His Blue Caps, whose

lead guitarist, Cliff Gallup, was his childhood idol. "I stayed loyal to the solos because they're such fun to play. It's just my interpretation, as close as I can get," he told in Chris Gill in *Guitar Player*. The album was "my tribute to Cliff, and the dedication to learning to play his solos when I was 14," he added. While these two albums were his worst-selling to date, he had little concern: "If I had those [radio] hits, I would be sorely tempted to be lazy and just do those," he told Jerry Shriver in *USA Today*. "Probably that will never happen because it's just not in my nature. I can't think of anything more boring than being a live jukebox."

When Beck returned to recording with 1999's *Who Else!*, the musical chameleon had added elements of techno music to his style. "There's so many amazing sounds out there that we could never have dreamed of ten years ago—great processed drum loops that sound better than any drummer," he explained to Clay Marshall in *Billboard*. He used even more of these elements in 2001's *You Had It Coming*, sounding "comfortable melding his adventurous fret work with studio wizardry," according to Steve Futterman in *Entertainment Weekly*. The track "Dirty Mind" earned the guitarist a third Grammy for Best Rock Instrumental, and "Plan B" from 2003's *Jeff* brought him a fourth award. His constant musical experimentation, he told Lisa Sharken in *Guitar Player*, was not a deliberate choice; "it's just what I absorb through listening to things. It's a perpetual thing. The time between records enables me to become somebody else."

Beck spent much of the mid-2000s touring, including dates with blues legend B. B. King, and released three live albums. The DVD version of 2008's *Performing This Week ... Live at Ronnie Scott's Jazz Club* was certified platinum with one million in sales, while the CD version generated Beck's fifth Grammy Award, for his cover of the Beatles' "A Day in the Life." The renewed interest in Beck's work was reflected in his 2009 induction into the Rock and Roll Hall of Fame as a solo artist. "I couldn't believe I was even nominated," the guitarist told Andy Greene on the *Rolling Stone* Web site. "I thought the Yardbirds [being inducted in 1992] was as close as I'd get to getting in. I've gone on long after that and gone through different musical changes. It's very nice to hear that people have been listening."

Audiences were still listening in 2010 when Beck released *Emotion & Commotion*, his first album to land in *Billboard*'s Top 15 in 25 years. It was another change of style for Beck, who recorded jazz standards with vocalists and even operatic pieces with an orchestra. "There's no substitute for a full string orchestra," he told Stephen Wilmot in the *Financial Times*. "I was fulfilling a dream—I wanted to do it back in 1966, but couldn't afford it.... It's a beautiful sound that can only be achieved with acoustic instruments." "Like a great opera singer," Art Thompson noted in his *Guitar Player* review, "Beck delivers every note with such intense feeling that you may not even care that there isn't an abundance of ripping lead work here." Beck believed that he did not always have to produce fireworks on the guitar to appeal to an audience: "You reach people with the right notes in the right way," he told David Fricke in *Rolling Stone*. "Million-mile-an-hour chops leave me cold. Vocalists don't go dididididid. Why should guitars?" As he explained to Widders-Ellis, "Emotion rules everything I do. I can switch on automatic and play, but it sounds terrible. I've got to be wound up, in the right mood."

The inexhaustible Beck was up for five Grammys in early 2011: Best Pop Collaboration with Vocals (with others), for "Imagine," from *The Imagine Project*; Best Pop Instrumental Performance, for "Nessun Dorma," from *Emotion & Commotion*; Best Rock Performance by a Duo or Group (with Joss Stone), for "I Put a Spell On You," from *Emotion & Commotion*; Best Rock Instrumental Performance, for "Hammerhead," from *Emotion & Commotion*; and Best Rock Album, for *Emotion & Commotion*.

Despite his emphasis on musical emotion over pyrotechnics, Beck was known for his technical virtuosity as well as his ability to produce unusual sounds. This was despite his refusal to use a pick, as most electric guitarists do, a style he learned from listening to 1950s country records: "I just did it because I wanted to know how it was done, but I never thought I'd ever put that style into practice," he told Sharken. Eventually, he added, "I simply couldn't see the sense of wasting all of the other fingers by holding a pick between your thumb and first finger. The loss of the pick was a blessing in disguise, really." Although he has admitted to sometimes feeling overshadowed by other musicians' successes, he told Fricke that he keeps his mother's advice in mind: "Don't criticize anybody else until you know you can do better. And even then, don't do it." In the end, he told Ludovic Hunter-Tilney in the *Financial Times*, "I'm proud to say I have made a decent living without a singer. I don't know if it was selfishness or just the desire to retain individual quality, but I'm glad I did it."

The "decent" living Beck earned by making music his own way included a sixteenth-century manor house in the English countryside that he bought in 1971 and restored, as well as an extensive collection of classic cars he rebuilt himself. Even after more than 45 years of acclaim for his musicianship, he continued practicing his guitar every day, sometimes for hours at a time. "There's always something in the guitar which never ceases to amaze me, some sick sound that I never heard before," he told Sharken. "That's what my job is, really. It's not playing fantastic runs and trying to dazzle everybody, it's coming up with some little cheesy trick. This is rock and roll." For him, the music is about the guitar, not the guitarist: "You've got to admit that it has been a pretty remarkable instrument, the electric guitar, since the 1930s," he told Hunter-Tilney. "If I do nothing at all I'd be happy if someone saw me play and took the guitar up. Job's done, really."

Selected discography

(With the Yardbirds) *For Your Love* (compilation; contributor to three tracks), Magic, 1965.

(With the Yardbirds) *Having a Rave Up*, Epic, 1965.

(With the Yardbirds) *The Yardbirds* (UK release; also known as *Roger the Engineer*), Epic, 1966, released with two fewer tracks in U.S. as *Over Under Sideways Down*, Epic, 1966.

(With the Jeff Beck Group) *Truth*, Sony, 1968.

(With the Jeff Beck Group) *Beck-Ola*, Sony, 1969.

(With the Jeff Beck Group) *Rough & Ready*, Epic, 1971.

(With the Jeff Beck Group) *The Jeff Beck Group*, Epic, 1972.

(With Beck, Bogert & Appice) *Beck, Bogert & Appice*, Epic, 1973.

Blow by Blow, Legacy, 1975.

Wired, Epic, 1976.

(With the Jan Hammer Group) *Jeff Beck with the Jan Hammer Group Live*, Epic, 1977.

There and Back, Epic, 1980.

Flash, Epic, 1985.

Jeff Beck's Guitar Shop, Epic, 1989.

Beckology (compilation), Epic, 1991.

(With Jed Leiber) *Frankie's House* (soundtrack), Epic, 1992.

(With the Big Town Playboys) *Crazy Legs*, Epic, 1993.

Best of Beck (compilation), Epic, 1995.

Who Else!, Epic, 1999.

You Had It Coming, Epic, 2001.

Jeff, Epic, 2003.

Live at B. B. King's Blues Club & Grill, Sony, 2006.

Official Bootleg USA '06 (live album), Sony, 2007.

Performing This Week ... Live at Ronnie Scott's Jazz Club (CD/DVD), Eagle Records, 2008.

Emotion & Commotion, Atco, 2010.

Sources

Books

Carson, Annette, *Jeff Beck: Crazy Fingers*, Backbeat Books, 2001.
Clayson, Alan, *The Yardbirds*, Backbeat Books, 2002.

Periodicals

Billboard, January 27, 2001, p. 12.
Entertainment Weekly, February 9, 2001, p. 78.
Financial Times, March 27, 2010, p. 11; September 30, 2010.
Guitar Player, January 1992, p. 25; April 1993, p. 38; May 1999, p. 44; December 2000, p. 98; September 2003, p. 52; June 2010, p. 62.
Independent, September 8, 2002.
New York Times, June 15, 1968, p. 38; November 15, 1989, p. B3;

People, October 30, 1989, p. 19.
Rolling Stone, July 29, 1976; October 16, 1980, p. 17; July 18, 1985; April 1, 1993, p. 15; March 4, 2010, p. 34.
USA Today, April 13, 2010, p. 7B.

Online

"Jeff Beck Opens Up About Rock and Roll Hall of Fame, Gigs With Clapton, Jeff Beck Group Reunion," *RollingStone,* http://www.rollingstone.com/music/news/15765/90870 (October 21, 2010).
"The Official Online Biog: Jeff Beck," Jeff Beck Web site, http://www.jeffbeck.com/jeff-bio.php (October 21, 2010).
"The Yardbirds: Biography," AllMusic, http://www.allmusic.com/artist/the-yardbirds-p5888/biography (October 21, 2010).

—Diane Telgen

Regina Benjamin

Carrie Devorah/WENN/Newcom

U.S. Surgeon General

Born Regina Marcia Benjamin, October 26, 1956, in Mobile, AL; daughter of Clarence (a government employee) and Millie (a waitress) Benjamin. *Education:* Xavier University, B.S., 1979; attended Morehouse School of Medicine, Atlanta, GA, 1980-82; University of Alabama, M.D., 1984; Tulane University, M.B.A., 1991.

Addresses: *Office*—Office of the Surgeon General, 5600 Fishers Ln., Rm. 18-66, Rockville, MD 20857. *Web site*—http://www.surgeongeneral.gov/.

Career

Associate dean for rural health, University of South Alabama College of Medicine, 1980s; physician, National Health Service Corps, Irvington, AL, 1987-90; opened private practice in Bayou La Batre, AL, 1990; founder and chief executive officer, Bayou La Batre Rural Health Clinic, c. 1991; U.S. Surgeon General, 2009—; vice admiral, U.S. Public Health Service Commissioned Corps, 2010—.

Member: Board of trustees, American Medical Association, 1995-98; president, Medical Association of the State of Alabama, 2002; Institute of Medicine at the National Academy of Science; board, Robert Wood Johnson Foundation; board, Kaiser Commission on Medicaid and the Uninsured; board, Catholic Health Association; board, Morehouse School of Medicine.

Awards: National fellow, Kellogg Foundation, 1993-96; Nelson Mandela Award for Health and Human Rights, Henry J. Kaiser Family Foundation, 1998;

National Caring Award, Caring Institute, 2000; fellow, American Academy of Family Physicians; Pro Ecclesia et Pontifice (Papal Cross), Roman Catholic Church, 2006; fellow, John D. and Catherine T. MacArthur Foundation, 2008; next generation leader, Rockefeller Foundation.

Sidelights

Regina Benjamin's appointment to the post of U.S. Surgeon General in 2009 by President Barack Obama capped a career already rife with professional accolades. A family-practice physician in the small town of Bayou La Batre, Alabama, Benjamin had been lauded in media profiles as far back as 1995 for her devotion to her patients; moreover, her clinic had been twice wiped out by hurricanes, and then destroyed entirely by fire just months after Hurricane Katrina. In announcing Benjamin's name as the next surgeon general, Obama asserted that Benjamin "represents what's best about health care in America—doctors and nurses who give and care and sacrifice for the sake of their patients," according to the *New York Times*.

Benjamin was born in 1956 in Mobile, Alabama, and grew up across Mobile Bay in the town of Daphne on a plot of land her family held for generations.

Her parents divorced when she was a toddler, and her mother, Millie, supported Benjamin and her brother by working as a waitress. "I didn't know I was poor until someone in junior high told me I was," Benjamin recalled in an interview with *People*'s Christina Cheakalos. "I grew up fishing and crabbing, so we always had plenty of good food."

After graduating from high school in nearby Fairhope in 1975, Benjamin entered Xavier University, a Roman Catholic institution in New Orleans. Asked in one interview why she was drawn to medicine, Benjamin replied that it was almost accidental that she wound up in the school's pre-med program, admitting "I had never seen a black doctor before I went to college," to Bob Dart of the *Atlanta Journal-Constitution*. She earned her undergraduate degree in 1979 and went on to Morehouse School of Medicine in Atlanta, where "David Satcher taught me community medicine," she told Dart, referring to the professor who would become U.S. Surgeon General in 1998. "He would take us out to all these little towns in Georgia."

Benjamin finished her medical degree at the University of Alabama in Birmingham in 1984, and went on to a residency in family practice at the Medical Center of Central Georgia in Macon. Her medical school tuition had been paid in part by a scholarship from the National Health Service Corps, which requires newly certified doctors to work in a medically underserved community for three years. Benjamin was assigned to a clinic in Irvington, Alabama, near the border with Tennessee.

Once her Health Service Corps obligation ended, Benjamin turned down lucrative job offers from big-city hospitals to return to the Mobile Bay region in 1990. She settled in tiny Bayou La Batre, a town far from the tourist routes whose economy is reliant on the commercial fishing and shrimping industry. The population of 2,500 is a multiracial mix—about half white, and the other half black, Hispanic, or Vietnamese immigrants. About 80 percent of the community's residents live below the federal poverty line. Bayou La Batre's main claim to fame was as the location for some shrimping industry scenes in the 1994 box-office hit *Forrest Gump*. "This is a community where folks are too poor to afford medical care, but too rich to qualify for Medicaid," she told Cheakalos in *People*.

As a private-practice physician, Benjamin had a difficult time earning a living as the town's sole healthcare provider, and oftentimes accepted payment in oysters or other catch. She worked emergency-room shifts at Mobile hospitals to make ends meet, and completed an accelerated weekend M.B.A. program at Tulane University in New Orleans. She learned about a 1977 federal law that provided funding for rural health clinics that operated in medically underserved areas, and eventually turned her practice into a nonprofit clinic. She still struggled to provide adequate care for her patients, often paying for prescription medicine out of her own pocket.

In 1998, the Bayou La Batre Rural Health Clinic was demolished in Hurricane Georges. For two years Benjamin treated patients at home, or out of her Ford pickup truck. Finally, she was able to rebuild the clinic on much higher spot thought to be free from flooding danger. The site proved no match for Hurricane Katrina, which slammed the Gulf Coast in August of 2005. The clinic was ruined, and most of Bayou La Batre's residents lost their homes. For six weeks, Benjamin treated patients at a makeshift clinic set up on the stage of a community center that served as the town's emergency shelter. She and her staff managed to enter the clinic ruins, but it "stank of shrimp, fish, and old crab," she wrote in an op-ed piece for the *New York Times* as Katrina's one-year anniversary neared. "If we didn't strip down the building within 48 hours, we would further lose the structure to mildew, so we set about gutting the place, removing everything that had sat below the five-foot water line."

Benjamin and her staff finally obtained a trailer from the Federal Emergency Management Agency (FEMA), and she took out a mortgage on her home in order to build a new clinic. It was set to reopen on January 2, 2006, when it was destroyed by fire. The clinic was once again rebuilt later in 2006. Benjamin was nearing the two-decade anniversary of serving the community in the summer of 2009 when President Barack Obama announced her name as his candidate for the next U.S. Surgeon General. The post, which comes with an officer's commission in the United States Public Health Service Corps, has commonly been doled out to prominent researchers or public-health advocates; Obama's selection of a family-practice physician in a struggling rural community was deemed a symbolic gesture for a president who came to office on campaign pledges to bring access to health care for all Americans.

In interviews that followed her selection, confirmation, and swearing-in ceremony, Benjamin has often remarked that she had lost both parents, and her brother, to diseases that were preventable or nonfatal with proper care. She also faced some negative comments about her role as the nation's top public health official because of her size. "I am like 67 percent of Americans who struggle with their weight," she said in response to detractors in an interview with Cynthia Gordy of *Essence*. "I know what it's like to be overly stressed, working two or three jobs.... I bring a sense of empathy and understanding when we're trying to implement health and exercise programs. Having gone through it gives me more credibility."

Sources

Periodicals

Atlanta Journal-Constitution, June 4, 2006, p. A1.
Ebony, March 1997, p. 86.
Essence, May 2010, p. 126.
New York Times, April 3, 1995; August 27, 2006; July 14, 2009.
People, May 13, 2002, p. 219.
USA Today, January 14, 2010, p. 8D.

Transcripts

All Things Considered, National Public Radio, January 7, 2006.

—*Carol Brennan*

Kathryn Bigelow

Andrew H. Walker/Getty Images

Film director, producer, and screenwriter

Born Kathryn Ann Bigelow, on November 27, 1951, in San Carlos, CA; married James Cameron (a film director), August 17, 1989 (divorced, 1991). *Education:* San Francisco Art Institute, BFA, 1972; studied at the Whitney Museum, New York, NY, 1972; Columbia University, MFA, 1979.

Addresses: *Agent*—Creative Artists Agency, 2000 Avenue of the Stars, Los Angeles, CA 90067.

Career

Film work includes: director, *The Set Up* (short), 1978; script supervisor, *Union City,* 1980; co-director and co-screenwriter, *The Loveless,* 1982; director and screenwriter, *Near Dark,* 1987; director and screenwriter, *Blue Steel,* 1989; director, *Point Break,* 1991; director, *Strange Days,* 1995; director, *Weight of Water,* 2000; producer and director, *K-19: The Widowmaker,* 2002; director, *Mission Zero,* 2007; producer and director, *The Hurt Locker,* 2008. Television work includes: director, *Wild Palms* (miniseries), 1993; writer, *Undertow* (movie), 1996; director of "Fallen Heroes: Parts 1 and 2," *Homicide: Life on the Streets,* NBC, 1998; director, "Lines of Fire," *Homicide: Life on the Streets,* NBC, 1999; director, "He Was a Friend of Mine," *Karen Sisco,* 2004. Film appearances include: *Born in Flames,* 1983. Began career as an artist, c. early 1970s-mid-80s; also directed music video for "Touched by the Hand of God," by New Order, 1987.

Awards: Silver Raven Award, Brussels International Festival of Fantasy Film, for *Near Dark,* 1988; Saturn Award for best director, Academy of Science Fic-

tion, Fantasy & Horror Films, for *Strange Days,* 1996; Film and Literature Award, Film by the Sea International Film Festival, for *The Weight of Water,* 2000; Human Rights Film Network Award, Venice Film Festival, for *The Hurt Locker,* 2008; SIGNIS Award, Venice Film Festival, for *The Hurt Locker,* 2008; Sergio Trasatti Award, Venice Film Festival, for *The Hurt Locker,* 2008; Young Cinema Award for best film, Venice Film Festival, for *The Hurt Locker,* 2008; Andrew Sarris Award, Columbia University Film Festival, for *The Hurt Locker,* 2009; Dallas Star Award, AFI Dallas International Film Festival, for *The Hurt Locker,* 2009; Austin Film Critics Award for best director, for *The Hurt Locker,* 2009; Boston Society of Film Critics Award for best director, for *The Hurt Locker,* 2009; Chicago Film Critics Association Award for best director, for *The Hurt Locker,* 2009; Golden Space Needle Award for best director, Seattle International Film Festival, for *The Hurt Locker,* 2009; Gotham Award (with others) for best film, Independent Film Project (IFP), for *The Hurt Locker,* 2009; Hollywood Film Award for director of the year, Hollywood Film Festival, 2009; Los Angeles Film Critics Association Award for best director, for *The Hurt Locker,* 2009; New York Film Critics Circle Award for best director, for *The Hurt Locker,* 2009; Satellite Award for best director, International Press Academy, for *The Hurt Locker,* 2009; Sierra Award for best director, Las Vegas Film Critics Society, for

The Hurt Locker, 2009; Southeastern Film Critics Association Award for best director, for *The Hurt Locker,* 2009; Toronto Film Critics Association Award for best director, for *The Hurt Locker,* 2009; Washington DC Area Film Critics Association Award, for *The Hurt Locker,* 2009; Tribute Award, Gotham Film Awards, IFP, 2009; Triumph Award for Outstanding Directing, ShoWest Convention, 2009; Academy Award for best achievement in directing, Academy of Motion Picture Arts and Sciences, for *The Hurt Locker,* 2010; Academy Award (with others) for best motion picture of the year, Academy of Motion Picture Arts and Sciences, for *The Hurt Locker,* 2010; ALFS Award for director of the year, London Critics Circle, for *The Hurt Locker,* 2010; BAFTA Film Award for best director, British Academy of Film and Television Arts, for *The Hurt Locker,* 2010; BAFTA Film Award (with others) for best film, British Academy of Film and Television Arts, for *The Hurt Locker,* 2010; Best Director Award, Santa Barbara International Film Festival, for *The Hurt Locker,* 2010; Broadcast Film Critics Association Award for best director, for *The Hurt Locker,* 2010; Directors Guild of America Award (with others), for outstanding directorial achievement in motion pictures, for *The Hurt Locker,* 2010; Kansas City Film Critics Circle Award for best director, for *The Hurt Locker,* 2010; Motion Picture Producer of the Year Award (with others) for theatrical motion picture, Producers Guild of America, for *The Hurt Locker,* 2010; National Society of Film Critics Award for best director, for *The Hurt Locker,* 2010; Online Film Critics Society Award for best director, for *The Hurt Locker,* 2010; Vancouver Film Critics Circle Award for best director, for *The Hurt Locker,* 2010.

Sidelights

In 2010, Kathryn Bigelow became the first woman to win a best director honor at the Academy Awards for her tense war drama, *The Hurt Locker.* She won numerous other honors for the film as well, including the best director award from the Directors Guild of America, which marked the first time a woman won that award as well. After beginning her career as an artist, Bigelow launched her directing career in 1978 and also wrote numerous screenplays for her films. Many of her films challenged the genre of which they were a part as well as gender stereotypes. Discussing her perspective on filmmaking with Dave Gardetta of the *Washington Post,* she spoke of "rules that are meant to be broken, boundaries that are meant to be invaded, envelopes meant to be pushed, preconceptions challenged." Among her other best known works are *Point Break, Strange Days,* and *K-19: The Widowmaker.*

Born on November 27, 1951, in San Carlos, California, she was the daughter and only child of a paint factory manager father and librarian mother. Raised in the rural community of San Carlos, she had an ideal childhood and grew up making art. She was perhaps inspired by her father who drew cartoons and wanted to be a cartoonist, but never achieved his goal. By the age of 14, she was already showing a keen interest in detail in painting. For example, Bigelow blew up small images culled from canvases of painters like Raphael and Rembrandt and painted them on 12-by-12-foot canvases. She began her post-high school education at the San Francisco Art Institute, where she studied painting for two years, graduating in 1972.

After winning a scholarship to the Independent Study Program at the Whitney Museum, Bigelow moved to New York City. There, she worked on her art in a studio located in a vault of a former Offtrack Betting building. She was influenced by French critics like Guy Debord, Jacques Lacan, and Jean Baudrillard, and interested in potentiality. Her work received the critical attention of such luminaries as Richard Serra, Robert Rauschenberg, and Susan Sontag. Of this time in her life, she told Jamie Diamond of the *New York Times,* "You were constantly thinking, what statement am I trying to make? And then Susan Sontag would come in and ask you the same question and you'd go, now wait a minute, I thought I had a logic for this." In this time period, Bigelow also became involved with the Art and Language group, a somewhat radical avant garde cultural/conceptual group, and served as an editor of *Semiotext (e),* a theoretical journal.

Over the years, Bigelow realized that while painting was fascinating for her, it left her isolated and aware of its elitism. She became interested in film, with all its socially equalizing potential. As her interest shifted to film, Bigelow entered Columbia University's graduate film school, where she studied scholarship and criticism with acclaimed director Milos Forman. The first film Bigelow directed, *The Set Up,* was a short released in 1978. The 20-minute-long film featured two men beating each other up while another person reads an essay on the character of violence. Bigelow then co-wrote and co-directed 1982's arty *The Loveless* with Monty Montgomery. The film told the story of bikers attacking a small town, an early indicator in a career-long interest in the action genre.

Leaving New York City for Hollywood in 1983, Bigelow wanted a career as a mainstream film director and soon landed a development deal. Her first solo feature film drew much attention. *Near Dark,* which she both wrote and directed, was released in 1987 by the De Laurentiis Entertainment Group shortly before the company went under. The film was a modern-day western, set in Oklahoma, which had elements of horror and centered around a blood-craving vampire family. Bigelow declined to call them vampires per se—as she avoided any mention of vampire cliches—and tried to play with the horror genre by eliminating the gothic elements to make *Near Dark* unconventional. Critics and audiences called a sequence in which the family took over a roadhouse and sucked the blood of its patrons both squeamish and enjoyable.

Discussing *Near Dark* and its genre, Bigelow explained to the *Washington Post*'s Gardetta, "The nice thing with a genre like horror is that it's a definite grid on which to hang a piece and give the audience a familiarity before you kind of subvert it. In the case of *Near Dark*, I was interested in this sort of marginal ad hoc family unit doing no more than trying to survive as any family unit will do. They're not like serial killers or someone killing for pleasure; they're killing for survival. And so I kept thinking of them as this marginal family structure—I wanted to see how they could function in an alternative universe."

Bigelow gained more fame—and controversy—for her next film, 1989's *Blue Steel*. She both wrote and directed the thriller, which focused on a female cop (played by Jamie Lee Curtis) falling in love with a killer. Bigelow faced resistance in part because a woman was at the center of the story. She explained her inspiration to Clifford Terry of the *Oregonian*, saying "Very simply, I wanted to make a women's action film. I'd seen it in a science fiction context, I'd seen it the context of comedy, but I'd never seen it in an action film."

Another aspect of *Blue Steel* which would become a hallmark of Bigelow's films was creative casting. She told the *Oregonian*'s Terry, "I also love to cast against type. Ever since Sergio Leone cast Henry Fonda as this man who shoots this eight-year-old kid in the face, that was it for me. That's when I said, 'Yeah.' So in *Blue Steel*, I cast Ron Silver, who's always been this kind of charming comedian, as the killer...." Bigelow followed *Blue Steel* with 1991's *Point Break*. The surf heist/police thriller starred Keanu Reeves and Patrick Swayze.

Bigelow received more attention for *Strange Days*, released in 1995. The futuristic noir film starred Ralph Fiennes as Lenny Nero, a former Los Angeles vice squad cop who worked on the black market selling what was known as "playback," a type of virtual reality experience sold on compact disc and offering users any sensation. He drew the line, how-

ever, at dealing "blackjack" (a product similar to snuff films), but unintentionally viewed the rape and murder of his friend, a prostitute named Iris, through a playback. The experience profoundly changed him and disturbed viewers. As she told Diamond of the *New York Times*, "There's a reflexive element in *Strange Days*. The spectacle is both medium and subject."

It was five years before Bigelow released another film, but she did work in television while developing her next project. She wrote a television movie, *Undertow*, which aired in 1996. She also directed several episodes of the Baltimore-set cop series, *Homicide: Life on the Streets*, which aired in 1998 and 1999. Her next film as a director, the little-seen *Weight of Water*, was released in 2000.

Bigelow followed *Weight of Water* with 2002's *K-19: The Widowmaker*, which she both produced and directed. Based on a real incident, the film starred Harrison Ford as the captain of a Russian submarine which carried nuclear missiles. The Russians nearly started a nuclear war by accident when a nuclear reactor on the submarine started melting down. Bigelow told the story from a Russian perspective and emphasized the courage and humanity of the men aboard. Of her interest in the story, she explained to Sandy MacDonald and Marla Cranston of the *Halifax Daily News*, "I just thought *K-19* was a profoundly interesting and intriguing story. It was an opportunity to put a human face on a culture we weren't exposed to during the Cold War, and it gave us an opportunity to look at ourselves through the eyes of the 'enemy.'"

After *K-19*, Bigelow directed the short film *Mission Zero*, which starred Uma Thurman and was released in 2007. She received the most acclaim of her career with her next film, *The Hurt Locker*, seen on the film festival circuit in 2008 and reaching American theaters in the spring of 2009. Set in at the beginning of the Iraq War of the early 2000s, *The Hurt Locker* focused on bomb technicians who dismantled the roadside IEDs planted by insurgents. At the center of the film was a maverick tech Sergeant James (played by Jeremy Renner), who shed his protective gear and took what some might consider unnecessary chances as he went about his sometimes-deadly duties. Bigelow shot the film in Jordan near the Iraq border, adding to the film's authenticity and power.

Discussing the character of James, Jennie Yabroff of *Newsweek* wrote that he "evokes iconic images of American masculinity.... But Bigelow sees the character less as a commentary on popular images of masculinity and more as an exploration of the modern hero. While exemplary at his job, James can barely function in noncombat zones." Bigelow told Yabroff, "He's evocative of a kind of John Wayne type, but updated to accommodate the complexities of this character, who is almost attracted to the world's most dangerous job." Bigelow concluded, "War's dirty little secret is that some men love it. I'm trying to unpack why, to look at what it means to be a hero in the context of 21st-century combat."

The Hurt Locker received some of the best reviews of Bigelow's career, though the film barely made back its $15 million budget. However, during the Hollywood awards season, the film was consistently nominated and received major awards. In addition to receiving several best film honors as a producer, Bigelow was given numerous awards for best director. Her wins at the Directors Guild of America Awards and the Academy Awards marked the first time a woman won each award. When Bigelow won the Oscar, she said, according to Carrie Rickey of the *Philadelphia Inquirer,* "This really is—there's no other way to describe it—the moment of a lifetime." Bigelow also dedicated her Oscar "to the women and men in the military who risk their lives on a daily basis.... May they come home safe."

Talking about her directing career as a whole as well as the doors that opened for her more easily than other female directors, Bigelow told Diamond of the *New York Times,* "I know that power is never given, only seized, and you have to decide to seize it and do it. But there is no formula. At 20, I was in the Whitney Museum with these chrome tubes. I could have gone in a myriad of directions. On the other hand, the only thing I was determined to do, ever since I was a child, was to make art."

Sources

Periodicals

Halifax Daily News (Nova Scotia, Canada), July 19, 2002, p. 25.
Los Angeles Times, December 23, 2009, p. S12.
Newsweek, June 29, 2009, p. 64.
New York Times, October 22, 1995, sec. 2, p. 13.
Oregonian (Portland, OR), April 10, 1990, p. C2.
Philadelphia Inquirer, March 8, 2010.
San Francisco Chronicle, July 19, 2002, p. D4.
Washington Post, October 17, 1995, p. C1.

Online

"Kathryn Bigelow," Internet Movie Database, http://www.imdb.com/name/nm0000941/ (March 8, 2010).

—A. Petruso

Patrick Blanc

Vittorio Zunino Celotto/Getty Images Entertainment/Getty Images

Botanist

Born June 3, 1953, in Paris, France; partner of Pascal Héni (a singer). *Education:* Universitè Pierre et Marie Curie, junior doctorate (*doctorat de troisième cycle*), 1978, Ph.D., 1989.

Addresses: *Home*—Crèteil, France. *Office*—Centre national de la recherche scientifique (CNRS), 3, rue Michel-Ange, 75794 Paris, France.

Career

Research scientist, National Center for Scientific Research, Paris, France, 1982—.

Sidelights

French botanist Patrick Blanc conceived a novel way to grow plants vertically, without soil, to achieve stunning effects on a monumental, often multistory scale. His *murs végétal,* or plant walls, have been installed in museums, luxury retail centers, and at other sites around the globe and have made Blanc a household name in France—and a cult figure for fans of "green" buildings worldwide. "Humanity is living more and more in cities, and at odds with nature," the scientist and designer explained to *New York Times* writer Kristin Hohenadel. "The plant wall has a real future for the well-being of people living in cities. The horizontal is finished—it's for us. But the vertical is still free."

Blanc was born in 1953 in Paris, and his fascination with nontraditional plants stretched back to his childhood: he had a fish aquarium, and was capti-

vated by the plants that were able to thrive inside of it despite the lack of soil. In his early teens, he began experimenting with philodendrons and rhododendrons, both hardy flowering plants, training them to grow vertically on a garden wall onto which he had constructed a mesh frame. His curiosity about plants that needed little soil or sunlight to grow led him to the study of botany in college, and he traveled to places like Malaysia and Thailand in the early 1970s to research flora that flourished on rocky terrain or under dense rainforest canopies. In 1978, he earned a junior doctorate from Paris' Universitè Pierre et Marie Curie (UPMC), the leading center of science education in France. The UPMC is also affiliated with the *Centre national de la recherche scientifique,* the country's esteemed National Center for Scientific Research, and Blanc began working as a researcher there in the early 1980s. He earned his doctorate in botany in 1989 with a dissertation on forest undergrowth in the tropics.

Blanc trademarked his *mur végétal,* or plant wall, in 1988, and showed it at Paris' Museum of Science and Industry that same year. He perfected the methods over the next few years to create a vertical garden at the 1994 International Garden Festival in Chaumont-sur-Loire, France, which caused a minor sensation and garnered a great deal of press. Paris city officials commissioned him to create one for a botanical garden in the city, and that led to collaborations with the architect Jean Nouvel for high-profile new buildings. One of the first was for the Cartier Foundation for Contemporary Art, a contemporary art museum in Paris where Blanc's vertical garden adorns the façade above the entrance.

There are many species of climbing plants, like ivy, but in some cases their root systems work their way into the actual building structure and can pull apart mortar and cement over the years. "Blanc devised a system in the 1990s that helps prevent that damage," explained Sonia Kolesnikov-Jessop in the *New York Times*. "A heavy-duty PVC sheet is riveted to a building's metal frame, adding rigidity to the structure and making it waterproof, while a felt layer made of polyamide is fixed to the PVC and acts as a water distributor, with the roots growing on the felt, without soil."

Blanc's creations are fed by a nutrient solution of dissolved minerals that runs through the pipe system. They are designed to last at least three decades, and many of the ones installed in the late 1990s or early '00s were still thriving a decade later. "People often have a hard time understanding that by using materials which are not biodegradable, it allows biology to install itself, and to last," he told Hohenadel in the *New York Times* interview. His novel green installations have been commissioned by the Marithè & François Girbaud retail chain; the Aquarium in Genoa, Italy; the 21st Century Museum of Contemporary Art in Kanazawa, Japan; and the Musèe de Quai Branly, a museum of indigenous arts in Paris. This last vertical garden is an especially noteworthy one: Nouvel was the project's chief architect and gave Blanc the task of creating the outside walls of the museum's administrative building. At more than 8,000 square feet and filled with 15,000 species of plants from around the world, the structure appears to be constructed entirely from plants.

Two of the largest *murs végétal* Blanc has created are in London; one is at the Athenaeum Hotel, which is an eight-story outdoor wall, and the other is at Westfield London, a major shopping center in the Shepherd's Bush neighborhood. In 2008 Blanc's first English-language book, *The Vertical Garden: From Nature to the City*, was published by W. W. Norton. He began to take commissions further afield, including one for a private academy in San Francisco, and a renovation at the luxury Emporium Shopping Centre in Bangkok, Thailand.

Blanc is a highly regarded figure in France and appears frequently in the media to comment on environmental design topics. Often described as an artistic visionary as well as a scientist, he is almost always photographed wearing green-hued apparel, and sports green highlights in his hair as well as a two-inch-long thumbnail enameled in a shade of particularly verdant green. His home in Crèteil, near Paris, contains several examples of his work as well as pet birds that fly freely overhead. He also shares it with his partner, Pascal Héni, the singer known as Pascal of Bollywood. Blanc hopes to one day bring his unique installations to places outside of the world of high-end retail spaces and luxury hotels, imagining plant walls installed at the high-rise housing projects outside Paris, for example, that have been a source of much social unrest. "No matter where you are in the world, people live more and more in towns," he theorized in an interview with *Design Week* writer Natasha Edwards. "People are increasingly cut off from nature, but, at the same time, we talk more and more about the problems of nature and the environment.... I think the planted walls bring a little optimism when you realise that, despite the setting, where nature has been most modified you can reintroduce not just nature, but an enormous diversity of species into the city."

Selected writings

Le mur végétal: de la nature à la ville, Editions Michel Lafon (Neuilly-sur-Seine, France), 2008, translated into English and published as *The Vertical Garden: From Nature to the City*, W. W. Norton (New York City), 2008.

Sources

Periodicals

Design Week, February 15, 2007, p. 13.
New York Times, May 3, 2007; May 27, 2010.

Online

Patrick Blanc Official Web site, http://www.murvegetalpatrickblanc.com/#/en/home (August 3, 2010).
"Redefining the Urban Jungle," *BusinessWeek Online*, http://www.businessweek.com/globalbiz/content/oct2006/gb20061004.tif_381966.htm (July 30, 2010).

—Carol Brennan

Amy Bloom

Author and psychotherapist

Born June 18, 1953, in New York, NY; daughter of Murray (a journalist and author) and Sydelle (a writer, teacher, and group therapist) Bloom; married Donald Moon (a professor), August 21, 1977 (divorced, 1993); married second husband (an architect), c. 2007; children: Alexander (stepson; first marriage), Caitlin, Sarah. *Education:* Wesleyan University, B.A., 1975; Smith College, M.S.W., 1978.

Addresses: *Agent*—William Morris Endeavor Entertainment, 1325 Avenue of the Americas, New York, NY 10019. *Office*—Random House, 1745 Broadway, New York, NY 10019. *Web site*—http://www.amybloom.com/.

Career

Private psychotherapy practice, Middletown, CT, 1981-c. 2007; began writing fiction, c. 1988; published first story in a Western Canadian feminist journal, 1991; published first short story collection, *Come to Me,* 1993; published first novel, *Love Invents Us,* 1996; served as judge for National Book Awards, 1996; writer and executive producer on *State of Mind,* c. 2007; published third novel *Where the God of Love Hangs Out,* 2010. Also taught at Yale and Smith College; contributed to periodicals including *Vogue, New Yorker,* and *Harper's Bazaar.*

Awards: O. Henry Award, for "Semper Fidelis," 1994.

Sidelights

Award-winning author Amy Bloom spent more than two decades working as a psychotherapist. Her fiction focused on the complexities and humor in interpersonal relationships, especially those of a sexual and romantic nature. Bloom was lauded by critics for her insights as an author and the well-designed nature of her prose. As Kate Medina, Bloom's editor at Random House, explained to Beth Brophy of *U.S. News & World Report,* "She can say more in less space than anyone I know. She tells the unvarnished truth, written with generosity and wisdom. People get tired of a whitewash." Critic Ron Charles believed Bloom was a gifted author. He wrote in the *Washington Post Book World,* "Bloom writes with extraordinary care about people caught in emotional and physical crosswinds: desires they can't satisfy, illnesses they can't survive, and—always—love that exceeds the boundaries of this world."

Born on June 18, 1953, in New York City, she was the daughter of Murray and Sydelle Bloom. Her father worked as a finance journalist and author while her mother was a magazine writer, teacher, and group therapist. Raised in Great Neck, Long Island, she received her education at Wesleyan College from which she earned her B.A. in 1975. She worked as a waitress as a young adult, and once studied theater, trained to become an actress, and worked in professional theater for several years. After marrying Donald Moon in 1977, she completed an M.S.W. at Smith College in 1978 and trained as a psychotherapist.

In 1981, Bloom opened a private psychotherapy practice in Middleton, Connecticut, but it was not her only professional focus. She began writing fiction the late 1980s, and initially focused on mysteries. Bloom explained to Valerie Takahama of the *Orange County Register*, "I understood how the rules work, and I thought I could probably master them. Inadequately, as it turned out." Bloom found her voice while writing short stories, and her first story was published in a Western Canadian feminist journal in 1991. She received $35 for her efforts. Her stories were soon being published regularly and included in anthologies like the *Best American Short Stories, 1991* and *Best American Short Stories, 1992.*

As Bloom began publishing, she did not find her training, work, and experiences as a therapist particularly impacted her writing; however, she did admit there was a connection between being a writer and a therapist as both focused on relationships. Bloom told Takahama of the *Orange County Register*, "I think that's the stuff that is interesting to me. What's interesting to me is people. What connects them and what divides them and how they tell the story of their lives and how we keep changing the story as we go along."

In 1993 Bloom published her first collection of short stories, *Come to Me*. The 12 stories included in *Come to Me* primarily focus on interpersonal relationships. For example, "Love Is Not a Pie" is about a young woman named Ellen who reflects on the realization that her recently deceased mother had a lover during her childhood and that her fiancée might not be the right man for her. "The Sight of You" also focuses on an affair as the married Henry DiMartino has a meaningful affair with Galen Nichols. He wants her to leave her husband, David, and for them to combine their families as Henry plans on seeking custody of his children. Galen imagining what her life would be like with Henry compels her to end the affair. Another story, "Silver Water," concerns Galen's unconditional love of her two daughters.

Reviewers lauded *Come to Me*, with Margaret Camp noting in the *Washington Post* that the stories "are like reconnaissance missions into the land of pos-

sible human relationships: They're fast, there's a lot of information to gather, it can be dangerous, and we're not always sure why we're there." Camp added, "Each is provocative and uniquely unconventional—some disturbingly so—emphasizing the psychological." In the *New York Times*, Margo Jefferson wrote, "At the end of *Dora: Analysis of a Case of Hysteria*, Freud writes of the flight into disease, and then of being 'reclaimed by the realities of life.' Claiming and being claimed by those realities is Amy Bloom's text: the realities of anger, sorrow, lust; of blind love, lame love, and halt love; of old love, new love—even true love."

Come to Me was nominated for a National Book Award in 1993. Bloom was one of five finalists for the honor, though its prominent status in the literary circle was lost on her. She told the *Orange County Register*'s Takahama, "I was delighted, but to be honest, I didn't know what it meant because this is not my world. I hardly knew about it." The following year, Bloom won an O. Henry Award for her story "Semper Fidelis."

In 1996 Bloom published her first novel, *Love Invents Us*, using the main character from the titular short story "Come to Me." The novel focuses on the life of Elizabeth Taub, from her affluent but empty childhood with indifferent parents, to her life as a suburban mother in her forties as she tries to locate love and make a family. Because her parents are distant and selfish, Elizabeth is forced to find affirmation elsewhere in school and through friendships with furrier Mr. Klein and an ill African-American woman named Mrs. Hill. Elizabeth also has an affair with her English teacher, Max Stone, beginning when she is 15 years old, and becomes romantically involved with a black basketball player at her school, Huddie Lester, who becomes her first boyfriend. While her relationships with these two men last for years, she conceives a child with the teacher's son and moves to the suburbs, and seems to have re-connected with Huddie.

While critics praised *Love Invents Us* and Bloom's skill as a writer, they found some flaws in the book, including the jarring shifts in perspective and an ending that many believed did not do the story justice. Still, Alicia Metcalf Miller of the Cleveland *Plain Dealer* called it "an almost spectacular first novel" and "an endearing story, both sweet and tough." Miller also noted "Her humor is shrewd, her insights luminous, her descriptions of physical passion arresting and rare." Some critics were bothered by the way Bloom drew Elizabeth, with Dolores Flaherty and Roger Flaherty of the *Chicago Sun-Times* writing, "she is a victim who continues to be compulsively amoral. She talks in a knowing manner about her past, but doesn't seem to learn anything from it."

By this time period, Bloom was also contributing a monthly sex advice column to *New Woman* magazine. The column was popular with the magazine's readers for its uncompromising, literate nature. She also contributed fiction to prestigious periodicals like the *New Yorker* and nonfiction to publications like *Vogue* and *Harper's Bazaar.* In addition, Bloom served as a judge for the National Book Awards in 1996. She and four other writers picked the finalists and winner in the fiction category from 250 novel and short-story submissions.

Bloom published her second short-story collection in 2000, *A Blind Man Can See How Much I Love You.* Lauded by critics, it was nominated for a National Book Critics Circle Award. The stories in *A Blind Man* are again primarily focused on interpersonal relationships but were more carefully composed and showed her growth as a writer. The titular story, for example, explored the complex relationship between a mother, Jane Spencer, and her daughter Jessie, as Jessie undergoes gender re-assignment surgery and the changes it causes in both of their lives. Two stories, "Night Vision" and "Light Into Dark," focus on the similarly complicated characters of Lionel and Julia. Julia is a white woman who is 21 years older than the African-American man Lionel, and was once his stepmother until the death of his father. Soon after his father's death they slept together, though the incident was long ago. One story focuses on how they will manage through a Thanksgiving dinner and how Lionel deals with memory.

Reviewing *A Blind Man Can See How Much I Love You,* Janet Maslin of the *New York Times* wrote, "Exotic intimacies color the sharply wrought tales in Amy Bloom's fine new collection. And they reveal themselves hauntingly as these tales unfold." Maslin also noted, "In a set of stories whose characters find themselves bridging various chasms—medical, sexual, racial—and casually breaking assorted taboos, Ms. Bloom writes warmly and astutely, with arresting precision, about the various adjustments that they make." Other critics, like Jere Real of the *Richmond Times Dispatch,* praised the wit Bloom imbued in her stories. Real commented, "the author [is] a perceptive observer who can combine a delineating understanding with a subtle sense of humor."

Bloom continued her psychotherapy practice for part of the early 2000s, taught at Yale, and spent a lot of time writing. In 2002, she published her first collection of nonfiction, *Normal: Transsexual CEOs, Crossdressing Cops, and Hermaphrodites with Attitude.* The tome was originally intended to be essays for the *New Yorker* but became 130 pages of character sketches and anecdotes that reveal much about the author. Many of her observations were considered insightful and observant, and focus primarily on hermaphrodites, cross-dressers, and transsexuals. Bloom writes about their lives and what she sees when she meets them in various life contexts. As Eric Hanson wrote in the Minneapolis *Star Tribune,* "At the core of *Normal* is Bloom's belief that normality doesn't exist, as much as some people might wish it otherwise." Hanson generally praised the book, noting "Bloom's storytelling talent is as obvious in these real-life stories as it is in her fiction, and her ear for dialogue is just as keen when the words are someone else's."

After *Normal,* Bloom published two best-selling books in three years. In 2007, she published her second novel, *Away.* Unlike much of her previous work, this novel is set in the past and is a story about an immigrant to the United States. Lillian Leyb, a young Jewish woman, immigrates from oppressive conditions in Russia in the mid-1920s that contributed to the murder of her entire family, to find a better life in New York City. There, she does whatever she has to survive and fit in, including learning English and pretending to be the mistress of her employer's gay son. Lillian's new life changes when she learns that her presumed-dead three-year-old daughter Sophie could still be alive in Russia. Lillian endures horrible circumstances, including sexual exploitation, as she travels west across the United States to reach the Bering Strait and cross into Soviet Russia, ready to give up her new life to find her daughter. As Ron Charles wrote in the *Washington Post Book World,* "Throughout this breathless story, Bloom blends her voice with her heroine's to create a deeply sympathetic narrative that's analytical but always inflected with Lillian's fervor."

In 2010, Bloom published the short-story collection, *Where the God of Love Hangs Out,* which included both new and previously published work. It again focuses on love relationships between people and the fallout of their actions or lack thereof. The erotic, often explicit, stories looked at people in their moments of heartbreak and wince-worthy behavior. Critics like Francine du Plessix Gray of the *New York Times* noted "The upbeat sassiness of tone is one of the many treasures of Bloom's new collection, which differs markedly from her previous ones...." In the four interconnected stories, for example, William and Clare are two imperfect friends/professors who are married to other people and leave their spouses for each other. They eventually divorce their spouses and marry each other, but William soon dies, leaving Clare a widow with a drinking problem. Reviewing the collection, Ann Oldenberg of Gannett News Service believed Bloom could have fleshed out the stories into multiple novels, but admitted "The writing here is compelling and beautiful." More enamored of *God of Love*, Gray of the *New York Times* generally shared Oldenberg's assessment, but noted "She writes in beautifully wrought prose, with spunky humor and a flair for delectably eccentric details."

Writing was not Bloom's only artistic venture in this time period. She was asked by a television producer for series ideas, and she came up with the premise behind the 2007 Lifetime series *State of Mind*, which focuses on five therapists and their convoluted lives. By the time the series aired, Bloom had left psychotherapy behind to focus on her creative endeavors, which were often tinged with darkness. As an author, Bloom explained to the *U.S. News & World Report*, "I have a dark kind of optimism. To me, a happy ending might be that everyone is still alive, or that no one is rotting away with Alzheimer's."

Selected writings

Short-story collections

Come to Me, HarperCollins (New York City), 1993.
A Blind Man Can See How Much I Love You, Random House (New York City), 2000.
Where the God of Love Hangs Out, Random House, 2010.

Novels

Love Invents Us, Random House, 1996.
Away, Random House, 2007.

Nonfiction

Normal: Transsexual CEOs, Crossdressing Cops, and Hermaphrodites with Attitude, Random House, 2002.

Sources

Periodicals

Chicago Sun-Times, March 22, 1998, p. 407; September 16, 2007, p. B9.
Denver Post, September 2, 2007, p. F16.
Gannett News Service, January 26, 2010.
Guardian (London, England), March 13, 2010, p. 10.
New York Times, August 16, 1993, p. C18; July 24, 2000, p. E8.
New York Times Book Review, February 7, 2010, p. 10.
Observer (England), September 2, 2007, p. 25.
Orange County Register, February 12, 1997.
Plain Dealer (Cleveland, OH), January 26, 1997, p. 12I.
Richmond Times Dispatch (VA), September 17, 2000, p. F4.
Star Tribune (Minneapolis, MN), October 27, 2002, p. 16F.
St. Louis Post-Dispatch (MO), September 24, 2003, p. E1.
Toronto Star, October 21, 2007, p. E4.
U.S. News & World Report, January 27, 1997, p. 69.
Washington Post, July 29, 1993, p. C2.
Washington Post Book World, August 19, 2007, p. 1.

Online

Contemporary Authors Online, Gale, 2010.

—*A. Petruso*

Chris Bradford

Chief Executive Officer of Valcent

Born c. 1937 in southwestern England.

Addresses: *Office*—27G Pennygillam Way, Pennygillam Industrial Estate, Launceston, Cornwall, PL15 7ED, United Kingdom.

Courtesy of Vorticom, Inc.

Career

Began career with family business Bradford & Sons, Ltd., mid-1950s; worked way up to director and manager of Crop Services and Horticultural Division, Bradford & Sons, Ltd., 1950s-76; moved to Canada and became division manager, Masterfeeds, Maple Leaf Mills, Ltd., 1976; chief executive officer, commodities company, and general manager, agricultural supply and animal feed manufacturing company, late 1970s-1984; founded consulting firm, 1984-97; returned to England to be business developer adviser and project coordinator for Business Link, 1997; manager, regional agricultural program, ca. late 1990s-2005; conducted market study on Valcent, 2005; became managing director of new European Valcent subsidiary, 2006—; president, chief executive officer, and director of Valcent, late 2000s—.

Sidelights

Corporate executive Chris Bradford serves as the president, chief executive officer (CEO), and director of green technology company Valcent Products, Inc., as well as the managing director of its United Kingdom-based subsidiary, Valcent Products (EU) Limited. Under Bradford's watch, Valcent cre-

ated an innovative vertical farming system, the VertiCrop High Density Vegetable Growing System, that has captured the interest of news organizations and environmental watchers worldwide. The system, which employs hydroponic techniques to grow crops stacked atop one another, allows the large-scale cultivation of agricultural crops that have traditionally required massive amounts of acreage with relatively small footprints and reduced levels of water waste. In late 2009, *Time* magazine recognized VertiCrop as one of the 50 Best Inventions of the 2009 for its potential to increase food supplies—a vital concern in the light of a rapidly expanding global population—without taking up large chunks of land.

Born in the southwest of England, Bradford attended the private preparatory institution Blundell's School in Tiverton, Devonshire. Rather than pursuing a university degree after completing his studies at Blundell's, however, Bradford took a job with his family's business, Bradford and Sons Limited, in the mid-1950s. Although primarily a supplier of building materials, Bradford's at that time operated a Crop Services and Horticultural division dedicated to the sale of agricultural products. Here Bradford made his mark, rising to become the director and manager of the department before its sale to an outside firm in 1976. Soon after this event, Bradford left the family business after some two decades to take a job with the Winnipeg, Manitoba, Canada-based company Maple Leaf Mills as the Masterfeeds division manager. Over the next several years he held a succession of high-level positions with Canadian agricultural businesses. He first became the CEO of an Ontario commodities company, leaving that role to become the general manager of a British Columbia agricultural supply and animal feed manufacturing firm. In 1984, Bradford translated his years of experience in the corporate world into a consulting practice that he founded in Vancouver. Over the next several years, he served as a consultant to the food processing industry, working with companies around the world, particularly in managing waste from food processing plants.

Bradford left his Canadian practice to return to England in 1997 when he took a position with Business Link, a small and medium business advisory service run by the British government. There, he acted as a business development adviser and project coordinator. His next role was as the manager of a joint government-business initiative that focused on raising consumer awareness of purchasing local foods and promoting the agricultural products of his native southwestern England. Bradford's earlier consulting work in Canada had put him in contact with Sweetwater Capital, a venture capital and financial services firm based in Vancouver. In late 2005, Sweetwater hired Bradford to analyze the potential British market for Valcent's Tomorrow Garden, a small pre-packaged plant biome intended for consumer use. His report led to the establishment of a European subsidiary of the Canada-based Valcent Products in August of the following year. Bradford became the new Valcent Products (EU) Limited's first managing director, and, later, the president and CEO of Valcent Products, Inc.

Spurred by the ideas of Columbia University environmental health professor Dickson Despommier, Valcent began work the following year on the experimental VertiCrop High Density Vegetable Growing System. Led by the European branch of the company in conjunction with Valcent's El Paso, Texas research laboratory, the initiative explored the possibilities of using hydroponic, or water-based, growing strategies to create a farm that stretched upward rather than outward. The idea quickly began to intrigue green-watchers, with Bryan Walsh of *Time* noting that when one considers "the fact that modern agriculture and everything associated with it—deforestation, chemical-laden fertilizers and carbon-emitting transportation—is a significant contributor to climate change … suddenly vertical farming doesn't seem so magic beanstalk in the sky."

In August of 2009, the first VertiCrop system began operations at Paignton Zoological and Environmental Park in Paignton, South Devon, England. Employing a moving array of vertically stacked hydroponic growing pods attached to conveyor belts, the 100-square-meter (about 1,075 square feet) VertiCrop system can produce as many as 11,000 heads of lettuce in less than a month while requiring only about two hours of operations and maintenance time each day. This fresh produce—which is planned to eventually include other greens, such as red chard and mizuna, as well as edible flowers, wheat grass, and barley—helps form part of the diets of the zoo's animals. "We can grow more plants in less room using less water and less energy," the zoo's curator of plants and gardens, Kevin Frediani, told the BBC News two months after the Paignton initiated the VertiCrop. "It will help to reduce food miles and bring down our annual bill for animal feed." Many, including Bradford, have noted that one of the VertiCrop's greatest advantages is its small physical footprint and relatively low water needs. "It doesn't require a green field site so it can be used in urban areas, in warehouses and in deserts," he explained in the same BBC News article.

The success of this first VertiCrop system drew media attention on both sides of the Atlantic, with *Time* hailing it as one of its 50 Best Inventions of 2009. In March of the following year, VertiCrop earned a nod as one of the top ten global innovations from LAUNCH, an international sustainability partnership between such government and business entities as NASA, USAID, the U.S. State Department, and Nike. Around the same time, Valcent announced the planned production of a smaller version of the widely hailed VertiCrop system called AlphaCrop. Designed for small commercial growers and home gardeners, the AlphaCrop allows the propagation of a wider variety of plants than does the larger VertiCrop and can employ either the VertiCrop's hydroponic system or more traditional growing materials, such as compost. As the human population continues to expand, making the need for food ever greater even as the amount of available land to support that growth declines, Bradford and Valcent's unique growing systems seem likely to remain in the news for some time to come.

Sources

Periodicals

Time, December 11, 2008; November 12, 2009.

Online

"Leadership Team," Valcent Products, Inc., http://www.valcent.net/s/Leadership.asp (March 11, 2010).

"Vertical Crop System is Piloted," BBC News, http://news.bbc.co.uk/2/hi/uk_news/england/devon/8282288.stm (March 11, 2010).

Additional information was obtained from press releases from Vorticom, Inc.

—*Vanessa E. Vaughn*

Libba Bray

Author

Born Martha E. Bray, March 11, 1964, in Alabama; daughter of a Presbyterian minister and an English teacher; married Barry Goldblatt (a literary agent); children: Josh. *Education:* University of Texas Austin, B.A., 1988.

Addresses: *Agent*—Barry Goldblatt LLC, 320 7th Ave., Ste. 266, Brooklyn, NY 11215. *Web site*—http:// libbabray.com/; http://libba-bray.livejournal.com/.

Career

Member of publicity staff, Penguin Putnam, New York City, 1980s; staff, Spier (an advertising agency), New York City, c. late 1980s through early 1990s; published *Kari,* part of the "Sweet Sixteen," romance series, 2000; signed publishing deal for trilogy, 2001; published first installment *A Great and Terrible Beauty,* 2003; published last installment, *The Sweet Far Thing,* 2007; published award-winning *Going Bovine,* 2009.

Awards: Award for best young adult novel of the year, New Atlantic Independent Booksellers Association, for *Rebel Angels,* c. 2005; Michael L. Printz Award, American Library Association, for *Going Bovine,* 2010.

Sidelights

Author Libba Bray found much success with her first trilogy of best-selling supernatural Victorian novels targeted at a teen audience. Beginning

with 2003's *A Great and Terrible Beauty,* readers and reviewers lauded the writer's interesting stories and attention to detail. Bray began her career as an aspiring playwright turned employee at a publisher and an advertising agency. After churning out a few titles for a teen novel series, Bray signed the deal that led to the publication of her own original work in the early 2000s. In 2009, Bray published an entirely different kind of teen novel, the Mad Cow Disease-driven and award-winning *Going Bovine.* Of her relationship with her chosen profession, the droll Bray told Claire E. White of *Writers Write,* "I'm one of those people who has to write. If I don't write, I feel itchy and depressed and cranky. So everybody's glad when I write and stop complaining already."

Bray was born on March 11, 1964, in Alabama, the daughter of a Presbyterian minister father and English teacher mother. The family moved to Texas when Bray was young. Reading, acting, and the theater were intense focuses of Bray's life as a child. She also cultivated an interest in science fiction and fantasy literature, among other pursuits. She told White of *Writers Write,* "I grew up on a diet of Sonic Drive-In tater tots, *Monty Python* reruns, *The Rocky Horror Picture Show* at midnight, and impromptu gatherings of the Unofficial Sardonic's Club."

An Anglophile with an interest in the Victorian era by the age of ten, she wanted to learn how to speak like the British and become their monarch. As she explained to Cecelia Goodnow of the *Seattle Post-Intelligencer*, "I think there's such an overlap between [Victorian] culture and Southern culture. There is repression and darkness and [a hint of] 'What's going on behind that respectable veneer?'"

As a teen, Bray faced the consequences of such cultural mores. When she was 14 years old, her parents were divorced and her father came out as a homosexual to his family. Yet the family kept his sexuality a secret so that he could keep his position with the church. (Bray's father died of AIDS in the mid-1990s.) Bray soon faced more personal challenges.

At 18 years old, Bray was in horrific car accident in which she suffered two broken legs, a permanently damaged left eye, multiple facial bone fractures, and a missing rib. It took 13 reconstructive surgeries over six years to put her back together. Of this challenging time in her life, Bray told the *Seattle Post-Intelligencer*'s Goodnow, "To lose your face—talk about a loss of identity—you look in the mirror, and you're not the same person anymore. You're the same on the inside, but not on the outside. It was very informative of the role appearances play in our society."

Writing proved a solace for Bray as well during this time period. She told Beth Bakkam of *The Writer*, "I began to keep a journal as a way … to say everything that needed to be said, to scream and rage and cry and howl—all the things I felt I couldn't do in my life."

During her recovery, Bray also studied theater at the University of Texas at Austin. There, she wrote some plays and saw some of them produced. She earned her B.A. in theater in 1988. After graduation, Bray moved to New York City to live with a friend who lost a roommate. She had $600 and hopes to become a professional playwright. As she told White of *Writers Write*, she moved to New York City with high hopes. Bray explained, "I blame it all on *That Girl*, a seminal show of my youth. I thought I would move to the big city and fly a kite down Fifth Avenue, and people would be charmingly exasperated by me. People do get exasperated with me, but they don't seem charmed. At the time, I was a playwright, and I thought I could move to New York, fall in with the Wooster Group and be 'discovered' as the next Edward Albee."

Instead, Bray took jobs in publishing and advertising with the intent of honing her writing skills. She began working at Penguin Putnam on the advertising staff soon after her move, then became a staff member at the advertising agency Spier, which specialized in book advertising, for three years. Bray eventually began writing fiction for teen paperback series like "Sweet Sixteen," including 2000's *Kari*. In 2001, she was able to land a publishing contract for a trilogy of novels that would cement her reputation as an author. Bray began writing the first installment in 2002.

The first novel in the series, 2003's *A Great and Terrible Beauty*, became an unexpected best seller and brought Bray's name to the public eye. Set in a girls' boarding/finishing school in Victorian England, *A Great and Terrible Beauty* was a supernatural mystery story about the strong friendship of a group of girls as well as a reflection on the life and mores of nineteenth century England. Led by 16-year-old free spirit Gemma Doyle, who attends Spence Academy in London with her friends, she must deal with her own powers, intrigue, and otherworldly villains as well as teenage angst in "The Realms," a mystical place. The otherworldly powers caused the death of Gemma's mother in India, an event Gemma sees in detail in a vision. Nicole Joseph of *Newsweek* called *A Great and Terrible Beauty* and its successors "an unusual mix of sci-fi, fantasy, and unalloyed romance."

Joseph also noted that the books "have a large and devoted following of teen girls who identify with the heroine Gemma Doyle…." Bray told Joseph that when developing these characters, she wanted to make them complex. Bray explained, "One of the things that I did want to do is have characters that are as complicated as the people I know. Often, when it comes to girls and women, we don't show the full emotional spectrum of what we experience; there's still a lot of fear about showing anger in women. If you think about when they show women on TV or in the movies, if they're angry, it's either like; 'oh isn't she cute, she's angry'—or it's scary, fatal attraction. There's no in-between." Critics responded positively to Bray's vision as well. *Publishers Weekly* called it a "riveting debut novel" and a "delicious, elegant gothic."

The sequel to *A Great and Terrible Beauty* was published in 2005 and debuted on the *New York Times* best-seller list at number four. In this book, *Rebel Angels*, Gemma and her friends confront the powers that led to her mother's proactive suicide by trying to locate a temple within the realm. They also work to tie up the realms' magical powers that were set free by Gemma at the end of *A Great and Terrible Beauty*. Class and gender issues are explored again, primarily through the relationships of Gemma and friends with their love interests.

Critics continued to praise Bray and *Rebel Angels,* though some thought it did not quite measure up to *A Great and Terrible Beauty. Publishers Weekly* noted that "Bray provides a satisfying ending, yet she implies a further struggle for power. Fans will want to stay tuned." Reviewing *Rebel Angels* in the *Sherbrooke Record,* Michelle Barker raved, "Bray's imagination knows no limits." She added, "Bray is a master when it comes to describing the subtle cruelties of young girls at boarding school. She has also captured the British history well, with its balls and class distinctions, its petty concerns over what the neighbours might think, the poverty of London as well as its riches."

The popularity of the incomplete trilogy led to a film deal for Bray in 2006. That year, she optioned the rights to the trilogy to Icon Productions with Charles Sturridge attached to direct the first film based on *A Great and Terrible Beauty.* Just as impressive, by 2007, more than 600,000 copies had been sold of *A Great and Terrible Beauty* and *Rebel Angels.*

The third installment of Bray's trilogy, *The Sweet Far Thing,* was published in 2007. This book proved hard for the author to write as she developed writer's block for a time. Bray told Sue Corbett of *Publishers Weekly,* "I can honestly say I've never worked so hard on anything in my life. Not even labor. That was awful, but it was over in seven hours." The result was a book that, at more than 800 pages, was twice as long as *A Great and Terrible Beauty* and had a complex plot which tied up the many storylines from the previous books.

Reviewers were generally impressed with *The Sweet Far Thing. Publishers Weekly* noted, "Bray poses ... vital questions without sacrificing the gothic undertones of the previous volumes—the body count is high, and the deaths, gruesome. That creepiness is balanced by the fully realized company of players...." Meredith Robbins of *School Library Journal* commented "the novel's fast-paced and exciting ending and Bray's lyrical descriptions of the decaying realms are sure to enchant readers who loved Gemma's previous exploits."

After completing the trilogy, Bray moved on to a different style of novel. Dubbed "an absurdist comedy" by *Publishers Weekly, Going Bovine* focused on the experiences of underachieving 16-year-old Cameron Smith. He works in a burger joint and contracts mad cow disease. After leaving the hospital—with only months to live—he is visited by an angel who sends him on a quest to find a cure and save the world. The angel could be real or a hallucination, but Cameron goes on a road trip across the United States with odd characters.

Critics noted that the 480-page *Going Bovine* was quite different from the trilogy, especially in its type of humor. Yet *Publishers Weekly* said to "[o]ffer this to fans of Douglas Adams's *Hitchhiker's Guide to the Galaxy* seeking more inspired lunacy." Lisa Von Drasek of the *New York Times Book Review* took a different perspective, writing "Libba Bray not only breaks the mold of the ubiquitous dying-teenager genre—she smashes it and grinds the tiny pieces into the sidewalk. For the record, I'd go anywhere she wanted to take me." *Going Bovine* won the author the 2010 Michael L. Printz Award from the American Library Association.

As an author, Bray explained to *The Writer*'s Bakkam that she felt compelled to write "[b]ecause I'm fascinated by the complications of the human heart, the ways in which people connect or try to connect and fail. Because I've always wanted to know the 'why' of things. Because I enjoy knowing I can craft whole answers out of sentence fragments that start with 'because.' It makes me feel mildly rebellious. And because I couldn't become the brooding, enigmatic guitar god I always wanted to be, frankly."

Selected writings

Novels

Kari, HarperTrophy (New York City), 2000.
A Great and Terrible Beauty, Delacorte Press (New York City), 2003.
Rebel Angels, Delacorte Press, 2005.
The Sweet Far Thing, Delacorte Press, 2007.
Going Bovine, Delacorte Press, 2009.

Short Story Collections

(Contributor) *The Restless Dead: Ten Original Stories of the Supernatural,* Candlewick Press (Cambridge, MA), 2007.
(Contributor) *Up All Night: A Short Story Collection,* Laura Geringer Books/HarperTeen (New York City), 2008.

Sources

Books

Writers Directory, 25th ed., St. James Press, 2009.

Periodicals

Newsweek, January 13, 2006.
New York Times, March 14, 2004, sec. 7, p. 19.
New York Times Book Review, February 14, 2010, p. 14.

Publishers Weekly, December 8, 2003, p. 62; August 1, 2005, p. 66; October 29, 2007, p. 57; November 12, 2007, p. 24; August 3, 2009, p. 46.
School Library Journal, January 2008, p. 114.
Screen International, July 24, 2006.
Seattle Post-Intelligencer, September 22, 2005, p. C1.
Sherbrooke Record (Quebec, Canada), May 13, 2008, p. 8.
Writer, May 2006, p. 66.

Online

Contemporary Authors Online, Gale, 2010.
"A Conversation with Libba Bray," *Writers Write,* http://www.writerswrite.com/journal/feb04/bray.htm (March 10, 2010).

—A. Petruso

Drew Brees

Andy Lyons/Getty Images

Professional football player

Born January 15, 1979, in Austin, TX; son of Chip (an attorney) and Mina (an attorney) Brees; married Brittany Dudchenko (a travel agent); children: Baylen (son). *Education:* Purdue University, B.S., 2001.

Addresses: *Agent*—Tom Condon, CAA Sports, 162 5th Ave., 7th Fl., New York, NY 10010. *Home*—New Orleans, LA. *Office*—c/o New Orleans Saints, 5800 Airline Dr., Metairie, LA 70003.

Career

Quarterback, Boilermakers, Purdue University, 1997-2000; quarterback, San Diego Chargers, 2001-06; quarterback, New Orleans Saints, 2006—. Co-founder, Brees Dream Foundation, 2003—.

Member: National Football League Players Association (executive committee, 2008—).

Awards: Texas 5A Offensive Player of the Year, 1996; Big Ten Player of the Year, 1998, 2000; Socrates Award Winner, *Sporting News* Radio, 1999; Maxwell Award for College Player of the Year, Maxwell Football Club, 2000; Academic All-American Player of the Year, College Sports Information Directors of America, 2000; NFL Comeback Player of the Year, *Pro Football Weekly*, 2004; named to Pro Bowl, National Football League, 2004, 2006, 2008; Walter Payton Man of the Year Award, National Football League, 2006; Player of the Year—Quarterback, NFL Alumni, 2006, 2009; 101 Award for NFC Offensive Player of the Year, Kansas City Committee of 101, 2006, 2008, 2009; FedEx Air Player of the Year, National Football League, 2006, 2008, 2009; Arthur S. Arkush Humanitarian Award, *Pro Football Weekly*, 2007; Don Newcombe Award, Los Angeles Opportunities Industrialization Centers, 2008; Horizon Award, U.S. Congress, 2008; Henry P. Iba Citizen Athlete Award, Rotary Club of Tulsa, 2009; named Pro Bowl starter, National Football League, 2009; Bert Bell Award for Player of the Year, Maxwell Football Club, 2009; Most Valuable Player, Super Bowl XLIV, National Football League, 2010.

Sidelights

At the end of the 2005 National Football League (NFL) season, quarterback Drew Brees looked to have an uncertain future. Not only had he failed to lead the San Diego Chargers to the playoffs, during the final game of the season he suffered a shoulder injury that required surgery and months of rehabilitation. The Chargers released him and Brees signed with the New Orleans Saints, who had the second-worst record in the league and were still making repairs to their stadium after it had been rendered unusable by Hurricane Katrina in late 2005. The move to New Orleans proved opportune: Brees led the surprising Saints to the playoffs in

2006 and again in the 2009-10 season, when they claimed Super Bowl XLIV over the Indianapolis Colts. Brees has been a leader in the city's recovery off the field as well, with his Brees Dream Foundation contributing millions of dollars to programs that benefit schools, children, housing, and other worthy causes in New Orleans.

Brees was born in 1979 in Austin, Texas, a football-mad state where his grandfather, Ray Akins, was a successful high school coach. His parents, Chip and Mina Brees, were both attorneys and sports enthusiasts; they taught Drew and his younger brother Reid baseball, football, and tennis. At 12, Brees was not only the state's highest-ranked tennis player for his age, he also set the record for most home runs in his city's Little League. "Growing up, I was more of a baseball player than a football player," he told *Sports Illustrated Kids.* "I played pitcher, shortstop, and third base." Although he often spent summers watching his grandfather's teams practice, Brees did not play tackle football until high school, where he worked his way from the freshman B-team to varsity starter in his junior year. During his two years quarterbacking Austin's Westlake High School, the team had an overall record of 28-0-1. During his junior year he had an knee injury during the state playoffs, but in 1996 Brees led Westlake to an undefeated season and a state championship, and was named Texas' 5A Offensive Player of the Year. He also lettered in basketball and baseball for his school's teams.

Despite throwing for 5,416 yards and 50 touchdowns in high school, Brees was not recruited by many elite college programs. Not only were coaches concerned about his knee injury, they felt that, at six feet tall, Brees did not have the build of a prototypical quarterback. Brees accepted a scholarship from Purdue University, a Big Ten school whose engineering programs had a better reputation than their football team. Under new coach Joe Tiller, the program began turning around with a spread offense that emphasized the passing game. Brees played sparingly his freshman year, but became Purdue's starting quarterback as a sophomore in 1998. He set several school records during the team's 8-4 regular season and, in a game against Wisconsin, set the NCAA record for pass attempts (83) and tied the record for completions (55). The Big Ten Offensive Player of the Year concluded the season by leading Purdue to a last-second victory over number four Kansas State in the Alamo Bowl. As a junior in the 1999 season, Brees led the Boilermakers to a 7-5 record, an Outback Bowl appearance, and a final ranking in top 25. With a 60.8 percent completion rate and over 3,909 yards passing, Brees himself placed fourth in the voting for the Heisman Trophy.

He could have turned professional, but decided to return for his final year so that he could complete his college degree.

During his senior year, Brees helped Purdue win their first Big Ten title and Rose Bowl berth since 1967. In a key game against Ohio State, Brees threw for three touchdowns in the fourth quarter for a come-from-behind victory over the perennial Big Ten powerhouse. For Brees, such situations were nothing to get excited about. "In the two-minute drill," *Sporting News* reporter Tom Dienhart quoted him as saying, "I just tell the guys to remain cool. That we are going to win this thing. The two-minute drill is my favorite part of practice, so I love running it in games." The Boilermakers finished the season with an 8-4 record, going 6-2 in the Big Ten and losing to Washington in the Rose Bowl. While Brees finished third in voting for the Heisman, he was once again named Big Ten Offensive Player of the Year, and also earned the Maxwell Award as the nation's best college player. Just as impressive were Brees' academic achievements. In 1999 he earned the first Socrates Award for excellence in academics, athletics, and citizenship, while in 2000 he was named Academic All-American Player of the Year and earned a NCAA postgraduate scholarship. While most elite college football players, if they graduate at all, take five years to earn a diploma, Brees took just four years to earn his bachelor of science degree in industrial management, which included difficult classes in calculus, physics, and economics. "Hopefully, I can set an example," he told Tim Layden of *Sports Illustrated.* "I can show that it's possible to play football at a high level, graduate, and still go on to the NFL."

Although Brees left Purdue holding most of the Big Ten's career and season passing records, some NFL scouts still doubted whether his skills would translate to the pro game. They considered him small for a quarterback and wondered whether his big numbers were due more to Purdue's system than his skills; however, the San Diego Chargers were impressed with his talent and drafted him with the first pick in the second round. Brees signed a four-year deal and saw little action in his rookie season, playing as a backup to Doug Flutie. He beat Flutie the following year in training camp and started all 16 games in 2002, passing for almost 3,300 yards and leading the Chargers to a respectable 8-8 record. He was not surprised at his success; as he told Vito Stellino in *Football Digest,* "I expect to win out there. I expect to drive us down the field and score a touchdown. I expect to make big plays. And when I don't, I'm upset about it. I won't cop out and say, 'Oh, I'm young—I have a lot to learn.' No, I can do it now." Nevertheless, the 2003 season turned into a disappointment, with Brees throwing more interceptions than touchdowns and the team falling to 4-12. Believing that Brees would not pan out as a pro, Chargers management drafted quarterback Philip Rivers in the first round to be their future signal caller. "It was devastating," Brees told Josh Elliott in *Sports Illustrated.* "I was angry. No one wants to hear that he's not wanted. But once I got past it, I knew I could only worry about things in my control."

Rivers held out during training camp, while Brees focused on improving his skills and conditioning. "I changed my mental approach and my preparation," he told *Sports Illustrated Kids.* With a list of food allergies that included dairy, wheat, gluten, eggs, and nuts, "I studied my diet and I started sleeping better. Everything I needed to be a good quarterback, I analyzed and tried to improve upon." He kept his starting job and soon there was talk of a quarterback controversy as Brees led San Diego to a division title with a 12-4 record. He threw for 3,159 yards and 27 touchdowns with only seven interceptions, and earned *Pro Football Weekly*'s NFL Comeback Player of the Year Award, as well as Pro Bowl status. Although San Diego lost in overtime in the first round of the playoffs, expectations were high for the 2005 season and for Brees, whom the Chargers had signed to a one-year contract extension. The team finished with a winning record of 9-7 but it was not good enough to make the playoffs. When Brees injured his shoulder diving for a fumble in the last game of the season, his career in San Diego was over. Brees signed as a free agent with the New Orleans Saints in 2006.

The Saints had a history of losing, with only one playoff win in the team's 39-year history. In 2005 they were unable to play in the Superdome because of Katrina damage and ended up with the league's second-worst record. Under new coach Sean Payton, however, Brees led a revitalized New Orleans offense that kept winning games throughout the 2006 season. Brees led the league with 4,418 passing yards, and the Saints' 10-6 record was good enough to give the team the second seed in the playoffs. They won their first game 27-24 over the Philadelphia Eagles, but were stymied by the Chicago Bears defense in the conference championship despite Brees' 354 yards and two touchdowns, losing 39-14. Nonetheless, fans were excited by their new quarterback, who ended the season as a member of the Pro Bowl with multiple offensive player of the year awards to his credit.

Not only did Brees spur a renaissance for the Saints, through his charity work he contributed to a comeback for their home city as well. When he first visited New Orleans only months after it had been devastated by Hurricane Katrina, the Saints staff "showed places that hadn't recovered," he recalled to Seth Wickersham in *ESPN The Magazine.* "They showed me how I could be a part of the city's rebuilding process. Now, some might be intimidated by that. My wife and I thought it was a calling." Through his Brees Dream Foundation, which he founded with his wife Brittany, the quarterback began contributing to charitable programs throughout the city. They gave 500 children new bikes and helmets; built playgrounds; restored athletic fields and facilities at schools damaged by Hurricane Katrina; and established afterschool, mentoring, and tutoring programs. Brees and his wife bought and refurbished a historic home in a flooded New Orleans neighborhood, and with the help of his Saints teammates and his Sigma Chi fraternity brothers, the quarterback rebuilt several homes in the city's damaged Ninth Ward as part of a Habitat for Humanity program. For his charitable efforts, the NFL gave him the Walter Payton Man of the Year Award in 2006.

Hopes were high for the Saints in the 2007 season, and Brees had another stellar year. He set an NFL record with 440 completions for the season, and finished with 4,423 yards and 28 touchdowns. The team had a challenging schedule, however, and finished with a 7-9 record. During the following season, Brees once again led the NFL, this time in both yards and completions. His season total of 5,069 yards was only the second time a quarterback had thrown more than 5,000 yards, and was only 15 yards short of tying Dan Marino's all-time record. While the Saints scored more points than any other NFL team in 2008, their defense also gave up a lot of points and the team finished out of the playoffs at 8-8. Although Brees was again named to the Pro Bowl and claimed several offensive player awards, he spent the off-season examining how he could improve his play and help his team win more games.

As practices began for the 2009 season, Brees gave his teammates wristbands reading "Finish Strong" and lived up to the slogan with his own punishing work ethic. "His drive for perfection is contagious," a teammate told David Fleming of *ESPN The Magazine.* "If he told me to jump off a cliff in order to win a game, I'd do it." The Saints got off to a strong start, winning their first five games by an average of 20 points on the way to a conference-best 13-3 record. During the regular season Brees broke a 27-year-old NFL record for passing accuracy, completing 70.62 percent of his throws, and led the league in passer rating (a measure of production and efficiency). He was just as accurate during the postseason, throwing eight touchdowns with no turnovers during the Saints' playoff run. New Orleans crushed the Arizona Cardinals 45-14, then outlasted the explosive Minnesota Vikings in overtime, 31-28, to win the conference. In Super Bowl XLIV against league powerhouse Indianapolis, the Saints got off to a slow start, falling behind 10-0 in the first quarter. Brees completed 32 of 39 passes for 288 yards and two touchdowns in leading the Saints to a comeback victory, 31-17, and was named the game's Most Valuable Player. One of the most memorable images that night was of the quarterback whispering to his year-old son, Baylen, as confetti rained down in celebration of their victory.

Brees could have taken a break after his Super Bowl win, but he continued working all out with his Brees Dream Foundation. "Some guys might be playing ten hours of Madden [football video game] today, which is cool," Peter King reported him as saying to a charity audience. "But this is my outlet. This is what I love to do." His activities included sponsoring a regular "Brees on the Seas" fishing event, which pairs NFL players with sick children; working with Visa's Financial Football program to teach kids about money management; and traveling with the USO to visit American troops in Afghanistan, Kuwait, and Japan. As of 2010, his foundation had contributed nearly $5 million to programs in New Orleans, San Diego, and the Purdue University area. Brees also hoped to inspire people with his 2010 memoir, *Coming Back Stronger: Unleashing the Hidden Power of Adversity*. While his book included his account of recovering from a severe shoulder separation in 2005, it also focused on the recovery of New Orleans, a city he felt had done more for him than he had done in return. While he hoped to continue his success with the Saints, Brees considered his work rebuilding New Orleans more important. "The strong sense of faith in this city makes you think this is destiny, that we're going to achieve what we set out to achieve," he told Fleming in *ESPN The Magazine*. "It's only a matter of time."

Selected writings

(With Chris Fabry) *Coming Back Stronger: Unleashing the Hidden Power of Adversity*, Tyndale House, 2010.

Sources

Books

(With Chris Fabry) Brees, Drew, *Coming Back Stronger: Unleashing the Hidden Power of Adversity*, Tyndale House, 2010.

Periodicals

ESPN The Magazine, October 28, 2002; May 22, 2008; July 3, 2008; January 25, 2010.
Football Digest, January 2003, p. 12.
New Orleans CityBusiness, 2007; 2008; 2009.
Sporting News, November 9, 1998, p. 54; October 23, 2000, p. 21; November 6, 2000, p. 58; November 27, 2000, p. 53; December 13, 2004, p. 37.
Sports Illustrated, December 7, 1998, p. 118; August 16, 1999, p. 56; November 15, 1999, p. 50; November 27, 2000, p. 54; April 30, 2001, p. 56; October 21, 2002, p. 64; November 15, 2004, p. 60; January 18, 2010, p. 54; February 11, 2010, p. 15.
Sports Illustrated Kids, December 3, 2008, p. 21; December 2009, p. 24.
Texas Monthly, January 2003, p. 82.
USA Today, August 25, 2005, p. 3C.

Online

Biography Resource Center Online, Gale Group, 2000.
Brees Dream Foundation, http://www.drewbrees.com (May 19, 2010).
"Drew Brees," National Football League Official Site, http://www.nfl.com/players/drewbrees/profile?id=BRE229498 (May 19, 2010).
"Drew Brees," Official Site of the New Orleans' Saints, http://www.neworleanssaints.com/team/roster/Drew-Brees/09634fe8-9ab7-4f47-a5ea-c0fb5ad343a9 (May 19, 2010).
"Player Bio: Drew Brees," Purdue Boilermakers, http://www.purduesports.com/sports/m-footbl/mtt/brees_drew00.html (May 19, 2010).

—*Diane Telgen*

Jan Brewer

AP Images/Ross D. Franklin

Governor of Arizona

Born Janice Kay Drinkwine, September 26, 1944, in Hollywood, CA; daughter of Wilford (a naval munitions supervisor) and Edna (a dress shop owner; maiden name, Bakken) Drinkwine; married John Brewer (a chiropractor); children: Ronald, John (deceased), Michael. *Education:* Received radiological technician certification, Glendale Community College, Glendale, CA, before 1970; also attended Los Angeles Valley College.

Addresses: *Home*—Glendale, AZ. *Office*—Governor of Arizona, 1700 West Washington, Phoenix, AZ 85007.

Career

Worked as a radiological technician c. 1970—c. 1983; member of Arizona House of Representatives, 1983-86; member of Arizona Senate, 1987-96, served as Republican majority whip, 1993-96; member of Maricopa County Board of Supervisors, 1996-2002, also served as board chairman; Arizona Secretary of State, 2002-09; governor of Arizona, 2009—.

Sidelights

For the first 26 years of her political career, Republican Janice K. Brewer served Arizona in various state and county offices with little national notice. After succeeding to the governor's office in 2009, however, she signed a controversial law which required police to stop anyone they suspected of being in the country illegally. Critics believed the new immigration law, the nation's most restrictive, would lead to increases in racial profiling and violations of civil liberties, and opponents advocated for boycotts of Arizona in protest. While Brewer drew national and even international protest for signing the bill, the action gained the approval of Arizona voters, who returned her to the governor's office in the election of 2010.

Brewer was born Janice Kay Drinkwine in California in 1944. Her parents had moved from Minnesota to Nevada during World War II so her father could take a job as a naval munitions officer. He developed lung disease from exposure to chemicals on the job, leading the family to move to California for the climate. Nevertheless, Wilford Drinkwine died within a year, when his daughter was only eleven years old. His widow Edna opened a dress shop, and her children spent many hours after school and weekends working alongside her. "She taught me that you always had to be honest, you always had to be loyal, and you always had to work hard," Brewer told Daniel Scarpinato in the *Arizona Daily Star.* The future governor earned certification as a radiological technician and, after marrying John Brewer, she worked to help finance his medical training. They moved to Arizona in the early 1970s, and while he built his chiropractic practice, she raised their three sons and became interested in their education. She began attending school board meetings, and "I said to my husband, John, 'Who are these people, and what are they doing?,'" she recalled to Scarpinato. She thought of running for the school board, but when her local state congressional seat became open, "I thought, 'Well, maybe I could have bigger a impact on education by going to the Legislature.'"

In 1983 Brewer ran as a Republican for a seat in Arizona's House of Representatives. Despite her political inexperience she won the election and served as a congresswoman for four years. In 1987 she ran for the State Senate and won again. She earned a reputation as a fiscal conservative with a concern for education and health issues, particularly mental health. While in Arizona's Senate, Brewer sponsored the first living will legislation in the country. From 1993 to 1996 she served as the Republican Majority Whip, charged with keeping party legislators in line with the leadership's objectives. According to Tom Patterson, majority leader during her term, "Brewer was a perfect fit for the whip position, given her natural ability to talk, cajole and, if necessary, compromise to achieve objectives," as he told Jeremy Duda and Christian Palmer of the *Arizona Capitol Times.*

Brewer left the legislature in 1996 to run for the Board of Supervisors of Maricopa County; Maricopa was one of the most populous counties in the U.S., encompassing metropolitan Phoenix and Brewer's hometown of Glendale. Like many of her neighbors, Brewer was appalled that the previous board had voted to increase sales taxes to fund the building of a stadium for Major League Baseball's Arizona Diamondbacks. When she came into office, the county was borrowing $165 million to cover cash needs; by the time she resigned in 2002, the trade journal *Governing* named Maricopa one of the two best-managed large counties in the United States. Other issues she worked on as a supervisor included increased funding for sheriffs and prosecuting attorneys, land conservation and preservation, and improved medical facilities and homeless shelters. Mental health issues were of particular importance to her, having seen one of her own sons hospitalized for mental illness. She served as chairman of the board of directors for Recovery Innovations of Arizona, a rehabilitation center for those suffering from chronic mental health or substance abuse problems. Other causes and commissions she served during her career included those supporting local military bases, a commission that worked at reducing crime, a government-business coalition to promote economic development, and several children's charities.

Brewer resigned from the Maricopa County Board in 2002 to run again for state office. In running for Arizona Secretary of State, she pledged to use technology to modernize the state's voting system, reduce voter fraud, and encourage greater voter turnout. After winning a close election by fewer than 40,000 votes, she looked for ways to streamline the voting process, eliminated punch-card ballots to comply with federal law, and increased access for disabled voters by supplying touch-screen devices to all districts. In 2004, Arizonans approved Proposition 200, which required prospective voters to show proof of citizenship when registering and identification at the voting booth. Brewer helped implement the law, defended it from court challenges, and set up an education program, including a telephone hotline, to make voters aware of the changes. She was re-elected Secretary of State in 2006, this time by a margin of almost 265,000 votes. During her second term she helped establish a system that allowed military voters overseas to cast absentee votes via Internet or fax. During her time as Secretary of State, Brewer also spearheaded a public-private partnership to allow seriously ill patients to file advanced medical directives online.

During her career in the Arizona legislature, Brewer repeatedly introduced a law that would have created a lieutenant governor position for Arizona. Her argument was that the existing system—in which the Secretary of State took over if the governor had to leave office—meant the voters might end up with a governor of the opposing party, or one with little executive or legislative experience. She was never able to get enough support for the proposal, which many of her colleagues came to call "Jan's Law," and ironically found herself in position to succeed to Arizona's governorship. After Democrat Barack Obama was elected President in 2008, he chose Arizona's Democratic Governor Janet Napolitano to serve as his Secretary of Homeland Security. As Secretary of State, Brewer succeeded to the governor's office in January 2009 when Napolitano resigned to join Obama's cabinet. State Republicans, frustrated by six years of gubernatorial vetoes, were excited at the prospect of holding the legislature and the governor's office.

Brewer came into office with Arizona, weakened by one of the country's highest foreclosure rates, facing an unprecedented budget deficit of almost $3.6 billion over the next 18 months. She immediately signed a bill cutting $580 million in spending, including a two percent cut to K-12 education, then traveled the state to introduce herself to voters and push a plan to balance the budget. To the shock of her Republican allies, that plan included a temporary one-cent raise in the state sales tax. "Was I going to do what was right?" Brewer told the *Arizona Daily Star*'s Scarpinato. "Or was I going to be a politician with the idea that I was going to cover my backside, if you will, and play magic?" She vetoed Republican bills she felt made overly drastic cuts to education and health care, and upset Democrats by proposing to cut personal and corporate tax rates to balance out the sales tax increase. By the end of 2009, many observers thought she would have difficulty retaining the governorship in the 2010 election.

The governor's political fortunes changed in April of 2010 when she signed Senate Bill 1070, a strict immigration bill which made being in the country illegally a criminal offense punishable by jail time. Legal immigrants were required to carry identification with them at all times, and police were required to stop and question anyone they suspecting of being an illegal. "It's the federal government's responsibility, of course, to secure our borders and to protect the people of Arizona," the governor later explained to Larry King on *Larry King Live.* "And they have laws that mandate that they do that. And they're not enforcing those laws." Because S.B. 1070 followed certain federal procedures and was similar to laws already enforced in the city of Phoenix, she added, "When we signed the bill we felt it was in good order and that it was constitutional." The law included provisions against racial profiling and Brewer planned to set up special training programs to educate law enforcement on how to follow it.

While Brewer expected some opposition to the passage of S.B. 1070, the national outcry it produced surprised her. The law made national headlines, for many observers believed it would encourage racial profiling and harassment of Latinos. Several groups initiated boycotts against the state: the city of Phoenix estimated they had lost $100 million in convention commitments within the first two months, and several entertainers promised not to perform in Arizona until the law was repealed. "I knew that [the law] would be … talked about and there would be a response for a couple days, but I had no idea it would elicit the response that it did," Brewer told Duda in the *Arizona Capitol Times.* "I think it was a little bit overwhelming to most people and it was based primarily on mischaracterization and mistruths about what the bill did." Seven court cases were filed challenging the law in the first three months, including one brought by the U.S. Department of Justice. Despite the national controversy, a majority of the Arizona public favored the law, and a legal fund Brewer set up to defend it in court garnered more than $1 million in contributions in under three months. A federal circuit court judge filed an injunction against parts of the law in July of 2010, and the court was still considering arguments in November of 2010. The governor and her supporters vowed to fight for the law all the way to the U.S. Supreme Court, if they had to.

Brewer's defense of Arizona's tough immigration law increased her standing with state voters. Voters also demonstrated resounding public support for her sales tax proposal, which garnered 64 percent of vote in a May 2010 election. With Brewer's popularity on the upswing, her high-profile primary opponents dropped out, ensuring an easy primary victory over a political novice. In November she ran against the state's Attorney General, Terry Goddard, a Democrat who opposed S.B. 1070. She suffered a disastrous opening to her single debate against him, when she stumbled over her opening statement and left a 16-second gap of silence; later she had to disavow her post-debate statement that border conflicts were producing headless bodies in the Arizona desert. Her opponents tried to build on these gaffes by spreading false rumors about her health and accusing state Republicans of violating campaign finance laws in support of her candidacy. Others called her hypocritical for decrying the federal government's stimulus bill while taking credit for the building projects it brought to Arizona. About the latter, the governor explained to John King on CNN that "we're going to be in debt forever, but we're certainly not going to cut off our nose to spite our face and not accept those dollars." On election day, Brewer easily won with 54 percent of the vote. "I think that it says that the voters, they know who Jan Brewer is and that she has shown leadership and that she's got a plan, and that together we're going to continue with Arizona's comeback," she told Duda of the *Arizona Capitol Times.*

Despite her election victory, Brewer still had challenges ahead of her. During her previous two years as governor Arizona had added $2 billion to state's debt, and the state's economy was not expected to rebound in the short term. Brewer noted that dealing with budget issues required the same care and pruning as her favorite hobby, gardening, and she was determined to keep working on the various issues facing her state, no matter the political pressures. On January 8, 2011, U.S. Rep. Gabrielle Giffords of Arizona was critically wounded in a mass shooting that killed six people. On January 11, Brewer signed emergency legislation that barred protests within 300 feet of a funeral and within an hour from its beginning or end. "This legislation will assure that the victims of Saturday's tragic shooting in Tucson will be laid to rest in peace with the full dignity and respect that they deserve," Brewer said in a statement, according to CNN.com. The action was in response to the Westboro Baptist Church's announcement that it will picket the funeral of Christina Green, the nine-year-old girl who was among six people killed during the attempted assassination of Giffords. "Since I've been governor, I moved forward and did what I thought was right," she told Rhonda Bodfield of the *Arizona Daily Star.*

"And I have not deviated an inch from what I thought was right for Arizona, and I think it paid off. People know that I am honest and that I care about the state and the people of Arizona. I'm a problem-solver, I'm not afraid of a challenge and I'm not a quitter."

Sources

Periodicals

Arizona Capitol Times (Phoenix), December 5, 2008; November 5, 2009; January 14, 2010; May 20, 2010; October 29, 2010; November 3, 2010.
Arizona Daily Star (Tucson), January 22, 2009; May 1, 2009; July 25, 2010; October 3, 2010.
Arizona Republic (Phoenix), July 14, 2010, p. A1; September 14, 2010; November 2, 2010; November 3, 2010.
Christian Science Monitor, July 15, 2010; September 3, 2010.
Los Angeles Times, June 4, 2010, p. A12; July 30, 2010, p. 1; September 19, 2010, p. A18.
Newsweek, August 16, 2010, p. 34.
New York Daily News, April 26, 2010.
New York Times, August 6, 2009, p. A14; April 25, 2010, p. A14; May 20, 2010, p. A16; September 4, 2010, p. A19.
Washington Post, April 24, 2010, p. A1; June 9, 2010, p. A1.

Online

"About Governor Jan Brewer," Arizona Governor Jan Brewer, http://azgovernor.gov/About_Gov.asp (November 19, 2010).
"Arizona enacts funeral protest legislation," CNN.com, http://www.cnn.com/2011/US/01/11/arizona.funeral.westboro/index.html?iref=allsearch (January 24, 2011).
Biography Resource Center Online, Gale Group, 2003.

Transcripts

John King, USA, CNN, October 28, 2010.
Larry King Live, CNN, July 30, 2010.

—*Diane Telgen*

Jeff Bridges

Actor

Jason LaVeris/FilmMagic/Getty Images

Born Jeffrey Leon Bridges, December 4, 1949, in Los Angeles, CA; son of Lloyd Vernet (an actor) and Dorothy Dean (an actress; maiden name, Simpson) Bridges; married Susan Geston (a photographer), 1977; children: Isabelle Annie, Jessica Lily, Hayley Roselouise. *Education:* Studied at the Berghoff Studios, New York, late 1960s.

Addresses: *Agent*—Creative Artists Agency, 2000 Avenue of the Stars, Los Angeles, CA 90067.

Career

Actor in films, including: *The Company She Keeps,* 1951; *Halls of Anger,* 1970; *The Yin and Yang of Mr. Go,* 1970; *The Last Picture Show,* 1971; *Bad Company,* 1972; *Fat City,* 1972; *The Iceman Cometh,* 1973; *The Last American Hero,* 1973; *Lolly-Madonna XXX,* 1973; *Thunderbolt and Lightfoot,* 1974; *Hearts of the West,* 1975; *Rancho Deluxe,* 1975; *King Kong,* 1976; *Stay Hungry,* 1976; *Somebody Killed Her Husband,* 1978; *Winter Kills,* 1979; *The American Success Company,* 1979; *Heaven's Gate,* 1980; *Cutter's Way,* 1981; *Kiss Me Goodbye,* 1982; *The Last Unicorn* (voice), 1982; *Tron,* 1982; *Against All Odds,* 1984; *Starman,* 1984; *Jagged Edge,* 1985; *8 Million Ways to Die,* 1986; *The Morning After,* 1986; *Nadine,* 1987; *Tucker,* 1988; *The Fabulous Baker Boys,* 1989; *See You in the Morning,* 1989; *Texasville,* 1990; *The Fisher King,* 1991; *American Heart,* 1992; *Fearless,* 1993; *The Vanishing,* 1993; *Blown Away,* 1994; *Wild Bill,* 1995; *The Mirror Has Two Faces,* 1996; *White Squall,* 1996; *The Big Lebowski,* 1998; *Arlington Road,* 1999; *Forever Hollywood,* 1999; *The Muse,* 1999; *Simpatico,* 1999; *The Contender,* 2000; *K-Pax,* 2001; *Scenes of the Crime,* 2001; *Masked and Anony-* *mous,* 2003; *Seabiscuit,* 2003; *The Door in the Floor,* 2004; *The Moguls,* 2005; *Tideland,* 2005; *Stick It,* 2006; *Surf's Up* (voice), 2007; *Cool School,* 2008; *How to Lose Friends & Alienate People,* 2008; *Iron Man,* 2008; *Crazy Heart,* 2009; *A Dog Year,* 2009; *The Men Who Stare at Goats,* 2009; *The Open Road,* 2009; *Tron Legacy,* 2010. Television appearances include: *Sea Hunt,* 2 episodes, 1958-60; *The Lloyd Bridges Show,* 3 episodes, 1962-63; *The Loner,* 1965; *The F.B.I.,* 1969; *Silent Night, Lonely Night* (movie), 1969; *The Most Deadly Game,* 1970; *In Search of America* (movie), 1971; *The Girls in Their Summer Dresses and Other Stories by Irwin Shaw* (movie), 1981; *Hidden in America* (movie), 2002. Narrator for television specials, including: *Raising the Mammoth,* 2000; *Lewis and Clark: Great Journey West,* 2002.

Awards: Saturn Award for best actor, Academy of Science Fiction, Fantasy, and Horror Films, for *Starman,* 1985; best male lead, Independent Spirit Awards, for *American Heart,* 1994; star on the Walk of Fame, 1994; Film Excellence Award, Boston Film Festival, 2000; Alan J. Pakula Award (with others), Broadcast Film Critics Association Awards, for *The Contender,* 2001; modern master award, Santa Barbara International Film Festival, 2003; career achievement award, National Board of Review, 2004; Donostia Lifetime Achievement award, San Sebastián International Film Festival, 2004; best actor award, Los Angeles Film Critics Association, for *Crazy Heart*, 2009; Academy Award for best actor, Academy of Motion Picture Arts and Sciences, for *Crazy Heart*, 2010; Critics Choice Award for best actor, Broadcast Film Critics Association Awards, for *Crazy Heart*, 2010; Golden Globe award for best performance in a drama, Hollywood Foreign Press Association, for *Crazy Heart*, 2010; best male lead, Independent Spirit Awards, for *Crazy Heart*, 2010; Desert Palm Achievement Award, Palm Springs International Film Festival, for *Crazy Heart*, 2010; SAG award for outstanding performance by a male actor in a leading role, Screen Actors Guild, for *Crazy Heart*, 2010.

Sidelights

Jeff Bridges was born into a family of actors and has been described by the Web site ShortList as being "a self-confessed product of Hollywood nepotism." He is the son of the late Lloyd Bridges, a character actor who became a star in the late 1950s as the main character in the nautical drama *Sea Hunt*. Bridges' brother is Beau Bridges, who is also an actor and who has a multitude of film and television credits including *The Fabulous Baker Boys* which the two brothers made together with Michelle Pfeiffer. Bridges grew up behind a camera and began his acting career at the very early age of six months when he was carried on screen by Jane Greer as a crying infant in one of the scenes in *The Company She Keeps*. Scott Bowles, writing for *USA Today*, reported that the "elder Bridges suggested someone pinch his son to get the tears flowing." Later he was a child actor on *Sea Hunt*. His biography for the Yahoo Movies Web site reported that Bridges told the London *Times* in 1999 about his guest appearances on *Sea Hunt*, "[My dad would] always say, 'Do you want this part? You'll be gone from school for a couple weeks.' And when you're eight years old, it's kind of fun."

Bridges' first big film role came in 1971 in *The Last Picture Show*. It was an adaptation of the award-winning novel by Larry McMurty that was directed by Peter Bogdanovich and featured an ensemble cast that included such luminaries as Cybil Shepherd, Timothy Bottoms, Cloris Leachman, Randy Quaid, Eileen Brennan, and Ben Johnson. In addition to Leachman winning the Academy Award for Best Supporting Actress, Bridges was nominated at the age of 23 for an Academy Award for Best Supporting Actor for his portrayal of the boyishly charming Duane Jackson. This was to be the first of his many nominations for an Academy Award.

After *The Last Picture Show*, Bridges went on to do a number of movies that displayed his considerable talent as an actor in quality productions. In 1972 he portrayed a struggling boxer in John Huston's *Fat City*, and a likable but untrustworthy con artist in the post-Civil War west in Robert Benton's *Bad Company*. In 1973 he played a stock car driver named Junior Jackson in director Lamont Johnson's *The Last American Hero*.

After finishing *The Last American Hero*, Bridges received a call from his agent saying that he had been offered a part in director John Frankenheimer's production of Eugene O'Neill's *The Iceman Cometh*. Bridges initially turned down the role. Five minutes after telling his agent that he did not want to accept the role he received a phone call from Lamont Johnson who proceeded to tell him in no uncertain terms that this was not an intelligent decision and that if he was really an actor he would take the role and do the job. In an interview with Audrey Kelly for *Fade In* Bridges described how making *The Iceman Cometh* helped him to finally decide to be an actor. Up until that time, he had not determined that he really wanted to be an actor. Bridges told Kelly, "So after that film where I had a really great experience with those guys, I thought, 'This is something that I can make my professional career and my other interests can all bring to that.'"

In 1974 Bridges worked with director Michael Cimino and fellow actor Clint Eastwood on *Thunderbolt and Lightfoot*. His performance demonstrated his range of acting ability and earned him a second nomination for an Academy Award for Best Supporting Actor. After his brilliant performance in *Thunderbolt and Lightfoot*, Bridges unfortunately participated in a number of film productions that damaged his growing stature as a talented actor who could competently get the job done and bring in box-office dollars. In 1976 he starred in a remake of *King Kong* that was a flop. Another dramatic failure was Cimino's production of *Heaven's Gate*. In a business where two expensive failures such as these can mean doom to an actor's career, Bridges continued to be offered work.

Bridges was able to resurrect his flagging acting career with solid performances in movies that spanned the decade of the 1980s. The first of these movies was director Taylor Hackford's production *Against All Odds* in which Bridges was reunited with Greer. It also starred Rachel Ward and James Woods. In 1984 Bridges earned his first nomination for an Academy Award for Best Actor for his portrayal of an Earth-bound alien in director John Carpenter's science fiction drama *Starman*. To prepare for his performance in *Starman* Bridges studied the movements of small children and animals. He also videotaped himself writhing on his floor to perfect the way that his alien would hatch. After *Starman*, Bridges starred in the movie that was his greatest box office hit up until that point. He co-starred with Glenn Close and played a businessman accused of murder in the legal thriller *Jagged Edge*. In 1988, Bridges starred as Preston Tucker in Francis Ford Coppola's *Tucker: The Man and His Dream*. Tucker was an American entrepreneur who tried to develop his own line of automobiles in the United States and was best known for the '48 Tucker Sedan. Production of the Tucker Sedan was shut down amidst allegations of stock market fraud in 1949 but many features of the Tucker Sedan are standard features in modern automobiles. In 1989, Bridges portrayed the character of Jack Baker in *The Fabulous Baker Boys*. In *The Fabulous Baker Boys* he played brother to his real-life brother, Beau.

Steve Wulf, writing for *Entertainment Weekly*, quoted film critic Pauline Kael as saying about Bridges, "He may be the most natural and least self-conscious screen actor who ever lived; physically, it's as if he had spent his life in the occupation of each character." It is almost a cliché to say that Bridges is one of the most under-appreciated actors in Hollywood. In 1991 Bridges starred with Robin Williams and Mercedes Ruehl in the urban fantasy *The Fisher King*. Critics were impressed and gave him acclaim for his role because he provided a counterpoint to Williams' energetic performance in the movie, but it was Ruehl who won an Academy Award for Best Supporting Actress for her portrayal of Bridges' girlfriend. After *The Fisher King* Bridges starred in *American Heart*, which was about an ex-convict who wishes to reconcile with his son. In 1993, *Fearless* was released. In this movie, Bridges played a man who survives an air disaster but is transfigured. The movie was nominated for an Academy Award, but Bridges was overlooked despite that. The author of his Yahoo Movies biography wrote, "*Fearless* was considered by many to be Bridges' finest, most courageous piece of work" up until that time.

Bridges next three movies did middling business. They were *Blown Away*, which came out in 1994 and in which Bridges co-starred with Tommy Lee Jones; *Wild Bill*, which was an eccentric "art western" that came out in 1995; and lastly Ridley Scott's *White Squall*. In 1996 Bridges starred in the romantic comedy *The Mirror Has Two Faces* with Barbara Streisand.

By the mid-1990s Bridges had three daughters with his wife Susan and was reluctant to take the role that next came his way. The Coen Brothers offered him the role of the Dude in the comedic movie *The Big Lebowski*. The Dude character is a reefer-toking,

White Russian drinking, hallucinating slacker with a penchant for bowling. The film was only mildly successful in the United States when it was first released but has since become a cult classic and has inspired Big Lebowski festivals.

In 1999, Bridges starred in a trio of movies. In *Arlington Road*, he portrayed a college professor who loses his FBI wife in a counter-terrorism operation. When new neighbors move in, the character is initially excited and then grows progressively more paranoid as he comes to believe that the neighbors may be terrorists. In *The Muse* Bridges played a screenwriter who introduces a friend of his to a woman played by Sharon Stone. Sharon Stone then becomes his friend's muse. The last movie of that year was also made with Sharon Stone and was called *Simpatico*. It was based on the play by Sam Shepherd.

In the year 2000, Bridges played the character of President Jackson Evans in the political drama titled *The Contender*. For his portrayal of the manipulative and shrewd president, Bridges was once again nominated for an Academy Award and once again did not win the award. After *The Contender* he portrayed a psychiatrist who comes to doubt his diagnosis of a delusional patient who believes himself an alien in *K-Pax*, which came out in 2001.

In 2003 Bridges starred in his first blockbuster. In *Seabiscuit* he played wealthy financier Charles Howard. The same year he starred in a comedy called *Masked and Anonymous* about an unknown singer-songwriter who stages a benefit concert. In 2005 he starred in Terry Gilliam's *Tideland*. After this came *Stick It*, a comedic movie about gymnastics. In 2007 he did voice work on the animated movie *Surf's Up*.

In 2008 came his second blockbuster, *Iron Man*. In the movie he portrayed Obadiah Stane. *Iron Man* tested Bridges' work ethic, which is to have fun and do as little work as possible. In the *Sunday Times* it is described how, when he showed up on the set of *Iron Man*, he discovered that while there was everything necessary for a movie including a release date, a cast, a crew, and cameras, there was no script. Every day the script was written for the day before shooting began. The experience on *Iron Man* showed how laid back Bridges really is. He rolled with the experience and decided that it was all play and things were fine.

In 2009 Bridges completed two movies. The first was the political satire *The Men Who Stare at Goats* which also starred George Clooney. The other movie, *Crazy Heart,* was originally destined to only be released on DVD until it was picked up and distributed by Fox Searchlight. In that film Bridges portrayed an alcoholic, washed-up singer named Bad Blake. For his portrayal of Bad Blake, Bridges won a Screen Actors Guild Award and a Golden Globe Award for Best Actor. He also won his first Academy Award, for Best Actor.

In addition to acting Bridges is also a musician who, in 2000, released his own album called *Be Here Soon.* He is an accomplished photographer and takes photographs to document the behind-the-scene actions on all of his movies. He has published a book of his photographs titled *Pictures.*

Bridges also helped to establish the End Hunger Network in 1983. This is a non-profit organization that was originally started to end world hunger. It has since switched its focus to end hunger in the United States. According to Bridges' Web site, 35 million people in the United States do not know where their next meal is coming from and 13 million of those people are children. The End Hunger Network provides informational videos and articles linked directly from Bridges Web site.

Family is very important to Bridges. Of his wife Susan, Bridges told N. F. Mendoza of *Reader's Digest,* "In the 28 years we've been married, we've done 50 movies together. I say 'we' because Sue deserves a credit, too. I'm the guy who makes the buck, but she's the one who takes care of everything else. I really am more in love with her than ever."

Sources

Books

Contemporary Theatre, Film, and Television, vol. 60, Thomson Gale, 2005.

Periodicals

Entertainment Weekly, February 23, 2001, p. 70.
Reader's Digest, February 2006.
Sunday Times (London, England), February 7, 2010..
USA Today, April 28, 2008, p. 1D.

Online

"Crossing Bridges," *Fade In,* http://fadeinonline.com/100228/articles/jeff_bridges/ (March 1, 2010).
"Jeff Bridges Interview," ShortList, http://www.shortlist.com/movies/article/jeff-bridges-interview/1 (March 1, 2010).
"Jeff Bridges," Yahoo Movies, http://movies.yahoo.com/movie/contributor/18000116.tif34/bio (March 5, 2010).

—*Annette Bowman*

Alton Brown

SHNS file photo courtesy of Food Network/Newscom

Television host and cookbook author

Born on July 30, 1962, in Los Angeles, CA; married Deanna; children: Zoey. *Education:* University of Georgia, B.A., c. 1984; New England Culinary Institute, Montpelier, VT, 1995.

Addresses: *Agent*—William Morris Agency, 1325 Avenue of the Americas, New York, NY 10019. *Web site*—http://www.altonbrown.com.

Career

Worked as cameraman and commercial director, 1980s-1990s. Host of television series, including: *Good Eats*, 1998—; *Iron Chef America*, 2005—; *Feasting on Asphalt*, 2006; *Feasting on Asphalt 2: The River Run*, 2007; *The Next Iron Chef*, 2007—; *Feasting on Waves*, 2008. Television guest appearances include: *Iron Chef America: Battle of the Masters*, 2004; *The Making of Iron Chef America*, 2004; *All-Star Grill Fest: South Beach*, 2007; *SpongeBob Squarepants*, 2008; *Dear Food Network: Thanksgiving*, 2008; *The Next Food Network Star*, 2009; *Ace of Cakes*, 2010. Author of cookbooks, including: *I'm Just Here for the Food: Food + Heat = Cooking*, 2002; *Alton Brown's Gear for your Kitchen*, 2003; *I'm Just Here for the Food: Food x Mixing + Heat = Baking*, 2004; *Feasting on Asphalt: The River Run*, 2008; *Good Eats: The Early Years*, 2009.

Awards: Award for best cookbook, James Beard Foundation, for *I'm Just Here for the Food*, 2003; American Food and Entertaining Award for cooking teacher of the year, *Bon Appetit*, 2004.

Sidelights

Although cookbook author and television chef Alton Brown is widely known for his appearances on a variety of popular Food Network programs, he began his career on the other side of the camera. After spending a decade working as a video director and cinematographer, Brown launched the long-running informational show *Good Eats* on the then-young cable Food Network in 1998 soon after completing culinary school. His triad of roles—writer, producer, and star—has made him a culinary figure recognized and respected by fans and foodies alike. A number of well-received cookbooks, including the James Beard Award-winning *I'm Just Here for the Food,* and expanded roles on such Food Network shows as *Iron Chef America* and *Feasting on Asphalt* have cemented Brown as one of television's most popular food personalities.

Born on July 30, 1962, in Los Angeles, California, Brown became interested in food and cooking at a young age. Growing up mostly in Georgia, where his parents owned a local radio station, he spent much of his childhood watching his mother and grandmother prepare food. As a student at Lithonia High School, Brown held part-time jobs in restaurant kitchens. After graduation, he enrolled in the drama program at Athens, Georgia's University of Georgia, continuing to moonlight as a restaurant cook while completing his drama degree, claiming in his Food Network Web site biography that his talents at the stove served handily "as a way to get dates." A job as a camera operator on fellow Athens residents R.E.M.'s "The One I Love" music video saw Brown's entry into the world of film and television in the mid-1980s. Over the next decade, the future television star made a living shooting video and film, perhaps most notably on director Spike Lee's 1988 film *School Daze*. However, Brown felt unfulfilled in his work and decided to forsake his career in favor of a stint at Vermont's New England Culinary Institute.

After graduating from culinary school in 1997, Brown spent several months working in restaurants before melding his love of food with his camera skills to create the television program *Good Eats*, a decision informed by his longtime boredom with what he considered poorly made television food programming. A combination of food documentary, science experiment, and cooking class, the show debuted on the Food Network in 1998 with an episode dedicated to the quintessential American Thanksgiving dinner. It won Brown an audience intrigued by his deep knowledge of food and culinary techniques as well as his quirky, offbeat presentation style. Becoming a regular series for the network the following year, *Good Eats* has proved to be one of the Food Network's most enduring offerings, with more than ten seasons in the can and new programs in production more than a decade after its debut.

In 2002, Brown branched into a different media with the publication of his first cookbook, *I'm Just Here for the Food*. Hailed for its "winning formula of pop culture combined with history, science and common sense" by *Publishers Weekly*, the work went on to earn Brown a prestigious James Beard Foundation Award in 2003. The newly minted author quickly followed up his debut with 2003's *Alton Brown's Gear for Your Kitchen* and 2004's *I'm Just Here for More Food: Food x Mixing + Heat = Baking*, both noted for interpreting Brown's distinctive television persona into the written word. His varied culinary output won Brown the 2004 Cooking Teacher of the Year award at the *Bon Appetit* American Food & Entertaining Awards.

Along with these efforts—and while continuing to create *Good Eats*—the busy chef found the time in 2004 to serve as the color commentator on *Iron Chef America: Battle of the Masters*, based on the popular Japanese competitive cooking program. The following year he resumed this role when *Iron Chef America* launched on the Food Network's regular primetime schedule, acting as one of the program's primary hosts during its multi-season run. In 2007, he also became the host of the related Food Network competition show, *The Next Iron Chef*.

Brown's next project allowed him to marry his love of food with another hobby: motorcycling. An avid biker, the chef starred in the Food Network's *Feasting on Asphalt*, a miniseries that followed Brown—and his bike—around the United States seeking out local roadside food establishments. The program's success during its initial 2006 run led to a second installment the following year, and a related miniseries titled *Feasting on Waves*. This third season, aired in 2008, found Brown travelling the Caribbean to profile island cuisines. That same year, Brown's companion book, *Feasting on Asphalt: The River Run*, appeared on bookstore shelves.

During 2009, Brown began attracting attention not only for what output of food knowledge, but also his shifting personal intake of food products—and his resulting 50-pound weight loss. Citing a desire not only to improve his own health but also to encourage the general public to develop healthier eating habits, the television personality slimmed down from an admitted 213 pounds over the course of several months by eliminating unhealthy foods from his diet. "I decided there were foods I was just not going to have," he explained to Joel Stein of *Time*. "I've probably had three tons of French fries in my life. I don't need any more French fries." Brown's much-altered physique perhaps unsurprisingly became the subject of an episode of *Good Eats* in which the host promoted the eating plan that had enabled him to lose a considerable amount of weight without officially dieting.

Unquestionably, Brown's decreasing size has not detracted from his popularity on a network unabashedly dedicated to the consumption of food. The fall of 2009 saw Brown return as the host of the Food Network's competitive reality program *The Next Iron Chef* as well as reprise his commentator role on *Iron Chef America*. A retrospective book on his signature program, *Good Eats: The Early Years*, reached shelves in October of that year. Although he described himself as simply a "really twisted home ec teacher" to *Cooking Light*'s Adrienne Martini, the Atlanta-based Brown seems likely to remain a popular cooking instructor both on the screen and the page for some time to come.

Selected writings

Cookbooks

I'm Just Here for the Food: Food + Heat = Cooking, Stewart, Tabori & Chang (New York City), 2002.

Alton Brown's Gear for your Kitchen, Stewart, Tabori & Chang, 2003.

I'm Just Here for the Food: Food x Mixing + Heat = Baking, Stewart, Tabori & Chang, 2004.

Feasting on Asphalt: The River Run, Stewart, Tabori & Chang, 2008.

Good Eats: The Early Years, Stewart, Tabori & Chang, 2009.

Sources

Books

Marquis Who's Who, Marquis Who's Who, 2009.

Periodicals

Publishers Weekly, April 15, 2002, p. 58.
Saturday Evening Post, September-October 2009, p. 25.
Time, December 14, 2009, p. 67.
Variety, May 10, 1999, p. 135.

Online

"Alton Brown," Food Network, http://www.foodnetwork.com/alton-brown/bio/index.html (February 24, 2010).

"Alton Brown," Internet Movie Database, http://www.imdb.com/name/nm0113002/ (February 25, 2010).

Biography Resource Center Online, Gale, 2007.

"Table Talk with Alton Brown," *Cooking Light,* http://www.cookinglight.com/cooking-101/meet-the-chef/table-talk-with-alton-brown-00400000.tif005709/ (February 25, 2010).

—Vanessa E. Vaughn

Samantha Brown

Television personality

Born Samantha Elizabeth Brown, March 31, 1969, in Dallas, TX; daughter of Christopher (a business owner) and Elsie Mae (an administrative assistant) Brown; married Kevin O'Leary (in information technology), October 28, 2006. *Education:* Syracuse University, B.F.A., 1992.

Addresses: *Home*—Brooklyn, NY. *Office*—The Travel Channel, 5425 Wisconsin Ave., Chevy Chase, MD 20815.

Career

Appeared in New York City off-Broadway productions, c. 1992-98, and in television commercials. Host of Travel Channel television shows, including: *Great Vacation Homes,* 1999; *Girl Meets Hawaii,* 2000; *Great Hotels,* 2002; *Passport to Europe,* 2004-05; *Great Cruises,* 2006; *Walt Disney World Christmas Day Parade* 2006; *Samantha Brown: Passport to Latin America,* 2007; *Walt Disney World Holidays,* 2007; *Passport to China,* 2008; *Samantha Brown: Passport to Great Weekends,* 2008; *Samantha Brown's Asia,* 2010; *Samantha Brown Fan-a-Thon,* 2010; *Samantha Brown: Inside the Suitcase,* 2010; *Samantha Brown's Vancouver,* 2010; *Samantha Brown's World of Sports,* 2010.

Sidelights

Samantha Brown attained celebrity status on The Travel Channel thanks to her friendly, energetic on-camera style. Brown's *Passport* series for the cable channel have gained her a loyal following, and her far-flung trips to exotic locales proved so popular that viewers sometimes download and copy her itineraries from the channel's Web site to retrace themselves, landmark by landmark. Most of the appeal of Brown's *Passport to Europe* and *Great Weekends* shows, asserted *San Francisco Chronicle* writer Spud Hilton, rests in "the unflappable and impossibly upbeat Brown bouncing from site to site, not lecturing about the place ... as much as learning about it—discovering it—along with viewers."

Brown was born in 1969 in Dallas, Texas, and her first major travel adventure came when her family moved cross-country to New Hampshire when she was seven years old. In the city of Dover her father started a building-materials supply firm, Conproco, and Brown grew up in coastal New Castle. She graduated from a private school in Derry, the Pinkerton Academy, in 1988, where she captained its cheerleading squad.

At Syracuse University in upstate New York Brown was a musical-theater major and, after earning her degree in 1992, moved to New York City to launch her career on Broadway. She never quite made it that far, spending the better part of the decade in off-Broadway plays, but she did train with Mouth, a sketch-comedy group that relied heavily on improvisational-style theater. She also appeared in television commercials, and a few she did for a cable-television provider, Century Cable in Los Angeles, as fictional spokesperson "Wendy Wire" would inadvertently propel her career forward: her perky demeanor caught the attention of a producer for The Travel Channel, who called her in to audition. Her debut on the network came in 1999 as the tour guide for *Great Vacation Homes,* followed by *Girl Meets Hawaii* a year later and *Great Hotels* in 2002.

Brown's *Passport to Europe* series, which debuted in December of 2004, helped make her a household name. Viewers liked her personable attitude and frisky energy, as did her bosses. "It was a little disturbing for me eight years ago to realize that there weren't that many hosts around who didn't act like Stepford Wives," she told Fort Wayne *Journal Gazette* writer Steve Penhollow. "I didn't want to go that way at all. I went the other way, and the Travel Channel loved that."

Passport to Europe ran for two seasons on The Travel Channel and followed Brown through 19 half-hour episodes that tracked her and a crew all the way from Finland, south to some Mediterranean locales, then as far west as Cornwall in the southwestern corner of England. The show developed a solid viewership, and some devotees considered Brown so trustworthy a source that the show's Web site posted itineraries that viewers could download to plan their own travels. As one of The Travel Channel's most trusted on-screen tour guides, Brown was sent to more exotic locales for the next series, *Passport to Latin America,* which began airing in 2007 with a full, 19-episode season. *Passport to China* debuted just in time for the Beijing Summer Olympic Games in 2008, showcasing a nation that just 30 years earlier had imposed draconian restrictions on travelers from Western nations. Individual American trekkers were not even allowed to travel inside China until 1980; in the decade before that, they were permitted to visit only as part of formal tour groups.

The Travel Channel's contractual requirements with the Chinese government included an all-Chinese technical crew and an official guide. Brown admitted that she initially feared her escort might censor any footage his superiors would consider inappropriate, but as she told John Bordsen in the *Charlotte Observer,* "by the end of the trip we were great friends. He was definitely on our side, which was neat to see. He would go to battle for us when policemen would come up and say, 'You're not supposed to be here,' and we'd have to show them the permits that were months in the making."

In the same interview, Brown also remarked that having a local video crew meant that all of their dining choices were exciting, authentic experiences. In fact, that is one of her standard suggestions to travelers on how to genuinely discover a new place. "Don't ask the concierge where to go for lunch," she told Hilton in the *San Francisco Chronicle* interview. "Ask your housekeeper. Ask the bellman." Asked in another article about the potential dangers of foreign travel, Brown admitted she had found herself in a dicey place or two on her many jaunts, but added, "my best advice is to trust the hairs on your neck," she told Cindy Kibbe, a reporter for the *New Hampshire Business Review.* "Trust your gut instincts. They are better than any guidebook or tour guide."

In 2008 The Travel Channel capitalized on Brown's high ratings with a second series, *Passport to Great Weekends.* After her 2006 marriage to Kevin O'Leary, a New York city-based information-technology specialist, Brown wanted to be able to travel some places with her husband, and staying closer to home also served to introduce Travel Channel viewers to noteworthy locales in their own backyard. As she told Myrtle Beach *Sun News* journalist Lisa Fleisher, the United States was a tremendously diverse place all by itself. "Every city, every destination has an enclave of immigrants, neighborhoods, that have settled there. And I think especially these days when traveling to Europe, traveling abroad has become so prohibitively expensive because of the dollar, it's really actually easy to look at our own country as places of international destinations."

Brown's work schedule has her on the road about ten months out of the year. She and O'Leary live in Brooklyn, but "I'm rarely home," she told Fleisher, the *Sun News* reporter. "I've got about three weeks of errands to run in two days." Once, she was trundling down one of her neighborhood's streets with an armload of boxes, dry cleaning, and groceries when a man spotted her and said, "'I watch you on TV all the time ... You're never home!'," she told Fleisher. "It would have been a perfect shot of what my home life is like."

Sources

Periodicals

Charlotte Observer (NC), August 3, 2008.
Journal Gazette (Fort Wayne, IN), July 13, 2008.
New Hampshire Business Review, July 4, 2008, p. 3.
New Hampshire Union Leader, June 5, 2007, p. A1.
San Francisco Chronicle, May 4, 2008, p. E3.

Sun News (Myrtle Beach, SC), April 30, 2008.

Online

Biography Resource Center Online, Gale, 2008.

"Samantha Brown," Travel Channel, http://www.travelchannel.com/TV_Shows/Samantha_Brown (June 30, 2010).

—*Carol Brennan*

Scott Brown

AP Images

U.S. senator

Born September 12, 1959, in Wakefield, MA; son of C. Bruce and Judith Brown; married Gail Huff, c. 1987; children: Arianna, Ayla. *Education:* Tufts University, B.A., 1981; Boston College Law School, J.D., 1985.

Addresses: *Office*—U.S. Senate, 317 Russell Senate Office Building, Washington, DC 20510.

Career

Worked as a model, 1980s; practiced real estate law, 1990s-2000s; assessor, Wrentham, Massachusetts, 1992-95; elected to Massachusetts House of Representatives, 1998; elected to Massachusetts Senate, 2004; elected to U.S. Senate, 2010.

Sidelights

Politician Scott Brown rose to national prominence when he won the Massachusetts Senate seat left vacant by the death of Ted Kennedy in a special election in January of 2010, the first time a Republican had done so in nearly three decades. News outlets seized on Brown's somewhat surprising victory as an expression of voters' disapproval of Democratic policy initiatives and of the Barack Obama administration as a whole. Writing shortly after the election, John Fritze and Kathy Kiely of *USA Today* observed that, regardless of the cause, "the down-to-the-wire election has given Democrats pause as House and Senate lawmakers nationwide prepare to face voters in the fall election." Brown's election significantly impacted Democratic plans for health care reform and has been acknowledged as a sign of rising conservative influence throughout the American electorate.

Born on September 12, 1959, Brown grew up in the Boston suburb of Wakefield, Massachusetts. During childhood he suffered a series of personal challenges; his parents divorced when Brown was still a toddler, and the youth experienced continued familial upheaval as each parent remarried three times. After graduating from Wakefield High School, the future public servant earned a bachelor's degree at Boston's Tufts University and then enrolled at Boston College Law School to continue his education along with serving in the Army National Guard. While working on his law degree, the 22-year-old Brown was named "America's Sexiest Man" by *Cosmopolitan* magazine, appearing nude in the publication's June 1982 issue. The nod led to a successful modeling career, and Brown spent the next several years working in the fashion industry. During this period, he met and married Boston television personality Gail Huff, with whom he later had daughters Arianna and Ayla.

By the early 1990s, Brown had given up his modeling career to return to the bar. He became a real estate attorney in his native Massachusetts, continued his service with the National Guard, and quietly entered politics. In 1992, he became the assessor of Wrentham, Massachusetts, and six years later was elected as a state-level representative. He won re-election to the Massachusetts House of Representatives before successfully campaigning for a seat in the state Senate during a special election in 2004. Despite being one of a tiny minority of Republicans in the legislative body, Brown again retained his seat through three election cycles.

Categorizing himself as "fiscally conservative and socially conscious," according to Brian Mooney of the *Boston Globe,* Brown has drawn attention for his blend of political and social views. Despite being an outspoken opponent of such issues as the legalization of gay marriage, the politician has also expressed qualified support for abortion rights and voted in favor of Massachusetts' 2006 health care reform initiative. Before 2009, Brown was arguably better known for stating in 2001 that it was "not normal" for Democratic state senator and lesbian Cheryl Jacques to have an adopted child with her partner, than for his legislative efforts.

When the death of long-serving U.S. Senator Ted Kennedy left one of Massachusetts' two Senate seats open in late 2009, national attention focused on the special election being mounted to fill the vacancy. An unusual set of political circumstances gave the race greater weight than such elections normally carry: Democrats held a filibuster-proof 60-seat supermajority in the U.S. Senate and were in the process of using that power to enact a controversial, large-scale health care reform package supported by the sitting Obama administration. Pundits quickly put forth that the Massachusetts special election would serve as a referendum on the issue, with the state's voters essentially choosing to support the national health reforms by electing a Democrat or putting a practical stop to the effort by choosing a Republican.

Despite the intense scrutiny focused on the race, Massachusetts Republicans had little expectation of winning the seat in the traditionally Democratic stronghold. Instead, party aides hoped to raise Brown's profile in order to position him as a viable contender for statewide office during the next regular election cycle. "If he got 40 percent," former Massachusetts Governor William Weld told Frank Bruni of the *New York Times,* "they would all have been covered in glory." Democrats nominated Massachusetts Attorney General Martha Coakley, expecting to claim an easy victory in the January election. However, Coakley soon proved to be a poor choice. She was an unenthusiastic campaigner who seemed ill at ease with voters, particularly in comparison to Brown's pickup-truck-driving everyman persona. The support of nationwide conservative groups and the burgeoning Tea Party movement also helped strengthen Brown's unlikely candidacy, and by the end of 2009 the race's outcome no longer seemed certain.

Although registered Democrats greatly outnumbered their Republican counterparts, Massachusetts' large population of independent voters made a Republican victory a legitimate possibility. As the date of the election neared, Brown pulled ahead in the polls, transforming his chances of victory from merely possible to feasible and, eventually, to likely. Despite last minute campaigning efforts by President Obama on Coakley's behalf, Brown retained an edge going into Election Day. When the polls closed on January 19, 2010, the state senator received a push up the political ladder to national office. Short weeks after the election, he was sworn in as the junior U.S. Senator from Massachusetts.

Brown quickly established himself as a centrist Republican who was willing to break with the party line, perhaps a nod to the relatively moderate bloc of independent voters who had brought him to office. Although he joined his fellow Republicans in lodging a vote against the finalized—and ultimately adopted—health care reform package, he became one of just five Republican senators to support a jobs bill passed by Congress in his very first Congressional vote in February of 2010. He went on to build a reputation as a centrist willing to work across party lines, drawing comparisons to fellow Northeastern Republican Senators Olympia Snowe and Susan Collins. "I am not quite sure what all the surprise is, and people wondering kind of like, 'wow, he's independent,'" Brown was quoted as commenting in a *New York Times* article by David M. Herszhenhorn. "I have always been this way. I am going to look at each and every bill and look at the merits of it."

Sources

Periodicals

Boston Globe, November 20, 2009.
New York Times, January 18, 2010; February 28, 2010; June 1, 2010.
USA Today, January 20, 2010, p. 2A; January 28, 2010, p. 9A.

Online

"Biography," Scott Brown Official Web site, http://scottbrown.senate.gov/public/index.cfm/biography (August 26, 2010).

"Senator is the Centerfold," *Cosmopolitan*, http://www.cosmopolitan.com/celebrity/news/scott-brown-nude-in-cosmo (August 26, 2010).

"Times Topics: Scott P. Brown," *New York Times*, http://topics.nytimes.com/top/reference/timestopics/people/b/scott_p_brown/index.html (August 26, 2010).

—Vanessa E. Vaughn

Kyle Busch

Professional race car driver

Born May 2, 1985, in Las Vegas, NV; son of Tom (an auto mechanic and amateur racer) and Gaye Busch; married Samantha Sarcinella, December 31, 2010.

Addresses: *Office*—Kyle Busch Motorsports, 351 Mazeppa Rd., Mooresville, NC 28115; c/o Joe Gibbs Racing, 13415 Reese Blvd. West, Huntersville, NC 28078. *Web site*—http://www.kylebusch.com/; http://www.kylebuschmotorsports.com/; http://www.kylebuschfoundation.org/; http://www.nascar.com/drivers/dps/kbusch01/cup/; http://twitter.com/kylebusch; http://www.facebook.com/KyleBusch.

Career

Began racing at the age of 13; competed in six Truck Series races for Rousch Racing, 2001; finished eighth in ASA (American Speed Association) standings, 2002; professional race car driver for Hendrick Motorsports, 2003-07; won first Nextel Cup Series race, 2005; signed with Joe Gibbs Racing, 2007; formed own truck series team through his company, Kyle Busch Motorsports, c. 2009; won Nationwide Series title, 2009; became first driver to win in the top three NASCAR series on one track in one weekend, 2010.

Awards: Raybestos Rookie of the Year Award, 2004; first place, Sony HD 500, California Speedway, 2005; first place, Checker Auto Parts 500, Phoenix International Raceway, 2005; first place, Lenox Industrial Tools 300, New Hampshire International Speedway, 2006; first place, Food Place 500, 2007; Aaron's 499, Talladega Speedway, 2008; Best Buy 400, 2008; first place, Coke Zero 400, 2008; Dodge Challenger 500, Darlington Raceway, 2008; Kobalt Tools 400, Atlanta Motor Speedway, 2008; first place, Toyota Save Mart 350, Infineon Raceway, 2008; first place, LifeLock.com 400, 2008; first place, Centurion Boats at the Glen, 2008; first place, Food City 500, 2009; Sharpie 500, 2009; first place, Shelby 427, 2009; first place, Crown Royal Presents the Russ Friedman 400, 2009; first place, Autism Speaks 400, 2010; first place, Crown Royal Presents the Health Calhoun 400, 2010; first place, Irwin Tools Race Night, 2010.

Sidelights

National Association for Stock Car Auto Racing (NASCAR) star Kyle Busch was known as a gifted race car driver but one with a temper and given to outbursts that have been to the detriment of his performance on the race track, his reputation, and his career as a whole. Known for his speed and aggressive tactics on the track, he had a number of firsts to his name. For example, Busch was the youngest driver ever to win a Nextel Cup Series level race and the first to win the races in the top three NASCAR series at one track in one weekend. Driving for Joe Gibbs Racing in Sprint Cup series and Nationwide series, he was also an owner of a Truck Series team that he raced for. Embracing his intense image, Busch told Nate Ryan of *USA Today*, "People are obsessed with everything I do. I enjoy it. I'm not here to be vanilla. What's the ice cream flavor all green and purple? That's me! Colorful." He also noted, "Everybody else wants to win, but I don't think they take it maybe as seriously or as hard as I do."

Born on May 2, 1985, in Las Vegas, Nevada, Busch was the son of Tom, an auto mechanic and amateur racer, and his wife, Gaye. He began driving a home-made go-kart when he was four years old. He and his elder brother Kurt (who also became a professional race car driver, winning the 2004 Sprint Cup championship) raced around their neighborhood on the vehicle. When Busch was 13 years old, he began racing in Legend Cars in Las Vegas. He won two Legend Car championships in Las Vegas; by the age of 15 he had compiled 65 Legend Car victories. By 2001, he was racing in late-model cars and won ten local races in Vegas. A junior in high school at the time, he also started in six Craftsman Truck Series races for Rousch Racing (which already employed his brother), finishing in the top ten twice. After the victories, NASCAR adopted a rule that stated that its top three national series, including the Truck Series, would only allow drivers over the age of 18 to compete. The rule led to the nullification of Busch's contract with Roush and a year out of the highest level of racing.

An exceptional student, Busch graduated from Durango High School, in Durango, Nevada, in 2002. Busch earned his high school diploma a year early so he could focus on his racing career. That year, he finished eighth in the ASA (American Speed Association) standings, a series for young racers. By 2003, Busch signed a new deal to race in a number of ARCA (Automobile Racing Club of America) and Busch series (the second tier of NASCAR stock car racing) events with Hendrick Motorsports, and was considered the next Jeff Gordon. Team owner Rick Hendrick told Lars Anderson of *Sports Illustrated*, "Kyle drives like he's 28, not 18. I'm glad I got him because when it comes to racing, he's as good as anybody I've seen at this age." Busch went on to win two ARCA events that year. He also started in seven Busch Series races for Hendrick Motorsports. His best finish was second at a race in Charlotte, North Carolina.

The following year, Busch was competing in both Busch Series and Nextel Cup Series (later known as the Sprint Series, the top tier of NASCAR stock car racing) events for Hendrick Motorsports. In his first full year of racing in the Busch Series, he won rookie of the year honors after finishing second in the standings. Busch also competed in six Nextel Cup Series races, making his debut in Las Vegas where he started eighteenth, but finished forty-first. His best finish of the year in the Nextel Cup Series was twenty-fourth at the Fontana Labor Day weekend race. Busch finished the Nextel Cup Series season in fifty-second place for series points.

Because of his showing in Nextel Cup races, Hendrick named him a full-time driver for 2005 in the team's number five car in that series. A true rookie in the Nextel Cup Series, he won two races that season. His first Nextel Cup victory came on September 4 at Fontana, while his second was on November 13 in Phoenix. With his first victory, he became the youngest driver ever to win a race in the Nextel Cup Series. Busch finished the season with nine top five finishes and thirteen top ten finishes. By season's end, he had finished twentieth in series points. By this time, however, his temper and ruthless driving style had made him one of the least popular drivers in NASCAR despite being one of the youngest drivers in the history of the highest level of NASCAR.

Busch continued to blossom as a driver in 2006 as he showed growth and a newfound maturity after a series of public displays of poor behavior. They included driving with a rowdy aggressiveness during the Daytona 500, having run-ins with then-Cup series champion Tony Stewart, and throwing a safety device at the car of another driver, Casey Mears, who unintentionally clipped Busch's car during a race, causing him to wreck and be unable to complete the race. Because of the latter incident, Busch was placed on probation for the rest of the season.

Busch made an effort to change but also understood why he did not fit in well with the NASCAR community. During the 2006 season, he told Anderson of *Sports Illustrated*, "There's no manual on how to become a NASCAR driver and how to interact with fans and other drivers. Everyone thinks I'm cocky and that I'm the same person as my brother … but no one has gotten to know me. I've tried to reach out and mingle with other drivers, but I don't have a lot in common with them. Plus—and this is just a fact—older guys don't like when you beat them."

Though Busch won only one race (July 16 in New Hampshire) in 2006, he had ten top five finishes and 18 top ten finishes. Busch also won one pole and the right to compete in the Chase for the Nextel

Cup at the end of the season. Busch ultimately finished tenth for the year. In 2007, Busch again showed significant improvement as a driver on the Nextel Cup Series. He won the Car of Tomorrow race in Bristol, Connecticut, and had eleven top-five finishes as well as 20 top ten finishes. Making the Chase for the Cup, he ultimately finished fifth in the series standings at the end of the season.

During the 2007 season, Busch and Hendrick Motorsports announced they were parting ways at season's end. Sick of Busch's antics, owner Rick Hendrick told the mercurial Busch that he was being let go as Hendrick was signing Dale Earnhardt, Jr., for his team. Busch signed with Joe Gibbs Racing for the 2008 season, replacing J. J. Yealey in the number 18 car. Driving exceptionally well and finding a better fitting, more comfortable home with Gibbs, Busch won eight races on the season and again made the Chase for the Cup. He ultimately finished tenth in series points. But the Sprint Cup series was not Busch's only racing focus. He also competed in the Nationwide Series (formerly known as the Busch Series), nabbing ten victories, as well as the Truck Series, with three victories. Busch's combined 21 victories in the three NASCAR national series were a new record. In 2008, he also set a record by becoming the first driver in the history of NASCAR to win three road races in one year. Because of his success, Busch's merchandise sales jumped more than 500 percent.

In 2009, Busch had four wins in the Sprint Cup series, including victories in Las Vegas, Richmond, and twice in Bristol. He also won the Gatorade Duel No. 2 before the season-opening Daytona 500, but had an accident on lap 125 and finished forty-first in the race. After 19 races, Busch was in the top ten of drivers standings but fell out of contention after finishing thirty-eighth in Indianapolis. He never clawed his way back to contention and ultimately finished thirteenth in series points at season's end. He also changed crew chiefs during the season, replacing his longtime chief Steve Addington with Dave Rogers. After the change, Busch finished eleventh at a race in Texas and showed a new resolve in his driving.

In 2009, Busch did win the Nationwide Series title and formed his own successful Truck Series team under the banner of his new company, Kyle Busch Motorsports. He raced in one truck (also sporting the number 18), while another driver raced in the other. Busch continued to drive in the Sprint Cup and the Nationwide Series for Joe Gibbs Racing, signing a multi-year contract extension with the company in January of 2010. At the beginning of the 2010 racing season, Busch seemed to be more calm, patient, and mature, in part the effect of team ownership but also because of his forthcoming marriage to former model and psychology student Samantha Sarcinella (the couple married on December 31, 2010). He was also seen as a contender for the Sprint Cup championship, though there were concerns he was overextending himself by competing in three different series and owning his own racing team.

Busch did not live up to his pre-season hype in the Sprint Cup series in 2010. He finished out of contention for the championship, though he had at least three wins in 36 starts. Late in the season, one of his best showings was at the Bank of America 500 in Charlotte, North Carolina, where he finished second. Nonetheless, he made more than six million dollars on the year. Busch did better in the Truck Series, where he was in competition for the owner's title. His number 18 Toyota truck was second in the standings by mid-November 2010. Because of his success, Busch lined up a major new sponsor for his Truck Series vehicle in five races in 2011: Dollar General. Busch also did well the Nationwide Series, where he had 13 victories and won Joe Gibbs Racing the owners' championship.

Despite such mixed results over the whole season, Busch demonstrated the depth of his talent on the track in August of 2010. At the Bristol Motor Speedway, he won events in Sprint Cup, Nationwide Series, and Truck Series in one weekend. The three victories at the same track in the same weekend were something that no other driver had done before him. Describing why Busch was such a successful driver, former NASCAR champion Jimmie Johnson told Anderson of *Sports Illustrated*, "Kyle has a great feel for his cars and just amazing car control. He can fly through the turns where other drivers will lift off the gas because they feel like they're losing control. The kid is totally fearless."

Sources

Books

Marquis Who's Who, Marquis Who's Who, 2010.

Periodicals

Bristol Herald Courier (VA), January 19, 2010.
Las Vegas Review-Journal (NV), December 12, 2009, p. 9C; December 27, 2009, p. 1C.
New York Times, November 21, 2010, p. 8.

Professional Services Close-Up, November 17, 2010.

Racer, October 2010, p. 7.

Republican (Springfield, MA), August 27, 2010, p. B04.

Richmond Times Dispatch (VA), September 10, 2010, p. D-01.

Sports Illustrated, September 1, 2003, p. Z7; September 18, 2006, p. 66; March 24, 2008, p. 104; May 17, 2010, p. 26.

USA Today, August 10, 2007, p. 12C; June 18, 2009, p. 8C.

Virginian-Pilot (Norfolk, VA), August 22, 2010, p. C1.

Online

"Kyle Busch #18," ESPN, http://sports.espn.go.com/rpm/driver?driverId=580 (November 25, 2010).

"Kyle Busch," NASCAR, http://www.nascar.com/news/headline/cup/kyle.busch.bio/ (November 25, 2010).

—A. Petruso

Gerard Butler

Actor

Born Gerard James Butler, November 13, 1969, in Glasgow, Scotland; son of Edward and Margaret Butler. *Education:* Glasgow University, D.Litt., 1992.

Addresses: *Agent*—Creative Artists Agency, 2000 Avenue of the Stars, Los Angeles, CA 90067. *Contact*—c/o Spanky Taylor, 3727 W. Magnolia Blvd., Ste. 300, Burbank, CA 91505. *Management*—Alan Siegel Entertainment, 345 N. Maple Dr., Ste. 375, Beverly Hills, CA 90210.

Career

Actor on stage, including: *Coriolanus*, Mermaid Theater, London, 1995; *Trainspotting,* Ireland and Fringe Festival, Edinburgh, 1996; *Snatch,* Soho Theater Company, 1998; *Suddenly Last Summer,* Donmar Warehouse, London, 1999. Television appearances include: *Little White Lies,* 1998; *The Young Person's Guide to Becoming a Rock Star,* 1998; *Lucy Sullivan Is Getting Married,* 1999-2000; *Attila,* 2001; *An Unsuitable Job for a Woman,* 2001; *The Jury,* 2002. Film appearances include: *Mrs. Brown,* 1997; *Tomorrow Never Dies,* 1997; *Fast Food,* 1998; *Talos the Mummy,* 1998; *The Cherry Orchard,* 1999; *One More Kiss,* 1999; *Please!,* 1999; *Harrison's Flowers,* 2000; *Dracula 2000,* 2000; *Jewel of the Sahara,* 2001; *Reign of Fire,* 2002; *Shooters,* 2002; *Lara Croft Tomb Raider: The Cradle of Life,* 2003; *Timeline,* 2003; *Dear Frankie,* 2004; *The Phantom of the Opera,* 2004; *Beowulf & Grendel,* 2005; *The Game of Their Lives,* 2005; *300,* 2006; *Butterfly on a Wheel* (also released as *Shattered*), 2007; *P.S. I Love You,* 2007; *Nim's Island,* 2008; *RocknRolla,* 2008; *Gamer,* 2009; *Law Abiding Citizen,* 2009; *Tales of the Black Freighter* (voice), 2009; *The Ugly Truth,* 2009; *The Bounty Hunter,* 2010; *How to Train Your Dragon* (voice), 2010.

Awards: Certificate of Bravery, Royal Humane Society, c. 1997; Spirit of Scotland Award—Screen, Glenfiddich Single Malt Whiskey, 2001; Bowmore Scottish Screen Award for best actor, *Sunday Times,* for *Dear Frankie,* 2005; MTV Movie Award for best fight, MTV, for *300,* 2007; World Stunt Award for action movie star of the year, World Stunt Foundation, 2007; International Star of the Year Award, *Variety,* 2009.

Sidelights

Growing up outside Glasgow, Gerard Butler dreamed of someday becoming an actor but thought it unlikely for a boy from Scotland. After leaving a law career behind to pursue his ambition, Butler has become an international film star known for his versatility. Whether singing in *The Phantom of the Opera,* fighting in *300,* or romancing the girl in *The Ugly Truth,* Butler has earned a reputation for intensity and charm. This charm has captivated his many fans, who display their dedication through numerous Web sites and fan conventions.

Butler was born in 1969 in Glasgow, Scotland's largest city. His parents divorced when he was only two, and Butler had no contact with his father until he turned 16. He and his older siblings were raised by his mother, who moved her children to Paisley, a mill town west of Glasgow that was within driving distance of the Scottish Highlands. The family often spent weekends in the Highlands, Butler told Andy Dougan in the Glasgow *Evening Times*. "You would see this spectacular scenery and couldn't help but think of the stories of [Scottish heroes] Robert the Bruce, William Wallace, and Bonnie Prince Charlie. You were just steeped in history and I always wanted to be involved in that sort of heroic adventure." As he related to *Esquire* contributor Cal Fussman, he spent much of his childhood "playing out movie scenarios in my head. I'd walk along the road, pretending like I was in the army, talking on the radio, and doing maneuvers. I dreamt a lot about performing in movies and living in fantasies." As a youth he also indulged in more physical activities: Scotland "was an amazing place to grow up," Butler told James Davidson in *Men's Health*. "Every day I was out playing with the other kids. There was a lot of fun, a lot of craziness, a lot of risk taking. We were always running over the railroad tracks and hanging off cliffs."

With few examples of successful Scottish actors before him (except Sean Connery, famous as the first James Bond), Butler put aside his dreams of acting to enter Glasgow University, where he became an outstanding law student. He was voted president of his class and earned a training position with a top firm. Nevertheless, he told Emily Mortimer in *Interview*, "I was miserable. I was drinkin' too much, and I knew in my heart that being a lawyer was not what I wanted to do." When he saw a performance of the hard-edged play *Trainspotting*, he had his "heart broken watching this guy play the lead, Renton, thinking, I know I can do this." After too many late nights and missed workdays in the law office, Butler was fired only a week before completing his law credentials. He took it as a sign and moved to London to pursue acting. "I had no connections, no experience, no training, and no prospects," he told Davidson. Although "moving to London was a huge risk," he continued, he believed that "I'm aiming for the stars. I'll worry about the details later."

The aspiring actor gave up drinking and worked a series of jobs while trying to find roles in the theater. Through a casting agent friend, Butler got a job distributing script pages for actor and director Steven Berkoff and talked his way into an audition. The result was a major role in a production of Shakespeare's *Coriolanus*. After learning he had scored the part, "walking home was probably the happiest moment of my life, when there's an energy in you that can't be put down," he told Fussman.

"I'd gone from handing out pages to getting the lead role." The following year he snagged the same role of Renton in *Trainspotting* that had inspired him to leave law. In 1997 he earned his first small film role in the historical drama *Mrs. Brown*, and soon he was getting regular work on television.

By 2000 Butler was earning his first leading roles in film and television. He starred as the titular vampire in *Dracula 2000*, produced by horror legend Wes Craven, and played Attila the Hun in the 2001 cable miniseries *Attila*. His creditable starring turns led to roles in bigger action-film productions. He fought off dragons in the 2002 flick *Reign of Fire*, romanced Angelina Jolie in 2003's *Lara Croft Tomb Raider: The Cradle of Life*, and traveled through time in the 2003 adaptation of Michael Crichton's bestseller *Timeline*. While none of these films were huge hits, more people began noticing Butler's appeal. Reviewing the *Lara Croft* sequel, *Salon* contributor Andrew O'Hehir remarked that "Butler is a bemuscled charmer with a mischievous twinkle and a Glaswegian burr who may provide this series with a dash of Harrison Ford energy that could keep it afloat for a while." *San Francisco Chronicle* critic Carla Meyer similarly noted that "Butler's craggy virility would appeal to a fair maiden of any century," in her *Timeline* review.

While Butler could have continued building his action movie credits, his next roles showcased a completely different side to his acting. First he had the high-profile title role in *The Phantom of the Opera*, the 2004 adaptation of Andrew Lloyd Webber's popular stage musical. Although Butler had little musical training besides a few years singing in a college rock band, he won the role of a deformed, tortured opera composer in love with a young singer. "For pleasure, I'd always preferred to sing ballads and more emotional music," he told Mortimer in *Interview*. "So, strangely enough, when *Phantom* came along, it just seemed to make sense." The movie received mixed reviews, as did Butler, whom some critics considered miscast as the older and horrifyingly ugly Phantom; others believed he acquitted himself well. *New York Times* critic A. O. Scott, for instance, wrote that "Butler has sufficient physical and vocal presence to give the phantom some dramatic weight," with his musical numbers displaying "some impressive singing."

The actor's next role was in the 2005 Scottish indie *Dear Frankie*, as a sailor who is hired by a woman named Lizzie to pretend he is her deaf son's father. Writing in the *San Francisco Chronicle*, Ruthe Stein noted that "Butler has Russell Crowe's rough-and-tumble manly appeal but is far better looking, especially without half his face covered by a mask. He's completely mesmerizing whether befriending Frankie or showing affection for Lizzie." The performance earned Butler a Bowmore Scottish Screen Award for best actor. Butler appeared in two more small films that year, starring in the soccer story *The Game of Their Lives* and as the legendary Scandinavian warrior Grendel in *Grendel & Beowulf*.

In 2007, Butler finally scored a breakthrough role in an international hit. Expectations were not high for the historical epic *300*, which was based on Frank Miller's graphic novel about the Battle of Thermopylae in the fifth century BCE. Butler played King Leonidas, leader of the 300 Spartans who were charged with repelling thousands of Persian warriors under the command of Xerxes. Although the film was filled with computer-generated imagery (CGI), Butler had to be in peak physical condition both for his fight scenes and for his skimpy costume. He trained for seven months, "just you against those weights," he told Craig McLean in the London *Sunday Times*. "Every time I was pumping, I was pulling in more energy, more determination, more focus, more power.... It was something that was more internal, too—it was about building character inside yourself." The violent, visually arresting film was a surprise smash, setting a record for the best March opening with more than $70 million in box office in its first weekend. The film became a worldwide blockbuster and made Butler a star. As Mick LaSalle noted in his *San Francisco Chronicle* review, "Butler must be singled out for praise.... Here, working with material worthy of him, he enters into the ancient psychology of the role and comes back every inch a king."

With the success of *300*, Butler could have become the next big action star, but he turned instead to films that provided him with a variety of roles. In the 2007 romantic drama *P.S. I Love You*, he starred with Oscar-winner Hilary Swank as a terminally ill husband who writes a series of letters to be delivered to his wife after his death. Much of his scenes were shown as flashbacks, during which he "manages to evince buckets of charm," according to David Noh in *Film Journal International*. The following year saw him in the family film *Nim's Island*, playing a marine biologist who lives with his daughter on an island in the Pacific. When he goes missing in a storm, his daughter enlists the help of her favorite adventure novelist, a homebody who motivates herself with images of her novels' hero (also played by Butler). Neither film was a hit, but both had respectable box office results.

Butler returned to the action genre with 2008's *RocknRolla*, one of British director Guy Ritchie's cult gangster movies. "Butler emerges as first among

equals in an impressive ensemble cast as One Two, a small-time hustler hoping to become a big-time entrepreneur by entering the booming London real-estate market," Joe Leydon wrote in *Variety*. The complicated criminal plot involves a Russian mobster, a Cockney crime lord, and a drug-addicted rock star. "Butler, from *300*, uses his burly, earthy gruffness to ground the movie, and he's surrounded by terrific actors," *Entertainment Weekly* critic Owen Gleiberman remarked.

Butler continued mixing it up in 2009, appearing in the successful romantic comedy *The Ugly Truth* with Katherine Heigl and the futuristic action thriller *Gamer*, which was a box-office disappointment. The project closest to his heart, however, was the revenge thriller *Law Abiding Citizen*, the first film from his Evil Twins production company, which he founded with manager Alan Siegel. Butler played Clyde, a man who is driven to punish the men who murdered his family, as well as the members of the legal system who let them escape justice. While originally Butler thought he would play the prosecutor who battles Clyde, "as time went on the more I was becoming seduced by the role of Clyde," he told Paul Greenwood in the Glasgow *Evening Times*. "I've often played the more heroic character with a more straightforward journey and I kind of wanted something I could get my teeth into." As a result, according to *Variety*'s Justin Chang, "it's Gerard Butler's juicy performance as a grieving father turned mass-murdering psycho genius that powers this self-serious pulp entertainment." While some critics faulted the movie's violence, Butler had no reservations about presenting mayhem and cruelty in this or any of his films. "Whether people love or loathe those movies, they'd be hard put to deny that there aren't some strong messages in there and deeper themes," he told Olivia Barker of *USA Today*. "I can't do it otherwise."

With almost $360 million in worldwide box office revenues during 2009—all for R-rated movies—Butler was singled out by *Variety* as their International Star of the Year. He continued his successes in 2010 with *The Bounty Hunter*, a romantic comedy with Jennifer Aniston which had a respectable box office take despite poor reviews, and the animated hit *How to Train Your Dragon*, in which he voiced a Viking warrior whose son befriends a dragon. The other projects he was filming during the year were predictably diverse: a film version of Shakespeare's *Coriolanus* (this time as the villain); a raunchy sketch comedy film with director Peter Farrelly (of *Dumb and Dumber* fame); and a biopic about a drug dealer turned preacher who worked to save Sudanese children from abduction by rebel military forces. On the producing side, he and his partners hoped to finally begin filming a biography of beloved Scottish poet Robert Burns. When it comes to his career, Butler told Ali Jaafar in *Variety*, "anytime they think they have me pegged as one thing, then the challenge for me is to get out and surprise myself. I feel I've only tapped into ten percent of what I can do."

Butler's success has brought him financial security and comfort, including homes in New York City, Los Angeles, and London; this fortune has inspired him to help others as well. As he wrote in *USA Today*: "For a good part of my life, I've been a bit of a rogue—not always living the best, healthiest, most responsible life. But I feel like I've turned myself around, gotten my personal life and career together, and I love what I do. Along with this contentment has come an increasing desire to give back to others." Butler has had a long-time involvement with the charity Kids Kicking Cancer, which uses martial arts techniques to help sick children deal with the emotional and physical challenges of their disease. He also became very involved with celebrity efforts to assist the victims of the 2010 Haiti earthquake, volunteering in Haiti with the nonprofit Artists for Peace and Justice and sponsoring a school there for five years. His ability to help people and maintain an interesting career outweighs any drawbacks of celebrity, he told Davidson. When things seem too stressful, he noted, "I try to love where I am and what I'm doing. I see it as an honor to do what I do for a living."

Sources

Books

Contemporary Theatre, Film, and Television, vol. 54, Gale, 2004.

Periodicals

Entertainment Weekly, March 23, 2007, p. 24; October 17, 2008, p. 78; July 31, 2009, p. 36.
Esquire, August 2009, p. 54.
Evening Times (Glasgow, Scotland), March 21, 2007; November 24, 2009.
Film Journal International, January 2008, p. 39.
Interview, December 2004, p. 64.
Men's Health, October 2008, p. 164.
New York Times, December 22, 2004.
San Francisco Chronicle, November 26, 2003, p. E1; March 4, 2005, p. E5; March 9, 2007, p. E1.
Sunday Times (London, England), March 4, 2007.
USA Today, August 26, 2009, p. 7B; April 13, 2010, p. 1D.
Variety, September 8, 2008, p. 20; October 19, 2009, p. 25; December 7, 2009, p. A10.

Online

Biography Resource Center Online, Gale Group, 2008.
"Gerard Butler," Internet Movie Database, http://www.imdb.com/name/nm0124930/ (June 24, 2010).
"Proving that there is life after Glasgow," Glasgow University, http://www.gla.ac.uk/services/alumni/lifeafterglasgow/ (June 24, 2010).
Review of *Lara Croft Tomb Raider: The Cradle of Life*, *Salon*, http://www.salon.com/entertainment/movies/review/2003/07/25/lara_croft/index.html?CP=IMD&DN=110 (June 24, 2010).

—*Diane Telgen*

Cassandra Butts

Senior advisor at Millennium Challenge Corporation

Born Cassandra Quin Butts, August 10, 1965, in New York, NY. *Education:* University of North Carolina—Chapel Hill, B.A., 1987; Harvard Law School, J.D., 1991.

Addresses: *Office*—Millennium Challenge Corporation, 875 Fifteenth St. NW, Washington, DC 20005-2221.

Career

Researcher, Africa News Service, 1987-88; legal counsel in the office of U.S. Senator Harris Wofford (D-PA), c. 1991; assistant counsel, NAACP Legal Defense and Educational Fund, early 1990s; senior advisor, U.S. Representative Dick Gephardt (D-MO), 1996-2004, and policy director for Gephardt's 2004 presidential campaign; vice president for domestic policy, Center for American Progress, 2004-08; senior policy advisor, Obama campaign, 2008; general counsel on the transition team for President-elect Barack Obama, 2008-09; deputy White House counsel for domestic policy and ethics, 2009; senior advisor to the chief executive officer, Millennium Challenge Corporation, 2009—.

Sidelights

Cassandra Butts is a former Harvard Law School classmate of U.S. President Barack Obama who was part of his close-knit circle of advisors and friends during the lead-up to his historic 2008 victory. As deputy White House counsel for domestic policy and ethics in the first year of his administration, she was one of several highly qualified African-American women named to key posts in the Obama Administration's White House. Butts described her longtime friend as an "interpreter," to David Remnick for his 2010 biography, *The Bridge: The Life and Rise of Barack Obama.* "To be a good interpreter means you need fluency in two languages, as well as cultural fluency on both sides. When you go to a foreign country and you don't know the language, your interpreter is someone you rely on, because he is your compass. Barack has been that for me from the time I met him."

Butts was born in 1965 in the borough of Brooklyn in New York City, and moved to Durham, North Carolina with her family at the age of nine. At the University of North Carolina at Chapel Hill, she was a political-science major who was active in the protests against apartheid in South Africa that swept across U.S. college campuses in the 1980s. After graduation, she worked as a researcher for the Africa News Service while she prepared for the law school admissions test and readied her applications. She earned a place at Harvard Law School and arrived there in the fall of 1988 as one of 500 students in the Class of 1991.

Butts and Obama met during their first week in Cambridge. "We met at the financial aid office at Harvard Law School," she recalled in an interview with the Public Broadcasting Service newsmagazine *Frontline*. "We were going through the process of filling out a lot of paperwork that would make us significantly in debt to Harvard for years to come. We bonded over that experience." They were two of about four or five dozen black students in their class, but Obama stood out from most of the incoming class because of his international background and work experience in Chicago as a community organizer. "The Barack that I knew at the time is fundamentally the Barack that you see today," she added. "He was incredibly mature."

Butts, Obama, and a few other classmates from various backgrounds formed a core of friends who shared some of the same progressive-minded outlook on politics, economics, and social policy. They studied and socialized together, sometimes "just sitting around and talking about how we were going to change the world," Butts told *Chicago Tribune* writers Mike Dorning and Christi Parsons years later. "How do you take this thing we're learning in law school and make a difference on the issues that we care about?"

After earning her Harvard Law degree, Butts won a Georgetown University fellowship to study women's law and public policy. In Washington, D.C., she worked as a legislative counsel to a Democratic senator from Pennsylvania, Harris Wofford. She also put her commitment to effecting change into practice as an attorney for the Legal Defense and Educational Fund of the National Association for the Advancement of Colored People (NAACP), a role in which she argued cases involving voting rights and school desegregation challenges in the courts. In 1996, she was hired by U.S. Representative Dick Gephardt of Missouri, who was the House Minority Leader at the time. Butts served as general counsel to the House Democratic Policy Committee, and advised Gephardt and other Democrats on legal strategies prior to and during President Bill Clinton's 1998-99 impeachment hearings in Congress. When Gephardt entered the race for the Democratic Party presidential nomination in 2003, she served as a policy director for the campaign, but Gephardt dropped out in early 2004.

From 2004 to 2008 Butts was a vice president for domestic policy with the Center for American Progress, a liberal think tank. She took a two-month leave to help Obama set up his new office in Washington when he was elected to one of Illinois' two Senate seats in 2004. She and other Harvard Law School '91 classmates became part of an inner circle of informal advisors as Obama was contemplating a run for higher office. As she recalled in the *Frontline* documentary, he "asked us to challenge him on what he would face in running for president, to really ask the tough questions ... so the issue of race was raised. And Barack did say that he wasn't interested in running as a black politician; he was going to run as a politician who is black."

Butts formally joined the Obama campaign as senior policy advisor in July of 2008. After the historic November win, Obama named her to his transition team as general counsel, and just before Christmas he announced her appointment as deputy White House counsel for domestic policy and ethics. She spent the first year of the Obama administration working on judicial nominations, and was a behind-the-scenes figure in the president's appointment of a New York Court of Appeals judge, Sonia Sotomayor, the first Hispanic associate justice on the U.S. Supreme Court.

In November of 2009 Butts moved to a new job, as senior advisor to the office of the chief executive officer at the Millennium Challenge Corporation. This was an independent government agency that developed recommendations on doling out U.S. foreign aid to eradicate poverty in developing nations. Her job change came just after the resignation of her immediate supervisor, White House counsel Gregory Craig, following a contentious debate over Obama's pledge to close the U.S. military detention facility at Guantanamo Bay, Cuba.

For many years, Butts held onto a unique artifact from her Harvard Law School era: the future president's textbook for a constitutional law class. Obama had borrowed a Miles Davis/John Coltrane album from her, and she held the book as collateral. In the *Frontline* interview, she admitted that she once harbored doubts whether Americans would elect a black person to lead the nation. "During the course of our friendship, Barack has always been the one to convince me that things are progressing and that we're at a place where we can do certain things," she said. "He convinced me that an African American person like Barack Obama could run and win the presidency of the United States.... Before I met Barack Obama, I never thought I would see it in my lifetime. But I'm happy to be in the moment."

Sources

Books

Remnick, David, *The Bridge: The Life and Rise of Barack Obama*, Random House, 2010, p. 190.

Periodicals

Chicago Tribune, January 14, 2007.
New Yorker, May 7, 2007, p. 48.
New York Times, December 24, 2006; June 4, 2008; November 24, 2008.

Online

"Cassandra Butts," WhoRunsGov.com, http://www.whorunsgov.com/Profiles/Cassandra_Butts (April 28, 2010).
"Interview: Cassandra Butts," *Frontline*, PBS.org, http://www.pbs.org/wgbh/pages/frontline/choice2008/interviews/butts.html (April 26, 2010).

—*Carol Brennan*

Magnus Carlsen

Chess player

Born November 30, 1990, in Tønsberg, Vestfold, Norway; son of Henrik (an information technology consultant) and Sigrun (a chemical engineer) Carlsen.

Addresses: *Contact*—c/o FIDE (Federation Internationale des Echecs), 9 Siggrou Ave., Athens, Greece 11743. *Web site*—http://www.magnuschess.com/.

Career

Began playing chess at the age of eight; became International Master, 2003; second youngest grandmaster in chess history, 2004; placed tenth at the FIDE World Cup, 2005; became number-one-ranked chess player in the world, 2009; coached by Garry Kasparov, 2009-10; became the youngest player ever to top the FIDE rankings, 2010.

Sidelights

Dubbed the "Mozart of chess," Magnus Carlsen became the number-one-ranked chess player in the world in 2009 and became the youngest player to top the FIDE (*Federation Internationale des Echecs*; the International Chess Federation) rankings in 2010. Carlsen was a child prodigy in the game and was coached by such prestigious players as Garry Kasparov. Known for his creativity as a player, Carlsen was expected to be a dominant force in chess for many years to come. He hoped to eventually become the chess world champion, a goal he could reach as early as 2011.

Born on November 30, 1990, in Tønsberg, Vestfold, Norway, he was the son of Henrik and Sigrun Carlsen. It was evident from an early age that Carlsen had a photographic memory as he could list all car brands by the age of two. His father used this ability to impress friends at parties as he had his young son recite the names and populations for each of the 430 districts in Norway. Carlsen's father, a club-level player, first introduced him to the game of chess when his son was five years old, though he did not become interested playing until the age of eight because his elder sister Ellen was becoming good at the game. It soon became apparent that Carlsen had a gift for the game because he was doing well at national tournaments, then beat his father at the age of ten. Carlsen did not start training seriously until the age of 12; his first coach was Simon Agdenstein, a grandmaster from Norway.

By 2003, Carlsen was an International Master of the game. To support his son's chess career, Henrick Carlsen landed a sponsorship from Microsoft, sold the family's second car, and rented out the family home so they could travel worldwide full time to play in tournaments. Over the next year or so, Carlsen gained more than 300 ratings points in a relatively short amount of time. He gained points by winning a Holland Grandmaster tournament in January of 2004 then placed well at a tournament in

Moscow. Carlsen also garnered the notice of the chess world in March of 2004 when he defeated former world champion Anatoly Karpov at a tournament in Reykjavik, Iceland, and played to a draw with another highly respected world champion, Garry Kasparov. Carlsen became the second youngest grandmaster in chess history at the age of 13 years and five months after he won the Dubai Open in April of 2004.

In 2005, Carlsen placed tenth at the FIDE (the governing body of the sport of chess) World Cup. Because of his finish, he qualified for the candidates' matches for the world championship. He was the youngest player to do so, but he did not win. Also in 2005, the newly retired Kasparov offered his services as a coach, but Carlsen turned him down so that he could control his own development. While Carlsen struggled in the first half of 2005, he continued to improve and, by the end of 2006, he was ranked 21st in the world after finishing eighth at the Tal Memorial tournament in Moscow.

Carlsen rapidly made progress as a chess player over the next few years, but by January of 2009, he was ready for Kasparov's coaching. As the pair began working together, Kasparov taught Carlsen the aggressive opening moves that were the hallmark of his playing career. Kasparov also added more calculation to Carlsen's moves. Carlsen's playing improved greatly under Kasparov's tutelage. By November of 2009, Carlsen had become the number-one-ranked chess player in the world after logging two final round wins at the Tal Memorial title despite suffering from the flu. He also won the world blitz title at that tournament. Later that year, his profile was raised higher when he competed in the London Chess Classic, the biggest tournaments in London in a quarter century.

On January 1, 2010, Carlsen became the youngest player ever to reach the top ranking on the FIDE best player list. Because of his progress, the expensive cost of his coaching, and perhaps a personality clash, he dropped the sometimes overbearing Kasparov as a coach in early 2010. While Carlsen's goal remained becoming the world champion, which was not possible until 2011 or 2012 at the earliest because of the FIDE system, he was not letting that quest consume him. Carlsen told Agence France Presse, "A lot of players have got lost waiting for world championship matches.... And for me, it's much easier to think that the World Championship is far in the future and I won't focus on it too much. As for now, I'm focusing more on playing in tournaments and on winning them and staying at the number-one rank."

Throughout his childhood, Carlsen continued to do schoolwork on the road when he was not at home in Lommedalen where he attended a private school. He spent only three to five hours a day studying or playing chess, much less than most elite players. Known for his engaging personality, he related to kids his own age but was also able to interact with adults with ease. Away from chess, he enjoyed sports like skiing, ski-jumping, soccer, squash, and tennis as well as playing games on the Internet.

As Carlsen grew into young adulthood, he graduated from high school and tried to remain balanced in his life. But his chess made him a celebrity in both Norway and around the world. In his home country, he appeared on talk shows and was often surrounded by fans. He explained to Simon Usborne of the *Independent Extra,* "In Norway, we are not good at many things, so when you win you become popular. And now chess has become popular, too, and people are changing their idea of the game." Carlsen also used his fame to become a model for a Dutch fashion brand, G-Star Raw. He appeared in ads for the clothes with American actress Liv Tyler.

Despite such opportunities, chess remained Carlsen's professional focus. Explaining Carlsen's importance to chess both in Britain and world wide, Malcolm Pein, the director of the London Chess Classic, told Usborne of the *Independent Extra,* "Carlsen is a vital part of raising the profile of chess. Chess has always been very popular—in Britain four million people play regularly, which is more than play cricket, but what we lack is good role models for young people who play in clubs and schools."

Sources

Periodicals

Agence France Presse, February 21, 2010; July 7, 2010.
BusinessWorld, February 10, 2006, p. S2/7.
Daily Telegraph (London, England), April 29, 2004, p. 27.
Guardian Unlimited (London, England), November 21, 2009; March 13, 2010.
Independent Extra (London, England), December 8, 2009, p. 6.
New York Times, December 10, 2006, sec. 1, p. 52; July 4, 2010, p. A16.
Ottawa Citizen, December 31, 2009, p. A8.
United Press International, March 18, 2004.

Online

"Magnus Carlsen," Chessgames.com, http://www.chessgames.com/perl/chessplayer?pid=52948 (July 26, 2010).

—A. Petruso

Aníbal Cavaco Silva

President of Portugal

AFP Photo/Dominique Faget/newscom

Born July 15, 1939, in Boliqueime, Loulé, Portugal; son of Teodoro Gonçalves Silva (a gas station owner) and Maria do Nascimento Cavaco; married Maria Alves (a professor), October 20, 1963; children: Patrícia, Bruno. *Education:* Technical University of Lisbon, degree in finance, 1964; University of York, Ph.D., 1973.

Addresses: *Home*—Lisbon, Portugal. *Office*—Palácio de Belém, Calçada da Ajuda, no. 11, 1349-022 Lisbon, Portugal.

Career

Served in the Portuguese army in Mozambique, early 1960s; teaching and research assistant in the Superior Institute of Economic and Financial Sciences, Technical University of Lisbon, 1966-68, then assistant professor, 1974-75; professor of economics, Catholic University of Portugal, after 1975, then professor at the School of Economics and Management, 2004-06; professor, New University of Lisbon, after 1979; director of research, Bank of Portugal, 1977-85, and advisor, c. 1996-2004; editor of Portugal's *Economy* magazine, DATE; elected to the Assembly of the Republic, 1980, 1985; served as minister of finance, 1980; elected head of the Partido Socialdemócrata (PSD), or Social Democratic Party, 1985, and served as prime minister, November 1985-October 1995; president of Portugal, 2006—.

Sidelights

Portugal's prosperity in the late twentieth and early twenty-first centuries has been widely credited to the leadership skills of former prime minister Aníbal Cavaco Silva. As head of the Social Democrat Party after 1985, he and his party became the first to secure a clear majority in the Assembly of the Republic since the restoration of democracy a decade earlier. The stern, sometimes dour-appearing economist returned to politics in 2006 when he won the presidency of Portugal. Writing of a 1987 campaign, when Cavaco again led his Social Democrats to victory at the polls and supporters waved the party's orange flags on Election Night, *Time*'s Howard G. Chua-Eoan noted that the prime minister "possesses an appetite for hard work and a confidence verging on arrogance. Fiendishly punctual, he ran his campaign so smoothly that journalists dubbed it 'Clockwork Orange.'"

Cavaco was born on July 15, 1939, in the town of Boliqueime in Loulé, one of several provinces in Portugal's torrid southern Algarve region. At the time, the country was six years into what would be a 41-year right-wing dictatorship—not unlike that of neighboring Spain, which endured a similar regime almost concurrently—under António de Oliveira Salazar, an economics professor who seized control of the country in 1933 with the help of the army.

Cavaco's father ran a gas station, but the family had much higher ambitions for their son. When the 13 year old failed a grade, they sent him to work on a farm for three months, hoping that some manual labor would inspire him to study harder. It did: Cavaco won entrance into the Technical University of Lisbon, where he earned a degree in finance, and was a national collegiate title-holder in hurdles. He also collected a few table-tennis championships. "I always try to be the best," *New York Times* journalist Edward Schumacher quoted him as telling one Portuguese newspaper. "It's not vanity. I take things very seriously."

Cavaco's academic career was something of a minor miracle: during his teen years, the country was one of the poorest in postwar Europe, with a per-capita income rate of less than $200 a year. Its illiteracy rate was estimated at about 40 percent. There were very few university slots available, and those were reserved for either the wealthy or for students who had earned near-perfect marks.

In 1964, Cavaco was awarded his degree from the Technical University, and then went on to fulfill his compulsory military service in Mozambique, which at the time was an overseas territory of Portugal. He brought his new wife, Maria Alves da Silva, with him, and then back in Lisbon in 1966 he took a job as a teaching and research assistant at his alma mater. In 1968, the couple departed for England so that Cavaco could pursue his doctorate in economics at the University of York. They returned five years later, just on the eve of Portugal's historic Carnation Revolution. Salazar had died in 1970, but a faction of left-leaning officers inside the military combined with an underground opposition movement and managed to peacefully overthrow his handpicked successor on April 25, 1975. This became a national holiday, commemorating the *Revolução dos Cravos*, or Carnation Revolution for the red flowers thousands of Portuguese carried out onto the streets in celebration when news of the ouster came over the radio.

There was a two-year transition period until Portugal's new constitution went into effect in 1976. It established a parliamentary democracy, with the political powers divided between four entities: the office of the president, who is directly elected; then a prime minister, whose party has won a majority of seats in the Assembly of the Republic and who rules with the help of a cabinet, called the Council of Ministers; the 250-seat Assembly itself; and finally an independent judiciary. In this document and subsequent amendments the military's power was severely curtailed, to prevent any restoration of a junta-style regime.

Cavaco became an assistant professor of economics at the Superior Institute of Economic and Financial Sciences in 1974, then taught at the Catholic University of Portugal after 1975. In 1977, he took a position as director of research for the Bank of Portugal, cementing his reputation as one of the country's brightest young economists. He also took a teaching post at the New University of Lisbon, one of several new colleges founded during this period to meet the strong demand for higher education. In the last years of the Salazar regime, Portugal had taken some important steps to modernize its economy and improve its national gross domestic product (GDP; a key indicator of a country's economic vitality). The largest companies and industries remained under the control of a handful of powerful families, but during the transitional period to democracy in 1974-76, most of these were seized and nationalized by the government.

After four decades of authoritarian rule, the Portuguese electorate began to consistently vote leftist politicians into office. The head of the Socialist Party, Mário Soares, served as prime minister from 1976 to 1978, and again in the early 1980s. But other political parties also gained a foothold, and the fractious atmosphere in the Assembly meant that several governments came and went in rapid succession. One of the new parties was the Partido Socialdemócrata (PSD), or Social Democratic Party. It was modeled on similar parties in Europe, but instead of the typical left-of-center orientation, Portugal's PSD veered to the right. One of its founders was Francisco Sá Carneiro, who came to office as prime minister in early 1980 after a general election; Cavaco ran that year as well, on the PSD ticket, and won a seat in the Assembly. Sá Carneiro appointed him as the new finance minister, but Cavaco's plan for drastic cutbacks in public service drew scorn, and he resigned in the final months of 1980. Sá Carneiro perished in a plane crash, and the leadership ranks of the party were embroiled in various squabbles for the next few years.

Cavaco grew dissatisfied with the PSD leadership under Francisco Pinto Balsemão, who in 1981 became Portugal's eleventh prime minister since the Carnation Revolution just seven years earlier. He also opposed a new Socialist-PSD coalition government that struggled to hold power after the 1985 general election. On June 2, 1985, Cavaco successfully won election to lead the PSD. After the October 1985 general election, he became prime minister of Portugal in yet another coalition government.

Cavaco had a radical vision for Portugal's economic future that few believed possible at the time. On the first day of 1986, both Spain and Portugal joined the European Economic Community as its eleventh and twelfth members; full membership was set for 1992, after both countries met stringent economic rules and guarantees that its institutions operated under fully democratic mandates. It was a time when some in Western Europe considered both countries of the Iberian Peninsula rather backwater places, staggering under moribund economic growth rates and their politics mired in an unwinnable contest between the hard-line left and holdouts from the fascist era. Yet over the next 17 months, Cavaco managed to implement several new policies that created a mini-boom in the Portuguese economy and, in the general elections held on July 19, 1987, the PSD won by a landslide, taking 148 of the 250 Assembly seats. It marked the first time than an actual majority government was able to take power in Portugal since the end of the dictatorship.

That July 1987 PSD victory was a jubilant moment in the country's history, with thousands streaming out once again onto Lisbon's grand main thoroughfare, the Avenida da Liberdade, but this time holding aloft the orange colors of the PSD logo instead of red carnations. "At midnight," reported Chua-Eoan in *Time*, "200,000 supporters waved orange balloons and held up portraits of their leader, Premier Aníbal Cavaco Silva. 'Cavaco, our friend!' they shouted. 'Portugal is with you!'" Cavaco spoke briefly, and cautioned the revelers, "tomorrow morning let us go back to work," according to another report, this one in the *Times* of London.

In his first years as prime minister, Cavaco secured important reforms from the Assembly, some enacted via constitutional amendments after referenda. One of them included a plan to privatize the state-held industries—in other words, selling them off to groups of private investors—and another was a series of changes to existing labor laws, which were vehemently opposed by the major trade unions. There was a series of strikes in 1988 and 1989, but Cavaco's labor-reform bill eventually went into effect, which marked a significant step forward in full integration into the newly created European Union (EU) and its Euro Zone, or single-currency area planned for the end of the next decade. In October of 1991, Cavaco and the PSD were given a prover-bial vote of confidence, as more than 50 percent of the Portuguese electorate cast their ballots for PSD candidates over the Socialist Party and its new chief, Jorge Sampaio.

During his near-decade in office, Cavaco and his cabinet ministers also secured funding from the United States, which operated an air base on one of Portugal's Azores Islands, located in the middle of the Atlantic Ocean and settled by Portuguese back in the fifteenth century. On other foreign-policy matters, there was a concerted effort to help Portugal's former colonies and overseas territories in Africa—Mozambique and Angola—and secure full independence for East Timor, which had been invaded by Indonesia shortly after it declared independence back in 1975. There was also a massive influx of available new funding from the EU coffers, which aided in Portugal's ongoing infrastructure improvements.

In January of 1995, as his ten-year mark as prime minister was nearing, Cavaco announced that he would step down as PSD chief and, with that, the post of prime minister. The country had achieved unprecedented prosperity during his party's era, and had finally lost its status as the poorest nation in the EU to Greece. He announced he would run as the PSD candidate for president of Portugal, but lost that 1996 contest to Sampaio, who had most recently served as mayor of Lisbon. Cavaco's resignation as PSD chief was considered a potentially risky change for the party, which had successful fended off the left to ensure Portugal's continued prosperity and stability. "The PSD is a sort of federation," explained political science professor Antonio Barreto to *Guardian* correspondent John Hooper, "which extends from very tough rightwing people—some of whom even look back nostalgically to the dictatorship—to social democrats of a sort who could be in the Liberal Democrats or even the Labour Party in Britain. All this has had to be held together by something, and that something was Cavaco."

Sampaio served two terms as president, and a Socialist also became prime minister with that party's victory in the 1995 general election. The PSD returned to power in the Assembly in 2002 with a coalition government formed with the People's Party, another rightist party. Portugal's constitution permitted Sampaio to serve only two consecutive terms, and Cavaco decided to run again in 2006, after having returned to his career in academia and with the Bank of Portugal. On January 22, 2006, he was elected as the nineteenth president of Portugal since 1974. He beat out an independent Socialist candidate along with Soares, the former Socialist chief and prime minister. With that, Cavaco became the first non-leftist to be elected Portugal's president since the end of the dictatorship.

Portugal's presidents serve five-year terms. They are granted relatively broad powers by the constitution, but rarely deploy them. Cavaco could have blocked an Assembly bill mandating a referendum vote on reproductive rights, for example, but did not. The 2008 law permitted termination of pregnancy in the first ten weeks, a controversial move in a country that is still predominantly Roman Catholic. When Pope Benedict XVI visited country's famous pilgrimage site of Fátima in 2010, he used it as a platform to voice the Church's opposition to Portugal's plan to legalize same-sex unions.

Cavaco and his wife, who wrote her doctoral dissertation on the work of nineteenth-century German poet Friedrich Höderlin, have two grown children. The president's official residence is the magnificent Belém Palace, a pink-stucco mansion dating back to 1559 that once housed Portugal's monarchs. Even its name, which is the Portuguese word for Bethlehem, reflects the country's deep roots in Roman Catholicism.

Sources

Periodicals

Guardian (London, England), February 18, 1995, p. 14.
National Review, November 6, 1987, p. 46.
New York Times, October 8, 1985; July 21, 1987.
Time, August 3, 1987, p. 31.
Times (London, England), July 21, 1987.

Online

"Biografia," President of Portugal, http://www.presidencia.pt/?idc=3 (July 8, 2010).

—*Carol Brennan*

William B. Chiasson

Chief Executive Officer of Leapfrog

Born c. 1953; son of Robert Breton (a zoologist) and Frances Marguerite (Kientzle) Chiasson; married Carol Eberhardt; children: Kathryn, Daniel. *Education:* University of Arizona, B.A., 1974; University of Southern California, M.B.A., 1976.

Addresses: *Office*—Leapfrog Enterprises Inc., 6401 Hollis St. #100, Emeryville, CA 94608. *Web site*—http://www.leapfrog.com/

Career

Worked as an accountant for Anderson and Co., 1976-79; served in varying positions, including vice president and controller, Baxter Healthcare, June 1979-January 1988; served in various positions, ending as senior vice president of finance and systems, Kraft Foods, 1988-98; chief financial officer, Levi Strauss, August 1998-December 2003; chief financial officer, LeapFrog, 2004-10, then president, March-September 2010, chief executive officer and member of the board of directors, March 2010—.

Member: Governing board of the Brookfield Zoo; board of trustees of Oakland Museum of California Foundation; John Muir Medical Center Foundation; Presidential Leadership Council of the University of Arizona.

Sidelights

William B. Chiasson is the chief executive officer of Leapfrog Toys. He previously worked as a financial officer for Baxter Healthcare, Kraft Foods, and Levi Strauss and Co. He is known for seeking out positions where he faces challenges and new opportunities. As Gregory J. Millman wrote in *All Business*, Chiasson "has a habit of seeking a challenge whenever he finds himself getting comfortable."

Chiasson was one of eight children born to Robert, a zoologist at the University of Arizona, and Frances Chiasson. Because of his father's job, which required fieldwork in remote locations, and his large family, Chiasson had a somewhat unconventional childhood. When Chiasson was a senior in high school, his father took the whole family to Africa, where Chiasson attended the University of Science and Technology in Ghana. He came back to the United States determined, he told Millman, "to get the best damn liberal arts education I could." He studied anthropology at the University of Arizona, learning about human behavior, then moved on to earn a masters in business administration at the University of Southern California. After graduating, he worked from 1976 to 1979 at the public accounting firm Anderson and Co. He remarked to Millman that this "was a good training ground, because it exposed me to a lot of different businesses and types of problems."

He then moved to Baxter Healthcare, working in financial positions with varying responsibilities, from 1979 to 1988; however, he told Millman, after working at Baxter for almost ten years, "I was getting too comfortable and wanted to get out of my comfort zone." As Millman summed up, "The key to understanding Chiasson is knowing that he likes problematic, uncomfortable situations so much that he goes out of his way to find them."

Chiasson moved to Kraft Foods in 1988, starting as vice president of financial planning and analysis, and was promoted through the ranks to vice president of finance for Kraft General Foods Canada, to vice president of finance and systems, then senior vice president of finance and systems. At the time that he joined the company, Kraft was a target for takeovers, so his first job was to develop contingency plans in case of a takeover event. Sure enough, shortly after he joined the company, the tobacco company Philip Morris made a bid, and after negotiatons, which went along the lines Chiasson had predicted, the companies were consolidated. Chiasson was doing well, but again, after ten years, he began feeling too comfortable and he wanted another challenge.

In 1998, Chiasson joined the San Francisco-based clothing company Levi Strauss and Co. as its chief financial officer. At the time, he wasn't looking for a new job, but he had to go to California for a wedding anyway, so when the company approached him with an offer, he stayed over for a few days to talk with them. Once again, he found himself interested in a new challenge. He told Millman he "got excited by the notion of a company trying to redefine itself into a real consumer products company." Although Levi had been a powerhouse in the jeans market in the past, by the mid-1990s it had lost touch with the changing tastes of its customers and it was struggling.

However, this time he failed to turn the company around. By 2003, Levi Strauss' market share had been suffering for some time, and the company's projections of a gain in sales by the end of 2002 failed to come true. In addition, the company was suffering from unresolved tax issues that went as far back as 1986. In 2003, Chiasson left Levi Strauss, amid talk about the company hiring a restructuring firm to reduce its load of debt and attempt to regain some of its lost sales. According to Jenny Strasburg in the *San Francisco Chronicle*, his departure was viewed as "not surprising, considering the depth of Levi's financial dificulties."

Chiasson joined the educational toy company Leapfrog in November of 2004, when he was appointed the company's chief financial officer. The company is known for its interactive toys, such as the Leap-Pad and Leapster, which help children learn to read and do math. The president and CEO of Leapfrog, Tom Kalinske, commented in a PR Newswire release that the company expected Chiasson to "contribute immediately and significantly to our ongoing intensive efforts to improve cost controls, forecasting and financial analysis." Chiasson re-

marked in the same press release, "I look forward to joining a company whose products have made a real difference in the lives of millions of children around the world.... This is a company with a great future, and I am glad to be a part of it." Chiasson told Ryan Kim in the *San Francisco Chronicle* that he believed educational technology did not diminish a child's educational experience by removing human interaction from it: "It is important to remember that technology is nothing until someone picks it up and interacts with it, so the process remains very much human-driven."

On February 25, 2010, Chiasson was appointed a member of Leapfrog's board of directors. In that same month he became the company's president and chief executive officer. In September of 2010, he stepped down from his position as president but continued to serve as chief executive officer and as a member of the board of directors. He had big plans for Leapfrog. In a 2010 interview with Dhanya Skariachan for Reuters, he said that he believed Leapfrog could increase its international business to 30 percent of sales within the next five years. At the time, it was making 20 percent of its sales outside the United States, mainly in France, Britain, Mexico, and Canada. Chiasson noted that the company would continue to focus on building sales in those countries, because "We are frankly underrepresented in those countries right now."

Sources

Periodicals

Business Wire, July 20, 1998.
Corporate Finance, December 2004, p. 20.
Financial Times, January 14, 2003, p. 28.
Investment Dealers' Digest, November 29, 2004.
Loan Market Week, December 8, 2003, p. 7.
PR Newswire, July 15, 1993; November 11, 2004.
Reuters, June 7, 2010.
San Francisco Chronicle, December 2, 2003, B1.

Online

"The New CFO," *All Business*, http://www.allbusiness.com/human-resources/employee-development/319863-1.html (November 15, 2010).
"Three Questions for Bill Chiasson, CEO, Leapfrog," *San Francisco Chronicle*, htp://articles.sfgate.com/2010-04-04/business/20834768.tif_1_gadgets-leapfrog-tag-reader (November 15, 2010).

"William B. Chiasson," *Forbes,* http://people.forbes.com/profile/william-b-chiasson/48802 (November 15, 2010).

"William Chiasson: Executive Profile & Biography," *BusinessWeek,* http://investing.businessweek.com/research/stocks/people/person.asp?personid=646960&ticker=LF:US (November 15, 2010).

—*Kelly Winters*

Chris Christie

© Saed Hindash/Star Ledger/Corbis

Governor of New Jersey

Born Christopher James Christie, September 6, 1962, in Newark, NJ; son of Bill and Sondra Christie; married Mary Pat Foster, 1986; children: Andrew, Sarah, Patrick, Bridget. *Education:* University of Delaware, B.A., 1984; Seton Hall University School of Law, J.D., 1987.

Addresses: *Office*—Office of the Governor, P.O. Box 001, Trenton, NJ 08625.

Career

Attorney, Dughi, Hewitt and Palatucci, 1987-2002; Freeholder, Morris County, 1995-97; United States attorney, New Jersey, 2002-08; governor, New Jersey, 2010—.

Member: Morris County Board of Chosen Freeholders (director, 1997), 1994-97.

Sidelights

After a successful run for class president in junior high school, Chris Christie's taste for political office was ignited, and it has not yet been quenched. For most of his life, New Jersey's 55th governor has been campaigning for office, either for himself or for others. A Republican candidate winning the top spot in the reliably liberal Garden State, where registered Democrats outnumber Republicans two to one, is nothing short of a coup; citizens and politicos nationwide watched the hotly contested race and its unlikely, yet somehow not unexpected, winner.

Born in Newark on September 6, 1962, the oldest of three children, Christie spent his early childhood in a fourth floor walk-up apartment across from West Side High School in Newark. His father, Bill, a Korean War veteran, worked full time at the Breyers ice cream plant during the day and took six years of night classes at Rutgers University with the G.I. Bill. The first of the family to attend college, Bill completed his accounting degree just weeks before his first child was born.

Christie's Italian mother, Sondra, whom he adored, also worked hard. The oldest child of a single mother, Sondra's high school earnings had been necessary to help support her younger siblings. She passed on her leadership skills and work ethic to her son even while on her deathbed. In 2004, Christie was called home from a conference by his brother because Sondra, a lifelong smoker, was finally succumbing to lung cancer and time was short. When Christie arrived, his mother asked him why he was not at work, urging him twice to go back.

After completing his studies at Rutgers and saving money for a house, Bill was able to afford to move his family to nearby Livingston in order to give them a nicer place to live with a better school system and more opportunities for the children. Christie attended Livingston High School, and by the time he was a senior, he had been elected president of his class for six years. The principal told John Martin of NJ.com that he believed Christie would eventually run for governor, "because he usually aspired to the top slot."

While in high school, in addition to serving as captain of the baseball team, Christie volunteered for Republican Tom Kean's gubernatorial campaign at the urging of his mother, who saw Christie's leadership skills. Although his father was a Republican, his mother was a Democrat. This was his first taste of public politics, but it would not be his last.

After graduating from high school, Christie entered the University of Delaware, completing a bachelor of arts in Political Science in 1984; unsurprisingly, he was also class president. As he likes to point out, the undergraduate years were the only time in his life when he did not live in the Garden State. Leaving was probably a good idea, however, as this is where he met his future wife, Mary Pat Foster, in his senior year. They were engaged nine months later.

As many political science majors do, Christie went on to law school after graduation. He completed his J.D. at Seton Hall University School of Law in 1987, the year after he married his college sweetheart. The couple made their first home in Summit, New Jersey, in a one-room apartment "so shabby her mother cried after seeing it," according to NJ.com's Martin. While Christie completed school, his new wife began her career as an investment banker, a career path she would stay on until the September 11, 2001, terrorist attacks caused the Christie family to reevaluate priorities. Mary Pat left Wall Street firm Cantor Fitzgerald.

After graduating from Seton Hall and passing the bar exam, Christie began work as an attorney with the Dughi, Hewit and Palatucci firm in Cranford, New Jersey. After six years with the firm, he was named partner in 1993. During this time, he helped Christie Whitman's Senate campaign in 1990. Although Whitman's bid was unsuccessful, the experience was an exceptional stepping stone for Christie. He and fellow campaigner William Palatucci became friends during the Whitman campaign, a relationship that would later give Christie a connection to George H. W. Bush's reelection campaign in 1992, and seven years later, George W. Bush's 1999 campaign, when Christie's political star would rise.

Although he lost his own bid for State Senate in 1993, in 1994 Christie ran his first successful public political campaign, becoming a member of the Morris County Board of Chosen Freeholders. In New Jersey, a freeholder is an elected, part time, county government official, the "freeholder" term a remnant from earlier centuries when only landowning men could hold office. He would serve on the board until 1997, acting as director of the board in his final year.

In 1995, before he had served as freeholder for an entire year, and two years before his term was up, Christie put in his bid for the New Jersey General Assembly, but was soundly defeated. Chastened, Christie did not venture out with personal political aspirations again until 1999, when he registered as a political lobbyist, representing the interests of New Jersey's General Public Utilities and Hackensack University Medical Center, among other groups.

His status as a lobbyist raised his profile considerably, and in 2002, Christie was appointed the United States attorney for New Jersey, the state's top federal prosecutorial position, under Attorney General Alberto Gonzales, a role Christie would play until resigning on December 1, 2008, to run for governor. Although his ascension raised some eyebrows and caused some tongues to wag—Christie had no previous experience as a prosecutor—his astonishing success in the position is undisputed. Jon Corzine, a U.S. Senator for New Jersey at the time and later the incumbent governor Christie ran against, supported his nomination to U.S. attorney. Opponents made hay with Christie's family connection to a high-ranking member of the Genovese organized crime family, Tino Fiumara, Christie's aunt's husband's brother, but the tenuous connection ultimately made little difference in public opinion.

As the U.S. attorney, Christie set to work cleaning up his beloved state of New Jersey, from gangs, terrorists, and human trafficking to polluters, corporate and political criminals in the state's notoriously dirty political environment. Before the end of his tenure, Christie had prosecuted 130 public officials for corruption. Astonishingly, all 130 people either pled guilty or were sentenced in court. Some of the higher-profile falls included Newark mayor Sharpe James, New Jersey state Senators Joe Coniglio and Wayne Bryant, real estate magnate Charles Kushner, and Essex County Executive and two-time senatorial candidate James Treffinger.

In two of his more notable cases in other areas, Christie prosecuted nearly 50 members of the dangerous Double II Bloods gang and about 1,500 people in a child pornography ring spanning the globe. He was also instrumental in bringing down the would-be terrorists in the failed 2007 attack on New Jersey's Fort Dix Army base.

Christie's overwhelmingly successful work won him accolades from ranking members of both political parties and every major New Jersey newspaper. His bid for governor, then, was logical. With Monmouth County Sheriff Kimberly Guadagno as his running mate—who would go on to become the first-ever lieutenant governor in the state—Christie mounted an uphill battle as a Republican candidate in solidly blue, liberal New Jersey. The dismal economy and New Jersey's outrageously high tax rate, however, proved to be a boon.

Normally, a Republican would not have had a chance, but hot on the heels of a primary win with 55 percent of the vote, Christie was running against Democrat incumbent Jon Corzine, who had been largely a disappointment even to staunch Democrats. Corzine, a former Goldman Sachs CEO who had been elected in large part due to his presumed financial and business prowess, found himself at a severe disadvantage in the 2009 election precisely because of his financial background; New Jersey was in complete disarray, with outrageous taxes and the economy bleeding jobs, not to mention a staggering $33 billion in debt.

According to an unnamed official in the *Weekly Standard*, Corzine's attempts to blame the economy were wrongheaded and simplistic. Under his watch, the spending had ballooned out of control. The state's "fiscal management had been so bad that [the Democrats] were using bonds to pay for ordinary operating expenses." Christie's record, by contrast, drew widespread comparisons to the popular tough-on-crime reformer Rudy Giuliani. As close to the election as July of 2009, 44 people, including officials and rabbis, were charged with bribery, further dragging down Corzine's public support.

In contrast to the multimillionaire Corzine, who far outspent his opponent using $30 million of his own money in addition to campaign contributions from other sources, Christie appealed to voters as a regular guy, a middle class family Jersey boy just like everyone else. According to NJ.com's Martin, during the campaign Christie told a voter bemoaning the high cost of living in the state, "Listen, I've got four kids between five and 15, so I'm going to be working for the rest of my life. I'm in the same boat you are."

Christie told the Newark *Star-Ledger*, as quoted in the *National Journal*, that "I will be a very different governor. I will wake up every morning with one mission: How do we make government smaller? How do we give tax money back to New Jersey?"

According to Gabriel Sherman of *New York* magazine, Corzine did not have positive messages to run on, so he had to "tarnish" Christie as his best political strategy, targeting the Republican's driving habits and an undisclosed loan to a friend in addition to hammering away at Christie's size. But even Corzine's numerous attacks on Christie's considerable girth—his longtime struggles with his weight are well known—ultimately was a $17 million failure the *New York Times* called a "relentless barrage of negative commercials." Christie ran his campaign by speaking directly to people and frankly answering questions, even tough ones. He prefers to speak off the cuff without a script, and colleagues remark on his exceptional memory.

Christie set up campaign headquarters in the staunchly liberal cities of Newark and Paterson, not because he expected to win the majority of the votes in the areas—and he was right—but because he wanted to "[lay] the groundwork for governing," according to Christie in an article by Michael Symons published in the *Asbury Park Press*. "I wanted everybody to know, whether you voted for me or not, I'm going to be your governor.... I was trying to send a signal to the people who live in the cities that I care about their problems and that whatever they think about Republicans before, we're dealing with a different kind of Republican now."

Not everyone responded well to Christie, however, as his views were more conservative than a typical New Jersey conservative could get on board with. The *National Review* described him as "short on charisma," further remarking that even the conservative columnist for the state's *Star-Ledger* said Christie was "running the worst campaign in New Jersey history."

Nevertheless, the referendum against Corzine prevailed, and Christie was elected with 49 percent of the vote, compared to 45 percent in favor of Corzine. Sworn in as New Jersey's 55th governor on January 19, 2010, at the Trenton War Memorial, Christie would hold the office until the next election in 2013. As governor, Christie pledged to work on behalf of schools, particularly in urban areas; affordable housing; and more favorable tax burdens and rates. He also pledged to eliminate the pork from state funding, cutting programs that do not work.

Christie and his wife have four children: Andrew, Sarah, Patrick, and Bridget. The family makes its home in Mendham Township, where the governor has coached his childrens' Little League baseball teams and taught them to follow in his footsteps as a proud Jersey boy Bruce Springsteen fanatic and diehard Mets enthusiast.

Sources

Books

Pritchard, Joshua. *Our States: New Jersey,* Great Neck Publishing, 2010, p. 1.

Periodicals

Economist, November 7, 2009, p. 45.
Forbes, April 27, 2009, p. 13.
National Journal, June 5, 2009.
National Review, October 5, 2009, p. 30.
New York, October 19, 2009.
New York Times, September 24, 2009.
Weekly Standard, March 30, 2009.

Online

"Chris Christie Official Bio," WTXF Fox, http://www.myfoxphilly.com/dpp/news/politics/Chris_Christie (February 5, 2010).

"Christie: A Need to Lead, Honed by Family and Success," NJ.com, http://www.nj.com/news/index.ssf/2009/05/christie_a_need_to_lead_honed.html (February 5, 2010).

"Christie Starts 1st Day as Governor in Newark, His Birthplace," *Asbury Park Press,* http://www.app.com/article/20100119.tif/NEWS0301/10011900.tif1/Christie-starts-1st-day-as-governor-in-Newark—his-birthplace (February 11, 2010).

"Christopher J. Christie," Internet Movie Database, http://www.imdb.com/name/nm2665166/ (February 5, 2010).

"Governor Chris Christie," Office of the Governor, http://www.state.nj.us/governor/about/ (February 5, 2010).

"Governor Christopher J. 'Chris' Christie (NJ)," Vote Smart, http://www.votesmart.org/bio.php?can_id=111064 (February 5, 2010).

"Times Topics: Christopher J. Christie," *New York Times,* http://topics.nytimes.com/top/reference/timestopics/people/c/christopher_j_christie/index.html (February 5, 2010).

—Helene Barker Kiser

Doo-Ri Chung

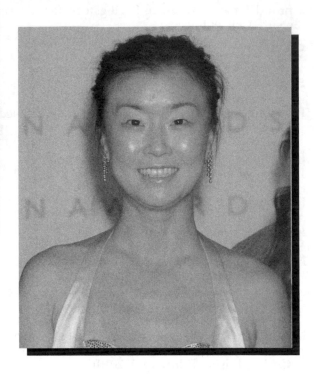

AP Images

Fashion designer

Born September 18, 1973, in South Korea; daughter of dry-cleaner business owners; immigrated to the United States, c. 1979; married Jeff Green (a fashion executive), 2006. *Education:* Parsons School of Design, B.F.A., 1995.

Addresses: *Home*—Bayonne, NJ. *Office*—Doori Clothing Company L.L.C., 99 Hook Rd., Sec. 5, Bayonne, NJ 07002. *Web site*—http://www.doori-nyc.com/.

Career

Began career as an assistant designer at Banana Republic, 1995; design assistant, Geoffrey Beene, 1995, then head designer; launched Doo.Ri label, 2001; expanded company with lower-priced Under. Ligne, 2009.

Awards: Designer of the Year Award, Parsons School of Design, 1995; Swarovski/Perry Ellis Award for Emerging Talent in Ready-to-Wear Women's Wear, Council of Fashion Designers of America, 2006; Fashion Fund Award, *Vogue*/Council of Fashion Designers of America, 2006.

Sidelights

Designer Doo-Ri Chung first gained notice for her elegant draped-jersey dresses during a presentation at the New York Fashion Week show in 2003. A year later, she was chosen as a finalist for *Vogue* magazine's new-designer contest, which gave her small New York City atelier some priceless free publicity. In 2006, Chung won the Swarovski/Perry Ellis Award for Emerging Talent from the Council of Fashion Designers of America and the coveted *Vogue*/Fashion Fund award. "My clothes aren't whimsical," she told *New York Times* writer David Colman. "They're analytical. I don't do retro. I don't believe in it."

Chung was born in South Korea in 1973 and came to the United States with her parents a few years later. The family settled in the Saddle River, New Jersey, area, where her mother and father ran a dry-cleaning business. As a child, Chung developed a fascination for the apparel that came in and out of the dry cleaning operation, and loved to sketch outfits in her spare time. She excelled at the Parsons School of Design in New York City, graduating with a fashion degree and the school's Designer of the Year Award in 1995.

Chung's first job out of Parsons was with Banana Republic, but in August of 1995 she turned up at a Fashion Mobile event run by New York City's *Paper* magazine, where up-and-coming designers could present their work to the edgy magazine and talent-spotters from Seventh Avenue, the locus of the American fashion industry. The grey cashmere dress

Chung showed that day was singled out by *New York Times* journalist Amy Spindler, who wrote that one of Seventh Avenue's best-known names, Geoffrey Beene, also checked out the Fashion Mobile event. After that, Beene's office contacted Chung for an interview. She and Beene—a veteran designer known for the seemingly effortless draping of his women's wear—"started talking about Ellsworth Kelly, MoMA, different artists we both liked," Chung recalled in an interview with *New York Times* writer Tammy La Gorce. "The next day, I got a call asking me when I could start."

Chung started as a second assistant under Alber Elbaz, who not long afterward left his role at Beene as the first assistant to take over at Guy Laroche, the French design house. She had a tough apprenticeship those first few years, Chung told *WWD*'s Meenal Mistry. The Moroccan-born Elbaz "had made it look so easy, and Mr. Beene was so used to having everything just so." She eventually rose to become head designer under Beene before leaving to start her own label, Doo.Ri, in 2001. Both Beene and her parents were enthusiastic and supportive of her plan: Beene donated sewing machines and other equipment, which she set up in the basement of her parents' new dry-cleaners' business in Paramus, New Jersey. For the next four years, Chung lived in New York City but made a reverse commute back to New Jersey for work. Her parents also loaned her $100,000 to start her business, on top of the money she had already saved working at Beene. "I couldn't have done what I did without them," she told the *Korea Times* in 2008 about her parents. "It's not just the money. Money is important, yes, but my mother helped me sew, my father picked up the clothes from the production house. They fed me."

Chung initially sold clothes out of a small boutique in SoHo, but she found the retail part of the business extremely difficult. In the end, she realized it had been a valuable experience to meet the actual customers of her women's wear. "I'm more accustomed to thinking about the clothes, about design, but they're thinking about their bodies, what will look good on them," she told La Gorce in the *New York Times* interview. Her first New York Fashion Week presentation was in February of 2003, when store buyers and fashion journalists converge to preview American designers' upcoming Fall/Winter lines. She earned favorable mention from *WWD*. "Pay attention, hipsters," the magazine alerted readers. "Cheung [sic] is designing with you in mind. For her first Doo.Ri. show, she turned out a lineup of beautiful draped dresses with string details, pleated tops and smart full skirts."

In late 2004, Chung was selected as one of ten finalists for the newly launched Fashion Fund Award sponsored by *Vogue* and the Council of Fashion Designers of America (CFDA). Designed to promote the work of talented newcomers, the award came with a flush of promotion inside the pages of *Vogue* and elsewhere in the media, and Chung was also tracked by filmmaker Douglas Keeve (*Unzipped*) for a 2005 documentary, *Seamless,* along with the design duo behind Proenza Schouler—the winners of the inaugural Fashion Fund Award—and Cloak's Alexandre Plokhov.

The publicity generated by the Fashion Fund Award and the documentary helped Chung secure a financial backer for her business, and she was able to move out of her parents' Paramus commercial space into an actual atelier in the Garment District. She continued to win accolades for her draped-jersey dresses and ensembles, with most articles citing the influence of Beene—who died in 2004—on her technical expertise. "Chung's clothes have never looked more beautiful," asserted *Washington Post* fashion writer Robin Givhan about Doo.Ri's Spring/Summer 2006 runway show at New York Fashion Week. "Chung has mastered the subtle art of draping, and her collection of silk jersey dresses combined sexiness, femininity, and a nod to the mystery of seduction."

Chung won a pair of important awards in 2006: in June, she was honored with the CFDA's Swarovski/Perry Ellis Award for Emerging Talent, and later that year she won the Vogue/CFDA Fashion Fund contest, which came with a $200,000 prize purse and a Lexus. In the years that followed, however, Doo.Ri struggled to stay afloat after the drastic drop in retail sales related to the economic meltdown of 2008. Chung had some success with a lower-priced label, Under.Ligne, launched in 2009, which is available at Nordstrom and specialty retailers. After accumulating some phenomenal successes during her first decade as a designer, she looked back a bit wistfully to those first years when she worked out of the Paramus dry-cleaners' business. "It was so much easier when I was designing in obscurity because I had this time to really grow," she told *Newsweek* writer Holly Peterson. "Now there is so much more scrutiny. People take apart my clothes and ask what direction I'm going."

Sources

Periodicals

Korea Times (Seoul, Korea), September 29, 2008.
Newsweek, December 26, 2005, p. 92.
New York Times, September 11, 2005; December 17, 2006.

San Jose Mercury News, June 11, 2006, p. 19D.
Washington Post, September 16, 2005, p. C1.
WWD, February 11, 2003, p. 15; May 30, 2006, p. 38S.

Online

"Doo-Ri Chung," Cityfile.com, http://cityfile.com/profiles/doo-ri-chung (June 29, 2010).

—*Carol Brennan*

Salvatore Cipriano

Chief Executive Officer of Better Made Snack Foods

Born c. 1941, in Michigan; son of Peter (a company executive) and Evelyne Cipriano.

Addresses: *Office*—Better Made Snack Foods, Inc., 10148 Gratiot Ave., Detroit, MI 48213.

Career

Executive with Better Made Snack Foods, Inc., since 1981; became chief executive officer, 2003.

Sidelights

Salvatore "Sam" Cipriano leads the business started by his father back in 1930, the Better Made potato chip brand. The beloved Detroit product is one of the few remaining regional snack-food makers in the United States, and has a devoted following in the Midwest for their light but flavorful flagship product. In 2009, Cipriano's company enjoyed revenues of $55 million, according to *Crain's Detroit Business*, with some of that coming from out of state. "We have a nice brand following from customers," he told Alexandra R. Moses in the *Grand Rapids Press.* "People that have grown up with Better Made are loyal."

One of three children in his family, Cipriano was born in the early 1940s, about a decade after his father, Peter, founded the company that became Better Made Snack Foods. The firm's original name, Cross & Peters Co., belied its deep roots to Detroit's Italian immigrant community. The elder Cipriano started the company in 1930 with Cross Moceri, whom he knew from their original hometown in Sicily. They set up their potato-chip manufacturing venture in a densely populated area on Detroit's east side that was home to many Italian Americans.

Potato chips were a fried snack food that first caught on with American consumers in the early decades of the twentieth century. The Cross & Peters factory kitchen fried thinly sliced potatoes, grown not far from their headquarters, in batches, then sent vendors out to hawk them on Belle Isle, a city park in the middle of the Detroit River that was a favorite weekend recreation spot for city residents. The company later gained a lucrative corner of the local movie-theater business in Detroit, selling them in wax-paper bags, then began grocery and convenience-store distribution routes in the city.

Cipriano spent a large part of his youth at the immense Better Made plant on Detroit's east side. "The potatoes used to come in sacks, and they'd stack 'em all up along on the other side of that wall there," he told Moses, the *Grand Rapids Press* journalist. "I'd climb up there and everybody'd yell at me." In the postwar years, Better Made thrived as one of the metro Detroit area's homegrown products, along with candy and ice-cream maker Sander's, Vernor's ginger ale, and Awrey Bakeries. In 1955, Peter Cipriano and Cross Moceri cut the ribbon on a state-of-the-art plant that remained in operation five decades later in Detroit's onetime Italian-immigrant community.

Better Made Chips gradually lost market share to Frito-Lay North America, which became part of the

Pepsi beverage empire in the 1960s. The muscle behind PepsiCo was able to seize increasingly larger segments of the snack food market, and scores of local potato-chip manufacturers across the country went out of business. In 1981, Peter Cipriano and Cross Moceri died within months of one another. They had left the business in the hands of sons from both families, but in 2003, the Ciprianos bought out the Moceri heirs and reorganized the company. Cipriano became chief executive officer of the newly named Better Made Snack Foods, Inc.

Cipriano, his brother Isidore, and sister Cathy Gusumano set out to capture a bigger share of the local market. They fixed some issues with the production line and delivery schedules, hired a sales team and new general manager, and began rolling out new products. By 2007, they held ten percent of the southeastern Michigan snack-food business, and began tentatively expanding to Ohio, Chicago, upstate New York, and even Canada. The company posted sales of $50 million in 2007, a tiny but impressive slice of the entire U.S. snack food industry's 2007 sales of $16 billion.

Better Made remains a unionized workplace in an era when there is one last automotive manufacturing plant left inside Detroit city limits, Chrysler's Jefferson-North Assembly facility. The Better Made plant factory can process 240,000 pounds of potatoes every day (about 400,000 potatoes), and many Better Made employees, like Cipriano, have spent the majority of their careers with the company. In 2007, when the company was named Snack Manufacturer of the Year by *Snack Food & Wholesale Bakery* magazine, Cipriano's sister pointed out to a reporter for the publication that the youngest truck driver at Better Made had been with them for 24 years.

Cipriano has overseen an expanded line of products, including popcorn, pretzels, tortilla chips, and even dips and salsas. The company also promotes what was once a setback for potato-chip manufacturers everywhere: during certain weeks in autumn, potatoes harvested contain more sugar. When the thin slices are fried, the sugar caramelizes, giving the product a darker shade and sweeter taste. Better Made turned the annual chemical blip into a new, limited-edition Rainbow potato-chip product. Another flavor in the Better Made lineup is named after Cipriano, Salvatore's Sicilian Style, which features a mix of parmesan, garlic, and onion.

Cipriano tries to source as much of his potatoes from Michigan farmers as possible, and the chips are still fried in trans-fat-free cottonseed oil, which gives them a lighter taste than competitors' products. "Potato chips get a bad rap," he told *Detroit News* writer Alexa Stanard. "A lot of people blame potato chips for obesity. But not all potato chips are created equally."

In his office at the plant, Cipriano displays the bygone tins—which used to keep the chips fresh in the era before nitrogen-gas-filled plastic bags—of more than 20 Detroit chipmakers that have gone out of business since his father and friend Cross Moceri began their business during the Great Depression. "We don't want to be the biggest chip company in the world," Cipriano told *Crain's Detroit Business* writer Brent Snavely. "We just want to be the best."

Sources

Crain's Detroit Business, October 3, 2005, p. 3; September 22, 2008, p. 18; May 17, 2010, p. 27.
Detroit News, October 17, 2006, p. 2C.
Grand Rapids Press, July 15, 2001, p. E7.
Snack Food & Wholesale Bakery, February 2007, p. 12.

—*Carol Brennan*

Arianne Cohen

Author and journalist

Born c. 1981; daughter of Arline Cohen. *Education:* Harvard University, B.A., 2003.

Addresses: *Office*—Bloomsbury Publishing, 175 Fifth Ave., New York, NY 10010. *Web site*—http://ariannecohen.com/.

Career

Journalist, *Cambodia Daily Newspaper,* Phonm Penh, Cambodia, c. 2003; moved to New York City, 2004; worked part-time at *Life,* c. 2004; launched freelancer writing and editing career, c. 2004; published first book, *Help, It's Broken!: A Fix-It Bible for the Repair-Impaired,* 2005; began editing "The Sex Diaries" column for *New York* magazine, 2007; published *The Tall Book: A Celebration of Life from on High,* 2009.

Awards: Mark of Excellence Award, Society of Professional Journalists, 2003.

Sidelights

Witty, six-foot-three-inch tall author Arianne Cohen has written humorous books on such subjects as home repair and being of above-average height, including 2009's *The Tall Book: A Celebration of Life from on High.* Also a freelance writer and editor for such publications as *New York* and the *New York Times,* she often tackled similar topics in her periodical work. Cohen was a champion swimmer in her youth, graduated from Harvard University, and claimed to have a much bigger personality because her height brings her much attention.

Born in the early 1980s, she is the daughter of Arline Cohen and raised in the suburbs of Albany, New York, primarily Delmar. Coming from a family with above-average height genes, Cohen was tall from an early age. By the time she was eight years old, she was five-foot-three-inches tall. She tried to look up books on tallness as a child, but could not find any, influencing her later literary work. By age eleven, Cohen was pressured to take growth inhibitors as her mother had. Cohen's mother started taking estrogen before she hit puberty which curbed her growth so she ended up a shade under six-feet tall. Cohen refused this treatment and grew to her expected natural height.

In her youth, Cohen found a use for her height in sports and dance. She did not fight the perception that tall people play basketball and played for a while. She also played tennis. Cohen had more success as a swimmer. She began swimming as an infant and competing as a youngster, becoming nationally ranked as a teenager. When she was 16 years old, Cohen earned three gold medals and two silver medals at the 15th Maccabiah Games, a sporting competition in Israel for Jewish athletes from around the world.

To compete and train as a swimmer, Cohen attended the Germantown Academy in Forth Washington, Pennsylvania, for high school. While a student-athlete, she worked part-time in restaurant and did some volunteer work. Entering Harvard University, Cohen was six-foot-two-inches tall and would grow another inch. She played water polo and was a member of the swim team. Cohen also took 35 classes in 29 departments and worked on the *Harvard Crimson* before completing her degree.

After graduating *magna cum laude,* Cohen moved to Cambodia to work as a journalist at the *Cambodia Daily Newspaper* in Phonm Penh. There, she became self-conscious about her height as she was often the tallest person most people there had ever seen. After a year, she moved back to the United States and settled in New York City in 2004. Cohen took a part-time job at *Life* magazine while working on a book about her experiences in Cambodia.

However, the first book Cohen published was not about her life as an expatriate but about minor household repairs. She was inspired to write the book after an incident in college in which she could not fix a broken window shade. Cohen bought her own tool kit and learned how to do such repairs. She eventually wrote a book on the subject of repairs, *Help, It's Broken!: A Fix-It Bible for the Repair-Impaired.* Published in 2005 to positive reviews, critics lauded the fact that she offered practical advice infused with an appropriate sense of humor.

While working on a second book, Cohen began freelance writing for such publications as *New York* magazine (for whom she edited the popular "Sex Diaries" column), *Marie Claire, Vogue,* and the *New York Times.* She also became a contributing editor at *Women's Day.* In 2007, Cohen published her second book, *Confessions of a High School Word Nerd: Laugh Your Gluteus* Off and Increase Your SAT Verbal Score.* Written with Colleen Kinder, the book featured humorous personal essays that used SAT vocabulary words and help readers increase their scores.

For her next writing project, Cohen returned to a topic important to herself: her height. Drawing on her years of experience as a tall person, she put together a proposal for a book about tall people and tall culture and easily landed a contract to write it. In 2009, Cohen published her fact-based but funny and irreverent book about being tall called *The Tall Book: A Celebration of Life from on High.* In the tome, she discussed the whole of the tall experience, including its advantages and disadvantages. For example, Cohen claimed that tall people make more money, have higher IQs, and longer life expectancies than those of average height.

Discussing the book with Lianna George of *Maclean's,* Cohen explained, "Height has really defined every aspect of my life, from which sports I participated in to who I dated to what I wore—because I couldn't wear most clothes—to even what profession I ended up in. There's been tons of research done on height and tall people but it was all tucked away in different corners of the world. I re-

ally wanted to create a bible for tall people—one book of foundational knowledge to really paint a picture of tall culture, because there really is a culture but it has never been written about."

Reviewers responded positively to *The Tall Book,* with Colleen Mondor of *Booklist* noting, "Plenty of food for thought here, especially among those whose heads have long been near the clouds." In support of *The Tall Book,* Cohen went on a book tour and continued to do speaking engagements. She also started a Web site, TallBook.com, to bring tall people together to share information about their challenges as well as their triumphs.

By the time *The Tall Book* came out, Cohen was making her home, at least part of the time, in Portland, Oregon. She remained based in New York City on a part-time basis as well. Cohen advised other authors to use writing as a means to solve their difficulties. She told Jeff Baker of the *Oregonian,* "Any issue you have, if you do a book about it, that's it. You're over it."

Selected writings

Help, It's Broken!: A Fix-It Bible for the Repair-Impaired, Three Rivers Press (New York City), 2005.
(With Colleen Kinder) *Confessions of a High School Word Nerd: Laugh Your Gluteus* Off and Increase Your SAT Verbal Score,* Penguin (New York City), 2007.
The Tall Book: A Celebration of Life from on High, Bloomsbury USA (New York City), 2009.

Sources

Periodicals

Booklist, January 1, 2007, p. 73; June 1, 2009, p. 15.
Denver Post, July 5, 2009, p. E13.
Maclean's, June 29, 2009, p. 18.
New York, November 2, 2009.
New York Times, May 22, 2005, sec. 11, p. 5; November 27, 2005, sec. 9, p. 14; August 22, 2008, p. A19.
Observer (England), May 31, 2009.
Oregonian (Portland, OR), July 3, 2009.
Times Union (Albany, NY), August 6, 1997, p. C7.
Vogue, April 2009, p. 96.

Online

"About Ari," Arianne Cohen's Official Web site, http://ariannecohen.com/about.html (May 10, 2010).

—*A. Petruso*

Miranda Cosgrove

Actress and singer

Born May 14, 1993, in Los Angeles, CA; daughter of Tom (a dry cleaning business owner) and Chris Cosgrove.

Addresses: *Office*—c/o Nickelodeon, 1515 Broadway, New York, NY 10036; c/o Columbia Records, 550 Madison Ave., New York, NY 10022-3211. *Web site*—http://www.mirandacosgroveofficial.com/us/home; http://www.facebook.com/MirandaCosgrove; http://twitter.com/MIRANDABUZZ.

Career

Began appearing in television commercials, 1996; made first appearance on television series, 2001; appeared in first regular series role on *Drake & Josh*, 2004; landed leading role in a television series with *iCarly*, 2007; signed with Columbia Records, 2008; signed promotional deal with Neutrogena skin care, 2010; released first solo album, *Sparks Fly*, 2010. Television appearances include: *Smallville* (pilot), The WB, 2001; *Drake & Josh*, Nickelodeon, 2004-07; *Grounded for Life*, 2004; *What's New, Scooby-Doo?*, 2004; *Lilo & Stitch* (voice), 2005; *Drake and Josh Go Hollywood* (movie), Nickelodeon, 2006; *iCarly*, Nickelodeon, 2007—; *Just Jordan*, Nickelodeon, 2007; *The Naked Brothers Band*, Nickelodeon, 2007; *Unfabulous*, Nickelodeon, 2007; *Zoey 101*, Nickelodeon, 2007; *iCarly: iGo to Japan*, Nickelodeon, 2008; *Merry Christmas, Drake & Josh*, Nickelodeon, 2008; *The Good Wife*, CBS, 2010. Film appearances include: *The School of Rock*, 2003; *Here Comes Peter Cottontail: The Movie* (voice), 2005; *Yours, Mine and Ours*, 2005; *Keeping Up with the Steins*, 2006; *The Wild Stallion*, 2009; *Despicable Me* (voice), 2010.

Awards: Young Artist Award for best performance in a TV series (comedy or drama)—leading young actress, Young Artist Foundation, for *iCarly*, 2009.

Sidelights

While actress Miranda Cosgrove came to fame as the star of the hit Nickelodeon series *iCarly*, she also had a burgeoning singing career and released her first full album in 2010, *Sparks Fly*. Like her television show, the album was extremely successful, debuting near the top of the *Billboard* album charts. Cosgrove first came to prominence for her role in the ensemble kid comedy *School of Rock*, and later had a memorable supporting role in another popular Nickelodeon series, *Drake & Josh*.

Cosgrove was born on May 14, 1993, in Los Angeles, California, the daughter of Tom and Chris Cosgrove. Her father owned a dry cleaning business. Cosgrove was discovered as a toddler when she was out with her parents at a restaurant. She was dancing and singing around the table, and was noticed by a talent agent. By 1996, Cosgrove was signed to an agent and began doing television commercials. Her first was for a soft drink commercial for Mello Yello when she was three years old.

But Cosgrove only worked occasionally as a small child, and did not pursue acting seriously until she was seven or eight years old. Among her first roles was providing the voice of five-year-old Lana Lang in the pilot of *Smallville* in 2001. Cosgrove also began singing at the age of five and learning to play guitar at the age of eight.

In 2003 Cosgrove moved to the big screen when she appeared in the comedy *School of Rock*. The film was set at an elite private school in New York City. Comic actor Jack Black played the lead, Dewey Finn, a down-on-his luck, music-obsessed headbanger who pretended to be his respected roommate Ned so that he can take a job as a substitute teacher and earn much-needed money after being kicked out of his own band. While teaching, Black's character molds his class of ten year olds into a backing band for himself as well as a support team so he can enter a battle of the bands contest.

Cosgrove was the youngest member of the cast, and played the extremely intelligent manager of the band. Her character was also supposed to be unable to sing, though the actress was already an accomplished singer. She had to take a lesson in how to sing badly to nail the role. Praising her and her castmates, David Ansen of *Newsweek* noted "The casting of the kids is spot on, from the prissy grade-grubber (Miranda Cosgrove) who becomes the band's super-efficient manager (having rejected the assignment of 'groupie')...."

Before filming *School of Rock*, Cosgrove had filmed a pilot for Nickelodeon. The show was *Drake & Josh* and it was picked up for production while she was completing *School of Rock*. Returning from *School of Rock*'s New York set to Los Angeles, Cosgrove immediately began working on the show. *Drake & Josh* focused primarily on the relationship between the titular stepbrothers, and Cosgrove played their younger sister, Megan Parker, a mischievous girl who regularly outsmarted her elder biological brother, Drake, and stepbrother, Josh.

During the five-year run of *Drake & Josh*, Cosgrove completed elementary school, then was home-schooled since she began working on a regular basis. She enjoyed working and did not always like having down time. She told Jonathan Dee of the *New York Times Magazine*, "Sometimes I get kind of bored if I go like a month or so and I'm not doing anything. At first I'm like, 'Cool, I have a little time off and I'll get to hang out with friends,' but then after a little while goes by I'm like, 'Oh,' and I really wish that I could go back and start doing work

again. It's just a blast to get to come in to the set and say hi to everyone and work with the people you know. After a few months it seems like everybody's family."

Cosgrove also took roles in other projects in this time period. She provided the voice of Munch in the 2005 children's film *Here Comes Peter Cottontail: The Movie*. Cosgrove had a featured role in another film released in 2005, the family comedy *Yours, Mine and Ours*, as well.

Drake & Josh was a hit, created and produced by Dan Schneider. It was not his only popular, successful show on Nickelodeon as he also was the force behind *All That*, *Zoey 101*, and *iCarly*. The last show was created specifically as a vehicle for Cosgrove, who impressed Schneider in her supporting work as Megan on *Drake & Josh*. On *iCarly*, she played the lead, Carly Shay, a teenager who lived with her elder brother, a hyperactive, eccentric struggling artist named Spencer, while their parents were serving in the military overseas. Cosgrove's Carly had her own web series, also titled *iCarly*, with her friends Freddy and Sam. The show touched on Carly's life at school and included real web videos contributed by viewers used in the fictional show's webcast.

The television show took the interactive element to an extra level by including viewer contributions on a Web site that shared the show's name and featured a design that made it look like Carly really ran the site—not Nickelodeon or Schneider. Of this element, Cosgrove told Bill Keveney of *USA Today*, "When I first heard about the idea, I thought it was so cool. If I were at home and watching TV, I'd want to send in a video." Producers combed through the submitted videos and picked a handful to edit and air on the actual Nickelodeon show each week. Within three weeks of *iCarly*'s debut, viewers had uploaded more than 10,000 videos to the show's Web site.

As *iCarly* began airing in 2007, Cosgrove was expected to become a breakout star. Dee wrote in the *New York Times Magazine*, "Having made her reputation playing second-banana, precocious-little-sister roles, sort of a preadolescent Eve Arden, Miranda seems poised to become a true, idiosyncratic beauty." Schneider confirmed Dee's impression, telling him "She's a star. She is one of the classiest little girls I've ever met. I don't believe I've ever heard her complain about anything. I don't think I've seen her in a bad mood once in my life, and I've done 61 episodes of television with her.... Miranda's the real deal; there's nothing Hollywood about her."

iCarly was an immediate smash for Nickelodeon, especially with tween and teen viewers. While *Drake & Josh* was one of the most popular live-action shows ever on the network, *iCarly* more than surpassed it to become the highest-rated live action show on Nickelodeon. By April of 2008, *iCarly* was averaging 3.5 million viewers per episode. Only the animated Nickelodeon series *SpongeBob SquarePants* attracted more viewers on the network at that time; *iCarly* was also surpassing *Hannah Montana,* the hit rival Disney Channel series, in the ratings. *iCarly*'s Web site was attracting 1.6 million visitors per month by April of 2008 as well. Because of the success of *iCarly,* Cosgrove and her co-stars were tapped to make several television movies, including 2008's *iCarly: iGo to Japan.* By 2009, new episodes of *iCarly* were attracting 5.6 million viewers, the show was averaging 26 million total viewers each week, and it was spawning lucrative merchandising. In 2010, one episode of the show attracted 11.2 million viewers, the series best to date.

Cosgrove did not just show off her acting talents on *iCarly*; she demonstrated her singing abilities as well. A promising recording artist by the time *Drake & Josh* ended its run and *iCarly* debuted, Cosgrove sang the theme song to her new series. The theme song also featured Drake Bell, who played her brother on *Drake & Josh*; Bell was a musician trying to launch his own music career. In April of 2008, Cosgrove signed with Columbia Records as Nickelodeon and the Sony Music Label Group launched a global partnership. Her first release was *iCarly—Music From and Inspired by the Hit TV Show,* featuring four songs by Cosgrove—including the theme song that hit the *Billboard* charts—as well as songs inspired by the series and tracks from other popular artists. As *iCarly—Music From and Inspired by the Hit TV Show* was released, Cosgrove told the Associated Press State & Local Wire, "For as long as I can remember I've dreamed of a career that included singing and acting, and it's so exciting that it's coming true now." By June of 2008, *iCarly—Music From and Inspired by the Hit TV Show* was the number-one album on the *Billboard Top Kid Audio* album chart and number two on the soundtrack albums chart.

Over the course of *iCarly*'s multiple seasons, Cosgrove and her co-stars grew up through their teen years in front of the camera. As they aged, the show paralleled their experiences, exploring the trials and tribulations accompanying such changes. Touching on this issue, Marjorie Cohen, the executive vice president of Nickelodeon, told Cristina Kinon of the New York *Daily News,* "We always want to serve our core audience and make sure that the stories are emotionally appropriate without making the kids look ridiculous—like being 16 but acting like 12 year olds. You don't want to push a kid to where they're uncomfortable, but there's a lot of fodder for kids this age and I don't think we'll ever run out."

During the run of *iCarly,* Cosgrove also took on other acting roles. In November of 2008, she reprised her role as Megan in the Nickelodeon movie *Merry Christmas, Drake & Josh.* Two years later, she played a teen Disney star in an episode of the hit CBS drama *The Good Wife.* Cosgrove also appeared in a few films, including 2009's *The Wild Stallion,* and provided the voice of Margo in the 2010 hit animated film *Despicable Me.*

By 2010, Cosgrove was making $180,000 per episode of *iCarly,* and the show was expected to air at least through 2011. Her career was reaching new heights in other ways as well. In February of 2010, Cosgrove signed as a brand ambassador for Neutrogena skin care. A few months later, Cosgrove released her first album, *Sparks Fly,* which featured the hit single "Kissin' U." The pop album was an immediate hit, debuting at number eight on the *Billboard* album charts. Cosgrove co-wrote a number of songs on the album, including "Kissin' U." She told Jason Lipshutz in the *Calgary Herald,* "Some people might think I'm just another actress putting out an album. But I wanted to prove that I'm more than that."

In the future, Cosgrove hoped to focus on feature films and have a career as solid as Rachel McAdams and Reese Witherspoon, both former child actresses who made successful transitions to adult roles. Cosgrove told Michael Cavna of the *Washington Post,* "I really would love to do a *Mean Girls* and a dramatic indie film—a lot of different things." Cosgrove also intended to go to college, perhaps in the fall of 2012. She told Alan Peppard of the *Dallas Morning News,* "I want to go to NYU really bad, but my parents want me to stay in LA. I think I'm going to end up at USC. I was thinking about maybe going there for two years, then going to New York." In addition to acting, Cosgrove had another post-college career goal. She added to Peppard, "I wouldn't mind being behind the camera."

Selected discography

(With others) *iCarly—Music From and Inspired by the Hit TV Show,* Columbia, 2008.
Sparks Fly, Columbia, 2010.

Sources

Periodicals

Associated Press State & Local Wire, May 22, 2008.
Buffalo News (NY), May 11, 2010, p. B1.

Calgary Herald (Alberta, Canada), May 9, 2010, p. D14.

Calgary Sun (Alberta, Canada), September 25, 2003, p. 58.

Creators Syndicate, July 8, 2010.

Daily News (NY), July 27, 2009, p. 69.

Daily Record, October 22, 2010, pp. 48-49.

Daily Variety, September 11, 2003, p. 10; October 5, 2007, p. A21.

Dallas Morning News, May 22, 2010, p. E1.

Edmonton Journal (Alberta, Canada), July 19, 2010, p. B4.

Gannett News Service, June 16, 2008.

Multichannel News, April 21, 2008, p. 10.

Newsweek, September 29, 2003, p. 54.

New York Post, September 30, 2007, p. 2; April 7, 2008, p. 77; November 7, 2008, p. 107; May 10, 2010, p. 69.

New York Times, September 7, 2007, p. E1; February 24, 2009, p. C1.

New York Times Magazine, April 8, 2007, p. 33.

Observer (England), May 3, 2009, p. 29.

PR Newswire, April 18, 2008; June 19, 2008; February 12, 2010.

USA Today, September 4, 2007, p. 10D.

VNU Entertainment News Wire, March 18, 2010.

Washington Post, November 6, 2007, p. C13; September 27, 2008, p. C7.

Online

"*The Good Wife* recap: Miranda Cosgrove tried to 'climb out of the Disney ghetto thing,'" *Entertainment Weekly,* http://watching-tv.ew.com/2010/11/17/the-good-wife-season-2-episode-7/ (November 18, 2010).

"Miranda Cosgrove," Internet Movie Database, http://www.imdb.com/name/nm1388927/ (November 15, 2010).

—*A. Petruso*

Scott Cowen

Eliot Kamenitz/The Times-Picayune/Landov

President of Tulane University

Born Scott S. Cowen, c. 1946 in Metuchen, NJ; son of Stanley and Helen Cowen; married Marjorie; children: four. *Education:* University of Connecticut, B.S., 1968; George Washington University, MBA, 1972, DBA, 1975.

Addresses: *Office*—218 Gibson Hall, Tulane University, 6823 St. Charles Ave., New Orleans, LA 70118. *Home*—Audubon Place, New Orleans, LA.

Career

Assistant professor of management, Bucknell University, 1974-76; joined the faculty of Case Western Reserve University, 1976; won fellowship from Ernst & Whitney, Cleveland, 1978-79; Eleanor F. and Philip G. Rust visiting professor, University of Virginia, 1982-83; dean, Weatherhead School of Management and Albert J. Weatherhead Professor of Management, Case Western Reserve University, 1984; Seymour S. Goodman Memorial Professor of Business, A.B. Freeman School of Business, Tulane University, 1998—; professor of economics, Tulane University, 1998—; president, Tulane University, 1998—. Author of books and articles including *Introduction to Business: Concepts and Applications,* 1981; *Information Requirements of Corporate Directors,* 1983; *Accounting Today: Principles and Applications,* 1995; *Innovation in Professional Education: Steps of a Journey from Teaching to Learning,* 1995.

Member: Board of directors, Forest City Enterprises, Inc., 1987—; board of directors, American Greetings Corporation, 1989—; board of directors, Jo-Ann Stores, 1989—; board of directors, Newell Rubbermaid, Inc., 1997—; chair, Southeast Regional Airport Authority, 2008; member, American Council on Education; board of directors, Council of Higher Education Accreditation; trustee, Jewish Federation of Cleveland; member, Leadership Council of the Council of Small Enterprises; board of directors, Mt. Sinai Medical Center; member, National Association of Independent Colleges and Universities; board of directors, National Merit Scholarship Corporation; board of directors, Ohio-Israel Chamber of Commerce.

Awards: CASE III Chief Executive Leadership Award, Council for Advancement and Support of Education, 2007; Ten Best College Presidents, *Time,* 2009; Loving Cup, *Times-Picayune,* 2010; fellow, American Academy of Arts and Sciences, 2010; Torch of Learning, Hebrew University; Torch of Liberty, Anti-Defamation League.

Sidelights

University administrator Scott Cowen has gained national attention for his leadership of New Orleans, Louisiana's Tulane University. Assuming the presidency in 1998, Cowen oversaw the institution during one of the city's most challenging periods: the arrival and aftermath of catastrophic 2005 Hurricane Katrina. With nearly three-quarters of Tulane's campus flooded by the storm, Cowen spearheaded efforts to quickly restore the grounds and reopen the school just one semester after Katrina's blow. These and other accomplishments—including a significant rise in student applications, the success of a hefty endowment drive, and numerous community service initiatives—have garnered Cowen praise from academia and media alike. In 2009, *Time* magazine named the administrator one of its ten Best College Presidents, with the magazine's Gilbert Cruz citing Cowen's status as "a deft academic leader and a committed civic booster."

The younger of the two children of Stanley and Helen Cowen, the future educational leader was born in the mid-1940s in Metuchen, New Jersey. Cowen enjoyed a comfortable, if not privileged, upbringing, taking regular summer vacations with his family to nearby Long Island Beach and attending local public schools. Although as a boy he had little interest in his studies, Cowen developed both the commitment to learning and the leadership skills that would shape his lifelong academic career by his teens. Recalling his time at Metuchen High School to Suzanna Johnson of Tulane's *Tulanian* magazine soon after ascending to the university's presidency, Cowen noted that he "was a competent student, but not a star. " The young man excelled in other ways, however, serving as class president, Student Council president, and captain of the school's Bulldogs football team. By the time graduation rolled around in 1964, Cowen's classmates had named him the class member who "Did Most for MHS While In School."

After earning his diploma, Cowen passed up an opportunity to study at an Ivy League college in order to enroll at the University of Connecticut, where he had been awarded a football scholarship. He continued his involvement in student organizations and sports, graduating with a bachelor's degree in 1968. Shortly after graduation, Cowen was drafted into the U.S. Army. Assigned to the infantry, he pursued officer training and served in various locations around the United States and abroad in Turkey over the next three years. "That turned out to be a very critical point in my life," Cowen told Johnson in the same *Tulanian* interview. "I began to take life much more seriously, began to reflect much more about what I wanted to do with my life." When his stint in the army ended in 1971, Cowen returned to graduate school at Washington, D.C.'s George Washington University, completing a master's in business administration in 1972 and a doctorate in business administration three years later.

His education concluded, Cowen joined the faculty of Lewisburg, Pennsylvania's Bucknell University as an assistant professor of management. He remained at Bucknell until 1976, when he joined Cleveland, Ohio's Case Western Reserve University. This move proved a significant one as Cowen's affiliation with the university continued for the next two decades. During 1978 and 1979, he held a fellowship sponsored by local accounting firm Ernst & Whitney. Two years later, he served as a co-author on his first academic book, *Introduction to Business: Concepts and Applications*. A second book, *Information Requirements of Corporate Directors*, followed in 1983, and two additional books following: *Accounting Today: Principles and Applications* in 1985 and *Innovations in Professional Education: Steps on a Journey from Teaching to Learning,* in 1995. During the 1982-83 academic year, Cowen served as the Eleanor F. and Philip G. Rust visiting professor at the University of Virginia's Colgate Darden Graduate School of Business Administration in Charlottesville, Virginia. The following year, he rose to become the Albert J. Weatherhead III professor of management and dean of Case Western Reserve's respected Weatherhead School of Management. Over the next several years, Cowen dedicated himself not only to the educational institution, but also to community involvement through directorship service on the boards of a number of area corporations and non-profit organizations.

During his lengthy tenure at Case Western, Cowen helped initiate a major expansion of the management school by attracting funding for the construction of a new building. Although planners had first considered simply adding on to the school's existing facilities, "it became clear that even if we might be able to accommodate one round of expansion by going that route, we wouldn't be able to accommodate a second or third. A new facility would allow that room for expansion," Cowen commented to G. M. Donley of the university's *Case Magazine*. After securing a significant endowment increase from the school's primary benefactor, Albert Weatherhead III, and raising funds from others including millions of dollars donated by the building's namesake, local philanthropist Peter B. Lewis, the dean approached world-renowned architect Frank Gehry to design Case Western Reserve's new building. Gehry, against Cowen's expectations, accepted the project; soon, plans for the school were underway. "We wanted the building to express physically the philosophy of the school," Cowen explained in the same *Case Magazine* article. "Even if you hate the design, it will make you question and think. The Weatherhead School has always had a reputation as very innovative—this is a statement to the business community to provoke people to think in new ways."

Despite these efforts, Cowen did not remain at Case Western long enough to see the fruits of his labor. In 1998—a year before the groundbreaking of the new building—Cowen left his deanship to become the fourteenth president of Tulane University, also receiving appointments as the Seymour S. Goodman Memorial Professor of Business at the institution's A.B. Freeman School of Business and as a professor of economics in the School of Liberal Arts. Even before Cowen assumed the school's top leadership spot, however, he began devising initiatives under the umbrella theme of "Tulane: A Renaissance of Thought and Action." Among these efforts were increased decentralization of academic administration, which granted deans of individual schools both more freedoms and more responsibilities; the launch of a major strategic planning process; the creation of university-wide gatherings aimed at generating a shared Tulane spirit; and the promotion of community service and involvement.

The work that attracted Cowen the most notoriety during the early years of his tenure, however, lay in a field in which he himself had collegiate experience: football. Frustrated by Tulane's exclusion from the prestigious—and lucrative—college football Bowl Championship Series, in 2003 Cowen led a group of five university leaders representing large, Division 1-A schools left out of the system. "We are going to work diligently with other presidents and the NCAA to see if we can change the nature of the Bowl Championship Series alliance and the way it has created financial haves and have-nots," Cowen told Ray Glier of the *New York Times.* "We want to change the behavior that has made it more entertainment-centric than student-centric…. Whether we can win the fight, I don't know, but it's a fight worth fighting." Cowen's efforts attracted nationwide attention, and by November of that year the opposing sides had agreed to compromise on a new, more inclusive system, which was introduced with the 2006 season.

Soon, a new and far greater challenge arose. Students had barely begun returning to campus in August of 2005 when Hurricane Katrina struck the Louisiana coast. After riding out the storm at Tulane, Cowen stepped up to promote the rejuvenation of not only the school's devastated campus but also the city as a whole. With the lingering destruction forcing students, faculty, and staff to scatter around the country during the fall semester, Cowen employed what Jennifer Reingold of *Fast Company* termed "equal parts grit, creativity, and optimism" to rebuild and reopen Tulane. The president and his team undertook stringent efforts to balance immediate, practical concerns, such as recovering student and staff records from flooded buildings and finding adequate student housing for formerly displaced students—a problem solved in part by leasing a cruise ship—with long-term plans to elevate Tulane's academic standing.

Some of these decisions required significant and often painful losses for the school, including the termination of some 180 clinical faculty members from a much-downsized medical school and the elimination and consolidation of several engineering programs in December of 2005. Because Cowen's Renewal Plan focused closely on rebuilding the school's undergraduate division, which the president viewed as Tulane's core strength, admissions to several graduate-level programs also ceased; yet even the undergraduate portion of the university underwent a major reorganization, with the university's long-standing Tulane College for men and Newcomb College for women abolished in favor of a new, co-ed Undergraduate College. Although these cuts kicked up considerable controversy, Tulane resumed classes in January of 2006 with a substantial portion of the previously displaced students returning to a still-battered New Orleans. Fund-raising efforts soon brought in returns well above their initial goals, and applications from prospective undergraduates poured in at steadily increasing rates.

Among Cowen's major post-Katrina initiatives was the adoption of a public service requirement as part of the university's core curriculum, a move that both required undergraduate students to undertake community service projects during all four years of their education and reflected Cowen's firm commitment to engaging in community rebuilding. "What happened to us was a once-in-a-lifetime tragedy. How we rebound from the tragedy is going to be so very important to the history of the city that if I can make a difference … that's a good use of time," he asserted to John Pope of the city's *Times-Picayune* newspaper. Even before Tulane reopened, Cowen had set aside funds for a charter school to serve the children of faculty members not only at his own institution, but at other colleges and universities in the area. New Orleans mayor C. Ray Nagin named Cowen as the chair to the education committee of the Bring Back New Orleans Commission in the days after Katrina, placing much of the future of the city's school system under the university administrator's guidance. Cowen emerged as a strong community leader committed to rebuilding his adopted hometown on a number of fronts.

In 2007, Cowen participated in the creation of two area service organizations, the Cowen Institute for Public Education Initiatives, dedicated to improving

New Orleans' public education system, and the Fleur-de-Lis Ambassadors program, which works to promote New Orleans' image and recovery throughout the United States. The following year, he became the chair of the Southeast Regional Airport Authority, charged with promoting the growth of New Orleans' Louis Armstrong International Airport. These diverse efforts garnered the community leader nationwide recognition. In 2009, *Time* magazine acknowledged Cowen as one of the nation's top university presidents, and the following year the *Times-Picayune* awarded him its annual Loving Cup award for contributions to New Orleans. Indeed, in spite of the city's continuing challenges, Cowen has remained positive about the possibilities present in the storm's aftermath. "To me it's an exciting time to be in New Orleans," he told *Weekend Edition*'s John Burnett in 2006, "no other major city that I know of in the United States in well over 100 years has the opportunities to redo themselves, to reinvent themselves, the way New Orleans has."

Selected writings

(With others) *Introduction to Business: Concepts and Applications*, West (St. Paul, MN), 1981.
(With others) *Information Requirements of Corporate Directors*, 1983.
(With others) *Accounting Today: Principles and Applications*, West, 1985.
(With others) *Innovation in Professional Education: Steps on a Journey from Teaching to Learning*, Jossey-Bass (San Francisco, CA), 1995.

Sources

Books

Marquis Who's Who, Marquis Who's Who, 2010.

Periodicals

Case Magazine, Fall 1998, pp. 44-48.
Fast Company, December 19, 2007.
New York Times, June 11, 2003; March 1, 2004; January 4, 2006; January 14, 2006.
Time, November 11, 2009.
Times-Picayune (New Orleans, Louisiana), April 4, 2010.
Tulanian, Summer 1998.

Online

"Biography," Office of the President, Tulane University, http://tulane.edu/administration/president/biography.cfm (June 1, 2010).
Cowen Institute for Public Education Initiatives, http://www.coweninstitute.com/ (June 1, 2010).
Fleur-de-Lis Ambassadors Program, Tulane University, http://fleurdelis.tulane.edu/index.html (June 1, 2010).
"Peter B. Lewis Building," Weatherhead School of Business, Case Western Reserve University, http://weatherhead.case.edu/about/facilities/lewis/ (June 1, 2010).

Transcripts

Weekend Edition, National Public Radio, August 26, 2006.

—*Vanessa E. Vaughn*

Sloane Crosley

Author

Born August 3, 1978; daughter of Denis (an advertising executive) and Derry (a special education teacher) Crosley. *Education:* Earned degree in creative writing from Connecticut College, 2000; attended Columbia University.

Addresses: *Home*—New York, NY. *Office*—c/o Author Mail, Riverhead Books/Penguin Group (USA), 375 Hudson St., 4th Fl., New York, NY 10014. *Web site*—http://sloanecrosley.com/

Career

Publicist, Vintage/Anchor Books, 2002-06, then deputy director of publicity 2006—; contributor to the *Village Voice*, 2004-06; freelance writer contributing to the *New York Times, Maxim, GQ, Esquire, New York Observer, Elle, Teen Vogue,* and *Playboy*; contributing editor and humor columnist, *The BlackBook.*

Sidelights

Sloane Crosley's debut collection of essays, *I Was Told There'd Be Cake,* landed on the *New York Times* best-seller list in 2008 and netted its young author a development deal with cable giant HBO. In 2010, notices for Crosley's second book, *How Did You Get This Number,* often mentioned that she was still working as a publicist for Vintage Books, a subsidiary of Alfred A. Knopf. London *Guardian* journalist Emma Brockes asked Crosley if, as a publishing-industry insider, she was ever tempted to write what she knew would sell well. "If I was

identifying a marketplace I'd write vampire books about Lincoln," Crosley quipped. "The two things that sell: vampires and Abraham Lincoln. And diets."

Much of Crosley's childhood, teen, and young-adult years are the fodder for her essays. Born in 1978, she grew up in suburban New York City, has an older sister, two supportive—and humorous—parents, and as a child was diagnosed with spatial dysphasia disorder, which means that she becomes lost quite easily. She had planned to become a writer at an early age, but after graduating from Connecticut College in 2000 with a creative writing degree, she was unable to find a steady magazine job in Manhattan. She once spent two weeks alone in New Hampshire writing a novel, but the manuscript failed to ignite any interest from literary agents. She wound up working for a literary agent, a boss who sometimes threw objects at Crosley in anger and frustration. The details of that job were revealed in the essay "The Ursula Cookie" in Crosley's first book, in which she attempts to bake a Christmas cookie in the shape of her loathed boss as a way to make amends.

In 2002 Crosley went to work at Vintage Books as a publicist. Two years later, she was making enough money to move from a shared apartment into her own studio, both on the Upper West Side just three blocks apart. "I locked myself out of both the old apartment and the new one in the same day," she told *Publishers Weekly*. "I sent a long e-mail about it to friends," which wound up in the inbox of a *Village Voice* editor, who told her he would run it if she put some more work into it. She did, and the essay appeared in the weekly paper in late May of 2004 under the title, "Goodbye, Columbus." As she remarks in her opening paragraph, most New Yorkers have a horrific moving-day story or two, but Crosley readily admitted that hers veered toward the moronic. She relives the day's events, which culminate in her locking herself out of her brand-new place, wearing flip-flops, after heading out to dispose of a single moving carton. Finally, two hours later, as Saturday evening descended, "I do it," she writes. "I call my parents collect from a pay phone. I think they think I'm in jail."

After that, Crosley began writing regularly for the *Village Voice*, and landed other freelance writing jobs, too. In early 2006, she was promoted to deputy director of publicity at Vintage Books, and later that year secured a deal with Riverhead Books for a collection of personal essays. *I Was Told There'd Be Cake* did not appear until the spring of 2007, about 18 months after her book deal was announced, and by that time Crosley had become a sort of overnight literary sensation in the Manhattan book-publishing/blogosphere worlds. In November of 2007, the *New York Observer* ran a lengthy profile on her headlined "The Most Popular Publicist in New York." In it, former Gawker.com contributor Leon Neyfakh asserted that Crosley "is more universally admired than anyone who's been working, dating and going to parties in this city for longer than a few months has any right to be. Against all odds, just about every book editor, magazine writer and media blogger in New York seems to think the world of Ms. Crosley—not an easy feat considering how much most of these people tend to snipe at each other."

The article was a tremendous publicity coup, and one that a book publicist like herself could only dream of pitching for a client's media rollout. "It was huge," she said of the 2,000-word profile in an interview with *San Francisco Chronicle* writer Reyhan Harmanci. "So embarrassing. And the publicist in me was like, it's so early!" Thanks to that advance buzz, *I Was Told There'd Be Cake* became a paperback best seller and aroused interest from development executives at HBO. "Crosley's a terrific essayist, and this is a debut book to be proud of," declared *Forbes* reviewer Michael Maiello. "The impulse is to demand a follow-up in the form of a longer memoir or maybe some fiction, but the scat-

tered details of Crosley's life that emerge" here, wrote Maiello, "imply that such forward-looking statements will jinx her."

The success of Crosley's book helped her land even better freelance writing jobs—for such behemoths as *Esquire, Maxim*, and *Teen Vogue*—while crafting another collection of essays. *How Did You Get This Number* was published to terrific fanfare in June of 2010. The first essay recounts the failure of what she hoped would be an adventurous solo trip to Lisbon—where she was endlessly lost and confounded by maps because of her disorder—and the collection concludes with a story about a miserably failed, yearlong romance. In that final essay, the most trenchant words of post-breakup advice she receives come from a shady dealer who may be helping furnish her apartment in stolen merchandise. "Crosley is like a tap-dancer, lighthearted and showmanlike, occasionally trite, but capable of surprising you with the reserves of emotion and keen social observation that motivate the performance," wrote Maria Russo in her *New York Times Book Review* assessment.

Crosley's acerbic style has often been compared to that of mid-twentieth century wit Dorothy Parker, and her impressive grasp of the personal-essay format usually invokes comparisons to David Sedaris. "It's the form that comes naturally to me," she told Brockes in the London *Guardian* interview. "The secret benefit is that there aren't that many essayists out there.... So I feel like if anyone makes a comparison, it's going to be good, because there are only 20 of us. There are very few terrible essayists that are well known."

Selected writings

Essays

I Was Told There'd Be Cake, Riverhead Books, 2008.
How Did You Get This Number, Riverhead Books, 2010.

Sources

Periodicals

Guardian (London, England), July 15, 2010, p. 12.
New York Observer, November 27, 2007.
New York Times Book Review, June 11, 2010.
Publishers Weekly, January 21, 2008, p. 164.
San Francisco Chronicle, April 18, 2008, p. E1.
WWD, June 15, 2010, p. 4.

Online

"Goodbye, Columbus," *Village Voice,* http://www. villagevoice.com/content/printVersion/183620/ (October 6, 2010).

"The Girl with the Most Cake," *Forbes,* http://www. forbes.com/2008/03/31/book-review-cake-oped-cz_mm_0401crosley.html (October 6, 2010).

Michael Crow

President of Arizona State University

Born in 1956 in San Diego, CA; married Sybil Francis; children: three. *Education:* Iowa State University, BA, 1977; Syracuse University, PhD, 1985.

Addresses: *Office*—Arizona State University, 300 E. University, ASU Foundation Bldg., 4th Fl., P.O. Box 877705, Tempe, AZ 85287-7705.

Career

Assistant professor of public administration, University of Kentucky, 1984-85; director, Institute for Physical Research and Technology, Iowa State University, 1988-91; associate vice provost for research and engineering, Columbia University, 1991-92; vice provost for research, Columbia University, 1992-93; vice provost for the university, Columbia University, 1993-98; executive vice provost, Columbia University, 1998-2002; president, Arizona State University, 2002—.

Sidelights

When Michael Crow became president of Arizona State University (ASU) in 2002, he inherited an institution that consistently ranked among *Playboy* magazine's top party schools. Crow had a different vision for the institution and launched several initiatives aimed at transforming ASU into what he dubbed the "New American University." Crow's conversion plan included turning ASU into a prominent research institution while improving academic quality and broadening access. He recruited noteworthy professors and National Merit scholars and launched the first college-based school of sustainability in the United States. As Crow worked to revamp ASU's mission, the world of academia took note. When *U.S. News and World Report* released its list of "2011 Up-and-Comers" among U.S. universities in its 2011 best colleges guidebook, ASU ranked second of the 20 universities—most of them private—that made the category.

Crow, the oldest of five, was born in San Diego in 1956. Because his father served in the U.S. Navy, the family moved frequently. Crow's mother died when he was young so he spent a portion of his childhood living with one of his aunts in Chicago. After graduating from high school, Crow headed to Iowa State University and lived an active campus life. He tutored football players, participated in the student government, did night watchman work, and competed on the track team. Crow graduated in 1977 with a dual major in political science and environmental studies. "If I could have taken 20 majors I would have," Crow told the *Business Journal*'s David Schwartz. "I was taking as many courses as I could."

Crow enjoyed college life so much he decided to pursue graduate studies and enrolled at the Maxwell School of Citizenship and Public Affairs at Syracuse University, earning a doctorate in public administration in 1985. His dissertation examined how the economic market and public policy influence knowledge-producing organizations, such as research and development labs. Next, Crow took a job as an assistant professor of public administration at the University of Kentucky before returning to his alma mater in Iowa to serve as director of the Institute for Physical Research and Technology at Iowa State. During his time there, Crow helped establish several new research facilities.

In 1991, Crow was lured to Columbia University to become the associate vice provost for research and engineering. The following year, he was made vice provost of research and in 1998 became executive vice provost. During the 1990s, Crow helped turn Columbia into a cutting-edge research institution through several revolutionary initiatives. Among his accomplishments, Crow facilitated the establishment of the Columbia Earth Institute, a conglomeration of several research facilities that began working together to better understand the earth and how humans affect change in an effort to foster more sustainable development. Crow also instituted Columbia Technology Ventures, a program aimed at turning technological academic research into practical industrial applications. The program generated significant funding for the university. In 2001, licensing and patent revenue at Columbia reached $170 million—topped only by the University of California system. There were some missteps, however. Crow failed with Fathom, an Internet-based learning platform designed to sell Columbia University lectures to the public in hopes of generating revenue. At Crow's behest, the university sank millions into the project before abandoning it.

In 2002, Crow became president of ASU and promptly laid out his agenda to transform the institution into the "New American University," a high-quality, accessible school where the academic focus is on developing solutions to the world's greatest challenges. One of the most noticeable changes included Crow's practice of merging different academic disciplines. He introduced several new interdisciplinary schools and in 2007 opened the School of Sustainability. "About half go into teaching and research and the other half want to go into problem-solving in NGOs, local governments and industry," Crow told Newsweek. "We're producing people with broad backgrounds who are problem solvers." In other cross-disciplinary changes, Crow disbanded the anthropology department and added mathematicians, political scientists, geographers, and sociologists to form the School of Evolution and Social Change.

Crow also worked to forge new initiatives between the university, local industry, and the government. Crow believed that innovation drives enterprise, so he wanted students to work on problems that occur in the real world. To this end, Crow helped establish the Flexible Display Center, which conducts research on the design and manufacture of full-color flexible display technologies. The center, in partnership with the U.S. Army, was working on the development of new electronic displays that could be used by soldiers, such as displays that could be rolled up and placed in a pocket when not in use. Crow also opened the Biodesign Institute, which conducts research in many areas that affect human health and the environment. Projects include finding sources for renewable energy, discovering new ways to clean harmful chemicals from drinking water, and designing technologies to detect biohazards.

The big question was whether the changes would pay off in the long run, said Charles Vest, president of the National Academy of Engineering. Speaking to Inside Higher Ed's Jack Stripling, Vest called Crow's approach an interesting experiment. "There's nothing that guarantees it's going to work," he said. "I think they're very idealistic, and they're trying to make a radical shift, and they know it. They see [this approach] as a path to leapfrog, but it's an experiment and it's got a big risk."

Another goal of Crow's was to keep the university accessible—even as research and innovation turned elite. As of 2009, ASU was the largest single public university in the United States, serving more than 67,000 students. Despite the success, Crow has not been without challenges, particularly in the area of the university's budget. In February of 2009, he ordered a furlough of employees as part of an $88 million package of budget cuts. Administrators had to take 15 days of unpaid leave, with all other staff taking 12 days. He also cut hundreds of staff positions.

The changes have undoubtedly improved the university's reputation. ASU made the 2008 National Science Foundation's list of top 20 research universities without a medical school. In 2010, ASU was named 81st on a list of the top 100 universities in the world by the Shanghai Jiao Tong University's Institute of Higher Education. Crow told Statepress.com reporter Philip Haldiman he was proud of his work at advancing the school's image. "We have kept this institution accessible, advanced its reputation, enhanced its impact and embedded it in the city," Crow said. "I hope that people will remember that whoever was running this place in the early 21st century moved the institution into that unique meaningful status."

Sources

Periodicals

Ascribe Higher Education News Service, March 29, 2002.

Business Journal (Phoenix, AZ), May 3, 2002, p. 46.

Minnesota Review, Fall 2009, pp. 53-61.

Newsweek, September 15, 2008, p. 81.

New York Times, May 14, 2009, p. A20.

States News Service, August 17, 2010.

Time, November 11, 2009.

Online

"As the Crow Flies," *Inside Higher Ed,* http://www.insidehighered.com/news/2010/07/16/crow (July 16, 2010).

"Michael Crow," Arizona State University, https://webapp4.asu.edu/directory/person/66195 (July 12, 2010).

"New American University Plan Ahead of Schedule," Statepress.com, http://www.statepress.com/archive/node/2606 (July 16, 2010).

"The Party's Over: ASU Drops to 20th on National 'Party School Survey,'" *Phoenix NewTimes* Blogs, http://blogs.phoenixnewtimes.com/valleyfever/2009/07/the_party_is_over_asu_drops_to.php (July 12, 2010).

—Lisa Frick

Andrew Cuomo

Attorney General of the State of New York

Born Andrew Mark Cuomo, December 6, 1957, in New York, NY; son of Mario (a lawyer and politician) and Matilda (maiden name, Raffa) Cuomo; married Kerry Kennedy, June 9, 1990 (divorced, 2003); children: Cara, Mariah, Michaela. *Education:* Fordham University, B.A., 1979; Albany Law School, J.D., 1982.

Addresses: *Office*—Office of the Attorney General, The Capitol, Albany, NY 12224-0341. *Web site*—http://www.ag.ny.gov/.

Career

Served as adviser and campaign manager for Governor Mario Cuomo, 1982-84; assistant district attorney, City of New York, 1984-85; partner, Blutrich, Falcone and Miller, 1985-88; managed Housing Enterprise for the Less Privileged (HELP), 1988-93; assistant secretary, U.S. Department of Housing and Urban Development, 1993-97; secretary, U.S. Department of Housing and Urban Development, 1997-2001; mounted failed gubernatorial campaign, 2002; Attorney General of the State of New York, 2007—. Editor of *Crossroads: The Future of American Politics*, 2003.

Awards: Outstanding Community Service Award, Latin Soul, 1988; Man of the Year Award, Coalition of Italo-American Associations, 1988; Ed Sulzberger Award, *Our Town*, 1989; Public Service Award, Council of Jewish Organizations, 1989; Distinguished Community Service Award, New York Uni-

versity, 1991; Bard Award, 1992; Albert Einstein Award, 1993; Encore Heart to Heart Award, 1994; Innovation in American Government Award, John F. Kennedy School of Government, Harvard University, 1996; Special Achievement Award in Government, National Italian American Foundation, 2001; Good Neighbor Award, ARC; National Puerto Rican Coalition Appreciation Award; Freedom and Justice Award, NAACP Alliance for Justice; Leadership in Public Service Award, Coalition of Italo-American Associations.

Sidelights

Government official Andrew Cuomo's three-decade political career has been marked by both considerable success and harsh defeats. A second-generation public servant who is the son of former New York Governor Mario Cuomo, Cuomo entered top-level politics by running the elder Cuomo's successful 1982 gubernatorial campaign. After practicing law for several years in New York City, the younger Cuomo then returned to public life in the 1990s, eventually rising to become secretary of United States Department of Housing and Urban Development (HUD) under then-President Bill Clinton. An aborted run for governor of New York in 2002 temporarily halted Cuomo's rise, but a successful bid for state attorney general four years later restored his political fortunes. As attorney general, Cuomo initiated several high-profile lawsuits, including an investigation into student loan practices, an anti-trust suit against technology company Intel, and an accusation of fraud against beleaguered financial giant Bank of America. Coupled with his political prominence, such efforts have kept Cuomo's name at the top of speculated lists for other high-level government jobs, including the U.S. Senate seat vacated by Secretary of State appointee Hilary Clinton in 2009. Although that post ultimately went to Kirsten Gillibrand, by the following year Cuomo had become a much-rumored candidate for the state's governorship.

Born on December 6, 1957, in the borough of Queens in New York City, Cuomo is the oldest child of Matilda and Mario Cuomo. Before entering politics during the 1970s, the elder Cuomo practiced law and the family maintained a comfortable, if not lavish, financial footing. While still a teenager, Cuomo became involved in his father's nascent political career. After graduating from high school, Cuomo enrolled at New York City's Fordham University, from which he earned his bachelor's degree in 1979. He then studied at Albany Law School while maintaining an interest in politics and working to support incumbent President Jimmy Carter during the contentious 1980 Democratic presidential primary race. Upon completion of his law degree in 1982, Cuomo returned to New York City and helped propel his father to the state's top executive job by "putting my posters up and pulling the other guy's down," explained the elder Cuomo to Kevin Sack of the *New York Times* in 1994. Cuomo accompanied his father to Albany to serve as a senior adviser—a job that came with great public notoriety but a salary of just one dollar per year. Not all of this attention was positive, however, as the youthful attaché began to develop a reputation as spoiled, hot-tempered, and arrogant. "Andrew believes in winning, that winning is its reward.... He plays the game of politics at the cutting edge. He's very charming and that masks an ability to be ruthless," commented former head of the Urban Development Corporation and 1982 campaign affiliate William Stern to the *New York Times'* Jeffrey Schmalz in 1986.

After two years at the state capital, Cuomo again went back to his native New York City. There, he worked to establish himself independently of his famous father by practicing law first as an assistant district attorney for the city and later as a partner at Blutrich, Falcone, and Miller, a private law firm noted perhaps more for its connections to the elder Cuomo than for its legal victories. In 1988, however, Cuomo left private practice altogether to focus his efforts on housing advocacy, an issue that largely defined his career over the next several years. His non-profit organization, the Housing Enterprise for the Less Privileged (HELP), worked to encourage housing development aimed at taking homeless people off the streets. Although some still leveled accusations of stubbornness and even strong-arming at Cuomo, his successes at bringing increased government funding to homeless issues were widely acknowledged.

Around the same time he began working full-time with HELP, Cuomo became involved with another member of a political family dynasty: Kerry Kennedy, the daughter of the late Senator Robert F. Kennedy. After meeting at a dinner party, the couple quickly developed a serious relationship and married in New York City in June of 1990 in what Maureen Dowd of the *New York Times* called "the union of the nation's two most renowed [sic] liberal Democratic clans." The marriage produced three daughters: twins Cara and Mariah in 1995 and Michaela in 1997.

By the early 1990s, Cuomo had become an acknowledged force for housing reform, heading up a commission on homelessness in New York City and continuing his efforts with HELP. This work attracted the attention of the Clinton Administration, and Cuomo was tapped to join the U.S. Department of Housing and Urban Development as an assistant secretary in 1993. Over the next several years, Cuomo lived in Washington, D.C., where he became one of Clinton's—and particularly Vice-President Al Gore's—close political associates. In 1996, Clinton named Cuomo to fill the top job at HUD when incumbent Henry Cisneros stepped down. Cuomo was the youngest person to ever hold the office of Secretary of HUD when he assumed the role in early 1997, and he quickly earned a reputation for efficient management of a government agency long known for mishandling its finances. "I am very impressed with the intensity and the diligence with which the Secretary is pressing for reform within the department. He takes the job very seriously," commented Representative Jerry Lewis to Lizette Alvarez of the *New York Times*. Cuomo continued to impress both high-ranking government officials and housing advocates during his tenure with his efforts to both control costs and expand the positive work done by the agency. "We can do real good things here for people," Cuomo told Alvarez. "When I got here we served 25,000 homeless people a year. We now serve 280,000 a year. Who gets a chance in their life to make that difference?"

After the Republican Party took control of the White House with the election of George W. Bush in 2000, Cuomo left Washington for New York. Soon, he announced his intention to stand for election in the 2002 gubernatorial election against Republican George Pataki, who had bested the elder Cuomo in 1994 and handily won re-election four years later. Cuomo's planned bid turned ugly before it even truly began, however, as many Democrats had already decided to support state Comptroller H. Carl McCall, who was striving to become New York's first black governor. McCall clearly earned the party's nod at the state's Democratic Convention in May of 2002—Cuomo failed to attend altogether—and just a week before the primary Cuomo announced that he was dropping out of the race. The uncontested McCall carried the primary nomination easily, but lacked equal success in the November general election; Pataki won a sweeping victory, and Cuomo seemed battered by the negative political climate that had characterized his bid. The following year brought the erstwhile candidate further troubles in the public eye, as the failure of his marriage became a heavily reported topic in the press. In July of 2003, Kennedy formally separated from her husband and announced her intentions to pursue a divorce. With his personal life overshadowing his public one, Cuomo largely slipped from the center of the political radar as some questioned whether he could recover from the double blow of his failed 2002 campaign and subsequent divorce.

However, Cuomo proved to be down but not out. He rebuilt his bridges with the state Democratic Party and began to reenter the political arena. By the time of the next major state elections in 2006, Cuomo had set his sights on the office of Attorney General, then occupied by the presumed Democratic nominee for governor, Eliot Spitzer. A lengthy primary season ensued, with Cuomo announcing his intentions to run over a year before the general election. Although the election was hotly contested, Cuomo won the party's nomination over closest contender Mark Green and advanced to the general election battle against Republican candidate Jeanine Pirro. The fierce battle ended in a wide victory for Cuomo, who found his prospects particularly boosted after allegations that Pirro had, among other unethical activities, tried to wiretap her own husband marred the Republican campaign. Cuomo assumed office as New York Attorney General in January of 2007.

His tenure as the state's top legal figure was marked by high-profile litigation against some of business and finance's main players. Citing his main priorities on the New York Attorney General's Web site as "social justice, economic justice, racial justice, the environment, and public integrity," Cuomo sought to continue the history of investigation established under Spitzer. His first major investigation came in

2007 as Cuomo delved into the student loan industry, uncovering a system that sent kickbacks to college financial aid advisers that referred student to particular lenders. These findings led to reforms throughout the student loan industry, and established Cuomo as a force to be reckoned with. The following year, the attorney general sparred with financial ratings agencies including Standard and Poor's, Moody's, and Fitch over what he believed were corrupt ratings practices that allowed companies to see their potential ratings before deciding to pay for them.

In March of 2009, Cuomo led efforts to require finance giant American International Group—better known as AIG—to reclaim large corporate bonuses and other employee perks paid even as the company took vast sums of money from the federal government under the Troubled Asset Relief Program (TARP). Later that year, he filed anti-trust charges against technology giant Intel, arguing that the company had used what Cuomo called, in an article by *BusinessWeek*'s Arik Hesseldahl, "bribery and coercion to maintain a stranglehold on the market." Short months later, Cuomo again took on Wall Street when he brought suit against Bank of America. Accusing the financial company of civil fraud, the attorney general claimed that Bank of America head Kenneth D. Lewis and other executives had misled shareholders regarding the extent of losses that the company suffered after its takeover of troubled investment powerhouse Merrill Lynch. Although Bank of America had reached an agreement over the matter with the federal Securities and Exchange Commission shortly before Cuomo filed his suit in February of 2010, he chose to press on with the matter—a decision that may have stemmed from widespread public sentiment against big banks that had largely been indicted for causing a global recession but themselves suffering only slightly from its consequences.

In addition to his legal efforts, Cuomo has remained a viable political player. After President-elect Barack Obama announced his choice of Hilary Clinton as Secretary of State, the attorney general became one of the acknowledged frontrunners for appointment to her soon-to-be-vacant seat in the U.S. Senate. In January of 2009, however, Governor David Paterson announced his appointment of the less well-known Gillibrand, an incumbent member of the House of Representatives from the Albany area. Yet, this choice did not check Cuomo's possible advancement to higher office. As early as summer of that year, rumors began to circulate that Cuomo was considering a run for the governorship despite the seat being held by fellow Democrat Paterson. Paterson's lack of popularity with voters contrasted sharply with Cuomo's generally positive levels of approval, and speculation that Cuomo was considering a primary challenge ran high. Although Cuomo continued to maintain that his primary focus lay in his role as attorney general, some acknowledged that a run had not been ruled out entirely. By early 2010, Cuomo had accumulated campaign funds in excess of $18 million and—particularly after Paterson announced that he would end his bid for re-election in late February of that year—seemed the most likely candidate to carry the Democratic nomination for the state's top job.

Selected writings

(Editor) *Crossroads: The Future of American Politics,* Random House (New York City), 2003.

Sources

Books

Marquis Who's Who, Marquis Who's Who, 2009.

Periodicals

New York Times, March 14, 1986; October 18, 1988; February 16, 1990; June 10, 1990; March 27, 1994; January 4, 1998; July 1, 2003; October 27, 2006; October 16, 2008; August 3, 2009; February 5, 2010.

Online

"About the Attorney General," Office of the Attorney General, http://www.ag.ny.gov/about.html (March 7, 2010).
"Andrew Cuomo," WhoRunsGov.com, http://www.whorunsgov.com/Profiles/Andrew_Cuomo (March 7, 2010).
"NY AG Cuomo Files Antitrust Lawsuit Against Intel," *BusinessWeek,* http://www.businessweek.com/the_thread/techbeat/archives/2009/11/ny_ag_cuomo_fil.html (March 7, 2010).
"Times Topics: Andrew M. Cuomo," *New York Times,* http://topics.nytimes.com/top/reference/timestopics/people/c/andrew_m_cuomo/index.html (March 7, 2010).

—Vanessa E. Vaughn

Viola Davis

Actress

Born August 11, 1965, in St. Matthews, SC; son of Dan (a horse groomer, race horse exerciser, warehouseman, and janitor) and Mary Davis; married Julius Tennon (an actor), June 23, 2003; children: two stepchildren. *Education:* Rhode Island College, B.F.A., 1988; Juilliard School, advanced diploma, c. 1992.

Addresses: *Management*—Principal Entertainment New York, 130 West 42nd St., Ste. #614, New York, NY 10036.

Career

Actress in stage productions, including: *Measure for Measure,* Trinity Repertory Company, Providence, RI, 1994; *Seven Guitars,* New York City, 1996; *God's Heart,* New York City, 1997; *Pericles,* New York City, 1998; *Everybody's Ruby,* New York City, 1999; *The Vagina Monologues,* New York City, 1999; *King Hedley II,* New York City, 2001; *Intimate Apparel,* Off-Broadway production, New York City, and Mark Taper Forum, Los Angeles, CA, 2004; *Fences,* New York City, 2010. Film appearances include: *The Substance of Fire,* 1996; *Out of Sight,* 1998; *Traffic,* 2000; *Kate & Leopold,* 2001; *The Shrink Is In,* 2001; *Antwone Fisher,* 2002; *Far from Heaven,* 2002; *Solaris,* 2002; *Get Rich or Die Tryin',* 2005; *Syriana,* 2005; *The Architect,* 2006; *World Trade Center,* 2006; *Disturbia,* 2007; *Doubt,* 2008; *Nights in Rodanthe,* 2008; *Beyond All Boundaries* (short film), 2009; *Law Abiding Citizen,* 2009; *Madea Goes to Jail,* 2009; *State of Play,* 2009; *Eat Pray Love,* 2010; *It's Kind of a Funny Story,* 2010; *Knight & Day,* 2010; *Trust,* 2010; *The Unforgiving Minute* (short film), 2010. Television appearances include: *New York Un-* *dercover,* 1996; *NYPD Blue,* 1996; *The Pentagon Wars* (movie), 1998; *Grace & Glorie* (movie), 1998; *City of Angels,* CBS, 2000; *Judging Amy,* 2000; *Amy & Isabelle* (movie), 2001; *The Guardian,* CBS, 2001; *Providence,* NBC, 2001; *Third Watch,* NBC, 2001; *CSI: Crime Scene Investigation,* CBS, 2002; *The Division,* 2002; *Father Lefty* (movie), 2002; *Law & Order: Criminal Intent,* NBC, 2002; *Hack,* 2003; *Law & Order: Special Victims Unit,* NBC, 2003-08; *The Practice,* ABC, 2003; *Century City,* CBS, 2004; *Jesse Stone: Stone Cold* (movie), 2005; *Threshold,* 2005; *Jesse Stone: Death in Paradise* (movie), 2006; *Jesse Stone: Night Passage* (movie), 2006; *Life Is Not a Fairytale: The Fantasia Barrino Story* (movie), 2006; *Without a Trace,* CBS, 2006; *Fort Pit* (movie), 2007; *Jesse Stone: Sea Change* (movie), 2007; *Traveler,* 2007; *Brothers & Sisters,* ABC, 2008; *The Andromeda Strain* (miniseries), 2008; *The United States of Tara,* Showtime, 2010. Film work includes: co-executive producer, *Driving Fish* (short film), 2002.

Member: Academy of Motion Picture Arts and Sciences, 2009—.

Awards: *Theatre World* Award, Theatre World Awards, Inc., for *Seven Guitars,* 1996; Obie Award, *Village Voice,* for *Everybody's Ruby,* 1999; Antoinette Perry Award for best actress featured role—play, American Theatre Wing and Broadway League, for

King Hedley II, 2001; Drama Desk Award for outstanding featured actress in a play, Drama Desk, for *King Hedley II,* 2001; Drama Desk Award for outstanding actress in a play, Drama Desk, for *Intimate Apparel,* 2004; Los Angeles Drama Critics Circle Award for lead performance, Los Angeles Drama Critics Circle, for *Intimate Apparel,* 2005; Black Reel Award for best supporting actress, Foundation for the Advancement of African-Americans in Films, for *Doubt,* 2008; Dallas-Fort Worth Film Critics Association Award for best supporting actress, Dallas-Fort Worth Film Critics Association, for *Doubt,* 2008; National Board of Review Award for best breakthrough performance—female, National Board of Review, for *Doubt,* 2008; Virtuoso Award, Santa Barbara International Film Festival, 2009; Antoinette Perry Award for best actress in a play, American Theatre Wing and Broadway League, for *Fences,* 2010; Drama Desk Award for outstanding featured actress in a play, Drama Desk, for *Fences,* 2010.

Sidelights

African-American actress Viola Davis first found success on the New York stage, winning two Tony Awards for her work in *King Hadley II* and *Fences.* While the stage was the actress' most comfortable milieu, she also had significant roles on film and television. Her best-known film roles included supporting parts in *Antwone Fisher* and her Academy Award-nominated turn in the drama *Doubt.* On television, Davis appeared in a number of well-received television movies, including *Amy & Isabelle,* while *The United States of Tara* provided her with her first acclaimed television series. Roger Ebert of the *Chicago Sun Times* wrote in 2009, "Davis is a great actor. If she is ever given a leading role in a movie, she will come to full glory, as she has on the stage.... She has a magnetism that allows her to illuminate an important scene, even when she has no dialogue...."

Born on August 11, 1965, in St. Matthews, South Carolina, she was the daughter of Dan and Mary Davis. When she was two months old, her family moved to Central Falls, Rhode Island. There, her father worked variously as a horse groomer for racetracks, exercise rider for racehorses, warehouseman, and janitor. Davis grew up in grinding poverty, living in condemned, rat-filled buildings and sometimes having no food, though her family was warm and loving. She found an escape in acting and writing from an early age, and her father, a storyteller who played blues guitar and harmonica, encouraged performing. Davis performed regularly by the time she was a student at Central Falls High School, including roles in *Runaways.*

Davis graduated from Central Falls High School, then entered Rhode Island College. She was part of a program to help disadvantaged students receive a higher education. She majored in theater but struggled at times because she was the only African-American student in the department. Unsure if she really wanted to be an actress and chafing at the department's policy of not casting parts color blind, she did not audition for many shows during her five years at the school though she did land a couple of leads.

Deciding to pursue acting seriously after earning her bachelor's degree, Davis applied for and entered the famed Juilliard School, one of the premiere training grounds for performing artists. She spent four years at the school, earning an advanced diploma and gaining attention for her talents. Over the years, Davis would return to Rhode Island, and take parts in productions of the Trinity Repertory Company. Among them was playing Isabella in a 1994 production of *Measure for Measure.*

Soon after, Davis was cast in a new play by esteemed playwright August Wilson. In *Seven Guitars,* Davis played Vera, a young woman who comes into her own and becomes her own person while living in Pittsburgh in the years after World War II. Davis stuck with the play through tryouts in four cities before the production made its way to Broadway in 1996. That year, Davis was nominated for her first Tony Award for her work in *Seven Guitars.* The actress received much acclaim for her work in the role, but admitted she was shocked by the prestigious nomination. She told William K. Gale of the *Providence Journal-Bulletin,* "I mean, I come from Central Falls. I did not, growing up, ever, ever dream I could be in this place." Though she did not win the honor, being nominated moved her career forward.

Davis' next lauded role came in 1999 with the Broadway production of *Everybody's Ruby.* Based on real events, Davis played Ruby McCollum, an African-American woman who was accused of murdering her abusive lover, a white man, in the early 1950s. Author Zora Neale Hurston, who was played in the production by Phylicia Rashad, covered the trial. Davis received rave reviews for her work in the role as well as an Obie Award. Asked how she approached the role of Ruby, who led a very different life than hers, Davis told John Castellucci of the *Providence Journal-Bulletin,* "You're impersonating someone, but to me, you're also revealing a part of humanity, which means you have to reveal a part of yourself on stage."

To this point in Davis' career, she had focused primarily on stage work, including appearances as Eleanor in the 1997 production of *God's Heart* and the 1999 production of *The Vagina Monologues,* both in New York City. She worked occasionally in film and television. Davis had small roles in films like 1996's *The Substance of Fire* and 1998's *Out of Sight.* Her television appearances to this point included guest spots on shows like *NYPD Blue* and *New York Undercover,* as well as roles in television movies like *The Pentagon Wars* and *Grace & Glorie.* In the early 2000s, however, she moved regularly between stage, film, and television, finding much success in all three genres.

In 2000, Davis had a featured role in the series *City of Angels.* She played nurse Lynette Peeler on the hospital drama, which was cancelled by CBS during its first year on the air because of poor ratings and generally negative reviews. After its cancellation, she took a role as a factory worker in the 2001 television movie *Amy & Isabelle,* which was produced by Oprah Winfrey's production company, Harpo Productions. Davis also had roles in two films of note, *The Shrink Is In* and *Kate & Leopold.* Yet Davis wanted to work on stage, telling Andy Smith of the *Providence Journal-Bulletin,* "I really feel the need to go back and do some theater. I'm jonesing for it. The money's good in TV, but there's nothing like theater for an actress."

Davis landed a major stage role in 2001, playing Tonya in the Broadway production of Wilson's play *King Hedley II.* The actress was honored with her first Tony Award for her work in the role of a woman deciding if she should have an abortion in Pittsburgh in 1985. She spent much of the next few years again working in film and television. She had roles in three films released in 2002: *Far from Heaven,* a memorable turn in the drama *Antwone Fisher,* and the moody remake of the science fiction drama *Solaris.* In addition to guest spots on various television series like *Law & Order: Criminal Intent* and *CSI: Crime Scene Investigation* in 2002, Davis also appeared in television movies like *Father Lefty* and began a recurring role on *Law & Order: Special Victims Unit* in 2003. Her next regular role on a television series came with the futuristic legal drama *Century City,* which was quickly cancelled after a spring run in 2004.

While the television series did not work out, Davis again found acclaim on the stage. She won several awards for her work as Esther Mills in the play *Intimate Apparel,* in both New York and Los Angeles productions in 2004. Set in 1905 in New York City, *Intimate Apparel* features Davis playing a 35-year-old woman who is plain and lonely, working as a seamstress of undergarments for women until she finds long-distance romance with a man working on the Panama Canal. Their relationship helps her blossom as a person. As Davis explained to Celia McGee of the New York *Daily News,* "Everyone around her is drawn to a beauty she wasn't aware she had. She is a gift."

After *Intimate Apparel,* Davis concentrated on film and television for the next six years. Her television work included appearances in a series of television movies: 2005's *Jesse Stone: Stone Cold,* 2006's *Jesse Stone: Night Passage* and *Jesse Stone: Death in Paradise,* and 2007's *Jesse Stone: Sea Change.* She also appeared in several other television movies, including *Life Is Not a Fairytale: The Fantasia Barrino Story,* which focused on the hardscrabble life story of the *American Idol* winner. In 2007, Davis returned to series television with a key role in the science fiction drama *Traveler,* but the series was canceled during its first season. The following year, Davis was cast in a miniseries remake of the science fiction classic, *The Andromeda Strain.* By 2010, Davis found success on series television when she joined the cast for the second season of the Showtime hit drama, *The United States of Tara,* which centered on a woman with multiple personality disorder.

Davis' film roles brought her even more acclaim. She appeared in the George Clooney vehicle *Syriana* in 2005, the thriller *Disturbia* in 2007, and, most notably, the film adaptation of the Pulitzer Prize-winning stage play *Doubt* in 2008. Set in 1964, *Doubt* focuses on accusations that a priest molested an African-American boy, the son of Davis' character, Mrs. Miller. A nun, played by Meryl Streep, wanted her help in stopping the priest. The role was considered one of the best available for African-American actresses in some time, and Davis beat out a number of her peers to land the supporting role.

Yet Davis had difficulties understanding Mrs. Miller and the choices that she made. Davis told David S. Cohen of *Daily Variety,* "The contemporary Viola wanted to come in and just tell the nun off. The other part of it was that I didn't have anything in my life that let me understand a black woman who would be willing to sacrifice her son to a teacher who might be molesting him." Working through the character and giving the performance of a lifetime, Davis was critically lauded for her work as Mrs. Miller. She was nominated for numerous awards, including an Academy Award, and won several, including a Black Reel Award.

After *Doubt,* Davis tried her hand at comedy, appearing in *Madea Goes to Jail* in 2009. She had a starring role as Ellen, an ex-prostitute and drug addict, in the Tyler Perry family comedy. Davis described the part to Cindy Pearlman in the *Chicago Sun Times,* explaining: "It was fun because she's in recovery, so I got to play that part, too. It's funny because it's a joy as an actress to play a drug addict or hooker. It's a joy to shoot a gun on screen. All the horrific things in life are wonderful to act." Davis went on to appear in the drama *State of Play,* with Russell Crowe and Ben Affleck in 2009, then returned to comedy with *Knight & Day,* in 2010. She also took roles in the anticipated film version of Liz Gilbert's memoir, *Eat Pray Love,* and the well-received independent comedy *It's Kind of a Funny Story,* both released in 2010.

Also in 2010, Davis returned to the stage in a Broadway revival of the marital drama *Fences,* by Wilson. She played Rose Maxson, the wife of Troy, played by Denzel Washington. In the play, set in Pittsburgh in 1957, the long-married couple, despite some marital strife, inspire each other's hopes in a world of dreams unfulfilled. The production was well reviewed by critics, and both Davis and Washington were nominated for Tony Awards. While Wilson wrote multi-dimensional African-American characters, Davis believed most black characters were not so well-rounded and did not accurately reflect her complex spirit. She told Dann Gire of the *Chicago Daily Herald,* "When you go to acting school, your job is to create a fully realized human being. What is a human being? A human being has dichotomies, contradictions, dualities.... They're never just one thing. What I see with so many African-American characters is that they're always one thing.... I don't see myself ever represented. I see a vast array of white women represented. I don't see me."

Sources

Periodicals

Camwest News Service, August 12, 2010.
Chicago Daily Herald, February 19, 2009, p. 18.
Chicago Sun Times, February 4, 2009, p. 30; February 22, 2009, p. D1.
Daily News (New York, NY), June 13, 2001, p. 41; April 14, 2004, p. 38.
Daily Variety, May 2, 2001, p. 15; March 16, 2004, p. 4; April 13, 2004, p. 10; August 17, 2006, p. 5; May 23, 2008, p. 3; October 28, 2008, p. A11.
Jet, December 11, 2000, p. 12.
New York Times, June 3, 2001, sec. 2, p. 7; May 23, 2010, p. AR1.
Providence Journal-Bulletin (RI), June 1, 1996, p. 1C; April 1, 1999, p. 1D; October 19, 2000, p. 1E; December 26, 2008, p. 6.
UPI, June 15, 2009.
Variety, November 25-December 1, 2002, p. 22; March 2-8, 2009, p. 17; September 26, 2010, p. 48.

Online

"Viola Davis," Broadway World, http://broadwayworld.com/people/Viola_Davis (November 22, 2010).
"Viola Davis," Internet Broadway Database, http://www.ibdb.com/person.php?id=37520 (November 22, 2010).
"Viola Davis (I)," Internet Movie Database, http://www.imdb.com/name/nm0205626/ (November 22, 2010).

—*A. Petruso*

Giada De Laurentiis

Chef and television personality

Born Giada Pamela De Benedetti, August 22, 1970, in Rome, Italy; daughter of Alex De Benedetti (an actor and producer) and Veronica De Laurentiis (an actress); married Todd Thompson (a clothing designer), May 25, 2003; children: Jade Marie. *Education:* University of California—Los Angeles, B.A., 1996; trained at Le Cordon Bleu, Paris.

Addresses: *Agent*—William Morris Endeavor Entertainment, 9601 Wilshire Blvd., 3rd Fl., Beverly Hills, CA 90210. *Home*—Pacific Palisades, CA. *Office*—c/o The Food Network, 1180 Avenue of the Americas, New York, NY 10036.

Career

Cook, Spago, Beverly Hills, CA and the Ritz-Carlton hotel chain, c. late 1990s; founded catering company, GDL Foods, c. late 1990s; food stylist, *Food & Wine* magazine, c. early 2000s. Television appearances include: *Everyday Italian* (host), 2003-08; *An Italian Christmas with Mario and Giada*, 2004; *Behind the Bash* (host), 2005-06; *Giada's Italian Holiday*, 2005; *Iron Chef America* (competitor), 2006; *Today* (contributor), 2006—; *Giada in Paradise*, 2007; *Giada's Weekend Getaways* (host), 2007—; *Giada at Home* (host), 2008—; *The Best Thing I Ever Ate*, 2009; *The Next Food Network Star* (guest judge), 2009. Author of cookbooks, including: *Everyday Italian: 125 Simple and Delicious Recipes*, 2005; *Giada's Family Dinners*, 2006; *Everyday Pasta*, 2007; *Giada's Kitchen: New Italian Favorites*, 2008; *Giada at Home: Family Recipes from Italy and California*, 2010.

Awards: Daytime Emmy for outstanding lifestyle host, National Academy of Television Arts and Sciences and the Academy of Television Arts & Sciences, 2008.

Sidelights

Giada De Laurentiis joins a long roster of kitchen professionals who became authentic celebrity chefs thanks to exposure on the Food Network. Her series *Everyday Italian* launched her career as doyenne of a mini-empire that includes best-selling cookbooks and a line of cookware introduced at mass retailer Target in 2010. She is also the scion of one of the most famous dynasties in Italian cinema as the granddaughter of legendary producer Dino De Laurentiis. "When I first wanted to do it, my grandfather thought I'd lost my mind," she confessed in an interview for *Redbook* with Jancee Dunn about her plan to become a chef. "A female wanting to cook! He said, 'You should just get married and have some kids. Don't you worry about a career.'"

De Laurentiis was born in 1970 in Rome, Italy, to Veronica De Laurentiis, an actress and the wife of Alex De Benedetti, an actor and producer. Veronica's father Dino had produced scores of cinematic masterpieces in Italy and then the United States, from Federico Fellini's *La Strada* to *Serpico* and *King Kong* in the 1970s. Giada—whose name means "jade" in Italian—also had a famous grandmother, Silvana Mangano, one of Italian cinema's top stars of the postwar period.

De Laurentiis' parents divorced around 1977 and Veronica moved her four children to the Los Angeles area, where her father Dino had relocated. De Laurentiis grew up in Beverly Hills and attended the single-sex Marymount High School on Sunset Boulevard. She recalled that as a child she enjoyed the stupendous Sunday dinners with all members of the extended De Laurentiis clan at their grandfather's nearby home, while on weekdays her mother let her and siblings Igor, Eloisa, and Dino Jr. help with meals. "We did a lot of mixing, sifting, and egg breaking, which we got all over the place," she told Carol Mithers in a *Town & Country* article. "We all felt grown-up, part of the adult world, because my mom allowed us to do it with her. I think that's why I fell in love with food—I was around it, smelling it, and it was associated with family and feeling good."

De Laurentiis' tight-knit family gave her two choices upon graduating from Marymount: "I always wanted to go to cooking school, but my family said, 'You gotta either go to college or work in the family business, the movies,'" she told *Self* magazine's Laura Brounstein. "I worked in wardrobe, set design, makeup. I even tried acting but was very uncomfortable doing it. So I went to college." After earning an undergraduate degree in social anthropology from the University of California at Los Angeles, she remained resolute about pursuing her dream and moved to Paris to enroll at the prestigious Le Cordon Bleu cooking school. The rigorous training she received there opened doors for her back home, and she worked for Wolfgang Puck's flagship Spago restaurant and at the Ritz Carlton hotel chain before starting her own catering company, GDL Foods.

As a caterer and private chef, De Laurentiis landed some impressive Hollywood clients, but it was a simple recipe she submitted to *Food & Wine*—where she occasionally worked as a food stylist—which ran with her picture and famous last name that brought her to the attention of executives at the Food Network. They asked her to send an audition tape, and she filmed herself making a peanut butter and jelly sandwich in her kitchen, which led to a contract to appear in a new show, *Everyday Italian,* that premiered on the Food Network in 2003. De Laurentiis admitted that her new role as a television chef was daunting at first. "Talking to other people while you're cooking, it doesn't come naturally," she told Dunn in the *Redbook* interview. "You're chopping, the timing is tricky, and then you have to explain it all and tell stories."

De Laurentiis improved with practice, however, and *Everyday Italian* began pulling strong ratings numbers in 2004. That led to a deal for her first cookbook, also called *Everyday Italian,* which became a *New York Times* best seller in the spring of 2005. De Laurentiis was stunned to find hundreds of fans waiting in line to meet her at book signings, and her name began cropping up in *Esquire* magazine in its routine surveys of appealing women in the public eye. Her rising profile led to more series and specials for the Food Network, such as *Giada's Weekend Getaways* and *Giada at Home,* which succeeded *Everyday Italian* in the fall of 2008.

Earlier in 2008 De Laurentiis took a brief break from her hectic schedule to sit out the final months of her pregnancy. Her first child, Jade Marie, was born in March of 2008, to De Laurentiis and her clothing-designer husband Todd Thompson. The couple married in 2003, but had been dating for more than a decade by then. "My goal in life was never marriage," she told *Town & Country*'s Mithers. "It was to take care of myself and make sure I did everything I wanted to do. In Europe, the man takes care of the woman. I watched that my whole life, and I knew I didn't want it for myself."

De Laurentiis' other cookbooks include *Giada's Family Dinners,* published in 2006, *Everyday Pasta* (2007), and 2008's *Giada's Kitchen: New Everyday Favorites,* all of which became best sellers. In early 2008, she began appearing on the new fourth-hour segment of NBC's long-running morning staple, the *Today* show, demonstrating recipes and tips for successful entertaining. De Laurentiis and her family live in the beachfront Los Angeles community of Pacific Palisades, where *Giada at Home* is taped. In the interview with Brounstein in *Self,* she admitted to an unusual method of relaxing from her multiple work commitments and heavy travel schedule—she unwinds in the kitchen. "Without cameras, cooking is no longer a job, it's my hobby," she said. "It's something I still enjoy doing. It lets me go into my own world, reflect, and relax."

Sources

Redbook, January 2008, p. 86.
Self, December 2008, p. 176.
Town & Country, January 2007, p. 120.
USA Today, May 13, 2005, p. 6D.

—Carol Brennan

Landon Donovan

Professional soccer player

Born Landon Timothy Donovan, March 4, 1982, in Ontario, CA; son of Tim Donovan (a pharmaceutical representative) and Donna Kenney-Cash (a special-education teacher); married Bianca Kajlich (an actress), December 31, 2006 (separated, 2009).

Addresses: *Agent*—Richard Motzkin, Wasserman Media Group, 10960 Wilshire Blvd., Ste. 2200, Los Angeles, CA 90024. *Office*—c/o Los Angeles Galaxy, 18400 Avalon Blvd., Ste. 200, Carson, CA 90746. *Web site*—www.landondonovan.com.

Career

Soccer forward or midfielder on U.S. national teams, including Under-17s, 1998-99, Under-23s, 1999-2004, U.S. Men's National Team, 1999—, and U.S. Olympic team, 2000. Professional soccer forward or midfielder with Bayern Leverkusen, Germany, 2000-05, on loan to San Jose Earthquakes, 2001-04, and Los Angeles Galaxy, 2005—; played on loan with Bayern Munich, Germany, 2009, and Everton, England, 2010.

Awards: Golden Ball for most valuable player of Under-17 World Championship, FIFA (Federation of International Football Associations), 1999; All-Star selection, Major League Soccer (MLS), 2001-10; All-Star Game most valuable player, MLS, 2001; Honda Player of the Year for best U.S. Men's National Soccer Team player, Fútbol de Primera, 2002-04, 2007-09; ESPY Award for top male soccer player, ESPN cable network, 2002; FIFA World Cup Best Young Player Award, FIFA, 2002; MLS Cup MVP, MLS,

2003; Male Athlete of the Year award, U.S. Soccer Federation, 2003-04, 2009-10; Major League Soccer Best XI (all-league team), MLS, 2003, 2008-10; ESPY Award for best MLS player, ESPN cable network, 2006-07, 2009-10; Golden Boot for most regular-season goals, MLS, 2008; Most Valuable Player, MLS, 2009; Honda Player of the Decade, Fútbol de Primera, 2009; ESPY Awards for Best Performance Under Pressure and Best Moment, ESPN cable network, 2010.

Sidelights

Landon Donovan is considered by many to be the greatest men's soccer player in American history. After joining the U.S. men's national soccer team as a teenager, he took fewer than ten years to become the United States' all-time leader in goals and assists in international play. In ten seasons he won three Major League Soccer (MLS) championships with teams in San Jose and Los Angeles and became the league's all-time scorer of playoff goals. In 2010, even casual fans of soccer learned his name after he scored a dramatic, game-winning goal in extra time to send the United States to the second round of the World Cup.

Donovan was born in 1982 in California, where he grew up with his twin sister Tristan and older brother Josh. His parents divorced when he was two years old and it was his older brother who taught him to play soccer in their back yard. Donovan was a high-energy child and soccer was a great outlet for his exuberance. At age five he joined a league for six and seven year olds and scored seven goals in his first game. "There's this incredible liberating feeling that you get right after you score a goal," he recalled to Joe Rhodes in *Los Angeles Magazine*. "I decided that I loved that feeling. It still gives me goose bumps every time."

Soccer was a big part of Donovan's life throughout his childhood, and he loved to win. "I was so competitive," he told Rhodes, "even more competitive than I am now. I loved playing soccer more than anything in the world. The reason I had good grades wasn't because I cared that much about school. It was because I wanted to get my homework out of the way and have more time for playing soccer." By age 15 he was invited to participate in Olympic developmental programs sponsored by U.S. Soccer. He attended a training program in Florida where he impressed coaches and earned a spot on the U.S. Under-17 team. He told Jill Lieber in *USA Today*, "A lot of other guys probably knew what was going on and thought, 'Shoot, I really have to try hard to make this team.' I couldn't have cared less," Donovan recalled. "That's when I play the best, when I'm just playing for fun." He missed most of his junior year of high school while playing on the Under-17 team, traveling around the world for tournaments, but the experience brought him to the attention of several soccer clubs overseas. He was a month shy of his 17th birthday when he became the youngest American ever to be offered a contract with a European club.

While Donovan's mother was initially opposed to the move, his father, a former semi-professional hockey player, believed the soccer star should have a chance to chase his dreams. He checked out the city and convinced Donovan's mother to let their son go, especially since Donovan was on target to earn his GED. The young player signed a four-year deal with Bayer Leverkusen in Germany that paid $400,000. The adjustment to living and playing in a foreign country was difficult, however, and Donovan languished on the team's reserve squad. "I definitely played horribly at first," the player told Marc Spiegler of *Sports Illustrated*. "I just couldn't understand why my game was not working…. Finally, I quit playing like a sissy and decided to fight and run." Although he worked on becoming a more physical player, the competition for playing time was fierce and after two years he still had not been called up to the main club. His homesickness and frustration did not affect his national team play; he

earned the Golden Ball for best player at the 1999 Under-17 World Cup and scored a goal as a reserve during the team's fourth-place run at the 2000 Olympics. Nevertheless, he kept being relegated further down Bayer Leverkusen's reserve list. He asked them to loan him to a team back in the United States, and they agreed.

Donovan began playing with Major League Soccer's San Jose Earthquakes in 2001. The team had finished with the worst record in the league the previous year, but Donovan helped them to a winning record and a playoff berth. During the playoffs he scored five goals in six games, including one in San Jose's MLS Cup victory. He was also named to the All-Star team that year, and earned most valuable player (MVP) status at the All-Star game by scoring four goals. He attributed his success to being at home and getting regular playing time: "I wanted to get out of Germany so bad. If I weren't playing in MLS, I wouldn't be with the national team," he told *Sports Illustrated*'s Grant Wahl, explaining that "I have grown so much from playing day in and day out."

In 2002 Donovan made his first appearance in the World Cup, soccer's most important tournament, which the Federation of International Football Associations (FIFA) holds every four years. Since placing third in the first World Cup in 1930, the United States team had enjoyed little success, not even qualifying for the tournaments held between 1954 and 1986. Despite American efforts to develop the sport—they hosted the tournament in 1994 and made it to the second round—their performance in the 1998 tournament was dismal, with three losses in three matches. For 2002 the team's goal was to make it out of the first round, but helped by Donovan's two goals, the United States had its best finish since 1930, reaching the tournament's round of eight. In group play, Donovan had a cross strike knocked in by a Portuguese player in their 3-2 victory over the perennial soccer power, as well as a goal against Poland. He also scored in their second-round game against rival Mexico. For his efforts, FIFA gave him the tournament's Best Young Player Award and honorable mention consideration for the All-World Cup team.

Although Donovan's star performance at the World Cup earned him more interest from European teams, he chose to return to MLS' Earthquakes for the 2002 season. "I'd rather be spending time here, making less money, and maybe not playing at the highest level in order to be near the people I love," he told Ashley Jude Collie in *Soccer Digest*. He explained that "as a forward, I haven't mastered this level, so what makes me think I can go where it's so much more competitive? ... I've learned that no matter how good a finisher you think you are, you could always be better." The perennial MLS all-star led the Earthquakes to the playoffs in 2002 and 2003; in the latter year they earned their second MLS Cup championship in three years. During the 2003 playoffs Donovan scored a winning overtime goal to get the team into the finals, then scored two goals in the 4-2 championship victory over the Chicago Fire. His awards for the 2003 season included MLS Cup MVP, MLS All-League status, Honda Player of the Year, and U.S. Soccer's Male Athlete of the Year award.

While the 2004 season was a down year for Earthquakes—they were eliminated in the first round of the playoffs—Donovan continued leading the U.S. team in international play. He played more minutes than any other team member and earned four goals and four assists in eight qualifying games. At the beginning of 2005 he returned to Germany for another stint with Bayer Leverkusen, but only started two games. "I was out of it mentally," the forward admitted to Lieber in *USA Today*. "I wasn't inspired to play anymore.... This is a game I played my whole life and loved. It's always been my way of expression. And meanwhile I'm 6,000 miles from home. I didn't want to be miserable. I'm 23, and I don't need to go through that." He asked to be released from his contract and signed instead with MLS' Los Angeles Galaxy, becoming the highest-paid player in the league with a reported four-year deal for $4.8 million. With 12 goals and ten assists in 22 regular-season games, Donovan led the Galaxy to a MLS title in 2005. He scored four goals in three playoff games, becoming the league's all-time playoff scoring leader in the process.

The same year he was outstanding in national team play, as well. In the CONCACAF Gold Cup, a tournament between national teams in North and Central America and the Caribbean, he scored three goals, including a shootout goal in the championship game that helped clinch a U.S. victory. Hopes were high for the U.S. team in the 2006 World Cup, as they entered with a FIFA ranking of fifth in the world. The pressure proved too much, however, as Donovan was held scoreless in his three starts and the team went out after the first round with one tie and two losses. The dismal performance affected his enthusiasm for the game until his then-wife, at the time a struggling actress, told him he should feel fortunate to make a living doing what he loved. The words changed his outlook, he explained to Joe Posnanski in *Sports Illustrated*: "I always worked very hard on the game, but, you know, soccer came pretty easily to me. I had to realize and accept that I

do have great responsibility. It's not just because I'm immensely talented and blessed with a gift physically. It's also because of the mental [feel for the game]. It would be horrible of me not to bring that out."

Donovan applied himself to becoming an even better soccer player. In 2007 he led the Galaxy in goals and assists in a down season, while in 2008 he earned the MLS Golden Boot for most goals scored. In 2009 he led the Galaxy back into the playoffs and was named league MVP for first time; late that year the club re-signed him to a four-year, $9 million contract. His international play was outstanding, as well. In 2007 he set a U.S. team record for goals scored in a year, leading the team to another Gold Cup victory. He scored two goals at the 2009 Confederations Cup, a FIFA tournament featuring the world's regional champions, helping the U.S. team to a runner-up finish, their best ever at a FIFA event. In early 2010 he played in England's Premier League on loan to Everton and finally proved he could compete with Europeans, being named the team's player of the month for January. Donovan was looking forward to the challenge of another World Cup, he told *New York Times* writer Jere Longman: "Now there's more responsibility. In my opinion, there's also greater opportunity. I enjoy the challenge of that now. In 2006, that became burdensome. I wasn't ready for it. Now I'm ready for it. I'm really excited for it."

In the 2010 World Cup held in South Africa, Donovan solidified his status as the heart of the U.S. team. In four games, he led the team with four goals and became the United States' all-time World Cup leader in matches played (12), goals scored (five), and consecutive games with a goal (three). His most notable goal was against Algeria, scored during injury time to give the United States a victory and their first group win in 80 years. The game was watched by a record number of fans in the United States, and Donovan was amazed by the response to the victory. "In the past, I just thought this is a game that we play," he told Kent Jones on MSNBC's *The Rachel Maddow Show*. "And at the end of the day, maybe it is. But the reality is, there are people who want to be inspired and people want a break from their everyday life so that they can just enjoy something and be proud to be an American. And hopefully, we gave that to them today." Although the United States lost their second-round match to Ghana in overtime—Donovan scored the only U.S. goal—it was clear the team's performance had made an impact on the American sports consciousness. "Since I've been back, it's been very clear that people were captivated by this team and what we were about," Donovan told Jose de Jesus Ortiz in the *Houston Chronicle*. "You see that in the All-Star Game, in our league games and certainly see that in the national level."

In the summer of 2010 Donovan resumed playing with the LA Galaxy, tying an MLS record with his tenth consecutive All-Star appearance and leading the team to a league-best finish. He was once again named to the MLS Best XI squad, and led the league in assists for the first time with 16. "I'm not the guy who can take the ball, dribble through everyone, and score. That's not me," he told Rhodes. "But I think I do other things that benefit the team, and I think that's why I've always been a winner. If a team tries to shut me down, then other guys are open and I'll find them." Despite their success in the regular season, the Galaxy fell short in the play-offs, losing in the conference championship to FC Dallas.

As he approached his 30s, Donovan felt he still had plenty of good games left to play; he had learned to bring his mental game up to the level of his physical skills. "I'm proving it to myself all the time," he told Posnanski. "I can play at a high level and bring the best out of myself no matter what the situation.... In the past I needed something to get me going. Now I know: If I want to have a good game, it's right here [inside]." As for future World Cups, he wrote on his Web site: "If I can do it physically, I think I can still be a top player. I know mentally what I'm capable of now. I think there's still a lot more room for me to grow mentally, and if I can keep up physically then I'll do it.... I'd love to play in another World Cup. You never know, maybe another two." In December of 2010, Donovan was named Male Athlete of the Year by the U.S. Soccer Federation for the fourth time. Shortly after the award announcement, Donovan declared his intent to rest during the MLS off season and not return for a second season with Everton.

Sources

Periodicals

Houston Chronicle, July 28, 2010, p. 1.
Los Angeles Magazine, September 2005, p. 68.
New York Times, May 19, 2010, p. B13.
San Jose Mercury News, July 22, 2010.
Soccer Digest, October-November 2002, p. 14.
Sports Illustrated, April 17, 2000, p. 45; October 29, 2001, p. R8; June 17, 2002, p. 38; April 5, 2004, p. Z7; June 7, 2010, p. 70.
USA Today, May 20, 2005, p. 1C.

Online

"Donovan Rules Out Everton Return," BBC Sport, http://news.bbc.co.uk/sport2/hi/football/teams/e/everton/9311063.stm (December 21, 2010).
"Landon Donovan and Abby Wambach Win 2010 Athlete of the Year," Soccer Nation, http://www.soccernation.com/landon-donovan-and-abby-wambach-win-2010-athlete-of-the-year-cms-842 (December 21, 2010).
"Landon Donovan," Major League Soccer, http://www.mlssoccer.com/player/landon-donovan (September 30, 2010).
"Recent Q&A," Landon Donovan Official Web site, http://www.landondonovan.com/donovan/index (September 30, 2010).

Transcripts

The Rachel Maddow Show, MSNBC, June 23, 2010.

—*Diane Telgen*

Anne L. Doubilet

Photographer

Photo courtesy of Anne Doubilet. Photo by Milbry Polk.

Born c. 1948; married David Doubilet, 1974 (divorced); children: Emily Dara. *Education:* Studies at Boston University, 1970.

Addresses: *Gallery*—MERI Gallery, 55 Main St., Blue Hill, ME 10003. *Home*—New York, NY. *Office*—c/o Explorers Club, 46 E. 70th St., New York, NY 10021.

Career

Underwater photography assistant, 1970s; freelance underwater photographer, early 1980s—; author of the children's book *Under the Sea from A to Z*, 1991; lecturer on marine environment issues; founder and owner, ALD Consulting.

Member: Board director, Explorers Club; board member, Wings WorldQuest.

Awards: Fellow, Explorers Club; Women Diver's Hall of Fame.

Sidelights

Anne L. Doubilet has devoted her life to capturing the realm that lies beneath the ocean's surface. A diver, photographer, and writer, Doubilet travels the world on various assignments and scientific expeditions, and has long ties with both the National Geographic Society and the Explorers Club of New York City. "I had my first Alice in Wonderland moment," she said, describing her inaugural dive as a young woman in the Bahamas to *Vogue*'s Eve MacSweeney. "I stepped off the side of the boat into crystalline turquoise and entered an enchanted realm."

Born in the late 1940s, Doubilet grew up in the Boston area but spent her summers along the Atlantic Ocean shore at her family's summer home on Cape Ann, near the Massachusetts border with New Hampshire. She loved swimming, roaming the beach, and collecting shells. "My parents did once send me to overnight camp in the mountains," she told MacSweeney, "and I was miserable." She was even unhappier at the age of eleven when she contracted St. Vitus' dance, a nerve disorder sometimes related to rheumatic fever, that left her paralyzed and confined to bed for a year. To pass the time, she spent hours "watching the sea from my window," she said in an interview that appeared on the Art of Exploration Web site. "I vowed that if and when I recovered I would learn to swim underwater to explore all the places I could then only dream about."

Doubilet's physical freedom was hampered again at the age of 19, when she was involved in a motorcycle accident in Boston. The college student endured several operations over the course of the next six years. "I almost lost my left leg," she told Mac-Sweeney in the *Vogue* article. "I found my place in the water because swimming is weightless."

In college, Doubilet studied literature and photography, but found her calling when she met her future husband, David Doubilet, who was emerging as a well-known underwater photographer. She earned her scuba-diving certification—a rigorous course for using the Self Contained Underwater Breathing Apparatus (SCUBA)—and made her first dive in the Bahamas. The pair married in 1974 and spent their honeymoon exploring the Red Sea, which separates the Arabian Peninsula from northeast Africa. She has described the Red Sea to *Vogue* as "the most exquisite paradise you could ever imagine," detailing how it was "teeming with corals and anemones and sharks swimming around; polka-dotted stingrays and schools of glassy sweepers; beautiful pink, purple, orange, lavender, and yellow soft corals gently waving back and forth in the currents."

By the early 1980s Doubilet was assisting her husband on underwater photo shoots and taking some of her own shots on the specialized camera equipment used in the field. David Doubilet gained renown for his images of the fearsome great white shark, and his wife became one of the first women permitted to descend in a cage to observe the beast. After having a daughter, she wrote a 1991 children's book, *Under the Sea from A to Z* which featured her photographs and was published by Random House. She also became a fellow of the rarified Explorers Club, a select group of pioneers linked to the National Geographic Society whose home is a treasure-laden clubhouse on New York's Upper East Side. Founded in 1904, the Explorers Club boasts a notable roster of members, from Roald Amundsen and Ernest Shackleton to Charles Lindbergh, Chuck Yeager, and Neil Armstrong. Famed anthropologist Jane Goodall and the first men to ascend Mount Everest, Edmund Hillary and Tenzing Norgay, have also been invited to become members; the Club did not permit women to join before 1981.

Explorers Club members like Doubilet have become ardent environmental activists after witnessing first-hand the impact of human carelessness on the planet. Coral reefs she photographed early in her career have disappeared, for example, and a 2008 exhibit of her photography at the National Arts Club titled *Coral and Ice: From the Ends of the Earth* showed in detail the destruction of the delicate reefs and the rapid changes in polar icebergs in just a few short years. Doubilet also lectures on various topics related to protecting the oceans, discussing the massive floating garbage island in the North Pacific and new cancers found in whales and other marine mammals because of toxins released into the oceans.

Doubilet is often invited to photograph scientific research expeditions. She wrote about one to the waters around Papua New Guinea for the *Explorers Journal,* a quarterly publication issued by the Explorers Club, which also ran the magnificent images she captured of a species of poisonous catfish called *Plotosus lineatus* but dubbed "ploto" by the members of the crew. "We set up a system of tag-team dives, each a half-hour in duration, so there will always be a pair of human eyes to observe and record plotos' behavior," she wrote of the experience. "Critical times for observing the fish are from 5:00 to 7:00 am and from 3:00 to 8:00 pm. Observers do not leave the dive site until a replacement team appears. Eyes must remain fixed on the plotos or the swarm may suddenly disappear into the murky background."

Doubilet is active in Wings WorldQuest, which provides grants to female explorers and scientific researchers. Her daughter Emily Dara Doubilet has also become an experienced diver and majored in environmental studies at Oberlin College. In her early sixties when interviewed for *Vogue* in 2009, Doubilet still spent many hours each year underwater and continued to display infectious enthusiasm about her life's work. After her Papua New Guinea trip, she ventured to the Arctic Ocean for another job. "To be able to see that much of the planet in the space of a few months was life-changing," she told MacSweeney. "Everything came into focus."

Sources

Periodicals

Explorers Journal, 2008, pp. 46-50.
Petersen's Photographic, June 1983, p. 68.
Vogue, August 2009, p. 154.

Online

"About," ALD Consulting, http://www.annedoubilet.com/ (March 1, 2010).
"The Art of Exploration: Anne Doubilet," Imagination Celebration Fort Worth (ICFW), http://www.icfw.org/AnneDoubilet-final_AnneDoubilet-final.qxd.pdf, (March 1, 2010).

—*Carol Brennan*

Arne Duncan

U.S. Secretary of Education

Born November 6, 1964, in Chicago, IL; son of Starkey (a professor) and Susan (founding director of a tutoring program; maiden name, Morton) Duncan; married Karen; children: Claire, Ryan. *Education:* Harvard University, A.B., 1987.

Addresses: *Home*—Arlington, VA. *Office*—U.S. Department of Education, 400 Maryland Ave. SW, Washington, DC 20202.

Career

Played professional basketball with the National Basketball League of Australia, 1987-91; tutor in Australia; director, Ariel Education Initiative, 1992-98; chief executive officer, Chicago Public Schools, 2001-08; U.S. Secretary of Education, 2009—.

Sidelights

Arne Duncan, a longtime friend of Barack Obama and head of the Chicago Public Schools, became Secretary of Education in the new president's cabinet in 2009. The Chicago native possesses a wealth of experience that dates all the way back to the tutoring program his mother ran on the city's South Side. Recalling a photo of him in his teens with some of his peers from the program in the late 1970s, he told *New Yorker* writer Carlo Rotella that some of those men had now fallen victim to urban violence. "As much as the success stories have shaped me and given me hope, those deaths might be an even bigger motivator," he reflected. "The guys who got killed were the guys who didn't finish high school. It was literally the dividing line between you live or you die. Nobody who went to college died young."

Born in 1964, Duncan was the eldest of three children in the family. His father was Starkey Duncan, a professor of psychology at the University of Chicago. His mother Sue was a Smith College graduate who had been invited to teach a Bible-study class at a predominantly black church near the Hyde Park neighborhood where the family lived. She quickly realized some of the nine-year-olds could not read, and set up a tutoring program for elementary-school students at 46th Street and South Greenwood Avenue. Duncan, his brother, and sister all worked there as tutors throughout their own school years, which were spent at the University of Chicago Lab School.

Duncan's mother was also a gifted athlete and passed on that trait to her son. He emerged as a first-class basketball player in his teens, recruited by colleges but also shooting hoops in pickup games at playgrounds across the South Side. Though his own enclave of Hyde Park, home to the University of Chicago campus, was relatively middle-class and diverse, much of the city's South Side looked like the rest of urban America. "A bunch of places where

I played were extraordinarily dangerous," he told Rotella in the *New Yorker* interview. "I couldn't fight. There were times when I was really scared, but that's where the best basketball was.... I learned to read people's character. I learned to trust certain people completely." Duncan's love of the game also served to introduce him to Craig Robinson, two years his senior, who went on to play for Princeton University. Robinson's sister, Michelle, also attended Princeton, then Harvard Law School. When she returned to Chicago, she met another Harvard Law grad who was working as a community organizer; that man was Barack Obama, her future husband.

Duncan played for Harvard University, serving as co-captain of the Crimson basketball team in his senior year. He majored in sociology and graduated magna cum laude in 1987. Hoping to play professionally for a few years, he tried out for the Boston Celtics, but failed to make the cut. Instead he was drafted by the National Basketball League (NBL) of Australia, and spent four years there playing for the Eastside Spectres of Melbourne and the Launceston Ocelots of the island province of Tasmania.

In Australia, Duncan returned to tutoring students, and when he decided to return to Chicago with his new bride in tow, he took a job as director of the Ariel Education Initiative. This had been founded by a friend from the Lab School and Princeton, John W. Rogers Jr., who had gone on to a successful career as an investment banker. By 1996, Rogers' efforts to help students at William Shakespeare Elementary School—one of the feeder schools for Sue Duncan's tutoring program in Kenwood—led to the founding of the Ariel Community Academy at the former site of Shakespeare Elementary, which became one of the top-performing schools in the city.

In 1999, Duncan's demonstrated track record at Ariel led to a job as deputy chief of staff to the superintendent—called chief executive officer—of the Chicago Public Schools (CPS). He also served as director of the system's network of magnet schools. Two years later, Chicago mayor Richard M. Daley appointed the then 36-year-old Duncan as the CPS's new chief executive officer. The promotion stunned the community, for Duncan had never even taught in the classroom, nor served as a school principal. As expected, he excelled in the job, serving eight years in a position where such tenure is rare. He linked up with the Teach for America program to recruit new teachers, closed some under-performing schools then reopened them with entirely new staff, and instituted superior data-tracking systems to more accurately measure student performance.

Duncan and his wife Karen were part of a social scene that included Barack and Michelle Obama; in fact, John W. Rogers' ex-wife, Desiree Rogers, would go on to serve as the Obama White House social secretary. Duncan met Obama in the late 1990s and the two regularly played basketball together to keep fit. Obama went on to win a U.S. Senate seat from Illinois in 2004, and launched his campaign for the Democratic presidential nomination in early 2007. Duncan became his advisor on education policy in the run-up to the historic 2008 win for Obama, who became the nation's first African-American president.

Not unexpectedly, on December 15, 2008, President-elect Obama named Duncan as his choice for secretary of the Department of Education, a cabinet-level post. The nomination was confirmed by vote of the U.S. Senate on January 20, 2009. Shortly after Duncan took office in Washington, his department received a significant influx of new federal funding, with Congress approving President Obama's American Recovery and Reinvestment Act (ARRA), a major economic-stimulus package that included $100 billion for education alone, giving Secretary Duncan control over the largest education budget in U.S. history.

Duncan's most formidable task was to correct the flaws in the controversial No Child Left Behind (NCLB) Act, signed by President George W. Bush into law in 2001 to remedy the uneven educational opportunities in U.S. schools. Duncan was reportedly given broad leeway by Obama to rewrite parts of NCLB, which may include revising rules on job security for teachers. Duncan's appointment as education secretary weathered some criticism from teachers' unions for his demonstrated support, back when he headed the CPS, for charter schools, merit pay for teachers, and a policy of removing ineffective educators from the classroom. Duncan and his wife moved from Chicago to Arlington, Virginia, for the cabinet job. His two children are enrolled in public schools in that community.

Sources

Periodicals

New Yorker, February 1, 2010, p. 24.
Time, April 27, 2009, p. 36; September 14, 2009, p. 26.

Online

"Arne Duncan, U.S. Secretary of Education—Biography," U.S. Department of Education, http://www2.ed.gov/news/staff/bios/duncan.html (July 30, 2010).

—*Carol Brennan*

Steve Earle

AP Images

Singer and songwriter

Born Stephen Fain Earle, January 17, 1955, in Hampton, VA; son of Jack (an air traffic controller) and Barbara (a homemaker) Earle; married Sandra Henderson, 1974 (divorced, 1976); married Cynthia Dunn, 1977 (divorced, 1980); married Carol-Ann Hunter, 1981 (divorced, 1987); married Lou-Ann Gill (married, 1987; divorced, 1988; remarried, 1993; divorced, 1997); married Teresa Ensenat, 1988 (divorced, 1992); married Allison Moorer (a country singer), 2005; children: Justin Townes (from third marriage), Ian (from fourth marriage), John Henry (from seventh marriage), and a fourth child.

Addresses: *Web site*—http://www.steveearle.com.

Career

Wrote songs for music publishers around Nashville, 1975-mid-80s; released debut EP *Pink & Black,* 1982; signed to Epic Records, 1983; dropped by Epic Records, 1984; signed to MCA Records, 1985; released debut album *Guitar Town,* 1986; Epic released *Early Tracks,* 1987; released MCA follow-up *Exit 0,* 1987; dropped by MCA, 1991; signed to Winter Harvest, 1995; released *Train a Comin',* 1995; signed to Warner Brothers, 1996; formed own E Squared record label and released *I Feel Alright,* 1996; published short story collection *Doghouse Roses,* actor in television show *The Wire,* 2002—; released *The Revolution Starts...Now,* 2004; host of *The Revolution Starts Now,* Air America radio show, 2004-07; playwright, off-Broadway play *Karla,* 2005; signed to New West Records, 2007; released *Washington Square Serenade,* 2007; host, Sirius Radio show, 2007—; released *Townes,* 2009.

Awards: Country Artist of the Year, *Rolling Stone* magazine, 1986; Lifetime Achievement award, BBC Radio 2, 2004; Grammy Award for best contemporary folk album, National Academy of Recording Arts and Sciences, for *The Revolution Starts...Now,* 2005; Grammy Award for Best Contemporary Folk/Americana Award, National Academy of Recording Arts and Sciences, for *Washington Square Serenade,* 2008; Grammy Award for Best Contemporary Folk/Americana Album, National Academy of Recording Arts and Sciences, for *Townes,* 2010.

Sidelights

Often called the "hardcore troubadour," Grammy-award-winning musician Steve Earle has built a long-lasting career on the strength of his country, roots, and rock songwriting and performing abilities as well as his riotous, rebellious persona. Known almost as well for his numerous failed marriages, run-ins with the law, and substance abuse problems as for his critically praised recordings, Earle has been a figure of greater or lesser sway in the music world since he began writing songs for other artists during the 1970s. First rising to fame when his major label debut, *Guitar Town,* hit shelves in 1986, Earle had more than his share of ups and downs over the years as he gradually lost and regained listeners' ears. After a triumphant comeback in the mid-1990s, the clean and sober artist won his first Grammy Award in 2005 for *The Revolution Starts...Now,* with additional Grammies for *Washington Square Serenade* and *Townes* following in 2008 and 2010, respectively. Earle is also an outspoken liberal and self-proclaimed socialist who hosted a program on erstwhile left-leaning radio station *Air America* for three years before becoming an on-air personality for satellite radio provider Sirius XM.

Born on January 17, 1955, at Fort Monroe in Hampton, Virginia, Earle was raised by his air traffic controller father Jack and homemaker mother Barbara outside San Antonio, Texas. As a boy, Earle struggled in school, making poor grades in math class and fruitlessly seeking ways to fit in. Even at the age of three, however, Earle was intrigued by music, and by the time he reached ninth grade had begun playing guitar; he also began experimenting with drugs, introduced to heroin by an uncle who was only a few years older. At the age of 14 Earle and a school friend dropped out of junior high and ran away to Houston. He briefly returned to the San Antonio area not long after, but he did not re-enter school, and instead began performing at coffeehouses and bars around Texas. While playing in Houston one night in 1972, Earle met Texas singer-songwriter Townes Van Zandt and formed a lasting friendship that greatly influenced both his lifestyle and his music.

In 1974 at the age of 19 Earle married for the first of several times, but short months later moved to the country music mecca of Nashville, Tennessee, without his bride in tow. He worked odd jobs and performed in local bands before landing a songwriting job for music publisher Sunbury Dunbar, penning tunes for other country performers for much of the remainder of the 1970s and, for publishers Roy Dea and Pat Clark, the early 1980s. In 1982, Earle made his recording debut with the EP *Pink & Black,* featuring backing band the Dukes. The EP attracted the attention of Epic Records, which signed the performer the following year. However, the ensuing recording sessions produced a collection of songs that Epic believed to be unmarketable, and no album had materialized by the time Epic dropped Earle from its roster in 1984.

Earle returned to writing songs, this time for music publisher Silverline Goldline. Through this position, he met a producer who convinced record label MCA to give Earle a chance. In 1986, MCA released Earle's full-length debut, *Guitar Town.* The album became an immediate critical and popular success, spawn-

ing successful singles "Guitar Town" and "Goodbye's All We Got Left," placing Earle firmly on the country music map. Writing in *TimeGuitar Town,* Jay Cocks noted that Earle's "voice has off-hand brute force when it has to bear down and unforced gentleness when it comes to business of the heart." This newfound notoriety spurred Epic to release his earlier recording session in 1987 under the title *Early Tracks.* That same year, Earle put out his true sophomore effort, *Exit 0,* again accompanied by the Dukes. Leaning more into rock territory than had his debut, *Exit 0* performed well critically but failed to live up to the commercial success of its predecessor.

His third album, 1988's *Copperhead Road,* continued this shift from country to rock. Country audiences began abandoning Earle even as rock audiences both in the United States and Europe took to his evolving sounds. The performer, however, faced continuing personal turmoil as drug and alcohol dependencies took their toll and his series of failed marriages mounted—four in all by the end of the decade. He was slapped with an assault charge after a New Year's Eve concert and spent 1990 on probation; his difficulties worsened with the commercial disappointment of his fourth album, *The Hard Way.* In 1991, MCA dropped Earle, and he embarked on a period of intense drug abuse. A 1994 arrest for heroin possession landed him in rehab, and the cleaned-up performer emerged in 1995 ready for a comeback.

Signing with small label Winter Harvest, Earle recorded an album of acoustic tracks titled *Train a Comin'.* Released in 1995 after a studio album break of five years, the album became a somewhat unexpected critical and popular success. "Earle is nothing short of a narrative master," raved Alanna Nash in *Entertainment Weekly.* A Grammy nomination for the album cemented Earle's comeback. A major label again came calling, and Earle soon signed with Warner Brothers. The company put out his next album, *I Feel Alright,* in 1996, the same year that the performer contributed the well-received anti-death penalty track "Ellis Unit One" to the *Dead Man Walking* soundtrack. Reinvigorated by these achievements, Earle released the reasonably well-received *El Corazón* in 1997 and the more successful *The Mountain* in 1999 with respected bluegrass artists the Del McCoury Band. "Earle taps a style of bluegrass neither frozen in the past nor experimenting with the future but simply played, without drams, on mandolins, banjos, guitars, fiddles, and upright basses. It's the kind of music that ... gets its real support from middle-American families.... [It is] a medium for fellowship, an escape from shallowness and insincerity in modern life," wrote William Hogeland in the *Atlantic.*

Earle entered the 21st century strong, picking up another Grammy nomination for *The Mountain,* this time for Best Bluegrass Album. In 2000, he released the roots rock album *Transcendental Blues* on his own E Squared label through Artemis Records. "This is the first mass-appeal record [Earle's] made since he's been healthy and focused," Artemis president Danny Goldberg told Jim Bessman of *Billboard.* That mass appeal translated into strong reviews and sales, with the album capturing the number-five spot on *Billboard's* Top Country Albums chart. The following year, Earle explored new forms of expression, releasing a collection of short fiction titled *Doghouse Roses* and performing in a small but recurring role as a drug addict in the acclaimed HBO prison series *The Wire.*

In the fall of 2002, Earle returned to music with the album *Jerusalem.* A politically charged effort influenced by the previous year's terrorist attacks on the United States, the album featured the controversial track "John Walker's Blues," a retelling of the story of John Walker Lindh, a young California man who had served with the Taliban. At times taking on Lindh's voice and at other times comparing him to Jesus, the song was decried by some critics, with John Elvin of *Insight on the News* deeming it "a decidedly unpatriotic and anti-Christian ode." Earle denied any anti-American slant, however, telling *Newsweek's* Jac Chebatoris that "I don't condone what [Lindh] did. But I have a 20-year-old son, which is my main connection to this, and I really do believe it could have been my son, or anybody's son. The way that John Walker arrived at Islam could have only happened here. It's a very American story. And when it's presented the way that it was in the media, I totally understand the average person reacting to it violently." In spite—or perhaps because—of the media controversy, however, *Jerusalem* performed well commercially, capturing the top slot of the *Billboard* Top Independent Albums chart and peaking at number seven on the Top Country Albums rankings. A film documenting his tour in support of *Jerusalem* titled *Just an American Boy* and complementary live album appeared the following year.

Earle's next release, *The Revolution Starts...Now,* again dealt with political issues. Released in August of 2004 during the run-up to a heated presidential contest pitting incumbent George W. Bush against Democratic challenger John Kerry, the album harshly criticized the Bush administration and its policies, particularly those relating to the ongoing war in Iraq. "There is little doubt that *The Revolution Starts...Now* will be viewed as the essential political statement of 2004," commented Christopher Walsh of *Billboard* upon its release. The Grammy committee also acknowledged the album's quality, giving Earle his first trophy for Best Contemporary Folk Album. At about the same time, Earle came to the airwaves in another way: as a host. He began presenting a Sunday night program, also called *The Revolution Starts Now,* on liberal radio outlet Air America. Combining music, guests, and political discussion, the program remained on the air until 2007, when Earle shifted to Sirius radio.

In 2005, Earle continued to expand in new directions. His one-act play, *Karla,* opened off-Broadway after originally being staged in Nashville in 2002. The play tells the story of the religious conversion and execution of convicted Texas murderer Karla Faye Tucker. *Karla* received generally positive notices for its delicate exploration of the sensitive topics of crime and death penalty. "Unlike his songwriting, which has taken a distinct political turn in the past few years," commented Bruce Weber in the *New York Times,* "[the play is] more philosophical than polemical, more rueful than argumentative." That same year, the singer married for the seventh time to fellow country singer and musician Allison Moorer. "But it's the first time I've ever been married sober," Earle told Weber in the same interview.

Moorer appeared on Earle's next album, 2007's *Washington Square Serenade.* A departure from the politically charged sounds that had characterized his previous two releases, *Washington Square Serenade* addressed the singer's freshly adopted hometown, New York City, and the discoveries that came with his new marriage. "*Washington Square Serenade* ultimately sounds a bit less focused than its immediate predecessors ... but it also finds Earle trying out some new tricks both as a performer and a songwriter, and it's exciting and encouraging to hear him exploring fresh turf after two decades of record-making," noted Mark Deming of the Allmusic Guide. The album garnered Earle another Grammy win, taking home the trophy for Best Contemporary Folk/Americana Album, and cracked the top ten of both the *Billboard* Country Albums and Top Independent Albums charts.

In 2009, Earle explored the songs of longtime influence Townes Van Zandt, who had died in 1997, with the tribute album *Townes.* A collection of 15 of Van Zandt's tunes, the album saw Earle "[favoring] a laconic delivery and arrangements that build organically from the accompaniment of his acoustic guitar," according to Brian Mansfield of *USA Today,* to create what Greg Kot of *Entertainment Weekly* characterized as "the kind of carefully considered settings they deserve." The album performed well both critically and commercially, debuting at number six on the *Billboard* Top Country Albums chart and giving the singer/songwriter a career high placement of number 19 on the *Billboard* 200. In January of the following year, Earle scooped up his third Grammy for Best Contemporary Folk Album for *Townes*.

Selected discography

Pink & Black (EP), 1982.

Guitar Town, MCA, 1986.

Early Tracks, Epic, 1987.

Exit 0, MCA, 1987.

Copperhead Road, MCA, 1988.

The Hard Way, MCA, 1990.

Shut Up and Die Like an Aviator, MCA, 1991.

Train a Comin', Winter Harvest, 1995.

(Contributor) *Dead Man Walking* (soundtrack), Columbia, 1996.

I Feel Alright, E Squared/Warner Bros., 1996.

El Corazón, E Squared/Warner Bros., 1997.

(With the Del McCoury Band) *The Mountain*, E Squared, 1999.

Transcendental Blues, E Squared/Artemis, 2000.

Sidetracks, E Squared/Artemis, 2002.

Jerusalem, E Squared/Artemis, 2002.

Just an American Boy (live), Rykodisc, 2003.

The Revolution Starts...Now, E Squared, 2004.

Live at Montreux 2005 (live), Eagle Records, 2006.

Washington Square Serenade, New West Records, 2007.

Townes, New West Records, 2009.

Selected writings

Doghouse Roses, Houghton Mifflin (New York, NY), 2001.

Sources

Books

Contemporary Musicians, vol. 43, Gale Group, 2004.
Marquis Who's Who, Marquis Who's Who, 2010.
St. John, Lauren, *Hardcore Troubadour: The Life and Near Death of Steve Earle*, HarperCollins, 2003.

Periodicals

Atlantic, October 1999, pp. 94-96, 98.
Billboard, June 10, 2000, p. 25; August 28, 2004, p. 45; May 30, 2009, p. 41.
Daily Variety, October 25, 2005, p. 5.
Entertainment Weekly, May 5, 1995, p. 71; January 12, 1996, p. 54; May 15, 2009, p. 59.
Insight on the News, August 19, 2002, p. 35.
Newsweek, April 17, 1995, p. 64; September 2, 2002, p. 69.
New York Times, October 22, 2005.
Sing Out!, Winter 2005, pp. 14, 56.
Time, September 8, 1986, p. 84.
USA Today, May 12, 2009, p. 5D.

Online

"Grammy Award Winners," Grammy.com, http://www2.grammy.com/GRAMMY_Awards/Winners/Results.aspx (June 4, 2010).
"Steve Earle Biography," Allmusic Guide, http://www.allmusic.com/cg/amg.dll?p=amg&sql=11:hiftxqe5ldhe~T1 (June 4, 2010).
"Steve Earle Launches a Show on Sirius," Soundboard Music Blog, *Orlando Sentinel*, http://blogs.orlandosentinel.com/entertainment_music_blog/2007/06/steve_earle_lau.html (June 4, 2010).
"Washington Square Serenade," Allmusic Guide, http://www.allmusic.com/cg/amg.dll?p=amg&sql=10:3ifwxzthldhe (June 4, 2010).

—*Vanessa E. Vaughn*

Johan Eliasch

AP Images

Chief Executive Officer of Head

Born Johan Carl Eliasch, February 15, 1962, in Sweden; son of doctors; married Amanda Gilliat (a photographer), 1988 (divorced, 2007); married Ana Paula Junqueira, July 2009; children: Charles, Jack (from first marriage). *Education:* Stockholm University, bachelor's degree; Royal Institute of Technology, Sweden, B.S., M.S.

Addresses: *Office*—Head International, Wuhrkopfweg 1, 6921 Kennelbach, Austria. *Web site*—http://www.head.com/.

Career

Chairman, Young Conservative Party Sweden, 1979-82; compulsory military service, King's Private Lifeguard, Stockholm, Sweden, 1980-81; employed at the Siemens Group, Stockholm, Sweden, 1982; employed at the Consensus Partners AB, Sweden, 1984; partner and director, The Tufton Group, London, 1985-91; chairman, London Films, c. early 1990s—, serving as executive producer on *Best of Friends*, 1991, *Lady Chatterley*, 1993, *Resort to Murder*, 1995, and *The Scarlet Pimpernel*, 1998, 2000; non-executive director, The Tufton Group, 1991-98; chairman, Equity Partners Group, London, 1991—; bought Head Tryolia Mares, 1995; chairman and chief executive officer, Head, 1995—; bought 400,000 acres of the Amazon rainforest, 2006; founded Cool Earth, c. 2006; senior deputy party treasurer, Conservative Party, United Kingdom, through 2007; served as the special representative of the prime minister on deforestation and clean energy, 2007—.

Sidelights

Swedish-born entrepreneur Johan Eliasch became a self-made millionaire as a turnaround specialist who saved a number of companies through various investment firms. Some of his major investments included London Films, a production and distribution company, and Head Tryolia Mares, an Austrian athletic firm. Because of his success with these companies, Eliasch became one of the wealthiest men in the United Kingdom, his home base after 1985. He also found acclaim socially as he counted members of the royal family and the U.K.'s political leaders among his friends. In the early 2000s, Eliasch became concerned with conservation and bought thousands of acres of Amazon rainforest as a means of preserving it.

Born on February 15, 1962, in Sweden, Eliasch was the son of two doctors and was raised in relative privilege. His maternal grandfather was a Swedish industrialist, though his will did not allow Eliasch (or any of his heirs) to inherit any money until he reached the age of 50. From an early age, Eliasch was not interested in medicine but in business. When he was 12 years old, he bought his first stock shares. They were in the mining company Atlast

Copco. Eliasch was athletic as a child, participating in numerous sports from an early age. He began skiing when he was three years old. Taking up golf, Eliasch won a golfing trophy when he was 14 years old. Also active in the winter sport of curling, he nabbed two awards in the sport by the time he was 18 years old.

A gifted student, Eliasch earned three degrees: a bachelor's in economics and business from Stockholm University and bachelor's and master's degrees in science (engineering) from Sweden's Royal Institute of Technology. During this time period, he was already politically active. He served as the chairman of the Young Conservative Party Sweden from 1979 to 1982. Eliasch completed his compulsory military service as a member of the King's Private Lifeguard in Stockholm from 1980 to 1981.

After finishing his degrees, Eliasch started working in business in 1982. He began working in finance, first with the Siemens Group, a German electronics company. He was a trainee in Siemens' Stockholm office. Eliasch then moved to the Swedish investment banking group Consensus Partners AB. Also in this time period, he lived briefly in New York City. There, he purchased a struggling cards company. Displaying the business skill that would become his hallmark, he turned the company around and sold it for a profit.

Like many aspiring entrepreneurs, Eliasch moved to London to take advantage of the potential for creating wealth in the Margaret Thatcher-led United Kingdom. Arriving in 1985, Eliasch founded the Tufton Group, a private equity firm that specialized in turning around ailing companies, with friends. He served as a partner and director of the company. Tufton was successful in its renewal of Scholl, which made health sandals, and Guild Entertainment, a film distributor. After a disagreement with his partners over the direction of the company, Eliasch left Tufton in 1991 to co-found a new private investment firm. (Eliasch remained non-executive director of the Tufton Group from 1991 to 1998, however.)

With advertising gurus Charles and Maurice Saatchi, Eliasch founded Equity Partners Group in 1991. Also based in London, Eliasch served as the chairman of the company. Equity Partners bought companies that were struggling and improved them through financial investments. Among Equity Partners' investments was London Films, a film and television production company. Eliasch also became the chairman of London Films. In this capacity, he served as executive producer on a number of productions, including 1991's *Best of Friends*, 1993's *Lady Chatterley*, and 1995's *Resort to Murder*. He also was the executive producer on the series *The Scarlet Pimpernel* in 1998 and 2000. By the early 2000s, London Films focused more on distribution than production as the former was a less risky proposition.

During this time period, Elias continued to display his athletic skill. Between 1994 and 1998, he took part in qualifying play for the British Open. His investments also reflected his sporting interests because in 1995, Eliasch gained control of Head Tryolia Mares for one million dollars. The Austrian-based company was once dominant in ski and tennis markets. Its founder, Howard Head, had invented the first composite tennis racquet. Head also made the first laminated metal ski. Before being bought by Eliasch, Head was owned and operated by Austria Tabak, a state-owned tobacco monopoly. It had been operating on a loss, losing more than 36 million pounds per year by the mid-1990s, and was burdened by a number of unprofitable divisions. As soon as Eliasch bought the company and took over, he named himself chairman and chief executive officer. He also made a number of major changes, explaining to Neil Hartnell of *SGB UK*, "It was a brand with global recognition that had fallen on hard times, and I saw the possibility of revitalizing it given the right ingredients."

While retaining the profitable Mares division which was the number-one scuba diving equipment producer worldwide, he strengthened the tennis and ski businesses by introducing innovations in these products. In 1996, Head introduced an extremely light and strong titanium and graphite racquet, the lightest and strongest available at the time. Within a few years, Head racquet sales doubled because of such products. For skiers, Head debuted a carving ski that was targeted at both average and expert skiers. Previously, such shaped skis were intended only for experts. This innovation lead to Head dominating the carving ski market worldwide and coming in number two for all skis by 1998.

As Head's owner, Eliasch was not afraid to make bigger changes as well. Head had been manufacturing sportswear and golf products, but with little success. He made the decision to license these lines to other companies. Also licensed out were Tyrolia skis and boots which did not sell as well as ski bindings made by the company. Eliasch's goal with all these moves was to make Head number one in each category.

Explaining his actions, Eliasch told Lisa J. Adams of the Associated Press, "Having an athletic background, it's a bit of a game. You want to beat the competition and excel. It's fun to come up with new products, see that you have an impact out in the market, and also change the course of things.... That gives me a buzz." His business acumen paid off with Head and his other investments. By 1999, Head products were number one or number two in their category and the company had been profitable for several years. That year, Eliasch showed his personal success, reaching 87 on the list of the 1,000 richest people living in the United Kingdom. His worth was then estimated at 250 million pounds.

One reason for Eliasch's success was not only his business acumen but his public relations abilities as well. Head tennis products were endorsed by some of the leading players in the sport including Bjorn Borg and Andre Agassi. In 2002, he arranged for John McEnroe and Borg to play each other in a charity match on the grounds of Buckingham Palace. The match benefitted the National Society for the Prevention of Cruelty to Children. Not only was the line-up impressive but so were the guests, including Charles Saatchi, race car driver Damon Hill, and model/media personality Claudia Schiffer. Eliasch also attended the match and remained in the public eye by personally congratulating each athlete who endorsed Head products when victorious. He also attended all major downhill skiing events and skied the course himself before the start of competition.

Eliasch invested in other sporting companies over the years, buying Penn, the American-based tennis ball and racquet company, in 1999 as well as Blax and Genesis snowboard brands. But by the early 2000s, Eliasch was regularly featured in the British press hobnobbing with Prince Andrew and British prime minister Tony Blair. Over the next few years, Eliasch focused more of his attention on politics in the United Kingdom, especially after becoming a British citizen in 2003. That year, for example, he gave 250 thousands pounds to the Conservative party, which was then not in power. The amount made Eliasch one of the largest donors to that party, though he had been donating smaller amounts since the early 1990s. In 2005 and 2006, Eliasch gave the party more money, including a one million pound emergency loan to allow the party to buy back its freehold (land and buildings on the land). He also served as the senior deputy party treasurer of the Conservative Party in this time period.

In 2006, Eliasch took on a new interest: conservation. Concerned about the logging and deforestation in the Amazon, he bought 400,000 acres of prime real estate in the middle of the Amazon rainforest from a logging company for eight million pounds to en-sure that plants and wildlife would be protected. Eliasch's purchase was seen as part of a new trend in conservation efforts. Instead of charities and other agencies working to convince developing countries to protect their natural resources, the wealthy would use their riches to rent or buy large plots of land in an effort to protect them when the locals could not or would not.

Explaining his purchase, Eliasch told Maurice Chittenden of the London *Sunday Times,* "The Amazon is the lung of the world. It provides 20% of the world's oxygen and 30% of the fresh water." Eliasch added, "In theory you can perhaps buy the Amazon for $50 billion (£28.5 billion). It would be a very quick payback because a hurricane like Katrina will cost them a similar amount in payouts. You can plot a direct correlation between cutting down trees which absorb carbon dioxide and the global warming and extreme conditions which lead to hurricanes like Katrina."

Eliasch did not buy the land, located about 1,600 miles northwest of Rio de Janeiro, solely to protect it. He also asked scientists to travel there and examine wildlife and plants. He hoped they might find medicinal extracts or make other scientific discoveries because of the area's biodiversity. Eliasch wanted to gain carbon credits for preserving the trees. He planned on using any money gained from carbon credits to buy more forest, to speak regularly on his environmental efforts worldwide, and hoped others would follow suit. He told Aida Edemariam of the London *Guardian,* "What I want to do is expand this, get other people interested in doing the same thing, and eventually preserve as much of the rainforest as posssible."

Eliasch's interest in politics and public policy continued to deepen over the years. In 2006, he set up a think tank, the Global Strategy Forum, with prominent Conservative Party member Michael Ancram. Eliasch also founded a trust, Cool Earth, to encourage others to buy parts of the Amazon, and donated more than 20 million pounds to green causes. In 2007, Eliasch stepped down from his position as deputy of the Conservative Party and joined the Labour Party government of Prime Minister Gordon Brown. Eliasch served as the special representative of the prime minister on deforestation and clean energy beginning in September of that year and immediately began conducting a review on deforestation and clean energy. Eliasch made the move in part because he believed that the Conservative Party was moving too far to the right under David Cameron. Eliasch remained in Brown's government until Conservative David Cameron became prime minister in May of 2010.

During this time period, however, Eliasch faced challenges in his business life. Head had thrived under his leadership for many years, but faced a significant decline in 2009 due to the worldwide recession. By that time, the company had been de-listed from the New York Stock Exchange for a year and saw its shares falling badly on the Vienna Stock Exchange as well. With high debts, Eliasch hoped to save his company by replacing unsecured loans with secured bonds. Head managed to remain viable into 2010, and sponsored downhill skiing star Lindsay Vonn during her Winter Olympic campaign that year. Though his various businesses, including Head, were important to Eliasch, he told Michael Binyon of the London *Times* that "These are my hobbies." Binyon concluded, "Even his frenetic energy running Head now seems a sideshow. His real job is saving the planet."

Sources

Books

Debrett's People of Today, Debertt's Peerage, Ltd., 2009.

Periodicals

Associated Press, July 12, 1998.

Daily Mail (London, England), July 12, 2006, p. 37; July 6, 2009, p. 33.

Daily News (New York), February 14, 2010, p. 64.

Evening Standard (London, England), July 3, 2002, pp. 25-26.

Guardian (London, England), April 4, 2006, p. 14.

Independent (London, England), February 12, 2003, p. 2; September 8, 2007, p. 6.

Mirror, April 1, 2006, p. 10.

Observer (England), March 26, 2006, p. 1.

Rubber & Plastics News, May 17, 1999, p. 1

SGB UK, August 19, 1999, p. 20.

Sunday Times (London, England), March 19, 2006, p. 9; September 9, 2007, p. 23; May 3, 2009, p. 2.

Times (London, England), April 23, 2007, p. 53.

—A. Petruso

Rahm Emanuel

White House Chief of Staff

Born November 29, 1959, in Chicago, IL; son of Benjamin (a pediatrician) and Marsha (a social worker) Emanuel; married Amy Rule; children: Zach, Ilana, Leah. *Education:* Sarah Lawrence College, B.A., 1981; Northwestern University, M.A., 1985.

Addresses: *Office*—The White House, 1600 Pennsylvania Ave. NW, Washington, D.C., 20500.

Career

Worked for Illinois Public Action Council, early 1980s; field organizer and fund-raiser for Paul Simon, U.S. Senator from Illinois, 1984; consultant for various political candidates, 1980s; staffer for Democratic Congressional Campaign Committee, c. 1988; senior adviser and chief fund-raiser, Chicago Mayor Richard M. Daley, 1989, 1991; national finance director for Clinton presidential campaign, 1992; White House staff, 1993-98 (final title was senior adviser to the president for policy and strategy); investment banker, Wasserstein Perella, Chicago, 1998-2002; elected to Congress, 2002; chairman of the Democratic Congressional Campaign Committee, 2005-06; House Democratic Caucus Chair, 2006-09; White House chief of staff, 2009—.

Awards: Great Laker Award, Healing Our Waters Great Lakes Coalition, 2007.

Sidelights

For years, as a congressman, presidential aide, and political operative, Rahm Emanuel cultivated a reputation as tough, rude, combative, demanding, obnoxious, intimidating, and effective. He helped U.S. President Bill Clinton get elected, survive numerous scandals, and enact key parts of his program. Emanuel's aggressive strategy helped Democrats take over Congress in 2006, unnerving Republicans, who realized "there was a killer at the helm of the Democratic Party," Emanuel biographer Naftali Bendavid told Susan Baer of the *Washingtonian.* "He really, really, really wants to win—whatever it is—and he'll go to extraordinary lengths to do it."

Impressed with Emanuel's success, new president Barack Obama chose him as his White House chief of staff. Political observers thought the choice shrewd, figuring the inspiring, idealistic Obama needed a practical fighter and deal-maker to balance his talents. The chief of staff job tested Emanuel as never before. With the public deeply divided and Congress often deadlocked, Obama and his administration often struggled to enact his ambitious agenda. By his second year in the Oval Office, some criticisms of the president's performance shifted to Emanuel, as commentators asked whether he had lived up to his fierce, successful reputation.

Emanuel was born in Chicago on November 29, 1959. He grew up in the Chicago suburb of Wilmette. His father, Benjamin, was a children's doctor who moved to the United States from Israel. His mother, Marsha, was a psychiatric social worker who was involved in civil-rights activism in the 1960s. "It was a loud household where the parents encouraged reading and debate [and] held monthly meetings at which anyone could say anything," Baer wrote in the *Washingtonian*. Two details from Emanuel's teenage years stand out. While working at an Arby's restaurant, Emanuel cut his right middle finger on a meat slicer and, when infection set in, the finger was later partially amputated. Also, his parents made their sons take ballet lessons, which Emanuel excelled at. The Joffrey School of Ballet offered him a scholarship, but Emanuel chose to attend Sarah Lawrence College instead.

All three sons have nationally prominent careers. Emanuel's oldest brother, Ezekiel Emanuel, chairs the bioethics department at the National Institutes of Health Clinical Center. His younger brother, Ari Emanuel, is a Hollywood agent who has inspired a TV character, the combative Ari Gold on *Entourage*. The Emanuels, four years apart in age, resemble one another, wrote Baer in the *Washingtonian*, in their "wiry frame and dark hair, ... the big personalities, the headstrong nature that lands each of them in the headlines and with their share of enemies."

Emanuel graduated from Sarah Lawrence College in 1981 and received a master's degree in speech and communication from Northwestern University in 1985. He worked for the Illinois Public Action Council, an activist group, in the early 1980s, then as a field organizer and fund-raiser for U.S. Senator Paul Simon. By 1988, he had joined the staff of the Democratic Congressional Campaign Committee, the organization dedicated to electing Democrats to the House of Representatives. That year, Emanuel pulled a stunt that helped develop his abrasive, combative reputation. Working on a congressional campaign in Erie County, New York, he commissioned a poll, hoping it would show that his candidate, David Swarts, was running a close race and could win if well-funded. Instead, the poll seemed to show the candidate losing by 17 points. An error was later discovered—Swarts was only down by five or six points—but it was too late to seize the opportunity. Emanuel and others took revenge by hiring a company called Enough Is Enough to send the pollster a dead fish in a box. "Sending the fish

to the pollster that he thought had failed sent a message about how public he can be about his displeasure," longtime Democratic adviser Stanley Greenberg explained to Ryan Lizza of the *New Yorker*, "and showed that he's willing to step beyond the normal bounds, that he's willing to be outrageous and he doesn't suffer fools."

Emanuel developed his talents as a political fund-raiser by working for Richard M. Daley's 1989 and 1991 campaigns for mayor of Chicago. Impressed, Bill Clinton asked Emanuel to raise donations for his presidential campaign. Emanuel's successful work kept Clinton's campaign afloat during the Democratic primaries in early 1992, when Clinton was nearly done in by an adultery scandal and questions about how he had avoided the military draft.

After Clinton won the presidency, Emanuel joined the White House staff. Though demoted after a conflict with the president's wife, Hillary Clinton, Emanuel did not quit, but earned his way back into favor by helping convince Congress to pass the North American Free Trade Agreement. He also helped pass the State Children's Health Insurance Program, which provides health insurance to seven million children. He became a top adviser to the president, with a small office right next door to Clinton's study. In 1998, he was one of several advisers counseling Clinton on how to survive special prosecutor Kenneth Starr's investigation of the president's extramarital affair with White House intern Monica Lewinsky. Later that year, Emanuel returned to Chicago to work as an investment banker for Wasserstein Perella. In three years, he earned $16 million handling mergers and acquisitions, mostly in the utilities industry. He ran for Congress in 2002 and was elected on his first try.

At a roast in Emanuel's honor in 2005, Obama, his future boss, summed up his reputation in few memorable jokes. Combining Emanuel's teenage dedication to ballet with a reference to a classic political book about the ruthless pursuit of power, Obama (according to Mark Leibovich of the *New York Times*) called Emanuel "the first to adapt Machiavelli's *The Prince* for dance" with a performance that included "a lot of kicks below the waist." Crossing Emanuel's reputation for using profanity with the seemingly grim story of his lost middle finger, Obama joked that the accident "rendered him practically mute."

In 2005, though he was only in his second term in Congress, Emanuel's political talents won him the chairmanship of the Democratic Congressional

Campaign Committee. "More than anyone else, [Emanuel] was responsible for restoring Democrats to power the following year," wrote Lizza in the *New Yorker*. Early in 2006, Emanuel gathered weary Democratic congressmen, some of them resigned to losing after Al Gore and John Kerry's presidential defeats, and convinced them that voters had turned so angry at President George W. Bush that Democrats could actually win the elections that year. He relentlessly recruited candidates, often courting conservative and moderate Democrats even if they opposed abortion, in districts where he thought liberals would do poorly. To counter Republican claims that Democrats were soft, he convinced several military veterans, law enforcement officers, and former sports stars to run for Congress as Democrats. He dropped support for candidates who did not raise enough money. He motivated his staff by declaring (according to Leibovich of the *New York Times*) that Republicans were "bad people who deserve a two-by-four upside their heads."

Emanuel's aggressiveness helped the Democrats score stunning victories in the November 2006 elections. They won a majority in the House for the first time since 1994. No incumbent House Democrats lost. The victorious Emanuel was elected the Democratic Caucus chair, the fourth highest leadership position in the House. He played an important role in passing the bank bailout, the Troubled Assets Relief Program, during the financial crisis in the fall of 2008. Emanuel was well-positioned to eventually become Speaker of the House. "I had my own personal desire of being the first Jewish speaker," Emanuel told Lizza of the *New Yorker*.

After Obama won the presidency, he persuaded Emanuel, a fellow Chicagoan, to resign from Congress and become his chief of staff. At first, Emanuel did not want the job, but he decided he could not pass up what was arguably the second-most-powerful position in the United States government. Political observers felt Obama was shrewdly choosing a top aide with different talents than his own. The president had only spent four years in the Senate, so Emanuel knew Washington better than he did. Obama gave Emanuel a major role in choosing almost all of his cabinet secretaries and top aides. He usually let Emanuel speak first and last at meetings.

To the surprise of many in Washington, Emanuel became one of the administration's best negotiators with Republicans in Congress. "He knows there is a time in this business to drop the switchblades and make a deal," U.S. Representative Adam Putnam, a Republican from Florida, told Leibovich of the *New*

York Times. Emanuel continued to work out at the House gym on Capitol Hill, where he would cut deals with congressmen. Emanuel also turned less feisty, adopting more of his boss' cool tone. "I'm not yelling at people; I'm not jumping on tables," he told Leibovich. "That's a campaign. Being the chief of staff of a government is different."

A year into Obama's presidency, however, political trends shifted. In January of 2010, Scott Brown, a Republican, unexpectedly won a special election for a U.S. Senate seat in Massachusetts, depriving Democrats of the 60-vote supermajority needed to end filibusters and pass most Senate legislation. Obama's top legislative priority, health-care reform, seemed in jeopardy. Critics unhappy with the administration's direction blamed Emanuel. Republicans complained he had not tried hard enough to forge bipartisan solutions to big issues, while Democrats thought he should have been more of a partisan fighter. Moderate Democrats in Congress felt Emanuel and Obama were asking them to move too far left, while liberals complained Emanuel had pushed the president to compromise on health care and had not pressured moderates enough. "For all the reputation of being able to bust knee caps, we haven't seen nos turned to yeses," one Democratic congressman told Peter Baker of the *New York Times*.

Those strategic debates got Emanuel in trouble in the media in early 2010. He held a confrontational meeting with some liberal Democrats who had run commercials attacking party moderates over health care. Enraged, he swore at the liberal activists and called them "retarded" (according to Baker of the *New York Times*). After criticism from advocates for the mentally challenged, including former Alaska Governor Sarah Palin, Emanuel apologized for using the derogatory term.

Emanuel defended the Obama Administration's record, pointing to early successes such as a fair pay act for female workers, expanded health care coverage for poor children, and new protections for credit-card users. He felt the Democrats could win by forcing Republicans to choose whether to cooperate with the president or say no to any progress in Washington. "You walk away? You're walking away from responsibility, and the public's angry at you," he explained to Baker of the *New York Times*. "You participate? Your base hates you."

In a surprising comeback, Democrats managed to pass Obama's health-care plan after lots of arm-twisting, deal-making, and legislative maneuvering. By the summer of 2010, that victory had not led to a turnaround in Obama's fortunes or Emanuel's reputation. Polls showed Americans remained skeptical of the new health-care law. Conservatives seemed more politically energized than liberals, leading most political commentators to forecast Democratic losses in the 2010 elections. The uncertainty and scrutiny highlighted a truth Emanuel knew well: He would be judged on whether he could help preserve the Democrats' record of legislative successes and victories at the polls.

Sources

Periodicals

Chicago Tribune, November 12, 2006.
New Yorker, March 2, 2009, pp. 24-29.

New York Times, January 25, 2009; February 2, 2010; March 8, 2010.
Washingtonian, May 2008.

Online

"Chief of Staff Rahm Emanuel," The White House, http://www.whitehouse.gov/administration/staff/rahm-emanuel (June 6, 2010).
"Times Topics: Rahm Emanuel News," *New York Times*, http://topics.nytimes.com/top/reference/timestopics/people/e/rahm_emanuel/index.html (May 30, 2010).

Transcripts

Frontline, Public Broadcasting System, June 2000.

—*Erick Trickey*

Nathan Fillion

Robert Pitts/Landov

Actor

Born Nathan Christopher Fillion, March 27, 1971, in Edmonton, Alberta, Canada; son of Bob (a teacher) and Cookie (a teacher) Fillion. *Education:* Attended University of Alberta, Edmonton, Alberta.

Addresses: *Agent*—Mark Schumacher, The Gersh Agency, 232 North Canon Dr., Beverly Hills, CA 90210. *Management*—3 Arts Entertainment, 9460 Wilshire Blvd., 7th Fl., Beverly Hills, CA 90212.

Career

Actor in films, including: *Strange and Rich,* 1994; *Saving Private Ryan,* 1998; *Blast from the Past,* 1999; *Dracula 2000,* 2000; *Water's Edge,* 2003; *Outing Riley,* 2004; *Serenity,* 2005; *Slither,* 2006; *White Noise 2: The Light,* 2007; *Waitress,* 2007; *Trucker,* 2008; *Wonder Woman* (voice), 2009; *Super,* 2010. Television appearances include: *Ordeal in the Arctic* (movie), 1993; *One Life to Live,* 1994-97, 2007; *Spin City,* 1996; *Total Security,* 1996; *Maggie Winters,* 1998; *Two Guys, a Girl and a Pizza Place,* 1998-2001; *The Outer Limits,* 1999; *King of the Hill* (voice), 2001; *Firefly,* 2002-03; *Pasadena,* 2002; *Alligator Point* (movie), 2003; *Buffy the Vampire Slayer,* 2003; *Miss Match,* 2003; *Hollywood Division* (movie), 2004; *Justice League,* 2005-06; *Lost,* 2006; *Drive,* 2007; *Desperate Housewives,* 2007-08; *Robot Chicken,* 2007, 2009; *Dr. Horrible's Sing Along Blog,* 2008; *PG Porn,* 2008; *61st Primetime Emmy Awards,* 2009; *Castle,* 2009—. Voice work for video games includes: *Jade Empire,* 2005; *Halo 3,* 2007; *Halo 3: ODST,* 2009; *Halo: Reach,* 2010.

Awards: Cinescape Genre Face of the Future Award for a male actor, Academy of Science Fiction, Fantasy, and Horror Films, USA, for *Firefly,* 2003; Feature Film Award for acting, Newport Beach Film Festival, for *Waitress,* 2007.

Sidelights

Nathan Fillion's character, Malcom Reynolds, said in an episode of *Firefly,* "Whoo-hoo! I'm right here! I'm right here! You want some of me? Yeah, you do! Come on! Come on!" and this exemplifies the actor who has appeared in numerous feature films, made-for-television movies, television series, and other productions. Fans of Nathan Fillion cannot get enough of him. He has an estimated 600,000 Twitter followers and, in the summer of 2010, a campaign began to have him host the popular late night television show *Saturday Night Live.* The charismatic actor once played the character of Joey Buchanan on the ABC soap opera *One Life to Live,* but it was his portrayal of Malcom Reynolds in the short-lived television series *Firefly* and the subsequent feature film *Serenity* that made him a cult icon.

Fillion was born in Edmonton, Alberta, Canada. He was the son of Bob and Cookie Fillion, who were both English teachers. Fillion's older brother Jeff also became an English teacher. His family instilled in him the importance of literacy and education. Along with his friend, P.J. Haarsma, who is an author, Fillion founded the non-profit organization

Kids Need to Read. Kids Need to Read gives gifts of inspiring books to schools, libraries, and literacy programs that have less access to books and are serving disadvantaged children. After Haarsma told Fillion about traveling around the country and speaking at schools where he discovered that some libraries cannot afford to buy books, the two started the organization. Fillion said he strongly believes that all children deserve the chance to read good books and was quoted on the Kids Need to Read Web site as saying, "It breaks my heart to think that there are kids out there, ready to have their imaginations lit on fire, excited and wanting to read, and facing naked shelves in their school or local libraries. Rather than complain or wait till the system stops failing our nation's children, this is a matter I feel we must take into our own hands." Kids Need to Read has teamed up with the American Library Association to make even more of an impact and help more children.

Fillion began acting while he was still in high school. At the University of Alberta he minored in drama and began to do stage work. He did improvisational work at the Rapidfire Theatre in Edmonton and appeared in various productions at Theatresports. While Fillion was still attending the University of Alberta, he began filming the made-for-television movie *Ordeal in the Arctic*. Fillion's first significant role was Master Warrant Officer Tom Jardine in that movie. Fillion next made an audition tape and was cast as Joey Buchanan in *One Life to Live*. He left college one semester away from graduating and moved to New York to accept the role. He worked on the soap opera for three years and, in 1996, was nominated for a Daytime Emmy Award in the category of "Outstanding Younger Actor". He left the show in 1997 to move to Los Angeles and pursue other acting opportunities but made a return guest appearance on *One Life to Live* in 2007 for the show's 9,999th and 10,000th episodes.

Moving to Los Angeles was a positive change for Fillion and opened up more chances for him to display his acting abilities. In 1998, he was cast in Steven Spielberg's hit war drama *Saving Private Ryan*. He played the small part of Private James Frederick "Minnesota" Ryan. He also had other supporting roles in movies and appearances in television series throughout the late 1990s and into 2000. One of these roles was in the television series *Two Guys, A Girl and a Pizza Place*. He was cast as Johnny Donnelly, the boyfriend of one of the main characters. When the show was renamed *Two Guys and a Girl*, his role was expanded and he became a regular on the show.

The year 2002 was a pivotal year for Fillion. This was the year that writer and director Joss Whedon expanded his Mutant Enemy Productions company to include a science fiction spaghetti western with an ensemble cast titled *Firefly*. Fillion was cast as the leading man in the short-lived television series that followed the renegade adventures of the crew of the Firefly-class spaceship named Serenity. Fillion played the role of Captain Malcom Reynolds. The show was originally written to explore the lives of a group of people who were living in a post-civil war era and surviving at the pioneering edges of civilization. The character of Malcom Reynolds was a former soldier who had fought on the losing side of the civil war. Fourteen episodes of the show were produced, but the show was cancelled by FOX after airing only eleven episodes because the show did not have strong enough Nielsen ratings. After the show was cancelled there was a huge fan-driven campaign to get the show back on the air. Whedon tried to get the show picked up by another network but was unsuccessful. The continuation movie *Serenity* was released in 2005; role-playing games and other products in the Firefly franchise have also been marketed to fans.

Working with Whedon was very beneficial for Fillion. In addition to working on *Firefly* and *Serenity*, Whedon cast Fillion in the last episodes of *Buffy the Vampire Slayer* as Caleb, a priest who went to the dark side. Whedon also cast Fillion as the anti-hero Captain Hammer, who is the arch nemesis of Dr. Horrible in the quirky short movie *Dr. Horrible's Sing-Along Blog,* released in the summer of 2008 over the Internet as a free download. After the initial release it became available for purchase through iTunes. Described as a musical tragicomedy in three acts *Dr. Horrible's Sing-Along Blog* won seven different awards, earned enough revenue for Whedon to recoup his initial investment of $200,000, made it possible for the crew and actors who initially volunteered their time to be paid, and showed the world that the Internet could be used in new and creative ways to distribute artistic and entertainment material.

Fillion has been continuously working in a variety of different productions. He has provided voiceovers on a variety of animated productions and video games, including: *King of the Hill, Jade Empire, Justice League, Robot Chicken*, and *Halo 3*. In *Halo 3* he performs the voice of a marine sergeant who identifies himself as "Reynolds" over the radio. Adam Baldwin and Alan Tudyk, who were also part of the *Firefly* cast, provided voice talent in *Halo 3* as well.

Fillion has appeared in numerous television series. In 2007 Fillion starred in the short-lived series *Drive* as the main character Alex Tully. The show was cancelled after only two episodes had aired because it did not get the desired ratings. In the autumn of 2007, Fillion appeared as a gynecologist named Dr. Adam Mayfair on the hit television series *Desperate Housewives.* During the 2006-07 season of *Lost* he made one appearance as the character of Kate's husband, Kevin. In 2009 Fillion first appeared in the role of Richard Castle in the ABC television series *Castle.* Castle is a wealthy mystery novelist who helps the New York Police Department solve crimes. As a promotion for the television show, ABC had a novel named *Heat Wave* ghost written and released as being written by the show's main character. It was initially available on the show's Web site. In the book's product description on the Web site Amazon, the fictional author Castle was described as being "the author of numerous bestsellers, including the critically acclaimed Derrick Storm series." It went on to relay that the character first published his first novel while in college and described that he lives in Manhattan and has a wife and daughter.

Keeping steadily present in feature films, Fillion garnered acclaim in several movies. In 2006 he starred in James Gunn's horror film *Slither* in which he played the character of Bill Pardy. For this role he received a *Fangoria* Chainsaw Awards nomination in the category of "Dude You Don't Wanna Mess With." He also starred in another horror film titled *White Noise 2: The Light.* In 2007, Fillion worked with director Adrienne Shelly on the romantic comedy *Waitress* which premiered at the Sundance Film Festival that year. He played the part of Dr. Pomatter, a gynecologist who has an affair with the main character Jenna, one of his pregnant clients. The role was considered very challenging because the character is seemingly in a happy marriage with an adoring wife and there appears to be no reason for the affair. Fillion had to make the character sympathetic to the audience despite this challenge. In 2009 the independent feature film *Trucker* was released. Fillion co-starred with Michelle Monaghan in this movie about a female independent trucker who suddenly has her life of freedom on the road interrupted when her estranged son comes and finds her. The boy's father is terminally ill and in the hospital and Monaghan's character must take on caring for her son. The movie received much critical acclaim and won awards at the Fort Collins TriMedia Festival, the Fort Lauderdale International Film Festival, and the San Diego Film Critics Society. Reuniting with Gunn in the movie *Super,* Fillion was cast as the Holy Avenger.

Bierly, reporting for *Entertainment Weekly,* quoted Whedon on Fillion as saying that he believed "he's Harrison Ford, if given a shot." In 2007 British artist Martin Firrell created an outdoor exhibit where he projected a likeness of Fillion onto one of London's oldest skyscrapers along with ruminations about the nature of heroism. Fillion was listed in 2007 in *Entertainment Weekly*'s "50 Actors We'd Watch in Anything" list. The Web site Sky TV named him as "TV's Ultimate Cult Hero." He was featured in *People*'s Sexy Men issue under the category of "Domestic Bliss/Guys Worth Running Home To." Fillion, who lives in Los Angeles, California, was quoted in the feature as saying, "There are black widow spiders in my backyard, coyotes walking down the streets, killer bees, rattlesnakes—there's so much around L.A. that'll kill you!" According to the Web site Ecorazzi, Fillion was seen purchasing a new electric car to drive around Los Angeles and quoted as saying "I found it! I found my spaceship! It's real and I'm getting it!"

Sources

Books

Contemporary Theatre, Film, & Television, vol. 54, Gale, 2004.

Periodicals

Entertainment Weekly, August 1, 2008, p. 30; April 2, 2010, p. 66.
Maclean's, December 3, 2007, p. 58.
People, November 26, 2007, p. 141.

Online

"50 Actors We'd Watch in Anything (Part 1)," *Entertainment Weekly,* http://www.ew.com/ew/gallery/0,,20190207.tif_16,00.html (August 28, 2010).
"About Dr. Horrible's Sing-Along Blog," Dr. Horrible's Official Fan Web Site, http://doctorhorrible.net/about/ (August 28, 2010).
Biography Resource Center Online, Gale, 2006.
"Firefly quotes," Firefly and Serenity Fan Web Site, http://www.browncoats.nl/bcquotes.htm (August 28, 2010).
"Heat Wave," ABC, http://abc.go.com/shows/castle/castle-novel (August 28, 2010).
"Heat Wave," Amazon, http://www.amazon.com/Heat-Wave-Nikki-Richard-Castle/dp/14013238.tif20 (August 28, 2010).
"Join the Campaign(s) to Get Nathan Fillion on *Saturday Night Live!*," *Wired,* http://www.wired.com/geekdad/2010/08/join-the-campaign-to-get-nathan-fillion-on-saturday-night-live/ (August 26, 2010).

"Joss Whedon Finally Wins Emmy, Dr. Horrible Interrupts Awards Show," Associated Content, http://www.associatedcontent.com/pop_print.shtml?content_type=article&content_type_id=2197707 (August 28, 2010).

"Joss Whedon Wins Emmy Award for Dr. Horrible," Suite 101, http://filmtvindustry.suite101.com/article.cfm/joss_whedon_wins_emmy_award_for_dr_horrible/ (August 28, 2010).

Kids Need to Read, http://www.kidsneedtoread.org/ (August 28, 2010).

"Nathan Fillion—Bio," Flixster, http://www.flixster.com/actor/nathan-fillian (August 28, 2010).

"Nathan Fillion Biography," Monsters and Critics, http://www.monstersandcritics.com/people/Nathan-Fillion/biography/ (August 28, 2010).

"Nathan Fillion Biography," Yahoo Movies, http://movies.yahoo.com/movie/contributor/18043719.tif96/bio (August 28, 2010).

"Nathan Fillion Gaga For Spaceship-Like Arcimoto Pulse Electric Car," Ecorazzi, http://www.ecorazzi.com/2010/08/25/nathan-fillion-gaga-for-spaceship-like-arcimoto-pulse-electric-car/ (August 28, 2010).

"Nathan Fillion is 'Super,'" *Entertainment Weekly*, http://popwatch.ew.com/2010/01/11/nathan-fillion-super/ (August 28, 2010).

"Nathan Fillion, Michelle Monaghan's *Trucker* Details," Movies Online, http://www.moviesonline.ca/movienews_18140.html (August 28, 2010).

"Nathan Fillion Talks About *Waitress*," About.com, http://movies.about.com/od/waitress/a/waitressnf42607.htm (August 28, 2010).

"Read with Nathan Fillion—Americal Libraries Magazine," TV.com, http://www.tv.com/read-with-nathan-fillion-and-american-libraries-magazine/webnews/127991.html?print=1&tag=actions; (August 26, 2010).

"TV's Ultimate Cult Hero: Nathan Fillion," Sky TV, http://tv.sky.com/tvs-ultimate-cult-hero-nathan-fillion (August 28, 2010).

—Annette Bowman

Béla Fleck

© 2010 Jordi Vidal/Redferns/Getty Images

Musician and songwriter

Born Béla Anton Leos Fleck, July 10, 1958, in New York, NY.

Addresses: *Contact*—Béla Fleck & the Flecktones, PO Box 91076, Nashville, TN 37209. *Web site*—http://www.belafleck.com/index.html; http://www.flecktones.com/.

Career

Became interested in banjo as a small child, c. early 1960s; given first banjo, 1973; joined first band, Wicker's Creek, c. mid-1970s; member of Tasty Licks, Boston, MA, c. 1976-c. 1979; released first solo album, *Crossing the Tracks*, 1979; member of Spectrum, Lexington, KY, c. 1979-81; member of New Grass Revival, 1981-88; formed Béla Fleck and the Flecktones, 1989; released first Flecktones album, *Béla Fleck and the Flecktones*, 1990; released solo album *Tales from an Acoustic Planet*, 1995; signed a recording deal with Sony Music, 2000; released classically oriented solo album, *Perpetual Motion*, 2001; traveled to Africa, 2005; put out a duet album with Chick Corea, *The Enchantment*, 2007; released result from Africa trip, *Throw Down Your Heart: Tales from the Acoustic Planet, Vol. 3—Africa Sessions*, 2009.

Awards: Grammy Award (with others) for best country instrumental performance, National Academy of Recording Arts and Sciences, for "Hightower," 1995; Grammy Award (with the Flecktones) for best pop instrumental performance, National Academy of Recording Arts and Sciences, for "The Sinister Minister," 1996; Grammy Award (with others) for best instrumental composition, National Academy of Recording Arts and Sciences, for "Almost 12," 1998; Grammy Award (with Alison Brown) for best country instrumental performance, National Academy of Recording Arts and Sciences, for "Leaving Cottondale," 2000; Grammy Award (with the Flecktones) for best contemporary instrumental jazz performance, National Academy of Recording Arts and Sciences, for *Outbound*, 2000; Grammy Award (with Edgar Meyer) for best instrumental arrangement, National Academy of Recording Arts and Sciences, for "Doctor Gradus ad Parnassum," 2001; Grammy Award for best classical crossover album, National Academy of Recording Arts and Sciences, for *Perpetual Motion*, 2001; Grammy Award (with the Flecktones) for best contemporary jazz album, National Academy of Recording Arts and Sciences, for *The Hidden Land*, 2006; Latin Grammy Award (with Chick Correa) for best instrumental album, Latin Academy of Recording Arts and Sciences, for *The Enchantment*, 2007; Grammy Award (with the Flecktones) for best pop instrumental album, National Academy of Recording Arts and Sciences, for *Jingle All the Way*, 2008; Grammy Award for best pop instrumental performance, National Academy of Recording Arts and Sciences, for "Throw Down Your Heart," 2009; Grammy Award for best contemporary world music album, National Academy of Recording Arts and

Sciences, for *Throw Down Your Heart: Tales from the Acoustic Planet, Vol. 3—Africa Sessions,* 2009.

Sidelights

Grammy Award-winner Béla Fleck is considered one of the best, most unique banjo players in the world. While he recorded and performed as a solo artist, he also was a member of several musical groups, including the New Grass Revival and Béla Fleck and the Flecktones, and worked across numerous musical genres from bluegrass to jazz to country, rock, and soul. He was the only musical artist to be nominated for Grammys in the jazz, bluegrass, pop, country, spoken word, Christian, composition, and world music categories—the most categories in Grammy history. In addition, the critically acclaimed Fleck was a composer who wrote for himself and others. Describing his talent, Geoffrey Himes of the *Washington Post* stated that "Fleck has redefined the possibilities of the banjo."

Born on July 10, 1958, in New York City, Fleck was given his unusual first name in honor of Hungarian composer Béla Bartók. Raised in New York, he played guitar in his youth. As a child growing up in the early 1960s, he became interested in playing banjo after hearing Flatt & Scruggs and their bluegrass sound while watching an episode of *Beverly Hillbillies.* (The duo wrote and played the television show's theme song, "The Ballad of Jed Clampett"; Earl Scruggs played the banjo on the number.) Fleck's grandfather brought him a banjo in 1973, and the instrument became the focus of his life. While a high school student at the High School of Music and Art in New York City, Fleck studied the French horn. Because of what the school deemed a lack of musical aptitude, he was placed in the chorus.

Taking private lessons on the banjo, Fleck explored the possibilities of the instrument and began using it to play bebop. He was guided on this musical journey by Tony Trischka, who was also pushing the boundaries of banjo, as well as Erik Darling and Mac Horowitz. He also joined his first band, Wicker's Creek, and gained musical influence from the many acts that he saw in New York City, including Stanley Clarke, jazz-fusion band Return to Forever, and jazz legend Chick Corea. He graduated from high school in 1976 and never looked back. Fleck explained to Jon Ferguson of the Lancaster, Pennsylvania, *Intelligencer Journal,* "I never had the ego to think anything would happen like what did happen. But I know that I couldn't put it down. It was just a simple passion. I neglected to apply to any colleges. I had nothing in mind I wanted to do when I got out of high school because all I was doing was playing the banjo."

Moving to Boston, Fleck joined the Tasty Licks. The group released two albums, *Tasty Licks* and *Anchored to the Shore.* Both were released on the Rounder label. While working with the Tasty Licks, Fleck began releasing his own solo albums, also through Rounder. His first solo album was 1979's *Crossing the Tracks.* It included a range of sounds and material, including bluegrass and a cover of "Spain" by Corea.

After the Tasty Licks broke up, Fleck played on the streets of Boston with bass player Mark Schatz for a summer. The pair then moved to Lexington, Kentucky, where they formed a group called Spectrum. The band played together until 1981 and released one album, *Opening Roll.* Later in 1981, Fleck joined the New Grass Revival, an established progressive bluegrass band. The group played not only bluegrass, but also blended rock and country music into their sound as well. They released a number of acclaimed albums, including *On the Boulevard* and *Hold to a Dream.* His work with this band established his credibility in the country and bluegrass genres, and brought more attention to his skill as a musician as the New Grass Revival toured nationally and internationally. He remained with the band until 1988.

Fleck also continued to release solo albums though the 1980s. While performing with Spectrum, he recorded his second solo album, *Natural Bridge,* which was released on Rounder in 1982. Other albums in this time period included 1983's *The Dreadful Snakes* and 1984's *Double Time.* Fleck received more attention for his 1988 release *Drive.* In addition to his solo recordings, he also worked with an acoustic supergroup called Strength in Numbers. Their 1989 album, *The Telluride Sessions,* chronicled their evolutionary sound.

In 1989, Fleck founded a new group, the genre bending, eclectic Béla Fleck and the Flecktones. Its members included the multi-instrumentalist Howard Levy, whom Fleck had met when the New Grass Revival appeared at the Winnipeg Folk Festival; bass player Victor Lemonte Wooten; and drummer Roy Wooten, who was Victor Wooten's brother and later became known as Future Man. (Roy Wooten was already developing the drumitar, which let him play the drums with his fingers on electronic drum pads placed on a guitar body slung over the shoulders.) Making their television debut on the PBS show *Lonesome Pines,* the Flecktones released their debut, a self-titled album, in 1990. Fleck himself financed the production, though it was later picked up and released by Warner Bros. It was nominated for a Grammy Award.

Moving away from the country-bluegrass sounds that dominated the Tasty Licks, the Flecktones focused on mixing jazz and bluegrass into what came to be known as "blu-bop." It was not their only musical focus as funk, world beats, and pop made their way into the mix over the years. From the first, the group was commercially successful and critically acclaimed for its musical diversity, eclectic nature, and category-defying output. Each album was a revelation, with 1991's *Flight of the Cosmic Hippo* coming next. The *Washington Post*'s Holmes noted that this album "emphasizes ... the four musicians' improvisatory talents—which are prodigious.... It's as if the methodology of jazz has been applied to a whole new musical vocabulary...." It was also nominated for a Grammy Award. Levy left Fleck's band in 1992, and it remained a trio until Jeff Coffin, a saxophonist, joined later in the 1990s.

Fleck and the Flecktones recorded and toured regularly throughout the 1990s and into the early 2000s. While early albums were recorded live in the studio, their productions eventually became as adventurous as their music and incorporated overdubbing into the process. Because of their success and the respect they garnered from other artists, later albums included impressive guest stars such as Corea, Branford Marsalis, Dave Matthews, and the Alash Group. One particularly important album for Béla Fleck and the Flecktones was 1998's *Left of Cool*, the first to be recorded with overdubs. The Flecktones toured on their own, but also opened for such groups as the Dave Matthews Band in 1996 and 1997. The Flecktones' shows were as eclectic as their musical blend. Live, the band favored improvisation and allowed their musical muse to guide their sound.

Fleck continued to record and perform as a solo artist as well. In 1995, he released *Tales from an Acoustic Planet*. This challenging album featured songs he had written over the previous 20 years, recorded with the help of numerous guest artists such as Corea, Marsalis, Matt Munde from Aquarium Rescue Unit, and Bruce Hornsby, as well as Victor Wooten and Future Man from the Flecktones. Describing the recording process, Fleck told *Billboard*, "Recording this album was so joyful that it never felt like work. Every situation was an adventure, and hearing the songs come alive with everybody's ideas and the musical input was just so exciting." The all-instrumental album was critically acclaimed, with *Billboard* noting "*Tales from the Acoustic Planet* avoids the obvious pitfall of becoming a pastiche. Instead, it sets the modern jazz stylings of the Flecktones in an acoustic framework." In 1999, he released *Tales from the Acoustic Planet Vol. 2, the Bluegrass Sessions*, which focused on his bluegrass roots and also featured many impressive guest artists.

In 2000, Fleck left behind his nearly decade-long relationship with Warner Bros. and signed a new deal with Sony Music that allowed work to be released on subsidiaries including Columbia, Sony Classical, and Sony. Fleck's first release under the deal was the 2000 Flecktones album *Outbound*. While it included what was the classic Flecktones mèlange of musical stylings as well as Fleck's signature creative banjo sound leading the way, it also featured and stressed the importance of notable guest artists, including acclaimed vocalists Shawn Colvin and Yes's Jon Anderson. *Outbound* was also recorded with more spontaneity than other Flecktones releases. Another important Flecktones album was 2003's *Little Worlds*, a three-disc set. Their stripped-down 2006 album *The Hidden Land* won a Grammy for a contemporary jazz album, while their first holiday album, 2008's *Jingle All the Way* won a Grammy for best pop instrumental album.

Fleck's solo output continued at a rapid rate, and was no less daring. In 2001, he ventured into classical music with *Perpetual Motion*. This critically acclaimed album won the Grammy for best classical crossover album. *Perpetual Motion* was created with the help of bassist/composer Edgar Meyer who began working with Fleck on a regular basis. The pair formed a duo around the bass and the banjo, and toured together. They released *Music for Two*, which demonstrated their live sound. In addition, Fleck and Meyer wrote and performed a double concerto for the bass, banjo, and the Nashville Symphony. It was first performed in November of 2003. In 2007, Fleck put out a duet album with Corea, who was a great influence on his music and sometimes collaborator on various projects. *The Enchantment* was well received.

In 2009, Fleck released the award-winning solo album *Throw Down Your Heart: Tales from the Acoustic Planet, Vol. 3—Africa Sessions*. It was considered an ambitious release as it featured collaborations with a number of African musicians from countries like Uganda, Senegal, South Africa, and Madagascar which were recorded on site in Africa in 2005. Through the album and the accompanying documentary film, *Throw Down Your Heart*, Fleck went on an exploratory adventure to discover the banjo's origins in Africa. Early versions of the banjo were crafted in Africa and brought to the United States by slaves. Fleck's experience was insightful and moving, and was reflected in the music created on the album. Among the highlights of *Throw Down Your Heart*, were the traditional medley "Ajula/ Mbamab," performed by Fleck and Gambia's Jatta Family, and "Djorolen" a duet with singer Oumou Sangare. Critics raved about *Throw Down Your Heart* as well as the documentary. Fleck toured in 2009 and 2010 with various African musicians who appeared on the album and some who did not.

Of his musical philosophy, Fleck told Jim Patterson of the Associated State & Local Wire, "If I can make the banjo work in any kind of music that it hasn't been in before, I feel a certain sense of accomplishment. If the banjo wasn't dumped on and discriminated against, I wouldn't have as much opportunity." Summarizing his penchant for exploring and mixing musical genres, he explained to Eyder Peralta of the Jacksonville *Florida Times-Union*, "I keep it varied. I have all types of things going on so I don't get bored."

Selected discography

(With the Tasty Licks) *Tasty Licks*, Rounder, 1978.
Crossing the Tracks, 1979.
(With the Tasty Licks) *Anchored to the Shore*, Rounder, 1979.
(With Spectrum) *Opening Roll*, Rounder, 1981.
(With Tony Trischka and Bill Keith) *Fiddle Tunes for Banjo*, Rounder, 1981.
Natural Bridge, Rounder, 1982.
(With Spectrum) *It's Too Hot for Words*, Rounder, 1982.
The Dreadful Snakes, Rounder, 1983.
(With Spectrum) *Live in Japan*, Rounder, 1983.
(With New Grass Revival) *Live*, Sugar Hill, 1983.
Double Time, Rounder, 1984.
Deviation, Rounder, 1984.
(With New Grass Revival) *On the Boulevard*, Sugar Hill, 1984.
Inroads, Rounder, 1986.
(With New Grass Revival) *New Grass Revival*, Capitol, 1986.
(With New Grass Revival) *Hold to a Dream*, Capitol, 1987.
Drive, 1988.
(With New Grass Revival) *Friday Night in America*, Capitol, 1989.
(With Strength in Numbers) *The Telluride Sessions*, MCA, 1989.
(As Béla Fleck and the Flecktones) *Béla Fleck and the Flecktones*, Warner Bros., 1990.
(As Béla Fleck and the Flecktones) *Flight of the Cosmic Hippo*, Warner Bros., 1991.
(As Béla Fleck and the Flecktones) *UFO TOFU*, Warner Bros., 1992.
(With Tony Trischka) *Solo Banjo Works*, Rounder, 1992.
(As Béla Fleck and the Flecktones) *Three Flew Over the Cuckoo's Nest*, Warner Bros., 1993.
Tales from the Acoustic Planet, Warner Bros., 1995.

(As Béla Fleck and the Flecktones) *Live Art*, Warner Bros., 1996.
(With others) *Tabula Rasa*, Water Lily Acoustics, 1996.
(With Edgar Meyer and Mike Marshall) *Uncommon Ritual*, Sony, 1997.
(As Béla Fleck and the Flecktones) *Left of Cool*, Warner Bros., 1998.
Tales from the Acoustic Planet Vol. 2, the Bluegrass Sessions, Warner Bros., 1999.
(As Béla Fleck and the Flecktones) *Outbound*, Columbia, 2000.
Perpetual Motion, Sony Classical, 2001.
(As Béla Fleck and the Flecktones) *Live at the Quick*, Columbia, 2002.
(As Béla Fleck and the Flecktones) *Little Worlds*, Columbia, 2003.
(With Edgar Meyer) *Music for Two*, Sony, 2004.
(As Béla Fleck and the Flecktones) *The Hidden Land*, Sony, 2006.
(With Abigail Washburn and the Sparrow Quartet) *The Sparrow Quartet*, Nettwerk Productions, 2006.
(With Chick Corea) *The Enchantment*, Concord, 2007.
(With Abigail Washburn and the Sparrow Quartet) *Abigail Washburn & the Sparrow Quartet*, Nettwerk Productions, 2008.
(As Béla Fleck and the Flecktones) *Jingle All the Way*, Rounder, 2008.
Throw Down Your Heart: Tales from the Acoustic Planet, Vol. 3—Africa Sessions, Rounder, 2009.

Sources

Books

Marquis Who's Who, Marquis Who's Who, 2010.

Periodicals

Associated Press, March 9, 2009.
Associated Press State & Local Wire, November 9, 2000.
Billboard, March 4, 1995.
Chicago Sun-Times, August 18, 2000, p. 8.
Florida Times-Union (Jacksonville, FL), March 26, 2004, p. WE-15; January 20, 2006, p. WE-13.
Intelligencer Journal (Lancaster, PA), February 12, 1999, p. 2.
Knoxville News-Sentinel (TN), April 2, 2009.
Mix, September 1, 2007, p. 111.
Ottawa Citizen, February 27, 2010, p. G1.
Record (Bergen County, NJ), August 23, 2000, p. Y1.
St. Louis Post-Dispatch (MO), May 31, 1996, p. 4E.
Virginian-Pilot (Norfolk, VA), December 31, 1996, p. E1; December 7, 2000, p. W1.

Washington Post, May 18, 1990, p. N26; September 20, 1991, p. N17.

Online

"Bela Fleck," Béla Fleck and the Flecktones, http://www.flecktones.com/page/Bela-Fleck (August 27, 2010).

"Biography," Béla Fleck—The Official Web Site, http://www.belafleck.com/bio.html (August 26, 2010).

"Discography," Béla Fleck—The Official Web Site, http://www.belafleck.com/discography.html (August 26, 2010).

—*A. Petruso*

Tyler Florence

Bobby Bank/WireImage/Getty Images

Chef and television personality

Born Kevin Tyler Florence, March 3, 1971, in Greenville, SC; married Christie Leer (divorced); married Tolan; children: Miles (first marriage), Hayden (son, second marriage), Dorothy Tyler (second marriage). *Education:* Graduated from Johnson & Wales University (with honors), 1991.

Addresses: *Office*—c/o Food Network Studios, 604 W. 52nd St., New York, NY 10019. *Web site*—http://www.tylerflorence.com/; http://www.foodnetwork.com/tyler-florence/index.html; http://twitter.com/tylerflorence.

Career

Worked as a chef at Aureole, Mad 61, and River Café, all New York, NY, 1992-95; executive chef, Cibo, New York, NY, 1995-98; began appearing on the Food Network, 1996; founded, created, and served as an executive chef at Cafeteria, New York, NY, 1998-2000; joined Food Network, 1999; host, *Food 911,* Food Network, 1999-c. 2003; host, *Tyler's Ultimate,* Food Network, 2003—; host, *How to Boil Water,* 2003—; debuted cooking line at Mervyn's, 2003; host of radio show *Food Talk,* WOR (New York City), 2006; signed endorsement deal with Applebee's, 2006; opened first kitchen retail shop, The Tyler Florence Shop, Mill Valley, CA, 2008; appeared on *Search for the Greatest American Recipe,* Food Network, 2009; host, *The Great Food Truck Race,* Food Network, 2010—; opened and served as chef at Wayfare Tavern in San Francisco, CA, 2010—; launched Spouts (a line of organic baby food), 2010.

Awards: Honorary Doctorate, Johnson & Wales University, 2004.

Sidelights

Celebrity chef and Food Network star Tyler Florence championed cooking accessible but flavorful recipes in real kitchens. Recognized by numerous publications like *Bon Appétit* and *Food & Wine* as a leading chef, he worked in several hip New York City restaurants before focusing on cooking shows, writing cookbooks, and entrepreneurial enterprises full time. In 2010, Florence opened his first signature restaurant, the Wayfare Tavern, in San Francisco. Describing his take on food, Jennifer Olvera of the *Chicago Sun-Times* wrote, "Florence is considered by many to be an authority on cooking with fresh, world-wise flavors." Florence himself told Tara Dooley of the *Houston Chronicle,* "I enjoy making pure, simple food."

He was born Kevin Tyler Florence on March 3, 1971, in Greenville, South Carolina. Florence's father worked in advertising, publishing, and radio, while his mother was the business manager for a local television station. While his parents were good cooks—especially his mother—he did not have a positive connection with food in all its variety from birth. When he was an infant, he was taken to an allergist and was diagnosed with severe food allergies. The young Florence was allergic to many foods and food groups, including dairy and chicken. He eventually grew out of all of his allergies during his childhood, developed a palate over time, and became interested in cooking by the age of 12.

By the time he was 15 years old, Florence was working in restaurants. He initially took a job at an eatery to pay for upkeep on the car he acquired, a 1965 Comet Capri. He began by washing dishes at a trendy restaurant in Greenville. Florence eventually moved into the kitchen, and was especially influenced by a chef he worked for early on, Donald Barickman, who imparted his knowledge about Southern food to the aspiring chef. After completing high school, Florence decided to train for a career as a chef and attended the College of Culinary Arts at Johnson & Wales University, located in Charleston, South Carolina. While a student, he worked in the kitchen of Magnolias and under Louis Osteen who was executive chef at the Charleston Grill in Charleston Place. In 1991, Florence graduated with honors. He continued to work in Charleston for a time, but by 1992, sought new challenges in New York City.

When he moved to New York City, Florence sought employment in the kitchen at Aureole. He landed a job by passing a test required of all aspiring chefs. Florence was subject to a five-day stage, which meant working in the restaurant for free during that time to demonstrate his skills and dedication. Because of the vast number of people doing the stage, they were all given mundane tasks like spending eight hours first carving stale baguettes into small logs then paring them down into perfect cylinders. The resulting cylinders were thrown away at the end of the day. Florence passed this test, was invited to work a sixth day, was hired on the seventh, and soon became a sous chef. He learned much from Aureole's chef, Charlie Palmer.

Florence went on to take jobs at other New York City restaurants, including Mad 61, where he worked for chef Marta Pulini, and River Café, where he worked for Rick Laakkonen. By 1995, Florence was serving as an executive chef at Cibo in New York City. The menu that he created featured modern American cuisine. Florence left Cibo in 1998 to create the menu and serve as an executive chef at Cafeteria, located in Chelsea. This restaurant served diner food done in hyper-modern style.

While working in New York City, Florence caught the attention of the Food Network, then a small but growing cable network devoted to food. He began

appearing on the network in 1996. Florence soon became a regular guest on Food Network shows like *Door Knock Dinners, Ready, Set, Cook!*, and *Chef du Jour*. Florence officially joined the Food Network in 1999 and soon became nationally famous as one of the network's signature chef/hosts. His first show was *Food 911*, which was on the air for about five years beginning in 1999. He appeared on the show first as a guest then became its host. On *Food 911*, he helped non-chefs with their culinary and recipe-related problems such as how not to overcook vegetables and how to repair sauces. With Florence's help and clear explanations, people were able to make impressive meals.

Discussing the unique nature of *Food 911*, Florence explained to Rick Nelson of the Minneapolis *Star Tribune*, "It's the only cooking show that takes cooking on the road. We show up at someone's home and turn their kitchen into a studio for the day, using their pots and pans. It's entertaining but it's also enormously practical. When we're done cooking, people say, 'Yeah, I can do this, it's the easiest thing in the world.' That's very satisfying."

By the time Florence was hosting *Food 911*, he had grown at ease in front of the camera. He told Jae-Ha Kim of the *Chicago Sun-Times*, "It took about two years of appearances before I didn't sweat like a pig when I was on camera. Now I feel very comfortable, and I don't have time to be nervous. I'm too busy making sure that my guests are comfortable. People get intimidated by cooking shows because they don't think they can duplicate what we do. We're not magicians. We've just had a little more practice in the kitchen." Florence also understood that his show was effective because he made his recipes and cooking demonstrations easy to follow.

Because of the demands of his work on Food Network, Florence left Cafeteria in 2000, though friends continued to operate it after his departure. He did not work in restaurants for a number of years as he focused on various Food Network shows, writing cookbooks, and building an empire. Florence's career reached new heights by 2003. That year, he launched a new show on Food Network, *Tyler's Ultimate*. This series featured a pure Florence take on food as he identified the best ingredients and recipes from around the world and created ultimate but accessible dishes from them. As he explained to Rosemary Black of the New York *Daily News*, "It's about how to make the best meat loaf or fried chicken or macaroni and cheese. It's about brilliant simple cooking, really." Florence also hosted another show on the network, *How to Boil Water*, which offered advice and recipes for the beginning cook.

In addition to new television programs, Florence introduced a line of cooking products at the department store Mervyn's and published his first cookbook in 2003 as well. Written with JoAnn Cianciulli, *Tyler Florence's Real Kitchen* reflected the attitude he emoted on his television appearances and featured culinary ideas from around the world. Reviewing the book, *Publishers Weekly* noted that "many of the recipes themselves are clever." They were also intended to be simple, appealing primarily to home cooks looking to prepare simple but interesting dishes. Michael Hastings of *Winston-Salem Journal* concluded, "*Tyler Florence's Real Kitchen* is not a cookbook for beginners. But for those at an intermediate level, with an adventurous palate and inclination to really getting into the kitchen and cook, the rewards can indeed be real good." It was a best seller.

Florence published his second cookbook in 2005, *Eat This Book: Cooking with Global Fresh Flavors*, and it continued to reflect his casual style but with a more personal touch. The recipes focused on American cuisine while incorporating ideas from other countries and cuisines to embellish American food. Reviewing *Eat This Book, Publishers Weekly* noted that "Florence's vast culinary knowledge translates well to the page, as nearly every entry includes practical, and often charming, personal commentary...." The *Chicago Sun-Times'* Olvera added, "His approach is conversational and down-to-earth, and the dishes, while largely straightforward, shoot for dazzling results." Florence told Olvera, "These recipes are well-worked and beautifully tested. They're a well-stamped passport of my cooking experiences, and they'll make you look like a superhero in the kitchen."

In 2006, Florence's career continued to expand. He published a third cookbook, *Tyler's Ultimate: Brilliant Simple Food to Make Any Time*, a tie-in to his popular Food Network show. Also positively reviewed, it focused on flavorful, straightforward recipes. Judith Sutton of *Library Journal* commented, "Florence has a friendly, unassuming style, and his enthusiasm is contagious." Also that year, Florence began hosting a weekday radio show, *Food Talk*, on WOR in New York City. He took over the show from another celebrity chef, Rocco DiSpirito. On *Food Talk*, Florence took calls from listeners about cooking questions and discussed food with guests like Michael Lomonaco and Mario Batali. In addition, Florence built on his name recognition by signing a deal with the restaurant chain Applebee's to add exclusive dishes created by Florence to its menu such as penne rosa with sweet Italian sausage and a bruschetta burger. He became the face of the chain

for several years, making several million dollars in the process, though some labeled him a sell-out for his work with Applebee's.

Florence took on new challenges in 2007. That year, he left New York City and moved to the Bay Area in California. He settled with his family in Mill Valley. In 2008, Florence published two new cookbooks, *Stirring the Pot*, and *Dinner at My Place*. The former focused on cooking techniques while the latter featured recipes he cooked for friends and family at home in Mill Valley. He also expanded his business empire by opening The Tyler Florence Shop, a kitchen retail store, in Mill Valley. He planned on opening another outlet online, then perhaps another storefront in a different city in California. His work with the Food Network still took much of his focus as he hosted *Search for the Greatest American Recipe* in 2009 and a new show *The Great Food Truck Race,* a reality food competition, beginning in 2010.

While Florence had many offers over the years to open his own signature restaurant, it was not until 2010 that he took the plunge. That year, he opened the Wayfare Tavern, located in the financial district of San Francisco, and served as its chef. Florence had planned to open two other restaurants in 2010, El Paseo in Mill Valley and the Tyler Florence Rotisserie & Wine in Napa. He hoped to launch other Tyler Florence Rotisserie & Wine locales in the United States, including at the new terminal of the San Francisco airport. While Florence had his own eateries, he continued to publish new books, including *Tyler Florence Family Meal*. Like his previous cookbooks, it was extremely well-received. Reviewing the book in the *Providence Journal-Bulletin*, Gail Ciampa wrote "*Tyler Florence Family Meal* ... is a love story starring both family and food: the comfort of being part of a happy, trusted unit and sharing that around a table is a cornerstone of American life."

Florence's popularity as a celebrity chef soon extended worldwide. Florence's Food Network series *Food 911* and *Tyler's Ultimate* also aired in other countries like Australia. He told GraceAnn Walden of the *San Francisco Chronicle*, "I'm moving toward a global brand, where we can launch our shows in every English-speaking nation in the world." His entrepreneurial zeal extended to other areas as well. Florence became interested in winemaking and was a winemaker. His own wine label was set to launch in October of 2010. He also had an iPhone app and launched his own line of organic baby food, Sprout, in May of 2010. Of this aspect of his career, Florence told Paolo Lucchesi of the *San Francisco Chronicle*, "The food community expects their chefs to be poor, little humble guys that hunt mushrooms by the third moonlight of the third full moon of the month. I've set myself up to have a vertically integrated, multitiered company."

Explaining his influences and motivations as a chef, Florence told the *Star Tribune*'s Nelson, "Everything I do inspires everything I do. I get a lot of influence from authentic food, something not translated by a chef into haute cuisine but rather something that's true to a region, something rough and simple and organic. I'm totally fascinated with food. It's the one link that connects everyone around the world. We may not speak the same language, but if I cook a good meal for you we will totally understand each other."

Selected writings

(With JoAnn Cianciulli) *Tyler Florence's Real Kitchen*, Clarkson Potter (New York City), 2003.

Eat This Book: Cooking with Global Fresh Flavors, Clarkson Potter, 2005.

Tyler's Ultimate: Brilliant Simple Food to Make Any Time, Clarkson Potter, 2006.

Stirring the Pot, Meredith Books (Des Moines, IA), 2008.

Dinner at My Place, Meredith Books, 2008.

Tyler Florence Family Meal, Rodale Books (Emmaus, PA), 2010.

Sources

Books

The Complete Marquis Who's Who, Marquis Who's Who, 2010.

Periodicals

Alameda Times-Star (Alameda, CA), April 23, 2003.
Business Wire, October 29, 2003; August 25, 2006.
Chicago Daily Herald, November 15, 2006, sec. FOOD, p. 1.
Chicago Sun-Times, September 20, 2000, sec. FOOD, p. 1; May 25, 2005, sec. FOOD, p. 1.
Daily News (New York, NY), April 26, 2006, sec. GOOD LIVING, p. 43.
Houston Chronicle, May 14, 2003, sec. FOOD, p. 1.
Library Journal, September 15, 2006, p. 84.
Philadelphia Inquirer, May 26, 2005, p. F4.
Post and Courier (Charleston, SC), April 29, 2001, p. D1.
Providence Journal-Bulletin (RI), October 6, 2010, p. 7.
Publishers Weekly, March 17, 2003, p. 68; December 6, 2004, p. 56.
San Francisco Chronicle, June 26, 2005, p. 49; April 22, 2010, p. E1.
San Jose Mercury News, October 21, 2008.
Star Tribune (Minneapolis, MN), October 2, 2003, p. 1T.
Winston-Salem Journal (Winston Salem, NC), May 7, 2003, p. E2.

Online

"Celeb Chef Tyler Florence Launches Organic Baby Food," *People* Celebrity Baby Blog, http://celebritybabies.people.com/2010/05/24/celeb-chef-tyler-florence-launches-organic-baby-food/ (November 15, 2010).

Contemporary Authors Online, Gale, 2007.

"Tyler Florence Bio," Food Network, http://www.foodnetwork.com/tyler-florence/bio/index.html (November 14, 2010).

"Tyler Florence," Internet Movie Database, http://www.imdb.com/name/nm1346162/ (November 14, 2010).

—A. Petruso

Jonathan Safran Foer

Author

Born February 21, 1977, in Washington, DC; son of a public relations executive and a legal researcher; married Nicole Krauss (a writer), 2001; children: two sons. *Education:* Princeton University, A.B., 1999.

Addresses: *Agent*—Nicole Aragi, Aragi Agency, 143 W. 27th St., Ste. 4-F, New York, NY 10001. *Home*—Brooklyn, NY.

Career

Worked as a receptionist at a public relations firm; other jobs include jewelry salesperson, morgue assistant, math tutor, and ghostwriter. Contributor to magazines, including the *Paris Review* and the *New Yorker*. Professor in the graduate creative writing program, New York University, 2009—.

Awards: National Jewish Book Award, Jewish Book Council, for *Everything Is Illuminated*, 2002; Young Lion Award, New York Public Library, for *Everything Is Illuminated*, 2003.

Sidelights

Jonathan Safran Foer's debut novel, *Everything Is Illuminated*, provoked a minor literary sensation when it was published in 2002. He was just 24 years old at the time, and the story's bifurcated narratives centering on a young American searching for his family's Jewish roots in Eastern Europe seemed to garner the author equal amounts of critical adoration and opprobrium. Foer's second novel, and then a 2009 treatise on meat-eating, elicited similar responses—which pleased the Brooklyn-based writer. "People don't care enough," Foer told Joshua Wolf Shenk, who interviewed him for *Mother Jones*. "They don't get worked up enough. They don't get angry enough. They don't get passionate enough. I'd rather somebody hate what I do than be indifferent to it."

Foer—whose surname is pronounced "four," like the number—was born in Washington, D.C., in 1977 into a family of three brothers. Neither parent followed artistic career paths, but Foer has said that the public-relations executive and a legal researcher were supportive and encouraged expressions of exuberance. "I was a flamboyant child," he admitted to another reporter, Lev Grossman of *Time*, asserting that his wardrobe was rife with "bow ties, big blazers, glittery stuff."

Unlike many future novelists, Foer was not an avid reader in his youth, but he was a prolific letter-writer. At Princeton University he majored in philosophy, but took a creative-writing class taught by Joyce Carol Oates, who encouraged him to pursue his craft further. In 1997, Foer traveled to Ukraine in order to retrace the history of his mother's Jewish family, who endured immense hardship during World War II. Foer's grandfather had avoided being sent to one of the concentration camps established by Nazi Germany to exterminate Europe's Jewish population when a neighbor came to his aid. Foer went there to unravel this mystery, and that journey became the fodder for his debut novel.

Before it emerged in that form, however, Foer used the story for his senior thesis submission, and it won the creative writing thesis prize at Princeton just before he graduated in 1999. A year later, Foer had an extravagantly fortunate break when one of his first short stories, "About the Typefaces Not Used in This Edition," was published in the Fall 2000 issue of the prestigious *Paris Review*. At this time, Foer was compiling a book of essays about the American artist Joseph Cornell, who died in 1972. Cornell created surrealist dioramas with found objects inside small wooden boxes; he was an extreme recluse for much of his life but has been hailed as one of the most original visionaries to come out of twentieth-century American art. Foer was fascinated by Cornell's art, and while still in college began asking established writers to create something inspired by a Cornell piece. In the end, he collected poems and fiction from Oates, Rick Moody, Siri Hustvedt, and Barry Lopez, among other prominent names, and the result was published in 2001 as *A Convergence of Birds: Original Fiction and Poetry Inspired by the Work of Joseph Cornell.*

Foer settled in the New York City area after graduating from Princeton and resumed turning his senior thesis into a novel. Along the way, he held a variety of jobs to make ends meet, including stints as a morgue assistant and math tutor. He ghostwrote a book about prostate cancer and was working as a receptionist at a public-relations firm when the sixth agent to whom he had sent the finished manuscript about his Ukraine trip agreed to sign him. That agent then sold the book to Houghton Mifflin, and the hardcover rights alone netted Foer $500,000. "Surprised is not even the right kind of word," he told Clark Collis, a journalist for the London *Observer.* "I was just the guy who picked up the phone, making $11,000 a year. I always had this number of $20,000 floating in my head. I thought that if I made that then I could go away to Spain for a couple of months."

Published in the spring of 2002, *Everything Is Illuminated* briefly landed on the *New York Times* best-seller list, but was one of the most heavily buzzed literary debuts of the year. The story's protagonist is named Jonathan Safran Foer and he is writing a novel based on his trip to visit the Ukrainian shtetl of his grandparents, which was leveled as Nazi troops marched across the Soviet Union in World War II. He sends pages of a fictional history of the village to his correspondent, Alex Perchov, whose family runs a Jewish-heritage travel business in Ukraine. Perchov, who dreams of moving to the United States, recounts the visit the fictional Foer made to find the woman who saved Foer's grandfather's life. On the trip to find the last living survivor of the vanished village of Trachimbrod, they were accompanied by Alex's own grandfather, who harbors some of the typical anti-Semitic views of his generation in this part of the world. Also with them is the supposedly blind grandfather's service dog, named Sammy Davis Junior Junior. "Any attempt to explain the complex narrative strategy of *Everything Is Illuminated* makes it sound more complicated than it is," wrote *New York Times* book reviewer Francine Prose. "Actually, it's not difficult to follow, since the structure reveals itself slowly, in stages, and each one of these small revelations is a source of surprise and pleasure. Indeed, one of the book's attractions is its writer's unusually high degree of faith in the reader's intelligence."

Other reviews of *Everything Is Illuminated* hailed Foer as a rising new star on the literary scene, finding particular praise for his mastery of dual narrative voices—one in the American novice's fable of Trachimbrod, the second in Alex's inventively mangled English as he recounts the events of the trip. "The manuscript he sends to Alex is a tiresomely familiar thing, a folklorical saga of life in the shtetl of Trachimbrod, full of lusty villagers and their quasi-magical adventures," wrote Salon.com's Laura Miller. "The Alex sections of the book feel utterly alive and teeter invigoratingly between hilarity and a terrible, creeping dread." The British magazine *New Statesman* slotted Foer's debut as its "Novel of the Week," with the critic Siddhartha Deb remarking that the novel, with its unusual format, "often comes close to reducing its subject matter to an endless commentary on how stories are told, but in the end it just about escapes the gravity well of postmodernism to produce a work of wit and invention."

Everything Is Illuminated sold well in hardcover form, and Foer earned another small fortune for the paperback and foreign rights; it was also optioned for the screen by actor Liev Schreiber, who shares Foer's Ukrainian-Jewish roots and made his directorial debut with the 2005 film adaptation. By that point, Foer had utterly scrapped his second novel, whose main setting was a museum devoted to an obscure American writer of the World War II era, except for one part about an elderly man who survived the Allied bombing of Dresden, Germany, during the war.

That character became the mute grandfather in *Extremely Loud and Incredibly Close,* Foer's 2005 novel. This time, the story is anchored by a more recent tragedy: the World Trade Center attack on September 11, 2001. Oskar Schell is a nine-year-old New Yorker who has lost his father in the attack, but months later, as the novel opens, he seems to show little sign of grief. Oskar is also a child prodigy, a talented inventor and inveterate letter-writer. Left on his own by his working mother and monitored by his grandmother, who lives across the street, the boy discovers a key with the name "Black" on it hidden deep inside his late father's closet. He sets out to interview every person named Black in New York City. Oskar's grandmother is separated from her husband, the survivor of the Dresden bombing who is saddled with his own anguish. Letters between the family members, including those of Oskar's father, tell the story. In the end, Oskar's grandfather finally begins to recount his own history. Foer admitted that centering a novel around 9/11 was risky, but as he explained to Grossman in the *Time* article, "so much of the reason I wrote the book was because I was tired of the tellings of [the Twin Tower bombings] having messages, having points. What I wanted was exactly to make something that didn't have a point: These are people who lost something, this is what it looks like."

Extremely Loud and Incredibly Close won Foer another round of mixed reviews from critics. In the *New Yorker,* John Updike remarked upon the book's unusual typography and layout, asserting that these "graphic embellishments reach a climax in the last pages, when the flip-the-pages device present in some children's books answers Oskar's yearning that everything be run backward—a fall is turned into an ascent. It is one of the most curious happy endings ever contrived, and unexpectedly moving." The *New York Times* book reviewer, Michiko Kakutani was less enthusiastic. "While it contains moments of shattering emotion and stunning virtuosity that attest to Mr. Foer's myriad gifts as a writer, the novel as a whole feels simultaneously contrived and improvisatory, schematic, and haphazard," Kakutani asserted.

Foer spent several years researching his third book, a nonfiction treatise titled *Eating Animals.* It was inspired, in part, by the birth of the first of his two sons with his wife, the novelist Nicole Krauss. Foer and Krauss had each been intermittent vegetarians since adolescence, but debated on what kind of diet was best for their toddler son. Foer began investigating the process by which meat and dairy products find their way to American tables, the majority of which is produced by major agribusinesses. The moral and ethical dilemmas of eating meat is also discussed, which prompts Foer to reflect on the obvious love and affection most middle-class consumers shower on their pets. "Every factory-farmed animal is, as a practice, treated in ways that would be illegal if it were a dog or a cat," Foer asserts in a *New York Times* article, wondering why many—himself included—so enjoy the taste of meat but are deeply averse to the details of the violence necessary to turn it into food.

Eating Animals stirred up some contentious debate in the media, and landed on the *New York Times* best-seller list. A *Times* of London reviewer, Neel Mukherjee, noted that "the information that emerges will shrivel your soul," and that some chapters "are so bleak and shocking that they will fill you with shame, horror, anger, and disgust." Writing in the *Christian Science Monitor,* Michael O'Donnell cited one passage in which Foer accompanied an animal-rights advocate as she trespassed into a live-turkey warehouse, where they "discovered a barn floor covered with tens of thousands of turkey chicks, many of them deformed, seriously injured, or expired." O'Donnell continues, "The book's tone evolves from twee precocity to stunned outrage to profound grief as Foer acquaints himself with the suffering endured by the tens of billions of animals bred for our food each year."

Foer has often stated in interviews that he had little ambition to write novels, and stumbled upon this career path in a most accidental way thanks to encouragement from Oates and other writers. "The thing I hate most in the world is any sort of association of writing with professionalism. It's the most insincere thing I can imagine, and it's done a lot of damage to American letters," he told *Esquire* in 2002, though he later took a teaching post at New York University's graduate-writing program. "M.F.A. programs tend to encourage thinking about writing as a profession. You aren't doing what you should be doing, which is figuring things out for yourself."

Selected writings

Novels

Everything Is Illuminated, Houghton Mifflin (Boston), 2002.
Extremely Loud and Incredibly Close, Houghton Mifflin, 2005.

Other

(Editor) *A Convergence of Birds: Original Fiction and Poetry Inspired by the Work of Joseph Cornell,* Distributed Art Publishers (New York City), 2001.
Eating Animals, Little, Brown (New York City), 2009.

Sources

Periodicals

Christian Science Monitor, November 17, 2009, p. 25.
Esquire, December 2002, p. 142.
Independent on Sunday (London, England), April 21, 2002, p. 12.
Mother Jones, May-June 2005, p. 78.

New Statesman, July 1, 2002, p. 55.
New York, October 26, 2009.
New Yorker, March 14, 2005, p. 138.
New York Times, April 14, 2002; March 22, 2005; October 11, 2009.
Observer (London, England), June 2, 2002, p. 28.
Time, March 14, 2005, p. 61.
Times (London, England), February 27, 2010, p. 8.

Online

"'Everything Is Illuminated' by Jonathan Safran Foer," Salon.com, http://www.salon.com/books/review/2002/04/26/foer (April 26, 2010).

—*Carol Brennan*

Steven J. Freiberg

Chief Executive Officer of E*TRADE

Born c. 1957; married; children: two. *Education:* Hofstra Universtity, Hempstead, NY, B.B.A, 1979, M.B.A., 1980.

Addresses: *Office*—E*TRADE Financial Corporation, 1271 Avenue of the Americas, New York, NY, 10022.

Career

Began as a management associate and worked in other positions, Citi Card Products Division, 1980-85; chief financial officer, Citi Card Products Division, 1985; chief financial officer, Citicorp Investment Services, 1987-91; member of task force to develop a five-year Global Consumer Strategic Plan, Citicorp, 1991; head of the distribution department, Florida Consumer Bank, 1991-95; chairman and chief executive officer, Citicorp Investment Services and Citicorp Insurance Group, 1995-97; chairman and chief executive officer, Citigroup Credit Card Division, 1997-2000; chairman and chief executive officer, Citicards, 2001-05; executive vice president, Citibank North America, 2005-09; chairman and chief executive officer, Citi Holdings Global Consumer, 2009; chief executive officer, E*TRADE Financial Corporation, 2010—.

Member: Board of directors, Mastercard U.S. region, 2001-06; chairman of the board, Mastercard U.S. region, 2004-06; board of directors, Mastercard Worldwide, 2006—; board of directors, Citibank; board of trustees, March of Dimes, 2009— board of directors, Direct Marketing Association; board of directors, Fi-

*Courtesy of E*TRADE Financial Corporation*

nancial Services Roundtable; NYC council co-chairman, Habitat for Humanity; board of directors, Upromise; National Republican Congressional committee; National Republican Senatorial Committee.

Sidelights

The U.S. banking and financial industry had little stability over the first decade of the twenty-first century. Stocks plummeted. The sub-prime mortgage industry went into overdrive. Banking and financial giants required a bailout from the federal government so that the shock wave of financial disaster would not sink the entire world into a massive recession. Very little stability could be found throughout the entire industry. Steven J. Freiberg, who had worked for more than 25 years in the credit card industry and been a stable fixture in the Citigroup Corporation, took the helm in April of 2010 of the E*TRADE Financial Corporation in this volatile atmosphere.

Freiberg graduated from Hofstra University's Frank G. Zarb School of Business with a bachelor of business administration degree in banking and finance in 1979 and completed a master of business administration degree in 1980. He joined the Citigroup

Corporation upon leaving college. His first position with Citigroup was as a management associate in the Card Products Division. In this division he quickly began to build a reputation for being a person who ran extremely efficient operations. By 1985 he had been promoted to the division's chief financial officer. From the Card Products Division, he was transferred within Citigroup to its Citibank Financial Account. This division of the company was Citigroup's early foray into online banking which at the time was still in its infancy.

Continuing to build skills that would later help him in the position of chief executive officer for E*TRADE, in 1987 Freiberg became the founding director of Citicorp Investment Services. Within Citicorp Investment Services, he held many different positions including chief financial officer, chief investment officer, and national sales director.

Adding another dimension to his reputation, he became known as a go-to person who could nurse troubled divisions of the company through difficult times and transitions. In 1991 when the United States was coming out of a worldwide recession, Freiberg joined a corporate-wide task force to develop a five-year Global Consumer Strategic plan for Citicorp and tackle perceived problems within the company and come up with a proactive plan to make the company more profitable. That same year he bravely looked the recession in the eye and transferred to Florida to run the Florida Consumer Bank. Creswell, writing for *New York Times*, described Freiberg's position and performance at Florida Consumer Bank as "taking over a money-losing Citigroup retail branch network in Miami in the mid 1990s and making it profitable within two years."

After turning around the Florida Consumer Bank, Freiberg returned to New York City. Still working steadily within the Citigroup Corporation, in 1995 he became the chief executive officer and the chairman for Citicorp Investment Services, a division that he had worked in previously, and he joined the Citigroup Insurance Group. John Reed, a chairman of Citigroup Corporation along with Sanford Weill, appealed to Freiberg in 1997 to return to the credit card division of Citigroup because the division was losing money. While Freiberg was in charge of the credit card division, it returned to profitability and the number of card accounts swelled to more than 125 million with approximately $140 billion dollars worth of loans that were outstanding. Freiberg also moved the credit card division in the direction of private-label cards and Citigroup became partners with such retailers as Sears, Home Depot, and Federated Department Stores. In 2000 Freiberg was also appointed chairman and chief executive officer of Citi Card.

In 2005, after a tumultuous five years within the Citigroup corporation that saw one co-chairman outmaneuver another and force him out of the company, Freiberg was promoted to the position of co-chairman of the Citigroup Global Consumer Banking group along with Ajay Banga. The two were to operate the division together, coming to their respective positions after a power upset within the company and the appointment of a new chief executive officer of the Citigroup corporation as a whole. Banja was to run the international portion of the Global Consumer Banking group while Freiberg was to run the North American division. Freiberg once again was called upon to utilize his accrued skills in finance, banking, investment, and credit, as well as his problem-solving capabilities and ability to run a tight ship. He was courageously taking on a very difficult job within the corporation at a time when there were growing challenges in the U.S. banking industry that were making it more difficult for banks to make a profit. Under Banjay and Freiberg's leadership the Global Consumer group grew to represent more than 50 percent of Citigroup's earnings.

In the spring of 2010 Freiberg was appointed the new chief executive officer for E*TRADE Financial Corporation. Freiberg, who had been a stable fixture for 30 years at Citigroup, was leaving for a new position outside of the company. The E*TRADE Financial Corporation is a holding company which offers online discounted brokerage services for self-directed investors. The company also offers banking and lending products such as checking and savings accounts, money market accounts, and certificates of deposit. Robert Druskin, chairman and interim chief executive officer of E*TRADE Financial Corporation at the time of Freiberg's appointment, was quoted by Amit Chowdhry of the Web site Pulse2 as saying, "Steve is an exceptional senior financial services executive who brings extensive experience in driving the strategic direction and management of a broad and diverse consumer financial services franchise." In the midst of uncertain and unstable financial times, some things did remain constant. When Freiberg took over E*TRADE the company was in trouble. In October of 2010, during the earnings conference call that E*TRADE made to all of its investors, Freiberg reported that the company had returned to profitability for its second consecutive quarter.

Sources

Periodicals

New York Times, August 31, 2005, p. C1.

Online

"Alumni Achievement Steven J. Freiberg," Hofstra University, http://www.hofstra.edu/pdf/Alumni/alu_Steven_Freiberg.pdf (November 28, 2010).

"E*TRADE Financial Corporation," Answers.com, http://www.answers.com/topic/e-trade-financial-corp (November 19, 2010).

"E*TRADE Financial Corp Q3 2010 Earnings Call Transcript," Morningstar, http://www.morningstar.com/earn-02/earnings--earnings-call-transcript.aspx/ETFC.shtml (November 19, 2010).

"Former Citigroup Exec Steven Freiberg Becomes CEO of E*TRADE," Pulse2, http://pulse2.com/2010/03/22/former-citigroup-exec-steven-freiberg-becomes-ceo-of-etrade/ (November 19, 2010).

"National Competition," Network for Teaching Entrepreneurship, http://www.nfte.com/what/judges (November 19, 2010).

"Steven Freiberg: Executive Profile & Biography," BusinessWeek, http://investing.businessweek.com/businessweek/research/stocks/priv...ivcapid=4204179&previousCapid=391687&previousTitle=CITIGROUP%20INC (November 19, 2010).

"Steven J. Freiberg," NNDB, http://www.nndb.com/people/027/00016852.tif0/ (November 19, 2010).

"Three New Trustees Named By March of Dimes Foundation," March of Dimes, http://www.marchofdimes.com/aboutus/49267_55473.asp (November 19, 2010).

—Annette Bowman

Nick Friedman and Omar Soliman

Courtesy of College Hunks Hauling Junk. Reproduced by permission.

Founders of College Hunks Hauling Junk

Both born c. 1982. *Education:* Friedman: economics degree, Pomona College, 2004; Soliman: business degree, University of Miami—Coral Gables, 2004.

Addresses: *Office*—College Hunks Hauling Junk, 4836 W. Gandy Blvd., Tampa, FL 33611.

Career

Friedman: economic research analyst, Marsh & McLennan Companies, Inc., 2004-05; president, College Hunks Hauling Junk, 2005—. Soliman: worked in marketing for a healthcare consulting company, c. 2004-05; chief executive officer, College Hunks Hauling Junk, 2005—. Both: founded College Hunks Hauling Junk, 2003, and revived company, 2005.

Sidelights

Nick Friedman and Omar Soliman are the founders of College Hunks Hauling Junk, a detritus-removal business that proved to be one of the surprising success stories of the post-2007 U.S. recessionary era. True to their company name, Friedman and Soliman actually started their company while in college, then revived it after they graduated and discovered they were ill-suited to the traditional corporate jobs they had taken. Friedman told Thomas Heath, a writer for the *Washington Post*, "We started out with the idea that clean-cut college guys doing the work, operating an unglamorous business with shirts tucked in and doing manual labor, had some allure to it."

Friedman and Soliman both grew up in the Washington, D.C., area and met at Sidwell Friends School, a private academy that catapulted to national notoriety during their time there when newly elected president Bill Clinton and his wife Hillary Clinton chose it for their daughter, Chelsea, who was three years ahead of the pair. When they graduated in 2000, Friedman headed to California to study economics at Pomona College, a private, liberal-arts school in Claremont. Soliman, meanwhile, enrolled at the University of Miami to study business.

The pair reunited in the summer of 2003, when they decided to start their own trash-hauling business. Soliman's mother owned a furniture store, and customers often asked her delivery personnel to take away their old items; this gave Soliman the idea of borrowing the van and putting out flyers for a junk-removal service they dubbed College Hunks Hauling Junk. They earned $9,000 that first summer, and Soliman's cell phone was still getting calls from potential clients when they returned to college in the fall.

After graduating from Pomona College in 2004, Friedman went to work at Marsh & McLennan Companies as an economic research analyst. Soliman, meanwhile, had used the idea of College Hunks Hauling Junk to write a business plan for one of his classes; he submitted it to a Leigh Rothschild Entrepreneurship Competition run by the University of Miami's business school, and it won first prize. Returning to the District of Columbia area, he took a marketing job with a healthcare consulting firm, but contacted Friedman about reviving the company in earnest in June of 2005. "We were basically working these nine-to-fives making entry-level salaries and working in these cubicles crunching numbers, and it really wasn't where we wanted to be," Soliman told *Success* magazine's Brenna Fisher, while Friedman told the reporter that "I remember e-mailing Omar to ask him what his time frame was in terms of getting out of the corporate world. And he e-mailed me back in all capital letters: 'MY TIME FRAME IS RIGHT NOW.'"

Buoyed by the $10,000 Rothschild prize and a loan from their parents, Friedman and Soliman bought a truck with enough space to offer their clients a full-load, half-load, or quarter-load rate for hauling away furniture or other unwanted items. They had it customized with their green and orange logo—a combination selected as homage to the University of Miami athletics program team colors—and the company slogan, "Let tomorrow's leaders haul your junk today!" They hired friends, relatives of friends, and University of Maryland students, whom they outfitted in spiffy uniforms of green polo shirt and durable khakis, topped off by an orange baseball cap. To fulfill the promise behind the company's name, they set a few minimum requirements—no visible tattoos or piercings—and of course hired women, too.

After a year in business, Friedman and Soliman had made $500,000—enough to take Soliman's business plan to the next level, which was franchising. Their revenues were plowed back into the company for legal fees necessary to set up the corporate paperwork and pay for a new telephone number, 1-800-JUNK-USA, which was already owned by a Michigan firm but was theirs for the price of $13,000. They also invested in a call center to handle the sudden flood of business. In 2007, College Hunks Hauling Junk opened its first franchise, in Orlando, Florida, and took in $1.1 million in revenues that year. In 2008, they moved their headquarters from suburban Maryland to the Tampa, Florida, area.

Interested parties, with demonstrated financial acumen, can buy a College Hunks Hauling Junk franchise for $35,000; the company handles all advertising and promotion, and takes a percentage of the franchisee's revenues. Customers pay a team $500 to cart away a full truckload; there is also a $99 single-item haul away offer and half-load and quarter-load pricing packages. Local franchisees try to recycle or donate as much of the loot as possible, for they must pay the local garbage dump by the pound to deposit that trash.

By 2010 Friedman and Soliman oversaw a company with nearly 30 franchise markets doing a healthy business. They were even forced to hire more experienced executives to help grow their company properly, which meant that Friedman, as president, and chief executive officer Soliman commanded some staffers old enough to be their parents. "That was actually really tough for us when we first started," Soliman admitted in an interview with Dalia Colon of the *St. Petersburg Times*. "The best advice is just to communicate in a way that's clear…. Just let them know what you're trying to do, and that usually tends to work."

Friedman and Soliman have won some high-profile television tie-ins for their increasingly successful start-up. College Hunks Hauling Junk have been featured on *The Oprah Winfrey Show* and the two bachelors even submitted to a dating segment on Bravo TV's *Millionaire Matchmaker* reality series in an episode that aired in January of 2010. Friedman took his date out to dinner, but Soliman invited his to come along on a job, an event that included the company's brightly colored delivery truck and matching green polo shirts for the two. Teased by friends after the show aired and chastised by the *Matchmaker* host Patti Stanger, Soliman said he only wanted to ensure that his date shared a similar work ethic to his own.

Both Friedman and Soliman are often asked for advice by recent college graduates searching for the right business opportunity. "Whatever you're going to do, make sure you have a vision that looks five or 10 years down the road," Soliman tells others, he reported to Fisher in the *Success* article. "Our vision is that, whether we fly into California or get off a plane in Chicago, we're going to see our orange-and-green trucks or our billboards and our marketing."

Sources

Periodicals

Inc., October 2009, p. 99.
New York Times, October 1, 2008.

St. Petersburg Times (FL), June 7, 2009, p. 1D; June 27, 2010, p. 1F.
Success, August-September 2008, p. 28.
Waste & Recycling News, March 15, 2010, p. 26.

Online

"Building Piles of Trash Into Heaps of Cash," Wash-BizBlog, *Washington Post,* http://www.washingtonpost.com/wp-dyn/content/article/2008/09/21/AR20080921.tif01372.html (August 18, 2010).

—Carol Brennan

Juliet Garcia

Photo courtesy of Dr. Juliet Garcia

President of the University of Texas at Brownsville

Born Juliet Villarreal, May 18, 1949, in Brownsville, TX; married Oscar E. García, 1969; children: two. *Education:* University of Houston, B.A., 1970, M.A., 1972; University of Texas at Austin, PhD., 1976.

Addresses: *Office*—Office of the President, University of Texas, 80 Fort Brown St., Brownsville, TX 78520.

Career

Instructor, Pan American University, 1972-74; instructor, Texas Southmost College, 1972-81; dean of arts and sciences, Texas Southmost College, 1981-86; president, Texas Southmost College, 1986-92; president, University of Texas at Brownsville, 1992—.

Member: Board of directors, Campus Compact; vice-chair, Carnegie Foundation for the Advancement of Teaching; board of directors, Ford Foundation; board of directors, JP Morgan Chase Rio Grande Valley; board of directors, Kennedy Memorial Foundation; board of directors, Public Welfare Foundation.

Awards: Hispanic Caucus Award, American Association of Higher Education, 1993; Outstanding Texas Leader Award, John Ben L. Sheppard Leadership Foundation, 1993; Women of Distinction, National Conference for College Women Student Leaders, 1995; VIDA Award, NBC/*Hispanic* magazine, 1995; John P. McGovern Award, American Association of Colleges of Nursing, 1998; inducted, Texas Women's Hall of Fame, 2000; Mujer Regional Award, National Hispana Leadership Institute, 2003; Hispanic Heritage Award for Education, 2006; Best College Presidents, *Time*, 2009.

Sidelights

When educational administrator Juliet Garcia was named president of community college Texas Southmost College in Brownsville, Texas, in 1986, she became the first Mexican-American woman to hold the top job at an American institution of higher education. Five years later, she became the president of the more extensive University of Texas at Brownsville after that university merged with Texas Southmost College in an innovative partnership that Garcia helped create. In the years since assuming that role, Garcia has earned the respect of her peers and attracted nationwide attention for her efforts to encourage educational opportunities for the many first-generation Hispanic students who attend her school, which is located just blocks from the U.S.-Mexico border. In 2009, her "community university" educational approach—a blend of the openness of a community college with the academic prowess of a university—earned Garcia a nod from *Time* magazine as one of the United States' ten best college presidents. "We're trying to send a very clear signal that the Latino human capital in this country simply needs access to the same opportunities that have been present for other people," explained Garcia to Gilbert Cruz in the accompanying *Time* profile. Garcia's work at the University of Texas also afforded her the chance to influence policy on a national scale when she served on President-elect Barack Obama's transition team as an education adviser in late 2008.

Garcia was born Juliet Villarreal, the second of the three children of a native Texan mother and a Mexican immigrant father on May 18, 1949, in Brownsville, Texas. Although neither of her parents attended college, they believed in the value of education and encouraged their children to strive for that goal. "They spent their lives making sure we developed a love for learning and set high expectations for my brothers and me to achieve," Garcia told Irene Kosela of *Texas Monthly.* The Villareals also worked to instill bilingualism in their household by speaking to their children in both English and Spanish. After Garcia's mother died when the future college president was but a young girl, her father assumed responsibility for rearing the family, setting expectations for his daughter as high as those for her two brothers in spite of the more traditional gender roles generally promoted by the era. Garcia attended local public schools, and enrolled at the University of Houston after completing her high school degree at Brownsville High School. At the University of Houston, she married fellow student and Brownsville native Oscar Garcia, with her father giving his blessing to the marriage only if his daughter promised to complete her university studies.

Garcia followed through with that promise, earning her bachelor's degree in speech and English in 1970. Both she and her husband continued with graduate studies at the University of Houston, with Garcia balancing a teaching fellowship with further academic work in speech and English. By the time she received her master's degree in 1972, Garcia had also become the mother of two. Degree in hand, the young educator and her family moved back to Brownsville. She soon found a job teaching at Pan American University, located in Edinburg, Texas, more than 50 miles from her home. The dual demands of her family and her lengthy commute were great, and Garcia soon left her position at Pan American in favor of one at Brownsville's Texas Southmost College, where she served as a full-time instructor for two years. The family then moved to

the state capital so Garcia could pursue doctoral studies at the University of Texas at Austin. There, she again served as a teaching assistant, garnered a Ford Foundation Fellowship in Doctoral Studies, and earned membership in the Phi Kappa Phi honors society.

After Garcia completed her doctorate in 1976, she and her family again returned to Brownsville where the newly minted Dr. Garcia rejoined the faculty at Texas Southmost College. In addition to teaching English courses, she made her first tentative steps into the world of educational administration by applying for the presidency of the institution despite being only 28 years old. Writing in *Leadership through Achievement*, Garcia later recalled that "I made it into the finalist group—largely because I was female. I knew it, and the search committee knew it. We all knew what the outcome would be and it was not a good experience. They asked all the wrong questions, including how old I was." Indeed, Garcia did not win the job; however, in 1979 she did gain an administrative position when she became the director of the school's Institutional Self-Study for the regional accreditation organization Southern Association of Colleges and Schools (SACS). In this role, Garcia spent more than a year coordinating the school's efforts to evaluate its educational offerings, including courses, facilities, and faculty and staff. Not long after completing this task, she was named the college's Dean of Arts and Sciences.

Garcia's tenure as dean was a successful one, and when the job of president again became vacant in 1986, she was invited to step into the role. She accepted, and in doing so became the first Mexican-American woman to helm a two- or four-year college in the United States. Drawing on her experience seeking SACS accreditation as well as her work as an academic dean, Garcia began implementing a series of campaigns aimed at raising money, expanding and improving the school's physical facilities, improving education offerings, and increasing student financial aid availability. Among her early efforts was the establishment of the Texas Southmost College Endowment Scholarship, a scholarship program that supported high-achieving students from the lower Rio Grande region. Before long, Garcia also began exploring a possible partnership between Texas Southmost College and the existing branch of the University of Texas in Brownsville. Observing that many students faced great difficulties transitioning from community college to a four-year university— on average, just under 20 percent of community college graduates go on to finish a bachelor's degree—Garcia decided to make the new University of Texas a supporting, welcoming environment for non-traditional students. "We proceeded to design what we call a community university," she explained to Patricia Valdata in *Diverse Issues in Higher Education*, "one that has the very best characteristics of a community college combined with the very best of a university, without all the bureaucracy that traditionally divides the two and causes that abyss."

In October of 1991, Garcia was named president of the new, merged institution. She assumed office in January of the following year, ushering in the combined community university program under which technical, vocational, and underclass courses are operated under the auspices of Texas Southmost College, while upperclassmen and graduate students study under the banner of the University of Texas. The result is an open-enrollment community college that allows students to naturally segue into a university setting to attain bachelors' or even masters' degrees with no transferring or culture shock. This innovative program, along with Garcia's trailblazing achievements for Mexican-American women, began to earn her considerable public recognition during the 1990s. *Hispanic Business* magazine named her as one of the United States' 100 most influential Hispanics in 1993, and the following year the American Association of Higher Education gave Garcia the Hispanic Caucus Award while the John Ben L. Sheppard Leadership Foundation granted her the Outstanding Texas Leader Award. In 1995, Garcia garnered a VIDA Award from NBC and *Hispanic* magazine. That year, she was also named a Woman of Distinction by the National Conference for College Women Student Leaders and one of the Most Influential Hispanic Women of Texas by *Texas Hispanic* magazine. Five years later, Garcia won admission to the Texas Women's Hall of Fame.

Garcia carried over the endowed Texas Southmost College scholarship program to the University of Texas campus when the two institutions merged, and by 2010 the fund had granted scholarships to some 9,500 local academic achievers. The success of the partnership can be readily seen in the development of its physical campus, degrees offered and awarded, and students served. Between her assumption of the presidency and 2010, Garcia oversaw the expansion of the campus from about 50 to more than 380 acres to encompass the needs of more than 4,000 additional full-time students. The university doubled its baccalaureate offerings and tripled its master's degree programs. Student achievement rates also grew dramatically, with associate's degree completion up 44 percent, bachelor's degree completion up 115 percent, and master's degree completion up a stunning 347 percent.

In early 2008, Garcia found her institution in the news for a topic that had little to do with its primary educational mission. Working to curtail illegal immigration over the U.S.-Mexico border, the U.S. Department of Homeland Security began work on a somewhat controversial stretch of fencing covering some 300 miles in May of that year. Residents and officials in border cities located near the fence alleged that the federal government had failed to consult them about the placement of the barrier. After the Texas Border Coalition, a collective representing communities and organizations near the U.S.-Mexico border, filed a lawsuit in Brownsville over the fence, Garcia testified in a Congressional hearing about its impact on the University of Texas' campus. Noting that the proposed 18-foot-high fence physically separated the school's technology center and golf course from the rest of its facilities—effectively locating them across the Mexican border—Garcia argued that the barrier could cause "serious harm to the university on many fronts," according to Randal C. Archibold and Julia Preston in the *New York Times*. That summer, the university and federal government reached an agreement to reinforce the security features of an existing fence rather than install the proposed one.

Later that year, Garcia again became involved with government, this time in a less contentious way. Shortly after Barack Obama was elected president in November of 2008, he named the university president to his transition team as an adviser to the Department of Education. Although Garcia had previously met Obama when the then-candidate visited the Brownsville campus earlier that year, she had not been directly involved in his campaign, making the appointment something of a surprise. The *Brownsville Herald*'s Emma Perez-Trevino quoted Garcia as stating, "I consider public service to be our highest calling, so I am greatly honored to have been invited to take part in the historic transition of our young democracy," in regard to the role. After completing her work on the transition team, Garcia returned to her administrative duties at the university. She also continued to deal with issues relating to the controversial border fence that ran through the campus by supporting the efforts of students and community organizers to plant flowers and decorative plants along both sides of the barrier. The *Brownsville Herald*'s Ildefonso Ortiz quoted Garcia as declaring, "We want everyone to be proud of their community. This should not be seen as a dividing fence.... We decided that the plant should be a sweet-smelling peaceful flower that would promote peace and unity." Later in 2009, *Time* magazine honored Garcia for her achievements when it named her one of the nation's ten best college presidents.

Sources

Books

Leadership Achievement, American Council on Education, 2005, p. 19.
Marquis Who's Who, Marquis Who's Who, 2010.
Notable Hispanic American Women, vol. 1, Gale Research, 1993.

Periodicals

Brownsville Herald, November 5, 2008; February 14, 2009; February 15, 2009; November 13, 2009.

Diverse Issues in Higher Education, November 16, 2006, p. 28.
New York Times, May 21, 2008.
Texas Monthly, February 2003.
Time, November 11, 2009.

Online

"President's Biography," University of Texas at Brownsville/Texas Southmost College, http://pubs.utb.edu/president/Bio.htm (March 12, 2010).

—*Vanessa E. Vaughn*

E. Gordon Gee

AP Images

President of Ohio State University

Born Elwood Gordon Gee, February 2, 1944, in Vernal, UT; son of an oil company employee and a teacher; married Elizabeth Anne Dutson (a professor of medical ethics), 1968 (died, 1991); married Constance Bumgarner (a professor of art education), 1994 (divorced, 2007); children: Rebekah (from first marriage). *Education:* University of Utah, B.A., 1968; Columbia University Law School, J.D., 1971; Columbia University Teachers College, Ed.D, 1972.

Addresses: *Home*—Columbus, OH. *Office*—Office of the President, Ohio State University, 205 Bricker Hall, 190 North Oval Mall, Columbus, OH 43210-1357.

Career

Judicial clerk, U.S. Court of Appeals for the Tenth Circuit, 1972-73; assistant dean for administration, S. J. Quinney College of Law, University of Utah, 1973-74; judicial fellow and senior staff assistant, U.S. Supreme Court, 1974-75; J. Reuben Clark Law School, professor and associate dean, Brigham Young University, 1975-79; dean and professor, West Virginia University Law School, 1979-81; president, West Virginia University, 1981-85; president, University of Colorado, 1985-90; president, Ohio State University, 1990-97, 2007—; president, Brown University, 1998-2000; chancellor, Vanderbilt University, 2001-07.

Sidelights

E. Gordon Gee returned to Ohio State University in 2007 to lead the school for his second term as president. He vowed to remain with the vast, publicly funded institution—the state's fourth-largest employer—until his eventual retirement. "I believe I have to earn that salary every day, so I work pretty hard," *USA Today* writer Eric Gorski quoted him as saying about his $1.5 million salary package, the highest paid to any president of a state school in the United States. "Ohio State belongs to the people of Ohio. If on any given day they don't believe I'm earning what I earn, I'll be pumping gas in Vernal, Utah."

Vernal is the Utah town where Gee was born in 1944 into a family descended from the original wave of religious refugees who settled the state. He was raised in the Mormon faith—more formally known as the Church of Jesus Christ of Latter-day Saints—by his parents, an oil-company employee and a teacher. A history major at the University of Utah, he also spent some time in West Germany and Italy to fulfill the Mormon Church's missionary requirement of its young-adult members. After graduating in 1968 he moved to New York City to earn a law degree from Columbia University, and also went on to earn a doctorate in education a year later.

As a graduate of an Ivy League law school, Gee had his choice of plum assignments, and chose a judicial clerkship with the U.S. Court of Appeals for the Tenth Circuit, which he began in 1972. He returned to his first alma mater, the University of Utah, to take a job as a assistant dean for administration at its S. J. Quinney College of Law, before departing for Washington when he landed a judicial fellowship at the U.S. Supreme Court for the High Court's 1974-75 term. The fellowship also came with a position as senior staff assistant, and in this capacity Gee clerked for Chief Justice Warren Burger.

Gee returned once more to Utah, taking a job as professor and associate dean at Brigham Young University's J. Reuben Clark Law School in 1975. That led to an offer four years later to become dean of the law school at West Virginia University; in 1981, he took over the presidency of the entire school, making the 37-year-old Gee one of the youngest university presidents in the country. In 1985, he was recruited by the University of Colorado to oversee its system of schools. Five years later, a search committee at Ohio State University offered him the president's job, and he spent eight years there, which would be the longest tenure of his career. In 1998, he was chosen as the seventeenth president of Brown University, an Ivy League institution in Rhode Island. It was a somewhat surprising choice by the Corporation, as Brown's combined executive committee and board of trustees is called, for Gee had no previous teaching or administrative experience in the Ivy League. It was also somewhat of a rarity for an Ivy League president to be without a Ph.D.

Gee spent a controversial two years in Providence leading a school that had been founded in 1764. There was criticism for his attempt to create a new interdisciplinary program in brain science, and at the small, elite school—where faculty were usually consulted on major changes in policy or direction—his emphatic management style rankled. In January of 2000, the *Chronicle of Higher Education* ran a lengthy profile on him, which offered him a platform to respond to detractors, but Kit Lively's article began by describing his penchant for greeting people with an enthusiastic "Hi there!" The article seemed to focus on proving what an odd fit the exuberant Gee was at elite, intellectual Brown. Lively's article appeared in the January 14, 2000, issue of the *Chronicle of Higher Education*, and on February 7 Vanderbilt University in Nashville an-

nounced Gee was to become the school's next chancellor. In the February 25 issue of the journal, Lively detailed the anger on Brown's campus over Gee's resignation, and discussed reports that the private Tennessee college had lured him with a salary package more than three times that of the $300,000 he earned as Brown's president.

Gee spent six years as Vanderbilt's chancellor, and once again faced a barrage of criticism for some controversial decisions, including dismantling the school's athletic department and placing it once again under university domain. The end of his tenure at the school came after a *Wall Street Journal* article that ran in September of 2006 about the free-spending ways of some college presidents; it reported that he had been able to spend $6 million renovating the university-owned president's mansion, and that employees there had reported to Vanderbilt's board that Gee's wife had used marijuana in the house, which she claimed was to alleviate symptoms of an inner-ear disorder. The couple filed for divorce a few months later.

In July of 2007, Ohio State University announced that Gee would return to lead the school that fall. Students, faculty, and alumni were overjoyed by the news, and at his first official visit back in Columbus he was greeted with unabashed enthusiasm. He also noted that his roots at OSU were more than professional: back in the early 1990s, his first wife, Elizabeth, had died of cancer. He had often commended the level of care she received at the university's highly regarded medical center, and the couple's daughter, Rebekah, went on to earn a medical degree and become a professor of medicine. She was still a teenager when her mother died, and both she and her father said that the OSU community were tremendously supportive during that difficult period, which Rebekah discussed in a 2010 segment on Ira Glass' public-radio documentary show *This American Life*.

In 2010, the annual *Chronicle of Higher Education* survey reported that Gee was the top-earning president of a public U.S. university. A few months earlier, *Time* magazine had ranked him as the U.S.'s best college president, detailing the long hours he put in, which included attending events on campus. OSU students, faculty, and alumni appear to adore Gee, who realizes that he continues to shatter expectations for what a college president should be. "People's expectation of a university president is a tall, gray-haired, gravelly-voiced stoic," he told Lively back in 2000 in the *Chronicle of Higher Education* profile. "And look at me. I'm very disappointed when I look in the mirror every morning, myself."

Sources

Periodicals

Chronicle of Higher Education, January 14, 2000, p. A38; February 25, 2000, p. A44.
Columbus Dispatch (OH), July 13, 2007; June 8, 2008.
New York Times, December 7, 2003.
Time, November 23, 2009, p. 44.

Online

"Office of the President" Ohio State University, http://president.osu.edu/ (June 30, 2010).
"Pay Raises Slow for Public University Presidents," *USA Today,* http://www.usatoday.com/news/education/2010-01-18-college-president-pay_N.htm (July 1, 2010).

—Carol Brennan

Sean Gerrity

Courtesy of American Prairie Foundation

President of the American Prairie Foundation

Born c. 1958.

Addresses: *Office*—American Prairie Foundation, P.O. Box 908, Bozeman, MT 59771. *Web site*—http://www.americanprairie.org.

Career

Founding partner, Catalyst Consulting Group, 1985; president, American Prairie Foundation, 2002—; involved with the American Leadership Forum (ALF) of Silicon Valley.

Sidelights

Sean Gerrity serves as president of the American Prairie Foundation (APF), a nonprofit land trust dedicated to preserving the vanishing American prairie. A former corporate consultant, Gerrity grew up in the city of Great Falls, Montana, and returned there after a successful career in California's Silicon Valley. APF's ultimate goal is to create the largest wildlife reserve in the lower 48 states—though this mission has sometimes placed the APF at odds with private landowners in the Northern Plains. "The land started going out of production long before we showed up," Gerrity explained to journalist Blaine Harden in an article that ran in the *Duluth News-Tribune*. "The only question is who is going to buy it."

Back in 1985, Gerrity co-founded the Catalyst Consulting Group with business partners Bill Underwood and Kayla Matson. The Santa Cruz-based firm focused on helping companies build brands, refocus their strategies, or prepare for expansion. They did this with novel team exercises that took participants into the great outdoors for rock-climbing expeditions combined with leadership-training classes. Catalyst accrued an impressive list of clients, many of them blue-chip Silicon Valley names, including Adobe, Oracle, Sun Microsystems, and eBay.

Gerrity's love of the outdoors and devotion to his home state led him back to Montana to help launch the American Prairie Foundation. Long before Montana entered the union, it was part of vast swath of steppes created in the wake of the formation of the Rocky Mountains after the last Ice Age. The relatively flat terrain, where few trees grew because of climate conditions, became home to a diverse grasslands ecosystem that stretched from the Canadian province of Saskatchewan all the way south to Texas; the Plains also extended eastward through Wyoming, the Dakotas, Nebraska, Kansas, Missouri, and Iowa. This isolated landscape also became home to massive herds of American bison—also called buffalo—which roamed freely and grazed the plentiful grasses. Their peak numbers are estimated to have reached 30 million before they were hunted almost to the point of extinction in the nineteenth and early twentieth centuries.

The remoter parts of Montana, Wyoming, and other Plains states east of the Rockies were settled by cattle and sheep ranchers. For decades, the livestock industry provided food for a growing U.S. population, but these fenced-off areas also encroached upon the natural prairie landscape, and the absence of free-ranging bison herds disturbed the ecosystem. Ranching itself eventually fell into decline. As Harden wrote in the *Duluth News-Tribune* article, by the end of the twentieth century the Northern Plains had few attractions for any species, human or otherwise. "The soil is bad, the weather is worse and the landscape achingly dull," Harden noted. "Collapsing barns punctuate a scraggly sea of brown grass and bleached boulders. The population peaked a century ago, and remaining ranchers cannot stop their children from running off to a less lonesome life."

In the late 1990s, the U.S.-based Nature Conservancy singled out a section of the Northern Plains in Montana as one of the sites best suited for candidacy as a protected area. Because of the great biodiversity the grasslands afforded, the World Wildlife Fund (WWF) became interested, and launched a conservation project. WWF's formal plan was authored by conservation biologist Curt Freese, and the Northern Plains Conservation Network became involved. All parties agreed to establish a prairie reserve in the Montana Glaciated Plains, and The Prairie Foundation was formally founded in June of 2001. Four years later, the organization morphed into the APF, with Freese as director and Gerrity serving as president.

The APF operates as a registered land trust and nonprofit organization. It solicits donations to acquire parcels of land, and then manages those acres. Some of its holdings include long-abandoned ranches, which Gerrity explained was related to the decline of cattle ranching in this part of the American West. "For the first time since World War I, neighbors aren't necessarily coveting each other's land," Gerrity told *Casper Star-Tribune* journalist Becky Bohrer. Private benefactors of the APF helped purchase these ranches, and by 2005 the APF was managing some 32,000 acres. "We will keep getting larger until it doesn't make sense anymore," he told Bohrer.

The APF's mission has been criticized by ranchers in the area, who resent the generous donations made by corporate titans like Ted Turner and Wall Street executives who love Montana's solitude and pristine vistas. When APF first began to gain national news media notice in 2005 and 2006, some $11 million had been raised. But Gerrity also told Hal Herring, who profiled the project for *Orion Magazine*, that many donations came from Montana residents who sent $50 checks made out to the APF. These are the supporters, he remarked, hopeful to create a place "they know they'll be able to take their grandchildren and show them what it was like when Lewis and Clark came up the Missouri River."

Gerrity and the APF hope to create the largest wildlife reserve in the lower 48 states. The group works with the U.S. Fish and Wildlife Service (FWS) and the Bureau of Land Management, both of which have extensive experience balancing the need for conservation against the rights of private interests. Gerrity dreams of creating a space almost as large as Yellowstone National Park, and a similar tourist destination, too. "What we are talking about with this project is a place of vastness, where people can find that spiritual connection to our native grasslands that's been lost," he told Herring in the *Orion Magazine* article. "If we can put all of this together, I can imagine this someday to be like visiting a coral reef—that kind of experience."

Some of the national media attention that focused on APF came after the nonprofit announced in 2005 that 16 bison had been released into the wild on APF lands, and calves were born in the spring of 2006 in Phillips County, Montana—a conservation milestone in the United States. Though there are an estimated half-million American bison left roaming the Great Plains, most of those populations are managed by conservation experts in a concerted effort to save the species; the herds have health issues such as brucellosis and have trouble maintaining population numbers without scientists' intervention. The five calves that were born on the APF trust lands were the first such births to free-ranging bison in the Northern Plains region since the 1880s. "These baby bison are entering this world just as the grass is starting to grow," Gerrity told the Web site Wildlife Extra. "They're already running around, playing and chasing each other."

Sources

Periodicals

Casper Star-Tribune (WY), November 14, 2005.
Duluth News-Tribune, August 6, 2006.
New York Times, November 17, 2005; January 27, 2006.

Online

"Five Calves Born to New 'Pure' Bison Herd in Montana," Wildlife Extra, http://www.wildlifeextra.com/go/news/extra-bison.html#cr (July 6, 2010).

"Our Background," American Prairie Foundation, http://www.americanprairiereserve.org/ourBackground.html (July 3, 2010).

"Prairie Dreaming," *Orion Magazine,* http://www.orionmagazine.org/index.php/articles/article/177/cr (July 6, 2010).

—*Carol Brennan*

Tavi Gevinson

Blogger

Born April 21, 1996; daughter of Steve (an English teacher) Gevinson.

Addresses: *Office*—c/o *Pop* Magazine, Bauer Media Group, Inc., 58 W. 40th Street, 5th Fl., New York, NY 10018. *Web site*—http://tavi-thenewgirlintown. blogspot.com/.

Career

Launched blog "Style Rookie" in March of 2008; signed deal with *Pop* magazine to cover New York Fashion Week, 2009.

Sidelights

Tavi Gevinson was just 13 years old when her fashion-oriented blog Style Rookie brought her international fame in 2009. With her concise commentary on the latest designer styles and trends and a steady, humorous tone, the Chicago-area teen first gained a cult following among fashion insiders, and in August of 2009 she appeared on the cover of arty *Pop* magazine; weeks later she was the most-talked about guest in the front rows of runway collections presented at New York Fashion Week.

Gevinson lives in the Chicago suburb of Oak Park, Illinois, in a household that also includes her English-teacher father, a mother, and at least two sisters. She launched "Style Rookie" on March 31, 2008, to photograph herself in the slightly outlandish, yet fashion-forward outfits she put together, cit-

AP Images

ing what she called a growing interest in fashion. At the time, she was just eleven years old. Some pieces she wore were from stores like H&M, others were borrowed from the closets of others in the house or "the family dress-up box," but Gevinson was also emerging as a savvy vintage shopper.

Fashion was the primary focus of Style Rookie, but Gevinson sometimes mentioned school assignments or family vacations in some posts. A cursory glance through her blog showed that despite her young age, she had a rather catholic range of tastes in reading materials and cultural markers for a middle-schooler, from foreign editions of *Vogue* to the computer game Snood. She listed albums by alt-rockers Wilco and the New Pornographers as among her favorites, posted a photo of Woody Allen's vintage comedy *Sleeper,* and even referenced the late-1990s cult-favorite television show *Freaks & Geeks.*

Style Rookie's first mention in the media came just three months after Gevinson launched the blog when a German publication profiled her. On July 22, 2008, The Cut—a fashion-oriented blog attached to *New York* magazine's Web site—ran a story on her titled "Meet Tavi, the 12-Year-Old Fashion Blogger," after citing her mention on a few other fashion blogs. "We're not sure if a 12-year-old is actually doing all this or if she's getting some help from a mom or older sister," wrote The Cut's editor, Amy Odell. "We're also not sure if we think she's the best thing since the Olsen twins," Odell noted, and invited readers to chime in. That prompted a flood of comments to The Cut's story, some of them quite harsh and a few speculating that Gevinson's was a "fake" blog as part of some as-yet-unrevealed marketing scheme. Gevinson was vacationing with her family in Michigan when the story broke, and admitted to being upset by some of the negative reactions. She took a few days off from blogging then returned to set the story straight. "As to whether or not my family helps me with this blog, no (though I do need to borrow some cash every now and then)," she asserted. "For a few of my first outfit posts I would ask my mom to snap a picture of me, but I can assure you that no one dresses me up (sometimes they are a little skeptical and I do get the *really?* look)."

Gevinson and her blog were featured in the *New York Times'* August 2008 *T Style* supplement, just before she started seventh-grade classes. The continued attention brought two new readers—Los Angeles-area designers Rodarte, which is the label run by sisters Kate and Laura Mulleavy. They sent Gevinson a pair of hand-knit leggings from their pricey, avant-garde collection and later told Evonne Gambrell of *Teen Vogue* why they were fans of Gevinson. "She's curious and discerning," the sisters said, as well as "a dreamer, and that definitely reminds us of ourselves when we were younger."

Gevinson's celebrity status reached epic proportions in August of 2009, when a fashion-forward publication, *Pop,* put her on its cover that month in a shoot styled by British artist Damien Hirst. She also landed a deal to cover New York Fashion Week for the magazine's Web site, and her father accompanied her on the trip to Manhattan. She sat in the front row at Marc Jacobs' presentation of his Spring/Summer 2010, and was photographed at after-parties that week. Her father was as surprised as anyone about his daughter's sudden fame. "I may have known," about her blogging, he told an Associated Press reporter, Amanda Kwan, for a story that originally ran in *USA Today.* "But to me it was a kind of a non-thing to know. I didn't look at it. I wasn't terribly interested in seeing it."

Later in 2009 Gevinson traveled to Tokyo as the guest of honor at a party given by the avant-garde Japanese design house Commes des Garçons, and appeared in a promotional video for a limited-edition line Rodarte designed for Target. In October, London's *Independent* ran a story on her and posed the question "Is This the Coolest Teenager in the World?" in its headline. At the end of the year, the *New York Times* featured a roundup of 2009's major style stories, and writer Eric Wilson delved into the new fashion bloggers and their presence at New York Fashion Week. He cited a comment by Anne Slowey of *Elle,* who had called Style Rookie "'a bit gimmicky' in an interview with *New York* magazine," Wilson wrote. "And in an instant, the subtext in her complaint was read by dozens of Ms. Gevinson's fans as an example of the tension between old media and new, when one leapfrogs ahead of the other."

Gevinson continued to occasionally miss school to cover runway shows. She turned up in Paris in January with daring newly dyed silver-blue hair for the French collections, again with her father in tow. Though some traditional print-media journalists remained skeptical about the now-14-year-old's credentials, one of the fashion industry's best-known publicists, Kelly Cutrone, reflected on the rise of a new frontier in media coverage for struggling fashion designers. "Do I think, as a publicist, that I now have to have my eye on some kid who's writing a blog in Oklahoma as much as I do on an editor from Vogue?," Cutrone said to Wilson in the *New York Times* article. "Absolutely. Because once they write something on the Internet, it's never coming down. And it's the first thing a designer is going to see."

Sources

Periodicals

Harper's Bazaar, January 2010, p. 43.
Independent (London, England), October 10, 2009, p. 28.
New York Times, December 27, 2009.
Observer (London, England), September 20, 2009, p. 19.
Teen Vogue, December 2009, p. 93.
Telegraph (London, England), February 3, 2010.
Times (London, England), October 8, 2009, p. 13.
USA Today, August 12, 2008.

Online

"Meet Tavi, the 12-Year-Old Fashion Blogger," The Cut, http://nymag.com/daily/fashion/2008/07/meet_tavi_the_12yearold_fashio.html (March 3, 2010).
"Mumbo Jumbo," Style Rookie, http://tavi-thenewgirlintown.blogspot.com/search?updated-max=2008-08-04T00%3A11%3A00-05%3A00&max-results=50 (March 3, 2010).

—*Carol Brennan*

Elizabeth Gilbert

Author

Born July 18, 1969, in Waterbury, CT; married Michael Cooper (divorced); married José Nunes (a gem trader and business owner), 2007. *Education:* Attended New York University.

Addresses: *Office*—c/o Viking-Penguin, 375 Hudson St., 4th fl., New York, NY 10014. *Web site*—http://www.elizabethgilbert.com/.

Career

Worked variously as bartender, waitress, and cowgirl, c. early to mid-1990s; began working as a journalist for magazines like *Spin* and *GQ*, c. mid-1990s; published first book, *Pilgrims*, 1997; found acclaim with first nonfiction work, *The Last American Man*, 2002; became international sensation with memoir *Eat, Pray, Love: One Woman's Search for Everything Across Italy, India, and Indonesia*, 2006; published second memoir, *Committed: A Skeptic Makes Peace with Marriage*, 2010. Also co-owner of Two Buttons (a retail store).

Awards: Pushcard Prize, Pushcart Press, for *Pilgrims*, 1997; John C. Zacharis First Book Award, *Ploughshares*/Emerson College, for *Pilgrims*, 1999.

Sidelights

While author Elizabeth Gilbert was an award-winning writer of fiction and honored for her nonfiction, it was her memoir, 2006's *Eat, Pray, Love: One Woman's Search for Everything Across Italy, India,*

Robert Pitts/Landov

and Indonesia, which made her world famous. In the best-selling book, she described her year of travels as she looked to heal from a difficult divorce. Gilbert also started a new relationship with a man she met during her travels which led to an unexpected second marriage. This transformation was discussed in her second memoir, 2010's *Committed: A Skeptic Makes Peace with Marriage*. Describing Gilbert's power as a writer, Jennifer Egan wrote in the *New York Times*, "Gilbert's prose is fueled by a mix of intelligence, wit, and colloquial exuberance that is close to irresistible, and makes the reader only too glad to join the posse of friends and devotees who have the pleasure of listening in."

Born July 18, 1969, in Waterbury, Connecticut, Gilbert was the daughter of a chemical engineer father and a nurse mother. She was raised on her parents' Christmas tree farm. Determined to be an author from an early age, she wrote as much as she could during her childhood, primarily focusing on short stories. (Her sister, Catherine Gilbert Murdock, also became a published author. Murdock wrote young adult novels such as *Dairy Queen*.) Gilbert attended New York University, where she studied political science and wrote short stories in her free time.

After leaving school, Gilbert traveled around the country and found employment as a bartender and waitress at various bars and diners. She was also a cowgirl in Wyoming. When she returned to New York City, Gilbert used the experiences she gained during her travels as the basis of her first short-story collection. Published in 1997, *Pilgrims* was the winner of the Pushcart Prize, the John C. Zacharis First Book Award, and was a finalist for the PEN/Hemingway Award. Critics raved about the unusual characters and situations found in the collection of people seeking self-definition, including the several westerns and the tale of Richard Hoffman and his bunny Bonnie in "The Famous Torn and Restored Lit Cigarette Trick." The story "The Finest Wife" was seen as a re-telling of the Wife of Bath's prologue in Geoffrey Chaucer's classic story collection *The Canterbury Tales*.

Reviewing *Pilgrims* in the *San Diego Union-Tribune Books*, Anne Marie Welsh wrote, "The stories are traditional in format, following the same reader-friendly arc as Chekhov, Flannery O'Connor, and Raymond Carver: exposition through conflict, to epiphanies as subtle as a shift in the wind. But the sharply delineated settings, the oblique intensity of the sexual longings, and the vigorous dialogue mark them of the moment. Gilbert's rough characters have an integrity that makes them memorable even when they're as unsavory as the incestuous stripper or a heroin-addicted nightclub singer."

While working on these stories, Gilbert supported herself by working as a journalist. She was a staff member of *Spin* magazine and writer-at-large for *GQ* magazine. In 1994, while writing for *Spin*, for example, she covered the women who followed rodeo riders in a story titled "Buckle Bunnies." She also wrote a highly regarded piece on singer Tom Waits for *GQ*. Over the years, Gilbert also contributed to the *New York Times Magazine*, *Harper's Bazaar*, and *Esquire*. A story she wrote about bartending for *GQ* eventually became the basis for the hit film *Coyote Ugly*. Gilbert was honored with three nominations for National Magazine Awards for her journalistic work.

Gilbert's primary focus in this time period, however, remained her fiction. In 2000, she published her first novel *Stern Men*. The comic story focused on the conflict between two men living on separate remote fishing islands—Fort Niles and Courne Heaven—located off Maine's coast told from the perspective of 18-year-old daughter of the second-best lobsterman in Fort Niles. The territorial wars between them over lobster proved brutal. *Stern Men* was selected as a notable book by the *New York Times*. Critics also responded positively, with John Stickney of the Cleveland *Plain Dealer* noting, "In *Stern Men*, Gilbert's training as a journalist is evident. She is able to render information both about lobster fishing and the plot and character twists with sharp and often hilarious detail. The dialogue is on the mark and the skilled portrait of this eccentric community places Gilbert among the likes of John Irving and E. Annie Proulx."

While fiction had been Gilbert's first love, she found more success writing nonfiction. Her first work of nonfiction was *The Last American Man*, published in 2002 and based on article she once wrote for *GQ*. It was honored with nominations for a National Book Award in nonfiction and a National Book Critics Circle Award in biography/autobiography, both in 2002. The book focused on Eustace Conway, a modern frontiersman who choose to live like Daniel Boone and Kit Carson on 1,000 acres in North Carolina to show there is an alternative way of living to save the world. Distancing himself from his suburban upbringing, Conway's resourceful, solitary way of living was described by Gilbert in the book. She also included information about historical figures who lived this way.

Many reviewers found much to like in *The Last American Man*, with Florence Shinkle of the *St. Louis Post-Dispatch* commenting, "The book would be a treat if it only told Conway's story." Shinkle adds, "Gilbert … gives us a fearlessly complete picture of Eustace and his estranged family. But beyond that, she hits the bulls-eye with her investigation into the probable nature of an American type that we're better off mythologizing than marrying." Elizabeth Bennett of the St. Petersburg Times concurred, concluding "*The Last American Man* takes a fresh, provocative look at everything from the American frontier and famous utopias to the current state of American manhood. Gilbert combines earthy language and spirited writing to come up with a book that explores some important questions about our culture and is also a delight to read."

Four years later, Gilbert garnered the most attention of her career with her memoir *Eat, Pray, Love: One Woman's Search for Everything Across Italy, India, and Indonesia*, published in 2006. It chronicled her own journey after a painful divorce from her first husband Michael Cooper and unfortunate rebound romance. She traveled alone to several countries for one year, looking to understand herself and her pain while seeking spiritual renewal. With seven million copies sold world-wide, the book was an international best-seller and was translated into 30 languages. *Eat, Pray, Love* was also adapted for a feature film in 2010 starring Julia Roberts and Javier Bardem and directed by Ryan Murphy.

While *Eat, Pray, Love*, was a runaway hit with readers (especially women), it received mixed reviews from some critics. In the *New York Times*, Egan commented, "Lacking a ballast of gravitas or grit, the book lists into the realm of magical thinking: nothing Gilbert touches seems to turn out wrong; not a single wish goes unfulfilled. What's missing are the textures and confusion and unfinished business of real life, as if Gilbert were pushing these out of sight so as not to come off as dull or equivocal or downbeat." Janet Maslin of the *New York Times* called it "mega-chatty" and "a book so user-friendly it made her feel like every reader's best pal." Despite such reviews, Gilbert believed the book resonated with female readers because, as she explained to Ellen McCarthy of the *Washington Post*, "You are actually really permitted to give yourself a little bit of time to contemplate what you would like the meaning of your life to be."

Though Gilbert had been working on a novel set in the Amazon, Gilbert's experiences with her boyfriend from *Eat, Pray, Love* pushed her in a different direction because, as she told McCarthy of the *Washington Post*, "What was happening was more interesting than what I had been thinking of inventing." She had a whole first draft of another memoir, but scrapped it in part because of its tonal resemblance to *Eat, Pray, Love*. Gilbert explained to Jeff Baker of the *Oregonian*, "It was in the same voice, but more clanging, like someone banging on sheet metal. It was just wrong. I needed to take a different approach."

Gilbert started over again and wrote a whole new version of what became *Committed: A Skeptic Makes Peace with Marriage*, published in early 2010, with added historical perspective. This book outlined what happened to Gilbert when she was compelled to marry her Brazilian-born Australian-citizen boyfriend José (known as Felipe in *Eat, Pray, Love* and with whom she founded the small retail store, Two Buttons) to avoid him being permanently deported. She looked at how she addressed her doubts and hesitations about marriage while also adding information about the history of marriage in many times, places, and cultures around the world.

Many lovers of *Eat, Pray, Love* were disappointed with *Committed*, as were many critics, though Gilbert told the *Washington Post*'s McCarthy, it is "exactly the book I wanted to write in exactly the voice I think is appropriate." Critics like the *New York Times*' Maslin were unimpressed, writing "In *Committed* the strain is palpable as the voice is cute, and the drama is virtually nonexistent.... That adorable mixture of spirituality and kitchen equipment was whisked by *Eat, Pray, Love* into an airy confection but falls flat as a pancake this time."

Gilbert's next book was expected to be a novel about gardening, being written at her home in rural New Jersey. The author was sometimes bothered by the fact that fans of *Eat, Pray, Love* were unaware of the well-received books she published before the memoir. Baker of the *Oregonian* quoted her as saying, "I'm proud of all of them, and you're getting the point most people have missed—I was a writer before *Eat, Pray, Love*, and I'll be a writer after it's over. It's what I want to do for the rest of my life."

She added to Christopher Borrelli of the *Buffalo News*, "What I want to say is my books are all there is. In terms of what I have to offer. Certainly in terms of spirituality. I am not going to have a talk show or start one, and no one has offered. Though I suppose if I wanted one I could push for one. And I am not angling to build a motivational empire. All I have are the conclusions I arrived at in my books. I am happy to share, but I am so grateful for my sanity."

Selected writings

Short story collections

Pilgrims, Houghton Mifflin (Boston, MA), 1997.

Novels

Stern Men, Houghton Mifflin, 2000.

Nonfiction

The Last American Man, Viking (New York City), 2002.
Eat, Pray, Love: One Woman's Search for Everything Across Italy, India, and Indonesia, Penguin (New York City), 2006.
Committed: A Skeptic Makes Peace with Marriage, Viking, 2010.

Sources

Books

Writers Directory, 25th ed., St. James Press, 2009.

Periodicals

Buffalo News, October 26, 1997, p. 7E; January 31, 2010, p. F11.
Houston Chronicle, January 5, 2010, p. 1.

New Yorker, January 11, 2010, p. 74.
New York Times, June 3, 2002, p. E6; February 26, 2006, sec. 7, p. 1; January 4, 2010, p. C1.
Oregonian (Portland, OR), January 31, 2010.
Ottawa Citizen, August 14, 1994, p. B6.
Philadelphia Magazine, February 2009.
Plain Dealer (Cleveland, OH), July 2, 2000, p. 10H.
San Diego Union-Tribune Books, November 9, 1997, p. 2.
St. Louis Post-Dispatch, May 19, 2002, p. F10; March 8, 2006, p. E1.

St. Petersburg Times (FL), June 2, 2002, p. 7D.
Washington Post, January 7, 2010, p. C1.

Online

Contemporary Authors Online, Gale, 2010.
"Elizabeth Gilbert," Elizabeth Gilbert's Official Web site, http://www.elizabethgilbert.com/bio.htm (March 9, 2010).

—*A. Petruso*

Julia Gillard

AP Images/Tertius Pickard

Prime minister of Australia

Born Julia Eileen Gillard, September 29, 1961, in Barry, Wales; immigrated to Australia, 1966; daughter of John (a psychiatric nurse) and Moira (a nursing home cook; maiden name, MacKenzie) Gillard. *Education:* Attended the University of Adelaide, c. 1980-82; University of Melbourne, J.D., 1987, B.A., 1990.

Addresses: *Home*—Altona, Victoria, Australia; Canberra, Australian Capital Territory (ACT), Australia. *Office*—Department of the Prime Minister and Cabinet, P.O. Box 6500, Canberra ACT 2600, Australia.

Career

President, Australian Union of Students, 1983-84; attorney, Slater & Gordon, 1987-90, partner, 1990-96; chief of staff to Australian Labor Party legislator John Brumby, 1996-98; elected to the Australian House of Representatives from Lalor, 1998, 2001, 2004, 2007, 2010; shadow minister for population and immigration, 2001-03; shadow minister for reconciliation and indigenous affairs, 2003-06; shadow minister for health, 2003-06; held several posts within the Australian Labor Party before being named deputy leader, 2006, and elected leader, 2010; deputy prime minister and Minister for Education, Employment, Workplace Relations, and Social Inclusion, 2007-10; prime minister of Australia, 2010—.

Sidelights

Julia Gillard made history in Australia in 2010 as the country's first female prime minister. The former labor lawyer and member of federal parliament became head of the Australian Labor Party in a surprise overnight party caucus in June, which prompted her predecessor, Prime Minister Kevin Rudd, to resign as head of government. Two months later, Gillard's party achieved a near-majority in parliamentary elections and she was sworn in for a second time. Gillard is not just the first woman to lead the Australian government, but is also the first unmarried prime minister in the 109-year history of the Commonwealth of Australia. "I expect there will be interest in me and my life," she told *Australian Women's Weekly* writer Bryce Corbett just before the August election, adding, "I think people will make decisions about my capacity to be prime minister in the things that I do as prime minister, rather than any private life issues. That comes with that practical Aussie sense."

Gillard is not an Australian by birth. Her parents, John and Moira, were from the Vale of Glamorgan area of Wales, where Gillard was born in 1961 on Barry Island, a spit of land on the Bristol Channel coast. She was the second of two daughters born to Moira and John, a police officer who came from a large family of coal miners. As a toddler Gillard came down with a severe case of bronchial pneumonia, and spent two weeks inside an oxygen tent in the hospital. Doctors warned the Gillards that their younger daughter would likely suffer periodic health crises, exacerbated by the damp Welsh climate, if they stayed in the area.

In the years following World War II, Australia endured dire labor shortages. The continent takes up 2.9 million square miles and is the sixth-largest country in the world, between Brazil and India. It became a self-governing commonwealth in 1901, and the boundaries and names of its federal states hearken back to their former colonial names. To encourage immigration, the Australian government established a program whereby British subjects were eligible for a £10 fare per adult via ship for the six-week journey; children traveled free. A four-year-old Gillard and her family left Wales in 1966, becoming one of the estimated one million "£10 Poms," as the emigrants were called. "Pom" is an Australian slang term used to denote those from the United Kingdom.

Gillard grew up near Adelaide, the coastal capital of the state of South Australia. In their suburban Kingswood home, Gillard recalled that their father was often gone for long stretches of time because of the hours he worked as a psychiatric nurse, often taking night shifts because of the better pay. "You look back on it now and you just can't imagine that anybody physically could keep up the pace of work that he used to," Gillard said in an interview for the television documentary show *Australian Story*, a staple of the Australian Broadcasting Corporation. "There were endless days where Alison and I'd have to be creeping around the house because dad was getting a few hours sleep before he went back to work."

Moira Gillard also worked to help support the family, spending her afternoons in the kitchen of a nursing home cooking the evening meal. Both Gillard and her sister attended Mitcham Demonstration School and Unley High School, where the future prime minister earned top grades and was a standout on the debate team. She chafed at some of the restrictions of the era, for the gender-equality movement was slow to arrive in the Australian educational system. "Mum and Dad, well before their time, always taught us we were as good as boys—that there was no hierarchy that had boys at the top of the hierarchy and girls somewhere else," she said in the *Australian Story* interview.

Gillard's parents were dedicated supporters of the Australian Labor Party (ALP), the major center-left party of Australian politics. One of the ALP's most influential figures was Gough Whitlam, who served as prime minister from 1972 to 1975. Whitlam managed to push through several important reforms during his tenure, including universal health coverage and an end to university fees, which enabled students from relatively modest households like Gillard's to go on to college. Whitlam faced so much opposition from more conservative factions in the federal parliament that he was removed from office by Australia's Governor-General—who represents the British monarch—and replaced by a rival in what was widely viewed as a shocking moment of political skullduggery and prompted a minor constitutional crisis, accompanied by large-scale street protests.

Gillard began classes at the University of Adelaide in 1979. At the time, Whitlam's successor, Malcolm Fraser, had been in office for two terms as head of government and chief of the Liberal Party of Australia, the country's center-right party. The Liberals would remain in office until 1983 and carried out major spending-reduction cuts. The Treasury minister, a Liberal Member of Parliament named John Howard, was a particularly reviled figure among university students for the major cutbacks he made in educational aid. Gillard became involved in the organized student protests against these budget cuts, and she rose to the post of president of the Adelaide University Union. She also became involved in the student wing of the ALP.

In 1983, Gillard was elected president of the Australian Union of Students (AUS) after moving to Melbourne, another major city, where she continued her education at the University of Melbourne. She earned her law degree in 1987 and joined the firm of Slater & Gordon in Melbourne. As an attorney she specialized in industrial law cases, representing trade unions in various court battles, and was made partner three years after she joined, making the 29 year old the youngest partner ever in Slater & Gordon history.

Gillard was pulled toward politics as she entered her thirties. Twice, she tried to run for office in Victoria, the state in which Melbourne is located, but failed to secure a spot on the ALP ballot in regional parliamentary elections. In 1996, she switched careers and went to work for John Brumby, a lawmaker in the Victorian Legislative Council, as chief of staff. At the time, Brumby was head of the Victoria ALP. By this point the national ALP had been ousted from power by the Liberal Party, which was now headed by Howard, the former Treasurer, who served as Australia's prime minister.

Since Gough's era the ALP had been split along the lines of two major factions: the Socialist Left and the Labor Right. Gillard was part of the Socialist Left, which promoted a progressive social agenda. She became active in the move to bring more women into the ALP political fold, especially as candidates at the state and federal parliamentary levels, and finally won a slot on the ALP ballot in the 1998 federal elections. She won a seat in the lower house of the Parliament of Australia, the House of Representatives, from Lalor, a Melbourne suburb that was a traditional ALP stronghold. In her first speech in the House, she laid out her commitment to the leftist ideals of the ALP. Her party rejected the Liberals' belief in "the survival of the fittest," she asserted, and instead "understands that, just like the most loving homes produce the confident kids who are able to face the world and take the risks necessary to get ahead, a nurturing and caring society is the best foundation for the individuals who will ensure Australia competes in the global market."

Known for her debating prowess since her Unley High School days, Gillard arrived in Canberra—the federal capital—with several years of litigation experience behind her. Howard's Liberal Party remained in office until 2007, and she gained national prominence for her spirited assails to the Prime Minister and his cabinet ministers during the daily Question Time session. She rose to hold several "shadow" cabinet posts, the term given to the opposition party's spokespersons on various issues, including shadow minister for population and immigration and shadow minister for reconciliation and indigenous affairs. From 2003 to 2006 she served as shadow minister for health, and in that role often sparred quite publicly with Howard's Health Minister, Tony Abbott.

Gillard was widely predicted to be a frontrunner for a shot at the ALP leadership in 2006, but chose not to run. Instead a career diplomat, Kevin Rudd, became the party leader, and named her to serve as his deputy. Nearly a year later, in late November of 2007, the ALP won so large a majority of seats in Australia's Parliament that the election was quickly dubbed a "Ruddslide" in the media. With that, Gillard became Rudd's deputy prime minister. Rudd also gave her enormous cabinet responsibilities, naming her to head a newly created Department of Education, Employment, and Workplace Relations.

Rudd also named Gillard to serve as Australia's first Minister for Social Inclusion, a department whose existence demonstrated the country's efforts to eradicate discrimination and bias. Nevertheless, Australia remained a step or two behind the rest of the industrialized world, and its politicians were known to make some shocking gaffes. One of them was Liberal MP Bill Heffernan, who several months before the November election told a magazine that Gillard—who had never married and had no children—was unfit for a leadership role because she was "deliberately barren." After a barrage of criticism—including a telephone rebuke from John Howard, still the Prime Minister—Heffernan publicly apologized to Gillard for his statements, which included the assertion that "if you're leader, you've got to understand your community," Heffernan said, according to the Brisbane *Courier Mail*. "One of the great understandings in a community is family and the relationship between mum, dads, and a bucket of nappies."

As Rudd's deputy, Gillard served as acting prime minister on several occasions when Rudd was out of the country. In 2009 and 2010, however, Rudd became embroiled in a series of leadership crises, including a decision to table an important piece of climate-change legislation, which had been a significant part of the ALP campaign platform. Rudd also earned scorn for a plan to levy a so-called supertax on profits earned by mining companies in Australia, arguing that prices on the commodities markets had soared in recent years and that the current business tax rate was inadequate.

Late on the evening of June 23, 2010, Rudd announced that he and Gillard would submit their names to a vote of 115 ALP lawmakers in a caucus vote; in the closed-door session, Rudd apparently backed down when it appeared he could not rouse sufficient support. Many Australians woke up on June 24 to news that Gillard was the new leader of the ALP, the first woman to head the party since its creation in 1891. Later in the day Rudd resigned as prime minister, and the Governor-General of Australia, Quentin Bryce, appointed Gillard as prime minister in one of the vestigial remnants of British crown power allowed by Australia's constitution.

After working to solve some of the crises of the Rudd government, including a compromise on the mining tax, Gillard announced elections would be held on August 21, 2010. She spent a month campaigning the entire continent, and faced Abbott, the former Health Minister who had become Liberal leader. Neither party won a majority of seats, resulting in a hung parliament for the first time in 70 years. Several Green Party legislators and a few independent MPs voiced their assent for a Gillard-led government, however, and Bryce—Australia's first female Governor-General—administered the oath of office to Gillard for a second time on September 14, 2010.

Both John and Moira Gillard lived to witness their daughter's triumph as Australia's first female prime minister. A few weeks after her swearing-in, Gillard moved into the official prime minister's residence in Canberra, a 1927 villa known as The Lodge, with her partner, Tim Mathieson, a hairdresser whom the Australian media quickly dubbed "First Bloke."

Sources

Periodicals

Australian Women's Weekly, August 25, 2010.
Courier Mail (Brisbane, Australia), May 2, 2007.
Guardian (London, England), August 14, 2010, p. 22.

Online

"About the PM," Prime Minister of Australia, http://www.pm.gov.au/Meet_the_PM/About_the_PM (October 6, 2010).

"Hon Julia Gillard MP, Member for Lalor (Vic)," Parliament of Australia, House of Representatives, http://www.aph.gov.au/house/members/firstspeech.asp?id=83L (October 6, 2010).

"Our Julia," *The Age,* http://www.theage.com.au/news/management/our-julia/2007/05/18/11789953.tif71860.html?page=fullpage#contentSwap2 (October 2, 2010).

Transcripts

Australian Story, Australian Broadcasting Corporation, March 6, 2006.

—*Carol Brennan*

Selena Gomez

Actress and singer

Born Selena Marie Gomez, July 22, 1992, in Grand Prairie, TX; daughter of Ricardo Gomez and Amanda Cornett.

Addresses: *Agent*—Creative Artists Agency, 2000 Avenue of the Stars, Los Angeles, CA 90067. *Office*—c/o Hollywood Records, 500 South Buena Vista St., Burbank, CA 91521. *Web site*—http://www.myspace.com/selenagomez; http://twitter.com/selenAgomeZ; http://www.facebook.com/Selena.

Career

Actress on television, including: *Barney & Friends*, PBS, 2001-03; *Walker, Texas Ranger: Trial by Fire* (movie), 2005; *Brain Zapped* (movie), 2006; *The Suite Life of Zack and Cody*, Disney Channel, 2006; *Arwin!*, Disney Channel, 2007; *What's Stevie Thinking?* (pilot), Disney Channel, 2007; *Hannah Montana*, Disney Channel, 2007-08; *Wizards of Waverly Place*, Disney Channel, 2007—; *Princess Protection Program* (movie), Disney Channel, 2009; *Sonny With a Chance*, Disney Channel, 2009; *The Suite Life on Deck*, Disney Channel, 2009; *Wizards of Waverly Place: The Movie*, Disney Channel, 2009. Film appearances include: *Spy Kids 3-D: Game Over*, 2003; *Another Cinderella Story*, 2008; *Horton Hears a Who!* (voice), 2008; *Arthur and the Revenge of Maltazard* (voice), 2009; *Ramona and Beezus*, 2010. Also a singer who recorded as a solo artist and with the band Selena Gomez & the Scene, 2009; named a UNICEF ambassador, 2009; launched fashion line, Dream Out Loud by Selena Gomez, 2010.

Awards: ALMA Award for actress in a television—comedy, National Council of La Raza, for *Wizards of Waverly Place*, 2009; Kids' Choice Award for favorite television actress, Nickelodeon, for *Wizards of Waverly Place*, 2009; Teen Choice Award for choice summer TV star: female, for *Princess Protection Program*, 2009; Young Artist Award for best performance in a TV movie, miniseries or special—leading young actress, Young Artist Foundation, for *Another Cinderella Story*, 2009.

Sidelights

The star of the hit Disney Channel series *Wizards of Waverley Place*, Selena Gomez not only was a gifted, up-and-coming young actress but a singer who released her first album in 2009. She began acting as a child in Texas and came to the attention of Disney executives at an open casting call. After moving to Los Angeles, Gomez landed the lead in *Wizards* and began appearing in high-profile television movies and films. While working, she used her spare time to record her album, start a fashion line, and pursue philanthropy, including serving as a UNICEF ambassador. Of her life, Gomez told Maxine Shen of the *New York Post,* "I don't really like to rest too much.... I do constantly like to work. I believe that it keeps me going and makes me happy."

Born on July 22, 1992, she was the daughter of Ricardo Gomez and Amanda "Mandy" Cornett. Her father was of Mexican descent and a native of New

Mexico, while her mother was of Italian extraction. Gomez was named after popular Tejano pop singer Selena Quintanilla Perez of whom her father was a big fan. Explaining her connection to the singer, Gomez told Andrea Peyser of the *New York Post* in 2008, "She passed away when I was two. I was the girl who visited her grave. I went to her house. She wanted to be an actress. I'm trying to be a singer.... We're so much alike in all these ways. I'm keeping her name alive."

Gomez's mother was only 16 years old when she gave birth to her daughter. Though her parents were married, they divorced when Gomez was five years old. She was raised in Dallas primarily by her mother, an amateur actress who appeared in local and community theater productions but sometimes lived paycheck to paycheck. Influenced by her mother's hobby, Gomez began acting as a child. She landed a regular role on the popular television series for preschoolers, *Barney & Friends*, after auditioning at an open call. Gomez played Gianna for two years, beginning in 2001. She credited the experience with teaching her much about acting. She told Richard Huff of the New York *Daily News*, "I learned a lot from that. I didn't know anything about 'Downstage,' or 'Go, camera left' or 'Go, camera right.'".

Over the next few years, Gomez acted on a limited basis, but as she explained to Huff of the *Daily News*, "I was just having fun with it, and it turned into something I was really passionate about." Gomez landed more work in Texas. In 2003, for example, she had a small role in the film *Spy Kids 3-D: Game Over*. Two years later, she played Julie, a bit part, in the television movie *Walker, Texas Ranger: Trial by Fire*. Gomez was educated in local public schools, including Danny Jones Middle School.

Discovered by Disney in a nationwide open casting call held in Austin, Texas, Gomez flew to audition for a pilot in California a few weeks later. Her mother made sure that Gomez remained grounded as fame neared. Gomez explained to *Inside Bay Area*'s Chuck Barney, "She has me do my own laundry and help out with the dishes and clean my room. Before we got to California, she told me, 'You're going to hear the word yes a lot. You're this. You're that. Yes-yes-yes. So I'm the one who's going to tell you no—only because I love who you are now, and I don't want you to change.'"

While Gomez landed the part, the pilot was not picked up, but her career began taking off with work on Disney Channel shows beginning in 2006.

She played Gwen in a guest spot on the long-running Disney Channel series *The Suite Life of Zack and Cody* in 2006. That year, she also played Emily Grace Garcia in the television movie *Brain Zapped*. Gomez recorded a song for the film as well. In 2007 and 2008, Gomez played Mikayla, in the Disney Channel hit series, *Hannah Montana*. Gomez's character was a mean singing rival to the titular character in several episodes.

The Disney Channel tried to find a starring vehicle for Gomez, who had permanently moved from Dallas to Los Angeles with her mother and stepfather. In 2007, she landed roles in two spin-off pilots—including the lead in *What's Stevie Thinking?*—but neither were picked up as a series. Later that year, Gomez had the first big break of her career when she was cast as Alex Russo in the Disney Channel series *Wizards of Waverly Place*. She had to audition three times to gain the role.

In *Wizards*, Gomez's character was a member of a New York City-based bicultural family, the Russos, that reflected her own ethnic heritage: an Italian-American father and a Mexican-American mother. The family operates a sandwich shop, but her television father also happens to be from a wizard family. His three children—Alex and her two brothers—are wizards with magical powers as well and undergo training under their father's tutelage. Gomez's Alex is rather rebellious in many aspects of her life, but a naturally talented wizard. She and her brothers use magic to help themselves, often with unintended consequences.

Explaining the appeal of *Wizards*, Gomez told Jennifer Frey of the *Washington Post*, "The reason why it's so successful, and especially for young kids, is because kids wish they could be invisible and kids wish they could rewind time. And we bring that on screen. I know I wished that when I was younger."

In 2008, Gomez branched out into big roles in films. That year, she played Mary in *Another Cinderella Story*, based on the classic fairytale. Also in 2008, she contributed a voice to the animated feature film version of *Horton Hears a Who!* Her Helga was the daughter of a character voiced by popular comedic actor Steve Carell. In 2009, Gomez provided the voice of Selenia in another animated feature, *Arthur and the Revenge of Maltazard*.

While continuing to appear on *Wizards of Waverly Place*, Gomez took leading roles in two Disney Channel movies in 2009. *Princess Protection Program* co-starred Demi Lovato, her closest friend, fellow

Texan, and the star of the Disney Channel series *Sonny With a Chance*. Gomez did a guest spot on *Sonny* as herself in 2009. Gomez and Lovato also had a web series together, *The Demi and Selena Show*.

In *Princess*, Gomez's Carter was a tomboy who helps Lovato's threatened Latina princess hide her identity and pretend to be a normal teenager. In turn, Lovato's character tries to convince her to glam up. Gomez explained to Lindsay E. Sammon of *Footwear News*, "I have to dress her down, and she tries to dress me up. [Demi's] character has never worn sneakers before, and I have her wearing Converse, while she tries to put me in heels. So it's cool to see the characters switch up."

Also in 2009, *Wizards of Waverly Place: The Movie* aired on Disney Channel. The movie was an extended adventure for Gomez's television series. Shot in Puerto Rico, Los Angeles, and New York City, the *Wizards* movie focuses on a family vacation gone awry when Gomez's Alex casts a spell that erases the day her parents met after her best friend Harper is left behind. The consequences are dramatic as the parents then do not know each other and their children might cease to exist. The movie also moves the series closer to the wizard competition that the three siblings must go through to see which one of them will end up inheriting the right to wizard powers as an adult.

Discussing the transformation of her character in the movie, Gomez told Melissa Rentería of *Conexión*, "It takes my character to a whole new level. It shows the sweeter side of Alex that you don't always see. She's a tomboy, very independent and strong. I am like her in that sense, but I don't think I'd get in as much trouble as her."

As Gomez's acting career took off, she continued to have an interest in singing as well. When she was 16 years old, she signed a recording deal with Hollywood Records, a subsidiary of Disney. While Gomez had contributed a few songs to various soundtracks over the years and performed the theme song to *Wizards*, she focused on making her first full-length album something on which to build a career. Not wanting to be a solo artist, she formed a band known as Selena Gomez & the Scene and began recording in her spare time.

She released her first album in 2009, the best-seller *Kiss & Tell*, and had hit singles with "Naturally" and "Falling Down." Featuring a sound influenced by techno, pop, and rock, it was lyrically inspired by Gomez's life at the time. She told Lauren Water-

man of *Teen Vogue*, "It's what I've gone through with heartache, friendships, and things like that. I want my fans to know me a little bit better after they hear this record." Gomez and her band also toured in support of *Kiss & Tell* in late 2009 and early 2010.

Gomez continued acting around the release and tour, filming the next season of *Wizards of Waverly Place* as well as a feature film, *Ramona and Beezus*. The film was based on the beloved children's book by Beverly Cleary and was scheduled for release in 2010. Gomez played Beatrice "Beezus" Quimby in *Ramona and Beezus*.

Away from acting and singing, Gomez was home-schooled and hoped to attend college (preferably Northwestern University) when *Wizards* finished its run. Her goal was to transition into an adult acting career away from series television. She was also an enthusiastic sports fan, especially NBA basketball and the San Antonio Spurs. In addition, she enjoyed cooking, photography, and fashion. She planned on launching her first clothing brand, Dream Out Loud by Selena Gomez in the fall of 2010. Gomez was especially active in charitable and philanthropic causes. In 2009, she was named ambassador to UNICEF and visited Ghana that year on her first mission. She is the youngest person ever to be named a UNICEF ambassador. Gomez was also involved with the Raise Hope for Congo charity, which helps raise awareness about violence against women in the Congo.

While her fame afforded many opportunities to help, it was still difficult for the young actress. Gomez told Bill Harris in the *Sarnia Observer*, "The hardest part for me is the fame part. I love that kids look up to me. But people start getting curious about personal life, which makes me kind of sad, because then I know it's not about the career any more, it's about who I'm friends with. That's a bit of a bummer. But that's OK, I know it comes with it."

Selected discography

(As Selena Gomez & the Scene) *Kiss & Tell*, Hollywood Records, 2009.

Sources

Periodicals

Columbus Dispatch (OH), September 5, 2009, p. 6D.
Conexión, August 27, 2009, p. 12CX.
Daily News (NY), October 10, 2007, p. 86.

East Valley Tribune (Mesa, AZ), December 12, 2009.

Footwear News, May 11, 2009, p. 20.

Inside Bay Area (CA), February 7, 2008.

Morning Call (Allentown, PA), February 13, 2010, p. E8.

Newsday (NY), October 11, 2009, p. 1.

New York Post, September 10, 2008, p. 55; June 17, 2009, p. 68; August 23, 2009, p. 3.

San Antonio Express-News, October 10, 2007, p. 1G; June 24, 2009, p. 1F.

Sarnia Observer (Ontario, Canada), June 19, 2009, p. B3.

Teen Vogue, June-July 2009, p. 98.

USA Today, June 23, 2009, p. 4D.

Washington Post, October 19, 2007, p. C7.

Women's Wear Daily, October 15, 2009, sec. 1, p. 12.

Online

"Selena Gomez," Internet Movie Database, http://www.imdb.com/name/nm1411125/ (March 3, 2010).

—*A. Petruso*

Mary Gordon

Educator

Born c. 1947 in Newfoundland, Canada. *Education:* Teachers' College, 1969.

Addresses: *Office*—c/o Roots of Empathy, 250 Ferrand Drive, Ste. 800, Toronto, ON Canada, M3C 3G8.

Career

Began working as a kindergarten teacher, 1969; founded Parenting and Family Literacy Centres, 1981; founded Roots of Empathy, 1996; founded Seeds of Empathy and published *Roots of Empathy: Changing the World Child by Child*, 2005.

Member: Executive board of directors, Ashoka Foundation.

Awards: Ashoka Fellow, 2002; member, Order of Canada, 2006; Public Education Advocacy Award, Canadian Teachers' Federation, 2009; Queen's Golden Jubilee medal.

Sidelights

Childcare expert and educator Mary Gordon is best known as the founder of the innovative educational programs Roots of Empathy and Seeds of Empathy. Formed in 1996 in Gordon's native Canada, Roots of Empathy aims to instill feelings of kindness and respect for others through understanding their feelings—in short, empathy—in elementary and middle school students through guided classroom observations of the relationship between infants and their parents. The Seeds of Empathy program provides much the same experience, but for younger children enrolled at childcare facilities. Since its formation, the Roots of Empathy program has reached young people in Canada, the United States, New Zealand, and the United Kingdom. It has attracted worldwide notice for its successes in building emotional literacy, with respected peace advocate the Dalai Lama recognizing it as a powerful tool for building world peace.

Gordon grew up in the Canadian province of Newfoundland as part of a large family. Her parents encouraged the development of civic pride and social consciousness in their children through such means as allowing discussion of ideas rather than of daily events at the family dinner table. "There was definitely a sense that you were a citizen," Gordon later recalled in a biography on the Ashoka Web site, "and that you were lucky for that." She attended teaching college and became a kindergarten teacher after completing her degree in 1969.

As a teacher, Gordon quickly realized that family interaction lay at the heart of childhood development. To encourage family support of young people, she founded Parenting and Family Literacy Centres in 1981, the first of their kind in Canada. Based in schools, these centers have grown greatly since their initial appearance in Toronto to encompass hundreds of schools throughout the province of Ontario, many of them in low-income, high dropout-risk areas. The success of these centers in Canada led to their use as a model in other countries, and Gordon herself has traveled to nations including South Africa in her role as a parenting expert.

Despite the spread of the Parenting and Family Literacy Centres, Gordon remains better known for her next creation: Roots of Empathy. Also based in Gordon's adopted hometown of Toronto, the Roots of Empathy program further built upon the educator's belief in the importance of family interaction in childhood development. Due to her years developing the Parenting and Family Literacy Centres, Gordon had a great deal of experience working with parents who treated their children poorly, neglecting or even abusing them. As David Bornstein explained in an online *New York Times* feature on Roots of Empathy, "Gordon had found many of [the parents] to be lacking in empathy for their children. They hadn't developed the skill because they hadn't experienced or witnessed it sufficiently themselves. She envisioned Roots as a seriously proactive parent education program—one that would begin when the mothers- and fathers-to-be were in kindergarten."

In order to introduce children to healthy, supportive family interaction, Gordon developed a program based on a series of monthly visits by an infant and one of his or her parents, typically the mother. Each infant is just two to four months old at the time of the first visit at the beginning of the school year. Classroom instructors conduct a 40-minute pre-visit lesson with students following Roots of Empathy's standard curriculum. During the 40-minute visit with the infant, students attempt to understand and describe the infant's feelings. "It's a launch pad for them to understand their own feelings and the feelings of others," Gordon told Bornstein in the same *New York Times* feature. "It carries over to the rest of class." A 40-minute post-visit lesson wraps up the cycle, which is repeated for each of the school year's nine months. Students participate in the program beginning in kindergarten through the seventh grade, giving them a long-term basis to develop emotional literacy skills.

Independent research has repeatedly shown that this educational program works, although Gordon is among the first to admit that empathy is not nec- essarily a skill that can taught, but rather one that is gained through exposure and personal emotional development. Writing for the *Huffington Post* in 2010, Gordon noted that studies have shown that "children experiencing Roots of Empathy have dramatically reduced levels of aggression and increased levels of social and emotional literacy. The program reduces bullying, creates a positive foundation for mental health, teaches children about responsible and responsive parenting, and creates an environment where vulnerable kids become more resilient and aggressive or dominant children become more inclusive.... Giving children Roots of Empathy is like providing societal rocket fuel so that empathy can thrive."

In 2005, Gordon published *Roots of Empathy: Changing the World Child by Child.* The book went on to become a Canadian best-seller and was named one of the top 100 books of the year by Canadian newspaper *Globe and Mail.* Writing in that newspaper, Keith Oatley declared the book "impressive" and praised the Roots of Empathy program as "a bold and wonderful idea." That same year, Gordon expanded the program to include younger children in a sister Seeds of Empathy program. By 2010, Seeds of Empathy had spread beyond Canada's borders, with schools in Seattle, Washington, becoming the first international affiliates.

Gordon's efforts have earned her numerous accolades. In 2002, she was made the first female Ashoka Canadian Fellow in recognition of her social entrepreneurship. She was invested as a member of the Order of Canada in 2006; that same year, Gordon was invited to speak with the Dalai Lama about her programs during a visit by the leader to British Columbia. Gordon has also received the Queen's Golden Jubilee medal and the 2009 Public Education Advocacy Award.

Gordon continues to work tirelessly for greater empathetic development both through her programs and by sharing her own personal expertise. In September of 2010, she spoke before the United Nations as part of a literacy symposium held for the United Nations International Literacy Day Celebration in New York City, marking the first time that emotional literacy was included in the event. During 2010–11, the Roots of Empathy program was anticipated to expand to new international locations, including Scotland, the Republic of Ireland, and Northern Ireland.

Selected writings

Selected writings

Roots of Empathy: Changing the World Child by Child, Thomas Allen & Son Ltd. (Markham, ON), 2005.

Sources

Periodicals

Globe and Mail, January 28, 2006, p. D4.
Time, May 24, 2010.

Online

"About Mary Gordon," Roots of Empathy, http://www.rootsofempathy.org/Mary.html (November 26, 2010).

"'Empathic Civilization': Building A New World One Child At A Time," *Huffington Post*, http://www.huffingtonpost.com/mary-gordon/empathic-civilization-bui_b_464359.html (November 26, 2010).

"Fighting Bullying with Babies," *New York Times*, http://opinionator.blogs.nytimes.com/2010/11/08/fighting-bullying-with-babies/ (November 26, 2010).

"History and Milestones," Roots of Empathy, http://www.rootsofempathy.org/history.html (November 26, 2010).

"Mary Gordon," Ashoka, http://www.ashoka.org/fellow/mgordon (November 26, 2010).

"Mary Gordon," PBS Global Tribe: Voices, http://www.pbs.org/kcet/globaltribe/voices/voi_gordon.html (November 26, 2010).

—Vanessa E. Vaughn

Toni Griffin

Urban planner

Born Toni L. Griffin, c. 1964, in Chicago, IL. *Education:* University of Notre Dame, B.Arch., 1986; Harvard University Graduate School of Design, Loeb Fellow.

Addresses: *Office*—City of Detroit, Planning and Development Department, 65 Cadillac Sq., Ste. 2300, Detroit, MI 48226.

Career

Architect, Skidmore, Owings & Merrill LLP, then associate partner, 1986-98; vice president for planning and tourism development, Upper Manhattan Empowerment Zone Development Corporation, 1998-2000; deputy director for neighborhood planning, Office of Planning, Washington, DC, 2000-02; deputy director for revitalization planning, Office of Planning, Washington, DC, 2000-05; vice president and director for design, Anacostia Waterfront Corporation, 2005-06; director, Division of Planning and Community Development, City of Newark, 2007—; adjunct associate professor of urban planning, Harvard University Graduate School of Design, 2009—; head of strategic planning team, City of Detroit, 2010—; founder and principal of eponymous consulting firm.

Member: American Institute of Architects, 1986-97; board of directors, Chicago Friends of Downtown, 1994-96; Mid-South Planning & Development Commission, Chicago, 1994-96; founder, Women in Planning & Development, 1994, then president 1996-97; Near North Redevelopment/Cabrini Green Hous-

ing Project, Chicago, 1995; Habitat for Humanity, Chicago, 1996; board of directors, Black Metropolis Convention and Tourism Council, 1996-97; advisory board, Cultural Facilities Fund, 1996-97; board member, U Street Theater Foundation, Washington, DC, 2005; Urban Land Institute, 2006; board member, Branch Brook Park Alliance, c. 2007—; board member, Newark Boys Chorus School, c. 2007—; board member, New Jersey Futures, c. 2007—; board member, Institute for Urban Design, 2010—.

Sidelights

Toni Griffin arrived in Detroit in 2010 to help reshape the ailing city for its fourth century. An urban planner with a background in architecture, Griffin came to the city with a resume that included stops in Harlem, Washington, D.C., and Newark, New Jersey. The Chicago native professed to being "a big city kid," according to Katie Wang of the Newark *Star-Ledger*. "I love big, urban, gritty cities. I love cities that are messy and eclectic. This is something to work with."

Born around 1964, Griffin spent her formative years on the South Side of Chicago and entered the University of Notre Dame, from which she earned a bachelor of architecture degree in 1986. She went to work for Skidmore, Owings & Merrill (SOM), a major international architectural firm based in Chicago, where she stayed for 12 years. SOM gained fame in the post-World War II years for constructing the "big box" glass-and-steel skyscrapers, including a pair of Windy City landmarks that were, for many years, among the world's tallest buildings—the Sears Tower and the John Hancock Center. But Griffin was assigned to a job involving neighborhood revitalization for areas of Chicago still lagging after some devastating riots back in 1968, which piqued her interest in urban planning issues.

Griffin eventually went on to a Loeb Fellowship at the Harvard University Graduate School of Design, and was hired by the Upper Manhattan Empowerment Zone Development Corporation, which was set up under a new 1994 federal law to restore blighted areas of urban America. The Upper Manhattan area was one of nine designated federal empowerment zones to receive special funding and tax incentives, and Griffin served as vice president for planning and tourism development until 2000. In this capacity, she helped create the Harlem heritage tourism initiative, capitalizing on the neighborhood's unique historic character as a center of African-American culture.

In 2000, Griffin moved to the Washington, D.C., area to work for the city's Office of Planning. She spent the next five years as deputy director for revitalization planning, and then took a key executive position with the Anacostia Waterfront Corporation, which worked to restore a 45-acre parcel of land along the Anacostia River, which joins with the larger Potomac River in the southeast part of the nation's capital. This was a historically black part of the District of Columbia and had long been neglected in favor of other sites and landmarks.

Griffin eventually set up her own private consulting firm, named after herself and dedicated to urban projects, and took a teaching post with the Harvard University Graduate School of Design. In May of 2007 she was hired by Newark's recently elected mayor, Cory A. Booker, as director of community development. Booker, not yet 40 years old, had won the support of residents of beleaguered parts of the city for actually living in the public-housing complexes or neighborhoods where a majority of drug-related crimes occurred.

Griffin's job on the city of Newark payroll required that she establish residency in the city, and she found an apartment in the first new luxury multi-unit residential buildings in the city in four decades. On the job, she helped end a reliance on the so-called Bayonne box, named after the New Jersey city but used elsewhere in the empowerment-zone era of rebuilding across the United States. These were three-story units, ideally suited for narrow urban lots and cheap to build. She invited architects to submit redesigns for some of the Newark blocks where they predominated.

Griffin's main task, however, was drawing up Newark's master plan, which had not been updated since the late 1970s. "It's like cleaning out your closet," she said of the Newark job in the interview with Wang for the Star-Ledger. "It gets messy before you get nice and tidy again. This is not an overnight project." When Griffin took the job, her former boss in Washington, Andrew Altman, told Wang that Griffin "has a great sense of how to put planning and design in service of revitalizing a city, and not many people know how to merge planning, design and economic development in a way that can produce meaningful change."

Griffin's credentials brought her to the attention of a search committee in the metropolitan Detroit area looking for someone to spearhead a joint effort to rebuild the hard-hit Rust Belt city. Detroit had been steadily losing residents since the 1950s, but it was also a city that once boasted extraordinarily high home-ownership rates thanks to the automotive and manufacturing industries that flourished in the early twentieth century. As a result, by the dawn of the twenty-first century the city had lost more than half its population, along with sorely needed property tax revenues. The city's population had peaked at a high of 1.8 million in 1950, but had shrunk to half that by 2010, the year Griffin was hired for the job.

Griffin accepted the offer from the office of Detroit Mayor Dave Bing to head up the new urban planning initiative, but the city, facing a budget deficit of $85 million in 2010, could not even afford to pay her salary or those of any consultants she chose for her team, so those costs were covered by the Kresge Foundation, a private philanthropic foundation with long ties to the metro Detroit area. Griffin's primary goal was coming up with a new land-use policy for the city, which might include the consolidation of some neighborhoods. Spread out over 139 square miles, one-third of Detroit's residential parcels are uninhabited—listed either as vacant lots or empty buildings, many in dangerous condition.

Some Detroiters feared the planned "downsizing" of the city, to conserve already-overstretched city services, might mean the forcible relocation of households, but a few months after Griffin took the job Bing's office assured residents that there would be no such measures. The new Detroit Strategic Framework Plan would take shape through a series of town hall meetings planned for September of 2010, carried out under Griffin's office. "One reason for the slow pedaling is that Detroiters are notoriously skeptical of land-use proposals, scarred by the memory of past efforts to move people out of their homes and neighborhoods in the name of improving the city," explained *Wall Street Journal* writer Alex P. Kellogg about any new land-use master plan for Detroit. "Among the casualties of those efforts were communities like Poletown, a Polish enclave cleared by eminent domain to make way for a General Motors plant in 1981, and Black Bottom, a poor black neighborhood."

Sources

Periodicals

Detroit Free Press, August 17, 2010.
Detroit News, August 17, 2010.
New York Times, March 27, 2005; November 30, 2008.
Star-Ledger (Newark, NJ), November 18, 2007.
Time, March 29, 2010, p. 4.
Wall Street Journal, August 18, 2010.

Online

"Money Talks, Detroit Silenced," *Michigan Citizen*, http://michigancitizen.com/money-talks-detroit-silenced-p8758-1.htm (August 17, 2010).
Toni L. Griffin Web Site, http://tonilgriffin.com/default.aspx (September 23, 2010).

—*Carol Brennan*

Robert M. Groves

UPI/Bill Greenblatt/newscom

Director of U.S. Census Bureau

Born c. 1949; married Cynthia; children: Christopher, Andrew. *Education:* Dartmouth College, A.B. (summa cum laude), 1970; University of Michigan, two M.A.s, 1973, Ph.D., 1975.

Addresses: *Office*—U.S. Census Bureau, 4600 Silver Hill Rd., Washington, D.C. 20233. *Web site*—http://www.census.gov/.

Career

Worked as prison guard at Vermont State Prison, Windsor, VT, 1968; assistant study director, Center for Political Studies at the Institute of Social Research, University of Michigan, Ann Arbor, MI, 1971; graduate research assistant for the sampling section of the Institute of Social Research, 1973-75; lecturer in the department of sociology, University of Michigan, 1975-76, then assistant professor 1977-83, then associate professor, 1983-90, then professor, 1990—; study director, Survey Research Center, 1975-80, then coordinator of research services, 1982-85, then senior study director, 1980-88, then program director (senior research scientist), 1988-95, then director, 2001—; associate director, Joint Program in Survey Methodology at the University of Maryland, University of Michigan, and Westat, 1990-92, then director, 1996-2001; research professor, University of Michigan, 2002—; director, U.S. Census Bureau, 2009—.

Awards: Mecklin Sociology Prize, Dartmouth College, 1970; Brittingham Scholar Award, University of Wisconsin, 1996; Innovator Award, American Association for Public Opinion Research, 2000; award for exceptionally distinguished achievement, American Association for Public Opinion Research, 2001; book award (with Mick P. Couper), American Association for Public Opinion Research, for *Nonresponse in Household Interview Surveys*, 2008; Julius Shiskin Award for Economic Statistics, National Association for Business Economists/Washington Statistical Society, 2008; Helen Dinerman Award, World Association for Public Opinion Research, 2010; O'Neil Award, New York Association for Public Opinion Research.

Sidelights

University of Michigan sociology professor Robert M. Groves came to national prominence in 1990 and again in 2009 for his work on the U.S. census. A respected researcher who focused on improving response rates for surveys, he came under controversy for his stint as associate director for the U.S. Census Bureau in 1990 for suggesting the bureau use statistical sampling to account for undercounted population areas. Despite this uproar, Groves became head of the bureau in 2009 and successfully oversaw the 2010 census.

Born around 1949, Groves was a native of Kansas City. After completing high school, Groves entered

Dartmouth College. While a college student, he worked as a prison guard at the Vermont State Prison in 1968. Groves received his bachelor's in sociology summa cum laude from Dartmouth College in 1970. He then moved on to the University of Michigan where he earned two master's degrees, one in statistics and the other in sociology, in 1973, and his Ph.D. in sociology in 1975. While a graduate student, he conducted research on political statistical data as an assistant study director for the Center for Political Studies at the Institute of Social Research. Groves was also a graduate research assistant for the sampling section of the Institute of Social Research.

With degrees in hand, Groves was hired by the University of Michigan as a lecturer in the sociology department in 1975. He became an assistant professor in 1977, an associate professor in 1983, then full professor in 1990. Over the years, Groves' research focused on methods for improving response rates for surveys. Because of his research interests, he also worked with the University of Michigan's Survey Research Center. He served as a study director from 1975 to 1980, then took over various posts of increasing responsibility, including serving as program director from 1988 to 1995.

Groves published journal articles and books regularly over the course of his career, including 1989's *Survey Errors and Survey Costs,* which was named one of the most influential books in survey research by the American Association for Public Opinion Research (AAPOR). He also co-wrote the award-winning *Nonresponse in Household Interview Surveys* with Mick P. Couper and won an APPOR award in 2008. In addition to publishing academic pieces, Groves assisted in the development of surveys for various entities including the American Lung Association, the U.S. Bureau of Justice Statistics, the National Institutes of Health, and the A. C. Nielson Company.

In 1990, Groves took on new challenges when he became the associate director of statistical design, standards, and methodology for the U.S. Census Bureau, on loan from his duties at Michigan. Working on the 1990 census, he came under fire because he, as well as other officials, recommended that this census be adjusted statistically to compensate for undercounting five million people. Many people who were undercounted were minorities who lived in urban areas. Because these often undercounted people tended to vote for Democrats, the idea of statistic compensation came under fire by Republicans as such numbers were used to appoint seats in the House of Representatives, draw Congressional boundaries, and allocate federal funds.

During the ensuing political debate, the Census Bureau's use of statistic compensation was overruled by the Robert Mosbacher, the Republican Commerce Secretary. In 1999, the Supreme Court ruled that statistical sampling could not be used for apportioning House seats but could be used to adjust the population count when re-drawing congressional boundaries and for appropriating funds. While the related court case was working its way through the court system, Groves had already returned to the University of Michigan, having gone back in 1992.

At Michigan, Groves resumed his professorship and work at the Survey Research Center. He also served as the associate director for the Joint Program in Survey Methodology from 1992 to 1996. The program was affiliated with the University of Michigan, the University of Maryland, and Westat. In 1996, Groves became the director of this program, a position he held until 2001. In this time period, Groves also became a research professor at the University of Maryland, a post he held beginning in 1995. In 2001, Groves became the director of the Survey Research Center at the University, while in 2002 he became a research professor for the University of Michigan, a position he held in addition to his other professorships and duties.

In April of 2009, Groves returned to national prominence when President Barack Obama nominated him to become the census director for the 2010 U.S. census. Groves' nomination was contentious as Republicans worried he again might try to use statistical sampling in census counts. Current Commerce Secretary Gary Locke assured them that there were no plans to use sampling for redistricting, though the process might be used in measuring census accuracy, for example. Because Groves was appointed so close to the 2010 census, he would have little time to make sampling part of the process. He had the power, however, to bring ideas like statistical adjustment to the forefront for future census surveys. Locke believed in Groves, telling Hope Yen of the Associated Press Financial Wire, "He is a respected social scientist who will run the Census Bureau with integrity and independence."

To squelch such controversy, Groves assured senators at his confirmation hearing in May 2009 that he would not use statistical sampling in the 2010 census. Because of ongoing concerns, his confirmation was put on hold by at least one Republican senator for months, though he was finally confirmed by the U.S. Senate on July 13, 2009. Groves began his term as director two days later. As the head of the Census Bureau, he hit the ground running to prepare for the 2010 census. Though he could not use sampling, Groves was charged with ensuring that minorities and residents of dense urban areas, who had been traditionally undercounted because of language problems and other issues, were counted. This issue remained controversial, but the federal government allotted about $250 million of one billion dollars in stimulus money for this effort.

In early 2010, Groves himself traveled by dogsled to Noorvik, Alaska, a 650-person Inuit village, to officially launch the census. It was not his only high-profile effort to raise awareness about the census. Groves also appeared on *The Daily Show* and taught children about the census by making an appearance with the *Sesame Street* character Count von Count. The U.S. Census Bureau also sponsored a NASCAR racing team for three races and aired an ad during the Super Bowl to raise awareness. The census went well, and, by July 2010, it was underbudget as it moved into quality assurance operations, including the checking of vacant households and verifying the existence of addresses.

The original cost of the 2010 census was estimated at $16 billion; however, Groves faced controversy when he announced that he would return at least $1.6 billion in operation savings. The final cost was expected to be only $14.5 billion, a figure that outraged some Congressman as the 2010 census was at least 54 percent more expensive than the 2000 version. Cost issues aside, Groves and the U.S. Census Bureau planned on presenting its findings on December 31, 2010. He also made plans for the next census, and hoped to add an online option for the 2020 census, though the whole process could not be digitized because of the nature of the data needed. As Groves explained to Haya El Nasser of *USA Today* of the digital process, "It won't solve all our problems. Some ideas will work. Some ideas won't."

Sources

Periodicals

Associated Press, April 2, 2009.
Associated Press Financial Wire, April 2, 2009.
Charleston Gazette (WV), January 17, 2010, p. 16A.
New York Times, May 16, 2009, p. A9; June 9, 2009, p. A26; July 17, 2009, p. A22.
Oklahoman (Oklahoma City, OK), May 4, 2010, p. 9A.
States News Service, August 10, 2010.
USA Today, July 7, 2010, p. 1A.
Waterloo Chronicle, January 25, 2010, p. 1.

Online

"Census Director Robert Groves presents status of 2010 Census to Michigan students, peers," *AnnArbor.com*, http://www.annarbor.com/news/census-director-robert-groves-presents-status-of-2010-census-to-michigan-students-peers/ (August 25, 2010).
"Curriculum Vitae: Robert M. Groves," University of Michigan Population Studies Center, http://www.psc.isr.umich.edu/people/cv/groves_robert_cv.pdf (August 25, 2010).
"Obama selects survey researcher Robert Groves for sensitive census post, annoying Republicans," Cleveland.com, http://www.cleveland.com/nation/index.ssf/2009/04/obama_selects_survey_researche.html August 25, 2010).
"Robert M. Groves, Director, U.S. Census Bureau," U.S. Census Bureau, http://www.census.gov/newsroom/releases/pdf/GrovesBio_on_letterhead.pdf (August 25, 2010).
"Robert M. Groves: Obama's Pick for Census Chief," *Time*, http://www.time.com/time/nation/article/0,8599,1889793,00.html (August 25, 2010).

—A. Petruso

Michael C. Hall

Cesar Cebolla/ALFAQUI/Newscom

Actor

Born Michael Carlisle Hall, February 1, 1971, in Raleigh, NC; son of William Carlyle (an IBM employee) and Janice (a high school counselor, maiden name Styons) Hall; married Amy Spanger (an actress), 2002 (divorced, 2007); married Jennifer Carpenter (an actress), December 31, 2008. *Education:* Earlham College, Richmond, Indiana, B.A., 1993; New York University, M.F.A., 1996.

Addresses: *Agent*—c/o Don Buchwald & Associates, 10 E. 44th St., New York, NY 10017.

Career

Actor in films, including: *Showboy,* 2002; *Paycheck,* 2003; *Gamer,* 2009; *East Fifth Bliss,* 2010; *Peep World,* 2010. Television appearances include: *Bereft* (movie), 2004; *Six Feet Under,* 2001-05; *Mysteries of the Freemasons* (narrator), 2006; *Dexter,* 2006—. Stage appearances include: *Henry V,* Public Theater, New York City, 1996; *Timon of Athens,* Public Theater, 1996; *Skylight,* Mark Taper Forum, Los Angeles, 1997-98; *Corpus Christi,* Manhattan Theatre Club, New York City, 1998; *Cymbeline,* Public Theater, 1998; *Macbeth,* Public Theater, 1998; *The English Teachers,* Manhattan Class Company, New York City, 1998-99; *Cabaret,* Roundabout Theatre, Broadway, New York City, 1999; *Wiseguys* (workshop), New York City, 1999; *Chicago,* Broadway, New York City, 2002; *Mr. Marmalade,* Laura Pels Theater, New York City, 2005.

Awards: Screen Actors Guild Award (with others) for outstanding performance by an ensemble in a drama series, Screen Actors Guild, for *Six Feet Un-*

der, 2003, 2004; Saturn Award for best actor in a television program, Academy of Science Fiction, Fantasy, & Horror Films, for *Dexter,* 2007; Satellite Award for best actor in a series—drama, International Press Academy, for *Dexter,* 2007; TCA Award for individual achievement in drama, Television Critics Association, for *Dexter,* 2007; Golden Globe Award for best performance by an actor in a television series—drama, Hollywood Foreign Press Association, for *Dexter,* 2010; Screen Actors Guild Award for outstanding performance by a male actor in a drama series, Screen Actors Guild, for *Dexter,* 2010.

Sidelights

Michael C. Hall is a man who has seen, been touched by, and impersonated death. He is an actor of exceptional talent who approaches the roles he portrays with an uncommon intelligence and his life experiences have given him a bank of understanding from which to draw from in order to bring life to the characters he portrays. His life has had drama in it including death in his family while he was a child and his own bout with cancer.

Hall was born in Raleigh, North Carolina, to William and Janice Hall. He was the second of two children but his sister died in infancy before his birth.

His father, who worked for IBM, died of prostate cancer when Hall was eleven years old. In an interview with Anne Stockwell for the *Advocate,* Hall said, "At that age … my father's death was a real maker. Certainly, for a young boy, there's no good age, but I think I was on the cusp of a time in my life where I was starting to reach puberty, to relate to my father—or as a result, I was becoming more like him. To have him [die].... Something gets frozen. As you revisit it for the rest of your life, it's sort of this slow but hopefully sure crawling-out of that frozen moment." In many odd ways death has defined Hall.

After the death of his father, Hall's mother went back to school and obtained her doctorate in education and became a guidance counselor. Because it was just the two of them, Hall's relationship with his mother was very close and strong. Hall attended Ravenscroft High School in Raleigh where he was a member of a chamber choir that toured Austria for ten weeks. In addition to singing in the choir, he also performed in several musicals. Most of the musicals were old standards like *Oklahoma, The Sound of Music,* and *Fiddler on the Roof.* Hall told Stockwell, "There was always an impulse to perform in one way or another. Most of my experiences performing growing up were doing musicals, singing, being in choirs—I sang in choirs when I was in college as well. I was a choir geek the first couple of years. Then I became a theater geek. I took an acting class my sophomore year and realized that in terms of [my] enthusiasm and aptitude, it was definitely the thing." After graduating from high school, Hall attended college at Earlham College in Richmond, Indiana. Originally he intended to become a lawyer, but changed his major and career plans during his undergraduate education to become an actor. After obtaining his bachelor's degree in 1993, he went on to do a masters of fine arts program at New York University.

While Hall was in New York for graduate school he found an agent and began performing in off-Broadway productions. He was an understudy for roles in *Henry V* and *Timon of Athens* at the New York Public Theater. He appeared in *Macbeth* and *Cymbeline* at the New York Shakespeare Festival. He appeared as the Apostle Peter in a homosexual-themed version of The Gospels titled, *Corpus Christi.* After this Hall appeared in Stephen Sondheim's workshop piece *Wiseguys,* directed by Sam Mendes. Mendes later cast Hall in *Cabaret.*

Mendes turned out to be a very beneficial contact for Hall. While Mendes was directing the film *American Beauty* he recommended Hall to Alan Ball who wrote *American Beauty* and later went on to create *Six Feet Under.* If Hall's relationship with death started before his birth with the death of his sister and then continued and was shaped by the death of his father, being cast as the character of David Fisher certainly extended this relationship. The character of David Fisher was a repressed gay man trying to come to terms with both his sexuality and his relationship with his dead father while running the family mortuary business that his father has left him. Hall's acting abilities on the television show not only gave him his first real on screen break, but also earned him an Emmy nomination in 2002 for outstanding actor in a drama series. The role in which Mendes cast Hall in *Cabaret* was that of the flamboyant Emcee. The character of David Fisher has been described as "closeted." James Donaghy writing for the *Guardian* has quoted Hall as saying, "Everything I opened up for *Cabaret,* I slammed shut for David." The theme of death and hiding emotions followed Hall into his next major project.

Hall's next major role was in the dark comedic television series for *Showtime* called *Dexter.* The character of Dexter Morgan is a blood-splattered forensics expert who lives and works in Miami. However, the blood splatters are not always a hazard of his job. Dexter Morgan is a serial killer. When the character was a very small child he was present at the brutal murder of his mother inside a shipping crate. The character and the character's brother were both present and left in the crate with the dead body of their mother. When the children were found by police officer Harry Morgan, they were traumatized and covered in blood. Harry decides to adopt the young Dexter.

In looking at the character of Dexter it is important to consider the character of Harry. As Dexter's adoptive father, he makes an unusual decision in the upbringing of his son as described in the character's history. When young Dexter begins to kill animals, Harry teaches Dexter how to kill and how not to get caught. Donaghy quoted Hall as saying about the character of Dexter, "Everything stems from the outside-the-box parenting style of his father. A man who sold Dexter on two ideas. One: He had no choice but to kill—that's what got into him too deeply and too early. And two: He had the capacity to do good." Donaghy quotes Hall as saying further, "It really was a simultaneously loving and manipulative act.... I probably think more about Dexter's father than Dexter does." Out of Harry's parenting comes what the character of Dexter calls "The Code of Harry" which is a code of conduct and a way for Dexter to pursue his desire to commit murder.

While a casual viewer of the television show could dismiss the character of Dexter as just another serial killer, the role is far more complicated. Hall told Claire Zulkey for the *Los Angeles Times* column "The Envelope," in regards to Dexter, "I think Dexter in spite of everything is an eminently relatable guy. We all have questions about our authenticity and have secrets that we keep that are potent in terms of our interior landscape. We all have a shadow side, maybe not as formidable on paper as Dexter's." Dexter does leave a trail of victims but he tries to only kill those individuals who escape justice. His victims include a child killer, a black widow, and a rapist-murderer. Further, he understands the mind of a serial killer and the patterning of blood splatters better than any other forensics expert. His sister, who is played by Hall's real life wife—Jennifer Carpenter—also works on the Miami-Dade police force and he has a familial relationship with her. The character of Dexter has a relationship and child with a woman named Rita who is the survivor of domestic abuse and prefers not to have sex, which is a decision that is fine with the character of Dexter who has difficulty relating to other people. Hall narrates the series in Dexter's deadpan voice and with his sometimes very insightful revelations about his own conflicted character. Speaking with CraveOnline, Hall said in regards to Dexter, "I think that's a part of my job, playing the character in spite of his claims of having a closed heart, to open my heart to him. The more I learn about Dexter as he learns about himself the more affection that I have for him, the more respect that I have for him too. We all have our shadow. His is about as formidable a shadow as you can imagine, but he's taking this unique responsibility for it. I admire him for that." The complexity of Dexter that includes both his humanity and his monstrosity makes the show's moral ambiguity fascinating. The series is always shocking and yet somehow believable in what it displays about the potentials of human behavior.

In addition to his portrayals on television series, Hall has also appeared in films. In 2003 he played an FBI agent hunting a computer engineer who was portrayed by Ben Affleck in director John Woo's film *Paycheck*. In 2004 he appeared in a made-for-television movie titled *Bereft*. In 2010 Hall worked on two films, *Peep World* and *East Fifth Bliss*.

In 2010 Hall earned two awards for the role of Dexter. He accepted the Golden Globe award for best performance by an actor in a television series—drama wearing a black knit hat. Gina Salamone writing for the New York *Daily News* quoted Hall as saying about the knit cap, "It's nice to have a justifiable excuse for accessorizing." Hall made no mention during his acceptance speech about the Hodgkin's lymphoma he was undergoing treatment

for, but his wearing of the knit cap put his battle with cancer front and center for everyone to see. Hodgkin's lymphoma is a type of cancer that affects the lymphatic system, part of the body's immune system. The announcement that Hall was diagnosed and being treated for Hodgkin's lymphoma was made on January 13, 2010, by his agent, only days before the Golden Globe ceremony. The type of lymphoma that Hall was diagnosed with is considered treatable and at the time of the announcement the cancer was in remission. According to Josh Grossberg of E! Online, Hall said in a statement, "I feel fortunate to have been diagnosed with an imminently treatable and curable condition, and I thank my doctors and nurses for their expertise and care."

Throughout Hall's appearances to accept both his Golden Globe Award and Screen Actors Award for outstanding performance by a male actor in a drama series, his wife has been by his side. Hall was married once before to Amy Spanger who was a cast mate in the musical *Chicago*. He was married to Spanger from 2002-07. Hall dated Carpenter, who plays Dexter's sister Deb, for about a year and a half before they married on December 31, 2008. Following the announcement of Hall's cancer, Carpenter told Access Hollywood, "Every second's special with him, it sounds corny but it's true. I'm very lucky."

The death of Hall's father and his tight relationship with his mother, his pursuit of acting, and his evident ability to reflect on his own internal thoughts are all things that have contributed to his ability to portray complicated characters who have secrets, are deeply conflicted, and are confronting the major issues of life. Even though Hall's cancer is in remission, it may still have an impact on him and be another potential life event that may inform the way that he approaches analyzing the psychology of the characters that he portrays. While his major roles thus far have been connected to death—a man whose family business is a mortuary and a forensics expert and serial killer—Hall brings a vibrant sense of reality to the characters that he portrays.

Sources

Books

Marquis Who's Who, Marquis Who's Who, 2010.

Periodicals

Advocate, June 8, 2004.
Guardian (London, England), July 7, 2007.
Los Angeles Times, July 7, 2007.

Online

"Dexter Season 2: Michael C. Hall Interview," CraveOnline, http://www.craveonline.com/entertainment/tv/article/dexter-season-2-michael-c-hall-interview-65323 (March 13, 2010).

"*Dexter*'s Michael C. Hall Has Cancer," *People*, http://www.people.com/people/article/0,,20336663.tif,00.html (March 13, 2010).

"Jennifer Carpenter on Husband Michael C. Hall's Cancer Battle: 'Every Second's Special,'" Access Hollywood, http://www.accesshollywood.com/jennifer-carpenter-on-husband-michael-c-halls-cancer-battle-every-seconds-special_article_27827 (March 13, 2010).

"Michael C. Hall and Jennifer Carpenter Are Married," E! Online, http://www.eonline.com/uberblog/watch_with_kristin/b78384_michael_c_hall_jennifer_carpenter_are.html (March 13, 2010).

"Michael C. Hall and Jennifer Carpenter at SAG Awards," *Examiner*, http://www.examiner.com/x-34874-Long-Island-Celebrity-Headlines-Examiner~y2010m1d24-Michael-C-Hall-and-Jennifer-Carpenter-at-SAG-Awards (March 13, 2010).

"Michael C. Hall, Globes winner for 'Dexter,' doing 'fine' in his battle with cancer," *Daily News*, http://www.nydailynews.com/entertainment/tv/2010/01/18/2010-01-18_michael_c_hall_globes_winner_for_dexter_doing_fine_in_his_battle_with_cancer.html (March 13, 2010).

"Michael C. Hall: Summary," TV.com, http://www.tv.com/michael-c.-hall/person/47125/summary.html (March 13, 2010).

—Annette Bowman

Bonnie Hammer

President of NBC Universal Cable

Born in 1950, in New York, NY; married Dale Huesner; children: two. *Education:* Boston University, B.A., 1971; M.A., 1975.

Addresses: *Office*—NBC Universal, 30 Rockefeller Plaza, New York City, NY 10112.

Charles Eshelman/FilmMagic/Getty Images

Career

Worked as a photojournalist; got started in television in Boston, mid-1970s-1984; director of development, Dave Bell Associates, 1985-87; programming executive, Lifetime network, 1987-89; vice president of original programming, USA Network, 1989-95, then vice president of original production, 1995-98; senior vice president, Sci-Fi programming and USA original productions, 1998-99; executive vice president and general manager, Sci-Fi Channel, 1999-01, then president, 2001-08; president, USA Network, NBC Universal, 2004-08; president of NBC Universal Cable, NBC Universal, 2008—.

Awards: Lillian Gish Award, Women in Film Festival, for documentary *Gangs: Not My Kid,* 1988; one of the 100 most powerful women in entertainment, *Hollywood Reporter,* 2006, 2007; Humanitarian Award, Anti-Defamation League, 2008; Vanguard Award, National Cable & Telecommunications Association, 2010.

Sidelights

Cable television executive Bonnie Hammer spent decades working her way up the entertainment ladder before becoming recognized as one of the industry's most powerful players. After beginning her media career as a photojournalist, Hammer made the leap into television in the mid-1970s, working on public television programming in the Boston area before shifting first into traditional network and later the cable television arenas. She served in successively more responsible roles before becoming head of the Sci-Fi Channel, boosting it to both critical acclaim and commercial success on the strength of programs such as *Battlestar Galactica.* Hammer's television savvy led to her continued rise when she was appointed the first president of the Sci-Fi Channel and, in 2008, head of NBC Universal's cable operations.

In her role as the president of NBC Universal Cable Entertainment and Universal Cable Productions, Hammer oversaw the growth the USA Network from a relatively sleepy cable outpost to a record-breaking ratings behemoth. By 2008, Hammer's flagship network had become so popular with viewers that its ratings topped those of the CBS-owned

CW Network—the first time that a cable network had attracted a larger audience than a traditional over-the-air offering. In late 2010, Hammer took on still greater responsibility in the corporate reorganization that was announced as the Comcast-NBC Universal merger awaited approval from government regulators. Under the new structure, Hammer was slated to oversee the operation and programming for a host of cable channels, including E!, G4, Chiller, and Sleuth alongside the USA Network and the renamed SyFy.

Born in 1950, Hammer grew up as the youngest of the three children of a Russian immigrant father and stay-at-home mother in Queens, New York. Her father started a successful pen company, enabling the family to enjoy a comfortable middle-class lifestyle. "My parents did great and provided well, and gave all their kids personal, moral, ethical values, not a belief that we were entitled to something," Hammer recalled in a profile on the Web site of the Paley Center for the Media. As a girl, Hammer regularly attended Broadway productions and took lessons in piano, voice, and drama, helping her form an early interest in the arts and entertainment fields, particularly in photography.

After completing high school, Hammer enrolled at Boston University to study communications. She earned a bachelor's degree in 1971, and began taking the first steps into her then-chosen profession of photojournalism by working in a local darkroom. However, Hammer soon decided that she wished to pursue graduate studies, managing to land a spot in her alma mater's already full program. By the time Hammer completed her master's degree in media and new technology in 1975, she had already shot photographs that had appeared in such major publications as the *Boston Herald*, the *Los Angeles Times*, and *Time* magazine.

Despite a burgeoning career as a respected photojournalist, Hammer took a detour that proved fateful in the mid-1970s when she accepted a job as a temporary production assistant on the PBS children's series *Infinity Factory*. Initially attracted by the prospect of making some extra money, she quickly became intrigued by the process of making television programs. Her work on *Infinity Factory* was far from glamorous; one of her main duties was cleaning up after a sheep dog. "When people whine about paying dues, I just think, 'You don't know how easy you've got it,'" she noted wryly in a 2000 interview with Deborah D. McAdams of *Broadcasting & Cable*.

With her graduate studies behind her, Hammer next took a job with local PBS affiliate WGBH's *This Old House* and *Zoom* before moving into private net-work programming in a position with a Boston-based morning talk show, *Good Day!*, that aired on the city's ABC affiliate. Speaking to *TelevisionWeek*'s James Hibberd in 2005, Hammer recalled, "I went from the public broadcasting arena ... where the kind of attitude was 'We don't care who watches as long as it's quality,' to the ABC affiliate, which was 'We don't care about the quality necessarily, as long as people watch.' So it was a great education on two really opposing points of view." By the mid-1980s, she had traded in New England for the West Coast, joining the development staff at Los Angeles' Dave Bell Associates. There, she oversaw the production of the program *Alive and Well*.

Hammer's work with Dave Bell Associates soon segued into a position as a junior programming executive with the then-relatively new women's cable network, Lifetime, back in New York City. "We'd do documentaries about women's issues on a shoestring budget and then sit in [a colleague's] apartment in the Village drinking a bottle of wine and watching the rough cuts," she recalled to Stuart Miller of *Broadcasting & Cable* in a 2007 interview. Despite the shoestring budgets and lack of a marketing plan, those Lifetime documentaries achieved respectable ratings figures and encouraged Hammer to stick with the fledging cable programming industry.

Although Hammer enjoyed her time with the Lifetime network, she left in 1989 to become a vice-president of original programming with the USA Network. The transition from the female-focused shows of Lifetime to the rough-and-tumble programming of the USA Network, then dominated by broadcasts of World Wrestling Federation (WWF), was a bumpy one. Then-network president Ron Perth assigned Hammer to take over the WWF programming much to her initial dismay. "I had never watched wrestling, and it was just so against anything I would ever consider doing," she explained to Hibberd in the same *TelevisionWeek* profile. Ever a risk taker, however, Hammer decided to give wrestling a chance and met with the WWF. She confessed her ignorance of the sport, but declared her intention to produce good, entertaining wrestling programming. The unlikely partnership became a fruitful one, with viewership of wrestling nearly tripling under Hammer's guidance.

Hammer remained with the USA Network through much of the 1990s, leaving only in 1999 to join the Sci-Fi Channel. Among her first major tasks at that network was rebranding the somewhat geeky image of science fiction programming to appeal to a broader audience. An opportunity to do just that soon landed on her desk when renowned director Steven Spielberg agreed to pen a miniseries for the network. Aired in December of 2002, "Steven Spielberg Presents: Taken" made the Sci-Fi Channel the highest-rated cable network during its two-week, 20-hour run. "We wanted to create an event, something other channels hadn't done before," Hammer said in a *Rocky Mountain News* story by Mark Wolf. "In a way, we're taking a risk, trying to go back to the old days when miniseries were short bursts of great programming that took over a channel for a week or so." The alien abduction-themed miniseries cost millions to make but reaped significant rewards for its home network, with the Sci-Fi Channel garnering an Emmy Award and winning over potential new viewers who had previously ignored its standard repeats of *Star Trek* episodes. Another science fiction miniseries, *Battlestar Galactica*, premiered on the channel in December 2003 to great success, ultimately becoming a long-running and critically lauded series.

In 2004, NBC Universal acquired both the Sci-Fi Channel and the USA Network. NBC Universal executives respected Hammer's proven abilities to rebrand cable networks and to build ratings, so they placed her in charge of both the Sci-Fi Channel and the USA Network. One of Hammer's first tasks as the head of the USA Network was to help it forge a new brand identity. Much as she had transformed the Sci-Fi Channel from a niche media outlet to one that appealed to a mainstream audience, Hammer sought to expand the viewership of the USA Network to appeal to those not already watching. Terming the networks' programming "meat and potatoes" in an article by John Dempsey of *Variety*, the new network president commented, "while our shows are reaching lots of eyeballs, I'm wondering if we shouldn't seek programming that's hipper and younger, that displays a little more diversity. Maybe a little less meat and potatoes and little more sushi and salsa?"

One of Hammer's first moves was to get it touch with her former contacts at the WWF. She successfully convinced them to bring wrestling back to the USA Network, giving the network a ratings boost and bringing together its somewhat scattered programming into a cohesive unit. Marked by such wide-ranging fare as wrestling; reality competition *Nashville Star*, which pitted budding country music performers against one another; comedic mystery series *Monk*, about an obsessive-compulsive detective; frequent reruns of shows from the *Law & Order* family; and even the annual Westminster Dog Show, the USA Network lacked a common programming thread.

To draw together this seemingly disparate programming, the USA Network launched the "Characters Welcome" campaign to position the network as the spot to watch shows about unusual but interesting characters. Programs such as *Monk*, *The Dead Zone*, and newcomer *Psych*, about an observant private detective who pretends to be psychic, became the USA Network's new standard-bearers, with *Psych* becoming cable's top-rated new program in its first season. "A USA show would be a fun way to escape, would not be depressing, would not be dark," she explained to Kate Aurthur of the *New York Times* soon after launching the "Characters Welcome" campaign.

Aiming to stay true to that concept over the next few years, Hammer approved the launch of several new shows, including *Burn Notice*, a series about an ex-spy seeking to rebuild his life in Miami after being "burned," or having his identity erased, by his former employer; *In Plain Sight*, a drama about a federal marshal balancing her responsibilities guarding participants in the federal witness protection program with her own family life; and *Starter Wife*, a program about the ex-wife of a studio executive struggling to make it as a writer and single mother. These new programs helped bolster the network's long-term ratings, and it eventually reclaimed its spot as the top-rated cable network. Hammer also remained a force at the Sci-Fi Channel. On the network, she oversaw the creation of another ambitious miniseries, *The Triangle*, about events in the Bermuda Triangle, and encouraged the development of less traditional science-fiction programming such as *Eureka*, a series about high-tech scientists working in Eureka, Oregon.

In 2008, the USA Network's often light-hearted continuing dedication to featuring unusual characters and its "Erase the Hate" public service campaign contributed to its president receiving a serious accolade: the Anti-Defamation League's Humanitarian Award. That same year, Hammer received another professional boost when NBC Universal expanded her role to include responsibility for the development of all entertainment programming across its cable channels. "It's an acknowledgement of the fantastic job she has done for the company since Day 1," NBC Universal president Jeff Zucker told Bill Carter of the *New York Times*. Despite significant shifts in the management landscape at NBC Universal following its planned acquisition by cable television provider Comcast in 2010, Hammer remained in a position of strength with the network. After the formal completion of the merger, she was slated to retain oversight of both SyFy and the USA Network as well as helm four additional cable networks under the NBC Universal Cable umbrella.

Sources

Books

Marquis Who's Who, Marquis Who's Who, 2010.

Periodicals

Broadcasting & Cable, June 19, 2000, p. 49; January 15, 2007, p. A6; October 22, 2007, p. 30.
MediaWeek, May 31, 2010, p. 24.
Newsweek, July 20, 2009, p. 55.
New York Times, December 4, 2005, p. AR26; March 25, 2008, p. C2; June 22, 2008, p. 24; November 19, 2010, p. B3.
Rocky Mountain News (Denver, CO), November 30, 2002, p. 16D.
TelevisionWeek, January 10, 2005, p. 42; June 27, 2005, p. 18.
USA Today, March 23, 2009, p. 6B.
Variety, June 14, 2004, p. 21; June 9, 2008, p. 55.

Online

"Bonnie Hammer," The Paley Center for the Media, http://www.shemadeit.org/meet/biography.aspx?m=130 (November 27, 2010).

—Vanessa E. Vaughn

Jeff Han

AP Images

Inventor and research scientist

Born Jefferson Y. Han, c. 1975. *Education:* Attended Cornell University, 1990s.

Addresses: *Office*—Perceptive Pixel, Inc., 111 Eighth Ave., 16th Flr., New York, NY 10011. *Web site*—http://www.perceptivepixel.com.

Career

Began career at BoxTop Interactive, Los Angeles, c. 1997; research scientist, New York University's Courant Institute of Mathematical Sciences, c. 2003-07; founded Perceptive Pixel, 2006.

Awards: Named one of the 100 most influential people in the world, *Time*, 2008; National Design Award, The Cooper Hewitt Museum, 2009.

Sidelights

The average person has never heard of Jeff Han, though they have probably seen his high-tech wizardry at work. Han invented the technology behind CNN's multi-touch sensor screen—or "Magic Wall"—that dazzled viewers during election coverage in 2008. During the election season, viewers watched as CNN correspondent John King issued news reports while standing before an eight-foot-long interactive electronic wall map. With the touch of a finger, King zoomed into battleground states and pulled up results, showed voter distribution pie charts, and offered projections. Han believes multi-touch screens are the wave of the future.

"Touch is one of the most intuitive things in the world," he told *Fast Company*'s Adam L. Penenberg. "Instead of being one step removed, like you are with a mouse and keyboard, you have direct manipulation. It's a completely natural reaction—to see an object and want to touch it."

Jefferson Y. Han, who goes by Jeff, was born around 1975. Han's parents grew up in Korea and moved to the United States in the 1970s to operate a deli in Queens, New York, which is where Han grew up. Early on, Han showed a propensity toward math and was light-years ahead of his peers when he entered kindergarten already knowing his multiplication tables. As a child, Han's fascination with electronics drove him to take apart every gadget or appliance he could find, including televisions and VCRs. By age six, he was proficient with a soldering iron. Han requested that his parents pay his allowance in quarters so he could blow it at the local arcade. He built his first laser at age 12 and spent his free time at Radio Shack reading technical manuals. At summer camp, Han was a hit with other campers, repairing broken Walkmen in exchange for soda.

Han attended the Dalton School, a private preparatory school located in Manhattan. After graduating in 1993, he enrolled at Cornell University, where he studied electrical engineering and computer science. Han never graduated because he left his senior year to join an upstart company that sought to exploit multiparty video chat technology Han had created. Based in Los Angeles, the company—called BoxTop Interactive—went belly up during the dotcom bubble bust of 2000.

Around this time, Han's father became ill so he returned to New York. Despite never having finished his degree, Han procured a research position at New York University's Courant Institute of Mathematical Sciences. During his time at NYU, Han was involved with defense department research ventures. One of the projects Han worked on involved trying to create a flying camera that would be able to navigate its own way. Another tech project Han worked on was trying to create an autonomous robot-type vehicle that could cross various landscapes. The military envisioned an unmanned combat vehicle capable of crossing everything from deserts and busy streets to mountain trails and jungles. The vehicle would have to accomplish this by learning from its experiences so it would know how to navigate whatever terrain was before it.

Han's life went in a different direction, however, when he experienced an "Ah-ha" moment while drinking a glass of water. This breakthrough led to the development of the multi-touch screen. As Han picked up the glass, he noticed that his fingertips imaged clearly though the glass, which had to do with the way the light diffused. He researched the optical phenomenon, which scientists call "frustrated total internal reflection." Speaking to CNN's Jeremy Bradley, Han recalled his breakthrough moment. "After you get an inspiration like that you run back to the lab where you have a lot of spare parts and all of a sudden, literally within days, you can start going to prototype. It was pretty neat."

Han created a prototype quickly. He attached LEDs to an acrylic screen and stuck an infrared camera behind it, allowing light to travel through the screen. Whenever he touched the screen, the light was diffused out and captured by the camera. Next, he had to create software to utilize the multi-touch screen. Touch screens were not new—ATMs had been using them for years—but the ATM touch screen can only take input from one finger, one point at a time. Han's new screen could take input from multiple fingers at a time but the software to run such a device did not exist. Han created image-processing software to interpret the scattering of light so the screen could be used for photo-handling, figure-drawing, and utilizing mapping programs.

Han unveiled his invention at the 2006 annual Technology, Entertainment and Design (TED) Conference, held in Monterey, California. His invention captured large audiences who gawked as he touched his display screen with both hands drawing figures, moving photos and manipulating images. The images were projected onto a giant screen, allowing everyone to see. Han flipped through photos as if they were actual prints on a tabletop. He enlarged some images and shrank others by pulling his two index fingers apart or bringing them together. He also played with a two-dimensional keyboard on the screen. In addition, he pulled up a satellite image of a mountainous landscape, then zoomed right in with the touch of his fingers. After the convention, TED posted a video of Han's demonstration on its Web site and it ended up on YouTube, where it received more than 250,000 views.

Han also took the technology to a military trade show, where CNN executives fell in love with it and saw an immediate use—thus the "Magic Wall" was born. During the 2008 election cycle, CNN utilized the touch screen to add some zing to its election coverage. *Saturday Night Live* even parodied the wall. The success, however, did not come without a lot of hard work. "I'm here seven days a week, and yeah, I stay up late," Han told Adam Lisberg of the *Daily News*. "But I grin every morning."

In 2006, Han founded Perceptive Pixel to manufacture and market his touch screens. Han's multi-touch devices reportedly sell for six figures. While the technology has mostly been utilized by military agencies interested in managing their intelligence data, Han believes the multi-touch interface will become more mainstream. He has been contacted by museums and 911 response units looking for ways to use multi-touch technology. In addition, film companies have expressed interest in it for use with storyboarding and medical researchers have wondered whether the touch screen might be a way to connect with autistic children. "We're just scratching the surface of what's possible with it," Han told CNN's Bradley. "We see huge growth in diverse areas such as creative applications, architecture, in education, in collaborative brainstorming, ideation processes—which starts to cover a huge range of companies."

Sources

Periodicals

Daily News, January 21, 2007, p. 25.
Washington Post, February 5, 2008, p. C1.

Online

"Can't Touch This," *Fast Company*, http://www.fastcompany.com/magazine/112/open_features-canttouchthis.html (April 16, 2010).

"The Inventor Behind CNN's Election 'Magic Wall,'" CNN.com, http://www.cnn.com/2008/TECH/11/04/magic.wall/ (April 16, 2010).

"Jeff Han's Multitouch Media Wall Takes Teamwork to the Future," *Popular Mechanics*, http://www.popularmechanics.com/technology/gadgets/news/4224762 (June 4, 2010).

"Jeff Han," *Time*, http://www.time.com/time/specials/2007/article/0,28804,1733748_1733754_1735325,00.html (April 16, 2010).

"TED: Jeff Han, A Year Later," *Wired*, http://www.wired.com/print/techbiz/people/news/2007/03/72905 (June 4, 2010).

—*Lisa Frick*

Woody Harrelson

Actor and activist

Born Woodrow Tracy Harrelson, July 23, 1961, in Midland, TX; son of Charles Voyde Harrelson (a professional gambler) and Diane Lou Oswald (a legal secretary); married Nancy Simon, June 29, 1985 (divorced, January 20, 1986); married Laura Louie (a personal assistant), December 28, 2008; children: Deni Montana, Zoe Giordano, Makani Ravello (second marriage). *Education:* Hanover College, B.A., 1983.

Addresses: *Office*—c/o Ziffren Brittenham Branca Fischer Gilbert-Lurie, 1801 Century Park West, Los Angeles, CA 90067-6406.

Career

Actor in television including: *Cheers*, NBC, 1985-93; *Bay Coven* (movie), 1987; *Killer Instinct* (movie), 1988; *Dear John*, 1989; *The Simpsons*, FOX, 1994; *Spin City*, 1996; *Frasier*, NBC, 1999; *Will & Grace*, NBC, 2001. Film appearances include: *Wildcats*, 1986; *Cool Blue*, 1990; *Doc Hollywood*, 1991; *Ted & Venus*, 1991; *White Men Can't Jump*, 1992; *Indecent Proposal*, 1993; *The Cowboy Way*, 1994; *I'll Do Anything*, 1994; *Natural Born Killers*, 1994; *Money Train*, 1995; *Kingpin*, 1996; *The Sunchaser*, 1996; *The People vs. Larry Flynt*, 1997; *Wag the Dog*, 1997; *Welcome to Sarajevo*, 1997; *The Hi-Lo Country*, 1998; *Palmetto*, 1998; *The Thin Red Line*, 1998; *Edtv*, 1999; *Play It to the Bone*, 1999; *Anger Management*, 2003; *Scorched*, 2003; *After the Sunset*, 2004; *Go Further*, 2004; *She Hate Me*, 2004; *The Big White*, 2005; *North Country*, 2005; *The Prize Winner of Defiance, Ohio*, 2005; *A Scanner Darkly*, 2006; *Battle in Seattle*, 2007; *The Grand*, 2007; *Management*, 2008; *No Country for Old Men*, 2007; *The Walker*, 2007; *Semi-Pro*, 2008; *Seven Pounds*, 2008; *Sleepwalking*, 2008; *Surfer, Dude*, 2008; *Transsiberian*, 2008; *2012*, 2009; *Defendor*, 2009; *The Messenger*, 2009; *Zombieland*, 2009; *Bunraku*, 2010. Stage appearances include: *Biloxi Blues*, New York City, 1984; *2 on 2*, Los Angeles, CA, 1989; *Zoo Story*, Los Angeles, CA, 1989; *Brooklyn Laundry*, c. 1991; *The Rainmaker*, Brooks Atkinson Theater, New York City, 1999; *On an Average Day*, West End production, London, 2002; *The Boys Next Door*, Off-Broadway production. Stage work includes: writer and producer, *2 on 2*, Los Angeles, CA, 1989; producer, *Zoo Story*, Los Angeles, CA, 1989; director, *This Is Our Youth*, Berkeley St. Theatre Upstairs, Toronto, 2003. Also co-owner of Prairie Pulp and Paper Company, Manitoba, Canada, c. 2000.

Awards: American Comedy Award for funniest newcomer—male or female, for *Cheers*, 1987; Emmy Award for outstanding supporting actor in a comedy series, for *Cheers*, 1989; MTV Movie Award (with Demi Moore) for best kiss, for *Indecent Proposal*, 1994; Bronze Wrangler (with others) for theatrical motion picture, Western Heritage Awards, for *The Hi-Lo Country*, 1999; Honorary Maverick Award, Woodstock Film Festival, 2003; Texas Hall of Fame inductee, 2003; Screen Actors Guild Award (with others) for outstanding performance by a cast in a motion picture, for *No Country for Old Men*, 2008;

Verona Love Screens Film Festival Award for best actor, for *The Walker*, 2008; National Board of Review Award for best supporting actor, for *The Messenger*, 2009; Phillip Borsos Award for best actor, Whistler Film Festival, for *Defendor*, 2009; Special Award for body of work in the last year, San Diego Film Critics Society, 2009; Independent Spirit Award for best supporting male, for *The Messenger*, 2010.

Sidelights

After his breakout role on the long-running situation comedy *Cheers*, actor Woody Harrelson built a varied film career playing roles from the comic to the dramatic and serious. Twice nominated for an Academy Award, he received rave reviews for his work in such varied films as *White Men Can't Jump, Natural Born Killers, The People vs. Larry Flynt,* and *The Messenger*. Outside of acting, Harrelson was a vegan and passionate environmental activist who also fought for the legalization of marijuana.

Born July 23, 1961, in Midland, Texas, he was the middle of three sons of Charles Voyde Harrelson and Diane Lou Oswald. His father left the family when Harrelson was seven years old, and his mother, a legal secretary, moved herself and her sons to Lebanon, Ohio, when he was 12. There, Harrelson—who was hyperactive and dyslexic—was raised by his mother, grandmother, and great-grandmother. Raised in a religious environment, Harrelson wanted to be a minister but had a tough streak. About this time in his life, Harrelson told Gail Buchalter of the *Houston Chronicle*, "I wanted to be a minister. I was the head of the youth group and used to lead Bible studies. But I also fought a lot. I would watch Steve McQueen on *Wanted Dead or Alive* and thought it was so cool the way he'd kick the chair out from under somebody. I would always fight for someone who couldn't protect himself—that's how I justified it to myself."

Harrelson became interested in acting while in high school in Ohio. He explained to Mike Higgins of the *Independent on Sunday*, "I was in the library at school one time when some buddies of mine from the football team said 'Come on Woody, do your Elvis.' Before I knew it I started singing 'Well bless my soul, what's wrong with me.' I jumped up on the table and was doing my little Elvis dance and everybody loved it. A girl from the theatre group asked me if I had ever thought about doing theatre—I was more of a jock, but I said I was interested." Performing soon became a focus in his life.

After high school, Harrelson attended Hanover College in Indiana on a Presbyterian Church scholarship. Though he lost his faith and was not a great student, he earned his bachelor's degree in theater arts and English in 1983, Harrelson moved to first to Houston then New York City to pursue stage work. While auditioning, he held 17 day jobs in 14 months, primarily because he kept getting fired. He soon landed a role as an understudy in *Biloxi Blues* in 1984. Harrelson's career took an unexpected turn when he landed a role on an already popular television situation comedy, *Cheers*, in 1985. After the unexpected death of actor Nicholas Colasanto who played the show's loveable bartender known as Coach, Harrelson was cast as the new bartender, a naïve Indiana farm boy living in the big city of Boston for the first time.

Describing the change, Harrelson told Jerry Buck of the Associated Press, "Nobody can really replace Nicholas Colasanto. He was a legend. But I think the producers and writers felt there was a void. They needed the energy of another character. There are a lot of similarities, but I don't think you can compare us. I think they had to bring in a little more comedy into it and give it a different perspective." Harrelson's character, Woody Boyd, soon became one of *Cheers'* most popular characters. For his work on *Cheers*, Harrelson was nominated for four Emmy Awards and won one Emmy for outstanding supporting actor in a comedy series in 1989.

While taping *Cheers* in Los Angeles, Harrelson continued to appear on stage there. He wrote, produced, and acted in his comedic play *2 on 2* as well as produced and acted in a production of *The Zoo Story* by Edward Albee. He also tried to launch a film career, but often found it difficult because of the demands of *Cheers*. Harrelson's first role of note came in the 1986 football comedy *Wildcats*, starring Goldie Hawn. Although 1990's *Code Blue* went straight to video, he gained more credibility with the 1991 Michael J. Fox comedy *Doc Hollywood* in which he played the small-town rival to Fox's character. Harrelson then had a starring role as a basketball hustler in the 1992 basketball comedy *White Men Can't Jump*.

Considered a box office draw because of *White Men*, Harrelson's film career took off in 1993, the same year *Cheers* was canceled. He had a hit with the 1993 drama *Indecent Proposal*—in which he played a man who sells a night with his wife for a million dollars to a billionaire—and a leading role as a serial killer in the 1994 dark satire *Natural Born Killers*. Critics lauded his work as mass murderer Mickey in *Killers*, which was directed by Oliver Stone, with *Chicago Sun-Times'* critic Roger Ebert writing, "Woody Harrelson and Juliette Lewis are both capable of being frightening, both able to project amorality and disdain as easily as Jack Lemmon projects ingratiation." Harrelson also received acclaim for playing modern-day cowboy Pepper Lewis in the comedy *The Cowboy Way.*

Harrelson's interests in this time period outside of film were varied as he spent some of his off-time appearing with his band, Manly Moondo and the Three Kool Kats, in the early 1990s and taught yoga with Ken Scott Nateshvar while filming his 1995 hit action comedy *The Money Train.* Harrelson was again teamed with *White Men* co-star Wesley Snipes and *Train* showed off their natural chemistry.

In the second half of the 1990s, Harrelson continued to stay on top of the box office with roles in such hits as the 1996 bowling comedy *Kingpin* and 1997 biopic *The People vs. Larry Flynt.* In the latter film, Harrelson played the controversial Flynt, founder of *Hustler* magazine. He was nominated for his first Academy Award nomination for best actor in a leading role for his work in *The People vs. Larry Flynt.* Harrelson also appeared in smaller films as well, playing a cancer doctor in the 1996 drama *The Sunchaser* and a journalist who adopted a child in 1997's antiwar drama *Welcome to Sarajevo.*

For the rest of the decade, Harrelson continued to mix both Hollywood films (1997's *Wag the Dog* and 1999's *Edtv*) with smaller films (1998's *The Hi-Lo Country* and 1999's *Play It to the Bone*). Even in a failed comic film noir like 1998's *Palmetto,* Harrelson shined, with Mick LaSalle of the *San Francisco Chronicle* writing, "The movie's best aspect is Woody Harrelson, who has established himself as a fine comic actor and a reliable screen personality."

While continuing to appear in films, Harrelson had not forgotten his early roots on stage. In 1999, he starred in the Broadway revival of N. Richard Nash's *The Rainmaker.* Three years later, Harrelson had a starring role in the West End production of *On an Average Day.* Between these years, he made very few films, though he did return to television on a multi-episode arc of the hit NBC comedy *Will & Grace,* as Grace's love interest.

In 2003, Harrelson returned to film acting and over the few years mixed the serious with the comic, and Hollywood films with smaller independent pictures. For every broad comedy like 2003's *Anger Management,* and 2004's *She Hate Me,* there were smaller-budgeted films like the 2004 relationship drama *After the Sunset,* and the 2006 mind-bending work of animation *A Scanner Darkly.* Harrelson also balanced out critically acclaimed dramas like 2007's *No Country for Old Men* with comedies like *Semi-Pro.*

Harrelson appeared in four films in 2009 which demonstrated the range of his acting. He played a lead in the hit zombie road comedy *Zombieland,* and a superhero wanna-be in *Defendor.* Harrelson also had a part in the smash post-apocalyptic action film, *2012.* In one of his most unexpected roles, Harrelson played Captain Tony Stone in the Iraq War drama *The Messenger.* While the actor was peace activist, playing a casualty notification officer who, along with a trainee/returning veteran (played by Ben Foster), informed families of the combat deaths of their loved ones proved deeply moving. Harrelson told Deborah Sontag of the *New York Times,* "I'm not a crier, but I probably cried dozens of times during this thing." He also told G. Allen Johnson of the *San Francisco Chronicle,* "I thought it was one of the most beautiful and powerful scripts I'd ever read, and I was really knocked out by it."

Critics responded positively to Harrelson's deep performance, with Johnson of the *San Francisco Chronicle* noting. "Harrelson summons humanity without politics ... in one of his best performances." In 2010, Harrelson landed his second Academy Award nomination for his supporting role in *The Messenger.* While he was honored with other nominations for his work as Stone, he won only the Independent Spirit Award.

Throughout his career, Harrelson stayed in the headlines for reasons other than acting as well. His professional gambler father was given a life sentence for allegedly murdering a federal judge on the order of a drug dealer. Harrelson fought for his father's release, believing his innocence in the matter but his father died in prison in 2007. The actor faced several arrests of his own, including a 1983 disorderly conduct charge and a 1996 marijuana possession charge. The latter was an act of civil disobedience meant to challenge a Kentucky state law which made no distinction between marijuana and hemp.

A longtime activist, Harrelson participated in a number of demonstrations and acts of support for marijuana and hemp legalization as well as environmental causes, including a 2001 bike tour down the West Coast of the United States. A documentary about this SOL (simple organic living) Tour was released in 2004, *Go Further.* Beginning in the 1980s, he also supported such groups as the Earth Communications Office and the American Oceans Campaign. In 2000, Harrelson became a co-owner of a non-wood pulp mill in Manitoba, the Prairie Pulp and Paper Company.

Harrelson's co-star in *The Rainmaker,* Jayne Atkinson, summed him as both an actor and a person to Robin Pogrebin of the *New York Times.* She said,

"He's much smarter than he looks. He's just a mischievous, adventurous human being. He definitely marches to the beat of his own distinct drum, but what I appreciate about the way he steps is that it's never to the detriment of others. It's about just being who he is."

Sources

Books

Marquis Who's Who, Marquis Who's Who, 2010.

Periodicals

Associated Press, December 27, 1985.
Chicago Sun-Times, August 26, 1994, p. 51.
Globe and Mail (Canada), February 18, 2010, p. R1.
Guelph Mercury (Ontario, Canada), July 11, 2003, p. B12.
Houston Chronicle, April 12, 1992, p. 20.
Independent on Sunday, July 28, 2002, p. 3.
National Post (Canada), August 31, 2000, p. C1; February 16, 2010, p. AL1.
New York Times, March 15, 1995, p. C3; October 31, 1999, sec. 2, p. 5; November 8, 2009, p. AR1.
Record (Bergen County, NJ), March 2, 2001, p. Y3.
San Francisco Chronicle, February 20, 1998, p. C3; October 2, 2009, p. F10; November 25, 2009, p. E2.
Seattle Post-Intelligencer, November 12, 2004, p. 32.
Toronto Star, April 2, 1993, p. C2.
Toronto Sun, November 19, 1995, p. S9; April 4, 1998, p. 42.
USA Today, August 2, 1991, p. 1D; July 25, 1996, p. 8B.
Vancouver Sun, July 12, 1994, p. C10.

Online

"Woody Harrelson," Internet Movie Database, http://www.imdb.com/name/nm0000437/ (March 8, 2010).

—A. Petruso

Heather Headley

Actress and singer

Born October 5, 1974, in Trinidad; daughter of Iric (a minister) and Hannah (a teacher) Headley; married Brian Musso (a professional football player), September 6, 2003; children: John David. *Education:* Attended Northwestern University, c. 1993-96.

Addresses: *Web site*—http://www.heatherheadley. com/; http://en-gb.facebook.com/pages/Heather-Headley/34333402.tif598; http://www.myspace. com/heatherheadley.

Career

Began acting and singing as a child; appeared in high school musicals; began professional stage acting career, c. 1996; released first album *This Is Who I Am*, 2002; made film debut in *Dirty Dancing: Havana Nights*, 2004; released first gospel album, *Audience of One*, 2009. Stage appearances include: *And the World Goes 'Round*, Marriott's Lincolnshire Theatre, Chicago, IL, 1996; *Ragtime*, Toronto, Ontario, Canada, 1996; *The Lion King*, New Amsterdam Theater, New York City, 1997-98; *Elaborate Lives: The Legend of Aida*, Alliance Theatre, Atlanta, GA, 1998; *Aida*, Chicago, IL, 1999, then Palace Theatre, New York City, 2000-01.

Awards: Tony Award for best actress in a musical, American Theatre Wing, for *Aida*, 2000; Drama Desk Award for outstanding actress in a musical, for *Aida*, 2000; Lady of Soul Award for best R&B/soul or rap new artist, *Soul Train*, 2003; Lady of Soul Award for best R&B/soul album of the year, *Soul Train*, for

This Is Who I Am, 2003; Grammy Award for best contemporary R&B gospel album, Recording Academy, for *Audience of One*, 2009.

Sidelights

Award-winning actress and singer Heather Headley received much acclaim for both her stage appearances as well as her albums. An immigrant from Trinidad who came to the United States in her teens, she was attending Northwestern University when she received the kind of break most actresses long for. Headley joined the Toronto cast of a popular Broadway musical, *Ragtime*, then won starring roles in two new major musicals, *The Lion King* and *Aida*. Leaving theater behind, Headley focused on a recording career, releasing two R&B/soul albums and a gospel album, 2009's *Audience of One*. Many critics praise the depth and emotional breadth of Headley's vocal prowess.

Headley was born on October 5, 1974, in Trinidad, the daughter of Iric and Hannah Headley. Her father was a minister in the Barataria Church of God while her mother taught school. Her father presided over a one-room church in Trinidad where Headley began singing as a toddler. She gave her first performance at the age of two. She would practice singing and playing piano for hours in the empty church. Headley joined the church choir and later performed in dramatic productions with a group affiliated with the church.

Headley's family moved to Fort Wayne, Indiana, when she was 15 years old because her father was assigned to a church there. A student at a local high school, she experienced some culture shock, especially due to her race. She told Jack Kroll and Veronica Chambers of *Newsweek*, "I had to learn this whole minority thing. I thought, 'Wait a minute, I'm the majority in Trinidad.' I had to deal with it." Despite such difficult adjustments, she was a member of her church's show choir, attended Northrup High School in Fort Wayne, Indiana, and was often given the lead in school musicals.

To further her education, Headley entered Northwestern University. There, she majored in communications and musical theater. She also appeared in productions of *Dreamgirls* and *And the World Goes 'Round* at the Marriott Lincolnshire Theatre. A review of the latter production commented on Headley's burgeoning talent. Hedy Weiss of the *Chicago Sun-Times* singled out the actress by writing, "note the striking Headley, with a torch singer sensibility."

Though she did not want to leave school, Headley dropped out of Northwestern at the end of her junior year in 1996 when unexpected opportunities came her way. She was asked to read for a workshop version of what would become a hit Broadway musical in *The Lion King*. Headley also was cast as the understudy Sarah to Audra McDonald in the Toronto version of the musical *Ragtime*. The young performer took the latter role and she performed the role of Sarah more than 20 times.

The production team behind *The Lion King* had not forgotten Headley, however, and she was asked to audition for the role of Nala for the Broadway production of the play based on the popular Disney animated film and featuring a score written by Elton John and Tim Rice. In 1997, Headley's career took a big leap forward when she won the part. Disney bought out her *Ragtime* contract, and the performer made her Broadway debut. Critics praised her talent, especially her rendition of the song "Shadowland."

Headley, however, found that appearing on Broadway was not exactly what she expected. She told Mary Campbell of the Associated Press Online, "I thought I would be sailing high on Broadway. I never thought it would be so frustrating. I go home at night and think about the show and get in the morning thinking, 'How can I make it better?' ... I'd go home and Nala would slap me around. I think I'm beginning to get the better of her; I'm getting more confidence."

Headley's impressive performance as Nala led to the chance to audition for the lead in the next musical written by John and Rice. She landed the title role in *Aida*, which was titled *Elaborate Lives: The Legend of Aida* during its pre-Broadway run in Atlanta in 1998. The rock musical was based on the opera by Giuseppe Verdi and was a hit even in its out-of-town showing there.

Discussing her career to this point, Headley told Steve Murray of the *Atlanta Journal and Constitution*, "It's been a quick three years, but it's my life, so I don't see it as something phenomenal or great. People are like, 'You've done two of the biggest musicals of the century in one year.' But I don't see it like that. For me, it's just 'My ankle hurts. This is killing me!' But I do consider it a blessing."

After some re-tooling in Atlanta and another re-working at another difficult out-of-town tryout in Chicago in 1999, *Aida* finally opened on Broadway in 2000 to much acclaim for Headley. She won both a Tony Award and a Drama Desk Award for her work in the role. While critics were not always kind to the production, Headley's performance as the Nubian princess who falls in love with her Egyptian captor Radames garnered much acclaim.

Reviewing *Aida* in the New York *Daily News*, Fintan O'Toole raved "In the title role, Heather Headley is quite splendid. She has the rare ability to suggest deep feelings with a look, a gesture, a turn of the head. Her movements have a commanding dignity, her voice a range that loops all the way from a roar of rage to a sigh of sorrow." Another reviewer, Robin Pogrebin of the *New York Times*, added "Ms. Headley alone ... is worth the price of admission."

For her part, starring in *Aida* meant that she focused solely on the work. She told the *New York Times'* Pogrebin "My social life is kaput for now. *Aida* is the boyfriend right now. I have no problem staying at home. The way I look at it, you're paying me to do something I do in the shower. I'm honored and blessed that at 25 I have this role. Not in a proud way, but in an awed, grateful way."

While still appearing in *Aida*, Headley decided to shift her focus to singing and began recording her first solo album. Released in 2002, *This Is Who I Am* fell into the R&B and soul categories, but was also a hit on the pop charts and spawned two top five dance hits with "He Is" and "I Wish I Wasn't." Various tracks were produced by such luminaries as Jimmy Jam & Terry Lewis as well as Shep Crawford.

Critics enthusiastically praised Headley's ability to make the transition to recording artist with Gail Mitchell of *Billboard* noting, "Making the adjustment from stage to studio in no way diluted the power of Headley's depth-defying voice, which can shift from passionate and vulnerable to down-home soul effortlessly." She made sure *This Is Who I Am* was not your typical contemporary R&B album, telling Misha Davenport of the *Chicago Sun-Times,* "I was determined that this album would be about me. It wasn't going to be about sex, money, credit cards, or cursing. Call it a political statement if you will, but this record reflects what I believe in." The album was eventually certified gold and earned Headley two Grammy Award nominations (including one for best new artist) and two Lady of Soul Awards.

Marrying former New York Jets football player Brian Musso in September of 2003, Headley continued to move between singing and acting in 2004. She garnered much positive critical attention for her version of "Your Song," which she played at the Kennedy Center Honors Salute to Elton John. Also that year, Headley took her first film role with a small part in *Dirty Dancing: Havana Nights.* She appeared on the film's soundtrack with several tracks, including "Represent, Cuba," as well.

In 2006, Headley released her delayed second album, *In My Mind.* She again worked with Jam & Lewis and Crawford as well as Warryn Campbell and Lil' Jon. The title song, "In My Mind," became a number-one hit on the dance charts. Another track, "Change," was inspirational in nature. Headley co-wrote the song, which foreshadowed the next phase of her recording career. While the performer was pleased with the album, critics were not kind. Mary Awosika of the *Sarasota Herald-Tribune* noting "One too many sluggish ballads traps Heather Headley's voice on her sophomore album *In My Mind.*"

After touring in support of *In My Mind*, Headley sought out different musical experiences. By 2008, Headley took on new challenges when she began performing with popular classical singer Andrea Bocelli. She appeared with him on his PBS special *Live in Tuscany* as well as on his world tour. Another of their performances together was featured on his live DVD release *Under the Desert Sky.*

Focusing again on her solo career, Headley began thinking about doing a full-length gospel album after recording the traditional spiritual "I Know the Lord Will Make a Way," for the compilation album *Oh Happy Day ...,* released on EMI Gospel/Vector. The strength of her performance compelled EMI Gospel label executives to ask her to record a gospel album of her own. In January of 2009, Headley released her third album *Audience of One.*

Changing direction from her first two releases, *Audience of One* was indeed a full-fledged gospel album. It reflected Headley's beginning as a singer in her father's church and included a song she sung as a child in Trinidad, "Jesus Is Love," done in duet with labelmate Smokie Norful. The title referred to the times when Headley would practice singing and piano in the church alone with God as the one member of her audience. The release of *Audience of One* also fulfilled a goal inspired in part by her mother who told her years ago to record a gospel album, as well as the singer's own deep faith. Headley co-wrote one song on *Audience of One*, the hymn-like "Zion."

Critics responded positively to the album, with Elysa Gardner of *USA Today* praising her "discipline and grace, which not only pleases the ear but also reinforces the sense of humility so central to these songs." In support of *Audience of One*, Headley did a tour of churches, including her own in Chicago, Harvard Bible Chapel. She also won a Grammy award, her first, for *Audience of One.*

Even amidst her busy schedule, Headley and her husband found time to start a family. The pair quietly welcomed the birth of their son, John David, on December 1, 2009. Outside of music, Headley was a humanitarian activist. For example, she had an educational campaign through the March of Dimes dubbed "I Want My Nine Months." But it was her singing and acting that took up most of her time and focus. Explaining her approach to her career, Headley told Janet Rausa Fuller of the *Chicago Sun-Times,* "I believe in being versatile as a performer.... I would hope to be like those Kevin Spaceys of the world, you know what I mean?"

Selected discography

(With others) *The Lion King Original Broadway Cast,* Walt Disney Records (Burbank, CA), 1997.
(With others) *Aida Original Broadway Cast,* Walk Disney Records, 2000.
This Is Who I Am, RCA (New York City), 2002.
In My Mind, RCA, 2006.

(Contributor) *Oh Happy Day ...*, EMI Gospel/Vector (Brentwood and Nashville, TN), c. 2008.
Audience of One, EMI Gospel (Brentwood, TN), 2009.

Sources

Periodicals

Associated Press Online, January 7, 1998.
Atlanta Journal and Constitution, October 28, 1998, p. 1C.
Billboard, October 5, 2002, p. 15; January 28, 2006.
Birmingham News (AL), April 9, 2006, p. 1F.
Chicago Daily Herald, February 6, 2004, p. 34.
Chicago Sun-Times, February 2, 1996, p. 31; July 30, 2000, p. 1; October 6, 2002, p. 1.
Daily News (NY), March 24, 2000, p. 58.
Jet, October 28, 2002, p. 46.
Newsweek, August 30, 1999, p. 61; April 3, 2000, p. 76.
New York Times, April 6, 2000, p. E1.
Sarasota Herald-Tribune (FL), February 3, 2006, p. 9.
St. Louis Post-Dispatch, April 23, 2006, p. F1.
USA Today, January 13, 2009, p. 6D.
Washington Post, January 13, 2009, p. C8.

Online

"Biography," EMIGospel.com, http://heatherheadley.emigospel.com/biography/ (March 3, 2010).
"Heather Headley," Internet Movie Database, http://www.imdb.com/name/nm0372186/ (March 3, 2010).
"Heather Headley: Journal," Heather Headley Official Web site, http://www.heatherheadley.com/journal.html (April 2, 2010).

—*A. Petruso*

Abbe Held

Creative director of Kooba

Born Abbe Held, c. 1966; daughter of Bonnie (maiden name, Kooba); married Scott; children: two daughters.

Addresses: *Office*—2652 Long Beach Ave., Los Angeles, CA 90058.

Career

Fashion merchandizer for DKNY; co-founder, co-president, and creative director of Kooba, 1998—.

Sidelights

Finding the perfect handbag to compliment one's wardrobe can be a very frustrating experience. A person can go from department store to department store and examine dozens of bags and still not find one that inspires a purchase. This was what happened to Abbe Held and she decided to do something about it. Kellye M. Garrett, writing for the New York *Daily News,* reported that "Held and her mother, Bonnie, went home and designed exactly what they wanted." Self-described accessory addicts, Held—who up until that time had been employed with DKNY doing fashion merchandising in their midtown showroom—and her mother decided that designing handbags would be fun. This was how Kooba, the accessories, clothing, and home furnishings line, was created.

The name Kooba comes from Held's mother's maiden name. Held wanted to create unique, beautiful, and functional handbags. She enjoyed shopping for vintage clothing and accessories, so Held created the line of handbags with unusual details. In an interview with Mariana Leung for the blog The Purse Page, Held explained, "Vintage shopping is a passion of mine that I inherited from my mom, Bonnie.... She taught me how to scour every corner to find that special piece. My favorite piece is an amethyst satin pouch that I found while shopping at a flea market in St. Tropez." Sometimes simple antique or retro items will provide the inspiration for ornamentation or styling on a handbag. Items such as old belt buckles or the lock on an old door have inspired custom decorations on her stylish handbags.

The Kooba line was started in 1998. The Kooba motto is "Stand apart. Love the difference." In fact the line was so distinctive and creative that within a season it was picked up by fashion conscious retailers like Barneys and Bergdorf Goodman, who were placing sold-out orders for Kooba bags and asking about the next season's collection. Sarah Bernard, writing for *New York* magazine, quoted Held as saying "We looked at each other like, 'Next collection?'" Many celebrities have been seen with the handbags slung over their shoulders. Sienna Miller bought a whipstitched bag and gave Kooba some popularity because she was photographed with the bag. One of the most successful handbags in the Kooba line is called the Sienna and is inspired by and named after Miller. Sophia Chabbott, reporting for *WWD,* quoted Lynn Pincus, the co-president of Kooba, as saying, "Our customer always likes to see their choices validated by celebrities." Pincus went on to say that the Sienna handbag was their first 'It' bag and that while they were already an established company it raised them to the next level of becoming a fashion icon. Among the other celebrities that own Kooba handbags are Julia Roberts, Jennifer Aniston, Avril Lavigne, Kristen Bell, Hayden Panettiere, Scarlett Johansson, and Jessica Biel. These fashion trendsetters help to create demand for the finely crafted handbags which rang in price from $200 to $800.

The Kooba handbag has become a fashion necessity. So much so that in an article for *WWD* written by Whitney Beckett, one of the respondents to the question of what she would get her mother for Mother's Day responded, "I actually buy my mother a Kooba handbag each year for Mother's Day. It is her one guilty pleasure she won't buy herself. Their bags allow her to feel sexy and young without being over the top." In 2007 Vicki M. Young, writing for *WWD*, reported "According to industry sources, Kooba's sales volume, still primarily based on its handbag collections, is expected to exceed $220 million this year. Sources described the company's growth rate in the last four years as 'extraordinary,' with the business quadrupling in volume."

The company has expanded into other products. In addition to the women's handbags the company produces, they branched out in 2007 into a line of casual clothing that consists primarily of tops and a line of men's bags that includes backpacks, messenger bags, and weekend bags. In 2009 the company introduced a line of women's footwear. Held told Julee Greenberg of *WWD*, in regards to the collection of contemporary tops, "When I started the bags, the idea came from the fact that I couldn't find exactly what I wanted in a bag. I saw a need in the market. So it's a bit of the same with the clothing. I wanted items like these, and I couldn't find them." Brenner Thomas, writing for the *Daily News Record* in regards to the line of men's bags, quoted Held as saying, "We make accessible, fashionable bags for women and no one was doing that in the men's market." This kind of business savvy and ability to recognize that there is a need in the marketplace has helped Held to make Kooba as successful as it has been. Held, who is currently listed as being the co-founder, co-president, and creative director of Kooba, has also initiated some very creative marketing for her line of handbags. Held has teamed up with the Bravo television network to promote a line of handbags. Kooba designed a special line of handbags for the television show *NYC Prep* which was a reality program that followed the lives of rich Manhattan high school students. Kooba also partnered with Beauty.com to create a giftbag set.

Kooba handbags have been so popular that a number of imitative knock-off brands have appeared. Held has had to protect her company and the creative licensing of her brand. In 2006, The Bag Lady Inc., parent company of the Kooba brand, filed a trade dress infringement lawsuit against the Accessory Network Group and Nordstrom Inc. Kooba handbags were so popular they came with a certificate of authenticity to ensure that they really were a Kooba bag.

Held lives in Greenwich Village with her husband, Scott, and their two daughters. Her mother is no longer involved with Kooba. Held continues to be the creative force behind this powerhouse company dedicated to haute couture.

Sources

Periodicals

Daily News Record, January 15, 2007, p. 22.
New York Times, April 13, 2009, p. B3.
WWD, February 28, 2005, p. 6S; March 6, 2006, p. 31; February 1, 2007, p. 10; October 18, 2007, p. 2; October 22, 2007, p. 26S; December 5, 2008, p. 13; May 7, 2008, p. 8; July 13, 2009, p. 9.

Online

"5 Questions for Kooba Designer, Abbe Held," The Purse Page, http://www.pursepage.com/other-designer-handbags/pursepage-exclusive-5-questions-for-kooba-designer-abbe-held.html (March 7, 2010).
"Abbe Held's Bold and Beautiful Home," *Page Six Magazine, New York Post*, http://www.nypost.com/pagesixmag/issues/20081102.tif/Abbe+Helds+Bold+and+Beautiful+Home?print=true (February 21, 2010).
"Interview: Kooba's Abbe Held," PurseBlog, http://www.purseblog.com/interview-koobas-abbe-held/ (February 21, 2010).
"Style: The Return of Jordache; Household Products that Energize," *New York* magazine, http://nymag.com/nymetro/shopping/fashion/features/4007/ (February 21, 2010).
"Voice of Authority Abbe Held," *Daily News*, http://www.nydailynews.com/archives/lifestyle/2000/11/05/2000-11-05_voice_of_authority_abbe_held.html (March 4, 2010).

—*Annette Bowman*

Tom Henderson

Courtesy of ShelterBox USA

Chief Executive Officer of ShelterBox

Born c. 1950; married; wife's name, Jane.

Addresses: *Office*—ShelterBox, Unit 1A Water-Ma-Trout, Helston, Cornwall TR13 0LW, United Kingdom. *Web site*—http://www.shelterbox.org/.

Career

Search-and-rescue diver with the Royal Navy; founder, ShelterBox, 2000, and chief executive, 2000—.

Awards: Officer of the Order of the British Empire, Queen Elizabeth II, 2010.

Sidelights

Tom Henderson is the founder and chief executive of ShelterBox, a nonprofit humanitarian aid organization. Since 2001 the charity has provided supplies to survivors of natural disasters such as the 2004 Indian Ocean tsunami and the 2010 Haitian earthquake. Each green plastic "shelter box" contains basic necessities for survival amidst chaos and rubble, including a large tent, tools, a cook stove, and water-purification tablets. "It's a simple package of aid delivered to the most needy people in the shortest amount of time," Henderson told CNN about ShelterBox's mission.

Henderson is a native of Cornwall, the section of Britain situated on its southwestern peninsula. He was a search and rescue diver for the Royal Navy

before returning to civilian life, where he became active in the Helston-Lizard Rotary Club near his hometown of Helston, Cornwall. One day in 1999, he was watching television footage about a natural disaster, and was disturbed by the images of international aid workers throwing food-relief packages on the ground, which the obviously traumatized and desperate victims then rushed to grab. "I decided there and then that I would try to make a difference in a more sensible and dignified way," Henderson said in the CNN interview. "I went to my study and I got a piece of paper out, and I wrote down 'shelter,' 'warm,' 'comfort,' and 'dignity.'"

Henderson knew that the majority of international relief efforts were concentrated on bringing food and medical supplies to survivors of mass-scale natural disasters, and saw that there were no exclusive providers committed to meeting basic shelter needs. At the meeting of his Helston-Lizard Rotary Club in April of 2000, he convinced fellow Rotarians to adopt this as its millennium project. He had already researched suppliers to find the best prices on durable goods that the new ShelterBox would require: a large plastic container, firstly, then enough supplies to aid ten people for up to six months. Contents included a large tent made by Vango, a Scottish manufacturer whose high quality products are a favorite of mountain climbers; ground sheets;

thermal blankets for cold-weather sites or mosquito nets for tropical climates; water purification tablets; some essential tools, like a hammer, saw, axe, small shovel, pliers; cooking pots, bowls, mugs, and basic utensils; and a stove that burns either wood or a variety of fuels. ShelterBoxes even contain crayons and coloring books for children, while the emptied box itself has been used for a variety of purposes, including a makeshift crib for infants.

The first ShelterBoxes were sent out in January of 2001 in response to a major earthquake in Gujarat, India, whose death toll reached more than 19,000. The nonprofit organization grew over the next few years as it was adopted by Rotary Clubs around the world, and had responded to 16 disasters by the time of the Indian Ocean tsunami in December of 2004. Less than a year later, Henderson's organization sent out its first major shipment to Americans in need after Hurricanes Katrina and Rita devastated New Orleans and the Gulf Coast.

Each ShelterBox, from assembly to delivery, costs between $700 and $1,000, depending on its origin and destination. Rotarians raise money to stock ShelterBox warehouses by promoting their work to schools, scouting troops, church groups, and other organizations. As ShelterBox's founder, Henderson makes some of these visits himself. In 2010, he spoke before students at a Roman Catholic school in Sarasota, Florida, and asked them if they knew how children in the Southern African nation of Swaziland lived. "St. Martha's students were quiet and focused as Henderson described children who physically fight to attend school, for only in school will they receive a meal," reported *Sarasota Herald Tribune* journalist Jennifer Shea, who quoted Henderson as telling the students that Swaziland's children "yearn for education and share meager supplies, so please continue to work with your teachers and friends to make a difference."

ShelterBox began packing relief supplies for Haitians just 12 minutes after the news of the Haitian earthquake in January of 2010. In most cases, the containers are offloaded from relief cargo planes in less than 72 hours. "Our boxes don't just create tent cities," Henderson told *Time*'s William Lee Adams. "They build communities. Within an hour of the tents going up, a mother starts hanging laundry lines and someone else sets up a minishop."

Henderson's nonprofit secured an important royal patron in 2007 when Camilla Parker-Bowles, the Duchess of Cornwall, agreed to become president of the charity. Two years later, Henderson was honored with the Order of the British Empire (OBE) in the annual New Year's Eve list of honors from Queen Elizabeth II. "On occasions like this everybody always [says] it's not a personal thing and I genuinely believe it," the British Broadcasting Corporation news organization quoted him as saying. "We work very hard with lots of people, from the trustees right down to our huge band of volunteers."

Henderson still lives in Cornwall, where the main ShelterBox headquarters are located in Helston. By 2010, 75,000 of its distinctive green boxes had been sent to survivors of more than a hundred catastrophic events. Some of them were high-profile ones, like the earthquakes in Haiti and Chile, but ShelterBox's special response teams of volunteers situated around the globe coordinated efforts for smaller-scale disasters, too. One of them was Tropical Storm Agatha, which struck Guatemala and El Salvador in May of 2010 and left 90,000 homeless. "It's all about shelter, warmth, comfort, and dignity," Henderson told CNN. "There are thousands of people dying every day. That's what drives us forward. This is not a job for us. It's a passion."

Sources

Periodicals

Sarasota Herald Tribune, February 25, 2010.
Tweed Daily News (Tweed Heads, Australia), March 10, 2010, p. 10.

Online

"About Us," ShelterBox, http://www.shelterbox. org/about.php (May 4, 2010).
"Home for 10 People … In a Portable Box," CNN. com, http://edition.cnn.com/2008/WORLD/europe/09/05/heroes.henderson/index.html (May 4, 2010).
"How ShelterBox Helps Haiti Earthquake Victims," *Time*, http://www.time.com/time/magazine/article/0,9171,1960259,00.html (June 2, 2010).
"ShelterBox Founder Appointed OBE," BBC News, http://news.bbc.co.uk/go/pr/fr/-/2/hi/uk_news/england/cornwall/8435025.stm (May 4, 2010).
"Tracking Aid to Haiti," CNN.com, http://www.cnn.com/2010/WORLD/americas/01/25/haiti.aid.track/index.html (June 2, 2010).

—*Carol Brennan*

Dan Hesse

Chief Executive Officer of Sprint Nextel

Born Daniel R. Hesse, c. 1954. *Education:* University of Notre Dame, B.A.; Massachusetts Institute of Technology, M.S.; MIT Sloan School of Management, M.S.; Cornell University, M.B.A.

Addresses: *Office*—c/o Sprint, 6200 Sprint Parkway, Overland Park, KS 66251-4300.

Career

Began working at AT&T and held a variety of management assignments such as network operations, network engineering, international services, human resources, strategic planning, product management, and sales, c. 1977-91; president and chief executive officer, AT&T Network Systems International, 1991-95; leader, AT&T Worldnet family of Internet services Online Services Group, 1995-97; president and chief executive officer, AT&T Wireless Services, 1997-2000; chairman, president, and chief executive officer, Terabeam Corporation, 2000-04; chairman and chief executive officer, Embarq Corporation, 2004-07; chief executive officer, Sprint Nextel Corporation, 2007—.

Member: Director, USCS International, Inc.; vice chairman, Cellular Telecommunications and Internet Association; independent director, member of compensation committee and member of finance committee, V.F. Corporation, 1999-2000; director, Utfors AB, 2000—; director, Proxim Wireless Corporation, 2004—; non-executive and independent director and member of personnel committee, 2005-07; director, Embarq Corporation, 2006-07; chief executive officer, president, director and chairman of executive committee, Sprint Nextel Corporation, 2007—; director, member of nominating and corporate governance committee, and member of compensation committee, Clearwire Corporation, 2008-10; National Board of Governors of the Boys and Girls Clubs of America; chairman, Pacific Region of Boys and Girls Club of America.

Awards: Brooks Thesis Prize for writing the outstanding masters thesis from all masters programs, MIT's Sloan School of Management; wireless industry person of the year, *RCR*; executive of the year, *Wireless Business and Technology*; leadership award, *Wireless Week*; Ellis Island Medal of Honor; most influential person in mobile technology, *Laptop* magazine, 2008.

Sidelights

Dan Hesse is a risk taker who puts himself into the arena to tackle problems. He not only takes on the rough and tumble business world, he does it in the cutting-edge industry of telecommunications. This attitude of fearlessness has helped him to win a variety of awards such as *RCR* magazine's "Wireless Industry Person of the Year" designation and *Wireless Business and Technology* magazine's "Executive of the Year."

After Hesse took over as the beleaguered Sprint Nextel Corporation's chief executive officer in September of 2007, he rolled up his sleeves, took a look around, and bravely faced the company's most serious challenges to becoming profitable once again. At the time Sprint Nextel Corporation had the worst customer service record of any telecommunications company and was losing customers at twice the rate of any other company in the business. Hesse made this a personal challenge and featured himself in a series of Sprint Nextel Corporation television commercials (according to a *New York Times* report) where he asked, "If you could change the way wireless companies did things, what would you do?" The commercials offered the direct and personal e-mail address dan@print.com. Other executives at Sprint Nextel were dubious and worried about putting their chief executive officer on the television as a target at which consumers could sling their complaints. Laura M. Holson, reporting for the *New York Times* one year after Hesse had taken over at Sprint, wrote, "he is making progress. In a report by Pali Research, Sprint has improved its customer care response times, ranking first in a survey of peers."

Customer service was not the only concern Hesse had to deal with at Sprint Nextel in that first year that he became the chief executive officer. The company also had 23 billion dollars in debt, a bank note for 600 million dollars coming due, and only three and a half billion dollars cash at hand. This was also 2008 when the banking and credit crisis were in full swing and refinancing and consolidating debt in the corporate sector was not as easy as in previous years. Further, the recession in the United States was becoming a depressing reality for many people who were not willing or able to part with extra money for the services Sprint Nextel offered. Hesse, drawing on his background, took these issues in stride.

In addition to his fearlessness, Hesse also has a solid education to draw from that he used to construct a plan to revive the company. Hesse obtained a bachelor of arts degree from the prestigious University of Notre Dame. While attending the Massachusetts Institute of Technology Hesse earned a master of science degree as well as a management degree. He was awarded the Brooks Thesis Prize for writing the best masters thesis from all of the masters programs while at MIT's Sloan School of Management. In addition to these degrees, he also received a master of business administration, with distinction, from Cornell University.

Working for Sprint Nextel was not Hesse's first job straight out of college. Hesse learned about the telecommunications industry through another company for whom he worked for 23 years. While he was employed at AT&T he learned about the concept of brand and the idea of building a brand. When he first became employed by AT&T that company was not well thought of in the industry and its sales were down. Over the course of his employment with AT&T he held management positions in several departments including network operations, network engineering, international services, human resources, strategic planning, and product management and sales. He moved into the upper echelons of AT&T when he served as the president and chief executive officer of AT&T Network Systems International. Later, from 1997-2000 he was the president and chief executive office of AT&T's Wireless Services.

In 2000, he left AT&T to become the chairman, president, and chief executive officer for the Terabeam Corporation, a wireless telecommunications service provider and technology company. He worked there for five years before moving on to be the chairman and chief executive officer of Embarq Corporation, a telecommunications services company. He also served as a member, chairman, or director on the board of directors of a number of telecommunications companies.

Hesse brought all of this education and experience to Sprint Nextel. He determined that to turn the company around, he needed to accomplish three goals. The first of these goals was to improve customer service. The second goal was to "build the brand." Building the brand involved reversing the negative image of Sprint and creating a more positive image. In an interview with Kai Ryssdal on *Marketplace* from American Public Radio, Hesse commented that building the brand took time but was ultimately so important that he said it was, "really nirvana." The third goal in Hesse's plan to turn around Sprint was to generate more cash, which could be accomplished by achieving the first two goals.

To build the Sprint brand not only did Hesse work on improving customer service, he also looked to find what would be the cutting edge of technology that he could use to create Sprint devices. In the summer of 2010 Sprint introduced the first 4G cellular phone called the Evo. A 4G phone at the time was five times better than a 3G phone. The Evo was loaded with extras like a camcorder, a high-resolution screen, and a camera. In addition to introducing the 4G phone, Hesse strived to have Sprint be at the forefront of rate plans and offers. The experience that Sprint offered its customers became so different from that which people experienced before Hesse took over as chief executive officer that the American Customer Satisfaction Index said that in the 16 years that the survey had been conducted only one other company had improved their customer satisfaction score to such a large extent. With almost everyone in the United States over the age of 12 already owning and carrying a cellular phone, Hesse used this combination of good customer service, cutting edge technology, and a variety of rate plans, offers, and services to acquire new customers and to have them feel satisfied with their experience with Sprint.

Sources

Periodicals

New York Times, June 9, 2008, p. C6; October 21, 2008, p. B3.

Online

"Dan Hesse," *Laptop,* http://www.laptopmag.com/business/feature/25-most-influential-people-in-mobile-technology.aspx?page=26#axzz199jxzUET (November 28, 2010).

"Dan Hesse's Bio," *Marketplace,* American Public Radio, http://marketplace.publicradio.org/display/web/2010/07/01/pm-corner-office-hesse-bio (November 17, 2010).

"Dan Hesse: Executive Profile & Biography," Bloomberg BusinessWeek, http://investing.businessweek.com/research/stocks/people/person.asp?personld=638178&ticker=S:US (November 17, 2010).

"Dan Hesse," Sprint, http://newsroom.sprint.com/article_display.cfm?article_id=1477 (November 17, 2010).

"Sprint's Wake-Up Call," Bloomberg BusinessWeek, (November 17, 2010). http://www.businessweek.com/magazine/content/08_09/b40730544.tif48185.htm (Novemebr 17, 2010).

Transcripts

Marketplace, American Public Media, July 1, 2010.

—*Annette Bowman*

Steven Holcomb

Newscom

Bobsled racer

Born April 14, 1980; son of Steven Holcomb. *Education:* University of Phoenix, B.S., c. 2011.

Addresses: *Contact*—Night Train Bobsled Team, P.O. Box 118, Oakley, UT 84055. *Web site*—http://stevenholcomb.com.

Career

Began as an alpine skiier; soldier, advancing to combat engineer, Utah Army National Guard, 1999-06; began bobsled racing, 1998; driver of an international level competition bobsled, 2002—.

Awards: Gold medal, World Cup, for two-man bobsled team overall, 2006-07; silver medal, World Cup, for four-man bobsled team overall, 2006-07; silver medal, World Cup, for two-man bobsled team overall, 2007-08; gold medal, World Cup, for four-man bobsled team, 2008-09; bronze medal, World Championships, for mixed bobsled team, 2008; bronze medal, World Championships, mixed bobsled team, 2009; bronze medal, World Championships, two-man bobsled team, 2009; gold medal, World Championships, four-man bobsled team, 2009; gold medal, Vancouver Olympic Games, four-man bobsled team, 2010.

Sidelights

Steve Holcomb had a vision. Perhaps this vision needed a certain amount of adjustment in a variety of ways, but it was a vision. Holcomb knew that he wanted to be a competitive athlete in the winter sports. For most athletes there is a correlation between vision and what they are capable of in two separate ways and this was especially true for Holcomb. Many sports trainers encourage the athletes that they work with to visualize themselves doing their particular sport and using this visualization to hone their skills and mentally practice for their sport. In addition, good eyesight simply enhances performance.

Holcomb originally started as an athlete in alpine skiing. He was involved in alpine ski racing for about ten years prior to switching to bobsled. The switch from one dangerous sport to another did not concern his family in and of itself. What bothered his father was that he had just sent a check for a semester's worth of tuition to the University of Utah prior to Holcomb deciding to change sports and head off to Europe to pursue this new ambition. In an article written for the *New York Times* by Jonathan Abrams, the elder Holcomb was quoted, while standing near the finish line at the Whistler Sliding Centre watching his son compete, as saying "Probably a good investment. It was money well spent, poorly." Holcomb can offer his father a repayment on that generous donation to the University of Utah; a repayment in gold. Holcomb's four-man bobsled team won the gold medal for the United States at the 2010 Vancouver Olympic games. This was the first time in 62 years that the United States won a gold medal in the bobsled event. The last person to head a team to accomplish that feat was Patrick Henry Martin in 1948 during the St. Moritz Olympic Games.

The attainment of the gold medal at the Vancouver games was the stuff of legends. Even the bobsled that Holcomb and his teammates designed which had been dubbed on the bobsled circuit the "Night Train" took on mythic proportions. It is a stunning sled. Sleek with a dull black finish, it was designed by race-car designer Bob Cuneo who spread rumors that the finish had been created by NASA to make the sled even faster. Holcomb described "Night Train" to Lisa Olson, a national columnist writing for the Web site Fanhouse, saying, "Technically, it's my wife. I'm married to it." Olson also reported that Holcomb had listed on his Facebook page under "Relationship Status" that he was "Married to Night Train Bobsled" and he would have taken the sled back to the Athletes' Village nightly if he could have.

The relationship that a bobsled driver has with the bobsled is unique. The object has to become an extension of the athlete's body. The driver has to feel the pressure of where the bobsled is in relation to the ice and space through their hands, arms, and legs. They have to know instantly whether they are steering the sled too high or too low. Physics will determine the ideal path for a 1,400-pound sled with four passengers and the most direct line to maneuver the course has to be determined and maintained. Being off by fractions of an inch at one point in a run if not corrected can become distorted into disaster. Bobsledding is a sport where honed physical skills and an almost supernatural intuition to mediate between the ice and the sled are required.

Writing for *Sports Illustrated*, David Epstein compared a bobsledder's intuition to a Jedi Knight's use of the mythical Force in *Star Wars*. In the first *Star Wars* movie, *A New Hope*, Obi-wan Kenobi is training Luke Skywalker to use the force with a lightsaber and a floating training ball that sends out electrical impulses. Luke is repeatedly zapped. Obi-wan then lowers the blast shield on Luke's helmet. Luke asks how he is supposed to fight if he cannot see and Obi-wan tells him to use the Force and that his eyes can deceive him. This is a good analogy for bobsledding where visual cues can actually impair the ability of the driver to maneuver the sled. Holcomb who has had vision problems since high school learned to steer a bobsled by the feel of the sled.

The NBC Olympics Web site reported that, prior to the Torino Olympic games, Holcomb was "legally blind without corrective lenses. If I don't wear my contacts, it's comparable to opening your eyes under water." Two years before the 2010 Vancouver games Holcomb considered dropping out of bobsledding because his vision had become so bad that even corrective lenses could no longer help. His vision at the time was 20-500 and he saw everything with glare and distortion. The degenerative eye disorder that Holcomb had is called keratoconus and it gradually distorts the cornea and destroys a person's eyesight. According to the National Keratoconus Foundation the disease affects one in every 2,000 people. In 2008, Holcomb opted for surgery.

Because Holcomb participated in the high risk sport of bobsledding, he could not use corrective eye glasses and a cornea implant would make his eyes too fragile to continue to be a bobsledder; nonetheless, Holcomb was on the list for a cornea transplant. After some research and consideration Holcomb and his coaches decided to have him undergo an experimental treatment called C3-R to correct his vision. In a press release from the Boxer Wachler Vision Institute, Dr. Boxer Wachler claimed, "Previously, the only treatment for severe Keratoconus was a cornea transplant. This is why C3-R is being seen as such a breakthrough. C3-R is non-surgical. It uses vitamin applications and light to strengthen the cornea. C3-R can cure the disease without the need for a cornea transplant. The treatment only takes 30 minutes and can be done in a doctor's office." After undergoing this experimental procedure and receiving insertable contact lenses to further improve his vision, Holcomb could get on with his ambitions of being a bobsled champion. Shortly after the procedure he and his Night Train team won the World Bobsled Championship. This was the first bobsled medal for the United States in more than 50 years.

For a while after the corneal treatment, which did involve placing permanent corrective lenses on Holcomb's eyes, his ability to steer a bobsled was ironically impaired. He had learned to feel his way through the bobsled runs. Holcomb told Abrams of the *New York Times* that, "I got away from driving by feel and started driving by visual cues. I took a few steps back for a couple weeks." In the same article, Brian Shimer, five-time bobsled Olympian and the U.S. bobsled team coach said, "My concern was that maybe he wouldn't be as good. He would see too much peripherally and get too much information." Holcomb handled this new challenge of enhanced vision in a few ways. He determinedly blocked out all unnecessary information, smudged his visor to blur his vision, and did not replace his helmet even though the visor was scratched. He also worked on envisioning in his imagination his team standing at the finish line as the winners of the event and then began to work his way mentally back through each of the turns in the run to prepare himself for each one in order. This technique worked and helped Holcomb to win the World Championship and the Olympic gold medal in the four-man bobsled event.

In addition to helping Holcomb to steer his team to victory, having the corrective surgery on his eyes also brought Holcomb out of his shyness to a degree. Shimer told Abrams, "A lot of times, he really couldn't see into crowds and who was surrounding him. Now, he doesn't have those problems and he's more aware of the world that's around him." Holcomb, while viewed as the reserved member of his team, has always gotten along very well with his teammates, including pushers Steve Mesler, Justin Olsen, and Curt Tomasevicz. The four are best friends and rarely separated. They share hotel rooms, car rides, and are crammed together inside a tight-fitting bobsled. Their routine on the day of races consists of reciting the lyrics to the song "All the Above" by the rapper Maino. Part of the song's lyrics are: "Tell me what do you see/ When you looking at me/On a mission to be/What I'm destined to be." Tomasevicz told Abrams, "We're like brothers."

In addition to bobsledding, Holcomb, whose nickname is "Holkie," is also considered to be something of a techie. According to a story on the Microsoft News Center Web site, Holcomb is a self described computer geek who has Microsoft Certified Professional training and has used computer games as part of his training for bobsledding. When Holcomb enrolled at the University of Utah before his bob sledding career took off, his ambition was to major in computer science; he plans to work in the IT industry after his bobsledding career is over. Holcomb is an avid video game player and plays video games prior to starting his bobsled training in order to improve his performance. Microsoft News Center quotes him as saying, "As soon as I was on the track, I noticed how much easier driving was—things moved slower, I could interpret everything that was going on, I could tune out everything that wasn't on the track. Sure enough, when I play video games my bobsledding improves."

Holcomb's other interests include cycling, reading, video editing, and his copper-colored Golden retriever named Bailey. The day that Holcomb and his teammates appeared on the *Today Show*, the program featured a segment called "Bow-to-WOW!" where dogs from a local animal shelter were to be featured for adoption. For Holcomb and Bailey it was love at first sight. On the Web site PeoplePets, Holcomb is quoted as saying, "It was like an instant connection. All the people there were like, 'Whoa, you tamed her.'" The host of the *Today Show* asked Holcomb if he was going to adopt Bailey and at first Holcomb said that he might and then later in the show he announced that he would adopt the dog. Holcomb had been looking for a dog for over a year since the death of his 14-year-old springer spaniel.

For this remarkable athlete from Park City, Utah, having a vision of himself standing with his bobsled teammates in the winner's circle became a reality at the Vancouver Olympic games. Prior to that, he and his team won several prizes in the World Cup competitions, but it was the 2010 Olympic gold medal that placed him firmly in the international spotlight and everyone will be watching to see what he does next. With his vision corrected, Holcomb can keep competing and he can look out upon the audience watching his breathtaking accomplishments.

Sources

Periodicals

New York Times, February 1, 2010, p. D4; February 28, 2010, p. 8.
PR Newswire, February 18, 2010.
Sports Illustrated, November 9, 2009, pp. 60-62.

Online

"Gold Medalist Bobsledder Reveals His Techie Side," Microsoft News Center, http://www.microsoft.com/presspass/features/2010/may10/05-24holcomb.mspx (June 2, 2010).
"'Night Train' Helps Bring Steven Holcomb, US Bobsledders to Light," Fanhouse, http://lisa-olson.fanhouse.com/2010/02/12/night-train-brings-holcomb-u-s-bobsledders-to-light/ (June 2, 2010).
"Olympic Gold Medalist Steven Holcomb Adopts a Golden Retriever!," PeoplePets, http://www.peoplepets.com/news/dogs/olympic-gold-medalist-steven-holcomb-adopts-a-golden-retriever (June 2, 2010).
"Steve Holcomb—Biography," NBC Olympics, http://www.nbcolympics.com/athletes/athlete=2328/bo/index.html (June 2, 2010).

"Steven Holcomb, Bobsleigh," Vancouver 2010, http://www.vancouver2010.com/olympic-bobsleigh/athletes/steven-holcomb_ath1023679 bT (June 2, 2010).

"Team Holcomb," Team Holcomb, http://steven holcomb.com/contactus.html (June 4, 2010).

—Annette Bowman

Bill Hybels

Minister and author

Born December 12, 1951, in Kalamazoo, MI; son of Harold (a business owner) and Gertrude (a homemaker; maiden name, VeldKamp) Hybels; married Lynne Barry (an author and speaker), May 18, 1974; children: Shauna, Todd. *Education:* Attended Dordt College, 1970-72; Trinity College, B.A., 1975.

Addresses: *Office*—c/o Willow Creek Community Church, 67 East Algonquin Rd., South Barrington, Il 60010. *Web site*—http://www.willowcreek.org/.

Career

Worked as a youth minister at a church in Park Ridge, IL, 1973-75; became an ordained interdenominational minister, 1975; co-founder and senior pastor, Willow Creek Community Church, South Barrington, IL, 1975—; chaplain, Chicago Bears, National Football League, 1982-87; co-founded Willow Creek Association, 1992; named one of the 25 most influential evangelists in America by *Time* magazine, 2005.

Awards: Honorary doctorate, Trinity International University.

Sidelights

The long-time senior pastor of the innovative Willow Creek Community Church in suburban Chicago, Bill Hybels challenged traditional norms in churches and developed a contemporary message and presentation intended to draw in nonchurchgoers and retain believers. Over the years, Willow Creek became the basis of a network of churches numbering more than 11,000 by 2007. He served as the leader of this network as well as actively participated in the training of 100,000 pastors each year. Also an author of many books on Christianity, Hybels emphasized real-world communication in his writings and teachings. In 2005, *Time* magazine named him one of the 25 most influential evangelists in the United States, noting that "Hybels was a pioneer in attracting an upscale, youthful following with an informal yet rousing and contemporary service."

Born on December 12, 1951, in Kalamazoo, Michigan, he was the son of Harold and Gertrude Hybels. His father owned a business, Hybels Produce Company, while his mother was a homemaker. The family attended Westwood Christian Reformed Church. As a teenager, Hybels received his education at Kalamazoo Christian High School and became more committed to Christianity after his father sent him to visit poor communities and missions in Europe, Africa, and the Middle East.

After graduating from Kalamazoo Christian in 1970, Hybels attended Dordt College, located in Sioux Center, Iowa, where he studied business for two years before deciding to change careers. He transferred to the Deerfield, Illinois-based Trinity College (later known as Trinity International University), from which he earned his bachelor's degree in Bible Studies in 1975. While in school, Hybels served as a youth minister at a church in Park Ridge, Illinois, from 1973 to 1975. He also married his wife, Lynne, in May of 1974. After graduating, Hybels became an ordained interdenominational minister in 1975.

Also in 1975, Hybels co-founded Willow Creek Community Church, originally located in Palatine, Illinois, with his new wife. The couple and others interviewed several hundred people about what they were looking for in a church before they held their first service. They were also inspired by Gilbert Bilezikian, who taught about church growth, and Robert Schuller, the minister at the Crystal Cathedral who emphasized self-empowerment. At first, Willow Creek rented space in a movie theater and Hybels was the only pastor and counselor. (The name Willow Creek comes from the name of the Palatine movie theater.) The Hybels went from door to door inviting people to come to their service.

When asked about his original idea for Willow Creek Community Church by Cathleen Falsani of the *Chicago Sun-Times*, Hybels explained that he envisioned something radical. He explained it "As a new and different way to do church, because I barely survived the church I grew up in. Not because I wasn't sensitive to things of God, it's just the structure of the church and the way church was done was very difficult for me to relate to. So when I started to imagine how church could be done differently, that was a very exciting thought."

While only 125 people attended the first service in October of 1975, weekly attendance reached 2,000 by 1977. When membership outgrew the theater in 1981, Willow Creek moved to South Barrington, Illinois, where it had bought land. By this time, church had developed a reputation for being quite different than a traditional church. Willow Creek was novel in its approach to attracting attendees (uncommitted Christians seeking information about Christianity) by using praise songs rooted in contemporary music and played by live bands. Hybels and his church also incorporated dramatic skits and videos as well as short sermons which emphasized practical application and understandable concepts and language. Underlining the importance of local mission, he worked to reach the so-called "unchurched," and wanted Christians to affect those around them.

Through Willow Creek, Hybels effectively launched a Protestant renewal that gave those questioning Christianity the space and anonymity to explore the faith, while committed Christians had dynamic services. He outlined his ideas about spiritual matters as well as church organization in the many books he wrote and published over the years, be-

ginning in the late 1970s with *Caution: Christians Under Construction*. Hybels put out a book at least once every few years, touching on topics such as sex, abortion, the workplace, and other Christian lifestyle topics. Hybels also reached some people in a completely different way. From 1982 to 1987, he served as the team chaplain for the Chicago Bears professional football team.

In 1992, Willow Creek began extensively expanding its network of churches, forming the Willow Creek Association as its evangelistic and teaching arm. The network soon extended worldwide, with the association providing resources for its member churches to offer contemporary worship services and relevant church life. Through Willow Creek's Church Leadership Conferences, which began in 1995, Hybels and his staff equipped pastors and lay leaders with the tools to lead their churches in renewal and develop a strategy for change that would not destroy the church. That is, to make even mainline denominational churches more relevant and contemporary in their focus and appeal.

Describing a 1998 Church Leadership Conference in which Hybels spoke on "The Way It Really Is," Judy Bradford of the *South Bend Tribune* explained "The Willow Creek way challenges every traditional notion of what worship is. Rather than congregants with heads down in a hymn book, they are looking up, reading lyrics off a screen. Rather than long sermons to make a point, drama makes it and a message delivers only the good news. Fancy, liturgical words are removed from worship: The person who just walked in off the street must understand."

In the mid- to late 1990s, Hybels came to national prominence as a spiritual counselor to then President Bill Clinton. Hybels met Clinton on a monthly basis to advise him on these matters. Describing his responsibilities, Vince Galloro of the *Chicago Daily Herald* quoted Hybels as saying, "Well, I think it's a very complex role that I'm playing. Sometimes I don't even understand exactly what God has in mind for the role I am to play there, because it's a mixture of a confidant, a mentor, a coach, a prophet, a friend." While their relationship was controversial—especially as many evangelical Christians disliked or distrusted Clinton—Hybels remained close to the president during his time in office. In 2000, Clinton even accepted Hybels' invitation to visit Willow Creek and spoke at the annual Leadership Summit to thousands of pastors both live and via satellite.

By 1998, Hybels' church saw in excess of 17,000 people in attendance weekly. Two years later Willow Creek boasted 20,000 parishioners and was seen as a leader in the "megachurch" movement. Hybels' church was located on a 155-acre compound with numerous buildings for group meetings, treatment programs, counseling, recording studios, theaters, various types of musical entertainment, libraries, and even stores. Willow Creek's foray into what had been considered secular amenities was considered part of Hybels' entrepreneurial vision and began drawing more and more attention to Hybels, his methodology, and his church.

In 2000, Hybels took his church in a new direction when he announced plans for a spiritual outreach to the four million people in Chicago and its suburbs who do not go to church and change the city for the better. Willow Creek was not to strive for this goal alone, but formed alliances with thousands of other pastors and churches in the area who shared this ideal and worked toward the objective of reaching each and every non-church attending person over the next few years. Hybels also wanted to expand Willow Creek as attendance increased, as the church's first aim was converting the half million people who lived within 30 miles of the church campus.

Some in the community expressed skepticism of Hybels' ambition, but the pastor told Teresa Mask of the *Chicago Daily Herald,* "Willow Creek has been a risk-taking church since its conception. We've been willing to do what we believe God has asked us to do for the last 25 years. Sometimes that winds up being very popular with people around the community. And sometimes not so much." He added, "Here's what I'm confident of: If we don't try, nothing will happen. If we do try, with God's help, something is going to happen. So, our intent is to try."

By 2005, Willow Creek was able to add a $72 million addition to its grounds that included a Christian book store, coffee bar, auditorium, children's ministry facilities, and dining area. That year, *Time* magazine recognized Hybels' contributions to the changing face of Christianity in the United States. While Willow Creek and its association had been long established, some observers, such as the *Grand Rapids Press* in 2005, noted that "His message is packaged in a performance-style service that draws criticism from outsiders but also pulls in more than 17,000 worshipers a week, making it one of the largest churches in America."

While reaching greater Chicago remained a focus, Hybels and Willow Creek also thought globally as well. Under Hybels' leadership, his wife and the church raised $600,000 for AIDS-related causes in Africa, for example. Over the next few years, Hybels continued to be considered one of the most influential Christians in the United States while challenging his churchgoers, pastors, and lay leaders. He spent much of the first decade of the 2000s, for example, working to bring minorities into his overwhelmingly white congregation and ensure that the institution would be welcoming to them. In 2010, Hybels' flock was comprised of about 20 percent minorities and he launched a specific campaign of race reconciliation in both Willow Creek's community as well as greater society.

Hybels remained convinced that churches like Willow Creek had a bright future, telling the *Chicago Sun-Times'* Cathleen Falsani, "I've never been more optimistic about the future of the local church than I am right now, because I think church leaders have finally come to understand that the wise thing to do is to recalibrate the methodology of the church for each societal change and each generational reality."

Outside of his ministry, Hybels enjoyed racing sailboats, flying planes, riding motorcycles, running, and playing racquetball. He never expected to become the head of a church and molder of a modern evangelical movement, telling the *Grand Rapids Press,* "I grew up thinking I'd go into the family business. I never intended to be a pastor. No one is more surprised by the path my life took than [me]."

Selected writings

Nonfiction

Caution: Christians Under Construction, Victor Books (Wheaton, IL), 1978.
Christians in the Marketplace, Victor Books, 1982.
Laws That Liberate, Victor Books, 1985.
One Church's Answer to Abortion, Moody Press (Chicago, IL), 1986.
Who You Are When No One's Looking, InterVarsity (Downers Grove, IL), 1988.
Seven Wonders of the Spiritual World, Word Books (Dallas, TX), 1988.
Christians in a Sex-Crazed World, Victor Books, 1988.
Authentic Christianity, Moody Press, 1989.
(With Stuart Briscoe and Haddon Robinson) *Mastering Contemporary Preaching,* Multnomah (Portland, OR), 1990.
Honest to God?: Becoming an Authentic Christian, Zondervan (Grand Rapids, MI), 1990.
(With Lynn Hybels) *Fit to Be Tied: Making Marriage Last a Lifetime,* Zondervan, 1991.

(With Rob Wilkens) *Descending into Greatness,* Zondervan, 1993.

(With Mark Mittelberg) *Becoming a Contagious Christian,* Zondervan, 1994.

The God You're Looking For, T. Nelson (Nashville, TN), 1997.

(With Lynn Hybels) *Making Life Work: Putting God's Wisdom into Action: With Questions for Reflection and Discussion,* InterVarsity, 1998.

(With Ken Blanchard and Phil Hodges) *Leadership by the Book: Tools to Transform Your Workplace,* W. Morrow (New York City), 1999.

Engraved on Your Heart: Living the Ten Commandments Day by Day, Victor (Colorado Springs, CO), 2000.

Courageous Leadership, Zondervan, 2002.

Courageous Faith Through the Year, InterVarsity, 2002.

(With Dale and Sandy Larsen) *Wisdom: Making Life Work: 6 Studies for Individuals or Groups with Leader's Notes,* InterVarsity, 2003.

The Volunteer Revolution: Unleashing the Power of Everybody, Zondervan, 2004.

Just Walk Across the Room: Four Sessions on Simple Steps Pointing People to Faith, Zondervan, 2006.

Holy Discontent: Fueling the Fire That Ignites Personal Vision, Zondervan, 2007.

Axiom: Powerful Leadership Proverbs, Zondervan, 2008.

Sources

Books

Marquis Who's Who, Marquis Who's Who, 2009.

Periodicals

Chicago Daily Herald, October 11, 1998, p. 2; September 18, 2000, p. 5; February 1, 2007, p. 3; August 10, 2007, p. 3; January 11, 2010, p. 3.
Chicago Sun Times, October 23, 2005, p. A9; October 24, 2005, p. 12.
Grand Rapids Press, March 5, 2005, p. E1.
Kalamazoo Gazette, February 27, 2005, p. A1.
South Bend Tribune (IN), October 30, 1998, p. C3.
Weekly Standard, September 11, 2000, p. 14.

Online

"Bill Hybels," *Time,* http://www.time.com/time/covers/11010502.tif07/photoessay/12.html (March 6, 2010).
"Can Megachurches Bridge the Racial Divide?," *Time,* http://www.time.com/time/magazine/article/0,9171,1950943,00.html (March 6, 2010).
Contemporary Authors Online, Thomson Gale, 2007.

—*A. Petruso*

Christian Jacobs and Scott Schultz

Creators of Yo Gabba Gabba!

Born Christian Richards Jacobs, January 11, 1972, in Rexburg, ID; married; children: four. Born Scott Schultz in 1972; married; children: four.

Addresses: *Office*—Wildbrain Entertainment, 15000 Ventura Blvd, Sherman Oaks, CA 91403. *Web site*—http://www.yogabbagabba.com/

Career

Jacobs: Played in the band The Aquabats, 1994—; Schultz: Played in a band called Majestic (now defunct). Both: Created children's television show *Yo Gabba Gabba!*, Nickelodeon and Nick Jr. networks, 2007—.

Sidelights

Christian Jacobs and Scott Schultz are the creators of the children's television show *Yo Gabba Gabba!*, which appears on the Nickelodeon and Nick Jr. networks. The show is known for its use of independent rock music, a format that appeals both to preschool kids and to their parents. It features five colorful creatures, as well appearances by musicians and actors including Jack Black, Andy Samberg, Elijah Wood, The Shins, MGMT, the Ting Tings, the Flaming Lips, the Killers, and Weezer. The show's "cool factor" has drawn a wide variety of celebrities to live performances—Christina Aguilera, Jason Bateman, and Dennis Quaid have all been spotted in the audience. A press release for the show in PR Newswire summed up, "Millions of preschoolers and their families have been beat-boxing, singing and dancing along to the infectious lyrics and high-energy soundtrack on the show."

Jacobs and Schultz are cousins by marriage. They both came from entertainment backgrounds. As a child Jacobs worked as an actor, appearing in commercials, television shows, and films, and Schultz spent much of his childhood touring with his father, who directed musical variety shows. They met when Jacobs' mother married Schultz's uncle. They quickly became friends and spent a lot of time surfing, skateboarding, and playing music together. They both played in bands. Schultz played in a band called Majestic, and Jacobs sang with the Aquabats, a band that was still active as of 2011.

The Aquabats were known for their entertaining live performances in which band members dressed up in colorful costumes and interacted with bizarre creatures during the set. In the late 1990s they had a couple of chances to turn their act into a television show, but the deals never came through. By 2001, both Schultz and Jacobs were new dads, and they were bored out of their minds by the shows that were available to preschoolers. Schultz told Rob Brunner in *Entertainment Weekly* that he and Jacobs thought, "Wow, we can do something way better than this." Even though the shows were very warm and safe-feeling for children, they were utterly boring to adults, Jacobs told Brunner, "There wasn't a lot for us dads to get excited about. It seemed like we needed to make something for our generation to relate to." As children, both Jacobs and Schultz had watched 1970s staples like the *Electric Company* and *H. R. Pufnstuf,* and they drew on those shows for inspiration. They also used their own experience—both are fathers of four kids—for ideas. Schultz told Kristin Rushowy in the *Toronto Star,* "You get to the point as a parent, you are going to get really mad and be frustrated, or you make up a really funny story that makes your kid laugh and eat his vegetables. Those are the types of things we wanted to present to the world, life lessons that are funny and fun." Schultz explained to Diane Toroian Keaggy in the *St. Louis Post-Dispatch,* "What we are doing is providing a huge range of musical styles that aren't being represented in kids' music and exposing them to a variety of different colors they've never seen before.... It's, 'Let's get bands we like and have them do a song kids can relate to and we can find common ground there.'"

They began working on ideas for a show, starting with characters named Muno and Brobee, who had been featured in the Aquabats' stage shows. In 2006 they borrowed money from friends, took out second mortgages, and they shot two pilot episodes. They needed a host for their show, and Schultz recalled a member from a band he had once known who might be a good fit. They drove to Los Angeles to meet him at the record store where he worked. Jacobs told Brunner, "He comes out and he's wearing this '70s getup, like he would have been on [the children's television show] *Electric Company* or in Sly Stone's band—a huge beard and a giant Afro and these rainbow-colored striped pants. He had a big smile on his face and said, 'Hey, how ya doing? I'm Lance.' It was like lightning struck."

The guy was Lance Robertson, and he decided to go with the flow and see what might happen with this television show. It followed the traditional children's television format of a host (DJ Lance Rock), upbeat music, and a group of charming, colorful monsters named Brobee, Foofa, Muno, Plex, and Toodee; however, it had a difference. As Carolyn Sayre noted in *Time,* "The songs are set to contagious hip-hop beats, and the animation is so retro it looks like a rave party for kids." They filmed the pilot episodes, but couldn't get any television networks interested in them. "We'd sent it around," Schultz told Rushowy, "but no one knows where those [DVDs] went, probably on the bottom of someone's desk—some intern." They began promoting the show themselves, handing out DVDs at concerts and posting clips on their Web site.

By word of mouth, news about the show spread, and their site got so many visitors that it crashed. Pretty soon they had a breakfast meeting scheduled with Brown Johnson, president of animation at Nickelodeon, but they were stuck in traffic and ended up arriving 45 minutes late. Jacobs told Brunner that it was "like, really, really not cool. We were biting our nails the whole way." Johnson, however, was charmed by their lack of polish, and told Brunner, "They rolled up in this really crappy nine-passenger band van. I fell in love with them. It was like having breakfast with puppies. Their excitement was so contagious and felt so pure and fresh." Johnson felt that the show idea was fresh, too, and by the end of the breakfast she offered them their own show with complete creative control.

Yo Gabba Gabba! premiered on August 20, 2007, produced by Wildbrain Studios, with a mix of five colorful creatures and 1980s rapper Biz Markie. The first episode featured Mark Mothersbaugh from the 1980s band Devo and actor Elijah Wood. A typical show featured hip-hop musician Biz Markie doing "Biz's Beat of the Day," teaching kids how to make hip-hop percussion sounds with their voices and Mothersbaugh drawing pictures in a "Mark's Magic Pictures" segment. Other segments include animation, life-size walking puppet characters, real kids, and guest actors teaching simple life lessons. The puppet characters are Foofa, a pink flower bubble; Muno, a red cyclops; Brobee, a little green monster; Toodee, a blue cat-dragon; and Plex, a robot. When the host yells "Yo Gabba Gabba!" they spring to life and sing, dance, and play. Behind the play are gentle lessons. As Johnson told Dave Itzkoff in the *New York Times,* "What may seem outwardly like a segment about beatboxing really has to do with counting and rhythm, and being able to imitate what someone is doing, and following directions. There's all sorts of hidden agendas there."

Reaction was mixed. Some parents loved it, while others said it was too strange and they would never allow their kids to watch it. The show took off, though, and by April of 2008 it was the number-one show in its time slot among kids aged two to five, with 21 million viewers. The show also generated 25 million video streams on the Nick Jr Web site in the fall of 2008. In 2008 the cast began doing road shows, which sold out, and in 2010 there was talk of a movie. The show was featured in *Time* and *Newsweek* as well as in the *New York Times.* Like most other kids' shows, this one quickly turned into a marketing bonanza, with spin-off books, toys, clothes, and accessories.

As a result of the show, some musicians found a second avenue of creativity in writing and performing for kids, something they would not have thought of doing before being featured on the show. Promoter Paul Stark told Toroian Keaggy, "There is a growing number of artists who have found this new audience. They may do a show the night before for adults and then come back the next afternoon for [a *Yo Gabba Gabba!* performance]." He added that some musicians ultimately make more money playing for children than they do playing for adults.

Stark remarked to Toroian Keaggy that some parents enjoyed the fact that they could still retain part of their life before children because of the show's live performances: "I do it for the kids. But yes, there is that extra benefit. Parents get to be part of a scene. They're still at the club listening to great music, only it's 3 in the afternoon." Jacobs, commenting on this crossover audience, told Brunner that in the past, parents and children had separate music and pastimes, "Whereas this show encourages a special bond between parent and child that I think is going to be valuable to the future. That might be kind of arrogant to say, but the fact that it's working makes me proud and kind of emotional. It's really magic."

Sources

Periodicals

Atlanta Journal-Constitution, October 23, 2010, p. D1.
Entertainment Weekly, March 12, 2010, p. 48.
License!, February 2008, p. 52.
People, September 13, 2010, p. 174.
PR Newswire, April 28, 2008, p. NA.
San Francisco Chronicle, August 17, 2007, p. E1.
San Jose Mercury News, August 20, 2007.
St. Louis Post-Dispatch, March 14, 2010, p. D1.
Time, May 26, 2008, p. 61.
Toronto Star, March 17, 2010, p. 5.

Online

"Charm the Children, Tickle the Parents," *New York Times,* http://www.nytimes.com/2007/08/12/arts/television/12itzk.html (November 15, 2010).
"Christian Jacobs and Scott Schultz," Wildbrain Entertainment, http://www.wildbrain.com/animation/abot_us/bios/pdf/director/Jacobs_Schultz_bio/.pdf (November 15, 2010).

—*Kelly Winters*

Ha Jin

Rogan Coles/Getty Images Entertainment/Getty Images

Author and professor

Born Xuefei Jin, February 21, 1956, in Jinzhou, Liaoning, China; son of Danlin (an army officer) and Yuanfen (a petty officer; maiden name, Zhao) Jin; married Lisha Bian, 1982; children: Wen (son). *Education:* Heilongjiang University, B.A., Heilongjiang, China, 1981; Shandong University, M.A., 1984; Brandeis University, Ph.D., 1992; Boston University, M.F.A., 1994.

Addresses: *Office*—Creative Writing Program, Boston University, 236 Bay State Road, Boston, MA, 02215.

Career

Published first collection of poems, *Between Silences: A Voice from China,* 1990; assistant professor of creative writing, Emory University, 1993-02; published first collection of short stories, *Ocean of Words: Army Stories,* 1996; published first novel, *In the Pond,* 1998; professor of creative writing, Boston University, 2002—; wrote libretto for opera *The First Emperor,* 2006.

Awards: PEN/Hemingway Award for first fiction, Hemingway Society and PEN New England, for *Ocean of Words: Army Stories,* 1997; Georgia Author of the Year Award for short fiction, Georgia Writers Association, for *Under the Red Flag,* 1997; Flannery O'Connor Award for Short Fiction, University of Georgia Press, for *Under the Red Flag,* 1998; National Book Award, National Book Foundation, for *Waiting,* 1999; PEN/Faulkner Award, PEN/Faulkner Foundation, for *Waiting,* 2000; Townsend Prize for

fiction, Georgia Perimeter College, for *The Bridegroom,* 2002; PEN/Faulkner Award, PEN/Faulkner Foundation, for *War Trash,* 2005; fellow of the American Academy of Arts and Sciences, 2005; three Pushcart Prizes for fiction.

Sidelights

Chinese-American author Ha Jin has gained great critical notice for his literary depictions of Chinese life and culture. Since the appearance of his 1990 debut poetry collection *Between Silences: A Voice from China,* Jin has published numerous volumes of poetry and short stories as well as delved into full-length novels and non-fiction. His sophomore novel, *Waiting,* garnered the National Book Award in 1999 and the PEN/Faulkner Award in 2000. Jin repeated his PEN/Faulkner win in 2005 for his novel *War Trash.* Despite Jin's success in his adopted United States, his work goes unread in his native China, where the government has banned the publication of some of his books. "If I wrote in Chinese, my books would be censored in China. It's crazy," he explained to Deborah Solomon of the *New York Times.* "That is why I write in English. Writing in English makes me feel crippled, but at least I know nothing will be cut."

Born Xuefei Jin on February 21, 1956, in Jinzhou, Liaoning, China, Jin is the eldest of the five children of Red Army officer Danlin Jin and his wife, petty officer Yuanfen (Zhao) Jin. Jin's childhood was a turbulent one. After China's Cultural Revolution—a decade-long period of social, political, and economic turmoil—began in the mid-1960s, his father was often away from home and his mother was arrested and forced into agricultural labor for a few years. With both parents gone, Jin and his siblings were left in the care of an older cousin, and the future author took on household responsibilities, such as cooking, at a young age. At the age of 13 or 14, Jin followed in his father's footsteps and enlisted in the People's Liberation Army, spending time in Korea and patrolling the border between northern China and the Soviet Union; however, because his maternal grandfather had been a small landowner, Jin found himself categorized as a counterrevolutionary despite his army service. He left the military after about six years, finding work as a telegraph operator at a railroad station. This job afforded him his first opportunity to study English by listening to a regular instructional radio program. "They would teach you to speak English by saying things like 'This is a table. Is that a chair? Long live, Chairman Mao!'" he recalled in the same *New York Times* interview.

Although Chinese universities had been closed for the duration of the Cultural Revolution, the end of this period led to their reopening in 1977. At 21 years old, Jin won acceptance to Heilongjiang University in northern China. As part of the application process, he identified five subjects that he hoped to study: classics, philosophy, world history, library science, and, only lastly, English. University officials funneled Jin in this last subject, and he thus began formal studies of the language. English soon proved to be a good fit, however, as Jin became fascinated by the works of American authors such as William Faulkner and Ernest Hemingway. After completing his degree at Heilongjiang University, Jin enrolled at Shandong University to pursue graduate studies in American Literature. He earned a master's degree in the subject before moving on to Brandeis University outside of Boston, Massachusetts, to pursue doctoral studies in 1985. During this period, Jin worked some odd jobs, including stints as a factory foreman and as a steakhouse waiter. "My English was so poor," he told Tony Emerson of *Newsweek International*, "the manager demoted me to busboy, to get me out of the way. I felt really bad."

Jin had planned to return to China upon receiving his doctorate to take a teaching position at Shandong University. However, the events at Tiananmen Square during the spring of 1989 changed his mind about returning to his native country. When these pro-democracy protests in Beijing turned violent, the expatriated student found himself stunned. Writing in the *New York Times* in 2009, he recalled, "we soldiers had always been instructed that our principal task was to serve and protect the people. So when the Chinese military turned on the students … it shocked me so much that for weeks I was in a daze." He decided to stay in the United States with his wife, and was joined by his young son, who had remained in China, soon after. Jin became an American citizen in 1998.

During his graduate studies, Jin published some poems in the *Paris Review,* and, in 1990, his first book of English-language poems, *Between Silences: A Voice from China,* appeared in print. Addressing themes of Chinese life and culture that would run throughout his body of work, Jin received positive notices for this early effort. "This is poetry unencumbered by self-consciousness, expressing the profundity of emotion with brutal honesty," declared Peggy Kaganoff of *Publishers Weekly*. After completing his doctorate at Brandeis in 1992, Jin became an assistant professor of creative writing at Emory University in Atlanta, Georgia; two years later, he also completed Boston University's creative writing program.

Continuing to write poetry and short stories that appeared in various publications, Jin accrued material for two new collections: a volume of poems titled *Facing Shadows* and one of prose called *Ocean of Words: Army Stories,* both published in 1996. The latter work drew on the author's experiences in the Chinese Army and won generally sound notices, later picking up a PEN/Hemingway Award. A follow-up volume of stories, *Under the Red Flag,* returned to China, exploring fictional events set in one small town during the Cultural Revolution. The collection earned Jin the Flannery O'Connor Award for Short Fiction, setting the stage for the release of his first novel, *In the Pond*. Termed a "wise and funny first novel that gathers meticulously observed images into a seething yet restrained tale of social injustice in modern China" by a *Publishers Weekly* reviewer, the book contributed to Jin's growing literary prestige.

In 1999, Jin published what has become his best-known novel, *Waiting*. The story of a Cultural Revolution-era Chinese army doctor forced into a loveless arranged marriage, the novel follows his two-decade-long efforts to divorce his wife—according to Chinese law, a couple must be legally separated for 18 years before divorcing—and to at last consummate his relationship with a nurse. Winning critical praise both for its plot and for what Megan Harlan of *Entertainment Weekly* called Jin's "unnerving insight," *Waiting* soon became one of the year's most lauded titles. "Although there is nothing inherently funny about two people being romantically thwarted for nearly two decades," commented *Time*'s Paul Gray, "*Waiting*, turns, page by careful page, into a deliciously comic novel. Ha Jin ... tells this tale in an impeccably deadpan manner." *Waiting* went on garner Jin a National Book Award and the first of two PEN/Faulkner Awards, making him the first Chinese-American author to be so honored.

Success did not slow Jin's written output, with another collection of his short stories appearing on bookshelves the following year. *The Bridegroom* returned to China to address policies and cultural practices unfamiliar—and perhaps even shocking—to American readers. Bianca Perlman of *Entertainment Weekly* praised the book for its "spare prose, subtle wit, and surprising plot twists [that] make for a read that is both quick and memorable"; however, Claire Messud of the *New York Times* took issue with some of that spare prose, observing that Jin's "literary vision, like his subjects thus far, is Chinese, and the English language not his calling but his arbitrary fate." Yet Messud also acknowledged that "his eye for detail, his great storytelling talent—these universal gifts suffuse his work and make *The Bridegroom* a genuine pleasure."

A third volume of poetry, *Wreckage*, and a shift from Emory to Boston University as a faculty member preceded Jin's third novel, 2002's *The Crazed*. Returning to the events of Tiananmen Square that had influenced him to remain in the United States more than a decade previously, Jin presented the story of a young scholar who, in the course of caring for a much-respected older professor, comes to reject the life of the intellectual in favor of one of action, only to become an inadvertent participant in the 1989 Beijing protests. According to Sudip Bose of the *Washington Times*, "the crazed in the title of Mr. Jin's subtle and compelling novel is not just Shenmin Yang, in the throes of a deathbed delirium, but also young Jian, whose idealism has been shattered and who, despite wanting always to remain clear of politics, unwittingly becomes a part of something far greater than his own hopes and dreams." Although *Waiting* was published in China, the country's government banned *The Crazed* outright.

Jin's next novel, 2004's *War Trash*, proved that he could challenge mores not only in China, but also in his adopted homeland. Describing the experiences of a Chinese prisoner of war held in American and South Korean war camps during the Korean War, the fictional memoir condemned American treatment of such POWs and spoke out against war in general. "I had planned *War Trash* as a short novel," Jin told Dwight Garner of the *New York Times Book Review*, "but somehow I couldn't stop.... Something inside me just came out, and later I realized what it was: fear. Because when I was a soldier in the Chinese Army, most of the soldiers were afraid of captivity more than death." *War Trash* garnered Jin his second PEN/Faulkner Award.

The author next found a creative outlet in two diverse projects. He wrote the libretto for the 2006 opera *The First Emperor*, the story of a real-life third-century Chinese emperor, which made its world premiere at New York City's Metropolitan Opera House. Writing for *Variety*, Eric Myers gave the piece a mixed review, but observed that "the libretto occasionally achieves some memorable poetic imagery," while *Hollywood Reporter*'s Frank Scheck wrote that Jin's "libretto is frequently awkward and mostly lugubrious." Better received was Jin's novel *A Free Life*, a partially autobiographical work published in 2007. Following the life of a Chinese immigrant to the United States who struggles to achieve success as a writer, the book represented Jin's first steps in telling a story with an American, rather than Chinese, setting. A non-fiction work titled *The Writer as Migrant* was published the following year and offered Jin's take on the process of writing about immigrants and some classic works in that tradition.

In November of 2009, Jin released his fifth short story collection, *A Good Fall*. Leaving China proper for the Chinatown located in Flushing, New York, the author explored cultural themes such as familial interaction and Americanization. Critics largely applauded the effort. "Jin's ear and eye for Chinese American life are acute," commented Donna Seaman in a *Booklist* review, "as is his sense of how one life can encompass a full spectrum of irony, desperation, and magic." A *Publishers Weekly* reviewer largely agreed, stating, "With startling clarity, Jin explores the challenges, loneliness, and uplift associated with discovering one's place in America." *Kirkus Reviews*, however, took a more measured stance, claiming that "Rich imagery ... displays the author's poetic gifts, but some of these tales belabor the obvious." With such long-running critical support, Jin was poised to remain one the United States' foremost literary voices on the Chinese-American experience for some time to come.

Selected writings

Between Silences: A Voice from China (poetry), University of Chicago Press (Chicago, IL), 1990.

Facing Shadows (poetry), Hanging Loose Press (Brooklyn, NY), 1996.
Ocean of Words: Army Stories, Zoland Books (Cambridge, MA), 1996.
Under the Red Flag (short stories), University of Georgia Press (Athens, GA), 1997.
In the Pond (novel), Zoland Books, 1998.
Waiting (novel), Pantheon (New York City), 1999.
Quiet Desperation (short stories), Pantheon, 2000.
The Bridegroom (short stories), Pantheon, 2000.
Wreckage (poetry), Hanging Loose Press, 2001.
The Crazed (novel), Pantheon, 2002.
War Trash (novel), Pantheon, 2004.
A Free Life (novel), Pantheon, 2007.
The Writer as Migrant (essays), University of Chicago Press, 2008.
A Good Fall (short stories), Pantheon, 2009.

Sources

Books

American Ethnic Writers, Revised, vol. 2, Salem Press, 2009, pp. 563-66.

Gale Contextual Encyclopedia of American Literature,, vol. 2, Gale, 2009, pp. 833-36.

Periodicals

Booklist, November 15, 2009, p. 20.
Entertainment Weekly, October 29, 1999, p. 106; October 6, 2000, p. 80.
Hollywood Reporter, January 15, 2007, p. 56.
Kirkus Reviews, October 1, 2009.
Newsweek, October 25, 2007.
Newsweek International, November 29, 1999, p. 73.
New York Times, October 22, 2000; October 10, 2004; April 10, 2005; May 31, 2009.
Publishers Weekly, August 24, 1990, p. 60; October 12, 1998, p. 58; September 21, 2009, p. 35.
Time, November 8, 1999, p. 144.
Variety, January 1, 2007, p. 36.
Washington Times, December 15, 2002, p. B6.

—*Vanessa E. Vaughn*

Judas Priest

Heavy metal group

Group formed in 1969 in Birmingham, England. Original members include: Kenneth "K.K." Downing (born October 27, 1951, in West Bromwich, England), lead guitar; Ian Hill (born January 20, 1952, in West Midlands, England), bass; Alan Atkins, vocals; John Ellis, drums. Current members include: Rob Halford (born August 25, 1951, in Birmingham, England), vocals; Glenn Tipton (born

October 25, 1949, in West Midlands, England), lead guitar; Scott Travis (born c. 1962), drums. Former members include: Les Binks, drums; David Holland, drums; Alan Moore, drums; Simon Phillips (born February 6, 1957, in London, England), drums; John Hinch, drums; Tim Owens (born September 13, 1967, in Akron, OH; married second wife, Jeanie; children: one daughter [first marriage]; one son [second marriage]).

Addresses: *Contact*—c/o Judas Priest Music, Ltd., 3rd Floor, 12 Oval Rd., Camden, London NW1 7DH United Kingdom. *Web site*—http://www.judaspriest.com/.

Career

Judas Priest formed with original members K.K. Downing, Ian Hill, Alan Atkins, and John Ellis, 1969; Atkins had been a member of another band named Judas Priest, pre-1969; Halford began career as theatrical lighting engineer, former member of band Hiroshima, joined Judas Priest when bands merged, 1973; John Hinch, another former member of Hiroshima, served as drummer for Judas Priest, 1973-74; Tipton joined Judas Priest, 1974; group signed with Gull (a British company), c. 1974; released debut, *Rocka Rolla*, 1974; Alan Moore served as drummer, 1974-77; signed with CBS Records, 1977; Simon Phillips served as drummer, 1977-78; Les Binks served as drummer, 1978-79; Dave Holland served as drummer, 1979-89; found success with release *Hellbent for Leather*, 1979; had first platinum album with *British Steel*, 1980; had string of hit albums in 1980s, including *Defenders of the Faith*, 1984; drummer Scott Travis joined Judas Priest, 1989; had gold album with *Painkiller*, 1990; Halford left band, 1990; fought American court case, c. early 1990s; hired Tim Owens to replace Halford, 1996; released first album with Owens, *Jugulator*, 1997; Owens forced out band in favor of Halford, 2003; Judas Priest released first studio album of new material after Halford's return, *Angel of Retribution*, 2005; won first Grammy Award, 2010.

Awards: Grammy Award for best metal performance, National Academy of Recording Arts and Sciences, for "Dissident Aggressor," 2010.

Sidelights

One of the most highly respected heavy metal bands of all time, Judas Priest brought the genre to new heights and helped craft its definitive sound. A leading band in the new wave of British heavy metal that emerged in the late 1970s and early 1980s, the band wore leather and chains and combined influences like fantasy, Goth, heavy riffs, and speed into a multi-guitar sound and theatrical stage presence. Though the band suffered setbacks in the 1990s, including the temporary defection of lead singer Rob Halford and a lawsuit, Judas Priest proved its staying power over the years. By 2010, Judas Priest had sold more than 30 million albums, singles, and videos. As Roy Wilkinson noted in the London *Guardian*, "Judas Priest helped form one of our planet's most enduring and pervasive musical forms."

Judas Priest originally formed in 1969 in Birmingham. The line-up included guitarist K.K. Downing, bassist Ian Hill, vocalist Alan Atkins, and drummer John Ellis. The band took its name from a Bob Dylan song, "The Ballad of Frankie Lee and Judas Priest." Atkins had previously been in another band named Judas Priest but the new band could not find another name. Within two years, Judas Priest began playing shows around England, though members could not settle on a vocalist and drummer. In 1973, the band solved the singer issue when it merged with Hiroshima, another band. Hiroshima's singer was Rob Halford, who had worked as a theatrical lighting engineer. Halford added his high tenor voice to the mix, giving Judas Priest its distinctive sound.

While Judas Priest picked up Hiroshima's drummer John Hinch, he did not remain in the line-up for the long term, though the lineup did tour in the United Kingdom, Germany, and the Netherlands. Another long term member was added in 1974, however, when guitarist Glenn Tipton, a former apprentice at British Steel, joined Judas Priest. Tipton and Downing both served as the band's lead guitarists, creating a sonic assault that came to define another aspect of the band's sound. The same year that Tipton joined, Judas Priest signed with Gull, a small British independent label. They released their first album in 1974, *Rocka Rolla*, and hit the road. An appearance at the Reading Festival introduced Judas Priest to a wider audience, one, unfortunately, they could not capitalize on with the release of *Sad Wings of Destiny*. Though 1976 album did not sell well and contributed to the band's ongoing financial problems, it had great reviews. These money issues were eventually solved by the album as it helped land the band a deal with a major record label.

In 1977, Judas Priest signed with CBS Records, the parent company of Columbia. They released their first album on the label that year, the aggressive *Sin After Sin*, produced by Roger Glover, the former bassist for Deep Purple. *Sin After Sin* featured the popular track "The Ripper." Another memorable cut was "Diamonds & Rust," a cover of a song by folk singer Joan Baez about her relationship with Dylan. While Judas Priest was able to capture its sound on recordings like 1978's *Killing Machine* and *Stained Class*, they had no hits. Still, their fan base had expanded enough that the band could tour in Europe, North America, and Japan.

By the group's tenth anniversary, Judas Priest finally found success on the charts. One of their 1979 releases, *Hellbent for Leather*, had a hit single in the United Kingdom. "Take on the World" reached the top ten in Britain. *Hellbent for Leather* reached the top 50 on the best-selling album charts in the United States. In support of the album, Judas Priest had its first headlining tour there, which proved memorable because Halford rode a Harley on stage each night. Their next album proved to be the group's breakthrough.

Released in April of 1980, *British Steel* became the band's first platinum album in the United States and their first top ten studio-produced album in the United Kingdom. It also reached number 34 in the United States on the *Billboard* album charts. This extremely influential record helped shape the genre of heavy metal in the 1980s and beyond, in part by moving past the genres' blues roots. Recorded at Tittenhurst Park in England, it was the second album produced by Tom Allom, who worked on eight live and studio albums with the band. *British Steel* produced several hits in the United States and the United Kingdom, including "Breaking the Law" and "Living After Midnight." The music video for "Breaking the Law" became a hit on MTV as well.

In support of *British Steel*, the band toured around the world, finding particular support at home. The 30-city tour of the United Kingdom sold out three months in advance. Building on the momentum, Judas Priest continued to produce important, successful albums over the next few years. *Point of Entry*, released in 1981, went gold in the United States and reached number 39 on the American album charts. The single "Heading Out to the Highway" was a hit video and popular on the radio. The band also toured relentlessly.

The 1982 album *Screaming for Vengeance* featured the only Judas Priest song to hit the *Billboard* Top 100 singles chart, "You've Got Another Thing Coming." While other albums sold better, *Screaming for Vengeance* was arguably the band's most popular hit as it reached number 17 on the American album charts. Judas Priest had a sold-out arena tour in support of

the album that featured pyrotechnic effects. The band's next album, 1984's *Defenders of the Faith*, went platinum on the basis of such tracks as "Freewheel Burning" and "Some Heads Are Gonna Roll." It reached number 18 on American album charts.

After touring in support of *Defenders of the Faith*, Judas Priest took a year off for the first time in 15 years. When they returned to recording, they tried to keep up with changing tastes in music by acknowledging the synthesizer-heavy sound of new wave music sweeping the world. *Turbo* had synthesized guitars and was a failure with most fans and critics. It did sell one million copies in the United States, primarily because of the power of the Judas Priest name. The band acknowledged its error by releasing *Priest ... Live!* in 1987, which included live versions of its best-selling songs thus far. Then, 1988's *Ram It Down* showed Judas Priest's ability to combine a bit of thrash metal to its raw heavy metal sound. The mix was successful as the album went gold and reached number 31 on American album charts. In 1989, Judas Priest finally found a drummer that could stick when they hired Scott Travis. The American had grown up in Virginia and had dreamed of being a member of the band since his teens.

With Travis on board, Judas Priest continued to top the charts with 1990's *Painkiller*. Another best seller, it reached number 26 on the album charts in the United States and went gold. However, the 1990s would prove difficult for the band. After the release of *Painkiller*, Halford left the band to work on solo projects, as well as taking part in the thrash metal band Fight, another band called Two, and another band called Halford. Judas Priest also spent three years fighting a controversial court case in this time period. The band had been accused of influencing suicide pacts since the mid-1980s. In this particular case, they were charged with including subliminal messages recorded backwards in several songs, and that these tracks caused two fans to attempt suicide. One of the young men, Raymond Belknap, was successful, while the other, James Vance, maimed himself and died several years later. The band eventually won a victory when the case was dismissed by a Nevada court in the early 1990s.

Judas Priest's recorded output was sporadic in the rest of the 1990s. Still without a lead singer and after Tipton released a solo project in 1996, the band began looking for a replacement for Halford. They found a lead vocalist in American Tim Owens, an office supply salesman and former law firm purchasing agent who fronted a Judas Priest tribute band as well as another band named Winter's Bane.

Owens was brought to the band's attention by Travis' girlfriend, who had seen his tribute band play and taped it. With Owens aboard, Judas Priest recorded and released 1997's *Jugulator*. They also began touring with the new line-up, releasing a live album in 1998, *98 Live Meltdown*. Sales of both albums, however, did not come close to matching Judas Priest in its heyday with Halford.

In the late 1990s, Owens' compelling story was being readied for a film which was originally supposed to include the input of Judas Priest. The band declined to remain involved when they were not given creative control, though the fictionalized *Rock Star* was released in 2001. Mark Wahlberg played the lead role, based on Owens. Judas Priest continued to record with Owens, producing a new studio album in 2001, *Demolition*, that sold poorly and was critically panned. By 2003, the band, including Halford and other former members, were working together to produce a definitive box set of Judas Priest's career. As they wrote liner notes and selected songs for what became a five-disc box set *Metalogy*, Halford got along better with his former bandmates than he had in years.

Owens was then forced out of Judas Priest in 2003 when Halford agreed to return to the band. At the same time, the band signed a new deal with Sony Music Entertainment, the parent company of Columbia, and began spending a significant proportion of the year on the road again. Judas Priest started recording new material as well, releasing *Angel of Retribution* in 2005. It reached number 13 on the *Billboard* album chart. Three years later, they put out *Nostradamus* which reached number eleven on the American charts. This ambitious release was a two-disc concept album based on the French physician, astrologer, and seer.

In 2009, Judas Priest released a live album drawn from the tours of the previous four years. *Touch of Evil: Live* did well, and landed the band its first Grammy Award for best metal performance for the song "Dissident Aggressor" in 2010. Preparing for the thirtieth anniversary of the release of *British Steel*, the band performed the complete album at stops on their 2009 tour of the United States and Japan. The band also celebrated the anniversary of *British Steel* with a new edition of the album that included two bonus tracks and a live DVD featuring performances from their 2009 tour.

There were no plans to end Judas Priest as most of its members reached or neared their sixties, despite more than 30 years of ups and downs. Discussing the band's longevity, Tipton told Victor R. Martinez of the *El Paso Times*, "If you ever said that to me in the beginning, I would have said you're crazy. But it has become my life, and you accept it. You get used to it. You get immune to it. It just seems right. It still seems right that Priest is up there. Our energy and enthusiasm is better than ever. I think it's because we genuinely love what we do."

Selected discography

Rocka Rolla, Gull, 1974.
Sad Wings of Destiny, Repertoire, 1976.
Sin After Sin, Columbia, 1977.
Killing Machine, Columbia, 1978.
Stained Class, Columbia, 1978.
Hell Bent for Leather, Columbia, 1979.
Unleashed in the East (Live in Japan), Columbia, 1979.
Hero, Hero, Columbia, 1979.
British Steel, Columbia, 1980.
Point of Entry, Columbia, 1981.
Screaming for Vengeance, Columbia, 1982.
Love Bites, Columbia, 1984.
Defenders of the Faith, Columbia, 1984.
Turbo, Columbia, 1986.
Judas Priest, Columbia, 1986.
Priest ... Live!, Columbia, 1987.
Ram It Down, Columbia, 1988.
Painkiller, Columbia, 1990.
Jugulator, Sanctuary Records, 1997.
98 Live Meltdown, Sanctuary Records, 1998.
Demolition, Atlantic/WEA, 2001.
Metalogy (boxed set), Sony, 2004.
Angel of Retribution, Epic, 2005.
Nostradamus, Sony, 2008.
Touch of Evil: Live, Epic, 2009.
British Steel: 30th Anniversary Edition, Columbia/Legacy, 2009.

Sources

Books

Baker's Biographical Dictionary of Musicians, Schirmer, 2001.
Contemporary Musicians, vol. 47, Gale Group, 2004.
St. James Encyclopedia of Popular Culture, St. James Press, 2000.

Periodicals

Beaver County Times (Beaver County, PA), August 14, 2010.
Calgary Sun (Alberta, Canada), May 17, 2010, p. 38.

Connecticut Post (Bridgeport, CT), September 29, 2005.

El Paso Times, July 30, 2004, p. 15T.

Guardian (London, England), May 21, 2010, p. 6.

New York Times, July 17, 1990, p. C13; July 27, 1997, sec. 2, p. 1.

Pittsburgh Post-Gazette (PA), August 14, 2008, p. W11.

Plain Dealer (Cleveland, OH), September 2, 2001, p. 11; July 20, 2003, p. J1.

PR Newswire, April 1, 2010.

St. Louis Post-Dispatch (MO), August 11, 2004, p. E3.

Sunday Telegram (MA), March 13, 2005, p. G6.

Toronto Star, August 23, 2001, p. A27.

Virginian Pilot, February 2, 2010, p. E4.

Online

"Biography,"KKDowning.net, http://kkdowning.net/kkdowning/biography.html (August 28, 2010).

"Judas Priest—Biography," Allmusic, http://www.allmusic.com/cg/amg.dll?p=amg&sql=11:kifrxqe5ldse~T1 (August 28, 2010).

—*A. Petruso*

Elena Kagan

U.S. Supreme Court Justice

Born April 28, 1960, in New York, NY; daughter of Robert (an attorney) and Gloria (a teacher; maiden name, Gittleman) Kagan. *Education:* Princeton University, A.B., 1981; Worcester College, Oxford University, M. Phil., 1983; Harvard Law School, Harvard University, J.D., 1986.

Addresses: *Office*—Supreme Court of the United States, 1 First Street, N.E., Washington, DC 20543.

Career

Clerked for Supreme Court Justice Thurgood Marshall, 1987; worked on presidential campaign of Michael Dukakis, 1988; associate, Williams & Connolly law firm, 1989-91; assistant professor, University of Chicago Law School, 1991-95, then tenured professor, 1995; associate White House counsel, then deputy assistant to the President for domestic policy, then deputy director of the Domestic Policy Council, Clinton administration, 1995-99; professor, Harvard Law School, 1999-2003, then dean, 2003-09; U.S. Solicitor General, 2009-10; U.S. Supreme Court Justice, 2010—.

Sidelights

Elena Kagan became the U.S. Supreme Court's fourth-ever female justice when she was sworn in as Associate Justice on August 7, 2010. The second Supreme Court justice appointed by the Obama administration, Kagan served as U.S. Solicitor General for about a year before her nomination to the nation's highest court. With a distinguished résumé including studies at Princeton University, Oxford University, and Harvard Law School, Kagan worked largely in government and academia throughout her career; unlike most Supreme Court Justices, she had practically no experience as a juror or even as a courtroom lawyer prior to her appointment to the Court.

This background raised many questions about her judicial philosophy and likely interpretation of the U.S. Constitution upon her nomination, as Kagan had not often publically discussed her perception of proper application of the law. "Elena is open-minded, pragmatic, and progressive," commented former acting solicitor general Walter Dellinger to the *New York Times'* reporting team of Sheryl Gay Stolberg, Katharine Q. Seelye, and Lisa W. Foderaro at the time of Kagan's nomination. "Each of those qualities will appeal to some, and not to others. Her open-mindedness may disappoint some who want a sure liberal vote on almost every issue. Her pragmatism may disappoint those who believe that mechanical logic can decide all cases. And her progressive personal values will not endear her to the hard right. But that is exactly the combination the president was seeking," Dellinger continued.

A native of New York City, Kagan was born on April 28, 1960, to attorney Robert Kagan and his wife, elementary school teacher Gloria Gittelman Kagan. She grew up with her parents and two brothers on Manhattan's Upper West Side, where the family attended the Lincoln Square Synagogue. Even as a girl, Kagan demonstrated the forcefulness of will and persuasive powers of a successful attorney. At the age of 12, she convinced the synagogue's rabbi, Shlomo Riskin, to perform a bat mitzvah—a traditional Jewish coming of age ceremony for a girl—despite the fact that Riskin, an Orthodox Jew, had never formally held one. "We crafted a lovely service, but I don't think I satisfied her completely," Riskin recalled to Foderado of the *New York Times.* "But she certainly raised my consciousness."

After graduating from New York City's Hunter College High School, Kagan enrolled at Princeton University to study history. She was a politically active student who worked as a press assistant on the failed 1980 campaign of Representative Elizabeth Holtzman, a strong women's rights advocate. Following Holtzman's defeat, Kagan penned an opinion piece for the college's *Daily Princetonian* newspaper in which she bemoaned that "there was no longer any place for the ideals we held.... I wonder how all this could possibly have happened and where on earth I'll be able to get a job next year," according to the *Washington Post* reporting team of Amy Goldstein, Carol D. Leonnig, and Peter Slevin. In fact, Kagan's concern over finding a job proved irrelevant; she instead received a Sachs scholarship and pursued graduate studies at England's Oxford University. She earned a master's degree in philosophy, and then returned to the United States to study law at Harvard University. Kagan graduated from Harvard Law School *magna cum laude* (with highest honors) in 1986.

Her next stop was in Washington, D.C., where she served as a legal clerk for Supreme Court Justice Thurgood Marshall. She hoped to eventually work for a Democratic presidential administration, and to that end joined the campaign of Democratic presidential nominee Michael Dukakis in 1988. When Dukakis lost the election to George H. W. Bush, Kagan took a job with private law firm Williams & Connolly; however, the private sector did not suit the future Justice, and she left in 1991 to become a faculty member at the University of Chicago's law school. She proved a popular instructor and received tenure in 1995.

Kagan gave up job security to accept the position with a Democratic administration that she had previously missed out on. She became an aide to President Bill Clinton's White House counsel, and later served as Clinton's Deputy Director of the Domestic Policy Council. In 1999, Clinton nominated Kagan for a federal judgeship; however, Congressional Republicans refused to grant her a hearing, and the post instead went to future Supreme Court Chief Justice John Roberts.

Denied a crack at being a jurist, Kagan returned to academia that same year when she accepted a position at her alma mater, Harvard Law. She quickly advanced from visiting professor to full professor to, in 2003, dean. The institution's first female dean, Kagan won the respect of the academic community for her ability to reconcile the warring conservative and liberal wings of the school's faculty. Simple gestures, such as offering free lunch, helped get philosophically opposed staffers to sit down and talk together, while larger efforts such as a grand event in honor of conservative Supreme Court Justice Antonin Scalia gained her respect on both sides of the ideological aisle. Kagan also undertook significant efforts to update the school's somewhat outdated curriculum, improve facilities, and encourage the hiring of new professors—a task that had been long stymied by ideological divides among the existing faculty. Her success in this last area was so great that the student-run *Harvard Law Record* lampooned her in an April Fool's Day headline declaring, "Dean Kagan Hires Every Law Professor in the Country," according to the *New York Times* profile by Stolberg, Seelye, and Foderaro.

In March of 2009, Kagan left her position at Harvard to become the nation's first female solicitor general. During her confirmation hearing in the U.S. Senate for the role, it became apparent that legislators considered her a probable future candidate for a seat on the Supreme Court. They asked many questions aimed at pinning down her unknown legal philosophy, only to receive studied, neutral responses from Kagan. "I do not think it comports with the responsibilities and role of the solicitor general for me to say whether I view particular decisions as wrongly decided or whether I agree with criticisms of those decisions," she explained, according to Robert Barnes of the *Washington Post.* Her unwillingness to take a stand on issues did not prevent her confirmation, however.

One the United States' top judicial offices, the Solicitor General is responsible for representing the federal government in cases heard before the Supreme Court and for assisting the Court in performing its duties by recommending cases to go before it, among other tasks. The office's close relationship with the nine-member Court has led to it being referred to as the "Tenth Justice." As solicitor general, Kagan at last argued her first case before a court and served as counsel of record for more than 100 merit briefs. Acting in her role as legal counsel for the government of the United States, Kagan argued six cases before the Supreme Court on issues including separation of church and state, federal election laws, free speech, and separation of powers.

After sitting Associate Justice John Paul Stevens announced his intention to retire, President Barack Obama considered several replacement candidates before nominating Solicitor General Kagan in May of 2010. Although Kagan lacked the courtroom experience common to the other eight sitting justices, she encountered relatively little significant opposition during her July of 2010 confirmation hearings. Observers noted that past Supreme Court justices have not always been drawn from the ranks of the judiciary; historical justices have included attorney generals, state and federal legislators, lawyers, and even a former president: William Taft, who was himself also Solicitor General. "It is hard to predict what it is about someone's background that will be important to them and how it will play out," explained Pamela Harris, the executive director of the Supreme Court Institute at Georgetown Law School, to Mallie Jane Kim in a *U.S. News and World Report* blog post. "So the best way to get a meld of different views on the court is to have a diversity of different backgrounds, different life experiences."

Because Kagan had no previous legal decisions upon which to base her likely judicial philosophy, analysts began mining other areas of her life in an attempt to predict how she might rule in a number of key areas. Kagan's past opposition to the U.S. military's "don't ask, don't tell" policy, for example, was interpreted as a sign that she would be unlikely to support a federal ban on gay marriage, while her middle-left policy advocacy on abortion during the Clinton era seemed to indicate that she would rule in moderately liberal ways upon that issue. What analysts most seized on was Kagan's history of pragmatism and consensus building, speculating that would prove to be a justice more interested in practical results than idealistic principles. Speaking about Kagan's history of policy advisement under Clinton, Supreme Court litigator and non-partisan blogger Tom Goldstein observed to Kim that Kagan "never ... says 'we just got to take a stand on principle, here.'" He explains, "I think she will be in the 'let's make this work' camp."

A lack of information about her legal beliefs perhaps helped Kagan win an easy confirmation as legislators found little to oppose in her background,

while the public let her nomination slip by with relatively little notice. Writing in the *Washington Post*, Paul Kane and Robert Barnes noted that "more than 20 percent of voters had no view of her, making her the least-known Supreme Court nominee in nearly two decades." The U.S. Senate formally approved Kagan's nomination to the Court by a vote of 63-37 on August 4, 2010. The vote largely followed party lines, with just five Republicans crossing the aisle to support Kagan's confirmation and one Democrat, Ben Nelson, voting to oppose it.

Although Kagan was formally sworn in by Supreme Court Chief Justice John Roberts on August 7, 2010, she did not begin practicing as an Associate Justice until the Court's next session began some two months later. Even then, the new justice's background as solicitor general impeded her ability to perform her new role; Kagan recused herself—or removed herself from deliberations on—nearly half of the Court session's scheduled 51 cases. This occurred because Kagan had herself been involved in writing the legal briefs for some of the cases set to be heard in the top court, or had been a part of the proceedings previously at a lower court level. Due to Supreme Court rules, this left a smaller court to hear these cases. Barnes noted in the *Washington Post* that such a situation was not unusual when a newly seated justice had previously been a solicitor general. "Thurgood Marshall ... recused himself from a large portion of cases his first and second years. But his legacy is more about the cases he helped decide than the ones he sat out," Barnes argued.

The continued recusals left Kagan's judicial philosophy still something of a mystery as the Court's session proceeded into 2011. Because Supreme Court justices serve lifetime terms, it seemed likely that Kagan would have several years, if not decades, to demonstrate her legal beliefs.

Sources

Books

Smelcer, Susan Navarro and Kenneth R. Thomas, "From Solicitor General to Supreme Court Nominee: Responsibilities, History, and the Nomination of Elena Kagan," *Congressional Research Service (CRS) Reports and Issue Briefs*, Congressional Research Service (CRS) and Issue Briefs, 2010.

Periodicals

New York Times, May 10, 2010; May 12, 2010.

Washington Post, March 6, 2009; May 10, 2010, p. A5; May 11, 2010, p. A1; August 6, 2010, p. A1; October 4, 2010, p. A15.

Online

"10 Factors That Could Shape Kagan's Supreme Court Decisions," *U.S. News and World Report,* http://www.usnews.com/news/articles/2010/06/30/10-factors-that-could-shape-kagans-supreme-court-decisions.html?PageNr=1 (November 24, 2010).

"Elena Kagan," WhoRunsGov.com, http://www.whorunsgov.com/Profiles/Elena_Kagan (November 24, 2010).

—Vanessa E. Vaughn

Rob Kalin

© *Ramin Talaie/Corbis News/Corbis*

Chief Executive Officer of Etsy

Born c. 1980; son of a teacher. *Education:* Attended School of the Museum of Fine Arts (Boston) and the Massachusetts Institute of Technology; earned individualized study degree from New York University, 2004.

Addresses: *Home*—Brooklyn, NY. *Office*—Etsy, Inc., 55 Washington St., Ste. 512, Brooklyn, NY 11201.

Career

Worked as a photographer in the late 1990s; woodworker; co-founder, Etsy, 2005, chief executive officer, 2005-08, and December 2009—, and board chair, 2005—.

Sidelights

Rob Kalin is the founder of Etsy, the startlingly lucrative online marketplace for handmade crafts. In its first half-decade in operation, Etsy accrued five million members and, by 2010, was tallying monthly sales past the $20 million mark. The success of the site, with its slogan "Buy, Sell, and Live Handmade," caught many e-commerce industry analysts by surprise, but Kalin knew he was creating something fresh. "We live in a culture of excess," he told *Financial Times* journalist Pan Kwan Yuk. "We want more and then throw it away faster and faster. When you buy something from Etsy, there's a story behind it ... there's a person behind it. By getting people to value handmade goods, hopefully we can also get them to consume better but less."

Kalin was born in the early 1980s and grew up in Boston as the son of a teacher and a father who taught him carpentry skills. By the time he reached his high-school years he was a talented photographer and earning money from this line of work, but his grades suffered and he finished high school with a D-minus grade-point average. His impressive photography portfolio, however, helped him get into a studio program at the Boston Museum of Fine Arts, and he also took classes at the prestigious Massachusetts Institute of Technology. At the age of 20 he moved to Brooklyn, worked at the famous Strand bookstore in the East Village, and enrolled at New York University as a classics major. He supported himself with carpentry jobs, too, but was so poor for a time he lived on a daily food budget of just $1.

Kalin's first foray into information technology came when his landlord in Brooklyn dared him to design a Web site for the Acme Bar and Grill, which the landlord also owned. "I didn't know anything about websites, but I learned HTML, and I built the basic site in four weeks," Kalin recalled in an interview with Donna Fenn for *Reader's Digest*. Discovering he had a knack for Web design, he took a job retooling the Web site for Get Crafty, an online community of crafters, in 2004. He realized that there was no comprehensive sales site for artisans of handmade objects, like himself and the custom items he created, which included a computer encased entirely in wood. He decided to build the e-commerce site himself.

The initial funding for Etsy came from a pair of woodworking clients of his, who put up the first $50,000. He teamed with two friends from NYU, Chris Maguire and Haim Schoppik, and started work on the project. Maguire and Schoppik "ended up basically moving into my apartment and we spent a solid six weeks working on it day and night," Kalin recounted to Teri Evans of the *Wall Street Journal*, noting that the path to going live was much slower than he had anticipated. "The last 10% it takes to launch something takes as much energy as the first 90%. The closer you get to it, the finish line keeps moving further and further."

Etsy was launched on June 18, 2005. The name, Kalin told Fenn in the *Reader's Digest* article, was a calculated move. "I wanted a nonsense word because I wanted to build the brand from scratch. I was watching Fellini's 8 1/2 and writing down what I was hearing. In Italian, you say etsi a lot. It means 'oh, yes.' And in Latin, it means 'and if.'" He has also said that the mission he envisioned for his start-up borrowed heavily from Leo Leonni's classic illustrated children's book from 1963, *Swimmy*, in which one small fish convinces his diminutive cohorts to swim together, so they look like one immense creature in order to fool the larger fish who feed on Swimmy and his ilk.

A seller with crafts could join Etsy for free, but there was a fee to list items for sale, then a 3.5 percent commission on every completed transaction. Etsy caught on quickly, and just two years after its launch reached the one millionth item-sold mark. Even the dramatic economic downturn in the U.S. economy that began in 2007 did not seem to affect the company's numbers, and Etsy even began to promote itself as an alternative to traditional employment for knitters and crocheters, clothing and accessory designers, printmakers and other visual artists, and all other makers of handmade items. Rob Walker, a writer on consumer topics for the *New York Times Magazine*, penned a feature on the Etsy phenomenon in December of 2007, which brought even more traffic to the site. "Browsing Etsy is both exhilarating and exhausting," Walker noted. "There is enough here to mount an astonishing museum exhibition. There is also plenty of junk. Most of all there is a dizzying amount of *stuff*, and it is simi-

larly difficult to figure out how to characterize what it all represents: an art movement, a craft phenomenon, or shopping trend."

Whatever Etsy was, its numbers appealed to venture capitalists, who handed Kalin and his cofounders some $30 million in funding for expansion between 2006 and 2009. The Etsy marketplace was so flooded with goods that it even spawned a "worst of" parody site—entirely unrelated to Etsy itself—called Regretsy. Etsy grew so quickly that Kalin and his 70 employees struggled to iron out the quirks, such as establishing a live call center to handle customer-service issues. The expanding Brooklyn loft that is home to the company holds a well-attended Monday-night craft lab in a mission to create a community, not just a successful e-commerce business. According to Kalin, the company reached the profitability point after just a few years in operation, and there are plans to take Etsy public with an initial public offering (IPO) of stock probably in 2012. "Etsy itself is hundreds of thousands of very small businesses and I want to be able to keep that intimacy," he told Evans in the *Wall Street Journal* article. "It means always keeping a human face on what we're doing. I don't want to hide behind a corporate firewall and start speaking with some third-person voice."

Sources

Periodicals

Financial Times, February 27, 2008, p. 16.
FSB, July 2009, p. 94.
Reader's Digest, December 2009.
New York Times Magazine, December 16, 2007.

Online

"Creating Etsy's Handmade Marketplace," *Wall Street Journal*, http://online.wsj.com/article/SB10001424.tif05270230.tif43703045.tif75152133.tif86088895.tif8.html?mod=WSJ_hp_editorsPicks (July 30, 2010).

—*Carol Brennan*

Patrick Kane

Professional hockey player

Born November 19, 1988, in Buffalo, NY; son of Patrick (in business) and Donna (in business; maiden name, Doyle) Kane.

Addresses: *Agent*—Pat Brisson, CAA Sports LLC, 2000 Avenue of the Stars, Los Angeles, CA, 90067. *Office*—c/o Chicago Blackhawks, 1901 W. Madison St., Chicago, IL 60612.

Career

Right wing, London Knights, Ontario Hockey League, 2007; chosen first overall in the National Hockey League draft, 2007; right wing, Chicago Blackhawks, 2008—. Member of U.S. national under-18 team, 2006; member of U.S. national junior hockey team, 2007; member of U.S. Olympic hockey team, 2010.

Awards: Gold Medal and All-Tournament honors, World Under-18 Championships, 2006; Bronze Medal and All-Tournament honors, World Junior Championships, 2007; Emms Family Award for rookie of the year, Ontario Hockey League, 2007; Calder Memorial Trophy for National Hockey League rookie of the year, Professional Hockey Writers' Association, 2008; voted NHL Western Conference All-Star starter, 2009; Silver Medal (with others), XXI Olympic Winter Games, 2010.

Sidelights

Patrick Kane lived every aspiring hockey player's dream in the 2010 Stanley Cup Finals when he scored the winning goal in overtime to give the Chicago Blackhawks their first National Hockey League (NHL) championship in almost 50 years. Although Kane was barely 21 years old at the time, the goal was just the latest in a long list of accomplishments. Despite being shorter and smaller than the average hockey player, he demonstrated that speed, skill, and will were the keys to success on the rink. "A lot of things drive me," the player told Tim Graham of the *Buffalo News.* "What it comes down to is I want to be the best."

Kane was born in hockey-mad Buffalo, New York, in 1988. Although he did not learn to skate until he was six, when he started playing hockey at age seven it was clear he had a natural feel for the game. He loved playing so much his parents enrolled him in several leagues at once. "My dad would push me so hard to get better," he recalled to Graham, and drove him to as many as four games in a day. By the time he was nine, Kane was so adept at scoring he was barred from playing with his own age group. He continuing scoring against older competition, and at age 14 he moved to Detroit to play in the Midwest Elite Hockey League. Moving in with his coach, former NHL player Pat Verbeek, helped him overcome his initial homesickness. He went on to score 83 goals and 77 assists, for a total of 160 points, in just 70 games during his one season with the Detroit Honeybaked team. Although he was only a high-school freshman, his performance earned him a college scholarship offer, as well as a place on the U.S. National Developmental Program in nearby Ann Arbor, Michigan.

Kane continued his torrid scoring pace as a member of various USA Hockey developmental squads. On the Under-17 team during the 2004-05 season, he led all players with 32 goals and 70 points in 63 games. He set a season scoring record as a member of the 2005-06 Under-18 team, with 52 goals and 102 points in 58 games. Some of those points came against college programs, playing NCAA players who were much older and bigger. "I think I kind of proved a lot of people wrong and proved to myself I can play this game in this body," he told Graham. There were few doubters left by the time he began playing for the United States in international competition. During the team's gold-medal run at the 2006 World Under-18 Championship, his seven goals and 12 points led all scorers and earned him all-tournament status. At the following year's World Junior Championships, Kane's nine points in seven games helped the United States earn a bronze medal, and he was again named to the all-tournament team.

Although Kane was offered scholarships from perennial NCAA hockey powerhouses Michigan and Boston University, he believed he could better develop as a player in the Ontario Hockey League (OHL), one of Canada's three junior developmental leagues. He finished his senior year of high school in London, Ontario, while playing for the London Knights. He captured the league's scoring trophy with 62 goals and 83 assists in 58 games, earning the OHL's Emms Family Award for rookie of the year. After the season he was eligible for the NHL Entry Draft, and commentators speculated whether his size—5'10" and 160 pounds—would cause teams to hold off on drafting him. Instead, Kane became only the sixth American to be taken with the first overall pick, going to the Chicago Blackhawks. "He's got great vision," Blackhawks coach Denis Savard later explained to Steve Silverman of the *Sporting News*. "He makes the beautiful pass. He obviously can shoot the puck. I just think he recognizes what's the best play. Out of ten choices, he'll probably make eight good ones, and that's pretty good." Kane told the *Buffalo News'* Graham, "This is

just another chapter in the books. Obviously, I have to prove myself at the next level and prove my size once again to prove people wrong."

Kane was only 18 when he started playing in the NHL; to help with the adjustment, he lived with the Blackhawks' then-assistant general manager, Stan Bowman, for the 2007-08 season. Although the Blackhawks missed the playoffs, Kane led the team in scoring with 21 goals and 72 points, his 51 assists setting the team's single-season rookie record. The performance helped him run away with the Calder Trophy for NHL rookie of the year. In his second season, he was a starter for the NHL All-Star game, earning the most votes in the Western Conference and notching one goal and one assist in the game. His 25 goals and 70 assists helped the Blackhawks make the playoffs, where he scored a hat trick in a series-clinching victory over Vancouver. The win sent them to the conference finals, where they lost to the Detroit Red Wings. Not long after, Kane became the youngest player to appear on the cover of an EA Sports' NHL video game.

Despite all of his success, Kane was still young, a fact that was brought home in summer 2009 after a conflict with a Buffalo cab driver over 20 cents led to an assault charge for Kane and his cousin. The player pled guilty to a misdemeanor charge, made a public apology, and tried to learn from the experience. "You have the microscope on you, and you have to watch what you do at all times," Kane told Terry Frei of the *Denver Post*, explaining that the conflict was "going to be with me, something I'm going to have to learn from.... I'm going to try to take a positive from a negative situation." The incident did not shake the Blackhawks' faith in their young star; they signed him to a five-year extension in December of 2009. He also earned a spot on the U.S. Olympic team for the 2010 Vancouver Games. During the team's silver-medal run, Kane scored two goals in the semifinal against Finland, and assisted on the game-tying goal in the gold-medal match. Although the team lost in overtime to Canada, Kane felt grateful just to enjoy the Olympic experience. "You get this close to the gold, you really do start to think about people who have supported you," he told David Haugh of the *Chicago Tribune*. "My grandpa, my parents, my sisters ... you want to thank them for sacrificing so much to get me here."

After the Olympics, Kane returned to the Blackhawks, where he had his best season yet. He led the Blackhawks with 30 goals and 88 total points, helping them to a Central Division title and second seed in the playoffs. During the first three rounds, Kane ranked fourth among all scorers with 20 points in

16 games, including a short-handed goal with seconds left to send Game 5 against the Predators into overtime, leading to an eventual Blackhawk victory and series lead. "You always feel like there's a next level and why not bring it out at a stage like this, the Stanley Cup finals," he told Haugh. "I can play even better." Although he had no points in the first two Finals games (both Chicago victories), he had eight points for the series, including two assists in game six before his overtime winner. Kane's winning shot took such a sharp angle that he was the only one to see it go into the net at first; by the time the referees checked the net and verified the score, Kane was already celebrating with his teammates.

When it was Kane's turn to take the Stanley Cup on its traditional summer tour, he took it to his hometown of Buffalo. "This year's going to be tough to top," the player told John Vogl in the *Buffalo News*. "I got to play in the Olympics, I got to play in the Stanley Cup final, and then obviously winning the Stanley Cup and scoring the goal to win it, I don't know if it gets much better." After taking the Cup to visit a local cancer hospital, he added that "there's always other things you can accomplish, and I think one of the biggest things, even coming here today, you want to make yourself a better person." Kane has supported medical charities and makes time for his young fans. He counts on his family, who often visit him in Chicago, to keep him grounded. The ups and down of hockey help as well; Kane and the Blackhawks experienced a slow start to the 2010-11 season, although the winger bounced back to become the second-fastest Blackhawk to reach the 250-point scoring milestone. In his fourth NHL season, he told Chris Kuc of the *Chicago Tribune*, "I have the puck a lot more, and I'm better defensively, that's for sure. I'm the same

player but growing in confidence and learning the game. I still have a little ways to go." Despite his success, he told Bucky Gleason in the *Buffalo News*, "deep down, if you ask my family and friends, I don't think I've changed. I'm still a kid at heart. I'm out there, a kid playing hockey."

Sources

Periodicals

Buffalo News, February 11, 2007; June 23, 2007; December 15, 2007; May 19, 2009; February 27, 2010; June 10, 2010; August 14, 2010; October 12, 2010.
Chicago Tribune, November 10, 2007, sec. Sports, p. 11; August 17, 2009; February 28, 2010; May 28, 2010; August 15, 2010; November 19, 2010.
Denver Post, October 11, 2009, p. F5.
New York Times, January 17, 2009, p. D6; August 28, 2009, p. B11; June 11, 2010, p. A25.
Sporting News, December 17, 2007, p. 66.
Sports Illustrated, June 7, 2010, p. 54.
USA Today, June 21, 2007, p. 10C; February 19, 2010, p. 3D.

Online

"Raising Kane," ESPN, http://sports.espn.go.com/chicago/columns/story?columnist=drehs_wayne&id=4175402 (November 3, 2010).
"Patrick Kane," Chicago Blackhawks Official Site, http://blackhawks.nhl.com/club/player.htm?id=8474141 (November 3, 2010).

—Diane Telgen

Mary Karr

Poet and memoirist

Born January 16, 1955, in Groves, Texas; daughter of J.P. (an oil worker) and Charlie Marie (an artist and business owner; maiden name, Moore) Karr; married Michael Milburn, 1983 (divorced, 1991); children: Devereux (son). *Education:* Attended Macalester College, St. Paul, MN, early 1970s; Goddard College, M.F.A., Plainfield, VT, 1979.

Addresses: *Office*—Syracuse University, Department of English, 401 Hall of Languages, Syracuse NY 13244.

Career

Published first poem in *Mother Jones* magazine, 1979; published first collection of poems, *Abacus*, 1987; joined English faculty at Syracuse University, 1991; published second collection of poems, *The Devil's Tour*, 1993; published first memoir, *The Liars' Club*, 1995; published third collection of poems, *Viper Rum*, 1998; published second memoir, *Cherry*, 2000; published fourth collection of poems, *Sinners Welcome* 2006; published third memoir, *Lit*, 2009.

Awards: Whiting Writers Award, Mrs. Giles Whiting Foundation, 1989; Bunting Fellowship, Radcliffe College, 1990; PEN/Martha Albrand Award, PEN American Center, for *The Liars' Club*, 1996; Carr P. Collins Prize, Texas Institute of Letters, for *The Liars' Club*, 1996; New York Public Library Award for *The Liars' Club*, 1996; Guggenheim fellowship for poetry, 2005; Pushcart Prize for nonfiction, 2007; Pushcart prize for poetry; fellow, National Endowment for the Arts.

Sidelights

Award-winning poet, memoirist, and professor Mary Karr has won over readers and critics alike with her vivid, intensely personal writing style. After attracting limited notoriety for her poetry, Karr came to the attention of a broad audience in 1995 with the publication of her *New York Times* best-selling memoir *The Liars' Club*. Her 2000 follow-up *Cherry* again stormed best-seller lists and received nods as one of the best books of the year from *Entertainment Weekly, US,* and Amazon. A third memoir, *Lit,* appeared to great esteem in November of 2009. Also a respected contemporary poet, Karr has published numerous volumes of poetry since the late 1980s, including *Abacus, The Devil's Tour, Viper Rum,* and *Sinners Welcome.* Her literary talents earned her a fellowship at Radcliffe College and the spot of Jesse Truesdell Peck Professor of Literature at Syracuse University, as well as Pushcart prizes and a Guggenheim Fellowship in Poetry. Despite this critical and popular success, Karr has remained modest about her achievements. "If you've been a poet for 20 years," she told Dwight Garner of *Salon,* "you don't expect anybody to read anything you write."

Born on January 16, 1955, in the small East Texas town of Groves—referred to as Leechfield in Karr's memoirs—the writer is the younger of the two daughters of oil refinery worker J.P. and his wife, artist and business owner Charlie Marie Karr. Karr's mother was an eccentric figure, particularly for the rural Texas of the 1950s: a former art student who had studied in New York City, she was married and divorced four times before marrying the man who became Karr's father, who was, as Karr put it in *The Liars' Club,* as "the proper blend of outlaw and citizen" to appeal to her somewhat wild mother. Although the marriage started off with reasonable success, the couple soon began fighting regularly, and Karr's mother developed a dependency on alcohol that heightened her already rather unstable mental condition.

As a result, Karr's upbringing was often tempestuous, marked by bad behavior and spankings, yet balanced by her family's determination to remain a unit. "Fact: as a child, I watched my mother set fire to all my toys then menace me with a butcher knife," she later wrote in the *New York Times.* "Fact: my mother adored me and even in our backwater town imbued me with the sensibility and curiosity to become an artist." Sexually assaulted at a young age by a neighbor and later a babysitter, and surrounded by familial strife, Karr found an outlet in literature. At the age of eleven, the future poet and memoirist presciently recorded in a notebook that her life's dream was to write poetry and autobiography.

As a teenager, Karr remained a committed reader even as her rebellious streak continued apace. She experimented with drugs and alcohol during high school, and eventually left both formal education and Texas to travel to Los Angeles with a group of friends. There, she spent about a year exploring the hippie and surfer subcultures of the early 1970s before again moving across the country, this time to enroll at St. Paul, Minnesota's Macalester College. She remained there for two years before dropping out to travel for a time. Despite her lack of a bachelor's degree, Karr talked her way into admission to a graduate-level creative writing program at Plainfield, Vermont's Goddard College. At Goddard, the young writer was influenced by the creative works of such writers as Tobias Wolff, Robert Bly, and Robert Haas. She completed her master of fine arts degree in 1979, and soon made her print debut with a poem in *Mother Jones* magazine. The following year, she settled in Boston, where she held a variety of non-literary jobs even as she pursued poetry on the side.

Karr's first published collection of poetry, *Abacus,* appeared in 1987. Writing in *Library Journal,* Ivan Argüelles observed that "Karr's work, though still uneven, has an edge," but gave the collection overall a middling review. The volume, along with poems published in literary and academic outlets, began to win the budding writer a degree of respect and notoriety among her peers. In 1990, she received a Bunting Fellowship at Harvard's Radcliffe College, which allowed her to focus more intently on her work. "I was in an academic ghetto in Boston, trying to publish enough to get a tenure-track position. I had just quit drinking, I had a small baby, and I was working about six different jobs.... To have the recognition of the Bunting program and the freedom to walk away from picking up Legos or folding laundry was a big deal for me," she told Ruth E. C. Prince of the *Radcliffe Quarterly* years later.

The fellowship proved a turning point in Karr's career; after its completion, she was hired as a tenure-track faculty member by Syracuse University, where she in time advanced to become the Jesse Truesdell Peck Professor of Literature. Two years later, Karr published her second poetry volume, *The Devil's Tour.* Characteristically focused on personal themes such as friends and family, the collection earned moderate critical praise. "Karr's strength lies in her delicate and meticulous control of detail.... While the poet's unflinching consciousness stands out in this text, the poetic voice is not completely developed," argued *Publishers Weekly.*

Despite this early focus on poetry, Karr's most popular works would come in another field. In 1995, she made her prose debut with the publication of *The Liars' Club.* A memoir of her childhood that took its title from the group of friends with whom her father regularly met to relax, drink beer, and tell stories, the work explored her family's unusual life in what Margot Mifflin of *Entertainment Weekly* called a "bold, blunt, and cinematic ... nothing short of superb" style. *The Liars' Club* quickly became a critical and popular success, climbing the ranks of the *New York Times* best-seller list—where it held sway for more than a year—and racking up sales in excess of a half million dollars in the United States alone. *The Liars' Club* went on to garner the PEN/Martha Albrand Award, the Texas Institute of Letters' Carr P. Collins Prize, and the New York Public Library Award; it also firmly established Karr as an important presence on the literary map of the era, catapulting her from little-known poet to established prose star.

Writing in *Texas Monthly* the year following *The Liars' Club*'s publication, Robert Draper characterized the book as "that rarest of publications, the literate pageturner." As such, it appealed to both serious and casual readers drawn in by Karr's humorous and at times scathing voice. Its success has been widely credited with kick-starting the revival of the memoir as a form of popular literature, a trend that has endured well into the 21st century. Nevertheless, Karr dismissed this claim to Garner somewhat dryly in the *Salon* interview by commenting, "I think memoir started with St. Augustine—not with me, and not with Oprah."

Although Karr may have herself remained modest about her work, critics and fans clamored for a follow-up. The newly minted memoirist instead returned to her first love with her third collection of poems, 1998's *Viper Rum*. In the *Chicago Review*, Barbara Jordan observed that "as a collection, *Viper Rum* finds its feet somewhere between the in-your-face stance of Karr's earlier work, and a new, what, openness? Largesse?" *Publishers Weekly* noted in its review that "the dark, knife-twisting wit Karr's greatly expanded audience has come to expect goes down with the burn of snakebite." The volume also reprinted Karr's 1991 *Parnassus* essay "Against Decoration," a sharp condemnation of the formalized and highly embellished but unemotional style of poetry that had risen to prominence over the previous several years, exemplified to Karr by the work of James Merrill and Amy Clampitt. Because of its harsh criticism against accepted form, the essay generated a great deal of discussion—and controversy—in the literary community at the time of its initial publication and again with its reprint.

In 2000, Karr returned with her much-anticipated second memoir, *Cherry*. Picking up the thread of her life during her middle school years, the book traced Karr's growth from preteen to young adult, focusing largely on her literary, intellectual, and sexual development. "Because Ms. Karr's parents ... are more marginal in this volume, because the events of Ms. Karr's teenage years are less overtly dramatic than those of her childhood, *Cherry* lacks, at first glance, the fierce singularity of *Liars' Club*," wrote Michiko Kakutani of the *New York Times*. "And yet after a somewhat hesitant start, she proves herself as fluent in evoking the common ground of adolescence as she did in limning her anomalous girlhood." This fluency again won over both critics and readers, who placed the book on several year-end best-of lists and sent *Cherry* up the best-seller lists, respectively.

Karr, who had converted to Catholicism after attending various churches for some time with her son as part of her continuing efforts to again stop drinking in the mid-1990s, chose to explore themes of religion and autobiography in her next work, the 2006 poetry collection *Sinners Welcome*. "The carnality of Catholicism appealed to me," Karr told Reyhan Harmanci of the *San Francisco Chronicle*. "An actual body on the cross, going through the repeated motions at Mass, all the things that cradle Catholics really resent," she explained. The volume roundly

drew critical accolades for displaying Karr's storytelling mastery in the poetic form, and for what *Publishers Weekly* dubbed her "clean, direct free-verse efforts."

The religious experience equally served as fodder for Karr's third memoir, *Lit*, published in the fall of 2009. Picking up where *Cherry* left off in her late teens, the book recounted Karr's college experiences; marriage to and subsequent divorce from poet Michael Milburn—called Warren Whitbread in the book—the birth of their son, Dev; the death of both of her parents; and Karr's own lengthy battle with alcohol and discovery of religion. Like her previous memoirs, *Lit* drew considerable praise for its unsparing yet often humorous depiction of Karr's struggles. "Karr has a unique ability to send up the irony-free culture of recovery while humbly testifying to its life-saving power," commented Mollie Wilson O'Reilly in *Commonweal*. Megan Hodge of *Library Journal* shared these positive sentiments, stating in her review, "that Karr survived the emotional and physical journey she regales her readers with to become the evenhanded, self-disciplined writer she is today is arguably nothing short of a miracle, and readers of her previous two books won't be disappointed." Although *Lit* failed to live up to the immense commercial success of *The Liars' Club*, it achieved respectable sales and took the number-two position on *Entertainment Weekly*'s best nonfiction of the year list.

With successful poetic and prose works under her belt, Karr has certainly more than achieved the childhood writing goal that she set for herself, and has become widely acknowledged as an important and influential contemporary literary figure. As a memoirist, she has already mined much of her life, but Karr seems likely to remain an important writer for some years to come.

Selected writings

Poetry

Abacus, Wesleyan University Press (Middletown, CT), 1987.
The Devil's Tour, New Directions (New York, NY), 1993.
Viper Rum, New Directions, 1998.
Sinners Welcome, HarperCollins (New York, NY), 2006.

Nonfiction

The Liars' Club, Viking (New York, NY), 2005.
Cherry, Viking, 2000.
Lit, HarperCollins, 2009.

Sources

Books

Contemporary Authors, New Revision Series, vol. 191, Gale, 2010, pp. 187-91.
Gale Contextual Encyclopedia of American Literature, vol. 2, Gale, 2009, pp. 852-55.
Karr, Mary, *Cherry*, Viking, 2000.
Karr, Mary, *Lit*, HarperCollins, 2009.
Karr, Mary, *The Liars' Club*, Viking, 1995.

Periodicals

Chicago Review, Summer 1998, p. 213.
Commonweal, October 23, 2009, p. 27.
Entertainment Weekly, July 14, 1995, p. 49; December 25, 2009, p. 106.
Library Journal, September 15, 1987, p. 84; October 1, 2009, p. 77.
New York Times, September 26, 2000, p. E7; September 14, 2008.
Publishers Weekly, March 15, 1993, p. 81; March 30, 1998, p. 78; October 2, 2000, p. 52; December 19, 2005, p. 42.
Radcliffe Quarterly, Spring 2003.
San Francisco Chronicle, March 2, 2006, p. H6.
Texas Monthly, September 1996, p. 106.

Online

"Mary Karr," English Department, Syracuse University, http://english.syr.edu/cwp/karr.htm (June 3, 2010).
"A Scrappy Little Beast," *Salon*, http://www.salon.com/may97/karr970521.html (June 1, 2010).

—*Vanessa E. Vaughn*

Garrison Keillor

Author and radio personality

Born Gary Edward Keillor, August 7, 1942, in Anoka, MN; son of John Philip (a railway mail clerk and carpenter) and Grace Ruth (a homemaker; maiden name, Denham) Keillor; married Mary C. Guntzel, September 1, 1965 (divorced, May 1976); married Ulla Skaerved (a social worker), December 29, 1985 (divorced, 1990); married Jenny Lind Nilsson (a violinist), 1995; children: Jason (from first marriage), Maia (from third marriage). *Education:* University of Minnesota, B.A., 1966, graduate studies, 1966-68.

Addresses: *Office*—Prairie Home Productions, LLC, 611 Frontenac Place, St. Paul, MN 55104. *E-mail*—phcmpr.org.

Career

Staff announcer, KUOM-Radio, 1963-68; producer and announcer, Minnesota Public Radio, 1971-74; host and principal writer, *A Prairie Home Companion,* 1974-87, 1993—; host, *Garrison Keillor's American Radio Company of the Air,* 1989-93; host, *Writer's Almanac,* 1995—; author of advice column "Mr. Blue," *Salon,* 1996-2001; actor, *A Prairie Home Companion,* 2005; syndicated columnist, *Salon,* 2005—; owner, Common Good Books, 2006—. Various television appearances, including: *A Prairie Home Companion: The Second Annual Farewell Performance* (host), 1988; *The Civil War,* 1990; *The Dakota Conflict* (narrator), 1993; *Redux Riding Hood* (narrator), 1997; *Hercules* (voice), 1998; *Afraid So* (voice), 2006; *Garrison Keillor's Independence Day Special: A Prairie Home Companion at Tanglewood* (host), 2006; *Garrison Keillor: The Man on the Radio in the*

Red Shoes (host), 2008. Narrator on recordings. Contibutor to various books and periodicals including *Atlantic Monthly, Harper's,* and the *New Yorker.*

Awards: George Foster Peabody Broadcasting Award, University of Georgia, for *A Prairie Home Companion,* 1980; Edward R. Murrow Award, Corporation for Public Broadcasting, 1985; Grammy Award for best nonmusical recording, National Academy of Recording Arts and Sciences, for *Lake Wobegon Days,* 1987; Ace Award, E.E. Times, 1988; Best Music and Entertainment Host Awards, 1988, 1989; medal for spoken language, American Academy of Arts and Letters, 1990; inducted into the Museum of Broadcast Communications and Radio Hall of Fame, 1994; National Humanities Medal, National Endowment for the Humanities, 1999; Berliner Morgenpost Reader's Prize, Berlin Film Festival, for *A Prairie Home Companion,* 2006.

Sidelights

In a headline for an article written by Nicholas Wroe of the *Guardian* Garrison Keillor was described as being a "Minnesota Zen Master." This description fits the quiet, Midwestern author. Keillor was born in rural Minnesota in a town named

Anoka. He was the third of six children and was raised within the Plymouth Brethren, a fundamentalist Christian sect that believes in prohibitions against things like dancing, television, and going to the movies. Keillor told Wroe about his childhood that he had "no choice but to accept that it was a very happy upbringing. I did grow up among fundamentalist people whose theology was very stark and absolute. But to their own children and relatives they were nothing but kind and generous and being among Christian people meant that cruelty was profoundly repressed. When outsiders look at this upbringing they look at the long list of prohibitions. But none of that bothers you as a child. You never went to movies or dances and so it seemed a perfectly reasonable way to grow up." Keillor has described the rural Minnesota of his youth as an idyllic place set back in time a few decades where farmers of Scandinavian descent still ploughed their fields with horses. From out of this Midwestern setting came a performer and writer who has been called one of the premier American satirical humorists of this age. Keillor has been compared to the likes of Mark Twain, E. B. White, and James Thurber. His homespun, folksy humor draws extensively from his background in Minnesota amongst the people of his youth.

Keillor led a rather cloistered life as a young child, describing himself in high school, to Wroe of the *Guardian*, as "a pale, awkward lad of no great acumen." Wroe also quotes Bill Pederson, a friend of Keillor's in high school, as saying that Keillor was both "very clever and very very kind. And he was well liked because he was such a nice kid. If I had been asked then which child would become a writer I would have said Gary. There was no question about that. But he was very quiet in high school and so the entertaining part has come out of the blue. That is not something he did when he was younger." Indeed Keillor's upbringing was an anathema to his eventual career. Jason Keillor, Keillor's son, said to Wroe about his father's success, "Suddenly he was speaking to a group of people that public radio had not previously appealed to. He had a dream in childhood that he never wavered from despite having parents who were very negative about anything related to entertainment. It was hardest for Garrison's father to say 'wow, you done great'. For a long time he disapproved of what [my father] was doing but after 25 or 30 years of success I think it did catch on with my grandparents eventually." Despite the disapproval of his family for anything to do with the entertainment industry or literature, Keillor set his sights on becoming a writer for the *New Yorker* which was a magazine that he developed a fondness for after discovering it in the public library

during high school. He also published his first poems in the school newspaper under the pseudonym of "Garrison Edwards."

While he was attending the University of Minnesota and earning a bachelor's degree in English, Keillor worked at the *Minnesota Daily* and KUOM, the University radio station. These two extracurricular activities helped him to develop skills for his later career. After graduating from college Keillor went to New York to try to find a job amongst the magazines and publishing companies on the East Coast. This trip convinced him that he wanted to be a writer but he wanted to stay in the Midwest. In an interview with Katie Bolick of the *Atlantic Unbound*, Keillor said, "I could see that New York is a tough place to be poor in, and then, too, I thought of myself as a [M]idwestern writer. The people I wanted to write for were back in Minnesota. So I went home." After returning to Minnesota Keillor achieved one of his goals and sold a story to the *New Yorker*.

The first story that Keillor sold to the *New Yorker* was "Local Family Keeps Son Happy," a 400-word mock newspaper article. *New Yorker* fiction editor Roger Angell told Wroe, regarding the story, "it was terrific. It was about the parents of this 16-year-old boy who were worried that he was rather quiet and unresponsive. So they moved in a local prostitute for him and his problems disappeared. One of her accomplishments was cooking 'fancy eggs' and he ended the piece with the recipe. I'd never seen anything like that before and it was just wonderful. We got in touch with him straight away and he began to send us great stuff." The relationship with the *New Yorker* proved to be both lucrative and fruitful. Keillor was able to earn a living from his writing because of the money he made from selling stories to the magazine. In 1974, the *New Yorker* sent him on an assignment to the Grand Ole Opry to write a story. While he was there, Keillor was inspired to create a type of old time radio program with musical performers, skits, and his now famous 20-minute monologues. Later that year, the first *A Prairie Home Companion* was broadcast from the Janet Wallace Auditorium at Macalester College in St. Paul, Minnesota.

A Prairie Home Companion has become a cultural icon. On the show Keillor not only showcases a variety of musicians who have played everything from folk to bluegrass to blues music, he also has created and expanded on the mythical small town of Lake Wobegon "where all the women are strong, all the men are good-looking, and all the children are above average." Lake Wobegon is to some degree patterned upon the Anoka of his childhood with its quiet, shy Scandinavian farmers, but it is a quirky place where used automobiles lately functioning as septic tanks are hauled down Main Street to the local dump as the homecoming queen in her finery makes her way up the street from the opposite direction aboard a flower-strewn memorial tank. It is the home of Keillor's many fictional sponsors such as Ralph's Pretty Good Grocery Store whose motto is "Remember, if you can't find it at Ralph's, you can probably get along without it," and Powdermilk Biscuits whose advertising tag is "Heavens, they're tasty." After premiering at the Janet Wallace Auditorium to a handful of people, the radio program moved to the World Theater in St. Paul, Minnesota in 1978. In 1980, the show was broadcast nationally for the first time.

In 1987 Keillor disbanded the radio program due to exhaustion, but after two years of not being on the air, Keillor created *Garrison Keillor's American Radio Company of the Air* which was broadcast from 1989-93 while *A Prairie Home Companion* was not being produced. In 1993, Keillor decided to move the show back to Minnesota and reinstate the name *A Prairie Home Companion*. In 1996 the show began to be broadcast internationally live over the internet and via satellite. While it may have started in a college auditorium and taken its name from a cemetery at Macalester College, the popularity of the program grew over the years and by 2009 reached approximately four million people weekly. The show has also broadcast from such famous venues as the Radio City Music Hall, the Hollywood Bowl, and the Fox in Atlanta.

Keillor continued to publish his writing while also writing for and performing in *A Prairie Home Companion*. Minnesota Public Radio published two collections of his *G. K. The DJ*, which was a collection of short fictional pieces, and *The Selected Verse of Margaret Haskins Durber*, which was a poetry collection. In 1983 Atheneum published a collection titled *Happy to Be Here: Stories and Comic Pieces*. After this he ventured into trying his hand at writing longer works of fiction.

Keillor's first attempt at a novel was a success. In 1985 *Lake Wobegon Days* was published and was a *New York Times* best-seller. It was the story of Lake Wobegon from the days of the French traders up until the modern era. Mary T. Schmich, writing for the *Chicago Tribune*, described the book as, "more tales about the routine oddities of life among the Irish, Norwegians, Swedes, Lutherans, and Catholics of his fictional town." She went on to say that the stories were humorous without being cutting

and were woven together in such a manner that they hung together and could not be dismissed as being a collection of humorous writings. According to Schmich, Keillor's small town of Lake Wobegon is "a town that lies not on any map but somewhere along the border of his imagination and his memory." More than two million copies of *Lake Wobegon Days* were sold.

Keillor's second novel, *WLT: A Radio Romance*, came out in 1991 after two other collections of shorter works called *Leaving Home: A Collection of Lake Wobegon Staories* and *We Are Still Married: Stories and Love Letters*. *WLT: A Radio Romance* is about two brothers in the golden era of radio who start up a radio station in 1926. The novel chronicles their lives and adventures and the growth of the station until television becomes popular and replaces radio as people's main entertainment. This novel—for a humorist author—was considered to be somewhat dark.

Keillor's third novel about Lake Wobegon, titled *Wobegon Boy* came out in 1997. The story of this novel follows John Tollefson as he leaves Lake Wobegon and takes a job at a radio station in upstate New York. The novel was criticized for not following Keillor's usual writing style and attempting to make the character more three dimensional as opposed to his usual two-dimensional caricatures that he has used as vehicles for his humorous vignettes.

In 2003 Keillor's semi-autobiographical novel *Love Me* was published. It follows the story of a writer who leaves his loyal wife and travels to New York so that he can pursue a life as a writer. At first he has success and then a second unpopular novel is published and he becomes the writer of an advice column. The novel was described by various reviewers as being wry, having humor and compassion, and a degree of cynicism.

Keillor's novels *Pontoon* and *Liberty: A Lake Wobegon Novel* continue the development of Lake Wobegon and its fictional denizens. In addition to his novels, Keillor has published several short-story collections, written young adult novels, authored children's books, produced an opera, penned a screenplay, performed on many sound recordings, and continued to contribute to various magazines and periodicals.

Keillor has had to weather many ups and downs in his personal life over the course of his years. He was married three times. His first wife was Mary C.

Guntzel to whom he dedicated *Love Me*. They had one child named Jason who works on "A Prairie Home Companion." His second wife, Ulla Skaerved, was a Danish exchange student at Keillor's Anoka High School; they became reacquainted at a reunion before marrying. His third wife was Jenny Lind Nilsson with whom he has a daughter named Maia. Keillor has moved from Minnesota to New York to Denmark, and back again. In 2001 Keillor underwent heart surgery at the Mayo Clinic in Rochester, Minnesota. Throughout all of his successes and changes in relationships and circumstances, he has remained the quiet, clever, funny radio host and author from Minnesota.

Selected writings

G.K. the DJ (collection), Minnesota Public Radio (St. Paul, MN), 1977.

The Selected Verse of Margaret Haskins Durber (poetry), Minnesota Public Radio, 1979.

Happy to Be Here: Stories and Comic Pieces, Atheneum (New York, NY), 1982; expanded edition, Penguin (New York, NY), 1983.

Lake Wobegon Days, Viking (New York, NY), 1985.

Leaving Home: A Collection of Lake Wobegon Stories, Viking, 1987.

We Are Still Married: Stories and Letters, Viking, 1989.

WLT: A Radio Romance, Viking, 1991.

The Book of Guys, Viking, 1993.

Cat, You Better Come Home (children), Viking, 1995.

The Old Man Who Loved Cheese (children), Little, Brown (Boston, MA), 1996.

(With Jenny Lind Nilsson) *The Sandy Bottom Orchestra*, Hyperion (New York, NY), 1996.

Wobegon Boy, Viking, 1997.

(Editor, with Katrina Kenison) *The Best American Short Stories: 1998*, Houghton Mifflin (Boston, MA), 1998.

Me: By Jimmy (Big Boy) Valente, Governor of Minnesota, As Told to Garrison Keillor, Viking, 1999.

A Prairie Home Companion Commonplace Book: 25 Years on the Air with Garrison Keillor, Highbridge (Minneapolis, MN), 1999.

Pretty Good Joke Book: Prairie Home Companion, Highbridge (Minneapolis, MN), 2000.

In Search of Lake Wobegon, Viking, 2001.

Lake Wobegon Summer, 1956, Viking, 2001.

(Editor) *Good Poems*, Viking, 2002.

Mr. And Mrs. Olson (libretto), produced in St. Paul, MN, 2002.

Love Me, Viking, 2003.

Homegrown Democrat: A Few Plain Thoughts from the Heart of America, Viking, 2004; updated edition, 2006.

A Prairie Home Companion (screenplay), Penguin, 2006.

Daddy's Girl, Hyperion Books for Children (New York, NY), 2005.

(Selector) *Good Poems for Hard Times*, Viking, 2005.

Pontoon, Viking, 2007.

Liberty: A Lake Wobegon Novel, Viking, 2008.

Life Among the Lutherans, Augsburg Books (Minneapolis, MN), 2009.

77 Love Sonnets, Common Good Books (Saint Paul, MN), 2009.

Pilgrims: A Wobegon Romance, Viking, 2009.

A Christmas Blizzard (novella), Viking, 2009.

Sound recordings

A Prairie Home Companion Anniversary Album, Minnesota Public Radio, 1980.

The Family Radio, Minnesota Public Radio, 1982.

News From Lake Wobegon, Minnesota Public Radio, 1982.

Prairie Home Companion Tourists, Minnesota Public Radio, 1983.

Ten Years on the Prairie: A Prairie Home Companion 10th Anniversary, Minnesota Public Radio, 1984.

Gospel Birds and Other Stories of Lake Wobegon, Minnesota Public Radio, 1985.

A Prairie Home Companion: The Final Performance, Minnesota Public Radio, 1987.

More News From Lake Wobegon, Minnesota Public Radio, 1988.

Lake Wobegon Loyalty Days: A Recital for Mixed Baritone and Orchestra, Minnesota Public Radio, 1989.

Local Man Moves to City, Highbridge, 1991.

News from Lake Wobegon, Highbridge, 1991.

More News from Lake Wobegon, Highbridge, 1991.

(With Frederica von Stade) *Songs of the Cat*, Highbridge, 1991.

Lake Wobegon U.S.A., Highbridge, 1993.

Garrison Keillor's Comedy Theatre: More Songs and Sketches from A Prairie Home Companion, Highbridge, 1997.

A Prairie Home Companion Pretty Good Joke Tape, Highbridge, 2000.

Definitely Above Average, Highbridge, 2001.

A Life in Comedy: An Evening of Favorites from a Writer's Life, Highbridge, 2003.

Prairie Home Christmas, Highbridge, 2007.

Even More Pretty Good Jokes, Highbridge, 2009.

Sources

Books

Authors and Artists for Young Adults, vol. 62, Thomson Gale, 2005.

Encyclopedia of World Biography Supplement, vol. 22, Gale Group, 2002.

Marquis Who's Who, Marquis Who's Who, 2009.

Periodicals

Chicago Tribune, March 15, 1987.
Guardian (London, England), March 6, 2004.

Online

Contemporary Authors Online, Gale, 2009.

"Garrison Keillor," Yahoo Movies, http://movies.yahoo.com/movie/contributor/18001076.tif12/bio (May 31, 2010).
"It's Just Work," *Atlantic Unbound,* http://www.theatlantic.com/past/unbound/factfict/gkint.htm (May 31, 2010).
A Prairie Home Companion, American Public Media, http://prairiehome.publicradio.org/ (May 30, 2010).

—Annette Bowman

Anna Kendrick

Actress

Born August 9, 1985, in Portland, ME; daughter of Will (a teacher) and Jan (an accountant) Kendrick.

Addresses: *Agent*—APA Talent and Literary Agency, 405 S. Beverly Dr., Beverly Hills, CA 90212.

Career

Actress on stage, including: *Annie Warbucks*, Maine State Music Theatre, Brunswick, ME, 1993; *High Society*, St. James Theatre, New York City, 1998; *A Little Night Music*, New York City Opera, New York City, 2003. Film appearances include: *Camp*, 2003; *Rocket Science*, 2007; *Twilight*, 2008; *Elsewhere*, 2009; *The Marc Pease Experience*, 2009; *Up in the Air*, 2009; *The Twilight Saga: New Moon*, 2009; *The Twilight Saga: Eclipse*, 2010; *Scott Pilgrim vs. the World*, 2010. Television appearances include: *The Mayor*, 2003; *Viva Laughlin*, 2007; *Fear Itself*, 2009.

Awards: Award for best supporting actress, Austin Film Critics Association, for *Up in the Air*, 2009; award for best supporting actress, National Board of Review, for *Up in the Air*, 2009; award for best supporting actress, Toronto Film Critics Association, for *Up in the Air*, 2009; rising star award, Palm Springs International Film Festival, for *Up in the Air*, 2010.

Sidelights

Oscar-nominated actress Anna Kendrick got her start on stage, earning a Tony Award nomination at the age of 12 for her role in the Broadway musical *High Society*. She was one of the youngest nominees in Tony history. As a teen, the stage actress moved to the silver screen and became an indie darling for her roles in *Camp* (2003) and *Rocket Science* (2007). During the late 2000s, Kendrick earned a considerable following as a supporting cast member in the highly successful *Twilight* vampire movie franchise.

Kendrick's breakout role came with 2009's *Up in the Air*, when the twentysomething gave an inspired performance, holding her own against veteran actor and screen heartthrob George Clooney. Kendrick's performance brought her an Oscar nomination and widespread critical acclaim. *New York Times* film critic Manohla Dargis put it this way: "One of the pleasures of *Up in the Air* is that its actresses—including Anna Kendrick … share the frame with Mr. Clooney as equals, not props. The ferocious Ms. Kendrick, her ponytail swinging like an ax, grabs every scene she's in."

Kendrick was born on August 9, 1985, in Portland, Maine, to Will and Jan Kendrick. Early on, she knew she wanted to be on stage. "I didn't know why," Kendrick told the *Sunday Mail*'s Barry Koltnow. "I wanted to sing and dance and perform. I wanted to perform and had no idea why." During her elemen tary school years, Kendrick found work close to home, appearing in stage productions in Portland and in nearby Biddeford, Maine. In 1993 she landed at the Maine State Music Theatre in nearby Brunswick, playing an orphan in the musical *Annie Warbucks*.

Kendrick yearned to do more so her parents started driving her down to New York City for auditions—the trip was more than 300 miles one way. As Kendrick grew older, her parents allowed her to take the bus to New York with her older brother because they could not always get off work to drive. Kendrick's mom worked as an accountant, while her father taught history. Kendrick came close to landing some prominent parts and made the final cut for the title role in the 1998 film adaptation of *Madeline*. She also came up short in her audition for a role in the PBS kids show *Zoom*.

Disappointed, Kendrick pressed on and scored an audition for a Broadway revival of the 1956 Cole Porter movie musical *High Society*, a hit that had featured Bing Crosby, Grace Kelly, and Frank Sinatra. Kendrick's brother accompanied her to the city for the tryout. Kendrick recalled the trip in an interview with Mark Ellwood of the *Daily News*. Kendrick told Ellwood that she ran into some trouble when she was asked to stay overnight. "And of course, we were planning on getting the Greyhound bus back that evening. So my parents had to fax a credit card to a hotel." Nervous at having their 12-year-old daughter and 14-year-old son spend the night alone in New York City, the Kendricks told their children to stay in their hotel room and not go anywhere but the audition. The temptation was too great and the siblings ventured down to Greenwich Village for breakfast before the audition.

The overnight was worth it, as Kendrick scored a singing part in *High Society*, a musical that tells the story of a Long Island socialite's romantic entanglements. Kendrick played the role of the heroine's little sister, Dinah, and appeared on stage in a pink tutu singing Porter's "I Love Paris," a song the famed composer had introduced in his 1953 Broadway musical *Can-Can*. As rehearsals got under way, Kendrick and her father moved to the New York suburbs to be closer to Broadway. Her teacher father tutored her on her schoolwork and her mother was able to visit on weekends.

High Society opened at Broadway's St. James Theatre in April of 1998 and closed that August after 144 performances. Kendrick was the only child in the production and appeared on stage during one-quarter of the show. Reviews were mixed. *New York Times* critic Vincent Canby lambasted the production, equating it to a "stage cartoon" that is "broad, flat, and gross." Canby went on, however, to note that Kendrick gave one of "the few legitimately decent performances." The theater world took notice and Kendrick earned a Tony Award nomination for best featured actress in a musical for her stellar portrayal of Dinah. Kendrick was the third-youngest Tony nominee in Broadway history. A few years later, she appeared in *A Little Night Music* at the New York City Opera. Though Kendrick ultimately ended up on the big screen, she told the *Daily News*' Ellwood that she was thankful to have started her acting career on the stages of New York instead of in Los Angeles' studios. "On a film set, you're sort of coddled, but when you're on stage, even as a 12-year-old, you're expected to be a professional and deliver every night."

Kendrick's shift from stage to film went fairly smoothly, particularly because she found the perfect transitional film in 2003's *Camp*, an indie comedy about a summer camp for kids who love musical theater. Kendrick had the opportunity to sing and dance in the film, which is what she had been doing on stage. One *Film Comment* critic noted that *Camp* included many showstoppers, yet Kendrick's "glass-breaking, back-stabbing rendition of the Stephen Sondheim chestnut 'Ladies Who Lunch' is on a whole other level." This clip became a favorite among YouTube audiences.

After *Camp*, Kendrick earned a prominent role in 2007's *Rocket Science*, a bittersweet comedy that debuted at the Sundance Film Festival to rave reviews, though box office sales were mediocre. The film is a coming-of-age story centering on the life of a brainy teen with a stutter named Hal—played by Canadian actor Reece Thompson. Hal is lured into joining his high school debate team when he falls for Kendrick's character—Ginny Ryerson—the frosty, fast-talking queen of the debate team. In the film, Kendrick stunned moviegoers with her hyper-articulate, mile-a-minute line delivery, meant to showcase her character's debate skills. The film was directed by Jeffrey Blitz, best known for his 2002 documentary *Spellbound*. Blitz won the Sundance Film Festival's directing award for his work on *Rocket Science*.

Kendrick's performance in *Rocket Science* caught the attention of veteran moviemakers Catherine Hardwicke, director of 2003's *Thirteen*, and Jason Reitman, director of *Thank You for Smoking* (2005) and *Juno* (2007). Both directors sought out Kendrick for their upcoming projects.

Hardwicke cast Kendrick in the first installment of the *Twilight* film series, which is based on the *Twilight* books by Stephenie Meyer. The vampire romance series chronicles the relationship between a human teen named Bella Swan and her vampire beau Edward Cullen. In the film series, Kendrick was cast as insecure chatterbox Jessica Stanley, a non-vampire and often jealous friend to Bella Swan. Kendrick's appearance in *Twilight*, released in 2008, gave her instant recognition among the tween-lit crowd.

By spring 2009, Kendrick was busy filming the sequel, *The Twilight Saga: New Moon,* in Vancouver, while simultaneously working with Reitman on *Up in the Air,* which was filmed primarily in St. Louis. Kendrick snagged a principal role in *Up in the Air.* This was also her first big studio picture.

In the Reitman film Kendrick plays Natalie Keener, a straight-A college grad who lands a job at a firm specializing in corporate downsizing. Clooney plays the role of her foil, Ryan Bingham. Bingham enjoys traveling and never having to lay down roots. He spends his time crisscrossing the nation firing employees for bosses who are not up to the task. A seasoned professional, Clooney's character prefers to speak to workers face-to-face. Kendrick's Natalie, however, has come of age in front of the computer and proposes, in an effort to cut costs, that the company begins laying off workers through videoconferencing via the Internet.

The film was based on Walter Kirn's 2001 novel *Up in the Air,* though the book did not include Kendrick's character. When Reitman wrote the screenplay, he created the character to offer an outlet for Clooney's character to discuss his philosophies. Reitman also relied on personal experience to help him create Natalie. Speaking to Barbara Vancheri of the *Pittsburgh Post-Gazette,* Kendrick explained how Reitman told her the character was born. "He mentioned that Natalie was based on a shocking amount of women in his life that he knows and loves very dearly who are almost too smart for their own good, and their greatest frustration in life is constantly being the smartest person in the room."

Up in the Air garnered six Golden Globe nominations, including best drama, as well as acting nominations for Clooney and Kendrick, though neither won. Reitman won a Golden Globe for best screenplay. Kendrick also received an Oscar nomination for best supporting actress, though the honor went to Mo'Nique for her role as the vile, abusive welfare mother in *Precious.*

Initially, Kendrick thought she had blown the audition for *Up in the Air* because Reitman seemed unimpressed at her tryout, though silently, he was rooting for her. It turned out that the director had written the part for her. Reitman told MTV's Eric Ditzian that he found Kendrick's performance in *Rocket Science* inspiring and thought to himself, "'This girl has a different voice from everyone of her generation.' ... [S]he's so witty and smart and sharp, and I needed a girl who could go toe-to-toe with George Clooney."

Kendrick continued her work with the Twilight franchise, and in June of 2010 *The Twilight Saga: Eclipse* was released. She also appeared in the 2010 action comedy *Scott Pilgrim vs. the World,* an Edgar Wright film adaptation of Bryan Lee O'Malley's comic book series Scott Pilgrim. Scott is an unemployed 22-year-old garage band bass guitarist who must defeat an endless stream of his new girlfriend's ex-boyfriends in order to win her heart. Kendrick played Scott's younger sister, Stacey. In 2010, Kendrick was also busy shooting a comedy with Seth Rogen.

As for the way her career has developed, Kendrick is pleased to have found success but also happy that she has not become as famous as her Twilight co-stars who are constantly mobbed in crowds. When MTV's Larry Carroll asked Kendrick what she would do if she became so famous she needed to hide, Kendrick replied, "I guess I would go home. I would go to Maine, which is pretty isolated, and I would bring the entire Criterion DVD collection, and, you know, obviously some device for playing it. What else? Oh, one of those nap spa robes from Brookstone. I would just live the rest of my life in the nap robe from Brookstone, watching Criterion DVDs."

Sources

Periodicals

Film Comment, May/June 2003, p. 6.

Los Angeles Times, January 6, 2010, p. S30.

Maine Sunday Telegram (Portland, ME), April 19, 1998, p. 1E.

New York Times, May 3, 1998; December 4, 2009.

Pittsburgh Post-Gazette, December 23, 2009.

Portland Press Herald (ME), May 5, 1998, p. 1A.

Sunday Mail (Queensland, Australia), January 3, 2010, p. 3.

Washington Post, August 17, 2007, p. C6.

Online

"Anna Kendrick of 'Up in the Air,' 'New Moon,' Glad She Started on New York Stage," *Daily News*, http://www.nydailynews.com/entertainment/movies/2009/12/12/2009-12-12_anna_kendrick_of_up_in_the_air_new_moon_glad_she_started_on_new_york_stage.html (May 10, 2010).

"'Twilight' Tuesday: Anna Kendrick Says It Was 'Easy to Get Googly Eyed' At Robert Pattinson," MTV, http://www.mtv.com/news/articles/1597526/20081021.tif/story.jhtml (May 10, 2010).

"'Up in the Air' Director Raves About Anna Kendrick: 'I Wrote This Role For Her,'" MTV, http://www.mtv.com/news/articles/1627465/20091202.tif/story.jhtml (May 12, 2010).

—*Lisa Frick*

James Keyes

Chief Executive Officer of Blockbuster

Bloomberg via Getty Images

Born James Willard Keyes, March 17, 1955, in Worcester, MA; son of Harold L. and Dorothy M. (Anderson) Keyes; married Margo Bernadette Ramirez, April 20, 1991. *Education:* College of the Holy Cross, B.A., 1977; Columbia University, M.B.A., 1980; attended the University of London.

Addresses: *Office*—Blockbuster, Inc., 1201 Elm St., Dallas, TX 75270.

Career

Director of corporate planning, Gulf Oil Corp., Pittsburgh, PA, 1980-85; vice president of national gasoline, the Southland Corp., Dallas, TX, 1985-93; joined Southland subsidiary 7-Eleven Inc. as senior financial officer, c. early 1990s, then chief financial officer, 1996-98, then executive vice president and chief operating officer, 1998-2000, then president and chief executive officer, 2000-05; chairman and chief executive officer, Blockbuster, Inc., Dallas, TX, 2007—.

Awards: Horatio Alger Award, 2005; Retailer inductee, Convenience Store Industry Hall of Fame, 2005.

Sidelights

Business executive James Keyes spent several successful years at the helm of 7-Eleven before becoming head of the struggling Blockbuster chain of media rental stores in 2007. He had moved through the ranks to become the president and chief executive officer of 7-Eleven in 2000, and his tenure was marked by sustained profitability. Keyes faced more challenges at Blockbuster, but kept the company afloat amidst a changing industry. Respected for his managerial skills and innovative mind, *Convenience Store News* called Keyes "strategic, bright, articulate, colorful and so quotable."

Born on March 17, 1955, in Worcester, Massachusetts, he was the son of Harold and Dorothy Keyes. He earned his B.A. in 1977 from the College of the Holy Cross. Keyes did post-graduate work at the University of London then went on to earn his M.B.A. from Columbia University in 1980. That year, Keyes joined Gulf Oil in Pittsburgh, Pennsylvania, as the director of corporate planning. He remained in the post for five years.

In 1985, Keyes moved to Dallas to take a position as vice president of national gasoline for the Southland Corp. He remained in the position until 1993. In the early 1990s, Keyes went to work for 7-Eleven, the popular chain of convenience stores, a subsidiary of Southland at that time. He began as senior financial officer then became chief financial officer in 1996. Two years later, Keyes was named chief financial officer. In 1998, he became the executive vice president and chief operating officer.

Keyes was named 7-Eleven's president and chief executive officer in 2000. It was a growing empire of 22,000 stores in 17 countries worth $29 billion as of 2001. That year, his leadership was challenged by the terrorist attacks of September 11, 2001. The demands of business included providing moral support to the large number of immigrants in their workforce and among their franchisees, as well as dealing with travel restrictions as 7-Eleven business took place all over the world.

Despite such problems, Keyes was known for his innovative in-store merchandising at 7-Elevens. Among his innovations was the introduction of new fresh foods like sandwiches, increased financial services for customers, and more technology investments to better track stock as well as meet the customers' wants and needs. He also led the company to 36 consecutive quarters of same-store sales gains and took the company private after 15 years of being publicly traded shortly before he retired in 2005 after 20 years of service. Also in this time period, he was the retailer inductee to the Convenience Store Hall of Fame.

Of his impact on 7-Eleven, Keyes told *Convenience Store News* days before his tenure ended, "I hope I will have played a role in the transformation of 7-Eleven and that people will look back and say, 'Jim was responsible for getting the company to turn the corner.' I don't know if I will be the one to take it to the next level or if my strength is in the change—creating the change. That remains to be seen."

In 2007, Keyes returned to the business world after a two-year hiatus when he joined the Dallas-based company Blockbuster, Inc., as its chairman and chief executive officer. He replaced John Antioco, who resigned following a pay dispute. Keyes had a three-year contract that paid him a salary of at least $750,000 annually.

When Keyes took over Blockbuster, it was a company facing numerous challenges. After years of being a dominant force in video, DVD, and game rentals, Blockbuster struggled to stay afloat in the age of instant digital downloads, Netflix (a company which rented media via mail with no return deadline), cheap rentals at Redbox locations, and inexpensive DVDs sold at Wal-mart and other discount stores. Blockbuster posted losses for nine of the previous ten years before Keyes took over the company and its then 8,000 stores.

Keyes believed that he could help the company survive. He told Cindy Spielvogel of *Video Business*, "We have a competitive advantage in that we're al-ready the recognized leader in the industry." He added, that he saw himself as a "stimulator of change" and wanted the company to both "do a better job in the four walls" and outside of them. Keyes concluded to Claude Brodesser-Akner of *Advertising Age*, "If you look at the entertainment marketplace, it's all about convenience and convenient access to media and entertainment. We have the opportunity to find ways to become more convenient and relevant to the customer."

During his tenure, Keyes continued his predecessor's plan to bring Blockbuster back to profitability by closing hundreds, if not thousands of stores each year, increasing some prices and reducing others, and emphasizing a Netflix-like service that allowed customers to order movies by mail then return them to stores. He also cut costs in other ways, like reducing personnel. To improve Blockbuster's market share, Keyes worked to ensure that the most in-demand titles were always in stock. He helped reduce the size of stores and introduce new store layouts that emphasized beverage sales and kids' areas and increased the amount of product for sale in each store. He oversaw the introduction of thousands of Blockbuster Express kiosks during 2010 as well.

By that year, however, it was clear that Keyes' leadership was not leading Blockbuster to profitability. By July of 2010, Blockbuster was facing several financial crises. The company hoped to do a stock split, but failed to do so, and was de-listed on the New York Stock Exchange shortly thereafter. In addition, its credit rating was lowered by a major credit agency. Blockbuster also had to re-structure its debt, with the support of debt holders, to ensure continued liquidity. This move bought Blockbuster enough time to survive, at least in the short term, though debt holders forced the company to hire a chief restructuring officer.

Keyes' contract was also renewed in that time period despite ongoing concerns that Blockbuster would be soon forced to file for bankruptcy. After years of struggling, however, Blockbuster finally filed for bankruptcy on September 23, 2010. The company stayed afloat and was able to keep most of its 3,500 stores open by working out a deal with lenders that saw most of its $1 billion in debt eliminated. As part of this deal, its lenders, led by investor Carl C. Ichan, would essentially own Blockbuster.

The company was going to continue to re-invent itself to ensure its long-term survival, though it was unclear if the new owners would retain Keyes. By

October of 2010, it was reported that Blockbuster's owners were looking for a new CEO, though Keyes was still a candidate to retain the post. No matter what Keyes remained optimistic about Blockbuster's future, telling Maria Halkias of the *Dallas Morning News*, "I have reaffirmed, to the board and our management team, my commitment to facilitate the recapitalization and to continue the business transformation of Blockbuster."

Sources

Books

Marquis Who's Who, Marquis Who's Who, 2009.

Periodicals

Advertising Age, March 31, 2008, p. 6.

Associated Press, November 17, 2007; January 9, 2008; September 15, 2009.
Associated Press Worldstream, July 10, 2002.
CIO Magazine, May 15, 2005.
Convenience Store News, December 19, 2005.
Dallas Morning News, November 18, 2001, p. 1A; July 2, 2010, p. D1; July 3, 2010, p. D1.
Houston Chronicle, July 3, 2007, p. 3.
New York Times, September 24, 2010, p. B3.
SNL Kagan Media & Communications Report, July 2, 2010.
Time, October 11, 2010, p. 38.
Video Business, July 9, 2007, p. 5.

Online

"Blockbuster starts search for new CEO report," Reuters.com, http://www.reuters.com/article/idUSTRE69B0KC20101012.tif (October 17, 2010).

—A. Petruso

Vinod Khosla

Newscom

Entrepreneur and business executive

Born January 28, 1955, in New Delhi, India; son of an officer in the Indian Army; married Neeru; children: four. *Education:* India Institute of Technology, B.Tech., 1976; Carnegie Mellon University, M.S., 1978; Stanford Graduate School of Business, M.B.A., 1980.

Addresses: *Office*—Khosla Ventures, 3000 Sand Hill Rd., Building 3, Ste. 190, Menlo Park, CA 94025. *Web site*—http://www.khoslaventures.com/index.html. *E-mail*—vk@khoslaventures.com.

Career

Co-founded Daisy Systems, 1980; left Daisy, 1982; co-founded Sun Microsystems, 1982, then briefly served as chief executive officer; left Sun, 1986; general partner, Kleiner, Perkins, Canfield, and Byers (KPCB), 1986; scaled back involvement with KPCB, 2004; founded venture capital firm Khosla Ventures, 2004; raised one billion dollars for two funds focusing on green technology and information technology, 2009.

Awards: Named the greenest billionaire by *Forbes* magazine, 2010.

Sidelights

Once dubbed "The Man with the Golden Touch" by *Forbes* magazine, venture capitalist and entrepreneur Vinod Khosla was known for his involvement in such companies as Sun Microsystems

and the highly regarded venture capital firm Kleiner, Perkins, Canfield, and Byers (KPCB). Though KPCB, he helped in the development of such successful start-ups as Cerent Corp. and Siara Systems. In 2004, Khosla scaled back his involvement in KPCB to focus on his own firm, Khosla Ventures, which emphasized green technology. As Dave Fetters wrote of Khosla in *Network Computing*, "Combining cunning business sense with amazing technological insight, Khosla has funded, and been part of, some of the top companies in the technology field."

Born on January 28, 1955, in New Delhi, India, he was the son of an Indian Army officer. From his earliest days, Khosla was interested in technology and hoped to one day start his own company. He would read rented American trade magazines (his family was too poor to buy them) and play around with gadgets such as circuit boards. He dreamed of moving to the United States and having his own business there. Khosla convinced his father to allow him to study engineering instead of join the military as his father wanted.

After earning his bachelor of technology degree in electrical engineering from New Delhi's Indian Institute of Technology in 1976, Khosla made progress toward his goal by moving to the United States with his long-time girlfriend (later wife), Neeru to continue his education. He earned his master of science degree in biomedical engineering from Carnegie Mellon University in 1978. He then entered Stanford University's Graduate School of business, earning his master's in business administration in 1980.

In 1980, Khosla and two others started their own company making computer-aided engineering software based on a platform they built themselves. Khosla wrote the business plan and Daisy Systems was founded. However, Khosla moved on in 1982, using the knowledge and experience he gained with Daisy on a new company. In 1982, Khosla was one of the co-founders of Sun Microsystems, which focused on generic technical work stations. There, he served as chief executive officer and helped the company become a pioneer in open systems and RISC processors. He remained with Sun, which became a billion dollar company, until 1986.

Khosla then became a general partner of KPCB of Menlo Park, California, though he remained on Sun's board of directors for some time. Khosla worked with the venture capital firm during his tenure at Sun Microsystems; KPCB was a major early investor. While employed at KPCB, he focused on creating value and positively affecting effective partnerships with startups, entrepreneurs, and partners in the firm.

For example: Khosla helped challenge Intel's dominance in microprocessors with the Nexygen/AMD; he took a role in the development of Juniper Networks and its high-speed Internet routers; and he was involved with the early advertising-based search strategy for Excite, an online search engine. Khosla also was involved in the fundings of such ventures as Cerent Corp., which helped increase internet traffic over networks and was eventually sold to Cisco Systems for $8 billion, as well as Siara Systems, which made high-speed and broadband fiber optic network equipment. Not every venture he was involved with succeeded. He was very active in Dynabook Technologies, a failed attempt at a laptop computer in 1989-90, as well as the Go Corporation, which tried to produce the first pen-operated computer.

Such failures did not dampen Khosla's enthusiasm for the venture capital business. As he explained to Katie Brown of *San Francisco Business Times,* "I think of technology as one of the most fun things there is. It's a lot more interesting than fiction—a lot more uncertain, a lot more real. It's kind of a whodunnit story, but it's how does it happen and what." During his tenure at KPCB, Khosla also became deeply involved with TiE, a nonprofit worldwide entrepreneur network founded in 1992. He was a charter member.

While remaining with KPCB as a partner on a part-time basis, Khosla founded his own venture capital firm, Khosla Ventures, in 2004. With this company, he had the freedom to support and fund projects that were more experimental as well as both for profit and social impact groups. He admitted he funded some ideas and ventures that were little more than science experiments, like a new type of LED lightning. Khosla also publicly supported green technology. He expressed an interest in alternative energy sources, a belief in independence from petroleum, and a realistic approach to environmental issues. He invested in a number of clean-energy and bio fuel start-ups through his firm, including those involved with cellulosic ethanol production.

Khosla faced controversy, however, because he publicly stated that he firmly did not believe that hybrid cars and hydrogen power would make a real dent in climate change. He was also criticized for saying that the use of such technology as solar panels in San Francisco was futile. Khosla was certain that only large-scale solutions that were economical would really work. Some investors came to believe in Khosla's support for green technology ventures as he raised more than one billion dollars by September of 2009 for two funds which were to invest in green technology and information technology. By 2010, Khosla was recognized as the greenest billionaire by *Forbes* magazine.

Over the years, Khosla also became passionate about social entrepreneurship in the areas of education, health, affordable housing, and most especially using microfinance as a means of alleviating poverty. To that end, he supported a number of microfinance groups in both Africa and India. They included the SHARE program (Society for Helping and Awakening Rural Poor Through Education), which helped provide both training to impoverished entrepreneurs living in rural areas as well as microloans. In addition, Khosla used his some of his multi-million dollar fortune to found his own vineyard, Three Dog Vineyards, which produced 1,000 bottles of cabernet sauvignon per year in the early 2000s.

Explaining his philosophy as an entrepreneur, Khosla told Constance Loizos of the *San Jose Mercury News,* "I don't think of myself as a business person. I never have. I mean, I know how to do that part; I know how to handle it. But I've never enjoyed it. I love technologies. I love the future. I love thinking about solutions. Then once I believe them, I love to evangelize."

Sources

Books

Marquis Who's Who, Marquis Who's Who, 2010.

Periodicals

Information Company, April 23, 2010.
InfoWorld, August 13, 1990, p. 106.
InfoWorld Daily News, February 26, 2007.
National Post (Canada), July 26, 1999, p. C12.

Network Computing, October 2, 2000.
New York Times, January 3, 2000, p. C1; April 12, 2004, p. C3; September 1, 2009, p. B1.
Ottawa Citizen, February 19, 2001, p. B12.
San Francisco Business Times, April 20, 1987, sec. 1, p. 14.
San Francisco Chronicle, December 31, 2007, p. C1.
San Jose Mercury News, February 14, 2004, p. 1C; October 15, 2006, sec. BU, p. 1.
United Press International, March 29, 1987.
USA Today, June 21, 1989, p. 2B.

Online

"Vinod Khosla," Khosla Ventures, http://www. khoslaventures.com/khosla/people_vk.html (May 10, 2010).

—*A. Petruso*

Kim Yu-Na

Figure skater

Born September 5, 1990, in Gyounggi-Do, South Korea; daughter of Kim Hyeon-seok (a business owner) and Park Mi-hee.

Addresses: *Contact*—c/o Toronto Cricket, Skating and Curling Club, 141 Wilson Ave., Toronto, Ontario M5M 3A3 Canada.

Career

Began skating at the age of six, c. 1996.

Awards: Silver medal in ladies figure skating, World Junior Championships, 2005; gold medal in ladies figure skating, World Junior Championships, 2006; bronze medal in ladies figure skating, World Championships, 2007; won the ladies figure skating title, Cup of Russia, 2007; won the ladies figure skating title, ISU Grand Prix Final, 2007; won the ladies figure skating title, ISU Grand Prix Final, 2008; won the ladies figure skating title, Skate America, 2008; won the ladies figure skating title, Cup of China, 2008; Best Skater Award in figure skating, Korean Skating Union, 2008; bronze medal in ladies figure skating, World Championships, 2008; placed second in ladies figure skating, ISU Grand Prix Final, 2009; won the ladies figure skating title, Skate America, 2009; won the ladies figure skating title, Four Continents Championship, 2009; gold medal in ladies figure skating, World Championships, 2009; won the ladies figure skating title, ISU Grand Prix Final, 2010; gold medal in ladies figure skating, Winter Olympics, 2010; silver medal in ladies figure skating, World Championships, 2010.

Cameron Spencer/Getty Images

Sidelights

Considered a national treasure by South Korea and the Korean people, figure skating champion Kim Yu-Na is known as "Queen Yu Na." A skater of power, elegance, and technical ability, she was the first Korean to win a gold medal in figure skating at the Olympic Games. Kim was also the first Korean figure skater to win an ISU (International Skating Union) Championsip—when she won the 2006 World Junior Championship—as well as the first to win the ladies competition in the 2008 World Figure Skating Championships. In part because of the depth of her fame in Korea—compounded by her many commercial and endorsement deals—Kim trained in Toronto with Brian Orser, a former figure skating champion, as her coach.

Kim was born on September 5, 1990, in Gyounggi-Do, South Korea, the daughter of Kim Hyeon-seok and Park Mi-hee. Her father was a business owner. Raised in Gunpo City, South Korea, she began skating in 1996. She skated for fun at first, but when she was seven years old a coach told her mother that she had talent. Kim then began skating seriously, though her mother struggled to pay for her lessons at times. Her mother devoted herself to her daughter's skating career, hiring coaches and using the family home as collateral for a loan to cover the high cost of training.

Using various coaches in South Korea, Kim began doing well in international competition when she hit her teens. In 2005, she won silver at the World Junior Championships. In 2006, she won the World Junior Championships, becoming the first figure skater from Korea to win an ISU championship. Deemed too young to compete in the 2006 Winter Olympic Games in Torino, Italy, she was selected to take part in the Olympic Torch Relay. Despite such honors, Kim was chafing in the strictness of her coaching and wanted to be more free. She also was suffering from repeated ankle and knee injuries, and displayed technical ability without much spirit in her skating as well as her life. Kim even stated that she hated skating, in part because of the growing weight of public expectation in Korea.

To deal with these problems, Kim traveled to Toronto to work with David Wilson, a skating choreographer, in the summer of 2006. She spoke no English, but hoped to evolve both as a skater and person. Wilson told Juliet Macur of the *New York Times*, "Her coach said to me back then that Yu-Na wanted to be a happy skater, so that's what we started working on. I remember even having to teach her how to hug me because she was so shy. She was always so stiff, like a telephone pole."

Wilson worked out of a rink at the Toronto Cricket, Skating, and Curling Club. The rink's skating director was Brian Orser, a Canadian silver medalist in men's figure skating at the 1984 and 1988 Winter Olympics. He also won a World Championship and skated with the Stars on Ice tour. Wilson asked for Orser's help in cleaning up her world championship-caliber skating skills, especially her jumps. Together, Wilson and Orser helped add some personality to her skating as well. Kim responded well to Orser's laid-back coaching style and openness to her ideas.

Because of this positive working relationship, Kim and her mother asked Orser to be her full-time coach. After turning her down several times, Orser finally agreed and Kim moved to Canada to train with him in late 2006. Discussing Kim, Orser told Morgan Campbell of the *Toronto Star*, "She's an overnight success and we just have to help it continue. I'm really fortunate to have someone of that level as one of my first students." Orser praised her talent, strong work ethic, and attention to detail. Under Orser, her training was intense as she spent up to 48 hours per week on her skating and related activities.

The work paid off as Kim soon became the full package as a skater. In the *New York Times*, Macur explained, "She became a beauty on the ice, skating quickly and seamlessly, with an ease to her movement and an edge to her jumps. During her triple lutz-triple toe loop combination—a move most women have not mastered—her height, precision and distance help raise her scores. And she does it all with a smile."

After she first moved to Canada, Kim still spent part of the year in South Korea, but she decided to spend nearly all her time in Canada and live there permanently with her mother, physical therapist, and agent in 2007. Figure skating is extremely popular in South Korea and success put the young teenager under intense media scrutiny there. Living in Toronto protected her from such rabid attention, though the local Korean community in Toronto still closely followed her career and Korean fans sometimes showed up to her practices. Kim began learning the English language to achieve fluency and to help with her ability to communicate during international competitions.

As she was making the transition from South Korea to Canada, Kim suffered a bulging disk in her back. She still competed and won the ISU Grand Prix Final in early 2007, but she then was forced to take six weeks off the ice undergoing therapy. Kim was expected to do well at the World Championships, where she won bronze, then won the Cup of Russia. In 2008, she won Skate America, the Cup of China, and the ISU Grand Prix Final. Though Kim was living in North America full time by this time, she still became the most famous celebrity in South Korea according to *Forbes Korea*. Also in 2008, *Korea Times* named her the person of the year. An older, more confident Kim capitalized on her fame by accepting numerous endorsements, primarily from Korean companies, and appeared in a number of television commercials for such Korean companies as Samsung and Hyundai.

In 2009, Kim placed second at the ISU Grand Prix Final, held in her native South Korea. She won Skate America and the Four Continents Championship in Vancouver. At the Four Continents Championship, she bested Japan's Mao Asada, who was the defending world championship and who won the ISU Grand Prix Final over Kim. At the 2009 World Figure Skating Championships, Asada was again Kim's primary rival and though the event was held in Los Angeles, Koreans around the world looked to her to win and defeat her Japanese rival as a means of holding up their national honor.

Before the end of Worlds, Soo Chang, who lived in New York City and worked at a beauty supply store in Koreatown, told Macur of the *New York Times*,

"Ooh, there is a lot of pressure for Kim Yu-Na to beat the Japanese girl this week, a lot of pressure. She is now our only hope to make our country proud." For her part, Kim saw Asada as neither her friend nor her enemy. She told Macur of the *New York Times*, "Someday, if we retire, we'll be able to meet more comfortably." Kim triumphed at Worlds, marking the first time a South Korean skater won the ladies singles title. She won with a record 207.71 points, the first time a woman broke more than 200 points under the new ISU scoring system. Asada finished third. Kim told the *Washington Post*, "Being the world champion was my dream and I did it here. So it's just amazing."

With the title of world champion in hand, Kim signed endorsement and commercial contracts worth more than three billion won ($2.6 million), primarily in Korea, in 2009. Showing the depth of her popularity in South Korea, Samsung Electronics began selling a cellular telephone called the Yu-Na's Haptic in May of 2009. In first 80 days, more than a half million of these phones were sold; one million were sold within seven months. Another sponsor, Maeil Dairy, saw record sales after featuring Kim in numerous television campaigns. Sales rose more than 19 percent and operating profits over 129 percent, showing the power of her popularity.

Due to her appearances in these and many other commercials, there was some concern that Kim could become overexposed and her celebrity value could diminish in the end in South Korea. One anonymous advertising agency official told Kim Hyun-cheol of the *Korea Times*, "Companies using sports stars in ad campaigns usually take risks if their results fall below expectations. But as for Yu-Na, they don't need to worry about it as long as she remains as invincible as she is now."

Though Kim received much economic benefit from Korean endorsements, they contributed to her extraordinary reputation in her native country in contrast to her more sedate life in Toronto. Orser told Macur of the *New York Times*, "When you're with her in Korea, it's like you're traveling with Princess Diana; Yu-Na's that famous there. But here, things are obviously quieter. It gives her a chance for a normal life. She can focus on what she has to do."

As a skater, Kim continued to dominate in 2010. She won the ISU Grand Prix Final, then shone at the 2010 Winter Olympics, where she was the favorite to win gold in the ladies competition. Skating error-free programs, she set personal bests in the short program, free skate, and total score, with 78.

50, 150.66, and 228.56 respectively. Her gold medal marked the first time that a Korean figure skater won the honor. Describing the importance of her victory, Jere Longman of the *New York Times* wrote, "What the audience of 11,771 at Pacific Coliseum had witnessed was an unprecedented combination of technical difficulty and willowy sophistication.... She held up under enormous pressure to succeed as an athlete, a cultural icon, and a vanquisher of competitors from Japan, which occupied the Korean peninsula for 35 years through the end of World War II."

At the Olympics, Orser was impressed by his student's growth and performance, telling Andrew Longmore of the London *Sunday Times*, "Yu-Na has gone into a class by herself not just technically, but artistically. When the music starts, she really draws you in. She loves being beautiful and moving beautifully." After her Olympic victory, Kim told Beverly Smith of the *Globe and Mail*, "I can't believe this day has finally come for me."

While other skaters who did well at the Olympics—like men's gold medalist Evan Lysacek—declined to compete at the 2010 World Championships in Turin, Italy, held just over a month after the Olympics, Kim wanted to defend her title as ladies World Champion. She did not do well in the short program, where she had major errors on basic elements like a spin and a spiral. Kim made two more errors in her free skate program, but the level of difficulty in her program helped her rebound to place second to Asada. Explaining her perspective on Worlds, Kim told the *New York Times*, "I am just really happy that I didn't make a mistake like that at the Olympics. This competition, I just wanted to enjoy it."

Away from the rink, Kim enjoyed surfing the web, listening to music, doing karaoke, and shopping. Her Olympic victory only added to her value for endorsements in South Korea. Kim and her mother also set up her own management company to act as her commercial agent and represent her interests when her lucrative contract with IB Sports expired at the end of April 2010. Called AT Sports, it took over her representation on May 1, 2010. However, it was on the ice where Kim was expected to have the most influence.

Describing Kim's power as a skater and place in the skating world, retired skater Scott Hamilton told Longman of the *New York Times*, "Yu-Na has only been at the top of her game for a couple of years. But if she's here another four years at this level, a lot of skaters would break down. They would try to up their games so much, there would be injuries. There's no weakness there. Compare her with anybody; she's got it all. Under any system, anywhere, any time, she'd win."

Sources

Periodicals

Associated Press, March 27, 2010.
Globe and Mail (Canada), February 26, 2010, sec. SPORTS, p. 6; March 27, 2010, p. S6.
Korea Herald, March 1, 2010.
Korea Times, June 19, 2007; October 20, 2009; February 26, 2010.
New York Times, March 27, 2009, p. B9; February 14, 2010, p. SP1; February 24, 2010, p. B10; February 27, 2010, p. D1; March 28, 2010, p. 8.
Sports Illustrated, March 8, 2010, p. 38.

Sunday Times (London, England), February 21, 2010, sec. SPORTS, p. 13.
Toronto Star, March 13, 2007, p. E5.
Vancouver Sun (British Columbia, Canada), February 6, 2009, p. E5.
Washington Post, March 29, 2009, p. D3.
YON—Yonhap News Agency of Korea, April 27, 2010.

Online

"Biography: Ladies: Yu-Na Kim," International Skating Union, http://www.isuresults.com/bios/isufs00007232.tif.htm (May 12, 2010).
"Yu-Na Kim, Figure Skating," Vancouver 2010 Winter Olympics, http://www.vancouver2010.com/olympic-figure-skating/athletes/yu-na-kim_ath1007461Hd.html (May 12, 2010).

—*A. Petruso*

Lady Antebellum

AP Images

Country-music group

Group formed in 2006 in Nashville, TN; members include Charles Kelley (born 1982, in Augusta, GA; married), vocalist; Dave Haywood (born 1982, in Augusta, GA), guitar; Hillary Scott (born April 1, 1986 in Nashville, TN), vocalist.

Addresses: *Record company*—Capitol Records Nashville, 3322 West End Ave., Nashville, TN 37203. *Web site*—http://www.ladyantebellum.com.

Career

Kelley and Haywood were members of various local bands including Inside Blue, Augusta, GA, 2000s; Scott was performing as a solo act, before 2006; Kelley, Haywood, and Scott formed Lady Antebellum, 2006; released debut album *Lady Antebellum*, 2008; released *Need You Now*, 2010.

Awards: Top new duo or group, Academy of Country Music, 2008; new artist of the year award, Country Music Association, 2008; single of the year award, Country Music Association, for "I Run to You," 2010; vocal group of the year award, Country Music Association, 2010; Grammy award for best country performance by duo or group with vocals, National Academy of Recording Arts and Sciences, 2010; top vocal group of the year, Academy of Country Music, 2010; single record of the year award, Academy of Country Music, for *Need You Now*, 2010; song of the year award, Academy of Country Music, for "Need You Now," 2010.

Sidelights

A country-music group might do just about anything to have their music heard and to reach an appreciative audience. For the musical group Lady Antebellum the worst gig that they ever played was at a combination gas station and restaurant in Milwaukee, Wisconsin. The performance was first thing in the morning to celebrate the start of deer hunting season. Vocalist Charles Kelley told Whitney Pastorek of *Entertainment Weekly*, "Everybody was sitting there eating. They didn't know who ... we were. It was funny." After winning the 2008 Academy of Country Music award for Top New Duo or Group and the 2008 Country Music Association Award for New Artist of the Year and having their self-titled debut album open at the number-one spot on the *Billboard* Top Country Albums chart, it was certain that this anonymity would not last.

Lady Antebellum was formed in 2006 after Hillary Scott recognized Kelly from a MySpace page and began to talk to Kelly and Dave Haywood at a Nashville music club. Josh Kelley, solo pop artist and brother of Kelley had just moved to Nashville. After his break through song "Only You," he encouraged his brother to follow his own ambition to be a musician. Haywood had played in local bands in the Augusta, Georgia area with the two Kelleys. The brothers and Haywood had known one another since middle school and all three had graduated from Lakeside High School. In an exclusive interview with Navideh Forghani for NBC Augusta, Kelley said, "We used to play when we were 14 years old at the Red Lion Pub." One of the bands that the Kelleys and Haywood had played in together was called Inside Blue. Kelley and Haywood had not really pulled their group together yet when they had that fateful meeting with Scott.

Scott is the daughter of country music singer Linda Davis who won a Grammy award in 1994 for a duet with Reba McEntire titled "Does He Love You." Scott suggested at that meeting that she, Kelley, and Haywood get together for a writing session. They did and discovered that they had creative synergy and a dynamic desire to perform. Haywood told Forghani, "We just had chemistry and connection. We wrote a lot of songs and started playing shows. I think it really hit me that we could make it work." Lady Antebellum was born. The group conceived their name because Kelley had been taking photographs of antebellum mansions all day. Kelley, who was never fond of the name, prefers the nickname that fans have given the group—Lady A. The group does have fans, many fans. On October 7, 2009, their debut album was certified platinum by the Recording Industry Association of America for having shipments of one million copies in the United States.

Lady Antebellum has been described as an "everyband" because they appeal to such a wide fan base. Brian Mansfield, writing for USA Today, quoted Mike Dungan the president and CEO of Capitol Records Nashville as saying about the group, "This is the Everyband. The fans seem to range from ten-year-olds up to Grandma. Their niceness and their ordinary citizenship ring true to everybody who sees them." Originally their admirers were of a younger group of country and western music fans who liked their three-part poppy harmonies and had been primed by such acts as Taylor Swift to give their music a listen.

Lady Antebellum's first two singles were "Love Don't Live Here" and "Lookin' for a Good Time," which were respectively about a break up and a one-night stand. These were themes that seemed to resonate with younger audiences. Since those first two singles, the group's fan base has expanded to include a more diverse group of country and western music fans. Kelley's vocals draw attention and admiration for their gravelly and heartfelt undertones, Scott's sweet voice appeals to younger girls,

and there is a subgroup of fans who enjoy Haywood's guitar-playing abilities. Having both male and female front people, there is a wider range of songs and themes that the group can express. On the band's official Web site, Scott is quoted as saying, "I think we're able to say so much more and reach so many more people.... When it's a song I'm singing lead on, Charles and Dave can go be buddy-buddy on stage. When Charles and I do a duet, we can, without being too theatrical, almost play out the songs and tell the story a little bit more, whether we're making it dramatic or fun or flirty." When the group's second album was released in January of 2010, it sold nearly a half-million copies in its first week. Two months after its initial release it had sold 1.2 million copies according to Nielsen SoundScan, as reported by Mansfield for USA Today.

The group has come a long way from playing at that gas station and restaurant in Wisconsin. The trio began performing in clubs in Nashville; their first big gig was opening for Josh Kelley. In 2007 Capitol Records of Nashville signed a contract with them. Shortly after that, adult contemporary artist Jim Brickman chose them to sing on his 2007 single "Never Alone" which reached number 14 on the Billboard Adult Contemporary charts. They released their debut single "Love Don't Live Here" in September of 2007 and it eventually reached number three on the Billboard Hot Country Songs chart. Their self-titled debut album was the first album ever by a new duo or group to debut at the number-one spot on the Billboard Top Country Albums chart. In 2008 the group was signed on to be the opening act for Martina McBride's Waking Up Laughing Tour.

In 2009 the single "Need You Now" was released as a lead-off single to their album of the same name, released in January of 2010. Four weeks after being released, the album "Need You Now" was certified as being platinum. During most of 2010 Lady Antebellum toured with Tim McGraw after spending a year opening for Kenny Chesney. The group has decidedly graduated from playing dive bars. They have played the Grand Ole Opry and in addition to McBride, McGraw, and Chesney, they have played with such notable musicians as Phil Vassar, Rodney Atkins, Carrie Underwood, and Keith Urban.

When the group first began, they needed quite a bit of help and money was very tight. Haywood told Forghani of NBC Augusta, "It was a huge risk financially. We were living in debt for about a year, trying to make it happen." Initially when they were on the road, the three members of the group kept costs down by sharing one cheap hotel room. About the sharing-a-room situation, Scott quipped to Mansfield of *USA Today,* "[Try] explaining that to Mom and Dad." Because of this initial roughing it, growing into their own as a band in front of their fans, and simply being on the road as an opening act or supporting another band, the trio has spent a great deal of time together. On the official Lady Antebellum Web site Haywood said, "the three of us are the closest we've ever been as friends. Out on the road, we've spent almost every single day together for the past three and a half years. So by the time we were writing songs for this record, I think we'd all learned how to interact with each other better. We can write songs individually, but we definitely have something special when we do it together, and that's gotten elevated. I know what Hillary is thinking, I know what Charles is thinking, and I think we play off each other a lot better."

Each of the three members of Lady Antebellum have a part to play in the success of the group as a whole. Mansfield wrote in *USA Today* that Haywood called Scott the "heart" of the group. "She guides us emotionally, writing songs with where she's been and things she's going through." Haywood described Kelley as having "an incredible work ethic. He's incredibly driven, always ready to write and play and work." In the same article, Kelley said that Haywood not only played guitar but was the one who "guides the ship. He's the musical leader. Dave lets us take the reins as far as the vocal melody, while he does the instrumentation and the chord structure. When we get stuck, he knows exactly how to get us out of it." The combination of the talents and inclinations of the three members of Lady Antebellum has made the group a success.

In addition to selling millions of albums and downloads and performing with top country and western stars, Lady Antebellum has won several awards beyond those collected in 2008. In 2009, they won the Country Music Association awards for the Single of the Year for "I Run to You" and the Vocal Group of the Year. They won a Grammy in 2009 for Best Country Performance by a Duo or Group for "I Run to You." In 2010 they won the Academy of Country Music awards for Top Vocal Group of the Year, Single Record of the Year, and Song of the Year. Their success they measure in that they are suddenly much more busy and getting better offers. Scott told Mansfield of *USA Today,* "Instead of visiting radio stations and sleeping in Motel 6's, [we're] doing Oprah and Ellen." They are now getting more offers to collaborate and write songs than they can handle. Kelley even once missed his wife's birthday because he had to go to a song-writing session.

These three busy and successful friends are still writing songs together and making music, but instead of sharing a motel room and playing low-status gigs they now have their own customized tour bus and they are dreaming of being a headline act on their own. On the bus, Scott gets the rear stateroom because of her collection of grooming supplies. Haywood and Kelley each have bunks that are outfitted with DVD players so that they can relax between shows. Their ambition is to headline at large arenas in the near future. Because of the quality of their music and its ability to potentially crossover into the pop music category, they are poised to become a superstar group. When "Need You Now" was first released, radio station programmers who worked in both the country and western music and pop music formats immediately seized on the album's playability in both markets and on multiple stations. This helped propel sales of the album. Even with this gargantuan success the members of Lady Antebellum try to maintain an attitude of gratitude and an appreciation for one another and the help that they received to achieve their success. Craig Shelburne writing for the Country Music Television Web site was told by Scott in an interview, "The three of us have dreamed about this our entire lives and feel so blessed to be able to wake up every day and do this for a living."

Selected discography

Lady Antebellum, Capitol Records Nashville, 2008.
Need You Now, Capitol Records Nashville, 2010.

Sources

Periodicals

Entertainment Weekly, January 29, 2010, p. 68; February 26, 2010, p. 48.
New York Times, January 9, 2009, p. C7; April 20, 2010, p. C3.
People, February 8, 2010, p. 51.
USA Today, January 26, 2010, p. 4D; March 10, 2010, p. 1D; April 19, 2010, p. 3D.

Online

"Capitol signs Lady Antebellum" Country Standard Time, http://www.countrystandardtime.com/news/newsitem.asp?xid=744&t=Capitol_signs_Lady_Antebellum (June 4, 2010).
"Exclusive: Augusta's Josh Kelley and Lady Antebellum," NBC Augusta, http://www.nbcaugusta.com/news/entertainment/18338164.tif.html (June 4, 2010).

"Lady Antebellum," All Music, http://www.allmusic.com/cg/amg.dll?p=amg&sql=11:0jfix qyridae~T1 (June 4, 2010).

"Lady Antebellum Discuss New Music, New Tour, New Friends at CMA Awards," Country Music Television Web site, http://www.cmt.com/news/country-music/1626380/lady-antebellum-discuss-new-music-new-tour-new-friends-at-cma-awards.jhtml (June 4, 2010).

"Lady Antebellum Dominates ACM Awards," *People,* http://www.people.com/people/article/0,,20361945.tif,00.html (June 3, 2010).

Lady Antebellum Official Web site, http://www.ladyantebellum.com (June 3, 2010).

—*Annette Bowman*

Lady Gaga

AP Images

Singer

Born Stefani Joanne Angelina Germanotta, March 28, 1986, in New York, NY; daughter of Joe (an internet entrepreneur) and Cynthia (an internet entrepreneur) Germanotta. *Education:* Attended New York University's Tisch School for the Arts.

Addresses: *Web site*—http://www.ladygaga.com.

Career

Began playing open mics around New York City, early 2000s; dropped out of New York University and worked as a go-go dancer, 2005; performed with glam rock bands Mackin Pulsifier and SGB, 2006; performed with Lady Starlight as Lady Gaga and the Starlight Revue, 2007; received songwriting contract, landed record deal, released debut album *The Fame,* 2008; released follow-up EP *The Fame Monster,* 2009.

Awards: Grammy Award for best dance recording, Recording Academy, for "Poker Face," 2010; Grammy Award for best electronic/dance album, Recording Academy, for *The Fame,* 2010.

Sidelights

Grammy Award-winning and multi-platinum selling pop sensation Lady Gaga exploded onto the music scene in 2008 with the hit single "Just Dance" after paying her dues on the club circuit in her native New York City. Known almost as much for her extravagant—even bizarre—costumes and

outlandish stage persona as for her dance-influenced tunes, the singer has been widely recognized as a force both in pop music and pop culture. Propelled by the success of "Just Dance," Lady Gaga's 2008 debut album *The Fame* peaked at number two on the *Billboard* 200 as well as charting around the globe. The album went on to earn the performer five Grammy nominations and two trophies for Best Dance Recording and Best Electronic/Dance Album in 2010. A follow-up EP, *The Fame Monster,* appeared in 2009 as a taste of the singer's planned sophomore full-length release.

Lady Gaga was born Stefani Joanne Angelina Germanotta on March 28, 1986, in the borough of Yonkers in New York City, the older of the two daughters of early internet entrepreneurs Joe and Cynthia Germanotta. The future music star became intrigued by pop and rock music as a child, enthralled equally by the danceable sounds of fellow New Yorker Cyndi Lauper and the guitar riffs of the Rolling Stones and the Beatles. Even as a youngster, Lady Gaga displayed a clear love for attention; commenting in her Web site biography, the singer noted, "I was always an entertainer. I was a ham as a little girl and I'm a ham today." While her education at the private all-girls Catholic school Convent of the Sacred Heart may not have offered Gaga much of an outlet for her performance urges, by the time she graduated from high school the entertainer had learned to play the piano, begun writing her own music, and appeared at local open mic nights. She drew particular inspiration from the glam rock sounds of such artists as David Bowie and Queen, later adopting her stage name from the Queen song "Radio Ga-Ga." Additionally, the young Lady Gaga also had a great interest in theater, performing in dramatic productions throughout her school career.

After earning her high school diploma, the nascent performer enrolled at New York University's prestigious Tisch School for the Arts. Lady Gaga's time at the institution proved short, however, as she decided that formal training was not what she needed to accomplish her goal: becoming a pop star. She dropped out of NYU in 2005, and quickly became a regular on the New York club scene, where she performed as a go-go dancer while holding down a day job at a music publisher. Along with this somewhat scandalous career move, Lady Gaga entered into an increasingly serious relationship with cocaine. This lifestyle later became a source of inspiration for *The Fame* album track "Beautiful, Dirty, Rich." "It's from my coke years," the singer later explained to Tom Lanham of Shockhound. "2005 was where it began, and I thought I was gonna die. I never really did the drugs for the high—it was more the romanticism of Andy Warhol and Mick Jagger and all the artists that I loved. I wanted to be them, and I wanted to live their life, and I wanted to understand the way that they saw things and how they arrived at their art…. It was one of the most difficult times in my life, but it was important for me to experience, since it unlocked parts of my brain." Eventually, the disapproval of her family, to whom Lady Gaga had remained close, encouraged her to give up drugs and focus on her craft.

By early 2006, Lady Gaga had begun singing with a couple of local glam rock bands in addition to appearing as a go-go dancer, and soon accidentally came across her first record deal when a Def Jam executive signed her on the spot after hearing her sing in the hallway outside his office. Although this contract ultimately came to nothing, the 19-year-old performer developed an acquaintanceship with music producer RedOne that would prove vital to her later career. She also became friends with New York City burlesque performer Lady Starlight, who served as something of a mentor for the young entertainer. The two began appearing together in 2007 under the moniker Lady Gaga and the Starlight Revue—the first instance of the singer using the Lady Gaga name publicly—and packed venues such as New York's Mercury Lounge, Bitter End, and Rockwood Music Hall. The at times extravagant performance art show hit the road, fascinating

audiences on both coasts and points in between. A wild performance by the troupe at Chicago's Lollapalooza Festival and coverage by Internet gossip blogger Perez Hilton helped raise Lady Gaga's public profile, and soon the singer landed another contract with a music label.

This time, however, the contract was as a songwriter, not as a vocalist. Snapped up by songwriter Rob Fusari for Interscope's new Streamline Records imprint, Lady Gaga began working on pop tunes with producer RedOne in Los Angeles. Her work attracted the attention of major publisher Sony/ATV, and soon the performer was penning tracks for such mainstream artists as the Pussycat Dolls, Britney Spears, and Fergie. The burgeoning musician soon met Akon, a successful crossover hip-hop singer, songwriter, and producer. He was impressed by both her songwriting and vocal talents and, by the end of 2007, had signed Lady Gaga to his own Kon Live Distribution imprint under the Interscope umbrella. Short months later, the singer released her debut single, "Just Dance," an homage to clubbing co-written with RedOne. The song ascended the *Billboard* Dance Music/Club Play Singles chart, peaking at number two before gradually rising to the top of the *Billboard* Pop 100, Hot 100, and Hot Digital Singles charts. In time, "Just Dance" became a bona fide international hit, residing atop the charts of no fewer than seven different countries.

With "Just Dance" making the rounds of clubs and radio airwaves, Lady Gaga set out on the road as a solo act for the first time, opening for 1980s pop icons New Kids on the Block on their much-publicized 2008 reunion tour. In September of that year, follow-up single "Poker Face" was released to great popular and critical success. Like its predecessor, the song reached the apex of the *Billboard* Hot 100, topped the trio of dance music charts, and landed on charts around the world. The next month, her full-length debut *The Fame* hit the streets. Writing in *Entertainment Weekly*, Mikael Wood observed somewhat ambivalently that "*The Fame* is remarkably (and exhaustingly) pure in its vision of a world in which nothing trumps being 'beautiful, dirty, and rich,'" while Alexis Petridis of the *Guardian* argued that, "Pop music doesn't have to be blindingly original or clever to work: it needs tunes, and Lady GaGa is fantastically good at tunes…. [V]irtually everything on *The Fame* arrives packing an immensely addictive melody or an inescapable hook, virtually everything sounds like another hit single." Lady Gaga's growing fan base embraced the album, sending to the number-two slot on the *Billboard* 100 and making it an international sensation.

Quickly, Lady Gaga became known as much for her extravagant fashion choices as for her dance/pop music. Having long held unusual sartorial tastes and drawing on her costuming abilities from her burlesque days, the performer adopted a mane of platinum blonde hair—a sharp contrast from her natural mousy brown locks—along with wild, glam rock-inspired makeup techniques, and outfits that ranged from provocative to truly outré. Appearing in such odd ensembles as a dress made entirely of bubbles and rarely wearing anything more modest than hot pants, Lady Gaga drew comparisons to another taste-challenging blonde pop star: Madonna. Writing about the performer's fashion choices in the *New York Times*, Guy Trebay noted that, "her singular innovation on the sincerest form of flattery has been to barge right past imitation to outright larceny.... She patches together what she finds in the cultural image bank.... [A]nd subjects herself to a real-time version of Photoshop, studiously and at times laboriously conjuring up an over-the-top creation built from bits of [performance artists Leigh] Bowery and [Klaus] Nomi and [singers Grace] Jones and [David] Bowie, but also Liberace, [performance artist] Joey Arias, and Kylie Minogue." Just as Lady Gaga drew on pop culture and fashion history for her unique look, she also influenced major fashion innovators including American icon Marc Jacobs and boundary-pushing British designer Alexander McQueen, who included her songs in his fashion shows. Yet, the performer remained relatively sanguine about the attention her outfits attracted. Speaking to *Entertainment Weekly*'s Whitney Pastorek, Lady Gaga commented on the public fascination with her signature trouser-less style: "Well, yeah, I take my pants off, but does it matter if your pants are off if you've got eight-inch shoulder pads on, and a hood, and black lipstick and glasses with rocks on them?"

Propelled by a larger-than-life persona and catchy hits, Lady Gaga soon proved herself a pop force to be reckoned with. *The Fame* went multi-platinum and spawned a third chart-topping single, "LoveGame," while the singer headlined increasingly large venues, taking her live spectacle around the world. The success of her debut led to its reissue in November of 2009, accompanied by an EP of new material titled *The Fame Monster*. Writing for Allmusic Guide, Stephen Thomas Erlewine commented, "*The Fame Monster* builds upon those strengths exhibited on *The Fame*, offering a credible expansion of the debut and suggesting [Lady Gaga's] not just a fleeting pop phenomenon." The release resonated with fans, spawning popular singles including "Bad Romance" and a track featuring fellow pop superstar Beyoncé Knowles, "Telephone." Lady Gaga's chart prowess also continued, with *The Fame Monster* topping *Billboard*'s Top Electronic Albums chart and hitting number five on the *Billboard* 100.

Also in late 2009, the Recording Academy nominated Lady Gaga for Grammys in five categories: Record of the Year for "Poker Face," Album of the Year for *The Fame*, Song of the Year for "Poker Face," Best Dance Recording for "Poker Face," and Best Electronic/Dance Album for *The Fame*. The artist, who performed the televised show's opening number along with idol Elton John, ultimately walked away with the latter two awards. Following her victories, the performer continued with a vigorous touring schedule, traveling through the British Isles, Australia, Japan, and Europe before returning to crisscross North America in the summer of 2010. However, Lady Gaga faced adversity as well as triumph. In March of 2010, her former collaborator Fusari sued the performer for $35 million, claiming that he was owed some 20 percent of her song royalties and 15 percent of merchandising proceeds among other funds under a 2006 contract that the two had signed to form Team Love Child LLC. Fusari, with whom Lady Gaga had also had a romantic relationship, alleged that the singer had paid him only $611,000, a fraction of the total sum he claimed was owed to him. Nevertheless, this law suit seemed unlikely to derail Lady Gaga's continuing rise to lasting superstardom; with a second full-length album planned for the future and legions of fans around the world, Lady Gaga has unquestionably attained the fame that she announced in the title of her debut.

Selected discography

The Fame, Interscope, 2008.
The Fame Monster (EP), Interscope, 2009.

Sources

Books

Herbert, Emily, *Lady Gaga: Behind the Fame*, Overlook Press, 2010.

Periodicals

Entertainment Weekly, October 31, 2008.
Guardian (London), January 9, 2009.
New York Times, December 27, 2009.

Online

Biography Resource Center Online, Gale, 2010.

"Lady Gaga," Allmusic Guide, http://www. allmusic.com/cg/amg.dll?p=amg&sql=11:hcfix zr5ldse (February 25, 2010).

"Lady Gaga: Biography," Lady Gaga Official Web site, http://www.ladygaga.com/bio (February 25, 2010).

"Lady GaGa: Bonus Quotes from the Dance-Pop Queen!," *Entertainment Weekly,* http://popwatch. ew.com/2009/02/09/lady-gaga-inter/ (March 18, 2010).

"Lady GaGa: No Pants, No Problem," ShockHound, http://www.shockhound.com/features/402-lady-gaga--no-pants--no-problem (March 18, 2010).

"Lady Gaga Sued for $35M by Producer," *Billboard,* http://www.billboard.com/news/producer-files-35m-suit-against-lady-gaga-10040769.tif25. story?tag=hpflash1# (March 18, 2010).

"The Fame Monster," Allmusic Guide, http://www. allmusic.com/cg/amg.dll?p=amg&sql=10:aifrxz9 sldhe (March 18, 2010).

—Vanessa E. Vaughn

Lori Lansens

Author

Born Lori Lansens, July 25, 1962, in Chatham, Ontario, Canada; daughter of an auto worker and a homemaker; married Milan Cheylov (an actor, producer, and director); children: a son and a daughter. *Education:* St. Clair College, Windsor, Ontario, Canada, B.A.

Addresses: *Agent*—Bukowski Agency, 14 Prince Arthur Avenue, Ste. 202, Toronto, Ontario, M5R 1A9, http://www.thebukowskiagency.com. *Web site*—http://www.lorilansens.com.

Career

Worked in classified advertising, *Globe and Mail*; waitress; published first novel, *Rush Home Road*, 2002. Actress in stage productions and television series, including: *Alfred Hitchcock Presents*, 1989. Screenwriter of various scripts, including: *He Ain't Heavy*, 1990; *South of Wawa*, 1991; *Jimmy's Coming*, 1992; *The Night I Was Wed*, 1994; *Under My Skin*, 1995; *Royal Diaries: Cleopatra—Daughter of the Nile*, 2000; *Marine Life*, 2000; *Wolf Girl*, 2001. Producer of various television and independent film productions, including: *He Ain't Heavy*, 1990; *Tessa*, 1992; *Jimmy's Coming*, 1992; *The Night I Was Wed*, 1994; *Under My Skin*, 1995. Director of independent films, including: *Tessa*, 1992; *The Night I Was Wed*, 1994.

Sidelights

Acclaimed novelist Lori Lansens has had what she described as a Cinderella story in the way that her fiction has suddenly come into the public awareness. A long time screenwriter, producer, and director, Lansens' first novel was published in 2002 by A. Knopf Canada and was premiered among its "New Faces of Fiction" series. Her writing has been compared to Alice Munro who lived near Lansens' hometown and who is among her favorite authors. Lansens admitted in an interview with Chalene Ross, writing for the online magazine *Skirt!*, that she has had a "fabulous lucky life" and went on to elaborate that the "first short story I ever wrote was published, the first screenplay I wrote was made into a movie, and my first novel was published." She also goes on to relay that after those firsts she had about a dozen short stories that were rejected; she worked for about five years on a screenplay that she could not get anyone to accept or finance a production of; and she tossed into a garbage bin more than 100 pages of a novel that was a work in progress that was not developing satisfactorily. Both Lansens and her husband, Milan Cheylov, are long time veterans of the entertainment industry and she is quoted by Ross as saying that their family motto is: "We've been up and we've been down."

Lansens grew up in Chatham, Ontario, Canada, and was the middle child of a homemaker and an auto worker. Chatham is a rural town that is close to the Canadian-American border. Lansens discovered when she was in the ninth grade that she very much enjoyed English as a school subject and that she liked to write. Her ambition was to be a writer but she did not think that this was possible because of her background. When she attended St. Clair College in Windsor, Ontario, Canada, she studied advertising and business. On her Web site she described her rationale for this choice as being that her "plan was to become a copy writer, to marry my passion for writing with a practical approach to make a living." Lansens did not set out to become a fiction writer. Little did she know that she would draw heavily from her childhood background to become a successful author. Lansens, writing for the *Globe and Mail* wrote that her first novel "*Rush Home Road* is set in a fictional version of my hometown in southwestern Ontario, near the border to Detroit." She wrote about "the people I'd studied since I was a child," the farms with their strawberries and corn, and "the fishy lake." This setting and Lansens' identity as a Canadian figure very prominently.

Another thing that has figured very prominently in regards to Lansens' success as an author is not a thing but is rather a person. Her husband was the one who, upon learning that she wanted to write, encouraged her to quit her job and do so. She met Cheylov when she was new to Toronto and working at the *Globe and Mail* in the classified advertising department. He was the friend of one of her college friends and they happened to run into one another at a local deli. As they began to talk about books, he asked her what she was reading and she showed him her copy of Mordechai Richler's *Cocksure*. He smiled and pulled from his bag the same novel. Lansens, on her Web site, describes her husband as "everything I wanted to be, confident and brash and ambitious, but above all, an artist." Her husband encouraged her writing, suggested and supported her taking acting lessons to help her with dramatic writing, and was alongside her as she spent two years pursuing an acting career. As he worked as an actor, producer and director, he guided and worked with her through various combinations of roles as a writer, producer and director of several independent films, including: *He Ain't Heavy, Tessa, South of Wawa, Jimmy's Coming, The Night I Was Wed, Under My Skin, Royal Diaries: Cleopatra—Daughter of the Nile, Marine Life,* and *Wolf Girl*. When her first short story—about an older man and an obese younger woman falling in love—was published, she credits sharing the accomplishment with her husband and describes it on her Web site as being "for both Milan and I, the sweetest victory."

While Lansens no longer lives in Canada, Chatham was the setting that informed the creation of the fictional Baldoon County where *Rush Home Road, The Girls,* and *The Wife's Tale* all take place. Lansens explained to Natasha Clark of *Elle.* magazine, "These three books represent a kind of trilogy to me. *Rush Home Road* is about leaving home. *The Girls* is about being at home. And *The Wife's Tale* is about leaving home and making shifts and changes."

The first novel in the trilogy was *Rush Home Road*. Prior to writing this novel, Lansens had written an original screenplay titled *Jesus Freaks*. She very much wanted to see this screenplay be made into a movie and pursued this ambition for five long years. During that time she edited and revised the screenplay, traveled back and forth across the United States pursuing potential partners and financiers in what she described on her Web site as "domino deals that tumbled, house-of-cards deals that collapsed." She gave up in frustration and her husband suggested that she try writing the novel that she had wanted to write for a long time as a break from the film industry. Lansens began to pen *Rush Home Road* and soon discovered that she was pregnant with her first child, a boy. Her husband was working very long hours at the time and Lansens became a self described "hermit". She isolated herself and worked long hours on the novel. At one point she realized that the only sound her son was hearing in utero was the constant tapping of the keys on her computer. She began to compose the novel out loud for his benefit.

Rush Home Road was praised by one of the resident scholars, Harriet Klausner, on the Web site AllReaders as "quite a fabulous historical tale." The story is set in the Canada Lakeview Trailer Park and is about a white woman named Collette who wants to go and live for the summer with a man that she has met and asks an elderly black woman named Adelaide Shadd to care for her daughter. Addy Shadd agrees to do this if she is compensated for caring for the five-year-old girl. Collette agrees and a bargain is struck. When the little girl Sharla Cody is brought to Addy's home, Addy discovers that the child is bi-racial and surmises that Collette has abandoned the girl.

Lansens' depiction of Sharla does not portray her as a "cute" or even lovable child. Addy likes her solitude. The two characters have to learn to care for one another. Addy showers love on Sharla and Sharla helps Addy as she becomes progressively more ill. Over the course of the novel both characters begin to heal from the past abuses that they have suffered as Addy tells Sharla of her childhood days in the fictional town of Rusholme. Rusholme's history was patterned after that of Chatham, which was an end point on the Underground Railway and was populated by runaway slaves. Throughout the novel, as Addy tells Sharla about her past, her account is framed by historical events like the Pullman porter movement and Prohibition. Jennifer Baker, writing for *Library Journal,* describes the novel by saying that there is "an ultimate message of hope" and this message redeems "the book from melancholy."

As Lansens toured to promote *Rush Home Road,* she was pregnant with her second child. She continued on book tours and took her two small children along with her. At that time she began work on a second novel, which she abandoned as she mothered her children. On her Web site she jokes that she "had a child on my breast, my hip, or my lap for four years." This intense physical relationship to her children and a story about the Bijani sisters, Iranian Siamese twins who underwent a failed surgery to separate, helped Lansens conceive her second novel. Eva MacSweeney of *Vogue* wrote that Lansens had read that the twins who had been conjoined at the head in the rare condition called craniopagus had "expressed the desire before they went under the knife that they really wanted to look into each other's eyes." This expressed desire stuck in Lansens mind and grew into the novel *The Girls.*

While *The Girls* is about a pair of conjoined twins, the book does not read like an account of a freak show. "Lansens has not sensationalized their story, but treated every aspect with sensitivity and dignity, providing only enough of the details to understand both the challenges and solutions 'the girls' achieved in their lives," wrote Pat Neuman in a review for the Web site Mostly Fiction. The twins in the novel, Rose and Ruby Darlen, are adopted by Lovey Darlen, a nurse on duty the night that their single teen-aged mother gave birth and abandoned them. The Darlen family moves to a farm that Lovey inherits and she raises the girls to either overcome or ignore their limitations so that they may have as normal a life as possible. The novel is written as a type of memoir in both Rose and Ruby's voices with alternating chapters. Each character has a distinct voice despite the fact that the characters are joined at the head and can feel one another blush. Lansens placed the setting for the girls' story in the same fictional small town territory as *Rush Home Road* because "Rose and Ruby may stand out and perhaps never fit it, but they would be familiar to everyone else. In a bigger city, I'd have constantly been dealing with astonishment over their appearance, instead of being able to get down deep into their lives," reported Rachel Giese for the CBC. Rose and Ruby's lives are depicted with all the normalcy of any young woman's life, including junk food, laptops, music, and a sexual encounter with a young man who is adventuresome enough to engage with the twins.

The third novel in Lansens' trilogy came out of her contemplations after moving from her beloved Canada to the San Fernando Valley in California. When she first moved to California she felt lost, lonely, and confused. She knew no one and every street that she traveled on was unfamiliar. She wanted to belong to the community but felt alienated. She watched people and thought about all the conversations that she had had with women over the years about such things as happiness, divorce, food, husbands, and sex. Out of her musings about how people redefine themselves came Mary Gooch, the main character of *The Wife's Tale.*

Gooch begins her story in the familiar fictional setting of Baldoon County where both *Rush Home Road* and *The Girls* were set; however, this character does not remain in Canada. When her coward of a husband, on the eve of their twenty-fifth wedding anniversary, deposits $25,000 in their account and disappears, the morbidly obese Gooch decides to leave her small town and track him down. The story takes Gooch to a suburban community in the San Fernando Valley.

Lansens' work and fiction are intimately entwined with her life, an unfolding story of both professional and domestic success. As of 2010, she lived in southern California with her husband and children and was working on her next novel.

Selected writings

Novels

Rush Home Road, Little, Brown (Boston, MA), 2002.
The Girls, A. Knopf Canada (Toronto, Ontario, Canada), 2005; Little, Brown (New York, NY), 2006.
The Wife's Tale, Knopf Canada, 2009; Little, Brown, 2010.

Sources

Periodicals

Elle, February 18, 2010.
Globe and Mail, May 20, 2009.
Library Journal, May 15, 2002, p. 125.
Vogue, June 2006.

Online

Contemporary Authors Online, Thomson Gale, 2007.

"Girl Guide," CBC, http://www.cbc.ca/arts/books/lansens.html (August 29, 2010).

"Lori Lansens," Internet Movie Database, http://www.imdb.com/name/nm0487080/ (August 29, 2010).

"Lori Lansens," Mostly Fiction, http://www.mostlyfiction.com/contemp/lansens.htm (August 29, 2010).

"Lori Lansens: New Faces in Fiction," Random House Canada, http://www.randomhouse.ca/newface/lorilansens.php (August 29, 2010).

Lori Lansens Official Web Site, http://www.lorilansens.com/ (August 29, 2010).

"*Rush Home Road* by Lori Lansens," AllReaders, http://www.allreaders.com/Topics/info_11666.asp (August 29, 2010).

"Writer Series: Interview with Lori Lansens," *Skirt!*, http://www.ventura.skirt.com/shes_so_skirt/writer-series-interview-lori-lansens (August 29, 2010).

—*Annette Bowman*

W. Howard Lester

Company executive for Williams-Sonoma

Born August 14, 1935, in Durant, OK; married Mary. *Education:* Attended the University of Oklahoma, 1950s.

Addresses: *Office*—Williams-Sonoma, Inc., 3250 Van Ness Ave., San Francisco, CA 94109.

Career

Began career as salesperson for International Business Machines (IBM), 1958; founded and sold three computer-services and computer software companies, 1962-74; executive vice president with Bradford National Corporation until 1976; formed investment group that purchased Williams-Sonoma, 1978, president and chief executive officer, 1979-2001, 2006-10, chairperson emeritus, 2010—.

Sidelights

W. Howard Lester spent decades building the Williams-Sonoma chain of gourmet kitchenware into a retail powerhouse. Five years after buying it in 1978, he took it public, and the infusion of cash from Wall Street fueled an expansion to 250 stores across the United States. Though he was not the founder of Williams-Sonoma, Lester's vision helped make the San Francisco-based chain virtually synonymous with high-end cookware and specialty-food items. "We looked around and noticed there wasn't a national kitchen store," he once told *HFN: The Weekly Newspaper for the Home Furnishing Network.* "The stores that were around looked tacky and didn't stand for anything."

Lester was born in Durant, Oklahoma, on August 14, 1935, and graduated from the public high school in Altus, Oklahoma. After a stint in the military and studies at the University of Oklahoma, he went to work for computer giant IBM in Oklahoma City. This was in the late 1950s, when IBM's focus was on developing large, expensive mainframe computers it then sold to governments and corporations. Banks were some of the first commercial clients that sales representatives like Lester targeted, and he eventually saw an opportunity for those same financial institutions to lease out their computer downtime to other businesses for handling automated tasks. "I talked the bank into developing a program to run all the billing and office work for doctors," Lester told Lucinda Watson and Joanne Parrent for the 2001 book *How They Achieved: Stories of Personal Achievement and Business Success.*

The idea quickly caught on, and Lester left IBM to start his own company with two other business partners. They were based in Dallas, because Republic Bank of Texas was their largest client, but later moved to Memphis, Tennessee, as they signed up more regional banks. He and his partners eventually sold the business, but Lester started a new venture to sell the software the banks used. In 1967, his company was bought by a larger, Los Angeles-based firm, and he moved to California to take a senior executive position. He stayed there five years before leaving Computer Sciences Corporation for New York City in early 1972. After buying a Pennsylvania company that made software for the banking industry and relocating it to Southern California, he sold Centurex to the Bradford National Corporation, a much larger concern. He stayed on another 18 months as an executive vice president at Bradford, which went on to win lucrative state contracts to process Medicaid claims.

Lester was about to celebrate his forty-first birthday in the summer of 1976 when he returned to California permanently, and to a new home he had built in Rolling Hills, a gated enclave on the Palos Verdes Peninsula. "For about six months I loved not working," he told Watson and Parrent. "I'd get up every day and I'd say, 'Boy, I can do anything I want today! I'm not answering phone calls, or worrying about something not happening.'" Then he quickly became bored with a routine centered around playing golf every day, and began looking for a new investment opportunity with a friend, James A. McMahan. Lester was uninterested in returning to the computer- or financial-services sectors, but he and McMahan discovered a struggling San Francisco retailer of high-end kitchenware.

Williams-Sonoma took its name from Chuck Williams, a building contractor and hardware store owner in Sonoma, California, with a passion for cooking. On a trip to France in the mid-1950s, Williams brought back a cache of premium French cookware he knew was utterly unavailable in United States and began selling it in his hardware store. He eventually left the hardware business and moved the kitchenwares store to San Francisco in 1958. A highly profitable catalog business was launched, aided by an heir to the Neiman Marcus department store empire who became a business partner. Williams-Sonoma had a handful of Bay Area stores when Lester and McMahan bought out the group of investors for $250,000 in 1978. "I just felt like we could do better," Lester told Daily Oklahoman writer Gypsy Hogan about the potential he saw in the company. "At a minimum it could be a business that would earn money and be a lot of fun—sell quality merchandise, and I'd get to travel the world with Chuck looking for new products."

In the food revolution that followed in the early 1980s, Williams-Sonoma emerged as the leading retailer of ultra-luxe kitchen gadgets, from a $675 ice-cream maker to the traditional hand-hammered copper-bottomed cookware favored by the world's leading chefs. An expanding, increasing sophisticated middle class in America developed an appreciation for all things gourmand, and Williams-Sonoma sold hard-to-find items like omelet pans, soufflé molds, duck presses, and even the first non-commercial cappuccino makers. Both the stores and the catalog did phenomenally well, and sales began to double annually. Lester took the company public in the summer of 1983, when shares began trading at $23 each.

The initial public offering, or IPO, helped Lester finance his strategy for Williams-Sonoma. By this time, the company also included The Pottery Barn, a dishware chain it bought from The Gap; a gardening catalog; and Hold Everything, another catalog project. All eventually became brick-and-mortar stores. Williams-Sonoma opened a major warehouse and distribution center for all the companies in Memphis, a geographic epicenter of sorts for the continental United States, while both Williams-Sonoma and Pottery Barn launched a major retail expansion across the country.

Lester stepped down as CEO in 2001, but came back at the age of 70 in July of 2006 to help right the company after some management wobbles. By that point the combined holdings of Williams-Sonoma, Inc., included 550 stores plus a new catalog company, West Elm. At the time, even the 91-year-old Chuck Williams was still at work, concocting recipes for the popular Williams-Sonoma cookbooks. Lester announced his second retirement in February of 2010 as his seventy-fifth birthday approached, but planned to remain on board as a consultant until the end of 2012. "It has been an extraordinary privilege to lead this wonderful company," he said, according to Home Textiles Today, and added it had been even more rewarding to witness "our 27,000 associates delight our customers every day and together take our vision to a place that we could have only dreamed. I continue to be amazed by the creativity and entrepreneurship that lives within our culture."

Sources

Books

Marquis Who's Who, Marquis Who's Who, 2010.
Watson, Lucinda, and Joanne Parrent, How They Achieved: Stories of Personal Achievement and Business Success, John Wiley and Sons, 2001, pp. 103-114.

Periodicals

Daily Oklahoman, September 6, 1998, sec. BUSINESS, p. 1.

HFN: The Weekly Newspaper for the Home Furnishing Network, June 7, 1999, p. 5; November 13, 2006, p. 10.

Home Textiles Today, February 8, 2010, p. 14.

Kansas City Star (MO), March 1, 2005, p. D14.

New York Times, July 30, 1986; January 7, 1993.

San Francisco Chronicle, January 10, 1996, p. C1; May 29, 1997, p. D3.

—*Carol Brennan*

Harvey Levin

Television personality

Born Harvey Robert Levin, September 2, 1950, in Los Angeles, CA; partner of a chiropractor. *Education:* University of California—Santa Barbara, B.A., 1972; attended the University of Wisconsin—Madison; University of Chicago, J.D., 1975.

Addresses: *Office*—TMZ Productions, Inc., 8033 Sunset Blvd., Ste. 875, Los Angeles, CA 90046.

Career

In private practice with Richards Watson Dreyfuss & Gershon, a Los Angeles-area law firm, after 1975; law professor, Whittier Law School, c. 1977-96; host of radio talk show, late 1970s; legal-affairs reporter, KNBC-TV, 1982-86; legal consultant, *The People's Court* and *Superior Court*, 1980s; legal-affairs reporter, KCBS-TV, 1988-97; executive producer, *Celebrity Justice*, 2002-05; creator and managing editor, TMZ.com, 2005—; host and executive producer, *TMZ on TV*, 2007—.

Awards: Won several Los Angeles-area Emmy awards for investigative reporting, 1980s and '90s.

Sidelights

Los Angeles-based former attorney and television producer Harvey Levin has cleverly merged both of those professions into TMZ.com, one of the Internet's most popular Web sites for celebrity news and gossip. In 2007, two years after launching TMZ. com, Levin turned the site into the half-hour daily program *TMZ on TV*. "We don't need to have Tom Cruise in the studio to talk about his next picture," Levin told the *Los Angeles Business Journal* about his media company's appealingly aggressive outsider status. "We don't care about that type of coverage. So, publicists don't have any power over us."

Levin was born in 1950 and graduated from high school in the San Fernando Valley community of Reseda in 1968, the same year he worked as a campaign volunteer for Democratic presidential candidate Robert F. Kennedy, who was assassinated on a night in early June when millions of high-school seniors in the United States had just received their diplomas. As a student at the University of California—Santa Barbara, Levin was active in various on-campus groups before earning his undergraduate degree in political science in 1972. He also worked on a campaign for stricter gun control laws in California in the wake of the Kennedy assassination.

Levin headed to the Midwest to enroll in the political-science graduate program at the University of Wisconsin—Madison, but he had also applied to some law schools. The University of Chicago Law School's dean had sent a letter inviting him for a visit to the campus if he was ever in the city. Levin was unhappy at the University of Wisconsin and arranged to drop out and take a political job in Sacramento. On a long layover in Chicago, he phoned the University of Chicago dean, and left the airport to visit the campus. Levin was admitted to the Law School the same day.

After earning his J.D. from the University of Chicago in 1975, Levin returned to California and worked in private practice after passing the state bar exam. He also began teaching at Whittier Law School and became embroiled in the historic Proposition 13 ballot issue. This was a referendum vote in the state of California involving property-tax limits, and the court challenges over it made national headlines as they wound their way to the U.S. Supreme Court. The Whittier Law School dean asked Levin to hold some town-hall meetings on the topic, which led to a local call-in radio show.

After leaving his law practice, Levin spent much of the 1980s as a legal-affairs reporter for KNBC, the Los Angeles NBC affiliate. He won a local Emmy award for investigative journalism for one series, "Duty to Defend," which exposed egregious flaws in the Los Angeles County Courthouse's use of court-appointed attorneys for indigent defendants. He was also the legal consultant to *The People's Court* television show and its knockoff, *Superior Court;* both were early examples of reality-television programming in which plaintiffs and defendants in small-claims court cases agreed to abide by the decision of a retired judge in a televised hearing.

In early 1988 Levin went to work at a KNBC rival station, KCBS-TV, as its legal affairs reporter, where he continued to earn professional kudos, including additional local Emmys for reports on medical malpractice and credit card fraud. Levin gained enormous attention in the midst of the media circus that was the O. J. Simpson trial, in which the former football star was charged with murdering his estranged wife and her friend. In the frenzy of news reports that followed the June 1994 slaying, Levin interviewed Nicole Brown Simpson's former therapist, who was promoting a self-help book, and then aired footage of the Los Angeles County prosecuting attorney allegedly searching O. J. Simpson's mansion 17 minutes before the search warrant was signed. The potential legal breach caused analysts to assert that entire case against Simpson might be dropped, but then the video time-stamp was revealed to be P.M., not A.M. Levin was forced to retract the story and apologize on the air for the error.

Levin moved on from KCBS to a new version of *The People's Court,* then launched *Celebrity Justice* in 2002. The half-hour show covered some of the most siz-zling stories at the intersection of show business and legal woes, such as the new molestation charges against pop star Michael Jackson in 2003. *Celebrity Justice* failed to attract enough viewers, however, and ended its run in 2005. In December of that year, Levin created TMZ.com, a Web site for celebrity gossip. The acronym referred to what entertainment-industry executives had decades before decided could be included in the term "Hollywood"—a "thirty-mile zone" that radiated out from the one-time headquarters of the Association of Motion Pictures and Television Producers at the intersection of Beverly and La Cienega boulevards.

TMZ.com scored a massive coup in its first year when it obtained the full transcript of a drunk-driving arrest report involving actor Mel Gibson in Malibu in July of 2006. The official report, released to the media, did not contain quotes of Gibson's expletive-laden, anti-Semitic and misogynist rants as recorded by the arresting officers, and TMZ's coup made it a new, suddenly powerful player on the tabloid-journalism scene. That document had been leaked from inside the Los Angeles County Sheriff's Department, but anyone could submit a tip to TMZ.com. Sometimes these were grainy cell-phone videos of celebrities misbehaving; other times the stories seemed to come from deep inside a contentious legal battle, such as the long-running divorce and custody dispute between actors Alec Baldwin and Kim Basinger; in April of 2007, TMZ.com received millions of hits for its audio clip of Baldwin leaving an angry voice-mail message on his eleven-year-old daughter's phone.

Levin turned TMZ into a television series, *TMZ on TV,* in September of 2007. Airing on the Fox Television network, the half-hour show featured the day's top entertainment-gossip stories but also revealed the behind-the-scenes editorial meetings between Levin—holding his ubiquitous beverage container—and his staffers. He spoke to students at his alma mater, the University of Chicago Law School, in a 2010 "Privacy and the Media" lecture. "My training as a lawyer is so much more valuable than any training I could have gotten as a journalist," he told the students, according to a University of Chicago press release. "We self analyze all the time. We are aggressive journalists and yet I will defend a celebrity's right of privacy."

Sources

Periodicals

Broadcasting & Cable, August 7, 2006, p. 3.

Guardian (London, England), July 1, 2009, p. 4.

Los Angeles Business Journal, June 16, 2008, p. 1.

New York Times, September 13, 2007; December 28, 2009.

Observer (London, England), October 25, 2009, p. 33.

Television Week, December 12, 2005, p. 6.

Variety, September 10, 2007, p. 25.

Online

"Harvey Levin, '75, of TMZ Tells Students Why His JD Matters," The University of Chicago Law School, http://www.law.uchicago.edu/news/harvey-levin-75-tmz-tells-students-why-his-jd-matters (November 11, 2010).

—*Carol Brennan*

Ronald Liebowitz

President of Middlebury College

Born Ronald David Liebowitz in 1957, in New York, NY; married Jessica; children: David Heschel, Shoshana, Ezra. *Education:* Bucknell University, Lewisburg, Pennsylvania, A.B., 1979; attended Middlebury College's language institute, 1980-81; Columbia University, PhD, 1985.

Addresses: *Office*—President's Office, Old Chapel, 9 Old Chapel Rd., Middlebury College, Middlebury, VT 05753.

Career

Began teaching geography at Middlebury College, 1984-88, then assistant professor, 1988-93, then full professor, 1993—; dean of faculty, Middlebury College, 1993-95, then vice-president, 1995-97, then executive vice-president and provost, 1997-2004, then acting president, 2002, then president, 2004—. Editor of books, including: *Gorbachev's New Thinking: Prospects for Joint Ventures,* 1988; *Perestroika and East-West Economic Relations: Prospects for the 1990s,* 1989; *Russia and Eastern Europe after Communism: The Search for New Political, Economic and Security Systems,* 1996.

Member: Board of directors, National Institute for Technology in Liberal Education, 2001—.

Awards: Fellowship, George F. Kennan Institute; fellowship, International Research and Exchange Board; fellowship, National Council on Soviet and East European Research; fellowship, Social Science Research Council; fellowship, Woodrow Wilson Center for International Scholars; Best College Presidents, *Time,* 2009.

Sidelights

University administrator and professor Ronald D. Liebowitz became Middlebury College's sixteenth president in 2004 after serving as part of the institution's social sciences faculty for two decades. Since his inauguration, Liebowitz has gained widespread national attention for his efforts to enact environmental reform at the small, liberal arts college he leads. Spurred by student requests for increased environmental stewardship, the president has pledged to make Middlebury's Vermont campus carbon-neutral by 2016. "This is one of the highest priorities for the country," commented Liebowitz to Bryan Walsh of *Time* in 2009. "It's key for colleges to take the lead and push the envelope. We need to give something back to society." In addition to his administrative duties, Liebowitz continues to instruct undergraduate geography courses. He is also a noted scholar on Russian and Eastern European political and economic geography who edited three scholarly works on changes in that region during and after the fall of communism.

Born in 1957 in the borough of Brooklyn in New York City, Liebowitz earned a bachelor's degree in economics and geography from Lewisburg, Pennsylvania's Bucknell University in 1979. After a stint studying Russian at Middlebury's language institute during the summers of 1980 and 1981, he pursued graduate studies in geography at New York City's Columbia University, eventually focusing his research on the economic and political aspects of the Soviet Union from the 1950s through the 1970s. Even before completing his doctorate in 1985, however, Liebowitz had returned to Middlebury, this time as an instructor in the school's geography department. In 1988, he advanced to the rank of assistant professor; five years later, he achieved a full professorship. At the same time, Liebowitz became Middlebury's Dean of Faculty, a position he held through 1995. During this period, the scholar served as editor and co-editor of two academic volumes that explored the economic and political changes taking place in the declining Soviet Union and nascent democratic stat that followed on its heels: 1988's *Gorbachev's New Thinking: Prospects for Joint Ventures* and 1989's *Perestroika and East-West Economic Relations: Prospects for the 1990s.*

In 1995, Liebowitz made his first foray into the upper echelons of higher education administration when he was named vice-president of Middlebury College. The following year, he again acted as a co-editor on a scholarly work dealing with contemporary Russian geopolitical issues, *Russia and Eastern Europe after Communism: The Search for New Political, Economic and Security Systems.* Liebowitz's administrative rise continued in 1997 when he received the appointment of executive vice-president and provost of the college. He retained this post for the next seven years, as well as serving as Middlebury's acting president from February to June of 2002 during the tenure of President John McCardell Jr. As an administrator, Liebowitz was responsible for the establishment of several new C.V. Starr-Middlebury study abroad centers in Europe, Latin America, Russia, and China, as well as promoting an increasingly international-focused curriculum at Middlebury with new offerings in languages and international politics and economics. Despite the demands of his administrative duties, Liebowitz remained in the classroom as well as, in 2001, becoming the inaugural chair of the board of directors of the National Institute for Technology in Liberal Education, an organization dedicated to the promotion of the use of new technologies in liberal art curricula at small colleges such as Middlebury. He also received fellowships from such respected bodies as the National Council on Soviet and East European Research, the International Research and Exchange Board, the Social Science Research Council, the George F. Kennan Institute, and the Woodrow Wilson Center for International Scholars.

When McCardell retired from office in 2004, Liebowitz was elevated to the presidency of Middlebury. "I am enormously pleased with the se-

lection of Ron Liebowitz as the president of Middlebury College," Europe Intelligence Wire quoted Churchill Franklin, chairperson of the college's board of directors, as commenting upon the announcement of the new president's appointment in April of 2004. "Ron has been an extremely dedicated and talented member of the Middlebury College community for 20 years.... Ron's dedication and commitment to Middlebury is very strong, and he has remained here where his efforts have been instrumental in making the College a leading presence in higher education." Liebowitz assumed the office in October of that same year, becoming only the third faculty member to hold Middlebury's top office in the institution's more than 200-year history.

Liebowitz soon proved himself to be an active leader, developing initiatives aimed at helping Middlebury both change with the times and reinforce its dedication to the tenets of a classic liberal arts education. His first major undertaking was the creation of a long-term strategic plan that was launched in 2006 under the title "Knowledge Without Boundaries." The following year, the president announced the creation of the Project on Creativity and Innovation in the Liberal Arts, a sweeping program aimed at encouraging students' intellectual creativity and experimentation.

However, the program which has earned Liebowitz and Middlebury the most attention has been the school's ambitious efforts to reduce its carbon footprint and increase environmental sustainability. Since Middlebury's students proposed a ten-year deadline for carbon neutrality in 2006, Liebowitz has worked to make that goal a reality. He signed the American College and University Presidents Climate Commitment in 2007, the same year that construction began on a biomass gasification plant, a nearly pollution-free system of producing energy. Middlebury has also installed energy efficient lighting, solar panels, and a wind turbine. Efforts such as these have made the campus one of the greenest in the country, and helped earn Liebowitz a nod from *Time* as one of the nation's ten best college presidents.

Such initiatives came with a hefty price tag, however, and during 2009 Middlebury faced increasing financial pressures resulting from the general economic downturn. With a commitment to need-blind admissions and education for all of its students regardless of their financial situation, the college experienced heightened demand for financial aid even as its endowment and other revenues fell. Faculty and administrators accepted pay freezes and cuts, while Middlebury began considering other ways to reduce costs and increase its income. Liebowitz suggested one potential field of growth to *Fortune*'s Eugenia Levenson: educational language software. "[W]e know there's a huge demand from diplomats and journalists who come to our language schools. It's not without risks. But the business model that we've been operating under is gone, and we have to start thinking a little bit differently."

Selected writings

(Editor) *Gorbachev's New Thinking: Prospects for Joint Ventures*, HarperCollins (New York City), 1988.

(Co-editor) *Perestroika and East-West Economic Relations: Prospects for the 1990s*, New York University Press (New York City), 1989.

(Co-editor) *Russia and Eastern Europe after Communism: The Search for New Political, Economic and Security Systems*, Westview Press (New York City), 1996.

Sources

Books

Marquis Who's Who, Marquis Who's Who, 2009.

Periodicals

Europe Intelligence Wire, April 16, 2004; October 4, 2004; February 23, 2007.
Fortune, April 10, 2009.
Time, November 11, 2009.

Online

"Carbon Neutrality," Middlebury College, http://www.middlebury.edu/sustainability/energy-climate (March 1, 2010).
"President's Biography," Middlebury College, http://www.middlebury.edu/about/president/bio (March 1, 2010).

— *Vanessa E. Vaughn*

Porfirio Lobo

President of Honduras

Born Porfirio Lobo Sosa, December 22, 1947, in Trujillo, Honduras. *Education:* University of Miami, M.B.A.; also studied in Moscow, 1980s.

Addresses: *Office*—Palacio José Cecilio del Valle, Blvd. Juan Pablo II, Tegucigalpa, Honduras.

AP Images

Career

Elected to the Honduran National Congress, 1990; president, National Congress, 2002-06; president of Honduras, 2010—.

Sidelights

In November of 2009, Porfirio "Pepe" Lobo was voted president of Honduras in a controversial post-coup election held five months after the country's military ousted the former president from office. When Lobo took over in January of 2010, he inherited a country in near shambles. The nation faced an economic crisis as well as political unrest. Millions of dollars of much-needed foreign aid had been cut off following the coup because donor nations failed to recognize the interim government. Lobo faced the monumental task of persuading the international community to accept his government's authority in an effort to restore foreign aid and rebuild the ailing economy. In addition, a nationwide resistance movement flourished with opposition leaders requesting that a constitutional assembly convene to remove Lobo from power and restore a "true" democratic government. The opposition re-

fused to accept Lobo's government, seeing it as nothing more than an extension of an illegitimate coup that had ousted a properly elected president.

Lobo was born on December 22, 1947, in Trujillo, Honduras, into a family of cattle-ranching landowners. He grew up on a ranch near Catacamas, Olancho, Honduras, in a region known for growing mass quantities of corn and beans. Early on, Lobo was fascinated by politics and became a youth political leader in Olancho. He traveled abroad to further his education, earning a master's degree in business administration from the University of Miami. Lobo also studied in Moscow during the Soviet era of communism and returned home a leftist. Over time, however, Lobo's views turned more conservative and he became a member of Honduras' National Party—a center-right conservative party. In 1990, Lobo gained election to the country's legislature, known as the National Congress. He rose through the ranks and served as president of the National Congress from 2002-06.

In 2005, Lobo ran for president against Manuel Zelaya, another popular member of the National Congress, though he ended up losing by 73,000 votes. Zelaya captured 49.9 percent of the vote to Lobo's 46.4. Lobo, however, ended up having another chance at the presidency four years later following a political crisis. It started in June of 2009 when some 200 Honduran soldiers entered Zelaya's home, held him at gunpoint, and exiled him to Costa Rica. Zelaya's ouster resulted from his attempt to call a constituent assembly to rewrite the constitution. Dissidents feared Zelaya wanted to remove the constitution's one-term limit in an effort to keep himself in power once his term expired. In addition, many politicians did not trust Zelaya's ties to left-wing leader Hugo Chavez, president of Venezuela.

After Zelaya was deposed from power, the National Congress appointed Roberto Micheletti interim president and he called for a presidential election in November of 2009. All five of Honduras' political parties took part in the contentious elections. Some 60 percent of registered voters turned out. When all the ballots were counted, Lobo emerged victorious, with 56 percent of the vote over Liberal Party candidate Elvin Santos, who garnered 38 percent of the vote. Following the Honduran election several Latin American countries, including Argentina and Brazil, declined to accept Lobo's government for fear other nations would follow and try to oust elected leaders.

According to the *Economist*, U.S. President Barack Obama advised nations to cautiously consider the implications of allowing such an ouster, noting that "it would be a terrible precedent if we start moving backwards into the era in which we are seeing military coups as a means of political transition." Obama condemned the coup, but later decided to recognize the government after the elections as a way to move forward with diplomatic relations. Soon after the United States restored diplomatic ties with Honduras, Colombia, Costa Rica, Panama, and Peru followed suit; however, as of July 2010, many nations, including Mexico, still refused to recognize the Honduran government and President Lobo was banned from the European Union-Latin America summit that year.

When Lobo took office on January 27, 2010, he faced a severe economic crisis. The country's economy had shrunk by three to four percent since Zelaya's ouster due to the loss of foreign aid prompted by his departure—with Honduras in such distress, other nations stopped the flow of foreign aid that had bolstered the lagging economy. Lobo looked to help the economy by restoring relations with other nations. By July 2010, he had reopened relations with 86 countries.

On the international stage, Lobo did well at restoring legitimacy to his government and nation. At home it was a different story. In June of 2010, on the one-year anniversary of the coup, hundreds of thousands of Hondurans took to the streets calling for Lobo's departure and demanding a constitutional assembly convene to form a new government. Besides rejecting the election and denouncing the coup that brought it to fruition, activists were fed up with the government and the wealthy minority whom they believed controlled the country. Many resistance leaders were attacked and Hondurans blamed the government. In the year following the coup, the Committee of Families of the Detained-Disappeared in Honduras reported 52 political murders and 300 serious human rights abuses—most aimed at well-known vocal activists. In addition, attacks on journalists rose after Lobo came to power. From March to June 2010, seven journalists were killed in Honduras.

Despite the risks, followers of the resistance movement remained unfazed. Lobo's term was set to expire in 2014, but opposition leaders hoped for an earlier departure. Speaking to the *Progressive*'s Kari Lydersen, resistance leader Dionisia Diaz put it this way, "We're not going to rest until we have our constitution, an assembly of the people, for the people, not for ten families. They're threatening to kill us, but we're not afraid; we're going to die one day anyway. Better to die in the struggle."

Sources

Periodicals

Economist, December 5, 2009, p. 43; January 23, 2010, p. 47; July 24, 2010, p. 40.
Progressive, September 2010, p. 30.
Washington Times (Washington, DC), November 30, 2009, p. A13.

Online

"Honduras Country Profile: Leaders," BBC News, http://news.bbc.co.uk/2/hi/americas/country_profiles/1225416.stm (July 24, 2010).
"Honduras's President-Elect Is Wealthy Farmer Who Moved From Left To Right," *Telegraph*, http://www.telegraph.co.uk/expat/expatnews/6691538/Hondurass-president-elect-is-wealthy-farmer-who-moved-from-Left-to-Right.html (July 24, 2010).
"Profile: Honduran New President Porfirio Lobo," *People's Daily Online*, http://english.people.com.cn/90001/90777/90852/6881274.html (July 24, 2010).

"Zelaya Rival Wins Honduran Poll," BBC News, http://news.bbc.co.uk/go/pr/fr/-/2/hi/ americas/8384874.stm (July 24, 2010).

—*Lisa Frick*

Demi Lovato

Actress and singer

Born Demetria Devonne Lovato, August 20, 1992, in Dallas, TX; daughter of Patrick Lovato and Dianna De La Garza (a cheerleader and country and western singer; maiden name, Hart).

Addresses: *Record company*—Hollywood Records, 500 S. Buena Vista St., Burbank, CA 91521. *Web site*—http://www.demilovato.com.

Career

Actress on television, including: *Barney and Friends,* c. 2002-03; *As the Bell Rings,* 2007; *Camp Rock,* 2008; *Princess Protection Program,* 2009; *Sonny with a Chance,* 2009—; *Camp Rock: The Final Cut,* 2010. Guest appearances on television programs, including: *Prison Break,* 2006; *Just Jordan,* 2007; *Grey's Anatomy,* 2010. As a singer she appeared as an opening act for the Jonas Brothers' *Burning Up Tour,* 2008; released albums *Don't Forget,* 2008; *Here We Go Again,* 2009. Opening act for Jonas Brothers' *3D Concert Experience,* 2009.

Awards: Teen Choice Award for female TV breakout star, *Teen People,* 2009; (with David Archuleta) Teen Choice Award for music tour, *Teen People,* 2009.

Sidelights

Demi Lovato knew that she wanted to be a professional performer from the age of five when she sang "My Heart Will Go On" in a Kindergarten talent show. Indeed she told Amanda Forr in an in-

Retna UK/Landov

terview for *Girl's Life* that she is "very ambitious. I've always known I was supposed to do this, ever since I was really, really young. I saw what I wanted in my dreams, and then I worked hard." As a very young child she spent years on the Texas beauty pageant circuit honing her skills as a performer. When she was only five years old she auditioned for the first time for *Barney and Friends.* However, she was not cast on the show from that audition because she could not read.

Lovato did eventually earn a role on the famed kids' television program and began appearing in season seven when she was ten years old. Lovato played the corrective-glasses-wearing Angela on *Barney and Friends* for two seasons. Her relationship with the show was life altering, not only because it gave her a chance to be a performer on a national children's television program, but also because it is where she met her best friend, Selena Gomez. The two met while in the casting call line for that audition and then worked together on the show. In an interview for *Entertainment Weekly* Leah Greenblatt quoted Selena Gomez as saying, "We were in line with 1,400 kids and we happened to be standing right next to each other. She had a little bow in her hair, and she turned around and she looked at me and said, 'Do you want to color?' She laid her blue jean jacket down and we started to color. And after that we had a couple of callbacks, and I saw her from the other side of the room and it was kind of a movie moment. We still joke about it. We were inseparable after doing two seasons together, and our moms are best friends now. Later, we homeschooled together, went on auditions together, everything. And her mom even took me to the audition that got me on the Disney Channel!" They have remained close friends and both work with the Disney Corporation.

Lovato has been guided in her career by her mother, Dianna De La Garza, and her stepfather, Eddie De La Garza, who is also her manager. Dianna is a former Dallas Cowboys cheerleader who has also performed as a country western singer. Lovato's mother has opened for such big name country and western stars as Reba McEntire, George Strait, and Hank Williams Jr. Dianna nurtured the talents of her three daughters. Lovato received music lessons in voice, piano, and guitar starting at a young age. Both of her sisters, Dallas Lovato and Madison De La Garza, act and sing as well. Dallas has appeared in episodes of Lovato's Disney channel series *Sonny With a Chance* and on *Wizards of Waverly Place*. Madison plays the daughter of Eva Longoria's character on *Desperate Housewives*.

After her stint with the purple dinosaur, Lovato was cast in occasional guest roles on a variety of programs including an episode of *Prison Break*, but her big break came at a Dallas Disney talent search. Her screen test lead her to be cast as Charlotte in a recurring series of five-minute vignettes called *As the Bell Rings* that run between the regular programs on the Disney network.

The Disney Corporation has always looked for performers that were versatile since the days of the original Mouseketeers and Annette Funicello. Since the early 1990s, Disney has been responsible for catapulting to fame such young stars as Britney Spears, Hilary Duff, and Miley Cyrus. After *As the Bell Rings* Lovato made appearances in some of the Disney network programs and then was cast in the television musical *Camp Rock* opposite the very popular Jonas Brothers, who are heartthrobs to the 'tween-aged population. Described by Greenblatt as "An enjoyable, fairly self-explanatory trifle (It's a summer camp! For rock!), the movie serves largely as a vehicle for its stars' song-and-dance routines, a sweet G-rated romance, and parent-pleasing lessons on self-esteem and friendship." Lovato's performance as Mitchie Torres created an image for her as a wholesome girl-next-door type of personality. Disney cemented this image by creating the character of Sonny Munroe for Lovato and giving her a sitcom titled *Sonny with a Chance*. Munroe is a sweet

girl from Wisconsin who lands a part on her favorite show and moves to Los Angeles. It is very similar to Lovato's own life story. Lovato was also cast in two other Disney Channel movies, *Princess Protection Program* and the sequel to *Camp Rock* called *Camp Rock: The Final Jam*.

Lovato's meteoric rise to teen stardom has not always been easy. She has been turned down for more parts than she has received, but she has persisted. Lovato expressed that she stays strong in part due to the support system around her, which includes her family, who all moved to Los Angeles so that she could play the part of Munroe. Her family and friends have helped her weather ugly episodes that have occurred as her fame grew.

When Lovato was in seventh grade in Colleyville, Texas, she was bullied by a group of fellow students who targeted her as her career began to take off. Lovato told Monica Rizzo in an article for *People*, "There was a petition called 'We Hate Demi.' They would text me and say, 'We're going to make your life a living hell.' I remember asking them, 'What did I do?' and no one could answer." The threats were reported to the school but nothing could be done because it was all verbal threats and nothing physical had occurred. One day some of the girls involved told Lovato that they were going to beat her up and they chased her into a bathroom. Lovato called her mother and asked that she be taken out of school. Her mother removed her from school and began to homeschool her. Since that very frightening incident, Lovato has also received hate mail from girl fans of the Jonas Brothers who have assumed that she is dating one of them because she appeared in the movie *Camp Rock* with them, has appeared in concert with them, and is friends with the three brothers. Rizzo quoted Joe Jonas as describing Lovato as being "well-poised and has so much confidence in herself." Lovato's poise and self esteem is a credit to the maturity of the young star. Rizzo quoted Lovato as saying in regards to the bullying, "I'll always be scarred from it. But you can't focus on those people or you won't get anywhere."

Lovato recognizes the importance of being versatile. She told Jaime J. Weinman of *Maclean's* that "The more that someone can do, the more opportunities it opens up for them." In addition to acting, she always wanted to be a professional singer and, because of her talents, Lovato was given a recording contract with Disney's musical recording company, Hollywood Records, and put on tour to open with the Jonas Brothers while they were in concert. Lovato's debut album, *Don't Forget*, was released in

2008 and impressively rose to the number-two spot on the *Billboard* 200 chart. Jon Caramanica, writing for the *New York Times*, described her debut album as having "flashes of hard rock and pop-punk," and "surprisingly sprightly and tough." Lovato's second album, *Here We Go Again* was released in 2009 and opened at the number-one spot on the *Billboard* 200. Lovato's first two CDs have been very popular with the tween crowd.

Lovato has worked her entire life to be a successful performer. Gary Marsh, president for entertainment at Disney Channels Worldwide, told Caramanica that when he asked Lovato if she was ready for fame that "she looked at me straight in the eyes and said, 'I was born ready.' Some of them say it, but I don't think they all mean it." Marsh added that Lovato has "a frightening sense of her destiny. She built her whole life so this moment could happen." For her second album, Lovato wrote an intense song about her estranged father, but she was willing to drop it from the album because she recognized that it might be more than her young audience could easily emotionally handle. Lovato was aware that she was a spokesperson for the Disney Corporation, which is centered around wholesome family entertainment. Lovato told Greenblatt, "I am a pop singer. And I'm not gonna try to be too 'Oh, I'm hardcore, I'm a rock girl.' No, I'm with the Disney Channel! But bubblegum isn't really my thing." This type of professionalism can be stifling even as it helps a career along. Caramanica wrote, "Even as her fame grows, ever present is the knowledge that in a couple of years, or maybe less, it will be time to prove herself all over again; tween-focused acts arrive with a built-in expiration date."

Lovato said to Caramanica, "If it takes me ten years to be the musician I want to be, great. I don't want it to be pandemonium for something I'm not proud of in a few years, I want to be able to tell my kids, 'This is the great work that I did,' instead of it being, 'I was great for six months and now I've got this great work that nobody saw because my fame died out.'" Lovato has been reported as saying that she is interested in taking time off from performing to study at the Berklee College of Music. She also recently broke out of children's television with a guest performance on the hit television series *Grey's Anatomy* in which she played a teenage girl who had been misdiagnosed as schizophrenic. Caramanica also described a rendition of one of her songs that he heard in concert when she came out for an encore as being "tactile and intense, far rowdier than the version she released as a single last year, and probably over the heads of many in the crowd. Still, it played like the shedding of an ill-fitting skin, revealing an eccentric young woman itching to get out, sending up smoke signals to those who might recognize them." Belinda Luscombe, in an article for *Time*, quoted Frederick Levy, a manager of child actors and the author of the book *Acting in Young Hollywood*, as saying, "Disney's an amazing cross-promoter. You will become a teen star. Then you'll have to work twice as hard to prove you are more."

Selected discography

Don't Forget, Hollywood Records, 2008.
Here We Go Again, Hollywood Records, 2009.

Sources

Books

Contemporary Musicians, vol. 67, Gale, 2010.

Periodicals

Girl's Life, February-March 2009.
Entertainment Weekly, October 3, 2008, pp. 44-47; November 21, 2008, pp. 80-90.
Maclean's March 23-30, 2009, p. 81.
New York Times, July 19, 2009, p. 1; July 31, 2009, p. C2.
People, April 13, 2009, pp. 121-22.
Time, November 2, 2009, pp. 50-52.

Online

"Demi Lovato," TVGuide, http://www.tvguide.com/celebrities/demi-lovato/bio/290381 (May 31, 2010).

—Annette Bowman

Mitch Lowe

Lucas Jackson/Reuters/Landov

President of Redbox

Born c. 1953.

Addresses: *Home*—Northern California. *Office*—Redbox Automated Retail, One Tower Ln., Ste. 1200, Oakbrook Terrace, IL 60181.

Career

Partner in a video store, early 1980s; creator of Video Droid vending machines, 1984; sold company to a Japanese investor, 1986; opened chain of Video Droid stores that expanded to nine outlets in northern California; vice president of business development, Netflix, c. 1999-2003; consultant, Redbox Automated Retail LLC, after 2003, then chief operating officer, May 2005-09, then president, April 2009—.

Sidelights

Mitch Lowe has guided Redbox Automated Retail, a chain of DVD rental kiosks, from its humble start in 2004 with a dozen vending machines inside fast food restaurants into one of the dominant players in the rental industry. Five years after its launch, Redbox had surpassed the 20,000-rental mark and was adding new kiosks at the rate of one every hour. Lowe is a former video store owner whose primary task is playing hardball with major movie studios for rental rights for new releases.

In media profiles, Lowe divulges few details about his personal life, save for the fact that his teenage children thought the DVD rental idea was unwise.

As a video store owner in the early 1980s, Lowe started a business that repurposed soft drink vending machines into videotape-rental devices. That venture failed, and by the early 1990s Lowe was operating a small chain of video rental stores in the Mill Valley/Marin County area north of San Francisco. In a 1991 *USA Today* article about his efforts to convince other independent stores to offer voter registration sign-ups at the counter, Lowe divulged he had spent several years as a draft dodger during the Vietnam War era, living in two Communist countries, Romania and Hungary. "I know this sounds corny, but this is an opportunity for us to give something back to the community," he told the paper's Richard Halstead about the historically low U.S. voter-turnout statistics, especially among young adults. "We talk big about democracy, but most of us don't follow through."

Lowe entered the retail video rental business early, in the early 1980s, but was dismayed by the high costs of staffing and stocking a store. He exited and went into business with three partners to create Video Droid in 1982, which adapted soft drink vending machines as a free-standing, automated video-rental device. The first three machines were placed in grocery stores and eventually grew to number around 60 in the Bay Area, but the concept failed to catch on with consumers. "People would just kind of walk by and say, 'Hmm. That's kind of interesting,' and not use it," he told the *Chicago Tribune*'s Julie Wernau.

Lowe retained the rights to the Video Droid name and used it when he re-entered the retail video rental market. By 1991, he had three stores, and doubled that number by 1996, when he was elected board chair of the Video Software Dealers Association. In 1998, with nine stores in the Marin County area posting total annual revenues of $3 million, he signed on with a pair of Silicon Valley software executives who created an online DVD rental business called Netflix. Lowe served as the company's vice president of strategic alliances, and his role involved negotiating deals with the major Hollywood studios for release rights of their movies.

Netflix became a massive success, which spelled the beginning of the end for the rental chains like Blockbuster who had come to dominate the market in the 1990s. Yet Lowe was still convinced that a self-service option would work, too. "I hate losing," he told Wernau, the *Chicago Tribune* journalist. "I hate the fact that I failed with what I thought was a great idea." In 2003, Lowe left Netflix to become a consultant to a venture proposed by executives of the McDonald's fast food chain. In a bid to increase foot traffic in their restaurants, McDonald's created a self-service DVD-rental device. It was rolled out in 2004 with a dozen kiosks, each holding about 500 DVDs, available for a $1 per-24-hour period rental fee to anyone with a credit card. Failure to return the DVD after 25 days meant that the customer's credit card would be charged the maximum, $25—about the cost of buying the DVD at a retailer like Target or Wal-Mart.

Lowe became chief operating officer of Redbox in the spring of 2005, and was made company president in April of 2009, not long after the McDonald's corporation divested its holdings in the venture and sold it to Coinstar, the self-service coin-counting machines that became ubiquitous in U.S. grocery stores earlier that decade. In Redbox's half-decade history, the company had doubled the number of its kiosks annually to reach 21,000 by the end of 2009. Redbox rental units are found in a large swath of the most populated areas of the United States in grocery stores like Kroger, or drugstore chains like Walgreen's, along with targeted 7-11 convenience stores.

As at Netflix, much of Lowe's job is devoted to negotiations with major movie studios. He had some success with Paramount and Sony to release new movies the same day they become available in stores for purchase, but a few of the other big studios balked, and wanted to force Redbox into deals that required the company to wait a minimum of 28 days before stocking new titles—the same period when just-released DVD sales are highest. Lowe launched a two-pronged strategy: he hired teams of up to 800 associates a day to descend on retailers like Best Buy to buy the DVDS on the day of release, at full price, and sought the help of a legal team with anti-trust experience to file litigation against Universal, Fox, and Warner. The lawsuit was a risky move, Lowe told *Crain's Chicago Business* writer John Pletz. "They're big corporations with a lot of power. It's not something we relish." He also cited that deals agreeable to both parties could prove lucrative for all. "We're a big customer," he told Pletz. "We're buying 300,000 to 500,000 copies of a single title. That's $3 to $5 million that we're putting down on the table."

DVD rental kiosks had captured an estimated 19 percent of the market by the end of 2009, and the sector was predicted to show steady growth over the next decade. Less than half of all rental transactions occurred at a traditional store, and Netflix and other by-mail providers enjoyed about 35 percent of the market. Redbox was one of several self-service kiosk rental options, but the aggressive rollout with Coinstar backing made it a nimble competitor to Blockbuster, which was introducing its own branded kiosks even while shuttering brick-and-mortar stores altogether. As Lowe once assessed, the overhead on such retail spaces could be crushing for a company in skittish economic times. After three decades in the home-entertainment business, he believed the major studios would eventually come aboard with Redbox's dollar-a-night fee. "If you make renting affordable and fun," he told *New York Times* writer Brooks Barnes, "people are going to watch a whole lot more movies than they did before."

Sources

Chicago Tribune, October 16, 2009.
Crain's Chicago Business, September 7, 2009, p. 3.
Home Media Magazine, August 3, 2009, p. 1.
New York Times, July 12, 2009; September 7, 2009; October 25, 2009.
USA Today, September 6, 1991.
Video Business, May 17, 1991, p. 18.
Wall Street Journal, November 30, 2009.

—*Carol Brennan*

Jane Lynch

Actress

Born July 14, 1960, in Dolton, IL; daughter of a banker and a homemaker; married Lara Embry (a psychologist), 2010. *Education:* Illinois State University, B.F.A., early 1980s; Cornell University, M.F.A., 1984.

Addresses: *Home*—Los Angeles, CA. *Office*—*Glee*, P.O. Box 900, Attn: Fox Broadcasting Publicity Dept., Beverly Hills, CA 90213-0900.

Career

Appeared in productions at the Chicago Shakespeare Theater, Steppenwolf Theater Company, Second City Touring Company, and the Annoyance Theatre; original cast member of the *The Real Live Brady Bunch*, Annoyance Theater, Chicago, 1990. Actress on television, including: *In the Best Interest of the Children* (movie), 1992; *The Big Time* (movie), 2002; *MDs*, ABC, 2002; *Two and a Half Men*, CBS, 2004-09; *The L Word*, Showtime, 2005-09; *Lovespring International*, Lifetime, 2006; *Separated at Worth* (movie), 2006; *Help Me Help You*, 2006-07; *Boston Legal*, 2006-08; *Criminal Minds*, CBS, 2006-08; *American Dad!*, 2007; *Area 57* (movie), 2007; *The Adventures of Captain Cross Dresser* (voice; movie), 2008; *Never Better* (movie), 2008; *Mr. Troop Mom* (movie), 2009; *Party Down*, 2009-10; *Glee*, FOX, 2009—. Guest appearances on television, 1993—. Film appearances include: *Taxi Killer*, 1988; *Vice Versa*, 1988; *Straight Talk*, 1992; *Fatal Instinct*, 1993; *The Fugitive*, 1993; *Touch Me*, 1997; *Best in Show*, 2000; *Color Me Gay*, 2000; *Red Lipstick*, 2000; *What Planet Are You From?*, 2000; *Martini*, 2001; *Nice Guys Finish Last*, 2001; *Collateral Damage*, 2002; *Hiding in Walls*, 2002; *Exposed*, 2003; *A Mighty Wind*, 2003; *How to Be a Hollywood Player in Less Than Ten Minutes*, 2004; *Lemony Snicket's A Series of Unfortunate Events*, 2004; *Little Black Boot*, 2004; *Memoirs of an Evil Stepmother*, 2004; *Sleepover*, 2004; *Surviving Eden*, 2004; *The 40-Year-Old Virgin*, 2005; *Bam Bam and Celeste*, 2005; *The Californians*, 2005; *Holly Hobbie and Friends: Surprise Party* (voice), 2005; *Promtroversy*, 2005; *Eye of the Dolphin*, 2006; *Fifty Pills*, 2006; *For Your Consideration*, 2006; *The Frank Anderson*, 2006; *Holly Hobbie and Friends: Christmas Wishes* (voice), 2006; *Talladega Nights: The Ballad of Ricky Bobby*, 2006; *Alvin and the Chipmunks*, 2007; *Holly Hobbie and Friends: Best Friends Forever* (voice), 2007; *I Do & I Don't*, 2007; *The List*, 2007; *Love Is Love*, 2007; *Smiley Face*, 2007; *Suffering Man's Charity*, 2007; *Walk Hard: The Dewey Cox Story*, 2007; *Adventures of Power*, 2008; *Alex's Halloween*, 2008; *Another Cinderella Story*, 2008; *Man Maid*, 2008; *The Rocker*, 2008; *Role Models*, 2008; *Space Chimps* (voice), 2008; *The Toe Tactic*, 2008; *Tru Loved*, 2008; *Big Breaks*, 2009; *Ice Age: Dawn of the Dinosaurs* (voice), 2009; *Julie & Julia*, 2009; *Post Grad*, 2009; *Weather Girl*, 2009; *Paul*, 2010; *Shrek Forever After* (voice), 2010.

Awards: Satellite Award for best actress in a supporting role in a series, mini-series, or motion picture made for television, International Press Academy, for *Glee*, 2009; (with co-stars) Screen Actors

Guild Award for outstanding performance by an ensemble in a comedy series, Screen Actors Guild, for *Glee*, 2009.

Sidelights

After years of sitcom guest roles and television commercial voiceovers, Jane Lynch vaulted onto Hollywood's A-list thanks to her lead in the hit FOX series *Glee* in 2009. As malevolent cheerleading coach Sue Sylvester, Lynch's character personifies a wide spectrum of villainous adults in the fictional high school universe of western Ohio's McKinley High, where the performing arts takes a second seat to athletics. "Lynch's role in *Glee*," wrote *Newsweek*'s Joshua Alston, "makes ideal use of her best assets: her ability to deliver a zinger like a close-range cannonball, and a smile that can easily communicate menace."

Lynch was born in 1960 and grew up in Dolton, Illinois, one of the southern Chicagoland suburbs. Her father was a banker, while her mother stayed home to care for Lynch and her brother. At Thornridge High School, Lynch tried out for and was cast in a play during her freshman year, but "I was so afraid of failing that I just walked away from it and joined the tennis team," she told *Chicago Tribune* writer Maureen Ryan. After graduating, she enrolled at Illinois State University as a communications major, but finally committed to a performing-arts career midway through and switched to the theater department. She went on to earn a graduate drama degree from Cornell University and lived in New York City for a time. Her first film role came in a 1988 Italian-made thriller, *Taxi Killer*, that appears to have gone unreleased. Her second screen job was a small part in *Vice Versa*, a comedy starring Judge Reinhold and Fred Savage.

After moving back to Chicago, Lynch immersed herself in the city's thriving subculture of classic and experimental theater. She performed with the Chicago Shakespeare Theater and the acclaimed Steppenwolf Theater Company, and honed her comedic talents with the touring company of the Second City improvisational theater troupe and at the Annoyance Theatre, a well-known site for absurdist drama and satirical spoofs. Like Second City, the Annoyance stage was an early training ground for several notable names in comedy; Lynch's fellow Annoyance alumni include Stephen Colbert, Andy Richter, and Amy Sedaris.

In June of 1990, Lynch debuted in what became one of the most popular and long-running productions on the Chicago experimental theater scene: Annoyance Theatre's *The Real Live Brady Bunch*. Recreating episodes from the nostalgic early-1970s sitcom on ABC, the spoof became a sensation that quickly garnered national press attention. Lynch played Carol Brady, the mom of one of television's most famous blended families. As Lynch recalled in an interview with Diane Anderson-Minshall in *Curve*, the low-budget production started as a sort of joke in which the cast decided to simply reenact entire *Brady Bunch* episodes garbed in the vivid vintage clothing of the era. On opening night, "we all got drunk. And we went to go do the show and there was a line around the block—the first night!" Lynch told Anderson-Minshall. "I remember the lights coming up and my heart was pounding ... my hands were shaking; I could not believe that all these people had come to see us. And it was sold out every week and it became like this phenomenon."

Lynch returned to New York City with the cast of *The Real Live Brady Bunch* when the show moved to the Village Gate Theater in late 1991. A year later, she landed a small role in a major Hollywood movie set in Chicago, the Dolly Parton comedy *Straight Talk*, and in 1993 won a part in the Harrison Ford thriller *The Fugitive*, part of which also takes place in the city. Around this same time she made her small-screen debut in a television movie that starred Sarah Jessica Parker as a mentally unstable woman who loses custody of her children, *In the Best Interest of the Children*. Relocating to Southern California in 1994, Lynch spent the rest of the decade making a living on the sitcom circuit. She appeared in guest roles on *Married with Children*, *Party of Five*, *3rd Rock from the Sun*, *Frasier*, and *Dharma & Greg*, among other hit shows.

Lynch's primary source of income, however, came from appearing in television commercials and doing voiceovers for radio ads. She stood on the edge of a cliff for Nexium, the acid-reflux pill marketed by pharmaceutical giant AstraZeneca, and played a concerned shopper in a series of ads for a major supermarket chain. "I have kind of a stock Midwestern mom voice," Lynch explained to Terry Gross, host of the National Public Radio interview series *Fresh Air*. "I loved it. It's a great gig."

In the same interview, Lynch also discussed her breakthrough role, which came in the 2000 "mockumentary" *Best in Show*. Written and directed by Christopher Guest, the spoof documentary film follows several show-dog owners who come to Philadelphia for the annual purebred canine competition. It was the follow-up to Guest's earlier cult-favorite comedies, *This Is Spinal Tap* and *Waiting for Guffman*. Guest occasionally directed television commercials and had worked with Lynch when she appeared in a commercial for Kellogg's Frosted Flakes cereal. A few months later, Lynch ran into Guest at a Los Angeles coffee house, and he told her he was in the pre-production stages for a new movie set in the world of high-stakes dog shows and suggested she come by his office later that day. Lynch left Guest's office with a role in *Best in Show.* "I was thrilled, because when I saw *Waiting for Guffman,* I about fell out of my seat," she told Gross in the *Fresh Air* interview, saying she had thought to herself, "please, please let me work this way. This is how I want to work. This is the way to do it, and this guy's got it down.... [I]t was really a dream come true—a ridiculous, preposterous dream come true."

Guest relies on a corps of highly trained, supremely confidant actors who are required to improvise much of their dialogue, and even contribute to decisions on set props and wardrobe. Lynch was cast as Christy Cummings, a professional dog trainer hired by Sherri Ann Cabot (Jennifer Coolidge). Coolidge's ditzy blonde character lives in palatial splendor as the much-younger wife of a very wealthy, seemingly senile man, with her pet poodle. Sherri Ann and Christy bond over the dog-training regimen and fall in love. "Jennifer Coolidge and I went to a Great Dane dog show before we started shooting," Lynch told Mark Olsen in *The Advocate.* "There were at least five or six lesbian couples with their dogs, and there are always three or four gay men. They're so obsessed with their dogs. It's a really interesting microcosm. Gays are big in the dog show world." Backstage "footage" captures the two sharing a spontaneous kiss after a trophy win as *Best in Show* heads for its titular finale, and the mockumentary's epilogue interviews Christy and Sherri Ann in their new offices talking about their new magazine aimed at lesbian owners of purebred dogs.

Christy Cummings was Lynch's breakout role, garnering a fair share of laughs in a film already filled with the typical mountain of jokes Guest elicited from his improv-savvy cast. "Lynch deployed deft timing and an undercurrent of wistful neediness to steal every scene she was in," asserted Olsen in *The Advocate.* Her success led to scores of film offers, and she was even cast in a short-lived hospital drama on ABC called *MDs.* She stopped doing commercials and voiceover work around 2003, the same year that Guest put her in another mockumentary, this one skewering the folk-music scene. Lynch played Laurie Bohner, a former adult-film star now fronting a revival of a wholesome ensemble with her husband, played by John Michael Higgins, who had also appeared in *Best in Show.*

Lynch also became a popular recurring character on the hit CBS sitcom *Two and a Half Men* as Dr. Linda Freeman, a caustic psychologist who treats all three

title characters—a young boy, his divorced father, and fast-living uncle. In early 2005, Lynch began appearing on the Showtime series *The L Word* as Joyce Wischnia, a tough attorney introduced to the storyline as part of a custody battle between a same-sex couple. "Joyce is one of those supremely confident, stop-at-nothing-to-win kind of people," Lynch told *Entertainment Weekly* writer Tim Stack. "You take Christy Cummings, grow her up about 20 years, and put her through law school. And about 20 years of therapy, too, where she builds up her self-esteem."

Lynch is among just a handful of openly gay female actresses working in mainstream film and television. Often asked about this in interviews, Lynch has said that she came to terms with her sexual orientation in her twenties, but did not tell her family for several more years. She did so in a letter that her therapist suggested she write, but not send. Lynch decided to send it, and was immensely relieved that "there was no drama around it," she told Gross in the *Fresh Air* interview. "It was really kind of a lovely moment where we all came together and said, you know, of course this doesn't mean anything, you know, we still love you."

In the summer of 2005, Lynch appeared in a supporting role in a new movie from writer-director Judd Apatow. In *The 40-Year-Old Virgin,* Lynch was cast as Paula, the frisky electronics-store manager to Steve Carell's title character. Carell's wife, Nancy Walls, knew Lynch from Chicago when both were at Second City. A year later, Lynch turned up in another Christopher Guest movie, *For Your Consideration,* and began appearing on *Criminal Minds,* the CBS crime drama. Increasingly high-profile roles came her way, including that of Dorothy McWilliams, the sister of television chef Julia Child, in flashback scenes in the 2009 movie *Julie & Julia.*

Julie & Julia was released in the summer of 2009, just a few months after the debut of *Glee* on FOX Television. The show proved a ratings hit almost immediately, and Lynch anchored the cast as cheerleading coach Sue Sylvester, who resents the funding given to the newly reconstituted show choir at William McKinley High School in Lima, Ohio. Her rival is the school's Spanish teacher Will Schuester (Matthew Morrison), who has volunteered to take an extracurricular job no one else wants as the supervisor of the school's once-great glee club. "Lynch steals every scene," wrote Alessandra Stanley in the *New York Times,* in her role of "the bullying, mannish and conniving coach of the pep squad, who plots to annihilate the glee club and its mild-mannered coach."

Glee's musical numbers—as the students cover pop songs for their show choir competitions—gave the series an edge that brought viewers back for the full season in the fall of 2009. After a three-month break, the series returned for a third and concluding installment of the first season on April 13, 2010, tacking on a video preview of next week's all-Madonna episode in which Lynch's Sylvester recreated, frame by frame, the pop singer's iconic video for her 1990 hit "Vogue." The storyline for the April 20 episode, where the video also appeared, featured two of Sylvester's cheerleaders attempting to give her a makeover, which leads to the fantasy video sequence.

Many of the show's fans—known as "Gleeks"—were stunned to learn that Lynch actually sang in the video; she also contributed her own vocals to the musical numbers in *A Mighty Wind*. Her Madonna cover was one of the most talked-about entertainment-news and blogosphere stories for the next week. Some of the reports also noted that Lynch had announced she was engaged to her partner, psychologist Lara Embry. "As a younger person," Lynch reflected back in the 2006 interview with Olsen for *The Advocate*, "I'd lie in bed at night and wonder, If I do make it and start getting work and people know who I am—how will I handle this? What will I do? I had some angst about it, and gratefully I haven't had to deal with that at all."

Sources

Periodicals

The Advocate, November 21, 2006, p. 42.
Chicago Tribune, May 17, 2009, sec. ARTS, p. 1.
Curve, November 2005, p. 28.
Entertainment Weekly, October 30, 2009, p. 24.
Newsweek, September 7, 2009, p. 52.
New York Times, April 11, 2010.
Time, May 18, 2009, p. 59.

Online

"Jane Lynch," Internet Movie Database, http://www.imdb.com/name/nm0528331/ (April 17, 2010).

Transcripts

Fresh Air, National Public Radio, November 4, 2009.

—*Carol Brennan*

Evan Lysacek

Figure skater

Alberto E. Rodriguez/Getty Images

Born June 4, 1985, in Chicago, IL; son of Don (a building contractor) and Tanya (Santoro) Lysacek.

Addresses: *Agent*—Yuki Saegusa, IMG, 767 Fifth Ave., 45th Fl., New York, NY 10153. *Contact*—Lynn Plage, LP Communications, 2505 S. Allison Ct., Denver, CO 80227. *Office*—Toyota Sports Center, 555 North Nash St., El Segundo, CA 90245. *Web site*—http://www.evanlysacek.com.

Career

Figure skater, c. 1993—; professional model, 2007—. Actor in short film *Skate Great!*, 2007; competitor on television program *Dancing with the Stars*, ABC-TV, 2010.

Awards: First place juvenile level, Junior Olympics, 1996; first place, North American Challenge, 1999; first place novice level, State Farm U.S. Championships, 1999; first place junior level, State Farm U.S. Championships, 2000; second place, World Junior Championships, 2001, 2003, and 2004; first place, Triglav Trophy, 2002; first place, Junior Grand Prix Finale, 2003; third place, Four Continents Championship, 2004; second place, Marshalls World Cup, 2004; first place, Four Continents Championships, 2005, 2007; first place, Marshalls Figure Skating Challenge, 2005; second place, NHK Trophy, 2005; second place, Smart Ones Skate America, 2005; third place, World Championships, 2005, 2006; third place, State Farm U.S. Championships, 2005; (with team) first place, Campbell's Cup, 2006; first place,

Cup of China, 2006; second place, Skate America, 2006; second place, State Farm U.S. Championships, 2006; fourth place, Winter Olympics, 2006; third place, World Championships, 2006; second place, Cup of China, 2007; third place, Grand Prix Finale, 2007; second place, Skate America, 2007; first place, State Farm U.S. Championships, 2007; third place, Four Continents Championship, 2008; first place, Japan Open, 2008; first place, third place, Skate Canada, 2008; third place, Skate America, 2008; first place, U.S. Championships, 2008; third place, AT&T U.S. Championships, 2009; second place, Cup of China, 2009; second place, Four Continents Championship, 2009; reader's choice skater of the year award, *SKATING* magazine, 2009; first place, World Championships, 2009; first place, World Team Trophy, 2009; first place, Skate America, 2009; first place, Grand Prix Final, 2009; second place, AT&T U.S. Championships, 2010; first place, XXI Olympic Winter Games, 2010.

Sidelights

As Olympic and world champion, Evan Lysacek (pronounced LIE-sah-check) hoped to bring new fans and increased respect to men's figure skating. Lysacek has brought his athleticism, strength, and consistent work ethic to a sport better known for its wild costumes, judging controversies, and female stars. "We've got a lot of sequins going on," the skater told John Henderson of the *Denver Post*. "I'm doing the best I can to change that and wear high-fashion designers and trying to get design out there and masculine clothing, a masculinity and a simplicity and put the focus on the skating instead of the glitter."

Born in 1985, Lysacek is the second of Don and Tanya Lysacek's three children and grew up in the Chicago area. He was eight when his grandmother gave him and his older sister ice skates for Christmas. Although the youngster loved hockey, he was not a natural on the ice. "I was told if I wanted to be a hockey player I should take some skating lessons," he recalled to *Columbus Dispatch* reporter Tom Reed. He enjoyed learning tricks so much that he began competing in figure skating. At his first national competition, Lysacek competed against boys two and three years older and placed first. "I didn't know exactly what it meant," he told Nancy Armour in the Bergen County, New Jersey *Record*. "At the time I was doing the Junior Olympics I thought, 'Well, I won that, how hard can it be to do this other Olympics? It's just another step.'" He won the U.S. national novice title in 1999 and junior title in 2000.

Lysacek began moving up the junior ranks despite having to adjust to continual growth spurts. (He eventually reached a height of 6'2", unusually tall for a figure skater.) In 2001, he was a last-minute replacement to the World Junior Championships team but ended up with the silver medal, a feat he repeated in 2003. That success did not immediately translate to the senior level; he placed no better than tenth in his first three U.S. Championships. Although Lysacek wanted to train with coach Frank Carroll in California, his mother insisted he finish high school first. After graduating with honors from Naperville's Neuqua Valley High School in 2003, he moved to California and the successes started building. He won his first international competition, the 2003 Junior Grand Prix Final, and another silver at World Juniors in 2004.

The following season Lysacek moved permanently into the senior ranks and quickly became one of the United States' most consistent skaters. He won the 2005 Four Continents Championship, moving from fifth to first after the free skate. He won his first U.S. Championship medal, a bronze, and at his first World Championship finished a surprising third. "I really came here just looking to learn and have a good time," the skater told Gary Mihoces in *USA Today*, adding that "I think that as the week went

on, I gained a lot of confidence." He followed that up with a victory in the U.S. Figure Skating Challenge, setting him up for the Olympics in 2006. His success "definitely gives me a lot of inspiration to go home and work really hard for next year, the Olympic year," he told the *St. Petersburg Times'* Dave Scheiber. "I really would love to come into the Olympics as a national champion."

In 2006, Lysacek finished less than a point behind champion Johnny Weir in the U.S. Championships, earning a spot on the Olympic team. His experience at Turin was difficult; he was tenth in the short program, and immediately afterwards fell ill with a stomach virus. Lysacek spent the next 48 hours receiving intravenous fluids so he could compete in the free skate. Although he was still vomiting the morning of the event, he ended up receiving a personal best score in his free skate and finished fourth. The experience provided a valuable lesson. "I thought the Olympics were about coming and being perfect, being the most trained, being in great shape, and not missing one jump," the skater told the *Tampa Tribune's* Bill Ward. "But I learned the Olympics are about courage, about going out and finishing a job you start." A few weeks later, Lysacek repeated as bronze medalist at the World Championships.

In 2007 Lysacek claimed his first U.S. Championship, nailing his first quadruple jump in competition and winning by 30 points. "You can't be a leader in the sport by skating hesitant," Lysacek told Jo-Ann Barnas of the *Detroit Free Press*. He landed the quad again to earn a new personal best and win a second Four Continents title, but at the World Championships he missed the landing and ended up fifth. "The jumps and stunts we are doing nowadays are like an extreme sport," the skater told Reed. "The days of doing five doubles and just skating to pretty music are over." He hoped his performances would help change the perception that figure skating was not a real sport. "In my fifth hour of training, when my lungs are burning and I have a gash on my knee and I've hit my head on the ice, I don't think it's a girlie sport," he added.

The 2008 season contained both triumphs and challenges. Lysacek repeated as U.S. champion; although he and Weir tied with identical scores, Lysacek's superior free skate earned him the title. Before he could compete in the World Championships, a training crash left him with a dislocated shoulder and elbow. After being sidelined for two months, he realized he needed a change. "I was way overbooked," he told Janice Lloyd in *USA Today*. "I had no time to breathe, no time to rest, barely enough time to train. Mentally, I just felt like I'd lost the love of skating." He spent three weeks training with Russian coach Tatiana Sarasova, experimenting with a different style of movement. He returned to California eager to continue training for international competition.

Lysacek endured early disappointment during the 2008-09 season. He placed third at the U.S. Championships, falling on his quad and skating without energy. He worked so much mid-season to improve his performance that he developed a stress fracture in his left foot. The injury meant dropping the quad from his World Championship programs. Nonetheless, he set a personal best in his free skate and finished first, becoming the first American to win the men's title since 1996. "It's been a slow build for me this season, but as I got here, I felt a new aura of confidence," he told the *New York Times*'s Juliet Macur. "I felt like a calm new person." Part of his success was due to performing near his Los Angeles home. "I wasn't thinking about winning or medaling. I just wanted to skate well in front of my hometown crowd," he told Kelly Whiteside in *USA Today*.

As a favorite for the 2010 Winter Olympics in Vancouver, Lysacek responded by training harder: "I am not naive," the skater told *USA Today*'s Vicki Michaelis. "I don't think because I won the world championship that I'm unbeatable. I think I need to be stronger and better." He worked on improving his choreography and artistry; usually, he told Michaelis, "I like to jump, jump, jump, spin, spin, spin. I want to sweat. I want to work. This has been a little more of a stretch." He was rewarded with first-time victories at the Skate America and Grand Prix competitions, but fell on a quadruple jump during U.S. Nationals and finished second to Jeremy Abbott. This qualified him for the Olympics, where his competition would include three former world champions, including 2006 Olympic champion Yevgeny Plushenko, who came out of retirement for the event.

At the 2010 Olympics Lysacek earned a career-best in his short program to keep within a point of leader Plushenko. He then set another personal best in his free skate, despite not including a quadruple jump in his program, and bested Plushenko by 1.31 points to earn the gold medal. There was controversy when Plushenko, who completed a quad and had no major mistakes in his free skate, declared that the judging was flawed and that he had deserved the gold. While Lysacek did not attempt a quad because of his foot problems, he had been rewarded for his superior spins and footwork, and what many com-

mentators considered a smoother and more consistent performance. As Lysacek told Henderson: "If it was a jumping competition, they'd give you 10 seconds to run and do your best jump. But it's a 4-minute, 40-second program and about sustaining that level of skating, excitement, and endurance from start to finish."

After the Olympics, Lysacek did not defend his World Championship title; instead, he began competing on ABC-TV's *Dancing with the Stars*. Paired with professional dancer Anna Trebunskaya, Lysacek performed various ballroom dances and scored well with both judges and the home audience. His skating training was less helpful than he expected, he told Pohla Smith in the *Pittsburgh Post-Gazette*: "I've actually had to abandon some of the skating things—the body posture is so different.... I started at zero." His team achieved the season's first perfect score, despite Lysacek spending half of each week on tour with "Stars on Ice." Although they ended up placing second, the skater told *TV Guide*'s Joyce Eng that they "were completely satisfied with the whole season and what we put into it. We didn't leave anything on the table."

As an Olympic champion and reality TV star, Lysacek has brought increased exposure to men's figure skating. He earned endorsement deals from Coke, AT&T, Total Gym, and Flexjet, as well as a modeling contract. While he did not retire from skating after 2010, he intended to explore other fields. His future could include acting; he appeared in the 2007 short film *Skate Great!* as a Russian former skating champion, and he has taken acting classes. He has also expressed interest in fashion, having worked with designers Christian Dior, Alexander McQueen, and Vera Wang on his skating costumes. Equally important to him has been his work with charities such as the Ronald McDonald House, Make-a-Wish Foundation, Figure Skating in Harlem, and the Special Olympics. Whatever the effort, Lysacek believed determination would prove key to his success: "Go and fight every day, no matter what's happened the day before or what might happen," he wrote on his Web site. "Don't think about the past or the future—stay in the present."

Sources

Periodicals

Chicago Tribune, March 17, 2007.
Columbus Dispatch, May 4, 2007.
Denver Post, February 8, 2007, p. D2; March 18, 2007, p. B8; February 19, 2010, p. C1.

Detroit Free Press, January 28, 2007.

Los Angeles Times, February 18, 2010.

New York, February 1, 2010.

New York Times, January 26, 2009, p. D2; March 27, 2009; February 19, 2010, p. B9; February 20, 2010, p. D1.

Pittsburgh Post-Gazette, April 28, 2010.

Record (Bergen County, NJ), January 9, 2006, p. S10.

Sports Illustrated, April 6, 2009, p. 20.

Sports Illustrated Kids, January 2010, p. 36.

St. Petersburg Times (St. Petersburg, FL), March 30, 2005, p. 7C.

Tampa Tribune, February 17, 2006, p. 1.

USA Today, March 18, 2005, p. 13C; February 17, 2006, p. 3F; January 28, 2008, p. 9C; October 31, 2008, p. 6C; March 27, 2009, p. 11C; October 27, 2009, p. 2C; January 18, 2010, p. 7C; February 2, 2010, p. 1C; February 19, 2010, p. 4D.

Online

"Athletes: Evan Lysacek," NBC Olympics, http://www.nbcolympics.com/athletes/athlete=2367/index.html(June 1, 2010).

Biography Resource Center Online, Gale, 2010.

"Dancing's Evan Lysacek: I'm 'Not Upset' That Len Said Nicole Should Win," *TV Guide,* http://www.tvguide.com/Dancing-Stars/Dancings-Evan-Lysacek-1019048.aspx (May 28, 2010).

Evan Lysacek Official Web site, http://www.evan lysacek.com (June 1, 2010).

—Diane Telgen

Hilary Mantel

AP Images

Author

Born Hilary Thompson, July 6, 1952, in Glossop, Derbyshire, England; daughter of Henry (a clerk) and Margaret Thompson; stepdaughter of Jack Mantel; married Gerald McEwen (a geologist), September 23, 1972 (divorced and remarried). *Education:* Attended the London School of Economics, c. 1970; Sheffield University, B.Juris, 1973.

Addresses: *Agent*—Bill Hamilton, A.M. Heath, 6 Warwick Ct., Holborn, London WC1R 5DJ, England. *Home*—Surrey, England. *Office*—c/o Fourth Estate, 77-85 Fulham Palace Rd., London W6 8JB, England.

Career

Social worker in a geriatric hospital, 1974-75; teacher of English, Botswana, 1977-82; first short story "Poor Children" published in the February 21, 1979, edition of *Punch* under the name Hilary McEwen; first novel, *Every Day Is Mother's Day*, published by Chatto and Windus, 1985.

Awards: Shiva Naipaul Memorial Prize for travel writing, *Spectator* magazine, 1987; fellow, Royal Society of Literature, 1990; Commander of the Order of the British Empire, 2006; Man Booker Prize, Man Group, for *Wolf Hall*, 2009; National Book Critics' Circle Award for fiction, for *Wolf Hall*, 2009.

Sidelights

Hilary Mantel won the 2009 Man Booker Prize for her novel *Wolf Hall*, a fictional reimagining of the events of the English Reformation in the early 1500s. An accomplished storyteller with a mordant wit to her prose, Mantel produced nine other novels before her prize-winning Tudor saga, which also garnered the year's top fiction honors from the U.S. National Book Critics' Circle organization. "Her book's main characters are scorchingly well rendered," asserted *New York Times* critic Janet Maslin in her review of *Wolf Hall*. "And their sharp-clawed machinations are presented with nonstop verve in a book that can compress a wealth of incisiveness into a very few well-chosen words."

Mantel was born in 1952 and spent the first years of her life in the area of Glossop, a town in England's Derbyshire county. Her parents were Irish Catholic immigrants who had come to the northern industrial city of Manchester to improve their fortunes; her father worked as a clerk, while her mother had started working at one of the region's many textile mills at the age of 12. Mantel was the first of their three children, but the marriage fell apart when her mother became involved with the lodger the family had taken in; the entire family relocated to nearby Cheshire county, and they all took the new stepfather's name, though there was never an actual divorce.

As a child, Mantel was smart, imaginative, and a devoted bookworm. She was sent to the Harrytown

Convent School outside Manchester, which only intensified the growing distance between her family's working-class origins and her own ambition. Her stepfather proved a particularly antagonistic relative, as Mantel recalled in an interview with James Campbell in the *Guardian*. "Things that I grew to be interested in through my teens were to him a cause for rows," she said. "Shakespeare—he couldn't believe that people really found pleasure in Shakespeare, and took it to be some sort of establishment conspiracy from which he was shut out."

Mantel's years at Harrytown and her first year at the London School of Economics would later provide the background for one of her later novels, *An Experiment in Love.* She spent just a year in London before transferring to Sheffield University to be near her boyfriend from back home. At Sheffield she studied law with the aim of becoming a barrister and graduated with bachelor of jurisprudence degree in 1973, but never entered the profession. Instead she became a social worker in a geriatric hospital, and quit that in 1975 in order to write full time; by this point she had also wed her longtime boyfriend, Gerald McEwen, who was starting his career as a geologist during this period.

Mantel wanted to write a novel about the French Revolution. Having little literary training, she enrolled in a creative-writing course, but exited after a few classes. "It was really for people who wanted their poem about their walk in the park to be printed in the local paper," she told *Times* of London writer Valerie Grove. "When the teacher asked what I was writing—my French Revolution novel— her eyes glazed over."

When Mantel's husband was offered a job in the southern African nation of Botswana, the couple moved there in 1977 and settled in for the next five years. Throughout most of the 1970s Mantel suffered from mysterious pains in her legs and a troubling lack of energy. Seeking medical help, she was diagnosed with depression and put on an increasing array of prescription medications, including valium. By the time she reached Africa, her physical condition had deteriorated to the point where she could do little all day but attempt to write her novel about the French Revolution. She had conducted copious amounts of research by then and brought it with her to Africa. "I saw myself as being very barely a writer of fiction," she told Campbell in the *Guardian* interview. "I didn't consider I had great powers of invention. I was fixated on documents and on ferreting out as much of the truth as I could. I thought of making things up as rather a bad thing to do."

Mantel finally diagnosed herself with endometriosis, a disorder of the female reproductive system, and in 1979 returned to London to undergo major surgery that ended her ability to conceive and carry a child. It was also a trying time in her marriage, and she and McEwen divorced but later reunited and remarried so that she could join him on his next job assignment, in Saudi Arabia. They lived there for four long years, a period which she described as one of intense isolation that bred in her a deep sense of paranoia.

That solitude, however, spurred Mantel to begin and finish her first novel after shelving the French Revolution project. *Every Day Is Mother's Day* was published in Britain by Chatto and Windus in 1985 and earned her some gratifyingly positive first reviews. She had based the darkly comic tale on her stint as a social worker in northern England around 1974. Its two characters were a reclusive mother-daughter pair, Evelyn and Muriel Axon. Evelyn once earned extra money from neighbors by promoting her ability to contact the dead. Muriel is grown but is possibly autistic, and her life improves vastly when she begins attending vocational-education classes, but then she becomes pregnant. "Everything works towards a hideous, murderous conclusion," asserted a *Times Literary Supplement* reviewer, Christopher Hawtree. "One relishes the prospect of Hilary Mantel's devising further tortures" for her vividly unlikable characters, Hawtree concluded.

Mantel seemed to take that advice and made the Axon home the center of her second novel, *Vacant Possession.* Set several years later, the 1986 work finds Muriel now adrift in an Thatcherite England of the 1980s, when government cutbacks closed scores of psychiatric facilities. A year later, Mantel won an inaugural travel-writing prize sponsored by the *Spectator* magazine after submitting a piece on her life in Saudi Arabia. That led to a job offer from the magazine and a new publisher, Viking, for her next novel, *Eight Months on Ghazzah Street.* The story centers on Frances Shore, a cartographer by training who is forced to stay home in their bland, windowless modern apartment all day when her husband takes a job in Saudi Arabia. Frances finds the other expatriate wives insufferable and attempts to befriend her Muslim female neighbors. "Mantel's tale of Francis' disorientation and discovery is horrifyingly gripping," opined Grace Ingoldby in the London *Sunday Times.* "Her narrative urges the reader to suspend normal life entirely until the book is read."

Between 1989 and 1998 Mantel produced five new novels. These include *Fludd,* a tale set among a Roman Catholic minority in 1950s England, and that

French Revolution novel, *A Place of Greater Safety*. *A Change of Climate* was published in 1994 and tracks the homecoming of a pair of married missionaries who suffered a horrific family tragedy while working in Botswana. *An Experiment in Love* is Mantel's tale of a young woman at the University of London in the early 1970s, while her 1998 novel, *The Giant, O'Brien,* is based on the true story of Charles Byrne, also known as Charles O'Brien, who died in London in 1783. The seven-foot, seven-inch Byrne was exploited by a physician of questionable ethics as he becomes a minor celebrity in London.

In 2003, Mantel published a revelatory memoir, *Giving Up the Ghost,* that earned terrific reviews. Slowing down the pace of her writing after that, she produced the novel *Beyond Black* in 2005, about a professional psychic and the woman who becomes her personal assistant. Mantel said she was inspired in part by her own visit to a medium following the sudden death of England's Princess Diana in 1997. "I was amazed by her persona—how carefully got up she was, in a kind of cocktail dress," Mantel recounted in an interview with Rachel Cooke in the *Observer*. "Then, in the foyer, I saw this other woman, tweaking a piece of cloth that hung over a portrait of the psychic on a easel. Psychic assistant, I thought. What kind of job is that? What is it like when they go home?" The novel was shortlisted for the 2006 Orange Prize for Fiction, awarded annually to a female writer for a full-length work in English.

It would be Mantel's massive, 532-page 2009 novel, however, that won her the top prize in U.K. letters, the Man Booker award. *Wolf Hall* draws heavily from the dramatic events in the reign of England's King Henry VIII in the first half of the sixteenth century. The Tudor monarch's first marriage to Spain's Catherine of Aragon failed to produce a male heir, and because divorce was prohibited by the Roman Catholic Church, Henry sought a dispensation from the Pope in Rome to divorce Catherine and marry Anne Boleyn. The Pope refused, which prompted Henry to break from Rome and establish the Anglican Church, which hewed more closely to the tenets of the Protestant Reformation sweeping through northern Europe at the time. Boleyn and two of Henry's most important advisors, Sir Thomas More and Sir Thomas Cromwell, all met their death by execution in the wake of Henry's increasingly authoritarian and tempestuous rule. History has generally assigned to More the role of the beleaguered, principled holdout, while casting Cromwell as the villain of the English Reformation.

Mantel's *Wolf Hall* seeks to reverse these characterizations by retelling the events of the 1520s and '30s from Cromwell's point of view. Cromwell was the king's chief minister and helped enact drastic measures against Roman Catholics in England before running afoul of other powerful figures at Henry's court, who resented his humble birth and rise to a baronetcy. The novel takes its title from the manor home of Jane Seymour, who became Henry's third wife and whose family had borrowed a significant sum from Cromwell. Seymour died after giving birth to Henry's only son, Edward VI, and Cromwell persuaded the king to marry a German princess, Anne of Cleves, in hopes of strengthening ties with the Protestant lands on the Continent. The match was an ill-advised one, and led to Cromwell's downfall. He was executed on the same day that Henry wed Catherine Howard.

Mantel's book, which took her a half-decade to write, earned glowing reviews. Writing in the *Atlantic,* Christopher Hitchens called it "a historical novel of quite astonishing power.... The means by which Mantel grounds and anchors her action so convincingly in the time she describes, while drawing so easily upon the past and hinting so indirectly at the future, put her in the very first rank of historical novelists." A review in the *Economist* hailed it as her "best novel yet," and went on to commend the way in which Mantel's "characters have a lifeblood of their own" as well as her "sustained use of the historic present tense, of which she is a master. Her prose is muscular, avoiding cod Tudor dialogue and going for direct modern English."

Wolf Hall concludes with the death of Thomas More in 1535. Mantel's exhaustive research yielded enough material to continue the saga in a sequel, tentatively titled *The Mirror and the Light*. Though her career had been slow to start, she possessed a trove of inspiration for future novels. "Once you're switched on to the trade of a writer, you don't really get holidays," she told Ramona Koval, a journalist with the Australian Broadcasting Corporation. "The best thing about being a writer I think is probably that every day presents material in a totally unpredictable way, and something that you see today may pay off in ten years time and it could breed a whole book or it could breed half a line. You've no way of knowing when the material crops up, you just have to harvest it and store it and hope for the best."

Selected writings

Novels

Every Day Is Mother's Day, Chatto and Windus (London), 1985, Owl Books (New York), 2000.

Vacant Possession, Chatto and Windus, 1986, Holt (New York), 2000.

Eight Months on Ghazzah Street, Viking (London), 1988, Holt, 1997.

Fludd, Viking, 1989.

A Place of Greater Safety, Viking, 1992, Athenaeum (New York), 1993.

A Change of Climate, Viking, 1994.

An Experiment in Love, Viking, 1995, Holt, 1996.

The Giant, O'Brien, Fourth Estate Ltd. (London), 1998.

Giving Up the Ghost (memoir), Fourth Estate Ltd., 2003.

Beyond Black, Fourth Estate Ltd., 2005.

Wolf Hall, Fourth Estate Ltd., 2009.

Sources

Periodicals

Atlantic, January 26, 2010.

Economist, October 10, 2009, p, 86.

Guardian (London, England), September 11, 2004, p. 31; November 19, 2005, p. 11.

New York Times, October 5, 2009.

Observer (London, England), April 24, 2005; April 19, 2009, p. 35.

Publishers Weekly, October 5, 1998, p. 60.

Sunday Times (London, England), May 15, 1988.

Times (London, England), April 25, 2009.

Times Literary Supplement, March 29, 1985, p. 341.

Online

"From 'Wolf Hall,'" *New York Review of Books,* July 17, 2008, http://www.nybooks.com/articles/archives/2008/jul/17/from-wolf-hall/?pagination=false (April 14, 2010).

Transcripts

The Book Show, Australian Broadcasting Corporation Radio National, October 21, 2008.

—*Carol Brennan*

Julianna Margulies

Actress

Born Julianna Luisa Margulies, June 8, 1966, in Spring Valley, NY; daughter of Paul (an advertising executive) and Francesca (a dance teacher) Margulies; married Keith Lieberthal (an attorney), November 10, 2007; children: Kieran. *Education:* Sarah Lawrence College, B.A., 1989.

Addresses: *Home*—New York, NY, and Livingston, NY. *Office*—c/o CBS Corporation, 51 W. 52nd St., New York, NY 10019-6188.

Career

Actress on television, including: *Law & Order*, 1993; *Murder She Wrote*, 1993; *ER*, NBC, 1994-2000, 2009; *Homicide: Life on the Street*, 1994; *Philly Heat*, 1994; *Jenifer* (movie), 2001; *The Mists of Avalon* (miniseries), TNT, 2001; *Hitler: The Rise of Evil* (movie), 2003; *The Grid* (miniseries), TNT, 2004; *Scrubs*, NBC, 2004; *The Lost Room* (miniseries), SyFy, 2006; *The Sopranos*, HBO, 2006-07; *Canterbury's Law*, FOX, 2008; *The Good Wife*, CBS, 2009—; *Sesame Street*, 2010. Film appearances include: *Out for Justice*, 1991; *Paradise Road*, 1997; *Traveller*, 1997; *A Price Above Rubies*, 1998; *The Newton Boys*, 1998; *What's Cooking?*, 2000; *Dinosaur* (voice), 2000; *The Big Day*, 2001; *Evelyn*, 2002; *Ghost Ship*, 2002; *Love Gets You Twister* (voice), 2002; *The Man from Elysian Fields*, 2002; *Slingshot*, 2005; *Beautiful Ohio*, 2006; *The Darwin Awards*, 2006; *Snakes on a Plane*, 2006; *City Island*, 2009. Stage appearances include: *Ten Unknowns*, Mitzi E. Newhouse Theater, Lincoln Center, New York, NY, 2000-01; *Intrigue with Faye*, MCC Theater, New York, NY, 2003; *Festen*, Music Box Theater, New York, NY, 2006.

Andrew H. Walker/Getty Images

Awards: Emmy Award for outstanding supporting actress in a drama series, Academy of Television Arts & Sciences, for *ER*, 1995; Q award for best supporting actress in a quality drama series, Viewers for Quality Television, for *ER*, 1995; SAG award (with others) for outstanding performance by an ensemble in a drama series, Screen Actors Guild, for *ER*, 1996, 1997; Q award for best actress in a quality drama series, Viewers for Quality Television, for *ER*, 1997; SAG award for outstanding performance by a female actor in a drama series, Screen Actors Guild, for *ER*, 1998, 1999; Golden Globe Award for best performance by an actress in a television series, Hollywood Foreign Press Association, for *The Good Wife*, 2010; SAG award for outstanding performance by a female actor in a drama series, Screen Actors Guild, for *The Good Wife*, 2010.

Sidelights

Actress Julianna Margulies may never be able to shed her image as beleaguered but resolute head nurse Carol Hathaway on the long-running NBC medical drama *ER*. She left the show after six seasons to pursue film and stage roles, but returned to prime-time television in 2009 with *The Good Wife*, one of the top-rated new shows of the year. "I couldn't stop turning the pages," Margulies told

USA Today journalist Donna Freydkin about her first encounter with the title role on the CBS drama about a woman whose marriage to a politician is tested by a salacious sex scandal. "It's very timely. What happens to the family? What are the repercussions? What do you say to each other? How do you even relate to each other?"

Margulies had an adventurous, unconventional childhood as the youngest of three daughters born to Francesca, a professional ballet dancer, and Paul, an advertising executive. The family had moved from New York City to Spring Valley, New York, before Margulies was born in June of 1966, but the marriage soon foundered, and her parents separated when she was still an infant. Her father moved to Paris for his job, while Francesca eventually found a place as a teacher at a school in Sussex, England; the trio of Margulies daughters shuttled back and forth across the English Channel and then the Atlantic Ocean when Paul eventually returned to New York City.

Margulies attended Green Meadow Waldorf School, a private school that followed the principals of nineteenth-century Austrian educator Rudolf Steiner. The Waldorf method emphasizes learning through the creative arts, including music and drama, and Margulies went on to a New Hampshire boarding school that also adhered to Steiner's principals. Following graduation, she entered Sarah Lawrence College near New York City to study art history, but was drawn to the performing arts and appeared in school plays.

After deciding to pursue acting as a career, Margulies struggled for a few years, working in the restaurant industry and taking jobs in television commercials—including one for McDonald's Hot Wings—to make ends meet. Her first break came when she appeared in a 1991 Steven Seagal movie, *Out for Justice*, which brought her to the attention of casting agents. Guest roles in episodes of *Law & Order* and *Murder, She Wrote* followed, but she had trouble landing steady work or winning over directors for leading roles. That changed in mid-1994, when she was cast in the pilot episode of a new television series for NBC called *ER*. Her character was the nurse-manager of the emergency room at a large Chicago hospital, and was involved in a troubled relationship with a handsome pediatrician on the ER staff played by George Clooney. In that first episode, Margulies' Carol Hathaway finishes her shift, then returns to the ER as a patient after attempting suicide. The show's writers originally set up a story arc that had Margulies' character die off, but after focus groups watched the show in secret

previews, the decision was reversed. Clooney called Margulies and left a message telling her that "Your character tested through the roof," she recalled in an interview with Dan Snierson of *Entertainment Weekly*, with Clooney adding, "Don't take another series!"

There was another offer that Margulies was weighing, a series set in the beach enclave of Malibu, but she took her new colleague's advice. She came back in *ER*'s third episode with her character's mental-health issues at least temporarily resolved but her romantic troubles still roiling. Over the rest of the first season, Nurse Hathaway tries to adopt a child, becomes engaged to another physician, and realizes she still harbors feelings for Dr. Doug Ross, the womanizing doctor played by Clooney. Margulies won an Emmy Award for Outstanding Supporting Actress in a Drama Series for that first season.

Margulies was thrilled with the professional achievement and financial stability offered by a hit television series, but sought to expand her roles before becoming too indelibly identified as Nurse Hathaway. *ER*'s producers reportedly offered her a contract worth $27 million to stay on through 2002, but she turned it down. The writing team eased her character out with a pregnancy that turned out to be twins; the father was Doug Ross, but Clooney was also leaving the show. The Thanksgiving-night episode in 1999 when Margulies' character delivered twin girls pulled in 30 million viewers, approximating a Super Bowl audience or a season finale of *American Idol*. During her six seasons on *ER*, the show was either the No. 1 or No. 2-ranked television series in ratings, trading off with *Seinfeld*; after she and Clooney left, it never reached the No. 1 spot again.

ER was filmed on a Warner Brothers studio lot in Burbank, California, but Margulies still kept an apartment in New York City. She moved back permanently after leaving the show and began to seek out feature-film and stage roles. Her television job had left her only enough time to do about one feature film a year, and her late-1990s big-screen appearances included *Paradise Road*, a 1997 drama set in a women's prisoner-of-war camp during World War II; a tale of a Hasidic Jew's marriage gone awry in *A Price Above Rubies*, which starred Renee Zellweger; and *The Newton Boys*, a 1920s crime-spree tale from director Richard Linklater.

On stage, Margulies appeared in *Ten Unknowns*, a new work from playwright Jon Robin Baitz that premiered at Mitzi E. Newhouse Theater at Lincoln

Center in 2000 and ran for several months. She co-starred with Donald Sutherland, Denis O'Hare, and Justin Kirk in the art-world drama about a once-acclaimed painter who vanished from the scene; the four-character play was described as "this season's mainstream cerebral hit" by *New York Times* critic Ben Brantley, who wrote approvingly of Margulies' performance as a graduate student enmeshed in the three men's interpersonal conflicts. "The luminous Ms. Margulies," Brantley asserted, "here becomes the girl everyone falls in love with in college, yet there's a grounding humanness about her, a glimmering insecurity."

Margulies struggled to find a film role that would suit her talents, and took television work in the interim. In 2001, she appeared as Morgaine, the protagonist and narrator of a long-awaited adaptation of Marion Zimmer Bradley's best-seller *The Mists of Avalon* for TNT. "I would love to do a big action film if the right one came along, but the one that came along for me was about a snake: there wasn't much acting to do," she told David Eimer in a *Times* of London interview. She was referring to the 1997 horror movie *Anaconda*, a part that helped turn Jennifer Lopez from a singer into a box-office draw.

Margulies took a lead in what many hoped would be a blockbuster thriller of 2002, *Ghost Ship*, but the at-sea supernatural thriller earned almost universally derisive reviews. "The vast movie-movie possibilities of pitting a group of people against the haunts of a cursed Italian luxury liner are completely scuttled," wrote Robert Koehler in *Daily Variety*, who contended the "horror pic collapses under the weight of its own dull conception and weak direction, dialogue and character portraits." In one of his scarce positive comments, Koehler noted that "Margulies manages to survive both ghost ship and movie, carving out a physical [performance] obviously modeled on Sigourney Weaver's school of tough-gal adventuring."

Margulies spent the remainder of the decade alternating between film, television, and stage roles. She was a counterterrorism expert in a 2004 TNT miniseries *The Grid*, appeared in a memorable two-episode story arc on the NBC sitcom *Scrubs*, and returned to Broadway as part of a solid ensemble cast in *Festen* in 2006. Between 2006 and 2007 she appeared in four episodes of the sixth and final season of the hit HBO drama *The Sopranos*, playing a New Jersey realtor who is first courted by lead mobster Tony Soprano (James Gandolfini), but then has an affair with his underling Christopher Moltisanti (Michael Imperioli). A *Sopranos* character was a plum role for any actor, but many of Margulies'

longtime fans were surprised when she appeared in the summer of 2006's most-hyped movie, *Snakes on a Plane*, as a flight attendant. "I didn't choose it because I was getting some intellectual thrill out of it," she told *Entertainment Weekly*'s Jennifer Armstrong. "I thought it would be a hoot, it was nice to pay the mortgage, and I got to work with Sam Jackson."

In 2009, nearly a decade after leaving *ER*, Margulies appeared in one of the final episodes of the series. "Old Times," the 328th episode in Season 15 of the longest-running medical drama in American television, showed her life in Seattle with Clooney's character, who also works at University of Washington medical center where Nurse Hathaway is now an organ-transplant coordinator. That followed a short-lived drama on the FOX network, *Canterbury's Law*, that was partially a victim of the 2007-08 Writers Guild of America strike. Margulies played the title character, an unlikable Rhode Island criminal defense attorney. Her character is married but unfaithful, and harbors a tragedy in her recent past. "*Canterbury's Law* may prove that her gifts as an actress far exceed the credit she has been given," asserted Ginia Bellafante in the *New York Times* about Margulies' performance. "Watching her here it is almost impossible to remember that she ever let George Clooney's Dr. Noncommittal treat her like an old footstool on *ER*. In some sense, then, she has arrived."

Margulies finally found the perfect middle ground between those two polarized casting stereotypes in *The Good Wife*, a new CBS series that debuted in September of 2009. Inspired by some political scandals in which married public figures were forced to resign because of allegations of extramarital dalliances, the pilot episode of the hour-long drama begins at one of those obligatory press conferences in which the husband (Chris Noth of *Sex and the City* and *Law & Order* fame) admits to using public funds to pay for escort services and resigns from his office of as attorney general for the state of Illinois in Chicago. He also faces a trial and prison sentence. At the podium, Peter Florrick's glum wife Alicia (Margulies) stands dutifully by his side. "Viewers are treated to the sort of vicarious retribution they don't get in real life," wrote *New York* magazine's Emma Rosenblum. "Right after the opening scene, the show cuts to a hallway outside the press conference, where the stunned Alicia stops dead in her tracks. When Peter turns to console her, she slaps him across the face."

The Good Wife pulled in a sizable audience for its Tuesday-night 10 p.m. time slot, regularly beating out the offerings on competing networks for a consistent lead during the fall and winter of 2009-10. "The intelligence and the subdued emotionalism of Margulies's performance lets you know that there is no neatness in Alicia's life," wrote *New Yorker* television critic Nancy Franklin. "She doesn't always say much, and there's no edge to her words when she does. But in every situation you can feel what she's going through, and the sacrifices she's continually forced to make." CBS ordered a second season of *The Good Wife* just a week before Margulies won her first Golden Globe award from the Hollywood Foreign Press Association for her title role.

The Good Wife is filmed in New York City, where Margulies lives with her attorney husband, Keith Lieberthal. In 2008 they bought a second home in upstate New York and welcomed a son, Kieran. "My reaction would have been to" end the marriage, she replied when Freydkin asked in the *USA Today* interview if she could imagine herself in Alicia's situation. "Until I put myself in her shoes—since I've been playing her—everything has changed."

Sources

Periodicals

Daily Variety, October 25, 2002, p. 5.
Entertainment Weekly, June 7, 1996, p. 12; May 26, 2006, p. 29.
InStyle, March 1, 2000, p. 452.
New York, September 21, 2009.
New Yorker, October 26, 2009, p. 94.
New York Times, March 9, 2001; March 17, 2008; September 22, 2009.
Times (London, England), August 25, 2001, p. 40.
USA Today, September 21, 2009.

Online

"Julianna Margulies," Internet Movie Database, http://www.imdb.com/name/nm0000523/ (February 2, 2010).

—*Carol Brennan*

Matthew K. McCauley

Chief Executive Officer of Gymboree

Born in 1973. *Education:* Brigham Young University, B.B.A., 1997

Addresses: *Office*—Gymboree Corporation, 500 Howard Street, San Francisco, CA 94105.

Career

Began retail career with Payless Shoe Source, 1990s; planning manager, The Gap, 2000-01, then manager of business solutions, 2001; joined Gymboree as director of allocation, 2001-03, then vice-president of planning and allocation, 2003-05, then senior vice-president and general manager, 2005; then president, 2005—; chief executive officer and chair of the board of directors, Gymboree, 2006—.

Sidelights

Corporate executive Matthew K. McCauley enjoyed a rapid rise in the world of retail leadership, becoming the chief executive officer (CEO) of national children's clothing chain Gymboree in 2006 while still in his early 30s. A few months later, the youthful executive was also named chairman of Gymboree's board of directors. During McCauley's first four years helming the company, it expanded dramatically both in terms of retail outlets and sales, with revenues ringing in at nearly $100 million higher for the fourth quarter of 2009 over the fourth quarter of 2005. These successes have been informed by McCauley's straightforward business philosophy, which he explained in a *San Francisco Business*

Times profile in 2007: "In business and personal life, I believe you have to want to make a difference in whatever you do."

Born in 1973, McCauley began his training for the corporate world while still in high school, learning the hard way that great effort was the key to success when he was knocked down by a competitor during a high school football game. He later recalled in a speech that "his coach had yelled at him, telling him never to ease up because, 'when you ease up, you get hurt,'" according to Nicole Maestri of the *New York Times*—a lesson that McCauley would later apply to weathering challenging retail conditions and widespread economic uncertainty. After graduating from high school, the future executive attended Brigham Young University in Provo, Utah, where he earned a bachelor's degree in business administration.

Degree in hand, McCauley began his retail career with discount footwear retailer Payless Shoe Source during the 1990s. By 2000, he had relocated to San Francisco, California, and made his entrance into the world of retail management when he became a planning manager for clothing behemoth The Gap, Inc. The following year, he was promoted to manager for business solutions for the company. However, his stint in that role proved brief when he left to join the staff of San Francisco-based children's clothing retailer Gymboree in July of 2001. McCauley spent the next two years as Gymboree's director of allocation, a position overseeing the distribution of various types and quantities of merchandise to each of the chain's nationwide retail storefronts. In 2003, McCauley advanced to upper echelons of

Gymboree's corporate leadership when he was named vice president of planning and allocation. His climb up the corporate ladder continued in 2005, when the youthful vice president became the company's senior vice president and general manager. McCauley's tenure in this role again proved a short one, as he was promoted to president of the company just three months after assuming the senior vice presidency.

Six months later, the corporate prodigy gained Gymboree's top slot when he was chosen to replace sitting CEO Lisa Harper, who was leaving the job to fill the newly created position of chief creative officer. "I am honored and excited to expand my role in the Company," McCauley commented in a press release distributed through PR Newswire. "Lisa has been an outstanding partner and mentor. I look forward to her continued support in the future." The new CEO assumed control of a sweeping retail chain with nearly 670 stores operating throughout North America under the Gymboree, Janie and Jack, and Janeville brands. Gymboree's decision to promote the relatively untested executive soon proved a fruitful one, however, with the company enjoying considerable sales growth during McCauley's first fiscal quarter at its helm. In July of 2006, the company again gave McCauley's career a boost when it named him chair of its board of directors upon Harper's retirement from that role.

From the beginning, McCauley promoted a plan of ambitious growth. His efforts to expand Gymboree's girls' clothing into a wider size range, increase the line's somewhat limited offerings in boys' clothing, and launch a lower-priced line called Crazy 8, coupled with what he later acknowledged was a difficult decision to shutter the company's underperforming adult Janeville outposts, contributed to dramatic, double-digit sales increases and stock price booms over the next several months. "Brash ambition coupled with operational discipline and a strong leadership team have transformed Gymboree from a persistent underperformer into a specialty retail powerhouse that continues to exceed Wall Street expectations," observed Sarah Duxbury of the *San Francisco Business Times* in 2007, attributing much of the chain's success to the vision of its new CEO and chairman. Indeed, under McCauley's leadership Gymboree continued to reap large financial gains until a general economic downturn in late 2008 stalled its progress.

Gymboree saw its first sales decline since its CEO's installation in early 2009 as part of an overall retail downturn spurred by poor economic conditions. In response to declining sales, McCauley announced far-reaching pay cuts by as much as 15 percent for many of its corporate and managerial employees in an effort to prevent layoffs and create additional funding for sales and marketing campaigns. "When things get tough, most companies cut marketing. We've done the opposite. We didn't want to sacrifice our long-term growth strategy," explained the CEO to Marilyn Much of *Investor's Business Daily*. "We told [employees] we'd continue to invest in the future and not lay people off, and if things go well we'll share the profits," he concluded. The strategy paid off, with sales soon beginning a rebound and McCauley fulfilling his profit-sharing guarantee to the workers who had received pay decreases. By the fourth fiscal quarter of 2009, Gymboree was again reporting year-over-year sales increases, albeit smaller than the booming figures of the past.

With its retail figures improving and its physical growth undeniable—nearly 300 new brick-and-mortar stores have opened since McCauley's appointment as CEO—Gymboree's continued success seems guaranteed even in the face of adverse market conditions. At least some of this success must be attributed to its driven, young CEO, who is perhaps uniquely suited to helping the company thrive in difficult financial times; speaking in the same *San Francisco Business Times* profile, McCauley commented, "I love fixing things. I love change. In this job I get to deal with a lot of change and fix a lot of stuff."

Sources

Books

Marquis Who's Who, Marquis Who's Who, 2009.

Periodicals

Investor's Business Daily, January 25, 2007, p. A6; October 7, 2009, p. A6.
New York Times, January 15, 2008.
PR Newswire, January 18, 2006; July 21, 2006.
San Francisco Business Times, May 4, 2006; October 5, 2007; November 30, 2007; August 7, 2008; December 16, 2008; February 4, 2010.

Online

"Corporate Governance: Board of Directors," Gymboree Corporation, http://ir.gymboree.com (March 4, 2010).

—*Vanessa E. Vaughn*

Stanley McChrystal

AP Images

U.S. Army General

Born Stanley Allen McChrystal, August 14, 1954; son of Herbert J. (a U.S. Army Major-General) and Mary Gardner (Bright); married Ann Corcoran, 1977; children: Sam. *Education:* United States Military Academy, B.S. 1976; United States Naval War College, M.A.; Salve Regina University M.S.; also attended Infantry Officer Basic and Advanced Courses, United States Naval Command and Staff College, and Harvard University Senior Service College Fellowship.

Addresses: *Contact*—Fort McNair, Washington, DC 20024.

Career

Began serving in United States Army as a Second Lieutenant, Weapons Platoon Officer, November 1976; promoted to First Lieutenant, 1978; attended Special Forces School, 1978-79; became Captain, 1980; promoted to Major, 1987; promoted to Lieutenant Colonel, 1992; promoted to Colonel, 1996; promoted to Brigadier General, 2001; promoted to Major-General, 2004; promoted to Lieutenant General, 2006; promoted to General, 2009, relieved of command, 2010. Served in Operation Desert Shield/Storm (Iraq) and Operation Enduring Freedom (Afghanistan).

Awards: Defense Distinguished Service Medal, 2010, Defense Superior Service Medal (with Oak Leaf Cluster), 2010, Legion of Merit (with 2 Oak Leaf Clusters), Bronze Star Medal, Defense Meritorious Service Medal, Meritorious Service Medal (with 3 Oak Leaf Clusters), Army Commendation Medal, Army Achievement Medal, Expert Infantryman Badge, Master Parachutist Badge, Ranger Tab, Special Forces Tab, Joint Chiefs of Staff Identification Badge, all U.S. Army.

Sidelights

U.S. Army General Stanley McChrystal was Commander of the Joint Special Operations Command in Iraq, and was the top commander of U.S. forces in Afghanistan. While pursuing the war in Afghanistan, he was noted for his emphasis on protecting civilians even if it meant a reduction in engagements with insurgents; reducing airstrikes to reduce casualties among civilians; and expanding the Afghan security forces. McChrystal was relieved of his command in late June of 2010, after disparaging remarks about the Barack Obama administration were attributed to him in an interview published in *Rolling Stone* magazine.

McChrystal was born on August 14, 1954. He was one of six children of Herbert J. and Mary Gardner McChrystal. His father, a Major-General in the U.S. Army, served in the wars in Korea and Vietnam, and all of the McChrystal children grew up to serve in the military or marry a member of the military. Speaking about his father, McChrystal recalled to a reporter for the *Sunday Times* that his father lived by a strict moral code: "I never, ever saw him do a wrong thing in my whole life."

Following his family's military tradition, McChrystal entered West Point in 1972 during the Vietnam War, and quickly gained a reputation as a partying rebel, accumulating a huge number of demerits for drinking and troublemaking, and spending most of his free time doing forced punishment marches in a paved courtyard known as The Area. In one incident, during which he staged a mock attack on a school building, using real guns and fake grenades, he was almost shot by police, who thought the attack was real.

McChrystal was also considered brilliant, and was made a battalion commander at the school, one of only 12. By the time he graduated, the Vietnam War was over and, like many of his fellow West Point students, McChrystal was disappointed that he would not be involved in the action. Looking for action, he entered the Special Forces and found his niche. A retired officer told a *Sunday Times* reporter, "He's lanky, smart, tough, a sneaky stealth soldier." Many of the details of his 33-year career are still classified.

In 1986 he became a regimental commander of the 3rd Ranger Battalion where he beefed up the Ranger training regime by adding mixed martial arts training, requiring all soldiers to be trained to shoot using night-vision gear, and making soldiers take long marches wearing heavy backpacks. While in the Rangers, McChrystal himself became known for his intense personal discipline, which he continued throughout his career. He would sleep only four or five hours a night, run seven or eight miles a day, and eat only one simple meal a day. He still had a tendency to push limits and make his own rules. In April of 2004, after former NFL star Corporal Pat Tillman was accidentally killed by his own troops in Afghanistan, McChrystal recommended that Tillman be awarded the Silver Star, implying that Tillman had been killed by enemy fire; he later wrote a memo to U.S. President George W. Bush, warning him not to mention the true cause of Tillman's death. Although the truth came out, the cover-up scandal did not affect McChrystal, who was promoted to Major-General shortly after Tillman died. In 2006, two years later, another scandal broke when reporters found that detainees at Camp Nama in Iraq had been abused and tortured. McChrystal, who had inspected the prison multiple times, was never disciplined for not stopping these activities.

Perhaps one of the reasons McChrystal escaped sanctions for these scandals was the fact that he was highly successful as head of the Joint Special Operations Command (JSOC) from 2003 to 2006. The JSOC is a team of elite terrorist-hunting forces, the U.S. military's most secretive branch. McChrystal enhanced the JSOC by recruiting computer specialists and employing their skills to hunt down terrorists using the Internet, cellphones, and other aspects of technology. A Special Forces commando told Michael Hastings in *Rolling Stone*, "The Boss would find the 24-year-old kid with a nose ring, with some … brilliant degree from MIT, sitting in the corner with 16 computer monitors humming. He'd say [to the commandos] 'Hey—you … muscleheads couldn't find lunch without help. You got to work together with these guys.'" As a result of this strategy, during McChrystal's tenure the JSOC killed and captured thousands of insurgents, including Abu Musab al-Zarqawi, the leader of Al Qaeda in Mesopotamia (Iraq). Forces under his command were also credited with capturing Saddam Hussein, the former dictator of Iraq.

By early 2009, opposition to the U.S. war in Afghanistan was growing worldwide. Many NATO countries had withdrawn from the war or had sharply reduced their troop numbers, leaving the United States to pursue operations there with very little help. U.S. President Barack Obama ordered the largest increase in U.S. troops in Afghanistan since the war began in 2001, sending 21,000 troops to Kabul. He also fired the current U.S. and NATO commander in Afghanistan, General David McKieran, and replaced him with McChrystal.

As commander in Afghanistan, McChrystal aimed to implement a military strategy known as counterinsurgency, in which members of the military live among the civilians in the country and rebuild its government from the inside out; as Hastings summed it up, "Think the Green Berets as an armed Peace Corps." After arriving in-county, McChrystal assessed the situation and issued a report, which was leaked to the press. The report stated that unless the United States sent 40,000 more troops to Afghanistan, the war was in danger of failing. President Obama was deeply angered by the leak, which he saw as an attempt to undermine his authority as Commander in Chief.

As commander in Afghanistan, McChrystal stopped the custom of flying flags at half mast each time a soldier was killed, perhaps wary of the effect this had on the morale of the surviving troops. He told a reporter for the London *Sunday Times,* "A force that's fighting a war can't spend all its time looking back at what the costs have been." Meanwhile, McChrystal became known for his strong opposition to civilian casualties in Afghanistan. According to Hastings, McChrystal called his theory regarding the effects of civilian casualties "insurgent math" because he believed that for every innocent person killed in a war, ten new enemies were created. He ordered convoys to cut incidents of reckless driving, limited the use of air power, and strictly reduced night raids. When civilians were killed, he apologized to Afghan President Hamid Karzai, even when, at times, his apologies angered NATO allies. McChrystal's ire at these incidents was legendary among his commanders. One U.S. official told Hastings, "For a while, the most dangerous place to be in Afghanistan was in front of McChrystal after a 'civ cas' incident." McChrystal was praised for the humanitarian value of these actions, but front-line soldiers viewed his orders to hold their fire as increasing their own risk of being killed and they were not happy. Even when McChrystal personally went out on combat raids with the soldiers in order to show them that he had solidarity with them, they continued to grumble about this policy.

In the fall of 2009, McChrystal annoyed the Obama administration again when he remarked at a London speech that Vice President Joe Biden's counterterrorism strategy was "shortsighted" and that it would lead to a state of "Chaos-istan," according to Michael Hastings in *Rolling Stone*. President Obama called McChrystal in to a meeting on Air Force One to express his displeasure.

While in Iraq, McChrystal had difficulty getting along with Karl Eikenberry, the U.S. ambassador to Afghanistan. Eikenberry was a retired three-star general who had served in Afghanistan in 2002 and 2005, but McChrystal did not appoint him viceroy of Afghanistan, instead giving the job to British Ambassador Mark Sedwill. In January of 2010, the disgruntled Eikenberry wrote a classified cable containing a harsh critique of McChrystal's war strategy. The cable was leaked to the press, and McChrystal viewed it as a betrayal by Eikenberry.

In the meantime, however, Obama analyzed the situation in Afghanistan and in early December of 2009, at a speech at West Point, he announced that the United States would send 30,000 more troops to Iraq, close to the 40,000 that McChrystal had recommended. The surge did not have the desired effect, and the war dragged on; by June of 2010 it had become the biggest war in American history, surpassing the Vietnam War, with no end in sight.

Despite his dressing-down by the President in 2009, McChrystal continued to express disdain for the Obama administration, and in June of 2010, in an interview with Hastings in *Rolling Stone,* he sarcastically answered a question about Biden, "Are you asking about Vice President Biden? Who's that?" One of McChrystal's top aides added, "Biden? Did you say: Bite Me?" Another aide called Jim Jones, a Cold War veteran and retired four-star general, a "clown" who remains "stuck in 1985," according to Hastings. Hastings also reported that McChrystal spoke scornfully about Richard Holbrooke, the Obama administration's special representative to Afghanistan.

As a member of the military, McChrystal had violated Article 88 of the Unified Code of Military Justice, which states: "Any commissioned officer who uses contemptuous words against the President, the Vice President, Congress, the Secretary of Defense, the Secretary of a military department, the Secretary of Transportation, or the Governor or legislature of any State, Territory, Commonwealth, or possession in which he is on duty or present shall be punished as a court-martial may direct." He was not court-martialed, but he was relieved of his command by Obama on June 23, 2010. His retirement ceremony, held a month later, included a 17-gun salute, an Army marching band, and a speech by the U.S. Secretary of Defense. According to Elisabeth Bumiller in the *New York Times*, he expressed regret during the ceremony, telling the audience, "Look, this has the potential to be an awkward or even a sad occasion. My service did not end as I would have wished." However, he also joked, "I have stories on all of you, photos on many. And I know a Rolling Stone reporter," causing the audience to break out into laughter and applause. In the end, he remarked, "If I had it to do over again, I'd do some things in my career differently, but not many. I believed in people and I still believe in them. I trusted and I still trust. I cared and I still care. I wouldn't have had it any other way."

Sources

Periodicals

Rolling Stone, July 8-22, 2010.

Online

"Biography of General Stanley McChrystal," Council on Foreign Relations, http://www.cfr.org/publication/19396/biography_of_general_stanley_mcchrystal.html (July 1, 2010).
"McChrystal Ends Service with Regret and a Laugh," *New York Times,* http://www.nytimes.com/2010/07/24/us/24mcchrystal.html?_r=1&ref=stanley_a_mcchrystal (August 27, 2010).

"Profile: Stanley McChrystal," *Sunday Times,* http:// www.timesonline.co.uk/tol/news/world/ afghanistan/article6860114.ece (July 1, 2010).

"Retirement Ceremony of General Stanley McChrystal," U.S. Department of Defense, http://www. defense.gov/speeches/speech.aspx?speechid= 1492 (August 1, 2010).

"Times Topics: Stanley A. McChrystal," *New York Times,* http://topics.nytimes.com/topics/ reference/timestopics/people/m/stanley_a_ mcchrystal/index.html (August 27, 2010).

—Kelly Winters

Nick McDonell

Author

Born Robert Nicholas McDonell, February 18, 1984, in New York, NY; son of Terry (a magazine editor) and Joan (a novelist) McDonell. *Education:* Harvard University, B.A., 2007.

Addresses: *Office*—c/o Grove/Atlantic, Inc., 841 Broadway, 4th Fl., New York, NY 10003.

Career

Signed book deal with Grove/Atlantic Press, 2001; published first novel, *Twelve*, 2002; freelance journalist for *Time, Harper's,* and the *Huffington Post*, 2008—.

Sidelights

Nick McDonell became the center of a minor literary sensation in 2002 when his debut novel, *Twelve,* was published just a few months after his eighteenth birthday. A recent graduate of one of New York City's toniest private schools, McDonell wrote the tale of debauchery and violence among Manhattan's moneyed teens the summer before his senior year. "I'm very wary of fame and all that," he told Simon Houpt in the *Globe & Mail* the week it was published. "The myth of the young writer is that they write this fantastic book, often about how messed up everything is—and then they go and ... and mess themselves up and have no soul. And I'm worried about all that, because smarter people than I have done that." To his credit, McDonell went on to graduate from Harvard University in 2007 and

pen two more moderately well-received novels before embarking on a career as a foreign correspondent with a specialty in war reportage.

McDonell was born on February 18, 1984, in New York City, to Joan McDonell, a novelist and poetry editor of *Harper's* magazine. She was married to Terry McDonell, who had launched *Outside* magazine back in 1977 after serving as managing editor of *Rolling Stone* back in its cutting-edge rock-journalism heyday. In the early 1990s McDonell's father became editor of *Esquire,* then moved on to top posts with *Men's Journal* and *Us* before taking the helm as managing editor of *Sports Illustrated* in 2002. By that point, the McDonells had divorced, but shared joint custody of a beach house in the Long Island enclave of the Hamptons.

McDonell attended the Buckley School, a private boys' academy on the Upper East Side. He later went to Riverdale Country School, another elite institution, where he was elected student-body president. A talented track and field jumper, he also played football but injured himself in his junior year, then went on to play on Riverdale's basketball team through the winter season. At the close of the school year, he was ordered by sports-medicine specialists to take the summer off from any strenuous activity that would permanently damage his leg. That summer, pent up at his family's Hamptons home, he decided to write a novel. "I wrote for five hours every day because I felt like I had to have a summer job and shouldn't just be a rich kid messing around, like the one I was writing about," he told Houpt in the *Globe & Mail* interview.

Twelve's title refers to a fictitious designer drug, one of several illicit substances whose sale and usage unites a group of dissolute New York City youth over the Christmas holiday break. Its central character is a drug dealer, Mike, who has postponed college for a year. His primary customers are former classmates and other students home for the holiday break from New England boarding schools and the elite private schools in the city. Mike's mother has died, and his father owns a restaurant that keeps him occupied for the better part of the day—and night. The lack of supervision is common, as is the unlimited source of funds for drugs, alcohol, designer clothes, and even weapons.

McDonell wrote a hundred pages, then asked his father to look at them. Terry McDonell, in turn, delivered the first chapters to Morgan Entrekin, a major literary starmaker in the publishing world. Entrekin immediately bought the as-yet-unfinished manuscript for his company, Grove Press, then took it to the Frankfurt Book Fair in the fall of 2001, where he sold the foreign rights and generated some book-industry buzz about the teen writer. Published in June of 2002, just after McDonell graduated from Riverdale Country, the fiction debut became "an international best seller, the kind of child-prodigy literary splash that elicits the most splenetic watercooler hostility," asserted Ariel Levy of *New York* magazine.

Twelve earned a mixed review from the *New York Times*, whose famously rigorous book critic, Michiko Kakutani, primarily faulted its over-the-top cinematic finish. Kakutani conceded, however, that McDonell "demonstrates a visceral storytelling talent," she wrote. "He gives us a palpable sense of the privileged but spiritually desolate world that his characters inhabit, without ever condescending to them, and he gives us some digitally clear snapshots of life in the upscale ZIP codes of millenial Manhattan."

McDonell received a great deal more press attention for his publishing debut than actual reviews of the book. Some of the articles cited the fact that his editor, Entrekin, had championed Bret Easton Ellis' much-hailed debut novel, *Less Than Zero*, back in the 1980s while still an lowly associate at Simon & Schuster. That novel became a sensation in 1985, published when Ellis was just 21 and still in college. A few commentators wondered if McDonell's family connections had helped him vault over the barrier to getting published and even landed him an all-important book-jacket blurb from legendary *Rolling Stone* journalist Hunter S. Thompson, a longtime friend of his father's. McDonell acknowledged that he had benefited from his parents' contacts, but defended himself against charges of nepotism in an interview with Tim Adams from the London *Observer*. "I have to hope these people who are helping me have integrity. I mean they do. I mean Hunter Thompson would quite happily say … 'I'm not giving you a quote' if he thought the book [was terrible], and Morgan is not going to publish it just because he knows me or likes me or something." Asked in other interviews what his peers thought of the book, McDonell told the *New York Times'* Charles McGrath that his former classmates were nonplussed. "About 50 percent of the people I met wanted to be investment bankers," he said. "And most of those who did want to write were poets, so it was all pretty supportive."

In the fall of 2002, McDonell enrolled at Harvard University. He spent part of the following summer as an intern at the Bangkok bureau of *Time*, and took the second half of his sophomore year off to write his next novel. *The Third Brother*, published by Grove in 2005, also features a protagonist named Mike. The novel focuses on his college-journalism internship in Hong Kong, where his boss sends him to Thailand to report on a certain class of young, risk-taking foreigners who travel there for the country's easy access to drugs. The second section of the novel chronicles Mike's return to New York City and the aftermath of 9/11; his parents—whose marriage was already troubled—have died in a house fire, apparently set by Mike's brother. He searches for his sibling in the chaotic days following the World Trade Center disaster. The third part knits several threads together as Mike—now back at college—ponders his future.

The Third Brother was one of the first batch of novels to use the 9/11 tragedy as a plot point. Reviewing it for *New York* magazine, Levy observed that McDonell "has attempted to write a grand novel, a dark family saga complete with murders and suicides and international intrigue, and it's a stretch." She went on to fault what she viewed as an overreliance on violent events to propel the plot forward, but granted that the still-young author had some strong points as a novelist. "The pacing, for example, is perfect," Levy wrote. "His descriptions of various things—the cafés on Khao San Road; the desperate yearning of the young for independence, experience, and drugs—are visceral and stirring. At times he achieves actual unsettling suspense." Other reviewers weighed in with similarly mixed judgments. Janet Maslin of the *New York Times* considered the national catastrophe too large a canvas for an inexperienced writer, remarking that McDonell "works best as a miniaturist, despite this book's overblown scale and underwhelming leaps through time and space. When Mike isn't busy contemplating nothing, he is a keen observer of internecine sparring, even those conflicts subtle enough to leave no scars."

In November of 2008, McDonell had a lengthy piece of journalism published in *Harper's* magazine. It delved into the ongoing conflict in the Darfur region of Sudan from the perspective of one of McDonell's professors at Harvard, Alex de Waal, a political scientist, land-mine expert, and human-rights crusader. McDonell recalled that de Waal's tales of adventures in Africa while on peacekeeping missions enthralled his students, but that the teacher was also a controversial figure on the geopolitical scene for his realistic perspective in recommending solutions to deeply entrenched conflicts in remote parts of the world. "De Waal's students were often just as critical," McDonell wrote in *Harper's*. "Confronted with the unpleasant idea that their activism might be pointless or even counterproductive, one or another of them would point fiercely at him from across the table and ask, 'Well what do you *want* us to do then?' In response to this unanswerable question, he would usually return as quickly as he could to his stories, mentioning perhaps the U.S. Marine who was eaten by a shark off the coast of Somalia."

In the rest of the article, McDonell recounted his travels with de Waal in Sudan, a journey rife with surreal experiences. He mined them further for his 2009 novel, *An Expensive Education*, which features a Harvard graduate on a secretive mission to Somalia, another war-torn African nation. Again, McDonell named his protagonist Michael, and this one is a low-level Central Intelligence Agency (CIA) operative whose family connections brought him to the spy agency. Michael Teak visits a Somali village where one of his Harvard friends was born; the village, suspected as a haven for a terrorist group, has been destroyed. Further enmeshed in the drama is Teak's former adviser at Harvard, the author of a prizewinning book that praises the same guerrilla movement and has earned its author the enmity of the CIA. "I wanted to create a world that's the interface between people who have real power and the world of college kids," McDonell explained to McGrath in the *New York Times* interview about his motivations in writing his third novel. He added

that the mood of unease that permeated Harvard around the time of the 2003 invasion of Iraq by American-led forces—which happened during his freshman year—was also a source of inspiration. "I had a sense that the war in Iraq was run by people not so different from myself," he told McGrath.

An Expensive Education earned terrific reviews, including comparisons to spy-fiction masters Graham Greene and John le Carré. The long-awaited film adaptation of *Twelve*, released in 2010, fared worse with critics, despite a top-flight cast that featured Chace Crawford of *Gossip Girl* fame and rapper 50 Cent. McDonell was not involved in the screenplay adaptation. After graduating from Harvard in 2007, he finished his third novel, then spent time in Iraq and Afghanistan as a journalist for *Time* and other publications. "I'm interested in why people, particularly people who are American and want to be involved in humanitarian prevention of war, behave the way they do," he told Chelsea L. Shover, a staff writer for the Harvard *Crimson*. "I'm interested in, for example, the way the International Criminal Court was set up, and why it has been set up the way it has, and the chasm between theoretical law and real-time politics that has opened up. I'm interested in things like that, the specifics of who and why and where."

Selected writings

Twelve, Grove/Atlantic (New York, NY), 2002.
The Third Brother, Grove/Atlantic, 2005.
An Expensive Education, Grove/Atlantic, 2009.

Sources

Periodicals

Entertainment Weekly, July 12, 2002, p. 42.
Globe & Mail (Toronto, Canada), June 22, 2002, p. 1.
New York, August 22, 2005.
New York Times, June 25, 2002; August 22, 2005; August 3, 2009.
Observer (London, England), June 16, 2002, p. 3.

Online

"The Activist," *Harpers*, http://www.harpers.org/archive/2008/11/0082260 (April 16, 2010).
"Fifteen Questions with Nick McDonell," *The Harvard Crimson*, http://www.thecrimson.com/article/2009/9/15/fifteen-questions-with-nick-mcdonell-nick/ (April 16, 2010).

—*Carol Brennan*

Bob McDonnell

Governor of Virginia

Born Robert Francis McDonnell, June 15, 1954, in Philadelphia, PA; son of John (a U.S. Air Force officer) and Emma McDonnell; married Maureen Gardner, 1976; children: Jeanine, Cailin, Rachel, Robert, Sean. *Education:* University of Notre Dame, B.B.A., 1976; Boston University, M.S.B.A., 1980; Regent University, Virginia Beach, VA, M.A.P.P. and J.D., 1989.

Addresses: *Office*—Office of the Governor, Patrick Henry Building, 3rd Fl., 1111 E. Broad St., Richmond, VA 23219.

Career

U.S. Army, 1976-81; Army Reserves, 1981-97; manager, American Hospital Supply Corporation, 1980-86; attorney, Virginia Beach Commonwealth, 1989-2005; delegate, Virginia House of Delegates, 1991-2005; attorney general, Commonwealth of Virginia, 2005-09; governor, Commonwealth of Virginia, 2010—.

Member: Board, Salvation Army; board, Teen Challenge; board, Ships at Sea.

Sidelights

When Bob McDonnell took office as Virginia's 71st Governor in 2010, he continued the record of open government and trustworthy rhetoric and behavior that propelled him to the office. He promptly posted a public list of all his campaign pledges, inviting Virginia residents to hold him accountable during his four years in office. A true bipartisan politician, a rarity who even critics agree "walks the walk," McDonnell has led a public life of uncompromised devotion to getting the job done in the best way possible, regardless of personal glory or private agenda, a man who is the same both in front of and away from the cameras.

Born in 1954 in Philadelphia, the young McDonnell, oldest of five children, became an adopted Virginian as a one year old. His father, John, had been a military man since Pearl Harbor, when he joined the Air Force, and the devoutly Catholic family relocated to Fairfax County. McDonnell's mother, Emma, worked at George Washington's Mount Vernon; as an adult, he would continue to claim Washington as a personal hero. With the exception of the six years his family spent in Germany where John was called to serve his country, McDonnell remained in Fairfax County until his college years; his father still lived in the same house in 2010. The future governor learned from a young age to value family, faith, military service, hard work, and his home state, all of which would receive top priority throughout his life.

At parochial Bishop Ireton High School in Alexandria, the popular, affable McDonnell played football as a wide receiver and defensive back. A former teammate told the *Richmond Times-Dispatch* that, during one game against the legendary, undefeated team that would inspire the 2000 film *Remember the Titans,* McDonnell, who earned Bishop Ireton's only points in this particular game, "was hit so hard that he vomited on the sidelines, but he was back in the game on the next play," an apt metaphor for McDonnell's hardworking later life.

Following in his father's military footsteps, McDonnell attended Notre Dame on a full Reserve Officers' Training Corps (ROTC) scholarship. After completing his management degree in 1976, and marrying former Washington Redskins' cheerleader Maureen Gardner, McDonnell served in the U.S. Army for 21 years, first on active duty until 1981, then as a reservist until retiring as Lieutenant Colonel in 1997. While on active duty, as a medical supply officer, he had the unusual distinction of earning a listing in the Guinness Book of World Records. To receive this recognition, McDonnell led his hospital unit's 32-hour long, 93.4 mile transport of a stretcher-bound, 120-pound woman.

While on active duty, McDonnell attended evening classes at Boston University in order to earn his Master of Science in Business Administration degree, which he completed in 1980. He was subsequently hired by American Hospital Supply Corporation, a Fortune 500 company, where he would quickly move up the corporate ladder, winning promotions and transfers to such major markets as Atlanta, Chicago, and St. Louis/Kansas City.

By 1985, however, fate converged to turn McDonnell in a different direction. First, he had become disillusioned with the corporate world, unsure of how his management career offered him the chance to live out his life with purpose. Second, the hospital supply industry was in flux, and the market stability was uncertain. Third, McDonnell's GI Bill education benefits were set to expire soon, and he would not have another chance to attend school tuition-free. The timing was right for the McDonnell family to return to Virginia, and as they had enjoyed the Hampton Roads area when McDonnell was stationed at Fort Eustis in Newport News, they made their home in Virginia Beach, where McDonnell enrolled in Pat Robertson's CBN (Christian Broadcasting Network) University, which would be renamed Regent University in 1990.

On this somewhat unusual educational choice, McDonnell explained to the *Richmond Times-Dispatch* that in addition to having chosen to attend both a faith-based high school and college, "I liked the fact that ... the public-policy area was focused on looking at the traditions and history that our Founders brought to the nation." He enrolled in the master's program in public policy and communications, and when Regent opened its law school, McDonnell enrolled in that too, eventually completing both his Master of Arts in Public Policy and his Juris Doctor in 1989. He was one of three students responsible for writing the brief which was the catalyst for Regent to be provisionally accredited by the American Bar Association.

While at Regent, McDonnell worked three jobs, one in sales for the *Virginian-Pilot* newspaper, one at a Christian toy business, and the last in the Reserves. During the summer of 1988, he interned with U.S. Representative Jerry Lewis of California on Capitol Hill for the House Republican Policy Committee, McDonnell's first taste of politics. He would not be far away from public life from that point forward.

For his 1989 thesis, McDonnell wrote *The Republican Party's Vision for the Family: The Compelling Issue of the Decade,* in which he argued that government should not interfere in the traditional family unit, for example, in providing tax credits for child care. In the gubernatorial campaign, McDonnell's opponent would seize upon this document and repeatedly attempt to paint McDonnell as hostile to working women and out of touch with modern society. McDonnell's supporters, however, pointed to his working wife, working daughters—including a combat veteran in Iraq—and long political record of employing and supporting women as proof that these accusations were untrue.

He completed his law studies in 1989 and promptly joined the Virginia Beach Commonwealth Attorney's office, where he learned to advocate for victims and underdogs and to crack down on criminals who were often let off with little punishment. His legal interests remained in these areas, with particular attention toward safety and prosperity for citizens of Virginia.

Recruited to run for the Virginia House of Delegates by then-Republican party chairman Kenneth Stolle, McDonnell agreed to throw his hat into the ring. In 1990, his first bid for public office, the unknown McDonnell defeated well-entrenched Democrat opponent Glenn McClanan—who had held the office for two decades and been unopposed for the second one—winning by knocking on doors, talking with people personally, and getting out the vote. He took office in the General Assembly in 1991 where he remained until 2005; in two decades, McDonnell has not been defeated in a bid for office.

In the mid-2000s, McDonnell was ready to move on from the General Assembly, and he ran for Attorney General in 2005. He and his opponent, Democrat Creigh Deeds, a Bath County attorney, were virtually tied in the closely watched race; it would eventually prove to be the closest race in the state's long history. No winner was declared on the November election night; in fact, multiple manual recounts were called before McDonnell was decisively declared the victor on December 24, 2005. Although two million votes had been cast, McDonnell won by a margin of just 360 votes.

During his term as Attorney General, McDonnell impressed people by his careful attention to detail and his efforts to understand the position and the people with whom he would be working. Focusing on stopping child sexual predators, Internet criminals, drug dealers, and drunk drivers, his tenure was a recognized success. Not only did he keep all his campaign pledges, he saw more than 87 percent of his legislative proposals passed in the General Assembly and all nine cases argued before the Supreme Court won.

Perhaps his nomination as the Republican gubernatorial candidate was to be expected, then, when the 2008 election was approaching. Virginia governors are subject to one four-year term limit, and the previous two governors, Mark Warner and Tim Kaine, both of whom were broadly popular, were Democrats, and McDonnell seemed to be a candidate who could turn the state around. What was more surprising was the identity of McDonnell's opponent—Creigh Deeds.

Because he ran unopposed for the Republican nomination—Lieutenant Governor Bill Bolling ran for reelection instead—McDonnell was able to focus his energy, message, and money on the general election from the beginning rather than facing the pressure of fighting among the party first. While this situation certainly gave him a head start, he also made good use of the solidarity of support behind him. Although his track record was one of unwavering social and economic conservatism, he redirected attention to the issues that Virginia voters—whether conservative, moderate, or liberal—cared most about: jobs, transportation, and education. Certainly, McDonnell's appeal stretched across party lines and incorporated the sizeable, crucial independent voter base; even lifelong Democrats such as African-American billionaire Sheila Johnson, co-founder of Black Entertainment Television, publicly supported McDonnell, not only for his keen business mind but also for "the strength of his character," according to the *National Review.*

While Deeds ran a largely negative campaign, McDonnell remained positive, upbeat, and on message. Campaigning statewide for nine months to speak to people from all localities and all walks of life, the affable McDonnell won over voters with his easy manner and genuine interest in hearing about their thoughts and struggles and offering his on-point attention to debating clear, specific plans for addressing those concerns. Although his roots were in metropolitan, upscale Northern Virginia, McDonnell was no stuffed shirt, traveling in a decidedly non-flashy Ford Expedition and dressing simply in khakis and button-down shirts, he spent more time listening than talking, as had always been his *modus operandi.* As a former colleague in the General Assembly told the *Richmond Times-Dispatch,* "I've never seen him lose his temper. I think it's his military background."

Or his faith, which has never been separate from his public life. An active, devout, and lifelong Catholic, McDonnell has remained aware of the fact that a public person professing to be a Christian bears a special burden of speech and behavior. Critics and supporters agree McDonnell has never waivered in this respect, and his bipartisan spirit has played out on numerous occasions. According to the *National Review,* McDonnell "eschewed ... polarizing rhetoric. He was unfailingly upbeat, respectful, and welcoming in his pronouncements, and was dignified and polished in his performances. This persona was not contrived, but rather reflected attributes McDonnell had exhibited throughout his public career." A few months after McDonnell took office in 2010, for example, Republican Attorney General Ken Cuccinelli sent a directive to Virginia colleges that homosexual employees could no longer be protected by non-discrimination policies. McDonnell, against his private feelings about homosexuality, was quick to reassure citizens that the only criteria for employment was job qualifications. And while McDonnell has been quick to disagree with President Barack Obama, he has been equally quick to point out those areas of agreement and common ground, notably in the shared desire that every child should have equal access to good education.

Unlike the first race against Deeds in 2005, the 2009 governor's election was not hotly contested; McDonnell beat out Deeds with 59 percent of the vote. He was sworn in as Virginia's 71st governor on January 16, 2010, and proceeded to live up to the expectation that he would bring his personal and professional consistency to bear, using his business and public policy backgrounds to their best advantage to lead the state during the challenging economic climate. His cabinet picks were made on qualifications, often without foreknowledge of the nominee's political party or the nominee's background in politics. As Delegate Jackson Miller told the *Washington Post*, the cabinet included business-oriented, results-oriented people who would rally the economy and create a strong job base. "This hits on all the main themes of his campaign."

In an interview with Cal Thomas on the Web site Townhall, McDonnell said he reads several newspapers and Internet sources to keep up with "what 85 percent of the people in Virginia are reading," and he reads "the Bible and books like *The Greatest Generation* by Tom Brokaw" for inspiration. He and his wife Maureen have been happily married since 1976 and have five adult children, Jeanine, Cailin, Rachel, Robert, and Sean, for whom family dinners were a strict priority while growing up. In addition to his political activity, McDonnell has served on several boards, such as for the Salvation Army, Teen Challenge, and Ships at Sea.

Sources

Periodicals

Economist, September 5, 2009, p. 54EU.
National Review, September 21, 2009, p. 27; November 23, 2009, p. 16.

Richmond Times-Dispatch, October 18, 2009.
U.S. News & World Report, November 3, 2009.
Virginian-Pilot, March 12, 2010.
Washington Post, February 7, 2010.

Online

"Bob McDonnell Speech: Republican State of the Union Response," *Huffington Post*, http://www.huffingtonpost.com/2010/01/27/bob-mcdonnell-speech-full_n_439508.html (March 16, 2010).
"Commonwealth Conservative," *Christian Leader*, http://www.regent.edu/publications/cl/features/ss_06/mcdonnell.cfm (March 16, 2010).
"Full Interview with Governor-Elect Bob McDonnell," Townhall, http://townhall.com/columnists/CalThomas/2009/12/04/full_interview_with_governor-elect_bob_mcdonnell (March 16, 2010).
Governor Bob McDonnell Web Site, http://www.bobmcdonnell.com (March 16, 2010).
"Governor Robert Francis 'Bob' McDonnell," Project Vote Smart, http://www.votesmart.org/summary.php?can_id=5170 (March 16, 2010).
"Regent Alum Bob McDonnell Wins Virginia Governor's Race," *Regent University News*, http://www.regent.edu/news_events/?article_id=551&view=full_article (March 16, 2010).

—*Helene Barker Kiser*

Bret Michaels

AP Images/Gus Ruelas

Singer and television personality

Born Bret Michael Sychak, March 15, 1963, in Butler, PA; son of Wally and Marjorie Sychak; children: Raine Elizabeth, Jorja Bleu (both with Kristi Gibson).

Addresses: *Office*—c/o B*M*B/Poor Boy Records, Inc., 23679 Calabasas Rd., PMB 346, Calabasas, CA 91302-1502. *Web site*—http://www.bretmichaels. com, http://www.facebook.com/BretMichaels.

Career

Co-founder of Paris (later known as Poison), 1984; lead singer, Poison, 1984—; moved to Los Angeles, 1984; Poison signed with Enigma Records, 1986; released first solo album, *Letter from Death Row*, 1998; star of reality series, *Rock of Love with Bret Michaels*, 2007-08; won *Celebrity Apprentice 3*, 2010; hosted Miss Universe Pageant, 2010. Television appearances include: *Unplugged*, MTV, 1991; *Billboard Live in Concert: Bret Michaels* (documentary), 1997; *Behind the Music*, VH1, 1999; *I Love the '80s*, VH1, 2002; *I Love the '70s*, VH1, 2003; *You Rock With ...*, 2003; *I Love the '90s*, VH1, 2004; *Nashville Star*, 2005; *Rock n' Roll Fantasy Camp*, 2006; *Poison: Live, Raw, and Uncut* (special), 2007; *Rock of Love with Bret Michaels*, VH1, 2007-08; *100 Greatest Hard Rock Songs* (host), 2008; *Rock of Love Bus with Bret Michaels* VH1, 2009; *Undatable*, 2010; *Celebrity Apprentice 3*, NBC, 2010; *Bret Michaels: Life As I Know It*, 2010. Film appearances include: *The Decline of Western Civilization Part II: The Metal Years* (documentary), 1988.

Awards: BMI Cable Award, for *Rock of Love with Bret Michaels*, 2008; Chair's Citation Award, American Diabetes Association, 2010.

Sidelights

While Bret Michaels came to fame in the 1980s as the charismatic lead singer of the best-selling hair metal band Poison, his career resurged in the early 2000s as a solo artist and reality television star. Beginning in 2007, Michaels starred in a series of highly rated reality shows for VH1 including *Rock of Love with Bret Michaels* and *Rock of Love Bus*. Using his reborn celebrity, Michaels toured and recorded both as a solo artist and with a reformed Poison. In 2010, the singer made headlines for a more sobering reason. A diabetic, he had an emergency appendectomy, brain hemorrhage, and stroke all within a few weeks. Despite being near death's door, Michaels made a quick recovery and returned to *Celebrity Apprentice 3* to win the competition.

He was born Bret Michael Sychak on March 15, 1963, in Butler, Pennsylvania, the son of Wally and Marjorie Sychak. When he was six years old, he was diagnosed with juvenile diabetes and began a life-long series of insulin shots to manage the condition. The condition ran in his family as a number of relatives, including his grandmother and great grandmother, also were diabetic.

Raised in Pennsylvania with two sisters, Michaels loved music from an early age and took vocal, guitar, and harmonica lessons as a child. He was in a garage band by the time he was in seventh grade, and began writing songs. Michaels formed the band Paris with bassist Bobby Dall and drummer Rikki Rockett in 1984. The trio soon changed their name to Poison and left Pennsylvania for Los Angeles. There, the band auditioned musicians for their guitarist slot, hiring C. C. Deville.

Poison began playing gigs in Los Angeles, working hard to promote themselves in the pay-to-play atmosphere that dominated the club scene there at the time. Michaels and his band mates already had taken on the glam style that came to define pop metal, including wearing eyeliner, ratted hair, and memorable outfits. But Michaels found life difficult at times as the band lived in a run-down warehouse and struggled to make ends meet.

By 1986, Poison was signed to the Enigma record label and released their first major album, *Look What the Cat Dragged In,* that summer. It was a hit, selling more than three million copies, and included two top 40 hits, "Talk Dirty to Me" and "I Won't Forget You." Michaels particularly attracted attention as Poison reached the pinnacle of its success.

Poison's best year was 1988 when *Open Up and Say...Ahh!* was released. This album sold more than five million copies and spawned four hits, including "Nothin' But a Good Time" and "Every Rose Has Its Thorn." The latter single became Poison's first number-one hit, and the song with which Michaels would be most closely identified for many years. He wrote the song in a laundromat in Dallas after his heart was broken by a girlfriend. Poison capitalized on its success by spending much of the next two years touring, most notably with former Van Halen front man David Lee Roth.

As Michaels was touring, recording, and leading the often frenetic lifestyle that came with his career, he had to test his blood sugar up to ten times per day. He told Marcia Mazur of *Diabetes Forecast,* "The more scheduled you can be, the better you control your diabetes, the better off you are. Unfortunately, I lead an irregular life. There's no schedule. But I do the best I can."

In 1990, Michaels and his band mates recorded *Flesh and Blood.* While the multiplatinum album produced the hits "Unskinny Bop" and "Something to Believe In," Poison began coming apart at its seams during the tour in support of it. Deville was a particularly difficult personality and an embarrassing appear-

ance on an MTV show—Deville performed a song with his guitar unplugged—led to a fight backstage among the members of Poison.

During the 1990s, Michaels often found life with Poison challenging and not only because the public's musical tastes were changing. After the release of the live album *Swallow This Live,* the band and Deville parted ways, primarily because of his addiction issues as well as a personality conflict. He was replaced first by Richie Kotzen, who played on the blues-based 1993 release *Native Tongue.* The album had only had a single hit ("Stand") and did not sell well despite generally positive reviews. After Kotzen was fired for becoming involved with the fiancée of Rockett, a third guitarist was hired, Blues Saraceno, who recorded *Crack a Smile* with Poison. (It was released in 2000 as *Crack a Smile ... and More!*) In 1994, Michaels also nearly died in a car accident.

By the end of 1996, Michaels and the rest of Poison reconciled with the newly clean DeVille, and the band toured again in 1999 and 2000. In the years in between, Michaels released his first solo album, 1998's *Letter from Death Row.* After the Poison reunion tour—which was cut short after an accident forced Dall to have major surgery—the band released another album *Power to the People.* It was not particularly successful.

While Dall recovered, Michaels continued to work on various projects of his own. Poison then reunited for another studio album, the unenthusiastically reviewed 2002 release *Hollyweird,* and a tour sponsored by VH1. By this time, Poison was regarded by many critics as a nostalgia band whose best years were past. Michaels disagreed, telling Ed Bumgardner of the *Winston-Salem Journal,* "Poison is proof that chemistry works. We've had our problems, some of them bad. But we have never broken up, despite what some people think or wish."

Michaels also recorded solo albums like 2003's *Songs of My Life* and 2005's *Freedom of Sound.* Michaels went on his first major solo tour in support of *Songs of My Life.* The latter album featured a country rock sound and had a country hit with "All I Ever Needed." That album was released the same year he appeared in the 2005 season of the reality competition *Nashville Star* as a judge. Also in 2005, Michaels became active in a campaign to raise awareness about juvenile diabetes. He created controversy when he began selling a T-shirt in support of the effort. The shirt had an image of a bare-chested Michaels and the number of times he had injected himself with insulin—more than 253,000 times.

During this time period, Michaels began appearing on a number of VH1 reality shows and specials as well. He contributed his opinions to such shows as 2002's *I Love the '80s*, 2003's *I Love the '70s*, and 2004's *I Love the '90s*. In 2007, Michaels landed his own reality dating show on the network; *Rock of Love with Bret Michaels* aired for two seasons. The show was a competition in which he tried to find a girlfriend among more than 20 competitors who would accept his rock-and-roll lifestyle.

Describing his conditions for doing *Rock of Love*, Michaels told Deborah Evans Price of *Billboard*, "There were a couple of things I asked for: I had to be able to play my solo music in the show and I had to do everything unscripted. I did not want to be told who I was. And I told them the show could not be shot in my house. It's extremely over the top. A couple of the girls got in actual fights.... It's crazy."

Both seasons of *Rock of Love* were extremely popular with audiences. The finale of the first season attracted 5.4 million total viewers. The premiere of season two in 2008 attracted 3.7 million viewers. The latter numbers were up more than 166 percent from the premiere of the first season.

Michaels was not done with Poison yet either. In 2006, the band again reunited, toured, and released a greatest hits album, *The Best of Poison: 20 Years of Rock*, that was a top 20 hit on the *Billboard* album charts. A new studio album of covers called *Poison'd* came out the following year and was another hit. It featured covers of songs by artists like the Rolling Stones, the Romantics, and the Marshall Tucker Band.

While Poison continued to find an audience, Michaels was a full-blown reality star. After starring in the second season of *Rock of Love*, he also hosted *100 Greatest Hard Rock Songs* in 2008. In 2009, he starred in a spin-off of *Rock of Love*, *Rock of Love Bus with Bret Michaels*. On this show, women competed to be his girlfriend while living on a tour bus and traveling across the United States. He also continued to release successful solo albums including the 2008 compilation *Rock My World* and 2010's *Custom Built*. The former album reached the top five of *Billboard*'s independent albums chart, while the latter was a chart-topping hit that featured a controversial duet with teen star Miley Cyrus, "Nothin' to Lose."

In 2010, Michaels took part in a different kind of reality show. This time he was a contestant in the reality competition *Celebrity Apprentice 3*, competing for the American Diabetes Association. During the run of the show, Michaels suffered a series of major health-related setbacks. On April 12, 2010, he had to undergo an emergency appendectomy. Less than ten days later, on April 21, he had a massive brain hemorrhage and was in critical condition for some time. Describing the initial pain, he told Anne Marie Cruz of *People*, "I thought someone shot me in the back of the head, like a burglar. It was the most severe, instant pain I've ever felt in my life."

Michaels recovered quickly, however, and despite suffering a small stroke, was able to return in time for the finale of *Celebrity Apprentice 3*. A finalist, he won the competition and raised $390,000 for his chosen charity. He also appeared on the finals of that season's *American Idol*. By the end of May 2010, Michaels was back touring in support of *Custom Built*.

Michaels continued filming another reality series, *Bret Michaels: Life As I Know It*, which he had begun shooting before his health problems. He declined to include those issues in the family focused series, telling Dalton Ross of *Entertainment Weekly*, "Some may say my medical problems are great TV. Not for me, it isn't. For ratings maybe, but not for my soul." The series aired in the fall of 2010. Michaels also hosted the Miss Universe Pageant and had another forthcoming reality series *Rock N' Roll Fantasy Camp*, which was scheduled to air later in 2010. In 2011, he and his Poison band mates were scheduled to go on a major tour with Mötley Crüe.

Of his philosophy toward life, Michaels told Terri D'Arrigo of *Diabetes Forecast*, "I'm the king of hard knocks, but I have a really fast learning curve. If I do something wrong, I just say, 'Okay, that didn't work,' and I fix it. That's my secret to life. Don't be scared, because even if you fail, you learn."

Selected discography

(With Poison) *Look But You Can't Touch*, 1983.
(With Poison) *Look What the Cat Dragged In*, Capitol, 1986.
(With Poison) *Open Up and Say...Ahh!*, Capitol, 1988.
(With Poison) *Flesh & Blood*, Capitol, 1990.
(With Poison) *Swallow This Live*, Capitol, 1991.
(With Poison) *Native Tongue*, Capitol, 1993.
Letter from Death Row, Unity Label Group, 1998.
(With Poison) *Crack a Smile ... and More!*, Capitol, 2000.
(With Poison) *Power to the People*, Cyanide Records, 2000.
(With Poison) *Hollyweird*, Cyanide Records, 2002.

Songs of Life, Poor Boy Records, 2003.
Freedom of Sound, Poor Boy Records, 2005.
(With Poison) *The Best of Poison: 20 Years of Rock,* EMI, 2006.
(With Poison) *Poison'd,* EMI, 2007.
Rock My World, VH1 Classic Records, 2008.
Custom Built, Poor Boy Records, 2010.

Sources

Periodicals

Billboard, June 16, 2007, p. 34; July 10, 2010, p. 43; July 24, 2010, p. 53; September 11, 2010, p. 20.
Diabetes Forecast, September 1989, p. 30; November 1993, p. 18; August 2007, p. 50; July 2010, p. 61.
Entertainment Weekly, June 4, 2010, p. 18.
Houston Chronicle, May 30, 2002, p. 5.
Internet Wire, June 25, 2010.
Knight Ridder/Tribune News Service, January 19, 2005.
New York Times, May 25, 2010, p. C2.
People, April 5, 2010, p. 94; May 17, 2010, p. 70; June 7, 2010, p. 29.
Pittsburgh Tribune-Review, June 20, 2007.
PR Newswire, February 13, 2007; October 2, 2007; January 15, 2008; July 16, 2008; September 30, 2010.
Sarasota Herald Tribune, August 18, 2006, p. 4.
St. Petersburg Times (St. Petersburg, FL), June 2, 2010, p. 2B.
Times Leader (Wilkes-Barre, PA), July 3, 2000.
UPI NewsTrack, April 23, 2010.
USA Today, July 8, 2008, p. 6D.
Winston-Salem Journal (Winston-Salem, NC), October 24, 2003, p. E1.
World Entertainment News Network, December 29, 2005; November 15, 2010.

Online

"Bret Michaels Biography," AllMusic, http://www.allmusic.com/artist/bret-michaels-p105600 (December 1, 2010).
"Bret Michaels Discography," AllMusic, http://www.allmusic.com/artist/bret-michaels-p105600/discography (December 1, 2010).
"Poison Biography," AllMusic, http://www.allmusic.com/artist/poison-p5162/biography (December 1, 2010).
"Poison Discography," http://www.allmusic.com/artist/poison-p5162/discography (December 1, 2010).

—A. Petruso

Jillian Michaels

Personal trainer and television personality

Born February 18, 1974, in Los Angeles, CA; daughter of JoAnn McKarus (a psychoanalyst). *Education:* Attended California State University—Northridge, early 1990s.

Addresses: *Home*—Los Angeles, CA. *Office*—c/o NBC Studios, 3000 W. Alameda Ave., Burbank, CA 91523.

Career

Worked as a bartender, early 1990s; became a personal trainer, early 1990s; worked at International Creative Management, c. 1994-97; trainer, *The Biggest Loser*, NBC, 2004-05, 2007—; cofounder, Empowered Media, Inc., 2008; host, *Losing It with Jillian*, NBC, 2010—; also appeared in a line of DVD workouts, including *30-Day Shred, Maximize,* and *No More Trouble Zones.*

Sidelights

Jillian Michaels emerged as a star in the reality-television genre with her tough-love approach to personal fitness on NBC's *The Biggest Loser*. Since the show's debut in 2004, Michaels has become one of America's most popular diet-and-exercise gurus, with multiple self-help books, workout DVDs, and even a line of nutritional supplements sold under her eponymous high-profile brand name. Her scare-tactic training style has earned her a legion of devoted followers—and critics—but Michaels says that as a formerly overweight person herself she is merely trying to help others succeed. "Underneath every self-destructive behavior is a self-esteem issue," she told Pauline Estrem in *Success*. "Those are symptoms of a deeper problem, and understanding the root of your self-esteem issues will help you rectify that symptom."

Michaels is a native of Los Angeles, born in 1974 and the only child of a mother who, as a psycho-analyst, recognized that her young daughter's neuroses might require professional help. As Michaels recounted in a cover-story interview with *Redbook* writer Abby Ellin, she was in therapy at the age of five. "You know how kids have night terrors? Mine were really bad," she said. "I thought sharks were coming out of the drain in the bathtub. I couldn't sleep at night, every night, waiting for aliens to come." When Michaels' parents divorced when she was 12, the turmoil prompted her to turn to food for solace. Her weight ballooned to 175 pounds, and her Southern California middle school classmates tormented her for it. "It was the one thing I would look forward to," she said in another interview, this one with *People* magazine's Monica Rizzo. "If I could just get through this one friggin' day at school, I'm gonna get a bag of Cheetos and watch *Punky Brewster.*"

Michaels' mother signed her up for therapy again, and also put her in karate classes. Michaels wound up working with the same martial-arts master for the next nine years, and that experience formed the core of her own fitness-training methods. She recalled one early round of sparring when her teacher "kept kicking me in the corner. When I started crying, he kicked me again. He was like, 'You can cry all you want, but you're eventually going to fight your way out of that corner,'" she explained to *Self* writer Erin Bried. "So I cleaned up my snot, got really [mad] and fought my way out of the corner. And that's what I do to my contestants."

Mastering karate gave Michaels the skills to survive middle school, too. At age 14, "I had a second-degree blue belt test and I broke two boards with my right foot," she told Leo Smith, a writer with the Los Angeles *Daily News*. "I walked into school the next day" with an entirely different attitude toward the kids who taunted her. "I realized it was the way I carried myself that changed everything." Michaels went on to earn a black belt in karate later in her teens, but still had interpersonal relationship issues. She fought with both of her parents, until finally her mother told her to move out of the house at 17. "I had a couple of dogs and a horse, and I became very close to them," she told Rizzo in the *People* interview. "They were really my only friends."

On her own, Michaels supported herself by working as a bartender and personal trainer, a profession she lucked upon when others at the gym she worked out at noticed her fitness and grueling workouts and asked her if that was what she did for a living. She took classes at California State University—Northridge, but never graduated. In the late 1990s, she switched gears and took a more traditional job, this one as a motion-picture packaging agent at the major Hollywood talent agency, International Creative Management (ICM). She was fired after three years, and happily went back into the fitness business. "I've never been quite so unhappy in my entire life," she said of her time at ICM, according to Daniel Jimenez, writing for the Web site YoungMoney. "But it was that stint in the entertainment industry that led me to *The Biggest Loser* because one of my clients was an agent at the agency where I used to work at, so he put me up for the show and the rest [is] history."

The Biggest Loser was NBC's newest entry into the reality-television category for the 2004 fall season. Its premise was to gather a group of overweight contestants who agreed to meet at a California ranch and give their lives over to personal trainers for a ten-week period. They competed on teams, and against one another, to shed the most pounds, with the first-prize winner receiving $250,000 at the finale. "I didn't want to do it. I didn't like the name of the show," Michaels recalled in the *Self* interview with Bried, but agreed to a meeting. The producers told her, she continued, "'We're going to give you these people. You're going to run their lives.' I was like, 'Oh, my God! Complete control?' It was too tempting!"

For the first two seasons on *The Biggest Loser*, Michaels coached the Red Team, with the competing Blue Team coached by Bob Harper, another Los Angeles-area fitness professional. The contestants on both sides endured a grueling regimen, with Michaels and Harper putting them through up to five hours of cardiovascular exercise daily. But Michaels quickly gained infamy for berating her team members to work harder, even at times seeming to relish the obvious physical and mental distress they were experiencing—though a team of medical professionals was on site to monitor the contestants' health. Critics were aghast, but the compelling weight-loss statistics helped *The Biggest Loser* garner, on average, between eight and ten million viewers weekly. Commenting on the viciously competitive nature of the show's set-up, *Entertainment Weekly* writer Gillian Flynn asserted "there's a loathsome, mock-the-fatty undertow to *Biggest Loser*," and noted that the hour-long program seemed cleverly edited to create scenes that "embody the can't-do attitude that's so often ascribed to heavy people."

In defending her training methods, Michaels often pointed out that weight gain is tied to an array of mental health issues, including the effects of long-term personal stress, depression, and poor self-esteem. "I don't believe in lazy," she asserted in a *Time* interview. "I think lazy is a symptom of something else that's wrong. Five or 10 lb. over your ideal aesthetic weight is normal. But when you're looking at 20-plus lb. over a healthy weight, that's not your body's metabolic set point, nor is it a question of laziness. You need to look a little deeper." Discussing the topic in the *Success* interview with Estrem, Michaels said that long-ago sparring session with her martial-arts instructor had served as a dramatic turning point in her life, and she wanted to impart that lesson to her clients. "So one of the things that I do with the people I work with is I make them fight their way out of the corner," she said. "I don't allow them to be victims, because if they're victims, they're not in control of their own destiny."

Michaels appeared on the first two seasons of *The Biggest Loser,* in its 2004 debut and again in the fall of 2005. In each of those seasons, one of her Red

Team contestants took first place. Michaels then took some time off to complete other projects, including a promotional push for her first book, *Winning by Losing: Drop the Weight, Change Your Life,* published by William Morrow in 2005. She returned for the start of the fourth season of *The Biggest Loser* in the fall of 2007, and during the fifth season *Biggest Loser: Couples* run in early 2008, the first-ever woman to win the top prize did so after switching to Michaels' Red Team. The sixth season featured Michaels training parent-child combination teams in *The Biggest Loser: Families.* A second version of the *Couples* format, which aired in early 2009, gave the NBC show some of its highest ratings since its debut.

Michaels' training methods result in dramatic weight loss for many contestants, but health experts have criticized the tactics as unsound and the show as exploitative. Even Michaels admitted in a 2009 interview with *New York Times* writer Edward Wyatt that the lure of the quarter-million-dollar payout turned the show into a numbers game at the dramatic weigh-in sessions; by that point, veterans of the show had come forward publicly, admitting to fasting and even shunning water on the day before stepping on the scale. "Contestants can get a little too crazy and they can get too thin," Michaels admitted, adding that the medical team ran regular tests to determine if contestants were cheating by taking diuretics or other drugs, which automatically disqualified them. "That is the worst part of the show. It's just part of the nature of reality TV."

Michaels' 2009 diet book, *Master Your Metabolism: The 3 Diet Secrets to Naturally Balancing Your Hormones for a Hot and Healthy Body,* was co-authored with Mariska van Aalst and became a best-seller. In the spring of 2010 Michaels debuted with her own show, *Losing It with Jillian,* on NBC. Its premise had Michaels moving into a house with an overweight family for a week in order to help them improve their diet and lifestyle. Six weeks later, she and the cameras returned to film their follow-up. Initially, the families were unaware that she would be moving in and staging an intervention of sorts. "Day one, the families hate me," Michaels told *Redbook*'s Ellin about the tension, confessing she sometimes had to sleep in the production trailer rather than the household's guest quarters. "Day one is screaming and confrontation. Day one is Biggest Loser Jillian. Day two is a little bit of Biggest Loser Jillian, and Day three she pretty much disappears. But I have to—these families are like, 'Oh, my God, [she] is crazy!' No one knows what they're getting into."

Michaels runs Empowered Media with her business partner, Giancarlo Chersich, a branding expert who once worked for the sportswear company Tommy Hilfiger. Her venture includes an expanding array of diet and exercise solutions, including a Nintendo Wii workout (*Jillian Michaels' Fitness Ultimatum*) and a line of nutritional supplements that have been the target of lawsuits, with some claimants asserting their ingredients are unsafe. Michaels herself came under scrutiny in the spring of 2010 when she told *Women's Health* magazine that while she would like to one day become a mother, she had no plans on becoming pregnant herself and would adopt. "I can't handle doing that to my body," she told writer Allyssa Lee. Michaels was savaged in cyberspace for the remark, with many mothers excoriating her for contributing to the myth that carrying a child would irrevocably alter a woman's body, but Michaels released a statement saying she suffered from endometriosis and other reproductive-health issues which made pregnancy medically unsafe for her.

In another sensitive matter, Michaels has won praise for admitting that she has dated, and been in love with, both men and women. She has two homes, one in the Hollywood Hills and a beachfront property in Malibu, and has a penchant for motorcycles she inherited from her dad. "What I love most about my job is that it gives me meaning," she told Jimenez in the YoungMoney interview. "I don't have any proof of an afterlife so as far as I know I need to make this one count the most. I need to find meaning in it. Getting letters from wives saying, 'Thank you so much for giving me my husband back' helps me sleep at night."

Selected writings

Winning by Losing: Drop the Weight, Change Your Life, William Morrow (New York City), 2005.
Making the Cut: The 30-Day Diet and Fitness Plan for the Strongest, Sexiest You, Crown (New York City), 2007.
(With Mariska van Aalst) *Master Your Metabolism: The 3 Diet Secrets to Naturally Balancing Your Hormones for a Hot and Healthy Body,* Crown, 2009.
The Master Your Metabolism Cookbook, Crown, 2010.
(With van Aalst) *The Master Your Metabolism Calorie Counter,* Three Rivers Press (New York City), 2010.

Sources

Periodicals

Daily News (Los Angeles, CA), November 5, 2009, p. L1.
Entertainment Weekly, December 17, 2004, p. 68.

New York Times, November 25, 2009; May 23, 2010.
People, June 21, 2010, p. 108.
Redbook, July 2010, p. 136.
Self, July 2009, p. 36.
Success, May 2010, p. 46.
Time, May 31, 2010, p. 2.
Variety, May 31, 2010, p. 9.
Women's Health, May 2010.

Online

"Jillian Michaels: The Biggest Motivator," Young-Money, http://www.youngmoney.com/personalities/262_879/ (November 12, 2010).

—*Carol Brennan*

Barbara and Richard Mikkelson

Founders of Snopes.com

Born Barbara Hamel in 1959 in Ontario, Canada; married David Mikkelson. Born David Mikkelson in 1960 in the United States; married Barbara Hamel.

Addresses: *Office*—c/o Snopes, P.O. Box 684, Agoura Hills, CA 91376. *Web site*—http://www.snopes.com.

Career

David Mikkelson: Worked as a computer programmer for an HMO; launched the Snopes Web site with Barbara Mikkelson, 1995.

Awards: National Association for Media Literacy Education, Media Literacy Media Award, 2007.

Sidelights

Barbara and David Mikkelson are the Los-Angeles-based founders of Snopes, a Web site that researches and debunks urban legends, rumors, e-mail chain letters, and modern myths. Founded in 1995, the site soon become a well-known source for information; ten years later, it was visited by thousands of people daily, including reporters for television and print media. The Mikkelsons investigate anything and everything, ranging from political smears to health claims to old wives' tales to terrorist threats. By 2009, their site had more than 6.2 million visitors per month. The influence of Snopes became so prevalent that some e-mail hoaxes pre-emptively claim they have already been checked out by the site in order to discourage readers from looking for verification on their own.

The Mikkelsons met each other in 1994 on a newsgroup—a type of online discussion group—that was devoted to urban legends. He was in Los Angeles, and she was in her hometown outside Ottawa, Canada. At the time, David was a computer programmer for an HMO. Both loved reading about and researching folklore. David Mikkelson told *Reader's Digest* writer David Hochman, "Our first date was me taking Barbara to the library at UCLA to go through old magazines." She moved to Los Angeles soon after that, and they were married.

Originally, they were busy on various online discussion groups, but as David Mikkelson told Mark Glaser in the *Online Journalism Review,* after a while, "It wasn't convenient to post individual answers to newsgroups every time someone asked about an urban legend, which suggested a Web site repository of such articles, which prompted the creation of Snopes.com."

They launched their own Web site in 1995, calling themselves the San Fernando Valley Folklore Society. At the time, they mainly pursued rumors about the Disney Corporation and various urban myths that were beginning to circulate on the Internet. The name Snopes is a family name of characters from the Southern writer William Faulkner's work; it was originally used as a handle by David Mikkelson on Internet forums. Although it has nothing to do with debunking rumors, it has now become commonly used as a synonym for fact finding and debunking.

In 2001, Snopes saw a huge increase in traffic after the terrorist attacks on New York and Washington, D.C. There were rumors of future attacks, and rumors about the terrorists—for example one rumor stated that the terrorist leader Osama bin Laden owned the Snapple beverage company, among others. The site's traffic registered more than two million hits on some days. There were so many questions about the wars in Iraq and Afghanistan, as well as terrorism, that the Mikkelsons began color-coding the questions, with red for false rumors, green for true, and yellow for rumors that they were still investigating. When they investigate a rumor, they use the Internet and libraries, and they often call government agencies such as the FBI for more information. When asked why she thought terrorism and wars had engendered so many rumors, Barbara Mikkelson told Julie Hinds in the *Detroit Free Press*, "This is part of how we deal with times of tragedy. Rumors reduce the unimaginable to something you can handle." The questions that generate the largest amount of traffic on the site are ones that have to do with personal safety or threats to the public. In November of 2001, some of the popular questions were, according to Hinds, "Can garlic and oregano treat anthrax? Did [boxer] Muhammad Ali make a crack about Hitler while visiting the World Trade Center? Have seven women died from sniffing perfume samples sent in the mail?" The answer to all of these questions was "No."

By 2003, the site was making enough money through advertising to allow David Mikkelson to quit his other job and devote himself to it full-time. The Mikkelsons also hired two employees to help with the volume of questions that were submitted to the site. By 2008, with a presidential election looming, including candidates who were not well-known, the rumors were flying and the Mikkelsons were receiving more than 1,000 submissions every day as people tried to sift the truth from rumors about such candidates as Barack Obama and Sarah Palin. Often the site's answers to these questions were controversial. Conservatives accused the Mikkelsons of being liberal, and liberals thought they had a conservative agenda. Mikkelson joked to a *New York Post* reporter, "We're apparently biased in every conceivable direction." In truth, since Barbara is still a Canadian citizen, she does not vote at all, and David is a registered independent who has never worked for a campaign, or donated money to a candidate. David told a reporter for the *New York Post*, "People are just looking for things to confirm what they're inclined to believe."

The Mikkelsons' center of operations is their home, a double-wide trailer set on a hillside in Los Angeles. The home is filled with magazines, dictionaries, almanacs, VHS tapes, DVDs, encyclopedias, and hundreds of books on arcane and obscure phenomena. They have five cats, which are sometimes included in the workload. Barbara told Hochman, "David and I work at opposite ends of the house. I once attempted to send him a note by sticking a Post-It on the side of one of the cats."

The Mikkelsons are not above having fun by trying to spread rumors of their own. Once, David tried to spread a rumor that Mr. Ed, the "talking horse" featured in the 1950s television show, was really a zebra. This rumor never took off, and he told Hochman, "You'd be surprised how hard it is to get traction with one of these. The things that take off have to hit a nerve we're all thinking about."

Brooks Jackson, owner of another fact-checking Web site, www.factcheck.org, told Brian Stelter in the *New York Times*, "The 'news' that is not fit to print gets through to people anyway these days, through 24-hour cable gasbags, partisan talk radio hosts and chain e-mails, blogs and Web sites…. What readers need now, we find, are honest referees who can help ordinary readers sort out fact from fiction." However, Barbara Mikkelson told Stelter, "When you're looking at truth versus gossip, truth doesn't stand a chance."

Sources

Periodicals

Detroit Free Press, November 6, 2001.
New York Post, September 14, 2008, p. 32.
New York Times, April 4, 2010, p. B1.

Online

"For Snopes.com, Debunking the Bambi Hoax Was All in a Day's Work," *Online Journalism Review*, http://www.ojr.org/ojr/glaser/10596926.tif46.php (November 15, 2010).
"Rumor Detectives: True Story or Online Hoax?" *Reader's Digest*, http:/www.rd.com/your-america-inspiring-people-and-stories/rumor-detectives-true-story-or-online-hoax/article122216.html (November 15, 2010).

Transcripts

CNN Sunday Morning, CNN, May 2, 2004.

—*Kelly Winters*

Rebecca Minkoff

Fashion designer

Born c. 1981 in San Diego, CA; married Gavin Bellour (an actor), 2009. *Education:* Attended the Fashion Institute of Technology, New York, NY.

Addresses: *Office*—Rebecca Minkoff, LLC; 33 W. 17th St., Fl. 6,New York, NY 10011. *Web site*—http://www.rebeccaminkoff.com.

Career

Internship with designer Craig Taylor, c. 2000; unveiled own clothing line, 2001; founded Rebecca Minkoff LLC and launched handbag line, 2005; reintroduced apparel line, rolling out complete ready-to-wear collection, 2009.

Member: Council of Fashion Designers of America, 2010—.

Awards: Power Women Award, New York *Moves* magazine, 2009.

Sidelights

In 2005, New York City upstart fashion designer Rebecca Minkoff unveiled her Morning After Bag—a classy satchel large enough to carry a toothbrush and a few other personal items a woman might need if she went out on a date and ended up spending the night with her beau. The bag landed on the pages of *Daily Candy,* a trendsetting newsletter for New Yorkers and the orders rolled in.

Stephen Lovekin/Getty Images Entertainment/Getty Images

Minkoff soon founded Rebecca Minkoff LLC and rolled out a complete line of handbags, which were quickly snapped up by Hollywood starlets like Hilary Duff, Lindsay Lohan, and Bijou Phillips. Those first several years, Minkoff's business doubled in growth each year. By 2010, Minkoff was the number-one independent fashion accessory designer in the United States with her designs featured in all of the top fashion glossies.

Minkoff was born in San Diego, California, and began sewing at age eight. At 13, she designed her own bat mitzvah dress. By the time Minkoff was in high school, her family had moved to Florida and her passion lay in dancing. Minkoff attended Gibbs High School, a performing arts school in St. Petersburg. Minkoff wanted to dance, but she was so tall that teachers were reluctant to use her in their productions, fearing she would stand out too much and throw off the stage symmetry with her towering head and long limbs. Instead, Minkoff was sent to the costume department, which turned out to be a blessing. There, Minkoff learned to make patterns and construct garments. As graduation approached in 1999, Minkoff knew college did not feel right. She felt ready to pursue a career in fashion design. Her brother was friends with designer Craig Taylor and arranged an internship for her.

Just 18 years old, Minkoff headed to New York City to work for Taylor. She also took night classes at the Fashion Institute of Technology but dropped out after three semesters, she told the Web site BagTrends. "I realized I knew what to do and while I might not be the best, I know how to promote myself. You can't be shy in this industry." In 2001, Minkoff launched her own clothing line. The first line she developed included just a few items—jersey dresses with revealing cutouts, short-length shorts, and draped tops, which she peddled at area boutiques.

Minkoff's big break came shortly after 9/11 when she sent one of her hand-sewn "I love New York" tees to family friend Jenna Elfman. The actress wore the shirt during an appearance on the *Tonight Show with Jay Leno*. Leno inquired about the shirt and Minkoff was soon overwhelmed with orders. "It was my jump start," Minkoff told Megs Mahoney Dusil of PurseBlog. "My boss told me to leave my job and go start my own line because I was so busy creating this shirt." The shirt also made it onto the pages of *US Weekly*. Minkoff took her boss' advice, quit her job, and devoted her time to making the T-shirts as fast as she could—cutting and sewing them from the floor of her New York apartment.

In time, Elfman asked Minkoff to design a handbag for an upcoming movie she was getting ready to film. Minkoff had not designed any bags but tackled the project for her friend and developed the Morning After Bag. In the end, there was a delivery holdup and the bag did not make it to the set on time. Minkoff had a few samples, however, and the bag received a write-up in *Daily Candy*. New Yorkers discovered the handbag and the orders rolled in. By 2005, Minkoff had given up on her clothing line to concentrate on her handbags, which were picked up by Anthropologie, Bloomingdale's, Saks Fifth Avenue, and Searle.

Minkoff's colorful Italian leather handbags tend to be functional, yet fashionable and slightly edgy. Many are two-toned. Minkoff finds inspiration from vintage bags, flea markets, old photos, and even people walking down the street. Someone's style will catch her eye and Minkoff will wonder if she can turn that person's look into a bag. To set her bags apart from the competition, Minkoff gives each bag a unique name. There is the Makeout Mini, the Hookup Tote, the Morning After Bag, and The Steady. In 2009, Minkoff introduced a diaper bag, complete with a lined changing pad, dubbing it the Knock Up Bag.

"I knew that to stand out I wanted to relate the bags to experiences that girls have and can identify with," Minkoff told Colleen Jenkins of the *St. Peters-*

burg Times. "I'm a romantic. So they are named after the different stages of love that people go through." Each Minkoff bag also comes with a picture of a sexy man and a phone number women can call to hear a message from the featured guy. Most Minkoff clutches and handbags retail for $195 to $595. Minkoff experienced explosive sales her first several years and, by 2007, the bags had reached retailers in Japan, Russia, Canada, and France.

In 2009, Minkoff turned to social networking to connect with customers in an effort to steer them toward stores to purchase her goods. She launched pages on Facebook and Twitter and created Minkette, a social networking Web site Minkoff uses to chat with customers and promote special sales and contests among members. She also posts celebrity clippings on the site. Once, the site promoted a picture of MTV reality star Lauren Conrad with Minkoff's Studded Rocker bag on her arm. The next day, Minkoff's top retailers ordered 300 of the bags to meet demand.

In 2009, Minkoff re-launched her eponymous clothing line. She dubbed her Spring 2009 collection "Almost Famous" because the designs were based on the fashion sense of roadies who tour alongside their boyfriends' bands. The jacket-heavy collection was manufactured in New York, where Minkoff hoped to keep operations indefinitely. For 2011, Minkoff planned to roll out a shoe line. Her goal was to one day become a complete lifestyle line for women. She envisioned flagship Rebecca Minkoff stores in Los Angeles and New York.

Sources

Periodicals

St. Petersburg Times, May 1, 2009, p. 24.
WWD, August 24, 2009, p. 9.

Online

"Company Timeline," Rebecca Minkoff, http://www.rebeccaminkoff.com/timeline/ (July 12, 2010).

"Meet Rebecca Minkoff," PurseBlog, http://www.purseblog.com/meet-the-designer/meet-rebecca-minkoff.html (July 12, 2010).

"Rebecca Minkoff," BagTrends, http://www.bagtrends.com/news_rebeccaminkoff.htm (July 12, 2010).

Rebecca Minkoff Web Site, http://www.rebeccaminkoff.com (July 14, 2010).

"Stylemaker: Rebecca Minkoff," BussBuss, http://www.bussbuss.com/bussbuss_articles/articles/001607.php (July 10, 2010).

—Lisa Frick

Elizabeth Mitchell

Actress

Born Elizabeth Joanna Robertson, March 27, 1970, in Los Angeles, California; daughter of Josephine (an attorney) Mitchell; married Christopher Soldevilla (a comedian), June 13, 2004; child: Christopher Joseph. *Education:* Stephens College, Columbia, MO, B.F.A., 1991; attended the British American Drama Academy.

Addresses: *Agent*—IFA Talent Agency, 8730 Sunset Blvd., Ste. 490; Los Angeles, CA 90069.

Career

Actress on television, including: *Loving,* 1994-95; *L.A. Firefighters,* 1996; *Comfort, Texas* (movie), 1997; *Gia* (movie), 1998; *Significant Others,* 1998; *Time of Your Life,* 1999-2000; *The Linda McCartney Story* (movie), 2000; *E.R.,* 2000-01; *Beast,* 2001; *Man and Boy* (movie), 2002; *Lyon's Den,* 2003; *Dale Earnhardt Story* (movie), 2004; *Grammercy Park* (movie), 2004; *Haskett's Chance* (movie), 2006; *Lost,* 2006-10; *Lost: Missing Pieces,* 2007-08; *V,* 2009—. Television guest appearances include: *Dangerous Curves,* 1993; *Cosby Mysteries,* 1994, *Sentinel,* 1996; *JAG,* 1997; *Spin City,* 2001; *Law & Order: Special Victims Unit,* 2003; *CSI: Crime Scene Investigation,* 2003; *Everwood,* 2004; *Boston Legal,* 2004; *House,* 2004. Film appearances include: *Frequency,* 1999; *Molly,* 1999; *Nurse Betty,* 2000; *Double Bang,* 2001; *Hollywood Palms,* 2001; *Santa Clause 2,* 2002; *Running Scared,* 2006; *Santa Clause 3: The Escape Clause,* 2006; *Answers to Nothing,* 2010.

Awards: Break Through of the Year Award, Hollywood Life Awards, for *Santa Clause 3: The Escape Clause* and *Lost,* 2007; Saturn Award for best sup-

porting actress, Academy of Science Fiction, Fantasy & Horror Films, for *Lost,* 2008; Ewwy Award for best supporting actress in a drama, *Entertainment Weekly,* for *Lost,* 2009.

Sidelights

Elizabeth Mitchell's career as an actress included many speculative and fantastical elements in the projects with which she has been involved. She has added complexity to the roles she portrayed, making the characters real. Her efforts have been noticed, earning her praise and the dream position for any actress of being simultaneously cast in important roles in two popular television series at the same time.

Monico Rizzo of *People* reported that Mitchell described herself as a nerd living in Dallas with "super-frizzy hair and terrible acne". When Mitchell was a small child one of the first big words that she learned was telekinesis. Believing in the possibility that she could move things with her mind, she focused on a pencil and tried repeatedly to make it move. While she was unsuccessful in her attempts to move the pencil, her imagination was expansive and she next tried to fly. Believing what she had read in comic books and fantasy novels about characters with super powers who could soar through the air, Mitchell gave it try by jumping off her bed. She landed hard on the floor and knocked the wind out of herself. "There's the child who really believes that if you move just the right way, you can go into another world. I'm that child," she told Dan Snierson of *Entertainment Weekly*.

Mitchell's imaginative journey into the world of acting began when she was a small child in Dallas, Texas, with a trip down the rabbit hole. She made her stage debut at the age of seven in a local production of *Alice in the Looking Glass* put on at the Dallas Theater center. Her mother, Josephine Marian Mitchell, and her step-father, Joseph Day Mitchell, encouraged Mitchell to pursue acting and work in the theater as she was growing up. Mitchell attended Booker T. Washington High School for the Performing and Visual Arts, a magnet school in the Dallas area that has a specialized curriculum to foster the artistic pursuits of its students. After graduating from high school in 1988, Mitchell attended Stephens College in Colombia, Missouri, and graduated in 1991 with a bachelor of fine arts degree. To further develop her craft as an actress, Mitchell flew across the Atlantic Ocean and studied acting at the prestigious British American Drama Academy in London.

Upon returning from England, Mitchell launched her television career when she was cast to play the role of Dinah Lee Mayberry on the ABC soap opera *Loving*. The actress who played the character before Mitchell had been buxom and sexy. The fans disliked Mitchell's portrayal of the character. In addition, Mitchell was a perfectionist and aggravated the writers of the show with her questions and suggestions. After four months, Mitchell was fired.

While being fired from *Loving* was a grounding moment for the actress, she rebounded and was cast in a succession of television roles and was an understudy in Edward Albee's off-Broadway production titled *Three Tall Women*. Her first television appearance after *Loving* was a one-time appearance in UPN's *Sentinel*. After this she landed a regular role in the FOX drama *L.A. Firefighters*. She played the unhappy wife of the firehouse captain whose dedication earns him the loyalty and respect of his crew but alienates him from his wife. Unfortunately the show was cancelled after only seven episodes. Next came a role as a fighter pilot facing court martial after having an affair with a married man on the NBC drama *JAG*.

Mitchell's breakthrough role came when she was cast in the HBO drama *Gia*. The made-for-television movie starred Angelina Jolie in the title role. The story was about the tragic life of Gia Carangi, a supermodel who died of AIDS in 1986. Mitchell played Carangi's makeup artist, a woman named Linda who was also the supermodel's on-again off-again lesbian lover. This was both Mitchell's first film role and her first onscreen nudity, which included a lengthy love scene with Jolie. Mitchell described kissing Jolie to Snierson as "Pillowy and fabulous. Honestly, you got lost in her lips. It was almost overwhelming." Mitchell handled the requirements of the role with a high degree of professionalism and her performance was judged as being stand out and earned her further work.

After *Gia* Mitchell played a regular role in the television show *Significant Others* and she was cast in a supporting role in the film *Molly* which was released in 1999. She played the character of Beverly Trehare. The year 2000 was a very busy year for Mitchell. She played the character Kim Legaspi who was Dr. Kerry Weaver's lesbian lover on the popular and acclaimed television series *E.R.* She appeared in the movie *Nurse Betty* as an actress playing a soap opera character. During the filming of her next movie, *Frequency*, in which she starred with luminary Dennis Quaid, she broke her nose on the set and earned respect because it did not slow her down or tarnish her attitude. Quaid told *People* magazine about the incident, saying that "She was positive about the whole thing. She's fantastic." Her parents were so proud of Mitchell's accomplishment as an actress that they stood outside of a theater in Dallas and asked people who had seen *Frequency* what they thought of her performance. Mitchell's acting credits continued to accrue for the year when she played Linda McCartney in the made-for-television movie *The Linda McCartney Story*. She became so immersed in the role and had such admiration for Linda McCartney, who was an animal rights activist, that Mitchell became a vegetarian.

In the year 2001, Mitchell starred with William Baldwin in another HBO movie titled *Double Bang*, a thriller about a police officer trying to get revenge for his partner's murder. After this she was cast in the ABC drama *Beast*, a short-lived series about a news station.

When Mitchell was cast to play the stern principal who does not believe in Santa Claus opposite Tim Allen in the movie *The Santa Clause 2*, she finally achieved the desirable status of being a face that was readily recognized by the public. In the film, Allen's Santa Claus gives Mitchell's character a gift that she secretly wanted as a child and did not receive. This warms the character's heart and she becomes Mrs. Claus. That same year Mitchell went out on her first date with her future husband Christopher Soldevilla, an actor and comedian who taught acting classes. They went to Topanga Canyon, walked as the sun was setting, and went swimming. After dating for two years they wed in 2004.

Because of the recognition that Mitchell garnered as a result of *The Santa Clause 2*, she was able to obtain more substantial roles in such popular shows as *Law & Order: Special Victims Unit, CSI: Crime Scene Investigation, Boston Legal, Everwood,* and *House.* She also was cast in the drama series *Lyon's Den* about a law firm and the relationships that occur between the partners and clerks. It was predicted to be a hit because Rob Lowe had been cast as one of the primary actors after leaving the popular series *West Wing,* but the show was cancelled after the pilot episode aired. Mitchell was also cast in a film titled *Running Scared.* After this she auditioned for *Lost.*

Lost was an American television series which originally aired on ABC from September 22, 2004 to May 23, 2010. The series followed the lives of the survivors of a commercial passenger plane that had been flying between Sydney and Los Angeles when it mysteriously crashed. The plane was ripped into sections, but many of the passengers survived, setting the stage for the story that took place on an island in the South Pacific. *Lost* was consistently ranked by U.S. critics on their lists of top-five series of the year. The first season garnered an average of 15.69 million U.S. viewers per episode on ABC. During its sixth and final season, the show averaged more than eleven million U.S. viewers per episode.

Lost was the recipient of many nominations throughout its run and won numerous industry awards, including the Emmy Award for U.S. prime time Outstanding Drama series in 2005. Mitchell auditioned for the role of Dr. Juliet Burke. At first, the character was not planned to have a significant and ongoing part. Later, after Mitchell had been cast and was playing Juliet, the character became a more prominent part of the story. When Mitchell read for the role she was given a script for an interrogation scene in which Juliet is telling the character of Jack to quit yanking on a chain and get off of the table that he is standing on. Damon Lindelof, one of the co-creators of *Lost,* told Snierson that Mitchell played the scene as both an interrogation and "like a mommy talking to a small child who's banging his head against the wall." Lindelof found her portrayal "disquieting." Being on *Lost* propelled Mitchell's career further; she received praise for the way she played Dr. Juliet Burke. Snierson described the character as "soothing, conflicted, clinical, ferocious, and maybe a

smidge flirty, while keeping her intentions murkier than swamp water." Mitchell received a Saturn Award for Best Supporting Actress on Television and an Ewwy Award for Best Supporting Actress in a Drama for her work on *Lost.* Mitchell, and the character of Juliet, was so beloved to everyone who worked on *Lost* that the producers decided to give the character the best send off that they could. They gave her a "finale" death in which the character sacrificed herself and was blown to bits by a hydrogen bomb.

In addition to having her character on *Lost* fly apart in a million pieces and reprising her role as Mrs. Claus in *Santa Clause 3: The Escape Clause,* Mitchell also became involved with the remake of the 1983 science fiction series *V.* When she first began to play FBI counter-terrorism agent Erica Evans, the rumors were dismissed that her character on *Lost* was going to be killed and she would be starring in the new series *V.* As *V* began its first season, the media was told that Mitchell was simply making a guest appearance. Later it was announced that she would indeed being playing the lead role in the new series. For awhile, Mitchell was cast in two popular television shows at the same time, one with strange conspiracies and the other with mysterious aliens from outer space who appear benevolent at first but are not.

As of 2010, Mitchell and her husband had one child and lived in a Victorian home on an island off the Washington coast. While it is much chillier in Washington state than Los Angeles or Oahu, Mitchell enjoyed spending time with her family. When not playing the cool counter-terrorism agent, the conflicted fertility doctor with varying loyalties, or the wife of Santa Claus, she was a mother to her son Christopher Joseph. Mitchell was grateful for her success. Always humble, she was happy to be dubbed "Geek Goddess" by Snierson and to be mobbed at the annual San Diego Comic Con. Never having Hollywood hopes when she was young, it was beyond what she aspired to when she first began in the theater. Mitchell has gone into that other world of the imagination.

Sources

Books

Contemporary Theatre, Film, and Television, Gale Group, vol. 51, 2003.

Periodicals

Entertainment Weekly, November 3, 2006, p. 27; November 6, 2009, p. 30.

People, May 22, 2000, p. 101; February 18, 2008, p. 145.
USA Today, November 8, 2006, p. 2D; November 10, 2009, p. 7D.

Online

Biography Resource Center Online, Gale, 2010.

"Elizabeth Mitchell," Internet Movie Database, http://www.imdb.com/name/nm0593310/ (December 26, 2010).
"Elizabeth Mitchell," Yahoo Movies, http://www.movies.yahoo.com/movie/contributor/18003112.tif55/bio (November 12, 2010).

—*Annette Bowman*

Scott Moir and Tessa Virtue

Scott Halleran/Getty Images

Ice dancers

Born Scott Moir, September 2, 1987, in London, Ontario, Canada; son of Joe (a drug company employee) and Alma (a skate instructor) Moir. Born Tessa Virtue, May 17, 1989, in London, Ontario, Canada; daughter of Jim (an attorney) and Kate Virtue.

Addresses: *Contact*—Arctic Edge Arena, 46615 Michigan Ave., Canton, MI 48188. *Contact*—Skate Canada National Office, 865 Shefford Road, Ottawa, Ontario, Canada K1J 1H9. *Home*—Canton, MI. *Web site*—http://virtuemoir.com.

Career

Moir: Began skating at the Ilderton Skating Club, Ontario, Canada; paired with Virtue as ice-dance partner, 1997; trained with Virtue at the Kitchener-Waterloo Skating Club, late 1990s; made debut at ISU World Championships, 2007; competed in Winter Olympics, Vancouver, Canada, 2010. Virtue: Began skating at the Ilderton Skating Club, Ontario, Canada; paired with Moir as ice-dance partner, 1997; trained with Moir at the Kitchener-Waterloo Skating Club, late 1990s; made debut at ISU World Championships, 2007; underwent leg surgery for chronic exertion compression syndrome, 2008; competed in Winter Olympics, Vancouver, Canada, 2010.

Awards: First place, Western Ontario Sectionals (junior), 2003; first place, Canadian Championships (junior), 2004; second place, Junior Grand Prix Final, 2004-05; silver medal, ISU (International Skat-

ing Union) World Junior Championships, 2005; first place, Junior Grand Prix Final, 2005-06; third place, Canadian Championships, 2006; third place, Four Continents Championship, 2005-2006; gold medal, ISU Junior World Championships, 2006; second place, Canadian Championships and Skate Canada International, 2006-07; third place, Four Continents Championship, 2006-2007; first place, Four Continents Championships, Canadian Championships and Skate Canada International, 2007-08; silver medal, ISU World Championships, 2008; second place, NHK Trophy, 2008; first place, Canadian Championships, 2009; second place, Four Continents Championships, 2009; bronze medal, ISU World Championships, 2009; first place, Skate Canada International, 2009-10; first place, Canadian Championships, 2010; gold medal, Winter Olympics, Vancouver, Canada, 2010; gold medal, ISU World Championships, 2010.

Sidelights

During the 2010 Winter Olympics held in their Canadian homeland, ice dancers Tessa Virtue and Scott Moir won gold, becoming the youngest ice-dance gold medalists in Olympic history and the first North Americans to win the event since its inception 30 years before. Virtue and Moir bested their U.S. archrivals and training mates Meryl Davis and Charlie White by nearly six whole points, flawlessly executing their high-risk lifts and amusing the crowd with their on-ice chemistry. One month later, Virtue and Moir captured their first global ice-dance title at the world championships in Turin, Italy, beating their U.S. archrivals by 1.40 points.

Because they were so young, the dazzling duo took the ice-dance world by surprise in 2010, skating with a maturity found in more tenured skaters. "People talk about us coming up the ranks quickly, and I guess that's because I suppose we are 20 and 22," Virtue told the *Globe and Mail*'s Beverley Smith shortly after their Olympic victory. "But it's been 13 years in the making. It's been a long road for us, and we've worked hard for this. We have a lot of experience. I think that helps us with maturity on the ice."

The Olympic champions began skating together in 1997: Virtue was seven; Moir was nine. They met at the Ilderton Skating Club in Ontario, Canada, where they were united by Moir's aunt Carol, a former competitive skater who coached both Moir and Virtue for singles competitions. Moir's aunt told *Maclean's* that Virtue was graceful, while her nephew was quite boisterous, so she figured the two would complement each other well.

Virtue was not Moir's first partner, he confessed to Lori Ewing of the *Hamilton Spectator*. "I had one partner before. But I screwed up the steps, and then she didn't want to skate with me again. I was eight. Then I found Tessa, and I screwed up the steps in the first competition and she stayed with me and that's when I knew I'd found one."

The youngest of four children, Virtue was born on May 17, 1989, in London, Ontario, Canada, to Jim and Kate Virtue. Initially interested in dance, Virtue began studying ballet at the age of three but decided to take up skating before a class field trip to a local arena because she feared she might be the only one stumbling around the ice. Once she started skating, she could not stop and by 1994, Virtue had joined the Ilderton Skating Club.

Moir, born on September 2, 1987, in London, Ontario, Canada, hails from a skating family. His mother, Alma, and her twin sister both worked as figure-skating instructors when Moir was young. Moir's father, Joe, coached hockey and worked for a drug company. Moir grew up in Ilderton in a house that backed to the local rink. Both of his older brothers skated competitively. Moir began skating because he wanted to play hockey but once he was paired with Virtue, his aspirations changed.

Soon, the couple surpassed the coaching of the Ilderton Skating Club and began training at the Kitchener-Waterloo Skating Club with veteran coach Paul McIntosh, who helped them improve their skating skills, carriage, and style. The families took turns driving the carpool, waking at 4 a.m. to make the more than 60-mile drive so the kids could be on the ice by 6:30 a.m. By the time they were teens, Virtue and Moir had moved to Kitchener to train, skating from 6 to 10 a.m. and then pushing through the school doors just as second period began.

Hoping to compete on the international level, Virtue and Moir relocated to Canton, Michigan, to train with Russian ice-dance coaches Marina Zoueva and Igor Shpilband. Virtue was 15. Her family purchased a home in Michigan and her mother quit her job with the Upper Canada Law Society so she could accompany Virtue; her father stayed behind in Canada.

When Virtue and Moir arrived in Michigan, they impressed their new coaches with their skating skills and raw talent. However, the new coaches realized they needed help with their lifts, so Virtue and Moir began training with acrobats and gymnasts from Cirque du Soleil. The hard work paid off and in 2006, the teenage skaters won the ISU (International Skating Union) Junior World Championships, the first Canadians to do so. In 2007, the teenagers made their debut at the senior world championships, finishing sixth. The following year, they won silver.

By now, Virtue and Moir were dreaming of the 2010 Olympics. Their goal was to make the Olympic team after being passed over in 2006. Their dream, however, hit a snag when Virtue came down with chronic exertion compression syndrome, which caused constant pain in her shins. Caused by overuse, the condition results in pressure building up in pockets within the nerves and muscles. Doctors gave Virtue two choices—quit skating or have surgery. "She thought about it for about two seconds," Kate Virtue told the *Globe and Mail*'s Gary Mason. "And then she said, 'What time can we do it?' She was 18 1/2 at the time and I remember it really bothering me because she had already sacrificed so much by then. I said to her, 'You don't have to do this, Tessa.' And she said: 'I do if I want to get to the Olympics.'"

Virtue had surgery in October of 2008. The procedure involved slicing open the sheath that surrounds the muscles in her lower legs, allowing more room for the muscle to expand. During her rehabilitation, she was not allowed to skate for two months, so in the fall of 2008, when Virtue and Moir should have been preparing for the upcoming season, they were separated. Moir began working on their routine using a sandbag or hockey stick for a partner, while Virtue recuperated. They also had to cancel an appearance at the Grand Prix, an international competition.

In an interview with Ewing—of the *Hamilton Spectator*—Moir discussed their painful time apart. "When you see someone every day for nine hours a day, it's a bit different. I was easily frustrated some days because I didn't have Tessa there. But at the same time, there was no lack of motivation 13 months out from the Olympics. To be out there and watching all these guys compete at the Grand Prixs kind of boiled my blood … so it wasn't that hard to stay motivated."

Virtue and Moir returned to the ice together to compete in the Canadian Championships in January of 2009. Virtue had been skating for only six weeks, yet the couple won the opening event—the compulsory dance portion—on their way to a gold in the competition. In February of 2009, they skated in the Four Continents Figure Skating Championship in Vancouver, marking their return to international competition. The duo took silver, with Virtue being treated by a medic after every skate. A month later they took bronze at the ISU World Championships doing a cutting-edge free skate to Pink Floyd.

Their goal for the year, though, was to prepare for the upcoming Winter Olympics in February of 2010, which would be held in Vancouver, Canada. Their routine for 2009-10 included a free dance to Gustav Mahler's *Symphony No. 5*. They skated their original dance to "Farrucas," a classic flamenco number by Pepe Rumero. The routine included the couple's trademark move—the "goose." The goose is a breathtaking, hands-free lift where Virtue places her knee on Moir's hunched shoulder blades while balancing on his back. At the release of the move, she free falls into his arms, while rotating. Initially, the couple was going to call it the eagle, but decided that was too American a symbol for a Canadian-created move, so they settled on goose.

In Vancouver, the competitors skated the compulsory dance first, followed by their original dance and then their free dance. Each event was held on a different night. Going into the free dance, Moir and Virtue were in first place with 111.15 points, followed by Americans Davis and White, who had

108.55 points. Davis and White skated ahead of the Canadians on the final night of the competition and nailed their routine, earning 107.19 points. Virtue and Moir knew the gold was in reach, but that they would have to execute a flawless program to secure a win. Though they should have been nervous, Moir told the *Globe and Mail*'s Smith that they were unexpectedly calm when they took the ice. "When the [free dance] music started, I felt so relaxed and we felt so together. In every moment we felt so confident, we knew it was ours. We knew that we had to take it."

And take it they did. During their four-minute free-dance routine, the Canadian couple brought the crowd to its feet with their unmatched display of athleticism and artistry. Virtue and Moir earned 110.42 points, finishing 5.83 points ahead of Davis and White. Afterward, Moir went back onto the rink in his street shoes and kissed the Olympic rings. Speaking to Mason of the *Globe and Mail*, Virtue's dad summed up his family's wondrous jubilation this way: "What are the odds of all the planets aligning at the moment they needed to peak in their sport at such a young age, in front of a Canadian crowd, at their first Olympics, and they nail it?"

A month later, the couple headed to Turin, Italy, to compete in the World Championships—an event they had yet to win. Once again, their biggest threat lay with the Americans, Davis and White. Though the couples are ice-dance rivals, they train together in Michigan, which makes them work harder. Speaking to the *Toronto Star*'s Rosie Dimanno, Virtue put it this way: "We're fortunate enough to train with Meryl and Charlie so we can compare ourselves on a daily basis. That really pushes us in training, seeing them do a run-through. There's that kind of battle."

As the World Championships got under way, Virtue and Moir faced a tough decision when rumors surfaced that the technical panel of judges might rule the goose illegal because of too many rotations, though no judges had balked at it during the entire Grand Prix season, or even at the Olympics. A few hours before the original dance competition, Virtue and Moir scrapped the lift from their routine because they did not want to risk a technical deduction.

Going into the free dance the last day of competition, Virtue and Moir held a two-point lead over Davis and White. They earned 110.03 during the free skate, but Davis and White notched a season-best score of 110.49 skating to the *Phantom of the*

Opera. Virtue and Moir lost the free skate medal by .46 points, but held on for the gold awarded to the pair with the most cumulative points. Virtue and Moir won with 224.43 points, besting the Americans by 1.40 points. Had they incorporated the goose into the original dance and received a deduction, they likely would not have won the world championships.

After winning the world championship, the couple took about a week off, then headed to Japan to appear in several Stars on Ice shows, using their free dance of Symphony No. 5 as an exhibition piece. They were also scheduled to appear in a cross-Canada tour with Stars on Ice through the spring. They planned to compete through at least the 2010-11 season and indicated they might hold on until the 2014 Winter Olympics in Sochi, Russia.

Sources

Periodicals

Globe and Mail (Canada), February 24, 2010, p. A1; March 2, 2010, p. O16; March 27, 2010, p. S8.

Hamilton Spectator (Ontario, Canada), January 16, 2009, p. SP2.

Toronto Star, February 5, 2010, p. S1; February 24, 2010, p. S3; March 26, 2010, p. S8; March 27, 2010, p. S1.

Online

"About Us," Tessa Virtue and Scott Moir Official Site, http://virtuemoir.com/about_us.php (June 3, 2007).

"Canada's Sweethearts: Tessa Virtue and Scott Moir," *Maclean's,* http://www2.macleans.ca/2010/03/01/canada0.000000E+002%99s-sweethearts/ (April 28, 2010).

"Scott Moir—Biography," NBC Olympics, http://www.nbcolympics.com/athletes/athlete=2382/bio/index.html (April 28, 2010).

"Tessa Virtue—Biography," NBC Olympics, http://www.nbcolympics.com/athletes/athlete=2381/bio/index.html (April 28, 2010).

—*Lisa Frick*

Greg Mortenson

Courtesy of Central Asia Institute

Philanthropist and author

Born in 1957, in MN; son of Dempsey (a missionary) and Jerene (a missionary and educator) Mortenson; married first wife (divorced); married Tara Bishop (a clinical psychologist); children: (second marriage) Khyber, Amira. *Education:* University of South Dakota, undergraduate degree, 1983.

Addresses: *Office*—Central Asia Institute, PO Box 7209, Bozeman, MT 59771. *Web site*—http://www. gregmortenson.com/, http://twitter.com/gregmort enson.

Career

Served in U.S. Army, 1977-79; worked as an emergency room nurse by early 1990s; inspired to build school in Korphe, Pakistan, 1993; founded Central Asia Institute, 1996; published first book, *Three Cups of Tea: One Man's Mission to Fight Terrorism and Build Nations—One School at a Time*, 2006; published *Stones into Schools: Promoting Peace with Books, Not Bombs, in Afghanistan and Pakistan*, 2009.

Awards: Commendation Medal, U.S. Army, 1975; David Brower Conservation Award, American Alpine Club, 1998; Peacemaker Award, Montana Community Medication Center, 2002; Golden Piton Award, *Climbing Magazine,* 2003; Vincent Lombardi Champion Award, 2003; Peacemaker of the Year Award, Benedictine Monks (Santa Fe, NM), 2003; Outdoor Person of the Year, *Outdoor Magazine,* 2003; Salzburg Seminar fellow, 2003; Freedom Forum Spirit Award, National Press Club, 2004; Jeanette

Rankin Peace Award, Institute for Peace, 2004; Anti-Terror Award, *Men's Journal,* 2005; Humanitarian of the Year Award for Montana, Red Cross, 2005; Alumni Achievement Award, University of South Dakota, 2006; Golden Fleur-de-lis Award, Comune Firenze, Italy, 2006; Paul Harris Award for Promoting Friendly Relations Among People, Rotary International, 2007; Award for Excellence in Mountain Community Service, Mountain Institute, 2007; Dayton Literary Peace Prize, 2007; Kiriyama Prize for nonfiction for *Three Cups of Tea: One Man's Mission to Fight Terrorism and Build Nations—One School at a Time,* 2007; Star of Pakistan, 2009.

Sidelights

The co-founder of the Central Asia Institute, philanthropist and activist Greg Mortenson has built a number of schools in Pakistan, Afghanistan, and other countries in Central Asia to improve the lives of remote villagers. Especially concerned with the education of girls and the positive effects such learning has on society as a whole, he also promoted community health and clean water projects. Mortenson wrote two best-selling books about his life and work, including *Three Cups of Tea: One Man's Mission to Fight Terrorism and Build Nations—One School at a Time* and *Stones into Schools: Promoting Peace with Books, Not Bombs, in Afghanistan and Pakistan.* As Donna Healey explained in an article on the Associated Press State & Local Wire, "In the fight against terrorism in Central Asia, he is convinced books will create more lasting change than bombs."

He was born in 1957 in Minnesota, the son of Dempsey and Jerene Mortenson. His parents were Lutheran missionaries who helped improve the lives of others. His father co-founded a teaching hospital in Tanzania, the Kilimanjaro Christian Medical Center, while his mother founded the International School Moshi. Mortenson spent the bulk of his childhood in Tanzania, on the slopes of Kilimanjaro. He lived there from 1958 to 1973.

As a child, Mortenson was already sensitive to the needs and suffering of others. His sister, Sonja Rauen, told Lisa Prue of the *Omaha World Herald,* that she saw him sharing cookies with beggars near their village when he was seven years old. Rauen marveled, "He didn't just give the beggar a cookie. He sat down with him and talked to him." Adventure was also key to his childhood. Mortenson climbed Mount Kilimanjaro when he was eleven years old.

Returning to Minnesota with his family in the early 1970s, Mortenson graduated from Alexander Ramsey High School (later known as Roseville Area High School) in 1975. Two years later, Mortenson joined the U.S. Army. He spent two years in the service, primarily stationed in Germany. For his service, Mortenson received the Army Commendation Medal. He then went back to the United States and entered the University of South Dakota. Mortenson earned his undergraduate degree in 1983. Moving to San Francisco, he worked as an emergency room nurse.

Mortenson's beloved sister, Christa, suffered from severe epilepsy her whole life and died from a seizure in July of 1992. The event profoundly affected Mortenson who climbed K2—located in Pakistan and the second highest mountain in the world—in 1993 to honor his sister's memory. Failing to reach the summit because a snowstorm blocked his group 1,000 feet from the top, he later became separated from them. Mortenson then got lost and became ill after the 78-day expedition.

Mortenson found shelter and support from the local Balti people in the remote village of Korphe. As explained to Sharon Schmickle of the Minneapolis *Star Tribune,* "They gave me everything they had—yak butter, tea, everything. They sat by my side and

fluffed up my mat." There, he also observed the primitive way the children were educated. All 84 students sat in the dirt of an orchard, writing with sticks in the sand and sharing six slate chalkboards. They also shared a teacher—who was paid a dollar a day—with another village. Mortenson explained to Richard Halicks of the *Atlanta Journal-Constitution,* "It was at that moment, when I saw those kids, I thought of my sister. I felt their fierce desire, their determination."

The state of education there changed Mortenson. He told the *Star Tribune*'s Schmickle, "I realized I hadn't come there to climb a mountain. I had come there to help these kids get a school." Mortenson promised to have a school built in the village for the children. The promise changed his life as he made the promotion of education, especially for girls, in Pakistan (and later other parts of Central Asia) the focus of his life.

After returning to the United States, Mortenson sold everything he had—a car and climbing gear—and cashed out a retirement account, which gave him about two thousand dollars. He continued to solicit donations for three years until he had enough to build the school. Some of the funds came from elementary school students at his mother's school in Wisconsin. In 1994, they gave over 62,000 pennies to help Mortenson build the school, prompting him to found the Pennies for Peace program to encourage the philanthropic efforts of children.

Returning to Korphe, Mortenson faced continued obstacles. Local officials proved difficult but Muslim clerics were more problematic because Mortenson wanted to educate girls as well as boys. When the school was being built, the villagers carried lumber for roof beams on their backs for 18 miles. Villagers also built the school themselves, often using locally available materials. When Mortenson's school opened, it served both sexes.

Continuing his mission, Mortenson founded the Central Asia Institute, based in his home city of Bozeman, Montana, in 1996 so he could build more schools. Because he lacked knowledge of fundraising early on, the financial support of Jean Hoerni, a physicist and pioneer in microchip technology, proved vital in establishing the foundation and funding the building projects. Each school cost approximately $12,000 to $25,000. The Central Asia Institute also played a hand in building water systems and founding community health programs. Pennies for Peace became a program of the institute after its founding.

One key point of Mortenson's school building project was a focus on education for girls. Each school built by the institute had an agreement with the village education committee in which the enrollment of girls increased by ten percent each year. Citing many studies, Mortenson believed that when girls reach at least a fifth-grade education level, the birthrate drops, the mortality rate of infants declines, and there is an improvement in quality of life overall for the people in the community as a whole. He explained to Healey of the Associated Press State & Local Wire, "You can hand out condoms, you can build roads, you can put in electricity, but, until the girls are educated, society really won't improve."

Sometimes Mortenson's efforts were not appreciated as he was kidnapped by the Taliban for eight days in a tribal area of Pakistan in 1996. After the September 11, 2001, terrorist attacks, Mortenson received threats from Americans because he was educating Muslim children. At various points, he was also investigated by the CIA and was the target of fatwehs from Islamic mullahs. Still, Mortenson visited 60 to 80 project sites per year and usually spent about six months of the year in Central Asia while his family—wife Tara Bishop and their two children—remained at home in Bozeman.

In the months after the 9/11 attacks in the United States, Mortenson was one of the few foreigners allowed in refugee camps located in Pakistan for Afghans fleeing war. He was able to observe their troubling condition first hand. He told Cynthia Boyd of the *St. Paul Pioneer Press*, "When I go there, I cannot eat or sleep for a couple of days. There is starvation. They have come off the trail of tears."

By 2003, the Central Asia Institute had an annual budget of $250,000, garnered from 1,600 donors, many of whom were women's groups who supported Mortenson's efforts to educate girls. The group had built 28 schools, primarily in northern Pakistan, which served 8,200 students by this time. The nonprofit also provided support for schools which served Afghan refugees. (After the terrorist attacks of September 11, the group began working in Afghanistan supporting and building schools there.) Mortenson continued to face personal danger while in the region as well. In 2003, Mortenson found himself in the middle of a firefight between Afghan warlords. He escaped by hiding in a truck full of animal hides that was headed for a leather-tanning factory.

As Mortenson continued to work with the Central Asia Institute, he published his first book, which told the story of his climb, the founding of the Central Asia Institute, and many of his early and personal challenges. Written with David Oliver Relin, a journalist, and published in 2006, *Three Cups of Tea: One Man's Mission to Fight Terrorism and Build Nations—One School at a Time* eventually reached number one on the *New York Times* best-seller list. In the book, Mortenson fully admitted his faults as well, admitting to Relin that he was often late for appointments, disorganized, and sometimes considered unreliable.

Of this aspect of his personality, Mortenson explained to Schmickle of the Minneapolis *Star Tribune*, "I said at the beginning that as great as some people think this work is, I have angered, disappointed and hurt a lot of people. I wrote [David Oliver Relin] a list, and I said I would like you to contact my critics.... Most of them didn't want to talk to him. My blessing is that I am cross-cultural, able to work with this society over there. But on the other hand, my way of dealing with things really drives a lot of people nuts.... You have to look at the results, I guess."

The runaway success of *Three Cups of Tea* changed Mortenson's life as thousands showed up for his book signings and lectures. The time he spent speaking to audiences in the United States left him exhausted and suffering from depression and panic attacks. Mortenson was even unable to play a direct role in the completion of a school in a remote area ten years in the making. Yet he continued to work for his Central Asia Institute and push through into new areas.

By 2009, Mortenson helped establish or provided support for at least 131 schools in rural areas of Afghanistan, Pakistan, Kyrgyzstan, and Mongolia. These schools educated 58,000 students, including 44,000 girls. For his efforts and much time spent in these regions (72 months in the field between 1993 and 2009), he earned the trust of many locals, including tribal chiefs and Islamic leaders as well as government officials. For Mortenson's efforts, several members of the House of Representatives nominated him for the Nobel Peace Prize in 2008 and 2009.

Also in 2009, Mortenson published several more books, including a picture book children's version of *Three Cups of Tea* titled *Listen to the Wind: The Story of Dr. Greg and "Three Cups of Tea."* He also put out a new book, *Stones into Schools: Promoting Peace with Books, Not Bombs, in Afghanistan and Pakistan.* This memoir which explains how the Central Asia Institute expanded in Afghanistan, offers his personal opinion on many leaders and ineffective government programs, muses on his personal sacrifices, and emphasizes the power of education to profoundly change lives. Like *Three Cups of Tea*, *Stones into Schools* was a best seller.

While Mortenson was proud of his work, he knew that it came at a cost to his health and for his own family, which included two young children. He told Sarah Hampson of the *Globe and Mail* in 2010, "I've been gone from my children for half their lives. I didn't get to see them learn to tie their shoes for the first time or the first time they rode their bicycles. I get criticized a lot." Yet, Hampson wrote, "nothing deters him from his mission."

Selected writings

Nonfiction

(With David Oliver Relin) *Three Cups of Tea: One Man's Mission to Fight Terrorism and Build Nations—One School at a Time*, Viking (New York City), 2006.

Stones into Schools: Promoting Peace with Books, Not Bombs, in Afghanistan and Pakistan, Viking (New York City), 2009.

For children

Listen to the Wind: The Story of Dr. Greg and "Three Cups of Tea," Dial (New York City), 2009.

Sources

Books

Marquis Who's Who, Marquis Who's Who, 2009.

Periodicals

Associated Press State & Local Wire, January 22, 2003.
Atlanta Journal-Constitution, April 16, 2006, p. 1F.
Globe and Mail (Canada), January 25, 2010, p. L1.
Houston Chronicle, February 12, 2010, p. 6.
New York Times, December 10, 2009, p. C1.
Omaha World Herald (NB), April 6, 2003, p. 1E.
Star Tribune (Minneapolis, MN), July 12, 2004, p. 7A; March 13, 2006, p. 11A.
St. Paul Pioneer Press (MN), October 22, 2001, p. A1.
Washington Post, February 11, 2009, p. C12.

Online

"Biography," Greg Mortenson Official Web site, http://www.gregmortenson.com/biography/ (March 6, 2010).
Contemporary Authors Online, Gale, 2010.

—*A. Petruso*

Jim Muller

Jim Bourg/Reuters/Landov

Physician and activist

Born James Edward Muller, February 6, 1943, in Lubbock, Texas; married Kathleen. *Education:* Notre Dame University, B.S., 1965, L.L.D, 1986; Johns Hopkins University, M.D., 1969; Kings College, D.S., 1994.

Addresses: *Office*—Voice of the Faithful, P.O. Box 423, Newton Upper Falls, MA 02464.

Career

Intern, Johns Hopkins Hospital, 1969-70, then resident, 1972-73; junior associate in medicine, Peter Brent Brigham Hospital, Boston, MA, 1976-81; founder, International Physicians for the Prevention of Nuclear War, 1980; associate in medicine, Brigham and Women's Hospital, Boston, MA, 1981-82, then associate physician, 1982-89; chief of cardiovascular division and co-director of institutional prevention of cardiovascular disease, Deaconess Hospital, Boston, MA, 1989-96; chief of cardiovascular division, University of Kentucky Medical Center, 1996—; founded Voice of the Faithful, 2002; professor of medicine, Harvard Medical School; associate director of the Center for Integration of Medicine and Innovative Technology, Massachusetts General Hospital.

Awards: Nobel Peace Prize (for International Physicians for the Prevention of Nuclear War), 1985; honorary doctor of laws degree, Notre Dame University, 1986.

Sidelights

Activist and physician Jim Muller has founded two groups: International Physicians for the Prevention of Nuclear War (IPPNW), which won a Nobel Peace Prize in 1985, and Voice of the Faithful, a response to the clergy abuse scandal within the Catholic Church. He is also a cardiologist and associate director at the Center for Integration of Medicine and Innovative Technology at Massachusetts General Hospital.

Muller grew up in a Catholic family—his aunt was a nun, and an uncle was a priest. When it came time for him to go to college, he chose the University of Notre Dame, a well-known Catholic university that also had an excellent science program. After graduating from Notre Dame, Muller entered medical school, where he read a book that made a deep impression on him. The book, *Sanity and Survival* by Jerome Frank, analyzed the Cold War and the constant threat of imminent nuclear destruction of the planet and humanity. Muller decided that in order to heal the dangerous rift between the Soviet Union and the United States, communication was necessary. He had studied Russian at Notre Dame (following a suggestion by his father after the Russians launched Sputnik, the first artificial satellite of

Earth), so he enrolled in an exchange program that would allow him to study in the Soviet Union for six months. While there, he found that Russian doctors were as opposed to the arms race as American ones were. He mulled this over until 1980, when he joined with doctors from around the world to form International Physicians for the Prevention of Nuclear War. They aimed to educate the public about the devastating, unwinnable consequences of nuclear war and to make the "option" of nuclear war unacceptable. Although Muller resigned from his position as the group's secretary in 1984, the group went on to win the Nobel Peace Prize in 1985.

Meanwhile Muller had begun his full-time career is as a physician specializing in cardiology. He is currently an associate director of the Center for Integration of Integration of Medicine and Innovative Technology at Massachusetts General Hospital. He has done extensive research on the onset of heart attacks and he teaches cardiology at the hospital clinic. Among other discoveries, he noted that most heart attacks occur in the early morning; that moderate drinkers have a higher heart-attack survival rate; and that people with cardiovascular disease benefit from drinking tea. He also found that there are different kinds of plaque in people's arteries; some types lead to heart attacks, while other types do not pose that risk.

In January of 2002, Muller's activist nature was re-awakened when a scandal involving child sex abuse by Catholic priests erupted in nearby Boston. Cardinal Bernard Law of Boston was accused of covering up child abuse by, and protecting, priest John Geoghan. Geoghan was only one of many: the truth was that there were hundreds of priests involved in the abuse, and thousands of victims. Muller was horrified. He told Jeff LaBrecque in the Johns Hopkins University Magazine, "I couldn't believe that an institution would cover up child sex abuse. We still went to church, but it wasn't the same church. We didn't know what to make of things, and we wanted to talk about it with other lay Catholics." Muller did not want to leave the church, which he saw as a vital part of his heritage and spiritual life.

In January of 2002 he met with a small group of other concerned people in his home church in Wellesley, Massachusetts. Within a year and a half, the group Voice of the Faithful (VOTF) grew to include 30,000 members worldwide. According to its Web site, the goals of the VOTF were to support survivors of clergy sexual abuse; to support priests of integrity; and to shape structural change within the Catholic Church. Its motto is "Keep the faith, change the church." As he explained to a reporter from the Cincinnati Enquirer, "We want to get to what we

think is the root of the problem and that's the Church structure." He added that the basis of the Church structure is "an underlying system of absolute power and no accountability by the Church hierarchy." He told the reporter that the early church was far more democratic, and that VOTF wanted to return to that model of Church structure: "We want the laity to have a stronger voice in how things are done in the church. We want transparency and accountability from the hierarchy." However, he does not have a clearly defined idea of the exact form structural change should take, preferring to let the people decide. He told Richard Conklin in the Notre Dame University Magazine, "we must keep 'structural change' undefined until its specifics can be determined by a lay voice that includes all spectrums." He hopes that the issue will be decided in a way that is acceptable to the entire spectrum of churchgoers—liberal, conservative, and middle-of-the-road.

The group pressured Law to resign, and he did so in December of 2002. In 2004 Muller and Charles Kenney published Keep the Faith, Change the Church, a book laying out the group's beliefs. Official church response to the group has been wary. Conklin quoted Jesuit scholar John O'Malley, who said, "There has never been a truly significant revolution from within the Catholic church by lay people." In addition, so far the group has attracted mostly older people who grew up in the years before the reforms of Vatican II; perhaps this is because younger people simply leave the church rather than remain in it hoping to reform it. As for leverage on the Church to make the urgency of their demands felt, Muller has advocated that parishioners stop donating to the church. Donations from members are, as Conklin noted, "the oxygen of the church."

Speaking to a Cincinnati Enquirer reporter about the future of VOTF, Muller said, "The Internet is a wonderful facilitator. When people say the laity doesn't have a chance against the hierarchy, I tell them: We have instruments now that we didn't have before.... We are bringing the power of the Internet to bear on the Church. The Internet is a great equalizer agent against a hierarchy."

Selected writings

(With Charles Kenney) Keep the Faith, Change the Church, Rodale (Emmaus, PA), 2004.

Sources

Periodicals

Johns Hopkins Magazine, April 2004.
Notre Dame Magazine, Winter 2002-03.

Online

"Voice of the Faithful: Seeking Changes in the Church," *Cincinnati Enquirer,* http://www.enquirer.com/editions/2003/08/17/editorial_wwwed1b17.html (August 25, 2010).

Voice of the Faithful Web Site, http://www.votf.org (August 25, 2010).

—*Kelly Winters*

Elon Musk

Vince Bucci/Getty Images

Entrepreneur

Born June 28, 1971, in South Africa; son of Errol (an engineer and consulting firm owner) and Maye (a model and dietician) Musk; married Jennifer Wilson (later known as Justine Musk, a fantasy novelist; separated, 2008); children: five sons (a set of twins and a set of triplets). *Education:* Studied at Queen's University, Kingston, Ontario, Canada, c. early 1990s; University of Pennsylvania, B.A. and B.S., c. 1995.

Addresses: *Office*—Space Exploration Technology Corp., 1310 East Grand Ave., El Segundo, CA 90245. *Office*—Tesla Motors, Inc., 1050 Bing St., San Carlos, CA 94070.

Career

Had internships at Microsoft and the Bank of Nova Scotia, c. late 1980s; programmer, Rocket Science (a video game developer), c. late 1980s; cofounder, chairman, chief executive officer, and chief technical officer, Zip2 Corp., 1995-99; co-founder, chairman, and chief executive officer, X.com (known as PayPal after c. 2000), 1999-2002; sold PayPal to eBay, 2002; co-founder, chairman, and chief executive officer, Space Exploration Technologies Corp., El Segundo, CA, 2002—; primary investor, chairman, and product architect, Tesla Motors, Inc., 2003—; founder and chairman, SolarCity, c. 2003—.

Member: Chairman, Musk Foundation; National Academy of Sciences; board of trustees, X-Prize Foundation.

Awards: Entrepreneur of the year, *Inc.* magazine, 2007; George Low Space Transportation Award, American Institute of Aeronautics and Astronautics, 2008.

Sidelights

Serial entrepreneur Elon Musk was the founder of such Internet companies as Zip2 Corp. and X.com, which later merged with PayPal and took on that company's name. He used the fortune that he made from these key businesses to found several other successful companies, including Space Exploration Technological Corp., known as Space X, Tesla Motors, and SolarCity. Through Space X he was able to launch the first privately developed liquid fuel rocket and saw the company as the future of space travel. Worth at least $325 million as of 2009, Musk was highly regarded for his wide-ranging intelligence, vision, ability to multitask, and unshakeable confidence.

Musk was born on June 28, 1971, in South Africa, the son of Errol and Maye Musk. His father was a South African engineer who owned a consulting firm as well as some mining and real estate interests while his mother was a Canadian model and dietician; they divorced when Musk was a young child. An enthusiastic learner, Musk loved to read from an early age. Also a video game fan, he began working on computer programs at the age of nine and published his first computer program when he was 12. It was software code for a video game, Blaster, which he sold for $500 to a gaming magazine. He and his younger brother, Kimbal, owned the third IBM personal computer in South Africa.

Musk also had entrepreneurial ambitions in his youth. At 13, he and Kimbal devised a plan to open up an arcade near their school in their home city of Pretoria. City officials told them they needed an adult's signature to gain a permit. Giving up on that dream, the brothers instead focused on selling homemade chocolates to schoolmates. Musk invested some of the money he made in the stock market, where he showed thousands of dollars in gains.

After gaining a Canadian passport (because of his mother's citizenship) when he was 16 years old, he moved to Canada to study at Queen's University in Kingston at the age of 17, in part to avoid compulsory service in the South African military. While a student there, he landed internships at a Canadian bank, the Bank of Nova Scotia, and Microsoft's Canadian marketing department. Musk also worked as a programmer for Rocket Science.

Musk soon landed a scholarship and transferred to the University of Pennsylvania. He first earned an undergraduate degree in economics from Penn's Wharton School of Business around 1995, then stayed another year to earn a bachelor's degree in physics. Musk moved to the West Coast to enter a Ph.D. program in physics with a focus on capacitors at Stanford University. He dropped out after two days to start his first company because he believed it afforded greater opportunity. As he told Brian Deagon of *Investor's Business Daily*, "I believed the Internet would dramatically change the future of humanity in a very positive way. I wanted to be a part of that."

In 1995, Musk was the co-founder of Zip2 Corp., with his brother Kimbal and others. (At various times, he also served as chairman, chief executive officer, executive vice president, and chief technical officer for the company.) Conceived of as a yellow pages for the Internet, Zip2 provided news of all types, city guides, ads, directories, and other related online content to various targeted cities, and Musk himself built some of the software for it.

Zip2 almost merged with CitySearch, another city guide company, in 1998, but the deal fell through because Musk did not trust CitySearch's chief executive Charles Conn and because of internal strife among executives at Zip2. While CitySearch was eventually forced into a merger with Ticketmaster Online, Zip2 was sold by Compaq for $307 million in cash in February of 1999. At the time, it was one of the biggest cash deals of its kind. Zip2 became the technology platform for Compaq's search engine Alta Vista. This transaction increased Musk's ambitions to create something new.

A multimillionaire from the Compaq deal, Musk soon moved on to his next venture. He co-founded and first served as the chairman of what was originally called X.com in 1999, backed by some of the major Silicon Valley technology venture capitalists. Musk's ambitious original idea was to offer, via the Internet, all types of financial services, including checking accounts, mortgages, insurance, mutual funds, and other investments. At the time, online banking had not been developed and was seen as a hard market to break into. Some observers wondered if Musk, who lacked banking experience save that brief college internship, could make X.com successful as a so-called World Wide Web Western Union.

Of this situation, Musk told Mark Gimein in the *Hamilton Spectator*, "I guess my talent/expertise is that I know how to build a killer Internet company with a solid foundation. I didn't know anything about the media business when starting Zip2, but figured it out along the way. Actually, I've found that being an outsider helps you to think creatively about improving the way things are done. When people have been doing things the same way for years, they stop questioning their methods even if they defy common sense."

When the much hyped X.com landed, it offered $20 to anyone who opened a free online checking account. Musk intended to make money through interest rate spreads as traditional financial service companies did. While X.com attracted 100,000 customers within two months, it was hard to make customers trust online banking. This situation worsened when it was revealed that hackers had gained access to accounts and completed illegal transfers.

In March of 2000, Musk merged X.com with another new online financial company, PayPal. PayPal had also launched in late 1999 and provided online payment services between people. Like X.com, PayPal was also attracting thousands of new customers. After the companies merged, PayPal moved into the business-to-consumer and business-to-business markets as well. Customers with X.com accounts could use money they deposited into their accounts to make instant payments to people and businesses that used PayPal, such as eBay, the online auction site. In June of 2000, X.com had 2.5 million unique visitors, and by October of 2000, had 300,000 accounts, demonstrating the attractiveness of the concept.

Musk soon came into conflict with X.com's chief executive officer and president, Bill Harris, who lasted only six months at the helm. In October of 2000, Musk announced that X.com could focus solely on payments between parties and soon after stated that the company would be known as PayPal. Much attention was paid to expanding business-to-business and business-to-consumer operations as well as growing internationally. Musk also ensured that customers had fraud protection and increased security features after negative publicity over major fraudulent transactions occurred.

Early in 2002, Musk took PayPal public, raising $750 million. Five months later, he sold it to eBay for $1.5 billion. Not interested in retirement, Musk moved on to his next challenge: outer space. In 2002, Musk became the founder, chief executive officer, chief technical officer, and head rocket designer for Space Exploration Technologies Corp. Better known as Space X, he used $50 million of his own money to found the company and accepted no outside investors.

Explaining the inspiration for Space X, Musk told Brian Deagon of *Investor's Business Daily*, "I've always been interested in space. I like to be involved in industries and sectors that are changing the world. Space is one of those things. After PayPal, I got interested in trying to figure out NASA's plans.... What hasn't government exploration progressed past Apollo? Why have we not gone back to the moon in 30 years? As I dove into this, it seemed the linchpin was cost. The fundamental issue was reliable, low-cost access to space."

Musk hoped that by severely cutting the cost of space travel, his business model—quite different than most space agencies and companies to date—would succeed. He used the most sophisticated lightweight materials available and a new engine that contributed to his cost efficiency. Shunning outside investors, he eventually put more than $100 million of his own money into Space X.

Originally, Space X focused on producing a two-stage space launch vehicle known as Falcon. Falcon was to put small satellites into low-earth orbit for a quarter of the price of the going rate. Musk origi-nally hoped to launch the Falcon 1 by the end of 2003, and had several customers under contract for multiple launches. He even signed a deal with the U.S. Air Force in April of 2005 for a series of launches worth up to $100 million.

However, delays in design and testing meant that Musk was unable to do test launches of the rocket needed to power the Falcon until 2006, years after his original scheduled launch. The first was a failure because the engine caught on fire. During the second test in March of 2007, his rocket Space-ShipOne went 180 miles above the Earth and reached only Mach 3 because of a mistake in the design of the fuel tank. However, his rocket had to reach Mach 25 to get to the appropriate orbit to launch satellites. The Falcon 1 finally went into orbit in September of 2008, marking the first time a privately developed liquid-fuel rocket orbited Earth.

Despite the setbacks he faced with the Falcon 1, Musk began building other more powerful rockets, such as the Falcon 9, while working on the Falcon 1. The Falcon 9 was intended to ferry astronauts and cargo to the International Space Station, perhaps beginning in 2011, as well as travel to other planets. This rocket had its first successful test launch on June 4, 2010, from Cape Canaveral, Florida. Musk also hoped to venture into commercial space tourism and other space ventures, like a manned colony on Mars. He told Brian Deagon of *Investor's Business Daily*, "We hope to colonize space, though yes, it might take 500 years."

While Space X remained his primary focus, Musk founded two other companies. He was the primary investor and chairman of SolarCity, a solar panel installation company. He invested $10 million and soon saw an immediate return on the money. Within a year of its founding, SolarCity became one of the largest installers of home solar panels in the United States. One of SolarCity's co-founders, Musk's cousin Lyndon Rive, told Max Chafkin of *Inc.*, "Our goal is to reduce the cost of solar so that everyone can adopt clean power. We definitely want to be a consumer brand."

More prominently, Musk served as the founder, principal owner and investor, chairman, and product architect for Tesla Motors, Inc., which produced the first all-electric sports car. Musk invested at least $55 million of his own money into the company. Tesla was able to deliver its first production vehicle, the Roadster, in December of 2007. The Roadster originally retailed for $100,000 and more than 1,000 names were on the waiting list before the vehicle even hit the showroom. The battery in the Roadster lasted 227 miles per charge and could go from zero to 60 in less than four seconds.

Don Sherman, the technical editor of *Automobile* magazine, test drove the Roadster in December of 2007 and was impressed. He told Joe Nocera of the *New York Times*, "My experience was highly positive. It was a very exciting, very interesting piece of work that I found quite appealing." As the Roadster was being brought to market, Musk and Tesla also began focusing on developing a sedan, dubbed Model S, that used the same efficient technology, but would be less expensive.

Because of his diverse successful business efforts, Musk was named entrepreneur of the year for 2007 by *Inc.* magazine. He also was a member of board of trustees of X-Prize Foundation and chairman of the Musk Foundation. Explaining why Musk was so successful Max Levchin, who co-founded X.com with him, told Max Chafkin of *Inc.*, "One of Elon's greatest skills is the ability to pass off his vision as a mandate from heaven. He is very much the person who, when someone says it's impossible, shrugs and says, 'I think I can do it.'"

Sources

Books

Gale Encyclopedia of E-commerce, Gale Group, 2002.
Marquis Who's Who, Marquis Who's Who, 2010.

Periodicals

American Banker, October 11, 2000.
Calgary Herald (Alberta, Canada), January 31, 2009, p. C13.
Canadian Business, February 7, 2000, p. 39.
GQ, February 2009, p. 74.
Hamilton Spectator (Ontario, Canada), September 6, 1999, p. A11.
Inc., December 2007, p. 115.
Investor's Business Daily, March 26, 2003, p. A6; November 17, 2004, p. A5; May 2, 2005, p. A4; December 22, 2005, p. A3.
New York Times, July 19, 2008, p. C1; February 16, 2010, p. D1.
San Francisco Chronicle, February 2, 1996, p. P3.
San Jose Mercury News (CA), August 13, 2000, p. 3F.
Sunday Times (London, England), January 4, 2009, pp. 6-7.
Toronto Star, October 12, 2009, p. B1.

Online

"Launch of SpaceX Falcon 9 Private Rocket a Success," *Washington Post*, http://www.washington post.com/wp-dyn/content/article/2010/06/04/AR20100604.tif03360.html (June 7, 2010).

—*A. Petruso*

Chris O'Donnell

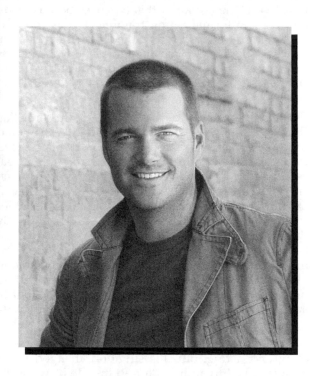

Actor

Born Christopher Eugene O'Donnell, June 26, 1970, in Winnetka, IL; son of William (a radio station owner) and Julie (a real estate agent) O'Donnell; married Caroline Fentress (an elementary school teacher), April 19, 1997; children: Lily Anne, Christopher Eugene, Jr., Charles McHugh, Finley, Maeve Frances. *Education:* Boston College, B.A., 1992; also attended University of California Los Angeles.

Addresses: *Office*—c/o *NCIS: Los Angeles,* Valencia Studios, 26030 Avenue Hall, Box 4, Valencia, CA 91355. *Management*—Untitled Entertainment, 1801 Century Park East, Ste. 700, Los Angeles, CA 90067.

Career

Began modeling, c. 1983; began appearing in television commercials, c. 1986. Actor on television, including: *Jack and Mike,* ABC, 1986; *The Practice,* ABC, 2003; *The Amazing Westermans* (movie), 2004; *Two and a Half Men,* CBS, 2004; *Head Cases,* FOX, 2005; *Grey's Anatomy,* ABC, 2006; *The Company* (miniseries), TNT, 2007; *NCIS: Naval Criminal Investigative Service,* 2009; *NCIS: Los Angeles,* CBS, 2009—. Work as an executive producer for television includes: *Miracle on the 17th Green* (movie), 1999; *The Triangle* (movie), 2001. Film appearances include: *Men Don't Leave,* 1990; *Fried Green Tomatoes,* 1991; *Scent of a Woman,* 1992; *School Ties,* 1992; *The Three Musketeers,* 1993; *Blue Sky,* 1994; *Batman Forever,* 1995; *Circle of Friends,* 1995; *Mad Love,* 1995; *The Chamber,* 1996; *In Love and War,* 1996; *Batman & Robin,* 1997; *The Bachelor,* 1999; *Cookie's Fortune,* 1999; *Vertical Limit,* 2000; *29 Palms,* 2002; *Kinsey,* 2004; *The Sisters,* 2005; *Kit Kittredge: An American Girl,* 2008; *Max Payne,* 2008; *Cats and Dogs: The Revenge of Kitty Galore,* 2010; *A Little Help,* 2010. Film work includes: producer, *Y2K,* 1999; executive producer, *The Bachelor,* 1999. Stage appearances include: *The Man Who Had All the Luck,* American Airlines Theatre, New York City, 2002.

Awards: Award for most promising actor, Chicago Film Critics Association, for *Scent of a Woman,* 1993; ShoWest Award for male star of tomorrow, ShoWest Convention, 1994; award for favorite supporting actor—sci-fi, Blockbuster Entertainment, for *Batman & Robin,* 1998; Caritas Award, Saint John's Health Center Foundation, 2009.

Sidelights

With his all-American looks, Chris O'Donnell came to fame as a film actor in the 1990s with roles in *Scent of a Woman, Batman Forever,* and *Circle of Friends.* Though he focused more on television than film in the early 2000s, he found success on the small screen as the co-star of the CBS drama *NCIS: Los Angeles.* O'Donnell was often surprised by his success, as he fell into his career after working as a teen model and appearing in a few television commercials. He told Cindy Pearlman in the Cleveland *Plain Dealer,* "It amazes me sometimes that I've come so far in this business because I really had no formal acting training. I guess there is something to be said for on-the-job training. I think of Jessica Lange, Al Pacino, and Gene Hackman as my professors. That's not a bad semester when it comes to learning!"

O'Donnell was born on June 26, 1970, in Winnetka, Illinois, a suburb of Chicago, the son of William and Julie O'Donnell. His father owned Wisconsin-based radio stations, while his mother worked as a real estate agent. O'Donnell was the youngest of seven children in his Irish-American family. He began modeling when he was 13 years old, after his elder sister Sally convinced a talent agent to meet him. By the time he was 16 years old, he was being cast in television commercials as well. He appeared in commercials for McDonalds and Brach's candy, among others. He took these jobs primarily for spending money. O'Donnell also made his television debut in an episode of the ABC drama *Jack and Mike* in 1986.

At 17, O'Donnell was ready to retire from both modeling and acting, but this situation changed when he was asked to audition for a film. He blew off the audition several times, but the casting director pursued him and his mother said she would buy him a new car if he went. O'Donnell landed the role, making his film debut in *Men Don't Leave* opposite Jessica Lange. He played her eldest son in the box office bomb but critical success.

Though O'Donnell continued to act, education also remained a priority. He graduated from Loyola Academy in Chicago, where he was active on the crew team. By the time *Men Don't Leave* was released in 1990, O'Donnell was a college student. He studied marketing at Boston College, earning his bachelor of arts degree in 1992. O'Donnell also attended the University of California at Los Angeles. He met his future wife, elementary school teacher Caroline Fentress, at Boston College; she was the sister of one of his roommates.

During his college years, O'Donnell only worked on a few films and was unsure if he could actually have a real career as an actor. He was cast in the 1991 release *Prince of Tides* as the son of a character played by Barbara Streisand, but lost the role when she insisted her real son appear opposite her. O'Donnell made three films released in this time period. They included critically acclaimed supporting roles in *Fried Green Tomatoes*, the 1991 adaptation of the popular novel by Fannie Flagg, and the 1992 prep school drama *School Ties*. O'Donnell's breakout role also came in 1992, *Scent of a Woman*.

Scent of a Woman starred acting legend Al Pacino as Lieutenant Colonel Frank Slade, an older, testy blind man. O'Donnell played Charles, a prep school student on scholarship who took a job as Slade's caretaker over one Thanksgiving weekend. Charles learned much about life from Slade, who became something of a surrogate father to his caretaker as Charles came from a broken home. In this Golden Globe award-nominated role, O'Donnell felt he was receiving an education from his co-star. He told James Ryan of the BPI Entertainment News Wire, "It was like taking an acting class from Al Pacino. You've got to be on your toes when you're acting with this guy. Sometimes he will just come up with stuff—improv—but that's what makes it so exciting."

With the success of *Scent of a Woman,* O'Donnell was labeled the next big thing. He felt he could focus on and have a career in acting, through his degree gave him a back-up plan if acting somehow did not work out. To maintain longevity, he tried to take on a variety of film roles. O'Donnell's next film was an adaptation of *The Three Musketeers.* Released in 1993, it starred then hot young actors Charlie Sheen and Kiefer Sutherland in leading roles, while O'Donnell played D'Artagnan.

After 1994's *Blue Sky,* O'Donnell starred in two very different romantic films. In 1995's coming-of-age film set in 1950s Ireland, *Circle of Friends,* O'Donnell played a handsome Irish college student who was the first love of Bernadette, a shy girl from the country played by Minnie Driver. Also released in 1995, the steamy *Mad Love* featured O'Donnell playing Matt, a repressed high school senior who finds freedom in polar opposite girlfriend Casey, played by Drew Barrymore. The manic depressive Casey ends up in a mental ward, but he breaks her out and they go on a road trip that shows them the limits of their love. Reviewing *Mad Love,* Emanuel Levy of *Daily Variety* commented, "O'Donnell impressively meets his greatest dramatic challenge to date."

With 1995's *Batman Forever,* O'Donnell's career reached new heights as he played the iconic character of Robin to Val Kilmer's Batman. He beat out Leonardo DeCaprio, Alan Cumming, Jude Law, Christian Bale, and Ewan McGregor to play the punkish version of the famous sidekick. With the success of this summer blockbuster, he was offered many commercial films with the potential for hundreds of millions in potential box office worldwide. But O'Donnell thought those kind of films would overexpose him in a short amount of time. He was choosy with his roles, and only took the films that interested him. One exception was the sequel to

Batman Forever, 1997's *Batman & Robin.* George Clooney replaced Kilmer as Batman, while O'Donnell reprised his role as Robin; however, O'Donnell did not enjoy the experience, likening this second film to a commercial for toys.

In between Batman films, O'Donnell took on two more demanding roles in 1996. With the dramatic thriller *The Chamber*, based on a novel by John Grisham, O'Donnell had one of his biggest roles to date and one of the first times he played a character who was his own age. The major Hollywood film focused on the efforts of O'Donnell's character, the idealistic young lawyer Adam Hall, who tried to get the execution of his estranged grandfather, the racist Sam Cayhall (played by Gene Hackman), postponed so that he could discover if his grandfather really was responsible for a 1967 bombing. O'Donnell found the filming challenging, telling Irv Letofsky of the *San Diego Union-Tribune*, "It's always exhausting making films ... a totally consuming thing. On a film like *Batman* I get a lot of days off because there are so many people in the film. But this one, it was the toughest role I've ever had and it was emotional and I had a lot of legal terms and phrases I've never used before." Also that year, O'Donnell had a featured role in *In Love and War,* as a young Ernest Hemingway when the author was a military ambulance driver in Italy during World War I.

To this point in his career, O'Donnell would travel to Los Angeles for work as needed but kept his home base in Chicago, where he had long-time friends and a simpler, less fame-oriented life. He told Barry Koltnow of the *Austin American-Statesman*, "This is a funny, weird business, but if you realize it's all about the work, then you can find happiness in Hollywood. So many people make it worse for themselves by seeking the spotlight. That part of the business is a joke. I understand the importance of promoting a movie, but when I'm not promoting a movie, I want to be away from it. I don't ever want to feel the pressure of having to play that glamour game."

O'Donnell began spending more time in Hollywood in the late 1990s and early 2000s as his career evolved, and eventually made Los Angeles his home base. He continued to appear in films like the 1999 Robert Altman film *Cookie's Fortune,* and the 2000 mountain climbing drama *Vertical Limit.* But O'Donnell took on new challenges when he began producing films and television movies. He worked on two films released in 1999. He was the producer of *Y2K,* and the executive producer of *The Bachelor.* O'Donnell also starred in the latter film, an updated remake of the classic Buster Keaton comedy *Seven Chances.* In addition, O'Donnell worked as an executive producer on two television movies: 1999's *Miracle on the 17th Green* and 2001's *The Triangle.*

The actor's personal life evolved as well as he married elementary school teacher Caroline Fentress in 1997, and he took nearly two years off from acting. The couple eventually had five children, and family life became extremely important to O'Donnell. After the birth of his first child, daughter Lily, in 2000, he became even more selective in the roles he took. By choice, his film career did not have the same trajectory in this time period and he worked irregularly on films in the early 2000s. His films of this time period included 2002's *29 Palms,* and the 2004 biopic *Kinsey.* O'Donnell also tried his hand at stage acting, making his Broadway debut in a revival of the Arthur Miller drama *The Man Who Had All the Luck* in 2002; however, much of his professional focus shifted to television with its predictable scheduling.

In 2003, O'Donnell made his first foray in television acting since the 1980s with a multiple-episode arc of the hit ABC legal drama *The Practice* playing a man accused of murdering his wife. He followed this with a role in the 2004 television movie *The Amazing Westermans* and a guest spot on the popular CBS situation comedy *Two and a Half Men,* which starred his former *Three Musketeers* co-star Sheen. O'Donnell had a deal to develop his own television projects, though few made it past the pilot stage. One show that was picked up was the short-lived 2005 FOX series, the quirky legal drama *Head Cases.* Also in 2005, O'Donnell appeared in the film, *The Sisters,* an adaptation of a play by Anton Chekhov.

Though O'Donnell's own series found limited success, he continued to take on memorable television roles including a multi-episode arc as a veterinarian in the popular ABC medical drama *Grey's Anatomy,* in 2006. He then had a featured role in the well-received TNT CIA spy miniseries *The Company* in 2007. O'Donnell's next projects were films, including two 2008 releases. The first was the children's film *Kit Kittredge: An American Girl,* which he agreed to do to please his eldest daughter. O'Donnell also made a film for an adult audience, the stylish drama *Max Payne.* In 2009, O'Donnell finally landed his first regular role in a series when he was cast as gifted undercover agent G. Callen in a new CBS military drama, *NCIS: Los Angeles.* The show co-starred rapper/actor LL Cool J and was such hit for the network that a syndication deal was signed after it was the air for only seven weeks. As *NCIS: Los Angeles,* found its audience, O'Donnell took roles in two films released in 2010: *A Little Help* and *Cats and Dogs: The Revenge of Kitty Galore.*

Of his life and career, O'Donnell told Kelley L. Carter of the Albany, New York *Times Union* in 2008, "I think it's funny the way life works. It was something I always wanted to do at an early age. And I can't believe I'm still doing it.... I'm pleased that I've been able to have the experiences that I've had in the business. And still get to have that other half of me, the traditional family life that I've always wanted."

Sources

Periodicals

24 Hours, January 19, 2010, p. 7.
Associated Press, May 6, 2002; September 23, 2005.
Austin American-Statesman, October 11, 1996, p. E3.
BPI Entertainment News Wire, December 31, 1992.
Chicago Sun-Times, July 26, 2003, p. 18; August 5, 2007, p. D3.
Daily Variety, May 26, 1995; November 4, 1999, p. 6; September 26, 2003, p. 1; September 14, 2005, p. 5.
Los Angeles Times, August 11, 2010, p. B1.
Pittsburgh Post-Gazette, January 28, 1997, p. D3.
Plain Dealer (Cleveland, OH), January 8, 1993, p. 3; December 3, 2000, p. 5I.
PR Newswire, October 20, 2009.
Redbook, June 1, 2010, p. 4.
San Diego Union-Tribune, October 6, 1996, p. E1.
Star Tribune (Minneapolis, MN), September 22, 2009, p. 1E.
Times Union (Albany, NY), July 3, 2008, p. P32.
Toronto Star, March 15, 1995, p. D1.
Toronto Sun, March 14, 1995, p. 55.
USA Today, January 28, 1993, p. 1D.
Variety, June 13-19, 2005, p. 40.
Vogue, August 2007, p. 154.

Online

"Chris O'Donnell," Internet Movie Database, http://www.imdb.com/name/nm0000563/ (November 18, 2010).

—*A. Petruso*

Kathryn Olson

Chief Executive Officer of the Women's Sports Foundation

Born c. 1961. *Education:* University of Illinois, B.S.; University of Chicago, M.B.A.

Addresses: *Office*—Women's Sports Foundation, 1899 Hempstead Turnpike, Ste. 400, East Meadow, NY 11554. *Web site*—http://www.womenssports foundation.org/.

Career

Worked in marketing at Quaker Oats Company, c. mid-1980s-c. mid-1990s; vice president of global marketing, Monsanto Life Sciences, c. mid-1990s; executive vice president for marketing, Nordstrom.com, 1998-2001; vice president of consumer marketing, William Wrigley Jr. Company, 2001-04; chief marketing officer, LeapFrog, Emityville, CA, 2004-07; trustee, Women's Sports Foundation, 2005—; chief marketing officer, Shutterfly, San Francisco, CA, 2007-10; chief executive officer, Women's Sports Foundation, 2010—.

Member: Board, Association of National Advertisers; board, Chicago Communities in Schools; Joffrey Ballet's women's board executive council; advisory board, Regen Living.

Awards: Named one of the most influential women in business, *San Francisco Business Times*, 2009.

Kevin Winter/Getty Images for The Noble Awards

Sidelights

Marketing executive Kathryn Olson has held numerous posts at high-profile companies including Quaker Oats, Wrigley, LeapFrog, and Shutterfly. In 2010, she took on new challenges by becoming the chief executive officer of a nonprofit, the Women's Sports Foundation. Olson hoped to draw on her business and marketing background to improve the finances of the struggling organization.

Born around 1961, Olson received her education at the University of Illinois. She earned her bachelor of science degree in marketing from its College of Commerce. Olson continued her education at the University of Chicago Graduate School of Business. From this institution, she earned her master's in business administration.

Professionally, Olson became based in Chicago and spent more than ten years working for the Quaker Oats Company. During her tenure, she was the director of marketing for Gatorade Europe for two years. She spent five years working on Gatorade Thirst Quencher, both domestically and worldwide. Olson also worked in marketing for Quaker's

Snapple line of lemonade and tea products. She landed numerous promotions and worked her way up through the company before leaving in the mid-1990s. Olson then had a tenure as the vice president of global marketing for Monsanto Life Sciences.

Returning to consumer products, Olson worked as an executive vice president for marketing at Nordstrom.com. She helped launch this venture, the Internet apparel Web site of the respected department store company, in 1998. In 1999, Olson oversaw Nordstrom.com's first ever national advertising campaign as part of the launch of a related Web site, Nordstromshoes.com, which claimed to be the largest shoe store in the world.

In 2001, Olson took a post at William Wrigley Jr. Company, the producer of various gum products like Eclipse, Orbit, Big Red, and Doublemint. At the company, she held the post of vice president of consumer marketing. She was in charge of marketing the company in the United States, which accounted for approximately one-third of the company's sales. She took the job in part because of new management and potential for growth. Olson came in at a time when Wrigley was changing its advertising and marketing approach to become more edgy and modern, approaches which helped improve sales.

Olson moved to the San Francisco Bay Area in 2004 to take on the newly created post of chief marketing officer for LeapFrog. This toy company produced learning platforms and products that were often technology-based and innovative. While at LeapFrog, Olson was charged with overseeing all the elements of marketing for the company worldwide. At the time, LeapFrog was expanding into a global education enterprise. She was also in charge of consumer insights, product direction, advertising, corporate communications, and licensing; however, in 2006, LeapFrog faced significant challenges with declining sales, and shook up both its product line and marketing strategies.

Olson left LeapFrog to become the chief marketing officer of Shutterfly in June 2007, shortly after it became a publicly traded company. This company offered online photography and other personal publishing services to consumers and businesses. During Olson's tenure, she helped turn the company into a premium brand. Taking charge of various marketing, merchandising, and customer experience aspects of Shutterfly, Olson was also involved with heading efforts to create new products and services, customer and consumer marketing, e-commerce, and merchandising. People were not only able to share their pictures online, but now could order prints online and pick them up at Target stores, and create personalized photo albums, as well as other products and services.

During Olson's tenure, Shutterfly saw record-breaking amounts of revenue, created in part by her efforts. Olson could also relate to consumers who used its products as she was an enthusiastic photographer in her own right. She told Kayla Platt of the *San Francisco Business Times*, "Taking a photo and sharing it with a friend is a very meaningful way to communicate." Olson also told Renee Kimmel of *Brandweek*, "People are passionate about our product. Shutterfly is very much geared towards the customer and we have a loyal customer base."

In April 2010, Olson took on new challenges when she became the chief executive officer of the Women's Sports Foundation, replacing Karen Durkin. Olson had been a trustee of the organization since 2005, and had once served as the chairperson of the governance committee. The Women's Sports Foundation had been founded in 1974 by star tennis player Billie Jean King to promote women and girls' participation in sports, as well as the importance of health and education. It was created by King in the wake of the passage of Title IX, a law which banned sexual discrimination in schools that received federal funds. Over the years, the Women's Sports Foundation focused its efforts on advocacy and research through programs like GoGirlGo!, which encouraged girls health throughout childhood and young adulthood. Though it was located in New York, Olson remained in San Francisco and opened a secondary office there.

When Olson took over, the Women's Sports Foundation was facing difficulties. In 2007, the organization received about $16 million in grants and contributions. By 2008, that figure was only $8 million. In 2009, it was halved again to about $4 million. As revenue fell, the organization's full-time staff went from 74 to about 28 in nine months during 2009 and 2010. King said that such staff losses actually benefitted the organization and were necessary no matter what the financial standing, and Olson planned no further cuts. In 2010, Olson hoped to raise $5 to $6 million, drawing on her corporate background to increase the amount raised. As she told Erik Brady of *USA Today*, "I'm very confident in the future of the foundation, or I wouldn't have taken on this role."

During her tenure, Olson hoped to continue to turn the foundation around, including ensuring that its advocacy and research efforts continued; however, the foundation's annual Billie Awards, which honored the best in media coverage and depiction of women and girls in sports, were suffering. The economic downturn forced the cancellation of the awards in 2009, while Elton John, who performed at other Billie Award ceremonies, was not available for the 2010 ceremony, compelling the foundation to again cancel them. Olson hoped the Billies would be held in 2011 in Los Angeles or San Francisco. The Women's Sports Foundation continued to hold its annual banquet in New York during this time period.

Over the years, Olson was active in charitable work by serving on nonprofit and industry-related boards, including tenures on the boards of the Association of National Advertisers, Chicago Communities in Schools, and the Joffrey Ballet's women's board executive council. Olson also served on the advisory board of Regen Living. This company was founded in 2009 and made personal electronics and home electronics all of which were powered by solar technology. In addition, Olson was recognized for excellence in her work. In 2009, Olson was named one of the most influential women in business by the *San Francisco Business Times*.

Sources

Periodicals

Advertising Age, March 18, 2002, p. 4; September 23, 2002, p. 3.
Brandweek, August 6, 2007, p. 40.
Business Wire, October 29, 1999; June 4, 2007.
Newsweek, June 2, 2008, p. E8.
Playthings, May 1, 2007, p. 28.
PR Newswire, September 27, 2004.
USA Today, June 30, 2010, p. 8C.

Online

"Chief Executive Officer," Women's Sports Foundation, http://66.40.5.5/About-Us/Who-We-Are/CEO.aspx (August 25, 2010).
"Chief Marketing Officer, Shutterfly," Infotrends, http://www.infotrends.com/public/Content/Events/bios/dius07/kolson.html (August 25, 2010).
"Former Shutterfly Exec is New Women's Sports Foundation CEO," *San Francisco Business Times,* http://www.bizjournals.com/sanfrancisco/stories/2010/03/29/daily70.html (August 25, 2010).
"Kathryn Olson Named CEO of the Women's Sports Foundation," Women's Sports Foundation, http://www.womenssportsfoundation.org/Content/Press-Releases/2010/Kathryn-Olson-Named-CEO-of-the-Womens-Sports-Foundation.aspx (August 25, 2010).
"Personal Power Innovator Regen Announces All-Star Board of Advisors," Regen, http://www.regenliving.com/about/#blog_post.php?id=72 (August 25, 2010).
"Shutterfly's CMO to Continue Photo Service's Appeal to Women," *San Francisco Business Times,* http://sanfrancisco.bizjournals.com/sanfrancisco/stories/2007/06/18/tidbits2.html (August 25, 2010).

—*A. Petruso*

Manny Pacquiao

Landry Major/Getty Images Sport/Getty Images

Professional boxer

Born Emmanuel Dapidran Pacquiao, December 17, 1978, in Kibawe, Philippines; married Jinkee; children: Jemuel, Michael.

Addresses: *Home*—General Santos, City, Philippines. *Web site*—http://www.mannypacquiao. ph. *E-mail*—info@mannypacquiao.ph.

Career

Began fighting on Vintage Sports Network's television program *Blow By Blow,* 1995; flyweight champion, World Boxing Council (WBC), 1997; flyweight champion, Oriental and Pacific Boxing Federation, 1997; super bantamweight champion, International Boxing Federation, 2001; featherweight champion, WBC, 2003; super featherweight champion, WBC and *Ring Magazine,* 2008; World lightweight champion, WBC, 2008; light welterweight champion, International Boxing Organization and *Ring Magazine,* 2009; World welterweight champion, World Boxing Organization, 2009; diamond belt champion, WBC, 2009.

Awards: Fighter of the decade, Boxing Writers Association Of America, 2000-09; athlete of the decade, Philippine Sportswriters Association, 2000-09; fighter of the decade, *HBO,* 2000-09; fighter of the year, *Ring Magazine,* 2006, 2008, and 2009; fighter of the year, Boxing Writers Association Of America, 2006, 2008, 2009; fighter of the year, BoxingScene. com, 2008, 2009; boxer of the year, *Sports Illustrated,* 2008; boxer of the year, WBC, 2008, 2009; fighter of the year, ESPN, 2009; knockout of the year, ESPN,

2009; best fighter, ESPY Awards, 2009; 100 most influential people, *Time,* 2009; fighter of the year, *Sports Illustrated,* 2009; knockout of the year, *Ring Magazine,* 2009.

Sidelights

A prize-winning boxer, the five-foot, six-inch tall Manny Pacquiao's nicknames are Pac-man and the Destroyer. Pacquiao is the first boxer ever to win seven world titles in seven different weight divisions. He has been described as being the toughest man alive, pound for pound. He has a record of 49 wins, three losses, and two draws. Thirty seven of his wins came about because of knockouts. He is a talented fighter who combines both speed and power to win in the ring. In addition to his titles he was named in 2009 by *Ring Magazine* as the fighter of the year.

Pacquiao was born to a very poor family in Kibawe in the Philippines and was the second of four children. After his abusive father left the family, Pacquiao was forced to drop out of school and work to support his family. He sold bread around the neighborhood. He also discovered early in life that he was a talented fighter. He used to fight for small sums of money. By the time he was 15 he was training seriously to be a boxer. He began his professional boxing career in 1995 at the age of 16. While only weighing 106 pounds, a combination of athletic training and working a construction job had made him very strong. His early fights were televised on the Vintage Sports Network's *Blow by Blow* show. On January 22, 1995, he fought his first professional fight against Edmund Ignacio. He won the match by the decision of the judges and became an instant celebrity on the show.

In December of 1998, Pacquiao won the WBA Flyweight Championship when he defeated Chatchai Sasakul in an eight-round bout. He held the title for a year. Despite his weight increasing from 106 to 113 pounds, in a fight with Rustico Torrecampo he lost via a third round technical knockout. Following this fight, Pacquiao made his U.S. debut in a match against the then-International Boxing Federation's super bantamweight champion, Lehlohonolo Ledwaba. He faced off with Ledwaba in 2001 at the MGM Grand in Las Vegas, where he won the fight and the title. He went on to defeat some of boxing's biggest names, including Marco Antonio Barrera of Mexico, Juan Manuel Marquez, and Eric Morales.

When it was determined that Pacquiao would fight American boxer Oscar De La Hoya, many observers speculated that Pacquiao was out of his league. De La Hoya had won ten titles in six weight classes and was a former Olympic gold medal winner. At the time he also outweighed Pacquiao by 20 pounds. When they met in the ring on December 13, 2008, in Las Vegas, the general opinion was that it was a severe mismatch. However, Pacquiao made headlines when he beat De La Hoya in an eighth-round technical knockout.

On May 2, 2009, Pacquiao won a title in a fifth weight class when he defeated Ricky Hatton. Hatton had held the International Boxing Organization's light welterweight title until the bout in Las Vegas with Pacquiao. Pacquiao handily beat him in a second-round knockout.

Pacquiao has a great deal of charisma. Tobias Xavier Lopez, writing for the Forth Worth, Texas *Star-Telegram*, quoted Bob Arum who said Pacquiao "is truly a crossover star. How many fighters of our time go on *Jimmy Kimmel Live* and go on *Good Morning America* and have a big article coming out in *Time* magazine? I think that is saying something." In a second visit to the *Jimmy Kimmel Live* show, before Kimmel could ask Pacquiao any questions, the audience began to chant, "Manny, Manny, Manny...."

Pacquiao represented his country at the 2008 Summer Olympic Games in Beijing, China, by carrying the Filipino flag in the opening ceremonies. He also has his image on a stamp.

Pacquiao has political aspirations and his name has been put forward as a potential candidate for president; however, his success in politics has not matched his success in the ring. In 2007 Pacquiao ran for Congress in the Philippines on President Gloria Macapagal-Arroyo's Free Filipino ticket. He lost to Darlene Antonio-Custodio of the National People's Coalition. Pacquiao only received approximately 35 percent of the vote. There were allegations that some of his supporters had channeled a portion of his campaign funds, which included Pacquiao's personal monies, into their own pockets. It was also speculated that he had lost the election because of his alliance with Arroyo who had been accused previously of election tampering. Pacquiao is once again running for a congressional seat, this time in the Sarangani Province, which had elections scheduled for May of 2010. He stated on the *Jimmy Kimmel Live* show that if he wins he is not certain that he will continue to fight.

Pacquiao was scheduled to fight Floyd Mayweather Jr. on March 13, 2010. The fight was canceled a few months prior when Pacquiao declined to be tested for drugs in an Olympic-style drug test, at Mayweather's request. The issue became inflamed when Pacquiao filed a lawsuit against Mayweather for defamation of his character because he would not submit to a drug test to determine if he was using performance-enhancing drugs. Further, in a brief article in the *New York Times* by Bob Arum, Pacquiao's boxing promoter called Mayweather, whom he used to represent, "a psychological coward who doesn't want to fight anybody who has a chance of beating him." On the *Jimmy Kimmel Live* show, Pacquiao asserted that Mayweather simply could be using the demand for drug testing as an excuse not to fight. He was quoted on ABS-CBN News online as saying "I think he's not ready for the fight. The job of the fighter is to train hard and fight in the ring. You do not need to change the rules because there's the Nevada Athletic Commission to implement the rules." Rather than fighting Mayweather, the date was kept and Pacquiao fought Ghanian boxer Joshua Clottey at Cowboys Stadium in Arlington, Texas, beating him and retaining his World Boxing Organization welterweight belt. Whether Pacquiao is singing a George Benson song on a live television show, running for political office, or fighting in the boxing ring, he is a dynamic figure.

Sources

Periodicals

Los Angeles Times, February 1, 2010.
New York Times, December 31, 2009, p. B13; January 8, 2010, p. B12; January 20, 2010, p. B14.
Time, March 19, 2009.

Online

"A Filipino icon, 'PacMan' Pacquiao has fans everywhere," *Star-Telegram,* http://www.star-telegram.com/2010/03/07/v-print/2020278/a-filipino-icon-pacman-pacquiao.html (March 7, 2010).
Biography Resource Center Online, Gale, 2009.
"Boxing Scene's 2009 Fighter of the Year: Manny Pacquiao," Boxing Scene, http://www.boxingscene.com/?m=show&id=24399 (March 10, 2010).
"Full Manny Pacquiao Biography," Perfect People, http://www.perfectpeople.net/biography/3222/manny-pacquiao.html (March 7, 2010).
"Manny Pacquiao Biography," Kidz World, http://www.kidzworld.com/article/13935-manny-pacquiao-biography (March 7, 2010).
"Manny Pacquiao is the Best Fighter at ESPY Awards 2009," Sirkulo, http://www.sirkulo.com/2009/07/manny-pacquiao-is-the-best-fighter-at-espy-awards-2009/ (March7, 2010).

"Pacquiao also wins fighter of decade," ESPN, http://sports.espn.go.com/sports/boxing/news/story?id=4875455 (March 10, 2010).
"Pacquiao and Roach scoop awards," ESPNSTAR, http://www.espnstar.com/other-sports/news/detail/item389700/Pacquiao-and-raoch-scoop-awards (March 10, 2010).
"Pacquiao returns to 'Kimmel' show, belts out another tune," ABS-CBN News, http://www.abs-cbnnews.com/sports/03/04/10/pacquiao-returns-kimmel-show-belts-out-another-tune (March 7, 2010).
"Ring Magazine Fighter of the Year," BoxRec, http://boxrec.com/media/index.php?title=Ring_Magazine_Fighter_of_the_Year& printable (March 10, 2010).
"SI.com's 2008 Boxing Awards," *Sports Illustrated,* http://sportsillustrated.cnn.com/2008/writers/chris_mannix/12/18/2008-boxing-awards/ (March 10, 2010).
"SI.com's 2009 Boxing Awards," *Sports Illustrated,* http://sportsillustrated.cnn.com/multimedia/photo_gallery/0912/boxing.awards.2009/content.1.html (March 10, 2010).
"Sports Illustrated Names Pacquiao 'Boxer of the Year'," Phil Boxing, http://philboxing.com/news/story-21269.html (March 10, 2010).

—*Annette Bowman*

Eduardo Padrón

President of Miami Dade College

Born c. 1946, in Cuba; divorced, 1980; children: Camilo (son). *Education:* Attended Miami Dade Community College, 1960s; Florida Atlantic University, B.S., 1960s; University of Florida, Ph.D., 1970.

Addresses: *Office*—Miami Dade College, 300 NE Second Ave., Miami, FL 33132-2204. *E-mail*—epadronmdc.edu.

Career

Joined Miami Dade College as economics instructor, early 1970s; president, Miami Dade College Wolfson Campus, 1980-95, president, Miami Dade College, 1995—.

Awards: Chief Executive of the Year, Association of Community College Trustees, 2002; Hispanic Achievement Award in Education, *Hispanic Magazine,* 2004; Charles Kennedy Equity Award, Association of Community College Trustees, 2008; Reginald Wilson Diversity Leadership Award, American Council on Education, 2008; Innovator of the Year, League for Innovation in the Community College, 2008; named one of the "Ten Best College Presidents," *Time,* 2009; Floridian of the year, *Florida Trend* magazine, 2009.

Sidelights

When Cuban expatriate Eduardo Padrón became president of Miami Dade College in 1995, he had one mission in mind—to open wide the doors to higher education, particularly to low-income and minority groups that often lack higher-ed accessibility. During the next 15 years, Padrón grew Miami Dade into the largest community college in the United States, graduating more black and Hispanic students than any other public institution. An astute administrator, the former economist faced criticism for some of his funding decisions, but in the end, Padrón remained steadfast in his mission and nonplussed by his detractors. As Padrón told the *Miami Herald*'s Mirta Ojito, "I have created an atmosphere at the college, where students of all races, from all over the world study and work in harmony, where everybody works together in the pursuit of a common agenda."

Padrón was born in Cuba around 1946 and spent his childhood in Santiago, Havana, and Cuabitas. His father worked for a British pharmaceutical company. Padrón's family initially supported Cuban Revolution leader Fidel Castro. Later, the family changed alliances after Castro's military regime took over. Worried about the future of their children, the family decided to send 15-year-old Padrón and his younger brother, Ernesto, to live with a family friend in Miami in July of 1961.

"We had to wait at the airport for a long time," Padrón recalled in an interview with the *Miami*

Herald's Ojito. "We were separated by a glass partition and we couldn't talk, but we touched each other through the glass. We were all crying." Before he left, Padrón's mother made him promise to go to college. Initially, Padrón struggled in school, he told Christine Armario of the Associated Press in an article published on the KCCI Web site. "I got to the school and I didn't understand a word and everything was alien to me." The experience left an indelible mark on Padrón, who has worked to ensure non-native English-speaking students at Miami Dade have the support they need to succeed.

Throughout high school, Padrón worked several jobs. He delivered newspapers and separated clothing at a dry cleaning business. As graduation approached, his counselor urged him to go to trade school—saying he was not college material—but Padrón refused to give up his mother's dream and was eventually accepted at Miami Dade College, which at the time had one campus and 5,000 students. After two years at Miami Dade, Padrón transferred to Florida Atlantic University and earned a bachelor's degree in economics. In 1970, he finished his doctorate in economics at the University of Florida. Padrón accepted a position with DuPont but some of his professors questioned his motivation for wanting to join a corporation. He decided to stay in Miami and got a job teaching economics at Miami Dade and in 1980 became president of the Wolfson Campus. Padrón worked his way through the ranks and in 1995 was elevated to the position of president, placing him in charge of all campuses.

When Padrón took over in 1995 he instituted a major belt-tightening that infuriated faculty members. The 1995-96 budget Padrón inherited included $3.3 million in cost overruns—a violation of state law that required the institution to have a reserve fund. In addition, the college was facing state funding cuts. To deal with those issues, Padrón made cuts and restructured the school's spending priorities. In March of 1996, he laid off 119 employees and eliminated 280 vacant positions. While no faculty members lost their jobs, they became leery of his swift managerial style, preferring to have more input. Padrón also consolidated the athletic programs from each campus and halted a $44 million project to double the size of the Medical Center Campus so he could use the money for other uses. It was a bold move because $2.8 million had already been spent on the project.

Padrón freed up enough money in the 1996-97 budget year to give staff members their first raises in four years. A majority of the faculty, however, did not feel comfortable with Padrón's style. Speaking to the *Miami Herald's* Jack Wheat, Padrón acknowledged the dissent. "The most important challenge I have faced as a president is not money, not technology, but the mindset of people about change."

Despite the tensions Padrón has endured with faculty, the community at large embraces Padrón. During the 1990s, he served as vice president of the local NAACP chapter. He also helped boost the city's economy by offering college campus space for the Miami International Book Fair, an annual event that brings millions into the city. Miami Dade students are also fans and so is Brian Keeley, CEO of Baptist Health South Florida, which relies on Miami Dade graduates to fill its healthcare openings. "Eduardo Padrón has had a profound effect on our local community and now on our economy," Keeley told Cynthia Barnett of the Web site Florida Trend. "It's probably fair to say he's touched everybody's life in south Florida—certainly more so than any other educator down here."

Over the years, Padrón has focused on improving access, retention and graduation rates. By 2010, Miami Dade College was the second-largest institution of higher education for undergraduates in the United States with more than 170,000 students attending classes at its eight campuses. In addition, Miami Dade was awarding more associate degrees than any other U.S. school. These numbers caught the attention of U.S. President Barack Obama, who has a goal for the United States to lead the world in college degrees by 2020 and he is looking to Padrón to lead the way. "President Obama has pointed out that we need to increase our education attainment rates to remain competitive as a country, and he's challenged us to do that," George Boggs, president of the American Association of Community Colleges told Armario in the KCCI article. "We'll be looking to Miami Dade and what they're doing to improve completion rates."

Sources

Periodicals

Miami Herald, March 1, 1996, p. 1B; March 2, 1997, p. 1B.
Miami New Times, May 7, 1998.

Online

"Eduardo Padrón, Floridian of the Year," Florida Trend, http://www.floridatrend.com/article.asp?aID=52170 (May 3, 2010).

"Miami Dade College: About MDC," Miami Dade College, http://www.mdc.edu/main/about/college_president.asp (May 3, 2010).

"Miami Dade College Flourishes Under Padrón's Watch," KCCI, http://www.kcci.com/education/23102084.tif/detail.html (May 3, 2010).

—*Lisa Frick*

Keke Palmer

Actress and singer

Born Lauren Keyana Palmer, August 26, 1993, in Robbins, IL; daughter of Larry and Sharon (a teacher) Palmer.

Addresses: *Contact*—Keke Palmer Fan Mail, William Morris Endeavor, 151 El Camino, Beverly Hills, CA 90212. *Web site*—http://kekepalmer.com.

Career

Actress in films, including: *Barbershop 2: Back in Business*, 2004; *Akeelah and the Bee*, 2006; *Madea's Family Reunion*, 2006; *Cleaner*, 2007; *The Longshots*, 2008; *Shrink*, 2009; *Madea Goes to Jail*, 2009. Television appearances include: *Cold Case*, 2004; *Strong Medicine*, 2004; *The Wool Cap* (movie), 2004; *ER*, 2005; *Keke and Jamal* (movie), 2005; *Knights of the South Bronx* (movie), 2005; *Law & Order: Special Victims Unit*, 2005; *Second Time Around*, 2005; *House of Payne*, 2007; *Jump In!* (movie), 2007; *True Jackson, VP*, 2008—.

Awards: Outstanding performance by a lead actress, Black Movie Awards, for *Akeelah and the Bee*, 2006; ShoWest rising star of the year award, ShoWest Convention, 2006; Image Award for outstanding actress in a motion picture, National Association for the Advancement of Colored People, for *Akeelah and the Bee*, 2007; Young Artist Award for best leading young actress in a feature film, Young Artist Foundation, for *Akeelah and the Bee*, 2007; Black Reel Award for best actress, Foundation for the Advancement of African Americans in Film, for *Akeelah and the Bee*, 2007; Image Award for outstanding perfor-

Pacific Rim Photo Press/Sthanlee B. Mirador/newcom

mance in a youth/children's program, series or special, National Association for the Advancement of Colored People, for *True Jackson, VP*, 2009, 2010; YoungStars Award, Black Entertainment Television, for *True Jackson, VP*, 2010.

Sidelights

At age nine Keke Palmer came out of nowhere to land a bit role in the 2004 comedy *Barbershop 2: Back in Business*. On the set, Palmer held her own against veteran actress Queen Latifah, who played her aunt. After the experience, Palmer knew she wanted to act and persuaded her parents to move to Hollywood, where she honed her acting skills in guest roles on *Cold Case*, *ER*, and *Law & Order: Special Victims Unit*. Palmer's breakthrough performance came in 2006 when she earned the titular role in *Akeelah and the Bee*, the story of an inner-city spelling bee champ. By 2008, Palmer had her own show on Nickelodeon, playing the headlining character on *True Jackson, VP*, which became an instant hit among the tween crowd and cemented Palmer's status as one of the most popular stars of her generation. Those who had worked with Palmer were not surprised by the extrovert's quick rise to fame. "She lights up the room, and she gives off an electricity that comes off the screen," Lionsgate Films production chief Mike Paseornek told *USA Today*'s Anthony Breznican.

Palmer was born to Sharon and Larry Palmer on August 26, 1993, in the Chicago suburb of Robbins, Illinois, where she spent her early years alongside her older sister, Loreal, and younger twin siblings. Palmer's given name was Lauren Keyana Palmer, but her older sister dubbed her Keke and the name stuck. Early on, Palmer felt driven to perform. At the age of five, she joined the church choir and became an instant sensation with her rendition of "Jesus Loves Me." In an interview with the *Chicago Tribune*'s Kelley L. Carter, Palmer's godmother, Nona Edison, recalled Palmer's early years singing in the church. "Keke, as a young child, always stood out." Edison went on to say that Palmer was never afraid to perform. "She's always had this fearlessness, that 'I could do this,' even at a very young age. She's very sure of herself and her place in the spotlight."

As a youngster, Palmer perfected her singing voice in her mother's home-recording studio. At nine, she went to Chicago and auditioned for a stage adaptation of *The Lion King*. "I didn't know anything about acting," Palmer told Jane Shin Park of *Teen Vogue*. "Singing was the huge thing in my life." Palmer, however, made it to the top 15 finalists before the casting director let her go, telling her parents she had talent but was too young for the production. "After that, I was like, 'I have to act!'" Palmer continued to bug her parents into letting her pursue an acting career and landed a role in *Barbershop 2* in 2004.

The experience of filming a movie cemented Palmer's desire to act and in November 2003, the family relocated to Hollywood. Within weeks, Palmer landed several high-profile gigs—including a national K-Mart commercial and a guest role on the CBS police drama *Cold Case*. In 2004, Palmer starred opposite William H. Macy in the Emmy-nominated made-for-TV movie *The Wool Cap*, playing a little girl who befriends a curmudgeonly mute man after her mother abandons her. Palmer was only ten when she shot the film, yet gave a performance beyond her years. For the role, Palmer earned a Screen Actors Guild nomination for best leading actress, becoming the youngest girl ever nominated for the leading actress award. Other SAG nominees that year included Charlize Theron, Hilary Swank, Glen Close, and Patricia Heaton.

Palmer earned her first lead role on the big screen after beating out 300 other hopefuls to play Akeelah Anderson in *Akeelah and the Bee*, the story of an inner-city eleven-year-old who dreams of competing at the national spelling bee. The 2006 film—which explored race and class—featured Laurence Fishburne as Akeelah's unforgiving coach and Angela Bassett as her worn-out single mother. Legendary *Chicago Sun-Times* film critic Roger Ebert took note of Palmer's breakthrough performance, writing that Palmer "becomes an important young star with this movie. It puts her in Dakota Fanning and Flora Cross territory, and there's something about her poise and self-possession that hints she will grow up to be a considerable actress."

Palmer earned several awards for her performance and was named the outstanding actress at the Black Movie Awards and the Black Reel Awards. Palmer told the Singapore *Straits Times*'s Tay Yek Keak that tackling the role of Akeelah proved inspirational for her own life. "I'm a person who's like Akeelah in the movie in that she believes in herself and thinks that she can do anything. That role made me feel that I can achieve anything. I hope that one day I can win an Oscar and a Grammy."

Along the way, Palmer returned to her musical roots and signed with Atlantic Records. She recorded a single, "All My Girlz," for the *Akeelah* soundtrack. In 2007, Palmer released a full-length pop/R&B album, *So Uncool*. In an effort to promote the disc, Palmer toured with the WNBA, singing half-time and post-game shows. Palmer's older sister, Loreal, shared several songwriting credits. Palmer left Atlantic and signed with Interscope Records after the album failed to chart.

In early 2007, Palmer starred in the Disney Channel original movie *Jump In!* alongside *High School Musical* phenom Corbin Bleu. Palmer played a double-dutch star who lures Bleu's character into joining her team. The film brought in 8.2 million viewers, setting a new record for a Disney Channel original movie premiere. Palmer contributed two songs to the soundtrack, including "It's My Turn Now," which charted on the *Billboard* Pop 100.

The year 2008 found Palmer back on the big screen playing real-life female quarterback Jasmine Plummer in *The Longshots,* a sports drama that followed Plummer's youth football career. Plummer was the first girl to compete in the Pop Warner national football tournament. In *The Longshots*, Palmer shared the set with Ice Cube, who played the role of Curtis Plummer, the endearing uncle who helped Plummer develop her quarterbacking skills.

In November of 2008, Palmer returned to television as the star of her own sitcom, *True Jackson, VP*. On the show, Palmer played 15-year-old True Jackson, vice president of the youth division of Mad Style, a New York City fashion firm. Five million viewers tuned in for the debut, making it Nickelodeon's most popular debut in history. Shortly after it hit the airwaves, *True Jackson* hit number three among ratings for kids ages 9-14. Palmer told the *Daily News'* Cristina Kinon that playing True Jackson fit well with her personality because she actually preferred comedy to drama. Palmer hoped the show, still in production in 2010, would have a long future. "I like making people laugh and making people happy. I just love it when I see people smile. I'm more of a comedian than a dramatic actress, I just happened to do a lot of drama roles."

Selected discography

So Uncool, Atlantic Records, 2007.

Sources

Periodicals

Chicago Tribune, August 22, 2008, sec. Tempo Movies, p. 1.

Daily News (NY), February 9, 2009, p. 66.

National Post (Toronto, Canada), April 25, 2006, p. AL4.

Scholastic Action, April 19, 2010, p. 4.

Straits Times (Singapore), September 2, 2006.

Teen Vogue, August 2008, p. 113.

USA Today, April 27, 2006, p. 5D.

Online

"Akeelah and the Bee," *Chicago Sun-Times,* http://rogerebert.suntimes.com/apps/pbcs.dll/article?AID=/20060427.tif/REVIEWS/60421002.tif/1001 (July 12, 2010).

"Biography," Official Web Site of Keke Palmer, http://kekepalmer.com/bio.htm (July 12, 2010).

"Keke Palmer Bio," Atlantic Records, http://www.atlanticrecords.com/kekepalmer/bio (July 12, 2010).

—*Lisa Frick*

Louise Penny

Author and journalist

Born in 1958, in Toronto, ON; married Michael Whitehead (a hematologist). *Education:* Ryerson Polytechnical Institute, B.A.A., 1979.

Addresses: *Agent*—Patricia Moosbrugger Literary Agency, 2720 Decker Ave. N.W., Albuquerque, NM 87107. *Home*—Quebec, Canada.

Career

Broadcast journalist, Canadian Broadcasting Corporation, 1979-2004; published first novel, *Still Life,* 2005.

Awards: Arthur Ellis Award for best first crime novel, Crime Writers of Canada, for *Still Life,* 2006; Agatha Award, Malice Domestic Ltd., for *A Fatal Grace,* 2008; Agatha Award, Malice Domestic Ltd., for *The Cruelest Month,* 2009.

Sidelights

Mystery writer Louise Penny began writing detective fiction after a long career in broadcast journalism. Her stories are set in a picturesque but rustic part of eastern Quebec and feature the unusual localized interplay of tensions between the province's Anglophone and Francophone citizens. "I think I was fortunate to have Quebec to write about," she told Don Graves in the *Hamilton Spectator* about her success. "For an international audience it's familiar enough to be comfortable, but exotic enough to be interesting. Clearly the French/

Courtesy of Louise Penny

English relations is great fodder for any writer. There's an old saying in journalism ... the protagonist is his own first customer."

Penny was born in Toronto in 1958 as the middle child in a family that included a pair of brothers. She spent much of her life in the Ontario provincial capital except for a few years when her parents relocated to Montreal. Much of her childhood, she admits, was spent with her nose in a book. "As punishment, when I was a child, my mother would send me out to play with other children," she confessed in an interview with Ann Patterson, a writer for the *Herald-Journal* of Spartanburg, South Carolina. "She knew all I really wanted to do was sit alone in my room reading."

Penny earned her undergraduate degree in radio and television from Ryerson Polytechnical Institute in Toronto in 1979 and joined the staff of the Canadian Broadcasting Corporation (CBC). Her first job was in her hometown, but she honed her reportage skills in Thunder Bay, a city that borders Lake Superior. Following that, she settled in Winnipeg, Manitoba, where she worked as a documentary producer and host of a CBC afternoon news show. She raised her profile further by moving to Quebec City, the capital of Quebec Province, to host the CBC's

English-language morning show. Like the province itself, Quebec City was firmly bilingual, but Penny's French skills were far from adequate when she settled there. "Within weeks," she wrote on her Web site, "I'd called Quebecers 'good pumpkins,' ordered flaming mice in a restaurant, for dessert naturally, and asked a taxi driver to 'take me to the war, please.' He turned around and asked 'Which war exactly, Madame?' Fortunately elegant and venerable Quebec City has a very tolerant and gentle nature and simply smiled at me."

In the final years of her 25-year career with the CBC, Penny hosted the *Radio Noon* show out of the network's Montreal studios. She retired in 2004 after marrying a Montreal physician and researcher, Dr. Michael Whitehead, and resolved to finish the novel she had dreamed of writing since her childhood. "Looking back I realize I've tried to write a book every decade of my life, and failed," she reflected in the interview with Graves for the *Hamilton Spectator*. "I think I was too callow, too self-absorbed when I was younger. In many ways, I was too fortunate. Not enough bad had happened."

Penny and her husband liked to visit a scenic part of Quebec known as the Eastern Provinces. The hilly, lake-dotted area is located east of Montreal and the St. Lawrence River and comprises an area that abuts Canada's border with Vermont, New Hampshire, and Maine. Her first novel, *Still Life*, was set in a remote little village like the ones she and her husband frequented, and it took her five years to finish. Her nearly half-decade of toil yielded no interest from publishers and agents, but fortunately found a more welcome reception when submitted to a contest for unpublished debut novels held annually by the Crime Writers' Association of Britain. That group bestows several different "Dagger" awards, but the Debut Dagger competition is open to unpublished authors only. Penny's first Three Pines story, featuring the calm, clever Chief Inspector Armand Gamache, was shortlisted for the 2004 Debut Dagger, which helped her find a literary agent. That representative, in turn, cut a deal with a British publisher for Penny's novel plus two more in a planned series.

Headline Books initially published *Still Life* in Canada in 2005, while Minotaur, an imprint of St. Martin's Press, acquired the U.S. publication rights. The story is set in the fictional town of Three Pines, near Montreal, and opens with the unexplained death of a retired schoolteacher known to all. Three Pines residents are shocked by the gruesome discovery of Jane Neal, felled by an arrow through her heart during hunting season. Miss Neal had taken up landscape painting after she retired, and found surprising success with the vistas she painted. Her friends in the close-knit town are horrified by her death, and a bit suspicious of the detective sent from Montreal to look into the case. This is Chief Inspector Armand Gamache, the lead homicide investigator for the Sûreté du Québec, or Quebec Provincial Police. Gamache receives notice of the murder, and makes his way to Three Pines with his lieutenant, Beauvoir. "Like Narnia, it was generally found unexpectedly and with a degree of surprise that such an elderly village should have been hiding in this valley all along," Penny writes in *Still Life*.

Gamache's detective intuition leads to a surprising discovery inside a Three Pines house. "It was like being in a cave, one of those wondrous caves explorers sometimes found filled with ancient symbols and depictions," he thought. "As with cave drawings, Gamache knew the history of Three Pines and its people was depicted here." The inspector's cool, methodical detective work also leads him to the unexpected killer, to the shock and relief of Three Pines' denizens.

Penny's debut won rave reviews, with many critics comparing her to Dame Agatha Christie, the twentieth century's doyenne of village-set murder mysteries. Writing in the *New York Times*, crime-fiction reviewer Marilyn Stasio lavished praise on Penny, calling her "an author whose deceptively simple style masks the complex patterns of a well-devised plot." Penny won the Arthur Ellis Award for best first crime novel from the Crime Writers of Canada.

Penny's next Three Pines tale, *Dead Cold*, was published in Canada in the fall of 2006, and in the United States the following spring under the title *A Fatal Grace*. This time, a widely disliked socialite dies by electrocution while at a curling event, a distinctly Canadian sport. Gamache must return to Three Pines once again to solve the mystery. Penny's second novel won the Agatha Award for best novel at the annual Malice Domestic convention of Agatha Christie fans. She won her second Agatha Award in 2009 for *The Cruelest Month*, in which a Three Pines resident dies during an amateur séance. Again, it earned terrific reviews. "Perhaps the deftest talent to arrive since Minette Walters, Penny produces what many have tried but few have mastered: a psychologically acute cozy," wrote a *Kirkus Reviews* contributor, using the mystery-genre term for a murder mystery in which the crime occurs outside of the narrative.

The "cozy" was perfected by Christie, who set her beloved stories in the sleepy, picturesque village that improbably also shelters a deviant murderer.

Other writers like Margery Allingham, Dorothy L. Sayers, and Ngaio Marsh also used this standard plot construction, but in a fast-paced contemporary era the cozy fell out of favor with readers, who seemed to prefer a new breed of gritty, urban-set dramas or ones in which the hunt for a serial killer preoccupied the lead detective. Writing in *Maclean's* about the popularity of Penny's books, Sarah Weinman called them "veritable throwbacks to the original golden age…. [I]n Penny's hands, this dated template seems fresh and new for several reasons—and not just because modern technologies such as cellphones and the Internet are woven into the stories." Weinman cited Chief Inspector Gamache as a major factor in the appeal of Penny's works, asserting that this crime-solver's "genuine affinity for Three Pines and its denizens place him far above stock characterization," Weinman noted. "By putting narrative trust in Gamache's hands, the reader is rewarded with airtight plotting and meticulously planted details."

Penny's fourth novel was *The Murder Stone*, published in Britain and Canada in the fall of 2008 and in the United States in early 2009 under the title *A Rule Against Murder*. This time, Gamache and his wife Reine-Marie are vacationing near Three Pines at a well-known wilderness lodge called Manoir Bellechasse. The lakefront resort has a "no-kill" policy, meaning that hunting and fishing are forbidden on its grounds. The other guests include members of an Anglophone family who are there for a reunion to honor their recently departed patriarch. They plan to unveil a new statue of him on the vacation grounds he loved, but it topples over and kills one of his daughters. Pressed into service, Gamache learns the Finney clan is a hotbed of dysfunction, with several potential culprits harboring a secret motivation for the crime. "Seamless, often lyrical prose artfully reveals the characters' flaws, dreams, and blessings," noted a *Publishers Weekly* contributor about Penny's novel.

Penny centers the plot of her fifth novel, *The Brutal Telling*, at a quaint bed-and-breakfast in Three Pines run by Olivier and Gabri, a same-sex couple whose jibes to one another about fulfilling "queer" stereotypes are a staple of the series. This time, a body turns up in one of their guest rooms, and Gamache is perplexed to find the corpse has apparently been moved more than once. "Gamache, to his considerable distress, will have to arrest a friend," noted a writer for *Kirkus Reviews*, who also called the author "a world-class storyteller." Critiquing this title for *Booklist*, reviewer Bill Ott commented on the consistent hailing of Penny as a modern-day Dame Agatha, a comparison he asserted "sells [Penny] short. Her characters are too rich, her grasp of nuance and human psychology too firm for the formula-bound Christie."

Penny was under contract to produce six novels in the Three Pines series. She is one of a handful of Canadian crime-tale authors whose works have achieved best-seller status on both sides of the U.S.-Canada border and across the Atlantic. Asked about her work habits by Patterson of the *Herald-Journal* interview, she explained she comes up with a basic outline, but "starts with 'why.' Why would someone kill? What would drive a person to do it? Then I build characters, then I work out how. Before I start I know who did it, why, all the main and most of the secondary characters, the red herrings and of course, the how." She also said she immerses herself in the project for quite a while. "I try to write 2,000 words a day. Each morning I read over what I've written, do a little tidying up, then start on the new pages," she told Patterson. "I write every day, from 10 a.m. until the 2,000 words are finished. Sometimes it's a few hours, sometimes it's much longer. I try to write every day. I think I'm fearful if I give it a break, the ideas, the muse, will leave."

Penny and her husband live in a small village near Quebec's international border at Vermont. "My dream, from lying in the bedroom as a child, was to live in the country and write books," she told the *Herald-Journal*'s Patterson. "And now I do. Not a day goes by I'm not astonished by my good fortune."

Selected writings

Still Life, Headline (London), 2005; St. Martin's Minotaur (New York City), 2005.

Dead Cold, Headline, 2006; also published as *A Fatal Grace*, St. Martin's Minotaur, 2007.

The Cruelest Month: A Three Pines Mystery, St. Martin's Minotaur, 2008.

The Murder Stone, Headline, 2008; also published as *A Rule Against Murder*, St. Martin's Minotaur, 2009.

The Brutal Telling, Minotaur Books (New York City), 2009.

Sources

Books

Penny, Louise, *Still Life*, St. Martin's Minotaur, 2005, pp. 14, 250.

Periodicals

Booklist, January 1, 2009, p. 54; October 15, 2009, p. 24.

Globe & Mail (Toronto, Canada), August 7, 2008, p. L2; December 19, 2009, p. T1.

Hamilton Spectator (Hamilton, Ontario), December 6, 2008, p. E7.

Herald-Journal (Spartanburg, SC), August 6, 2006.

Kirkus Reviews, January 1, 2008; November 15, 2008; September 15, 2009.

Maclean's, November 5, 2007, p. 93.

New York Times, July 23, 2006; February 8, 2009.

Publishers Weekly, March 12, 2007, p. 40; June 25, 2007, p. 54; January 7, 2008, p. 39; November 10, 2008, p. 34.

Online

"About Louise Penny," LouisePenny.com, http://www.louisepenny.com/louise.htm (February 3, 2010).

—*Carol Brennan*

Phoenix

Rock group

Group formed in the early 1990s in Versailles, France; members include Laurent Brancowitz, guitars; Deck D'Arcy, bass; Thomas Mars (children: [with filmmaker Sofia Coppola] Romy [daughter]), vocals; Christian Mazzalai, guitars.

Addresses: *Record company*—Glassnote Music, 770 Lexington Ave., New York, NY 10065. *Web site*—http://www.wearephoenix.com.

Career

Formed while attending school in Versailles, France, early 1990s; released debut single on own Ghettoblaster label, 1998; signed with Source Records, released single "Heatwave," 1999; released debut album, *United*, 2000; released *Alphabetical*, 2004; released *Live! Thirty Days Ago*, 2005; released *It's Never Been Like That*, 2006; released *Wolfgang Amadeus Phoenix*, 2009.

Jen Maler/Retna UK/Landov

Awards: Grammy Award for best alternative music album, Recording Academy, for *Wolfgang Amadeus Phoenix,* 2010.

Sidelights

The Grammy-award-winning rock group Phoenix emerged as a force in electro-rock in their native Europe during the early 2000s. Comprising members Thomas Mars, Deck D'Arcy, Christian Mazzalai, and Laurent "Branco" Brancowitz, the 1980s-influenced band got their start playing at local venues around France before coming to the attention of Parisian music label Source Records. After serving as a backing band for popular label mates Air, Phoenix released its debut album, *United,* on both sides of the Atlantic in the year 2000. Two albums, 2004's *Alphabetical* and 2006's *It's Never Been Like That* followed before the band recorded what would become their breakthrough hit, *Wolfgang Amadeus Phoenix.* A critically acclaimed effort that reached number two on the *Billboard* Top Independent Albums chart and cracked the Top 40 of the *Billboard* 200, the album went on to win the Grammy for Best Alternative Music Album in January of 2010 and spawned the popular single "1901." The success of *Wolfgang Amadeus Phoenix* propelled the group to headliner status, with Phoenix topping the bill at London's Field Day Festival and appearing at prominent indie rock festivals such as Bonnaroo and Coachella. In addition to their musical notoriety, Phoenix has also gained attention for Mars' long-standing romantic partnership with director Sofia Coppola, with whom he had a daughter in November of 2006.

Phoenix had its first stirrings during the 1980s when eleven-year-old school friends Mars and D'Arcy began writing music in their native Versailles, France—perhaps inspired by the fact that Versailles was, as D'Arcy told Roman Coppola in *Index,* "Boring. At least we had lots of time to work on the band because there was nothing else for us to do." By high school, the pair had become acquainted with classmate Mazzalai, and a bond based on mutual musical interests quickly emerged. The three started playing together, with Mars handling vocals, D'Arcy on bass, and Mazzalai playing guitar. "I showed Thomas and Deck that I could play the Pixies' song 'Where Is My Mind?' on guitar," the latter recalled in the same *Index* interview. "But when I was 16, the chord sequence was too hard for me to play standing up, so I had to do it sitting down. Honestly, I think I joined the band just to hang out with them."

From the beginning, the band dabbled in electronic music, relying on keyboard sounds and other studio-based techniques rather than driving guitars

and live shows. In 1995, Mazzalai's older brother Brancowitz joined the burgeoning group on guitar after his band Darlin'—which also featured the two members of French breakout electronic group Daft Punk—broke up, and the lineup was complete. Perhaps unexpectedly, the French group has always written and performed its songs in English. Speaking to Melena Ryzik of the *New York Times,* vocalist Mars explained, "It's much easier to sing in English because it seems that all the words are more separate; they don't have to blend. In French just the way you build a phrase, they all have an effect on each other. So when we write lyrics, my favorite part is when you delete the in-betweens so that it's almost some sort of weird cryptic form of poetry that doesn't make sense."

During the latter part of the 1990s, the band left the studio to begin playing cover songs at bars around France. The cover circuit did not suit them, however, and after a couple of years the group adopted the name Phoenix and released a limited edition single on its own Ghettoblaster label. Channeling punk rock and 1970s German electronic, the single showcased Phoenix's diverse influences and attracted the attention of Source Records, the musical home of French electronic duo Air. By 1999, Phoenix had signed to Source and begun to gain exposure as Air's backing band for performances on British television. Source released the group's formal debut, the disco-influenced "Heatwave," that same year. American electronic label Astralwerks picked up the group and a year after the release of "Heatwave," Phoenix presented their full-length debut, *United,* on Astralwerks/Source. Taking the production reins in their own hands, the group spent two months in the studio honing their electronic pop sound with what critics largely deemed great success. The group's *Contemporary Musicians* biography quoted Pitchfork Media as declaring the album "one of the most confoundingly brilliant debuts of the year," while Jason Birchmeier of Allmusic Guide dubbed it "an uncanny yet earnest showcase of what makes pop/rock pop without the gaudy trendiness that now makes the 1980s seem so distasteful."

United also gained the group more popular success, with British media outlets and listeners particularly embracing Phoenix's brand of vaguely retro electropop. The album's lead single, "Too Young," went into rotation on major British radio stations XFM, Virgin Radio, and London Live as well as picking up a nod from influential BBC Radio 1 disc jockey Jo Wiley as Record of the Week in May of 2000. Taste-making music paper *Melody Maker* proclaimed the group its New Band of the Week, while music magazine *Uncut* christened its debut the Album of the Week. "No young British band are making music quite like this—a definite retro rock-based feel but with a very 'now' production," argued music promoter Roland Hill in *Music & Media*. "These are early days but I think Phoenix have great potential and make great radio records," he concluded. "Too Young" also hit the airwaves in France and Norway, while its music video graced MTV Europe, Holland's TMF, and France's M6, assuring Phoenix widespread European exposure despite their admitted reluctance to tour. The group was also bolstered by the attention it garnered from the appearance of "Too Young" in the Sofia Coppola film *Lost in Translation*. Coppola, an early fan of Phoenix, had become acquainted with the group when Mars sang on the soundtrack for her previous film, *The Virgin Suicides*; she and the singer ultimately formed a romantic relationship.

Next up for Phoenix was the sophomore effort *Alphabetical*, an album at once more polished and laid-back than its debut. Drawing on influences ranging from hip-hop to synth pop to create a modern take on 1980s adult contemporary pop, *Alphabetical* was released on Astralwerks in March of 2004 after an extended two-year writing and recording process. It generally received critical favor, although Phoenix remained largely unknown on the American music scene—a state perhaps compounded by their practically non-existent North American touring presence. However, the group did make stops around Europe, and some of these were collected on the 2005 live collection *Live! Thirty Days Ago*. Offering an earful of the band's more guitar-based live sound, the album represented a significant departure from the smoothly produced studio tracks that had infused *United* and *Alphabetical*. "What's so attractive and unique about Phoenix's studio records … doesn't translate so well on-stage," sighed Andy Kellman of Allmusic Guide in his review of the collection. A brief tour of North America followed on the heels of this live release, offering audiences a chance to compare the group in-person to their studio personas.

Ultimately, this more contemporary rock & roll sound became the basis for Phoenix's third album, 2006's *It's Never Been Like That*. Mostly leaving behind the disco-influenced electronic beats of its earlier releases, the group sought a cleaner, simpler sound by holing up in Berlin with no prepared material and a tighter recording schedule. These efforts brought Phoenix into closer sync with the guitar-laden sounds that had gained popular ascendancy with the rise of bands such as the Strokes. "This earnest attempt at a costume change fails," commented Pitchfork Media's Rob Mitchum, "but at the same time creates the uncomfortable dynamic that

makes it Phoenix's best album." For the first time, the group's music resonated with broader American audiences, who pushed the album to a modest number 23 on the *Billboard* Top Heatseekers charts. After *It's Never Been Like That*, the group took a lengthy hiatus as front man Mars and his girlfriend Coppola had their first child, a daughter Romy, named for Coppola's brother, Roman.

Regardless of their absence from the public eye, Phoenix continued to write music in anticipation of their fourth album. By 2008, the group had completed its contract with record label EMI and began experimenting with recording music free of label influences with producer Philippe Zdar. In an interview with Pitchfork Media's Ryan Dombal in June of 2009, Mars explained, "we were tired of things that were a little too respectful and elegant…. Also, we were freer because there were no record companies involved. For the first time, we controlled the way we wanted fans to discover the music. So as soon as the record was done we gave the song '1901' away for free. We got such a great response and knew right away that something was happening." The musical result of that new outlook, *Wolfgang Amadeus Phoenix*, appeared on indie label Glassnote in May of 2009. Immediately the album began to attract enthusiastic notices, with fans and critics alike flocking to the esoterically poppy "1901" and "Lisztomania." Writing in *Rolling Stone*, Rob Sheffield proclaimed, "the band sounds more musically confident than ever…. The ten songs are sleek and clean," while Edna Gundersen of *USA Today* applauded "Thomas Mars' sunny croon and the Paris rock quartet's peppy, addictive melodies."

Bolstered by this critical acclaim, Phoenix made the rounds of American television, appearing on *Saturday Night Live* and *Late Night with David Letterman*. Notable appearances at major music festivals such as Tennessee's Bonnaroo followed hard on the heels of the album's release, and widespread public exposure also came through a Cadillac commercial featuring *Wolfgang Amadeus Mozart* single "1901." Widely hailed for its hip musical aesthetic, the album garnered a prestigious Grammy nomination later in 2009. In January of the following year, Phoenix picked up the Grammy for Best Alternative Music Album over such musical luminaries as Depeche Mode and the Yeah Yeah Yeahs. Speaking about the group's Grammy win to Ryan Dombal of Pitchfork Media, Mars commented, "It's weird because it's very nice, but you feel some sadness to it, too. It's hard to enjoy the moment. It felt like we're already on the other side of something, so the four of us are all trying to protect each other."

Despite their mixed feelings about their Grammy success, Phoenix had little reason to fear disappearing from the public eye in the months following their win. A lengthy series of mostly sold-out shows in the United States, Mexico, Japan, Australia, and Europe through the winter of 2010 led up to spring and summer appearances at major American music festivals Coachella and Bonnaroo, Germany's Southside Fest and Hurricane Fest, Belgium's Rock Werchter, and London, England's Field Day Festival. Indeed, the previously road-shy band continued to plow through a packed touring schedule, accompanied on the American leg of their tour by openers Two Door Cinema Club. Nevertheless, Phoenix still found time to pursue new projects, with a collaboration between the group and Coppola on a film adaptation of the *Wolfgang Amadeus Phoenix* track "Love Like a Sunset" on the books for the future. Also on the horizon for Mars was a second child with Coppola, due sometime in 2010.

Selected discography

United, Astralwerks/Source (New York City and Paris), 2000.
Alphabetical, Astralwerks (New York City), 2004.
Live! Thirty Days Ago, Astralwerks, 2005.
It's Never Been Like That, Astralweks, 2006.
Wolfgang Amadeus Phoenix, Glassnote (New York City), 2009.

Sources

Books

Contemporary Musicians, vol. 59, Thomson Gale, 2007.

Periodicals

GQ, December 2009, p. 292.
Index, June/July 2004.
Music & Media, July 15, 2000, p. 6.
New York Times, March 7, 2010.
Rolling Stone, May 26, 2009.
Thrasher, September 2006, p. 192.
Time, December 11, 2006, p. 101.
UPI NewsTrack, December 16, 2009.
USA Today, May 26, 2009, p. 08D.

Online

"Live! Thirty Days Ago," Allmusic Guide, http://www.allmusic.com/cg/amg.dll?p=amg&sql=10:hpfuxqlsldfe (March 15, 2010).
"Phoenix," Allmusic Guide, http://www.allmusic.com/cg/amg.dll?p=amg&sql=11:difyxqlkldde~T1 (March 15, 2010).
"Phoenix: It's Never Been Like That," Pitchfork Media, http://pitchfork.com/reviews/albums/9030-its-never-been-like-that/ (March 15, 2010).
"Phoenix," Pitchfork Media, http://pitchfork.com/features/interviews/7667-phoenix/ (March 15, 2010).
"Phoenix's Thomas Mars on Grammy Win: 'It Sounds Like a Joke,'" Pitchfork Media, http://pitchfork.com/news/37770-phoenixs-thomas-mars-on-grammy-win-it-sounds-like-a-joke/ (March 15, 2010).
"United," Allmusic Guide, http://www.allmusic.com/cg/amg.dll?p=amg&sql=10:djfrxqukldke (March 15, 2010).

—*Vanessa E. Vaughn*

Mark Pincus

Chief Executive Officer of Zynga

Born February 13, 1966, in Chicago, IL; son of Theodore Henry Pincus and Donna Foreman. *Education:* University of Pennsylvania, B.S.E., 1988; Harvard University, M.B.A., 1993.

Addresses: *Office*—Zynga Game Network, Inc., 365 Vermont St., San Francisco, CA 94103.

Career

Analyst, Lazard Freres & C.C., 1988-90; associate, Asian Capital Partners, 1990-91; telecommunications executive in Englewood, Colorado, 1993-94; vice president, Columbia Capital, 1994-95; co-founder, Freeloader, Inc., 1995, and chief executive officer, 1995-97; founder of SupportSoft and tribe. net; founder, Zynga Game Network, 2007, and chief executive officer, 2007—.

Sidelights

Mark Pincus is the founder and chief executive officer of Zynga, the stunningly successful developer of online games for Facebook and other social-networking Web sites. Zynga's Farmville application for Facebook users is one of the most successful interactive pastimes ever created: Every month, about 83 million "farmers" plant and harvest virtual crops via their Facebook account. "At first we didn't realize how big social gaming could be," Pincus confessed to public television talk-show host Charlie Rose in late 2009. "But once we launched our first game and we saw how viral it

could be and how many people would want to come and play games together, we started to see how big the audience could get."

Born in Chicago in 1966, Pincus is the son of a public relations executive and attended the city's elite Francis W. Parker School, a private academy in the Lincoln Park neighborhood. He earned an economics degree from the University of Pennsylvania in 1988 and went to work on Wall Street as an analyst at Lazard Freres, the investment banking firm. In 1990, he moved to Hong Kong to take a job with Asian Capital Partners, a Singapore bank. Returning to the United States, he entered Harvard Business school, from which he earned a master's in business administration in 1993. He spent time in the Denver, Colorado, area as a telecommunications-industry executive before joining Columbia Capital in Alexandria, Virginia, in 1994 as a vice president of a venture-capital firm that funded communications industry start-ups.

In late 1995 Pincus co-founded Freeloader, Inc., which offered a new "push" technology to avoid high-usage charges for Internet surfers in the first years of the World Wide Web, when dial-up, or landline connections were still the primary way to access cyberspace. While simple Web pages loaded relatively quickly in those days, Internet users who wanted to download larger files, such as images or media clips, could expect to be online for hours waiting for a download to complete over the slow modem speed. Pincus' cleverly named service permitted Web surfers to download data while offline to their hard drive, thus to avoiding high usage charges from their Internet service provider. Freeloader was so successful that the company grew exponentially in a matter of months, and it was sold to a more established company, Individual Inc., in June of 1996 for $38 million.

Pincus and Freeloader's co-founder, a former America Online engineer named Sunil Paul, moved to the heart of the burgeoning information-technology industry near the San Francisco Bay area, Silicon Valley, with the plan to expand Freeloader even further. There were internal fissures at Individual Inc., however, and some executives were unhappy with the acquisition and its prospects. Pincus and Paul declined an offer to buy back their company, and Freeloader was shut down in the spring of 1997. By then, the push technology was on the verge of becoming outdated anyway thanks to new high-speed Internet-connection options.

Pincus went on to start other companies, including SupportSoft, which offered major corporations and consumers third-party online support, and tribe.net, an online community that connected users via common interests that was launched in the summer of 2003. It competed with Friendster, an early entrant into the social-networking field that was quickly supplanted by MySpace. That site, in turn, lost users to Facebook, which was started at Harvard College by a student, then expanded to other schools in the Ivy League before rolling out to other U.S. colleges and universities. In mid-2006, Facebook began allowing anyone over the age of 13 to join, and membership skyrocketed. In May of 2007, the company began permitting third-party software developers to create applications for Facebook, and Pincus seized on the chance to create a new type of online gaming community.

Back in 1998, Pincus was interviewed by *Inc.* magazine about the rise and fall of Freeloader, and journalist Stephanie Gruner noted that Pincus brought Zinga, his American bulldog, with him to the café where they met. That became the name of Pincus' newest venture, Zynga Game Network, which was launched in early 2008. Early games offered were versions of popular board games like Risk, but a Texas Hold 'Em poker application caught on quickly, followed by Mafia Wars. Pincus explained the last one to Charlie Rose in the television interview.

"'Mafia Wars' is a game where you form a mafia with your friends," he said. "The key difference is that you are relying on your friends. You're collaborating together throughout the game. There's features like 'declare war' where if somebody attacks you, you can declare war on them and it tells all your friends to come help you."

In that same interview, Pincus estimated that of the 400 million active Facebook users in late 2009, about 60 million played Mafia Wars, Farmville, Café World, or other popular Zynga applications. Around this same time Zynga received a major influx of fresh capital from Digital Sky Technologies, a Russian investment house, and began to use the funds to expand into the smartphone market. The deal represented a major coup for Pincus, who had been known in the tech world more for the failure of his ventures than for their ultimate success.

Asked by the *New York Times'* Adam Bryant about his executive management skills, Pincus claims to draw upon the lessons he learned back at the Parker School in Chicago, when he played on a soccer team that advanced all the way to the state quarterfinals one year despite a perennial underdog status. He can judge a new hire's future performance quickly, he told Bryant. "There are people who don't want to screw up, and so they just pass the ball right away. Then there are the ones who have this kind of intelligence, and they can make these great plays. These people seem to have high emotional intelligence. It's not that they're a star player, but they have decent skills, and they will get you the ball and then be where you'd expect to put it back to them. It's like their head is really in the game."

Sources

Books

Marquis Who's Who, Marquis Who's Who, 2009.

Periodicals

Advertising Age, November 16, 2009, p. 22.
FSB, May 1, 2004, p. 88.
Inc., May 19, 1998, p. 88.
New York Times, January 31, 2010.
Washington Techway, January 17, 2000, p. 23.

Transcripts

Charlie Rose Show, PBS, December 29, 2009.

—*Carol Brennan*

Sebastián Piñera

President of Chile

Born Miguel Juan Sebastián Piñera Echenique, December 1, 1949, in Santiago, Chile; son of José Piñera Carvallo (a diplomat) and Magdalena Echenique Rozas; married Cecilia Morel Montes, 1973; children: Magdalena, Cecilia, Sebastián, Cristóbal. *Education:* Pontifical Catholic University of Chile, degree in economics, 1971; Harvard University, M.A., Ph.D, c. 1975.

Addresses: *Home*—Santiago, Chile. *Office*—Palacio de la Moneda, Morandé 130, Santiago Centro, Chile.

Career

Professor of economics, early 1970s-1990; founder, Inversiones Bancard Ltda. (a credit card company), late 1970s; Senator of Chile, 1989-98; president of the National Renewal Party, 2001-04; president of Chile, 2010—.

Awards: Raul Iver Oxley Prize, Pontifical Catholic University of Chile, 1971.

Sidelights

In 2010 Sebastián Piñera became first conservative political figure to lead Chile in more than two decades. The South American nation of 17 million has traditionally voted center-left governments into power since the end of a brutal dictatorship, but Piñera's election as president marked a new era for one of the most prosperous countries in Latin America. Images from his inauguration in March of 2010 became the focus of international news stories, for the ceremony was nearly derailed by a serious aftershock from a devastating late February earthquake.

Piñera was born in 1949 in Santiago, Chile's capital, as one of five children in a family of Spanish-Basque heritage. His father, José Piñera Carvallo, served as Chile's ambassador to Belgium when Piñera was a child, and then the family lived in New York City for a time when the elder Piñera was posted to the United Nations. He attended a Roman Catholic high school in Santiago and went on to the Pontifical Catholic University of Chile, earning an undergraduate degree in economics in 1971. Returning to the United States, he completed his master's and doctoral degrees in economics at Harvard University.

Piñera was in graduate school in 1973 when Chile's democratically elected president, the socialist Salvador Allende Gossens, died shortly after a right-wing military coup at the presidential palace. A military junta led by General Augusto Pinochet Ugarte ruled Chile for the next seven years; in 1980 a new constitution went into effect and Pinochet began an eight-year term as president, which he then attempted to extend. The Pinochet regime was tied to widespread human rights abuses that affected a large swath of Chilean families, and the scars from the period lingered long after Pinochet stepped down in 1990.

Back in Chile in 1976, Piñera became a professor of economics at several schools, including his alma mater, the Pontifical Catholic University, and the University of Chile. He also founded a company, Inversiones Bancard Ltda., that introduced the first credit cards to Chile in the late 1970s. His business empire expanded to include part of Línea Aérea Nacional de Chile, or LAN Airlines, and one of Chile's major television networks, Chilevisión.

In December of 1989, Piñera won a seat in the Senate of Chile, representing East Santiago. After allying with *Renovación Nacional*, or National Renewal Party, a center-right organization, he made his first bid for higher office in 1992 in his attempt to win the party's nomination for the coming presidential election. When his Senate term expired in 1998, he became the National Renewal Party's frontrunner in the coming election, but lost to Ricardo Lagos, the candidate from the main center-left party, *Partido por la Democracia*, or Party for Democracy.

Piñera ran again in 2005, but lost to Michelle Bachelet, the Socialist Party candidate who became the first woman ever to lead Chile. Bachelet's father had been an officer in the Chilean armed forces and died in custody after Pinochet came to power; Bachelet and her mother were detained for a time and tortured during interrogation.

In the years following the end of the Pinochet era, Chile's economy boomed. Some of this was tied to its position as the world's biggest copper producer, while fish, wine, timber, and other natural resources were also major exports for the global market. Through his investments, Piñera had become one of Chile's wealthiest citizens, with *Forbes* estimating his personal fortune at $2.2 billion in 2010 from his holdings in LAN, Chilevisión, and other properties. In the 2009 presidential election, he spent heavily as the candidate of the conservative *Coalición por el Cambio*, or Coalition for Change. His main challenger was Eduardo Frei Ruiz-Tagle of Concertación; Frei's father—Chile's president before Allende—had also died under suspicious circumstances during the Pinochet era.

One of Piñera's television campaign ads showed a same-sex couple, which caused a stir in the country, which remains ardently Roman Catholic. Some of the parties that belong to the Coalition for Change oppose divorce and birth control, or are the political base for figures who served under Pinochet. In a televised debate, Piñera vowed that he would not appoint any former Pinochet-era politicians to his cabinet if elected. "One of the main reasons I opposed the military government was because I knew human rights were being violated," he said in the debate, according to a report by Juan Forero in the *Washington Post*. "We won't have ministers from the military government in our cabinet."

Piñera failed to win a majority in the first round of voting on December 13, 2009, and faced off against Frei in the runoff on January 17, 2010. Piñera won with 51 percent of the vote, and became the first conservative politician elected to lead Chile since 1958. His business ties presented a possible conflict of interest, and he divested some of his holdings into a blind trust—though he refused to give up ownership of Colo-Colo, a professional soccer team. The inauguration was scheduled for March 11, but on February 27 Chile was struck by a massive earthquake of an 8.8 magnitude that provoked a tsunami on its Pacific coastline and leveled an estimated 500,000 homes. There was widespread looting, and Bachelet's lame-duck government was criticized for its slow response.

On the day of Piñera's inauguration, the country was struck by another earthquake, this one of 7.2 magnitude, that occurred just as he and his entourage were arriving at the National Congress building in the port city of Valparaíso. After his swearing-in ceremony, the National Congress building was evacuated and Piñera traveled to the city of Rancagua, epicenter of the aftershock, to survey the damage. He pledged to commit major resources to the rebuilding effort, which some predicted could cost as much as $30 billion and prove a major setback to the country's economic growth of the past decade. Piñera, noted a writer for the London *Independent*, "is assuming office amid a tremendous outpouring of solidarity and patriotism. Chileans have donated millions of dollars to help survivors and everywhere in the capital, Santiago, there are red, white, and blue flags. If the president can harness this goodwill and national defiance in the face of adversity, it could propel his government forward."

Sources

Periodicals

Independent (London, England), March 12, 2010, p. 30.
New York Times, March 10, 2010.
Washington Post, January 18, 2010, p. A10.

Online

"Profile: Sebastian Pinera," BBC News, http://news.bbc.co.uk/2/low/americas/8461261.stm (April 12, 2010).

"Sebastián: Mi Biografía," Bienvenida la Nueva Forma de Gobernar, http://www.pinera2010.cl/sebastian/ (April 14, 2010).

"The World's Billionaires: #437 Sebastian Pinera," *Forbes*, http://www.forbes.com/lists/2010/10/billionaires-2010_Sebastian-Pinera_YLRC.html (April 14, 2010).

—*Carol Brennan*

Maria Pinto

Bonnie Trafelet/MCT/Landov

Fashion designer

Born c. 1957, in Chicago, IL; daughter of Costantino (a sanitation worker) and Virginia (a caterer and store owner) Pinto. *Education:* School of the Art Institute of Chicago, B.F.A., 1990; also attended Parsons School of Design and the Fashion Institute of Technology.

Addresses: *Office*—Maria Pinto, 133 N. Jefferson St., 6th Fl., Chicago, IL 60661.

Career

Worked at her family's Chicago-area restaurants, 1975-87; design assistant for Geoffrey Beene, c. 1990; launched own line of accessories and eveningwear, 1991; filed for bankruptcy, 2002; relaunched eponymous line, 2004; opened Chicago boutique, 2008; became member of the Council of Fashion Designers of America (CFDA), 2009; closed business, 2010.

Sidelights

Designer Maria Pinto was already highly regarded among Chicago's more fashion-forward women for her streamlined but luxurious clothes, but catapulted to national fame when Michelle Obama began wearing her dresses on the campaign trail. Pinto's eponymous company garnered immense publicity when the future First Lady took the stage at a Minnesota rally in June of 2008 to congratulate her husband Barack Obama at a major milestone in his campaign when he became the presumptive Democratic presidential nominee. That

purple sheath dress she wore, asserted *Chicago Tribune* journalist Wendy Donahue, "broadcast Obama's taste—and Pinto's talent—to the world."

Pinto came to the fashion business relatively late in life, graduating from the prestigious School of the Art Institute in Chicago in 1990, when she was in her early thirties. The last of seven children in an Italian-American family and a twin, she spent the first years of her life in Chicago's Chinatown neighborhood before her family moved to the suburbs. After graduating from Palatine High School, Pinto worked in the restaurant her mother Virginia, a caterer, had opened in West Dundee in 1975, inside her homemade pasta shop. Mama di Pinto's closed in 1981, the same year that Pinto's older brother Silvio opened a new space in the River North neighborhood of downtown Chicago. Pinto was a partner in the restaurant, called Signi Dorati—Italian for "Golden Dreams"—and would help manage it in its six years of operation on North Wells Street. It closed in 1987, and Pinto's brother died of cancer a year later.

Pinto was a talented seamstress who had been sewing her own clothes and making outfits for her friends and family since her early teens. The shuttering of the restaurant forced her to consider her career options, and she finally decided to finish a fine-art degree at the School of the Art Institute of Chicago. After graduating in 1990, she moved to New York City, where she took classes at the Parsons School of Design and the Fashion Institute of Technology in New York City while working as an assistant at Geoffrey Beene. Pinto's first creations were small scarves for suit pockets, and she had some success selling these at local boutiques after she returned to Chicago. A friend loaned her $20,000 to launch her company out of her downtown loft, and the scarves evolved into a line of sumptuously embellished stoles and wraps for dressy occasions. The high-end retailer Bergdorf Goodman began carrying her wares in 1991, and Pinto expanded into a full line of eveningwear. By the end of the decade, her company, which remained privately held, was estimated to be bringing in roughly $4 million in revenue. In January of 2002, however, she was forced to file for bankruptcy after a serious slide in consumer spending that followed the 9/11 attacks; furthermore, Pinto had discovered a key employee had embezzled some $300,000 from the company coffers.

Reenergizing her creative spirit through painting, Pinto marshaled some experts and investors to finance a comeback. This time, her backers received a stake in the company, which was relaunched under the Maria Pinto name in 2004. Once again, she started out designing eveningwear, then began adding more daytime looks. Buyers from Saks Fifth Avenue, Barneys New York, and luxury Fifth Avenue department store Takashimaya all signed on, and Pinto's line was also carried at the Chicago boutique Ikram, named after its fashion-forward proprietor Ikram Goldman. Oprah Winfrey wore Pinto designs, the majority of which were made in Chicago by the team of talented seamstresses Pinto employed.

Pinto met the future First Lady during her first year back in business. Michelle Obama, a Harvard-trained lawyer and at the time a vice president with the University of Chicago Hospital system, "came in just like everyone else and said: 'I need a few dresses. I need a suit for work,'" Pinto recalled in an interview with New York Times journalist Susan Saulny. In early 2007 her new client's husband, U.S. Senator Barack Obama, announced his bid to secure the Democratic Party presidential nomination, and Michelle Obama cut back on her career to hit the campaign trail. Her boldly hued dresses and coats piqued interest from reporters, and Pinto's name was one of several designers released by the press office of the Obama campaign in response to queries about Mrs. Obama's attire.

On February 25, 2008, Michelle Obama appeared on the cover of Newsweek wearing one of Pinto's silk sheath dresses. On June 3, 2008, with the most important state primaries locked up, the Obamas appeared onstage at an event in St. Paul, Minnesota, embraced, and gave one another the famous knuckle bump just before the senator accepted the party nomination. Mrs. Obama was wearing a purple sheath from Pinto's line, and the resulting controversy over the couple's gesture helped put Pinto's dress on the front page of newspapers across the country. Two months later, Michelle Obama took the stage to deliver a speech at the Democratic National Convention wearing a teal dress by Pinto, which again appeared in the next day's headlines and most-viewed stories in cyber-journalism.

Pinto had been planning to open a boutique in Chicago, and rolled out a lavish space in Chicago's Fulton River District two weeks before the Democratic convention. Her company's sales increased 40 percent from 2008 to 2009, and she was invited to become a member of the Council of Fashion Designers of America (CFDA). In September of 2009, she presented her first runway show at New York Fashion Week, which WWD described as "a tango-inspired collection full of drama and color; bold silk flowers on blouses and dresses and some of the best leathers in town, particularly in sexy jackets and a chic sheath." Pinto was heartened by the industry accolades, but perplexed by the lack of follow-through. "I was like, where are the orders?," she told Saulny in the New York Times, adding she knew "this is not a good sign."

In February of 2010, Pinto announced she was closing her business and filing for bankruptcy. Her boutique, which had opened just 18 months earlier to immense publicity, was the site of a weeklong sale, and Pinto told journalists she was heading to Spain for a month. She planned to consider her options in the art world and fashion when she returned. "I know I'll do something again," she told WWD's Beth Wilson. "Life is chapters and this is the next chapter."

Sources

Periodicals

Chicago Tribune, June 27, 1998, sec. BUSINESS, p. 1; August 22, 2004; October 19, 2008, sec. STYLE, p. 4.
Crain's Chicago Business, February 18, 2008, p. 18.
New York Times, August 14, 2008; April 30, 2010.
Toronto Star, August 22, 2008, p. L1.
Virginian Pilot, January 7, 2009, p. E3.

WWD, October 20, 2004, p. 11; August 22, 2008, p. 11; September 18, 2009, p. 11; February 16, 2010, p. 24; March 11, 2010, p. 5.

Online

"Biography," Maria Pinto Official Web Site, http://www.mariapinto.com/about (April 17, 2010).

—*Carol Brennan*

Michael Pollan

Author and journalist

Born February 6, 1955, on Long Island, NY; son of Stephen M. (a financial consultant and author) and Corky (an editor and journalist) Pollan; married Judith Belzer (an artist); children: Isaac. *Education:* Bennington College, B.A., 1977; attended Oxford University; Columbia University, M.A., 1981.

Addresses: *Agent*—The Steven Barclay Agency, 12 Western Ave., Petaluma, CA 94952. *Home*—California. *Office*—Berkeley Graduate School of Journalism, 121 North Gate Hall, University of California—Berkeley, Berkeley, CA 94720-5860.

Career

Reporter, *Vineyard Gazette,* 1973; assistant editor (summers), *Village Voice,* 1974-76; assistant editor, *Politicks & Other Human Interests,* 1977-78; associate producer, Gateway Productions (a documentary film company), 1978; associate producer, *Straight Talk* (a daily public affairs talk show), 1980; senior editor, *Channels Magazine,* 1981-83; senior editor, *Harper's Magazine,* 1983-85, then executive editor, 1985-94; contributor, *New York Times Magazine,* 1988—, and contributing editor, 1995—; Knight Professor of Journalism and director of Knight Program in Science and Environmental Journalism, Graduate School of Journalism, University of California—Berkeley, 2003—. Contributor to periodicals, including *Esquire, Condé Nast Traveler, Vogue, New York Times Magazine, Mother Jones, Gourmet, Vogue, Travel & Leisure, House & Garden, Gardens Illustrated, New York Times Book Review, Metropolitan Home, Los Angeles Times Book Review, Smithsonian,* and *Gardens Illustrated.*

Member: Fellow, New York Institute of the Humanities; board of advisors, Center for Urban Education about Sustainable Agriculture.

Awards: Reuters-World Conservation Union Global Award for Excellence in Environmental Journalism, 2000, for "Playing God in the Garden," 2000; James Beard Award for Best Magazine Feature Article, James Beard Foundation, for "Sustaining Vision," 2002; Best Food Writing book award, for *The Omnivore's Dilemma,* 2006.

Sidelights

Author and journalist Michael Pollan topped the *New York Times* nonfiction best-seller list for several weeks in 2008 with his book *In Defense of Food: An Eater's Manifesto.* In it, he offers a discourse on contemporary American eating habits, some of which he explored in his previous tome, *The Omnivore's Dilemma: A Natural History of Four Meals.* A contributing editor with the *New York Times Magazine* since 1995, Pollan and his writings have been instrumental in creating a movement to eat more locally grown, non-processed foods. He is particularly critical of major agribusiness concerns, which he views as having deep, unethical ties to the U.S.

regulatory agencies charged with promoting healthy eating habits. "One of the problems is that the government supports unhealthy food and does very little to support healthy food," he asserted in a *Mother Jones* interview with Clara Jeffery. "We subsidize high fructose corn syrup. We subsidize hydrogenated corn oil. We do not subsidize organic food. We subsidize four crops that are the building blocks of fast food."

Pollan was born in 1955 to Corky Pollan, an editor who would spend much of her career with *New York* magazine, writing its popular "Best Bets" column. His father, Stephen M. Pollan, was a professor of business, real-estate consultant, and financial advisor who co-authored several popular personal finance books, including *Die Broke: A Radical Four-Part Financial Plan,* that became a bestseller after its 1997 publication.

Pollan spent his childhood in the Farmingdale and Syosset communities on Long Island, though his parents later settled in Sharon, Connecticut. He grew up with sisters Lori, Dana, and Tracy, the last of whom went on to appear in film, stage, and television productions before marrying the actor Michael J. Fox. At Bennington College in Vermont Pollan studied English, and then did a stint at Oxford University before entering Columbia University's graduate program, which granted him an M.A. in English literature in 1981.

By that point Pollan already had some extensive experience in journalism. After high school he worked for the *Vineyard Gazette* on Martha's Vineyard, and spent a couple of summers in the mid-1970s as an assistant editor at the *Village Voice.* He worked in television briefly before becoming a senor editor at *Channels Magazine,* a highly regarded publication that covered the television industry in the early boom years of cable. In 1983, he became a senior editor at *Harper's Magazine* as it was about to undergo significant modernization and reformatting. He became executive editor in 1985 and, with managing editor Lewis H. Lapham, the renewed *Harper's* went on to win six prestigious National Magazine Awards. Pollan's first published title was *The Harper's Index Book,* a 1987 compilation of the popular "Harper's Index" feature in the magazine, which he had complied for many years.

Pollan's first solo work set the future direction of his career. *Second Nature: A Gardener's Education* was published by Atlantic Monthly Press in 1991 and won critical acclaim. His essay-length discourses touch upon the various aspects of gardening his-

tory, the struggles to tame his parcel of Connecticut land, and the barrage of specialty catalogs for the modern gardener. He discusses how some common weeds came to North America—tumbleweed, for example, came from the seeds that nineteenth-century Russian immigrants brought with them to start flax farms on the High Plains—and divulges he has spent time in his yard looking for valuable composting traces of the cows who once inhabited his property, a former dairy farm. In one chapter, Pollan traces the history of the rose, which Maxine Kumin called "an absolute tour de force," in her laudatory review for the *New York Times.* Kumin wrote, "it enlarged my world view. As Mr. Pollan examines the social hierarchy of the old rose we traverse the Roman Empire, the Middle Ages, the Renaissance and the period of the Enlightenment with five major species, known across Europe."

Pollan had already begun to explore Western civilization's obsession with taming nature in articles for the *New York Times Magazine.* An essay he penned in time for Memorial Day weekend of 1989 titled "Why Mow?" prompted a flurry of reader responses published the following week. As Pollan had already noted in the essay, Americans had a particularly strong attachment to their grass lawns. "Nowhere in the world are lawns as prized as in America," he writes, theorizing that they serve as a sort of unifying force in such an inhomogeneous nation. "France has its formal, geometric gardens, England its picturesque parks, and America this unbounded democratic river of manicured lawn along which we array our houses."

In the article, Pollan also wrote of his father's own rebelliousness back on Long Island in the late 1950s, when he tired of mowing the lawn every week and decided to do it just once a month—which prompted open hostility from their neighbors. Once Pollan grew up and bought his own home in Connecticut's Housatonic Valley, he admitted he initially enjoyed the chore, then "came to resent the four hours that my lawn demanded of me each week," he confesses. "I tired of the endless circuit, pushing the howling mower back and forth across the vast page of my yard, recopying the same green sentences over and over: 'I am a conscientious homeowner. I share your middle-class values.'"

In 1995 Pollan became a contributing editor at the *New York Times Magazine.* His next book, *A Place of My Own: The Education of an Amateur Builder,* chronicled his experiences in building a small writing studio on his Connecticut property as he and his wife were expecting their first child. "It is also a wry and touching examination of the values of 'dadness'" noted Mary Loudon in a London *Times* review, "the sort of dadness that prizes manual and physical capability above intellectual prowess, and of which children are inordinately proud."

Pollan returned to the topic of plants and gardening in 2001 with *The Botany of Desire: A Plant's-Eye View of the World.* Here he dissects the history of humankind's domestication of four popular plant species that each represent a single human desire: the sweetness provided by an apple; the tulip's beauty; an ability to exert control as characterized by cultivation of the potato, and ebriety—the opposite of sobriety—that comes from *cannabis sativa,* or marijuana. In the essay on the potato, Pollan delves into the controversy spurred by genetically modified foods. Writing in the *New York Observer,* Ursula Buchan found Pollan's latest effort "an immensely readable, thought-provoking and unusual—indeed, uncategorizable—book.... He is fortunate in benefiting from a lack of competition in the field he has chosen for himself, for most garden writers could not begin to write such a book. Perhaps, like the plants he describes, Michael Pollan has made his own luck. But in his case, it was conscious."

Pollan's interest in the sociological aspects of agriculture expanded into a more fully researched consideration of what we eat and why. In 2006 his newest work, *The Omnivore's Dilemma: A Natural History of Four Meals,* won scores of awards, including one from the James Beard Foundation for best food writing of the year. Its title, using the scientific, Latin-root term for a creature that eats all types of food, was borrowed from Dr. Paul Rozin, a longtime University of Pennsylvania scholar whose research focuses on humans and their psychological relationship to food. The "omnivore's dilemma" was Rozin's term for the anxiety that such a vast array of food choices causes modern consumers, who worry about certain foods being detrimental to their health as well as the possibly toxic sources of the fish, meat, and vegetables.

Pollan set out to dissect four different meals, and his research took him to several corners of the United States. He went to South Dakota to buy his own steer, then met up with it again at a Kansas slaughterhouse, to which it had traveled by truck and arrived standing in a thick carpet of its own excrement and that of the other transported cattle. This was part of the first section, which examined the major agribusiness giants that produce ingredients for a typical fast-food meal. Next, Pollan investigated the burgeoning organic-food industry as exemplified by the Whole Foods grocery-store chain. After that, he slit the throat of a chicken he later ate at a Virginia farm that specializes in genuine "locavore" cuisine. Finally, Pollan prepares a meal from items he gathered himself, including a wild boar he shot and killed. "Walking with a loaded rifle in an unfamiliar forest bristling with the signs of your prey is thrilling," he wrote in an excerpt that appeared in the *New York Times Magazine.* "It embarrasses me to write that, but it is true."

Friends with more expertise had helped him learn to hunt, and others aided with the butchering. Pollan invited them all for dinner, serving the pork with greens he grew himself, and his guests pronounced it delicious. "I prized too the almost perfect transparency of this meal, the brevity and simplicity of the chain that linked it to the natural world," he wrote. "Scarcely an ingredient in it had ever worn a label or bar code or price tag, and yet I knew almost everything there was to know about its provenance and price," Ultimately, he conceded that "there was nothing very realistic about this meal. Yet as a sometimes thing, as a kind of ritual, a meal that is eaten in full consciousness of what it took to make is worth preparing every now and again, if only as a way to remind us of the true cost of our food, and that, no matter what we eat, we eat by the grace not of industry but of nature."

The Omnivore's Dilemma was a bestseller, as was Pollan's next book, *In Defense of Food: An Eater's Manifesto,* which appeared in 2008. Like his father's famously catchy "die broke, live rich" guide, Pollan devised a slogan: "Eat food. Not too much. Mostly plants." In this work, he dissects the history of processed and convenience foods in the American diet and the increasingly fruitless ways in which scientists and the food industry have conspired to promote healthier eating habits. One section examines what is known as the French Paradox: the French enjoy their vaunted cuisine, which is quite high in animal fats, yet are on average slimmer and less prone to cardiovascular-disease than Americans. The French Paradox had less to do with numbers than some important cultural differences, Pollan explained to Neal Conan of National Public Radio's *Talk of the Nation.* "They don't snack as much as we do," he said. "They think eating in your car, which we do with, you know, alarming frequencies, is really disgusting. They eat on smaller plates, smaller portions. They eat together."

Pollan condensed much of what he had discovered as a food writer into *Food Rules: An Eater's Manual,* which was published by Penguin in 2009. It serves as a quick-read guide to 64 basic tenets of healthy eating, plus some common-sense injunctions, such as Rule No. 11: "Avoid foods you see advertised on television." He had been working on these "rules" for a few years by then, and the guidelines draw upon biology and folklore, too. He discussed one with Conan in the *Talk of the Nation* interview, cautioning readers not to "eat anything that won't eventually rot." Food that decays, he explained, is good. "Other species that are still in touch with their instincts like bacteria and things like that and fungi are interested in that food. The reason a Twinkie has a shelf life that can be counted in years is that none of the microorganisms we share this planet with have any interest whatsoever in a Twinkie."

Pollan teaches journalism in the graduate program at the University of California—Berkeley, where he directs the Knight Program in Science and Environmental Journalism. In 2010, he answered readers' questions for a special *Time* magazine feature, and asked if he has any bad eating habits. "I like French fries, and I probably shouldn't eat them very often," he admitted. "I actually came up with a rule: Eat all the junk food you want as long as you cook it yourself. One reason we struggle with obesity today is that special-occasion foods like French fries, cakes, and cookies have become so easy to obtain."

Selected writings

(With Eric Etheridge) *The Harper's Index Book*, illustrated by Martim Avillez, introduction by Lewis H. Lapham, Holt (New York City), 1987.
Second Nature: A Gardener's Education, Atlantic Monthly (New York City), 1991.
A Place of My Own: The Education of an Amateur Builder, Random House (New York City), 1997.
The Botany of Desire: A Plant's-Eye View of the World, Random House, 2001.

The Omnivore's Dilemma: A Natural History of Four Meals, Penguin (New York City), 2006.
In Defense of Food: An Eater's Manifesto, Penguin, 2008.
Food Rules: An Eater's Manual, Penguin, 2009.

Sources

Books

Pollan, Michael, *In Defense of Food: An Eater's Manifesto*, Penguin, 2008.
Pollan, Michael, *Food Rules: An Eater's Manual*, Penguin, 2009.

Periodicals

Mother Jones, March-April 2009, p. 32.
New York Observer, May 28, 2001, p. 24.
New York Times, June 9, 1991.
New York Times Magazine, May 28, 1989; March 26, 2006.
Time, February 1, 2010, p. 4.
Times (London, England), June 28, 1997, p. 9.

Online

"Nutritionist Michael Pollan Accepts No Imitations," *Talk of the Nation*, National Public Radio, http://www.npr.org/templates/story/story.php?storyId=98690109.tif (June 21, 2010).

—Carol Brennan

Jeff Probst

Jason LaVeris/FilmMagic/Getty Images

Television host

Born Jeffrey Lee Probst, November 4, 1962, in Wichita, Kansas; son of Jerry (a business executive) and Barbara (a homemaker) Probst; married Shelley Wright, 1996 (divorced, 2001). *Education:* Attended Seattle Pacific University, early 1980s.

Addresses: *Agent*—William Morris Endeavor Entertainment, 9601 Wilshire Blvd., Beverly Hills, CA 90212.

Career

Host of television series, including: *Backchat*, 1994-95; *Sound fX*, 1994; *Family Business*, 1996; *Rock & Roll Jeopardy*, 1998-2001; *Dave Barlia: Extreme Stuntman*, 1999; *Hollywood on Trial*, 1999; *Survivor*, 2000—; *60th Primetime Emmy Awards*, 2008. Television appearances, including: *Face of a Stranger* (movie), 1991; correspondent on *Access Hollywood*, 1996; *CBS Cares*, 2001-09; *Fillmore!*, 2002; *Live with Regis and Kelly*, 2004-09; *MLB vs. Survivor*, 2007; *Big Night of Stars*, 2008; *I Get That a Lot*, 2009; *Head Case*, 2009; *Live for the Moment*, 2010. Actor in films, including: *The A-List*, 2001. Director of films, including: *Finder's Fee*, 2001. Producer for television, including: *Survivor*, 2006—; *MLB vs. Survivor*, 2007; *Live for the Moment* (executive producer), 2010.

Awards: Emmy Award (with others) for outstanding non-fiction program, Academy of Television Arts and Sciences, for *Survivor*, 2001; Emmy Award for outstanding host for a reality or reality-competition program, Academy of Television Arts and Sciences, for *Survivor*, 2008, 2009; best director,

Seattle International Film Fest, for *Finder's Fee*, 2001; best screenplay for a feature film, Method Film Fest, for *Finder's Fee*, 2001.

Sidelights

Emmy-winning television personality Jeff Probst may be most familiar to audiences as the host of pioneering reality competition *Survivor*, but he has contributed to the screen in a variety of other capacities, including producer, writer, director, and actor. During the 1990s, Probst hosted FX's *Backchat* and *Sound fX* as well as VH1's *Rock & Roll Jeopardy*, and appeared as a correspondent on entertainment news program *Access Hollywood*. Additionally, he wrote and directed the 2001 independent film, *Finder's Fee*, which garnered Probst awards at the Seattle International Film Festival and Method Film Fest.

The eldest of the three sons of Jerry and Barbara Probst, the future television host was born on November 4, 1962, in Wichita, Kansas. He grew up mostly in Wichita before moving with his family to the Seattle, Washington, area during high school. While in high school, he performed in school plays, sang in a local rock band, and earned a letter in golf. After graduation, he attended Seattle Pacific University, dropping out after three-and-a-half years despite the disapproval of his parents. "To their credit, they never did anything but support us kids, even when their first son did something that would make most parents say, 'Absolutely not!'" Probst later recalled to Beth Douglass Silcox of *Success*.

His first steps into the world of television came when Probst began hosting gardening and car programs for local channel KRIO-TV and, later, producing and narrating sales and marketing videos for aircraft manufacturer Boeing, where his father worked as an executive. His career truly began to take shape, however, after Probst left the West Coast for New York City. There, he landed gigs hosting the FX channel's *Backchat*, a program that responded to viewer mail, and the music-themed program *Sound fX*. Both of these shows ran live, giving Probst what he later acknowledged to Angela Phipps Towle of *Back Stage West* was valuable preparatory experience for *Survivor*. "[Live television] was probably the best training ground in terms of thinking on your feet," he explained. "It puts you in this way of thinking—which is four steps ahead, always." Additionally, Probst hosted the short-lived FX driving test reality show, *Family Business*.

By the late 1990s, Probst had begun appearing on programs for channels other than FX. He signed on as a regular correspondent for entertainment news show *Access Hollywood* in 1996, and a couple of years later was tapped as the host of VH1 game show *Rock & Roll Jeopardy*. After wrapping *Rock & Roll Jeopardy*, Probst entered a self-enforced hiatus. "I turned down nine jobs over 18 months, hoping for something better," he later recalled to *Salon*'s Janelle Brown. That something better came along when Probst heard *Survivor* executive producer Mark Burnett discussing plans for the upcoming show on the radio. Probst contacted Burnett and landed an interview to become the program's host. Although Burnett believed that Probst's studio-based background made him an unlikely candidate for the job, the potential host "spent the last 15 minutes [of the interview] basically on my knees, ripping up my résumé and telling him not to count me out," he told Brown in the same interview. This effort paid off, and three months later Burnett offered Probst the job.

Survivor debuted to great success in 2000, initiating a trend of reality programming that dominated television schedules for the rest of the decade. Despite the immediate success of the show, Probst faced criticism for his role; the Knight Ridder/Tribune News Service groused, "With a personality that's more TV studio than base camp, Probst was like sand in suntan oil, the group's Where's Waldo figure who kept popping up when you least wanted to see him." The beleaguered host soldiered on, however, eventually winning over fans and critics alike.

In 2001, Probst had found the time to write and direct his first feature film, *Finder's Fee*. The story of a New Yorker who discovers a wallet containing a winning lottery ticket just before taking part in a dramatic poker game, *Finder's Fee* debuted to mixed reactions at the Seattle International Film Fest, where it went on to earn a nod for Best Picture and, for Probst, Best Director. That same year, Probst shared his first Emmy as part of the team behind *Survivor*.

The active host channeled some of *Survivor*'s mass appeal into public service efforts. He was active in numerous charitable organizations, including the St. Jude Children's Research Hospital, the Alliance for Children's Rights, and the Elizabeth Glaser Pediatric AIDS Foundation. In 2002, Probst and other *Survivor* executives worked with the latter organization to establish an auction of *Survivor* memorabilia to benefit the charity, with Probst also acting as a spokesperson for the foundation's college outreach program.

The host remained a fixture of *Survivor*, traveling with the castaways to far-flung locations around the globe each season and developing into a celebrity in his own right. Probst became a regular fill-in host for Regis Philbin opposite Kelly Ripa on the morning program *Live with Regis and Kelly* and attracted the attention of celebrity gossip magazines when he began dating *Survivor* contestant Julie Berry in 2005. The relationship helped fuel rumors that Probst was considering leaving the popular program after its twelfth season, but he somewhat unexpectedly renewed his contract in late 2005. "I literally travel around the world, meet fascinating people, am part of a great social experiment—and get paid for it," he explained to *Entertainment Weekly*'s Dalton Ross. "It really was, this is your one life, what do you want to do with it?"

In 2008, Probst was a prominent figure at the annual Primetime Emmy Awards, both co-hosting the program alongside fellow reality show veterans Heidi Klum, Howie Mandel, Ryan Seacrest, and Tom Bergeron, and earning his first individual Emmy as the inaugural winner in the Outstanding Host For a Reality or a Reality Competition Program category. Despite negative critical reviews of the co-hosts' performance, Probst emerged from the experience in good spirits. Speaking to *People*'s Cynthia Wang shortly after the event, he enthused, "I am so proud of [the award]. I'm not embarrassed to say I left it out on the coffee table!" The following year, Probst repeated his victory.

Survivor's twentieth season hit the airwaves in February of 2010, with Probst returning as both host and executive producer. At about the same time, CBS announced the long-running host was officially on board through the two seasons scheduled to air in late 2010 and early 2011. "Even in my wildest dreams, I couldn't have predicted we'd still be going strong ten years later," Probst commented to *Daily Variety*. With more than a decade of highly visible television work under his belt, Probst seems likely to himself continue to go strong for some time to come.

Sources

Books

Contemporary Theatre, Film and Television, vol. 50, Gale Group, 2003.

Periodicals

American Fitness, July-August 2002, p. 16.
Back Stage West, November 30, 2002, p. 12.
Daily Variety, February 10, 2010, p. 12.
Entertainment Weekly, December 23, 2005, p. 27.
Knight Ridder/Tribune News Service, June 6, 2000.
Success, March 2010, p. 70.
Variety, July 16, 2001, p. 21.

Online

Biography Resource Center Online, Gale, 2006.
"Jeff Probst Biography, " InBaseline, http://www.inbaseline.com/person.aspx?view=BioSummary&person_id=3955203 (May 25, 2010).
"Jeff Probst Celebrates Emmy with New Survivor," *People*, http://www.people.com/people/article/0,,20229369.tif,00.html (May 28, 2010).
"Jeff Probst," Internet Movie Database, http://www.imdb.com/name/nm0698251/ (May 25, 2010).
"Jeff Probst is not an idiot," *Salon*, http://dir.salon.com/ent/movies/int/2002/05/08/probst/index.html (May 25, 2010).
"Jeff Probst's Charity Work, Events and Causes." Look to the Stars, http://www.looktothestars.org/celebrity/451-jeff-probst (May 25, 2010).
"Out Wit, Out Play, Out Last... Out Bid! Survivor: Marquesas Props And Memorabilia To Be Sold On eBay To Benefit The Elizabeth Glaser Pediatric AIDS Foundation," Charity Wire, http://www.charitywire.com/charity60/03145.html (May 25, 2010).
"Probst Survives Critics at the Emmys," E! Online, http://www.eonline.com/uberblog/b30200_probst_survives_critics_emmys.html (May 28, 2010).

—*Vanessa E. Vaughn*

Datuk Seri Mohamed Najib Tun Abdul Razak

Goh Seng Chong/Bloomberg/Getty Images

Prime minister of Malaysia

Born July 23, 1953, in Pahang Darui Makmur, Pahang, Malaysia; son of Tun Abdul Razak (a politician); married Datin Sri Rosmah Mansor; children: five. *Education:* University of Nottingham (Nottingham, England), bachelor's degree, 1974.

Addresses: *Office*—Office of the Prime Minister of Malaysia, Main Block, Perdana Putra Building, Federal Government Administrative Centre, 65202 Putrajaya, Malaysia.

Career

Public relations manager, Petronas, 1974-76; elected to Malaysia's parliament representing Pahang state, 1976-82; appointed deputy minister of Energy, Telecommunications, and Post, 1978-80; deputy minister of Education, 1980-81; deputy minister of Finance, 1981-82; Menteri Besar (chief minister), Pahang state, 1982-86; member of the State Assembly, Bandar Pekan, 1982-86; minister of Culture, Youth, and Sports, 1986-90; minister of Defense, 1990-95, 1999-2008; minister of Education, 1995-99; deputy prime minister of Malaysia, 2004-09; minister of Finance, 2008—; prime minister of Malaysia, 2009—.

Awards: Man of the Year Award, *New Straits Times,* 1990; Knight Grand Cross, 1992; Distinguished Service Award, Singapore, 1995.

Sidelights

Datuk Seri Mohamed Najib Tun Abdul Razak took office as Malaysia's sixth prime minister on April 3, 2009. Himself the son of the nation's second prime minister and the nephew of its third, the highly conservative Razak entered politics while in his early 20s when he was elected to his father's former parliament seat upon the latter's death. He later served in a number of Malaysian political posts before ascending to the nation's top political office, including Minister of Defense, Minister of Education, and Deputy Prime Minister. This rise did not come without controversy, as Razak became embroiled in the scandal surrounding the murder of the young Mongolian woman Altantuya Shaariibuu in 2007 while he was serving as deputy prime minister. Razak's possible involvement in the events surrounding the woman's death never drew formal censure, and his political career soon recovered sufficiently that he stood unopposed for the nation's premiership following the departure of previous Prime Minister Tun Abdullah Ahmad Badawi as head of the long-ruling political party United Malays National Organisation (UMNO). In addition to his role as prime minister, Razak has served as Malaysia's Finance Minister since September of 2008.

Born on July 23, 1953, in Pahang Darui Makmur, Pahang, Malaysia, Razak is the eldest son of politician Tun Abdul Razak. As a child, Razak attended Kuala Lumpur's prestigious St. John's Institution before traveling to England to attend Malvern Boy's College in Worcestershire. After completing his secondary education at that institution, he enrolled at the University of Nottingham in Nottingham, England, to study industrial economics. After completing his degree with honors in 1974, Razak returned to Malaysia and embarked on a career in business. His first position was as a public relations manager for Malaysian national oil company Petronas, then a brand new concern. Two years later, the young executive's father died and the 23-year-old Razak successfully stood for his father's parliamentary seat, becoming the nation's youngest member of Parliament.

Soon, the newly minted politician began acquiring important government posts. He served as the Deputy Minister of Energy, Telecommunications, and Post between 1978 and 1980, when he became the Deputy Minister of Education. The following year, he shifted to Deputy Minister of Finance. In 1982, Razak won elective office in the Malaysian state of Pahang; he later became the state's Menteri Besar, an executive position roughly comparable to a governor. He was returned to his national seat in 1986, and soon became the Minister of Culture, Youth, and Sports. The politician proved an active figure in this role, encouraging the development of Malaysian athleticism through the implementation of a National Sports Policy and instituting cash prizes for successful Malaysian Olympians. Razak remained in this position until 1990, when he was named the nation's Minister of Defense. Over the next several years, he worked to modernize the Malaysian armed forces by adopting a variety of specialized aircraft, artillery, and radar systems.

After five years with the Ministry of Defense, Razak shifted gears to become the Minister of Education. Under his guidance, the ministry created a series of major educational reforms as part of the sweeping Education Act 1996. The law increased education access for Malaysians, requiring that instruction take place in the common language and creating national exams and curricula, and has been widely regarded as a step forward for the country's education system. Despite this success, the minister saw his public popularity decline; in 1999, he won reelection to his parliamentary seat by a razor thin margin, a steep decline from his previous wide victories. Although the politician held onto his seat, he left his post at the Ministry of Education to return to the Ministry of Defense, taking up the lead role that he had held a decade previously. Razak again turned his attention to the modernization of the Malaysian military, remaining in this role until 2004, when he ascended to become the nation's Deputy Prime Minister.

In 2007, Razak made headlines around the world not for his involvement in politics, but for his alleged connections to a scandalous Malaysian murder investigation and subsequent trial. The story dated back to 2004, when Abdul Razak Baginda, an adviser to Razak, began an extramarital affair with Altantuya Shaariibuu, a part-time model who originally hailed from Mongolia and resided outside of Malaysia. The relationship went on for several months, during which time Baginda and Shaariibuu reportedly traveled around Europe finalizing details of the purchase of three submarines by the Malaysian government from French-Spanish military manufacturer Armaris. Razak was the nation's Minister of Defense and therefore he had regular contact with Baginda, who sometimes negotiated arms deals on his behalf; a photograph reportedly shows that the three had spent an evening together at a Parisian nightclub, although Razak later denied any acquaintanceship with Shaariibuu. According to a friend of Shaariibuu's speaking to Arnaud Dubus of the Bangkok, Thailand newspaper *The Nation,* the Mongolian woman "showed me the picture. She said that one of the men was her boyfriend, Abdul Razak Baginda, and the other the big boss, Najib Razak. I asked her if they were brothers because of the names, but she said no, that Najib Razak was the prime minister."

Shaariibuu was certainly mistaken about Razak's actual government position, but perhaps not about her acquaintanceship with him; a private investigator later alleged—but quickly retracted—that Shaariibuu and Razak had also had an on-again, off-again romantic entanglement. Later in 2005, Baginda ended his relationship with Shaariibuu, who began blackmailing him. Baginda—a high-profile think tank director and security expert—paid off Shaariibuu for a few months, but ceased to give in to her demands for hush money by early spring of 2006. In October of that year, Shaariibuu sought out her former lover in Kuala Lumpur to ask for a substantial sum of money she believed was due to her as a commission for her involvement in the transaction with Armaris. She apparently began to badger Baginda for her share of the hefty sum, which she estimated at half a million U.S. dollars.

By October 18, events had reached a boiling point. Baginda got in touch with Musa Safrie, a close associate of Razak and head of the Malaysian Special Branch, an intelligence operation attached to the nation's Royal Malaysian Police and responsible for the Defense Minister's personal protection. The next day, two Special Branch officers, Azilah Hadridan and Sirul Omar, came to Baginda's home to force Shaariibuu to cease her protestations against him. What followed sparked a national media sensation: the officers took Shaariibuu away from the home, shot her twice, and then destroyed her body with C4 explosives in a jungle outside of the capital. Her remains were found there about three weeks later. Dubus argued that the defense minister tried to stage a cover up of the murder, claiming in the *Nation* that Razak sent Baginda a text message stating, "I will see the inspector-general of police at 11am today.... The problem will be solved. Be cool," soon after the affair came to the attention of Kuala Lumpur police. Nevertheless, Baginda and the two officers were swiftly arrested, plunging Malaysia into its most scandalous, politically charged trials in many years.

As evidence in the murder trial began to build, opposition voices such as former deputy prime minister Anwar Ibrahim—who had himself been the subject of a contentious lawsuit some years previously—began to question Razak's possible involvement in the murder. "We are interested to know whether there is any political link to the murder," defense lawyer Zulkifli Noordin told Thomas Fuller of the *New York Times* in June of 2007. "Why were all the people involved linked to No. 2 [Razak]?" A potentially damning answer came during the trial the following month, when the existence of the photo depicting the Deputy Prime Minister, Baginda, and the murdered woman was put forth. The revelation that Shaariibuu's entry into Malaysia had apparently been scrubbed from immigration records further spurred speculation of a high-level government cover-up. Razak continued to deny any involvement with Shaariibuu and the ruling government party seemed to escape negative effects from the trial for some time. Yet as Malaysian fuel and durable goods prices went up considerably in a short time, that popularity took a sharp decline. The opposition party won a number of seats in elections held in the spring of 2008, and the Deputy Prime Minister's reputation seemed to come into serious question when a private investigator working for Baginda at the time of the murder made the explosive claims that Razak had been having an affair with Shaariibuu. Almost as scandalous as the investigator's claims was his prompt retraction and exit from Malaysia. In October of 2008, a judge threw out the case against Baginda—the two Special Branch officers were eventually convicted and sentenced to death—and official speculation about Razak's potential involvement ended.

At about the same time, the Deputy Prime Minister's political fortunes began looking up. UMNO party leader and prime minister Abdullah Ahmad Badawi announced his plans to step down, clearing the way for Razak to ascend to the nation's top office. The lifelong politician successfully carried party elections in March, and became Malaysia's sixth prime minister the following month. "The appointment of Mr Najib will appease the distraught party hardliners who have been baying for blood since last year's disastrous performance at the national polls," commented Luke Hunt in a *Times Online* article. Nevertheless, Hunt quoted Universiti Sains Malaysia professor Vejai Balasubramanium as arguing, "Gaining acceptance from the ordinary man in the street will be a tall order.... [Razak] has said he will try and appeal to all, that sounds nice but at the moment it's just words."

Indeed, Malaysian politics underwent a period of considerable turbulence at the time of the new prime minister's ascension. Increasing numbers of Malays threw their support behind the opposition party, and opposition leader Anwar Ibrahim found himself again the subject of allegations of sodomy. Razak forced an elected opposition official from his post in the Malaysian state of Perak, but this action was soon overturned by a judge. Accusations of cronyism and politicking also tarnished the premiership and the UMNO. By July of 2009, Razak attempted a populist move by eliminating some of Malaysia's long-standing regulations restricting ownership of Malay companies by foreigners and ethnic Chinese, Indian, or other Malay citizens. Some among the Prime Minister's own conservative party resisted the policy change, although such efforts contributed to a rise in Razak's general popularity among the Malay people. Nevertheless, Malaysian politics remained highly contentious into 2010, with continued political sparring between the ruling party and the coalition of opposition voices led by Ibrahim. As Ibrahim's sodomy trial began in February of that year, the opposition leader declared his intention to have Razak subpoenaed for questioning about his possible involvement in maliciously encouraging Ibrahim's accuser to make his allegations; groups including Amnesty International expressed their support for Ibrahim, claiming the trial was politically motivated. Regardless of the outcome of the trial, Razak seems likely to remain a figure of both political prominence and public discussion in the years to come.

Sources

Books

Marquis Who's Who, Marquis Who's Who, 2009.

Periodicals

Nation (Bangkok, Thailand), March 13, 2009.
New York Times, June 1, 2007; June 18, 2007; July 10, 2007; July 6, 2008; October 9, 2008; October 31, 2008; March 20, 2009; May 12, 2009; July 1, 2009; March 6, 2010
Time, July 5, 2007.

Online

"Biography," Office of the Prime Minister of Malaysia, http://www.pmo.gov.my/?menu=page&page=1926# (March 16, 2010).

"Malaysia," International Bureau of Education, UNESCO, http://www.ibe.unesco.org/International/ICE/natrap/Malaysia.pdf (March 16, 2010).

"Najib Rajak sworn in as new Malaysian Prime Minister," *Times Online,* http://www.timesonline.co.uk/tol/news/world/asia/article6026896.ece (March 16, 2010).

—Vanessa E. Vaughn

Jason Reitman

AP Images

Filmmaker

Born October 19, 1977, in Montreal, Quebec, Canada; son of Ivan Reitman (a filmmaker) and Geneviève Robert (an actress and director); married Michele Lee, September 5, 2004; children: one daughter. *Education:* University of Southern California, B.A.; also attended Skidmore College.

Addresses: *Agent*—William Morris Endeavor Entertainment, 9601 Wilshire Blvd., 3rd Fl., Beverly Hills, CA 90210. *Web site*—http://twitter.com/jasonreitman.

Career

Began appearing in and working on his father's films, 1988; began making own films, 1998; released feature debut, *Thank You for Smoking*, 2005; directed two episodes of *The Office*, NBC, 2007, 2008. Film work included serving as production assistant, *Kindergarten Cop*, 1990; director, producer, and writer, *Operation*, 1998; director and writer, *H*, 1999; director, executive producer, and writer, *In God We Trust* (short film), 2000; director and writer, *Gulp*, 2001; director and writer, *Uncle Sam*, 2002; director and writer, *Consent* (short film), 2004; director and writer, *Thank You for Smoking*, 2005; director, *Juno*, 2007; director, producer, and writer, *Up in the Air*, 2009; producer, *Jennifer's Body*, 2009; executive producer, *Chloe*, 2009; executive producer, *Ceremony*, 2010; producer, *Jeff Who Lives at Home*, 2011. Film appearances include: *Twins*, 1988; *Ghostbusters II*, 1989; *Kindergarten Cop*, 1990; *Dave*, 1993; *Fathers' Day*, 1997; *Operation*, 1998; *In God We Trust*, 2000; *Gulp*, 2001.

Member: Academy of Motion Pictures Arts and Sciences.

Awards: Audience Award, Aspen Shortfest, for *In God We Trust*, 2000; Audience Award (with others) for best short film, for *In God We Trust*, 2000; Best Short Award, New York Comedy Festival, for *In God We Trust*, 2000; Golden Space Needle Award for best short film, Seattle International Film Festival, for *In God We Trust*, 2000; Grand Jury Award for best narrative short, Florida Film Festival, for *In God We Trust*, 2000; Jury Award for comedy—best of category, Aspen Shortfest, for *In God We Trust*, 2000; Short Film Award, Austin Film Festival, for *In God We Trust*, 2000; Moxie! Award for best contemporary short comedy, Santa Monica Film Festival, for *In God We Trust*, 2001; Jury Award for best short short, Aspen Shortfest, for *Consent*, 2004; Golden Space Needle Award for best short, Seattle International Film Festival, for *Consent*, 2004; Audience Award, Norwegian International Film Festival, for *Thank You for Smoking*, 2006; Grand Prix, Alpe d'Huez International Comedy Film Festival, for *Juno*, 2006; National Board of Review Award for best directorial debut, for *Thank You for Smoking*, 2006; Sierra Award for best screenplay, Las Vegas Film Critics Society, for *Thank You for Smoking*, 2006; Audience Award, Stockholm Film Festival, for *Juno*, 2007; Audience Choice Award for best feature, St. Louis International Film Festival, for *Juno*, 2007; Best Film Award, Rome Film Fest, for *Juno*, 2007; Independent Spirit Award for best screenplay, for

Thank You for Smoking, 2007; Chairman's Vanguard Award, Palm Springs International Film Festival, for *Juno,* 2008; Grammy Award (with others) for best compilation soundtrack album for motion picture, television, or other visual media, National Academy of Recording Arts and Sciences, for *Juno,* 2009; Special Prize of the Young Jury, Gijón International Film Festival, for *Juno,* 2007; Canadian Comedy Award for best direction—film, for *Juno,* 2008; Christopher Award (with others) for feature films, for *Juno,* 2008; Austin Film Critics Award (with Sheldon Turner), best screenplay—adapted, for *Up in the Air,* 2009; British Academy of Film and Television Arts Film Award for best screenplay—adapted, for *Up in the Air,* 2010; Chicago Film Critics Association Award (with Sheldon Turner), best screenplay—adapted, for *Up in the Air,* 2009; National Board of Review Award (with Sheldon Turner), for best screenplay—adapted, for *Up in the Air,* 2009; Golden Globe Award (with Sheldon Turner), best screenplay—motion picture, for *Up in the Air,* 2010; Critics Choice Award (with Sheldon Turner), best screenplay—adapted, Broadcast Film Critics Association, for *Up in the Air,* 2010; Director of the Year Award, Palm Springs International Film Festival, for *Up in the Air,* 2010; Writers Guild of America Award (Screen) for best adapted screenplay (with Sheldon Turner), for *Up in the Air,* 2010.

Sidelights

Academy Award-nominated filmmaker Jason Reitman is responsible for some of the most thought-provoking films of the early 21st century. His three films—*Thank You for Smoking, Juno,* and *Up in the Air*—were talky, thoughtful comedies that allowed audiences to discover a story, digest it in their own way, and come to their own interpretation of its meaning. Inspired by filmmakers like Alexander Payne, Reitman's films focused on characters who were good people with major imperfections and a significant area of ignorance about themselves or life. As Reitman explained to Sharon Waxman of the *New York Times,* "I like tricky films, difficult films." Bob Thompson of Canwest News Service added that Reitman's films were "subversively droll pictures that aren't as obvious as they seem to be."

Born on October 19, 1977, in Montreal, Quebec, Canada, he was the son of filmmaker Ivan Reitman and French-Canadian actress/director Geneviève Robert. Reitman and his two younger sisters, Catherine and Caroline, were raised somewhat strictly with clear rules, even after a move to Beverly Hills, California. After the move, Ivan Reitman became one of the hottest filmmakers in Hollywood, the producer of *Animal House* and the director of such popular comedies as *Ghostbusters* and *Meatballs.* While stars like Arnold Schwarzenegger and Howard Stern regularly visited the Reitman family home, young Reitman had small roles in many of his father's films including 1988's *Twins,* 1989's *Ghostbusters II,* 1990's *Kindergarten Cop,* and 1993's *Dave.* Reitman also worked on a number of his father's films in various capacities, including serving as a production assistant on *Kindergarten Cop.*

Reitman was expected to follow his father's footsteps from an early age. He told VNU Entertainment News, "My whole life, people told me I was going to be a director. I'd walk around sets and grips would tell me, 'Hey! There goes my future boss!' In high school, I made videos and stuff, but by the end of high school I was scared of being a director. The going perception of children of filmmakers was that they were talentless spoiled brats who had drug problems and were ungrateful for how fortunate their lives were. So I went into college and actually did go premed. Nobody ever questions that decision."

Thus, after Reitman graduated from the Harvard-Westlake School in North Hollywood, California, in 1995, he spent a year studying pre-med at Skidmore College. He had poor grades, however, and returned to Los Angeles because he realized he was not called to have a medical career. Reitman completed college at the University of Southern California (USC) where he majored in English. By this time, he accepted his fate. He told Sharon Waxman of the *New York Times,* "I wanted to be a filmmaker. It was everything to do in my heart but didn't, because I didn't want to deal with the comparison."

While a student at USC, Reitman began making and appearing in short films. His first was 1998's *Operation,* a 20-minute dark comedy that focused on stealing kidneys for the black market. He raised the money to finance the film by creating a coupon calendar that would appeal to a campus audience and selling these advertisements to local businesses. Reitman made $8,000 through calendar sales and used the funds to make *Operation.*

After 1999's short film *H,* Reitman's next short, 2000's *In God We Trust,* garnered much attention and acclaim. The winner of numerous honors at film festivals, it focuses on a man who dies after getting hit by a truck. While in purgatory, he finds out that eternity works on a point system based on one's actions on Earth. He missed heaven by 12 points. *In God We Trust* was also shown on HBO.

While making short films, Reitman also directed television commercials and some of his spots won awards. He followed *In God We Trust* with 2001's *Gulp,* 2002's *Uncle Sam,* and 2004's *Consent.* Like *In God We Trust, Consent* won several awards from film festivals. While working on these films, Reitman was working on what would become his first feature.

In 2005, Reitman's first full-length film was released, *Thank You for Smoking,* which was based on the novel by Christopher Buckley. He was given the book in the late 1990s and immediately felt connected to the text. After his career moved to the next level, *Thank You for Smoking* became his ideal debut feature film. Reitman explained to Liam Lacey of the *Globe and Mail,* "As I began making short films and I got an agent and he began sending me scripts that were available (all awful), it became clear to me that *Thank You for Smoking* was exactly what I wanted to say as a director. I have a slight authority problem. Not in a skinhead kind of way, but I don't want to be told what to do. I loved that this book said, 'If you want to smoke, smoke; if you don't, don't.' The book is not about tobacco, but about the mania for telling people how to live."

Reitman also described *Thank You for Smoking* as "un-Hollywood" in the same interview. The project took several frustrating years to get off the ground because no studio would back Reitman—even with his pedigree and track record with commercials and short films. It was eventually made for $10 million from independent producer David Sacks (who made a fortune with PayPal). A hit at the Sundance Film Festival, *Thank You for Smoking* was also the subject of a bidding war at the Toronto Film Festival that ensured the film had wide release. *Thank You for Smoking* centered on big tobacco lobbyist Nick Naylor (played by Aaron Eckhart) as a means of satirically exploring the culture of political correctness, unethical reporters, and the long arms of the tobacco lobby.

While *Thank You for Smoking* was an art house hit, Reitman's next film found an even bigger audience and gave him much more credibility. He directed 2007's *Juno,* with a screenplay written by Diablo Cody. The film focused on a teenage girl, the titular Juno (played by Ellen Page) who finds herself pregnant and decides to give her baby up for adoption. She finds what she thinks is the ideal couple but learns that only the mother is truly committed to the changes that having a child will bring. Because of the deft handling of the teen's pregnancy, many people on both sides of the abortion debate embraced the film and its message. *Juno* made $213 million worldwide and landed Reitman his first Academy Award nomination (for best director).

Reitman believed *Juno* was popular because of its ability to touch audiences. He explained to Hap Erstein of the *Palm Beach Post,* "I'm proud that it seems to move people. At the end of the day, I want to make people laugh and I hope to move people too. That's a tough accomplishment, and it seems to have happened with this film." Critics lauded the film, with Joe O'Connell of the *Dallas Morning News* noting that *Juno* "conjures a perfect tone of sweetness, edge, and emotional truth."

In 2009, Reitman released his third film, *Up in the Air.* It received multiple Academy Award nominations including best director, producer, and screenwriter for the emerging filmmaker. Reitman spent three years working on the script, which was based on the 2001 novel of the same name by Walter Kirn. *Up in the Air* centered on Ryan Bingham (played by George Clooney), a businessman with no close ties because he chooses to spend most of his time on the road helping to downsize companies and giving motivational speeches. Along the way, his way of life and lack of personal growth are challenged by his remaining family, a female traveler who seems to have similar values, and changes to his trade brought by an ambitious young colleague, Natalie (played by Anna Kendrick). Much of Bingham's business focuses on firing people and Natalie devises a way of firing people online via video conference, thus eliminating Bingham's lifeblood: travel.

Reitman was thoughtful in his explanation of what drew him to the novel. He told Anthony Breznican of the Gannett News Service, "All of us have things to say and we just don't know how. Movies are kind of my way of dealing with my inner questions." Reitman continued, "Are we an island or not? That's the simple, classic version of it. More than the value of being connected to the world, what is your responsibility to be connected to the rest of the world?"

Another memorable aspect of *Up in the Air* was Reitman's use of people who had really lost their jobs in most of the firing segments. While filming in St. Louis and Detroit—two areas of the United States devastated by the economic downturn of the early twenty-first century—the filmmakers selected a number of people to go on camera and recreate their reactions to being fired. Reitman explained to David Carr of the *New York Times,* "The second they heard the language of firing, you could just see it. Their eyes would turn, their posture would change, their face would go sallow. One girl broke into hives. It just happened, and they would be in the moment."

In addition to making films, Reitman also directed two episodes of the hit NBC comedy *The Office* in 2007 and 2008. He worked as producer or executive producer on a number of other films as well. For example, he was the producer of the 2009's *Jennifer's Body,* a horror comedy written by *Juno* screenwriter Cody; however, it was a failure with critics and at the box office. Reitman also was an executive producer on the 2009 romantic thriller *Chloe* and the 2010 film *Ceremony.* Away from the film industry, Reitman performed DJ mashups with friend Mateo Messina (who composed music for both *Thank You for Smoking* and *Juno*) under the name Bad Meaning Bad in clubs around Los Angeles. Their shows were fun and often featured self-deprecating humor. Reitman also used Twitter to keep in touch with fans and share his sense of humor.

Describing Reitman's power as a filmmaker, David Poland, a long-time film industry reporter for the Web site MovieCityNews, told Gannett News Service's Breznican that Reitman emphasized "kindness while tackling subjects that feel edgy. That is what all the great directors who have commercial followings have done. No director—save [Orson] Welles—can be judged based on just three films. Jason Reitman has a long career ahead of him. But he already seems to understand actors and how to offer them to audiences in a way that is both familiar and unique."

Sources

Periodicals

Calgary Sun (Alberta, Canada), March 7, 2010, p. E6.
Canwest News Service, December 1, 2009.
Dallas Morning News, December 14, 2007.
Gannett News Service, September 1, 2009; February 18, 2010.
Globe and Mail, March 24, 2006, p. R34.
New York Times, September 10, 2005, p. B9; November 29, 2009, p. AR1.
Palm Beach Post (FL), April 20, 2008, p. 1J.
Toronto Sun, March 24, 2006, p. E18.
VNU Entertainment News Wire, February 20, 2008.

Online

"Jason Reitman," Internet Movie Database, http://www.imdb.com/name/nm0718646/ (July 26, 2010).

—*A. Petruso*

Lela Rose

Astrid Stawiarz/Getty Images

Fashion designer

Born Lela Helen Rose, c. 1969; daughter of Edward (an investment banker) and Deedie (an art collector) Rose; married Brandon Lee Jones (an investment banker), June 26, 1999; children: Grey (son), Rosie. *Education:* University of Colorado, B.A., 1991; Parsons the New School for Design, A.A.S., 1994.

Addresses: *Home*—New York, NY. *Office*—Lela Rose, 224 W. 30th St., New York, NY 10001.

Career

Design assistant, Christian Francis Roth, c. 1994; design assistant fabric buyer and researcher, Richard Tyler/Lisa Trafficante, c. 1994-96; launched eponymous ready-to-wear line, 1996; showed first runway collection, February 2004; introduced bridal line, 2006; introduced line of signature footwear at Payless Shoes, 2007.

Sidelights

Lela Rose's clothing company benefited from an enormous boost of free publicity when First Daughters Barbara and Jenna Bush both chose her designs for their father's 2001 presidential inauguration. Rose's frothy, candy-colored dresses and skirts owe tremendous allegiance to her Texan roots, but the designer wears her own creations every day on her Manhattan bicycle commute from home to office. "I feel like I'm really the customer for our clothing," she told *Austin American-Statesman* writer Jenny Miller. "I could live in a dress. Even when it's cold out in the morning, I just put on tights. We have pockets in pretty much every single dress we do. You can put keys in there, your lipstick."

Rose was in her mid-twenties when she started her company in 1996. She grew up in Highland Park, a wealthy enclave of Dallas. Her father, Edward "Rusty" Rose, made his fortune in investment banking, while mother Deedie Rose was a well-known figure in the Dallas cultural scene as a patron of the arts. Rose studied art at the University of Colorado at Boulder, and after earning her undergraduate degree in 1991 moved to New York City to enroll in the School of Fashion program at Parsons School of Design.

While still at Parsons Rose landed a job with Christian Francis Roth, the new wunderkind designer of the early 1990s, and honed her skills further as a design assistant and then fabric buyer for another buzz-worthy designer of that decade, Richard Tyler. "I had decided on the ten companies I wanted to work for," Rose recalled in an interview with Ruth La Ferla of the *New York Times*, adding she had designed what she imaged as a clever resumé in order to stand out from all the other eager applicants. "I had sewn little buttons up along the top," she confessed.

Rose eventually left Richard Tyler to start her own company, whose first collection she presented at a small event inside New York City's Royalton Hotel. Her new designs usually debuted at trunk shows staged in conjunction with small boutiques and the high-end retailers that sold her wares, like Saks Fifth Avenue and Nordstrom. Rose's ultra-feminine dresses were a hit with young, well-heeled women like herself on both coasts—and in her home state—but her line remained mostly under the radar and received scant attention in the fashion press. That changed dramatically in 2001 when the two Texas-born twin daughters of President-elect George W. Bush, 19-year-olds Jenna and Barbara, chose Rose to design outfits for the January inauguration. The president-elect and Rose's father were longtime associates, and had once been part of group of investors who owned the Texas Rangers, the Major League Baseball franchise in the Dallas-Fort Worth area.

Rose put the brunette Barbara in a combination of pink, black, and white, and designed a lighter ensemble of ivory, green, and orange for the blonde Jenna. "They've worn my designs before, but this is the first time I've designed things exclusively for them," Rose told *WWD* writer Rusty Williamson. "For the inauguration, we needed to find something in-between, styles that aren't too suity but fun and young. They will cast a mature and sophisticated image." Interest in Rose's designs spiked considerably after that, and there was another round of publicity a year later when Barbara Bush interned at Rose's company during one of her summers off from Yale University.

Rose presented her first full runway show during New York Fashion Week in February of 2004, at which American designers show their upcoming Fall/Winter lines to the fashion press and store buyers. At her next outing in September for the Spring/Summer presentations, she earned more positive assessments. "Rose has been guilty of immersing herself in too much tulle and cupcake" in her previous collections, asserted Ginia Bellafante in a *New York Times* critique. The journalist praised a steadily advancing maturity in her designs along with what Bellafante called "a new quirkiness" in her work.

Rose's girlish eveningwear designs segued naturally into a bridal division she launched in the fall of 2006. A year later, she signed a deal to create a line of footwear for the Payless chain, which underwrote her runway show in September of 2007 during New York Fashion Week. "For us, it is the added name recognition that is the most amazing thing," Rose said about the Payless collaboration in an interview with *New York Times Magazine* writer Eric Wilson. "It's like I had an advertising budget, which of course I don't. It's fabulous."

In 2008, Rose's bridal line received another terrific boost when Jenna Bush asked her to design the bridesmaids' dresses for her May wedding at the Bush family ranch in Crawford, Texas. Rose also had her own Texas wedding back in 1999 when she married investment banker Brandon Jones, also a Lone Star State native, in Dallas. The church altar was flanked by a pair of immense oak trees in keeping with the tree theme she chose for the event. The reception was held at the Dallas Museum of Art, and the 600 guests each went home with a sapling to plant. Rose also had four canine attendants in her bridal party, and is often photographed with Stitch, a Norwich terrier she named in homage to the 2002 animated feature film *Lilo & Stitch*.

Rose and Jones have two young children and live in Lower Manhattan's busy Tribeca neighborhood. The designer rides a custom-made three-wheeled bicycle to her work studio and showroom—a distance of three miles each way—sometimes with both children and dog in the enormous basket and usually in a dress of her own design. While often mistaken for a Southern-belle socialite with a little dress business, Rose has built up a certain steely resolve since she first went looking for a job with a button-bedecked resumé in hand. "It takes enormous tenacity to run a fashion business in New York," she told La Ferla in the *New York Times*. "You don't want to be pushy, but if you easily back off when someone says no, there's no way you're going to make it in this business."

Sources

Austin American-Statesman, May 4, 2007, p. 14.
Houston Chronicle, June 1, 2006, p. 6.
New York Times, April 9, 1996; September 8, 2002; September 11, 2004.
New York Times Magazine, September 9, 2007.
Town & Country, February 2000, p. 130.
USA Today, April 23, 2008, p. 4D.
W, June 2006, p. 66.
WWD, January 4, 2001, p. 5.

—*Carol Brennan*

Philip Rosedale

ABACAUSA.com/Giancarlo Gorassini/newscom

Chief Executive Officer of Linden Lab

Born in 1968, San Diego, CA; married. *Education:* University of California—San Diego, B.S.

Addresses: *Office*—Linden Lab, 945 Battery St., San Francisco, CA 94111.

Career

Founded database company, mid-1980s; founded Automated Systems Management, 1993; company bought by RealNetworks, 1996; vice president and chief technical officer, RealNetworks, c. 1996-99; entrepreneur with venture capital firm Accel Partners, 1999; founder, Linden Lab, 1999; chairman of the board, Linden Lab, 1999—; chief executive officer, Linden Lab, 1999-2008; 2010—.

Awards: One of the 100 Most Influential People, *Time* Magazine, 2007.

Sidelights

American Internet entrepreneur Philip Rosedale was best known as the founder of the online virtual world Second Life and of its parent technology company Linden Lab. Since beginning his career in the computer industry during the 1990s, Rosedale has served in executive-level positions with media streaming giant RealNetworks and Linden Lab, as well as acting as a consultant. His work with Second Life has won him widespread notice, including a nod from *Time* as one of 2007's most influential people; writing for the magazine in a pro-file of Rosedale, Suzanne Vega declared that Second Life was "like a TV show with an added dimension. All of us in our imaginary bodies, sharing an invented reality."

Born in San Diego, California, in 1968, Rosedale is the eldest of the four children of an English teacher and a retired pilot and architect. As a child, he became fascinated by the emerging world of computer technology, and his parents encouraged this interest by buying an Apple home computer for Rosedale during his middle school years. From the beginning, Rosedale experimented with ways to present the real world through virtual means. "I made trees growing on screen. That's when I realized you could simulate nature," he later explained in a biography on the All American Speakers Web site. Rosedale's early efforts soon became more sophisticated, and he founded a database company while still in his teens.

After completing a bachelor's degree in physics at the University of California at San Diego, Rosedale moved to the burgeoning tech hub of San Francisco. There, he established Automated Systems Management, a company that created a video conferencing software called FreeVue for the then-new online market. Soon, RealNetworks purchased the small company and brought Rosedale on board as a staffer. He rose to become Real's Vice-President and Chief Technical Officer, overseeing the development of products including RealVideo, RealSystem 5.0, and RealSystem G2.

Despite these successes, Rosedale continued to await an opportunity to pursue a longtime dream: creating a virtual world. "I've been intrigued since an early age by the possibility of using networking and computers to create a special kind of space between people that captures our passion to communicate, express ourselves, and pursue our dreams," he told Phil LoPiccolo of *Computer Graphics World* in 2004. Technological limitations hampered this goal until the late 1990s, when the development of more powerful video cards and increasingly fast Internet connection speeds made Rosedale's dream feasible.

Inspired by the carefree atmosphere of the Burning Man festival, Rosedale quit his job at RealNetworks, moved to San Francisco, and signed on with the venture capital company Accel Partners—a project partially funded by Lotus founder and former RealNetworks' board member Mitch Kapor—as an entrepreneur-in-residence in 1999. "I was struck by the fact that people were willing to make social connections to each other [at Burning Man]. Just standing there in Burning Man, you are willing to talk to people that you would never talk to just standing on a street in New York or San Francisco," Rosedale told *Information Week* in 2008. Backed by funds from Accel and by his own earnings from FreeVue, Rosedale launched the technological company Linden Lab, which takes its name from the street where the company's offices were located.

The new company became the breeding ground for Rosedale's most famous creation, Second Life. A virtual online world, the interactive landscape—inspired by science fiction author Neal Stephenson's so-called "Metaverse"—allows users to create avatars, or electronic versions of themselves, and engage in community features and activities. Like the real world, Second Life offers members the opportunity to own (virtual) land, operate a business, and engage in money-making transactions using site-specific currency called Linden dollars. This system has led to both positive and negative player feedback. "In 2003, we had a tax revolt," Rosedale ruefully recalled to Spencer Reiss of the *Technology Review* in 2005. "Our version of the Washington Monument was replaced by a giant tower of tea crates. We got the message: there are no taxes now."

Yet the presence of online money-based transactions has equally allowed Second Life users to generate real-world income through a system of Second Life-to-United States currency conversion. According to *Newsweek*'s Brad Stone, "single mom Munchflower Zaius, for example, designs decorative cyberclothes and skins and makes a high five-figure income selling them to Second Life citizens. 'I put in a 40-hour week.... I have fun, but for the most part, it's become a full-time job,'" explained Zaius, "who is so famous in the virtual world she prefers to use her Second Life name and keep her real name private," wrote Stone. Membership in Rosedale's online community grew over time to number in the millions, although admittedly only a minority of those users actively participates at any given time.

By 2008, however, Second Life's growth had begun to slow, and Rosedale stepped down as CEO of Linden Lab to allow a more experienced corporate hand to guide the company. Former digital communications CEO Mark Kingdon signed on Linden Lab's new CEO, with Rosedale remaining as chairman of the board. Even as this transition took place, Second Life gained the attention of a new audience: the United States Congress. Concerned about the possibilities of criminal groups using virtual worlds such as Second Life to plan nefarious activities such as terrorist attacks and money laundering, the House of Representatives called in Rosedale and other virtual world experts to discuss the communities' online policing efforts. "It is likely that virtual world activities are somewhat more policeable and the law somewhat more maintainable within virtual worlds," claimed the Second Life founder, according to a *CioInsight* story. "The virtual world has a degree of accountability ... and traceability which actually in many ways is better than the real world."

Second Life continued to grow under the leadership of its new CEO, despite complaints by disgruntled users over rising in-game fees for virtual property, goods, and services. In June of 2010, a corporate shakeup saw Rosedale resume his previous position as CEO of Linden Labs upon the exit of Kingdon; however, this position was intended to be an interim one, with Rosedale likely to step down again once a suitable candidate to guide the company's operations was found.

Sources

Periodicals

CioInsight, April 2, 2008.
Computer Graphics World, July 2004, p. 80.
Computer Weekly, April 29, 2008.
Inc, January-February 2009, p. 17.

Information Week, March 18, 2008.

Newsweek, October 17, 2005, p. 12.

New York Times, January 18, 2010; February 28, 2010; June 1, 2010.

PC Magazine Online, April 1, 2008.

Technology Review, December 2005, p. 34.

Online

"Biography of Philip Rosedale," All American Speakers, http://www.allamericanspeakers.com/sportspeakers/printerbio.php?speaker_id=6969 (August 29, 2010).

"Executive Profile: Philip Rosedale," *Business Week,* http://investing.businessweek.com/research/stocks/private/person.asp?personId=720162&privcapId=2532360&previousCapId=2532360&previousTitle=Linden%20Research,%20Inc (August 29, 2010).

"Management," Linden Lab, http://lindenlab.com/about/management#rosedale (August 29, 2010).

"TIME 100—Philip Rosedale," *Time,* http://www.time.com/time/specials/2007/article/0,28804,1595326_1615737_1615877,00.html (August 29, 2010).

—*Vanessa E. Vaughn*

Mark Ruffalo

Actor

Born Mark Alan Ruffalo, November 22, 1967, in Kenosha, WI; son of Frank (a painting contractor, inventor, and entrepreneur) and Marie (a hairstylist and restaurant manager) Ruffalo; married Sunrise Coigney (an actress and retail owner), June 11, 2000; children: Keen, Bella Noche, Odette. *Education:* Attended the Stella Adler Conservatory, Los Angeles, CA.

Addresses: *Management*—Robert Stein Management, 345 N. Maple Dr. #317, Beverly Hills, CA 90210.

Career

Actor, c. 1989—; also worked as a bartender and co-founded the Orpheus Theatre Company. Stage appearances include: *Avenue A,* Cast Theatre, Los Angeles, CA, 1990; *Betrayal by Everyone,* Met Theatre, Los Angeles, CA, 1993; *Still Life with Vacuum Salesman,* Cast Theatre, 1994; *Tent Show,* Cast Theatre, 1994; *This Is Our Youth,* INTAR Theatre, 1996, then McGinn-Cazale Theatre, New York City, 1998-99; *Betrayed by Everyone,* Los Angeles, CA, 1997; *The Moment When,* Playwrights Horizons Theatre, New York City, 1999-2000; *Waiting for Godot,* Page 93 Theatre Company, Los Angeles, 2002; *Awake and Sing!,* Belasco Theatre, New York City, 2006. Film appearances include: *Rough Trade,* 1992; *A Song for You,* 1993; *A Gift from Heaven,* 1994; *Mirror, Mirror 2: Raven Dance,* 1994; *There Goes My Baby,* 1994; *Mirror Mirror III: The Voyeur,* 1995; *Blood Money,* 1996; *The Dentist,* 1996; *The Destiny of Marty Fine,* 1996; *The Last Big Thing,* 1996; *54,* 1998; *Safe Men,* 1998; *A Fish in the Bathtub,* 1999; *How Does Anyone Get Old?* (short film), 1999; *Ride with the Devil,* 1999; *Committed,* 2000; *You Can Count on Me,* 2000; *Apartment 12,* 2001; *The Last Castle,* 2001; *Windtalkers,* 2002; *XX/XY,* 2002; *In the Cut,* 2003; *My Life Without Me,* 2003; *View from the Top,* 2003; *13 Going on 30,* 2004; *Collateral,* 2004; *Eternal Sunshine of the Spotless Mind,* 2004; *We Don't Live Here Anymore,* 2004; *All the King's Men,* 2006; *Just Like Heaven,* 2005; *Rumor Has It...,* 2005; *Reservation Road,* 2007; *Zodiac,* 2007; *Blindness,* 2008; *The Brothers Bloom,* 2008; *What Doesn't Kill You,* 2008; *Where the Wild Things Are,* 2009; *Date Night,* 2010; *The Kids Are All Right,* 2010; *Shutter Island,* 2010; *Sympathy for Delicious,* 2010. Film work includes: writer, *The Destiny of Marty Fine,* 1996; executive producer, writer, *We Don't Live Here Anymore,* 2004; director and producer, *Sympathy for Delicious,* 2010. Television appearances include: *CBS Summer Playhouse,* CBS, 1989; *Due South,* 1994; *On the Second Day of Christmas* (movie), 1997; *Houdini* (movie), 1998; *The Beat,* UPN, 2000; *Independent Lens* (documentary), 2008.

Awards: Best actor award, Montréal World Film Festival, for *You Can Count on Me,* 2000; New Generation Award, Los Angeles Film Critics Association, for *You Can Count on Me,* 2000; Special Jury

Prize—dramatic, Sundance Film Festival, for *Sympathy for Delicious*, 2010; best supporting actor award, New York Film Critics Circle, for *The Kids Are All Right*, 2010.

Sidelights

Best known for his work in such films as *You Can Count on Me, XX/XY, Zodiac,* and *The Kids Are All Right,* actor Mark Ruffalo has built an impressive career and demonstrated his versatility as a performer. Sometimes compared to a young Marlon Brando, Ruffalo played both leads and character roles, infusing them with depth and a memorable quality. He began his career on stage in Los Angeles, and returned to theater roles regularly over the course of his career. Describing Ruffalo, playwright, screenwriter, and director Kenneth Lonergan told Mal Vincent of the *Virginian-Pilot,* "He's very peculiar and very appealing. He's drawn to playing the sort of person who is very open and simultaneously very distressed."

Born on November 22, 1967, in Kenosha, Wisconsin, he was the son of Frank and Marie Ruffalo. Both of his parents were Italian American; his father worked as a painting contractor, inventor, and entrepreneur while his mother was a hairstylist and restaurant manager. When Ruffalo was 13 years old, his family, which included three younger siblings, moved to Virginia Beach, Virginia, where he spent the rest of his childhood. He attended First Colonial High School in Virginia Beach, where he was a wrestler and became interested in acting while taking a drama class. After graduating from high school, Ruffalo joined his family in San Diego, California, where they had recently moved. He soon left San Diego behind and moved to Los Angeles to pursue acting.

As soon as he moved to Los Angeles, Ruffalo appeared in a national commercial for acne medication. While Ruffalo also studied the craft of acting at the Stella Adler Conservatory (later known as the Stella Adler Academy of Acting and Theatre), he struggled to find professional work and his parents and a grandmother helped him out. He told Eirik Knutzen of the Copley News Service, "They gave me all the emotional and financial support they possibly could. They wouldn't let me quit trying to be an actor, and their checks usually came in just before they cut off my telephone service or electricity. I can't thank them enough." To support himself financially, Ruffalo worked as a bartender for nearly nine years, at Small's and other Los Angeles-area clubs.

In 1990, Ruffalo made his professional stage debut in the Cast Theatre production of *Avenue A.* He went on to appear in at least 30 more theater productions in Los Angeles in the 1990s. Among his roles was a Met Theatre production of *Betrayal by Everyone* in 1993, and Cast Theatre productions of both *Still Life with Vacuum Salesman* and *Tent Show* in 1994. In 1997, he appeared in a one-act play called *Betrayed by Everyone.* Ruffalo was also the co-founder of the Orpheus Theatre Company in Los Angeles. In addition to acting, he also was a writer, director, producer, lighting artist, and set builder for the group.

While his acting received great reviews, Ruffalo landed few television or film roles. He later claimed that he went on at least 800 auditions for film and television roles before he made it as an actor. He was cast in small and bit parts in films however, such as 1992's *Rough Trade,* 1993's *A Song for You,* and 1994's *Mirror, Mirror 2: Raven Dance.* Ruffalo had four film roles in 1996 with *The Destiny of Marty Fine, Blood Money, The Dentist,* and *The Last Big Thing.* He also wrote *The Destiny of Marty Fine,* which was first runner-up at the Sundance Film Festival. In 1998, he appeared in the disco-oriented *54,* as well as 1999's *A Fish in the Bathtub* and *Ride with the Devil.* The latter film was a western set in the Civil War-era directed by Ang Lee. Ruffalo's television roles included guest spots in shows like *Due South* in 1994, and roles in television movies like 1997's *On the 2nd Day of Christmas* and 1998's *Houdini.*

Frustrated by the progress of his career in the late 1990s, Ruffalo was nearly ready to quit when he landed his first break. Lonergan played a key role as Ruffalo was cast as Warren Straub in Lonergan's play *This Is Our Youth,* which was produced at the INTAR Theatre in 1996. Ruffalo moved to New York in this time period and reprised the role in the New York production, which was directed by Lonergan at the McGinn-Cazale Theatre in New York City from 1998 to 1999 to much acclaim. Ruffalo's turn in the play helped him land the male lead in a film scripted by Lonergan, *You Can Count on Me,* which was released in 2000.

In the low-budget *You Can Count on Me,* Ruffalo played Terry Prescott, the hippie brother of a single mother, played by Laura Linney, whose appearance in her life deeply affects her and her son. His performance won rave reviews and awards from the Montréal Film Festival and the Los Angeles Film Critics Association. It also took his career to the next level as Hollywood finally took notice of the hard-working actor. Yet, as he explained to Mal Vincent of the *Virginian-Pilot,* "All this is something to take in stride. It's taken so long to get to this point. I've been through the mill. This is no overnight success." After *You Can Count on Me,* he immediately directed a play at a Los Angeles theater.

Also in 2000, Ruffalo had his first starring role in a television series. He played Zane Marinelli, an off-beat New York City beat cop in the UPN drama *The Beat*. The Barry Levinson-created show not only explored Marinelli's life at work with his more straight-edged partner Mike Dorigan (played by Derek Cecil) but also his life outside of the precinct, including his tumultuous sex life. *The Beat* was short-lived. After the first 13 episodes of *The Beat* were filmed, Ruffalo appeared in a production at Playwrights Horizons, titled *The Moment When*. While Ruffalo worked in television on occasion over the years, he focused much of his attention on the big screen with some stage plays worked in as well. He appeared in many other films of note, both Hollywood blockbuster releases and independent films.

Just as Ruffalo's career was taking off, however, he suffered a personal setback in the summer of 2001. He was diagnosed with a brain tumor after filming 2001's *The Last Castle*, and had to drop out of the film *Signs*. Joaquin Phoenix took the role in the M. Night Shyamalan-directed film, released in 2002. The tumor was found to be benign, though he suffered from partial facial paralysis and memory loss for a time. The tumor helped give Ruffalo a new appreciation for life and his career. Before the tumor, Ruffalo felt he had sense of entitlement about acting and did not fully appreciate his recent success. During his recovery and after, he understood that he might not be able at act again, giving him a deeper appreciation of his career and success and empowered him to make careful choices in film roles.

After recovering, Ruffalo continued to build his career. Describing him as an actor, Cathy Horyn of the *New York Times Magazine* noted, "few performers possess their characters with more natural grace. Not only does Ruffalo make it look easy, he also manages to access emotions with a freedom unavailable to many of his better-known contemporaries, making him closer to the older generation of actors—especially the young Brando—for whom anger or sexual tension could often be registered with astonishing stillness."

His next film of note was an independent drama, 2002's *XX/XY*. This so-called romantic tragedy featured Ruffalo as an egotistical filmmaker who leaves the safe haven of college and discovers life is much more difficult. Also in 2002, he played Vladimir in a Page 93 Theatre Company production of *Waiting for Godot*. In 2003, Ruffalo appeared in three acclaimed films, including *My Life Without Me* and *In the Cut*. The former was about a dying young woman who wants to leave a legacy to her family. The latter was a sexual drama based on the novel by Susanna Moore and directed by Jane Campion. Ruffalo played Malloy, a very sexual New York homicide detective, to much critical praise.

In 2004, Ruffalo had four major films released, which demonstrated the breadth of his acting abilities. The drama *We Don't Live Here Anymore* focused on difficulties in marriage and adultery, while the Charlie Kaufman-penned comedy *Eternal Sunshine of the Spotless Mind* was a box-office success starring Jim Carrey. Ruffalo also appeared in two Hollywood blockbusters, *13 Going on 30*, a comedy staring Jennifer Garner, and the Michael Mann thriller, *Collateral*, which featured him playing an undercover agent and co-starred Jamie Foxx and Tom Cruise. He appeared in two more blockbuster films in 2005, the romantic comedy *Just Like Heaven* and *Rumor Has It....*

While Ruffalo appeared in the respected political drama *All the King's Men* in 2006, he also landed his first Tony Award nomination that year for his portrayal of Moe Axelrod in the Belasco Theatre production of *Awake and Sing!* It was his Broadway debut and he was nominated in the Supporting or Featured Actor in a Drama category. His next film was also a major Hollywood production, 2007's *Zodiac*, directed by David Fincher and based on the real life investigation into a serial killer who struck the San Francisco area in the 1970s. He continued to challenge himself as an actor, appearing in the independent con man comedy *The Brothers Bloom*, released in 2008, and the big-budget adaptation of the classic children's novel, 2009's *Where the Wild Things Are*. During this time period, in December of 2008, Ruffalo suffered another personal blow when his brother Scott was found outside of his home in Beverly Hills with a gunshot wound to his head. Scott Ruffalo eventually died of the injury and the circumstances of his death remained unresolved.

Ruffalo dropped out of his scheduled role in the independent film *Greenberg* and was replaced by Ben Stiller. He also took some time away from acting, but in 2010, his career reached new heights. That year, his directorial debut, *Sympathy for Delicious*, was released. The film focused on a paraplegic who gains the ability to heal but cannot heal himself, and Ruffalo had a starring role in the film. Also in 2010, he had a supporting role in the Martin Scorsese thriller *Shutter Island*, as well as a featured role in the romantic comedy *Date Night*. Most acclaimed was his work in the art house hit *The Kids Are All Right*, in which he played a freewheeling restaurant owner who meets the teenagers he sired by donating his sperm to sperm bank. His Paul becomes involved in their family—their mothers are lesbians in a long-term relationship—and nearly breaks it apart. For his work, Ruffalo received the New York Film Critics Circle Award for best supporting actor.

In 2010, Ruffalo was filming *Margaret,* directed by Lonergan and scheduled for release in 2011, and *The Avengers,* scheduled for release in 2012. Ruffalo was supposed to play the iconic character Bruce Banner/The Hulk in the latter film. Of his attitude towards his craft, Ruffalo told Jay Stone of the *Ottawa Citizen,* "I used to torture myself about acting. I used to think you weren't a good actor unless you were absolutely tortured 100 percent of the time. And now I think 50 percent of the time is enough."

Sources

Periodicals

Associated Press, May 22, 2006.
Calgary Sun (Alberta, Canada), July 4, 2010, p. E6.

Canwest News Service, September 5, 2008; January 28, 2010; July 9, 2010.
Chicago Sun-Times, September 16, 2005, p. 30.
Copley News Service, March 27, 2000; November 6, 2000; March 16, 2007.
Daily Telegraph (London), October 15, 2010, p. 29.
New York Times Magazine, November 9, 2003, p. 72.
Ottawa Citizen, September 2, 2004, p. E8.
Toronto Star, July 3, 2010, p. E3.
Toronto Sun, April 20, 2004, p. 47; September 23, 2006, p. 56.
UPI, December 11, 2008.
Vancouver Sun (British Columbia, Canada), September 5, 2003, p. D7.
Virginian-Pilot (Norfolk, VA), June 18, 2002, p. E1.

Online

"Mark Ruffalo," Internet Movie Database, http://www.imdb.com/name/nm0749263/ (November 21, 2010).

—*A. Petruso*

Ken Salazar

U.S. Secretary of the Interior

Aaron M. Sprecher/Bloomberg via Getty Images

Born March 2, 1955, in Alamosa, CO; son of Enrique (a rancher) and Emma (a rancher) Salazar; married Hope; children: Melinda, Andrea. *Education:* Colorado College, B.A., 1977; University of Michigan Law School, J.D., 1981.

Addresses: *Office*—U.S. Department of the Interior, 1849 C Street, NW, Washington, DC 20240.

Career

Attorney specializing in water issues, 1981-87 and 1994-98; farmer and partner, El Rancho Salazar, c. 1980s-90s; business owner, including radio stations in Pueblo and Denver, Colorado, c. 1980s-90s; chief legal counsel to governor of Colorado, 1987-90; executive director, Colorado Department of Natural Resources, 1990-94; attorney general of Colorado, 1999-2005; U.S. Senator, 2005-09; U.S. secretary of the interior, 2009—.

Awards: Profiles in Courage award, Conference of Western Attorneys General, early 2000s.

Sidelights

The day President Barack Obama announced he was nominating Ken Salazar as U.S. Secretary of the Interior, Salazar wore a cowboy hat and string tie to his introduction. That symbolism says a lot about how Salazar approaches politics. A moderate Democrat from rural Colorado, Salazar combines a Westerner's swaggering independence with a love of the land to find a middle ground on debates about protecting the environment and encouraging development on federal lands. His personality and politics proved popular in Colorado, whose people elected him to the U.S. Senate and twice voted him the state's attorney general. But it has led him to a sometimes controversial tenure as interior secretary. After the BP oil spill fouled the Gulf of Mexico in 2010, Salazar was criticized for not moving more boldly to reform the troubled department.

Though Salazar sometimes refers to himself as Mexican American, his ancestors came to the American West more than 400 years ago, before the United States or Mexico were countries. They emigrated from Spain and were among the first settlers of Santa Fe, New Mexico, in 1598. For five generations, the Salazars have farmed the same land in the San Luis Valley of Colorado.

Born in Alamosa, Colorado, in 1955, Salazar grew up on his family's potato farm and ranch, El Rancho Salazar, near Manassa. He lived in a house with no electricity or telephone and learned farming from his family. Though his parents did not graduate from college, Salazar and his seven brothers and sisters all became college graduates. He earned a bachelor's degree in political science from Colorado

College in 1977, then went on to the University of Michigan Law School, from which he graduated in 1981.

Salazar began his career as an attorney specializing in water and environmental issues in Colorado. Salazar and his wife also became owners of several businesses, from a Dairy Queen to radio stations in Denver and Pueblo. He also became a partner with his family in El Rancho Salazar. In 1987, he joined the cabinet of Colorado governor Roy Romer as chief legal counsel.

In 1990, Salazar became executive director of the Department of Natural Resources, a position he held until 1994. In that job, he defended Colorado's agreements with other states over water resources and reformed the state's regulations of the oil, gas, and mining industries. He also wrote a 1992 amendment to the state constitution that created the land conservation effort Great Outdoors Colorado.

After 1994, Salazar returned to his private law practice for four years. But politics beckoned before long. He ran for the job of Colorado attorney general in 1998 and won, taking office the following year. Again he focused on land and water issues, creating an environmental crimes unit; however, Salazar sometimes clashed with environmentalists. For instance, he resisted efforts to add the black-tailed prairie dog to the endangered species list. He also worked to strengthen and enforce the state's consumer protection laws and established special units to prosecute fugitives and gang members.

In 2004, Salazar ran for the U.S. Senate and defeated Republican candidate Pete Coors, a beer company executive. As a senator, he quickly positioned himself not as a liberal Democrat, but as a representative of the West. "The America where I grew up is vanishing today, left behind by a Washington, D.C., that has lost touch with what is important to the people of the heartland," he argued in his first speech to the Senate, in March of 2005 (as quoted by Alex Altman of *Time* magazine). "I fear that rural Colorado, like the rest of rural America, has become 'the Forgotten America.'"

In the Senate, Salazar advocated conserving water resources and pressed for more research into how climate change would affect the water supply; however, he defended water projects conducted by the U.S. Army Corps of Engineers against environmentalists' efforts to subject them to new regulations. He fought the administration of President George W. Bush over its plans to approve com-

mercial oil-shale development on federal lands in the West, arguing that not enough was yet known about how much water and electricity the work would consume and how much carbon emission it would produce.

Salazar also pushed for the federal government to support more renewable energy projects. In 2005, he cosponsored an unsuccessful bill that would have required the government to create a plan to reduce the nation's oil consumption. "We need to be honest with ourselves and the American people about our energy future," he said in a 2008 Senate speech (as quoted by Altman in *Time* magazine). "We simply cannot drill our way to energy independence." That year, he signed on to a bipartisan compromise energy plan that would have increased funding and tax incentives for renewable energy and also allowed more offshore drilling. The plan did not pass.

When Obama was elected president in November of 2008, he asked Salazar to join his cabinet as interior secretary. Obama knew Salazar well. They had both entered the Senate in 2005 and had been neighbors in the same townhouse building in Washington. Obama's choice of Salazar continued a long tradition of the Interior Department being headed by a Westerner. The department oversees about 20 percent of the land in the United States, about a half-billion acres. Much of it is in the West, so the department's decisions about the use of natural resources on federal land directly affect many Westerners' lives.

Obama was also making a shrewd political calculation. Salazar's ability to win elections as a Democrat in Colorado, which often leans Republican, was valuable to Obama's party as it tried to expand its appeal. The Salazar family name has been "shorthand for a big-thought Democratic Party strategy of carrying the West," wrote Kirk Johnson of the *New York Times*. "The Salazar formula: rural and urban coalitions around centrist, libertarian-tinged politics, mixing support for gun rights with an ability to look natural in a cowboy hat."

Everyone knew Salazar's new job would be tough. The Interior had become the federal government's most scandal-plagued department. Its twin missions, to protect federal lands and also increase the amount of royalties the lands generate from oil and gas mining, often come into conflict with each other. Many Interior employees had been accused of improper relationships with mining businesses. Some celebrated Salazar as a good choice for the job, saying he was highly ethical and could strike a balance between the department's goals. "He is a very ethical person, and I think he'll need that at Interior, because built into that place are latent conflicts," said Troy Eid, the U.S. attorney for Colorado (as quoted by Chris Frates on the Web site Politico).

However, some environmentalists were disappointed that Salazar beat out their favorite candidate, Arizona congressman Raul Grijalva, for the job. They thought Salazar compromised too often with industry. "He is a right-of-center Democrat who often favors industry and big agricultural interests in battles over global warming, fuel efficiency, and endangered species," Kieran Suckling, executive director of the Center for Biological Diversity, told John M. Broder of the *New York Times*.

In his first year in office, Salazar focused on goals such as encouraging offshore wind projects. As expected, he pursued a middle ground that left environmentalists complaining he had not acted boldly enough to protect natural resources, while oil and timber companies argued he had regulated them too strictly. Salazar defended the need to allow companies to drill and mine for coal, oil, and gas while also increasing support for wind and solar power. "We continue to produce conventional energy for the nation because we need to do that while we transition over to a new energy economy," Salazar told Broder and Ben Werschkul of the *New York Times*. "We also have completely turned the page on a new beginning with respect to renewable energy. We are harnessing the winds offshore and the sun of the desert in the Southwest and biomass and geothermal throughout the country."

Salazar vowed stronger scrutiny of oil and gas leases on public lands, saying the Bush Administration had made Interior a "candy store" for oil companies, according to Broder of the *New York Times*. "The previous administration's 'anywhere, anyhow' policy on oil and gas development ran afoul of communities, carved up the landscape, and fueled costly conflicts that created uncertainty for investors and industry," he said. "We need a fresh look—from inside the federal government and from outside—at how we can better manage Americans' energy resources."

The Interior Department moved slowly under Salazar to change one aspect of its regulation of the oil industry. Obama had asked Salazar to reform the Minerals Management Service, the agency that regulated offshore drilling. Audits and congressional hearings had revealed several scandals in the agency, from outright corruption to too-close relationships with the energy companies it regulated. But little changed in the Minerals Management Service in the first year and a half of the Obama Administration, a failure that soon became embarrassing.

In April of 2010, an oil rig exploded in the Gulf of Mexico. A massive oil leak flowed unchecked from below the rig for months. Suddenly, Salazar and Obama faced serious questions about the Minerals Management Service's regulation of oil drilling. Salazar decided in May to reorganize the agency, splitting it into three offices. But Obama pushed him to do more, admitting at a press conference that he felt the reform of the service was proceeding too slowly. In June, Obama sent a former prosecutor, Michael R. Bromwich, to oversee the reorganization of the minerals service and take charge of one of its successors, the Bureau of Ocean Energy Management. Observers felt it was a sign that the president was unhappy with Salazar's leadership on the issue, because the move came just a month after Salazar had assigned two aides to reorganize the agency. Salazar argued that faster reforms of the agency would not have prevented the spill.

Salazar had to tone down his cowboy rhetoric during the Gulf oil spill crisis, even though it expressed the frustration many Americans felt. Soon after the explosion, he promised to "keep the boot on the neck" of BP, the company that leased the rig (according to Campbell Robertson, Clifford Krauss, and Broder of the *New York Times*). He meant that the government would pressure BP to find a way to plug the leaking well and clean up the mess. Obama criticized Salazar's choice of words during a press conference. Later, Salazar threatened to take over the effort to stop the spill, but had to back down the next day and admit that BP had the best technology for stopping the leak.

In October of 2010, after the BP crisis was over, Salazar ended a months-long moratorium on issuing new offshore oil drilling permits, declaring that the Interior Department had made progress in reducing the risks of deepwater drilling. Otherwise, Washington observers noted that Salazar kept a lower profile after the spill while other members of the administration took the lead on environmental issues. Nor did Salazar get involved in the 2010 elections in Colorado, even though his brother, John Salazar, a congressman, was in a tight race for reelection. Salazar's position in the Obama Administration hurt his brother with voters in his conservative district, and his brother lost the race to the Republican candidate. That setback may hurt Salazar's reputation as a Democrat who knows how to appeal to voters in the West.

Sources

Periodicals

New York Times, December 18, 2008; January 7, 2010; May 24, 2010; July 12, 2010; October 14, 2010.
Time, December 18, 2008.
Washington Post, October 12, 2010; October 22, 2010.

Online

"About Secretary Salazar," U.S. Department of the Interior, http://www.doi.gov/whoweare/secretarysalazar.cfm (November 8, 2010).
"Department of Interior: Ken Salazar," Politico, http://www.politico.com/news/stories/0109/17245.html (November 8, 2010).
"Ken Salazar News," *New York Times*, http://topics.nytimes.com/top/reference/timestopics/people/s/ken_salazar/index.html (November 8, 2010).
"Ken Salazar," WhoRunsGov, http://www.whorunsgov.com/Profiles/Ken_Salazar (November 26, 2010).
"The New Team," *New York Times*, http://projects.nytimes.com/44th_president/new_team/show/ken-salazar (November 8, 2010).
"Salazar Plots Cautious Course at Interior," *New York Times*, http://thecaucus.blogs.nytimes.com/2009/12/01/salazar-plots-cautious-course-at-interior/ (November 8, 2010).
"Tea Party Triumphs in Rural Colorado," *New York Times*, http://thecaucus.blogs.nytimes.com/2010/11/03/tea-party-triumphs-in-rural-colorado/ (November 26, 2010).

—*Erick Trickey*

Alejandro Sanz

Raul Urbina/Getty Images Entertainment/Getty Images

Singer and songwriter

Born Alejandro Sánchez Pizarro, December 18, 1968, in Cadiz, Spain; son of Jesús Sánchez Madero (a professional guitarist) and María Pizarro Medina (a homemaker); married Jaydy Michel (a model), December 1998 (divorced, 2005); children: Manuela (with Michel), Alexander (with Valeria Rivera).

Addresses: *Contact*—Warner Music Latina, 3400 W. Olive Ave., Burbank, CA 91505. *Web site*—http://www.alejandrosanz.com.

Career

Began guitar lessons at age seven; started writing songs as a teen, releasing *Los Chulos Son Pa Cuidarlos* at 16, 1989; signed with Warner, 1991; released first studio album, *Viviendo de Prisa* (Living In A Hurry), 1991; recorded first song in English, 2001; released eighth studio album, *Paraíso Express* (Paradise Express), 2009.

Awards: Latin Grammy Award for record of the year, song of the year, album of the year and best male pop vocalist, Latin Academy of Record Arts & Sciences, for "El Alma al Aire" and *El Alma al Aire* (The Bared Soul), 2001; Latin Grammy Award for album of the year, Latin Academy of Record Arts & Sciences, for *MTV Unplugged*, 2002; Latin Grammy Award for record of the year and song of the year, Latin Academy of Record Arts & Sciences, for "Y Solo Se Me Ocurre Amarte" (All I Can Do Is Love You), 2002; Latin Grammy Award for record of the year, song of the year, album of the year, best male

pop vocalist, and best engineered album, Latin Academy of Record Arts & Sciences, for *No Es lo Mismo* (It's Not the Same), 2004; Grammy Award for best Latin pop album, National Academy of Recording Arts & Sciences, for *No Es lo Mismo* (It's Not the Same), 2004; Latin Grammy Award for record of the year and song of the year, Latin Academy of Record Arts & Sciences, for "Tu No Tienes Alma," 2005; Latin Grammy Award for record of the year and song of the year (with Shakira), Latin Academy of Record Arts & Sciences, for "La Tortura," 2006; Grammy Award for best Latin pop album, National Academy of Recording Arts & Sciences, for *El Tren de los Momentos*, 2008.

Sidelights

With 16 Latin Grammy Awards and worldwide album sales topping 25 million, Spanish pop superstar Alejandro Sanz is undoubtedly the most commercially successful Spanish singer of his generation. During the early 1990s, Sanz became a sensation among fellow Spaniards for his albums, which he filled with romantic ballads delivered in his flamenco-styled gravelly tenor. By decade's end, Sanz had crossed over into the Latin market and entered the U.S. market in 2001, when he recorded his first song in English. Two decades after his first album's release, Sanz remained popular as he continued to record songs with mass appeal. Writing in the *Dallas Morning News,* music critic Mario Tarradell commended Sanz for consistently delivering albums that "stretch the boundaries of Latin pop." Tarradell noted that Sanz had an exceptional gift for musical reinvention. "He frequently toys with melodies, opting for minor chord changes that give his music a late-night jazzy vibe. As a vocalist, he's prone to flamenco-style wails instead of smooth crooning. And he's not afraid to experiment with rhythms, from salsa to hip-hop."

Sanz's given name was Alejandro Sánchez Pizarro. He was born December 18, 1968, in Cadiz, located in the southernmost province of Spain, though he grew up in Madrid. Each summer, Sanz vacationed in southern Spain in the area his parents—Maria Pizarro Medina and Jesús Sánchez Madero—were raised. This region, known as Andalusia, is where flamenco originated. Madero passed his love of music on to his son. He had spent his life trying to find his way as a musician and enjoyed mild success managing cabaret acts. He worked as a door-to-door book salesman to make ends meet.

Influenced by his father, Sanz took an early interest in music and began guitar lessons at seven, intent on mastering the demanding flamenco style of play. Sanz once infuriated his mother so much with his incessant playing that she destroyed his guitar because he kept the family awake with his strumming. Eventually, Sanz gave up on learning flamenco when he realized how committed he would have to be to master the art form. The flamenco vibe, however, remained firmly rooted in his sound as Sanz developed as a musician. Sanz began recording his own songs at 13 with the aid of two cassette recorders, which allowed him to create multi-tracks of his voice and guitar. "It sort of came out of being bored," Sanz told Tarradell. "I was alone and bored. I wasn't much into playing with friends, so I started playing the guitar."

At age 16, Sanz adopted the name Alejandro Magno (Alexander the Great) and used the moniker for his first album, *Los Chulos Son Pa Cuidarlos,* an experimental collection of songs merging flamenco guitar with techno beats. The album, released under the Spanish label Hispavox, failed to impress listeners of either genre. Undaunted, Sanz continued to pursue music and honed his skills performing at local Madrid venues. During the 1980s Sanz performed his music at strip joints, entertaining audiences between the main acts.

Sanz entered college in Madrid—at his parents' request—but stayed with music on the side, landing a job at a small record label in Madrid, which let him write songs for its artists. Along the way, Sanz befriended Latin music insider Miguel Angel Arenas and persuaded Arenas to share a demo of his songs with others in the music business. Arenas shopped the demo, which led to a deal with Warner. In 1991, Sanz released *Viviendo de Prisa* (Living In A Hurry) under his own name. The album sold slowly at first, but sales took off after Sanz played at a televised UNICEF charity concert in Madrid. The debut went on to sell a million copies in Spain, where it topped the album chart and put Sanz's career on the fast track. He followed with *Si Tú Me Miras* (If You Look At Me) in 1993 and *3* in 1995. The songs on these first albums focused on romance and brought Sanz a large following of female fans who were smitten by both his good looks and poetic lyrics.

Sanz's fourth studio album—*Más* (More; 1997)—solidified his status as Spain's reigning pop idol. *Más* sold more than two million copes in Spain and proved popular in Mexico, buoyed by such hits as "Amiga Mia," which topped *Billboard*'s Latin Pop Songs chart, and "Corazón Partío," which hit number three. Sanz struck gold with 2000's *El Alma al Aire* (The Bared Soul), which sold 200,000 copies in Spain its first day and went on to sell a million copies by week's end, setting a new Spanish record for first-week sales. The album brought Sanz four Latin Grammy Awards, including album of the year honors. After the album's release, Sanz embarked on a 34-concert tour through nine Latin American countries and the United States. The tour was sold out, with ticket sales hitting 350,000.

In 2001, Sanz broadened his musical spectrum, recording two songs with the Irish folk rock band The Corrs—one of them in English. The songs were added to a special edition re-issue of *El Alma al Aire* and were released to promote an all-stadium tour of Spain Sanz was scheduled to play. While the English song helped broaden Sanz's fan base, he told *Billboard*'s Howell Llewellyn that he had no intentions of recording an entire album in English. "If I ever do that all I can promise is that it will be because of an artistic urge and not for marketing reasons. I don't sing 'pretty,' I give it all my soul. That's why I'm not interested in releasing on the Internet—music isn't the same if you can't touch it as a finished record."

By 2000, Sanz had captured a worldwide following but continued to have trouble breaking into the U.S. market. On the West Coast, the Spanish-language radio stations favored artists from Mexico; on the East Coast, salsa reigned. In 2001, Sanz made a play for the U.S. market with the release of *MTV Unplugged,* an album of live acoustic recordings of his biggest hits recorded at the Gusman Center in Miami and backed by an extensive string section. Sanz was the first Spanish artist invited to play on the MTV show. Sanz told the *Washington Post*'s Richard Harrington that the experience of performing live on the show influenced his style. "It was a rediscovery of how to perform, and also how to record music with live musicians. That was the spirit of the music in its pure form, though [it is ironic] that the more people who are playing, the more simple it is."

When the album of the show was released, it became an instant success. The most popular song was "Y Solo Se Me Ocurre Amarte" (All I Can Do Is Love You), written for his wife and daughter. Sanz married Mexican model Jaydy Michel in 1998 and their daughter, Manuela, followed in 2001. They later divorced. *MTV Unplugged* spent 50 weeks on *Billboard*'s Latin Pop Albums chart, peaking at number one. Sanz went on to win three Latin Grammy Awards for the album, including album of the year. "Y Solo Se Me Ocurre Amarte" won both record and song of the year honors.

In 2003, Sanz went a new direction in his music, releasing the edgier, more emotional *No Es lo Mismo* (It's Not the Same) in which he explored hip-hop, rock, and Cuban influences. In working to create an album that departed from his signature romantic-flamenco-ballad style, Sanz brought in legendary rock bassist Anthony Jackson, who had played alongside Madonna and Steely Dan. To the mix he added Cuban jazz drummer Horacio Hernandez, (who had played with Carlos Santana), Spanish flamenco guitarist Paco de Lucía, and Cuban-American rapper GQ. By bridging several musical styles, the album appealed to a broader audience.

In addition, Sanz steered away from focusing his lyrics on love and romance and included a track titled "Sandy a orilla do mundo" (Sandy at the Shoreline of the World), a heartbreaker about a 2002 oil spill that had tarnished Spain's coast. Sanz went political with "Labana," a song about Cuban oppression. The album's cover photo included a shot of Sanz in a sleeveless shirt meant to showcase the tattoo on his arm—a rendition of the famed bull from Pablo Picasso's antiwar masterpiece "Guernica." Sanz chose to feature the tattoo as a symbol of his opposition to the war in Iraq. The album was a hit with first-week sales of one million.

In an interview with the *Miami Herald*'s Jordan Levin, Sanz discussed his new sound. "I couldn't do the same music I'd already done, and I couldn't do the music everyone else was doing. I think one of an artist's obligations is to surprise people a little. Imagine that when you get a record you already know what it will sound like. That's not good, really." *No Es lo Mismo* hit number two on the *Billboard* Latin Pop Albums chart but demonstrated its wider appeal by charting on the *Billboard* 200. Sanz went on to capture five Latin Grammy Awards for the album, as well as his first Grammy Award for best Latin pop album.

In 2005, Sanz broadened his fan base when he contributed his singing and songwriting to Latin star Shakira's sixth studio album on a number titled "La Tortura." Released as a single, "La Tortura" received notoriety for becoming one of the few Latin songs to ever earn mainstream success. It charted in countries around the world, including Hungary, Germany, and the United States. Sanz notched two Latin Grammy Awards for "La Tortura," including song and record of the year. He followed with 2006's *El Tren de los Momentos*, for which he won a Grammy Award for best Latin pop album.

In 2009, Sanz released *Paraíso Express* (Paradise Express). More of a pop-rock album, it included a duet with R&B star Alicia Keys on the uptempo lead single "Looking for Paradise." The collaboration evolved from an accidental encounter. "I ran into her in New York on a friend's boat, and I began playing guitar, she began singing, and there was this magic that had everyone gaping," Sanz told the *Miami Herald*'s Levin. "So we decided we had to do something together, because this kind of magic is so rare." Sanz and Keys were right about the magic—"Looking for Paradise" hit number one on the *Billboard* Latin Pop Songs chart. In the song, the artists sing in both Spanish and English, taking turns crooning about what paradise means for them.

Sanz's two decades of success evolved out of his strong work ethic. Among industry insiders, Sanz was known as a workaholic and perfectionist—an artist who perpetually composes and practices his songs, sometimes until dawn. Speaking to *Billboard*'s Llewellyn, Warner exec Sal Tagarro once recalled an incident in which Sanz kept hotel guests awake with his saxophone until the early morning hours. Sanz joked about the incident with Llewellyn. "They rang me from reception to say they had received complaints. I asked, 'What instrument was it?' and the receptionist said, 'A trumpet, I think.' I said, 'Ah, well, it's not me then,' and put the phone down."

For Warner, signing Sanz has been a worthwhile venture, with worldwide album sales topping 25 million on the backs of eight studio albums and several compilations. "Warner knew from the beginning that it had a great artist," Sanz's longtime manager, Rosa Lagarrigue, told Llewellyn. "Virtually everybody in Spain now views him as a near-genius."

Selected discography

(As Alejandro Magno) *Los Chulos Son Pa Cuidarlos,* Hispavox, 1989.
Viviendo de Prisa (Living In A Hurry), WEA Latina, 1991.
Si Tú Me Miras (If You Look At Me), WEA Latina, 1993.
3, WEA Latina, 1995.
Más (More), WEA Latina, 1997.
El Alma al Aire (The Bared Soul), WEA Latina, 2000.
MTV Unplugged, WEA Latina, 2001.
No Es lo Mismo (It's Not the Same), WEA Latina, 2003.
El Tren de los Momentos, Warner, 2006.
Paraíso Express (Paradise Express), Warner, 2009.

Sources

Periodicals

Billboard, February 28, 1998; June 16, 2001, p. 43; May 10, 2003; November 7, 2009.
Dallas Morning News, July 2, 1998, p. 5C; May 7, 2004, sec. GUIDE, p. 25.
Los Angeles Times, October 19, 2003, p. E49.
Miami Herald, October 19, 2003, p. 5M; November 10, 2009, p. A8.
Philadelphia Inquirer, November 5, 2005, p. C6.
Washington Post, April 23, 2004, p. T6.

—Lisa Frick

John Sexton

President of New York University

Born John Edward Sexton, September 29, 1942, in New York, NY; first marriage annulled; married Lisa Ellen Goldberg (a philanthropic executive; died, 2007); children: Jed, Katie. *Education:* Fordham University, B.A., 1963, M.A., 1965, Ph.D., 1978; Harvard Law School, J.D. (magna cum laude), 1979.

Addresses: *Home*—New York, NY. *Office*—New York University, 70 Washington Square S., New York, NY 10012.

Career

Debate coach, St. Brendan's High School, 1961-75; instructor in religion, St. Francis College, 1966-75, and chair of religion department, 1969-75; founded John Sexton Educational Center (a test-preparation franchise), 1974; Supreme Court editor, *Harvard Law Review*, c. 1979; clerk for two U.S. Court of Appeals judges, 1979-80, and for U.S. Supreme Court Chief Justice Warren Burger, 1980-81; professor, New York University School of Law, 1981-88, then dean, 1988-2002; president, New York University, 2002—.

Sidelights

As president of New York University, John Sexton has worked to reposition the largest private university in the United States into a global powerhouse in academia. A few years after taking over in 2002, Sexton launched an ambitious program to set up a full liberal arts college under the NYU name in Abu Dhabi, the United Arab Emirates city-state. As he told *New York* magazine writer Zvika Krieger, "our strategy arises organically from New York City itself, which is the first miniaturization of the world."

Sexton possesses a dazzling array of personal and professional achievements dating all the way back to his childhood in the Belle Harbor beachfront community in Queens. In the early summer of 1953, an eleven-year-old Sexton noticed all the neighborhood women trekking to the beach with their children for the day lugging their beach umbrellas and lounge chairs. He offered to store the beach props in his parents' garage for a flat fee all summer. "Then I recruited these two ten year olds to carry the stuff out on a stretcher, and I stood there like Rommel," he recalled in an interview with *New York Times Magazine* writer James Traub, referring to the famous German field marshal of World War II. "I cleared $3,000 during the summer," he added, noting that that figure was $500 more than a newly minted law school graduate at a top Manhattan firm.

Sexton was a top debater at Brooklyn Preparatory School, a rigorous Roman Catholic all-boys high school, and won a national debating championship. He went on to Fordham College in the Bronx, another New York institution run by members of the Jesuit religious order, but his interest in schoolwork flagged after he took an unpaid position as debate-team coach at the single-sex Roman Catholic high school his sister attended. He wound up graduating from Fordham University in 1963 with a history degree and a 2.1 grade-point average, but he led St. Brendan's to five Interscholastic National Debate Championship titles.

In 1966, Sexton took a job teaching at a small Catholic school in Brooklyn, St. Francis College, as he pursued his Ph.D. in the history of American religion at Fordham. In 1974, while still teaching at St. Francis, he founded a successful chain of test-preparation schools that readied students for the Law School Aptitude Test (LSAT). In yet another twist on his already impressive credentials, Sexton finally gave in to pressure from his more accomplished friends and applied to the nation's top law schools. When he failed to make the cut at prestigious Harvard Law School, one of those friends interceded with the admissions dean, and Sexton began classes in Cambridge in 1976.

First-year law students commonly take a tough civil procedure class, which introduces them to the U.S. legal system inside the courtroom. At Harvard, a top expert in the field, Arthur R. Miller, taught civil procedure. Early on, "Sexton ended up sparring with Miller for most of the 50-minute class, making up mind-bending legal hypotheticals, contradicting Miller's assumptions, and even trading scholarly insults in an academic version of a Brooklyn street fight," wrote *BusinessWeek*'s John Hechinger. During Sexton's second year at Harvard, Miller invited him to substitute-teach the class for him when he was out of town; the two later co-authored a law school textbook on civil procedure.

Sexton graduated with his Harvard Law School degree in 1979 and landed, not surprisingly, with the best clerkship in the country for a new juris-doctor holder: to the Chief Justice of the U.S. Supreme Court, Warren Burger. In 1981 Sexton joined the faculty of New York University School of Law, which was emerging that decade as one of the top law schools in the country. Just seven years later, he became dean of the NYU law school, and its rankings soared even higher under his tenure.

Long known for his competitive streak, Sexton began his new job with a determination to set new

fund-raising records at NYU's law school. NYU's School of Law also established an innovative global law program during his 14 years as dean. In the spring of 2001, his name was announced as the next president of New York University. "N.Y.U. is already taken seriously as a research and teaching institution," he told *New York Times* writer Karen W. Arenson. "Now it is time to turn it into something special, a school that is going new places that everyone will have to follow." Taking over in the spring of 2002, he began implementing his highly successful fund-raising and expansion strategies on a much larger level. In his first eight years on the job, Sexton had brought in $2.5 billion to NYU's endowment fund, or roughly a million dollars a day.

Sexton's grand plan for New York University drew upon the prestige a college degree from a top American university conferred upon its holder overseas. With scores of international students applying to NYU and the Ivy Leagues, schools sought to meet the demand by opening foreign campuses in Asia and the Middle East. Sexton conceived of an entirely separate, but equal, campus in the United Arab Emirates' city-state, Abu Dhabi. The project was kicked off by a $50 million gift to NYU from Abu Dhabi's Crown Prince Sheikh Zayed bin Sultan Al Nahyan, and the plan alarmed some faculty members, who feared that the NYU name was being tarnished by lure of petrodollars. Sexton saw NYU Abu Dhabi as just the first phase of his scheme. "We're building Abu Dhabi as part of a circulatory system on six continents," he told Hechinger in *Business Week*. "You choose a continent for your next semester as easily as you choose a course."

With his aversion to business attire and penchant for hugs instead of handshakes, Sexton barely fits the mold of the traditional college president. He still teaches undergraduate courses, even commuting to Abu Dhabi for one of the first ones on the new campus. He has two grown children and a Havanese-breed dog he named Legs, after the initials of his late wife, Lisa E. Goldberg Sexton, whom he met at Harvard Law. In 2009, the *New York Times* interviewed him for a feature in which famous New Yorkers are quizzed about their Sunday routine. He told reporter Lisa W. Foderaro in 2009 that he still attends Sunday Mass and now lunches on salads. "I've lost 30 pounds since June 2," he told her. "I announced to the leadership team—the deans and senior vice presidents—to show them that we can control the budget, that I was going to control myself and that by Sept. 2 I would have lost 30 pounds. I reached that goal by August."

Sources

BusinessWeek, May 31, 2010, p. 72.
New York, April 13, 2008.

New York Times, May 9, 2001; September 13, 2009.
New York Times Magazine, May 25, 1997.

—*Carol Brennan*

Bruce Springsteen

AP Images

Singer and songwriter

Born Bruce Frederick Joseph Springsteen, September 23, 1949, in Freehold, NJ; son of Douglas Frederick (a bus driver) and Adele (a secretary; maiden name, Zerilli) Springsteen; married Julianne Phillips (an actress), May 13, 1985 (divorced, March 1, 1989); married Patti Scialfa (a singer), June 8, 1991; children: (second marriage) Evan James, Jessica Rae, Sam Ryan. *Education:* Attended Ocean County Community College.

Addresses: *Office*—c/o Columbia Records, 550 Madison Ave., 24th Fl., New York, NY 10022. *Web site*—http://www.brucespringsteen.net/.

Career

Member of the band The Castiles, 1965-67; member of Child (later known as Steel Mill), 1969-71; member of Dr. Zoom and the Sonic Boom, 1971; member of the Bruce Springsteen Band, 1971; signed recording contract with Columbia Records, 1972; released debut album, *Greetings from Asbury Park, NJ*, 1973; had first hit album with *Born to Run*, 1975; became rock superstar with *Born in the U.S.A.*, 1984; parted with E Street Band, 1989; released folk album, *The Ghost of Tom Joad*, 1995; reunited with E Street Band, c. 1999; released popular album *The Rising*, 2002; performed at Super Bowl half-time show, 2009.

Awards: Best international solo artist, British Phonographic Industry, 1986; Academy Award for best music—original song, Academy of Motion Picture Arts & Sciences, for "Streets of Philadelphia," 1994; Golden Globe Award for best original song—motion picture, Hollywood Foreign Press Association, for "Streets of Philadelphia," 1994; ASCAP Award for most performed songs from motion picture, American Society of Composers, Authors, and Publishers, for "Streets of Philadelphia," 1995; Grammy Award for best song written specifically for a motion picture or for television, National Academy of Recording Arts & Sciences, for "Streets of Philadelphia," 1995; Grammy Award for best contemporary folk album, National Academy of Recording Arts & Sciences, for *The Ghost of Tom Joad*, 1995; Polar Music Prize, Royal Swedish Academy of Music Award, 1997; inductee, Rock and Roll Hall of Fame, 1999; Grammy Award for best male rock vocal performance, National Academy of Recording Arts & Sciences, for *The Rising*, 2002; Grammy Award for best rock song, National Academy of Recording Arts & Sciences, for "The Rising," 2002; Grammy Award for best rock album, National Academy of Recording Arts & Sciences, for *The Rising*, 2002; Grammy Award (with Warren Zevon) for best rock performance by a duo or group with vocal, National Academy of Recording Arts & Sciences, for "Disorder in the House," 2003; Grammy Award for best solo rock vocal performance, National Academy of Recording Arts & Sciences, for "Code of Silence," 2004; Grammy Award for best solo rock vocal performance, National Academy of Recording Arts & Sciences, for "Devils and Dust," 2005; Grammy Award for best traditional rock album, National Academy of Recording Arts & Sciences, for *We Shall Overcome: The Seegar Sessions*, 2006; Grammy Award for best long form music video, National Academy of Recording Arts & Sciences, for *Wings for Wheels: The Making of Born to Run*, 2007; inductee, New Jersey Hall of Fame, 2008; Critics Choice Award for best song, Broadcast Film Critics Association, for "The Wrestler," 2009; Grammy Award for best rock song, National Academy of Recording Arts & Sciences, for "Girls in Their Summer Clothes," 2009; Kennedy Center Honors, 2009; Grammy Award for best solo rock vocal performance, National Academy of Recording Arts & Sciences, for "Working on a Dream," 2010.

Sidelights

Known as "The Boss," American rock musician Bruce Springsteen was highly regarded for his deep and articulate songs about working class and small town life. Also respected for his epic live shows, he won numerous awards and honors for his work. Springsteen emerged as an underground force in the 1970s and became a superstar in the 1980s with such releases as *Born in the U.S.A.*, which was one of the best-selling rock albums of all time. While he continued to record in the 1990s, it was not until the early 2000s that Springsteen emerged with powerful, popular releases like *The Rising*.

Describing Springsteen's importance to rock music when he was inducted into the Rock and Roll Hall of Fame, Andrew S. Hughes of the *South Bend Tribune* wrote, "Perhaps more than any other rock musician of the twentieth century, Springsteen has held fast to the principle of change. With each album and tour, he became someone else, sometimes in small increments, sometimes with far-reaching leaps. At the same time, he also embodied rock 'n' roll's past. His music contains elements of each major pop music movement since the 1950s but eschews nostalgia to reinvent the music as his own style."

Born on September 23, 1949, in Freehold, NJ, he was son of Douglas and Adele Springsteen. His father was a bus driver who also did odd jobs and was a gifted pool player while his mother worked as a secretary. His Roman Catholic working-class family had Irish, Italian, and Dutch ethnic roots. Raised in Freehold with his two sisters, Springsteen attended Catholic schools and was an altar boy. He became interested in music at the age of seven when he saw Elvis Presley singing on television. By 13, Springsteen was playing the guitar he bought for $18. As a teenager, he was a member of the garage band The Castiles, first as lead guitarist and later as lead singer. The group recorded two original songs co-written by Springsteen but they were never released.

After graduating from high school, Springsteen attended Ocean County Community College for a semester. He left school when a producer from New York City offered him a record deal, which never materialized. Though his father did not particularly support a career in music, Springsteen continued to pursue his passion in his early twenties as a member of the hippie rock band Child, later known as Steel Mill. This band, which stayed together between 1969 and 1971, included Steve Van Zandt and other musicians who would be a part of his E Street Band. Shortly after Steel Mill was disbanded by Springsteen, he quickly went through two more bands, Dr. Zoom and the Sonic Boom and the Bruce Springsteen Band. He ended both bands by the fall of 1971 to focus on his solo career.

In 1972, Springsteen signed an unbeneficial management contract with Laurel Canyon Productions, a management company run by Mike Appel and Jim Cretecos. The agreement gave Laurel Canyon the exclusive rights to his songs, a decision he would later regret. Through Appel, Springsteen auditioned for and landed a solo recording contract with Columbia Records with a royalty rate favorable to his management company. He recorded his first two albums released in 1973 with the help of his backup group, the E Street Band. While both *Greetings from Asbury Park, NJ* and *The Wild, the Innocent & the E Street Shuffle* were critical favorites, music fans did not find them as appealing and sales were poor. Springsteen was still developing his music and songwriting style on these albums, but he also realized that his strength was in live shows. To that end, he worked to make his stage shows a spectacle which attracted the attention of critics and audiences alike.

Springsteen began breaking through with his next album, 1975's *Born to Run*, which was a critical and commercial success. It reached the top ten of the charts shortly after its release and the title track was Springsteen's first hit single. With the popularity of the tour that followed as well as his status as a cult star, Springsteen appeared on the covers of *Newsweek* and *Time* simultaneously in 1975. However, the progress of his career slowed for several years because of a legal battle with Appel.

An independent auditor report in 1976 stated that Appel's contract with Springsteen was exploitative. The relationship between manager and artist continued to disintegrate when Appel refused to allow Springsteen to work again with Jon Landau, who had helped produce *Born to Run*. Springsteen sued his manager on several counts, including fraud. Appel countersued and won the right to prohibit Landau and Springsteen from working together. Because Springsteen would not record with Appel's choice of producer, a legal injunction prevented him from recording until the spring of 1977. Instead, he toured and wrote new songs.

The case was settled out of court with Appel paid a lump sum and Springsteen retaining the rights to his songs as well as an upgraded contract with Columbia. His next album reflected the turmoil of his life during the previous years, emphasizing the need to keeping moving forward. Springsteen released 1978's *Darkness on the Edge of Town*, and critics were impressed by how much growth he showed as an artist. He still struggled to find a steady audience for his releases, however. While 1980's double album *The River* was popular commercially with two million copies sold and two hit singles ("Hungry Heart" and "Fade Away"), the 1982 alienated folk album *Nebraska* was only accepted by critics. However, Springsteen's live shows had become legendary for their length—often at least four hours long—and their passion.

Everything changed for Springsteen in 1984. That year, he released *Born in the U.S.A.*, which produced seven top ten singles and sold more than ten million copies in the United States. The album and its iconic, relatively simple songs made Springsteen a superstar. *Born in the U.S.A.* spent two years on the charts, including a long stint at number one. Yet Springsteen himself later admitted he had problems with the album. He told Mark Binelli of *Rolling Stone*, "I was always unsatisfied with that album. That was one I really struggled with and never felt like I got the whole thing right. But your own wrestling in that department doesn't really have anything to do with the way something is received, or the way your fans hear it."

In the afterglow of *Born in the U.S.A.*, Springsteen again toured extensively and married his first wife, actress Julianne Phillips. The marriage was short-lived however, and Springsteen's next album, 1987's *Tunnel of Love* featured his very personal reflections on the difficulties of love. The album spawned three hit singles, including the title track and "Brilliant Disguise." After 1988's *Chimes of Freedom*, Springsteen tried to rework his use of the E Street Band live but decided in November of 1989 to part with them.

Springsteen then rebounded personally with a second marriage to one of his back-up singers, Patti Scialfa, in 1991. The couple eventually had three children. Thus, Springsteen's albums released in 1992, *Lucky Town* and *Human Touch*, were more upbeat and generally popular with audiences. *Human Touch* featured pop songs that especially connected with listeners and sold well. *Lucky Town* was favored by critics who appreciated his thoughts on adulthood. Taking on new challenges in this time period, Springsteen also recorded the soundtrack to the film *Philadelphia* in 1993 and won numerous honors, including an Academy Award and a Grammy Award, for the song, "Streets of Philadelphia."

The singer continued to be contemplative in the mid-1990s with the release of 1995's *The Ghost of Tom Joad*. The folk album was inspired by the Dale Maharidge book, *Journey to Nowhere: The Saga of the New Underclass*. Populist in sentiment, it was one of the first albums by Springsteen in years not to reach platinum status. However, he did won a Grammy for best folk album for the release. Springsteen followed *Tom Joad* with 1998's *Tracks*, a career retrospective. Returning to the road with the E Street Band for the first time in a decade, Springsteen toured for several years through 2000. They began the tour in New Jersey, where they had 15 sold-out shows. Springsteen was also inducted into the Rock and Roll Hall of Fame in 1999, with Bono from U2 giving his induction speech.

Continuing to work with the artists who made up the E Street Band, Springsteen recorded and released 2002's *The Rising*. Working with a new producer (Brendan O'Brien), it was his first new album in seven years and his first full album to fully feature the E Street Band since *Born in the U.S.A.* *The Rising* was also his first hit with both critics and audiences in some years. In *Rolling Stone*, Binelli commented, "*The Rising* is as expansive and uplifting as Springsteen's best work with the E Street Band, accentuating in particular the band's gospel roots."

While Springsteen and the E Street Band returned to the road in support of *The Rising*, his next release was again in the folk vein, 2005's *Devils and Dust*. Unlike his previous folk released, this album debuted at number one. Continuing to challenge himself, Springsteen's next album, 2006's *We Shall Overcome: The Seeger Sessions*, was recorded much more quickly than usual.

In 2007, Springsteen released *Magic*, again recorded with the E Street Band. Another number-one album, this record featured more accessible songs and a major tour with the E Street Band. After recording an award-winning song for the independent film *The Wrestler* in 2008, Springsteen again worked with the E Street Band on his next album, the 2009 hit *Working on a Dream*. Showing his ongoing stature as an icon of American music, Springsteen headlined that year's Super Bowl halftime show and toured with the E Street Band. They were also headliners at the Bonnarro Music Festival in Tennessee. In addition, Springsteen received the Kennedy Center Honors in 2009.

As Springsteen entered his sixties, he appreciated his continued success and understood himself. He told David Fricke of *Rolling Stone*, "I'm not worried now about who I am. My identity, what people are connecting with—those things are set pretty firmly. I have an audience, of some kind. I also have a world of characters and ideas I have addressed for a long time. By now, at my age, those things aren't supposed to inhibit you. They are supposed to free you." Later in the interview, Springsteen concluded, "I'll put *The Rising, Magic,* and the new one against any other three records we've made in a row, as far as sound, depth and purpose, of what they're saying and conveying. It's very satisfying to be able to do that at this point in the road."

Selected discography

Greetings from Asbury Park, NJ, Columbia (New York City), 1973.
The Wild, the Innocent & the E Street Shuffle, Columbia, 1973.
Born to Run, Columbia, 1975.
Darkness at the Edge of Town, Columbia, 1978.
The River, Columbia, 1980.
Nebraska, Columbia, 1982.
Born in the U.S.A., Columbia, 1984.
Live: 1975-1985, Columbia, 1986.
Tunnel of Love, Columbia, 1987.
Chimes of Freedom, Columbia, 1988.
Lucky Town, Columbia, 1992.
Human Touch, Columbia, 1992.
Philadelphia, Epic (New York City), 1993.

Greatest Hits, Columbia, 1995.
The Ghost of Tom Joad, Columbia, 1995.
Tracks, Columbia, 1998.
The Rising, Columbia, 2002.
Devils & Dust, Columbia, 2005.
We Shall Overcome: The Seeger Sessions, Columbia, 2006.
Magic, Columbia, 2007.
Working on a Dream, Columbia, 2009.

Sources

Books

Contemporary Musicians, vol. 63, Gale, 2008.

Periodicals

Rolling Stone, August 22, 2002; February 5, 2009.
San Diego Union-Tribune, May 26, 2000, p. E1; July 22, 2002, p. D1.
Slate Magazine, October 2, 2007.
South Bend Tribune (IN), March 14, 1999, p. E4.
Toronto Star, January 10, 1996, p. D1.

Online

"Bruce Springsteen: Biography," *Rolling Stone,* http://www.rollingstone.com/artists/brucespringsteen/biography (March 10, 2010).
"Bruce Springsteen: Discography," *Rolling Stone,* http://www.rollingstone.com/artists/brucespringsteen/discography (March 10, 2010).

—A. Petruso

Curtis Stone

Chef

Born November 4, 1975, in Melbourne, Australia; son of William (an accountant) and Lorraine "Lozza" (a florist) Stone. *Education:* Attended Victoria University.

Addresses: *Agent*—William Morris Endeavor Entertainment, 9601 Wilshire Blvd., 3rd Fl., Beverly Hills, CA 90210. *Home*—London and Los Angeles.

Career

Left school to become an apprentice chef at the Savoy Hotel, Melbourne, Australia, 1993; sous chef, the Grill Room at Cafe Royal, London, England, mid-1990s; sous chef, Mirabelle, London, late 1990s; head chef, Quo Vadis, London, c. late 1990s-2003; head chef, Restaurant 301, London. Host on television, including: *Dinner in a Box,* 2002; *Surfing the Menu,* 2003-04; *My Restaurant Rules,* 2004; *Take Home Chef,* 2006-07. Celebrity contestant on *The Apprentice,* 2010; guest appearances on numerous other television shows.

Sidelights

Australian Curtis Stone is a television celebrity, cookbook author, and accomplished chef. He emphasizes using local ingredients that are in season, organic, and at their freshest, as well as keeping preparation simple. He has appeared on several television shows and is the author of four cookbooks. On The Learning Channel (TLC) Web site, he summed up his philosophy of food: "If you get your hands on good ingredients and treat them properly, you don't need to do much."

Stone grew up in Melbourne, Australia, with his mother, Lorraine "Lozza" and his brother Luke. His father, William, did not live with them, but Stone had a good relationship with him. He appreciated his mother's hard work, as a single parent, in raising him: taking him and his brother to school, going to work, and coming home and making dinner for them. Lorraine was strict but loving, and Stone remained close to her as an adult. He told Paul Connolly in the *Sydney Morning Herald,* "She's a pretty straightforward person and realistic, and we've never had any secrets from each other. She's also got a great sense of humour and we've always had a lot of fun together."

Stone told Connolly that his mother was "a terrible cook and would overcook everything. She'd put the potatoes and green beans in the same pot and steam the hell out of it. But she was a good baker and I can vividly remember waiting around for her to finish so I could lick the spoon and go to work on the bowl."

His paternal grandmother was an excellent cook, however, and his mother's parents grew their own fresh vegetables and made delicious meals with them. He loved to spend time with his grandparents in the kitchen. "They gave me a passion for food," he told Connolly. He secretly dreamed of a career as a chef but thought he wouldn't make a decent living at it, so he reluctantly considered business, and even law. Cooking nonetheless won out, and when he was 18, Stone left school at Victoria University to pursue a career in culinary arts with his mother's approval and support. His first job was as an apprentice at the Savoy Hotel; after gaining experience there and becoming qualified as a chef, he left to travel around Europe with a friend. By the time he reached London, he was broke and needed work, but he decided not to take just any job. He went to Chef Marco Pierre White's kitchen at the Grill Room at Cafe Royal and made an offer to White: he would work for him for free if White would train him. He worked free for one month, then was hired. He worked there for two years, taking in everything the legendary White had to teach him.

He then moved on to work as sous chef at Mirabelle, and contributed to the restaurant's successful *Mirabelle Cookbook*. He worked there for two years, then moved on to Quo Vadis, where White made him the head chef. At Quo Vadis he attracted a lot of favorable attention and was included in a book about London's famous chefs, *London on a Plate*. He worked there until 2003, when, partly as a result of the publicity attending *London on a Plate*, he left to do his first television show, the 15-episode series in Britain, *Dinner in a Box*. He then filmed *Surfing the Menu*, which began in 2003 and lasted for four seasons in 26 countries. In 2004, he was host of a restaurant reality series in Australia, *My Restaurant Rules*. He has also had guest appearances on numerous other shows, including NBC's *Today Show*, *Martha Stewart*, the *Ellen DeGeneres Show*, the *Fox Morning Show*, and *Entertainment Tonight*. He has also appeared on *Biggest Loser* and *Celebrity Apprentice*.

In 2006 Stone began hosting the show *Take Home Chef* on the TLC network. The premise of the show was that Stone would find random shoppers at the grocery store, and offer to help them choose groceries and a menu for their evening meal, then go home with them and cook, making a delicious surprise meal for their loved one. The show was successful not only in the United States, where it was filmed, but also in Europe and Asia.

In a review in *Popmatters*, Bill Gibron discussed the reasons for the show's success: unlike other shows that might present a multitude of recipes in 30 min-

utes, or that used processed ingredients only slightly perked up with fresh ones, Stone emphasized making one delicious meal. Gibron noted, "Even though his dishes sound exotic, Stone doesn't 'dumb it down' for his always amazed host. He creates four-star eatery fare in easy-to-emulate steps, appears open to answering questions, and never complicates an entree to show off." He added, "While Stone doesn't go so far as to dismiss outright the microwave or MSG, he means to convert us to the fresh and fragrant. And so he does."

On his Web site, Stone explained why he loves his work so much: "Ever since I was young I've always been fascinated with food—whether it was making marmalade with my Nan and Grandad or fudge with my Granny. I've always realized it was food that brought my family and friends closer together. I often hear people say that they don't have the time to cook. Well, actually, a good home cooked meal can take less time than waiting for a take-in pizza! And be a lot more fun. It's one of life's' great pleasures."

Selected writings

Surfing the Menu Cookbook, ABC Books (Melbourne, Australia), 2004.
Surfing the Menu Again Cookbook, ABC Books, 2005.
Cooking with Curtis, Whitecap Books (Vancouver, Canada), 2006.
Relaxed Cooking with Curtis Stone: Recipes to Put You in My Favorite Mood, Clarkson Potter (New York City), 2009.

Sources

Curtis Stone's Facebook Page, http://www.facebook.com/pages/Curtis-Stone/83100856.tif091?v=info (August 24, 2010).
"Curtis Stone's Favourite Women," *Sydney Morning Herald*, http://www.smh.com.au/lifestyle/people/curtis-stones-favourite-women-20091005.tif-gioi.html (August 25, 2010).
"Meet Curtis Stone," TLC Web Site, http://tlc.discovery.com/fansites/takchomechef/bio.html (August 24, 2010).
"Take Home Chef," *Popmatters.com*, http://www.popmatters.com/tv/reviews/t/take-home-chef-060620.shtm (August 25, 2010).

—Kelly Winters

Aksel Lund Svindal

Alpine skier

Born December 26, 1982, in Lørenskog, Norway; son of Bjørn (an accounting executive) and Ina (maiden name, Lund) Svindal.

Addresses: *Home*—Kjeller, Norway. *Web site*—http://www.aksellundsvindal.com.

Career

Alpine skier on FIS World Cup circuit, 2001—.

Awards: Silver medal in combined, International Ski Federation (FIS) Alpine Skiing World Championships, 2005, gold medals in downhill and giant slalom, 2007, and gold medal in super combined and bronze medal in super-G, 2009; champion in super-G, FIS Alpine Skiing World Cup, 2005-06, 2008-09, champion in giant slalom and super combined, 2006-07, overall champion, 2006-07 and 2008-09; Male Athlete of the Year Award, Norwegian Sports Gala, 2008; Role Model of the Year Award, Norwegian Sports Gala, 2009; gold medal in super-G, silver medal in downhill, and bronze medal in giant slalom, XXI Olympic Winter Games, Vancouver, Canada, 2010.

Sidelights

In 2007, Norwegian skier Aksel Lund Svindal (pronounced "SVIN-dahl") seemed headed for a second season atop alpine skiing's World Cup standings when he suffered a horrible accident while training in Colorado. After spending months healing and rehabilitating, he returned to the sport in 2008 to capture his second World Cup overall title. With the addition of three medals at the 2010 Vancouver Olympics, Svindal staked his claim to being one of the world's best alpine skiers.

Svindal was born on December 26, 1982, in Lørenskog, a city east of the Norwegian capital of Oslo. His father, Bjørn, owned an accounting firm and his mother, Ina, once skied on the European Cup circuit. Young Aksel was only three years old when he received his first set of skis and soon he was learning the sport on the slopes of Geilo, Norway, where his grandparents kept a cabin.

Svindal was eight years old when tragedy struck his family: his mother died of complications from childbirth, with her infant son dying soon after. Svindal's grandparents helped Bjørn raise Aksel and his younger brother, Simen, and encouraged them both to keep skiing. At 15, Svindal moved to Oppdal, one of Norway's foremost ski resorts, where he attended a special high school that allowed him to work on his skiing skills. During his teenage years Svindal earned a place on the Norwegian Junior Team. He competed at home and around Europe, earning several top ten finishes in various alpine events. These included the slalom, in the which the skier must navigate around several closely set gates; the giant slalom, which is run on longer courses with the gates set further apart; the super giant slalom (also called super-G), which has fewer gates and is run faster; and the downhill, which is run at the highest speeds on steep courses with very few gates.

Svindal was 19 years old when he finished high school and decided to devote himself to skiing. He competed in his first World Cup race during the 2001-02 season, and finished the year by capturing one gold, one silver, and two bronze medals at the Junior World Ski Championships in Italy. He earned his first World Cup podium finish in 2003, finishing second in a combined downhill and slalom event in Austria. That year he also competed in his first FIS World championships, a meet held every two years, which does not count toward the overall World Cup standings. Svindal entered three events and finished fifth in the giant slalom.

At the next FIS world championships in 2005, an improving Svindal competed in all five events: slalom, giant slalom, super-G, downhill, and combined slalom/downhill. He finished twelfth in the slalom, but earned top ten finishes in his other races, including a silver medal in the combined. It was the prelude to his breakthrough season of 2005-06. He earned his first World Cup victories—in the super-G at Lake Louise, Canada, and the downhill at Are, Sweden—and had three additional top-three finishes in super-G, giant slalom, and combined events. He won the World Cup super-G title and finished second in the overall World Cup standings behind Austrian Benjamin Raich, a four-time Olympic medalist. Svindal also competed in the 2006 Winter Olympics in Turin, Italy. He entered all five alpine events but crashed in the slalom and combined. He finished twenty-first in the downhill, and claimed fifth in the super-G and sixth in the giant slalom.

Svindal became a dominating racer during the 2006-07 season. He won early races in the super combined and giant slalom, and added eleven top-ten finishes throughout the rest of the year. He was the only racer to compete in all 36 World Cup races that season, and earned points in all but four of them. In the final meet of the season at Lenzerheide, Switzerland, he captured victories in the downhill, super-G, and giant slalom to vault to the top of the World Cup standings. He finished fifteenth in the slalom to clinch the overall World Cup top ranking, in addition to the season's giant slalom and super combined titles. At the 2007 World Championships in Sweden, Svindal started all five races and won the downhill and the giant slalom.

Svindal opened the 2007-08 season with two victories in his first four starts. He was hoping to continue his success at Beaver Creek, Colorado, when he suffered a horrible accident on November 27, 2007. He was training for the downhill when he lost control on the difficult Golden Eagle jump and crashed. "I remember thinking, I have never gone this fast at Beaver Creek," he told John Branch in the *New York Times.* "Then I hit the jump." He landed hard on his back and got tangled in a fence. He fractured facial bones and chipped a tooth, but doctors were most concerned about the wound caused by landing on his ski. It created a six-inch gash on his left buttock that was so deep that surgeons operated to make sure no internal organs had been damaged. He remained in the hospital for nearly a month after the crash.

In the three months he spent recuperating from his accident, Svindal lost more than 30 pounds of muscle. Nevertheless, he was determined to make a comeback in time for the 2008-09 World Cup season. He trained hard and had three top-15 finishes in his first four starts. He then returned to the site of his accident at Beaver Creek and won both the downhill and the super-G. "This win doesn't change anything about my attitude towards the overall World Cup, it's still too early to think about it," the skier told *CBC Sports.* "For the moment I'm just too excited to think much about what's coming up." Although he had bad luck and scored no points in his slalom races during the season, he won the final downhill of the season and finished second in the last super-G race to claim the World Cup overall and super-G titles. His 1,009 points gave him a two-point margin of victory over Raich, and marked the closest World Cup overall finish ever. At that season's World Championships in France, he earned a gold in super combined, a bronze in super-G, and had top eleven finishes in giant slalom and downhill. His favorite memory of the season was his triumphant comeback in Colorado, however. "Nothing comes close to Beaver Creek," he told John Branch in the *New York Times.* "That was the moment."

Svindal was forced to take time off from training in November of 2009 to rest a sore knee and recover from the flu, but he was soon back out on the slopes and considered a medal contender for the 2010 Winter Olympics, held in Vancouver, Canada. In his first race, the downhill, he earned the silver medal, finishing just 0.07 seconds behind winner Didier Defago of Switzerland. The medal allowed him to relax during his next event, the super-G; as he told NBC Sports, "I felt like it was the last thing I was thinking at the start gate, 'You already have a silver and it can only get better so enjoy this and give it all you have. Don't hold anything back.'" On an icy track that confounded other racers, Svindal claimed the gold medal with a top speed of more than 70 miles per hour. The skier led the field by almost 0.4 of a second after the downhill portion of the super combined, but wiped out during the slalom portion. He came back in the giant slalom race, claiming a bronze to earn a complete set of Olympic medals. He finished the 2009-10 season with three more World Cup podium finishes, good enough to finish fourth in the overall Cup standings despite having lost time to injury.

While Svindal has enjoyed success in his sport, medals are not what drives him to keep skiing. "There have been changes, but the basics are the same," he wrote on his Web site. "It doesn't matter if you're 1st or 30th in the world. Your focus is on your sport and how to get better at it." To improve his performance, Svindal does a lot of weight training, biking, and running to supplement his ski training. Although he has days "when being an athlete feels like work and not your passion," as he wrote on his Web site, "then I think about the urge to always want to ski faster and [be] better." Many elite skiers compete well into their thirties, and Svindal has similar goals: "I'm healthy and I have fun; I hope I can do it for many years," he remarked on his Web site. Although he might go back to school after retiring, he has "no idea what I will do when I'm done," he noted. "I hope something fun."

Sources

Periodicals

New York Times, November 29, 2007, p. D4; March 15, 2009, p. 8; November 25, 2009, p. B11.
Sports Illustrated, March 10, 2010, p. 53.

Online

"Aksel Lund Svindal Bio," NBC Olympics Vancouver 2010, http://www.nbcolympics.com/news-features/news/newsid=259167.html (May 4, 2010).

Aksel Lund Svindal Official Site, http://www.aksellundsvindal.com/ (May 4, 2010).

"Americans Super, Finish Two-Three Behind Svindal," NBC Olympics Vancouver 2010, http://www.nbcolympics.com/news-features/news/newsid=430722.html#americans+super+finish+three+behind+svindal (May 4, 2010).

"Biography: Aksel Lund Svindal," Federation Internationale de Ski, http://www.fis-ski.com/uk/604/613.html?competitorid=59877&sector=AL&type=st-WC (May 4, 2010).

Biography Resource Center Online, Gale, 2009.

"Miller, Svindal, Swiss are the Big Alpine Winners," NBC Olympics Vancouver 2010, http://www.nbcolympics.com/news-features/news/newsid=453590.html#miller+svindal+swiss+alpine+winners (May 4, 2010).

"Svindal Scores Spectacularly Sans Super-G Scouting," NBC Olympics Vancouver 2010, http://www.nbcolympics.com/news-features/news/newsid=431982.html#svindal+scores+spectacularly+sans+super+g+scouting (May 4, 2010).

Transcripts

CBC Sports, Canadian Broadcasting Corp., December 6, 2008.

—Diane Telgen

Channing Tatum

Actor and model

Born Channing Matthew Tatum, April 26, 1980, in Cullman, AL; son of a salesman; married Jenna Dewan (an actress), July 11, 2009. *Education:* Attended Glenville State College, Glenville, WV.

Addresses: *Agent*—William Morris Endeavor, 9601 Wilshire Blvd. 3rd Fl., Beverly Hills, CA 90210. *Management*—Management 360, 9111 Wilshire Blvd., Beverly Hills, CA 90210. *Web site*—http://channingtatumunwrapped.com/; http://twitter.com/channingtatum.

Career

Worked as a model, beginning in 2000; appeared in music video for Ricky Martin's "She Bangs," 2000; appeared in television commercials, including Mountain Dew, Pepsi, and American Eagle, beginning c. 2002; launched acting career, 2005. Film appearances include: *Coach Carter*, 2005; *Havoc*, 2005; *Supercross*, 2005; *War of the Worlds*, 2005; *A Guide to Recognizing Your Saints*, 2006; *She's the Man*, 2006; *Step Up*, 2006; *Battle in Seattle*, 2007; *The Trap*, 2007; *Step Up 2: The Streets*, 2008; *Stop-Loss*, 2008; *Fighting*, 2009; *G.I. Joe: The Rise of Cobra*, 2009; *Public Enemies*, 2009; *Dear John*, 2010; *Morgan and Destiny's Eleventeenth Date: The Zeppelin Zoo*, 2010. Television appearances include: *CSI: Miami*, CBS, 2004. Also worked as a construction worker, mortgage broker, salesman, club dancer, and employee at a pet nursery.

Awards: Best Actor Award (with others), Gijón International Film Festival, for *A Guide to Recognizing Your Saints*, 2006; Special Jury Prize—Dramatic (with others), Sundance Film Festival, for *A Guide to Recognizing Your Saints*, 2006; Teen Choice Award for movies—choice breakout (male), for *She's the Man*, 2006; Teen Choice Award for choice movie: dance (with Jenna Dewan), for *Step Up*, 2007; Teen Choice Award for choice movie actor: drama, for *Stop-Loss*, 2008.

Sidelights

Actor Channing Tatum came to prominence in 2006 for his starring role in the hit dance film *Step Up*. The handsome but physically imposing actor often played troubled young men and soldiers, showing off his considerable athletic skills in the process. Tatum began his career as a model and appeared in memorable television commercials before making the transition to film roles. Among his other best-known films were *She's the Man*, *Stop-Loss*, *G.I. Joe: Rise of the Cobra*, and *Dear John*.

Tatum was born on April 26, 1980, in Cullman, Alabama, a small town outside of Birmingham. His father owned a roofing company until an accident forced him to change occupations and he became a traveling building supplies salesman. While Tatum spent much time with extended family in Alabama throughout his childhood, he was primarily raised in Mississippi and Florida. As a child, Tatum suffered from dyslexia and attention deficit disorder but was rambunctious and his parents used sports to focus his considerable energy. He participated in track and field, baseball, and soccer, but found his true passion in football. When he reached ninth grade, his parents gave him an option to go to military school or private school. Tatum chose military school. There, football became a focus of his life and he showed considerable talent in the sport. He also began doing martial arts, which became another passion of his.

During high school, Tatum set a goal of winning a football scholarship to college. He won a partial scholarship to play football for Wake Forest but his grades were not good enough for him to enter the school. He then took a scholarship at a small school, Glenville State College in West Virginia. The experience was not what he expected, telling Lisa Depaulo of GQ, "I liked the people and the players and stuff, but I got there and I was like, this is not what I wanted. The reality started to sink in about, you know, doing football as a *job*."

Feeling unsatisfied, Tatum left college after a year. He then held a series of day posts including construction worker, mortgage broker, salesman at a department store cologne counter, and employee at a puppy and kitten nursery while living in Miami, Florida. He also got paid to dance at a club in Tampa Bay, Florida. In 2000, Tatum's life found direction when he realized he could model. A friend, Vincent DePaul, asked him to appear in a fashion show for *Men's Health* at Level Nightclub in Miami. Tatum agreed and the appearance launched his modeling career. He soon modeled for publications like *Ocean Drive* magazine and companies such as Abercrombie & Fitch, Nautica, The Gap, Aeropostale, Dolce & Gabbana, and Emporio Armani.

Also in 2000, Tatum appeared in the music video for the Ricky Martin hit single, "She Bangs," which helped move his career along. By 2002, he was taking roles in television commercials, including ads for Pepsi, Mountain Dew, and American Eagle. Tatum moved from modeling to acting to seek new challenges. He found modeling limiting in its appeal, while acting opened new doors. To prepare for an acting career, he studied the craft at the Deena Levy Theatre Studio while appearing in commercials. Of his days studying acting, he told Patricia Sherdian of the *Pittsburgh Post-Gazette*, "I just literally fell in love. It's that cliche thing. I found my calling or my calling found me sort of thing.... You know, I live, breathe, and die for it."

Tatum's first acting role came in an episode of the hit CBS drama *CSI: Miami* in 2004. The following year, he took small roles in the films *Coach Carter, Supercross, War of the Worlds,* and *Havoc.* In *Coach Carter,* Tatum showed off his basketball skills. He would draw on his athletic ability in other films, including 2006's *She's the Man,* in which he displayed his soccer abilities while playing Duke, a college student who found it difficult to talk to girls.

In 2006, Tatum had a breakout year. While he demonstrated his capacity to do drama with a bigger role as a street tough in the critical hit *A Guide to Recognizing Your Saints,* Tatum became a star for his work in *Step Up,* a dance-oriented drama. Playing street ruffian turned dancer Tyler Gage gave him the opportunity to display both his athletic aptitude as well as his silky smooth dance moves. After several more featured film roles, including 2007 releases *Battle in Seattle* and *The Trap,* Tatum played Gage again in the 2008 sequel *Step Up 2: The Streets.*

Also in 2008, Tatum appeared in *Stop-Loss,* marking the first time he played a soldier, something he had considered doing in real life. Of the role, he told the *Pittsburgh Post-Gazette*'s Sheridan, "*Stop-Loss* was a real departure for me. I think it was a selfish reason at first to explore a childhood fantasy. I really wanted to play a soldier and do it well for them." Tatum played a soldier again in the 2009 critically panned summer blockbuster *G.I. Joe: The Rise of Cobra.* The film was based on the *G.I. Joe* comics and remained true to its source. While his 2009 film *Fighting* was not military-oriented, it did allow Tatum to again show off his athletic talents. He played Shawn MacArthur in the indie hit drama.

After playing gangster Pretty Boy Floyd in the 2009 film *Public Enemies,* Tatum turned to dramatic romance with 2010's well-received *Dear John.* Based on a novel by Nicholas Sparks, it focused on the twists and turns of a bittersweet, if not tragic, love affair between Tatum's John Tyree, a soldier, and deep, well-intentioned rich girl Savannah Curtis (played by Amanda Seyfried). Critics praised his work in the role with Jay Stone writing in the *Vancouver Sun,* that Tatum is "a physically imposing actor with sensitive green eyes who seems just right for the part of a former bad boy hellraiser now settled into the demands of duty, be they for Savannah or Uncle Sam."

Now an in-demand actor, Tatum had a number of films lined up for release in 2010 and 2011, including *Morgan and Destiny's Eleventeenth Date: The Zeppelin Zoo,* Roman battle epic *The Eagle,* and *The Son of No One.* Hollywood insiders believe that Tatum could become a major star. Producer Lauren Shuler Donner told Depaulo of *GQ* that she thinks he has what "all our big superstars have: an unpredictableness. Like Russell Crowe and Mel Gibson. There's an unpredictableness inside that makes them mesmerizing to us, and Chan has that." Of his life, career, and success, Tatum emphasized to Depaulo, "I got crazy lucky. Like, sometimes I think I won the lottery or something."

Sources

Periodicals

Canwest News Service, January 27, 2010.
Chicago Sun Times, August 2, 2009, p. D1.
Details, January-February 2010, p. 68.
GQ, August 2009, p. 68.
New York Times, August 11, 2006, p. E10.
Pittsburgh Post-Gazette, March 24, 2008, p. C1.
Toronto Sun, March 25, 2006, p. 57.
Vancouver Sun (British Columbia, Canada), February 5, 2010, p. D3.

Online

"Channing Tatum," Internet Movie Database, http://www.imdb.com/name/nm1475594/ (July 27, 2010).

—*A. Petruso*

Third Day

Christian-rock group

Group formed in 1992 in Marietta, GA; members include Tai Anderson (born June 11, 1976; married Shannon; children: five), bass; David Carr (born November 15, 1974; married Jennifer; children: a son, other children), drums; Mark Lee (born May 29, 1973; married Stephanie; children: two), guitar; Mac Powell (born on December 25, 1972; married Aimee, July 1996; children: five), vocals, guitar.

Addresses: *Agent*—Creative Artists Agency, 3310 West End Avenue, 5th Fl., Nashville, TN 37203. *Management*—Red Light Management, 39 Music Square East, Nashville, TN 37203. *E-mail*—thirddayredlightmanagement.com. *Record company*—Essential Records, 741 Cool Springs Blvd., Franklin, TN 37067. *Web site*—http://www.thirdday.com.

Career

Formed group in Marietta, GA, 1992; Brad Avery joined group, 1995; signed with gray dot records and released debut album, *Third Day*, 1995; signed with Reunion Records, re-released debut, 1996; released *Conspiracy No. 5*, 1997; signed with Essential Records, 1999; released *Time*, 1999; released *Offerings: A Worship Album*, 2000; released *Come Together*, 2001; released *Offerings II: All I Have to Give*, 2003; released *Wire*, 2004; released *Live Wire*, 2004; released *Wherever You Are*, 2005; released *Christmas Offerings*, 2006; released *Chronology Volume 1* and *Chronology Volume 2*, 2007; released *Revelation*, 2008; Avery left group, 2008; released *Live Revelations*, 2009.

Awards: Best video from a new artist in the contemporary Christian category, *Billboard* Music Video Award, for "Consuming Fire," 1996; Dove Awards

for best rock album, Gospel Music Association, for *Conspiracy No. 5*, 1998, for *Time*, 2000, and for *Come Together*, 2002; Dove Awards for best rock recorded song, Gospel Music Association, for "Alien," 1998, for "Sky Falls Down," 2001, for "Come Together," 2002, and for "40 Days," 2003; Dove Awards for special event album of the year (with others), Gospel Music Association, for *Exodus*, 1999, for *City on a Hill—Songs of Worship and Praise*, 2001, for *City On A Hill—Sing Alleluia*, 2003, and for *The Passion of the Christ: Songs Inspired by the Film*, 2005; Dove Award for artist of the year, Gospel Music Association, 2001; Dove Awards for group of the year, Gospel Music Association, 2001, 2002, and 2003; Dove Awards for praise and worship album of the year, Gospel Music Association, for *Offerings—A Worship Album*, 2001, and for *Offerings II—All I Have to Give*, 2004; Dove Award for long form music video of the year, Gospel Music Association, for *Third Day Live in Concert—The Offerings Experience*, 2002, and for *Third Day Live In Concert, The Come Together Tour*, 2004; Grammy Awards for Best Rock Gospel Album, National Academy of Recording Arts and Sciences, for *Come Together*, 2002, and for *Wire*, 2004; Dove Award for rock/contemporary album of the year, Gospel Music Association, for *Wire*, 2005; Grammy Award for Best Pop/Contemporary Gospel Album, National Academy of Recording Arts and Sciences, for *Wherever You Are*, 2006; Dove Award for pop/contemporary recorded song of the year, Gospel Music Association, for "Cry Out to Jesus," 2006; Dove Award for Christmas album of the year, Gospel Music Association, for *Christmas Offerings*, 2007; American Music Award for Favorite Inspirational Artist, ABC, 2008; Dove Awards for pop/contemporary album of the year and recorded music packaging of the year, Gospel Music Association, both for *Revelations,* 2009; Grammy Award for Best Rock or Rap Gospel Album, National Academy of Recording Arts and Sciences, for *Live Revelations,* 2009; inducted into Georgia Music Hall of Fame, 2009.

Sidelights

With four Grammys and two dozen Dove Awards to their credit, Christian rock group Third Day has become one of the leading performers in American gospel music. Pairing hard-driving Southern rock with heartfelt lyrics about struggle, love, and the power of faith, the group has regularly topped the Christian music charts, with some of their albums reaching the top ten of *Billboard*'s mainstream charts as well. The group attributed their crossover appeal to their focus on producing good music, even if there is an agenda behind it. "I think it's sad if you're doing anything creative if you don't have a goal," bass player Tai Anderson told John Blake of the *Atlanta Journal-Constitution.* "People assume we're going to try to get them saved or beat them up with the Bible, but that's not the way we approach music. We're a Christian band trying to produce music for a non-Christian world."

Third Day had its genesis in a garage band formed by singer Mac Powell and guitarist Mark Lee while they were both high school seniors in the Atlanta suburb of Powder Springs. Powell soon left the group, however, believing it did not fulfill God's purpose for him. Lee also had similarly strong feelings about his faith, and when he contacted his former band mate about creating a Christian band, the two began writing songs together. They added a keyboard player, Billy Wilkins, and decided to name their band Third Day to commemorate the time elapsed between Christ's death and resurrection. They started small, playing acoustic sets at Sunday schools and church youth groups. It was at a church event in 1992 where they met drummer David Carr and bassist Anderson, high schoolers who were backing a family singing group. The musicians hit it off and soon were playing together and recording demos.

Wilkins left the group in 1993, and over the next two years the four members of Third Day played shows around metro Atlanta while trying to save enough money to record a demo. In 1994, while still high school and college students, the band recorded their first full-length demo; still, they felt something was missing from the group. They recruited guitarist Brad Avery, whom they had heard playing around town. He joined the lineup in 1995, the same

year Third Day hired a booking agent and began playing venues around the southeast. They sold particularly well at Atlanta's Strand Theatre, where the management signed them to a small, independent label they had started. The self-titled *Third Day* sold so well the label could not keep up with demand, leading the group to sign with Reunion Records, at the time a division of Arista. The group recorded two more songs for the CD's major label reissue in 1996. Their sound was reminiscent of Southern rock bands like Lynyrd Skynyrd, with bluesy elements that led some critics to compare them to popular 1990s rockers Hootie & the Blowfish. The single "Nothing At All" even made an appearance on mainstream rock radio stations.

Part of Third Day's early success was due to their efforts touring and building grassroots support for the band. In 1996 they made their first main-stage festival performance and appeared on their first national tour, opening for the Australian group Newsboys. For their first headline tour, they went to smaller venues in 65 American cities, keeping ticket prices low and selling out shows. Not only were fans taking notice of the group, so was the industry: they were nominated for the Gospel Music Association's Dove Award for best new group and won a *Billboard* Music Video Award for "Consuming Fire." Still, they felt they had something to prove with 1997's *Conspiracy No. 5:* "We were anxious to show the world how much we had improved since our first record, which was compiled over the band's first few years together," the group noted on their Web site. With a harder edge to its sound, the album earned them comparisons to grunge rockers Pearl Jam as well as a Grammy nomination and their first two Dove Awards: rock album of the year and rock song (for "Alien"). The song "My Hope Is You" became a favorite as they toured in support of the album throughout 1997 and 1998. In 1998 they also contributed to *Exodus,* a compilation of worship songs that won a Dove for special event album.

After 18 months of touring, Third Day brought out their next album, *Time,* in 1999. The album topped the Christian album charts, while the single "I've Always Loved You" scored the group's first Christian number-one hit. The album was nominated for a Grammy and earned the Dove Award for album of year. The following year the group recorded the worship record *Offerings,* a collection of live tracks and new songs that was intended for use in churches and was offered with a "worship kit" that included lyrics and music so that songs could be used in a service. The album "teems with passion and spiritual commitment," Deborah Evans Price noted in *Billboard,* highlighting its "beautiful praise and worship songs as well as tunes that stretch the boundaries of worship music in a wonderful way." While the band thought they would be lucky if *Offerings* sold half as well as their other albums, on the strength of songs like "King of Glory" the album became their first to achieve gold status, or sales of half a million. By 2004 it had sold a million copies, earning platinum status.

Third Day had a breakout year in 2001. Not only was *Offerings* selling well, they were attracting crowds as large as 15,000 to special worship concerts. (A video of the tour, *Third Day Live in Concert—The Offerings Experience,* would win a Dove for Long Form Video.) They swept the Dove Awards in 2001, earning Artist of the Year, Group of the Year, Worship Album of the Year, Rock Song of the Year for "Sky Falls Down," and Special Event of the Year for their contributions to *City on a Hill—Songs of Worship and Praise.* Even as *Offerings* was nominated for a Grammy, the band released *Come Together,* with its timely call for unity. The album earned Third Day its first Grammy for Rock Gospel Album, as well as Doves for Rock Song (for the title track) and Rock Album. The group was once again Dove's Group of the Year, while Powell earned the Male Vocalist of the Year citation, an honor rarely bestowed to group singers. The title track was a hit, and while the album only reached number two on the Christian charts, it reached 31 on the mainstream *Billboard* Top 200 charts, a new high for the group. They hoped to appeal to a broader audience beyond the Christian market: "Christianity was never supposed to be about the religious status quo," Anderson told the *Atlanta Journal-Constitution*'s Blake. "Jesus was a radical rebel and that's what led to his death. If a young person is really looking to be different, identify with Christian music."

In 2003 Third Day released a second worship album, *Offerings II: All I Have to Give.* Powell told *Billboard*'s Price that the album was "probably one of the most rockin' records that we've recorded," explaining that "our definition of worship is probably a bit broader than a lot [of] people's definition. "The album included the Christian number-one hits "You Are So Good To Me" and "Sing a Song," and the band again held special worship concerts in support of the album. One of these concerts was broadcast in theaters nationwide. The group continued growing their audience with their 2004 album *Wire,* which reached number one on the Christian chart and number 12 on the Top 200 album chart. The group had performances on national TV and were featured performers at the 2004 Republican National Convention. Reviewers compared their sound to U2 and Bruce Springsteen, and the album earned both Grammy and Dove Awards. A concert album plus video version of *Live Wire* earned platinum video status with more than 100,000 copies sold.

Third Day continued building on their success with the 2005 album *Wherever You Are,* which debuted at number one on the Christian charts and number eight on the mainstream Top 200. On the strength of the hits "Mountain of God," "Tunnel," and "Cry Out to Jesus," which spent ten weeks atop the Christian singles chart, the album stayed on the Christian album charts for nearly two years and earned the group their third Grammy Award. The group followed up with the 2006 specialty album *Christmas Offerings* and a two-volume greatest hits set, 2007's *Chronology.* After 15 years in the business, Third Day had one platinum and five gold albums, more than 20 Christian number-one singles, more than 20 Dove Awards, and a legion of fans who called themselves "Gomers," after a song about the Biblical figure on the group's second album.

Despite their success, 2008 brought major changes for the group. For the album *Revelation,* they left Atlanta to record in Los Angeles for the first time with a producer known for his work with rock and country superstars. Recording the album was a challenge, but worth the effort: "I feel like we started more insecure than ever and we left more confident than ever," Anderson told *Billboard*'s Price, while guitarist Lee added that the new producer "came in and made us work hard and think really hard about how we're doing this and what matters in the end." Before the record was even released, however, Third Day announced that Avery was leaving the group to pursue solo projects. They declined to replace him and the four remaining members went on tour in support of *Revelation,* which included three top ten Christian hits. The song "Call My Name" topped the charts for six weeks; the album itself reached number six on *Billboard*'s Top 200 chart. The group's success continued as the band won Favorite Contemporary Inspirational Artist at the 2008 American Music Awards. They toured in 2009 and recorded the *Live Revelations* album plus video, which earned them a Grammy for Best Rock/Rap Gospel Album.

While the group paid tribute to their Christian faith in their music, they demonstrated it in their charity involvement as well. They took a trip to Lesotho in southern Africa to see the effects of the HIV/AIDS epidemic, and sponsored several other projects on the continent through their Come Together Fund. Third Day began the fund by donating one dollar from each ticket sold to their concerts to grassroots projects around the world. These projects have included disaster relief on the Gulf Coast and in Haiti; building and health projects in Africa and India; and partnerships with the charities Habitat For Humanity and World Vision. Through frequent tours, the group raised more than a million dollars in donations during a four-year period.

All four members of Third Day are married with children, and live in the Atlanta suburbs when not on the road. Their faith is what ties them together; although all come from different Christian denominations, they overlook such small differences to focus instead on what they share. Regular prayer sessions on the road keep them focused: "Our faith is that rock that we can go back to when we're facing challenges," Anderson told Eileen McClelland in the *Houston Chronicle.* "There have been a lot of challenges over the years, and it would have been easy to just come to blows." Instead, Third Day has grown from a band put together by school buddies into one of gospel music's most successful groups. "We certainly don't take it for granted," Anderson continued. "It so surpasses anything we ever dared to dream.... The whole time just to be able to do it, to play music, to have people seem to care and sing along, it's huge. You can't beat it."

Selected discography

Third Day, gray dot, 1995, reissued with extra tracks, Reunion, 1996.
Conspiracy No. 5, Reunion/Silver, 1997.
(Contributor) *Exodus,* Rocketown Records, 1998.
Time, Essential, 1999.
(Contributor) *City on a Hill: Songs of Worship and Praise,* Essential, 2000.
Offerings: A Worship Album, Essential, 2000.
Come Together, Essential, 2001.
(Contributor) *City on a Hill: Sing Alleluia,* Essential, 2002.
Offerings II: All I Have to Give, Essential, 2003.
(Contributor) *The Passion of the Christ: Songs Inspired by the Film,* Lost Keyword, 2004.
Wire, Essential, 2004.
Live Wire, Essential, 2004.
Wherever You Are, Essential, 2005.
Christmas Offerings, Essential, 2006.
Chronology, Volume 1 (1996-2000), Essential, 2007.
Chronology, Volume 2 (2001-2006), Essential, 2007.
Revelation, Essential, 2008.
Live Revelations, Essential, 2009.

Sources

Books

Contemporary Musicians, vol. 34, Gale Group, 2002.

Periodicals

Atlanta Journal-Constitution, January 24, 2001, p. E1; June 22, 2001, p. P3; June 19, 2002, p. F1.
Billboard, March 29, 1997, p. 9; August 12, 2000, p. 40; March 22, 2003, p. 14; April 21, 2007, p. 20; June 7, 2008, p. 22.
Houston Chronicle, November 14, 2002, p. 6; May 6, 2004, p. 15.
Record (Bergen County, NJ), September 29, 2006, p. G16.

Online

"Third Day," AllMusic Guide, http://www.allmusic.com/cg/amg.dll?p=amg&sql=11:knfixqqgldae (May 25, 2010).
"Third Day Enters Georgia Hall of Fame," The Weekend 22 Countdown, http://www.weekend22.com/music.cfm?newsid=813 (May 25, 2010).
Third Day Official Web Site, http://www.thirdday.com (May 25, 2010).

—*Diane Telgen*

Betty Thomas

Actress and director

Born Betty Thomas Nienhauser, July 27, 1948, in St. Louis, MO. *Education:* Ohio University, Athens, OH, B.F.A., 1969.

Addresses: *Agent*—Creative Artists Agency, 2000 Avenue of the Stars, Los Angeles, CA 90067.

© Reuters/Robert Galbraith/Corbis

Career

Taught high school art, Chicago, IL, c. 1969-1975; waitress at Second City, Chicago, IL, c. 1975-78. Actress in films, including: *Chesty Anderson U.S. Navy,* 1976; *Jackson County Jail,* 1976; *Last Affair,* 1976; *Tunnel Vision,* 1976; *Loose Shoes,* 1980; *Used Cars,* 1980; *Homework,* 1982; *Troop Beverly Hills,* 1989. Television appearances include: *Fun Factory,* 1976; *Dog and Cat* (movie), 1977; *C.P.O. Sharkey,* 1978; *Outside Chance* (movie), 1978; *Nashville Grab* (movie), 1981; *Hill Street Blues,* 1981-87; *Twilight Theater* (movie), 1982; *When Your Lover Leaves* (movie), 1983; *ABC Afterschool Specials,* 1985; *Prison for Children* (movie), 1987; *Tracey Ullman Show,* 1989. Director of various television projects, including episodes of: *Doogie Howser, M.D.,* 1989; *Hooperman,* 1989; *Mancuso, FBI,* 1989-90; *Parenthood,* 1990; *Dream On,* 1990-92; *Midnight Caller,* 1991; *Shannon's Deal,* 1991; *Sons and Daughters,* 1991; *Arresting Behavior,* 1992; *On the Air* (miniseries), 1992; *Couples* (movie), 1994; *My Breast* (movie), 1994; *Late Shift* (movie), 1996; *Silicon Follies* (movie), 2001; *R3* (documentary), 2003; *Senor White* (movie), 2003; pilot episode of *Loop,* 2006; *That Guy* (movie), 2006; *Dash for Cash* (movie), 2007. Director of films, including: *Only You,* 1992; *The Brady Bunch Movie,* 1995; *Private Parts,* 1997; *Doctor Doolittle,* 1998; *28 Days,* 2000; *I Spy,* 2002; *John Tucker Must Die,* 2006;

Alvin and the Chipmunks: The Squeakquel, 2009. Producer of a variety of film and television projects, including: *Can't Hardly Wait* (film), 1998; *Charlie's Angels* (film; executive producer), 2000; *Silicon Follies* (television movie; executive producer), 2001; *I Spy* (film), 2002; *Surviving Christmas* (film), 2004; *Guess Who* (film; executive producer), 2005.

Awards: Emmy Award for best supporting actress in a drama series, Academy for Television Arts and Sciences, for *Hill Street Blues,* 1985; Q Award for best supporting actress in a quality drama series, Viewers for Quality Television, for *Hill Street Blues,* 1986; Emmy Award for outstanding individual achievement in directing in a comedy series, Academy for Television Arts and Sciences, for *Dream On,* 1990; Audience Award, Karlovy Vary International Film Festival, for *Private Parts,* 1997; DGA Award for outstanding directorial achievement in dramatic specials, Directors Guild of America, for *Late Shift,* 1997; Dorothy Azner Directors Award, Women in Film Crystal Awards, 2001.

Sidelights

At an imposing six feet and one inch tall with gangly limbs, an expressive face, and a larger than life manner, Betty Thomas seemed destined to do comedy. Born in St. Louis, Missouri, she attended Ohio University where she obtained a bachelors degree in fine arts. After college she moved to Chicago where she was a high school art teacher in the Chicago Public Schools. Thomas wanted to earn extra money to take a trip to Europe so she began working as a waitress. Not working in just any restaurant, bar, or hotel, she landed a job at the Second City Improvisational Club in Chicago. Since it opened in 1959, Second City had consistently been a starting point for comedians, award-winning actors, directors, and others in show business. In the mid-1970s when Thomas began waitressing, Second City had become a source of cast members for *Saturday Night Live* and *SCTV*, which borrowed many of the writing and performing techniques pioneered by Second City and other improv groups. Thomas was encouraged to take an improvisational acting class. After she received disapproval within the public school system for being outspoken on social and sexual issues, she found a more productive outlet for her humor and opinions when she joined the Second City Comedy troupe. After working with the troupe for three years in Chicago, she moved out to Los Angeles when Second City expanded. While that branch of Second City did not survive, Thomas' career in show business was far from over.

Thomas played Bridget Bert Richards in a comedic and deeply satirical film that came out in 1976 titled *Tunnel Vision* which was about a committee investigating an uncensored television network. Clint Weiler, writing for the Internet Movie Database, commented that it "launched the careers of some of the greatest comedians of all time." Within the cast were such luminaries as Howard Hesseman, Gerrit Graham, John Candy, Al Franken, Laraine Newman, Chevy Chase, and many others.

That same year Thomas also had roles in *Jackson County Jail*, *Last Affair*, and *Chesty Anderson U.S. Navy*. Thomas played a waitress in the drama *Jackson County Jail*. Intended to be an independent, X-rated film, the financial backers of *Last Affair* withdrew support and the film was released without any sexually explicit footage. She then played the character of a party guest in the comedy *Chesty Anderson U.S. Navy* and added to her resume and comedy credentials. Also in 1976 Thomas played an ugly housewife in a series of sketches on the short-lived daytime game show titled *Fun Factory*.

From 1976 until 1980 Thomas was able to get small parts in a variety of television productions such as *Outside Chance*, *Dog and Cat*, and *C.P.O. Sharkey*. In 1980, Thomas played the part of Bunny in the feature film *Used Cars*, directed by Robert Zemeckis

and starring Kurt Russell. Next Thomas played the part of a biker chick in a series of sketches that comprised a feature length presentation released in movie theaters titled *Loose Shoes*. It starred many up-and-coming and prominent comedians such as Bill Murray and Hesseman.

While Thomas was able to gain steady employment in show business, she had not found the breakout role that would propel her to stardom. The role of police officer Lucille Bates on the dramatic police drama *Hill Street Blues* was Thomas' eventual breakout role. Over the course of the series, the character of Lucy Bates went from being an inexperienced rookie cop to a command sergeant on the force. Thomas showed a different side to her acting abilities from that which had previously been displayed. Her portrayal of the no-nonsense Bates was gritty and complex. Thomas received seven nominations for an Emmy for best supporting actress for her work on *Hill Street Blues*. She won the primetime Emmy from the Academy of Television Arts and Sciences in 1985. She also won a Viewers for Quality Television Award for her portrayal of Sergeant Lucy Bates.

While Thomas was working on *Hill Street Blues* she spent hours observing the directors who worked on the show. She wanted to try to direct an episode but never was given the opportunity by Steven Bochco, executive producer of the show; however, Bochco did give her the opportunity to direct three episodes of the television series *Hooperman*. This began her career as a director. After *Hooperman*, she directed two episodes of *Doogie Howser, M.D.* including the premiere of the show. After this she continued to direct episodes of a variety of different television series.

Thomas caught the attention of the critics with her work as a director on the short-lived ABC series *Arresting Behavior*. After her work on the pilot episode of *Arresting Behavior*, she directed 13 episodes of the HBO series *Dream On*. The series centered around the character of Martin Tupper whose reactions to events in his life were illustrated with old movie clips. Thomas won her second Emmy for her work as a director of *Dream On*. Thomas' feature film directorial debut was in 1992 with the romantic comedy titled *Only You*. The film starred Andrew McCarthy and Kelly Preston and went straight to video without ever having a theatrical release.

In 1994 Thomas directed a made-for-television movie for CBS titled *My Breast* based on a best-selling book by Joyce Wadler. Wadler was a successful women's magazine writer who discovered a lump in her breast and went through surgery to have the cancer removed. The story follows her personal, emotional response and interpersonal travails as she goes through the experience of having the cancer treated. Meredith Baxter played the role of Wadler. Thomas again received praise from the critics for her directorial work.

In 1995 Thomas' big directorial break came by way of an offer to remake into a movie the 1970s television series *The Brady Bunch*. She was given the small sum—by Hollywood standards—of 12 million dollars to complete the project. The movie starred Shelley Long and Gary Cole as the parents of the Brady family. The story involved a plot by an evil neighbor who wished to turn the entire subdivision that the Brady family lived in into a shopping mall but the Bradys are holdouts who refuse to sell their house. The neighbor researches and discovers that the Bradys owe 20 thousand dollars in back taxes on the house and he creates a situation where they will have to sell the house or have it taken from them by foreclosure. The kids come up with a plan to raise the money and eventually the Brady family ends up on a talent show, which they win, saving the neighborhood. Making an interesting directorial choice, Thomas decided to have the Bradys portrayed as they were in the 1970s but to have the story set in the 1990s. The resulting culture clash provided a brilliant element of humor that was simultaneously satiric and honored the old television series. This combination made the movie very successful and it grossed more than 60 million dollars. With the success of *The Brady Bunch Movie* Thomas was in the enviable position of having directed one of the highest-grossing movies made by a female director.

In 1996 Thomas directed a television movie for HBO titled *Late Shift*. The movie was based on a book about the choosing of the successor to late night comedian and talk show host Johnny Carson. It fictionally portrayed the rivalry between Jay Leno and David Letterman concerning who would take over *The Tonight Show.*

Her next feature film, *Private Parts*, was based on the life and work of Howard Stern. James Bowman, writing for *American Spectator*, described the film as "refreshing." He went on to say "it never pretends to seriousness. Like Woody Allen's early *Everything You Always Wanted to Know About Sex*, it is a procession of gags loosely tied together by their relation to the figure of the nebbishy hero." The movie was seen to hold together well because the jokes in it resonated in the culture of the time. Because of new

cultural rules about sexual harassment *Private Parts* was seen as an honest expression of repressed humor. Thomas won an award for *Private Parts* at the Karlovy Vary International Film Festival.

After *Private Parts* Thomas directed a remake of *Doctor Dolittle* starring Eddie Murphy in the lead role. In the remake the veterinarian not only talks to animals, he also offers them counseling. There is a drunken monkey and a dog with obsessive compulsive disorder. While *Doctor Dolittle* was not a favorite with critics it still did well at the box office and spun off a series of sequels. That same year, 1998, Thomas also produced her first film, *Can't Hardly Wait*.

In 2000 Thomas produced the major movie release *Charlie's Angels* and directed *28 Days* which starred Sandra Bullock as a newspaper columnist with a drinking problem who is forced to enter rehab to deal with her alcoholism after crashing a limousine. The film brought in box office sales of more than 62 million dollars while costing approximately 43 million dollars to make. It was not seen as a critical success.

Thomas again worked with Murphy on yet another remake of a television show in 2002 which she produced and directed. This time Murphy was paired with Owen Wilson for the remake of *I Spy*. The original television series was a spy comedy starring Robert Culp and Bill Cosby. Wilson and Murphy recreated these roles. Elvis Mitchell, writing for the *New York Times,* dismissed the movie by saying that the casting was "absurd" because Thomas was "shoehorning two actors who are born scene-stealers—Eddie Murphy and Owen Wilson—into a buddy comedy."

In 2004 Thomas produced *Surviving Christmas* which starred Ben Affleck. Hitting her comedic stride once again, Thomas returned to directing in 2006 with the teen comedy *John Tucker Must Die*. The movie was a dark comedy about a teen basketball star who is dating several girls at the same time. The girls discover that they are all dating him and plot revenge against him. Justin Chang, writing for *Variety*, described Thomas' directing style as "snappy" and "engaging." He went on to say that "she doesn't even try to pass off this glossy, enjoyable comic fantasy as a credible slice of high school life, and she casts a sympathetic net around all her characters, mainly by letting their charisma speak for itself."

Thomas' next successful feature film was about three singing chipmunks. The movie *Alvin and the Chipmunks: The Squeakquel* grossed more than 443 million dollars worldwide. Thomas used her improvisation talents from her days of comedy to tweak and finalize the CGI scenes in the live action sequences to make the movie action smoother. Her hard work paid off and the movie was a success. She was invited back to make the third installment of the Alvin and Chipmunks live action CGI series. Initially she signed on to direct *Alvin and the Chipmunks 3* but in October of 2010 she left the project.

A veteran of the entertainment industry with strong instincts and an animated personality, Thomas has taken on some unusual roles and projects. She has bucked conventional thinking, illuminated the humor in stories and characters that would otherwise be flat, and brought out the poignancy in difficult situations through her onscreen storytelling.

Sources

Periodicals

American Spectator, May 1997, p. 69.
Animation Magazine, December 2009-January 2010, 23, p. 20.
New York Times, July 18, 1997; November 1, 2002, p. B1.
Variety, July 31-August 6, 2006, 403, pp. 19, 24.

Online

28 Days, Internet Movie Database, http://www.imdb.com/title/tt0191754/business (November 27, 2010).

"Betty Thomas: Biography," MSN Movies, http://movies.msn.com/celebrities/celebrity-biography/betty-thomas.1/ (November 26, 2010).
"Betty Thomas," Yahoo Movies, http://movies.yahoo.com/movie/contributor/18000208.tif54/bio (November 12, 2010).
"Biography for Betty Thomas," Internet Movie Database, http://www.imdb.com/name/nm0858525/bio (November 16, 2010).
Chesty Anderson U.S. Navy, Internet Movie Database, http://www.imdb.com/title/tt0074308/fullcredits#cast (November 26, 2010).
"Director Betty Thomas Walks Away From Alvin And The Chipmunks," CinemaBlend, http://www.cinemablend.com/new/Director-Betty-Thomas-Walks-Away-From-Alvin-And-The-Chipmunks-3-21235.html (November 27, 2010).
Fun Factory, TV.com, http://www.tv.com/the-fun-factory/show/5537/summary.html (November 26, 2010).
A Labor of Love, Internet Movie Database, http://www.imdb.com/title/tt0249672/ (November 26, 2010).
My Breast, Yahoo Movies, http://movies.yahoo.com/movie/18087140.tif98/details (November 26, 2010).
"Plot Summary for *Dream On,*" Internet Movie Database, http://www.imdb.com/title/tt0098780/plotsummary (November 26, 2010).
Tunnel Vision, Internet Movie Database, http://www.imdb.com/title/tt0075357 (November 26, 2010).

—Annette Bowman

Joyce Tischler

Founder of Animal Legal Defense Fund

Born c. 1956 in New York, NY; married a stained-glass artist (widowed, 2003); children: a daughter. *Education:* Queens College, City University of New York, B.A., 1974; University of San Diego School of Law, J.D., 1977.

Addresses: *Office*—Animal Legal Defense Fund National Headquarters, 170 East Cotati Ave., Cotati, CA 94931.

Career

Founder of Animal Legal Defense Fund, 1979; executive director of ALDF, 1979-2004; general counsel of ALDF, 2005—.

Awards: Excellence in the Advancement of Animal Law Award, American Bar Association Tort Trial and Insurance Practice Section (TIPS) Animal Law Committee, 2009.

Sidelights

Known as the "Mother of Animal Law," Joyce Tischler is the founder of the Animal Legal Defense Fund. She has worked to implement laws protecting animals from cruelty and neglect, and to educate the public about the rights of animals. When she began her work, the practice of animal law was nonexistent, and through her efforts, it has become mainstream.

Tischler's love of animals was apparent from an early age. Growing up in the New York borough of Queens with her two older siblings and a dog

Courtesy of Joyce Tischler, Animal Legal Defense Fund

named Princess, Tischler brought home any other stray animals she found in her neighborhood. She told Leslie Jay in *QMag,* "As soon as I could walk around the block, I was finding injured birds and bringing home cats I thought were homeless. When I was six and my turtle died, I held a formal funeral."

She decided at an early age to become a lawyer, and attended Queens College in New York City with this plan in mind. She majored in political science, but she retained her interest in animals and their welfare. Outside the campus library, she noticed little wooden shelters for stray cats, and the people who came to feed them every day. She joined their ranks, and worked to get the strays spayed, neutered, and adopted out to new homes. The veterinary bills mounted, and a sympathetic professor helped organize a "Campus Cats" fund-raiser to pay the costs.

Tischler graduated with her bachelor's degree in 1974, and went to the University of San Diego School of Law. While at the university, she was a member of the *San Diego Law Review,* the Steering Committee on Women in the Law, and the Environmental Law Society. She was also a student member of the faculty appointments committee. After graduating in 1977, she moved to the San Francisco Bay area and took a job with a law firm that did real estate transactions.

She was still passionately interested in animal rights, but at the time, there was no law firm dedicated to this work. In her spare time, she kept in touch with lawyers and others who shared her interest, and in 1979, she cofounded the Animal Legal Defense Fund. It was the first national, nonprofit legal organization dedicated to issues involving animals. She had no money, so it was a volunteer effort that she did in her spare time. She told Michael Duffy in the *Sydney Morning Herald* that she saw her organization as a natural outgrowth of the civil rights movements that blossomed in the 1960s and 1970s. These movements aimed to protect minorities, women, children, and people with disabilities. Tischler told Duffy, "Each of these movements turned to the use of the law, and growing up in that atmosphere caused many of us to become social and legal activists. A natural outgrowth of this kind of lawyering is the animal law movement."

Tischler also commented that, like many in her generation, she was deeply influenced by *Animal Liberation,* a 1975 book by Australian philosopher Peter Singer. Singer advocated that animals should be treated as if they have rights, based on the fact that they feel pain and they suffer when they are mistreated. Tischler told Duffy that Singer's impact "cannot be overstated. We went from being mere 'animal lovers' to a movement with a strong philosophical foundation."

In 1981, Tischler became involved with her first animal rights case. A friend at the Animal Protection Institute told her that the U.S. Navy was killing hundreds of wild burros that were wandering around on the airfield at China Lake in the Mojave Desert. Tischler filed a suit against the Navy and won a temporary restraining order. After eight months of negotiations with the Navy, many of the burros were removed; the shooting stopped.

The Animal Protection Institute offered Tischler a job, but she asked for a grant instead. She received $5,000, and became the first full-time employee of the ALDF. For the first ten years of the organization's existence, money was sparse and Tischler ran up a lot of credit card debt. Gradually, however, things turned around, and by August of 2009 it had a $4 million budget.

The ALDF has since been involved in rescuing animals from people who were keeping them in deplorable conditions; removing chimpanzees from

trainers who beat them; determining the outcome of animal custody fights; and arbitrating disputes between landlords and tenants, among other issues. The organization provides free legal help in the prosecution of people charged with animal abuse, and it lobbies for stronger laws that protect animals. It also encourages enforcement of laws that already exist, and provides education to the public about animal rights.

In 2009, Tischler was honored with the Excellence in Animal Law Award. This award, given by the American Bar Association Tort Trial and Insurance Practice Sector, recognizes exceptional work by a leader of a bar association's animal law committee in advancing the humane treatment of animals.

In 2010, the ALDF and other groups filed a lawsuit against the oil company BP after a massive spill in the Gulf of Mexico. BP was burning off some of the spilled oil, resulting in the incineration of endangered sea turtles. The lawsuit stopped the burning.

Tischler told *QMag*'s Jay that she is excited about how far animal law has come since she was in law school: "Today, animal law is taught in 100 law schools. Law students tell me they're going to law school in order to practice animal law. Some of the largest firms in the United States are offering their services to us to do pro bono work, which stretches our resources. I'm very optimistic about the future of animal law; it's mainstream now."

Tischler was a vegan and did not eat or use any products from animals. She was widowed in 2003, when her husband, a stained-glass artist, died of lung cancer. As of 2010, she lived with her teenaged daughter and many animal companions in Cotati, California.

Sources

Online

"California Lawyer Joyce Tischler Honored for Advancement of Animal Law," California Bar Association, http://www.abanow.org/2009/07/california-lawyer-joyce-tischler-honored-for-advancement-of-animal-law/ (August 1, 2010).

"Joyce Tischler," Animal Legal Defense Fund Web Site, http://www.aldf.org/article.php?id=587 (August 1, 2010).

"Lawyer Takes a Stand for the Voiceless," *Sydney Morning Herald,* http://www.smh.com.au/opinion/society-and-culture/lawyer-takes-a-stand-for-the-voiceless-20100806.tif-11oi9.html (August 20, 2010).

"Legal Eagle Joyce Tischler '74 Flies in the Faceof Convention to Create Precedents for Animal Rights," *QMag*, http://www.qc.cuny.edu/communications/qmag/Documents/QMagWinter08_09.pdf (August 1, 2010).

—Kelly Winters

Akio Toyoda

President of Toyota Motor Corp.

Born May 3, 1956, in Nagoya, Japan; son of Shoichiro Toyoda (an automotive executive); married Hiroko; children: one son, one daughter. *Education:* Keio University, undergraduate degree, 1979; Babson College, M.B.A., 1982.

Addresses: *Office*—Toyota Motor Corp., 1 Toyota-cho, Toyota, Aichi 471-8571 Japan.

Career

Began career at an investment banking firm in New York City, 1982; joined Toyota Motor Corp., Japan, 1984; worked in Toyota Motor sales beginning in 1992, and factories through 1997; deputy manager, Toyota Motor Corp., 1997-98; executive vice president of New United Motor Manufacturing, Inc., part of Toyota Motor Corp., Fremont, CA, 1998; elected to the board of directors and named a general manager of Toyota Motor Corp., 2000; president, Gazoo Media Service, 2000; managing director, Toyota Motor Corp., 2002-03, then senior managing director, 2003, head of Asian operations, 2003-05, executive vice president, 2005-09, president, 2009—.

Sidelights

In 2009, Akio Toyoda became the youngest-ever president of Toyota Motor Corporation, one of the most highly respected automotive companies in the world. His grandfather founded the company in 1937. After Toyoda took the helm of Toyota, he faced unexpected challenges as certain defects in the

Jon Didier/Toyota Motor Corporation via Getty Images

company's most popular cars came to light in late 2009 and early 2010. It seemed that executives at Toyota were less than honest about the problems with the cars, and Toyoda was compelled to apologize publicly on several occasions as well as appear before a committee of the U.S. House of Representatives to answer questions about his company. While Toyoda's place at Toyota seemed secure, the future of the car manufacturer was more murky.

He was born on May 3, 1956, in Nagoya, Japan, the eldest son of Shoichiro Toyoda, who served as the president of Toyota Motor Company in the 1980s and early 1990s. The automotive manufacturer was founded by Kiichiro Toyoda, his grandfather, and was an off-shoot of an automatic loom manufacturing company founded by Toyoda's great-grandfather, Sakichi Toyoda, in the early 1900s. Toyota was run primarily by successive generations of the Toyoda family in the twentieth century. (The company's name is slightly different from the family name because the number of strokes needed to spell out Toyota in Japanese is luckier than Toyoda.)

Toyoda earned an undergraduate law degree from the highly regarded private Keio University in 1979. During his college years, he admitted to focusing more on playing field hockey than studying. Moving to the United States to continue his education, he earned his master's in business administration from Massachusett's Babson College (the alma mater of Edsel Ford II, also an automotive executive) in 1982.

Toyoda began his professional career working as an investment banker in New York City and Great Britain before joining Toyota Motor Corporation in 1984 as a junior manager. He was the first member of his family to take the entrance exam for Toyota employees. Toyoda subsequently held positions at a Toyota factory, in finance, and at the Production Research Office. There, he worked with engineers who developed Toyota's vaulted manufacturing methods. In 1992, Toyoda began working in sales, where he encouraged efficiency within the company. Under his own volition, he began intensely studying work flow in the repair department and removed inefficiencies. Toyoda's extraordinary efforts to improve flow were not always appreciated by dealers and sales executives and led to a three-week hospitalization of Toyoda for exhaustion in 1993.

After this setback, Toyoda founded the Office of Business-Revolution Promotion to promote efficiency in the distribution and dealer system. Though many sales people still had doubts about Toyoda, he and his team were given a chance by Motoo Katsumata, who owned a massive Toyota sales network near Japan. Katsumata became a supporter of Toyoda after he and his group streamlined operations at a brand-new $120 million vehicle distribution center. After six intense months, Toyoda and his people had cut staff and the number of assembly lines needed as well as sped up car deliveries from one week to only three days.

While Toyoda was gaining ground, Toyota itself was faltering under the overwhelmed leadership of his uncle, Tatsuro Toyoda. After Tatsuro Toyoda suffered a stroke in 1995 and was forced to step down, non-Toyoda family member Hiroshi Okuda took over. Okuda began modernizing the company and winning back market share. Toyoda prepared to perhaps take over Toyota himself some day. By the mid-1990s, Toyoda was employed at the Toyota Motor factories, where he remained until January of 1997. Toyoda then became a deputy general manager at Toyota with the title general manager of the Team CS Creation Department for the Domestic Sales Operations Supporting Division. He spent a little more than a year in the post.

In April of 1998, Toyoda was named the executive vice president of the New United Motor Manufacturing, Inc. The Fremont, California-based company was a joint venture between Toyota and General Motors founded in 1984. By this time, it was believed that Toyoda was being groomed to become the president of Toyota. Taking over this position was intended to prepare him for the presidency of the company. For much of his tenure, he served as vice president for production control and quality assurance. In 1999, he helped develop an agreement to jointly develop new technologies like fuel cells. He later played a key role in talks on the production of a gasoline-electric hybrid.

Also in 1998, Toyoda helped bring Toyota to the Internet for the first time with Gazoo, a move that proved unexpectedly successful despite the opposition of many Toyota executives. Toyoda used some of his own money to start the venture and buy computers. Though Gazoo initially focused on helping Toyota owners schedule repairs at dealers, it soon became a referral service for consumers looking to buy cars. By 2000, Gazoo was selling many different items, such as mutual funds and compact discs, in addition to cars. Toyoda used the Web site to gain knowledge about the true wants and desires of consumers. By 2000, it was the most popular auto-related Web site in Japan.

Toyoda continued to move toward the company's presidency by joining Toyota's board of directors (as its youngest member) and being named a general manager of the company in 2000, in part because of the success of Gazoo. He remained in his post in the United States for a brief time after these promotions. For his part, Toyoda had an ambition that focused more on his family's legacy than becoming Toyota's president. He told Norihiko Shirouzu of the *Contra Costa Times*, "Whether I am going to be president in the future or not, it's the founding family's mission to keep setting direction for the company."

While there was continued debate over whether Toyoda should take over the company, his mentor, Fujio Cho, succeeded Okuda as president of Toyota. Also in this time period, a biography about Toyoda, *The Next One*, was published in Japan. Toyoda continued to impress with the success of Gazoo in Japan. To that end, Toyota helped found and owned 75 percent of a new company, Gazoo Media Service. Toyoda became president of Gazoo Media Services in October of 2000. This new outfit sold and maintained computer terminals in car dealerships and convenience stores to link directly to Gazoo.

By the early 2000s, Toyoda's future as a forthcoming president of Toyota seemed more clear. In 2002, he began serving as a managing director of Toyota

Motor Corp., and in 2003, was named a senior managing director. He primarily focused on helming the e-Toyota business as well as the company's operations in Asia in general and China in particular. Continuing to be innovative, Toyoda worked on developing an e-mail terminal feature for vehicles and was a leader in a new project to produce passenger cars in China. From 2003 to 2005, Toyoda served specifically as the head of Asian operations for Toyota. When one operation in China was not proving workable, he made a deal to remove Toyota from that agreement and forged a better partnership with the China FAW Group Corp.

By 2005, Toyota was the most profitable car manufacturer in the world. Early in the year, Cho announced his retirement as president and was replaced by Katsuaki Watanabe. (Cho remained chairman of the board.) At the same time, Toyoda was named an executive vice president, a signal that he was in line to become Toyota's president in the near future. Toyoda was in charge of purchasing, quality, product management, information technology, and intelligent transport services. He also had a forward-thinking vision for the company, understanding that Toyota had become the leader of the automotive world (by unit sales if not corporate philosophy) and must act like the global powerhouse it had become.

Toyoda had a chance to show his vision when he took over as the head of Toyota's Japanese sales unit in 2007. Market share in Japan had fallen relative to other manufacturers and he was charged with making changes to turn the numbers around. Toyoda soon had bigger concerns. In December of 2008, Watanabe faced criticism of his choices as a leader amidst a deepening world financial crisis which negatively affected Toyota's profitability. As Watanabe was being pushed out, Toyoda was emerging as the next president of Toyota. The change in leadership was announced in January of 2009, with Toyota chairman Cho telling Hans Greimel of the *Automotive News*, "Innovative and youthful ideas will be required. We need a new generation to make bold change and reform."

In June of 2009, Toyoda officially became the president of Toyota Motor Corporation. He was only 53 years old and the youngest ever to hold the position in the history of the company. Though his managerial skills were given as the primary reason for his promotion, some critics believed, however, that he was given the post primarily because of his pedigree and not his qualifications. The Japanese media called him "the prince." When Toyoda took over, the car company was still in crisis because of a global economic recession that hit such manufacturers particularly hard. He vowed to address these difficulties and serve as an ideal leader of Toyota. He also stated, according to Greimel of the *Automotive News*, "We are now faced with unprecedented difficulties that come along only once in 100 years. I need to focus on the rapidly changing environment." Among his first steps was reviewing the company's product line-up, curbing rapid expansion, and focusing on core values like making sturdy, inexpensive cars.

Toyoda soon faced an even bigger problem when reports of major defects with certain Toyota models surfaced in the fall of 2009. On several models made by Toyota and its luxury subsidiary Lexus, cars accelerated without warning. Once they were accelerating, it was often hard to stop them. At first, Toyota said the accelerator stuck because of problems with floor mats. Later, another mechanical explanation was given related to the gas pedal itself. Toyota denied any electronic problems, though James E. Lentz, the top Toyota executive in the United States, was eventually forced to admit it was a possibility. Problems surfaced with other Toyota models, most notably braking problems on the Prius hybrid.

Toyota tried to avoid a massive recall and allegedly covered up the extent of the problem, which included millions of cars. By early 2010, however, it became clear that there was more to the problem than Toyota was admitting and the recall of affected vehicles began. During this public relations crisis, Toyoda was silent for weeks and there were questions about his leadership abilities. He began speaking publicly in early February of 2010. At a press conference, Toyoda was vilified by the Japanese media for speaking English in a halting fashion—despite the fact that he was fluent—and for not bowing deeply enough.

Later that month, Toyoda agreed to appear in a hearing before the U.S. government's House Committee on Oversight and Government Reform, despite an initial refusal. Toyoda believed that Toyota's senior executives in the United States would be better placed to speak there. He was also not legally bound to appear because he was not an American citizen. During his appearance, he apologized for his company's handling of the problems and believed the rapid rate at which the company had grown contributed to a culture in which safety took a back seat to profits. His explanation drew mixed reviews, but Toyoda pledged that the problems would be fixed.

Away from work at Toyota, Toyoda had an interest in cars and racing. In 2007 and 2009, he participated in a 24-hour endurance race at Nurburgring in

Germany. Toyoda was a member of the team that drove a Lexus LF-A supercar and finished fourth in the 2009 race. He wanted to be a race car driver as a boy, but his family would not let him. They also would not let him become a taxi driver, another youthful goal. Of his 2007 racing experience, Kwan Weng Kin of the Singapore *Straits Times* quoted Toyoda who wrote in his blog that "Just before crossing the finishing line, I could barely see in front of me because of my tears. I was so moved."

Sources

Books

Marquis Who's Who, Marquis Who's Who, 2010.

Periodicals

Associated Press, June 25, 2009.
Automotive News, January 17, 2000, p. 76; September 25, 2000, p. 3; April 12, 2004, p. 8; February 19, 2007, p. 14; October 29, 2007, p. T192; January 26, 2009, p. 4; February 15, 2010, p. 46.
Contra Costa Times (CA), May 16, 2000, p. B2.
Daily Yomiuri (Tokyo, Japan), February 27, 2010, p. 7.
Edmonton Journal (Alberta, Canada), July 30, 2010, p. G2.
Globe and Mail (Canada), January 12, 2009, p. B6; June 23, 2009, p. B15.
Guardian (London, England), May 24, 2000, p. 31.
Guardian Unlimited (London, England), February 23, 2010.
Japan Economic Newswire, April 8, 2003.
Los Angeles Times, February 6, 2010, p. B1; February 25, 2010, p. A1.
National Post's Financial Post & FP Investing (Canada), July 25, 2007, p. FP6.
New York Times, February 10, 2005, p. C4.
Nikkei Weekly (Japan), July 6, 1991, p. 8; April 6, 1998, p. 8.
Ottawa Citizen, February 10, 2010, p. B3.
Pantagraph (Bloomington, IL), November 9, 2000, p. C9.
Straits Times (Singapore), February 1, 2009.
Yomiuri Shimbun (Japan), January 13, 2009.

—*A. Petruso*

Buddy Valastro

Charles Eshelman/WireImage/Getty Images

Baker and television personality

Born Bartolo Valastro Jr., March 3, 1977, in Hoboken, New Jersey; son of Bartolo Sr. (a baker) and Mary Valastro; married Lisa, c. 2001; children: Sofia, Buddy Jr., Marco.

Addresses: *Office*—Carlo's Bake Shop, 95 Washington St., Hoboken, NJ 07030. *Web site*—http://www.carlosbakery.com.

Career

Owner and master baker, Carlo's Bakery, Hoboken, NJ, 1994—. Star of television shows *Cake Boss*, 2009—, *Cake Boss: Next Great Baker*, 2010-11, and *Kitchen Boss*, 2011.

Member: Retail Bakers of America.

Awards: Winner, *Food Network Challenge,* Wedding Cake Surprise challenge, 2009.

Sidelights

As the star of the TLC reality series *Cake Boss,* baker Buddy Valastro has become nationally recognized for his beautiful, elaborately detailed cakes. It was more than his ability to re-create the Leaning Tower of Pisa or a life-sized NASCAR race car in pastry that made the show one of the network's most popular, however. As the head of a family business that involved his mother, his four sisters, and assorted brothers-in-law and cousins,

Valastro presides over a fast-paced, passionate, and sometimes contentious workplace. "We blow up, we go a little nuts," the baker told Tammy La Gorce in the *New York Times.* "But at the end of the day we're family, and I love my family." He added, "It's important to me to show America there are still people who do what I do, where everything is from scratch. It's a tribute to my father, a way to honor his memory."

Bartolo "Buddy" Valastro Jr. was born in 1977 in Hoboken, New Jersey, where his father ran Carlo's City Hall Bake Shop, better known as Carlo's Bake Shop. Bartolo Sr. emigrated from Sicily at age 13, apprenticed himself to the shop's original owner, and bought out the business in 1964. Buddy Junior started in the family business at age eleven, after his father caught him lighting fires and made him start working weekends to stay out of trouble. On that first day, he related to *New York Daily News* contributor Rachel Wharton, "I asked, 'Oh, am I gonna make a wedding cake?' And my father said, 'No, you're gonna wash the sink.' I had to learn every single aspect of the bakery, so I started at the bottom. It made me realize how important every part of it is to the system." He eventually became his father's apprentice, learning to make cakes from scratch and sculpt flowers out of sugar, and was decorating wedding cakes by age 15.

Valastro was only 17 years old when he left school to run the family business. "I knew I was going to go into the business, I just didn't know I was going to so soon," he recalled to Kristina Lopez of the Web site Fancast. After his father died of cancer three weeks after being diagnosed, "it was kind of like one of those things I had to do. By the time [his illness] started happening, I already had my mind and my focus on the business more than schoolwork." Although he never had any formal culinary training, Valastro learned enough from his father and his own hard work to make himself a success. "A lot of people don't know much about baking," he told Nanci Hellmich in *USA Today*. "They either wing it or use box or bag mixes. I do test batch after test batch like a mad scientist." His recipes resulted in beautiful works of pastry that tasted just as good as they looked. "By refrigerating them and covering them in fondant, we seal in the moisture," he explained to Hellmich. "The cake and the cream infuse each other. It's like a marinade. It never dries out."

Valastro's work first began receiving national notice in bridal magazine photo spreads. Another wedding cake was featured in an episode of HBO's acclaimed series *The Sopranos*, while in 2006 viewers of NBC's *Today* Show chose his entry to be featured in a live wedding on the show. In December of 2008, a circus-themed cake he made for Britney Spears' birthday was featured on ABC's *Good Morning America*. He participated in several episodes of *Food Network Challenge*, finally winning a $10,000 prize in March 2009 for the "Wedding Cake Surprise" episode. Not long after, cable network TLC announced the new series *Cake Boss* would follow Valastro's work at Carlo's Bake Shop. "My passion is uniting Old World recipes with modern techniques, and I can't wait to share what we're doing," the baker told James Hibberd in the *Hollywood Reporter*.

Cake Boss showed average working days at Carlo's Bake Shop as well as the unique challenges presented by the specialty cakes Valastro was creating. One episode, for instance, featured Valastro taking a field trip to New York City's Museum of Natural History to research an ancient mammal resembling a giant rhino; he then made a cake resembling the creature for the museum's Extreme Mammal exhibit. Whatever he was working on, Valastro's days often included arguments with his sisters, who managed the storefront, and emergency fixes after employees made mistakes. As his cakes grew increasingly complex, something as simple as delivering the cake provided the greatest challenge. "I'm still learning things as I go along, even though I'm the cake boss," Valastro told Lopez. "You see what you can do to

fix it and what's going to work or what's not going to work." The more outlandish the request, the harder Valastro works to meet it. As he told Mike Kerwick of the Bergen County *Record*: "That's how I'm wired. I make things work. I don't back down. I figure out challenges. I go straight at it."

In 2010, Valastro began touring the United States in support of his first book, a combination recipe book and memoir titled *Cake Boss: Stories and Recipes from Mia Famiglia*. Interspersed among stories of how Valastro Sr. worked hard to achieve the American dream and how his son took the bakery to another level of success were family recipes popular at the bakery, such as his father's cannoli. Much like the book, Valastro's "Bakin' with the Boss" Tour combined interactive baking and decorating demonstrations with tales of the baker's family and life at Carlo's. The "Cake Boss" only visited 17 cities, however, for Valastro had to return to work on a new TLC series. *Cake Boss: Next Great Baker* premiered in December of 2010 and featured Valastro hosting a elimination competition between ten aspiring bakers for a cash prize and a job at Carlo's Bake Shop. The show was renewed in 2011 for a second season. In addition, Valastro was signed to star in *Kitchen Boss*, a daytime show on TLC. On this show, Valastro showcased family recipes and had special guests, including family members.

By mid-2009, Carlo's Bake Shop was producing upwards of 60 wedding cakes, 500 birthday cakes, 2,000 cupcakes, and thousands of pastries every week. Huge lines of fans appeared at the shop, waiting to sample his wares. "The thing I didn't know that [the show] was going to do is bring families together each week," Valastro told Kerwick. "You go outside in that line and it's all families. They'll say, 'Your show is the only show that we can agree on as a family.'" Because of his increased success, Valastro secured a new baking facility of more than 30,000 square feet to expand his business into mail order. The new building, he told Lois Weiss in the *New York Post*, would allow him to serve customers worldwide while maintaining a quality product: "I want people to taste a cake they got in the mail just like something they ate in Carlo's."

The new building also allowed him to continue filming *Cake Boss*, which remained an important part of his business. "I want to educate people," he told Wharton. "I want them to know that there are these old-school bakers out there and that baking is an art, that I'm a baker and proud of it." Although he enjoyed the increasing visibility his show brought the bakery, he noted that providing a quality product was always his main goal. As he told Hellmich:

"Sure, I have a hit TV show, but it's the little things you do every day, day in and day out, to touch other people that make you special."

Selected writings

Cake Boss: Stories and Recipes from Mia Famiglia, Free Press (New York City), 2010.

Sources

Periodicals

Hollywood Reporter, March 25, 2009, p. 3.
New York Daily News, May 30, 2009.
New York Post, October 5, 2010.
New York Times, July 5, 2009, p. 10.
People, July 19, 2010, p. 144; November 17, 2010, p. 14.
Record (Bergen County, NJ), October 11, 2010, p. F1.

USA Today, July 29, 2009, p. 1D; November 3, 2010, p. 4D.

Online

"Cake Boss's Buddy Valastro Dishes on the New Season," Fancast, http://www.fancast.com/blogs/2009/tv-news/cake-bosss-buddy-valastro-dishes-on-the-new-season (October 26, 2009).
"TLC Orders New Buddy Valastro Series Kitchen Boss," *TV Guide*, http://www.tvguide.com/news/tlc-kitchen-boss-1027332.aspx?rss=keywords&partnerid=yahoo&profileid=omg (February 1, 2011).
"TLC Renews Cake Boss: Next Great Baker," OMG! Yahoo!, http://omg.yahoo.com/news/tlc-renews-cake-boss-next-great-baker/54599 (February 1, 2011).

—Diane Telgen

Ron Vigdor

Image courtesy of BornFree

President of BornFree

Born c. 1970; married; children: two sons.

Addresses: *Office*—2263 North West Boca Raton Blvd., Ste. 202, Boca Raton, FL 33431.

Career

Worked for family investment firm, founded telecommunications company and Internet service provider, late 1980s; worked with GPS company Sky Watch and online retail service company Kyozou, early 2000s; co-founder and president of BornFree, 2005—.

Member: Board of directors, the X-Change Corporation.

Sidelights

Entrepreneur and corporate executive Ron Vigdor is best known as one of the three founding partners and president of BornFree, a company that produces BPA-free baby bottles, sippy cups, and other goods for small children. Since the formation of BornFree in 2006, the company has expanded from a simple operation run out of Vigdor's home to a lean but far-reaching enterprise with products distributed at mass retailers such as Whole Foods Market, Babies "R" Us, and Target. Profits for 2010 were anticipated to top $25 million, a testament to the founders' keen eye for a business opportunity and the changing demands of the American marketplace.

"I've learned that to launch a successful brand, you need to create an innovative product that fills a niche and be first to market with your concept.... Launching BornFree taught me that when you have an innovative product, you have to do whatever it takes to bring the product to market," Vigdor explained to the editors of the online *New York Times* small business feature series "You're the Boss" in 2010.

A U.S. citizen, Vigdor was born around 1970. He began his career working for his family's international trading and investment company; by the late 1980s, the budding entrepreneur had entered the emerging world of technology, founding both a company that provided Internet access and one that offered long-distance calling cards. He also developed business relationships with telecommunications firms and business investment companies in South America and the Caribbean at about this time.

As the growth of the Internet contributed to an explosion of e-commerce, Vigdor largely turned his financial and management attentions to that outlet. He became involved with online retail firm Kyozou, which was founded in 2003 to provide automated services such as listing, inventory control, and shipping for businesses selling goods through popular auction sites such as eBay. Vigdor also worked with the GPS vehicle locator system Sky Watch, which allows customers to remotely locate and disable vehicles, including cars and boats, via satellite.

The success of Vigdor's early business ventures allowed him to provide start-up capital for what has become his best-known venture, BornFree. During 2005, Galia Lemel, wife of Kyozou president Gil Lemel, became concerned about the possible effects of the plastics component bisphenol A—commonly called BPA—after seeing a report about it on Israeli television. Although BPA had been a major building block of plastics since approval in the 1960s, emerging science suggested that BPA may cause behavioral problems along with abnormal development of internal reproductive and hormonal systems, and that the chemical can leach from items such as baby bottles into the liquid contained within them. This leaching could allow the chemical to be ingested by infants still forming internal systems, worrying parents and providing an incentive for someone to create baby bottles without the controversial chemical.

In 2005, Lemel began discussions with Vigdor and his business partner and brother, Dan Vigdor, about manufacturing a BPA-free alternative to traditional baby bottles. With Sky Watch's success tepid at best, Vigdor had become interested in beginning a milk-delivery service for babies. A father of two sons, Vigdor had been previously unaware of the potential dangers of BPA; however, he soon recognized a good business opportunity. "Being fathers ourselves ... we became extremely concerned about the safety of our children, and all children, when we learned about the potentially dangerous effects of BPA-infused plastics," he explained to natural baby care Web site SafeMama in 2008. "We realized that we could give society something worthwhile—a safe solution to feeding our children—while creating a business model. The bridge from e-commerce to baby bottles was intuitive because of our interest in how technology interacts with our daily lives and mass market."

By early 2006, BornFree had begun marketing BPA-free baby bottles on the Internet. Lemel's business connections in Israel led to the company manufacturing the bottles in that nation for about $5 each. The bottles were then sold in a two-pack for $20, a significantly higher price than the $7 or $8 charged by major manufacturers such as Evenflo for a three-pack of BPA-plastic bottles. Sales started slowly, but began to pick up as the business partners and the scientific community spoke out about BPA-related concerns. Grocery chain Whole Foods Market re-moved all baby products containing BPA from its inventory, and by the end of the year had replaced them with BornFree goods. Soon, Canada banned the use of BPA in baby products, and other mass retailers followed Whole Foods' example by pulling the products from their shelves. The difference in cost proved to be somewhat irrelevant as worried parents strove to protect their children from the increasingly maligned chemical compound. "I'd rather be a little careful and pay a few extra dollars for some new bottles than have a potential harmful issue," explained mother Melissa Bazarian to Renae Merle and Ylan Q. Mui of the Washington Post.

This widespread shift away from plastics containing BPA created high market demand for BornFree's uniquely BPA-free products. "We are manufacturing as fast as we can right now in Israel to keep up with demand, and we are flying in products day in and day out," Vigdor told Sarah Gardner of American Public Media's Marketplace. BornFree grew rapidly, doubling in size by the end of 2007 and setting up offices in Boca Raton, Florida. In order to keep costs low, the company pursued another modern business practice: outsourcing. Although BornFree had about 150 employees by mid-2010, only a small minority of those workers were part of the company's corporate offices. Instead, most administrative functions—from human resources to public relations—were managed by a raft of outside companies.

In the spring of 2010, Vigdor became involved in another business: the X-Change Corporation. A multimedia and e-commerce company, the X-Change Corporation provides such services as a bilingual home shopping network and a mobile entertainment service aimed at North American Hispanic markets. Vigdor became the company's Treasurer and a member of its Board of Directors upon its relaunch in March of 2010, joining the corporation at a time of great expansion as it worked to acquire the telecommunications businesses Cybertel USA, Inc., and Genesis-Key, Inc.

Sources

Periodicals

Forbes, June 2, 2008.
PR Newswire, March 10, 2010.
South Florida Sun-Sentinel (Fort Lauderdale, FL), April 23, 2007; May 15, 2007.
Washington Post, August 22, 2007.

Online

"Building a Better Baby Bottle," Crain's New York Business, http://www.crainsnewyork.com/article/20100528.tif/SMALLBIZ/10052984.tif0 (November 27, 2010).

"The Dad Behind the Bottle: Ron Vigdor of Born-Free Interview," Lilsugar, http://www.lilsugar.com/BornFree-BPA-Free-Bottles-8819814 (November 27, 2010).

"How Can ShaveMate Compete with Gillette?," *New York Times,* http://boss.blogs.nytimes.com/2010/04/28/how-can-shavemate-compete-with-schick-and-gillette/ (November 27, 2010).

"Interview with BornFree President Ron Vigdor," SafeMama, http://safemama.com/2008/01/24/interview-with-bornfree-president-ron-vigdor/ (November 27, 2010).

"In With the Out(sourcing)," *Entrepreneur,* http://www.entrepreneur.com/humanresources/hiring/article204654.html (November 27, 2010).

"No More Baby Steps for BornFree," Portfolio, http://www.portfolio.com/views/blogs/heavy-doses/2010/08/02/baby-bottle-maker-bornfree-grows-on-fears-over-bpa-chemical (November 27, 2010).

"The X-Change Corporation Announces Acquisition of Cybertel USA, Inc.," PRWeb, http://www.prweb.com/releases/2010/09/prweb4537934.htm (November 27, 2010).

Transcripts

Marketplace, American Public Media, April 18, 2008.

—*Vanessa E. Vaughn*

Tom Vilsack

U.S. Secretary of Agriculture

Born on December 13, 1950, in Pittsburgh, PA; son of Bud (a real estate agent and insurance salesperson) and Dolly (a homemaker) Vilsack; married Ann Christine Bell, August 18, 1973; children: Jess (son), Douglas. *Education:* Hamilton College, B.A., 1972; Albany Law School, J.D., 1975.

Addresses: *Office*—U.S. Department of Agriculture, 1400 Independence Ave. S.W., Washington, DC 20250.

Career

Attorney in private practice in Mount Pleasant, IA, after 1975; elected mayor of Mount Pleasant, 1987; elected to the Iowa Senate, 1992, reelected 1994; elected governor of Iowa, 1998, reelected, 2002; counsel, Dorsey & Whitney (law firm), 2007-09; national co-chair, Hillary Rodham Clinton for President, 2007-08; confirmed by the U.S. Senate and sworn in as U.S. Secretary of Agriculture, 2009.

Sidelights

Former Iowa governor Tom Vilsack joined U.S. President Barack Obama's cabinet in 2009 as the newest U.S. Secretary of Agriculture. Previously, Vilsack had campaigned tirelessly for Hillary Rodham Clinton during her failed bid to capture the 2008 Democratic Party presidential nomination, which followed his own brief run for the White House. "This has been a great experience," Jeff Zeleny in the *New York Times* quoted him as saying when he dropped out of the 2008 race. "When you start out life in an orphanage and you run for president of the United States, that's what this country is supposed to be about."

Vilsack was born in 1950 and spent the first 15 months of his life in a Roman Catholic orphanage in Pittsburgh, Pennsylvania, where his mother had given up the infant she originally named Kenneth. He was adopted by a couple, Bud and Dolly Vilsack, and grew up with a sister. Bud was a real estate agent and insurance salesperson, but the family had persistent money troubles; Dolly drank heavily, and occasionally overdosed on prescription medications. "She'd go up in the attic and lock herself up there for weeks, and all you'd hear would be the dropping of liquor bottles on the floor," Vilsack recalled in a 2008 interview with *GQ*'s Lisa DePaulo. Finally, he told DePaulo, his mother had an epiphany and quit drinking altogether; after that, they had a much better relationship. "She taught me the capacity of the human spirit to overcome anything," he said.

Vilsack met his future wife at Hamilton College in Clinton, New York, and wed Christie Bell in 1973. He went on to Albany Law School, then settled in Bell's hometown of Mount Pleasant, Iowa, a town south of Iowa City with a population of about 7,000.

Over the next decade he honed his skills as a trial lawyer in private practice with his father-in-law and became active in various community organizations.

Mount Pleasant made national headlines in December of 1986 when a disgruntled citizen walked into a City Council meeting with a handgun and began shooting. The mayor was killed and two council members were wounded. Vilsack was persuaded to run for office to fill the mayoral vacancy, and kept the job for next six years. In 1992, he ran for a seat in the Iowa Senate and won; he was reelected in 1994.

In 1996, after a decade in politics and with the older of his two sons about to graduate from high school, Vilsack announced his intention to quit politics to spend more time with his family. His brother-in-law, Tom Bell, was stunned by this news, and urged him to reassess his political future. Bell even suggested that Vilsack enter the next gubernatorial contest—despite the fact that Iowans had not sent a Democrat to that office since 1966. The next day, Bell died of a heart attack at the age of 50, and Vilsack reconsidered his decision.

Vilsack entered the 1998 gubernatorial race and won the Democratic primary by four percentage points. Pollsters considered him a long shot for the office, betting instead on the Republican named Jim Lightfoot who had Congressional experience, but an old family connection gave Vilsack a surprise boost: back in 1974, the late Tom Bell had served on a Congressional impeachment-inquiry staff during the Watergate crisis with a fellow law school graduate named Hillary Rodham. The First Lady, by then married to U.S. President Bill Clinton but a longtime friend of Vilsack's in-laws, helped the Democratic candidate raise some much-needed campaign funds and even showed up at the Vilsack for Governor pre-election night rally in Iowa. He wound up beating Lightfoot by nearly six percentage points to become the first Democratic governor of the state since 1969.

Vilsack was reelected in 2002 and mentioned as a possible running mate for John Kerry in Kerry's 2004 presidential bid. In 2006, he opted not to run for a third term—Iowa has no term limits for this office—and on November 30, 2006, announced he was entering the race for the 2008 Democratic Party presidential nomination. His campaign centered on two primary issues: an immediate pullout of U.S. troops in Iraq, and a retooled Department of Energy that would become the Department of Energy Security instead, focused on reducing American dependence on foreign oil with the help of biofuels.

On February 23, 2007, Vilsack announced his withdrawal from the race, citing his campaign committee's mounting debts and the increasing difficulty of raising money in a crowded field. "I came up against something for the first time in my life that hard work and effort couldn't overcome," the *New York Times*'s Zeleny quoted him as saying. "I just couldn't work harder, couldn't give it enough."

Soon after that announcement, Vilsack joined Hillary Clinton's campaign as national co-chair. She was expected to win the Iowa Democratic Presidential Caucus in January of 2008 thanks to his help—Vilsack had left the governor's office with an approval rating of nearly 70 percent—but Obama won the first of these influential state-primary victories. Clinton folded her campaign in June after losing the California primary to her main rival for the Democratic nomination. A steadfast party supporter, Vilsack then campaigned for Obama in the lead-up to the candidate's historic November election victory.

The Secretary of Agriculture cabinet post has, since its creation back in the 1880s, usually been given to a politician from a Great Plains state, where economic livelihoods are intrinsically tied to agricultural production and government policies. President-elect Obama declared that Vilsack was his choice for the job on December 17, 2008, and the former governor was confirmed by unanimous Senate vote on January 20, 2009.

Vilsack's role as Secretary of Agriculture is to work with the White House on setting U.S. policies on crops, grain tariffs, subsidies to farmers, and various nutrition-related issues. In February of 2010, he joined the Obama administration's organized campaign to combat rising childhood obesity statistics. "I was an overweight kid," he confessed to *Washington Post* journalist Jane Black. "I can remember back in those days there weren't the strategies that there are today to deal with those issues. So my parents put this very nasty cartoon of a very overweight young kid with a beanie cap and pasted it on the front of the refrigerator. So every time I opened the refrigerator I had to look at that picture.... I don't want youngsters to go through what I went through."

Sources

GQ, March 2008, p. 264.
New York Times, November 12, 1998; June 27, 2004; February 24, 2007; December 17, 2008; November 17, 2009.
USA Today, March 16, 2009, p. 4B.
Washington Post, February 11, 2009, p. F1; February 8, 2010.

—*Carol Brennan*

Lindsey Vonn

Alpine skier

Born Lindsey Caroline Kildow, October 18, 1984, in St. Paul, MN; daughter of Alan Kildow (an attorney) and Linda Krohn (an attorney); married Thomas Vonn (an alpine skier), September 29, 2007.

Addresses: *Contact*—Sue Dorf and/or Mark Ervin, IMG, 767 Fifth Ave., New York, NY 10153. *Home*—Vail, CO. *Web site*—http://www.lindseyvonn.com.

Career

Competitive alpine skier, 2000—; competed in first World Cup race, 2000; made Winter Olympics debut in Salt Lake City, Utah, 2002; competed at the Winter Olympics in Torino, Italy, 2006; breakthrough came in 2007-08 season when she earned enough points to win the World Cup overall title; competed at Winter Olympics in Vancouver, Canada, 2010; had standout season in 2009-10 when she had eleven World Cup race victories, setting a new American record.

Awards: Won Italy's Trofeo Topolino, 1999; gold medal in slalom and super-G, U.S. National Championships, Alyeska, AK, 2004; Olympic Spirit Award, 2006; Minneapolis *Star Tribune* sportsperson of the year, 2008; downhill and overall champion, FIS Alpine World Cup, 2008; downhill, super-G, and overall champion, FIS Alpine World Cup, 2009; Skieur d'Or award, International Association of Ski Journalists, 2009; Beck International Award, U.S. Ski and Snowboard Association, 2010; gold medal in women's downhill and bronze medal in super-G, Winter Olympics, Vancouver, Canada, 2010; downhill, super-G, combined, and overall champion, FIS Alpine World Cup, 2010.

John Barrett/Newscom

Sidelights

American ski champ Lindsey Vonn became the most successful downhill ski racer in U.S. history in March of 2010 when she won her third consecutive overall World Cup title on the heels of an Olympic gold medal performance a month before. Vonn captured the overall title after winning her 33rd World Cup race, breaking the U.S. record for career World Cup wins set by Bode Miller.

A gritty, risk-taking skier, Vonn stood out on the junior circuit. She started skiing World Cup events at age 16, competed in her first Olympics at 17, and reached the World Cup podium at 19. "She's one of the best skiers I've ever seen in the world," Canadian alpine racer Karen Percy Lowe told the *Globe and Mail*'s Dawn Walton shortly before the 2010 Olympic games. "Her confidence and her strength and her commitment off the hill and just in the course is just amazing. I just have never seen that before."

Vonn's maiden name was Kildow—she competed under that name in the 2002 and 2006 Olympics. She was born Lindsey Caroline Kildow on October

18, 1984, in St. Paul, Minnesota, to Alan Kildow and Linda Krohn. The oldest of five and big sister to triplets, Vonn was skiing by age three. Her grandfather skied competitively and her father once reigned as a U.S. national junior champ before a knee injury ended his career. Eager to have his firstborn carry on the family tradition, Alan Kildow took his preschool-aged daughter to the ski mountain at Buck Hill, Minnesota, for lessons with Austrian coach Erich Sailer. At first peek, Sailer was unimpressed with Vonn and felt sorry for his former student. "I thought, 'Poor father,'" Sailer recalled in an interview with the *Star Tribune*'s Jim Souhan. "She moved like a turtle."

Within a few years, however, Vonn showed staggering improvements under Sailer's disciplined guidance. By the time Vonn was seven, Sailer had her skiing through 400 slalom gates every evening under the Buck Hill floodlights. She burned endless hours each week winding through the gates over and over again. Vonn did not mind the regimen because she was already thinking about the Olympics. As Clay Latimer noted in the *Rocky Mountain News*, Vonn's teacher once asked her to write about a dream and Vonn wrote that she aspired to "win more skiing medals than any other woman ever has." By age nine, Vonn was traveling to Europe with Sailer to train on tougher mountains and compete in international events.

In time, the turtle transformed into a skiing sensation, forcing Vonn to race kids several years older in order to have any real competition. "That was not the greatest way to make new friends," Vonn recalled in an interview with the *International Herald Tribune*'s Bill Pennington. "I would finish a race and all the 14 year olds at the bottom would be crying because a 10 year old had beaten them."

At age ten, Vonn found further encouragement when she met legendary U.S. skier Picabo Street at a ski shop in Minneapolis. Vonn received an autographed photo of Street, who was a rising star on the World Cup circuit. Vonn placed the photo of her idol on her bedroom wall. After meeting Street, Vonn realized she could do more than just have fun with skiing—she realized she could have a career as a ski racer.

As Vonn progressed and found success, her father dreamed bigger and bigger dreams—he envisioned his daughter becoming an Olympic alpine champ. In pursuing this dream, Alan Kildow moved his daughter so she could train on larger mountains. The 300-vertical-foot runs of Buck Hill were fine for

slalom training but not for alpine skiing. At eleven, Vonn and her mother wintered in Colorado so she could train on the speedier slopes of Ski Club Vail. Her father and siblings stayed in Minnesota but by the next year, the entire family had relocated to Colorado so Vonn could train there. Vonn also continued traveling to Europe for competitions and began homeschooling because her training schedule prevented her from attending school regularly. At 14, Vonn won Italy's Trofeo Topolino, the most prestigious youth ski games in the world. The event is often referred to as the "Junior-Junior Worlds." No U.S. female skier had ever won the event.

In 2000, Vonn competed in her first World Cup race, tackling the giant slalom in Park City, Utah. In 2002, Vonn made the U.S. Olympic ski team and competed alongside Street in Salt Lake City, Utah. Street remembered her brief encounter with Vonn many years before and took the Olympic first-timer under her wing. Vonn, just 17, competed in the "combined"—an alpine event that includes one downhill and two slalom runs on the same day. The skier with the best aggregate time wins. Vonn finished sixth in the combined event at an Olympics that proved disappointing for the U.S. women's ski team. No one medaled; not even Street. During the games, Vonn met her future husband—Thomas Vonn—a member of the U.S. men's ski team.

The next few years were filled with peaks and valleys. At the 2003 U.S. National Championships held in Whiteface, New York, Vonn placed second in the downhill and third in the super-G. The following year, she skied her way to first in the slalom and super-G. Then she struggled through 2005, missing the podium at the 2005 World Championships in Bormio, Italy, though she was favored to medal. Vonn placed ninth in her first event, the super-G. She crashed the next day during a practice run, experienced a meltdown and placed fourth in both the downhill and the combined.

At the time, Vonn was going through some personal struggles. Her father wanted her to follow his training program, while more and more she favored the advice of her boyfriend, Thomas Vonn, for whom her father did not care. Vonn knew her father's unwavering dedication had brought her a long way, but she decided she needed to take flight on her own and ended up cutting ties with her dad in the months following the disastrous World Championships. Her parents had already divorced by then.

Focused and back in form, Vonn made the cut for the 2006 Olympics. Favored in the downhill, super-G and combined, Vonn arrived in Torino,

Italy, in February of 2006 and began preparing for competition. During a training run as Vonn sped through the downhill course at more than 60 miles per hour, she lost her balance, flew ten feet into the air and smacked her head on the ice-packed snow before tumbling helplessly down the mountain. Vonn left the slope in a helicopter, which airlifted her to a local hospital. The video footage of the crash received extensive media play and witnesses went on the air speculating about injuries, including blown-out knees and a broken back and pelvis. Miraculously, Vonn suffered only extensive bruising. Aided with a heavy dose of painkillers, she went back to the top of the mountain 48 hours later, finishing the downhill in eighth place.

As Vonn explained to Barry Svrluga of the *Washington Post*, the accident served as a turning point in her career. "It was kind of a defining moment for me, personally. That was the first time I had ever thought that I might not be able to ski again because of what the doctors were saying. It really was a wake-up call. I never wanted to miss another opportunity, and I never wanted to be in the finish and think that I could've done better or could've worked harder."

Motivated by the setback, Vonn trained harder and became known for her six-hour workouts seven days a week. During the off-season, Vonn hardly skis, instead spending her time on agility training, biking, and lifting. Once the preseason skiing starts, she is capable of putting down ten training runs, whereas many competitors are spent after five. She married her boyfriend in a September 2007 wedding, which her father did not attend. Ski-wise, Vonn had a breakout season in 2007-08 and captured her first overall World Cup championship, becoming the first U.S. woman to do so since Tamara McKinney did it in 1983. Vonn repeated the win in 2008-09. The award goes to the skier with the most cumulative points won in races from October through March. Many elite skiers consider winning the World Cup overall title more prestigious than Olympic gold because the winner must master and outski opponents in each of the five disciplines—slalom, giant slalom, super-G, combined, and downhill.

In 2010, Vonn once again made the U.S. Olympic ski team and entered the games amid much hype. Because of Vonn's cover-girl face and magnetic personality, NBC chose to feature her in its Olympic ads and *Sports Illustrated* featured the five-foot-ten-inch, 160-pound blonde in its Olympic preview edition. Vonn often skis with her blond ponytail tucked back in a miniature American flag. Vonn went to the Olympics to compete in five events—the downhill, super-G, combined, slalom, and giant slalom. Favored to win every race, Vonn drew comparisons to swimmer Michael Phelps as commentators speculated about how many golds she would walk away with. Statistics were not on her side; no U.S. skier had ever won more than two medals in a single Olympics.

Vonn entered the games with a bruised shin, yet she fearlessly attacked Whistler Mountain. She put down a monumental run in her first event, the downhill, and won gold, beating U.S. rival Julia Mancuso by .56 seconds. It was the first-ever Olympic downhill gold for a U.S. woman. Vonn also won bronze in the super-G. She had the lead in the giant slalom when she crashed and broke a finger. In her final race—the slalom—she straddled a gate, earning a disqualification as flakes fell in the air, creating a soft track many racers struggled with. In the end, Vonn was pleased with her performance. "I'm definitely really happy with everything I've done here," Vonn told the *Washington Post*'s Svrluga. "I got the gold medal that I came here for." She went on to tell Svrluga that her goal was never five gold medals. "Of course I wanted to try. And looking back, four medals were very realistic. But nothing goes the way you want it to. Nothing's ever perfect."

A month after the games, Vonn traveled to Germany to ski the final races of the World Cup season. She won the super-G, notching her eleventh World Cup race victory of the season and setting a new American record for most wins in a season. Vonn ended the 2009-2010 race period winning World Cup titles in the super-G, downhill, and combined events, as well as her third consecutive overall title.

While Vonn possesses the raw talent and drive necessary for success in her sport, she credits her husband with providing the technical expertise and psychological support that has kept her on top. Thomas Vonn takes care of equipment evaluations and offers his wife tactical advice. Speaking to the *Rocky Mountain News*, Vonn confided in her luck at having her husband by her side. "When I'm traveling and tired and grumpy he's always there to make me feel better. Whenever I have a question I can always go to him—whether it's my training schedule, whether I should race in this race or should use these skis.... It's very rare that you have a person there to help you with that."

Sources

Periodicals

Globe and Mail (Canada), February 4, 2010, p. S1.
International Herald Tribune, February 6, 2010, p. S11.
Rocky Mountain News (Colorado), November 18, 2006.

Star Tribune (Minneapolis, MN), February 20, 2002, p. 1A; February 5, 2006, p. 1A; December 25, 2008, p. 1C.

Washington Post, February 10, 2010, p. D1; February 27, 2010, p. D5.

Online

Lindsey Vonn Official Web site, http://www.lindseyvonn.com (April 16, 2010).

"Vonn Wins Third Straight World Cup Title," ESPN, http://sports.espn.go.com/oly/skiing/news/story?id=4988519 (May 14, 2010).

"A World Champ From Buck Hill," *Wall Street Journal,* http://online.wsj.com/article/SB12356987.tif32432892.tif45.html (May 31, 2010).

—*Lisa Frick*

Christoph Waltz

Actor

Born on October 4, 1956, in Vienna, Austria; son of Johannes Waltz (a set designer) and Elisabeth Urbancic (a set designer); married first wife (divorced); married second wife; children: four. *Education:* Max Reinhardt Seminar, Vienna, Austria; Lee Strasberg Institute, New York, New York.

Addresses: *Agent*—International Creative Management, 10250 Constellation Blvd., Los Angeles, CA 90067.

Career

Actor on television, including: *Der Einstand* (movie), 1977; *Feuer!* (movie), 1979; *Parole Chicago*, 1979; *Die Weltmaschine* (movie), 1981; *Dr. Margarete Johnsohn* (movie), 1982; *The Mysterious Stranger* (movie), 1982; *Der Sandmann* (movie), 1983; *Ein Fall für zwei*, 1985; *Lenz oder die Freiheit* (miniseries), 1986; *Derrick*, 1986, 1988; *Der Alte*, 1986, 1990; *Tatort*, 1987, 2006, 2008; *The Alien Years* (movie), 1988; *Das andere Leben*, 1987; *Goldeneye*, 1989; *The Gravy Train* (miniseries), 1990; *The Gravy Train Goes East* (miniseries), 1991; *5 Zimmer, Küche, Bad*, 1992; *Die Angst wird bleiben* (movie), 1992; *König der letzten Tage* (miniseries), 1993; *Jacob* (movie), 1994; *Tag der Abrechnung—Der Amokläufer von Euskirchen* (movie), 1994; *Catherine the Great* (movie), 1995; *Die Staatsanwältin* (movie), 1995; *Man(n) sucht Frau* (movie), 1995; *Prinz zu entsorgen* (movie), 1995; *Der Tourist* (movie), 1996; *Du bist nicht allein—Die Roy Black Story* (movie), 1996; *Kommissar Rex*, 1996; *Faust*, 1997; *Maître Da Costa*, 1997; *Schimanski*, 1997; *Das Finale* (movie), 1998; *Einsteins Ende* (movie), 1998; *Mörderisches Erbe—Tausch mit einer Toten* (movie), 1998;

Rache für mein totes Kind (movie), 1998; *Schock—Eine Frau in Angst* (movie), 1998; *Vickys Alptraum* (movie), 1998; *Dessine-moi un jouet* (movie), 1999; *Das Teufelsweib* (movie), 2000; *Der Tanz mit dem Teufel—Die Entführung des Richard Oetker* (movie), 2001; *Engel sucht Flügel* (movie), 2001; *Riekes Liebe* (movie), 2001; *Dienstreise—Was für eine Nacht* (movie), 2002; *Weihnachtsmann gesucht* (movie), 2002; *Der Fall Gehring* (movie), 2003; *Jagd auf den Flammenmann* (movie), 2003; *Jennerwein* (movie), 2003; *Tigeraugen sehen besser* (movie), 2003; *Zwei Tage Hoffnung* (movie), 2003; *Mörderische Suche* (movie), 2004; *Schöne Witwen küssen besser* (movie), 2004; *Die Patriarchin* (miniseries), 2005; *Der Elefant—Mord verjährt nie*, 2005; *Die Spezialisten: Kripo Rhein-Main*, 2006; *Franziskas Gespür für Männer* (movie), 2006; *Polizeiruf 110*, 2006; *Stolberg*, 2006; *Der letzte Zeuge*, 2007; *Der Staatsanwalt*, 2007; *Die Verzauberung* (movie), 2007; *Die Zücher Verlobung—Drehbuch zur Liebe* (movie), 2007; *Unter Verdacht*, 2007; *Das Geheimnis im Wald* (movie), 2008; *Das jüngste Gericht* (movie), 2008; *Die Anwälte*, 2008; *Todsünde* (movie), 2008. Actor in films, including: *Feuer und Schwert—Die Legende von Tristan und Isolde*, 1982; *Wahnfried*, 1986; *Quicker than the Eye*, 1988; *St. Petri Schnee*, 1991; *Zycie za zycie*, 1991; *Ein Anfang von etwas*, 1994; *Our God's Brother*, 1997; *Love Scenes from Planet Earth*, 1998; *Sieben Monde*, 1998; *Die Braut*, 1999; *Falling Rocks*, 2000; *Ordinary Decent Criminal*, 2000; *Queen's Messenger*, 2000; *Death,*

Deceit, & Destiny Aboard the Orient Express, 2001; *Dorian*, 2001; *She*, 2001; *Der alte Affe Angst*, 2003; *Herr Lehmann*, 2003; *Schussangst*, 2003; *Lapislazuli—Im Auge des Bären*, 2006; *Inglourious Basterds*, 2009; *The Green Hornet*, 2010.

Awards: Adolf Grimme Award for fiction/entertainment, for *Der Tanz mit dem Teufel—Die Entführung des Richard Oetker*, 2002; Golden Camera for best actor, for *Der Fall Gehring*, 2004; best actor, Cannes Film Festival, for *Inglourious Basterds*, 2009; Golden Globe for best supporting actor, Hollywood Foreign Press Association, 2009; SAG Award for outstanding performance by a male actor in a supporting role, Screen Actors Guild, 2009; BAFTA Award for best supporting actor, for *Inglourious Basterds*, 2010; Academy Award for best supporting actor, Academy of Motion Picture Arts and Sciences, for *Inglourious Basterds*, 2010.

Sidelights

Academy Award-winning actor Christoph Waltz enjoyed a lengthy career in his native Europe where he graced television programs, feature films, and theatrical productions before gaining sudden popularity and critical acclaim in the United States thanks to his work in director Quentin Tarantino's 2009 World War II epic *Inglourious Basterds*. The Austrian actor's portrayal of SS officer Colonel Hans Landa propelled him to massive critical success, with Waltz scooping up a nod for Best Actor at that year's Cannes Film Festival as well as the Golden Globe, SAG Award, and Oscar for Best Supporting Actor. His increased profile and widely recognized talents quickly earned him a role as the villainous Chudnofsky in 2010 superhero flick *The Green Hornet*, with continued appearances in Hollywood blockbusters seemingly guaranteed.

Born on October 4, 1956, in Vienna, Austria, Waltz comes from a family with a long history in show business. His parents, Johannes Waltz and Elisabeth Urbancic, worked as set designers, while all four of his grandparents had been actors. By his late teenage years, Waltz had entered into the family business, eventually studying acting both at Vienna's respected Max Reinhardt Seminar and the Lee Strasberg Institute in New York City. Although the young Austrian spoke excellent English, Scott Roxborough observed in the *Hollywood Reporter* that "Ironically ... he was discouraged from trying for a U.S. career by an agent who warned him that, as an Austrian, Waltz would spend the rest of his life playing Nazis in war movies." Instead, Waltz returned to his native Europe and began building a career in film and television. Among his early ef-

forts were roles in such German-language television productions as *Der Einstand* (The Beginning), *Feuer!* (Fire!), and *Die Weltmaschine* (The World Machine) during the late 1970s and early 1980s and a co-starring appearance in 1982's *Feuer und Schwert—Die Legende von Tristan und Isolde* (Fire and Sword—The Legend of Tristan and Isolde). The actor also regularly performed on the stage with a number of theater troupes and graced some of the continent's most respected venues, including Vienna's Burgtheater, Zurich's Schauspielhaus Zurich, and the Salzburg Festival, over the next several years.

By the 1990s, Waltz's television roles had grown in size if not in artistic challenge; he played the major character Hans-Joachim Dorfman in the 1990 comedic BBC miniseries *The Gravy Train* and its 1991 follow-up *The Gravy Train Goes Easy* while continuing to make steady appearances on Austrian and German broadcasts. He also landed numerous film roles, including starring turns in 1997's *Our God's Brother*, 1998's romantic comedy *Das merkwürdige Verhalten geschlechtsreifer Großstädter zur Paarungszeit* (Love Scenes from the Planet Earth), and 2000's thriller *Falling Rocks*. That same year, Waltz made his directorial debut at the helm of television film *Wenn man sich traut* (A Question of Confidence). The new millennium brought Waltz continued European success as he appeared in a triad of 2001 films—*Dorian*, *She*, and *Death, Deceit & Destiny Aboard the Orient Express*—before returning to a balancing act of appearing in German-language film and television while living with his wife in London, England. Among his performances of the early 2000s were turns in *Der Tanz mit dem Teufel—Die Entführung des Richard Oetker* (The Dance with the Devil—the Kidnapping of Richard Oetker), which won a prestigious Adolf Grimme award in 2002, and in crime film *Der Fall Gehring*, which garnered the actor a Golden Camera prize.

Even this respectable resume, however, was outshined by what became Waltz's international breakthrough performance in the Quentin Tarantino film *Inglourious Basterds*. An ensemble piece set in World War II-era France, the story featured Waltz as Jew-hunting Nazi military officer Colonel Hans Landa opposite American star Brad Pitt's Nazi-hunting Lt. Aldo Raine. Notable for both his eloquence and cold-bloodedness, the character of Landa was widely recognized as the film's most memorable: a terrifying yet suave killer who shifted effortlessly between German, English, French, and Italian. Waltz immediately captured the hearts of critics, picking up the award for Best Actor at the film's Cannes Film Festival debut and winning enthusiastic notices around the globe. "Waltz stands head and shoulders above the rest with a lusty performance in the juiciest role," commented Todd McCarthy of *Variety*, while David Edelstein of *New York* magazine characterized his performance as "elegant and insinuating."

The high levels of anticipation built by *Inglourious Basterds'* warm Cannes reception translated into equal box-office success, with the film debuting at the top of the U.S. charts in August of 2009 and thus helping introduce its previously little-known antagonist to widespread American audiences. Just as critics and fans clamored to praise Waltz as the heart of the film, the actor acknowledged Tarantino's selection of him for the role of Landa as a reboot of his career, not only for its impact on his notoriety but also on his own enjoyment of and belief in his craft. "Quentin is not a prolific writer, he is not a fantastic writer—but he is the ideal actors' writer," Waltz told the BBC. "He created this immense universe and invited me to participate." His interpretation of that universe continued to win critical acclaim into the following year, with Waltz earning several major awards for his performance, including a Golden Globe, SAG Award, and BAFTA Award. He closed out the awards season in March of 2010 with another success when he scooped up the trophy for Best Supporting Actor at the Academy Awards. Speaking in his acceptance speech, the acclaimed actor stated that "this is your welcoming embrace and there's no way I can ever thank you enough, but I can start right now. Thank you."

Although Waltz's much-lauded turn in *Inglourious Basterds* was behind him, his star seemed on the rise as 2010 progressed. He turned in a performance as the antagonist in director Michel Gondry's *The Green Hornet* opposite such bankable stars as Cameron Diaz and Seth Rogen that was slated for release during the holiday season, and was rumored to be a part of the casts of two dramas planned to reach theaters in 2011: drama *Water for Elephants* alongside *Twilight* heartthrob Robert Pattinson and actress Reese Witherspoon, and the Kevin Costner-helmed *A Little War of Our Own*, which would return Waltz to the World War II-era of *Inglourious Basterds*.

Sources

Periodicals

Entertainment Weekly, August 21, 2009, p. 93.
Hollywood Reporter, July 10, 2009, p. 8.
New York, August 24, 2009.
Variety, May 25, 2009, p. 13.

Online

"Christoph Waltz," Allmovie, http://www.allmovie.com/artist/christoph-waltz-221135/bio (March 10, 2010).
"Christoph Waltz Biography," InBaseline, http://www.inbaseline.com/person.aspx?view=BioSummary&person_id=1063550&print=1 (March 10, 2010).
"Christoph Waltz," Internet Movie Database, http://www.imdb.com/name/nm0910607/ (March 10, 2010).
"Christoph Waltz: 2010 Oscar Acceptance Speech," Alt Film Guide, http://www.altfg.com/blog/awards/christoph-waltz-oscar-acceptance-speech-493/ (March 8, 2010).
"In profile: Best supporting actor," BBC News, http://news.bbc.co.uk/2/hi/entertainment/8539509.stm (March 9, 2010).

—*Vanessa E. Vaughn*

Alexander Wang

Fashion designer

Born May 17, 1984, in San Francisco, CA. *Education:* Attended Parsons The New School For Design, 2002-04.

Addresses: *Home*—New York, NY. *Office*—Alexander Wang, 386 Broadway, 3rd Fl., New York, NY 10013.

Career

Intern, *Vogue, Teen Vogue,* and with the Derek Lam and Marc Jacobs labels, c. 2002-04; launched limited line of knitwear under the label Alexander Wang, 2004; expanded to full line of ready-to-wear, 2006; added accessories line, 2008; launched T by Alexander Wang, 2009; launched footwear and eyewear collections, 2010.

Awards: Fashion Fund prize, Council of Fashion Designers of America/*Vogue*, 2008; Swarovski Award for emerging women's wear designer, Council of Fashion Designers of America, 2009; Swarovski Award for accessories designer of the year, Council of Fashion Designers of America, 2010.

Sidelights

By the age of just 26, American fashion designer Alexander Wang had won a trifecta of prestigious Council of Fashion Designers of America (CFDA) awards for his women's wear and accessories. The financial success of this California native—one of a new generation of Asian American

Jamie McCarthy/WireImage/Getty Images

all-stars in the fashion industry—with his eponymous brand seems all the more remarkable for the fact that Wang's sales figures rose in what was inarguably a devastating retail climate after the 2008 economic recession. Both Anna Wintour of *Vogue* and *Women's Wear Daily* were enthusiastic early champions of Wang's appealing designs, which build upon "often unpretty elements that somehow end up looking nonchalantly stylish and chic," declared *WWD*'s Venessa Lau.

Born in San Francisco in 1984, Wang is the son of Taiwanese parents. He has a brother and two sisters, but also an inordinately high number of female cousins—17 in all—and credits this with some of his interest in fashion. Setting his sights on a design career at an early age, he tried out several potential degree-granting schools via their summer programs, including London's Central Saint Martins College of Art and Design and the Otis College of Art and Design in Los Angeles, before settling on Parsons The New School for Design in New York City. He headed there after graduating from the private Drew School in San Francisco.

Wang staged his first fashion show at the age 15 at his brother's wedding reception, which was his brother's idea. In 2002, the year Wang graduated from Drew, he staged a second presentation, this one at his mother's birthday party celebration in Shanghai, complete with a runway and hired models. In New York, Wang wound up spending only two years at Parsons, but accrued crucial hands-on experience in design and marketing via internships at *Vogue, Teen Vogue,* and with designers Derek Lam and Marc Jacobs.

In 2004, Wang launched a limited line of women's wear with a few cashmere hoodies that featured novel prints of glamorous faces on the back. His brother and sister-in-law funded that venture. "We had six samples," as he recalled in an interview with Derick Chetty for the *Toronto Star,* "and my sister-in-law and brother ... said, let's just drive to the stores and approach them ourselves. We sold the first pieces on consignment and they sold out and we were like, 'Wow, we actually sold something.'"

Wang's first foray garnered some impressive press attention, including a mention in the *New York Times* Styles section. He gradually expanded the knitwear line until he was ready to present a full collection of ready-to-wear at New York Fashion Week in September of 2006, where designers present their upcoming Spring 2007 lines to fashion journalists and store buyers. Over the next few seasons, he struggled along, earning occasionally tepid reviews, but Wintour, the legendary *Vogue* editrix known for spotting new talent, was a steady supporter.

At New York Fashion Week in February of 2008, Wang finally scored enthusiastic accolades for a collection that hit a winning formula, mixing a rock-star ethos with his signature knitwear. Seven months later, at the September New York collections, he won an effusive review from the pen of Robin Givhan, the Pulitzer Prize-winning fashion writer for the *Washington Post.* Givhan termed his latest runway show "a perfect convergence of atmosphere, clothes and styling.... The models stalked out looking like they'd had a long, hard night and had gone to sleep with the taste of liquor and cigarettes still on their lips. The models wore black leather jackets pieced with denim, blazers paired with bloomer shorts, and gray jersey sweat pants with embroidered tank tops. All you could think was that you wanted to go to wherever they had just been."

Two months later, Wang picked up his first major honor from the Council of Fashion Designers of America (CFDA), which awarded him the coveted CFDA/*Vogue* Fashion Fund prize. The following

June, he won the CFDA Swarovski Award for emerging women's wear designer. By then, he had added a line of accessories and T-shirts, called T by Alexander Wang, that each proved surprisingly strong sellers during a time of plummeting returns for U.S. fashion houses. By 2010, when he won a third CFDA award for his accessories, Wang's company was estimated to be pulling in $25 million a year. It was still a family owned business, and his brother Dennis and sister-in-law Aimie both hold senior executive posts.

Wang is credited with coining the term "MOD," or "Model Off Duty." Counting several models, including Erin Wasson, as his friends, Wang often drew upon their casual, nonworking attire as inspiration for his own designs. Wang's term gained such currency that *Vogue* even ran a feature story using the MOD headline in the spring of 2009. "People tried to get me to license that!," Wang confessed to Chetty in the *Toronto Star* interview. "I was describing a movement, that high-low look and where it came from. These girls come from humble beginnings and didn't read fashion magazines and ... they are thrown into this world and they are given all kinds of luxurious things and they mix it all together."

In 2010, Wang's company rolled out eyewear—adding to an already successful footwear line—and planned to open its first store in New York City. There was also an online store in the works whose sales were predicted to reach stratospheric heights. Wang was still surprised by his good fortune after so few years in the business. In one interview with Lau for *WWD,* he recalled trotting those first cashmere-hoodie samples around New York City in a rolling suitcase. "They would tell us that the buyer wasn't there when we knew we were talking to her. It's funny because now we have stores calling us, the same ones that turned us down."

Sources

Periodicals

Globe & Mail (Toronto, Canada), July 24, 2010, p. L1.
New York Times, September 4, 2010.
Toronto Star, July 29, 2010, p. L4.
W, September 2009, p. 168.
Washington Post, September 10, 2008, p. C1.
WWD, January 3, 2005, p. 6; September 7, 2006, p. 10; May 2008, p. 33; August 6, 2008, p. 4.

Online

"Alexander Wang," *New York* magazine, http://nymag.com/fashion/fashionshows/designers/bios/alexanderwang/ (October 5, 2010).

—*Carol Brennan*

Shaun White

Scott Halleran/Getty Images

**Professional snowboarder
and skateboarder**

Born Shaun Roger White, September 3, 1986, in San Diego, CA; son of Roger (a water department worker) and Cathy (a waitress) White.

Addresses: *Contact*—United States Skiing and Snowboarding Association, 1 Victory Ln., Box 100, Park City, UT 84060. *Web site*—http://www.shaunwhite.com/.

Career

Became professional snowboarder for the Burton Snowboarding team, 1999; joined the Tony Hawk Gigantic Skateboard Tour, 2002; became a professional skateboarder, 2003; won U.S. Open Slopestyle Championship, 2004; appeared in the documentary *The White Album*, 2004; won all five U.S. Grand Prix Superpipe events, 2005-06; member of the U.S. snowboarding team at the Winter Olympic Games in Turin, Italy, 2006; competed at two stops on the Dew Tour, 2006; competed on the AST Dew Tour, 2007; member of the U.S. snowboarding team at the Winter Olympic Games in Vancouver, Canada, 2010.

Awards: Silver medals in superpipe and slope, Winter X Games, 2002; gold medal in slopestyle, Winter X Games, 2003, 2004, 2005, 2006; gold medal in halfpipe, Winter X Games, 2003, 2006; ESPY Award for best male action sports athlete, ESPN, 2003, 2006, 2008; gold medal in vert, Summer X Games, 2005; ESPY Award for best U.S. Olympian, 2006; Teen Choice Award, sports-choice action sports, Fox Net-

work, 2006; gold medal in men's halfpipe, Winter Olympic Games, 2006; gold medal in vert, Summer X Games, 2007; gold medal in men's halfpipe, Winter Olympic Games, 2010.

Sidelights

Known as the Flying Tomato, Shaun White is an accomplished snowboarder and skateboarder. He twice won Olympic gold as a snowboarder as well as numerous other competitions. White also set the standard for snowboard tricks. While White was primarily known for his snowboarding, he also was talented on the skateboard and won several Summer X Games gold medals. With his easy-going personality and devil-may-care attitude, White was sought after by sponsors and earned millions of dollars in endorsements each year.

Born on September 3, 1986, in San Diego, California, he was the son of Roger and Cathy White. His father had the talent to become a professional surfer, but the lack of parental support killed his dreams. His maternal grandparents competed in pro roller derby. Though he later became a professional athlete, White was born with a genetic heart defect and had to have open heart surgery when he was six months old. White struggled during his first year of life but soon became interested in action sports.

White focused on snowboarding, skateboarding, and surfing, and was a natural at all of them. He learned to snowboard and skateboard in part from his older brother, Jesse, who also became a professional snowboarder and later acted as his brother's agent. White told Brian E. Clark of the *San Diego Union-Tribune,* "Jesse (who rides for Burton) taught me all the grabs and spins. He told me to do stuff, and I'd go try it and maybe land it." Jesse White was impressed by his little brother who could land snowboarding jumps on his second day on the board. White's older sister Kari also competed professionally as a snowboarder.

When White was seven years old, his parents enrolled him in Windell's Snowboard Camp in Mount Hood, Oregon. Tim Windell, the camp director, recognized that White had a special talent and helped him develop it. White also earned his first sponsorship at seven with Burton who developed an appropriately sized snowboard for him. By the age of 12, his parents took out a home equity loan so White and his brother could afford to travel to Europe and Japan and compete.

In 1999, White became a professional snowboarder for the Burton Snowboarding team. He was soon recognized as an up-and-coming phenomenon, competing in events around the world while being homeschooled by his mother on the road. White appreciated the sacrifices his parents made, telling Don Norcross of the *San Diego Union-Tribune,* "That's the biggest thing, I've had support from my parents to drive me to the mountains, pay for all my (lift) tickets, hotels, food, everything. Pretty amazing."

In December of 2000, the young teenager unexpectedly finished second in superpipe at the Breckenridge, Colorado stop of the Vans Triple Crown of Snowboarding title. White won the first two rounds of the contest, losing to Todd Richards, a veteran snowboarder, in the final run. In February of 2001, White took fifth place in the Winter X Games. During other 2000-01 competitions, White continued to finish regularly in the top ten. He often traveled with his parents and two siblings at this stage in his career. Being hyped as the future of snowboarding, White was already becoming a celebrity and landed endorsements. To that end, he lent his image to the development of his video character in the PlayStation game *CoolBoarders4.*

While White's talent was undeniable and he was seen as one of the best in the world by 2002, he was not selected for the U.S. Olympic snowboarding team in 2002. Though he was disappointed because he was so close to making the team, White continued to shine at the highest levels. White won silver in both superpipe and slopestyle at the 2002 Winter X Games. He also competed at the World Snowboarding Championships that year. By this time, he began competing in skateboarding events as well, appearing with the Tony Hawk Gigantic Skateboard tour in 2002. White turned professional as a skateboarder in May of 2003.

That year, White became the first non-motocross athlete to compete in both the Winter X Games and the Summer X Games. He won gold in both slopestyle and half pipe in the Winter X Games of 2003. He also had a decent showing in his first Summer X Games, finishing sixth in vert. White showed that he could pull amazing tricks on the skateboard just as he did on the snowboard. While he was able to land a 720, he did not get high scores from the judges because of the lack of quality in his technical moves. White also needed to improve his grinds and flip tricks. Well-respected skateboarder Bob Burnquist told Kevin Pearson of the Riverside, California *Press Enterprise,* "Shaun has a lot to learn. He is so good and he has his spins down because of his snowboarding background. If he learns some lip tricks and mixes it up, he can win it." White, however, intended to focus on snowboarding for now but wanted to spend more time skateboarding when he could.

By this point in his career, White was still a typical teenager who played videogames, watched movies, slept late, and ate pizza. Yet he landed high-profile sponsorships from Target, PlayStation, Mountain Dew, and Oakley, and was making at least a million dollars per year. While taking independent study classes through Carlsbad High School, White's wealth allowed him to own two homes, an expensive Lexus, and to win ESPY Award for best male action sports athlete. Influenced by skateboarding great and neighbor Tony Hawk, White tried to remain humble and unaffected by the fame. He told Norcross of the *San Diego Union-Tribune,* "When you talk to Tony, he's just like this normal, mellow guy. He's not some untouchable star. That's what I try to pass forward. When I see some little kid too embarrassed to talk to me, I'll say hi to him."

In 2004, White became the youngest snowboarder to win the U.S. Slopestyle Championship and won gold in slopestyle at the Winter X Games. Yet he suffered a setback that year when he injured his right knee during the superpipe competition at the X Games when he landed awkwardly. He underwent arthroscopic knee surgery and tried to compete at the U.S. Open Snowboarding Championships six weeks later, but again hurt the knee. White suffered a deep bone bruise, stopped competing for a time, and impatiently underwent physical therapy for six months. The injury made him appreciate his sport all the more. He told Norcross of the *San Diego Union-Tribune,* "I swear, at that point (when recovering for the second time), I never loved snowboarding more. It just hit me real hard. Before that, I never couldn't snowboard." After he healed, White began skateboarding and competed in the 2004 Summer X Games. That year, he also shot a documentary about himself, *The Shaun White Album.*

White returned to form in 2005, winning gold in slopestyle at the Winter X Games. Firmly entrenched as a star by this point in his career, observers lauded the quality of his victories and fluidity of White's snowboarding moves. John Marshall wrote in the *Hamilton Spectator,* "It's not just that he wins. It's how he does it. While others force tricks, contorting their bodies in different directions to gain an edge, White flows from move to move with a grace that makes it look as though he's not even trying. It's made White the rock star of X, the one fans and athletes love to watch." In addition, White triumphed at the 2005 Summer X Games on the skateboard, winning his first gold in vert.

White's dominance continued for the next few years. From 2005 to 2006, White won all five U.S. Grand Prix Superpipe events, leading up to the Winter Olympics. He also nabbed gold in both slopestyle and halfpipe at the 2006 Winter X Games. A short time later, he was selected for the U.S. Olympic team and traveled to Turino, Italy, to compete in snowboarding events. White unexpectedly fell on his first run in the men's snowboard halfpipe at the Olympics. He explained to Bill Ward of the *Tampa Tribune,* "I was just dropping in [to the halfpipe] and it just hit me, 'Wow, we're at the Olympics' and I've never felt like that before. I was standing up there at the top looking at the crowd—I wasn't even looking at the halfpipe walls—and I was like 'Whoa, gnarly!'" White recovered to make a strong second run to make the finals and easily won gold in the event with an impressive score of 46.8 out of 50.

After the Olympics, White felt somewhat burned out on snowboarding, so he spent more time skateboarding and tried competing in some skateboarding events. That summer, he participated in a few stops on the Dew Tour, finishing last at one event then turning around and winning another. After these events, White decided to take the rest of the year off from competing to recharge. In 2007, White returned to the AST Dew Tour. On his skateboard,

he won the vert event at at least three different stops on the tour. He also won gold in vert at the Summer X Games. White's victories in skateboarding events were surprising considering he spent November through April snowboarding while other skateboarders continued to train. White explained to Ross Siler of the *Salt Lake City Tribune,* "My whole winter season those guys go to the ramps every single day while I'm gone. And it's terrible because I know it in the back of my head."

While White competed in both snowboarding and skate boarding events in 2008, he gained more notoriety for a new video game. He played a big role in the development of the *Shaun White Snowboarding* game created by Ubisoft Montreal. For the game, White performed all his tricks in front of the camera so that his moves could be accurately reproduced. Critics responded positively to the game, with Robert McGinty of the *Florida Times-Union* writing, "It's no frills, just fun and heaps better than that odd selection of Wii games now on shelves, and that makes this game a winner. Just like Shaun White."

By 2009, White was considered one of the most marketable winter sport athletes and earned an estimated eight to ten million dollars per year in endorsements for companies like Hewlett-Packard (HP), Red Bull, Target, and Oakley. He also had his own clothing lines for Burton Snowboards and Target. Jack Burton Carpenter, the owner of Burton snowboards, told David Ebner of the *Globe and Mail,* "He's become a superstar and plays that role better than anybody ever has. Craig [Kelly] was big, Terje [Haakonsen] was huge, but Shaun's on a whole other level. Those guys were never on the cover of *Rolling Stone.*"

In 2010, White again was selected to the U.S. Olympic snowboarding team for the winter games held in Vancouver, British Columbia, Canada. He repeated as the gold medal winner in the halfpipe with ease before his last run. White then used his last run to try and land a Double McTwist. He tried it and landed it, then told Mike Lopresti of *USA Today,* "It took blood, sweat and tears to land it.... It is my friend and my enemy. I always felt like I wanted to put everything on the table. That's what that last run was about … showing everyone in the world on this big stage what I could do." Soon after the Olympics, White began working with Ubisoft on another video game, *Shaun White Skateboarding,* which was expected to be released in time for holiday shopping in 2010. It was White's first skateboarding video game.

After winning his second Olympic gold, White said he might compete in the 2014 Olympics in Sochi, Russia. He explained to Lopresti of *USA Today,* "Being me is a strange thing sometimes. I have fun, I have dreams, I have goals and I'm just now trying to do them." He added that next, he would "Sleep, and then take on the world."

Sources

Books

Marquis Who's Who, Marquis Who's Who, 2010.

Periodicals

Associated Press, February 19, 2010.
ENP Newswire, March 8, 2010.
Florida Times-Union (Jacksonville, FL), January 21, 2009, p. E-3.
Globe and Mail (Canada), February 12, 2009, p. E13.
Hamilton Spectator (Ontario, Canada), February 2, 2005, p. SP10.
New York Magazine, March 15, 2010.
People, March 15, 2010, p. 74.
Press Enterprise (Riverside, CA), August 21, 2003, p. C10.
Salt Lake Tribune, February 13, 2006, p. C1; September 21, 2007.
San Diego Union-Tribune, February 12, 2001, p. D10; January 28, 2002, p. C4; August 15, 2003, p. D1; August 5, 2004, p. D5; January 28, 2005, p. D6.
Tampa Tribune (FL), February 13, 2006, sec. SPORTS, p. 1
Toronto Sun, November 16, 2008, p. E18.
USA Today, February 19, 2010, p. 2D.

—A. Petruso

Robin Wright

Charley Gallay/Getty Images for Chanel

Actress

Born Robin Virginia Gayle Wright, April 8, 1966, in Dallas, TX; daughter of Fred (a pharmaceutical executive) and Gayle (a cosmetics executive; maiden name, Gaston) Wright; married Dane Witherspoon (an actor), 1986 (divorced, 1988); married Sean Penn (an actor), April 27, 1996 (divorced, 2009); children: (from second marriage) Dylan Frances, Hopper Jack.

Addresses: *Agent*—William Morris/Endeavor, 9601 Wilshire Blvd., 3rd Fl., Beverly Hills, CA 90210.

Career

Actress on television, including: *The Yellow Rose*, 1983; *Home* (movie), 1987; *Santa Barbara*, NBC, 1984-89; *Empire Falls*, 2005. Film appearances include: *Hollywood Vice Squad*, 1986; *The Princess Bride*, 1987; *Denial*, 1990; *State of Grace*, 1990; *The Playboys*, 1992; *Toys*, 1992; *Forrest Gump*, 1994; *The Crossing Guard*, 1995; *Loved*, 1996; *Moll Flanders*, 1996; *She's So Lovely*, 1997; *Hurlyburly*, 1998; *Message in a Bottle*, 1999; *How to Kill Your Neighbor's Dog*, 2000; *Unbreakable*, 2000; *The Pledge*, 2001; *The Last Castle*, 2001; *Searching for Debra Winger*, 2002; *White Oleander*, 2002; *The Singing Detective*, 2003; *Virgin*, 2003; *A Home at the End of the World*, 2004; *Max*, 2005; *Nine Lives*, 2005; *Sorry, Haters*, 2005; *Breaking and Entering*, 2006; *Room 10*, 2006; *Hounddog*, 2007; *Beowulf*, 2007; *What Just Happened*, 2008; *New York, I Love You*, 2008; *A Christmas Carol*, 2009; *The Private Lives of Pippa Lee*, 2009; *State of Play*, 2009; *The Conspirator*, 2010. Also appeared on Broadway in *Talley's Folly*, 2010.

Sidelights

Though often cited by film directors as one of Hollywood's most under-utilized talents, Robin Wright has built up a small but critically acclaimed body of work on the big screen. She was the fluffy blonde heroine of the 1987 fantasy fairy-tale *The Princess Bride*, then played *Forrest Gump*'s unrequited love in the 1994 box-office hit. Some of her professional life has been subsumed by the personal: she has two children by actor-director Sean Penn, with whom she had a two-decade relationship. The couple divorced in 2009 following years of tabloid rumors that theirs was one of Hollywood's most tempestuous marital unions. "I've always been an elusive person," Wright admitted to London *Sunday Times* writer Ryan Gilbey. "Maybe because it's the only way to keep yourself sacred. If you blow yourself out on too many movies and magazine covers, you just get chewed up and spat out."

Wright was born in Dallas, Texas, in 1966, as the second of Gayle and Fred Wright's two children. Her father worked in the pharmaceutical industry, but the couple's marriage did not last, and Gayle moved with her young son and daughter to California, where they initially settled in Woodland Hills in the San Fernando Valley suburbs of Los Angeles. Gayle remarried and enjoyed a flourishing career as a sales agent for Mary Kay Cosmetics, a multilevel marketing organization whose tiers she scaled to reach the coveted top-producers' rank, which came with the emblematic custom-pink Cadillac. Wright's mother was also a house flipper, buying properties and renovating them, which enabled the family to eventually settle in the posh San Diego-area enclave of La Jolla.

At the age of 14, a Wright was roller-skating when a talent agent spotted her. That led to some modeling work and a few auditions. She made her television debut in 1983 in two episodes of *The Yellow Rose,* a nighttime soap on NBC that was essentially a knockoff of the popular *Dallas* drama on the rival CBS network, but the series was cancelled after one season. After graduating from high school—where she was elected homecoming queen—Wright traveled through Europe and alighted in Paris to try her luck modeling there. It was a difficult time for an already rootless young woman, and Wright found herself overwhelmed by the modeling business. "I'd hear the most awful things," she told Gilbey in the *Sunday Times* interview, recalling remarks about her physique. "There's no respect for you as a human being. You're a commodity."

Back in California, Wright returned to auditioning for roles. She had already decided to step off that career path and was working as a waitress in Hawaii when she learned she had won a part on *Santa Barbara,* a new daytime drama on NBC that debuted in July of 1984. She was cast as Kelly Capwell, a typical soap-opera heroine upon whom calamity after calamity is visited. The hour-long series was noted for its lush production values and Wright's Capwell, the quintessential long-legged California blonde, was one of the show's most popular characters. She spent four years on *Santa Barbara* and was nominated for three Daytime Emmy Awards as Best Ingénue.

Wright made her feature film debut in a dark exploitation drama called *Hollywood Vice Squad.* She starred in the 1986 movie, which was directed by Penelope Spheeris, as a runaway who becomes involved in the pornography industry. The storyline was almost directly lifted from a 1979 movie called *Hardcore,* which starred George C. Scott. Scott's real-life wife, Trish Van Devere, co-starred with Wright in the later film as the mother who searches for her missing daughter among some of the more debauched corners of Southern California.

Wright's major break came when director Rob Reiner cast her in the title role of a planned big-budget fairy tale, *The Princess Bride.* The 1987 movie

also starred handsome Cary Elwes as Westley, the stable boy Princess Buttercup loves, along with impish Wallace Shawn and wrestler Andre the Giant. It was a highly coveted role for a young female actor among a seasoned cast, and dozens of ingénues had not made the cut. Wright recalled being so nervous before her first meeting with Reiner that she meditated for 15 minutes in her car before she went inside. "On the walk up to the house I stuffed Kleenex in my pockets to help my sweaty hands," she told *People*'s Margot Dougherty.

The Princess Bride did not garner much critical acclaim, but went on to achieve cult-film status. Nevertheless, Wright was pegged as an up-and-comer in Hollywood, and landed another coveted role in a 1990 crime drama, *State of Grace.* The film starred Sean Penn—who had recently emerged from his highly publicized marriage to the pop singer Madonna—as a police informant who infiltrates his former New York City gang outfit. Again, it was an all-star cast, with Gary Oldman, Ed Harris, Burgess Meredith, and John Turturro; Wright played the sister of the malevolent brotherly duo who head up the Irish-American criminal outfit. Penn's character becomes romantically involved with her, and the film helped make him a bona-fide star after a few embarrassing years of being tagged "Mr. Madonna."

Wright had recently exited her own marriage to actor Dane Witherspoon, who had appeared on *Santa Barbara* with her, and she and Penn's on-screen romance spilled over into real life. In 1991, the couple's daughter, Dylan Frances, was born, followed by a son they named Hopper Jack two years later in honor of Penn's close friends, actors Dennis Hopper and Jack Nicholson. Wright put her career on hold, turning down meaty roles in *Jurassic Park, The Firm,* and *Batman Forever.* Finally, in 1994 she returned to the screen in *Forrest Gump,* the top-grossing movie of the year and based on the 1986 novel by Winston Groom. Tom Hanks played the title role, cast as a young man, possibly developmentally challenged, who falls in love with the sad little girl next door. Forrest grows up to serve in Vietnam and finds himself in the midst of pivotal events in mid-twentieth century U.S. history—a plot device filmmakers exploited via clever special-effects tricks. Reviewing it for *Time,* Richard Corliss called *Forrest Gump* "a smart, affecting, easygoing fable with plenty of talent on both sides of the camera.... Wright's Jenny is a frail soul in tailspin, a battered child in a beautiful woman's body. And Forrest is her redeemer. The suspense of the movie is whether she will allow him to save her."

Wright appeared opposite Nicholson in 1995's *The Crossing Guard,* directed by Penn. She earned critical accolades, but the couple broke up not long after its release. Penn was then nominated for an Academy Award for his role in the death-row drama *Dead Man Walking,* but as the Oscar ceremony neared, Wright was rushed into surgery for an emergency gallbladder issue. Penn was a no-show at the awards that night after having rushed to her side, and he and Wright married three months later.

In the interim, Wright had made *Moll Flanders,* another literary adaptation. She played the titular heroine, a seventeenth-century orphan who rises to great heights through her combination of beauty and cunning. The sweeping saga received little attention, hitting theaters during the summer blockbuster season of *Mission Impossible* and *Twister.*

Critics gave Wright a second look in 1997 with *She's So Lovely,* a moody drama from the pen of acclaimed writer-director John Cassavetes, who had died several years earlier; Cassavetes' son Nick directed the long-anticipated project. Wright played Maureen, who has a tempestuous and long-running romance with Eddie, played by Penn. Eddie is mentally unstable, and both are carousers; he disappears for a few days, and she dallies with a neighbor—James Gandolfini, later to become famous as HBO's Tony Soprano—whom Eddie then attacks. Eddie spends several years in a psychiatric-care facility, then returns to steal Maureen away from her husband, played by John Travolta. "One of the few things that makes *She's So Lovely* worth seeing is the way Robin and Sean look at each other on screen," asserted Stuart Jeffries in the *Guardian.* "There's hungry desire there." Most critics, however, were baffled by the dark story, which was nevertheless a classic Cassavetes movie. Such wrenching, realistic domestic dramas had once brought audiences into theaters, but that era was a quarter-century before.

Wright decided to try a more conventional screen role, this time opposite Kevin Costner in the 1999 romance *Message in a Bottle.* A fairly standard Hollywood tearjerker, the story centered around her character, a Chicago divorcee, who finds a letter in a bottle on a Cape Cod beach. Her newspaper boss encourages her to track down the story, which leads her to Costner's character, a lonely North Carolina widower and sailboat builder, and to a tentative romance. "Wright Penn conveys a sense of fierce self-reliance and toughness that works against the viewer's ability to get under her skin and feel her vulnerability, pain and giddy hope," declared *Variety*'s Todd McCarthy.

Wright went on to appear in the 2000 M. Night Shyamalan blockbuster *Unbreakable* as the wife of Bruce Willis' character, and then in *The Pledge* a year later, this one directed by her husband. She earned good reviews for another so-called "chick flick," 2002's *White Oleander,* then appeared with Robert Downey Jr. in *The Singing Detective* and Irish action star Colin Farrell in *A Home at the End of the World* in 2003 and 2004, respectively. She starred in one of director Anthony Minghella's final works, *Breaking and Entering,* with Jude Law as part of another dysfunctional film household.

Wright's own household had been beset by various woes in the years since she teamed up with Penn: in 1993, a brushfire claimed their Malibu house, destroying nearly everything. In May of 1996 she was carjacked in her own driveway in Santa Monica, with two teens demanding her Toyota Land Cruiser; she managed to convince them to let her remove her son and daughter, ages five and seven, first. "It was totally terrifying," she told Josephine Fairley, a journalist with the Melbourne *Sunday Herald Sun.* "Something like that turns your life around. We'd been talking about moving to San Francisco for five years—and that clinched it." The couple moved to a remote area of Marin County that is also home to Grateful Dead co-founder Phil Lesh and rocker Huey Lewis.

Despite the change of scenery, Wright's marriage to Penn was often rumored to be in its final death throes. Between 2007 and 2009 the couple filed for divorce three times, but finally formally divorced at the end of 2009. That same year, Wright returned to the screen for her first starring role in five years in *The Private Lives of Pippa Lee,* an adaptation of a novel by Rebecca Miller. Wright played the title character, whose dramatic life story is told through flashbacks in which *Gossip Girl* star Blake Lively played the teenaged Pippa. Pippa runs away from home at the age of 16 and leads a somewhat debauched Manhattan life before marrying a much older man, a literary-world celebrity played by Alan Arkin. The movie follows Pippa's fears, after a move to the suburbs with her now 80-year-old husband, that she is having a nervous breakdown. Once again, the critics were not very enthusiastic, but most faulted the meandering material, not Wright's talents on screen. "Pippa," remarked *Village Voice* writer Melissa Anderson, "played by Wright Penn in near-permanent Stepford Wife mode, isn't much more than a vehicle for false epiphanies and forced rapprochements—a plastic protagonist with all the nuances of any given character found in the midday-programming slot of WE TV."

Wright's post-divorce filmography included some high-profile projects: in 2010, she appeared in *The Conspirator,* a Robert Redford movie about the plotters behind the assassination of Abraham Lincoln, and she was scheduled to make her first screen appearance with Brad Pitt in *Moneyball,* an adaptation of Michael Lewis' best-selling nonfiction book about baseball's Oakland A's, in 2011. She also jumped the hurdle to live performance with an appearance in a revival of Lanford Wilson's Pulitzer Prize-winning play *Talley's Folly* at the end of the 2010-11 Broadway season. "I feel like I'm just beginning," Wright told *Vogue*'s John Powers back in 2006. "The kids are grown, and I feel like I'm ready. I turned 40, and at that age you get over the petty fears that are ultimately just self-absorption."

Sources

Guardian (London, England), November 6, 1998, p. 10.

People, October 12, 1987, p. 64; January 25, 1999, p. 107.

Sunday Herald Sun (Melbourne, Australia), January 10, 1999, p. 12.

Sunday Times (London, England), July 5, 2009, p. 8.

Time, August 1, 1994, p. 52.

Variety, February 8, 1999, p. 74.

Village Voice, November 24, 2009.

Vogue, September 2006, p. 515.

W, October 2000, p. 130.

—*Carol Brennan*

Viktor Yanukovych

Bloomberg via Getty Images

President of Ukraine

Born Viktor Fedorovych Yanukovych, July 9, 1950, in Makiivka, Donetsk Oblast, Ukraine; son of Fedor (a machinist) and Olga (a nurse) Yanukovych; married Lyudmyla Oleksandrivna; children: Oleksandr, Viktor. *Education:* Attended Donetsk Polytechnic Institute after 1974; Ukrainian Academy of Foreign Trade, correspondence degree in mechanical engineering, 1980; degree in international law, 2001.

Addresses: *Office*—Office of the President, 11 Bankova str., Kiev 01220, Ukraine.

Career

Worked as an electrician and mechanic, c. 1973-75; head of the motor-transport pool for Ordzhonikidze Coal, mid-1970s; Yenakiieve transportation authority, chief manager after 1980; also with Donbasstransremont, Ukrugolpromtrans, and Donetskavtotrans; Donetsk Oblast Administration, vice head, 1996-97; Donetsk Oblast governor, 1997-2002; prime minister of Ukraine, 2002-04; elected to Verkhovna Rada, 2006, 2007; head of the Party of Regions until 2010; elected president, 2010—.

Sidelights

Ukrainian president Viktor Yanukovych made one of the most surprising political comebacks in the post-Soviet world after effigies of him were burned by protesters during the 2004-05 Orange Revolution. In the dramatic events of those weeks, Yanukovych was finally forced to concede the presidential election to the clear winner and his archrival, Viktor Yushchenko. Writing in the *New York Times* on the eve of Yanukovych's 2010 victory to oust the incumbent, Clifford J. Levy described him as a politician once "derided as a barrel-chested party boss and Kremlin stooge," but one whose political resurrection "has capitalized on the nation's deep disillusionment with a limp economy and the Orange leaders, who promised to modernize the country and move it away from Moscow."

Yanukovych was born on July 9, 1950, in Makiivka, Ukraine. At the time, this was the Ukrainian Soviet Socialist Republic and was part of the Soviet Union, the world's first communist state. The fertile Ukraine, on the far eastern edge of Europe, had traditionally served as a buffer state between Europe and the autocratic empires of the East. Ukraine had a longstanding enmity with its larger, more powerful neighbor, and usually resisted Russia's attempts to subjugate its people, lands, and rich natural resources. In the 1920s and '30s, when Ukrainian farmers stubbornly refused to abide by Soviet land-collectivization decrees, the country experienced widespread famine.

Yanukovych's mother was a nurse of Ukrainian origin who died when he was two. His father, Fedor, worked as a machinist and shared quarters with his own mother, who raised Yanukovych. Andrew Wilson, who wrote the definitive book on the 2004-05 political crisis, *Ukraine's Orange Revolution,* described Yanukovych's childhood home as "no more than a wooden barracks," and quoted from one interview that Yanukovych gave in which he said, "I came from a very poor family and my main dream in life was to break out of this poverty." As a teen, Yanukovych fell in with a local gang and began committing burglaries and holdups. This was actually a political crime of sorts, because the goals of the 1917 Revolution were to eliminate iniquities in society, thereby eliminating the need for property crime. In 1967 he was arrested, tried, and convicted. A general amnesty shortened his three-year prison sentence, but he was arrested again in 1970 for armed robbery. Yanukovych's political rivals have claimed that the array of criminal charges against him may have included sexual assault and manslaughter.

Over the course of his political career periodic rumors have surfaced that Yanukovych was possibly recruited to work for the KGB, the Soviet secret police, either while in prison or after his release in 1972 or 1973. His political enemies have made such claims because of the unusual expunging of his criminal record a few years after his release, when he sought to join the Communist Party. By this point Yanukovych had made a concerted effort to reform, working as a lowly mechanic and then electrician while completing his education at the Donetsk Polytechnic Institute. Any ties to the KGB were unproven, and in his book Wilson instead attributes the trajectory of Yanukovych's post-prison career to the patronage of politician Georgii Beregovoi, a former Soviet cosmonaut and major Ukrainian hero of the era. Beregovoi appears to have interceded with authorities on Yanukovych's behalf in a 1978 bid to have a court expunge his criminal record. The two prison sentences were an obstacle to Yanukovych's application to join the Communist Party, a necessary step for a professional career of any merit in the Soviet era.

Yanukovych hailed from the heavily industrialized province of Donetsk Oblast in the eastern part of Ukraine. He worked for the state-run Ordzhonikidze Coal concern in the mid-1970s, earned a degree in mechanical engineering, and was hired as chief manager of the transportation authority in Yenakiieve, a coal-mining town also in Donetsk in 1980, the same year he was accepted for membership in the Communist Party. Over the next decade, as Soviet leader Mikhail Gorbachev came to power and ushered in a new era of sweeping reforms, the eastern Ukrainian mining regions continued to prosper with the help of subsidies from Moscow. Once the Soviet Union fell apart and Ukraine became an independent nation in 1991, the region was thrown into economic turmoil. This "Donbas," or Donets River basin, abuts Russia and during the Soviet era the Russian language was predominant. Yanukovych grew up speaking Russian, fully mastering Ukrainian only years later after rivals mocked his grammatical errors. As a politician, Yanukovych would draw much of his support from this gritty, industrial swath of Ukraine.

In the summer of 1996, just as Ukraine was about to celebrate the five-year anniversary of its independence, Yanukovych was named vice head of the Donetsk Oblast administration. A year later, he was appointed governor of Donetsk Oblast. He became active in a newly formed political party, the Party of Regional Revival of Ukraine, created to represent Russian-speaking Ukrainians in the Verkhovna Rada, or Ukrainian Parliament, in the capital of Kiev. The party struggled in its first few years, but reorganized as the Party of Regions in 2001 and gained strength after allying with Ukrainian president Leonid Kuchma, once a high-ranking member of the Ukrainian branch of the Communist Party. Kuchma had been elected president in 1994 with widespread popular support, but there were calls for him to step down as evidence of broad political corruption began to tarnish Ukraine's reputation on the global economic front.

Yanukovych's name was attached to Kuchma's most distasteful political scandal in 2000, when transcripts of secret recordings of Kuchma's telephone conversations were made public. In one, Kuchma discusses a Donetsk region judge with Yanukovych, then the Donetsk Oblast governor. The judge had made an unfavorable ruling in a libel case involving Kuchma and a political opponent, and Kuchma suggests the judge should be tortured. In November of 2002, Kuchma appointed Yanukovych to serve as prime minister. He spent two years on the job, a tenure notable because of a specific incident of corruption, when the state sold a major steel plant to a private investor named Rinat Akhmetov and others, including Kuchma's son-in-law. The plant was acquired for $811 million, though a foreign investor had offered nearly twice that.

These and scores of other incidents—including the mysterious death of prominent journalist Georgiy Gongadze, a vocal critic of Kuchma who was kidnapped and beheaded—galvanized opposition to Kuchma. A new political force emerged, headed by a young, handsome economist named Viktor Yushchenko. Yushchenko had served as head of the National Bank of Ukraine and even a stint as prime minister before Yanukovych's term in office. In 2002,

Yushchenko's new multiparty alliance, Blok Nasha Ukrayina, or Our Ukraine Bloc, gained a majority of seats in the Rada. Yushchenko became the Bloc's presidential candidate in the run-up to the 2004 election, facing off against Yanukovych, the Party of Regions choice.

Yanukovych's candidacy had the support of both Kuchma and Russia's president, Vladimir Putin, who visited Ukraine before first round of voting on October 31. The presidential race had already gained widespread international attention because of Viktor Yushchenko's sudden appearance in public—after disappearing for a few days for medical treatment—with his face scarred by dark cysts. Yushchenko reported that on September 5, he had dined with the Security Service of Ukraine, or S.B.U., and fell grievously ill soon afterward. Toxicology reports linked it to dioxin, a potentially lethal poison that is a byproduct of pesticide manufacturing. Medical experts believed Yushchenko had not died from it because he had vomited later that night, but his face remained disfigured and he endured intense back pain on the campaign trail.

Ukraine's constitution mandates that a presidential candidate must win at least 50 percent of the vote to win the election. If no single candidate achieves that, then a runoff election is to be held between the two candidates with the greatest number of votes. The results of the first round of voting on October 31 were extremely close, with Yanukovych behind Yushchenko by about 179,000 votes. Neither squeaked past 40 percent of the vote, however, which necessitated a runoff. That took place on November 21, and turnout was noticeably higher at the polls. It was on this election day that Yanukovych's detractors claimed that vote rigging and vote fraud had taken place; however, the Central Election Commission announced that Yanukovych had won with 49 percent of the vote versus Yushchenko's 46 percent—a decision that prompted widespread protests.

Yushchenko and another popular politician, Yulia Tymoshenko, led the opposition and spoke before massive crowds that gathered in Kiev's Independence Square near government buildings as November turned to December. Yanukovych was cast as the villain of the Orange Revolution—named after Yushchenko's Our Ukraine signature campaign color—and the country was paralyzed for weeks. In a surprise move, the Supreme Court of Ukraine overturned the results of the November 21 runoff and scheduled a new one for December 26. In that contest, Yushchenko beat Yanukovych by a clear majority of almost three million votes, and Yanukovych finally resigned as prime minister. Yushchenko was inaugurated on January 23, 2005, with Tymoshenko becoming his prime minister.

Yanukovych became head of the opposition in the Rada. Though there had been high hopes after the initial excitement of the Orange Revolution, Yushchenko and Tymoshenko disagreed on several key matters, and had difficulty governing effectively. Yanukovych, meanwhile, sought increased support from Akhmetov, Ukraine's richest tycoon, who was thought to have paid for an American political consultant named Paul J. Manafort to revive Yanukovych's career. Manafort had previously worked with former U.S. Senator Bob Dole, who tried unsuccessfully to oust President Bill Clinton from the White House in the 1996 presidential election. Manafort's consulting firm had also been involved in campaigns for Arizona Senator John McCain. With Manafort's help, Yanukovych made an effective comeback, positioning himself and his party as an alternative to the status quo. "The country is going from crisis to crisis," he told London *Sunday Times* journalist Mark Franchetti. "People look back now and see that under my leadership things were much better than they are now."

In Verkhovna Rada elections held in March of 2006, Yanukovych's Party of Regions won 186 of the 450 seats, giving it a 32 percent majority. As party leader, Yanukovych should have been appointed as prime minister, but Yushchenko stalled. When members of the Rada's Tymoshenko and Our Ukraine Blocs attempted to disrupt the formal procedure to confirm Yanukovych as prime minister, the august Kiev chamber was the site of a brawl between lawmakers. Finally, on August 4, 2006, Yushchenko asked Yanukovych to form a government.

Ukrainian political dramas are seemingly unending. The squabbling and skullduggery between widely disparate factions means that little change can be affected at the legislative level. An exasperated Yushchenko dissolved parliament in March of 2007, and Yanukovych's supporters defied the dissolution order for weeks. In new parliamentary elections held in September of 2007, Yanukovych's Party of Regions lost 11 seats, and he resigned as prime minister on December 18. Tymoshenko succeeded him and lasted on the job until March of 2010.

Presidential elections are held in Ukraine every five years. Yanukovych was again the Party of Regions candidate, and Tymoshenko his closest challenger; the now nearly discredited Yushchenko was also on the ballot as an independent. Pre-election public-opinion polls heavily favored Yanukovych as the winner. In the most notorious incident from an otherwise smoothly conducted campaign and election, Yanukovych refused to debate Tymoshenko live in a scheduled television event, which prompted her to call him a coward. "I'm told it's useless and wrong to argue with a woman," Yanukovych said, according to *Time International*'s Kiev correspondent, James Marson. "And if she is a woman, she should go to the kitchen."

In preliminary voting on January 17, 2010, Yanukovych won with 35 percent of the vote, ten points ahead of Tymoshenko. In the February 7 runoff, he won with 48 percent against her 45 percent. He was inaugurated as Ukraine's fourth president on February 25, 2010. While international observers commended the nation—not yet past the two-decade mark as an independent, democratic state—for switching political moods so dramatically between the 2004 and 2010 presidential contests, Yanukovych viewed his political comeback as preordained. "The orange revolution has long been over," he told Franchetti, the *Sunday Times* journalist, back in 2006. "It was a populist coup staged by people who made a lot of empty promises and brought Ukraine to the brink of catastrophe."

Sources

Books

Wilson, Andrew, *Ukraine's Orange Revolution*, Yale University Press, 2005, pp. 7-8.

Periodicals

New York Times, February 7, 2001; January 17, 2006; September 30, 2007; January 15, 2010.
Sunday Times (London, England), March 12, 2006, p. 26.
Time International, February 15, 2010, p. 26.

—*Carol Brennan*

Gerard Yosca

Evan Agostini/Getty Images

Jewelry designer

Born c. 1955; married Susan; children: Gabby.

Addresses: *Studio*—Gerard Yosca Jewelry, 256 West 38th St., 8th Fl., New York, NY 10018. *Web site*—http://www.yosca.com.

Career

Primary designer and owner of Yosca Jewelry, Inc., 1983—.

Sidelights

Gerard Yosca is a fashion designer who has worked in the fashion world tirelessly for more than 27 years. His primary focus is on jewelry designs and accessories. His work is constantly changing, bold, and experimental. Over the years his jewelry designs have been described as being lavish, earthy, and baroque. The Web site Charm and Chain described his work as "inspiring an infectious sense of whimsy that won the jewelry world over." Mattie Roberts, writing as a special contributor to *Dallas Morning News,* quoted Yosca as saying, "The only faux pas with jewelry is not wearing any."

Yosca originally trained to be a fine arts painter, but started Gerard Yosca Jewelry, Inc. in 1983. Yosca Jewelry, Inc. was a family business. His wife, Susan, joined him in the business three years later when the two of them married and they have run the company together ever since. He has described their re-

lationship as one where they have very clearly defined roles and they do not bring their work home with them. He is the primary designer and, while Susan at times has helped with the designs, she is very good at the business side of the company. Yosca has described times when their daughter, Gabby, has also helped in the business, doing small tasks such as rearranging displays. Yosca told Roberts, "We do run the business like a family. Everyone is respected. I take it as an honor that I provide for the families of the people who work for me."

Yosca is considered a fashion icon and he creates the prototypes for all of his designs. He saw it as part of his occupation to continually develop a "look" and to constantly be innovating. Within his business, he put his own hands to the materials and used all the tools of his trade—blow torch, file, and saw. He and his wife had many lean years where he did not have the luxury of drawing up his designs and sending them off to a model maker so he learned to craft the models himself. In his interview with Roberts, Yosca called those years "the pasta years." Yosca employs approximately 20 people and a crew of freelance artists who recreated all of his designs meticulously by hand. Yosca Jewelry, Inc. is renowned for its level of craftsmanship.

Yosca believed that a designer was only the sum of their experience and that instant success for a designer was not always a good thing. A designer needs time to build their business and get a sense of their own personal vision, otherwise their product may not have longevity. Yosca told Roberts, "We are craftsmen, and it's important for young designers to remember that. It can take years to develop a look. After 25 years' designing, I'm still refining my look." But Yosca has enjoyed moments where success propelled his business forward.

A frenzy over one of Yosca's designs occurred when the magazine *InStyle* featured one of his barrettes in its beauty best buys section in the March 1998 edition. The phone began to ring nonstop. Edward St. George, hairstylist for the popular program *Friends*, told Michelle Leder of *Crain's New York Business* that he was using the barrettes on the actresses "in almost every episode. There's nothing else like this out there." A store owner in Montana called Ms. Yosca to tell her that the actress Demi Moore had come into her store and purchased 24 of the barrettes. Leder quoted a spokeswoman for *InStyle* as saying, "People see something on a celebrity, and they buy it because it makes them feel like stars themselves." Yosca told Leder, "It's almost like we've become Beanie Babies for adults." The popularity of the butterfly barrettes doubled the company's sales that year to more than $2 million. Yosca has been credited with being an innovator who created a unique design in the butterfly barrette design as well.

Yosca was very much an innovator and drew inspiration for his designs from the world around him. Sometimes he got ideas from flea markets in New York where his studio was located and incorporated elements from vintage jewelry or enameled pots. He also has a keen sense of color and is credited with bringing back the use of vibrantly colored enamel jewelry to the fashion world. He produced five lines per year and his designs have incorporated semi-precious stones, metal, enamel, feathers, and wood. His designs are so unique that he has had to fight to maintain control of them. In 1990 a company called Bijoux Terner USA attempted to manufacture and sell earrings based on one of his designs and Yosca Jewelry, Inc. won an injunction against them to prohibit them from manufacturing the earrings.

Yosca has worked to make accessories more of a focus on fashion runways and to elevate the status of fashion accessories in general. Toward this aim, he was an emeritus board member on the Council of Fashion Designers of America. He has stated that he believes that there really is no limit to how much jewelry and accessories that a person could wear. He recommends that no one wear one designer from head to foot and that if they are wearing a particular outfit from a designer they should break it up with elements from someone else's work. Yosca said to Roberts that, when a person is composing an outfit and choosing accessories, they "need one thing that's just a little weird, a little off." Holly Haber, writing for *WWD*, quoted Yosca as saying, "By mixing things around, you amplify.... It's wearing the wrong thing or putting things together that just wouldn't go.... When you wear something unexpected, it looks young.... [I]t's charming." He believes that a person should only wear things they think are fabulous and they should let their personality shine through in whatever they wear.

Sources

Periodicals

Crain's New York Business, September 14, 1998, p. 12.
Dallas Morning News, February 2, 2005.
WWD, May 5, 1989, p. 6; March 23, 1990, p. 7; March 7, 2005, p. 19; March 17, 2005, p. 100S.

Online

"Gerard Yosca," Charm and Chain, http://www.charmandchain.com/pages/gerard-yosca (May 16, 2010).
Gerard Yosca Studio, http://www.yosca.com/ (May 16, 2010).

—*Annette Bowman*

Obituaries

Francisco Ayala

Born Francisco de Paula Ayala Garciá-Duarte, March 16, 1906, in Granada, Spain; died November 3, 2009, in Madrid, Spain. Novelist and literary scholar. Francisco Ayala, a novelist, scholar, critic, and sociologist, was considered one of the most distinguished intellectuals of twentieth-century Spain. The last survivor of the group of Spanish poets, artists, and writers known as the "Generation of '27," he was the author of more than 50 novels and short story collections, in addition to his essays on films and his scholarly work in sociology.

Because he fought for the Republic in the Spanish Civil War, he lived much of his life in exile, not returning to Spain until after dictator Francisco Franco died. Much of his work is related to the themes of abuses of power, and critics saw some of his stories as criticisms of Franco's government. His style tended toward realism and often dealt with Ayala's lack of faith in human nature. Near the end of his life, he said, as quoted in the London *Times,* "it's the same barbarity that beats a child to death as drops bombs on hundreds of people or cities. War can be repeated indefinitely; human beings haven't essentially changed."

Born in 1906 in Granada, Spain, Ayala began writing at an early age. At 14, he moved to Madrid with his family, and only five years later, his first novel, *Tragicomedia de un hombre sin espíritu* (Tragicomedy of a man without spirit), was published. As an undergraduate at Madrid University, he became a critic for *Revista de occidente* (The western review), a modernist journal started by philosopher José Ortega y Gasset that criticized Spain's conservative literary culture. Ayala graduated with a degree in law in 1929, after which he spent time studying sociology and philosophy in Berlin. He married Chilean Etelvina Silva Vargas, whom he met in Berlin, in 1931. In 1932, he received his doctorate from and took a position lecturing in law at Complutense University in Madrid. His writings focused on his scholarly pursuits for the next several years.

In 1936, the Spanish Civil War broke out. Ayala had been lecturing in Argentina, but he returned home to fight for the Republican government. Ayala's father and brother were jailed and executed by Franco's Nationalists. Ayala continued to work for the Republicans, serving in several high-level positions, including becoming the diplomatic envoy to Czechoslovakia. In 1939 the Republican government fell to Franco's forces and Ayala went into exile. He returned to Argentina, where he taught at Universidad de la Plata. While there, he founded the literary magazine *Realidad* (Reality), which published writers such as Jorge Luis Borges and Julio Cortázar.

Ayala became a citizen of Argentina and continued to write fiction and scholarly works. His short story collection *Los usurpadores* (published in English as *The Usurpers*), was published in 1949 and is one of his best-known works. The collection features some of his most famous stories, including the Kafkaesque tale "The Bewitched," in which a man petitions for the help of a king only to discover that the king is mentally unfit to rule and physically incapable. The man realizes that no help will ever come. The same collection includes a story of a rabbi who converts to Catholicism, and is so fanatic about his new faith that when his daughter is arrested for criticizing his work, he denies her. Another short story collection, *La cabeza del cordero* (The lamb's head"), was published the same year.

In 1950 Ayala moved to Puerto Rico where he founded a cultural magazine, *La Torre.* While there, he published a sociology textbook, *Introducción a las ciencias sociales* (Introduction to the social sciences), which became his first work to be published in

Spain under Franco's regime. In 1955 he moved to the United States where he spent the next 20 years teaching at various universities including Princeton, Rutgers, New York University, Bryn Mawr College, Brooklyn College, City University of New York, and University of Chicago, where he taught Spanish literature. Despite his long stay in the United States, few of his novels published during this time are available in English translation.

Franco died in 1975 and the dictatorship of Spain collapsed, allowing Ayala to return home. The years that followed brought Ayala recognition from the literary establishment for his work. He was often expected to be a contender for the Nobel Prize. Though he never received that honor, he was awarded the Miguel de Cervantes literary prize, the Spanish-language equivalent of the Nobel. He was elected to the Spanish Royal Language Academy and won the Prince of Asturias Prize for Letters.

Ayala's first wife died in 1990, and in 1999 he married Carolyn Richmond, who was the English-language translator of *The Usurpers*. In 2006, when Ayala turned 100, he was invited to dinner with King Juan Carlos and Queen Sofia of Spain. Though the year was full of seminars and conferences at which Ayala was acknowledged, the author knew his life was ending. He was, by turns, appreciative and tired. "It's not often someone witnesses a century of life, and especially with a conscience more or less alert," he was quoted as having said in the *New York Times*. "This is a privilege nature has bestowed on me." The London *Times* quoted one of Ayala's more somber statements: "I have lived too long and intensely and written too much."

Though he remained mentally alert until the end of his life, even updating his Facebook page, he never fully recovered from a bout of bronchitis, and died at his home in Madrid on November 3, 2009, at the age of 103. He is survived by his second wife, his daughter by his first marriage, a grandchild, and three great-grandchildren. **Sources:** *Los Angeles Times,* November 17, 2009; *New York Times,* November 5, 2009; *Times* (London), November 13, 2009; *Washington Post,* November 4, 2009.

—*Alana Joli Abbott*

Gene Barry

Born Eugene Klass, June 14, 1919, in New York, NY; died of congestive heart failure, December 9, 2009, in Woodland Hills, CA. Actor. A many-decades veteran of television, the silver screen, and the theater, Gene Barry's diverse roles ran the gamut from the dapper cowboy Bat Masterson and millionaire crime fighter of *Burke's Law* to the homosexual club owner Georges in *La Cage aux Folles* and the scientist Clayton Forrester in *The War of the Worlds*. Barry's versatility made him a believable, compelling, and beloved character no matter the medium or the genre.

Born Eugene Klass in New York in 1919, he would later change his name to the more show biz-friendly version for which he became known and remembered: Gene as a nickname for Eugene, and Barry as homage to the celebrated actor John Barrymore. Barry grew up in Brooklyn with his siblings and parents, jeweler Martin Klass and his wife, Eva, and attended the New Utrecht High School. Possessed of a musical ability from his youth, Barry played violin and sang; he won a singing contest that earned him both a scholarship to the Chatham School of Music and a position as a singer on the New York radio station WHN.

The singing ability would eventually lead Barry to the stage, where he would debut in the musical *Pins and Needles* before first appearing on Broadway in 1942 in *Rosalinda*. He would go on to perform several roles, both musical and non-musical, in stage productions, including opposite Mae West in the 1944 production of *Catherine Was Great*, before switching to straight Hollywood acting as a contract actor for Paramount in 1951.

Barry's big screen break came in 1953, with H. G. Wells' science fiction classic *The War of the Worlds*. Although it would remain his best-known role, it was hardly Barry's favorite. According to the *Washington Post*, Barry described this role as "just acting to special effects all over the place. We never knew where we were in that." Films such as *Soldier of Fortune*, in 1955, *China Gate* in 1957, and *Thunder Road* in 1958 followed.

His first major television role would be the title character of *Bat Masterson*, a job he nearly turned down because he did not want to be typecast and dismissed as just another television cowboy. However, once he learned that Masterson dressed as a dandy, complete with a derby hat, tailed coat, and gold-tipped cane, he was hooked. *Bat Masterson* ran from 1958 to 1961 and made Barry a natural choice for famed producer Aaron Spelling's first venture, *Burke's Law*. Again in the title role, Barry played the millionaire womanizer and Los Angeles chief of detectives who arrived at crime scenes in a chauffeured Rolls-Royce.

After Barry's run as Burke ended in 1966, a variety of television roles followed throughout the '60s, '70s, and '80s, including *The Name of the Game* from 1968-1971 and *The Adventurer* from 1972-1973, as well as appearances in *The Twilight Zone, The Love Boat, Fantasy Island,* and *Murder, She Wrote.* Barry also did voice-over commercial work for such companies as Miller beer and Haggar clothing. For a time, Barry was concerned about being typecast as the debonair leading man, telling the *Washington Post* he would ask his agent, "'Can't you get me a part of a vulnerable human being?' I was operating on 20 percent of the spectrum."

Although he was a winner of a Critic's Circle Award for the stage production of *Idiot's Delight* and is perhaps better remembered for his role in *The War of the Worlds*, Barry was nominated for a Tony Award for the role he personally considered his career's best, the homosexual nightclub owner in Allen Carr's 1983 Broadway production of *La Cage aux Folles.*

Carr asked Barry to audition for Georges, the first role for which Barry had had to audition in three decades, and he was cast opposite George Hern after Barry's standing ovation-worthy audition performance. The groundbreaking musical marked the first time in Broadway history that the leading couple was homosexual. Part of the appeal of this controversial couple was due to Barry's honest and heartfelt performance. The *Los Angeles Times* quoted Barry explaining in an interview, "I didn't camp him up. ... I played him sensitively, caringly ... loving my son like any father loves his son," and the *New York Times* also quoted Barry saying, "I'm not playing a homosexual—I'm playing a person who cares deeply about another person."

At the close of his acting career, Barry's roles included a musical comedy show at the Oak Room of Manhattan's Algonquin Hotel and a cameo appearance in *The War of the Worlds* 2005 remake with Tom Cruise. He was active in Democratic politics and was present with Robert Kennedy on the night of the senator's assassination.

The former Betty Kalb, his wife of 58 years—they met during *Catherine Was Great* rehearsals and married in 1944—preceded him in death in 2003. A short time after this loss, Barry was diagnosed with Alzheimer's disease. His family moved him into the Sunrise Assisted Living center in Woodland Hills, California, in the early summer of 2009, where the socialization opportunities were able to improve his mental capacity.

Barry died at the center on December 9, 2009, from congestive heart failure. He is survived by his sons, Michael and Fred; his daughter, Elizabeth; three grandchildren, and two great grandchildren. Like Georges in *La Cage aux Folles,* Barry was a "very loving and generous father," his son, Michael, told the *Los Angeles Times,* adding "and he was handsome, charming, and funny until the end." **Sources:** *Los Angeles Times,* http://www.latimes.com/news/obituaries/la-me-gene-barry11-2009dec11,0,6406555.story?track=rss&utm_source=feedburner&utm_medium=feed&utm_campaign=Feed%3A+latimes%2Fnews%2Fobituaries+%28Los+Angeles+Times+-+Obituaries%29&utm_content=Google+Reader (September 16, 2010); *New York Times,* http://www.nytimes.com/2009/12/11/arts/television/11barry.html?_r=2&partner=rss&emc=rss (September 16, 2010); *Times* (London), http://www.timesonline.co.uk/tol/comment/obituaries/article6953791.ece (September 16, 2010); *Washington Post,* http://www.washingtonpost.com/wp-dyn/content/article/2009/12/10/AR20091210.tif04080.html?wprss=rss_metro/obituaries (September 16, 2010).

—*Helene Barker Kiser*

Arthur Bartlett

Born Arthur Eugene Bartlett, November 26, 1933, in Glens Falls, NY; died of complications from Alzheimer's disease, December 31, 2009, in Coronado, CA. Founder of Century 21 Real Estate. Arthur Bartlett started the world's largest real-estate franchising company, Century 21, from a small office in Santa Ana, California. Within a decade of its founding in 1971, the empire he created with a business partner came to dominate the real-estate brokerage business and became a model for the entire franchising industry. Bartlett's obituary notice in *Franchising World* hailed him as "the pioneer of conversion franchising. Instead of recruiting retirees from other fields with little experience and a large learning curve, the partners tapped people in the real estate industry and existing real estate company owners, which resulted in dynamic growth."

A native of Glens Falls, New York, Bartlett was born in 1933 and moved out West with his family, who settled in Long Beach, California. As a teen he worked scores of jobs, but demonstrated a successful knack for sales. He sold suits while studying at Long Beach City College and then joined the Campbell's Soup Company. By the early 1960s, he had earned his California real estate license and was working for the state's top realtor, Forest Olson, out of its San Fernando Valley office. Promoted to branch manager and then district manager, Bartlett realized he missed the competitive atmosphere of sales, and founded Four Star Realty in Santa Ana, California, in the mid-1960s. He also created a company, Comps, Inc., that offered real-estate professionals up-to-date numbers on "comparables," or what homes had sold for in the area recently.

In 1971 Bartlett teamed with a former colleague from Forest Olson, Marshall Fisher, who had some franchising experience in the real-estate business. They designed Century 21 as a national chain of independent real-estate brokers. By paying an upfront fee and hanging a Century 21 sign on their office, brokers could benefit from a national advertising budget, training, and other operating costs that were shared among franchisees. In turn, Bartlett and Fisher collected a commission on homes sold by Century 21 brokers. This was a particularly challenging business strategy, for franchising had proven successful in some segments—fast food, for example—but less so in others. Moreover, they were persuading established owner-operators to essentially "pay top dollar for the privilege of running the very businesses they started," a 1985 *New York Times* article by Philip S. Gutis noted. "You have to be a supersalesman to convince someone with a big ego that he needs your services," Bartlett told Gutis.

But the Century 21 idea proved enormously successful. In their first six years of operation, Bartlett and Fisher signed up more than 6,000 brokers, and the revenues skyrocketed. Century 21 became a publicly traded company in 1977, and two years later was sold to the Trans World Corporation, the holding company of airline T.W.A., for $89 million. Bartlett stayed on another year as board chair and chief executive officer before leaving to seek new franchise opportunities. Neither Mr. Build, a home-improvement general-contracting business, nor Triex, a national used-car franchise company, caught on the way Century 21 had, but Bartlett remained committed to the franchise model. "Correct or not, consumers have confidence in the big, brand name," the *Los Angeles Times* quoted Bartlett as saying back in 1982. "Franchising has been the savior of free enterprise in this country. It has given the small businessman a way to survive."

Bartlett spent his retirement years in the San Diego area, where he was active in a number of local charitable organizations. Camp Able, a program for disabled youth, was on the verge of closing down until Bartlett learned about its situation and began a philanthropic effort to save it. Bartlett's Century 21 empire continued to thrive, too. It was eventually acquired by Realogy, which also owns ERA, Coldwell Banker, Sotheby's International Realty, and other properties.

Afflicted with Alzheimer's disease in his later years, Bartlett passed away on December 31, 2009, at the age of 76 at his home in Coronado, California. His first wife, Collette Cupiss Bartlett, predeceased him. Survivors include their daughter, Stacey Bartlett Renshaw; his second wife, Nancy Sanders; his stepson Larry Wells; one granddaughter, and three stepgrandchildren. His brother, Ray Bartlett, told *San Diego Union-Tribune* journalist Blanca Gonzalez that his sibling had "always been a salesman." Ray Bartlett elaborated, "He started out in junior high. He made potholders and had a group of kids selling them. He always had a lot of ideas." **Sources:** *Franchising World,* February 2010, p. 79; *Los Angeles Times,* January 6, 2010; *New York Times,* January 20, 1985; January 7, 2010; *San Diego Union-Tribune,* January 6, 2010.

—*Carol Brennan*

Aage Bohr

Born June 19, 1922, in Copenhagen, Denmark; died September 8, 2009, in Copenhagen, Denmark. Physicist. Aage Bohr, a nuclear physicist and son of Niels Bohr, is one of only seven parent-child combinations to have each won a Nobel Prize. His father won the physics Nobel in 1922, shortly after Bohr was born, and Bohr himself won the same prize, shared with two other physicists, in 1975.

Much of Bohr's career was dedicated to changing the conventional model of the atomic nucleus. He collaborated with Dr. Ben Mottelson and corresponded frequently with Dr. James Rainwater, developing the now mainstream idea that nuclear components can be ellipsoid in their arrangement, rather than evenly dispersed in a spherically symmetrical form. The three scientists were credited with discovering a connection between collective and particle motion in the nucleus of the atom.

Born in Copenhagen, Denmark, Bohr was the fourth child of Niels and Magrethe Norlund Bohr. From an early age, he was surrounded by well known scientists, including Wolfgang Pauli, Werner Heisenberg, and Yoshio Nishina, among others, who became like uncles to the Bohr children. He attended Sortedam Gymnasium in Copenhagen and studied informally at the Copenhagen Institute of Theoretical Physics, where his family lived. (The school was later renamed the Niels Bohr Institute after Bohr's father.)

Bohr began his studies at the University of Copenhagen in 1940, despite Germany's occupation of Denmark. As the years progressed, however, the deportation of Denmark's Jews was ordered, and the Bohr family was smuggled out of the country. They escaped to Sweden in a fishing boat, crossing the Oresund Strait. Bohr's father was brought to Britain by the Royal Air Force, and the two physicists joined the British Department of Scientific and Industrial Research in London. From there, they eventually made their way to the United States.

Niels Bohr joined the Manhattan Project under the code name Nicholas Baker; Bohr served as his father's secretary and assistant, working as Jim Baker. Some anecdotes tell of Bohr serving as an interpreter for his father, who was prone to mumbling. Both Bohr and his father cautioned Allied leaders on the use of the atomic bomb, due to the far reaching complications the weapon would have. After the bombs were dropped on Japan in 1945 and the war ended, the Bohrs were able to return to Denmark, where Bohr continued his studies.

After receiving his master's degree from the University of Copenhagen in 1946, Bohr joined the Institute for Advanced Study in Princeton, New Jersey, and the following year attended Columbia University on a fellowship. He was married to Marietta Soffer, with whom he had three children, in 1950. That same year, he returned to Denmark and published his first paper on the nature of the shape of the atomic nucleus.

Bohr became a research fellow at the Niels Bohr Institute and was named a professor of physics at the University of Copenhagen in 1956. He also became involved with the Nordisk Institut for Teoretisk Atomfysik (Nordita), where he served on the board from 1957 through 1975. After his father's death, Bohr was made the director of the Niels Bohr Institute, a position that he held from 1962 to 1970. He became the director of Nordita in 1975, a position he held until he retired in 1981.

From the time he returned to Denmark until we was awarded the Nobel prize in 1975, Bohr worked with Dr. Ben Mottelson, a naturalized Dane, to develop and refine the ideas Bohr had started developing in his 1950 paper. The pair worked together for 25 years, producing a theory that could be tested and verified through experimentation. With Mottelson, Bohr published the two-volume monograph, *Single-Particle Motion* and *Nuclear Deformations* that described their expanded theories on nuclear structure, in 1969 and 1975. "The conformity between theory and experiment was so complete that there could be no doubt of the accuracy of the theory," the Royal Swedish Academy of Sciences wrote in the Nobel prize announcement, as reported by the *New York Times*. The statement continued, "This gave stimulus to new theoretical studies, but above all to very many experiments to prove the theoretical predictions.... This dynamic development very soon led to a deepened understanding of the structure of the atomic nucleus."

Though the Nobel Prize is his highest achievement, Bohr received several other honors over the course of his career. He was awarded the Dannie Heineman Prize in 1960, the Pope Pius XI Medal in 1963, the Atoms for Peace Award in 1969, the Orsted Medal in 1970, the Rutherford Medal in 1972, the John Price Wetherill Medal in 1974, and the Ole Romer Medal in 1976. Bohr was elected to six academies of science in Europe, the National Academy of Science in the United States, and received honorary degrees from several universities.

In addition to his love of physics, Bohr had a great appreciation for classical music and played the piano. His first wife died in 1978, and Boh married Bente Meyer in 1981. Bohr died September 8, 2009, in Copenhagen, Denmark, at the age of 87. He is survived by his second wife and three children from his first marriage: Vilhelm, Tomas, and Margrethe. **Sources:** *Chicago Tribune*, September 11, 2009, sec. 1, p. 35; *Contemporary Authors Online*, Gale, 2009; *Los Angeles Times*, September 18, 2009; *New York Times*, September 11, 2009; *Times* (London), September 11, 2009; *Washington Post*, September 13, 2009.

—*Alana Joli Abbott*

Norman Borlaug

Born Norman Ernest Borlaug, March 24, 1914, in Saude, IA; died of cancer, September 12, 2009, in Dallas, TX. Agronomist. "More than any other single person of this age, [Norman Borlaug] has helped provide bread for a hungry world," the Nobel committee said of agricultural innovator Borlaug when they presented him with the Nobel Peace Prize in 1970, according to the *New York Times*. "We have made this choice in the hope that providing bread will also give the world peace." Borlaug has become known as the father of the "Green Revolution," and has been credited with saving "more lives than any other person who has ever lived" when he was presented with the Congressional Gold Medal.

Also awarded the Presidential Medal of Freedom, Borlaug was one of the five people in history to win all three honors.

Though in later years his innovations in the field of agriculture came under criticism from environmental activists, Borlaug developed strains of wheat and rice that increased production by more than double using only one percent more land to do it. His work in Mexico, India, and Pakistan staved off predictions of widespread starvation and famine that had been predicted to occur between the 1940s and 1960s. His techniques allowed those nations to become self-sufficient in their grain production, no longer requiring tremendous imports from the rest of the world.

Born on his grandfather's farm near the small town of Saude, Iowa, Borlaug was the grandson of Norwegian immigrants. He attended classes in a one-room schoolhouse, and early on expressed a curiosity in why some crops grew better in some places than in others. He was encouraged by a teacher to continue studying agriculture in an age where most farm children dropped out of school; his grandfather wanted Borlaug to have the chance at a good education, however, and encouraged him to attend college. Due to the effects of the Great Depression, Borlaug first raised money for his education as a farm worker, and later, when he began attending the University of Minnesota, he worked in a coffee shop and as a food server in a sorority to support himself.

Borlaug was impacted tremendously by the effects of the Great Depression on the people around him. "He often said that his dedication to solving issues of world hunger grew out of the bread lines and the suffering of the people that he saw during the Depression," Edwin Price, director of the Norman Borlaug Institute for International Agriculture at Texas A&M University, told the *Washington Post*. When he had to take a leave of absence from college due to his funding running out, he worked with the Civilian Conservation Corps, where he served as a group leader for many refugees of the Dust Bowl. The recruits were starving; "I saw how food changed them, and this left scars on me," Borlaug was quoted as having said in the London *Times*. In 1937, Borlaug graduated with a degree in forestry and intended to pursue that career until meeting Elvin Charles Stakman, a plant pathologist working on developing a strain of wheat that would be resistant to a fungus called rust. Borlaug pursued graduate studies under Stakman, earning both his master's and doctoral degrees before taking a job with DuPont.

Though he considered enlisting during World War II, Borlaug was told DuPont would be doing research to aid in the war effort and that his work would be put to better use on the home front. He worked on developing watertight sealants, adhesive gum that could resist salt water, and canteen disinfectant for the U. S. Army. After the war ended, Borlaug made the choice to leave the commercial work force and join a project funded by the Rockefeller Foundation to combat starvation in Mexico. Frustrated by conditions and lack of support from local farmers, as well as a falling out with his supervisor, Borlaug pressed the group to attempt "shuttle breeding," planting the same strain in two different locations, doubling the growing season. The idea was a breakthrough and led to the development of further cross-fertilized successful wheat strains.

Due to heavy use of chemical fertilizer, which at the time was thought to be the best way to increase production, some of the Mexican wheat strains found the wheat growing too large to be supported by the stalks. Borlaug was stymied until he crossed the wheat with a Japanese dwarf variety. The semi-dwarf result was highly successful in Mexico and led to that nation becoming self-sufficient. Approximately ten years later, as war broke out between India and Pakistan, the same breed of wheat was introduced, despite reluctance of local farmers to risk their crops on what they viewed as a scientific experiment. Between 1965 and 1967, the crops in India exploded, with one year's crop being 98 percent larger than the previous year's. Pakistan eventually imported the seeds as well, leading both nations to become self-sufficient. The crossing of the dwarf strain was also vital in increasing rice production in east Asia.

Though he was awarded the Nobel Peace Prize in 1970, Borlaug's work came under criticism in the 1980s due to environmental discoveries about chemical fertilizers. The destructive nature of DDT particularly inspired activists to attack Borlaug's methods. Social activists felt the style of agriculture introduced by Borlaug supported big business over small farmers, and made nations too dependent on a single crop. Though Borlaug eventually acknowledged some of the issues, particularly concerning potentially harmful fertilizers and pesticides, he remained a critic of methods that encouraged use of fertilizers like cow manure, which he felt would require more land—and more grain—to produce, limiting its feasibility in supporting an ever-growing population. That population growth was what Borlaug identified as the real threat to both the environment and the political stability of the world.

Despite the criticism, Borlaug continued to work, struggling to make inroads in war-torn Africa. Sponsored by the Nippon Foundation, Borlaug helped to introduce short-strawed, drought-resistant wheat to Ghana and Sudan. But the lack of infrastructure and the continual political upheaval in Africa made Borlaug's efforts there far less successful than they had been in Asia.

From 1984 until he was well into his 90s, Borlaug was an active faculty member and researcher at Texas A&M university. He died at his Dallas, Texas, home due to complications of cancer. He is survived by his children, Jeanie and William, and several grand- and great-grandchildren. **Sources:** *Chicago Tribune*, September 14, 2009, sec. 1, p. 20; *Los Angeles Times*, September 14, 2009; *New York Times*, September 14, 2009; *Times* (London), September 14, 2009; *Washington Post*, September 14, 2009.

—*Alana Joli Abbott*

Dennis Brutus

Born Dennis Vincent Brutus, November 28, 1924, in Salisbury, Southern Rhodesia (now Zimbabwe); died of prostate cancer, December 26, 2009, in Cape Town, South Africa. Poet and activist. Although he himself was no athlete, South African poet and social activist Dennis Brutus found a strong voice in publicizing the injustices of apartheid—the decades-long officially sanctioned racial separation in South Africa—and outspokenly fighting against it, through the sports arena. One of the most famous faces of the apartheid era, Brutus' efforts were directly responsible for the Olympic suspension of South Africa from 1964 to 1992 for the country's unabashed racialism, drawing international attention to apartheid's legal oppression of the South African people.

Born in 1924 in Salisbury, Southern Rhodesia, an area now known as Harare, Zimbabwe, Brutus moved with his South African parents to Port Elizabeth in the Eastern Cape Province of South Africa when he was just four years old. Because he was of mixed ancestry—French and Italian in addition to African—the racial code of South Africa labeled him as "colored." A brilliant student, Brutus was offered a full scholarship to study at University of Fort Hare from which he graduated in 1947 with distinction after majoring in English. The following year, South Africa's National Party instituted apartheid.

After completing his studies, Brutus spent several years as a school teacher in colored high schools. He was also heavily involved in social work, along with writing difficult, symbolic poetry. Only years later, while in prison as a political criminal, would he begin to write the more accessible lines that, while still politically charged, were more easily understood and more widely read. Even then, because his published work was banned in his native country, few South Africans knew of his poetry until decades later.

Disgusted with the growing government-sponsored racial discrimination in his country, Brutus became more and more politically active. Although a lackluster athlete himself, the sports fan in his soul grew increasingly troubled by the disservice done to South Africa's athletes and teams when talented black athletes were rejected and less capable white athletes accepted in their places, and in 1959, he co-founded the South African Sports Association. The Association's task was first to lobby—unsuccessfully—the sports organizations for internal voluntary change.

In 1962, Brutus moved on to co-found, and serve as president of, the more proactive and visible South African Non-Racial Olympic Committee. The Committee lobbied international Olympic committees to ban South Africa from participating because of its adherence to the policies of apartheid; the country was subsequently banned from Olympic participation beginning with the 1964 games in Tokyo, a ban that would not be rescinded until after apartheid crumbled in 1990, allowing an integrated team of South Africans to compete at the 1992 Olympic Games in Barcelona.

The visibility and relative success of Brutus' organization made him a significant political target. For example, in 1960, the government banned him from meeting with more than two non-relatives at a time, including social occasions. In 1963, Brutus defied this ban by meeting with a group of people, including a Swiss journalist, causing his arrest and sentence to 18 months imprisonment. Brutus attempted to escape by fleeing bail, but he was caught and returned by Portuguese secret police at the Mozambique border. While attempting to escape again, he was shot at point-blank range in the back and nearly died from the wound while waiting for an ambulance that would take a black person.

Brutus was not able to recover completely from the wounds before being sent to the Robben Island prison colony, where he endured five months of solitary confinement and many more months of backbreaking labor. The neighboring cell housed another famous political prisoner of apartheid, Nelson Mandela. While in prison, Brutus wrote many poems, two volumes of which were published before he was freed. According to the London *Times*, "Imprisonment proved crucial in his development as a poet." In all, he would eventually author 14 books, including one published under the pseudonym John Bruin, and would be awarded a lifetime achievement award from the Department of Arts and Culture of South Africa.

Upon Brutus' release in the mid-1960s, he was placed under a five-year house arrest, but he negotiated with the government to be given an exit visa, which would allow him to leave South Africa in 1966 and not return. After a few years in Britain, Brutus made his way to the United States in 1971, teaching in the African studies and English departments at universities like the University of Denver, Northwestern University, and the University of Pittsburgh while continuing to speak out against the South African government. In 1982 Brutus was almost deported because he did not possess the required paperwork, but a judge eventually ruled that political asylum was necessary as his life could be forfeited if he were returned to South Africa.

Twenty-five years after he was forced to leave his country, Brutus returned home to South Africa. Upon his return, he remained active in both politics and literature and was an annual contributor to Poetry Africa, an annual literary festival.

At the age of 85, Brutus died quietly at home in Cape Town on December 26, 2009, after a battle with prostate cancer. Two years before his death, he declined an invitation to be inducted into the South African Sport Hall of Fame, desiring no honor from those whom he termed "unapologetic racists," according to the *New York Times*. The *Los Angeles Times* added his comments that "It is incompatible to have those who championed racist sport alongside its genuine victims." He is survived by his wife, the former May Jaggers, to whom he had been married for 59 years; eight children, nine grandchildren, and four great-grandchildren. **Sources:** *Los Angeles Times*, http://www.latimes.com/news/obituaries/la-me-dennis-brutus29-2009dec29,0,308274.story?track=rss&utm_source=feedburner&utm_medium=feed&utm_campaign=Feed%3A+latimes%2Fnews%2Fobituaries+%28Los+Angeles+Times+-+Obituaries%29&utm_content=Google+Reader (September 16, 2010); *New York Times*, http://www.nytimes.com/2010/01/03/world/africa/03brutus.html?_r=1&partner=rss&emc=rss (September 16, 2010); *Times* (London), http://www.timesonline.co.uk/tol/comment/obituaries/article6976893.ece (September 16, 2010).

—*Helene Barker Kiser*

Rafael Caldera

Born Rafael Antonio Caldera, January 24, 1916, in San Filipe, Yaracuy, Venezuela; died of Parkinson's disease, December 24, 2009, in Caracas, Venezuela. Politician. Twice-elected president of Venezuela, albeit with terms two decades apart, 1969 to 1974 and 1994 to 1999, Rafael Caldera led his native country out of dictatorship and into democracy. During his second term, he issued a pardon for a political zealot upstart who had attempted a 1992 coup against the then-current government; this man would succeed Caldera as the notorious long-running president, Hugo Chavez.

Caldera was born in 1916 in San Felipe in the Yaracuy state of Venezuela; his mother died when he was still an infant, so his attorney father allowed him to be raised by an aunt, Eva Rodriguez de Liscano, who moved with the seven-year-old Caldera to Caracas where he would receive a Jesuit education. The future president would remain a faithful Catholic all his life.

At 15, he was ready to enter the university in Caracas and he enrolled to study law in 1931, eventually graduating with a political science degree. The following year he served as the general secretary for the Catholic youth organization and founded a Christian social movement. His Catholic beliefs were even more entrenched following a 1933 trip to Italy. By 1936, his political convictions were solidified when he founded a moderate organization that broke away from the national leftist student federation, a move which fed directly into his postgraduate position as department head of the national labor office under General Eleazar Lopez Contreras. Caldera had attracted the notice of Contreras through a series of newspaper articles the 20 year old had penned on the need for a new labor code.

In 1939, Caldera put his labor knowledge to use in the writing of his dissertation thesis, for which he earned his doctorate in political science with highest honors. Four years later, he was appointed as a university chair in law and social sciences, and would lecture on those topics for a quarter of a century. Prior to this appointment, in 1941, Caldera was appointed as a state deputy to congress as part of the Accion Nacional, for which he also served as general secretary. In 1945, the Accion Democratica (AD), a new social democracy party, recruited him to its ranks in public prosecutions as it overthrew the General Isaias Medina Angarita government.

His time with AD was short-lived, however, as he and leader Romulo Betancourt had a divergence of opinion, and in 1946, Caldera co-founded the social

Christian democrat party of Copei—the Venezuelan initials stand for "organizing committee for independent political elections"—with other educated Catholics as a moderate offering to stand against the left-wing party in leadership. As a Copei presidential candidate, Caldera made an unsuccessful bid for the office in 1947 against the AD candidate; however, Caldera did represent the Copei party in congress in 1948 and served as general secretary of the party until 1969 when he ran, this time successfully, for president; he had run and lost in both 1958 and 1963. In 1958, he was a signer of the Punto Fijo pact, creating a system for democratic elections in the wake of General Marcos Perez Jimenez's fall from power.

As president during his first term from 1969 to 1974, Caldera worked to steer Venezuela's economy away from what the London *Times* called "its almost exclusive dependence on oil, which accounted for about 90 percent of foreign exchange revenues." He would run at other times for a second term, but would be defeated by the AD candidate, and would not win reelection for two decades until being elected to a second term in 1994. In the meantime, the AD party had been all but dissolved because of corruption, and Caldera himself had left the Copei party he founded to create the National Convergence party, which backed his successful reelection bid.

For his second term, Caldera inherited a country torn by multiple coup attempts and the impeachment of a corrupt president. Although a principled, earnest, and honest man, Caldera eventually became a wildly unpopular leader. In addition to the political turmoil, Venezuela was reeling from years of poor economic management so dire it caused a state of emergency declaration and the widespread failure of Venzuelan banks.

As the figurehead, Caldera was blamed. So although it came as no surprise that he was defeated for the presidency after this term, nor that the defeat was to a militant, anti-party candidate, it was surprising that the victor was Hugo Chavez, who had been imprisoned for an attempted coup in 1992 against then-President Carlos Andres Perez and pardoned by none other than Rafael Caldera. The London *Times* commented, "this act of magnanimity cleared the way for the final destruction of the political system he had painstakingly helped to construct."

After battling Parkinson's disease, Caldera died in Caracas on December 24, 2009, at the age of 93. He is survived by his wife, Alicia Pietri, three sons, and three daughters. Upon Caldera's death, his family members made clear through the press that they would decline any commemorative activities or homage originating from the Chavez government. **Sources:** *Los Angeles Times,* http://www.latimes. com/news/obituaries/la-me-rafael-caldera25-2009dec25,0,5535003.story (September 16, 2010); *New York Times,* http://www.nytimes.com/2009/12/25/world/americas/25caldera.html (September 16, 2010); *Times* (London), http://www.timesonline.co.uk/tol/comment/obituaries/article6969744.ece (September 16, 2010); *Washington Post,* http://www.washingtonpost.com/wp-dyn/content/article/2009/12/24/AR20091224.tif02777.html (September 16, 2010).

—*Helene Barker Kiser*

Jim Carroll

Born James Dennis Carroll, August 1, 1949, in New York, NY; died of a heart attack, September 11, 2009, in New York, NY. Poet and musician. Only after poet Jim Carroll had established himself as a literary voice did he publish the work for which he is best known: a collection of prose memoirs titled *The Basketball Diaries.* The book revealed Carroll's descent from being a star basketball player in high school to becoming addicted to drugs and working as a thief and prostitute. The autobiography was praised by critics and became a staple on college campuses; it was later adapted as a movie starring Leonardo DiCaprio.

Celebrated as a poet and praised by peers including Jack Kerouac, Allen Ginsberg, and William S. Burroughs, Carroll wrote and published prose and poetry throughout his career. He also performed spoken-word pieces, forming his own band and recording the punk classic "People Who Died." Carroll was one of the first poets to perform spoken-word pieces on the television networks MTV and VH1. Later in his writing career, he began to produce fiction; his novel, *The Petting Zoo,* was scheduled to be released by Viking in November of 2010.

Born in New York City in 1949, Carroll grew up in a legacy of Irish-American bartenders. He began writing early, encouraged by parochial school teachers to keep a journal. As a teen, he was praised for the work he had produced by Jack Kerouac, who is widely quoted as having said, according to the *Washington Post,* that at 13, Carroll "writes better prose than 89 percent of the novelists working today." Carroll's talent for writing was not the only thing that gained him attention as a teen, however. His ability on the basketball court won him a scholarship to the elite Trinity High, setting the stage for his memoirs, *The Basketball Diaries.*

At age 18, Carroll's first book of poetry was published. *Organic Trains* won praise from critics; poet Ted Berrigan called Carroll "the first truly new American poet" in his review in *Culture Hero* (according to Carroll's *Los Angeles Times* obituary). That same year, 1967, the first short pieces that would eventually become *The Basketball Diaries* began to appear in *The Paris Review.* Carroll, who had been accepted into Wagner College and Columbia University, dropped out to spend more time in the music and art scene, becoming friends with Bob Dylan, Andy Warhol, Robert Mapplethorpe, and Patti Smith. Carroll wrote dialogue for Warhol's films and worked as a studio assistant for artist Larry Rivers.

While being engaged in the art scene, Carroll continued to write poetry. His *4 Ups and 1 Down* was published in 1970; *Living at the Movies* came out in 1973. As described in *The Basketball Diaries,* however, Carroll had descended into a life of drug use and prostitution, and in 1973, he moved to the West Coast, hoping to end his addiction to heroine. He moved to a coastal artistic enclave in Bolinas, California, where he was encouraged by Patti Smith to become involved in spoken-word poetry. The punk band Amsterdam joined his project and they formed the Jim Carroll Band. Keith Richards of the Rolling Stones found their sound appealing and recommended them for a contract with his label.

In 1978, *The Basketball Diaries* was published to tremendous praise. The book begins when Carroll is only 13 years old, but has already started to become addicted to various drugs. It ends with Carroll completely addicted with his life falling apart, depicting a bleak outlook on his future. Also in 1978, Carroll married Rosemary Klemfuss, who also served as his lawyer, though their relationship ended in divorce in the late 1980s.

Given the success of *The Basketball Diaries,* Carroll later picked up his memoirs where *The Basketball Diaries* left off, chronicling his next two years in *Forced Entries: The Downtown Diaries, 1971-1973.* Christopher Lehmann-Haupt, a critic for the *New York Times,* wrote of the second installment (according to the *Washington Post*), "Whether or not one believes Jim Carroll's redemption, his two diaries constitute a remarkable account of New York City's lower depths. At the very least, they should serve further to demystify the usefulness of drugs to writers."

In the meantime, he continued to work on his music. His debut album, *Catholic Boy,* was released in 1980, and several other albums followed. Carroll continued to produce music for the rest of his career, though he turned more toward spoken-word poetry in his later years. He wrote lyrics for other musicians and returned to his poetry, with *The Book of Nods, Fear of Dreaming,* and *Void of Course* published throughout the 1980s and 1990s. In 1995, the film version of *The Basketball Diaries* renewed interest in Carroll's work. DiCaprio, as the star of the film, attended book signings with Carroll to promote the author's work. But despite the actor's popularity, "it was Carroll the crowds clamored for," a reporter wrote in *Entertainment Weekly* (according to the *Los Angeles Times*).

Late in his career, Carroll became interested in producing fiction. His first novel, *The Petting Zoo,* was begun in the early 1990s and was scheduled to be published posthumously in 2010. At only 61 years of age, Carroll suffered from a heart attack that ended his life. He is survived by his brother, Thomas, of Stony Point, New York. **Sources:** *Chicago Tribune,* September 15, 2009, sec. 1, p. 22; *Contemporary Authors Online,* Gale, 2009; *Los Angeles Times,* September 14, 2009; *New York Times,* September 14, 2009; *Times* (London), September 15, 2009; *Washington Post,* September 15, 2009.

—*Alana Joli Abbott*

Vic Chesnutt

Born James Victor Chesnutt, November 12, 1964, in Jacksonville, FL; committed suicide, December 25, 2009, in Athens, GA. Singer and songwriter. The object of what could be described as a cult following, the subject of a documentary film, and the singer/songwriter for an astonishing output of record albums—15 in fewer than two decades—Vic Chesnutt's extraordinary music career both began and ended with tragedies.

Born in 1964 in Jacksonville, Florida, Chesnutt grew up with his adoptive family in Zebulon, Georgia. Young Chesnutt learned to play the guitar through lessons with his grandfather. One of the chief lessons was transposing the chords of the song "Sweet Georgia Brown" into every key on the scale; playing a song in this way develops an ear for the music, a knowledge of music theory and composition, and an advanced technical skill, all of which would come into play in Chesnutt's later music career.

As a teenager, Chesnutt performed as part of several local, amateur bands. His youth was not a carefree one, however, and Chesnutt was a drinker as a teenager. At the age of 18 in 1983, while driving drunk, he rolled his car into a ditch and was paralyzed from the waist down with limited use of his arms and hands. According to the *New York Times*, Chesnutt told Terry Gross, the host of National Public Radio's program *Fresh Air*, that the accident and subsequent paralysis paradoxically started his seriousness about his career even as his physical ability to play his instrument was limited. "It was only after I broke my neck and even like maybe a year later that I really started realizing I had something to say."

Switching away from the complicated chords and musical sequences his hands could no longer move to play, Chesnutt's distinctive style of simple chords accompanied by morbidly humorous lyrics emerged. As many musicians do, Chesnutt first moved to Nashville before settling in the university town of Athens, Georgia, where he would live the rest of his life. There, in the mid-1980s, in addition to performing as part of a band called the La-Di-Das, he began to play regular gigs—in a wheelchair—at the bar/nightclub/concert venue 40 Watt Club.

As luck would have it, indie rock musician Michael Stipe, of the vanguard band R.E.M., happened to see Chesnutt perform one of these gigs in 1988, and so struck was Stipe that he would become a major promoter and fan, producing Chesnutt's demo collection which would become his first album, the 1990 *Little*, as well as later recordings. Chesnutt's major label debut was 1996's *About to Choke*.

Chesnutt did not gain widespread popularity among general music listeners, but he had an enormous fan base in the alternative/indie population, including notable musicians and bands both in and out of that genre, from Lampchop to Widespread Panic to Elf Power, as well as to members of both Fugazi and Thee Silver Mt. Zion. Other musicians outside the genre also came to appreciate Chesnutt's songwriting, such as jazz guitarist Bill Frisell with whom Chesnutt recorded, Smashing Pumpkins, Madonna, Hootie and the Blowfish, Indigo Girls, and R.E.M., who each recorded their versions of Chesnutt songs.

In 1993, Chesnutt was the subject of a documentary film titled *Speed Racer: Welcome to the World of Vic Chesnutt*. His songs were also the inspiration for the 1996 collaborative album *Sweet Relief II: The Gravity of the Situation*, the proceeds of which were donated to the nonprofit Sweet Relief Musicians Fund, an organization and foundation that helped musicians in need of support and financial assistance for medical bills.

In near-constant pain and without health insurance, Chesnutt was intimately concerned with the subject of affordable and accessible health care. According to an interview in the *Los Angeles Times*, Chesnutt said that although he was not well-spoken or eloquent on the matter, his situation had become nearly all-consuming.

"I was making payments, but I can't anymore and I really have no idea what I'm going to do. It seems absurd they can charge this much. When I think about all this, it gets me so furious. I could die tomorrow because of other operations I need that I can't afford." Chesnutt was also a vocal supporter of medical marijuana for pain management.

His final public appearance was on December 1, 2009, at the Echoplex in Los Angeles, California, where he was promoting his release titled *At the Cut*. On Christmas Day of 2009, Chesnutt was pronounced dead at Athens Regional Medical Center in Athens, Georgia. Earlier that week, he had overdosed on muscle relaxants, the final of multiple suicide attempts over the years, and he briefly languished in a coma before passing away at age 45. He is survived by his wife and bass player, Tina Whatley Chesnutt, and his sister, Lorinda Crane.

Friend, producer, and filmmaker Jem Cohen told the *Los Angeles Times* that Chesnutt's "is not a story of a rock star being on heroin or even drinking themselves down. The real story is about someone who struggled against amazingly difficult odds for many years and managed to transcend those odds with almost unparalleled productivity and creativity and power in his work." **Sources:** *Los Angeles Times*, http://articles.latimes.com/2009/dec/26/local/la-me-vic-chesnutt26-2009dec26 (September 16, 2010); *New York Times*, http://www.nytimes.com/2009/12/26/arts/music/26chesnutt.html (September 16, 2010); *Times* (London), http://www.timesonline.co.uk/tol/comment/obituaries/article6970850.ece (September 16, 2010); *Washington Post*, http://www.washingtonpost.com/wp-dyn/content/article/2009/12/26/AR20091226.tif01693.html?amp;wprss=rss_metro/obituaries (September 16, 2010).

—*Helene Barker Kiser*

Nick Counter

Born James Nicholas Counter III, March 21, 1940, in Phoenix, AZ; died November 6, 2009, in Los Angeles, CA. Attorney. Labor attorney Nick Counter, who served as the president of the Alliance of Motion Picture and Television Producers (AMPTP) for 27 years, helped to change the way Hollywood labor deals were negotiated. Through his efforts, a unified organization made of more than 350 producers, from small independent groups to media conglomerates, successfully negotiated deals with writers, actors, teamsters, musicians, film crews, and other Hollywood professionals for nearly three decades.

During his tenure as president of AMPTP, he presided over 400 labor contracts. Most of his years went smoothly, the exception being two long labor strikes by the Writers Guild of America (WGA) in 1988 and 2007. He largely stayed out of the public eye, working behind the scenes until trouble caused him to step into the media spotlight.

Born in Phoenix, Arizona in 1940, Counter moved with his family to Colorado at a young age, where his father worked at a steel mill. In the summers, Counter worked at the same mill, watching as his father rose from mill worker into management positions until he was vice president. Counter's experience in the mill made him interested in labor issues. The *Los Angeles Times* quoted him as having said, "What I learned was that unions come about because of bad management."

His interest in labor law did not become a career path right away. During high school he was a star football player and amateur boxer. He earned a full scholarship to play halfback at the University of Colorado, where he studied electrical engineering. After graduating, he decided to focus on law, and attended Stanford University's law program. He became a labor attorney in Los Angeles and, in 1982, he was asked to work with a newly formed alliance of producers. He anticipated joining the team for three years before getting back to his own practice; instead, he became the major voice of the AMPTP.

When the AMPTP was founded, many of the competing studios and production companies in Hollywood had abandoned working as a team, instead trying to negotiate contracts on their own. Counter brought companies into the alliance, stressing the importance of showing a unified front when dealing with the Hollywood unions. He was often praised for his ability to handle so many diverse groups, particularly as the task became more challenging as media venues expanded and conglomerates diversified their interests. But although he earned the respect of his peers and colleagues, he was sometimes criticized for his negotiation tactics. He was known to stare down and insult union officials, sometimes rebuking them in public or to the media. But despite these techniques, he rarely lost his temper. He would also be openly emotional and appreciative of his opponents; in 2004, for example, he praised director Dan Petrie, father of the former WGA president, at the WGA negotiations.

Counter's first major challenge happened in 1988, when the WGA went on strike for 22 weeks. The result of that strike was that Counter began negotiations earlier, hoping to hash out the details of contracts and rates well before a strike would be inevitable. The system worked for nearly 20 years, until again the writers went on strike in 2007. Worried about new media, such as free Internet broadcasts for which they received no compensation, the writers stayed on strike for 100 days, shutting down most of Hollywood. The WGA depicted Counter as deaf to their pleas; some senior studio executives were also unhappy with Counter's performance, feeling that Counter had underestimated how dedicated the writers were to their cause. Counter was encouraged to retire after concluding talks with the Screen Actors Guild following the writers' strike. The negotiations with the actors took nearly a year, during which the actors worked without contract, but was resolved in 2009. Counter retired, leaving the AMPTP in the hands of Carol Lombardini, with whom he worked closely, in February of 2009.

In November of 2009, Counter collapsed in his home in Los Angeles. He was taken to the hospital, where he died at the age of 69; no cause of death was announced. He is survived by his wife and two children. The family asked that rather than receiving flowers, mourners contribute to the Motion Picture and Television Fund or the Entertainment Industry Foundation, two philanthropic organizations Counter had supported over the course of his career. He had also served as trustee for 14 union health and pension funds.

At the announcement of his death, both opponents and allies shared their thoughts about Counter's character. "Although we sat on opposite sides during labor negotiations, Nick was a friend, man of honor and worthy adversary, doing his best to represent his constituents," Directors Guild of America Secretary-Treasurer Gilbert Cates and National Executive Director Jay D. Roth said in a statement quoted by the *Los Angeles Times*. "Ultimately, Nick would always listen, evaluate, and try to understand where we were coming from and look for a way to find a deal that worked for both parties," Cates and Roth said. AMPTP President Lombardini told the *Los Angeles Times*, "Nick's passing is a profound loss for the entire entertainment community.

We will all remember Nick for his passionate leadership, which was always guided by a resolute sense of fair play and an earnest desire that everyone come out a winner." **Sources:** *Los Angeles Times,* November 7, 2009; *New York Times,* November 9, 2009; *Washington Post,* November 9, 2009.

—*Alana Joli Abbott*

Albert Crewe

Born Albert Victor Crewe, February 18, 1927, in Bradford, England; died of Parkinson's disease, November 18, 2009, in Dune Acres, IN. Physicist. Dr. Albert Crewe made major breakthroughs in the field of physics when he developed a high-resolution electron microscope that enabled him to create still images of atoms. His achievements in the field enabled developments in computers, cell biology, and catalysis that had previously been impossible. The still images were a tool to further the understanding of the building blocks of matter, from living cells to metals.

In addition to the still images, Crewe also developed a way to record images of atoms in motion. The film he created with his lab gave scientists a new way to understand how atoms interact.

Born in Bradford, England, to a poor family, Crewe only achieved moderate grades as a young boy. As a teen, however, he passed a nationwide entrance exam which enabled him to attend college, something never before achieved by a member of his family. From high school, he won a scholarship to the University of Liverpool. He earned his doctorate in physics from that university in 1951. He began his career working with atom smashers, or particle accelerators, which involve controlling beams of particles for experiments.

Crewe's work in England was on the cutting edge of the field, and in 1955, he was invited to join the physics faculty at the University of Chicago. He began as a visiting research associate and was soon offered a position as an assistant professor. In 1958, he was brought in to the Argonne National Laboratory to lead a research team working to develop an advanced particle accelerator. The government-supported lab offered him more opportunities for advancement, and he quickly became the director of the particle accelerator division, overseeing 100 engineers. In 1961, before he became a citizen of the

United States, he was promoted to the position of director for the entire laboratory, a position he held for six years as an assistant professor who had not yet received tenure.

Due to his contributions to research at Argonne, Crewe's citizenship was expedited—according to his son, his citizenship test involved only one civics question. His studies involved electron microscopy, in which beams of electrons are used to create images. Although electrons are particles, they have the properties of waves, just as light does. Unlike light, however, electron waves are very short. It was this property that Crewe worked with in order to enable him to see atoms. Because atoms are too small to see with visual light, Crewe needed to develop a machine that would allow him to use electrons to create the image.

The idea for how to create his powerful microscope came to him after a conference in England. Having forgotten to buy a book to read for his flight home, he began sketching out different ways he could improve the microscopes he was currently using. Of his two ideas, one had already been tested, which he discovered when he returned home to Chicago. The other, however, was a new concept, and his lab pursued that design. His goal was to design something that could have a resolution high enough to view a single angstrom, which is a measurement of about a third of the diameter of a carbon atom. To accomplish this, Crewe developed a special electron source giving him access to electrons with nearly identical wavelengths. He could use this source to send a beam of electrons into an object, focusing it at a much smaller target—such as an atom—than had previously been possible. The way the electrons scattered created the image. Crewe further improved both the microscope lens and detection technologies. Once his technique was developed, and his microscopes had managed resolutions of several angstroms, Crewe applied ultra-high-vacuum technologies to create an image contrast at ten times the level before achieved. This made it possible to see details that had previously been far too small to see.

Crewe and his team succeeded in 1970, when the scanning transmission revealed images of uranium and thorium atoms magnified one million times. In his report, according to *The Washington Post,* he wrote that "the bright spots" in the image were "probably single atoms." His report, "Visibility of Single Atoms" was published in *Science.*

In 1975, Crewe continued to expand the field's ability to see atoms when he recorded the first motion pictures of atoms. The film he produced was shown on Chicago television, hosted by movie critic Gene Siskel. While the accomplishment was praised, Siskel admitted that he wouldn't pay to watch it.

Crewe became the dean of physical sciences at the University of Chicago from 1971 to 1981, and he continued to work on electron microscope research throughout the 1980s. Over the course of his career, he held 19 patents and published 275 research papers. In addition to developing his own enhancements on electron microscopes, he consulted with Hitachi Corporation. He retired from the University of Chicago in 1996 as a professor emeritus.

Crewe met his wife, Doreen Blunsdon, the summer of 1946, while he was an undergraduate visiting Cornwall. The pair married in 1949 and reached their sixtieth wedding anniversary before Crewe's death on November 18, 2009, at the age of 82 from Parkinson's disease. In addition to his wife, Crewe is survived by four children and ten grandchildren. **Sources:** *Los Angeles Times*, November 27, 2009; *New York Times*, November 21, 2009; *Washington Post*, November 26, 2009.

—*Alana Joli Abbott*

Alicia de Larrocha

Born Alicia de Larrocha y de la Calle, May 23, 1923, in Barcelona, Spain; died September 25, 2009, in Barcelona, Spain. Pianist. In a career that spanned three quarters of a century, Spanish pianist Alicia de Larrocha was critically acclaimed not only for her interpretations of classical composers, but also for her performances of works by native Spanish composers. By grouping the often-neglected Spanish composers, such as Albéniz and Granados, with Beethoven and Mozart, her performances brought attention and respectability to their music. "At the outset of her career few pianists outside Spain played this repertory, and none with de Larrocha's empathy and panache," wrote a contributor to the London *Times*.

Under five feet tall, and shrinking to a height of four foot five by the end of her career, de Larrocha had small hands. Despite that she showed flawless technique. In her later career her repertoire was limited because she could no longer reach a full tenth on the keyboard. Her style was considered graceful, poetic, and interpretive, rather than grandiose, though she performed many of the great romantic pieces well at the beginning of her career. Her attention to detail, however, made her an ideal performer of Mozart and enabled her to highlight lesser-known works.

Born in 1923 in Barcelona, de Larrocha begged to begin learning piano at the age of three. Her aunt, a piano teacher, found her first attempts at the keyboard competent enough that she introduced de Larrocha to renowned teacher Frank Marshall, who felt de Larrocha was too young to begin studying. In a fit of protest—according to the *New York Times*, she "banged her head on the floor until Marshall relented"—de Larrocha won herself a teacher, and she made her concert debut at the young age of five. The performance, which took place at the World's Fair in Barcelona in 1929, launched her career.

By the time she was six, de Larrocha was invited to play at Barcelona's Paulau de la Musica. At nine years of age, de Larrocha made her first recording after she was invited by singer Conchita Supervia to take a turn at the microphone. Though she could barely reach the pedals on the piano, de Larrocha recorded two of Chopin's works, which were well reviewed. Two years later, she performed as a soloist in a Mozart concerto with the Madrid Symphony Orchestra.

Spain's Civil War in 1936 left de Larrocha without a teacher; Marshall was a target of Loyalists and had to flee the country. The young performer continued her studies on her own for the next three years, and she continued to study under Marshall when he returned in 1939. In the next three years, de Larrocha became well known in Spain, performing to crowded halls, but it was not until 1947 that she was well known beyond her home nation. That year, she went on her first European tour and performed in Paris, Geneva, and Brussels.

In 1950, de Larrocha married fellow pianist and student of Marshall, Juan Torra. (Some sources say they were married in 1958; Torra died in 1982.) The pair worked together to run Marshall's academy when their mentor died in 1959. Though de Larrocha made time for family and teaching, she continued to develop her career, making her first United States appearance with the Los Angeles Philharmonic in 1955. She performed in New York that same year. In the late 1950s, she frequently appeared as a chamber musician and performed with such musicians as cellist Gaspar Cassadó, Victoria de los Angeles, and Montserrat Caballé. In addition, she performed with the elite Emerson, Guarneri, and Tokyo string quartets, the English Chamber Orchestra, and the New York Philharmonic.

Though she largely recorded in Spain with Hispavox, which licensed her recordings to American companies, she eventually signed with the British Decca label and continued to record through 1990. From 1965 until her retirement in 2003, de Larrocha made annual trips to the United States to perform at recitals or with chamber orchestras. She began receiving awards in 1961, when she was given the Paderewski Memorial Medal. Over the course of her career, she received four Grammys, the Grand Prix du Disque twice, the Medallo d'Oro for artistic merit, and the Spanish National Assembly's gold medal for artistic achievement, which was presented to her by King Juan Carlos. She was admitted to the Spanish Royal Academy of Fine Arts, San Fernando, in 1988, making her the second woman ever to be included.

In later years, de Larrocha's health declined, particularly after breaking her hip in 2007. She died on September 25, 2009 at the age of 86 in a hospital in Barcelona, and is survived by her son, Juan, and her daughter, Alicia. In the *New York Times*, de Larrocha's concert manager Herbert Breslin was quoted as having said in 1978, "There are two kinds of repertory Alicia plays. Things she plays extremely well, and things she plays better than anyone else. But what I think makes her a phenomenon is that she doesn't give the impression of being a great personality. She's cool as a cucumber. Onstage, she doesn't even like to look at the audience. So what the public is responding to is something in the music." **Sources:** *Los Angeles Times*, September 27, 2009; *New York Times*, September 26, 2009; *Times* (London), September 28, 2009.

—Alana Joli Abbott

Larry Gelbart

Born February 25, 1928, in Chicago, IL; died of cancer, September 11, 2009, in Beverly Hills, CA. Screenwriter. Though best known for his work on the television show *M*A*S*H*, Larry Gelbart wrote scripts for radio, television, film, and stage over the course of his 60-year career, including the book for the Broadway musical *A Funny Thing Happened on the Way to the Forum* and the classic film *Tootsie*, for which he was a co-writer. Gelbart received Tony awards, an Emmy, two Oscar nominations, and awards from the Writers Guild of America. His words were delivered by such comedians as Bob Hope, Jack Paar, and Joan Davis, and other writers he worked with included lauded playwright Neil Simon and comedy filmmaker Mel Brooks.

For four years, between 1972 and 1976, Gelbart served as the principal writer for *M*A*S*H*, writing the pilot and writing and directing 97 episodes before deciding to leave the show. Though Gelbart went on to pursue other projects, the television program remained on the air for seven more seasons and was one of the top-rated shows by both audiences and critics. Gelbart wrote about his experiences as a writer for *M*A*S*H* and several of his other projects in his memoir *Laughing Matters*.

Born in Chicago, Illinois, Gelbart was the son of immigrants: his father was from Latvia and his mother was from Poland. Gelbart spoke only Yiddish until he was four. In 1942, when Gelbart was 14, the family moved to Los Angeles. His father, a barber, took on several clients associated with Hollywood, including comedian Danny Thomas. Without consulting Gelbart, his father declared to Thomas that his son was a comedy writer, and Thomas agreed to look at a sketch written by the then-16-year-old Gelbart. Writing in his memoir (according to the *Los Angeles Times*), Gelbart described at that the time, "my only real 'gift' was for showing off, doing imitations, putting together sketches, speeches, monologues at Fairfax High School." But despite his qualms, Gelbart wrote a sample for Thomas, who passed it on to the radio show's head writer. Soon after, the teen Gelbart had to balance his studies with part-time work as a comedy writer for the radio show, *Maxwell House Coffee Time*. At 18, Gelbart was a staff writer for the radio program *Duffy's Tavern*.

Drafted into postwar military service, Gelbart was able to continue honing his skills. Rather than being sent overseas, he was able to live at home, writing for the Armed Forces Radio Service variety show, *Command Performances*. The star-studded program opened an opportunity for Gelbart to move from radio into television with coworkers including Bob Hope. He later joined the staff of Sid Caesar's *Caesar's Hour*, where he worked with Neil Simon and a young Woody Allen. He shared three Emmy nominations with the writing staff.

After getting married to Broadway actress Patricia Marshall in 1956, Gelbart decided to write for the stage. His first attempt, *The Conquering Hero*, for which he wrote the book, was such an abysmal failure that it closed after only eight performances. But Gelbart continued on, teaming up with Burt Shevelove to co-write the book for *A Funny Thing Happened on the Way to the Forum*. Based on the satires of Plautus and featuring music and lyrics by Stephen Sondheim, the show was an instant classic, starring Zero Mostel and staying on stage for more than 1,000 performances. Shevelove and Gelbart shared a Tony for the book, and the musical itself won five others, including the Tony for best musical.

Gelbart alternated his stage and film writing, co-writing the scripts for *The Notorious Landlady* and *The Wrong Box* during a period where he and his family moved to London for several years. Though they had initially moved to follow *Forum* to the London stage, they ended up staying for nine years. Gelbart wrote for British television and Italian film as well, though his works were short-lived. However, it was during the stay in London that Gelbart was contacted by producer Gene Reynolds about developing a series based on the novel and film *M*A*S*H*. The program was pictured as a comedy that would deal with the serious issues of the Korean War, bringing laughs and drama to American audiences. The blend of laughter and tragedy appealed to Gelbart, and the success of the series reflected that it also worked for an American television audience.

After four years working on the series, Gelbart returned to writing for stage and film, including the George Burns film *Oh, God!*, in which Burns stars as the deity, and *Tootsie*, starring Dustin Hoffman as an out-of-work actor who masquerades as a woman to find work. Despite the success of *Tootsie*, Gelbart was reportedly frustrated with the number of rewrites the script went through before it was finally completed.

Gelbart also wrote the books for Broadway's *Sly Fox, Mastergate,* and *City of Angels*. The last, which featured a score by Cy Coleman, is a noir musical featuring the double stories of a mystery novelist and the mystery novelist's hard-boiled main character. The musical won six Tony Awards, one of them going to Gelbart for the best book for a musical. In addition to his stage and film work, Gelbart continued to write for television, though he never again reached the same level of success he had with *M*A*S*H*.

Gelbart was reported dead in an Internet hoax in December of 2008. He found out about it online, like everyone else, and promptly responded to the postings, "Does that mean I can stop exercising?" In a conversation with the *Los Angeles Times*, he quipped, "I was dead, but I'm better now."

Gelbart was diagnosed with cancer in 2009, and he died in September at his home in Beverly Hills, California, at the age of 81. He continued to write up until the three weeks before his death. Survivors include his wife, their two children, two stepsons, six grandchildren, and two great-grandchildren. **Sources:** *Chicago Tribune,* September 12, 2009, sec. 2, p. 11; *Contemporary Authors Online,* Gale, 2009; *Los Angeles Times,* September 12, 2009; *New York Times,* September 12, 2009; *Times* (London), September 14, 2009; *Washington Post,* September 11, 2009.

—*Alana Joli Abbott*

Israel M. Gelfand

Born Israel Moiseevich Gelfand, September 2, 1913, in Krasnye Okny, Ukraine; died October 5, 2009, in New Brunswick, NJ. Mathematician. While most modern mathematicians specialize in increasingly specialized theoretical and esoteric areas, or work to solve famous mathematical puzzles, Israel Gelfand was among the dying breed of generalists, interested in practical, varied, and wide-ranging uses for math and math concepts, such as those required for now-standard MRI and CT scans in medical applications. According to Rutgers University colleague Vladimir Retakh in the *Washington Post,* Gelfand was considered the "greatest mathematician of the last half of the 20th century." In the *New York Times,* Retakh added, "He was probably the last of the greatest who worked in almost every area of mathematics."

Born in 1913 in Okny, Ukraine, Gelfand did not complete high school or earn an undergraduate degree; instead, his educational background was largely a self-taught one. Gelfand's mill-operator father had a mill assistant, and in the eyes of the then-Soviet Socialist Republic country, this made the family capitalists by definition, causing Gelfand to be expelled from technical school before he had finished ninth grade. Learning never lost its appeal, however, and when he was hospitalized at age 15 for appendicitis, he requested a calculus textbook, which he read and completely mastered during his 12-day stay.

In 1930, while still a teenager, Gelfand moved to Moscow to find employment. At Moscow State University, mathematics seminars were regularly in session, and the unschooled but brilliant Gelfand regularly took part while working odd jobs to support himself. His intelligence did not escape the notice of the famous mathematician Andrei Kolmogorov, and in 1932, despite his Jewish heritage and his lack of formal schooling, the young Gelfand was admitted directly to the graduate school, where he first earned a regular doctorate followed by a higher doctorate. According to the London *Times,* fellow student Vladimir Arnold reported that if Professor Kolmogorov and Gelfand found themselves in the mountains, "Kolmogorov would start scaling the highest peaks, while Gelfand would start building roads."

Although his valued intelligence protected him from the worst fates of the Jews during the World War II years, the rampant anti-Semitism around him did cause him to be forced out of both the Steklov Institute and Moscow State University and into a lesser position at the Institute of Applied Mathematics. Additionally, although he was admitted to the Soviet Academy of Sciences as a corresponding member in 1953, he did not receive full membership status recognition until 1984.

In 1943, Gelfand recreated the mathematics seminars that had opened so many doors for him, but in the legendary weekly seminars he conducted until the 1990s, when he began them anew at Rutgers, the participants—students and professors alike—were more involved in unscripted mathematical conversation than in listening to a lecture. Edward Frenkel, a University of California-Berkeley mathematician who worked with Gelfand in Moscow, described the atmosphere to the *Los Angeles Times* as an hours-long, social gathering. "He would walk the aisles, stop and chat with people, interrupt and ask questions, pull a member of the audience to the blackboard and ask them to repeat what had just been said or to find a mistake in it. His interest was always in the development of the next generation of mathematicians."

Gelfand began a similar seminar in mathematical biology when his young son was diagnosed with leukemia, but he did not reestablish this series after leaving Moscow. In 1989, he spent a brief year in Massachusetts at both Harvard University and the Massachusetts Institute of Technology, finally setting at Rutgers University in New Jersey where he remained for the rest of his life.

In the 1990s, in addition to reestablishment of the mathematics seminars, Gelfand created a correspondence program for rural teenagers who would otherwise have no access to training in mathematics, offering opportunities for study and personal growth. "Mathematics is a way of thinking in everyday life," he told the *New York Times.* "It is important not to separate mathematics from life."

In addition to his work which later became the framework for now commonplace medical imaging applications, Gelfand's work in representation theory was a crucial part of quantum physics, and his early work in the Weiner Taubman theory ushered classical analysis to functional. Gelfand reportedly thought of himself as being the mathematician equivalent of Mozart, whose greatness is recognized in the sum total of his body of work, not in individual compositions; indeed, Gelfand's prolific writings total 3,000 pages.

For his extraordinary work in mathematics, Gelfand was the recipient of several awards, including the Wolfe Prize, the Steele Prize, the Kyoto Prize, three Orders of Lenin, and a grant by the John D. and Catherine T. MacArthur Foundation. He was also awarded honorary degrees from such institutions as Oxford University and was a foreign member of the American Mathematical Society, the London Mathematical Society, the Royal Society of Sciences, and the U.S. National Academy of Sciences.

Gelfand and his first wife, Zorya Shapiro, had three sons before divorcing. One son, Aleksandr, died in childhood of leukemia. Gelfand remarried, and he and second wife Tatiana, who was also a mathematician, had a daughter. He died at Robert Wood Johnson University Hospital in New Brunswick, New Jersey, on October 5, 2009; he was 96. Gelfand is survived by his wife, sons Sergei and Vladimir, daughter Tatiana, four grandchildren, and three great-grandchildren. **Sources:** *Los Angeles Times,* http://www.latimes.com/news/nationworld/ nation/la-me-israel-gelfand11-2009oct11,0,2421446. story (March 18, 2010); *New York Times,* http:// www.nytimes.com/2009/10/08/science/08gelfand. html?_r=1&partner=rss&emc=rss (March 18, 2010); *Times* (London), http://www.timesonline.co.uk/ tol/comment/obituaries/article6879978.ece (March 18, 2010); *Washington Post,* http://www.washing tonpost.com/wp-dyn/content/article/2009/10/11/ AR20091011.tif01927.html?wprss=rss_metro/ obituaries (April 7, 2010).

—*Helene Barker Kiser*

Vitaly L. Ginzburg

Born Vitaly Lazarevich Ginzburg, October 4, 1916, in Moscow, Russia; died of a heart attack, November 8, 2009, in Moscow. Physicist. Russian physicist Vitaly L. Ginzburg played a key role in his country's development of its first hydrogen bomb. Working with the famed Soviet scientist Andrei Sakharov, Ginzburg concocted the correct recipe for the thermonuclear explosive device's fuel supply, which resulted in the first successful test in August of 1953. Many years later, Ginzburg shared a Nobel Prize in physics for his other area of research, super-conductivity.

Ginzburg was born in the pre-Soviet era, when Imperial Russia still used the so-called Old Calendar, also known as the Julian calendar and which dated back to the Roman era. Therefore the date of his birth appears as either September 21, 1916 (Old Calendar) or October 4, 1916 (New Calendar) of the Gregorian system adopted by most of Europe in the 1600s. He grew up in Moscow, the soon-to-be new capital of Soviet Russia, in a Jewish family of professionals. It was a time of world war and great political and social turmoil, however, and Ginzburg did not begin his formal schooling until the age of eleven. A few years later, his school was closed down, but a family connection helped him land a job as a laboratory assistant. He went on to Moscow State University, earning advanced degrees, the last of which was a doctorate in science in 1942, the same year he joined the Communist Party.

By that point, the Soviet Union was mired in another world war, and the resulting postwar battle for control over the spoils of Europe became known as the cold war. The United States and the Soviet Union vied for status as a global superpower, and an arms race began in earnest, with each country stockpiling a vast array of nuclear weapons. The Americans developed the first atomic bomb, and Soviet leader Josef Stalin marshaled the country's prodigious resources to build a Soviet hydrogen bomb with immense explosive capacity.

Scientists working on this project needed top security clearance, and Ginzburg's intellectual gifts likely helped him land a place on the bomb team in 1950 despite the fact that his wife had once been arrested in an anti-Stalin plot. He worked with Sakharov, widely revered as the father of the Soviet H-bomb, and devised a nuclear fuel recipe that used tritium, an isotope of hydrogen. "Ginzburg's insight was that it could be made, within the device, by bombarding solid lithium deuteride with neutrons," explained Frank Close in the *Guardian*.

Soviet scientists and other classes of professionals were occasionally targeted by Communist Party officials and the authoritarian state's pervasive secret service; in some cases these were regular purges of Jewish leaders in their fields. Ginzburg was removed from the H-bomb team for a time in the early 1950s, but Stalin's death in 1953 prevented any further consequences. "It was a tremendous luck that the great leader did not have enough time to carry

out what he had planned to do and died, or was killed," that March, Ginzburg recalled in an autobiographical statement he wrote years later for his Nobel Prize ceremony, according to his *New York Times* obituary. "In the former U.S.S.R. many people (at any rate, my wife and I) have up till now been celebrating this day as a great festival."

Ginzburg was able to return to the H-bomb team and inducted into the Russian Academy of Sciences. In a separate area of research, he and theoretical physicist Lev Davidovich Landau unlocked the secret of how superconductivity worked. This led to experiments with magnetic fields of immense size, and then the development of the first superconductive wire in the early 1960s. "Superconductivity has vast implications in technology, being used in powerful electromagnets, such as are found in MRI scanners in hospitals, in magnetic levitation systems for high-speed transport, and in the world's largest cryogenic facility—the 27[kilometer] ring of super-conducting magnets of the Large Hadron Collider, the particle accelerator, at Cern in Geneva," Close wrote in Ginzburg's *Guardian* obituary.

For many years Ginzburg taught at Moscow State University and, after 1971, served as director of the I. E. Tamm Theory Department at the Lebedev Physical Institute of the Russian Academy of Sciences. His H-bomb team colleague, Sakharov, fared less well in the post-Stalin Soviet Union: Sakharov became a prominent voice in the anti-nuclear movement and spent six years under virtual house arrest in the city of Gorky, which was closed to outsiders.

In 2003 the Nobel committee awarded Ginzburg that year's prize in physics, along with Landau—who had died in 1968—another Russian physicist named Alexei Abrikosov, and Anthony Leggett, a British scientist, for their work on the theory of superconductivity. Ginzburg submitted a long, 14,000-word autobiography for the august prize ceremony in Stockholm, in which he recounted the climate of fear and persecution he and others had toiled under for their country during the tense years of the cold war. Later, he used his position to criticize the rising influence of the Russian Orthodox Church in the post-Soviet era. He died of a heart attack in Moscow at the age of 93 on November 8, 2009. Survivors include his wife, Nina, and a daughter from his first marriage. "The forces of democracy," he wrote in his Nobel Prize essay, as quoted in his *Guardian* obituary, "have saved civilized society and nowadays both nazism and communism have almost sunk into oblivion." **Sources:** *Guardian* (London), November 15, 2009; *New York Times*, November 10, 2009; *Times* (London), November 10, 2009, p. 61.

—*Carol Brennan*

Alfred Gottschalk

Born March 7, 1930, in Oberwesel, Germany; died of complications following an automobile accident, September 12, 2009, in Cincinnati, OH. Rabbi. Alfred Gottschalk was a leading figure in American Reform Judaism as president of Hebrew Union College-Jewish Institute of Religion (HUC), the foremost training ground for rabbis in this branch of Judaism. The scholar, rabbi, and administrator presided over many sweeping changes during his 25-year tenure as head of the oldest Jewish seminary in the Western Hemisphere, including the ordination of the first female rabbi in the United States and the admission of openly gay and lesbian students into rabbinical-studies programs.

Gottschalk's life and career was shaped by the Holocaust. He was born in the northern German town of Oberwesel in 1930, where his family's roots stretched back to the 1500s. Before he turned three, Adolf Hitler and the Nazi Party rose to power, and Germany began enacting anti-Semitic laws that dispossessed Jews of their property rights, careers, citizenship, and finally their freedom; some six million of Europe's Jews would perish in Nazi concentration camps between 1933 and 1945, when World War II finally came to an end. Gottschalk was eight years old in November of 1938 on the infamous *Kristallnacht,* or Night of Broken Glass, when Jewish synagogues across Germany were targeted by organized mob violence. The sacred Torah scrolls of the Oberwesel synagogue were thrown into the Rhine River, but Gottschalk's grandfather fished them out, gave them to him, and said, "One day you will put it together again," according to Elaine Woo in the *Chicago Tribune.*

Gottschalk's father emigrated first, leaving Germany for New York City, and Gottschalk and his mother followed a year later. The family settled in Brooklyn, where Gottschalk taught himself English by watching movies from funds he earned shining shoes. He became a naturalized citizen in 1945 while a student at Boys High School in Brooklyn, and decided to become a rabbi around this same period, when the full horror of the Holocaust was revealed

to the Jewish diaspora; 55 members of his family had died, along with the majority of their neighbors in Oberwesel.

After earning his undergraduate degree from Brooklyn College in 1952, Gottschalk enrolled at the Hebrew Union College (HUC) in Cincinnati, Ohio. He was ordained a rabbi in 1957 and went on to complete his doctoral studies at the University of Southern California in Jewish thought and biblical studies in 1965. A teaching post at the Hebrew Union College's California outpost led to a promotion as dean of the Los Angeles HUC campus, and he oversaw a major initiative to build a new campus nearer to the University of Southern California and the forging of an academic partnership between the two institutions.

In 1971, Gottschalk was chosen by the HUC's board of governors to become the school's sixth president. Formally known as the Hebrew Union College-Jewish Institute of Religion after a 1950 merger between the Cincinnati and New York City schools, the HUC organization was a major force in Reform Judaism, which is the most liberal of the three Jewish sects, after the Orthodox and Conservative wings. Reform Judaism is also the most common denomination of American Jews, and the HUC had long been the center for the movement, which began in Germany but gained momentum in the United States in the 1870s. "The purpose of Jewish learning is to create a human being who is a Jew, passionately attached to the knowledge and values of the past and deeply involved in the burning present and in the life of his people," Gottschalk told the *New York Times* in an article about his selection as the new HUC president.

Gottschalk continued a long tradition of adapting to modern life that is the cornerstone of Reform Judaism. In June of 1972, he ordained Sally Priesand as the first woman rabbi in mainstream Judaism in the United States. The history-making ordination provoked intense criticism from leaders of the Orthodox and Conservative wings, but the Jewish Theological Seminary of America—the home of the Conservative branch—eventually followed suit and ordained a female rabbi in 1985. Gottschalk also promoted the investiture of the first female cantor in American Reform Judaism, Barbara Herman, in 1975, and later permitted openly gay and lesbian students to enroll at the HUC, which eventually led to a 1990 vote at the 101st Central Conference of American Rabbis to permit gay and lesbian Jews to enter the Reform rabbinate.

In 1996 Gottschalk retired as president of the HUC, but served as chancellor of the school for the next four years. He later served as president of the Museum of Jewish Heritage in New York City. In October of 2008 he was involved in a car accident, and died almost a year later of injuries from it on September 12, 2009, in Cincinnati, Ohio; he was 79. Survivors include his second wife, Deanna Zeff Frank, a son and daughter from his first marriage, Marc and Rachel, five grandchildren, two stepsons, and four step-grandchildren.

Gottschalk played a vital role in the creation of the U.S. Holocaust Memorial Museum, which opened on Washington, D.C.'s National Mall in 1993. Back in the 1970s he had been appointed to a commission that was charged with planning a monument for victims of the Holocaust, but argued that a museum was in order. "Other members of the memorial council suggested he 'lighten up,'" wrote Douglas Martin in the *New York Times*, to which he responded, "I didn't travel this far to lighten up." **Sources:** *Chicago Tribune*, September 18, 2009, sec. 1, p. 32; *The Forward*, September 25, 2009; *New York Times*, June 4, 1971, p. 12; September 15, 2009; *Washington Post*, September 17, 2009.

—*Carol Brennan*

Esther Hautzig

Born Esther Rudoman, October 18, 1930, in Vilnius, Lithuania; died of congestive heart failure and Alzheimer's disease, November 1, 2009, in New York, NY. Author. Esther Hautzig is best remembered for a 1968 memoir of her life as a teenager during World War II. Her Lithuanian Jewish family was fortunate to escape the Holocaust, but endured tremendous hardship as exiles in Siberia, where they lived in an unheated hut and scrounged for enough food to avoid starvation. In *The Endless Steppe*, Hautzig sought to depict her life as one nevertheless marked by typical events common to the life of any young teen. "I went to school there, made friends, learned how to survive no matter what life brought," she once wrote elsewhere, according to the *Washington Post*.

Hautzig was born Esther Rudoman in 1930 in what was then Vilna, Poland, but later became the capital of modern-day Lithuania as the renamed city of Vilnius. Hers was an affluent family who was part of the city's flourishing Jewish community, which had made Vilna the center of Jewish learning and culture in that part of the world on the eve of World War II. Like others, the Rudomans were unnerved by developments in Western Europe, as Nazi Ger-

many began restricting German Jews' civil rights and then sending them to labor camps in Poland, a practice that followed for every country the Nazi army invaded in its quest to conquer all of Europe.

In June of 1940, the eastern part of Poland was invaded by Soviet troops as part of a German-Soviet agreement. The world's first Communist nation seized Lithuania's assets wholesale, and middle-class families like the Rudomans were deemed capitalist conspirators and deported to Siberia for re-education through hard labor. The ten-year-old Hautzig and her family, including her aging grandparents, spent weeks locked inside a crowded cattle car as it wended its way through the Russian steppes to Siberia. In the town of Rubtsovsk, Hautzig's grandfather was separated from the family and died in a camp; Hautzig's mother went to work in a gypsum mine while Hautzig and her grandmother worked as farm laborers. Finally, intervention by foreign diplomats helped end their status as prisoners, and they were allowed to live in the village on their own. They lived in an unheated hut and spent much of the war scavenging for food in a climate where few nourishing crops could grow. Hautzig's father, meanwhile, was drafted into the Red Army.

When the war ended, Hautzig's family returned to Poland, and learned that most of their surviving family was gone: the 1940 Russian invasion had been followed, a year later, by a Nazi one, and most of Lithuania's Jews perished in concentration camps. Of the 57,000 Jews in the city on the eve of the war, just 3,000 remained in Vilnius. Among the missing was her mother's brother, Ela-Chaim Cunzer, a beloved uncle of Hautzig's who had actually turned up at their house on the day the Soviets came to arrest the Rudomans. Hautzig's mother, Raya, told the Soviet officials she did not know him, hoping to spare him from arrest.

The Rudomans went to Sweden, and from there the 17-year-old Hautzig applied for and was granted a student visa for the United States. On board a ship called the *Drottninghom* she met Walter Hautzig, a concert pianist from Vienna, who became her husband three years later. Hautzig completed her schooling at Brooklyn's James Madison High School and went on to Hunter College, but was discouraged from becoming a teacher because of her heavily accented English. For a number of years she worked as a secretary at G. P. Putnam's, the publishing house, while becoming a mother to a son and daughter. Her first book, *Let's Cook Without Cooking*, was a children's title that appeared in 1955. She also drew upon the craft skills she honed in Rubtsovsk for another how-to book for young readers, *Let's Make Presents*.

In 1958, a prominent U.S. politician, Adlai Stevenson, visited several Soviet cities, including Rubtsovsk. Impressed by the two-time Democratic presidential candidate's written accounts of the Siberian town, Hautzig wrote to him to tell him of her experiences, and it was Stevenson who suggested she commit her own recollections to paper. The result was *The Endless Steppe*, published by HarperCollins in 1968. It earned excellent reviews as well as comparisons to Anne Frank's *The Diary of a Young Girl*, another memoir of a young Jewish teen during World War II with a more tragic outcome.

Hautzig visited Vilnius in the early 1990s—despite her mother's caution to avoid her once-idyllic childhood home—to successfully hunt down a single picture of her late uncle that the family knew probably still existed somewhere in his application to the University of Vilna. She also wrote a few other books, including a 1990 memoir, *Remember Who You Are*, before her death from congestive heart failure and complications from Alzheimer's disease on November 1, 2009, at New York Presbyterian Hospital. She was 79 and is survived by her husband, her son David, her daughter Deborah, and three grandchildren. **Sources:** *Los Angeles Times*, November 12, 2009; *New York Times*, April 21, 1996; November 4, 2009; *Washington Post*, November 12, 2009.

—Carol Brennan

Paula Hawkins

Born Paula Fickes on January 24, 1927, in Salt Lake City, UT; died from complications after a stroke, December 4, 2009, in Orlando, FL. Politician. Prior to the late twentieth century, women had to have a father or husband in politics to be taken seriously when running for public office. In 1980 Paula Hawkins broke that trend, becoming the first woman without family ties to be elected to a full term in the Senate. A conservative Republican from Florida, she served under then-President Ronald Reagan from 1981 to 1987, championing family and children's causes.

Born in 1927 in Salt Lake City, Utah, Hawkins grew up Mormon in the "Beehive State," but her childhood was not idyllic. In a 1984 Senate hearing, she revealed that she had been sexually molested as a child. After she graduated from high school, she attended Utah State University from 1944 to 1947 and also did some work as a model. She married Gene

Hawkins, an electrical engineer, and the couple moved to Florida in 1955, where they would live the rest of their life together.

After the cross-country relocation, Hawkins was active both in raising her three children and in her local community. In later years, as a senator, she would vocally support legislation that would financially benefit women's pension and retirement funds to acknowledge and recognize the years they spent at home, raising their children and caring for their families, instead of earning a paycheck by being in the workforce. She was a GOP committee member, director of the Rural Telephone Bank Board, and vice president of Air Florida.

In 1972, she was elected to her first term on the Florida Public Service Commission, with a second term following in 1976. On the commission, she was widely known and respected as a great consumer advocate. She first ran for Senate in 1976, but was unsuccessful, and she also put her hat in the ring for Florida's lieutenant governor in 1978. It was not until Ronald Reagan rode the tidal wave of support into office that her bid for higher public service was successful. Hawkins was confirmed in the Senate in 1981.

Her historic win was even more impressive because the Hawkins campaign was not a wealthy one. For example, instead of a teleprompter, her staff unrolled the paper towels on which her speeches were written, so she could read the rolls as she talked.

When she arrived in Washington, the fitness conscious Hawkins insisted that the until then all-male environment of the Senate gym adjust to accommodate the presence of women during the day, which effectively forced swim trunks to be required attire. This was a remarkable feat, considering the fact that these were the days when it was still appropriate for a national network television reporter to ask Hawkins during a news conference who would do her laundry since she was too busy working in Congress. Her short reply, according to the *New York Times*, was "I don't really think you need to worry about my laundry. O.K.?"

The conservative, family oriented Hawkins was no feminist, but she worked tirelessly to support and affirm women's rights and strong parent-child relationships. Among her causes was legislation that eased the way for single women, whether divorced or widowed, to join the traditionally male workforce. In addition to elevating the importance of a mother's years at home raising children, she was a vocal supporter of offering the now-common tax breaks for child care expenses. In 1982, Hawkins' voice aided in the passage of the national clearinghouse for information to help in the identification and location of missing children, the Missing Children's Act.

Despite her credentials and support for women's issues, she was not widely supported by more liberal women's groups, including the influential National Organization for Women, largely because of her traditional beliefs about family and gender roles. For example, Hawkins was not interested in becoming a member of the Congressional Women's Caucus because she did not believe the issues it concerned itself with—including equitability of retirement benefits and child care concerns —were women's issues but family ones. The *New York Times* acknowledged her comments to the *Washington Post* that such issues have "emasculated the male." She did not hold a pro-choice position on abortion, because it went against the nature of human life. According to the *Washington Post,* Hawkins did not support the Equal Rights Amendment because "I predicted that it would bring about the downfall of the father's responsibility to support the family."

Hawkins was not successful in her bid for reelection, and then-Governor of Florida, Bob Graham, a Democrat, won her seat in 1986. Hawkins might have had better luck in the election had an earlier accident not necessitated back surgery in the middle of the campaign. In 1982, Hawkins had been struck by a heavy backdrop during a television taping, an accident that knocked her unconscious, contributing to complications from back injuries in a car accident from years before, which caused her to suffer from severe, lifelong pain. In 1986, her back surgery was a significant factor in her ability to travel and campaign properly.

In 1998, Hawkins suffered a stroke which left her partially paralyzed. She fell in late 2009 and was hospitalized in an Orlando hostpital, where she died on December 4 at the age of 82. Hawkins is survived by her husband, her daughters, Genean and Kelly; her son, Kevin; eleven grandchildren, and ten great-grandchildren. **Sources:** *Los Angeles Times,* http://www.latimes.com/news/obituaries/la-me-paula-hawkins7-2009dec07,0,7260840.story?track= rss&utm_source=feedburner&utm_medium= feed&utm_campaign=Feed%3A+latimes%2Fnews %2Fobituaries+%28Los+Angeles+Times+-+Obitu aries%29&utm_content=Google+Reader (September 16, 2010); *New York Times,* http://www.nytimes. com/2009/12/05/us/05hawkins.html?_r=1&part ner=rss&emc=rss (September 16, 2010); *Washington Post,* http://www.washingtonpost.com/wp-dyn/ content/article/2009/12/04/AR20091204.tif04335. html?wprss=rss_metro/obituaries (September 16, 2010).

—*Helene Barker Kiser*

Tommy Henrich

Born Thomas David Henrich, February 20, 1913, in Massillon, OH; died December 1, 2009, in Dayton, OH. Professional baseball player. While not a legend like teammates Joe DiMaggio, Lou Gehrig, and Yogi Berra, Yankees right-fielder Tommy Henrich was the player the team counted on when the game was a tough one. Nicknamed "Old Reliable" for his uncanny ability to play best when it counted most, a title he also deserved off the field, Henrich helped the Yankees win multiple World Championships and pennants and was himself both a five time All-Star and an American League record-setter.

Born in 1913 in the football town of Massillon, Ohio, Henrich, who bucked the local trend by rooting for the New York Yankees, did not have an easy time finding decent baseball fields where he lived so he could play and hone his growing skill. In fact, as a youth, he had to play high school softball, finally joining a town baseball team. From there, he was recruited by the Cleveland Indians in the autumn of 1933 to play for its minor league teams.

Henrich was able to shine in this role, batting more than .300 in all three seasons and distinguishing himself on the field as well; however, by 1937 the Indians had still not promoted him from the minors. Afraid he would continue to languish on the farm teams, watching his career go nowhere fast, the frustrated Henrich wrote to Kenesaw Mountain Landis, the then-baseball commissioner, in an attempt to ascertain whether or not his treatment by the Indians was fair and proper. In April of that year, Landis determined that Henrich was in fact being treated unfairly and, more importantly, released him to sign with another team.

The Yankees were happy to sign Henrich with a $20,000 bonus, and Henrich could not believe his good fortune to sign with the team he had idolized since he was a boy of eight years old, the team on which his favorite player, Babe Ruth, had made a name for himself. Even better, Henrich would inherit Ruth's former right field position from Ruth successor George Selkirk, and would play next to center field legend DiMaggio, who the *Washington Post* reported describing Henrich as baseball's smartest player.

Henrich rose to the challenge, continually working to improve himself by studying the technique of other players, learning about the effect of wind currents on the ball, and paying close attention to what was happening on the field. According to the *Washington Post*, Henrich once said, "Catching a fly ball is a pleasure. But knowing what to do with it after you catch it is a business."

Henrich made it his business, with his quick thinking and faster playing, especially when the team was in a pinch. According to teammate and third baseman Bobby Brown in the *Los Angeles Times*, "If we were ahead 10-1 or 10-2, he was just average. If we were behind 10-1 or 10-2, same thing. But get him in a big game and he was terrific." Brown went on to tell the *New York Times*, "He was his best in the big games, and he never made a mistake in the outfield."

This ability to pull out all the stops when big plays were needed was what earned him his moniker. During an overtime game against the Philadelphia Athletics, both teams were unable to break the tie and the Yankees had to hurry to catch a train, so time was of the essence. According to the *New York Times*, Henrich told a reporter for the *Chicago Sun-Times* that after his hit won the game for the Yankees, radio broadcaster Mel Allen quipped "Good old reliable Henrich. Looks like we'll catch the train after all."

He was Old Reliable off the field as well, and was the rare professional ball player who was known for his strength of moral character. With the exception of a three-year hiatus from baseball, during which Henrich was called to serve in the U.S. Coast Guard in World War II, "Old Reliable" never left the Yankees, playing on the team for eleven seasons. He was benched several times due to injuries, including knee surgery in 1940. Even that turn of events turned out lucky for him, as he met and married his future wife and lifelong companion, Eileen O'Reilly, one of the nurses who took care of him during and after the surgery.

Henrich retired for the Yankees in 1950 with a career batting average of .283, 183 home runs, and 795 RBIs, and having played for both Joe McCarthy and Casey Stengel. After retiring, he stayed to coach the team, including new center fielder Mickey Mantle, who was just 19 years old. Henrich also coached

briefly for both the New York Giants and the Detroit Tigers. He was a gifted singer, one part of a championship barbershop quartet, and would happily and skillfully entertain his teammates with song. According to Berra, speaking in an official statement from the team in the *Los Angeles Times*, "Being around Tommy made you feel good.... He was a proud man, and if you knew him, he made you proud too."

Preceded in death by his wife of more than 60 years, who died just a few months earlier in March 2009, Henrich passed away in Dayton, Ohio, on December 1, 2009, at the age of 96. He had been the oldest living Yankee and the last remaining member of 1930s Yankee teams. Henrich is survived by his daughters, Patricia, Mary, and Ann; his sons, Tom and Paul; three grandchildren, and three great-grandchildren. **Sources:** *Los Angeles Times*, http://www.latimes.com/news/obituaries/la-me-tommy-henrich2-2009dec02,0,3900105.story?track=rss&utm_source=feedburner&utm_medium=feed&utm_campaign=Feed%3A+latimes%2Fnews%2Fobitua}ries+%28Los+Angeles+Times+-+Obituaries%29&utm_content=Google+Reader (September 16, 2010); *New York Times*, http://www.nytimes.com/2009/12/02/obituaries/02henrich.html?_r=2&partner=rss&emc=rss (September 16, 2010); *Washington Post*, http://www.washingtonpost.com/wp-dyn/content/article/2009/12/02/AR20091202.tif03995.html?wprss=rss_metro/obituaries (September 16, 2010).

—*Helene Barker Kiser*

Mahlon Hoagland

Born Mahlon Bush Hoagland, October 5, 1921, in Boston, MA; died September 18, 2009, in Thetford, CT. Biochemist. During the 1960s, when the study of DNA was at the forefront of biological and medical research, Mahlon Hoagland's discovery of transfer RNA (tRNA) provided the key information on how the genetic information stored in DNA was converted to the proteins necessary for proper cell function. After spending his career in biological research, Hoagland went on to a second career, writing accessible and lucid books on biological topics for a lay audience.

Born in 1921, Hoagland was the son of Hudson Hoagland, co-founder of the Worcester Foundation for Experimental Biology. His research physiologist father spent many long hours in the laboratory, and although Hoagland shared his father's interest in science in general and biology in particular, he did not want to be slave to the grueling schedule of a research scientist, and he decided to study medicine instead. After high school, Hoagland attended Williams College for one year, then transferred to Harvard University.

His college years in the 1940s put Hoagland in school during World War II, timing that coincided with a program allowing students to begin medical school without first completing an undergraduate degree program. He graduated with his M.D. in 1948, but did not serve in the military or begin a career as a pediatric surgeon as expected. While treating a baby, Hoagland contracted tuberculosis, and the disease so weakened him that he was forced to shift his career plans. Following in his father's footsteps after all, Hoagland ultimately focused on biological research. The timing serendipitously put him right in the center of cutting edge research on DNA.

While the existence of DNA had been determined in the 1800s by Johann Friedrich Miescher, the understanding of its structure and its role in biology was not understood until the 1950s and 1960s. Without the component known as transfer RNA (tRNA), discovered by Hoagland in conjunction with Paul Zamecnik at Massachusetts General Hospital in 1958, the DNA could not be used properly by cells; the tRNA function is to transfer the amino acids to appropriate places in protein chains, the ribosome.

Hoagland and Zamecnik's research first showed how amino acids acquired energy by enzyme catalysts, proving the theory through the use of radioactive labels in a cell-free system constructed from rat liver elements. This research led to the isolation and identification of the necessary molecule tRNA, the missing link bridging the gap from amino acid to ribosome, in order that the genetic codes in the cells could be carried by messenger RNA and used by the body. Colleague James Watson, who shared the 1962 Nobel Prize in medicine for discovering DNA's structure and who worked with Hoagland at the Cavendish Laboratory at Cambridge University, told the Los Angeles Times that Hoagland and Zamecnik "deserved to win the Nobel Prize for their fundamental work on tRNA."

After his work with tRNA, Hoagland continued research in other areas, including beryllium, coenzyme A, and liver regeneration. He would also become an outspoken proponent of the need for research funding to ensure medical advancement, helping to form the Delegation for Basic Biomedical Research with several Nobel laureate members, to lobby Congress for support. In 1970, he moved from Massachusetts General to become the scientific director for the Worcester Foundation his father had co-founded. He retired in 1985; the Foundation became part of the University of Massachusetts Medical School in 1997.

Retirement for Hoagland meant a shift to different work, not a cessation of work. He took up the mantle of author, penning multiple books on biology for general audiences as well as the award-winning textbook The Way Life Works, for which Bert Dodson created original watercolors, and which won the 1996 American Medical Writers Book Award. Teaching was important to Hoagland—he was the microbiology department head of Dartmouth Medical School and associate professor of microbiology at Harvard Medical School—and he believed textbooks were often unnecessarily dense and complex. Thoru Pederson, Hoagland's colleague, described his colorful and engaging writing to the New York Times, saying Hoagland was "an extremely skillful exponent of the joy of scientific discovery for lay audiences."

In his spare time, he enjoyed sculpting, using wood as the medium to create many figures, including women and children, seagulls, and, perhaps unsurprisingly, the DNA double helix. Hoagland married Elizabeth Stratton in 1943 and the couple had four children together, one of whom, daughter Susan, predeceased him. The Hoaglands divorced, and he married Olley Virginia Jones, a bookseller, who died just a few months before he did.

At the end of his life, Hoagland was diagnosed with cardiovascular disease and kidney failure. At his request, he opted to remain out of the hospital, doing without food and water so he could die peacefully at home in Thetford, Vermont. He passed away after nine days, on September 18, 2009, surrounded by family; he was 87. He is survived by his daughters Judy and Robin, his son Mahlon "Jay" Jr., his stepsons Jeff, Jonathan, Jim, and Jeremy; his stepdaughter Jennifer, four grandchildren, and two great-grandchildren. **Sources:** *Los Angeles Times*, http://www.latimes.com/news/nationworld/nation/la-me-mahlon-hoagland17-2009oct17,0,4143793.story (March 18, 2010); *New York Times*, http://www.nytimes.com/2009/10/02/us/02hoagland.html?partner=rss&emc=rss (March 18, 2010); *Washington Post*, http://www.washingtonpost.com/wp-dyn/content/article/2009/10/05/AR20091005.tif03571.html?wprss=rss_metro/obituaries (March 18, 2010).

Helene Barker Kiser

Thomas Hoving

Born Thomas Pearsall Field Hoving, January 15, 1931, in New York, NY; died of lung cancer, December 10, 2009, in New York, NY. Museum director. Thomas Hoving spent an energetic decade transforming the staid Metropolitan Museum of Art in New York City into a dynamic, pace-setting leader in the museum world. Hired in 1967 when he was just 36, "Hoving introduced shops and restaurants to the Met," noted his *Times* of London obituary, "transforming it from a cultural haven to an infotainment mecca, and was more than any single museum director responsible for drawing millions to gaze at art by staging blockbuster exhibitions."

Born in 1931 in New York, Hoving grew up in a rarified, bygone midcentury Manhattan. On his mother's side, he was a descendant of one of the first U.S. postmasters general; his father was a successful retail executive with Bonwit Teller before he became president of Tiffany & Company. The Hovings divorced when their son was five, and he went on to rack up a problematic disciplinary record in his teen years as he moved from one private school to another. At Princeton University, he settled down and majored in fine art, graduating summa cum laude in 1953. After a three-year stint in the U.S. Marines, he announced his intention to pursue a graduate degree in art history. His father objected and refused to fund the plan, but Hoving won a fellowship at Princeton and earned both a master's degree and his doctorate.

James J. Rorimer, the director of the Metropolitan Museum of Art, heard Hoving give a lecture at the Frick Collection in 1959, and offered him a job as junior curator at The Cloisters, a reassembled abbey from France that, in its new location in Washington Heights' Fort Tryon Park, housed the Met's medieval art collection. Hoving quickly made a name for himself in the art world when he managed to land a near-priceless artifact for The Cloisters, a large, intricately carved 12th-century altar cross of walrus ivory from the Bury St. Edmunds Abbey in England.

In 1965, Hoving was promoted to chief curator for medieval artifacts at the Met. He left a year later when John Lindsay became mayor of New York City and offered him the job of Parks Commissioner. His tenure in that post set the stage for his future career at the Met: Hoving made controversial decisions that, in the end, proved enduringly popular. He halted Sunday automobile traffic in Central Park and, borrowing a term from the counterculture of the era, staged "happenings" in the park, including a concert by the rock group the Grateful Dead. Central Park's first bike lanes were also created during Hoving's era.

Because the Met backs up onto Central Park, Hoving's role as Parks Commissioner also gave him a seat on the museum's board of trustees. When Rorimer died suddenly in March of 1967, Hoving won the support of the board in his bid to succeed his mentor. He was just 36, making him the youngest director in the institution's history, and quickly announced his intention to turn the Met into a much livelier place while advancing its status as a world-class museum and city landmark.

Hoving began organizing major exhibitions that drew large crowds and were heavily promoted. There was "The Great Age of Fresco: Giotto to Pontormo" in 1968, 1969's controversial multimedia exhibit "Harlem on My Mind," and "The Impressionist Epoch" in 1974. But Hoving's biggest coup was bringing the rare artifacts from the tomb of ancient Egypt's fabled boy king, "Treasures of Tutankhamun," to the United States. The dazzling objects, discovered only in the 1920s and some made of solid gold, were displayed in five U.S. cities before coming to the Met in 1978, shattering attendance records for the museum and generating tremendous popular interest.

Hoving faced down critics who claimed he overcommercialized the museum experience, festooning the Met's façade with showy banners announcing the new exhibitions and adding a gift shop stocked with exhibition-themed merchandise, but these practices became standard in the museum world. Serious collectors and scholars derided his tactics as more suitable to that of a circus promoter, but Hoving liked to assert that "great art should be shown with great excitement," according to his *New York Times* obituary.

During his decade on the job, Hoving made several notable—and expensive—acquisitions at the Met, vastly improved the museum's holdings in African and Islamic art, courted major bequests from donors, and hired fashion doyenne Diana Vreeland to run what had been a moribund Costume Institute. He also enlarged the Met's entrance steps, making them a favorite gathering spot for New Yorkers and visitors alike. Much of this was detailed in his 1993 memoir, *Making the Mummies Dance: Inside the Metropolitan Museum of Art*, which became a *New York Times* best-seller.

Hoving stepped down as director of the Met in 1977 to take a job at the University of Pennsylvania's Annenberg School of Communications, which fell through. The remainder of his career was spent as an art consultant, writer, correspondent for ABC's *20/20*, and editor of *Connoisseur* magazine. Diagnosed with lung cancer, he died at his New York City home on December 10, 2009, at the age of 78. Survivors include his wife, Nancy Bell Hoving, and his daughter, Petrea. "We are still working out of the model he set," the director of the Los Angeles County Museum of Art, Michael Govan, told *Los Angeles Times* writer Suzanne Muchnic about Hoving's renegade decade helming the Met. "Beyond blockbusters, it's the fundamental assumption that our museums have to be open and accessible to the public. That's his legacy, and it's a very important one." **Sources:** *Los Angeles Times*, December 11, 2009; *New York Times*, December 11, 2009; *Times* (London), December 15, 2009, p. 50; *Washington Post*, December 12, 2009.

—Carol Brennan

Jeanne-Claude

Born Jeanne-Claude Denant de Guillebon, June 13, 1935, in Casablanca, Morocco; died of a brain aneurysm, November 18, 2009, in New York, NY. Artist. Working for many years as a silent collaborator, Jeanne-Claude was instrumental to the vision and works of her husband, the artist Christo, throughout their marriage. Jeanne-Claude took on the role of the business manager for the pair's environmental spectacles. From wrapping the Reichstag in Berlin to planting 3,000 umbrellas in California and Japan, Christo and Jean-Claude made art on a large scale.

Like her husband, Jeanne-Claude went only by her first name. Beginning in 1961, the pair began creating large-scale art, always from their own budgets. To raise funds for their productions, they sold many of Christo's initial sketches for their projects, using exhibitions to raise not only money, but awareness about their future works.

Born on the same day as her future husband on June 13, 1935, Jeanne-Claude was the daughter of a French officer serving in Casablanca, Morocco. She received her education in France and Switzerland, earning a degree in Latin and philosophy from the University of Tunis in 1952.

She met Christo Javacheff, who was then still using his last name, in 1958 in Paris. He was a Bulgarian refugee, but had already started art projects that in-

volved wrapping objects, furniture, and oil drums. Jeanne-Claude was intended to marry Philippe Planchon, whom her parents felt was a better choice for her than a refugee artist. Jeanne-Claude and Christo had an affair before Jeanne-Claude's marriage, however, so that when she married Planchon, she was already pregnant. After only three weeks, Jeanne-Claude abandoned her marriage to continue her relationship with Christo. She gave birth to their son, the poet Cyril Christo, in 1960.

Though Jeanne-Claude had never intended to be an artist, she was caught up in Christo's projects. "I became an artist out of love for Christo," she was quoted as having said in the *Los Angeles Times*. "If he had been a dentist, then I would have become one, too." They launched their first major project together after the birth of Cyril, using the wrapping techniques Christo had already been working on when they met. The couple stacked oil barrels and packages wrapped with tarpaulin and rope in Cologne harbor. The following year, they blocked a major street in Paris with similar oil barrels, calling the work "Wall of Oil Barrels, Iron Curtain." The police were summoned, and Jeanne-Claude became the voice of the pair, trying to convince officials that the installation should remain in place for just a few hours.

The temporary nature of the displays of Christo and Jeanne-Claude were a trademark of their style. From their beginning years through when they hired a crew to help them install the displays, the works of art were never intended to be permanent. The *Los Angeles Times* quoted one of Jeanne-Claude's recollections of telling a worker on the New York installation "The Gates" why the projects were temporary. "I told him to think of a rainbow. And he grabbed my arm and says, 'I think I got it. If the gates were there all the time, after a while nobody would be looking at them and the magic would be gone.' And I said, 'You've got it better than most art historians.'"

Christo and Jeanne-Claude moved to New York in 1964 and became American citizens. They had gallery exhibitions to show the works they had in progress, selling sketches, collages, scale models, and objects by Christo to fund their next work. With their boundless imaginations, raising funds could be a challenge, especially with projects as large scale as wrapping one million square feet of Australian coastline, which they accomplished in 1969 on Little Bay in Sydney, in a display called "Wrapped Coast." A similar project called "Surrounded Islands" involved floating woven polypropylene fabric around the 11 islands in Miami's Biscayne Bay in 1983.

Some of the most famous projects by the pair, who were sometimes referred to as "The Christos," include 1970's "Valley Curtain," in which they hung 400-yard nylon curtain across a valley in Colorado; "Running Fence," a 1976 display of a fluttering fabric fence 24 miles long on the California hillsides; a display that involved the Pont Neuf bridge in Paris wrapped with gold material; and "Umbrellas," which featured 3,000 custom built umbrellas erected in California and Japan. The last became famous in part because, when the wind picked up, one of the umbrellas lifted off and killed an audience member. "The Gates," a 2005 installation in New York's Central Park, was more than 20 years in the making. They first pitched the idea—an installation of thousands of saffron colored, banner-like panels—to Parks Commissioner Henry Stern in 1979.

The Christos often met with hesitation from local authorities and officials about their works, despite the draw of the crowds. In the two weeks that "The Gates" was open, it had five million viewers. Despite the popularity, some officials have considered the installments to be less art and more spectacle or stunt. Other critics, however, have recognized the progress made by Jeanne-Claude and Christo in expanding the art field. *Washington Post* art critic Blake Gopnik wrote that the pair "have made some of the most important and impressive artworks of the last 40 years.... Never before in the history of Western art has sheer scale been so completely conquered as a medium for art."

Jeanne-Claude was a silent partner in the collaboration until 1995, when the pair changed their credits to "Christo and Jeanne-Claude," and Jeanne-Claude received credit for all the previous works retroactively. The artist suffered a brain aneurysm in 2009, and she died at the age of 74, mid-project. Her husband Christos pledged to finish their two works-in-progress: "Over the River," which was planned to be built over parts of the Arkansas River in Colorado; and "The Mastaba," to be built in the United Arab Emirates. **Sources:** *Los Angeles Times,* November 20, 2009; *New York Times,* November 20, 2009; *Times* (London), November 21, 2009; *Washington Post,* November 20, 2009.

—Alana Joli Abbott

Jennifer Jones

Born Phylis Lee Isley, March 2, 1919, in Tulsa, OK; died of natural causes, December 17, 2009, in Malibu, CA. Actress. Jennifer Jones won an Academy Award in 1944 for her first feature role as the saintly nun in *The Song of Bernadette.* She went on to a stellar career as one of Hollywood's biggest stars of the 1950s, but some film critics assert her career was unduly stifled by her interfering husband, studio mogul David O. Selznick. Jones later married industrialist and art collector Norton Simon, and enjoyed a lengthy second career as the guardian of his collection at the Pasadena Art Museum.

Jones was born Phylis Isley in Tulsa, Oklahoma, in 1919, to parents who ran a traveling vaudeville tent show. Her first performances were on its stage, and she went on to Northwestern University in suburban Chicago before enrolling at the American Academy of Dramatic Arts in New York City. There she met her first husband, the actor Robert Walker, and they married in 1939 before heading to Hollywood. Unable to launch their respective film careers, the couple returned to New York City after the first of their two sons was born.

Jones was working as a millinery model when she arrived at the New York City office of film producer David O. Selznick to test for a role. Selznick was one of the most powerful figures in the entertainment business at the time, having scored a major hit with 1939's Civil War epic, *Gone with the Wind.* Jones did not win the title role in *Claudia,* but Selznick signed her to a contract anyway and began planning her career. He found the ideal star-making property for her in the story of a young farm girl, Bernadette Soubirous, who claimed to have seen visions of the Virgin Mary near her home in Lourdes, France, in the 1850s. Soubirous became a nun, Lourdes emerged as a pilgrimage site for devout Roman Catholics, and *The Song of Bernadette* turned Jennifer Jones—as the Twentieth Century-Fox studio dubbed their newest star—into a household name overnight.

Jones' auspicious screen debut earned her an Academy Award nomination for Best Actress, which she won. Another nominee that year was screen veteran Ingrid Bergman, who famously said "I cried all the way through *Bernadette* because Jennifer was so moving and because I realized then I had lost the award," according to the *Los Angeles Times.* Jones followed that triumph with a wartime tearjerker, *Since You Went Away,* which also starred her husband, but their real-life marriage was foundering. Her boss, Selznick, was a notorious womanizer who pursued her; Selznick's wife, daughter of Metro-Goldwyn-Mayer founder Louis B. Mayer, eventually filed for divorce after Jones left Walker. The couple wed in 1949 on a yacht off the French Riviera.

Jones went on to several memorable roles, including the love interest between Gregory Peck and Joseph Cotten in a 1947 western, *Duel in the Sun,* which earned her another Oscar nomination. "Selznick, who hoped to capture the epic glory of his *Gone with the Wind,* made the film in Technicolor at huge expense," wrote Adam Bernstein in the *Washington Post.* "It became a cult favorite, mocked by some as 'Lust in the Dust' for its bombastic score and ludicrously steamy ending: The two faithless lovers (Jones and Peck) die in a mire of blood and mud."

Selznick guided Jones' career into some notable duds, too. There was a stilted *Madame Bovary* in 1949, and one British production that he demanded be partially reshot in Hollywood, which prompted a court case. Jones fared better as the Eurasian doctor with whom William Holden is smitten in 1955's *Love Is a Many-Splendored Thing,* earning her fourth Oscar nomination, but she turned down roles in *On the Waterfront* and *East of Eden* on her husband's advice. Critics were aghast when he slotted her into a role meant for a much younger actress in a 1962 adaptation of the F. Scott Fitzgerald classic *Tender Is the Night.*

Jones was unhappy in her marriage, but even sadder when Selznick died in 1965. There were suicide attempts, and her first husband, Robert Walker, died quite young in 1951 after his own career was blemished by substance abuse. Jones and Selznick had a daughter, Mary Jennifer Selznick, who committed suicide in 1976 by jumping from a high-rise building in downtown Los Angeles. Tragically, just two years earlier Jones had made her last movie appearance in the disaster movie *The Towering Inferno* in which her character tumbles from the world's tallest skyscraper.

Jones married industrialist Norton Simon in 1971, who had made his first fortune in the canning industry. Simon went on to build an impressive art collection, and Jones worked with him as an unofficial curator until his death in 1993. He bequeathed much of the collection to the Pasadena Art Museum, which was later renamed the Norton Simon Museum, and Jones served on its board for many years. She died of natural causes at her home in Malibu on December 17, 2009, at the age of 90. One son from her first marriage, the actor Robert Walker Jr., survives her. His brother Michael Walker, also an actor, died in 2007.

Jones was an early devotee of yoga, and persuaded Norton Simon to visit India with her, which spurred him to begin collecting Asian art. Audiences loved Jones for her role as the sainted Bernadette, and seemed to sympathize with the difficulties she faced in her personal life. "When you're young, you're full of hope and dreams," she once reflected, according to the *New York Times.* "Later you begin to wonder. I did *The Song of Bernadette* without knowing what was going on half the time." **Sources:** *Los Angeles Times,* December 18, 2009; *New York Times,* December 18, 2009; *Times* (London), December 19, 2009, p. 79; *Washington Post,* December 18, 2009, p. B05.

—*Carol Brennan*

Ted Kennedy

Born Edward Moore Kennedy, February 22, 1932, in Boston, MA; died of brain cancer, August 25, 2009, in Hyannis Port, MA. U.S. Senator. During a Senate career spanning nearly half a century, Edward "Ted" Kennedy built bipartisan coalitions that allowed him to push through legislation and shape national policy in the areas of health care, education, civil rights, and immigration. Nicknamed the "Lion of the Senate" for his legislative prowess, Kennedy was an extraordinary deal-maker. Over the course of his career, the long-standing Massachusetts senator grew into a political heavyweight, yet his early years on Capitol Hill were overshadowed by his older brothers—President John F. Kennedy (JFK) and Senator Robert Kennedy. Both were assassinated in the 1960s, leaving Ted Kennedy as the only surviving brother of one of the United States' most legendary families. Though Kennedy did not match his brothers' political legacies, he nonetheless made a mark on the national scene.

Kennedy was born on February 22, 1932, in Boston, Massachusetts. He was the youngest of nine and the fourth of four boys born to Irish Catholics Rose Fitzgerald Kennedy and Joseph P. Kennedy Sr., a self-made millionaire and prominent East Coast Democrat. Joe Kennedy Sr. set high expectations for his children and encouraged his sons to enter politics. The senior Kennedy had served in President Franklin D. Roosevelt's administration.

The Kennedy family enjoyed great wealth. As a youngster, Kennedy moved between the family homes in Boston, New York, London, and Palm Beach, Florida. He attended ten preparatory schools and graduated from Milton Academy, located near Boston, in 1950. Following in the footsteps of his older brothers and father, Kennedy enrolled at Harvard University but was expelled for cheating on a Spanish test. He enlisted in the U.S. Army and spent two years stationed in Paris. His older brother, Joe Jr., had served in the U.S. Navy during World War II and died when his plane was shot down.

In 1953, the army discharged Kennedy and he re-entered Harvard, where he studied political science and earned a spot on the football team. He graduated in 1956 and pursued a law degree from the University of Virginia. After graduating in 1959, he worked as an assistant district attorney in Boston. Along the way, Kennedy was sucked into politics on the coattails of his brothers. In 1958, Kennedy worked on JFK's Senate campaign. In 1960 he toured the western United States, stumping for his brother's successful presidential run.

JFK was sworn into office in January of 1961, leaving his Senate seat vacant. In 1962, a special election was held to fill the seat and Edward Kennedy entered the fray. Kennedy was barely 30 years old—the minimum requirement to serve in the U.S. Senate. His opponent poked fun at his youth, inexperience, and lack of judgment—as exemplified by his Harvard expulsion. Kennedy, nonetheless, weathered the primary and won the election. He kept the seat until his death.

When Kennedy began service in the Senate in 1962, he encountered many friendly faces in Washington. JFK was in the White House and Robert Kennedy was the U.S. Attorney General. The Kennedy family's political victories were soon marred by tragedy. In November of 1963, JFK was assassinated. In 1964, Kennedy survived a plane crash that killed an aide as well as the pilot. With a broken back, he campaigned for re-election while recuperating in the hospital. In 1968, Robert Kennedy was assassinated on the eve of his victory in the California Democratic presidential primary.

After a period spent mourning in seclusion, Kennedy emerged as the family patriarch, playing a role in the lives of his brothers' left-behind children. Most political analysts believed Kennedy would one day wind up in the White House. Kennedy's reputation, however, was irrevocably tarnished in 1969 following an incident in Chappaquiddick, Massachusetts, when Kennedy drove his car off a narrow wooden bridge killing passenger Mary Jo Kopechne. Kopechne had worked on Robert Kennedy's presidential campaign. Kennedy waited nearly ten hours before reporting the accident to police. He later testified that he tried to dive under the water and save her but suffered from a concussion that blurred his thinking. Kennedy pled guilty

to leaving the scene of an accident. His license was revoked for a year and he received a suspended jail sentence. Authorities suspected alcohol may have played a role in the accident.

In 1980, Kennedy challenged incumbent President Jimmy Carter for the Democratic presidential nomination, though his campaign never really got off the ground as questions about Chappaquiddick continued to emerge. After realizing he would never make it into the White House, Kennedy decided to focus his efforts on the Senate and became a powerful voice for liberals.

Over the course of his career, Kennedy helped orchestrate the passage of many laws. He enjoyed legislative victories with the Civil Rights Act of 1964; the Voting Rights Act of 1965; the 1990 Americans with Disabilities Act, which Kennedy sponsored; and the 1993 Family and Medical Leave Act. He also promoted legislation that increased the minimum wage. In addition, Kennedy led the battle to end the draft and fought for legislation granting 18 year olds the right to vote.

Kennedy's concern extended beyond the borders of the United States. He opposed apartheid and urged Congress to impose sanctions on South Africa. He pressed for peace in Northern Ireland, condemned the Vietnam War, and voted against entering the war in Iraq. In 1997, Kennedy reached across party lines to team with Republican Senator Orrin Hatch to enact a health-insurance program for low-income children. Kennedy sponsored the bill, known as the State Children's Health Insurance Program, or SCHIP. In 2001, Kennedy worked with Republican President George W. Bush to pass No Child Left Behind, which called for educational reform.

In May of 2008, Kennedy was diagnosed with a malignant brain tumor but returned to Washington seven weeks later to help pass Medicare legislation. He was a strong advocate for President Barack Obama's health-care reforms and in July of 2009 led the Senate's Health, Education, Labor and Pensions Committee, which he chaired, into passing the proposed overhaul, thus sending it to the floor for debate, where it eventually passed.

Kennedy died on August 25, 2009, after spending nearly 47 years in the Senate. He is survived by his second wife, Victoria Ann Reggie Kennedy—whom he married in 1992—and their children, Curran and Caroline Raclin. Survivors also include his first wife, Virginia Joan Bennett, and their children, Patrick, Kara, and Edward Jr. They married in 1958 and divorced in 1983. Kennedy was buried at Arlington National Cemetery, near his slain brothers. **Sources:** *Chicago Tribune,* August 27, 2009, sec. 1, pp. 15-17; *Los Angeles Times,* August 26, 2009, pp. A1, A20-21; *New York Times,* August 27, 2009, pp. A1, A16-20; *People,* September 14, 2009, pp. 94-102.

—Lisa Frick

Leon Kirchner

Born January 24, 1919, in New York, NY; died of congestive heart failure, September 17, 2009, in New York, NY. Composer. Pulitzer Prize-winning composer Leon Kirchner worked outside of the mainstream ideas of musical composition in the late twentieth century. Combining electronic sounds with traditional string quartet music in his 1967 Third String Quartet earned him the first Pulitzer ever to go to a piece of music using electronics.

Kirchner's compositions stretch across a career of nearly six decades, many of which he also spent as a professor. He influenced many Harvard University musicians during his academic career there, working with young composers such as John Adams and Richard Wernick, as well as performers including violinist Lynn Chang and cellist Yo-Yo Ma. He served as a conductor for the Harvard Chamber Orchestra and was a pianist in his own right.

Born in the borough of Brooklyn in New York City in 1919, Kirchner had already begun studying piano by the time he was four years old. At the age of nine, Kirchner moved with his family to Los Angeles. He attended Los Angeles City College, where he began composing, earning the attention of Ernst Toch, who recommended him to study with Arnold Schoenberg at the University of California. Kirchner was influenced by many composers who had fled Hitler's Germany. Though Kirchner won the George Ladd Prix de Paris in 1942, he was unable to go to Paris to study due to World War II.

Kirchner worked under Ernest Bloch at the University of California at Berkeley, though his studies were interrupted by a stint in the army during World War II and a hiatus during which he worked with Roger Sessions in New York. After receiving his graduate degree, he was offered a position at Mills College, which he accepted. Though Kirchner had been recommended to the position by Igor Stravinsky, the older composer later advised him

not to take the job and instead focus on his compositions. "At the time I really didn't understand what he meant, but now ... well, I'm ambivalent," Kirchner once said to the London *Times,* as reported in his *New York Times* obituary. Throughout his academic career, Kirchner struggled to balance his focus on composing with his duties as a teacher.

Despite his own hesitations about his teaching career, Kirchner was an influential and important instructor for many young musicians. He combined musical analysis and performance in his courses at Harvard University, where he taught from 1961 until his retirement from academia in 1989. Kirchner founded and conducted the Harvard Chamber Orchestra, a group comprised of musicians from throughout the Boston area. Though music critics did not always praise Kirchner's work as a conductor, his interpretations of Beethoven, Brahms, and Mahler shed new light on the major works of those composers.

As a composer, Kirchner viewed the art of composition as a struggle, according to his former student John Adams, who told the *New York Times,* "I got the feeling that composing wasn't meant to be a painful activity, a ferocious wrestling match with inner demons." Kirchner's style changed over the years from large-scale works that were extremely expressive to more compact pieces. The sound of his early works was influenced by Bartok and Schoenberg, while later works combined the electronic sounds for which he earned the Pulitzer. A 2006 string quartet lasts only 12 minutes, but integrates many of the musical concepts that Kirchner developed over the course of his career.

Kirchner's single opera, *Lily,* premiered in 1977 at the New York City Opera. Based on *Henderson the Rain King,* a novel by Saul Bellow, the opera took nearly 18 years to compose and was roundly panned by critics, who considered it a failure. Though Kirchner held out hope that a revival might change the minds of the critics, he also used many of the musical themes and ideas from *Lily* in other works.

After his retirement from academic life, Kirchner composed the large-scale work "Of Things Exactly as They Are," which was performed by the Boston Symphony Orchestra in 1997 and was considered a high achievement by critics. Kirchner continued composing throughout his life, with his final orchestral work, "The Forbidden," premiering at a Boston Symphony Orchestra performance in 2008.

Criticizing the notion that music could be reduced to a science, Kirchner was quoted in the *Washington Post* as having written that "idea, the precious ore of art, is lost in the jungle of graphs, prepared tapes, feedbacks, and cold stylistic minutiae." In the *New York Times,* the composer once said, "Music is a science, but a science that must make people laugh and dance and sing."

Kirchner died of congestive heart failure at the age of 90 at his home in the borough of Manhattan in New York City. Married to Gertrude Schoenberg (who is of no relation to the composer of the same last name) in 1949, he outlived his first wife by ten years. He is survived by his companion, Sally Wardwell, two children, and a stepdaughter. **Sources:** *Los Angeles Times,* September 21, 2009; *New York Times,* September 18, 2009; *Washington Post,* September 20, 2009.

—*Alana Joli Abbott*

Jack Kramer

Born John Albert Kramer, August 1, 1921, in Las Vegas, NV; died of soft tissue cancer, September 12, 2009, in Los Angeles, CA. Professional tennis player. Jack Kramer dominated the sport of tennis in the mid-twentieth century as a player, promoter, and official. In his twenties he took several Wimbledon and U.S. National titles before turning pro. "Known for his 'big game,' a serve-and-volley attack complemented by a stinging forehand that presaged the modern attacking style, Kramer emerged as a brilliant amateur player in the years after World War II," asserted *New York Times* writer Richard Goldstein. Kramer is also remembered as the first player to wear shorts at Wimbledon's Centre Court back in 1947.

The son of a Union Pacific Railroad brake operator, Kramer was born in 1921 in Las Vegas, Nevada, and began to excel in the game after his family moved to the Los Angeles area. They lived in Montebello, located between East Los Angeles and the city of Whittier, and he was chosen as a junior member of the U.S. team for the Davis Cup international tournament in 1939, the same year he graduated from Montebello High School.

Kramer attended the University of Southern California and served in the U.S. Coast Guard during World War II. In 1940, 1941, and 1943 he won U.S. men's doubles titles, and when international play resumed following the end of the war, he and Ted Schroeder won the 1946 men's doubles title at the

Davis Cup event. Also in 1946, he and Tom Brown took the doubles trophy at Wimbledon, and later that summer he beat Brown for the men's singles title at the U.S. Nationals at Forest Hills, Queens, the precursor to the U.S. Open.

The year 1947 was the peak of Kramer's prowess as a player. He helped the U.S. team win another Davis Cup, and beat Brown again, this time at Wimbledon, for the men's singles title; he also won the doubles title with Robert Falkenburg. The singles match against Brown was particularly notable for Kramer's demolition of his rival in less than an hour, and it marked the first time a male player wore shorts at Wimbledon's Centre Court, where England's royal family has a special box from which to view the tournament. Again, in late August at Forest Hills Kramer retained his U.S. men's singles title by beating Frank Parker.

Tennis was still an amateur sport in this era—players won trophies at the U.S. Nationals and Wimbledon, but no money. Kramer worked in a meatpacking plant to support his family, and once even sold his car to pay the travel costs to bring his wife Gloria to watch him at Wimbledon. He decided to turn pro, and set up an event at New York City's Madison Square Garden against Bobby Riggs, one of the top players of the 1930s who had been playing the professional circuit for several years by then. Kramer's debut as a pro was scheduled for December 26, 1947, and more than 15,000 tennis fans trudged through more than two feet of snow in what was known as the Great Blizzard of 1947, to see the match. Kramer lost to Riggs, but they took their show on the road in a 1948 tour in which Kramer beat Riggs 69 times out of 89 games.

Kramer also played for money against Pancho Gonzalez, a fellow Californian who was one of the top players of the 1940s, but an arthritic back finally ended his playing career in 1954. He created the Kramer Tour, which brought the sport to dozens of medium-sized American cities in the mid-1950s, and it was such a financial success that he was able to lure some of the best foreign players to join the pro circuit, including Wimbledon champions. For more than a decade Kramer was the most powerful figure in the sport, even after the new "Open" era began in 1968 when international tennis officials finally agreed to permit pros to play for prize money in Wimbledon and other Grand Slam contests.

In 1972, Kramer became one of the founders of the Association of Tennis Professionals (ATP) and served as its first executive director. This was the men's-only pro association and its players staged a notable boycott of Wimbledon a year later over a decision made by the All England Club, which staged the tournament, to disqualify a female Yugoslavian player named Nikola "Niki" Pili. As head of the ATP Kramer was blamed for instigating the boycott, and he lost his job as a Wimbledon commentator for the British Broadcasting Corporation (BBC) as a result of the fracas.

Generations of promising tennis players grew up with the signature white "Jack Kramer" wood racket made by Wilson, the sporting-goods giant. It became one of the top-selling tennis rackets of all time, and helped earn Kramer and his family a small fortune. He also owned various businesses in southern California, including the Los Serranos Golf and Country Club near Chino Hills.

Kramer became a widower in 2008. He died on September 12, 2009, at the age of 88, in Los Angeles, from soft-tissue cancer, just two months after the initial diagnosis. His five sons—Robert, David, John, Michael, and Ron—survive him, as do several grandchildren. He wrote a 1979 autobiography with journalist Frank Deford, *The Game: My 40 Years in Tennis,* in which he defended himself against charges he dominated tennis during that heady period before the Open era. "I don't suppose any one man ever so controlled a professional sport as I did," he reflected, according to Goldstein in the *New York Times.* "But if I ran it, I didn't run it into the ground. In the late 1950s, I had as many as seven players a year making $50,000 or more—and how many football or baseball heroes were making $50,000 then?" **Sources:** *Los Angeles Times,* September 14, 2009; *New York Times,* September 14, 2009; *Times* (London), September 15, 2009; *Washington Post,* September 14, 2009.

—Carol Brennan

Edwin Krebs

Born Edwin Gerhard Krebs, June 6, 1918, in Lansing, IA; died of heart failure, December 21, 2009, in Seattle, WA. Scientist. Like many trailblazers before him, Nobel Prize-winning doctor and scientist Edwin Krebs had to wait some time for recognition of his discoveries, but the honor did finally come. He shared the Nobel honor for medicine with Edmond H. Fischer in 1992, the year after Krebs retired at the age of 74 and decades after the two began the research in 1955. Together, the researchers discovered the cellular reaction that led to an understanding of the process of enzyme use by and through which human cells change, a process which proved to be a foundation for all cell function.

Born in 1918 in Lansing, Iowa, the third son of a Presbyterian minister and a schoolteacher, Krebs moved with his family many times during his childhood and considered the town of Greenville, Illinois, to be home. Krebs was a bright and eager student who spent his free time creating gunpowder from ingredients out of a brother's chemistry set or purchased at the town drug store; however, his scientific interest did not stretch any farther or deeper until years later.

Krebs' father died when he was 15, and his mother moved them to Urbana, Illinois, to be near Krebs' two older brothers who were both enrolled in the University of Illinois, where Krebs would also later matriculate and graduate in 1940. Because he was enrolled in what was known as the "individual curriculum" program, his broad, varied coursework in math and science would have allowed him to find success either in chemistry or medicine, either of which Krebs believed would offer him the chance to make money good enough for a secure life, something many who grew up in the years of the Great Depression found of utmost importance.

The choice between the two was made for him when he received a scholarship offer. Krebs entered the Washington University of St. Louis medical school, graduating in 1943 and training in internal medicine. While at Washington, he met and married Virginia, a nurse at the university. World War II interrupted his studies and Krebs served in the United States Navy as a medical officer for a time before returning to St. Louis. While in the Navy, Krebs' ship was docked in Seattle for a time, and he fell in love with the city which would soon become his chosen home.

After his tour of duty ended in 1946, he was unable to immediately continue his medical training residency due to a two-year waiting period, so he began to work with future Nobel Prize-winning biochemistry researchers Carl and Gerty Cori. This experience with the husband-and-wife team led Krebs to turn permanently to laboratory work instead of direct patient care. In 1948, he was invited to join the newly established medical school at the University of Washington, and he happily went to Seattle where he would spend the remainder of his career, except for an eight-year hiatus at the University of California, Davis.

In Seattle, Krebs began his collaboration with Fischer in 1955, when the two researchers discovered they were both working to understand how muscles acquire energy to contract. It was in searching for that source of energy that the pair discovered the reaction that spawned a branch of research that, according to Nobel Prize committee member Hans Wigell in the *Washington Post*, "took off like a rocket. Now ten percent of all biology articles in journals like *Nature* or *Science* deal with their field." The discovery also earned them the Nobel Prize for medicine in 1992, after the weighty importance of their discovery was finally understood.

According to Fischer in the *Los Angeles Times*, the research led them to "stumble on a reaction that regulates the activity of a muscle enzyme. We had no idea how widespread the reaction would be." The reaction turned out to be a crucial part of the process for changes in cells, which has led to other discoveries related to such far-reaching areas as cancer and diabetes development, organ transplants, nerve diseases, heart conditions, hormones, metabolism, and genetics. Indeed, a full one percent of the human genome produces the enzyme for the process Krebs and Fischer isolated, a process known as phosphorylation.

Krebs left Washington for UC Davis in 1968 to become the department of biological chemistry's founding chairman, but he returned in 1977 as the chairman of Washington's department of pharmacology, remaining there until his retirement.

In addition to the Nobel Prize in medicine, which he won at the age of 74, Krebs was a recipient of the Columbia University Louisa Gross Horwitz Prize, the Albert Lasker Basic Medicine Research Award, and the Canadian Gairdner Foundation Award. He was also a member of the scholarly research association the National Academy of Sciences.

Although Krebs officially retired from the University of Washington in 1991, he continued to walk from his home to the campus every day in order to meet with graduate students and research fellows. He died of complications from heart failure on December 21, 2009, in Seattle; he was 91. Krebs is survived by his wife of 64 years, two daughters, one son, four grandchildren, and six great-grandchildren. **Sources:** *Los Angeles Times,* http://www.latimes.com/news/obituaries/la-me-edwin-krebs29-2009dec29,0,5192367.story?track=rss&utm_source=feedburner&utm_medium=feed&utm_campaign=Feed%3A+latimes%2Fnews%2Fobituaries+%28Los+Angeles+Times+-+Obituaries%29&utm_content=Google+Reader (September 16, 2010); *New York Times,* http://www.nytimes.com/2009/12/25/health/25krebs.html?partner=

rss&emc=rss (September 16, 2010); *Washington Post,* http://www.washingtonpost.com/wp-dyn/content/article/2009/12/30/AR20091230.tif02877.html?wprss=rss_metro/obituaries (September 16, 2010).

—*Helene Barker Kiser*

H. C. Robbins Landon

Born Howard Chandler Robbins Landon, March 6, 1926, in Boston, MA; died November 20, 2009, in Rabastens, France. Musicologist. H. C. Robbins Landon, known as "Robbie" to friends and audiences, was a popular musicologist well known for his in-depth research of Haydn and his writings for lay readers about Mozart, Beethoven, and other composers. His ability to make music seem interesting made him a well-known figure for European radio and television audiences.

Landon's research helped restore many previously unknown pieces of Haydn's works, reintroducing them into popular performance. He was involved in reconstructing fragments and unfinished works, as well as organizing productions of Haydn operas and symphonies at festivals and for recordings. Landon worked on documentaries and provided commentary on orchestral broadcasts by the BBC. Widely published, Landon worked as a professor in the United States and Europe, sharing his knowledge both in the classroom and on syndicated television and radio programs.

Born in Boston, Landon grew up in the more rural Lancaster, Massachusetts, with his family. Music was encouraged early on and, as early as 13, Landon fell in love with the music of Haydn. Listening to radio broadcasts from New York while he attended boarding school in North Carolina, Landon decided that he wanted to pursue a study of music. He told a teacher who encouraged his interest, particularly in Haydn.

"He told me that Haydn needed a Gesamtausgabe," Landon was quoted as having recalled in the *New York Times.* "I said, 'What's a Gesamtausgabe?' He explained that it was a complete edition of a composer's works and everyone has one: Mozart, Beethoven, Brahms, even Buxtehude. But not Haydn." Landon went to Swarthmore College, where he learned composition under Harl McDonald, before moving to Boston University so he could study under Haydn scholar Karl Geiringer. From Geiringer, he learned to value musicology combined with music performance.

After graduating in 1947, Landon moved to Vienna, where he volunteered to work as a researcher for the U. S. Army, allowing him to combine his own interests with military service and avoid being drafted. He wrote the official history of the liberation of Italy and the Fifth Army, and he studied music on his own time. Upon his return to Boston, he became one of the founders of the Haydn Society, which was formed with the intent of publishing a complete edition of Haydn's works and making recordings of performances available to the public. In 1949, Landon returned to Vienna, where he began a commercially successful recording program that enabled him to further pursue his research. He was adept at cutting red tape, despite the political divisions of Eastern Europe at the time. He became a correspondent to the London *Times, Musical America,* and other American publishers, using that status to clear his way behind the Iron Curtain. A *Times* contributor described him as tireless, and wrote that "to arrive in a library he had recently explored was to encounter a trail of exhausted but respectful librarians."

In the 1940s, Landon edited critical editions of Haydn's works, which led up to his landmark work *The Symphonies of Joseph Haydn.* Published in 1955, the tome includes discussion of all 107 works, set in a chronological context. He subsequently wrote about Haydn's Masses, and published Haydn's operas in new editions. Alongside these published works, he organized performances of the pieces for recording. He also assisted the Vienna Philharmonic in interpreting Haydn's 56th symphony, discovering that the horn parts were originally written for horns pitched an octave higher than the modern instruments.

In the 1960s, Landon moved to Italy and continued to write articles, spending winters in Vienna. The Haydn Society eventually established its center in Vienna as well, producing previously unrecorded symphonies by Haydn, Haydn's Masses, and performances of Mozart's "Idomeno" and his Mass in C minor. Landon was involved with productions of Haydn's works at the Holland Festival, and between 1969 and 1973, he oversaw a recording of Haydn's symphonies for Decca, performed by Antal Dorati. He searched for fragments of Haydn's works, reconstructing them so deftly that scholars were left scratching their heads at where Landon's work began. Landon was quoted as having said in the *New York Times,* "There were many symphonies that

even if you wanted to do them, you couldn't because there was no score and no parts.... So my task was to start preparing editions, and now of course they are all issued and they sell very well." During the 1970s, Landon taught at universities in the United States; in 1975, he moved to Vienna so that he could focus on writing his biography of Haydn, *Haydn: Chronicle and Works,* published in five volumes from 1976 to 1980.

Landon served as an honorary professorial fellow and the John Bird Professor of Music at University College Cardiff in Wales during the 1970s. In the 1980s, he settled in France, where he spent more time studying Mozart and countering popular legends about the composer brought about through the play *Amadeus,* and the movie adaptation. In the 1990s, he worked with John Julius Norwich on a five-part television series detailing Venice's musical history, *Maestro.*

Landon was taken in by a hoax in his later years, partly due to his enthusiasm for finding forgotten works by Haydn. In 1993, he was presented six piano sonatas that were said to be lost pieces by Haydn. Landon and other musicologists were taken in, supporting the pieces as authentic, until further study made Landon doubt his initial statements. The pieces were eventually proved to have been written by a modern German composer.

Over the course of his career, Landon received honorary fellowships and doctorates of music from several institutions. He received the Verdienstkreuz für Kunst und Wissenschaft from the Austrian government and the Gold Medal of the City of Vienna. His autobiography, *Horns in High C,* was published in 1999. Landon died on November 20, 2009, in his home in Rabastens, south of Toulouse, France; he was 83. **Sources:** *New York Times,* November 26, 2009; *Times* (London), November 25, 2009; *Washington Post,* November 26, 2009.

—Alana Joli Abbott

Claude Lévi-Strauss

Born November 28, 1908, in Brussels, Belgium; died of cardiac arrest, October 30, 2009, in Paris, France. Anthropologist. A philosopher and a sociologist, Claude Lévi-Strauss challenged the status quo of the field of anthropology with new theories on mythic thinking. He was convinced from both field studies and from the research of others that the people of pre-literate cultures did not behave vastly different from people from scientifically oriented cultures. In a series of books and lectures, he described a grammar of myth that showed a structured way of understanding the world for peoples previously viewed by the establishment as savage and less intelligent than their Western counterparts.

Though Lévi-Strauss' ideas met with criticism from the establishment as reductionist theories that promoted cultural relativism, his impact on the field was profound. He did not invent structuralism—the idea that words are defined by their relation to others in the same language system, rather than independently—but he was one of the earliest to apply that linguistic idea to the values and beliefs of different cultures. According to the *Los Angeles Times*, Lévi-Strauss once wrote that his writings were "an attempt to show that there are laws of mythical thinking as strict and rigorous as you would find in the natural sciences."

Lévi-Strauss was the son a French painter who was working on portrait commissions in Brussels, Belgium, where Lévi-Strauss was born in November of 1908. Though his family was not religious, Lévi-Strauss was given a bar mitzvah in order to please his grandfather, who was a rabbi. During his early years, music was present throughout his home, and his childhood environment was generally artistic. Lévi-Strauss was taught violin—his great-grandfather had been a violinist in the court of King Louis-Philippe—and learned to compose at an early age. He also enjoyed collecting objects and putting together dissimilar pieces from secondhand stores to compare them. His family's collection of antiques was much later displayed in the Musée de Cluny in Paris.

During his younger years, Lévi-Strauss was introduced to the ideas of Freud and Marx, who had a huge impact on his understanding of the world. During his studies at the University of Paris, Lévi-Strauss produced his first publication, a political piece about Gracchus de Babeuf, a French revolutionary. Lévi-Strauss also studied Kant, completing a degree in philosophy and taking his exams alongside Simone Weil, who became a noted philosopher.

After earning his degree, Lévi-Strauss taught at the Lycée Janson de Sailly, a high school in Paris, where other teachers included Simone de Beauvoir and Jean-Paul Sartre. He also became familiar with Maurice Merleau-Ponty, who alongside de Beauvoir was an important friend and influence on Lévi-Strauss'

work. After a short service in the military and an attempt to become a politician, Lévi-Strauss took a teaching position at the University of São Paulo in Brazil. He took trips into the countryside in an effort to learn about the indigenous cultures and developed an interest in anthropology. The experience had a huge impact on Lévi-Strauss, who wrote that he felt like a sixteenth-century explorer, and that the landscape seemed mythical. After a short return to France to offer an exhibition of the objects he collected in Brazil, he left his teaching position and focused on fieldwork. In 1939, he returned to France with the intention of staying for further study, but he was drafted to become a liaison officer between the French and British during World War II. After requesting a discharge, Lévi-Strauss attempted to find work as a teacher again, not realizing the risk to himself as a Jewish-born citizen. When he was invited to become a visiting professor in New York, he took the opportunity and worked at the New School for Social Research.

It was in New York where he first became introduced to the ideas of structuralism. Russian-American scholar Roman Jakobson described the concepts to him, and Lévi-Strauss saw his own ideas reflected back in an actual academic discipline. "At the time I was a kind of naive structuralist, a structuralist without knowing it," Lévi-Strauss was quoted as having said in the London *Times*. Lévi-Strauss stayed in New York as the cultural counselor for the French Embassy. There he wrote his first major work, *The Elementary Structures of Kinship*.

For several years, alongside teaching, Lévi-Strauss continued to publish works on structural anthropology and kinship systems. In the 1960s, he shifted to studying religious representations. His book *The Savage Mind* was a major work in challenging the idea of pre-literate cultures as intellectually inferior. He pursued his ideas of a science of mythology in his four part series *Mythologiques,* which collected many of the myths he had learned in the Americas and analyzed them as a system. The studies and writings for the quartet of books happened over a period of 20 years, during which, Lévi-Strauss said, according to the London *Times*, "I would get up at dawn, drunk with myths—truly I lived in another world."

Mythologiques uses many of the ideas that Lévi-Strauss became known for, particularly in contrasting ideas, such as raw and cooked. He explored philosophical differences between boiling and roasting, drew connections between myths, and further detailed ideas of kinship. The series not only analyzed American mythologies, but drew conclusions about cultures throughout the world.

In 1982, Lévi-Strauss retired from his position at the Collège de France, but continued to write. He produced essays that completed the ideas he began in his *Mythologiques,* as well as two essays published in the early 1990s that discussed non-anthropological interests. In 2008, Lévi-Strauss' 100th birthday was celebrated in 25 countries; a selection of his works was chosen for inclusion in the Pléiade collection in France.

Lévi-Strauss died on October 30, 2009, less than a month short of his 101st birthday. Over the course of his career, he received many awards and accolades, including honorary degrees from various prestigious universities, the Gold Medal for research, and the Grande Croix de la Légion d'Honneur. **Sources:** *Los Angeles Times,* November 4, 2009; *New York Times,* November 4, 2009; *Times* (London), November 4, 2009; *Washington Post,* November 5, 2009.

—*Alana Joli Abbott*

James R. Lilley

Born James Roderick Lilley, January 15, 1928, in Qingdao, Shandong Province, China; died of prostate cancer, November 12, 2009, in Washington, DC. Diplomat. James R. Lilley had a long and distinguished career as a diplomat, intelligence officer, and policymaker in the Sino-American relations of the cold war era. A veteran of the Central Intelligence Agency (CIA) who later became U.S. ambassador to China, Lilley helped negotiate both the official and backstage responses to the Chinese government's crackdown on protesters in Tiananmen Square in the spring of 1989. "As the key U.S. official on the ground, he maintained lines of communication even in the most critical period, while also forcefully conveying U.S. concerns," wrote the *Guardian*'s Kerry Brown about his role. "That America was able to continue talking to China after the massacre, at a time when both sides could have descended into a new cold war, was in no small part due to Lilley."

Lilley's family ties to China stretched back a dozen years before his birth, when his father was posted to Shanghai as an executive with the Standard Oil Company. Lilley was born in 1928 in a Chinese coastal resort town, and he and his older brother were raised with the help of a Chinese caregiver, and thus learned the Mandarin language at an early age. The family, which would also include a sister, returned to the United States in 1940, just a year before America entered World War II when Japanese fighter planes bombed a U.S. military installation at Pearl Harbor, Hawaii.

Completing his education at the private Phillips Exeter Academy in New Hampshire, Lilley enlisted in the U.S. Army in 1945, the final year of the war, following his much-adored older brother Frank, who had helped train Chinese anti-Communist forces overseas. His brother was then posted to the Japanese city of Hiroshima, devastated by the world's first nuclear weapon in August of 1945 and under subsequent U.S. military occupation; several months later, Lilley's brother committed suicide. Frank Lilley "was a pacifist and idealist at heart," explained Andrew Nagorski in *Newsweek International,* and the atomic bomb and its aftermath "plunged [him] into a fatal depression. As a result, his younger brother concluded it was better to eschew 'romanticism and excessive emotion,' and pursued a steadfastly pragmatic career in public service," Nagorski wrote, quoting from Lilley's 2004 memoir, *China Hands.*

Lilley went on to graduate from Yale University and then earned a master's degree in international relations from George Washington University. He followed that with advanced language instruction in Chinese at Hong Kong University and Columbia University before joining the ranks of the Central Intelligence Agency in 1951. For the next two decades he served as an operative in several Asian nations at the height of cold-war tensions and the U.S. effort to oust a Communist insurgency in Vietnam. In 1975, Lilley was named the national intelligence officer for China, and in the early 1980s was appointed to a seat on the National Security Council by President Ronald Reagan.

In 1986, Reagan sent Lilley to Seoul, South Korea, to serve as U.S. ambassador to the country, which was undergoing a dramatic change from military dictatorship to genuine democracy. Lilley also served for a time as the unofficial U.S. ambassador to Taiwan, an island which remained adamantly opposed to the mainland Chinese Communist government and was a cautious U.S. ally. "Gruff with a no-nonsense manner and a keen eye for detail that peppered his reports from the field," asserted his *Washington Post* eulogist John Pomfret, "Lilley was singular in the fractious world of China-watching in that he was respected by both Communist China and Taiwan and across the political spectrum at home." In 1989, President George H. W. Bush named Lilley to serve as the new U.S. ambassador to China; the two men had known one another for several years, dating back to Bush's service as CIA station chief in Beijing.

Lilley arrived in Beijing just as international attention began to focus on a growing group of student protesters in a large public space in the city, Tiananmen Square. The demonstrators ignored warnings to disperse. "Lilley was familiar with the students' grievances: only days after arriving in Beijing in 1989, he took to riding his bicycle on the streets to glean firsthand knowledge of what was going on," noted David Stout in the *New York Times*. Finally, television camera crews captured Chinese Army tanks rolling into the square, and the protest ended in violence and an unknown number of deaths. International reaction was strong, but Lilley counseled against taking any permanent action against China's hard-line rulers. "History has proved Bush and Lilley right," remarked Brown in the *Guardian*. "China did not, as many feared at the time, turn in on itself and pull back from further change."

Lilley formally retired from government service in 1991, and died at a Washington hospital of complications related to prostate cancer on November 12, 2009; he was 81. Survivors include his wife, Sally Booth Lilley, whom he had married in 1954, and their three sons, Jeffrey, Doug, and Michael, plus six grandchildren. His son Jeffrey served as co-author of the 2004 memoir, *China Hands,* in which Lilley asserted in a brief but cogent kernel of wisdom (according to Nagorski), "China is what it is, not as we want it to be." **Sources:** *Guardian* (London), January 15, 2010, p. 44; *Newsweek International,* June 21, 2004, p. 69; *New York Times,* November 16, 2009; *Washington Post,* November 14, 2009.

—Carol Brennan

Daniel Melnick

Born April 21, 1932, in New York, NY; died of lung cancer, October 13, 2009, in Los Angeles, CA. Producer. In a career that ran the gamut from television to film to theater, and from the serious to the offbeat, celebrated producer Daniel Melnick was a risk taker, unafraid to tap controversial or risqué subject matter. Over four decades, his television shows won multiple Emmy Awards, and his films won dozens of Academy Awards.

He was born in 1932 to Benjamin Melnick, a Russian immigrant who was killed in a car accident when his son was just nine, and his wife Celia. Melnick attended the New York High School of Performing Arts, then went on to New York University but did not complete a degree. After a stint in the U.S. Army, where he produced entertainment for the troops stationed in Oklahoma and at Fort Dix in New Jersey, he married composer Richard Rodgers' daughter, Linda, in 1955. Although the couple would divorce in 1971, the union produced a son, Peter, who also became a composer. Melnick did not remarry, although a later relationship produced a daughter.

Melnick's first formal position in the industry was as a staff producer on the CBS network in 1954, the youngest producer on staff. He moved to ABC soon after, and his production credits as vice president of programming included *The Flintstones, The Fugitive, The Untouchables,* and *77 Sunset Strip.* With Leonard Stern and David Susskind, Melnick formed a production company, Talent Associates, which in the 1960s would produce *N.Y.P.D.* for the ABC network as well.

His breakout television hit was yet to come with CBS. He had a keen eye for trends and a knack for working with talented people. In an interview with the *New York Times* (as quoted in the *Los Angeles Times*) he said, "What I try to do is identify and work with the most talented people I can get." Melnick sought to capitalize on the 1960s popularity of both James Bond, the serious spy, and Inspector Clouseau, the bumbling detective, asking writers Mel Brooks and Buck Henry to collaborate on an idea that would combine the best of both characters. The product of this effort was the multiple Emmy Award-winning series *Get Smart,* which starred Don Adams. Melnick, with partner Susskind, would earn an Emmy for the 1966 television program *Ages of Man* starring Sir John Gielgud and for 1967's *Death of a Salesman* starring Lee J. Cobb, both of which aired on CBS.

By the 1970s, however, Melnick was ready to move to the silver screen, producing Sam Peckinpah's disturbing and controversial *Straw Dogs* in 1971. In 1972, he produced the *That's Entertainment* musical series, *The Sunshine Boys,* and *Network* as head of worldwide production for MGM studios. At the end of the decade, Melnick had moved to Columbia studios, serving briefly as president of the company in 1978 when the former president, David Begelman, resigned, embroiled in an embezzlement scandal. At Columbia, Melnick produced the cutting edge *Kramer vs. Kramer, The China Syndrome,* and *Midnight Express.*

Not one to be pigeonholed, Melnick's genre interests were far-reaching, and in the late 1970s and 1980s he also produced *All That Jazz, Altered States, Making Love, Footloose, Roxanne, Air America,* and

L.A. Story for other studios, including Warner Brothers and 20th Century Fox, some under the umbrella of his independent production company IndieProd Company Productions. *Blue Streak*, in 1999, was his final film. According to journalist and film historian Aljean Harmetz, quoted in the *New York Times*, "Melnick has always ridden the cutting edge of new Hollywood trends without ever losing his balance or getting blood on his feet." Studio executive Sherry Lansing, quoted in the *Los Angeles Times*, described Melnick as "an extraordinary producer and an extraordinary executive. He always thought out of the box and was never afraid to take a risk. His films stand the test of time."

Perhaps the only area in which Melnick's Midas touch failed was in theater. In 1965, he produced the Broadway musical *Kelly*, about a man who jumps off the Brooklyn Bridge and survives. The stellar flop opened and closed on the same night. According to his son, Peter, in the *New York Times*, "That was not his favorite moment in history, but he wore it with grace."

Besides his career in production, in 1997, Melnick joined the board of telecommunications company ComTec International. He was also a dedicated art collector. Johnny Carson, Chevy Chase, Barry Diller, Steve Martin, Carl Reiner, and Neil Simon were regular attendees at the monthly poker games Melnick hosted, where the world-famous industry personalities and players would enjoy themselves immensely.

At the end of his life, Melnick's general health declined, and he suffered from several ailments, including lung cancer, before his death at home in Los Angeles on October 13, 2009; he was 77. He is survived by his son, Peter; daughter, Gabrielle Wilkerson-Melnick; and two grandchildren. **Sources:** *Los Angeles Times*, http://www.latimes.com/news/obituaries/la-me-daniel-melnick15-2009oct15,0,6172008.story?track=rss (March 18, 2010); *New York Times*, http://www.nytimes.com/2009/10/17/movies/17melnick.html?partner=rss&emc=rss (March 18, 2010); *Times* (London), http://www.timesonline.co.uk/tol/comment/obituaries/article6886046.ece (March 18, 2010); *Washington Post*, http://www.washingtonpost.com/wp-dyn/content/article/2009/10/19/AR20091019.tif03387.html?wprss=rss_metro/obituaries (March 18, 2010).

—*Helene Barker Kiser*

Jack Nelson

Born John Howard Nelson, October 11, 1929, in Talladega, AL; died of pancreatic cancer, October 21, 2009, in Bethesda, MD. Journalist. Credited with putting the *Los Angeles Times* on the short list of the country's must-read newspapers, Pulitzer Prize-winning journalist Jack Nelson was relentless when it came to getting to the bottom of a story. From an exposé of a Georgia hospital to coverage of the civil rights movement to the first big scoop of the Watergate scandal, Nelson was the consummate investigative reporter over a newspaper career spanning 55 years.

Born in 1929, Nelson was the first of three children born to Howard and Barbara. He grew up helping his father (who would later become a shoe salesman) run a fruit store, using his natural ability to engage with people and his sense of humor to coax people in to buy. According to colleague Richard Cooper in the *Los Angeles Times*, Nelson tied this early foray in sales to his later skill in journalism, saying the requirements were similar, because "you had to be able to sell yourself to people, convince them that they should answer your question or show you the records."

Nelson's later childhood was spent in Georgia and Mississippi. In 1947, he graduated from Notre Dame High School in Biloxi, where he had been sports editor of the school paper, and went immediately to work for the *Biloxi Daily Herald*, where he quickly earned the nickname of "Scoop" for his exposure of corruption. He spent two years in the U.S. Army as a sergeant, writing news releases, and upon his discharge in 1952, he took a position at the *Atlanta Constitution*, where he published a harrowing tale of abuse of mentally ill patients at the Milledgeville Central State Hospital, including nonconsensual drug trials, nurses performing major surgery, and on-duty physician substance abuse, a story which earned him the 1960 Pulitzer Prize.

In 1965, Nelson was recruited by *Los Angeles Times* publisher Otis Chandler in a deliberate effort to expand coverage of the southern region of the country. This put Nelson, a southerner, in a unique position to investigate and publicize the growing civil rights movement. His writing earned widespread notice and readership; prior to his tenure, only the *New York Times* had a southern bureau. A colleague at the *Los Angeles Times*, former managing editor George Cotliar, described Nelson's hard-hitting and timely approach as one in which he "just annihilated every other paper. He was ahead of everyone on everything." Cotliar described him as "the toughest, hardest-charging, finest reporter I've known in my 40 years in the business."

One of Nelson's earliest offerings for the *Los Angeles Times* covered the March 7, 1965, attack on civil rights marchers in Selma, Alabama, an event that would go down in history as "Bloody Sunday." Governor George Wallace specifically attacked Nelson in his comments about the unrest. Other major investigations by Nelson during this time provoked the ire of FBI director J. Edgar Hoover because the stories exposed the FBI's unconventional tactics for dealing with the Ku Klux Klan. Nelson also broke the story of the truth behind the slaying of black student protestors in what would be known as the Orangeburg Massacre. While the police claimed a sort of self-defense for the killings, Nelson published the medical report findings that the victims were shot in the back of the head and wounded on their feet.

In the early 1970s, after he had joined the Washington Bureau and the President Richard M. Nixon scandal was breaking, Nelson managed to score an interview with eyewitness and former FBI operative Alfred Baldwin, who described the now-infamous break-in at the Democratic National Committee headquarters, inextricably binding the White House to the burglary. A judge issued a gag order on the story, but the Supreme Court ruled in the newspaper's favor, and the front page of the *Los Angeles Times* on October 5, 1972, carried the piece.

In 1975, Nelson was the natural choice to head the Washington bureau as chief, a position he would hold until he stepped down in 1996, continuing to serve as chief Washington correspondent and founding member of the Reporters Committee for Freedom of the Press until his retirement in 2001. During his tenure, the bureau rose from a 15-reporter and three-editor office to a 36-reporter and seven-editor powerhouse, one of the most elite, well-respected Washington bureaus in the country. A reporter's reporter, Nelson encouraged the brand of investigative work that had built his career. Instead of directing the reporters under him, he operated as one of them. He took the job, according to the *New York Times*, not because he was interested in being an executive, but because, as he put it, he "could get a lot more reporters to give the politicians a hard time."

Former rival Gene Roberts Jr., told the *Los Angeles Times* that "just his work at the *Constitution* would be a distinguished career for most journalists. Then add that he was one of the most effective reporters in the civil rights era, all before you even get to him being bureau chief in Washington. All in all, I would say he was one of the most important journalists of the 20th century." The *Washington Post* quoted Nelson's successor as bureau chief, Doyle McManus, as saying Nelson believed "the main thing people want from newspapers is facts—facts they didn't know before, and preferably facts that somebody didn't want them to know. Jack was tolerant of opinion writers; he respected analysis writers, and he even admired one or two feature writers. But he believed the only good reason to be a reporter was to reveal hidden facts and bring them to light."

In addition to his prolific career in newspapers, Nelson penned or co-authored several books, including *The Censors and the Schools*, 1963; *The Orangeburg Massacre*, 1970; *The FBI and the Berrigans*, 1972; *High School Journalism in America*, 1974; and *Terror in the Night*, 1993. A principal on the PBS television show *Washington Week in Review*, Nelson was also a Nieman Fellow and a Shorenstein Fellow at Harvard University.

Diagnosed with pancreatic cancer, Nelson died at home in Bethesda, Maryland, on October 21, 2009, at the age of 80. Preceded in death by one son, he is survived by his second wife Barbara Matusow, his daughter, his son, six grandchildren, and five great-grandchildren. **Sources:** *Los Angeles Times*, http://www.latimes.com/news/obituaries/la-me-jack-nelson22-2009oct22,0,4611751.story?track=rss (March 18, 2010); *New York Times*, http://www.nytimes.com/2009/10/22/business/media/22nelson.html?partner=rss&emc=rss (March 18, 2010); *Washington Post*, http://www.washingtonpost.com/wp-dyn/content/article/2009/10/21/AR20091021.tif01040.html?wprss=rss_metro/obituaries (March 18, 2010).

—Helene Barker Kiser

Patriarch Pavle

Born Gojko Stojcevic, September 11, 1914, in Kucani, Slavonia (then part of Austria-Hungary); died of cardiac arrest, November 15, 2009, in Belgrade, Serbia. Leader of the Serbian Orthodox Church. A respected theologian who became the leader of the Serbian Orthodox Church, Patriarch Pavle served as head of the Church for 19 years. His term was made difficult by the violence that plagued the Balkan region during the 1990s. Known for urging the differing factions toward peace, the Patriarch broke the formal political neutrality of the Church ten years after he was elected into office.

The Patriarch was sometimes criticized for siding too closely with Serbian leaders and causes over the plights of Croatian or Bosnian Catholics and Muslims. Though he met with leaders of other faiths to condemn the rampant hatred in their region, he was manipulated by Slobodan Milosevec, the president of Serbia and Yugoslavia at the time. Occasionally seeming to side with Milosevec, the Patriarch called for the president's resignation in 2000, helped organize the revolt that deposed Milosevec, and led efforts to restore Serbian churches after Milosevic left office.

Born Gojko Stojcevic, Pavle was the child of peasants in the village of Kucani, then part of Austria-Hungary. His parents died when Pavle was young, and he was raised by an aunt. He attended school in the village, in larger Tuzla, and later in Belgrade. Though he did poorly in his religion courses, he decided to attend the Orthodox seminary at Sarajevo in Bosnia, where he studied for six years. He left the seminary to teach at Belgrade University, first in medicine and later, theology. He also became the secretary to the Minister of Church Affairs.

During the occupation of Serbia by the Nazis, Pavle went home to Slavonia. He was soon assigned to a position in Belgrade, where he was tasked with clearing buildings ruined in the war. During the Bulgarian occupation, he worked at several different monasteries, teaching children who had taken refuge with the Church. He fell ill during his travels, having contracted tuberculosis. His health was so poor that he was told he would die from it, but after the war was over, he regained his health.

In 1948, Pavle received his monastic name and was tonsured a monk at Blagovestenje monastery. He was sent to Raca monastery to serve both as a monk and as a teacher in the local town. In the 1950s, he left Serbia for two years to attend the Theological Academy in Athens, where he earned his doctorate in New Testament and Liturgy. Upon his return to Serbia, he was consecrated Bishop of Raska and Prizen, allowing him to return to the same region he had served from Raca. He was responsible for overseeing all of southern Serbia and Kosovo. These were diverse regions at the time where many Muslim and non-Orthodox citizens lived. While Bishop, Pavle struggled against the communist government, trying to restore the Serbian Orthodox churches in his region and build new ones. He traveled throughout his region, not only as Bishop, but also as a lecturer.

Pavle's election to the head of the church, the Archbishop of Pec, Metropolitan of Belgrade and Karlovci, and Patriarch of Serbia, was very controversial. In 1990, the former leader of the church, Patriarch German, was in poor health. Because he could not maintain his duties, an election was held, despite protests of those who felt a new leader should not be elected until the former Patriarch had died, since the position is traditionally held for life. Pavle was thought the least likely of the three candidates to be elected, but after he was chosen, he began his term with the humility that was one of his defining features.

The fall of communism allowed Pavle to welcome the United States branch of the Serbian Orthodox Church, the Free Serbian diocese, back into the larger organization. But the changing politics also brought challenges, most notably the violence of ethnic hatred that plagued the Balkan region for much of the 1990s. Though Pavle called for peace, he often showed support for the Serbian leaders, turning a blind eye to Serbia's own crimes against other groups in the region. Early on, Pavle followed orders from Milosevic to encourage students to end their protests against the government. But later, Pavle apologized for his course of action, and by the late 1990s, he began to side with the anti-government protesters. Offering a few words of praise for Milosevic in 1999, he urged Milosevic to step down in 2000 after a bombing by the NATO forces had hampered the president's attempts to manage separatists in Kosovo.

In 2007, Pavle fell ill and, as in the case of his predecessor, the church considered appointing a new Patriarch. The decision was overturned, and Pavle remained the head of the church during his final two years of poor health before his death on November 15, 2009; he was 95.

According to the *Los Angeles Times*, Serbian President Boris Tadic said that Pavle's death was a "huge loss." The Serbian government declared a three-day period of national mourning. **Sources:** *Los Angeles Times*, November 16, 2009; *New York Times*, November 16, 2009; *Times* (London), November 18, 2009; *Washington Post*, November 18, 2009.

—*Alana Joli Abbott*

Irving Penn

Born June 16, 1917, in Plainfield, NJ; died October 7, 2009, in New York, NY. Photographer. In a long career that elevated fashion and portraiture photography to an art form, Irving Penn's unique perspectives produced some of the twentieth century's most recognizable images. From the pages of *Vogue* to the tribespeople of New Guinea, celebrated artist Pablo Picasso, Hell's Angels motorcyclists, Clinique products, and literal trash in the streets, Penn's images simultaneously captured the beauty and essence of his diverse subjects.

Born in 1917, Penn was the first of two sons born to Harry, a watchmaker, and Sonia, a nurse. He grew up in Philadelphia and attended the Pennsylvania Museum School of Industrial Art, now known as University of the Arts, from 1934 to 1938, where he studied graphic and industrial design, drawing, and his first love—painting. His teacher was *Harper's Bazaar*'s Alexey Brodovitch, who was impressed enough with Penn's work that Penn was invited to be his summer intern for 1937 and 1938, joining the paid staff in New York after completing school. Penn would purchase his first camera with the money he earned drawing shoes for *Harper's*.

By 1941, however, Penn was less interested in graphic design and more interested in painting, so he packed up and went to Mexico to work on canvas. Unfortunately, although he was competent, his talent did not match his desire, so he returned to the United States in 1943 to pursue other avenues of creativity; he would return to painting in his later years in 1985 as a personal project. But in 1943, he joined *Vogue* as assistant to then-art director Alexander Liberman. Penn's task was to supervise creation of the magazine covers, but the photographers were not enthusiastic about the sketches he drew. Liberman encouraged Penn to take the photographs himself, and Penn happily complied. His first effort, an arrangement of accessories, appeared on the October 1, 1943, cover of *Vogue*, the first of more than 150 covers he would shoot for the magazine.

After a brief tour in 1944 and 1945 during World War II driving an ambulance in Italy, and taking photographs for the American Field Service, Penn returned to *Vogue* as a staff photographer. During this time, he developed what would become a signature style in uncluttered and elegant fashion photography. In 1948, he also began taking portrait photographs of celebrities such as Pablo Picasso, Truman Capote, or the Duchess of Windsor, in which the subject was wedged into a corner—many of his portraits would become the most famous photographs of the subjects—as well as controversial photographs of Peruvians, New Guineans, and members of other worldwide cultures wearing traditional garb, images that some called exploitative. These led to a series of photographs of western and European figures, posed with simple items indicating their trade, a rolling pin, perhaps, or a fish.

The *Los Angeles Times* noted that his work was the first to be both of commercial and artistic significance, and that his process was always the same: "isolating his subject, allowing for scarcely a prop and building a work of graphic perfection through his printing process." Perhaps due to his background in graphic design and his keen painter's eye, his photographs, no matter the subject, could all be fairly described as still lifes. As the *New York Times* noted, "Instead of offering spontaneity Mr. Penn provided the illusion of something fixed, his gaze precisely describing ... in a way that could almost mesmerize the viewer." The publication went further to describe Penn's images as part of a "quest to undercut fashion's standards of perfection, and to find beauty in the disdained, overlooked, or overripe.... In an otherwise pristine still life of food, he included a house fly, and in a 1959 close-up, he placed a beetle in a model's ear."

The consummate perfectionist, Penn, according to the London *Times*, "only ever worked in situations in which he could minutely control every variable in the photographic process," and he even traveled with his own studio. His eye was legendary, as were his expectations. According to an interview with fashion editor Babs Simpson in *Vanity Fair*, quoted in the *Los Angeles Times*, "First, you had to buy 500 lemons for him to pick the perfect one. Then he had to take 500 shots of that lemon until he got the perfect one."

Beginning in the 1960s, Penn began to experiment with a development process from the late 1800s and early 1900s, using platinum instead of silver. This process made the photographs appear denser and richer, almost velvety, and Penn would continue to use and perfect this process until the end of the century, even for his more base subjects, such as cigarette butts and other sidewalk litter.

During his decades-long career, his photographs earned shows at the Museum of Modern Art (the first photographs ever exhibited by MoMA), the Metropolitan Museum of Art, the J. Paul Getty Museum, the Victoria and Albert Museum, and others. In 1990, several of his photographs were acquired by the National Portrait Gallery and the Smithsonian; in 1996, Penn gave 130 prints to the Chicago Art Institute along with his archives; and in 2007, 67 of his portraits went to the Morgan Library & Museum. Multiple books of his photographs have appeared over the years, including *Moments Preserved* in 1960; *Worlds in a Small Room* in 1974; and *Still Life* in 2001.

Preceded in death by his beloved wife of 42 years, former Swedish ballerina and one-time Penn model Lisa Fonssagrives, Penn died at his Manhattan home on October 7, 2009, at the age of 92. He is survived by his brother, film director (*Bonnie and Clyde*) Arthur Penn; son Tom; stepdaughter Mia Fonssagrives-Solow; three grandchildren; and eight great-grandchildren. **Sources:** *Los Angeles Times,* http://www.latimes.com/entertainment/news/arts/la-me-irving-penn8-2009oct08,0,1536282.story (March 18, 2010); *New York Times,* http://www.nytimes.com/2009/10/08/arts/design/08penn.html?partner=rss&emc=rss (March 18, 2010); *Times* (London), http://www.timesonline.co.uk/tol/comment/obituaries/article6866550.ece (March 18, 2010); *Washington Post,* http://www.washingtonpost.com/wp-dyn/content/article/2009/10/07/AR20091007.tif03848.html?wprss=rss_metro/obituaries (March 18, 2010).

—*Helene Barker Kiser*

Sol Price

Born January 23, 1916, in New York, NY; died of natural causes, December 14, 2009, in La Jolla, CA. Founder of Price Club. Sol Price pioneered the concept of the big-box, membership-only discount retail store. His Price Club chain, launched in California in 1976, was the model for both Sam's Club and Costco, and the latter competitor acquired Price's company in the early 1990s. "I don't want to sound dumb, but my idea was simple," the *Los Angeles Times* quoted him as once saying. "All I wanted to do was sell for the lowest price possible."

Price was born in 1916 in New York City and grew up in the Bronx. His parents were Russian Jewish émigrés who both toiled in the city's garment industry before starting their own small clothing-manufacturing enterprise; however, his father's health was compromised by tuberculosis and the family moved to California in the late 1920s. Price graduated from San Diego High School at age 15 and went on to earn his undergraduate degree from the University of Southern California, and then a law degree. He was rejected for military service because of a vision problem, but during World War II trained maintenance workers at Convair, which built fighter planes for the U.S. military and was later acquired by General Dynamics. During this period he maintained his law practice, seeing clients and appearing in court in the morning hours, then working the afternoon shift at Convair's San Diego plant.

The war brought an influx of defense workers to Southern California's burgeoning aerospace industry, many of whom were on the government payroll.

Sensing an opportunity to capture this consumer segment, Price started a retail chain called FedMart in 1954 with a few other investors. It sold food, gasoline, and even liquor to federal employees and their families for a membership fee of $2 a year. FedMart eventually expanded to 40 stores across the southwestern United States, offering cut-rate prices for select merchandise that Price bought at wholesale. In 1974, a German retail magnate, Hugo Mann, bought a majority stake in FedMart for $22 million, but Price and Mann—founder of the successful Wertkauf chain of discount department stores—clashed, and Price and both of his sons, who had joined their father's business, were soon ousted. A few years later, FedMart went out of business, and the store sites were acquired by an emerging Minnesota retailer called Target.

Price teamed with his son Robert to start a new venture, Price Club, in 1976. The first store was a cavernous former airplane hangar in San Diego once used by aviation mogul Howard Hughes. The Price Club was initially designed to lure small-business owners who were interested in buying in bulk, but failed to catch on and lost $750,000 in its first year in operation. Price then decided to make the $25 annual membership fee available to anyone, and the idea caught on. He opened new stores across the western United States, often sited at out-of-the-way parcels of land that he had bought for a bargain. The no-frills stores did not even accept credit cards for a number of years. "Vast, concrete-floored and teeming with shopping carts, Price Clubs exuded a certain spartan cachet," wrote *New York Times* journalist Margalit Fox. "Industrial shelves were stocked with a variety of products, including cigarettes, auto parts, alcohol, clothing, Robert Ludlum paperbacks, Rolex Oyster watches, 10-pound bags of rice and gallon jars of mayonnaise."

As with FedMart, Price was considered the cut-rate villain by other retailers because Price Club's model was so successful—and its merchandise so cheap. "Initially, many producers, sometimes pressured by traditional retailers, rejected selling their products to Fed-Mart and Price Club," wrote Peter Eisner of the *Washington Post.* "Price responded by creating his own store brands, guaranteeing equal quality at a lower price." His single misstep was to fail to recognize the threat from Sam's Club—whose founder, Sam Walton of Wal-Mart fame, freely admitted to having copied Price's model—and Costco, which was founded in the early 1980s by a former stock clerk at a FedMart store. Price merged his stores with Costco in 1993 and exited the business.

Though he was in his seventies by then, Price was not yet ready to retire. With his son Robert he founded PriceSmart, a chain of discount retail stores that operates in Panama, Nicaragua, Jamaica, and other places in Central America and the Caribbean as well as in Guam and the Philippines. He also established a charitable foundation that donated heavily to various causes in the San Diego area, including a generous revitalization project for one of the city's most blighted areas, City Heights. FedMart, Price Club, and PriceSmart were all known for paying their employees relatively high wages and offering terrific benefits. Price liked to assert he read the *Daily Worker*, the newspaper of the Communist Party USA, instead of the *Wall Street Journal* every morning, and contributed greatly to the campaigns of Democratic Party heavyweights.

Price was married to Helen Moscowitz in 1938, with whom he had two sons. She died in 2008. Price passed away at his home in La Jolla, California, of natural causes on December 14, 2009. He was 93. His sons Robert and Laurence survive him, as do five grandchildren and four great-grandchildren. "He's the smartest man I've ever known," Costco's co-founder, Jim Sinegal, told Andrea Chang in the *Los Angeles Times*. Sinegal had risen from a stockroom position at FedMart in his teens to a management job before starting his own empire. "He was probably the most creative guy in retail in the 20th century." **Sources:** *Los Angeles Times*, December 15, 2009; *New York Times*, December 16, 2009; *Washington Post*, December 15, 2009.

—*Carol Brennan*

Trevor Rhone

Born March 24, 1940, in Kingston, Jamaica; died of a heart attack, September 15, 2009, in Kingston, Jamaica. Playwright and screenwriter. For more than three decades, Trevor Rhone worked to bring Jamaican life to stage and screen, both for Jamaican audiences and for the world. Best known for his co-written film, *The Harder They Come*, Rhone is credited with introducing international audiences to reggae before most people were aware of Bob Marley. His works use Jamaican dialect to reflect the culture the plays present. Jamaican actress Leonie Forbes, a long-time friend of Rhone's, told the *New York Times*, "He loved the music of our language." Another Jamaican actress, Fae Ellington, said in the same article, "If he wrote five words for you, they were the best five words." Actor Alwyn Scott said in the London *Times*, Rhone "captured the voice and attitude and culture of so many Jamaicans."

Focusing on the social conflicts that Jamaica experienced after it gained its independence from England in 1962, Rhone's plays offer satirical commentary on both the political and personal lives of Jamaican characters. Rhone also focused on creating black characters that were not negative or stereotypical due to the lack of roles for black actors in classic theater. Several of Rhone's works have been integrated into school curriculums in the Caribbean.

Born in Kingston in 1940, Rhone was brought up in Bellas Gate, a poor rural village where his father worked as a farmer. He did not see a play until he was 14 years old. In 1959, Rhone received a scholarship that allowed him to travel to England, where he attended the Rose Bruford College in Kent to study theater.

After returning to Jamaica, Rhone applied for a position to teach drama. Upon his arrival at the Ministry of Education for his interview, the receptionist made him wait on a bench in the hallway because he was black. Despite that incident, Rhone did become a teacher at a missionary school and later became a schoolmaster at Kingston College and worked as a lecturer at the University of the West Indies.

Rhone's first major play, *Smile Orange* (1971), is a dark comedy that takes a critical look at the tourism industry in Jamaica. The characters are underpaid black workers at a resort where they primarily cater to rich white tourists. The workers remain in degrading positions, often coming to hate themselves, because they need the money. While bleak, the play offers commentary on how the tourism industry impacts the self-image of the Jamaicans in service positions. Rhone adapted the play for film three years later and directed the work for the screen.

The stage version of *Smile Orange* came out the same year that *The Harder They Come* debuted on screen. Based on the true story of a Jamaican criminal killed by police in 1948, the movie featured reggae musician Jimmy Cliff as a would-be singer who becomes a notorious outlaw. After killing a police officer, he is celebrated as a hero among Jamaica's poor. The view of urban Jamaican life was one of the first to reach international audiences, and the film won an award at the Venice Film Festival in 1973.

Rhone used his own experiences as a teacher at a missionary school for *School's Out*. Like *Smile Orange, School's Out* brings heavy criticism on cultural problems in Jamaica, this time focusing on the education system that seems to be falling apart. The missionary school where the play is set is suffering from severely declining standards: conservatives praise the old days when only the elite were allowed education while doing nothing to fix the current system, and undereducated new hires bring in more semi-literate workers while alienating the good teachers who remain. Symbolically, a toilet remains broken and the absent headmaster's door never opens. Though focusing on the school where it is set, critics have drawn an analogy between the situation at the school and the state of affairs in Jamaica after the nation gained its independence in 1962.

Rhone continued to write throughout his life. In 2002, his stage-memoir *Bellas Gate Boy* premiered at the Calabash Literary Festival. The play shows Rhone's pride in his own upbringing and celebrates the positive aspects of his rural childhood home. In addition to its initial performance, the memoir was adapted as a book, and Rhone took it on tour as a one-man show. In 2003, Rhone's romance *One Love* debuted, starring Ky-mani Marley, the son of musician Bob Marley.

In addition to his writing and teaching careers, Rhone was the founder of the Barn Theater, a small converted garage that could seat an audience of 120 people. Many of Rhone's plays were performed there, and his performances packed the seats. Closed in 2007, the Barn Theater had a major influence on the culture of Jamaica, welcoming audience members who did not usually attend theater performances to see reflections of themselves on stage. Many actors who performed Shakespeare would play Jamaican characters at the Barn Theater.

Rhone died of a heart attack at the age of 69, a day after he visited his old hometown of Bellas Gate and saw the graves of his mother, father, and aunt, as well as a primary school he had founded. He is survived by his wife, Camilla King, three children, and a grandchild. **Sources:** *Contemporary Authors Online,* Gale, 2009; *Los Angeles Times,* September 25, 2009; *New York Times,* September 21, 2009; *Times* (London), September 24, 2009; *Washington Post,* September 17, 2009.

—*Alana Joli Abbott*

Oral Roberts

Born Granville Oral Roberts, January 24, 1918, in Ada, OK; died of pneumonia, December 15, 2009, in Newport Beach, CA. Televangelist. At the height of his ministry, charismatic televangelist Oral Roberts was bringing in $100 million in annual donations to his ministry from the faithful who believed God would reward them richly for their financial contributions. The first to use the television medium and organized, targeted direct mail campaigns, Roberts was, in the 1970s, the most recognized religious leader in the world after Billy Graham. In his career spanning seven decades, he also founded the Oklahoma university that bears his name; founded a now-defunct medical center; preached worldwide in person and on television, including to multiracial crowds in the years of segregation; and had dozens of publications translated into 100 languages.

Born in 1918 in rural Pontotoc County, Oklahoma, near Ada, Roberts was the youngest child born to Ellis, a part time preacher in the Pentecostal Holiness church, and Claudius, his part-Cherokee wife. Roberts, who had a stutter, and his three older brothers and older sister grew up in strict poverty on the family farm. When he was 16 years old, he contracted so severe a case of tuberculosis that he was bedridden for half a year; it was expected he would not live. Providentially, George Moncey, a faith healer, was holding tent services near Ada, and Roberts travelled to hear him speak.

On the trip to the service in 1935, according to Roberts' autobiography, named after the phrase which would become known as his religious philosophy tagline, *Expect a Miracle,* Roberts claimed to have heard the voice of God, telling him that he would be healed and that his calling was also to heal others and to start a university for God. Whether or not Roberts in fact heard the voice of God, both predictions came true. He was healed of both his tuberculosis and his stutter after Moncey's service, and in 1963, Oral Roberts University would open its doors in Tulsa, Oklahoma.

Two years after the healing service, Roberts himself gave his first public sermon. He studied at Oklahoma Baptist University and Phillips University, and pastored churches in Oklahoma, North Carolina, and Georgia, before buying a tent in 1948 to become a traveling preacher, having founded the Oral Roberts Evangelistic Association. Over the decades, thousands claimed to have been healed as a direct result of his touch, but no case was ever medically proven—or disproven.

His "prosperity gospel" and hands-on faith healing were embraced by millions who flocked to hear him in person and, later, in 1954, on television. Roberts was the first of his time to recognize the power and reach of television to promote his message and ministry, and through his repeated requests to "send a letter to Oral Roberts," according to the *Los Angeles Times,* from which he was able to design a computerized direct mailing and solicitation database with help from IBM, one of the first of its kind.

In 1963, Roberts founded Oral Roberts University in Tulsa, Oklahoma, which was accredited in 1971. In 2009, the university, the largest one of its type in the world, boasted 3,000 students. In 1968, Roberts left the Pentecostal Holiness denomination for the mainstream Methodist church, which gave him an even wider, more socially acceptable audience and he also became a household name with lavish television specials featuring secular performers of the day, including Johnny Cash, Robert Goulet, and many others. In 1978, construction began on the City of Faith Medical Center, but it closed in 1989, taking public opinion about Roberts down as well, a downfall from which he would never recover.

In fact, his popularity—and his credibility—not only waned but plummeted in the late 1980s, when he publicly declared that if he was unable to raise several million dollars for City of Faith scholarship money by the end of the tax year, God would call him home. The money was raised, but Roberts became fodder for mockers both inside and outside the church. His ministry, under his leadership, was never decisively proven to be run improperly, but his lavish personal lifestyle, one which included luxury homes, cars, and clothing, led to widespread skepticism that was nevertheless not fully overcome. In fact, a 1987 Gallup Poll discovered 72 percent of Americans disapproved of Roberts, only slightly lower than the percentage who disapproved of fellow televangelist Jim Bakker after his sex scandal.

In the wake of his nosedive in popularity, the medical and dental schools in the City of Faith closed, the law school was sold, and hundreds of employees were let go. By 2007, he was even removed from the board of Oral Roberts University, in part due to a financial scandal involving his son, Richard, then-university president, although Roberts returned as co-president, a rallying figurehead, after Richard left.

This was not the first heartache involving one of Roberts' children. He married schoolteacher Evelyn Lutman Fahnestock in 1938, and the couple had four children. Daughter Rebecca was killed in a 1977 plane crash along with her husband, leaving three children orphaned; son Ronnie shot himself in 1982; and son Richard's financial mismanagement threat-

ened the stability and longevity of the university in the 2000s. Richard's ex-wife, in 1983, had already embarrassed the family by publishing a memoir about the Roberts' lavish lifestyle.

According to biographer David Harrell, quoted in the *Los Angeles Times,* "All of Oral Roberts' life was controlled by two primal drives—a relentless restlessness and a sense of divine calling. They were perhaps the same drive in secular and religious versions."

On December 15, 2009, Roberts died at the hospital in Newport Beach, California, following a fall and complications from pneumonia. Preceded in death by his wife of 66 years, a daughter, and a son, Roberts is survived by his son, Richard; his daughter, Roberta; 12 grandchildren, and several great-grandchildren. By the time of his death, the *New York Times* reported that Roberts had, according to Oral Roberts University materials, "personally laid his hands on more than 1.5 million people during his career, reached more than 500 million people on television and radio, and received millions of letters and appeals," including Presidents Kennedy, Nixon, and Carter, and musician John Lennon. **Sources:** *Los Angeles Times,* http://www.latimes.com/news/obituaries/la-me-oral-roberts16-2009dec16,0,3407 978.story?track=rss&utm_source=feedburner&utm_ medium=feed&utm_campaign=Feed%3A+latimes %2Fnews%2Fobituaries+%28Los+Angeles+Times+-+Obituaries%29&utm_content=Google+Reader (September 16, 2010); *New York Times,* http://www.nytimes.com/2009/12/16/us/16roberts.html?part ner=rss&emc=rss (September 16, 2010); *Times* (London), http://www.timesonline.co.uk/tol/comment/obituaries/article6959387.ece (September 16, 2010); *Washington Post,* http://www.washing tonpost.com/wp-dyn/content/article/2009/12/15/AR20091215.tif03225.html?wprss=rss_metro/obituaries (September 16, 2010).

—*Helene Barker Kiser*

Nan Robertson

Born Nancy Robertson, July 11, 1926, in Chicago, IL; died of heart disease, October 13, 2009, in Rockville, MD. Journalist. Pulitzer Prize-winning journalist Nan Robertson, whose career was established by her honest, unflinching examination of such topics as discrimination against women, alcoholism, and toxic shock syndrome, was known for her raw narrative style and attention to detail in the service of the story, even at the risk of great personal embarrassment or exposure.

Born in 1926 to Frank and Eva Morrish Robertson, the future journalist never wavered in her career ambition. She grew up in Chicago and, after completing school, entered Northwestern University, graduating in 1948 with a bachelor's degree in journalism from the college's Medill School of Journalism. She went to work in the newspaper business immediately, acting as a European correspondent for several publications, including *Stars & Stripes*, the *Milwaukee Journal*, and the *New York Herald Tribune*.

In 1955, Robertson joined the staff of the *New York Times*. Despite her experience and credentials, Robertson was placed where female reporters were generally relegated—the "women's pages," specifically the fashion department, where she remained until moving to the metropolitan staff in the city room as a general assignment reporter in 1960, where she was recognized by those editors as being equal to or better than the mostly male reporters. However, this respect would not last long; in 1963, she moved to the Washington bureau, and in the process was nearly put back to square one.

Gender discrimination was rampant throughout the hallowed halls of the newspaper, and in 1972, Robertson was one of 50 women who protested, in writing, the treatment differentials, including significant salary disparities. The following year, seven named female plaintiffs brought a class action lawsuit against the *New York Times* on behalf of 550 female reporters; the case was settled out of court in 1978 for $350,000 and a pledge that management would make sweeping changes and implement affirmative action guidelines. Although Robertson herself was not among the named plaintiffs, she chronicled the story in her 1992 book, *The Girls in the Balcony*, the only written record of the case available because the court documents were sealed at the settlement.

The book's title came from the practice at the National Press Club, where major addresses were given by powerful and well-known people, both national and international, of relegating female reporters to a balcony so cramped that the women were forced to stand; chairs would not fit in the space. Adding insult to injury, the women were not permitted to ask questions or address the speakers in any way, and they were required to enter and exit though the club's back door. Women had been barred completely until 1955, and were not able to become members under 1971.

After a decade in the Washington bureau, Robertson left in 1973 to become the Paris correspondent, but by 1975, her alcoholism was so out of control—she had begun drinking after completing college—that she left her post and checked into a treatment program, later suffering a nervous breakdown as well. Always the journalist, Robertson transformed the struggle into the well-regarded book, *Getting Better: Inside Alcoholics Anonymous*, which in 1988 was the first significant book written about the organization and its efforts.

The alcoholism recovery was followed by a greater trial, the sudden onset in 1981 of the rare toxic shock syndrome, a condition which hospitalized Robertson for nearly three months and caused her to lose the tips of all eight fingers to gangrene. In 1983, Robertson was awarded the Pulitzer Prize in feature writing journalism for her *New York Times* article chronicling the near-fatal experience and her long, arduous recovery. "Toxic Shock" described, in characteristically unflinching detail the ordeal, which had struck without warning after a Thanksgiving holiday meal. Had her condition, which had only recently been named, not been immediately recognized by an infectious disease specialist, and her subsequent care in the hospital not been excellent, Robertson would most certainly have died.

As it was, the amputation of her fingertips meant she was left unable to perform basic self-care, let alone use a typewriter, and this was her greatest fear. She undertook physical therapy with such single-mindedness and dogged sense of purpose that she was able to overcome the physical disability and return to her life, literally and figuratively. The prizewinning article, which marked her return to journalism and allowed her skill to be appropriately recognized, was published in the *New York Times* in September of 1982, ending "My deepest fear did not materialize. I have typed the thousands of words of this article, slowly and with difficulty, once again able to practice my craft as a reporter. I have written in—at last—with my own hands."

After her recovery, she returned to the newspaper, covering cultural affairs. Robertson retired from the *New York Times* in 1988, but she did not leave journalism completely behind. Instead, she embarked on somewhat of a second career, teaching journalism students at the University of Maryland in Bethesda from 1994 to 1999 as the inaugural Eugene L. Roberts visiting professor of journalism. She had also been a MacDowell Colony Fellow and Woodrow Wilson National Fellow. In addition to the Pulitzer Prize, she was recognized by the International Women's Media Foundation and the Washington Press Foundation lifetime achievement award.

At the time of her death from heart disease on October 13, 2009, she was in the Collingswood Nursing and Rehabilitation Center in nearby Rockville; she was 83. Preceded in death by two husbands—second husband Stanley Levey died in 1971 and third husband William Warfield Ross died in 2006 (Robertson and first husband Allyn Baum divorced)—Robertson is survived by her sister Jane, five stepchildren, and nine step-grandchildren. **Sources:** *Los Angeles Times*, http://www.latimes. com/news/obituaries/la-me-nan-robertson15-2009oct15,0,7924258.story?track=rss (March 18, 2010); *New York Times*, http://www.nytimes.com/ 2009/10/15/business/media/15robertson. html?partner=rss&emc=rss (March 18, 2010); *Washington Post*, http://www.washingtonpost.com/wp-dyn/content/article/2009/10/14/AR20091014. tif03268.html?wprss=rss_metro/obituaries (March 18, 2010).

—*Helene Barker Kiser*

Willy Ronis

Born August 14, 1910, in Paris, France; died September 12, 2009, in Paris, France. Photographer. French photographer Willy Ronis snapped some of the most iconic images of twentieth-century Paris. Usually described as the least well-known among a passel of great French photojournalists whose work revolutionized the medium, Ronis outlived Henri Cartier-Bresson, Brassaï, Robert Doisneau, and his other peers. "Ronis became the chronicler and creator of a romantic vision of Paris now firmly lodged in the public imagination," noted his *Times* of London obituary. "His is eternally a city of street urchins and knife grinders, of jolly moustachioed diners and—in perhaps his best-known picture—of young lovers gazing across misty rooftops."

Ronis was born in the fabled City of Light in 1910 to parents who had both fled anti-Semitic violence in their respective countries of Poland and Lithuania. His father was a photographer who set up a portrait studio in Montmartre, but Ronis inherited his piano-teacher mother's musical gifts and aspired to a career in music. He played the violin for many years, hoped to become a composer, and even paid for further studies by playing in a restaurant orchestra. His parents urged him to study law at the Sorbonne, but he was unhappy there. He returned from compulsory military service in 1932 when his father became ill in order to take over management of the studio. Four years later, his fa-

ther died and the business soon closed. Ronis was uninterested in the bulk of the income-producing work a photography studio needed, such as family portraiture and passport photos—and preferred to wander the streets of Paris with his Rolleiflex camera instead.

Ronis made his name as a freelance photojournalist by capturing images from various news stories of the late 1930s in France, a period of political turmoil and dramatic labor actions, including a months-long strike at the Citroën automobile plant. In 1940, neighboring Nazi Germany invaded France, and Ronis fled to the as-yet-unoccupied region of Provence in southern France. His Jewish heritage put him in grave danger of being deported to the German-run concentration camps in Eastern Europe, and after the Nazis moved to occupy all of France in 1942 he went into hiding.

The remainder of Ronis' life would be divided into alternating periods in Paris—where he lived in the working-class neighborhoods in the eastern part of the city—and in Provence, where he eventually acquired property in a picturesque area near Avignon. It was in the south that he met his future wife, the painter Marie-Anne Lansiaux, who shared his strong leftist political sympathies. After the war's end, he returned to photojournalism full-time, and set forth his strategies in the 1951 book *Photo-Reportage: The Hunt for Images*. Scenes of life in post-war Paris appeared in a new collection three years later, *Belleville-Ménilmontant,* the name of the Paris neighborhoods where he preferred to live and work. For many years Ronis worked for the agency Rapho, whose stable of notable photographers included Brassaï and Doisneau. Brassaï was known for capturing the seedier side of Paris, especially after dark, while Doisneau made his name with images that were more playful or romantic, such as his famed *Kiss by the Hotel de Ville* in 1950. Ronis delivered some similarly iconic images, including the 1957 *Les Amoureux de la Bastille*, which presented a magnificent view of Parisian rooftops around the Place de la Bastille while a couple on the left of the frame nuzzle one another.

In the United States, Ronis' work was published in *Life* magazine and heralded in an exhibit at the Museum of Modern Art in New York City curated by Edward Steichen, "Five French Photographers," which featured his images along with those of Brassaï, Doisneau, Cartier-Bresson, and Izis Bidermanas. In 1957 he was honored with a gold medal at the Venice Biennale. Later in his career he taught photography at art schools in Avignon and Marseilles, and occasionally worked in fashion for French *Vogue* and other publications. He and Lansiaux had one child, a son, who died in a 1988 accident; in her later years Lansiaux was stricken with Alzheimer's disease and her husband took a series of haunting photographs of her in the final stages of the disease before her 1991 death.

After skydiving at the age of 85 and taking a photograph of himself mid-jump, Ronis was slowed by age and forced to abandon the street photography that he had enjoyed for the past six decades. In 2005, he was honored with a retrospective at the Paris' Hôtel de Ville, which drew large crowds in an autumn season in which the city was disrupted by deadly riots; Parisians of all ages seemed nostalgic for the bygone city his work immortalized, such as the little boy running down the street with a baguette nearly as long as he is tall. Ronis died in Paris on September 12, 2009, at the age of 99. "It is my contemporaries who most interest me, ordinary people with ordinary lives," Ronis told the *New York Times* a few years before his death. "I have never sought out the extraordinary or the scoop. I looked at what complemented my life. The beauty of the ordinary was always the source of my greatest emotions." **Sources:** *New York Times*, September 18, 2009; *Times* (London), September 14, 2009; *Washington Post*, September 23, 2009.

—Carol Brennan

Soupy Sales

Born Milton Supman, January 8, 1926, in Franklinton, NC; died October 22, 2009, in New York, NY. Comedian. Estimating that he had received 20,000 cream pies in the face—shaving cream pies with a lot of crust and no tin plates gave the most desirable results—over the course of his career in show business, Soupy Sales was one of the most popular personalities of the 1960s, so much so that he was a legend who had developed a cult following. From his live stand up routines to live television, millions of viewers of all ages were entertained by Sales' brand of wacky humor and slapstick comedy.

One of three boys born to Irving and Sadie Supman, Milton Supman grew up in Franklinton, North Carolina, part of the only Jewish family in the area. His last name was frequently mispronounced as Soupman, earning him the lifetime nickname Soupy. Irving ran a dry goods store in town until his death when Sales was just five, prompting Sadie and her sons to relocate to Huntington, West Virginia, where

Sales would spend the remainder of his youth. In high school, Sales honed his acting talent and stage presence in the school drama productions, and his schoolmates voted him most popular boy.

After completing high school, Sales joined the Navy and fought in World War II, entertaining his shipmates with comedy routines broadcast over the onboard public address system. After serving his term, he was discharged and returned to West Virginia where he enrolled in Marshall College, earning a bachelor's degree in journalism in 1949. After college, his first professional job in the industry was as a scriptwriter for a Huntington radio station; he was soon promoted to disc jockey.

In the early 1950s, however, Sales left West Virginia and took a job in Cleveland, Ohio, where the station manager christened him Soupy Hines. However, when he moved to WXYZ-TV in Detroit in 1953, the station manager in Michigan changed it to Soupy Sales after actor Chic Sale, so Sales would not be confused with the station's major advertiser, Heinz.

His first show, *Soupy Sales Comics* was successful enough that he earned a prime time spot for *Soupy's On*, which was acquired as a replacement for *Kukla, Fran and Ollie* in 1955 by ABC and renamed *The Soupy Sales Show*. Its star and namesake was soon launched to stardom, and despite the fact that critics widely panned the show as mediocre or just plain dumb, it was the number-one show in 1962 and remained an undisputed hit for most of the decade. Notable Sales-created characters were Wyatt Burp, Philo Kvech, Pookie, White Fang, Black Tooth, and Peaches, and Americans everywhere imitated his dances, known as the Soupy Shuffle and the Mouse, the latter of which spawned a top-ten song in 1965.

In 1950, Sales received his first pie in the face as part of a spoof of the James Stewart film *Broken Arrow*. Sales would later switch to cream pies, his signature bit, an experience that celebrities such as Frank Sinatra, Burt Lancaster, Mickey Rooney, Sammy Davis Jr., Tony Curtis, Shirley MacLaine, and Dick Martin came to expect when they appeared on his show. According to the *New York Times*, Sales expected certain characteristics from a pie. "You can use whipped cream, egg whites or shaving cream, but shaving cream is much better because it doesn't spoil. And no tin plates. The secret is you just can't push it and shove it in somebody's face. It has to be done with a pie that has a lot of crust so that it breaks up into a thousand pieces when it hits you." The *Los Angeles Times* added the information that the explosion was necessary to the comedy so the viewer could "see the person's face and see it take away his dignity."

Not only did Sales raise pie throwing to an art form, he was considered a leading expert in the field; no one else, after all, could claim to have been hit with tens of thousands of pies. In 1974, a sailor was court-martialed for having thrown a pie into his commanding officer's face, and the defense called Sales as an expert witness, testifying that the prank was just that—a joke, and was not in any way an assault. Despite Sales' pleas and an offer to perform for the naval base, the military court did not see the humor.

The Federal Communication Commission also did not see the humor when at the close of the January 1, 1965 show, with one minute remaining, Sales told the children watching to get into their parents wallets, send him the bills, and he would send them a postcard from Puerto Rico. A viewer complained that he was encouraging children to steal and the show was taken off the air for one week, prompting an avalanche of complaints. The *Los Angeles Times* noted that Sales recalled the situation as "the most brilliant minute of ad-lib in television history because it proved how powerful the medium is."

After new episodes of the show ended, Sales went on to be a panelist on *What's My Line?*, a featured performer on *Sha Na Na* during the 1970s, and to host a radio show on WNBC New York in the 1980s. He also appeared in a Broadway show and in several movies on the silver screen. His memoir, *Soupy Sez!*, was published in 2001.

Of his time in live television, the *New York Times* quoted Sales' comments in his memoir: "Our shows were not actually written, but they were precisely thought out. But the greatest thing about the show, and I think the reason for its success, was that it seemed undisciplined. The more you can make a performance seem spontaneous, the better an entertainer you are."

Suffering from multiple ailments, Sales died at Calvary Hospital in the New York City borough of the Bronx on October 22, 2009; he was 83. Sales is survived by his second wife, Trudy; two sons from his first marriage to Barbara Fox, Tony and Hunt; and four grandchildren. **Sources:** *Los Angeles Times,* http://www.latimes.com/news/obituaries/la-me-soupy-sales23-2009oct23,0,699167.story (March 18, 2010); *New York Times,* http://www.nytimes.com/2009/10/24/arts/television/24sales.html?partner=

rss&emc=rss (March 18, 2010); *Washington Post,* http://www.washingtonpost.com/wp-dyn/content/article/2009/10/23/AR20091023.tif04095.html?wprss=rss_metro/obituaries (March 18, 2010).

—*Helene Barker Kiser*

Paul A. Samuelson

Born Paul Anthony Samuelson, May 15, 1915, in Gary, IN; died December 13, 2009, in Belmont, MA. Economist. Described by the London *Times* as a "great wit," possessing "dazzling learning, insight, energy, aplomb, modesty, profundity, and an amazing inventiveness," Nobel Prize-winning economist Paul Samuelson was hardly a stuffy academic far removed from society and the plight of the working class. On the contrary, his finger on the pulse of that aspect of the United States contributed to his astonishing and groundbreaking understanding of the economic principles that drive society, for better or for worse.

Born in 1915 in the then-thriving steel town of Gary, Indiana, Samuelson grew up in a community of Jewish immigrants from Poland who as a group were upwardly mobile; however, Samuelson's father Frank, a pharmacist, and mother Ella, lost most of their money after World War I and so began the family's own Great Depression before the rest of the country. The Samuelsons moved to Chicago, where young Paul enrolled in Hyde Park High School and his mathematical and puzzle-solving ability was made known. He even helped his algebra teacher choose stocks to buy, although this was not a successful venture.

Samuelson enrolled in the University of Chicago when he was just 16 years old, and the *New York Times* reported that after an economics lecture on Thomas Malthus, who studied the links between poverty and population, he was hooked: "I was born as an economist on Jan. 2, 1932." His personal experience with middle class families coming to the door begging for a single potato to ward off starvation gave him a heart to understand poverty and unemployment in a way that most academics and economists, who lived well above the rest of society, did not.

It was natural, then, for Samuelson to be drawn to the work of John Maynard Keynes, who proposed that government must get involved in matters of economic import, whether through tax cuts or reduced interest rates or government spending. Samuelson would first be introduced to Keynesian economics while a student at Harvard, where he matriculated after graduating from Chicago with his bachelor's degree in 1935. The idea that some level of unemployment was impossible to avoid was at first repugnant to him, but after spending his summers from college unemployed and watching his friends search unsuccessfully for any employment whatsoever, he changed his mind, saying, according to the *New York Times*, "Why do I want to refuse a paradigm that enables me to understand the Roosevelt upturn from 1933 to 1937?"

At Harvard, Samuelson continued to make waves with his bold and forward-thinking ideas and principles, making as many friends as enemies—including the chair of the Harvard economics department—as he spent his years earning both his master's degree in 1936 and his doctorate in 1941. His doctoral dissertation was published by Harvard University Press in 1947, earning him both accolades and the first-ever John Bates Clark Medal, an award established that year by the American Economic Association to honor the exceptional work and promise of an economist under the age of 40.

When he completed his studies, Harvard offered him an instructorship, and although he accepted the position, a month later he left for the Massachusetts Institute of Technology, where he would remain for the duration of his career until his retirement in 1985. Harvard did not urge Samuelson to stay on, despite his success—he was also a member of the Harvard Society of Junior Fellows—and it was widely believed to be at least in part due to his Jewishness. But Samuelson was content to take his wife, fellow economics student Marion Crawford, who he married in 1938, and move to MIT to eventually head the economics department.

During the war years, Samuelson worked in the Radiation Laboratory to help develop computers that tracked aircraft, and he also consulted with the War Production Board. After the war ended, he immediately returned to the classroom and the teaching he loved, becoming full professor in 1947. In fact, as chair of the department in later years, his greatest pleasure was in helping to develop good faculty.

He and his wife would eventually have six children, the latter half in a set of triplets, and the family was sending hundreds of diapers to be laundered weekly. Friends quipped that he ought to write a book to earn the money to pay for the laundry service. Samuelson decided to write an economics textbook explaining Keynesian principles in a clear, compelling, visually appealing, and even humorous way. The book, 1948's *Economics: An Introductory Analysis* would go on to be a veritable blockbuster, selling four million copies in 40 languages in almost 20 editions, the best-selling textbook in American history. In addition to paying for the diapers, the book's proceeds made Samuelson a multi-millionaire.

According to the *Washington Post*, Samuelson said of his book, "I knew it was a good book, but what I didn't realize would be its lasting power. [I tried to make economics] understandable and enjoyable." Not only did he succeed in this venture, but the textbook would contribute in large part to his winning of the 1970 Nobel Prize in economics, sealing his fate as the economic voice of generations, many of whom read his column in *Newsweek* from 1966 to 1981.

An advisor to President John F. Kennedy, Samuelson declined an official political appointment, wanting to be sure he could always say exactly what he believed to be true. In addition to his other achievements, Samuelson was awarded an MIT Institute Professorship, was honored with the 1991 Paul A. Samuelson Professorship in Economics, and the recipient of the 1996 National Medal of Science presented by then-President Bill Clinton. He was the student, professor, and classmate of many Nobel laureates, and president of both the American and International Economic Societies as well as the Econometric Society.

Well-liked and a profoundly cheerful man, Samuelson was active long into his later years, playing regular tennis matches and enjoying others' company and conversation. On December 13, 2009, Samuelson died at home in Belmont, Massachusetts, at the age of 94. His first wife, Marion, predeceased him in 1978, and he had remarried Risha Eckhaus a few years later. She survived him, in addition to two daughters and four sons from his first marriage, a stepdaughter, and 15 grandchildren. His nephew, Lawrence Summers, served as the chief economic advisor to U.S. President Barack Obama. **Sources:** *Los Angeles Times,* http://www.latimes.com/news/obituaries/la-me-paul-samuelson14-2009dec14,0,368061.story?track=rss&utm_source=feedburner&utm_medium=feed&utm_campaign=Feed%3A+latimes%2Fnews%2Fobituaries+%28Los+Angeles+Times+-+Obituaries%29&utm_content=Google+Reader (September 16, 2010); *New York Times,* http://www.nytimes.com/2009/12/14/business/economy/14samuelson.html?partner=rss&emc=rss (September 16, 2010); *Times* (London), http://www.timesonline.co.uk/tol/comment/obituaries/article6955107.ece (September 16, 2010);

Washington Post, http://www.washingtonpost.com/wp-dyn/content/article/2009/12/13/AR20091213.tif02810.html?wprss=rss_metro/obituaries (September 16, 2010).

—*Helene Barker Kiser*

Shelden J. Segal

Born Sheldon Jerome Segal, March 15, 1926, in New York, NY; died of congestive heart failure, October 17, 2009, in Woods Hole, MA. Scientist. With a firm belief that women should have complete control over their own reproduction, embryologist and biochemist Sheldon "Shelly" Segal devoted most of his career to developing long-lasting, effective contraceptives. Perhaps best known for his work with Norplant, Segal's decades of contraceptive research has benefited more than 120 million women worldwide.

Born in 1926, Segal spent his youth in the area, attending Erasmus Hall High School. When he was just 16 years old, during World War II, Segal joined the Navy and was sent overseas on a troop transport vessel, but the Japan bombings and end of the war caused the vessel to be sent to Bikini Atoll for nuclear testing instead of to Japan for combat. He left the Navy after rising to the rank of lieutenant, junior grade. After returning to the United States, Segal enrolled first in Dartmouth College, where he completed his bachelor's degree in 1947, followed by the University of Iowa, where he completed his doctoral degree in embryology and biochemistry in 1952. In 1961, he married Harriet Feinberg, who would eventually be known in her own right as novelist Harriet Segal. Their marriage lasted 48 years, ending with his death.

In 1956, Segal would begin his career with the Population Council, an organization devoted to reproductive health and general well-being of people worldwide, where he directed the biomedical laboratories until 1978. Immediately, he became involved in research for a contraceptive alternative to the birth control pill. Although the pill was effective in preventing pregnancy when used properly and according to directions, not all women were able to use it without negative side effects, which included weight gain, depression, bleeding, and risk of cancer. In addition, the pill must be taken daily, so its effectiveness was reduced when women were not diligent about taking the pill as scheduled and accidentally skipped a day or two. Segal's team devoted the next 24 years to developing a contraceptive that was equally effective but less dependent on user memory, cheaper, and without as many side effects.

The result of these years was Norplant. Consisting of six silicone capsules containing levonorgestrel, a progestin hormone, the contraceptive was surgically implanted in a woman's arm. Effective for at least five years after implantation, Norplant both prevented the woman's ovulation cycle and the sperm's entry through the cervix's thickened mucus.

Approved by the Food and Drug Administration (FDA) in 1990, Norplant would remain available worldwide until being withdrawn from the United States market in 2002. Its success was hampered by several issues, including the side effects the contraceptive turned out to cause in some women, such as headaches and nausea, hair loss, bleeding, and depression, some of which were similar side effects to those caused by the pill. By 1996, Wyeth Pharmaceuticals, the manufacturer, had been sued by more than 50,000 users of Norplant who claimed the clearly labeled packages did not provide enough warning about the potential side effects. Wyeth never lost in court, although the company did settle 36,000 cases.

Segal was horrified when Norplant was used to further restrict reproductive freedom, completely contrary to his original intent. Some state governments attempted to offer incentives to poor and single women who agreed to use the contraceptive, some advocated widespread use of the drug to prevent teenage pregnancy, and some judges ordered abusive mothers to have the device implanted. While it did not surprise Segal that the use of Norplant would be so negative, he was surprised that it was so in the United States. In an open letter to the *Washington Post* in 1990, Segal wrote "Norplant should never be used for any coercive or involuntary purpose. It was developed to enhance reproductive freedom, not to restrict it.... Those who suggest using Norplant for involuntary or coercive sterilization or birth control will find me leading the opposition."

Segal and his team later developed a contraceptive known as Norplant II or Jadelle, which also contained levonorgestrel but in two rods instead of six capsules. Jadelle was also approved by the FDA, and while it has been used by the U.S. Agency for International Development, it was never marketed directly to women in the United States. Other contraceptives developed by Segal include the levonorgestrel-releasing intrauterine device (IUD) Merina and copper-bearing vaginal rings.

In 1978, Segal left the Population Council for the Rockefeller Foundation's population sciences division, but he returned to the Population Council in 1991 as institutional review board chairman and distinguished scientist. In addition to his laboratory research, Segal was co-author of *Is Menstruation Obsolete?* (1999), *Hormone Use and Male Andropause: A Choice for Women and Men* (2003), and *Under the Banyan Tree: A Population Scientist's Odyssey* (2003). In all, Segal authored 300 publications during his career and served as advisor to the United Nations Population Fund, the World Bank, the World Health Organization, the U.S. Congress, and the European Parliament.

On October 17, 2009, Segal succumbed to congestive heart failure at his home in Woods Hole, Massachusetts; he was 83. He is survived by his wife, Harriet; his daughters Amy, Jennifer, and Laura; and seven grandchildren. **Sources:** *Los Angeles Times,* http://www.latimes.com/news/nationworld/nation/la-me-sheldon-segal23-2009oct23,0,3518412.story (March 18, 2010); *New York Times,* http://www.nytimes.com/2009/10/21/health/21segal.html?partner=rss&emc=rss (March 18, 2010); *Washington Post,* http://www.washingtonpost.com/wp-dyn/content/article/2009/10/21/AR20091021.tif04031.html?wprss=rss_metro/obituaries (March 18, 2010).

—*Helene Barker Kiser*

Eunice Kennedy Shriver

Born Eunice Mary Kennedy, July 10, 1921, in Brookline, MA; died after a series of strokes, August 11, 2009, in Hyannis, MA. Activist. Eunice Kennedy Shriver was one of the last surviving siblings from the U.S.'s most famous—and tragedy-plagued—political dynasty. Three of her brothers died young—one in World War II, another while a sitting U.S. president, and a third felled on the campaign trail—and the large, Irish-American Roman Catholic family endured several other untimely losses. Shriver never held political office herself, but proved a major force in American society as an advocate for the developmentally disabled. "She should have been president," her nephew, environmental activist Robert Kennedy Jr. once said about her, according to the *Los Angeles Times.* "She is the most impressive figure in the family."

Shriver was the fifth of nine children born to Rose Fitzgerald Kennedy, the daughter of Boston's one-time mayor, and her financier-husband Joseph P. Kennedy, Sr. She was born at home in Brookline, Massachusetts, in 1921 into a family of wealthy, attractive overachievers whose athletic pursuits sharpened the competitive streak their parents encouraged. In 1938, the year Shriver turned 17, her father was appointed U.S. ambassador to England, where she finished her education. She spent some time at a Roman Catholic college for women, Manhattanville College in New York, before moving to California to study sociology at Stanford University. Like her next-eldest brother John, she suffered from an adrenal imbalance called Addison's disease, and was further plagued by ulcers and colitis for much of her life.

After graduating from Stanford in 1944, Shriver worked at the U.S. State Department and the Department of Justice, and later became a social worker in Chicago. In 1953, she wed Yale Law School graduate Robert Sargent Shriver Jr. at St. Patrick's Cathedral in New York City before 1,700 guests. It was during this decade that her brother John (known as "Jack") and her younger brothers Robert and Edward each entered the political arena, and she campaigned for all of them. Jack was elected to the White House in 1960, and made "Bobby" his Attorney General; "Ted," the youngest Kennedy son, was elected to the U.S. Senate.

Shriver's father had hoped that his oldest son, Joseph Jr., would become president, but Joe Jr. died in combat in World War II in 1944. That was the first public misfortune for the Kennedy clan, but privately they mourned an earlier loss—that of the eldest Kennedy daughter, Rosemary, in 1941, who was born with a moderate form of mental retardation. The family had always included her in all their activities, but she grew more willful in her early twenties and their father decided to permit doctors to perform a prefrontal lobotomy on her with the hope of easing her mood swings. The result was disastrous, for Rosemary lost much of her verbal faculties and ability to care for her most basic personal needs. She was secreted away to an institution run by Roman Catholic nuns, and her brothers and sisters were discouraged from having any more contact with her in the belief that this would confuse her.

Joe Kennedy, Sr. was said to have deeply regretted his decision over the surgery. He had already established a charitable foundation in memory of his eldest son, and in 1958 asked Shriver and her husband to run it and direct its resources toward research into and aid for Americans with developmental disabilities. When Jack Kennedy was sworn into office as U.S. president in 1961, he authorized the creation of a panel on mental retardation. That led, in turn, to the founding of National Institute of Child Health and Human Development (NICHD) in 1962 within the federally funded National Institutes of Health. By now Shriver was running the Foundation herself, after her husband became the first director of another Kennedy Administration creation, the Peace Corps, and had a growing family that would eventually number five children. Famously determined and rarely slowed by her own health issues, Shriver was a skillful persuader. Jack once said to Bobby, whom he had made his Attorney General, "Let's give Eunice whatever she wants so I can get on with the business of government," as her *Los Angeles Times* obituary reported.

With Jack's blessing, Shriver wrote a 1962 article for the widely read *Saturday Evening Post* about Rosemary, though she did not mention the lobotomy. The confession about the Kennedy secret was later considered an important turning point in the public perception of mental retardation, which still had great stigma attached to it. Often afflicted families were deeply ashamed and the prevailing wisdom was that the developmentally disabled were better off in institutions or hidden inside the home.

Like all the Kennedys, Shriver believed in the healing power of fresh air and physical exercise. The family sailed, skied, engaged in rambunctious touch football games, and these activities only expanded in scope with the growing number of second-generation offspring. Shriver was determined to bring that same competitive exhilaration to the developmentally disabled. This was a renegade idea, for medical experts believed that such children and adults might injure themselves, or not be able to fully accept the idea of losing an athletic contest. Shriver started the first summer camp for developmentally disabled children at her Maryland home in the early 1960s. By 1968, her idea had expanded to the First International Special Olympics Summer Games, where attendees from 26 states and Canada competed in track and field events and swimming; their travel costs were covered by the Kennedy Foundation.

That first Special Olympics received a significant amount of attention because of the Kennedy name, but also took place just weeks after Shriver's brother Bobby was killed while campaigning for the Democratic Party nomination in 1968; this was five years after Jack's assassination in 1963 in Dallas. There were subsequent tragedies in the growing Kennedy clan over the next few decades, but also many new triumphs. Shriver's daughter, Maria, became a television journalist and wed actor Arnold Schwarz-

enegger, who was elected governor of California in 2003. The Shrivers' four sons all entered public service or were elected to public office.

Shriver's health failed in the last few years of her life after a series of strokes. She died at Cape Cod Hospital in Hyannis, Massachusetts, on August 11, 2009, at the age of 88. Her husband survives her, as do sons Robert III, Timothy, Mark, and Anthony, along with daughter Maria and 19 grandchildren. Her brother Ted died two weeks later, leaving just Jean Kennedy Smith, the former U.S. ambassador to Ireland, as the sole remaining Kennedy sibling. Ted was eulogized for his efforts for health-care reform in America, but he had once said of his sister that she had, in the end, accomplished much more than any electoral triumph or legislative victory. "You talk about an agent of change," he said of Eunice, according to her *New York Times* obituary. "If the test is what you're doing that's been helpful for humanity, you'd be hard-pressed to find another member of the family who's done more." **Sources:** *Los Angeles Times*, August 12, 2009, pp. A1, A24; *New York Times*, August 12, 2009, p. A19; *People*, August 24, 2009, p. 96; *Washington Post*, August 12, 2009.

—Carol Brennan

Theodore R. Sizer

Born Theodore Ryland Sizer, June 23, 1932, in New Haven, CT; died of colon cancer, October 21, 2009, in Harvard, MA. Educator. Convinced that the top-down design of modern-day schools were a major cause of students' failure to learn anything of value, lifelong educator Theodore "Ted" Sizer devoted his career to education reform. Founder of the Coalition of Essential Schools, Sizer worked to change American education at its core through his tireless examination of and support for real and lasting education in the tradition of John Dewey.

Born in 1932 to his Yale art historian father, Sizer grew up in bulldog country, graduating from Yale in 1953 with a bachelor's degree in English. A self-described mediocre student, he left the academic world for a time to serve in the U.S. Army as an artillery officer. This experience was in large part responsible for forming the core of Sizer's beliefs and lifelong reform efforts.

In the military, mistakes can literally cost lives. Accordingly, no matter the education level of the soldiers, it was essential that they be well-trained to be reliable, responsible team members who could be counted on to deliver as expected. Sizer discovered that when his largely uneducated troops were treated in an egalitarian manner, they were entirely teachable; each soldier would rise to the level of the bar set for expected performance.

Sizer completed his time in the Army and briefly taught at high schools in Massachusetts and Australia before marrying Nancy Faust in 1955 and returning to school himself. He enrolled in Harvard, completing a master's degree in teaching in 1957 and a doctoral degree in education and American history in 1961. He joined the Harvard faculty after graduation, rising to Dean of the Graduate School of Education in 1964, where he remained until 1972 when he left to take the headmaster position at the preparatory school Phillips Academy. He would eventually return to Harvard as a visiting professor in the late 1990s.

After several years at Phillips, Sizer conducted an exhaustive multi-year study, begun in 1981, of high schools nationwide. This study, sponsored in part by the National Association of Independent Schools and the National Association of Secondary School Principals, further convinced Sizer of the failure of the American school system, rooted as it was in the outdated tradition of federal governmental directives which treated all students with a normalized, one-size-fits-all approach and therefore expected standardized testing, grades, and too-large groupings of students by little more than age. Low expectations had created the dismal state of the educational system, Sizer believed, in which students were not expected to connect anything of importance to their lives.

In 1984, the first volume of Sizer's book trilogy would be published, *Horace's Compromise: The Dilemma of the American High School*, followed by *Horace's School: Redesigning the American High School* in 1992 and *Horace's Hope: What Works for the American High School* in 1996, which chronicled the frustrated attempts of fictional English teacher Horace Smith to truly educate his students within the confines of the outdated and restrictive educational system. The compromise was the unspoken agreement that if the students behaved themselves, the teachers would not require or expect much of them.

According to the *New York Times*, Sizer's philosophy of education could be summed up by these lines from his most famous book, *Horace's Compromise*: "Horace Smith and his ablest colleagues may be the key to better high schools, but it is respected adolescents who will shape them.... Inspiration, hunger:

these are the qualities that drive good schools. The best we educational planners can do is to create the most likely conditions for them to flourish, and then get out of their way."

In response, the Coalition of Essential Schools was born in 1984, comprising a dozen member schools at its beginnings. By the early 2000s, there were 600 Essential Schools worldwide, both public and private, all committed to the same democratic principles. Those principles stem from the central idea that every member of a school is an equal, with a specific role to play. A teacher is most effective in the role of facilitator, mentor, and coach, and the students themselves are workers who are expected to devote themselves toward mastery of the core subject matter.

In 1993, Sizer joined Brown University as the founder and director of the Annenberg Institute for School Reform. Five years later, he and his wife co-principaled the Devens, Massachustts, Francis W. Parker Charter Essential School. In addition to the Horace trilogy, Sizer was author or co-author of several other volumes, including *Secondary Schools at the Turn of the Century*, 1964; *Places for Learning, Places for Joy: Speculations on American School Reform*, 1973; *The Students Are Watching*, 1999; *The Red Pencil: Convictions from Experience in Education*, 2004; and *Keeping School: Letters to Families from Principals of Two Small Schools*, 2004.

After battling colon cancer for some time, Sizer died on October 21, 2009, at his home in Harvard, Massachusetts; he was 77. He is survived by his wife, Nancy; his sons Theodore II and Hal; his daughters Judith and Lyde; and ten grandchildren. **Sources:** *Los Angeles Times*, http://www.latimes.com/news/obituaries/la-me-ted-sizer24-2009oct24,0,3562085.story?track=rss (March 18, 2010); *New York Times*, http://www.nytimes.com/2009/10/23/education/23sizer.html?partner=rss&emc=rss (March 18, 2010); *Washington Post*, http://www.washingtonpost.com/wp-dyn/content/article/2009/10/22/AR20091022.tif04839.html?wprss=rss_metro/obituaries (March 18, 2010).

—*Helene Barker Kiser*

Elisabeth Söderström

Born May 7, 1927, in Stockholm, Sweden; died of a stroke, November 20, 2009, in Stockholm, Sweden.

Soprano. For five decades, Elisabeth Söderström entranced opera audiences with her sensitive portrayals of a variety of roles and her rich vocal performances. Her repertoire included more than 60 roles in ten languages from a variety of composers including Mozart, Strauss, Tchaikovsky, Janacek, and Rachmaninov. She performed throughout Europe and the United States, regularly appearing at the Metropolitan Opera in New York and England's Glyndebourne Festival.

Söderström believed in the power of music as a medium for storytelling. She was modest about her own vocal quality, despite critics finding it distinctive. Along with her performance career, Söderström spread her love of music through a television program about classical music. Her song recitals often included lectures about the pieces she performed. "In my own country I try to spread opera wherever I can—in factories, prisons, hospitals, mental institutions," she was quoted as having said in the *Washington Post.* "I'm preaching, I admit it." Söderström was fluent in five languages, and, according to a writer for the London *Times,* "she spoke with penetrating insight and irresistible humour."

The daughter of a music-loving businessman and his Russian wife, Söderström was born in Stockholm in 1927. The family encouraged music; Söderström's father took her to performances by important singers when she was a youth. At 14, Söderström began singing and seriously studying music. She hoped to become an actress but she was rejected from the Stockholm Academy of Dramatic Arts. Her voice earned her a place in the Royal Academy of Music and Opera School in her native Stockholm.

At the age of 20, Söderström made her debut performance, playing the title female role in Mozart's *Bastien und Bastienne* at the Drottningholm Court Theater. Three years after her debut, she joined the Royal Swedish Opera, where she remained for more than 30 years. In 1955, she made her premiere performance outside of Sweden, playing Pfitzner's Ighino in *Palestrina* at the Salzburg Festival. Her role as the Composer in Strauss' *Ariadne auf Naxos* was first seen at the Glyndebourne Festival in 1957, and it became one of the favorites of that festival for years.

In 1959, Söderström gave her first performance at the Metropolitan Opera in New York, the same year she performed all three leading female roles in *Der Rosenkavalier* by Strauss. This feat showed Söderström's skilled versatility. She performed frequently at the Met for several years until, in 1964,

she returned to Sweden to spend more time with her young children. By 1969, she had returned to touring, singing with the Royal Opera at Covent Garden in London. Her portrayal of Mélisande in Debussy's *Pelléas et Mélisande* became the definitive rendition for many opera critics, and marked a high point in Söderström's career.

Already well established and respected, Söderström reached out to a wider audience in the 1970s by performing three heroines in operas by Janacek. Recording these performances under Australian conductor Charles Mackerras, Söderström became a favorite of the conductor, who asked her back to sing several Janacek roles for a variety of performances. These and Söderström's other recordings reflect the variety of roles she has performed over the course of her career. She has sung the music of Monteverdi, Mozart, Zemlinsky, Rachmaninov, and Shostakovich.

In the 1970s, Söderström wrote an autobiography, discussing her performances, life as a musician, and her philosophics on music. "All my life I have striven to show that it is not in the slightest unnatural to express yourself in song," She was quoted by the *Washington Post* as having written in her 1978 autobiography. She wrote that she hoped to "find a balance between music, words and gestures [to achieve] the work of art."

In 1983, Söderström returned to the Met, performing Strauss and Marschallin. Söderström continued performing regularly into her 60s, retiring from performing life in the late 1980s. From 1993 through 1996, she took a position as the director of Drottingholm Court Theater, the group with which she had originally made her debut. She came out of retirement in 1991, at 71 years old, to perform the part of the Countess in Tchaikovsky's *The Queen of Spades*, a role normally reserved for contraltos, at the Met.

In the late 2000s, Söderström suffered a stroke, from which she never fully recovered. The complications resulted in her death on November 20, 2009, at the age of 82. She is survived by her husband, retired Swedish naval officer Sverker Olow, their three sons, and her grandchildren. Söderström was honored throughout her career, receiving the Royal Court Singer title in Sweden and the Honorary Academian of the Swedish Royal Academy of Music. She was also made an honorary Commandeur de l'Ordre des Arts et des Lettres in France and an honorary Commander of the Order of the British Empire. **Sources:** *Los Angeles Times,* November 23, 2009; *New York Times,* November 22, 2009; *Times* (London), November 23, 2009; *Washington Post,* November 22, 2009.

—Alana Joli Abbott

Richard Sonnenfeldt

Born Heinz Wolfgang Richard Sonnenfeldt, July 23, 1923, in Berlin, Germany; died of a stroke, October 9, 2009, in Port Washington, New York. Interpreter. Just seven years after fleeing his native Germany to escape the Nazi persecution and mass extermination of his people, Richard Sonnenfeldt served as chief interpreter for and interrogator of some of the most notorious Nazi officers at Nuremberg. Speaking on behalf of those who had been forever silenced, the young Sonnenfeldt proved himself a professional and trustworthy translator during the famed 1945 war crimes trials.

Sonnenfeldt was born in 1923, the older of two sons born to physicians Walter and Gertrude. He grew up in the northeast town of Gardelegen. In 1938, his parents, fearing for the family's safety in the growing tide of persecution with Hitler's ascension to power, sent Sonnenfeldt and his brother Helmut to an English boarding school in Kent; however, in 1940, Sonnenfeldt was declared an enemy alien and was forcibly deported to Australia; Helmut, who was only 14, was able to remain at school.

Sonnenfeldt was not exiled for long as he was able to successfully argue in a letter to British Prime Minister Winston Churchill that his Jewish heritage made him an enemy of the Nazis. He was dropped off the ship in India and allowed to leave, so he found employment at a radio factory where he earned the money to join his family. The following year, in 1941, the Sonnenfeldt family, who had escaped to United States via Sweden, were reunited in Baltimore, Maryland. Sonnenfeldt became an American citizen and joined the Army, with which he fought in the Battle of the Bulge in 1944 and 1945, and set his own eyes on the abandoned Dachau concentration camp and its newly liberated prisoners.

When the war ended, Sonnenfeldt was shipped to Austria as part of a U.S. armored unit. Out of the motor pool, General William J. Donovan, who was head of the Office of Strategic Services (the early incarnation of the CIA, Central Intelligence Agency), chose Sonnenfeldt to be an interpreter for the American legal team conducting the Nuremberg war crimes trails of more than 20 men, a group which would include such infamous persons as Albert Speer, head of Germany's war manufacturing; Joachim von Ribbentrop, Nazi foreign minister; Reich minister Rudolf Hess; Hans Frank, governor of Nazi Poland; Ernst Kaltenbrunner, head of Nazi security; and Hermann Goering, Hitler's second in command and named successor.

Although he was young, just 22 at the time, and he had no special training or experience, Donovan chose Sonnenfeldt for the simple fact that he could be clearly understood. Although his native language was German, he spoke English fluently and with an American's accent. First, Sonnenfeldt's duties were simply to serve as interpreter for prosecutor John Amen, but he proved himself so skilled and so trustworthy that he was soon allowed to formulate and ask his own questions during the proceedings as an interrogator. The *New York Times* reported that, in the case of Goering, who Sonnenfeldt insulted by pronouncing his name as "gering," meaning "little nothing" Sonnenfeldt quickly became bold enough to snap, "When I speak, you don't interrupt me. You wait until I'm finished. And then when you have to say something, I will listen to you and decide whether it's necessary to translate it."

Sonnenfeldt rose to chief interpreter because his translations were the only ones that were not disputed. In fact, Sonnenfeldt's friend, law professor and author John Q. Barrett, told the *New York Times* that Sonnenfeldt was recognized as "the person who could really thrust and parry with the prisoner in his native tongue," and this was in part what made him so successful in the position. Further, despite his personal background and experience, he did not treat the trails as a personal vendetta. The newspaper quoted Sonnenfeldt in his autobiography as saying "Of course, I felt great satisfaction to be at Nuremberg, but my mind was more on doing my job than avenging a personal past in Nazi Germany. As to punishing the defendants for what they had done to humanity—that was the assigned task of the tribunal."

Although the legal team pleaded with him to stay until the end of the trials, Sonnenfeldt returned to Baltimore to enroll in Johns Hopkins University, where he earned a degree in electrical engineering. After graduating, he accepted a position with the color television development team at the Radio Corporation of America (RCA). After RCA, Sonnenfeldt moved on to several executive positions in other companies, including NASA, NBC television, and a newspaper printing plate producer, and was also dean of Brooklyn Polytechnic Institute's Graduate School of Management in the 1980s.

In his spare time, when not playing bridge or chess, Sonnenfeldt longed for the ocean. In fact, even while in his seventies, he three times crossed the Atlantic as captain of his 45-foot sailboat. Toward the end of his life, Sonnenfeldt wrote and spoke regularly about his memoirs of Nuremberg. His autobiography, *Witness to Nuremberg* was released in 2006, prompting a 2007 interview with widely watched Charlie Rose on the Public Broadcasting Service (PBS). Suffering from complications after a stroke, Sonnenfeldt died at home in Port Washington, New York, on October 9, 2009; he was 86. He was preceded in death by first wife Shirley in 1979 and is survived by his brother, Helmut; his second wife, Barbara; his sons, Michael and Lawrence; his daughter Ann; and his stepdaughters Elizabeth, Catherine, and Maggi. **Sources:** *Los Angeles Times*, http://www.latimes.com/news/obituaries/la-me-richard-sonnenfeldt14-2009oct14,0,6819391.story?track=rss (March 18, 2010); *New York Times*, http://www.nytimes.com/2009/10/13/nyregion/13sonnenfeldt.html?partner=rss&emc=rss (March 18, 2010); *Times* (London), http://www.timesonline.co.uk/tol/comment/obituaries/article6884388.ece (March 18, 2010); *Washington Post,* http://www.washingtonpost.com/wp-dyn/content/article/2009/10/13/AR20091013.tif03327.html?wprss=rss_metro/obituaries (March 18, 2010).

—*Helene Barker Kiser*

Mercedes Sosa

Born Haydée Mercedes Sosa, July 9, 1935, in San Miguel de Tucumán, Argentina; died from complications of kidney disease, October 9, 2009, in Buenos Aires, Argentina. Singer. In a career that spanned more than half a century, Argentine folk singer Mercedes Sosa, affectionately nicknamed "La Negra" because of her indigenous mestizo French and Indian ancestry and dark skin and hair, acted as "voice of the voiceless" in her political songs defending the poor and lifting up the oppressed. Winner of multiple Latin Grammy Awards and collaborator with such worldwide music industry giants as Joan Baez, Sting, Luciano Pavarotti, Shakira, Charly Garcia, and Andrea Bocelli, "It's hard to overestimate her popularity and importance as a standard-bearer of folk music and political engagement through folk music," according to ethnomusicologist Jonathan Ritter in the *Los Angeles Times.*

The desolate region of San Miguel de Tucumán in rural northwestern Argentina gave the people who lived there more proximity, both geographically and influentially, to Bolivia's native peoples and culture than to the faraway urban Argentine capital of Buenos Aires. Here, on July 9, 1935, Haydée Mercedes Sosa was born to a day laborer father and washerwoman mother, her home's location "an advantage for someone who wanted to be a folk singer," Sosa

said in the *Washington Post.* Indeed, being a folk singer was always in Sosa's future plans. When she was 15 she entered a singing contest for a radio station and won with a song called "I'm Sad," giving her the confidence to follow her dream.

While the lyrics of Sosa's songs were markedly political, she did not specifically define herself as a political activist but rather as an artist who shed light on political issues and concerns. In the 1960s and 1970s, Sosa was at the forefront of the "Nueva Cancion" (New Song) school, a blended political and folk music movement that she and her then-husband, guitarist Manuel Oscar Matus, had helped found in the late 1950s. Left-leaning by nature, the movement was largely defined by musicians with Marxist beliefs who used their platform as public artists to bring attention to the plight of lower class workers and peasants.

While many musicians worldwide were performing songs with similar themes, Sosa's brand of folk music, and her continued popularity, endured as art because she brought something else to the table. Unlike other protest songs of the period, which were often little more than direct politics, Sosa's offerings—drawn from many writers as Sosa herself was not a songwriter—overflowed with poetry. By 1976, however, it was difficult and dangerous to be a political activist of any form in Argentina, as the military junta which had seized power after Juan Perón's death was engaged in what would be known as the Dirty War, in which tens of thousands of perceived government enemies were "disappeared." Sosa did not back down from her politically charged lyrics, and if anything she became more specifically political and critically outspoken. Subsequently, her music was banned from both radio and television, and she was subjected to the humiliation of an onstage body search by security during one concert in La Plata. Later concerts were cancelled due to bomb threats, and she was subsequently banned from further performances.

By 1979, the silenced Sosa was exiled, during which time she had been so unhappy and distressed that even her vocal ability abandoned her for a time, and she was unable to sing. She spent the next three years living out of a suitcase in Spain and France before returning to Argentina to see the dictatorship fail and her own status skyrocket. Popular before her exile, her albums after her return sold hundreds of thousands of copies and her concerts regularly drew crowds in the tens of thousands. Her fame became worldwide; in 1987, she received a standing ovation at Carnegie Hall in which the cheers and applause lasted a staggering ten minutes. The fact that she sang only in her native language was not in any way a barrier for her global audiences. According to a review in *Esquire*, quoted in the *Washington Post*, Sosa "requires no translation. Hers is the song of all those who have overcome their fear of singing out."

Sosa's first album was released in 1962; during her career, she would release more than 70 albums. Her best-known song, her signature, was the nostalgic "Gracias a la Vida." Her final album, *Cantora*, was posthumously awarded the 2009 Latin Grammy for best folk album, the fourth time her music was honored with the award. (Her albums had previously won the best folk album Latin Grammy award in 2000, 2003, and 2006.) A tour to promote her new album had been planned, but was cancelled when Sosa's health declined.

At a Buenos Aires clinic on October 4, 2009, Sosa died of complications due to kidney disease and liver and lung problems. She was 74 years old. Testament to what she meant to the people of her country, Buenos Aires cancelled all artistic activities scheduled for that day; her body lay in state at the Argentine Congress building in the capital city. The *New York Times* quoted the Argentine newspaper *Clarín* calling Sosa "nothing more and nothing less than the most important Argentine singer in history." Preceded in death by second husband and manager Pocho Mazzitelli, she is survived by her only child, son Fabián Matus. **Sources:** *Los Angeles Times,* http://www.latimes.com/news/obituaries/la-me-mercedes-sosa5-2009oct05,0,4831419.story?track=rss (March 18, 2010); *Malianteo,* http://www.malianteo.com/en/general/calle-13-y-mercedes-sosa-ganan-varios-latin-grammy (April 17, 2010); *New York Times,* http://www.nytimes.com/2009/10/05/arts/music/05sosa.html?partner=rss&emc=rss (March 18, 2010); *Times* (London), http://www.timesonline.co.uk/tol/comment/obituaries/article6862067.ece (March 18, 2010); *Washington Post,* http://www.washingtonpost.com/wp-dyn/content/article/2009/10/04/AR20091004.tif00918.html?wprss=rss_metro/obituaries (March 18, 2010).

—*Helene Barker Kiser*

Percy E. Sutton

Born Percy Ellis Sutton, November 24, 1920, in San Antonio, TX; died December 26, 2009, in New York,

NY. Politician. The son of a former slave and attorney to the infamous Malcolm X, Percy Sutton spent decades fighting against racism and discrimination. His tireless efforts resulted in personal and political success, blazing a trail for many future aspiring African Americans to follow.

Born in 1920 in San Antonio, Texas, to Samuel, a former slave turned segregated school principal, and Lillian, a teacher, Sutton was the youngest of 15 children. He grew up in nearby Prairie View, Texas, traveling with his father to deliver milk from the family farm to the poor. The elder Sutton was also the owner of a funeral home, skating rink, and mattress factory, and he sold real estate as well. It was Sutton's parents' hardworking example and dedication to education that led all 12 of their surviving children to eventually attend college.

These were not the only qualities Sutton learned from his father, who told his children, according to the *New York Times*, "Suffer the hurts, but don't show the anger, because if you do, it will block you from being able to effectively do anything to remove the hurts."

Two events in his youth sealed his fate as a risk-taker and a proponent of racial equality. At the age of 12, Sutton sneaked onto a passenger train bound for New York, and had to sleep under a 155th Street sign when he arrived; his family did not punish their young adventurer. The following year, Sutton was handing out National Association for the Advancement of Colored People (NAACP) information, and a policeman questioned his presence in the white neighborhood and then beat him.

When he was older, Sutton was a stunt flyer and attended several colleges—Prairie View A&M, Tuskegee University, and Hampton University, but did not complete a degree. He wanted to enlist in World War II but was turned away in Texas so he went to New York where he enlisted with the all-black Tuskegee Airmen.

After his tour of duty and return to the states, the G.I. Bill paid for him to attend law school, and because his grades had been good, he was accepted to Columbia Law School. Sutton was unable to continue at Columbia, however, because of his work schedule—the 4:00 pm to midnight second shift at the post office and the after midnight to 8:30 a.m. third shift on the subway. Once he transferred to Brooklyn Law School, he began classes an hour later, at 9:30 a.m.. This schedule continued for three years. His wife, Leatrice, with whom he had a son,

Pierre, could not take Sutton's schedule, and she filed for divorce in 1950. Sutton married second wife Eileen and they had a daughter, Cheryl, but this marriage was very brief, and he remarried Leatrice in 1952.

When Sutton completed law school, he re-enlisted in the military to fight in the Korean War as part of the Air Force, under the mistaken impression he had failed the bar exam. When he returned stateside in 1953, Sutton established his law offices in Harlem, but it took some time for his practice to get going and he had to take odd jobs, such as scrubbing floors, to take care of his family. Eventually, he became known as a good civil rights attorney, representing hundreds of people who had been arrested in Southern protests and demonstrations and serving as president of the New York chapter of the NAACP. Famously, he appointed himself Malcolm X's attorney after Sutton heard him speaking on 125th Street and 7th Avenue, a position that did not end with the activist's murder, because Malcolm's body was refused burial by multiple cemeteries. Sutton also continued to represent Malcolm's widow and grandson.

In addition to his law practice, Sutton set his sights on the political arena, running seven times unsuccessfully for the New York Assembly before winning the seat in 1964. Two years later, he was appointed by Manhattan City Council to replace the promoted borough president, and he was reelected to that position in both 1969 and 1973, the highest ranking African-American elected official in New York state at the time. In 1977, Sutton set his sights on becoming New York City mayor, but despite fighting a hard and smart race, attempting to appeal to both whites and blacks, the deeply entrenched racism finally caused him to be unsuccessful in his bid. According to the *New York Times*, Sutton called this "the most disheartening, deprecating, disabling experience."

Sutton also attempted to fight racism through the news media, by partnering in the purchase of *The New York Amsterdam News* newspaper and radio station WLIB-AM in 1971, followed by WBLS-FM in 1974. Eventually, he would own part of 18 radio stations and two television cable franchises as part of Inner City Broadcasting, which also bought the Harlem Apollo Theater in a 1981 bankruptcy sale. He also served as a political mentor to the Rev. Jesse Jackson, the Rev. Al Sharpton, and others. According to the *Washington Post*, Sharpton said of Sutton, "He personified the black experience of the 20th century. He started the century where blacks were victims. We ended as victors."

On December 26, 2009, Sutton died in a Manhattan nursing home at the age of 89. He is survived by his wife, Leatrice; his son, Pierre; his daughter, Cheryl; and four grandchildren. **Sources:** *Los Angeles Times*, http://www.latimes.com/news/obituaries/la-me-suttonobit28-2009dec28,0,4353183.story?track=rss&utm_source=feedburner&utm_medium=feed&utm_campaign=Feed%3A+latimes%2Fnews%2Fobituaries+%28Los+Angeles+Times+-+Obituaries%29&utm_content=Google+Reader (September 16, 2010); *New York Times*, http://www.nytimes.com/2009/12/28/nyregion/28sutton.html?partner=rss&emc=rss (September 16, 2010); *Washington Post*, http://www.washingtonpost.com/wp-dyn/content/article/2009/12/27/AR20091227.tif01729.html?wprss=rss_metro/obituaries (September 16, 2010).

—*Helene Barker Kiser*

Patrick Swayze

Born August 18, 1952, in Houston, TX; died of pancreatic cancer, September 14, 2009. Actor and dancer. Known best for his iconic roles as a heartthrob in the movies *Dirty Dancing* and *Ghost*, actor and dancer Patrick Swayze surprised critics throughout his career by refusing to be typecast. Named *People* magazine's sexiest man in the world in 1991, Swayze did not want to be known as an action guy, romantic lead, or a dancer. Instead, he took roles that went against his previous performances, appearing as a surfer thief in *Point Break*, a doctor in the drama *City of Joy*, a drag queen in *To Wong Foo, Thanks for Everything, Julie Newmar*, and an FBI agent partnered with a double agent in the television series *The Beast*. In a 1989 interview with the *Chicago Sun-Times* (as reported in his *New York Times* obituary) Swayze said, "The only plan I have is that every time people think they have me pegged, I'm going to come out of left field and do something unexpected."

Though he could not escape the controversies that plague Hollywood stars, Swayze fought off a drinking problem, largely with the help of his childhood-sweetheart and wife of more than 30 years, Lisa Niemi. In 2000, he had to land a plane he was flying in an Arizona housing development due to a sudden depressurization in the cabin, which led bystanders to think he was flying while intoxicated. Instead, he was said to have suffered from hypoxia and possible carbon-monoxide poisoning. But though he struggled with depression after the death of his father and the suicide of his sister, Niemi made sure he got help. Even after being diagnosed with pancreatic cancer in 2008, Swayze kept a hopeful attitude, determined to live his life fully to the end.

Swayze was the second of five children born to Jesse, a cowboy, and Patsy, a dance instructor, Swayze. Patsy Swayze, along with running a ballet school, was a professional choreographer who, over the course of her career, choreographed films for actors including John Travolta. Swayze was taught to dance at his mother's school from an early age, something that earned him merciless teasing from his peers. However, he was also an exceptional athlete; by the time he was in high school, in addition to dancing, he played football, ran track, and was studying martial arts. His athletics won him a scholarship to San Jacinto College in Houston, where he grew up, but after two years, Swayze dropped out to begin a professional acting and dancing career.

When he was 19, Swayze fell for one of his mother's students, Niemi, four years his junior. After working as Prince Charming in the touring *Disney on Parade* ice show, Swayze moved to New York, and Niemi joined him after she graduated from high school. Both Swayze and Niemi earned positions with the Joffrey Ballet. Swayze later took a position in the Elliot Feld Ballet Company as a principal dancer, but a knee injury he had suffered playing football prevented him from continuing his career as a ballet dancer.

Though troubled by having to quit ballet, something he told *People* magazine he regretted throughout his career, Swayze found work on stage, taking a role as a dancer in *Goodtime Charley* before landing the lead role in *Grease*. The role earned Swayze some attention from Hollywood, so he and Niemi, who had married him in 1975, moved to Los Angeles. Swayze was cast in *Skatetown U.S.A.* (a movie he once told *Entertainment Weekly* he'd rather have forgotten), played a serious guest role in *M*A*S*H*, and was cast in *The Outsiders*. Though the last film began to show his potential, it was his role in the miniseries *North and South*, about the Civil War, that earned him his first real Hollywood recognition.

In 1987, Swayze reached stardom when he played the lead role of a dance instructor from the wrong side of the tracks at a pricey resort in *Dirty Dancing*. Starring opposite Jennifer Gray, Swayze impressed audiences with his charm and athleticism in dancing, as well as his chemistry with the younger lead. Though it was not expected to be a hit, *Dirty Danc-ing* had huge and lasting appeal, eventually becoming the first film to sell a million copies on VHS. Swayze performed all his own dancing and stunts.

Swayze turned down a reported seven million dollars to film a sequel (though he later made a small appearance in the 2004 spin-off, *Dirty Dancing: Havana Nights*), because he did not want to be locked into the same types of role. Instead, he performed in two smaller movies: *Next of Kin*, in which he played a rough-and-tumble police officer, and the critically panned *Road House*, which long afterward had a large presence on late-night cable television. His career looked to be on a downward slope until he was cast as the romantic lead in *Ghost*, a film in which he played a murdered investment banker who must solve his own murder. He communicates to his fiancé, played by Demi Moore, through a reluctant medium performed by Whoopi Goldberg.

Ghost launched Swayze back into stardom, earning him his second Golden Globe nomination (his first was for *Dirty Dancing*). But again, Swayze took off-the-wall roles that did little to help his career. With the exception of *To Wong Foo, Thanks for Everything! Julie Newmar*, which earned him his third Golden Globe nomination, few of his roles earned him critical attention. That was reportedly fine with Swayze, who was quoted in the *Chicago Tribune* as having said that he was "fed up with that Hollywood blockbuster mentality." He took roles in the cult film *Donnie Darko*, the 2005 film *Keeping Mum*, and the Jessica Biel film *Powder Blue*, which was released in 2009. He also filmed a movie with Niemi, *One Last Dance*, in 2003, based on a play they wrote together about aging dancers. In addition to his film work, he appeared in the Broadway revival of *Chicago* and a West End production of *Guys and Dolls*.

After filming a pilot for a new A&E series, *The Beast*, Swayze was diagnosed with pancreatic cancer. Unwilling to let the disease defeat him, he persuaded the network to allow him to film the first season while undergoing treatments. Despite his pain, he still performed all his own stunts. The series was cancelled after its first season due to Swayze's illness. Swayze's battle against cancer also led to a memoir that he co-wrote with Niemi, celebrating their life together. Swayze died on September 15, 2009, just weeks before the memoir was released. **Sources:** *Chicago Tribune*, September 15, 2009, sec. 3, pp. 1, 6; CNN.com, http://www.cnn.com/2009/SHOWBIZ/Movies/09/15/patrick.swayze/index.html (September 15, 2009); *Entertainment Weekly*, September 25, 2009, pp. 22-29; E! Online, http://www.eonline.com/uberblog/b144155_patrick_swayze_hollywoods_dirty_dancer.html (September

14, 2009); E! Online, http://www.eonline.com/uberblog/b144181_ghost_dirty_dancing_stars_shine_on.html (September 14, 2009); *Los Angeles Times*, September 15, 2009; *New York Times*, September 15, 2009; *People*, September 28, 2009, pp. 76-86; *Times* (London), September 16, 2009.

—*Alana Joli Abbott*

Mary Travers

Born November 7, 1936, in Louisville, KY; died of leukemia-related complications, September 16, 2009, in Danbury, CT. Singer. Recognizable by what a *Los Angeles Times* reporter called her "clarion" voice, Mary Travers was a third of the iconic folk trio, Peter, Paul, and Mary. The group, which won multiple Grammy awards, was one of the most popular in the folk movement during the 1960s and remained recognizable during their 40 years of touring. Their best-known songs include "If I Had a Hammer," "Puff the Magic Dragon," "Blowin' in the Wind," "I Dig Rock and Roll Music," and "Leaving on a Jet Plane."

Known as much for their politics as for their music, Peter, Paul, and Mary were active in the civil rights and the anti-war movements of the 1960s. They performed at Dr. Martin Luther King, Jr.'s march in Washington at which he delivered his "I Have a Dream" speech. Throughout her life, Travers continued to be active in causes, working on a mission in El Salvador and speaking out against U.S. involvement in Central America.

Born in 1936, Travers was the daughter of two newspaper writers who moved from Kentucky to Greenwich Village, New York, when Travers was very young. Her mother, Virginia Coigney, often took her to folk-music performances in the bohemian neighborhood. Travers attended both progressive and private schools in Greenwich Village, studying under musician Charity Bailey from as early as kindergarten. That upbringing gave Travers something unique in the folk scene that emerged from Greenwich Village during the 1950s: she was actually from the neighborhood, rather than migrating there from outside the area.

As a teen, Travers attended Elisabeth Irwin High School, where she joined the Song Swappers, a folk-music group that sang backup for legendary folk musician Pete Seeger. But despite her involvement in the Song Swappers and an appearance in a Broadway chorus, Travers had no plans to sing professionally. For Travers, it was just a part of life. "The music was everywhere," she said in the *New York Times* in 1994. "You'd go to a party at somebody's apartment and there would be 50 people there, singing well into the night."

Regardless of her intentions, Travers was drawn further into the folk movement. She began singing with Noel Paul Stookey, an electric guitarist who performed at the Gaslight as both a musician and stand-up comedian. Folk manager Albert Grossman introduced Travers to Peter Yarrow, hoping to form a trio in the vein of the formerly popular Weavers or the Kingston Trio. Travers suggested Stookey as the third member of the group, and Peter, Paul, and Mary was formed. Their first performance took place at the Bitter End in 1961, and their eponymous album was released to immediate acclaim in 1962. It remained on the Top 10 chart for ten months.

The trio's popularity continued to grow through the early 1960s with the albums *Moving* and *In the Wind*. The latter album featured a cover of Bob Dylan's "Blowin' in the Wind," bringing Dylan's almost inapproachable sound to a more-mainstream audience. Dylan, who shared Grossman as a manager, was grateful for the trio's support and gladly had them cover his "Don't Think Twice It's Alright" on a later album.

As the civil rights and anti-war movements progressed, protest took on an angrier sound, and much of the folk-music scene lost its momentum. Despite the change, Peter, Paul, and Mary remained popular, and they criticized rock music for not having the same quality of lyrics that had been present in the folk scene. Their satirical tune "I Dig Rock and Roll Music" poked fun at the Beatles and the Mamas and the Papas, and made it into the Top 10 in the charts. Their cover of John Denver's "Leaving on a Jet Plane" was their last hit, reaching the No. 1 spot in 1969.

In 1970, after releasing their children's album *Peter, Paul, and Mommy*, which won them their fifth and final Grammy, the group split up to give each member a chance at a solo career. Though Travers released five albums over the next eight years, none of them reached the same popularity as her work with Peter, Paul, and Mary. During those years, Travers also starred in a BBC television series and a U.S. radio program, trading in the mysterious persona Grossman had recommended she take by not speaking when the trio performed. She convinced

Bob Dylan to grant her a rare interview. In 1978, Yarrow asked Travers and Stookey to have a reunion concert at an anti-nuclear benefit, and the three began performing together again semi-regularly, appearing together over the next 25 years and releasing new albums.

Travers married four times and had two daughters. In 2004, she was diagnosed with leukemia. After undergoing a successful bone marrow transplant, she was hopeful that her cancer was in remission. But complications with the chemotherapy made her health deteriorate over the next few years. In 2009, Yarrow announced via radio that she would no longer be able to perform. Travers died on September 16, 2009, surrounded by her family. She is survived by her husband and two daughters. **Sources:** *Chicago Tribune*, September 17, 2009, sec. 1, p. 25; CNN.com, http://www.cnn.com/2009/SHOWBIZ/Music/09/17/obit.mary.travers/index.html (September 18, 2009); *Los Angeles Times*, September 17, 2009; *New York Times*, September 17, 2009; *Times* (London), September 18, 2009; *Washington Post*, September 17, 2009.

—Alana Joli Abbott

Richard T. Whitcomb

Born Richard Travis Whitcomb, February 21, 1921, in Evanston, IL; died of pneumonia, October 13, 2009, in Newport News, VA. Scientist. Through careful observation of the air moving around jets as they approached the sound barrier, scientist, engineer, and lifelong aviation enthusiast Richard Whitcomb redesigned aircraft to eliminate much of the air drag that previously slowed planes down. The improved efficiency in military performance eventually extended to commercial aircraft as well. Indeed, the Smithsonian Institution's senior curator of aeronautics, Tom Crouch, told the *New York Times* that Whitcomb's "intellectual fingerprints are to be found on virtually every major high-speed commercial and military aircraft flying today."

Born in 1921, Whitcomb, who was one of three children born to Frederick, an engineer who had been a World War I balloon pilot, and Gladys, spent his early years in Evanston, Illinois. He moved with his family, which included a sister and a brother, to Worcester, Massachusetts, where Whitcomb would spend the remainder of his youth and young adult years. In Worcester, Whitcomb commandeered the basement for his personal laboratory, where he set to work building model airplanes. These models were neither a boy's simple, artistic pastime, nor were they merely decorative. Instead, Whitcomb's planes could fly and fly well, at double the rate of speed normally seen from model planes with rubber band-powered propellers.

Enrolling in Worcester Polytechnic Institute, Whitcomb completed his mechanical engineering degree in 1943 and applied for a research position at Langley Memorial Aerodynamic Laboratory. He had read about the lab's research in *Fortune* and wanted to be a part of it. At the time, Langley was governed by the National Advisory Committee for Aeronautics (NACA), but long before his retirement in 1980, NACA was taken over by the National Aeronautics and Space Administration (NASA).

At the time when Whitcomb came on board at Langley, most planes were cigar-shaped. This design did allow the craft to break the sound barrier—as with Chuck Yeager's famous orange Bell X-1—but not with any ease in maneuverability. This lack of capability made it so that fighter jets were forced to choose between two levels of performance, supersonic speed or excellent handling. By attentively studying the body design and supersonic wind tunnel simulations, with an uncanny understanding of how the air flowed around the jets in flight, Whitcomb's first major discovery came in 1951: the "Coke bottle."

Whitcomb saw clearly that when a jet approached the sound barrier, the ride became very choppy, due in large part to the air drag that slowed down the plane in the same way heavy snow will slow down a plow. This was due in part to the sleek, straight, bullet design of the craft, slowed down by the wings. Whitcomb closely and repeatedly observed the air moving over the craft, and determined that a redesign of the fuselage to more resemble the shape of a Coke bottle—what would be called a "wasp waist" design or the "area rule"—would significantly reduce the drag, allowing the craft to fly faster and with greater efficiency. The 1951 design increased the jet speed 25 percent but did not use greater engine power to do so. For this breakthrough, Whitcomb was honored with the National Aeronautic Association's Collier Trophy for the most significant aeronautical advance of the year in 1955. The delay between implementation and award was due to the fact that the discovery was withheld from public knowledge until 1955 for reasons of military security and classified information.

Whitcomb's next two discoveries were made in the 1970s, both involving aircraft wings. First, he created what would be known as the supercritical wing, redesigning the wings to be flat on the top and curved on the underside. This innovation also improved aircraft efficiency, because planes could now fly at speeds up to 100 miles per hour more than before, with no increase in engine power. This discovery, which was implemented on most aircraft from that point forward, resulted in a savings of hundreds of thousands of hours and billions of dollars in fuel. For this accomplishment, Whitcomb was awarded the National Medal of Science in 1973. A few years later, he further tweaked the wing design, creating small panels that attached to the wingtips—"winglets"—to further reduce drag and subsequently increase efficiency.

A true workaholic who loved his job, Whitcomb did not even cash his paychecks with any regularity, preferring instead to use them as bookmarks. Whitcomb virtually lived at the office, regularly working double shifts and sleeping on a cot for a few hours near the wind tunnel before rising to begin the research again. His research was largely intuitive rather than arrived at through extensive testing and trials; he had an innate understanding of the movement of air molecules. According to the *New York Times*, Whitcomb explained, "I didn't run a lot of tests to arrive at an idea, and I didn't run a lot of mathematical calculations. I'd just sit there and think about what the air was doing, based on flow studies in the wind tunnel." He told the *Washington Post* that he had always been driven "to find a better way to do everything. A lot of very intelligent people are willing to adapt, but only to a certain extent. If a human mind can figure out a better way to do something, let's do it. I can't just sit around. I have to think."

After retirement, he worked as a consultant for several companies and for NASA, which called Whitcomb "the most influential aeronautical engineer/researcher of the jet age," in the *New York Times*. In addition to the Collier Prize and the National Medal, Whitcomb was inducted into the National Academy of Engineering and the National Inventors Hall of Fame.

Never married, except to the work he loved his whole life, Whitcomb died of pneumonia on October 13, 2009, in Newport News, Virginia, at the age of 88. He is survived by his sister Marian, his brother Charles, his stepbrother Kenneth, and his nephew David. **Sources:** *Los Angeles Times*, http://www.latimes.com/news/nationworld/nation/la-me-richard-whitcomb19-2009oct19,0,3160769.story (March 18, 2010); *New York Times*, http://www.nytimes.com/2009/10/26/us/26whitcomb.html?partner=rss&emc=rss (March 18, 2010); *Washington Post*, http://www.washingtonpost.com/wp-dyn/content/article/2009/10/15/AR20091015.tif03894.html?wprss=rss_metro/obituaries (March 18, 2010).

—*Helene Barker Kiser*

Edward Woodward

Born Edward Albert Arthur Woodward, June 1, 1930, in Croydon, Surrey, England; died of pneumonia, November 16, 2009, in Truro, Cornwall, England. Actor. British actor Edward Woodward took a staggering number of roles during his long career, but may be best remembered for his starring role in the original 1973 suspense film *The Wicker Man*. A decade later, Woodward won critical acclaim for as *The Equalizer,* a CBS drama that won him a Golden Globe Award for Best Performance by an Actor in a Television Series.

Like many of the best British actors of his generation, Woodward came from humble roots. He was born in 1930 and grew up in Croydon, near London, the son of a metal worker, and gave up a college journalism course to enter the Royal Academy of Dramatic Art (RADA) when he won a scholarship to the prestigious school. There was also a dalliance with a career as a professional soccer player, and it took him nine years from his first stage appearance—at Castle Theater's production of *A Kiss for Cinderella* in Farnham in 1946—to make it to the London stage as he honed his craft in English touring companies, which relied heavily on the Shakespeare repertoire. His London stage debut was in a 1955 drama by R. F. Delderfield, *Where There's a Will*, at the Garrick Theatre, and he reprised the role of Ralph Stokes in the film version that same year.

Woodward made his Broadway debut in a 1963 drama, *Rattle of a Simple Man,* and was directed by Noel Coward himself in *High Spirits,* which won the Tony Award for Best Musical of 1964. In 1967, Woodward debuted as *Callan* in a wildly popular new British television series about a deadly counterintelligence agent and trained assassin. "Woodward's downbeat portrayal of the seedy, ruthless intelligence agent, who had been conceived by the writer James Mitchell as an antidote to the glamour of James Bond, caught the public imagination and drew huge audiences," noted the *Times* of London. "The stony-faced and hardhearted Callan's dramatic foil was the pathetic, obsequious and malodorous Lonely, played by Russell Hunter." The show proved such a hit that there was an outcry and even London graffiti proclaiming "Callan Lives!" when it ended its four-season run in 1972.

Woodward's other enduring role was in *Wicker Man* as the uptight police sergeant Neil Howie who is sent to investigate the disappearance of a little girl on a remote island off the coast of Scotland. A staunch Christian, Sergeant Howie is appalled by the carefree lifestyle of the residents, who seem to be practicing ancient pagan rites under the spell of a nefarious overlord played by Christopher Lee. In the end, the unmarried detective finds himself imperiled as the islanders appear to prepare for their secretive annual springtime fertility rite.

A few years later, Woodward appeared in the title role as Harry *Breaker Morant,* an acclaimed drama based on the true story of an Australian officer court-martialed during the Boer War. At the age of 55 the actor found himself in a surprising lead role for a new American television series, *The Equalizer,* which ran on CBS from 1985 to 1989. He was cast as Robert McCall, a retired intelligence agent based in New York City who uses his espionage skills and high-tech weaponry to help those whom justice has failed. *The Equalizer* enjoyed solid ratings and gave Woodward a new generation of fans in North America; he even made *People* magazine's annual "Sexiest" list and won a Golden Globe Award from the Hollywood Foreign Press Association.

Woodward battled with weight and health issues in his later years. A heavy smoker, he suffered two heart attacks in 1996 before undergoing bypass surgery. In 2003 he was diagnosed with prostate cancer, and died at the Royal Cornwall Hospital in Truro on November 16, 2009, after a bout with pneumonia. He was 79 years old. Survivors include his first wife, the actress Venetia Barrett, whom he wed in 1952 and with whom he had three children—Tim, Peter, and Sarah—and his second wife, Michele Dotrice, with whom he had a daughter, Emily. After several decades in the entertainment business, Woodward once estimated he had made between two and three thousand appearances on television alone, in addition to roles on stage and in film. "I think there is a strange immediacy to it," he once said of the small screen, according to his *Washington Post* obituary. "I suppose there is also the feeling that it is the largest medium by far for information, education and above all, entertainment. And after all, that's what an actor's life is all about. Getting work and entertaining people." **Sources:** *Guardian* (London), November 16, 2009, p. 32; *Independent* (London), November 17, 2009, p. 34; *New York Times,* November 17, 2009; *Times* (London), November 17, 2009, p. 51; *Washington Post,* November 17, 2009.

—Carol Brennan

2011 Nationality Index

This index lists all newsmakers alphabetically under their respective nationalities. Indexes in softbound issues allow access to the current year's entries; indexes in annual hardbound volumes are cumulative, covering the entire *Newsmakers* series.

Listee names are followed by a year and issue number; thus **1996**:3 indicates that an entry on that individual appears in both 1996, Issue 3, and the 1996 cumulation. For access to newsmakers appearing earlier than the current softbound issue, see the previous year's cumulation.

AFGHAN
    Karzai, Hamid 1955(?)- **2002**:3

AFRICAN
    Brutus, Dennis 1924-2009
        Obituary **2011**:4

ALGERIAN
    Bouteflika, Abdelaziz 1937- **2010**:2
    Zeroual, Liamine 1951- **1996**:2

AMERICAN
    Aaliyah 1979-2001 **2001**:3
    Abbey, Edward 1927-1989
        Obituary **1989**:3
    Abbott, George 1887-1995
        Obituary **1995**:3
    Abbott, Jim 1967- **1988**:3
    Abdul, Paula 1962- **1990**:3
    Abercrombie, Josephine 1925- **1987**:2
    Abernathy, Ralph 1926-1990
        Obituary **1990**:3
    Abraham, S. Daniel 1924- **2003**:3
    Abraham, Spencer 1952- **1991**:4
    Abrams, Elliott 1948- **1987**:1
    Abrams, J. J. 1966- **2007**:3
    Abramson, Lyn 1950- **1986**:3
    Abzug, Bella 1920-1998 **1998**:2
    Achtenberg, Roberta **1993**:4
    Ackerman, Will 1949- **1987**:4
    Acuff, Roy 1903-1992
        Obituary **1993**:2
    Adair, Red 1915- **1987**:3
    Adams, Amy 1974- **2008**:4
    Adams, Don 1923-2005
        Obituary **2007**:1
    Adams, Patch 1945(?)- **1999**:2
    Adams, Scott 1957- **1996**:4
    Adams, Yolanda 1961- **2008**:2
    Adams-Geller, Paige 1969(?)- **2006**:4
    Addams, Charles 1912-1988
        Obituary **1989**:1
    Adelson, Jay 1970- **2011**:1
    Adler, Jonathan 1966- **2006**:3
    Adu, Freddy 1989- **2005**:3
    Affleck, Ben 1972- **1999**:1

AFI **2007**:3
Agassi, Andre 1970- **1990**:2
Agatston, Arthur 1947- **2005**:1
Agee, Tommie 1942-2001
    Obituary **2001**:4
Agnew, Spiro Theodore 1918-1996
    Obituary **1997**:1
Aguilera, Christina 1980- **2000**:4
Aiello, Danny 1933- **1990**:4
Aikman, Troy 1966- **1994**:2
Ailes, Roger 1940- **1989**:3
Ailey, Alvin 1931-1989 **1989**:2
    Obituary **1990**:2
Ainge, Danny 1959- **1987**:1
Akers, John F. 1934- **1988**:3
Akers, Michelle 1966- **1996**:1
Akin, Phil
    Brief entry **1987**:3
Alba, Jessica 1981- **2001**:2
Albee, Edward 1928- **1997**:1
Albert, Eddie 1906-2005
    Obituary **2006**:3
Albert, Marv 1943- **1994**:3
Albert, Stephen 1941- **1986**:1
Albom, Mitch 1958- **1999**:3
Albrecht, Chris 1952(?)- **2005**:4
Albright, Madeleine 1937- **1994**:3
Alda, Robert 1914-1986
    Obituary **1986**:3
Alexander, Jane 1939- **1994**:2
Alexander, Jason 1962(?)- **1993**:3
Alexander, Lamar 1940- **1991**:2
Alexie, Sherman 1966- **1998**:4
Ali, Laila 1977- **2001**:2
Ali, Muhammad 1942- **1997**:2
Alioto, Joseph L. 1916-1998
    Obituary **1998**:3
Allaire, Jeremy 1971- **2006**:4
Allaire, Paul 1938- **1995**:1
Allard, Linda 1940- **2003**:2
Allen, Bob 1935- **1992**:4
Allen, Debbie 1950- **1998**:2
Allen, Joan 1956- **1998**:1
Allen, John 1930- **1992**:1
Allen, Mel 1913-1996
    Obituary **1996**:4
Allen, Ray 1975- **2002**:1

Allen, Steve 1921-2000
    Obituary **2001**:2
Allen, Tim 1953- **1993**:1
Allen, Woody 1935- **1994**:1
Allen Jr., Ivan 1911-2003
    Obituary **2004**:3
Alley, Kirstie 1955- **1990**:3
Allgaier, Justin 1986- **2011**:3
Allison, Jr., Herbert M. 1943- **2010**:2
Allred, Gloria 1941- **1985**:2
Allyson, June 1917-2006
    Obituary **2007**:3
Alsop, Marin 1956- **2008**:3
Alter, Hobie
    Brief entry **1985**:1
Altman, Robert 1925- **1993**:2
Altman, Sidney 1939- **1997**:2
Alvarez, Aida **1999**:2
Ambrose, Stephen 1936- **2002**:3
Ameche, Don 1908-1993
    Obituary **1994**:2
Amory, Cleveland 1917-1998
    Obituary **1999**:2
Amos, Tori 1963- **1995**:1
Amos, Wally 1936- **2000**:1
Amsterdam, Morey 1912-1996
    Obituary **1997**:1
Anastas, Robert
    Brief entry **1985**:2
Ancier, Garth 1957- **1989**:1
Andersen, Chris 1978- **2010**:2
Anderson, Brad 1949- **2007**:3
Anderson, Gillian 1968- **1997**:1
Anderson, Harry 1951(?)- **1988**:2
Anderson, Laurie 1947- **2000**:2
Anderson, Marion 1897-1993
    Obituary **1993**:4
Anderson, Poul 1926-2001
    Obituary **2002**:3
Anderson, Tom and Chris
    DeWolfe **2007**:2
Andreessen, Marc 1972- **1996**:2
Andrews, Lori B. 1952- **2005**:3
Andrews, Maxene 1916-1995
    Obituary **1996**:2
Angelos, Peter 1930- **1995**:4
Angelou, Maya 1928- **1993**:4

Benchley, Peter 1940-2006
  Obituary **2007**:1
Benes, Francine 1946- **2008**:2
Bening, Annette 1958(?)- **1992**:1
Benjamin, Regina 1956- **2011**:2
Bennett, Joan 1910-1990
  Obituary **1991**:2
Bennett, Michael 1943-1987
  Obituary **1988**:1
Bennett, Tony 1926- **1994**:4
Bennett, William 1943- **1990**:1
Benoit, Joan 1957- **1986**:3
Benson, Ezra Taft 1899-1994
  Obituary **1994**:4
Bentley, Dierks 1975- **2007**:3
Bentsen, Lloyd 1921- **1993**:3
Bergalis, Kimberly 1968(?)-1991
  Obituary **1992**:3
Bergen, Candice 1946- **1990**:1
Berger, Sandy 1945- **2000**:1
Bergeron, Tom 1955- **2010**:1
Berkley, Seth 1956- **2002**:3
Berle, Milton 1908-2002
  Obituary **2003**:2
Berle, Peter A.A.
  Brief entry **1987**:3
Berlin, Irving 1888-1989
  Obituary **1990**:1
Berliner, Andy and Rachel **2008**:2
Berman, Gail 1957(?)- **2006**:1
Berman, Jennifer and Laura **2003**:2
Bern, Dorrit J. 1950(?)- **2006**:3
Bernanke, Ben 1953- **2008**:3
Bernardi, Herschel 1923-1986
  Obituary **1986**:4
Bernardin, Cardinal Joseph
  1928-1996 **1997**:2
Bernhard, Sandra 1955(?)- **1989**:4
Bernsen, Corbin 1955- **1990**:2
Bernstein, Elmer 1922-2004
  Obituary **2005**:4
Bernstein, Leonard 1918-1990
  Obituary **1991**:1
Berresford, Susan V. 1943- **1998**:4
Berry, Chuck 1926- **2001**:2
Berry, Halle 1968- **1996**:2
Besser, Richard 1959- **2010**:2
Bethe, Hans 1906-2005
  Obituary **2006**:2
Bettelheim, Bruno 1903-1990
  Obituary **1990**:3
Beyonce 1981- **2009**:3
Bezos, Jeff 1964- **1998**:4
Bialik, Mayim 1975- **1993**:3
Bias, Len 1964(?)-1986
  Obituary **1986**:3
Bibliowicz, Jessica 1959- **2009**:3
Biden, Joe 1942- **1986**:3
Bieber, Owen 1929- **1986**:1
Biehl, Amy 1967(?)-1993
  Obituary **1994**:1
Bigelow, Kathryn 1951- **2011**:1
Bigelow, Kathryn 1952(?)- **1990**:4
Bikoff, J. Darius 1962(?)- **2007**:3
Bikoff, James L.
  Brief entry **1986**:2
Billington, James 1929- **1990**:3
Birch, Thora 1982- **2002**:4
Bird, Brad 1956(?)- **2005**:4
Bird, Larry 1956- **1990**:3
Bishop, Andre 1948- **2000**:1

Bishop, Joey 1918-2007
  Obituary **2008**:4
Bissell, Patrick 1958-1987
  Obituary **1988**:2
Bixby, Bill 1934-1993
  Obituary **1994**:2
Black, Carole 1945- **2003**:1
Black, Cathleen 1944- **1998**:4
Black, Jack 1969- **2002**:3
Black Eyed Peas **2006**:2
Blackmun, Harry A. 1908-1999
  Obituary **1999**:3
Blackstone, Harry Jr. 1934-1997
  Obituary **1997**:4
Blaine, David 1973- **2003**:3
Blair, Bonnie 1964- **1992**:3
Blakey, Art 1919-1990
  Obituary **1991**:1
Blanc, Mel 1908-1989
  Obituary **1989**:4
Blass, Bill 1922-2002
  Obituary **2003**:3
Bledsoe, Drew 1972- **1995**:1
Blige, Mary J. 1971- **1995**:3
Bloch, Erich 1925- **1987**:4
Bloch, Henry 1922- **1988**:4
Bloch, Ivan 1940- **1986**:3
Block, Herbert 1909-2001
  Obituary **2002**:4
Bloodworth-Thomason, Linda 1947-
  1994:1
Bloom, Amy 1953- **2011**:3
Bloomberg, Michael 1942- **1997**:1
Blume, Judy 1936- **1998**:4
Blumenthal, Susan J. 1951(?)- **2007**:3
Bly, Robert 1926- **1992**:4
Blyth, Myrna 1939- **2002**:4
Bochco, Steven 1943- **1989**:1
Boehner, John A. 1949- **2006**:4
Boggs, Wade 1958- **1989**:3
Bogle, Bob 1934-2009
  Obituary **2010**:3
Bogosian, Eric 1953- **1990**:4
Bohbot, Michele 1959(?)- **2004**:2
Boiardi, Hector 1897-1985
  Obituary **1985**:3
Boies, David 1941- **2002**:1
Boitano, Brian 1963- **1988**:3
Bolger, Ray 1904-1987
  Obituary **1987**:2
Bollinger, Lee C. 1946- **2003**:2
Bolton, Michael 1953(?)- **1993**:2
Bombeck, Erma 1927-1996
  Obituary **1996**:4
Bonds, Barry 1964- **1993**:3
Bonet, Lisa 1967- **1989**:2
Bonilla, Bobby 1963- **1992**:2
Bon Jovi, Jon 1962- **1987**:4
Bonner, Robert 1942(?)- **2003**:4
Bono, Sonny 1935-1998 **1992**:2
  Obituary **1998**:2
Bontecou, Lee 1931- **2004**:4
Boone, Mary 1951- **1985**:1
Booth, Shirley 1898-1992
  Obituary **1993**:2
Bopp, Thomas 1949- **1997**:3
Borel, Calvin 1966- **2010**:1
Borlaug, Norman 1914-2009
  Obituary **2011**:1
Borofsky, Jonathan 1942- **2006**:4
Bose, Amar
  Brief entry **1986**:4

Bosworth, Brian 1965- **1989**:1
Bosworth, Kate 1983- **2006**:3
Botstein, Leon 1946- **1985**:3
Boudreau, Louis 1917-2001
  Obituary **2002**:3
Bourdain, Anthony 1956- **2008**:3
Bowe, Riddick 1967(?)- **1993**:2
Bowen, Julie 1970- **2007**:1
Bowles, Paul 1910-1999
  Obituary **2000**:3
Bowman, Scotty 1933- **1998**:4
Boxcar Willie 1931-1999
  Obituary **1999**:4
Boxer, Barbara 1940- **1995**:1
Boyer, Herbert Wayne 1936- **1985**:1
Boyington, Gregory Pappy
  1912-1988
  Obituary **1988**:2
Boyle, Gertrude 1924- **1995**:3
Boyle, Lara Flynn 1970- **2003**:4
Boyle, Peter 1935- **2002**:3
Boyle, T. C. 1948- **2007**:2
Boynton, Sandra 1953- **2004**:1
Bradford, Barbara Taylor 1933- **2002**
  :4
Bradley, Bill 1943- **2000**:2
Bradley, Ed 1941-2006
  Obituary **2008**:1
Bradley, Todd 1958- **2003**:3
Bradley, Tom 1917-1998
  Obituary **1999**:1
Bradshaw, John 1933- **1992**:1
Brady, Sarah and James S. **1991**:4
Brady, Tom 1977- **2002**:4
Brady, Wayne 1972- **2008**:3
Braff, Zach 1975- **2005**:2
Brando, Marlon 1924-2004
  Obituary **2005**:3
Brandy 1979- **1996**:4
Bratt, Benjamin 1963- **2009**:3
Braun, Carol Moseley 1947- **1993**:1
Bravo, Ellen 1944- **1998**:2
Bravo, Rose Marie 1951(?)- **2005**:3
Braxton, Toni 1967- **1994**:3
Bray, Libba 1964- **2011**:1
Brazile, Donna 1959- **2001**:1
Breathed, Berkeley 1957- **2005**:3
Brees, Drew 1979- **2011**:2
Bremen, Barry 1947- **1987**:3
Bremer, L. Paul 1941- **2004**:2
Brennan, Edward A. 1934- **1989**:1
Brennan, Robert E. 1943(?)- **1988**:1
Brennan, William 1906-1997
  Obituary **1997**:4
Brenneman, Amy 1964- **2002**:1
Brewer, Jan 1944- **2011**:4
Breyer, Stephen Gerald 1938- **1994**:4
Bridges, Jeff 1949- **2011**:1
Bridges, Lloyd 1913-1998
  Obituary **1998**:3
Brillstein, Bernie 1931-2008
  Obituary **2009**:4
Brinker, Nancy 1946- **2007**:1
Brinkley, David 1920-2003
  Obituary **2004**:3
Bristow, Lonnie 1930- **1996**:1
Brite, Poppy Z. 1967- **2005**:1
Brockovich-Ellis, Erin 1960- **2003**:3
Brody, Adrien 1973- **2006**:3
Brokaw, Tom 1940- **2000**:3
Bronfman, Edgar, Jr. 1955- **1994**:4
Bronson, Charles 1921-2003

Obituary **1995**:4
Cosgrove, Miranda 1993- **2011**:4
Costas, Bob 1952- **1986**:4
Costner, Kevin 1955- **1989**:4
Counter, Nick 1940-2009
    Obituary **2011**:3
Couples, Fred 1959- **1994**:4
Couric, Katherine 1957- **1991**:4
Courier, Jim 1970- **1993**:2
Courtney, Erica 1957- **2009**:3
Cousteau, Jean-Michel 1938- **1988**:2
Covey, Stephen R. 1932- **1994**:4
Cowen, Scott 1946- **2011**:2
Cowley, Malcolm 1898-1989
    Obituary **1989**:3
Cox, Courteney 1964- **1996**:2
Cox, Richard Joseph
    Brief entry **1985**:1
Cozza, Stephen 1985- **2001**:1
Craig, James 1956- **2001**:1
Crais, Robert 1954(?)- **2007**:4
Cram, Donald J. 1919-2001
    Obituary **2002**:2
Crandall, Robert L. 1935- **1992**:1
Cranston, Bryan 1956- **2010**:1
Craven, Wes 1939- **1997**:3
Crawford, Broderick 1911-1986
    Obituary **1986**:3
Crawford, Cheryl 1902-1986
    Obituary **1987**:1
Crawford, Cindy 1966- **1993**:3
Cray, Robert 1953- **1988**:2
Cray, Seymour R. 1925-1996
    Brief entry **1986**:3
    Obituary **1997**:2
Creamer, Paula 1986- **2006**:2
Crenna, Richard 1926-2003
    Obituary **2004**:1
Crewe, Albert 1927-2009
    Obituary **2011**:3
Crichton, Michael 1942- **1995**:3
Cronkite, Walter Leland 1916- **1997**:3
Crosby, David 1941- **2000**:4
Crosley, Sloane 1978- **2011**:4
Crothers, Scatman 1910-1986
    Obituary **1987**:1
Crow, Michael 1956- **2011**:3
Crow, Sheryl 1964- **1995**:2
Crowe, Cameron 1957- **2001**:2
Cruise, Tom 1962(?)- **1985**:4
Crumb, R. 1943- **1995**:4
Crump, Scott 1954(?)- **2008**:1
Cruz, Nilo 1961(?)- **2004**:4
Cruzan, Nancy 1957(?)-1990
    Obituary **1991**:3
Cryer, Jon 1965- **2010**:4
Crystal, Billy 1947- **1985**:3
Cugat, Xavier 1900-1990
    Obituary **1991**:2
Culkin, Macaulay 1980(?)- **1991**:3
Cunningham, Merce 1919- **1998**:1
Cunningham, Michael 1952- **2003**:4
Cunningham, Randall 1963- **1990**:1
Cunningham, Reverend William
    1930-1997
    Obituary **1997**:4
Cuomo, Andrew 1957- **2011**:1
Cuomo, Mario 1932- **1992**:2
Curran, Charles E. 1934- **1989**:2
Curren, Tommy
    Brief entry **1987**:4
Curry, Ann 1956- **2001**:1

Curtis, Ben 1977- **2004**:2
Curtis, Jamie Lee 1958- **1995**:1
Cusack, John 1966- **1999**:3
Cyrus, Billy Ray 1961(?)- **1993**:1
Cyrus, Miley 1992- **2008**:3
Dafoe, Willem 1955- **1988**:1
Dahmer, Jeffrey 1959-1994
    Obituary **1995**:2
Daily, Bishop Thomas V. 1927- **1990**
    :4
D'Alessio, Kitty
    Brief entry **1987**:3
Daly, Carson 1973- **2002**:4
Daly, Chuck 1930-2009
    Obituary **2010**:3
D'Amato, Al 1937- **1996**:1
Damon, Johnny 1973- **2005**:4
Damon, Matt 1970- **1999**:1
Danes, Claire 1979- **1999**:4
Dangerfield, Rodney 1921-2004
    Obituary **2006**:1
Daniels, Faith 1958- **1993**:3
Daniels, Jeff 1955- **1989**:4
Danticat, Edwidge 1969- **2005**:4
Danza, Tony 1951- **1989**:1
D'Arby, Terence Trent 1962- **1988**:4
Darden, Christopher 1957(?)- **1996**:4
Darling, Erik 1933-2008
    Obituary **2009**:4
Daschle, Tom 1947- **2002**:3
Davenport, Lindsay 1976- **1999**:2
David, George 1942- **2005**:1
David, Larry 1948- **2003**:4
Davis, Angela 1944- **1998**:3
Davis, Bette 1908-1989
    Obituary **1990**:1
Davis, Eric 1962- **1987**:4
Davis, Geena 1957- **1992**:1
Davis, Miles 1926-1991
    Obituary **1992**:2
Davis, Noel **1990**:3
Davis, Ossie 1917-2005
    Obituary **2006**:1
Davis, Paige 1969- **2004**:2
Davis, Patti 1952- **1995**:1
Davis, Raymond, Jr. 1914-2006
    Obituary **2007**:3
Davis, Sammy, Jr. 1925-1990
    Obituary **1990**:4
Davis, Terrell 1972- **1998**:2
Davis, Todd 1967- **2010**:1
Davis, Viola 1965- **2011**:4
Dawson, Rosario 1979- **2007**:2
Day, Dennis 1917-1988
    Obituary **1988**:4
Day, Pat 1953- **1995**:2
Dean, Howard 1948- **2005**:4
Dean, Laura 1945- **1989**:4
Dearden, John Cardinal 1907-1988
    Obituary **1988**:4
DeBakey, Michael 1908-2008
    Obituary **2009**:3
DeBartolo, Edward J., Jr. 1946- **1989**
    :3
DeCarava, Roy 1919- **1996**:3
De Cordova, Frederick 1910- **1985**:2
Dee, Sandra 1942-2005
    Obituary **2006**:2
Deen, Paula 1947- **2008**:3
Dees, Morris 1936- **1992**:1
DeGeneres, Ellen **1995**:3

de Kooning, Willem 1904-1997 **1994**
    :4
    Obituary **1997**:3
De La Hoya, Oscar 1973- **1998**:2
Delany, Dana 1956- **2008**:4
Delany, Sarah 1889-1999
    Obituary **1999**:3
de la Renta, Oscar 1932- **2005**:4
De Laurentiis, Giada 1970- **2011**:1
DeLay, Tom 1947- **2000**:1
Dell, Michael 1965- **1996**:2
DeLuca, Fred 1947- **2003**:3
DeLuise, Dom 1933-2009
    Obituary **2010**:2
De Matteo, Drea 1973- **2005**:2
DeMayo, Neda 1960(?)- **2006**:2
de Mille, Agnes 1905-1993
    Obituary **1994**:2
Deming, W. Edwards 1900-1993
    1992:2
    Obituary **1994**:2
Demme, Jonathan 1944- **1992**:4
Dempsey, Patrick 1966- **2006**:1
De Niro, Robert 1943- **1999**:1
Dennehy, Brian 1938- **2002**:1
Dennis, Sandy 1937-1992
    Obituary **1992**:4
Denver, Bob 1935-2005
    Obituary **2006**:4
Denver, John 1943-1997
    Obituary **1998**:1
De Palma, Brian 1940- **2007**:3
de Passe, Suzanne 1946(?)- **1990**:4
Depp, Johnny 1963(?)- **1991**:3
Dern, Laura 1967- **1992**:3
Dershowitz, Alan 1938(?)- **1992**:1
Deschanel, Zooey 1980- **2010**:4
Desormeaux, Kent 1970- **1990**:2
Destiny's Child **2001**:3
Deutch, John 1938- **1996**:4
Devine, John M. 1944- **2003**:2
DeVita, Vincent T., Jr. 1935- **1987**:3
De Vito, Danny 1944- **1987**:1
Diamond, I.A.L. 1920-1988
    Obituary **1988**:3
Diamond, Selma 1921(?)-1985
    Obituary **1985**:2
Diaz, Cameron 1972- **1999**:1
DiBello, Paul
    Brief entry **1986**:4
DiCaprio, Leonardo Wilhelm 1974-
    1997:2
Dickerson, Nancy H. 1927-1997 **1998**
    :2
Dickey, James 1923-1997 **1998**:2
Dickinson, Brian 1937- **1998**:2
Dickinson, Janice 1953- **2005**:2
Diddley, Bo 1928-2008
    Obituary **2009**:3
Diebenkorn, Richard 1922-1993
    Obituary **1993**:4
Diemer, Walter E. 1904(?)-1998 **1998**
    :2
Diesel, Vin 1967- **2004**:1
DiFranco, Ani 1970(?)- **1997**:1
Diller, Barry 1942- **1991**:1
Diller, Elizabeth and Ricardo
    Scofidio **2004**:3
Dillon, Matt 1964- **1992**:2
DiMaggio, Dom 1917-2009
    Obituary **2010**:2

2011 Nationality Index

DiMaggio, Joe 1914-1999
  Obituary **1999**:3
Di Meola, Al 1954- **1986**:4
Dimon, Jamie 1956- **2010**:3
Dinkins, David N. 1927- **1990**:2
Disney, Lillian 1899-1997
  Obituary **1998**:3
Disney, Roy E. 1930- **1986**:3
Dith Pran 1942-2008
  Obituary **2009**:2
Divine 1946-1988
  Obituary **1988**:3
Dixie Chicks **2001**:2
Doctorow, E. L. 1931- **2007**:1
Doherty, Shannen 1971(?)- **1994**:2
Dolan, Terry 1950-1986 **1985**:2
Dolan, Tom 1975- **2001**:2
Dolby, Ray Milton
  Brief entry **1986**:1
Dole, Bob 1923- **1994**:2
Dole, Elizabeth Hanford 1936- **1990**
  :1
Dolenz, Micky 1945- **1986**:4
Domar, Alice 1958- **2007**:1
Donahue, Tim 1950(?)- **2004**:3
Donahue, Troy 1936-2001
  Obituary **2002**:4
Donghia, Angelo R. 1935-1985
  Obituary **1985**:2
Donnellan, Nanci **1995**:2
Donovan, Landon 1982- **2011**:4
Donovan, Shaun 1966- **2010**:4
Dorati, Antal 1906-1988
  Obituary **1989**:2
Dorris, Michael 1945-1997
  Obituary **1997**:3
Dorsey, Thomas A. 1899-1993
  Obituary **1993**:3
Doubilet, Anne 1948- **2011**:1
Doubleday, Nelson, Jr. 1933- **1987**:1
Douglas, Buster 1960(?)- **1990**:4
Douglas, Marjory Stoneman
  1890-1998 **1993**:1
  Obituary **1998**:4
Douglas, Michael 1944- **1986**:2
Douglas, Mike 1925-2006
  Obituary **2007**:4
Dove, Rita 1952- **1994**:3
Dowd, Maureen Brigid 1952- **1997**:1
Downey, Bruce 1947- **2003**:1
Downey, Morton, Jr. 1932- **1988**:4
Downey, Robert, Jr. 1965- **2007**:1
Dr. Demento 1941- **1986**:1
Dr. Dre 1965(?)- **1994**:3
Dravecky, Dave 1956- **1992**:1
Drescher, Fran 1957(?)- **1995**:3
Drexler, Clyde 1962- **1992**:4
Drexler, Millard S. 1944- **1990**:3
Dreyfuss, Richard 1947- **1996**:3
Drysdale, Don 1936-1993
  Obituary **1994**:1
Duarte, Henry 1963(?)- **2003**:3
Dubrof, Jessica 1989-1996
  Obituary **1996**:4
Duchovny, David 1960- **1998**:3
Dudley, Jane 1912-2001
  Obituary **2002**:4
Duff, Hilary 1987- **2004**:4
Duffy, Karen 1962- **1998**:1
Dukakis, Michael 1933- **1988**:3
Dukakis, Olympia 1931- **1996**:4
Duke, David 1951(?)- **1990**:2

Duke, Doris 1912-1993
  Obituary **1994**:2
Duke, Red
  Brief entry **1987**:1
Dunagan, Deanna 1940- **2009**:2
Duncan, Arne 1964- **2011**:3
Duncan, Tim 1976- **2000**:1
Duncan, Todd 1903-1998
  Obituary **1998**:3
Dunham, Carroll 1949- **2003**:4
Dunham, Katherine 1909-2006
  Obituary **2007**:2
Dunlap, Albert J. **1997**:2
Dunn, Jancee 1966- **2010**:1
Dunne, Dominick 1925- **1997**:1
Dunst, Kirsten 1982- **2001**:4
Dunwoody, Ann 1953- **2009**:2
Dupri, Jermaine 1972- **1999**:1
Durocher, Leo 1905-1991
  Obituary **1992**:2
Durrell, Gerald 1925-1995
  Obituary **1995**:3
Duval, David 1971- **2000**:3
Duvall, Camille
  Brief entry **1988**:1
Duvall, Robert 1931- **1999**:3
Dworkin, Andrea 1946-2005
  Obituary **2006**:2
Dyer, Wayne 1940- **2010**:4
Dykstra, Lenny 1963- **1993**:4
Dylan, Bob 1941- **1998**:1
Earle, Steve 1955- **2011**:2
Earle, Sylvia 1935- **2001**:1
Earnhardt, Dale 1951-2001
  Obituary **2001**:4
Earnhardt, Dale, Jr. 1974- **2004**:4
Eastwood, Clint 1930- **1993**:3
Eaton, Robert J. 1940- **1994**:2
Eazy-E 1963(?)-1995
  Obituary **1995**:3
Eberhart, Richard 1904-2005
  Obituary **2006**:3
Ebersole, Christine 1953- **2007**:2
Ebert, Roger 1942- **1998**:3
Ebsen, Buddy 1908-2003
  Obituary **2004**:3
Eckert, Robert A. 1955(?)- **2002**:3
Eckhart, Aaron 1968- **2009**:2
Ecko, Marc 1972- **2006**:3
Eckstine, Billy 1914-1993
  Obituary **1993**:4
Edelman, Marian Wright 1939- **1990**
  :4
Ederle, Gertrude 1905-2003
  Obituary **2005**:1
Edmonds, Kenneth Babyface
  1958(?)- **1995**:3
Edwards, Bob 1947- **1993**:2
Edwards, Harry 1942- **1989**:4
Efron, Zac 1987- **2008**:2
Eggers, Dave 1970- **2001**:3
Ehrlichman, John 1925-1999
  Obituary **1999**:3
Eilberg, Amy
  Brief entry **1985**:3
Eisenman, Peter 1932- **1992**:4
Eisenstaedt, Alfred 1898-1995
  Obituary **1996**:1
Eisner, Michael 1942- **1989**:2
Eisner, Will 1917-2005
  Obituary **2006**:1
Elders, Joycelyn 1933- **1994**:1

Eldridge, Roy 1911-1989
  Obituary **1989**:3
Elfman, Jenna 1971- **1999**:4
Ellerbee, Linda 1944- **1993**:3
Elliott, Missy 1971- **2003**:4
Ellis, David 1971- **2009**:4
Ellis, Perry 1940-1986
  Obituary **1986**:3
Ellison, Larry 1944- **2004**:2
Ellison, Ralph 1914-1994
  Obituary **1994**:4
Ellroy, James 1948- **2003**:4
Ells, Steve 1965- **2010**:1
Elway, John 1960- **1990**:3
Emanuel, Rahm 1959- **2011**:2
Eminem 1974- **2001**:2
Engelbreit, Mary 1952(?)- **1994**:3
Engibous, Thomas J. 1953- **2003**:3
Engler, John 1948- **1996**:3
Engles, Gregg L. 1957- **2007**:3
Englund, Richard 1932(?)-1991
  Obituary **1991**:3
Engstrom, Elmer W. 1901-1984
  Obituary **1985**:2
Engvall, Bill 1957- **2010**:1
Ensler, Eve 1954(?)- **2002**:4
Ephron, Henry 1912-1992
  Obituary **1993**:2
Ephron, Nora 1941- **1992**:3
Epps, Omar 1973- **2000**:4
Epstein, Jason 1928- **1991**:1
Epstein, Theo 1973- **2003**:4
Erdrich, Louise 1954- **2005**:3
Ertegun, Ahmet 1923- **1986**:3
Ervin, Sam 1896-1985
  Obituary **1985**:2
Esiason, Boomer 1961- **1991**:1
Estefan, Gloria **1991**:4
Estes, Pete 1916-1988
  Obituary **1988**:3
Estevez, Emilio 1962- **1985**:4
Estrich, Susan 1953- **1989**:1
Etheridge, Melissa 1961(?)- **1995**:4
Evanovich, Janet 1943- **2005**:2
Evans, Dale 1912-2001
  Obituary **2001**:3
Evans, Janet 1971- **1989**:1
Evans, Joni 1942- **1991**:4
Evans, Nancy 1950- **2000**:4
Evans, Robert 1930- **2004**:1
Eve 1978- **2004**:3
Evers-Williams, Myrlie 1933- **1995**:4
Ewing, Patrick 1962- **1985**:3
Eyler, John. H., Jr. 1948(?)- **2001**:3
Factor, Max 1904-1996
  Obituary **1996**:4
Fagan, Garth 1940- **2000**:1
Fairbanks, Douglas, Jr. 1909-2000
  Obituary **2000**:4
Fairstein, Linda 1948(?)- **1991**:1
Falco, Edie 1963- **2010**:2
Falconer, Ian 1960(?)- **2003**:1
Falkenberg, Nanette 1951- **1985**:2
Fallon, Jimmy 1974- **2003**:1
Faludi, Susan 1959- **1992**:4
Falwell, Jerry 1933-2007
  Obituary **2008**:3
Fanning, Dakota 1994- **2005**:2
Fanning, Shawn 1980- **2001**:1
Faris, Anna 1976- **2010**:3
Farley, Chris 1964-1997 **1998**:2
Farmer, James 1920-1999

Obituary **2000**:1
Farmer, Philip José 1918-2009
   Obituary **2010**:2
Farrakhan, Louis 1933- **1990**:4
Farrell, Perry 1960- **1992**:2
Farrell, Suzanne 1945- **1996**:3
Farrow, Mia 1945- **1998**:3
Fassa, Lynda 1963(?)- **2008**:4
Fast, Howard 1914-2003
   Obituary **2004**:2
Faubus, Orval 1910-1994
   Obituary **1995**:2
Fauci, Anthony S. 1940- **2004**:1
Faulkner, Shannon 1975- **1994**:4
Faust, Drew Gilpin 1947- **2008**:1
Favre, Brett Lorenzo 1969- **1997**:2
Favreau, Jon 1966- **2002**:3
Fawcett, Farrah 1947- **1998**:4
Fehr, Donald 1948- **1987**:2
Feinstein, Dianne 1933- **1993**:3
Feld, Eliot 1942- **1996**:1
Feld, Kenneth 1948- **1988**:2
Feldman, Sandra 1939- **1987**:3
Feldshuh, Tovah 1952- **2005**:3
Fell, Norman 1924-1998
   Obituary **1999**:2
Felt, W. Mark 1913-2008
   Obituary **2010**:1
Fender, Leo 1909-1991
   Obituary **1992**:1
Fenley, Molissa 1954- **1988**:3
Fenwick, Millicent H.
   Obituary **1993**:2
Fernandez, Joseph 1935- **1991**:3
Ferraro, Geraldine 1935- **1998**:3
Ferrell, Trevor
   Brief entry **1985**:2
Ferrell, Will 1968- **2004**:4
Ferrera, America 1984- **2006**:2
Fertel, Ruth 1927- **2000**:2
Fetchit, Stepin 1892(?)-1985
   Obituary **1986**:1
Fey, Tina 1970- **2005**:3
Fidrych, Mark 1954-2009
   Obituary **2010**:2
Fieger, Geoffrey 1950- **2001**:3
Field, Patricia 1942(?)- **2002**:2
Field, Sally 1946- **1995**:3
Fielder, Cecil 1963- **1993**:2
Fields, Debbi 1956- **1987**:3
Fields, Evelyn J. 1949- **2001**:3
Fieri, Guy 1968- **2010**:3
Fierstein, Harvey 1954- **2004**:2
Filo, David and Jerry Yang **1998**:3
Finley, Karen 1956- **1992**:4
Finnamore, Suzanne 1959- **2009**:1
Fiorina, Carleton S. 1954- **2000**:1
Fireman, Paul
   Brief entry **1987**:2
Firestone, Roy 1953- **1988**:2
Fischer, Bobby 1943-2008
   Obituary **2009**:1
Fish, Hamilton 1888-1991
   Obituary **1991**:3
Fishburne, Laurence 1961(?)- **1995**:3
Fisher, Carrie 1956- **1991**:1
Fisher, Mary 1948- **1994**:3
Fisher, Mel 1922(?)- **1985**:4
Fitzgerald, A. Ernest 1926- **1986**:2
Fitzgerald, Ella 1917-1996
   Obituary **1996**:4
Fitzgerald, Patrick 1960- **2006**:4

Flanders, Ed 1934-1995
   Obituary **1995**:3
Flatley, Michael 1958- **1997**:3
Flavor Flav 1959- **2007**:3
Flay, Bobby 1964- **2009**:2
Fleck, Bela 1958- **2011**:3
Fleischer, Ari 1960- **2003**:1
Fleiss, Mike 1964- **2003**:4
Fleming, Art 1925(?)-1995
   Obituary **1995**:4
Fleming, Claudia 1959- **2004**:1
Fleming, Renee **2001**:4
Flockhart, Calista 1964- **1998**:4
Flood, Curt 1938-1997
   Obituary **1997**:2
Florence, Tyler 1971- **2011**:4
Florio, James J. 1937- **1991**:2
Flutie, Doug 1962- **1999**:2
Flynn, Ray 1939- **1989**:1
Flynt, Larry 1942- **1997**:3
Foer, Jonathan 1977- **2011**:2
Fogelberg, Dan 1951-2007
   Obituary **2009**:1
Foley, Thomas S. 1929- **1990**:1
Folkman, Judah 1933- **1999**:1
Fomon, Robert M. 1925- **1985**:3
Fonda, Bridget 1964- **1995**:1
Foo Fighters **2006**:2
Foote, Horton 1916-2009
   Obituary **2010**:2
Foote, Shelby 1916- **1991**:2
Forbes, Malcolm S. 1919-1990
   Obituary **1990**:3
Forbes, Steve 1947- **1996**:2
Ford, Faith 1964- **2005**:3
Ford, Gerald R. 1913-2007
   Obituary **2008**:2
Ford, Glenn 1916-2006
   Obituary **2007**:4
Ford, Harrison 1942- **1990**:2
Ford, Henry II 1917-1987
   Obituary **1988**:1
Ford, Tennessee Ernie 1919-1991
   Obituary **1992**:2
Ford, Tom 1962- **1999**:3
Ford, William Clay, Jr. 1957- **1999**:1
Foreman, Dave 1947(?)- **1990**:3
Foreman, George 1949- **2004**:2
Forsythe, William 1949- **1993**:2
Foss, Joe 1915- **1990**:3
Fosse, Bob 1927-1987
   Obituary **1988**:1
Fossett, Steve 1944- **2007**:2
Fossey, Dian 1932-1985
   Obituary **1986**:1
Foster, David 1950(?)- **1988**:2
Foster, Jodie 1962- **1989**:2
Foster, Phil 1914-1985
   Obituary **1985**:3
Foster, Sutton 1975- **2003**:2
Foster, Tabatha 1985-1988
   Obituary **1988**:3
Foster, Vincent 1945(?)-1993
   Obituary **1994**:1
Fox, Matthew 1940- **1992**:2
Fox, Matthew 1966- **2006**:1
Fox, Vivica 1964- **1999**:1
Foxworthy, Jeff 1958- **1996**:1
Foxx, Jamie 1967- **2001**:1
Foxx, Redd 1922-1991
   Obituary **1992**:2
France, Johnny

Brief entry **1987**:1
Francis, Philip L. 1946- **2007**:4
Franciscus, James 1934-1991
   Obituary **1992**:1
Frank, Barney 1940- **1989**:2
Frank, Robert 1924- **1995**:2
Franken, Al 1952(?)- **1996**:3
Frankenheimer, John 1930-2002
   Obituary **2003**:4
Frankenthaler, Helen 1928- **1990**:1
Frankfort, Lew 1946- **2008**:2
Franklin, Aretha 1942- **1998**:3
Franklin, Kirk 1970- **2010**:2
Franklin, Melvin 1942-1995
   Obituary **1995**:3
Franks, Tommy 1945- **2004**:1
Franz, Dennis 1944- **1995**:2
Franzen, Jonathan 1959- **2002**:3
Fraser, Brendan 1967- **2000**:1
Fraser, Claire M. 1955- **2005**:2
Frazier, Charles 1950- **2003**:2
Freeh, Louis J. 1950- **1994**:2
Freeman, Cliff 1941- **1996**:1
Freeman, Jr., Castle 1944- **2010**:2
Freeman, Morgan 1937- **1990**:4
Freiberg, Steven 1957- **2011**:4
Freleng, Friz 1906(?)-1995
   Obituary **1995**:4
French, Marilyn 1929-2009
   Obituary **2010**:2
French, Tana 1973- **2009**:3
Freston, Kathy 1965- **2009**:3
Friedan, Betty 1921- **1994**:2
Friedman, Milton 1912-2006
   Obituary **2008**:1
Friedman, Rose 1910-2009
   Obituary **2010**:4
Friend, Patricia A. 1946- **2003**:3
Frist, Bill 1952- **2003**:4
Fudge, Ann 1951- **2000**:3
Fulbright, J. William 1905-1995
   Obituary **1995**:3
Fulghum, Robert 1937- **1996**:1
Fuller, Millard 1935-2009
   Obituary **2010**:1
Funt, Allen 1914-1999
   Obituary **2000**:1
Furchgott, Robert 1916-2009
   Obituary **2010**:3
Furman, Rosemary
   Brief entry **1986**:4
Furyk, Jim 1970- **2004**:2
Futrell, Mary Hatwood 1940- **1986**:1
Futter, Ellen V. 1949- **1995**:1
Gabor, Eva 1921(?)-1995
   Obituary **1996**:1
Gacy, John Wayne 1942-1994
   Obituary **1994**:4
Gaines, William M. 1922-1992
   Obituary **1993**:1
Gale, Robert Peter 1945- **1986**:4
Gallagher, Peter 1955- **2004**:3
Gallo, Robert 1937- **1991**:1
Galvin, John R. 1929- **1990**:1
Galvin, Martin
   Brief entry **1985**:3
Gandolfini, James 1961- **2001**:3
Gandy, Kim 1954(?)- **2002**:2
Ganzi, Victor 1947- **2003**:3
Garbo, Greta 1905-1990
   Obituary **1990**:3

Garcia, Andy 1956- **1999**:3
Garcia, Cristina 1958- **1997**:4
Garcia, Jerry 1942-1995 **1988**:3
  Obituary **1996**:1
Garcia, Joe
  Brief entry **1986**:4
Garcia, Juliet 1949- **2011**:1
Gardner, Ava Lavinia 1922-1990
  Obituary **1990**:2
Gardner, David and Tom **2001**:4
Gardner, Randy 1957- **1997**:2
Garner, Jennifer 1972- **2003**:1
Garnett, Kevin 1976- **2000**:3
Garofalo, Janeane 1964- **1996**:4
Garr, Teri 1949- **1988**:4
Garrison, Jim 1922-1992
  Obituary **1993**:2
Garson, Greer 1903-1996
  Obituary **1996**:4
Garzarelli, Elaine M. 1951- **1992**:3
Gates, Bill 1955- **1987**:4
Gates, Melinda 1964- **2010**:4
Gates, Robert M. 1943- **1992**:2
Gathers, Hank 1967(?)-1990
  Obituary **1990**:3
Gault, Willie 1960- **1991**:2
Gayle, Helene 1955- **2008**:2
Gebbie, Kristine 1944(?)- **1994**:2
Gee, E. 1944- **2011**:3
Geffen, David 1943- **1985**:3
Gehry, Frank O. 1929- **1987**:1
Geisel, Theodor 1904-1991
  Obituary **1992**:2
Geithner, Timothy F. 1961- **2009**:4
Gelbart, Larry 1928-2009
  Obituary **2011**:1
Gellar, Sarah Michelle 1977- **1999**:3
Geller, Margaret Joan 1947- **1998**:2
Gentine, Lou 1947- **2008**:2
George, Elizabeth 1949- **2003**:3
Gephardt, Richard 1941- **1987**:3
Gerba, Charles 1945- **1999**:4
Gerberding, Julie 1955- **2004**:1
Gere, Richard 1949- **1994**:3
Gergen, David 1942- **1994**:1
Gerrity, Sean 1958- **2011**:3
Gerstner, Lou 1942- **1993**:4
Gertz, Alison 1966(?)-1992
  Obituary **1993**:2
Gerulaitis, Vitas 1954-1994
  Obituary **1995**:1
Getty, Estelle 1923-2008
  Obituary **2009**:3
Getz, Stan 1927-1991
  Obituary **1991**:4
Gevinson, Tavi 1996- **2011**:1
Giamatti, A. Bartlett 1938-1989 **1988**:4
  Obituary **1990**:1
Giamatti, Paul 1967- **2009**:4
Giannulli, Mossimo 1963- **2002**:3
Gibson, Althea 1927-2003
  Obituary **2004**:4
Gibson, Kirk 1957- **1985**:2
Gibson, William Ford, III 1948- **1997**:2
Gifford, Kathie Lee 1953- **1992**:2
Gilbert, Elizabeth 1969- **2011**:1
Gilbert, Walter 1932- **1988**:3
Gilford, Jack 1907-1990
  Obituary **1990**:4
Gill, Vince 1957- **1995**:2

Gillespie, Dizzy 1917-1993
  Obituary **1993**:2
Gillespie, Marcia 1944- **1999**:4
Gillett, George 1938- **1988**:1
Gilruth, Robert 1913-2000
  Obituary **2001**:1
Gingrich, Newt 1943- **1991**:1
Ginsberg, Allen 1926-1997
  Obituary **1997**:3
Ginsberg, Ian 1962(?)- **2006**:4
Ginsburg, Ruth Bader 1933- **1993**:4
Gioia, Dana 1950- **2008**:4
Gish, Lillian 1893-1993
  Obituary **1993**:4
Giuliani, Rudolph 1944- **1994**:2
Gladwell, Malcolm 1963- **2010**:3
Glaser, Elizabeth 1947-1994
  Obituary **1995**:2
Glass, David 1935- **1996**:1
Glass, Ira 1959- **2008**:2
Glass, Philip 1937- **1991**:4
Glasser, Ira 1938- **1989**:1
Glaus, Troy 1976- **2003**:3
Glazman, Lev and Alina Roytberg **2007**:4
Gleason, Jackie 1916-1987
  Obituary **1987**:4
Glenn, John 1921- **1998**:3
Gless, Sharon 1944- **1989**:3
Glover, Danny 1947- **1998**:4
Glover, Savion 1973- **1997**:1
Gobel, George 1920(?)-1991
  Obituary **1991**:4
Gober, Robert 1954- **1996**:3
Goetz, Bernhard Hugo 1947(?)- **1985**:3
Goizueta, Roberto 1931-1997 **1996**:1
  Obituary **1998**:1
Gold, Thomas 1920-2004
  Obituary **2005**:3
Goldberg, Gary David 1944- **1989**:4
Goldberg, Leonard 1934- **1988**:4
Goldberg, Whoopi 1955- **1993**:3
Goldblum, Jeff 1952- **1988**:1
Golden, Thelma 1965- **2003**:3
Goldhaber, Fred
  Brief entry **1986**:3
Goldman, Duff 1974- **2010**:1
Goldman, William 1931- **2001**:1
Goldman-Rakic, Patricia 1937- **2002**:4
Goldwater, Barry 1909-1998
  Obituary **1998**:4
Gomez, Lefty 1909-1989
  Obituary **1989**:3
Gomez, Selena 1992- **2011**:1
Gooden, Dwight 1964- **1985**:2
Gooding, Cuba, Jr. 1968- **1997**:3
Goodman, Benny 1909-1986
  Obituary **1986**:3
Goodman, Drew and Myra **2007**:4
Goodman, John 1952- **1990**:3
Goody, Joan 1935- **1990**:2
Goody, Sam 1904-1991
  Obituary **1992**:1
Gorder, Genevieve 1974- **2005**:4
Gordon, Dexter 1923-1990 **1987**:1
Gordon, Gale 1906-1995
  Obituary **1996**:1
Gordon, James 1941- **2009**:4
Gordon, Jeff 1971- **1996**:1
Gordon, Michael 1951(?)- **2005**:1

Gore, Albert, Jr. 1948(?)- **1993**:2
Gore, Albert, Sr. 1907-1998
  Obituary **1999**:2
Gore, Tipper 1948- **1985**:4
Goren, Charles H. 1901-1991
  Obituary **1991**:4
Gorman, Leon
  Brief entry **1987**:1
Gossett, Louis, Jr. 1936- **1989**:3
Gottlieb, William 1917-2006
  Obituary **2007**:2
Gottschalk, Alfred 1930-2009
  Obituary **2011**:1
Gould, Chester 1900-1985
  Obituary **1985**:2
Gould, Gordon 1920- **1987**:1
Gould, Stephen Jay 1941-2002
  Obituary **2003**:3
Goulet, Robert 1933-2007
  Obituary **2008**:4
Grace, J. Peter 1913- **1990**:2
Grace, Topher 1978- **2005**:4
Graden, Brian 1963- **2004**:2
Grafton, Sue 1940- **2000**:2
Graham, Bill 1931-1991 **1986**:4
  Obituary **1992**:2
Graham, Billy 1918- **1992**:1
Graham, Donald 1945- **1985**:4
Graham, Heather 1970- **2000**:1
Graham, Katharine Meyer 1917- **1997**:3
  Obituary **2002**:3
Graham, Lauren 1967- **2003**:4
Graham, Martha 1894-1991
  Obituary **1991**:4
Gramm, Phil 1942- **1995**:2
Grammer, Kelsey 1955(?)- **1995**:1
Granato, Cammi 1971- **1999**:3
Grandin, Temple 1947- **2006**:1
Grange, Red 1903-1991
  Obituary **1991**:3
Grant, Amy 1961(?)- **1985**:4
Grant, Cary 1904-1986
  Obituary **1987**:1
Grant, Charity
  Brief entry **1985**:2
Grant, Rodney A. **1992**:1
Graves, Michael 1934- **2000**:1
Graves, Nancy 1940- **1989**:3
Graves, Ron 1967- **2009**:3
Gray, Hanna 1930- **1992**:4
Gray, John 1952(?)- **1995**:3
Gray, Macy 1970(?)- **2002**:1
Gray, Spalding 1941-2004
  Obituary **2005**:2
Grazer, Brian 1951- **2006**:4
Graziano, Rocky 1922-1990
  Obituary **1990**:4
Green, Richard R. 1936- **1988**:3
Green, Seth 1974- **2010**:1
Greenberg, Hank 1911-1986
  Obituary **1986**:4
Greenberg, Robert 1940(?)- **2003**:2
Green Day **1995**:4
Greene, Brian 1963- **2003**:4
Greenspan, Alan 1926- **1992**:2
Greenwald, Julie 1970- **2008**:1
Gregoire, Chris 1947- **2010**:2
Gregorian, Vartan 1934- **1990**:3
Gregory, Cynthia 1946- **1990**:2
Gregory, David 1970- **2010**:2
Gregory, Dick 1932- **1990**:3

Gregory, Rogan 1972- **2008**:2
Grier, Pam 1949- **1998**:3
Griffey, Ken Jr. 1969- **1994**:1
Griffin, Kathy 1961- **2010**:4
Griffin, Merv 1925-2008
  Obituary **2008**:4
Griffin, Toni 1964- **2011**:3
Griffith, Melanie 1957- **1989**:2
Griffiths, Martha 1912-2003
  Obituary **2004**:2
Grisham, John 1955- **1994**:4
Groban, Josh 1981- **2009**:1
Grodin, Charles 1935- **1997**:3
Groening, Matt 1955(?)- **1990**:4
Gross, Terry 1951- **1998**:3
Grove, Andrew S. 1936- **1995**:3
Groves, Robert 1949- **2011**:3
Grucci, Felix 1905- **1987**:1
Gruden, Jon 1963- **2003**:4
Grusin, Dave
  Brief entry **1987**:2
Guccione, Bob 1930- **1986**:1
Guccione, Bob, Jr. 1956- **1991**:4
Guest, Christopher 1948- **2004**:2
Guggenheim, Charles 1924-2002
  Obituary **2003**:4
Gumbel, Bryant 1948- **1990**:2
Gumbel, Greg 1946- **1996**:4
Gund, Agnes 1938- **1993**:2
Gunn, Hartford N., Jr. 1926-1986
  Obituary **1986**:2
Gupta, Sanjay 1969- **2009**:4
Gutmann, Amy 1949- **2008**:4
Guyer, David
  Brief entry **1988**:1
Gwynn, Tony 1960- **1995**:1
Gyllenhaal, Jake 1980- **2005**:3
Gyllenhaal, Maggie 1977- **2009**:2
Haas, Robert D. 1942- **1986**:4
Hackett, Buddy 1924-2003
  Obituary **2004**:3
Hackman, Gene 1931- **1989**:3
Hackney, Sheldon 1933- **1995**:1
Hagelstein, Peter
  Brief entry **1986**:3
Hagen, Uta 1919-2004
  Obituary **2005**:2
Hagler, Marvelous Marvin 1954-
  1985:2
Hahn, Jessica 1960- **1989**:4
Hair, Jay D. 1945- **1994**:3
Ha Jin 1956- **2000**:3
Hakuta, Ken
  Brief entry **1986**:1
Halberstam, David 1934-2007
  Obituary **2008**:3
Haldeman, H. R. 1926-1993
  Obituary **1994**:2
Hale, Alan 1957- **1997**:3
Hale, Clara 1905-1992
  Obituary **1993**:3
Hale, Victoria 1961(?)- **2008**:4
Haley, Alex 1924-1992
  Obituary **1992**:3
Hall, Anthony Michael 1968- **1986**:3
Hall, Arsenio 1955- **1990**:2
Hall, Gus 1910-2000
  Obituary **2001**:2
Hall, Michael 1971- **2011**:1
Halston 1932-1990
  Obituary **1990**:3
Hamels, Cole 1983- **2009**:4

Hamilton, Laurell K. 1963- **2008**:2
Hamilton, Margaret 1902-1985
  Obituary **1985**:3
Hamilton, Scott 1958- **1998**:2
Hamm, Jon 1971- **2009**:2
Hamm, Mia 1972- **2000**:1
Hamm, Paul 1982- **2005**:1
Hammer, Armand 1898-1990
  Obituary **1991**:3
Hammer, Bonnie 1950- **2011**:4
Hammer, Jan 1948- **1987**:3
Hammer, M. C. **1991**:2
Hammond, E. Cuyler 1912-1986
  Obituary **1987**:1
Hammond, John 1910-1987
  Obituary **1988**:2
Hampton, Lionel 1908-2002
  Obituary **2003**:4
Han, Jeff 1975- **2011**:2
Hanauer, Chip 1954- **1986**:2
Hancock, Herbie 1940- **1985**:1
Hand, Elizabeth 1957- **2007**:2
Handler, Chelsea 1975- **2009**:3
Handler, Daniel 1970- **2003**:3
Handler, Ruth 1916-2002
  Obituary **2003**:3
Hanks, Tom 1956- **1989**:2
Hanna, William 1910-2001
  Obituary **2002**:1
Hannah, Daryl 1961- **1987**:4
Hannigan, Alyson 1974- **2007**:3
Harbert, Ted 1955- **2007**:2
Hardaway, Anfernee 1971- **1996**:2
Harden, Marcia Gay 1959- **2002**:4
Hargitay, Mariska 1964- **2006**:2
Haring, Keith 1958-1990
  Obituary **1990**:3
Harker, Patrick T. 1958- **2001**:2
Harkes, John 1967- **1996**:4
Harmon, Mark 1951- **1987**:1
Harmon, Tom 1919-1990
  Obituary **1990**:3
Harrelson, Woody 1961- **2011**:1
Harriman, Pamela 1920- **1994**:4
Harriman, W. Averell 1891-1986
  Obituary **1986**:4
Harris, Barbara **1996**:3
Harris, Barbara 1930- **1989**:3
Harris, E. Lynn 1955- **2004**:2
Harris, Ed 1950- **2002**:2
Harris, Emmylou 1947- **1991**:3
Harris, Katherine 1957- **2001**:3
Harris, Patricia Roberts 1924-1985
  Obituary **1985**:2
Harris, Thomas 1940(?)- **2001**:1
Harry, Deborah 1945- **1990**:1
Hart, Carey 1975- **2006**:4
Hart, Johnny 1931-2007
  Obituary **2008**:2
Hart, Kitty Carlisle 1910-2007
  Obituary **2008**:2
Hart, Mary
  Brief entry **1988**:1
Hart, Melissa Joan 1976- **2002**:1
Hart, Mickey 1944(?)- **1991**:2
Hartman, Phil 1948-1998 **1996**:2
  Obituary **1998**:4
Harvard, Beverly 1950- **1995**:2
Harvey, Paul 1918- **1995**:3
Harvey, Steve 1956- **2010**:1
Harwell, Ernie 1918- **1997**:3
Haseltine, William A. 1944- **1999**:2

Hassenfeld, Stephen 1942- **1987**:4
Hastert, Dennis 1942- **1999**:3
Hastings, Reed 1961(?)- **2006**:2
Hatch, Orin G. 1934- **2000**:2
Hatch, Richard 1961- **2001**:1
Hatcher, Teri 1964- **2005**:4
Hatem, George 1910(?)-1988
  Obituary **1989**:1
Hathaway, Anne 1982- **2007**:2
Hautzig, Esther 1930-2009
  Obituary **2011**:3
Hawk, Tony 1968- **2001**:4
Hawke, Ethan 1971(?)- **1995**:4
Hawkins, Jeff and Donna Dubinsky
  2000:2
Hawkins, Paula 1927-2009
  Obituary **2011**:4
Hawkins, Screamin' Jay 1929-1999
  Obituary **2000**:3
Hawn, Goldie Jeanne 1945- **1997**:2
Hayes, Helen 1900-1993
  Obituary **1993**:4
Hayes, Isaac 1942- **1998**:4
Hayes, Robert M. 1952- **1986**:3
Hayes, Woody 1913-1987
  Obituary **1987**:2
Haysbert, Dennis 1954- **2007**:1
Hayse, Bruce 1949(?)- **2004**:3
Hayworth, Rita 1918-1987
  Obituary **1987**:3
Headroom, Max 1985- **1986**:4
Healey, Jack 1938(?)- **1990**:1
Healy, Bernadine 1944- **1993**:1
Healy, Timothy S. 1923- **1990**:2
Heard, J.C. 1917-1988
  Obituary **1989**:1
Hearst, Randolph A. 1915-2000
  Obituary **2001**:3
Heat-Moon, William Least 1939-
  2000:2
Heaton, Patricia 1958- **2010**:4
Heche, Anne 1969- **1999**:1
Heckerling, Amy 1954- **1987**:2
Heckert, Richard E.
  Brief entry **1987**:3
Hefner, Christie 1952- **1985**:1
Heid, Bill
  Brief entry **1987**:2
Heifetz, Jascha 1901-1987
  Obituary **1988**:2
Heigl, Katharine 1978- **2008**:3
Heinricher, Jackie 1961- **2010**:1
Heinz, H.J. 1908-1987
  Obituary **1987**:2
Heinz, John 1938-1991
  Obituary **1991**:4
Held, Abbe 1966- **2011**:1
Held, Al 1928-2005
  Obituary **2006**:4
Helgenberger, Marg 1958- **2002**:2
Heller, Joseph 1923-1999
  Obituary **2000**:2
Heller, Walter 1915-1987
  Obituary **1987**:4
Helms, Bobby 1936-1997
  Obituary **1997**:4
Helms, Jesse 1921- **1998**:1
Helmsley, Leona 1920- **1988**:1
Heloise 1951- **2001**:4
Helton, Todd 1973- **2001**:1
Hemingway, Margaux 1955-1996
  Obituary **1997**:1

Henderson, Rickey 1958- **2002**:3
Hennessy, John L. 1952- **2002**:2
Henning, Doug 1947-1999
  Obituary **2000**:3
Henrich, Tommy 1913-2009
  Obituary **2011**:4
Henry, Carl F.H. 1913-2003
  Obituary **2005**:1
Hensel Twins **1996**:4
Henson, Brian 1964(?)- **1992**:1
Henson, Jim 1936-1990 **1989**:1
  Obituary **1990**:4
Hepburn, Katharine 1909- **1991**:2
Herbert, Don 1917-2007
  Obituary **2008**:3
Hernandez, Lazaro and Jack
  McCollough **2008**:4
Hernandez, Willie 1954- **1985**:1
Hero, Peter 1942- **2001**:2
Hershberger, Sally 1961(?)- **2006**:4
Hershey, Barbara 1948- **1989**:1
Hershiser, Orel 1958- **1989**:2
Herz, Rachel 1963- **2008**:1
Herzog, Doug 1960(?)- **2002**:4
Hesse, Dan 1954- **2011**:4
Heston, Charlton 1924- **1999**:4
Hewitt, Jennifer Love 1979- **1999**:2
Hewlett, William 1913-2001
  Obituary **2001**:4
Heyer, Steven J. 1952- **2007**:1
Hiaasen, Carl 1953- **2007**:2
Highsmith, Patricia 1921-1995
  Obituary **1995**:3
Hilbert, Stephen C. 1946- **1997**:4
Hilfiger, Tommy 1952- **1993**:3
Hill, Andrew 1931-2007
  Obituary **2008**:3
Hill, Anita 1956- **1994**:1
Hill, Faith 1967- **2000**:1
Hill, George Roy 1921-2002
  Obituary **2004**:1
Hill, Grant 1972- **1995**:3
Hill, J. Edward 1938- **2006**:2
Hill, Lauryn 1975- **1999**:3
Hill, Lynn 1961(?)- **1991**:2
Hillegass, Clifton Keith 1918- **1989**:4
Hills, Carla 1934- **1990**:3
Hills, L. Rust 1924-2008
  Obituary **2009**:4
Hilton, Perez 1978- **2010**:3
Hines, Gregory 1946- **1992**:4
Hinton, Milt 1910-2000
  Obituary **2001**:3
Hirschhorn, Joel
  Brief entry **1986**:1
Hirshberg, Gary 1954(?)- **2007**:2
Hirt, Al 1922-1999
  Obituary **1999**:4
Hiss, Alger 1904-1996
  Obituary **1997**:2
Ho, Don 1930-2007
  Obituary **2008**:2
Hoagland, Mahlon 1921-2009
  Obituary **2011**:2
Hockfield, Susan 1951- **2009**:2
Hodges, Carl 1937- **2008**:1
Hoff, Syd 1912-2004
  Obituary **2005**:3
Hoffa, Jim, Jr. 1941- **1999**:2
Hoffman, Abbie 1936-1989
  Obituary **1989**:3
Hoffman, Dustin 1937- **2005**:4

Hoffman, Philip Seymour 1967-
  2006:3
Hoffs, Susanna 1962(?)- **1988**:2
Hogan, Ben 1912-1997
  Obituary **1997**:4
Hogan, Hulk 1953- **1987**:3
Holbrooke, Richard 1941(?)- **1996**:2
Holcomb, Steven 1980- **2011**:2
Holden, Betsy 1955- **2003**:2
Holder, Jr., Eric H. 1951- **2009**:4
Holl, Steven 1947- **2003**:1
Hollander, Joel 1956(?)- **2006**:4
Holliday, Chad 1948- **2006**:4
Holmes, John C. 1945-1988
  Obituary **1988**:3
Holtz, Lou 1937- **1986**:4
Holyfield, Evander 1962- **1991**:3
Hooker, John Lee 1917- **1998**:1
  Obituary **2002**:3
hooks, bell 1952- **2000**:2
Hootie and the Blowfish **1995**:4
Hope, Bob 1903-2003
  Obituary **2004**:4
Horne, Lena 1917- **1998**:4
Horner, Jack 1946- **1985**:2
Hornsby, Bruce 1954(?)- **1989**:3
Horovitz, Adam 1968(?)- **1988**:3
Horowitz, Paul 1942- **1988**:2
Horowitz, Vladimir 1903-1989
  Obituary **1990**:1
Horrigan, Edward, Jr. 1929- **1989**:1
Horvath, David and Sun-Min Kim
  2008:4
Horwich, Frances 1908-2001
  Obituary **2002**:3
Hosseini, Khaled 1965- **2008**:3
Houseman, John 1902-1988
  Obituary **1989**:1
Housenbold, Jeffrey 1969- **2009**:2
Houston, Cissy 1933- **1999**:3
Houston, Whitney 1963- **1986**:3
Hoving, Thomas 1931-2009
  Obituary **2011**:4
Howard, Desmond Kevin 1970-
  1997:2
Howard, Dwight 1985- **2010**:1
Howard, Ken 1944- **2010**:4
Howard, Michelle 1960- **2010**:2
Howard, Ron **1997**:2
Howser, Dick 1936-1987
  Obituary **1987**:4
Hubbard, Freddie 1938- **1988**:4
Hudson, Dawn 1957- **2008**:1
Hudson, Jennifer 1981- **2008**:1
Hudson, Kate 1979- **2001**:2
Hudson, Rock 1925-1985
  Obituary **1985**:4
Huerta, Dolores 1930- **1998**:1
Huffman, Felicity 1962- **2006**:2
Hughes, Cathy 1947- **1999**:1
Hughes, John 1950-2009
  Obituary **2010**:4
Hughes, Karen 1957- **2001**:2
Hughes, Mark 1956- **1985**:3
Hughes, Sarah 1985- **2002**:4
Hughley, D.L. 1964- **2001**:1
Huizenga, Wayne 1938(?)- **1992**:1
Hull, Jane Dee 1935- **1999**:2
Hullinger, Charlotte
  Brief entry **1985**:1
Hundt, Reed Eric 1948- **1997**:2
Hunt, Helen 1963- **1994**:4

Hunter, Catfish 1946-1999
  Obituary **2000**:1
Hunter, Evan 1926-2005
  Obituary **2006**:4
Hunter, Holly 1958- **1989**:4
Hunter, Howard 1907- **1994**:4
Hunter, Madeline 1916(?)- **1991**:2
Hurd, Mark 1957- **2010**:4
Hurt, William 1950- **1986**:1
Huston, Anjelica 1952(?)- **1989**:3
Huston, John 1906-1987
  Obituary **1988**:1
Hutchins, Carleen 1911-2009
  Obituary **2010**:4
Hutton, Timothy 1960- **1986**:3
Hwang, David Henry 1957- **1999**:1
Hyatt, Joel 1950- **1985**:3
Hybels, Bill 1951- **2011**:1
Hyde, Henry 1924- **1999**:1
Hynde, Chrissie 1951- **1991**:1
Iacocca, Lee 1924- **1993**:1
Ice Cube 1969- **1999**:2
Ice-T **1992**:3
Ifill, Gwen 1955- **2002**:4
Iger, Bob 1951- **2006**:1
Iglesias, Enrique 1975- **2000**:1
Ilitch, Mike 1929- **1993**:4
Immelt, Jeffrey R. 1956- **2001**:2
Imus, Don 1940- **1997**:1
Inatome, Rick 1953- **1985**:4
Indigo Girls **1994**:4
Ingersoll, Ralph II 1946- **1988**:2
Inkster, Juli 1960- **2000**:2
Inman, Bobby Ray 1931- **1985**:1
Interior, Lux 1946-2009
  Obituary **2010**:1
Iovine, Jimmy 1953- **2006**:3
Ireland, Patricia 1946(?)- **1992**:2
Irvin, Michael 1966- **1996**:3
Irving, John 1942- **2006**:2
Irwin, Bill **1988**:3
Irwin, Hale 1945- **2005**:2
Irwin, James 1930-1991
  Obituary **1992**:1
Isaacson, Portia
  Brief entry **1986**:1
Isaacson, Walter 1952- **2003**:2
Ito, Lance 1950(?)- **1995**:3
Iverson, Allen 1975- **2001**:4
Ives, Burl 1909-1995
  Obituary **1995**:4
Ivins, Molly 1942(?)- **1993**:4
Jablonski, Nina G. 1953- **2009**:3
Jackson, Alan 1958- **2003**:1
Jackson, Bo 1962- **1986**:3
Jackson, Cordell 1923- **1992**:4
Jackson, Janet 1966(?)- **1990**:4
Jackson, Jesse 1941- **1996**:1
Jackson, Jesse, Jr. 1965- **1998**:3
Jackson, Lisa P. 1962- **2009**:4
Jackson, Michael 1958- **1996**:2
Jackson, Phil 1945- **1996**:3
Jackson, Samuel L. 1949(?)- **1995**:4
Jackson, Thomas Penfield 1937- **2000**
  :2
Jacobs, Christian 1972-. See
  Christian Jacobs and Scott Schultz
Jacobs, Joe 1945(?)- **1994**:1
Jacobs, Marc 1963- **2002**:3
Jacobson, Nina 1965- **2009**:2
Jacuzzi, Candido 1903-1986
  Obituary **1987**:1

Jahn, Helmut 1940- **1987**:3
James, Etta 1938- **1995**:2
James, Jesse 1969- **2004**:4
James, LeBron 1984- **2007**:3
James, Rick 1948-2004
  Obituary **2005**:4
Jamison, Judith 1944- **1990**:3
Jane, Thomas 1969- **2010**:3
Janklow, Morton 1930- **1989**:3
Janney, Allison 1959- **2003**:3
Janzen, Daniel H. 1939- **1988**:4
Jarmusch, Jim 1953- **1998**:3
Jarrett, Keith 1945- **1992**:4
Jarrett, Valerie 1956- **2010**:4
Jarvik, Robert K. 1946- **1985**:1
Jay, Ricky 1949(?)- **1995**:1
Jay-Z 1970- **2006**:1
Jeanne-Claude 1935-2009
  Obituary **2011**:3
Jefferts Schori, Katharine 1954- **2007**
  :2
Jeffords, James 1934- **2002**:2
Jeffrey, Mildred 1910-2004
  Obituary **2005**:2
Jemison, Mae C. 1956- **1993**:1
Jen, Gish 1955- **2000**:1
Jenkins, Sally 1960(?)- **1997**:2
Jennifer Boulden and Heather
  Stephenson 1973- **2010**:2
Jennings, Waylon 1937-2002
  Obituary **2003**:2
Jeter, Derek 1974- **1999**:4
Jewel 1974- **1999**:2
Jillian, Ann 1951- **1986**:4
Jin, Ha 1956- **2011**:3
Jindal, Bobby 1971- **2006**:1
Jobs, Steve 1955- **2000**:1
Joel, Billy 1949- **1994**:3
Joffrey, Robert 1930-1988
  Obituary **1988**:3
Johansson, Scarlett 1984- **2005**:4
John, Daymond 1968- **2000**:1
Johnson, Abigail 1961- **2005**:3
Johnson, Betsey 1942- **1996**:2
Johnson, Beverly 1952- **2005**:2
Johnson, Diane 1934- **2004**:3
Johnson, Don 1949- **1986**:1
Johnson, Earvin Magic 1959- **1988**:4
Johnson, Jack 1975- **2006**:4
Johnson, Jimmie 1975- **2007**:2
Johnson, Jimmy 1943- **1993**:3
Johnson, John H. 1918-2005
  Obituary **2005**:4
Johnson, Kevin 1966(?)- **1991**:1
Johnson, Keyshawn 1972- **2000**:4
Johnson, Lady Bird 1912-2007
  Obituary **2008**:4
Johnson, Larry 1969- **1993**:3
Johnson, Michael **2000**:1
Johnson, Philip 1906- **1989**:2
Johnson, Randy 1963- **1996**:2
Johnson, Robert L. 1946- **2000**:4
Johnson, Shawn 1992- **2009**:2
Johnson, Van 1916-2008
  Obituary **2010**:1
Jolie, Angelina 1975- **2000**:2
Jonas Brothers **2008**:4
Jones, Arthur A. 1924(?)- **1985**:3
Jones, Bill T. **1991**:4
Jones, Cherry 1956- **1999**:3
Jones, Chuck 1912- **2001**:2
Jones, E. Fay 1921-2004

  Obituary **2005**:4
Jones, Edward P. 1950- **2005**:1
Jones, Etta 1928-2001
  Obituary **2002**:4
Jones, Gayl 1949- **1999**:4
Jones, Jennifer 1919-2009
  Obituary **2011**:4
Jones, Jerry 1942- **1994**:4
Jones, Marion 1975- **1998**:4
Jones, Norah 1979- **2004**:1
Jones, Quincy 1933- **1990**:4
Jones, Sarah 1974(?)- **2005**:2
Jones, Tommy Lee 1947(?)- **1994**:2
Jones, Van 1968- **2010**:3
Jong, Erica 1942- **1998**:3
Jonze, Spike 1961(?)- **2000**:3
Jordan, Barbara 1936-1996
  Obituary **1996**:3
Jordan, Charles M. 1927- **1989**:4
Jordan, James 1936(?)-1993
  Obituary **1994**:1
Jordan, King 1943(?)- **1990**:1
Jordan, Michael 1963- **1987**:2
Jordan, Vernon, Jr. 1935- **2002**:3
Jorgensen, Christine 1926-1989
  Obituary **1989**:4
Joseph, Wendy Evans 1955(?)- **2006**
  :2
Jovovich, Milla 1975- **2002**:1
Joyce, William 1957- **2006**:1
Joyner, Florence Griffith 1959-1998
  1989:2
  Obituary **1999**:1
Joyner-Kersee, Jackie 1962- **1993**:1
Judd, Ashley 1968- **1998**:1
Judge, Mike 1963(?)- **1994**:2
Judkins, Reba
  Brief entry **1987**:3
Julavits, Heidi 1968- **2007**:4
July, Miranda 1974- **2008**:2
Junck, Mary E. 1948(?)- **2003**:4
Jurgensen, Karen 1949(?)- **2004**:3
Justin, John Jr. 1917- **1992**:2
Justiz, Manuel J. 1948- **1986**:4
Kael, Pauline 1919-2001 **2000**:4
  Obituary **2002**:4
Kagan, Elena 1960- **2011**:4
Kahane, Meir 1932-1990
  Obituary **1991**:2
Kahn, Madeline 1942-1999
  Obituary **2000**:2
Kalin, Rob 1980- **2011**:3
Kallen, Jackie 1946(?)- **1994**:1
Kamali, Norma 1945- **1989**:1
Kamen, Dean 1951(?)- **2003**:1
Kanakaredes, Melina 1967- **2007**:1
Kandel, Eric 1929- **2005**:2
Kane, Patrick 1988- **2011**:4
Kanokogi, Rusty
  Brief entry **1987**:1
Kapor, Mitch 1950- **1990**:3
Karan, Donna 1948- **1988**:1
Karmazin, Mel 1943- **2006**:1
Karr, Mary 1955- **2011**:2
Kasem, Casey 1933(?)- **1987**:1
Kashuk, Sonia 1959(?)- **2002**:4
Kaskey, Ray
  Brief entry **1987**:2
Kassebaum, Nancy 1932- **1991**:1
Kathwari, M. Farooq 1944- **2005**:4
Katz, Alex 1927- **1990**:3
Katz, Lillian 1927- **1987**:4

Katzenberg, Jeffrey 1950- **1995**:3
Kaufman, Charlie 1958- **2005**:1
Kaufman, Elaine **1989**:4
Kavner, Julie 1951- **1992**:3
Kaye, Danny 1913-1987
  Obituary **1987**:2
Kaye, Nora 1920-1987
  Obituary **1987**:4
Kaye, Sammy 1910-1987
  Obituary **1987**:4
Kazan, Elia 1909-2003
  Obituary **2004**:4
Keating, Charles H., Jr. 1923- **1990**:4
Keaton, Diane 1946- **1997**:1
Keaton, Michael 1951- **1989**:4
Keeling, Charles 1928-2005
  Obituary **2006**:3
Keeshan, Bob 1927-2004
  Obituary **2005**:2
Keillor, Garrison 1942- **2011**:2
Keitel, Harvey 1939- **1994**:3
Keith, Brian 1921-1997
  Obituary **1997**:4
Keith, Louis 1935- **1988**:2
Kelleher, Herb 1931- **1995**:1
Kellerman, Jonathan 1949- **2009**:1
Kelley, DeForest 1929-1999
  Obituary **2000**:1
Kelley, Virginia 1923-1994
  Obituary **1994**:3
Kelly, Ellsworth 1923- **1992**:1
Kelly, Gene 1912-1996
  Obituary **1996**:3
Kelly, Jim 1960- **1991**:4
Kelly, Maureen 1972(?)- **2007**:3
Kelly, Patrick 1954(?)-1990
  Obituary **1990**:2
Kelly, R. 1968- **1997**:3
Kelly, William R. 1905-1998 **1998**:2
Kemp, Jack 1935- **1990**:4
Kemp, Jan 1949- **1987**:2
Kemp, Shawn 1969- **1995**:1
Kendrick, Anna 1985- **2011**:2
Kendricks, Eddie 1939-1992
  Obituary **1993**:2
Kennan, George 1904-2005
  Obituary **2006**:2
Kennedy, John F., Jr. 1960-1999 **1990**
  :1
  Obituary **1999**:4
Kennedy, Rose 1890-1995
  Obituary **1995**:3
Kennedy, Ted 1932-2009
  Obituary **2011**:1
Kennedy, Weldon 1938- **1997**:3
Kenny G 1957(?)- **1994**:4
Keno, Leigh and Leslie 1957(?)- **2001**
  :2
Kent, Corita 1918-1986
  Obituary **1987**:1
Keough, Donald Raymond 1926-
  1986:1
Keplinger, Dan 1973- **2001**:1
Kerger, Paula A. 1957- **2007**:2
Kerkorian, Kirk 1917- **1996**:2
Kerr, Clark 1911-2003
  Obituary **2005**:1
Kerr, Cristie 1977- **2008**:2
Kerr, Jean 1922-2003
  Obituary **2004**:1
Kerr, Walter 1913-1996
  Obituary **1997**:1

Kerrey, Bob 1943- **1986**:1
Kerrigan, Nancy 1969- **1994**:3
Kerry, John 1943- **2005**:2
Kesey, Ken 1935-2001
  Obituary **2003**:1
Kessler, David 1951- **1992**:1
Ketcham, Hank 1920-2001
  Obituary **2002**:2
Kevorkian, Jack 1928(?)- **1991**:3
Keyes, Alan 1950- **1996**:2
Keyes, James 1955- **2011**:3
Keys, Alicia 1981- **2006**:1
Kidd, Jason 1973- **2003**:2
Kidd, Michael 1915-2007
  Obituary **2009**:1
Kid Rock 1972- **2001**:1
Kilar, Jason 1971- **2010**:1
Kilborn, Craig 1964- **2003**:2
Kilby, Jack 1923- **2002**:2
Kiley, Dan 1912-2004
  Obituary **2005**:2
Kilgore, Marcia 1968- **2006**:3
Kilmer, Val **1991**:4
Kilpatrick, Kwame 1970- **2009**:2
Kilts, James M. 1948- **2001**:3
Kim, Eugenia 1974(?)- **2006**:1
Kim Barnouin and Rory Freedman
  1971- **2009**:4
Kimmel, Jimmy 1967- **2009**:2
Kimsey, James V. 1940(?)- **2001**:1
King, Alan 1927-2004
  Obituary **2005**:3
King, Bernice 1963- **2000**:2
King, Coretta Scott 1927- **1999**:3
King, Don 1931- **1989**:1
King, Larry 1933- **1993**:1
King, Mary-Claire 1946- **1998**:3
King, Stephen 1947- **1998**:1
Kingsborough, Donald
  Brief entry **1986**:2
Kingsley, Patricia 1932- **1990**:2
Kings of Leon 1982- **2010**:3
Kingsolver, Barbara 1955- **2005**:1
Kinison, Sam 1954(?)-1992
  Obituary **1993**:1
Kinney, Jeff 1971- **2009**:3
Kiraly, Karch
  Brief entry **1987**:1
Kirchner, Leon 1919-2009
  Obituary **2011**:1
Kirk, David 1956(?)- **2004**:1
Kirkpatrick, Jeane 1926-2006
  Obituary **2008**:1
Kissinger, Henry 1923- **1999**:4
Kissling, Frances 1943- **1989**:2
Kistler, Darci 1964- **1993**:1
Kitaj, R. B. 1932-2007
  Obituary **2008**:4
Kite, Tom 1949- **1990**:3
Kitt, Eartha 1927-2008
  Obituary **2010**:1
Klass, Perri 1958- **1993**:2
Klein, Calvin 1942- **1996**:2
Kline, Kevin 1947- **2000**:1
Kloss, Henry E.
  Brief entry **1985**:2
Kluge, John 1914- **1991**:1
Knievel, Evel 1938-2007
  Obituary **2009**:1
Knievel, Robbie 1963- **1990**:1
Knight, Bobby 1940- **1985**:3
Knight, Philip H. 1938- **1994**:1

Knight, Ted 1923-1986
  Obituary **1986**:4
Knight, Wayne 1956- **1997**:1
Knotts, Don 1924-2006
  Obituary **2007**:1
Knowles, John 1926-2001
  Obituary **2003**:1
Koch, Bill 1940- **1992**:3
Koch, Jim 1949- **2004**:3
Kohnstamm, Abby 1954- **2001**:1
Kolff, Willem 1911-2009
  Obituary **2010**:2
Koogle, Tim 1951- **2000**:4
Koons, Jeff 1955(?)- **1991**:4
Koontz, Dean 1945- **1999**:3
Koop, C. Everett 1916- **1989**:3
Kopits, Steven E.
  Brief entry **1987**:1
Koplovitz, Kay 1945- **1986**:3
Kopp, Wendy **1993**:3
Koppel, Ted 1940- **1989**:1
Kordich, Jay 1923- **1993**:2
Koresh, David 1960(?)-1993
  Obituary **1993**:4
Korman, Harvey 1927-2008
  Obituary **2009**:2
Kornberg, Arthur 1918(?)- **1992**:1
Kors, Michael 1959- **2000**:4
Kostabi, Mark 1960- **1989**:4
Kostova, Elizabeth 1964- **2006**:2
Kovacevich, Dick 1943- **2004**:3
Kozinski, Alex 1950- **2002**:2
Kozol, Jonathan 1936- **1992**:1
Kramer, Jack 1921-2009
  Obituary **2011**:1
Kramer, Larry 1935- **1991**:2
Kramer, Stanley 1913-2001
  Obituary **2002**:1
Krantz, Judith 1928- **2003**:1
Krause, Peter 1965- **2009**:2
Kravitz, Lenny 1964(?)- **1991**:1
Krebs, Edwin 1918-2009
  Obituary **2011**:4
Krim, Mathilde 1926- **1989**:2
Kroc, Ray 1902-1984
  Obituary **1985**:1
Krol, John 1910-1996
  Obituary **1996**:3
Kroll, Alexander S. 1938- **1989**:3
Krone, Julie 1963(?)- **1989**:2
Kruk, John 1961- **1994**:4
Krupp, Fred 1954- **2008**:3
Krzyzewski, Mike 1947- **1993**:2
Kubler-Ross, Elisabeth 1926-2004
  Obituary **2005**:4
Kubrick, Stanley 1928-1999
  Obituary **1999**:3
Kudrow, Lisa 1963(?)- **1996**:1
Kullman, Ellen 1956- **2009**:4
Kulp, Nancy 1921-1991
  Obituary **1991**:3
Kunitz, Stanley J. 1905- **2001**:2
Kunstler, William 1919-1995
  Obituary **1996**:1
Kunstler, William 1920(?)- **1992**:3
Kuralt, Charles 1934-1997
  Obituary **1998**:3
Kurzban, Ira 1949- **1987**:2
Kurzweil, Raymond 1948- **1986**:3
Kushner, Tony 1956- **1995**:2
Kutcher, Ashton 1978- **2003**:4
Kwoh, Yik San 1946(?)- **1988**:2

Kyser, Kay 1906(?)-1985
  Obituary **1985**:3
LaBeouf, Shia 1986- **2008**:1
Lachey, Nick and Jessica Simpson
  2004:4
LaDuke, Winona 1959- **1995**:2
Lady Antebellum 1982- **2011**:2
Lady Gaga **2011**:1
Laettner, Christian 1969- **1993**:1
Lafley, A. G. 1947- **2003**:4
LaFontaine, Pat 1965- **1985**:1
Lagasse, Emeril 1959- **1998**:3
Lahiri, Jhumpa 1967- **2001**:3
Lahti, Christine 1950- **1988**:2
Laimbeer, Bill 1957- **2004**:3
Lake, Ricki 1968(?)- **1994**:4
Lalas, Alexi 1970- **1995**:1
Lam, Derek 1966- **2009**:2
Lamb, Wally 1950- **1999**:1
Lamour, Dorothy 1914-1996
  Obituary **1997**:1
L'Amour, Louis 1908-1988
  Obituary **1988**:4
Lancaster, Burt 1913-1994
  Obituary **1995**:1
Lancaster, Jen 1967- **2010**:2
Land, Edwin H. 1909-1991
  Obituary **1991**:3
Lander, Toni 1931-1985
  Obituary **1985**:4
Landers, Ann 1918-2002
  Obituary **2003**:3
Landon, Alf 1887-1987
  Obituary **1988**:1
Landon, H. C. Robbins 1926-2009
  Obituary **2011**:3
Landon, Michael 1936-1991
  Obituary **1992**:1
Landrieu, Mary L. 1955- **2002**:2
Landry, Tom 1924-2000
  Obituary **2000**:3
Lane, Burton 1912-1997
  Obituary **1997**:2
Lane, Diane 1965- **2006**:2
Lane, Nathan 1956- **1996**:4
Lang, Eugene M. 1919- **1990**:3
Lange, Jessica 1949- **1995**:4
Lange, Liz 1967(?)- **2003**:4
Langella, Frank 1940- **2008**:3
Langer, Robert 1948- **2003**:4
Langevin, James R. 1964- **2001**:2
Langston, J. William
  Brief entry **1986**:2
Lanier, Jaron 1961(?)- **1993**:4
Lansbury, Angela 1925- **1993**:1
Lansdale, Edward G. 1908-1987
  Obituary **1987**:2
Lansing, Sherry 1944- **1995**:4
Lantos, Tom 1928-2008
  Obituary **2009**:2
Lanza, Robert 1956- **2004**:3
LaPaglia, Anthony 1959- **2004**:4
Lardner Jr., Ring 1915-2000
  Obituary **2001**:2
Larian, Isaac 1954- **2008**:1
Larroquette, John 1947- **1986**:2
Larson, Jonathan 1961(?)-1996
  Obituary **1997**:2
LaSalle, Eriq 1962- **1996**:4
Lasseter, John 1957- **2007**:2
Lauder, Estee 1908(?)- **1992**:2
Lauper, Cyndi 1953- **1985**:1

Lauren, Dylan 1974- **2010**:3
Lauren, Ralph 1939- **1990**:1
Lawless, Lucy 1968- **1997**:4
Lawrence, Martin 1966(?)- **1993**:4
Laybourne, Geraldine 1947- **1997**:1
Lazarus, Charles 1923- **1992**:4
Lazarus, Shelly 1947- **1998**:3
Lear, Frances 1923- **1988**:3
Leary, Denis 1958- **1993**:3
Leary, Timothy 1920-1996
    Obituary **1996**:4
LeBlanc, Matt 1967- **2005**:4
Lederman, Leon Max 1922- **1989**:4
Lee, Brandon 1965(?)-1993
    Obituary **1993**:4
Lee, Chang-Rae 1965- **2005**:1
Lee, Henry C. 1938- **1997**:1
Lee, Jason 1970- **2006**:4
Lee, Pamela 1967(?)- **1996**:4
Lee, Peggy 1920-2002
    Obituary **2003**:1
Lee, Sandra 1966- **2008**:3
Lee, Spike 1957- **1988**:4
Legend, John 1978- **2007**:1
Leguizamo, John 1965- **1999**:1
Lehane, Dennis 1965- **2001**:4
Leibovitz, Annie 1949- **1988**:4
Leigh, Dorian 1917-2008
    Obituary **2009**:3
Leigh, Janet 1927-2004
    Obituary **2005**:4
Leigh, Jennifer Jason 1962- **1995**:2
Lelyveld, Joseph S. 1937- **1994**:4
Lemmon, Jack 1925- **1998**:4
    Obituary **2002**:3
Lemon, Ted
    Brief entry **1986**:4
LeMond, Greg 1961- **1986**:4
L'Engle, Madeleine 1918-2007
    Obituary **2008**:4
Leno, Jay 1950- **1987**:1
Leonard, Elmore 1925- **1998**:4
Leonard, Sugar Ray 1956- **1989**:4
Leopold, Luna 1915-2006
    Obituary **2007**:1
Lepore, Nanette 1964(?)- **2006**:4
Lerner, Michael 1943- **1994**:2
Lerner, Sandy 1955(?)- **2005**:1
Leslie, Lisa 1972- **1997**:4
Lester, W. 1935- **2011**:3
Letterman, David 1947- **1989**:3
Levi, Zachary 1980- **2009**:4
Levin, Gerald 1939- **1995**:2
Levin, Harvey 1950- **2011**:4
Levin, Ira 1929-2007
    Obituary **2009**:1
Levine, Arnold 1939- **2002**:3
Levine, James 1943- **1992**:3
Levinson, Arthur D. 1950- **2008**:3
Levinson, Barry 1932- **1989**:3
Levitt, Arthur 1931- **2004**:2
Levitt, Helen 1913-2009
    Obituary **2010**:2
Lewis, Edward B. 1918-2004
    Obituary **2005**:4
Lewis, Edward T. 1940- **1999**:4
Lewis, Henry 1932-1996
    Obituary **1996**:3
Lewis, Huey 1951- **1987**:3
Lewis, John 1920-2001
    Obituary **2002**:1
Lewis, Juliette 1973- **1999**:3

Lewis, Kenneth D. 1947- **2009**:2
Lewis, Loida Nicolas 1942- **1998**:3
Lewis, Ray 1975- **2001**:3
Lewis, Reggie 1966(?)-1993
    Obituary **1994**:1
Lewis, Reginald F. 1942-1993 **1988**:4
    Obituary **1993**:3
Lewis, Richard 1948(?)- **1992**:1
Lewis, Shari 1934-1998 **1993**:1
    Obituary **1999**:1
LeWitt, Sol 1928- **2001**:2
Lewitzky, Bella 1916-2004
    Obituary **2005**:3
Leyland, Jim 1944- **1998**:2
Lhuillier, Monique 1971(?)- **2007**:4
Liberace 1919-1987
    Obituary **1987**:2
Libeskind, Daniel 1946- **2004**:1
Lichtenstein, Roy 1923-1997 **1994**:1
    Obituary **1998**:1
Lieberman, Joseph 1942- **2001**:1
Liebowitz, Ronald 1957- **2011**:1
Lightner, Candy 1946- **1985**:1
Liguori, Peter 1960- **2005**:2
Lilley, James 1928-2009
    Obituary **2011**:3
Lilly, John C. 1915-2001
    Obituary **2002**:4
Lil Wayne 1982- **2009**:3
Lim, Phillip 1974(?)- **2008**:1
Liman, Arthur 1932- **1989**:4
Liman, Doug 1965- **2007**:1
Limbaugh, Rush **1991**:3
Lin, Maya 1960(?)- **1990**:3
Lincoln, Blanche 1960- **2003**:1
Lindbergh, Anne Morrow 1906-2001
    Obituary **2001**:4
Lindros, Eric 1973- **1992**:1
Lindsay, John V. 1921-2000
    Obituary **2001**:3
Lindsay-Abaire, David 1970(?)- **2008**
    :2
Lines, Ray 1960(?)- **2004**:1
Ling, Bai 1970- **2000**:3
Ling, Lisa 1973- **2004**:2
Linklater, Richard 1960- **2007**:2
Linney, Laura 1964- **2009**:4
Lipinski, Tara 1982- **1998**:3
Lipkis, Andy
    Brief entry **1985**:3
Lippman, Laura 1959- **2010**:2
Lipsig, Harry H. 1901- **1985**:1
Lipton, Martin 1931- **1987**:3
Lisick, Beth 1969(?)- **2006**:2
Lithgow, John 1945- **1985**:2
Little, Benilde 1959(?)- **2006**:2
Little, Cleavon 1939-1992
    Obituary **1993**:2
Litzenburger, Liesel 1967(?)- **2008**:1
Liu, Lucy 1968- **2000**:4
Lively, Blake 1987- **2009**:1
Livingston, Ron 1968- **2007**:2
LL Cool J 1968- **1998**:2
Lobell, Jeanine 1964(?)- **2002**:3
Locklear, Heather 1961- **1994**:3
Lodge, Henry Cabot 1902-1985
    Obituary **1985**:1
Loewe, Frederick 1901-1988
    Obituary **1988**:2
Lofton, Kenny 1967- **1998**:1
Logan, Joshua 1908-1988
    Obituary **1988**:4

Lohan, Lindsay 1986- **2005**:3
Long, Nia 1970- **2001**:3
Long, Shelley 1950(?)- **1985**:1
Longo, Robert 1953(?)- **1990**:4
Lopes, Lisa 1971-2002
    Obituary **2003**:3
Lopez, George 1963- **2003**:4
Lopez, Jennifer 1970- **1998**:4
Lopez, Mario 1973- **2009**:3
Lopez, Nancy 1957- **1989**:3
Lord, Bette Bao 1938- **1994**:1
Lord, Jack 1920-1998 **1998**:2
Lord, Winston
    Brief entry **1987**:4
Lords, Traci 1968- **1995**:4
Lott, Trent 1941- **1998**:1
Louganis, Greg 1960- **1995**:3
Louis-Dreyfus, Julia 1961(?)- **1994**:1
Louv, Richard 1949- **2006**:2
Lovato, Demi 1992- **2011**:2
Love, Courtney 1964(?)- **1995**:1
Love, Susan 1948- **1995**:2
Loveless, Patty 1957- **1998**:2
Lovett, Lyle 1958(?)- **1994**:1
Lovley, Derek 1954(?)- **2005**:3
Lowe, Edward 1921- **1990**:2
Lowe, Mitch 1953- **2011**:2
Lowe, Rob 1964(?)- **1990**:4
Lowell, Mike 1974- **2003**:2
Lowry, Adam and Eric Ryan **2008**:1
Loy, Myrna 1905-1993
    Obituary **1994**:2
Lucas, George 1944- **1999**:4
Lucci, Susan 1946(?)- **1999**:4
Luce, Clare Boothe 1903-1987
    Obituary **1988**:1
Lucid, Shannon 1943- **1997**:1
Lucke, Lewis 1951(?)- **2004**:4
Ludacris 1977- **2007**:4
Ludlum, Robert 1927-2001
    Obituary **2002**:1
Lukas, D. Wayne 1936(?)- **1986**:2
Lupino, Ida 1918(?)-1995
    Obituary **1996**:1
LuPone, Patti 1949- **2009**:2
Lutz, Robert A. 1932- **1990**:1
Lynch, David 1946- **1990**:4
Lynch, Jane 1960- **2011**:2
Lyne, Susan 1950- **2005**:4
Lynn, Loretta 1935(?)- **2001**:1
Lysacek, Evan 1985- **2011**:2
Mac, Bernie 1957- **2003**:1
MacCready, Paul 1925- **1986**:4
MacDonald, Laurie and Walter
    Parkes **2004**:1
MacDowell, Andie 1958(?)- **1993**:4
MacFarlane, Seth 1973- **2006**:1
Machover, Tod 1953- **2010**:3
Mack, John J. 1944- **2006**:3
Mackey, John 1953- **2008**:2
MacKinnon, Catharine 1946- **1993**:2
MacMurray, Fred 1908-1991
    Obituary **1992**:2
MacNelly, Jeff 1947-2000
    Obituary **2000**:4
MacRae, Gordon 1921-1986
    Obituary **1986**:2
Macy, William H. **1999**:3
Madden, Chris 1948- **2006**:1
Madden, John 1936- **1995**:1
Madden, Steve 1958- **2007**:2
Maddow, Rachel 1973- **2010**:2

Maddux, Greg 1966- **1996**:2
Madonna 1958- **1985**:2
Maglich, Bogdan C. 1928- **1990**:1
Magliozzi, Tom and Ray **1991**:4
Maguire, Tobey 1975- **2002**:2
Maher, Bill 1956- **1996**:2
Mahony, Roger M. 1936- **1988**:2
Maida, Adam Cardinal 1930- **1998**:2
Mailer, Norman 1923- **1998**:1
Maiman, Theodore 1927-2007
  Obituary **2008**:3
Majerle, Dan 1965- **1993**:4
Malda, Rob 1976- **2007**:3
Malden, Karl 1912-2009
  Obituary **2010**:4
Malkovich, John 1953- **1988**:2
Malloy, Edward Monk 1941- **1989**:4
Malone, John C. 1941- **1988**:3
Malone, Karl 1963- **1990**:1
Maltby, Richard, Jr. 1937- **1996**:3
Mamet, David 1947- **1998**:4
Manchin, Joe 1947- **2006**:4
Mancini, Henry 1924-1994
  Obituary **1994**:4
Manheimer, Heidi 1963- **2009**:3
Maniscalco, Chuck 1953- **2010**:3
Mankiller, Wilma P.
  Brief entry **1986**:2
Mann, Sally 1951- **2001**:2
Manning, Eli 1981- **2008**:4
Manning, Peyton 1976- **2007**:4
Mansfield, Mike 1903-2001
  Obituary **2002**:4
Mansion, Gracie
  Brief entry **1986**:3
Manson, JoAnn E. 1953- **2008**:3
Manson, Marilyn 1969- **1999**:4
Mantegna, Joe 1947- **1992**:1
Mantle, Mickey 1931-1995
  Obituary **1996**:1
Mapplethorpe, Robert 1946-1989
  Obituary **1989**:3
Maraldo, Pamela J. 1948(?)- **1993**:4
Maravich, Pete 1948-1988
  Obituary **1988**:2
Marchand, Nancy 1928-2000
  Obituary **2001**:1
Marchetto, Marisa Acocella 1962(?)-
  2007:3
Marcus, Stanley 1905-2002
  Obituary **2003**:1
Mardin, Brice 1938- **2007**:4
Margolis, Bobby 1948(?)- **2007**:2
Margulies, Julianna 1966- **2011**:1
Marier, Rebecca 1974- **1995**:4
Marin, Cheech 1946- **2000**:1
Marineau, Philip 1946- **2002**:4
Maris, Roger 1934-1985
  Obituary **1986**:1
Mark, Mary Ellen 1940- **2006**:2
Marky Mark 1971- **1993**:3
Maroon 5 **2008**:1
Marriott, J. Willard 1900-1985
  Obituary **1985**:4
Marriott, J. Willard, Jr. 1932- **1985**:4
Marsalis, Branford 1960- **1988**:3
Marsalis, Wynton 1961- **1997**:4
Marshall, Penny 1942- **1991**:3
Marshall, Susan 1958- **2000**:4
Marshall, Thurgood 1908-1993
  Obituary **1993**:3
Martin, Agnes 1912-2004

Obituary **2006**:1
Martin, Billy 1928-1989 **1988**:4
  Obituary **1990**:2
Martin, Casey 1972- **2002**:1
Martin, Dean 1917-1995
  Obituary **1996**:2
Martin, Dean Paul 1952(?)-1987
  Obituary **1987**:3
Martin, Judith 1938- **2000**:3
Martin, Lynn 1939- **1991**:4
Martin, Mary 1913-1990
  Obituary **1991**:2
Martin, Steve 1945- **1992**:2
Martinez, Bob 1934- **1992**:1
Marvin, Lee 1924-1987
  Obituary **1988**:1
Mary Mary 1972- **2009**:4
Mas Canosa, Jorge 1939-1997 **1998**:2
Mashouf, Manny 1938(?)- **2008**:1
Master P 1970- **1999**:4
Masters, William H. 1915-2001
  Obituary **2001**:4
Matalin, Mary 1953- **1995**:2
Mathews, Dan 1965- **1998**:3
Mathias, Bob 1930-2006
  Obituary **2007**:4
Mathis, Clint 1976- **2003**:1
Matlin, Marlee 1965- **1992**:2
Matlovich, Leonard P. 1944(?)-1988
  Obituary **1988**:4
Matthau, Walter 1920- **2000**:3
Matthews, Chris 1945- **2010**:1
Matthews, Dave 1967- **1999**:3
Matthias, Rebecca 1953- **2010**:1
Mattingly, Don 1961- **1986**:2
Matuszak, John 1951(?)-1989
  Obituary **1989**:4
Mauldin, Bill 1921-2003
  Obituary **2004**:2
Maxwell 1973- **2010**:4
Maxwell, Hamish 1926- **1989**:4
Mayer, John 1977- **2007**:4
Mayes, Frances 1940(?)- **2004**:3
Maynard, Joyce 1953- **1999**:4
Mays, Billy 1958-2009
  Obituary **2010**:4
McAfee, George 1918-2009
  Obituary **2010**:2
McAuliffe, Christa 1948-1986
  Obituary **1985**:4
McBride, Martina 1966- **2010**:1
McCain, John S. 1936- **1998**:4
McCall, Nathan 1955- **1994**:4
McCarron, Chris 1955- **1995**:4
McCarthy, Carolyn 1944- **1998**:4
McCarthy, Cormac 1933- **2008**:1
McCarthy, Jenny 1972- **1997**:4
McCartney, Bill 1940- **1995**:3
McCartney, Linda 1942-1998
  Obituary **1998**:4
McCauley, Matthew 1973- **2011**:1
McChrystal, Stanley 1954- **2011**:3
McCloskey, J. Michael 1934- **1988**:2
McCloskey, James 1944(?)- **1993**:1
McCloy, John J. 1895-1989
  Obituary **1989**:3
McColough, C. Peter 1922- **1990**:2
McConaughey, Matthew David
  1969- **1997**:1
McCourt, Frank 1930- **1997**:4
McCrea, Joel 1905-1990
  Obituary **1991**:1

McDermott, Alice 1953- **1999**:2
McDonald, Camille 1953(?)- **2004**:1
McDonell, Nick 1984- **2011**:2
McDonnell, Bob 1954- **2011**:2
McDonnell, Mary 1952- **2008**:2
McDonnell, Patrick 1956- **2009**:4
McDonnell, Sanford N. 1922- **1988**:4
McDonough, William 1951- **2003**:1
McDormand, Frances 1957- **1997**:3
McDougall, Ron 1942- **2001**:4
McDuffie, Robert 1958- **1990**:2
McElligott, Thomas J. 1943- **1987**:4
McEntire, Reba 1954- **1987**:3
McFarlane, Todd 1961- **1999**:1
McFerrin, Bobby 1950- **1989**:1
McGillis, Kelly 1957- **1989**:3
McGinley, Ryan 1977- **2009**:1
McGinley, Ted 1958- **2004**:4
McGoohan, Patrick 1928-2009
  Obituary **2010**:1
McGowan, William 1927- **1985**:2
McGowan, William G. 1927-1992
  Obituary **1993**:1
McGrath, Judy 1953- **2006**:1
McGraw, Phil 1950- **2005**:2
McGraw, Tim 1966- **2000**:3
McGraw, Tug 1944-2004
  Obituary **2005**:1
McGreevey, James 1957- **2005**:2
McGruder, Aaron 1974- **2005**:4
McGuire, Dorothy 1918-2001
  Obituary **2002**:4
McGwire, Mark 1963- **1999**:1
McHale, Joel 1971- **2010**:4
McIntyre, Richard
  Brief entry **1986**:2
McKee, Lonette 1952(?)- **1996**:1
McKenna, Terence **1993**:3
McKinney, Cynthia A. 1955- **1997**:1
McKinney, Stewart B. 1931-1987
  Obituary **1987**:4
McLaughlin, Betsy 1962(?)- **2004**:3
McMahon, Ed 1923-2009
  Obituary **2010**:3
McMahon, Jim 1959- **1985**:4
McMahon, Vince, Jr. 1945(?)- **1985**:4
McMillan, Terry 1951- **1993**:2
McMillen, Tom 1952- **1988**:4
McMurtry, James 1962- **1990**:2
McMurtry, Larry 1936- **2006**:4
McNamara, Robert S. 1916- **1995**:4
McNealy, Scott 1954- **1999**:4
McNerney, W. James 1949- **2006**:3
McRae, Carmen 1920(?)-1994
  Obituary **1995**:2
McSally, Martha 1966(?)- **2002**:4
McVeigh, Timothy 1968-2001
  Obituary **2002**:2
Meadows, Audrey 1925-1996
  Obituary **1996**:3
Meier, Richard 1934- **2001**:4
Meisel, Steven 1954- **2002**:4
Melendez, Bill 1916-2008
  Obituary **2009**:4
Mellinger, Frederick 1924(?)-1990
  Obituary **1990**:4
Mello, Dawn 1938(?)- **1992**:2
Mellon, Paul 1907-1999
  Obituary **1999**:3
Melman, Richard
  Brief entry **1986**:1
Melnick, Daniel 1932-2009

Obituary **2011**:2
Melton, Douglas 1954- **2008**:3
Meltzer, Brad 1970- **2005**:4
Mendoza, Lydia 1916-2007
  Obituary **2009**:1
Mengers, Sue 1938- **1985**:3
Menninger, Karl 1893-1990
  Obituary **1991**:1
Menuhin, Yehudi 1916-1999
  Obituary **1999**:3
Merchant, Ismail 1936-2005
  Obituary **2006**:3
Merchant, Natalie 1963- **1996**:3
Meredith, Burgess 1909-1997
  Obituary **1998**:1
Merkerson, S. Epatha 1952- **2006**:4
Merrick, David 1912-2000
  Obituary **2000**:4
Merrill, James 1926-1995
  Obituary **1995**:3
Merritt, Justine
  Brief entry **1985**:3
Messick, Dale 1906-2005
  Obituary **2006**:2
Messing, Debra 1968- **2004**:4
Metallica **2004**:2
Meyer, Stephenie 1973- **2009**:1
Meyers, Nancy 1949- **2006**:1
Mfume, Kweisi 1948- **1996**:3
Michaels, Bret 1963- **2011**:4
Michaels, Jillian 1974- **2011**:4
Michelman, Kate 1942- **1998**:4
Michener, James A. 1907-1997
  Obituary **1998**:1
Mickelson, Phil 1970- **2004**:4
Midler, Bette 1945- **1989**:4
Mikan, George 1924-2005
  Obituary **2006**:3
Mikkelson, Barbara 1959-. See
  Barbara and Richard Mikkelson
Mikkelson, Richard 1959-. See
  Barbara and Richard Mikkelson
Mikulski, Barbara 1936- **1992**:4
Milano, Alyssa 1972- **2002**:3
Milbrett, Tiffeny 1972- **2001**:1
Milburn, Rodney Jr. 1950-1997 **1998**
:2
Millan, Cesar 1969- **2007**:4
Milland, Ray 1908(?)-1986
  Obituary **1986**:2
Millard, Barbara J.
  Brief entry **1985**:3
Miller, Andre 1976- **2003**:3
Miller, Ann 1923-2004
  Obituary **2005**:2
Miller, Arthur 1915- **1999**:4
Miller, Bebe 1950- **2000**:2
Miller, Bode 1977- **2002**:4
Miller, Dennis 1953- **1992**:4
Miller, Frank 1957- **2008**:2
Miller, Merton H. 1923-2000
  Obituary **2001**:1
Miller, Nicole 1951(?)- **1995**:4
Miller, Rand 1959(?)- **1995**:4
Miller, Reggie 1965- **1994**:4
Miller, Roger 1936-1992
  Obituary **1993**:2
Miller, Sue 1943- **1999**:3
Mills, Malia 1966- **2003**:1
Mills, Wilbur 1909-1992
  Obituary **1992**:4
Milosz, Czeslaw 1911-2004

Obituary **2005**:4
Mindell, Jodi 1962- **2010**:4
Minkoff, Rebecca 1981- **2011**:3
Minner, Ruth Ann 1935- **2002**:2
Minnesota Fats 1900(?)-1996
  Obituary **1996**:3
Minsky, Marvin 1927- **1994**:3
Misrach, Richard 1949- **1991**:2
Mitchard, Jacquelyn 1956- **2010**:4
Mitchell, Arthur 1934- **1995**:1
Mitchell, Elizabeth 1970- **2011**:4
Mitchell, George J. 1933- **1989**:3
Mitchell, John 1913-1988
  Obituary **1989**:2
Mitchell, Joni 1943- **1991**:4
Mitchelson, Marvin 1928- **1989**:2
Mitchum, Robert 1917-1997
  Obituary **1997**:4
Mizrahi, Isaac 1961- **1991**:1
Moakley, Joseph 1927-2001
  Obituary **2002**:2
Moby 1965- **2000**:1
Modano, Mike 1970- **2008**:2
Mohajer, Dineh 1972- **1997**:3
Molinari, Susan 1958- **1996**:4
Monaghan, Tom 1937- **1985**:1
Mondavi, Robert 1913- **1989**:2
Monica 1980- **2004**:2
Mo'Nique 1967- **2008**:1
Monk, Art 1957- **1993**:2
Monroe, Bill 1911-1996
  Obituary **1997**:1
Monroe, Rose Will 1920-1997
  Obituary **1997**:4
Montalban, Ricardo 1920-2009
  Obituary **2010**:1
Montana, Joe 1956- **1989**:2
Montgomery, Elizabeth 1933-1995
  Obituary **1995**:4
Moody, John 1943- **1985**:3
Moody, Rick 1961- **2002**:2
Moog, Robert 1934-2005
  Obituary **2006**:4
Moon, Warren 1956- **1991**:3
Moonves, Les 1949- **2004**:2
Moore, Ann 1950- **2009**:1
Moore, Archie 1913-1998
  Obituary **1999**:2
Moore, Clayton 1914-1999
  Obituary **2000**:3
Moore, Demi 1963(?)- **1991**:4
Moore, Julianne 1960- **1998**:1
Moore, Mandy 1984- **2004**:2
Moore, Mary Tyler 1936- **1996**:2
Moore, Michael 1954(?)- **1990**:3
Moore, Rachel 1965- **2008**:2
Moose, Charles 1953(?)- **2003**:4
Moreno, Arturo 1946- **2005**:2
Morgan, Dodge 1932(?)- **1987**:1
Morgan, Robin 1941- **1991**:1
Morgan, Tracy 1968- **2009**:3
Morita, Noriyuki Pat 1932- **1987**:3
Moritz, Charles 1936- **1989**:3
Morris, Dick 1948- **1997**:3
Morris, Doug 1938- **2005**:1
Morris, Henry M. 1918-2006
  Obituary **2007**:2
Morris, Kathryn 1969- **2006**:4
Morris, Mark 1956- **1991**:1
Morris, Robert 1947- **2010**:3
Morrison, Sterling 1942-1995
  Obituary **1996**:1

Morrison, Toni 1931- **1998**:1
Morrison, Trudi
  Brief entry **1986**:2
Morrow, Rob 1962- **2006**:4
Mortensen, Viggo 1958- **2003**:3
Mortenson, Greg 1957- **2011**:1
Mosbacher, Georgette 1947(?)- **1994**
:2
Mos Def 1973- **2005**:4
Mosley, Walter 1952- **2003**:4
Moss, Cynthia 1940- **1995**:2
Moss, Randy 1977- **1999**:3
Motherwell, Robert 1915-1991
  Obituary **1992**:1
Mott, William Penn, Jr. 1909- **1986**:1
Mottola, Tommy 1949- **2002**:1
Mourning, Alonzo 1970- **1994**:2
Moyers, Bill 1934- **1991**:4
Moynihan, Daniel Patrick 1927-2003
  Obituary **2004**:2
Mraz, Jason 1977- **2010**:2
Mulally, Alan 1945- **2010**:3
Mulcahy, Anne M. 1952- **2003**:2
Muldowney, Shirley 1940- **1986**:1
Mulkey-Robertson, Kim 1962- **2006**
:1
Muller, Jim 1943- **2011**:3
Mullis, Kary 1944- **1995**:3
Mumford, Lewis 1895-1990
  Obituary **1990**:2
Muniz, Frankie 1985- **2001**:4
Munter, Leilani 1976- **2010**:4
Murdoch, Rupert 1931- **1988**:4
Murkoff, Heidi 1958- **2009**:3
Murphy, Brittany 1977- **2005**:1
Murphy, Eddie 1961- **1989**:2
Murphy, Kathleen A. **2009**:2
Murray, Arthur 1895-1991
  Obituary **1991**:3
Murray, Bill 1950- **2002**:4
Musburger, Brent 1939- **1985**:1
Muskie, Edmund S. 1914-1996
  Obituary **1996**:3
Mydans, Carl 1907-2004
  Obituary **2005**:4
Nader, Ralph 1934- **1989**:4
Nagin, Ray 1956- **2007**:1
Nair, Mira 1957- **2007**:4
Nance, Jack 1943(?)-1996
  Obituary **1997**:3
Napolitano, Janet 1957- **1997**:1
Nardelli, Robert 1948- **2008**:4
Nas 1973- **2009**:2
Natsios, Andrew 1949- **2005**:1
Nauman, Bruce 1941- **1995**:4
Navratilova, Martina 1956- **1989**:1
Neal, James Foster 1929- **1986**:2
Nechita, Alexandra 1985- **1996**:4
Neeleman, David 1959- **2003**:3
Ne-Yo 1982- **2009**:4
Neiman, LeRoy 1927- **1993**:3
Nelson, Byron 1912-2006
  Obituary **2007**:4
Nelson, Gaylord A. 1914-2005
  Obituary **2006**:3
Nelson, Harriet 1909(?)-1994
  Obituary **1995**:1
Nelson, Jack 1929-2009
  Obituary **2011**:2
Nelson, Rick 1940-1985
  Obituary **1986**:1
Nelson, Willie 1933- **1993**:4

Nemerov, Howard 1920-1991
  Obituary **1992**:1
Neuharth, Allen H. 1924- **1986**:1
Nevelson, Louise 1900-1988
  Obituary **1988**:3
Newhouse, Samuel I., Jr. 1927- **1997**:1
New Kids on the Block **1991**:2
Newman, Arnold 1918- **1993**:1
Newman, Joseph 1936- **1987**:1
Newman, Paul 1925- **1995**:3
Newman, Ryan 1977- **2005**:1
Newsom, Gavin 1967- **2009**:3
Newton, Huey 1942-1989
  Obituary **1990**:1
Nichols, Mike 1931- **1994**:4
Nicholson, Jack 1937- **1989**:2
Nick Friedman and Omar Soliman 1982- **2011**:3
Nielsen, Jerri 1951(?)- **2001**:3
Nipon, Albert
  Brief entry **1986**:4
Nirvana **1992**:4
Nissel, Angela 1974- **2006**:4
Nixon, Bob 1954(?)- **2006**:4
Nixon, Pat 1912-1993
  Obituary **1994**:1
Nixon, Richard 1913-1994
  Obituary **1994**:4
Nocera, Fred 1957- **2010**:3
Nolan, Lloyd 1902-1985
  Obituary **1985**:4
Nolte, Nick 1941- **1992**:4
Noonan, Peggy 1950- **1990**:3
North, Alex 1910- **1986**:3
North, Oliver 1943- **1987**:4
Northrop, Peggy 1954- **2009**:2
Norton, Andre 1912-2005
  Obituary **2006**:2
Norton, Edward 1969- **2000**:2
Norville, Deborah 1958- **1990**:3
Notorious B.I.G. 1973(?)-1997
  Obituary **1997**:3
Nottage, Lynn 1964- **2010**:1
Novak, Robert 1931-2009
  Obituary **2010**:4
Noyce, Robert N. 1927- **1985**:4
'N Sync **2001**:4
Nunn, Sam 1938- **1990**:2
Nussbaum, Karen 1950- **1988**:3
Nye, Bill 1955- **1997**:2
Nyro, Laura 1947-1997
  Obituary **1997**:3
Oates, Joyce Carol 1938- **2000**:1
Obama, Barack 1961- **2007**:4
O'Brien, Conan 1963(?)- **1994**:1
O'Connor, Cardinal John 1920- **1990**:3
O'Connor, Carroll 1924-2001
  Obituary **2002**:3
O'Connor, Donald 1925-2003
  Obituary **2004**:4
O'Connor, John 1920-2000
  Obituary **2000**:4
O'Connor, Sandra Day 1930- **1991**:1
O'Day, Anita 1919-2006
  Obituary **2008**:1
O'Donnell, Chris 1970- **2011**:4
O'Donnell, Rosie 1962- **1994**:3
O'Keefe, Sean 1956- **2005**:2
Olajuwon, Akeem 1963- **1985**:1
Olbermann, Keith 1959- **2010**:3

Oldham, Todd 1961- **1995**:4
O'Leary, Hazel 1937- **1993**:4
Olin, Ken 1955(?)- **1992**:3
Oliver, Daniel 1939- **1988**:2
Olmos, Edward James 1947- **1990**:1
Olopade, Olufunmilayo 1957(?)- **2006**:3
Olsen, Kenneth H. 1926- **1986**:4
Olsen, Mary-Kate and Ashley 1986- **2002**:1
Olsen, Sigrid 1953- **2007**:1
Olson, Billy 1958- **1986**:3
Olson, Johnny 1910(?)-1985
  Obituary **1985**:4
Olson, Kathryn 1961- **2011**:3
O'Malley, Susan 1962(?)- **1995**:2
Onassis, Jacqueline Kennedy 1929-1994
  Obituary **1994**:4
O'Neal, Shaquille 1972- **1992**:1
O'Neil, Buck 1911-2006
  Obituary **2007**:4
O'Neill, Ed 1946- **2010**:4
O'Neill, Paul H. 1935- **2001**:4
O'Neill, Tip 1912-1994
  Obituary **1994**:3
Ono, Yoko 1933- **1989**:2
Orbach, Jerry 1935-2004
  Obituary **2006**:1
Orbison, Roy 1936-1988
  Obituary **1989**:2
O'Reilly, Bill 1949- **2001**:2
Orman, Suze 1951(?)- **2003**:1
Ormandy, Eugene 1899-1985
  Obituary **1985**:2
Ornish, Dean 1953- **2004**:2
Orr, Kay 1939- **1987**:4
Osborne, Joan 1962- **1996**:4
Osgood, Charles 1933- **1996**:2
Osteen, Joel 1963- **2006**:2
O'Steen, Van
  Brief entry **1986**:3
Ostin, Mo 1927- **1996**:2
Ostroff, Dawn 1960- **2006**:4
Otte, Ruth 1949- **1992**:4
OutKast **2004**:4
Ovitz, Michael 1946- **1990**:1
Owens, Buck 1929-2006
  Obituary **2007**:2
Owens, Delia and Mark **1993**:3
Oz, Mehmet 1960- **2007**:2
Paar, Jack 1918-2004
  Obituary **2005**:2
Pacelle, Wayne 1965- **2009**:4
Pacino, Al 1940- **1993**:4
Pack, Ellen 1963(?)- **2001**:2
Packard, David 1912-1996
  Obituary **1996**:3
Padron, Eduardo 1946- **2011**:2
Page, Bettie 1923-2008
  Obituary **2010**:1
Page, Geraldine 1924-1987
  Obituary **1987**:4
Pagels, Elaine 1943- **1997**:1
Paglia, Camille 1947- **1992**:3
Paige, Emmett, Jr.
  Brief entry **1986**:4
Paige, Rod 1933- **2003**:2
Paisley, Brad 1972- **2008**:3
Pakula, Alan 1928-1998
  Obituary **1999**:2
Palahniuk, Chuck 1962- **2004**:1

Palance, Jack 1919-2006
  Obituary **2008**:1
Paley, William S. 1901-1990
  Obituary **1991**:2
Palin, Sarah 1964- **2009**:1
Palmeiro, Rafael 1964- **2005**:1
Palmer, Jim 1945- **1991**:2
Palmer, Keke 1993- **2011**:3
Palmer, Violet 1964(?)- **2005**:2
Palmisano, Samuel J. 1952(?)- **2003**:1
Paltrow, Gwyneth 1972- **1997**:1
Panetta, Leon 1938- **1995**:1
Panettiere, Hayden 1989- **2008**:4
Panichgul, Thakoon 1974- **2009**:4
Panofsky, Wolfgang 1919-2007
  Obituary **2008**:4
Pantoliano, Joe 1951- **2002**:3
Papp, Joseph 1921-1991
  Obituary **1992**:2
Paretsky, Sara 1947- **2002**:4
Parker, Brant 1920-2007
  Obituary **2008**:2
Parker, Colonel Tom 1929-1997
  Obituary **1997**:2
Parker, Mary-Louise 1964- **2002**:2
Parker, Sarah Jessica 1965- **1999**:2
Parker, Suzy 1932-2003
  Obituary **2004**:2
Parker, Trey and Matt Stone **1998**:2
Parker, Willie 1980- **2009**:3
Parks, Bert 1914-1992
  Obituary **1992**:3
Parks, Gordon 1912-2006
  Obituary **2006**:2
Parks, Rosa 1913-2005
  Obituary **2007**:1
Parks, Suzan-Lori 1964- **2003**:2
Parsons, David 1959- **1993**:4
Parsons, Gary 1950(?)- **2006**:2
Parsons, Richard 1949- **2002**:4
Parton, Dolly 1946- **1999**:4
Pascal, Amy 1958- **2003**:3
Pass, Joe 1929-1994
  Obituary **1994**:4
Pastorius, Jaco 1951-1987
  Obituary **1988**:1
Pataki, George 1945- **1995**:2
Patchett, Ann 1963- **2003**:2
Paterno, Joe 1926- **1995**:4
Patrick, Danica 1982- **2003**:3
Patrick, Robert 1959- **2002**:1
Patterson, Richard North 1947- **2001**:4
Patton, John 1947(?)- **2004**:4
Paul, Les 1915-2009
  Obituary **2010**:4
Pauley, Jane 1950- **1999**:1
Pauling, Linus 1901-1994
  Obituary **1995**:1
Paulsen, Pat 1927-1997
  Obituary **1997**:4
Paulucci, Jeno
  Brief entry **1986**:3
Pausch, Randy 1960-2008
  Obituary **2009**:3
Pavin, Corey 1959- **1996**:4
Paxton, Bill 1955- **1999**:3
Payne, Alexander 1961- **2005**:4
Payton, Lawrence 1938(?)-1997
  Obituary **1997**:4
Payton, Walter 1954-1999
  Obituary **2000**:2

Pearl, Minnie 1912-1996
  Obituary **1996**:3
Pearl Jam **1994**:2
Peck, Gregory 1916-2003
  Obituary **2004**:3
Pedersen, William 1938(?)- **1989**:4
Peebles, R. Donahue 1960- **2003**:2
Peete, Calvin 1943- **1985**:4
Peete, Holly Robinson 1964- **2005**:2
Pei, I.M. 1917- **1990**:4
Peller, Clara 1902(?)-1987
  Obituary **1988**:1
Pelosi, Nancy 1940- **2004**:2
Peltier, Leonard 1944- **1995**:1
Peluso, Michelle 1971(?)- **2007**:4
Pendleton, Clarence M. 1930-1988
  Obituary **1988**:4
Penn, Irving 1917-2009
  Obituary **2011**:2
Penn, Kal 1977- **2009**:1
Penn, Sean 1960- **1987**:2
Penn & Teller **1992**:1
Pennington, Ty 1965- **2005**:4
Penske, Roger 1937- **1988**:3
Pep, Willie 1922-2006
  Obituary **2008**:1
Pepper, Claude 1900-1989
  Obituary **1989**:4
Percy, Walker 1916-1990
  Obituary **1990**:4
Perdue, Frank 1920-2005
  Obituary **2006**:2
Perelman, Ronald 1943- **1989**:2
Perez, Rosie **1994**:2
Perkins, Anthony 1932-1992
  Obituary **1993**:2
Perkins, Carl 1932-1998 **1998**:2
Perlman, Steve 1961(?)- **1998**:2
Perot, H. Ross 1930- **1992**:4
Perry, Carrie Saxon 1932(?)- **1989**:2
Perry, Harold A. 1917(?)-1991
  Obituary **1992**:1
Perry, Luke 1966(?)- **1992**:3
Perry, Matthew 1969- **1997**:2
Perry, Tyler 1969- **2006**:1
Perry, William 1927- **1994**:4
Pesci, Joe 1943- **1992**:4
Peter, Valentine J. 1934- **1988**:2
Peters, Bernadette 1948- **2000**:1
Peters, Mary E. 1948- **2008**:3
Peters, Tom 1942- **1998**:1
Petersen, Donald Eugene 1926- **1985**:1
Peterson, Cassandra 1951- **1988**:1
Peterson, Roger Tory 1908-1996
  Obituary **1997**:1
Petty, Tom 1952- **1988**:1
Peyton, Elizabeth 1965- **2007**:1
Pfeiffer, Michelle 1957- **1990**:2
Phair, Liz 1967- **1995**:3
Phelan, John Joseph, Jr. 1931- **1985**:4
Phelps, Michael 1985- **2009**:2
Phifer, Mekhi 1975- **2004**:1
Philbin, Regis 1933- **2000**:2
Phillips, John 1935-2001
  Obituary **2002**:1
Phillips, Julia 1944- **1992**:1
Phillips, Sam 1923-2003
  Obituary **2004**:4
Phoenix, Joaquin 1974- **2000**:4
Phoenix, River 1970-1993 **1990**:2
  Obituary **1994**:2

Piazza, Mike 1968- **1998**:4
Pickett, Wilson 1941-2006
  Obituary **2007**:1
Picoult, Jodi 1966- **2008**:1
Pierce, David Hyde 1959- **1996**:3
Pierce, Frederick S. 1934(?)- **1985**:3
Pierce, Mary 1975- **1994**:4
Pierce, Paul 1977- **2009**:2
Pilatus, Robert 1966(?)-1998
  Obituary **1998**:3
Pilkey, Dav 1966- **2001**:1
Pincay, Laffit, Jr. 1946- **1986**:3
Pinchot, Bronson 1959(?)- **1987**:4
Pincus, Mark 1966- **2011**:1
Pink 1979- **2004**:3
Pinker, Steven A. 1954- **2000**:1
Pinkett Smith, Jada 1971- **1998**:3
Pinto, Maria 1957- **2011**:2
Pipher, Mary 1948(?)- **1996**:4
Pippen, Scottie 1965- **1992**:2
Pirro, Jeanine 1951- **1998**:2
Pitt, Brad 1964- **1995**:2
Pittman, Robert W. 1953- **1985**:1
Piven, Jeremy 1965- **2007**:3
Plater-Zyberk, Elizabeth 1950- **2005**:2
Plato, Dana 1964-1999
  Obituary **1999**:4
Pleshette, Suzanne 1937-2008
  Obituary **2009**:2
Plimpton, George 1927-2003
  Obituary **2004**:4
Plotkin, Mark 1955(?)- **1994**:3
Poehler, Amy 1971- **2009**:1
Poitier, Sidney 1927- **1990**:3
Politkovskaya, Anna 1958-2006
  Obituary **2007**:4
Pollack, Sydney 1934-2008
  Obituary **2009**:2
Pollan, Michael 1955- **2011**:3
Popcorn, Faith
  Brief entry **1988**:1
Pope, Generoso 1927-1988 **1988**:4
Porco, Carolyn 1953- **2005**:4
Porter, Sylvia 1913-1991
  Obituary **1991**:4
Portman, John 1924- **1988**:2
Portman, Natalie 1981- **2000**:3
Posen, Zac 1980- **2009**:3
Post, Peggy 1940(?)- **2001**:4
Poston, Tom 1921-2007
  Obituary **2008**:3
Potok, Anna Maximilian
  Brief entry **1985**:2
Potok, Chaim 1929-2002
  Obituary **2003**:4
Potter, Michael 1960(?)- **2003**:3
Potts, Annie 1952- **1994**:1
Pough, Richard Hooper 1904- **1989**:1
Pouillon, Nora 1943- **2005**:1
Povich, Maury 1939(?)- **1994**:3
Powell, Colin 1937- **1990**:1
Powell, Lewis F. 1907-1998
  Obituary **1999**:1
Pratt, Jane 1963(?)- **1999**:1
Predock, Antoine 1936- **1993**:2
Preminger, Otto 1906-1986
  Obituary **1986**:3
Presley, Lisa Marie 1968- **2004**:3
Presley, Pricilla 1945- **2001**:1
Presser, Jackie 1926-1988
  Obituary **1988**:4

Pressler, Paul 1956(?)- **2003**:4
Preston, Billy 1946-2006
  Obituary **2007**:3
Preston, Robert 1918-1987
  Obituary **1987**:3
Prevor, Barry and Steven Shore **2006**:2
Price, Lisa 1962- **2010**:2
Price, Sol 1916-2009
  Obituary **2011**:4
Price, Vincent 1911-1993
  Obituary **1994**:2
Pride, Charley 1938(?)- **1998**:1
Priestly, Jason 1970(?)- **1993**:2
Prince 1958- **1995**:3
Prince, Faith 1959(?)- **1993**:2
Prinze, Freddie, Jr. 1976- **1999**:3
Pritzker, A.N. 1896-1986
  Obituary **1986**:2
Probst, Jeff 1962- **2011**:2
Probst, Larry 1951(?)- **2005**:1
Proctor, Barbara Gardner 1933(?)- **1985**:3
Profet, Margie 1958- **1994**:4
Proulx, E. Annie 1935- **1996**:1
Prowse, Juliet 1937-1996
  Obituary **1997**:1
Prusiner, Stanley 1942- **1998**:2
Pryce, Deborah 1951- **2006**:3
Pryor, Richard **1999**:3
Public Enemy **1992**:1
Puccio, Thomas P. 1944- **1986**:4
Puck, Theodore 1916-2005
  Obituary **2007**:1
Puck, Wolfgang 1949- **1990**:1
Puckett, Kirby 1960-2006
  Obituary **2007**:2
Puente, Tito 1923-2000
  Obituary **2000**:4
Pujols, Albert 1980- **2005**:3
Puleston, Dennis 1905-2001
  Obituary **2002**:2
Puryear, Martin 1941- **2002**:4
Puzo, Mario 1920-1999
  Obituary **2000**:1
Pynchon, Thomas 1937- **1997**:4
Quaid, Dennis 1954- **1989**:4
Quayle, Dan 1947- **1989**:2
Queen Latifah 1970(?)- **1992**:2
Queer Eye for the Straight Guy cast **2004**:3
Querrey, Sam 1987- **2010**:3
Questrom, Allen 1940- **2001**:4
Quill, Timothy E. 1949- **1997**:3
Quindlen, Anna 1952- **1993**:1
Quinlan, Karen Ann 1954-1985
  Obituary **1985**:2
Quinn, Anthony 1915-2001
  Obituary **2002**:2
Quinn, Jane Bryant 1939(?)- **1993**:4
Quinn, Martha 1959- **1986**:4
Quivers, Robin 1953(?)- **1995**:4
Rabbitt, Eddie 1941-1998
  Obituary **1998**:4
Radecki, Thomas
  Brief entry **1986**:2
Radner, Gilda 1946-1989
  Obituary **1989**:4
Radocy, Robert
  Brief entry **1986**:3
Raimi, Sam 1959- **1999**:2
Raimondi, John

Brief entry **1987**:4
Raines, Franklin 1949- **1997**:4
Raitt, Bonnie 1949- **1990**:2
Raitt, John 1917-2005
   Obituary **2006**:2
Ramey, Estelle R. 1917-2006
   Obituary **2007**:4
Ramirez, Manny 1972- **2005**:4
Ramo, Roberta Cooper 1942- **1996**:1
Ramone, Joey 1951-2001
   Obituary **2002**:2
Rand, A. Barry 1944- **2000**:3
Randall, Lisa 1962- **2009**:2
Randall, Tony 1920-2004
   Obituary **2005**:3
Randi, James 1928- **1990**:2
Raphael, Sally Jessy 1943- **1992**:4
Rapp, C.J.
   Brief entry **1987**:3
Rascal Flatts **2007**:1
Rashad, Phylicia 1948- **1987**:3
Raskin, Jef 1943(?)- **1997**:4
Rauschenberg, Robert 1925- **1991**:2
Raven 1985- **2005**:1
Rawlings, Mike 1954- **2003**:1
Rawls, Lou 1933-2006
   Obituary **2007**:1
Ray, James Earl 1928-1998
   Obituary **1998**:4
Ray, Rachael 1968- **2007**:1
Raye, Martha 1916-1994
   Obituary **1995**:1
Raymond, Lee R. 1930- **2000**:3
Reagan, Ronald 1911-2004
   Obituary **2005**:3
Reasoner, Harry 1923-1991
   Obituary **1992**:1
Redenbacher, Orville 1907-1995
   Obituary **1996**:1
Redfield, James 1952- **1995**:2
Redford, Robert 1937- **1993**:2
Redig, Patrick 1948- **1985**:3
Redman, Joshua 1969- **1999**:2
Redmond, Tim 1947- **2008**:1
Redstone, Sumner 1923- **1994**:1
Reed, Dean 1939(?)-1986
   Obituary **1986**:3
Reed, Donna 1921-1986
   Obituary **1986**:1
Reed, Ralph 1961(?)- **1995**:1
Reed, Robert 1933(?)-1992
   Obituary **1992**:4
Reese, Della 1931- **1999**:2
Reese, Tracy 1964- **2010**:1
Reeve, Christopher 1952- **1997**:2
Reeves, Keanu 1964- **1992**:1
Reeves, Steve 1926-2000
   Obituary **2000**:4
Regan, Judith 1953- **2003**:1
Rehnquist, William H. 1924- **2001**:2
Reich, Robert 1946- **1995**:4
Reichs, Kathleen J. 1948- **2007**:3
Reid, Harry 1939- **2006**:1
Reilly, Charles Nelson
   Obituary **2008**:3
Reilly, John C. 1965- **2003**:4
Reiner, Rob 1947- **1991**:2
Reiser, Paul 1957- **1995**:2
Reitman, Jason 1977- **2011**:3
Remick, Lee 1936(?)-1991
   Obituary **1992**:1
Rendell, Ed 1944- **2010**:1

Reno, Janet 1938- **1993**:3
Retton, Mary Lou 1968- **1985**:2
Reubens, Paul 1952- **1987**:2
Reverend Ike 1935-2009
   Obituary **2010**:4
Rey, Margret E. 1906-1996
   Obituary **1997**:2
Reynolds, Paula Rosput 1956- **2008**:4
Reznor, Trent 1965- **2000**:2
Rhodes, Dusty 1927-2009
   Obituary **2010**:3
Ribicoff, Abraham 1910-1998
   Obituary **1998**:3
Ricci, Christina 1980- **1999**:1
Rice, Anne 1941- **1995**:1
Rice, Condoleezza 1954- **2002**:1
Rice, Jerry 1962- **1990**:4
Rice, Susan E. 1964- **2010**:3
Rich, Buddy 1917-1987
   Obituary **1987**:3
Rich, Charlie 1932-1995
   Obituary **1996**:1
Richards, Ann 1933- **1991**:2
Richards, Michael 1949(?)- **1993**:4
Richardson, Steve 1939- **2010**:4
Richmond, Julius B. 1916-2008
   Obituary **2009**:4
Richter, Charles Francis 1900-1985
   Obituary **1985**:4
Rickover, Hyman 1900-1986
   Obituary **1986**:4
Riddle, Nelson 1921-1985
   Obituary **1985**:4
Ridge, Tom 1945- **2002**:2
Rifkin, Jeremy 1945- **1990**:3
Riggio, Leonard S. 1941- **1999**:4
Riggs, Bobby 1918-1995
   Obituary **1996**:2
Rigopulos, Alex 1970- **2009**:4
Riley, Pat 1945- **1994**:3
Riley, Richard W. 1933- **1996**:3
Rimes, LeAnn 1982- **1997**:4
Riney, Hal 1932- **1989**:1
Ringgold, Faith 1930- **2000**:3
Ringwald, Molly 1968- **1985**:4
Riordan, Richard 1930- **1993**:4
Ripa, Kelly 1970- **2002**:2
Ripken, Cal, Jr. 1960- **1986**:2
Ripken, Cal, Sr. 1936(?)-1999
   Obituary **1999**:4
Ritchie, Dennis and Kenneth
   Thompson **2000**:1
Ritter, John 1948- **2003**:4
Ritts, Herb 1954(?)- **1992**:4
Rivera, Geraldo 1943- **1989**:1
Rivers, Joan 1933- **2005**:3
Rizzo, Frank 1920-1991
   Obituary **1992**:1
Robards, Jason 1922-2000
   Obituary **2001**:3
Robb, Charles S. 1939- **1987**:2
Robbins, Harold 1916-1997
   Obituary **1998**:1
Robbins, Jerome 1918-1998
   Obituary **1999**:1
Robbins, Tim 1959- **1993**:1
Roberts, Brian L. 1959- **2002**:4
Roberts, Cokie 1943- **1993**:4
Roberts, Doris 1930- **2003**:4
Roberts, Julia 1967- **1991**:3
Roberts, Nora 1950- **2010**:3
Roberts, Oral 1918-2009

Obituary **2011**:4
Roberts, Steven K. 1952(?)- **1992**:1
Roberts, Xavier 1955- **1985**:3
Robertson, Nan 1926-2009
   Obituary **2011**:2
Robertson, Pat 1930- **1988**:2
Robinson, David 1965- **1990**:4
Robinson, Earl 1910(?)-1991
   Obituary **1992**:1
Robinson, Eddie 1919-2007
   Obituary **2008**:2
Robinson, Frank 1935- **1990**:2
Robinson, Max 1939-1988
   Obituary **1989**:2
Robinson, Sugar Ray 1921-1989
   Obituary **1989**:3
Robinson, V. Gene 1947- **2004**:4
Roche, Kevin 1922- **1985**:1
Rock, Chris 1967(?)- **1998**:1
Rock, John
   Obituary **1985**:1
Rock, The 1972- **2001**:2
Rockwell, David 1956- **2003**:3
Roddenberry, Gene 1921-1991
   Obituary **1992**:2
Roddick, Andy 1982- **2004**:3
Rodin, Judith 1945(?)- **1994**:4
Rodman, Dennis 1961- **1991**:3
Rodriguez, Alex 1975- **2001**:2
Rodriguez, Narciso 1961- **2005**:1
Rodriguez, Robert 1968- **2005**:1
Roedy, Bill 1949(?)- **2003**:2
Roemer, Buddy 1943- **1991**:4
Rogers, Adrian 1931- **1987**:4
Rogers, Fred 1928- **2000**:4
Rogers, Ginger 1911(?)-1995
   Obituary **1995**:4
Rogers, Roy 1911-1998
   Obituary **1998**:4
Rogers, William P. 1913-2001
   Obituary **2001**:4
Roizen, Michael 1946- **2007**:4
Roker, Al 1954- **2003**:1
Roker, Roxie 1929(?)-1995
   Obituary **1996**:2
Rolle, Esther 1922-1998
   Obituary **1999**:2
Rollins, Henry 1961- **2007**:3
Rollins, Howard E., Jr. 1950- **1986**:1
Romano, Ray 1957- **2001**:4
Romijn, Rebecca 1972- **2007**:1
Romo, Tony 1980- **2008**:3
Roncal, Mally 1972- **2009**:4
Rooney, Art 1901-1988
   Obituary **1989**:1
Roosevelt, Franklin D., Jr. 1914-1988
   Obituary **1989**:1
Rose, Axl 1962(?)- **1992**:1
Rose, Charlie 1943- **1994**:2
Rose, Lela 1969- **2011**:1
Rose, Pete 1941- **1991**:1
Rosedale, Philip 1968- **2011**:3
Rosenberg, Evelyn 1942- **1988**:2
Rosenberg, Steven 1940- **1989**:1
Rosendahl, Bruce R.
   Brief entry **1986**:4
Rosenfeld, Irene 1953- **2008**:3
Rosenthal, Joseph 1911-2006
   Obituary **2007**:4
Rosenzweig, Ilene 1965(?)- **2004**:1
Rosgen, Dave 1942(?)- **2005**:2
Ros-Lehtinen, Ileana 1952- **2000**:2

Ross, Herbert 1927-2001
  Obituary **2002**:4
Ross, Percy
  Brief entry **1986**:2
Ross, Steven J. 1927-1992
  Obituary **1993**:3
Rossellini, Isabella 1952- **2001**:4
Rossner, Judith 1935-2005
  Obituary **2006**:4
Rosten, Leo 1908-1997
  Obituary **1997**:3
Roth, Philip 1933- **1999**:1
Roth, William Victor, Jr. 1921-2003
  Obituary **2005**:1
Rothenberg, Susan 1945- **1995**:3
Rothstein, Ruth **1988**:2
Rothwax, Harold 1930- **1996**:3
Rourke, Mickey 1956- **1988**:4
Rouse, James 1914-1996
  Obituary **1996**:4
Rove, Karl 1950- **2006**:2
Rowan, Carl 1925-2000
  Obituary **2001**:2
Rowan, Dan 1922-1987
  Obituary **1988**:1
Rowe, Jack 1944- **2005**:2
Rowe, Mike 1962- **2010**:2
Rowland, Pleasant **1992**:3
Rowley, Coleen 1955(?)- **2004**:2
Rowley, Cynthia 1958- **2002**:1
Roybal-Allard, Lucille 1941- **1999**:4
Royko, Mike 1932-1997
  Obituary **1997**:4
Rozelle, Pete 1926-1996
  Obituary **1997**:2
Rubin, Jerry 1938-1994
  Obituary **1995**:2
Rudd, Paul 1969- **2009**:4
Rudner, Rita 1956- **1993**:2
Rudnick, Paul 1957(?)- **1994**:3
Rudolph, Wilma 1940-1994
  Obituary **1995**:2
Ruehl, Mercedes 1948(?)- **1992**:4
Ruffalo, Mark 1967- **2011**:4
Ruffin, David 1941-1991
  Obituary **1991**:4
Rumsfeld, Donald 1932- **2004**:1
Runyan, Marla 1969- **2001**:1
RuPaul 1961(?)- **1996**:1
Ruppe, Loret Miller 1936- **1986**:2
Rusk, Dean 1909-1994
  Obituary **1995**:2
Russell, Keri 1976- **2000**:1
Russell, Kurt 1951- **2007**:4
Russell, Mary 1950- **2009**:2
Russell, Nipsey 1924-2005
  Obituary **2007**:1
Russert, Tim 1950-2008
  Obituary **2009**:3
Russo, Patricia 1952- **2008**:4
Russo, Rene 1954- **2000**:2
Russo, Richard 1949- **2002**:3
Rutan, Burt 1943- **1987**:2
Ryan, Meg 1962(?)- **1994**:1
Ryan, Nolan 1947- **1989**:4
Ryder, Winona 1971- **1991**:2
Saberhagen, Bret 1964- **1986**:1
Sachs, Jeffrey D. 1954- **2004**:4
Safire, William 1929- **2000**:3
Sagal, Katey 1954- **2005**:2
Sagan, Carl 1934-1996
  Obituary **1997**:2

Sagansky, Jeff 1952- **1993**:2
Sajak, Pat
  Brief entry **1985**:4
Salazar, Ken 1955- **2011**:4
Salbi, Zainab 1969(?)- **2008**:3
Saldana, Zoe 1978- **2010**:1
Salerno-Sonnenberg, Nadja 1961(?)-
  1988:4
Sales, Soupy 1926-2009
  Obituary **2011**:2
Salk, Jonas 1914-1995 **1994**:4
  Obituary **1995**:4
Salzman, Mark 1959- **2002**:1
Sammons, Mary 1946- **2007**:4
Sample, Bill
  Brief entry **1986**:2
Sampras, Pete 1971- **1994**:1
Sams, Craig 1944- **2007**:3
Samuelson, Paul 1915-2009
  Obituary **2011**:4
Sanchez, Loretta 1960- **2000**:3
Sanders, Barry 1968- **1992**:1
Sanders, Bernie 1941(?)- **1991**:4
Sanders, Deion 1967- **1992**:4
Sandler, Adam 1966- **1999**:2
Sanger, Steve 1946- **2002**:3
Saporta, Vicki
  Brief entry **1987**:3
Sapphire 1951(?)- **1996**:4
Saralegui, Cristina 1948- **1999**:2
Sarandon, Susan 1946- **1995**:3
Sarazen, Gene 1902-1999
  Obituary **1999**:4
Satcher, David 1941- **2001**:4
Satriani, Joe 1957(?)- **1989**:3
Saul, Betsy 1968- **2009**:2
Savage, Fred 1976- **1990**:1
Savalas, Telly 1924-1994
  Obituary **1994**:3
Sawyer, Diane 1945- **1994**:4
Scalia, Antonin 1936- **1988**:2
Scardino, Marjorie 1947- **2002**:1
Scavullo, Francesco 1921-2004
  Obituary **2005**:1
Schaap, Dick 1934-2001
  Obituary **2003**:1
Schaefer, William Donald 1921- **1988**
  :1
Schank, Roger 1946- **1989**:2
Scheck, Barry 1949- **2000**:4
Scheider, Roy 1932-2008
  Obituary **2009**:2
Schembechler, Bo 1929(?)- **1990**:3
Schenk, Dale 1957(?)- **2002**:2
Schiavo, Mary 1955- **1998**:2
Schilling, Curt 1966- **2002**:3
Schirra, Wally 1923-2007
  Obituary **2008**:3
Schlessinger, David
  Brief entry **1985**:1
Schlessinger, Laura 1947(?)- **1996**:3
Schmelzer, Sheri 1965- **2009**:4
Schmidt, Eric 1955- **2002**:4
Schmidt, Mike 1949- **1988**:3
Schnabel, Julian 1951- **1997**:1
Schneider, Rob 1965- **1997**:4
Schoenfeld, Gerald 1924- **1986**:2
Scholz, Tom 1949- **1987**:2
Schott, Marge 1928- **1985**:4
Schreiber, Liev 1967- **2007**:2
Schroeder, Barbet 1941- **1996**:1
Schroeder, William J. 1932-1986

  Obituary **1986**:4
Schulberg, Budd 1914-2009
  Obituary **2010**:4
Schultes, Richard Evans 1915-2001
  Obituary **2002**:1
Schultz, Howard 1953- **1995**:3
Schultz, Scott 1972-. See Christian
  Jacobs and Scott Schultz
Schulz, Charles 1922-2000
  Obituary **2000**:3
Schulz, Charles M. 1922- **1998**:1
Schumacher, Joel 1929- **2004**:3
Schuman, Patricia Glass 1943- **1993**
  :2
Schwab, Charles 1937(?)- **1989**:3
Schwartz, Allen 1945(?)- **2008**:2
Schwartz, David 1936(?)- **1988**:3
Schwarzenegger, Arnold 1947- **1991**
  :1
Schwarzkopf, Norman 1934- **1991**:3
Schwimmer, David 1966(?)- **1996**:2
Schwinn, Edward R., Jr.
  Brief entry **1985**:4
Scorsese, Martin 1942- **1989**:1
Scott, Gene
  Brief entry **1986**:1
Scott, George C. 1927-1999
  Obituary **2000**:2
Scott, H. Lee, Jr. 1949- **2008**:3
Scott, Jill 1972- **2010**:1
Scott, Pamella 1975- **2010**:4
Scott, Randolph 1898(?)-1987
  Obituary **1987**:2
Sculley, John 1939- **1989**:4
Seacrest, Ryan 1976- **2004**:4
Sears, Barry 1947- **2004**:2
Sebelius, Kathleen 1948- **2008**:4
Sebold, Alice 1963(?)- **2005**:4
Secretariat 1970-1989
  Obituary **1990**:1
Sedaris, Amy 1961- **2009**:3
Sedaris, David 1956- **2005**:3
Sedelmaier, Joe 1933- **1985**:3
Sedgwick, Kyra 1965- **2006**:2
See, Lisa 1955- **2010**:4
Segal, Shelden 1926-2009
  Obituary **2011**:2
Segal, Shelli 1955(?)- **2005**:3
Seger, Bob 1945- **1987**:1
Seidelman, Susan 1953(?)- **1985**:4
Seidenberg, Ivan 1946- **2004**:1
Seinfeld, Jerry 1954- **1992**:4
Selena 1971-1995
  Obituary **1995**:4
Selig, Bud 1934- **1995**:2
Semel, Terry 1943- **2002**:2
Senk, Glen 1956- **2009**:3
Seo, Danny 1977- **2008**:3
Serra, Richard 1939- **2009**:1
Serrano, Andres 1950- **2000**:4
Serros, Michele 1967(?)- **2008**:2
Sethi, Simran 1971(?)- **2008**:1
Sevareid, Eric 1912-1992
  Obituary **1993**:1
Sevigny, Chloe 1974- **2001**:4
Sexton, John 1942- **2011**:4
Seyfried, Amanda 1985- **2009**:3
Shabazz, Betty 1936-1997
  Obituary **1997**:4
Shaich, Ron 1953- **2004**:4
Shakur, Tupac 1971-1996
  Obituary **1997**:1

Shalala, Donna 1941- **1992**:3
Shalikashvili, John 1936- **1994**:2
Shandling, Garry 1949- **1995**:1
Shanley, John Patrick 1950- **2006**:1
Sharkey, Ray 1953-1993
    Obituary **1994**:1
Sharpe, Sterling 1965- **1994**:3
Sharpton, Al 1954- **1991**:2
Shaw, Artie 1910-2004
    Obituary **2006**:1
Shaw, Carol 1958(?)- **2002**:1
Shaw, William 1934(?)- **2000**:3
Shawn, Dick 1924(?)-1987
    Obituary **1987**:3
Shawn, William 1907-1992
    Obituary **1993**:3
Shea, Jim, Jr. 1968- **2002**:4
Sheedy, Ally 1962- **1989**:1
Sheehan, Daniel P. 1945(?)- **1989**:1
Sheen, Charlie 1965- **2001**:2
Sheen, Martin 1940- **2002**:1
Sheffield, Gary 1968- **1998**:1
Sheindlin, Judith 1942(?)- **1999**:1
Sheldon, Sidney 1917-2007
    Obituary **2008**:2
Shepard, Alan 1923-1998
    Obituary **1999**:1
Shepard, Sam 1943- **1996**:4
Shepherd, Cybill 1950- **1996**:3
Sherman, Cindy 1954- **1992**:3
Sherman, Russell 1930- **1987**:4
Shields, Brooke 1965- **1996**:3
Shields, Carol 1935-2003
    Obituary **2004**:3
Shilts, Randy 1951-1994 **1993**:4
    Obituary **1994**:3
Shimomura, Tsutomu 1965- **1996**:1
Shirley, Donna 1941- **1999**:1
Shocked, Michelle 1963(?)- **1989**:4
Shoemaker, Bill 1931-2003
    Obituary **2004**:4
Shore, Dinah 1917-1994
    Obituary **1994**:3
Shreve, Anita 1946(?)- **2003**:4
Shriver, Eunice 1921-2009
    Obituary **2011**:1
Shriver, Lionel 1957- **2008**:4
Shriver, Maria
    Brief entry **1986**:2
Shue, Andrew 1964- **1994**:4
Shula, Don 1930- **1992**:2
Shulman, Julius 1910-2009
    Obituary **2010**:4
Shyamalan, M. Night 1970- **2003**:2
Sidney, Ivan
    Brief entry **1987**:2
Sidransky, David 1960- **2002**:4
Siebert, Muriel 1932(?)- **1987**:2
Sigmund, Barbara Boggs 1939-1990
    Obituary **1991**:1
Silber, Joan 1945- **2009**:4
Silber, John 1926- **1990**:1
Silva, Daniel 1960- **2010**:1
Silverman, Jonathan 1966- **1997**:2
Silverman, Sarah 1970- **2008**:1
Silvers, Phil 1912-1985
    Obituary **1985**:4
Silverstein, Shel 1932-1999
    Obituary **1999**:4
Silverstone, Alicia 1976- **1997**:4
Simmons, Adele Smith 1941- **1988**:4
Simmons, Laurie 1949- **2010**:1

Simmons, Russell and Kimora Lee
    2003:2
Simmons, Ruth 1945- **1995**:2
Simon, Lou Anna K. 1947- **2005**:4
Simon, Paul 1928-2003
    Obituary **2005**:1
Simon, Paul 1942(?)- **1992**:2
Simone, Nina 1933-2003
    Obituary **2004**:2
Simpson, Lorna 1960- **2008**:1
Simpson, Wallis 1896-1986
    Obituary **1986**:3
Simpson-Wentz, Ashlee 1984- **2009**:1
Sinatra, Frank 1915-1998
    Obituary **1998**:4
Sinclair, Mary 1918- **1985**:2
Singer, Bryan 1965- **2007**:3
Singer, Isaac Bashevis 1904-1991
    Obituary **1992**:1
Singer, Margaret Thaler 1921-2003
    Obituary **2005**:1
Singleton, John 1968- **1994**:3
Sinise, Gary 1955(?)- **1996**:1
Sirica, John 1904-1992
    Obituary **1993**:2
Siskel, Gene 1946-1999
    Obituary **1999**:3
Sizer, Theodore 1932-2009
    Obituary **2011**:2
Skaist-Levy, Pam and Gela Taylor
    2005:1
Skelton, Red 1913-1997
    Obituary **1998**:1
Skinner, B.F. 1904-1990
    Obituary **1991**:1
Skinner, Sam 1938- **1992**:3
Slater, Christian 1969- **1994**:1
Slater, Rodney E. 1955- **1997**:4
Slatkin, Harry 1961(?)- **2006**:2
Slaughter, Karin 1971- **2010**:3
Slick, Grace 1939- **2001**:2
Slotnick, Barry
    Brief entry **1987**:4
Smale, John G. 1927- **1987**:3
Smigel, Robert 1959(?)- **2001**:3
Smiley, Jane 1949- **1995**:4
Smiley, Tavis 1964- **2010**:3
Smith, Anna Deavere 1950- **2002**:2
Smith, Anna Nicole 1967-2007
    Obituary **2008**:2
Smith, Buffalo Bob 1917-1998
    Obituary **1999**:1
Smith, Emmitt **1994**:1
Smith, Frederick W. 1944- **1985**:4
Smith, Howard K. 1914-2002
    Obituary **2003**:2
Smith, Jack 1938- **1994**:3
Smith, Jeff 1939(?)- **1991**:4
Smith, Jerry 1943-1986
    Obituary **1987**:1
Smith, Jimmy 1928-2005
    Obituary **2006**:2
Smith, Kate 1907(?)-1986
    Obituary **1986**:3
Smith, Kevin 1970- **2000**:4
Smith, Lanty 1942- **2009**:3
Smith, Roger 1925- **1990**:3
Smith, Samantha 1972-1985
    Obituary **1985**:3
Smith, Will 1968- **1997**:2
Smith, Willi 1948-1987
    Obituary **1987**:3

Smits, Jimmy 1956- **1990**:1
Smoltz, John 1967- **2010**:3
Smoot, George F. 1945- **1993**:3
Smyth, Russell P. 1958- **2009**:4
Snead, Sam 1912-2002
    Obituary **2003**:3
Snider, Dee 1955- **1986**:1
Snider, Stacey 1961(?)- **2002**:4
Snipes, Wesley 1962- **1993**:1
Snoop Doggy Dogg 1972(?)- **1995**:2
Snow, Hank 1914-1999
    Obituary **2000**:3
Snow, John W. 1939- **2006**:2
Snow, Tony 1955-2008
    Obituary **2009**:3
Snowe, Olympia 1947- **1995**:3
Snyder, Jimmy 1919-1996
    Obituary **1996**:4
Snyder, Mitch 1944(?)-1990
    Obituary **1991**:1
Snyder, Ron 1956(?)- **2007**:4
Sobieski, Leelee 1982- **2002**:3
Sobol, Donald J. 1924- **2004**:4
Soderbergh, Steven 1963- **2001**:4
Solis, Hilda 1957- **2010**:1
Som, Peter 1971- **2009**:1
Somers, Suzanne 1946- **2000**:1
Sondheim, Stephen 1930- **1994**:4
Sontag, Susan 1933-2004
    Obituary **2006**:1
Soren, David
    Brief entry **1986**:3
Sorkin, Aaron 1961- **2003**:2
Sorvino, Mira 1970(?)- **1996**:3
Sothern, Ann 1909-2001
    Obituary **2002**:1
Sotomayor, Sonia 1954- **2010**:4
Souter, David 1939- **1991**:3
Southern, Terry 1926-1995
    Obituary **1996**:2
Sowell, Thomas 1930- **1998**:3
Spacek, Sissy 1949- **2003**:1
Spacey, Kevin 1959- **1996**:4
Spade, David 1965- **1999**:2
Spade, Kate 1962- **2003**:1
Spader, James 1960- **1991**:2
Spahn, Warren 1921-2003
    Obituary **2005**:1
Sparks, Nicholas 1965- **2010**:1
Spears, Britney 1981- **2000**:3
Spector, Phil 1940- **1989**:1
Spelke, Elizabeth 1949- **2003**:1
Spelling, Aaron 1923-2006
    Obituary **2007**:3
Spelling, Tori 1973- **2008**:3
Spellings, Margaret 1957- **2005**:4
Spergel, David 1961- **2004**:1
Spheeris, Penelope 1945(?)- **1989**:2
Spiegelman, Art 1948- **1998**:3
Spielberg, Steven 1947- **1993**:4
Spillane, Mickey 1918-2006
    Obituary **2007**:3
Spitzer, Eliot 1959- **2007**:2
Spitzer, Silda Wall 1957- **2010**:2
Spock, Benjamin 1903-1998 **1995**:2
    Obituary **1998**:3
Spong, John 1931- **1991**:3
Spray, Ed 1941- **2004**:1
Sprewell, Latrell 1970- **1999**:4
Springsteen, Bruce 1949- **2011**:1
Sprouse, Stephen 1953-2004
    Obituary **2005**:2

St. James, Lyn 1947- **1993**:2
Stack, Robert 1919-2003
    Obituary **2004**:2
Stafford, Jo 1917-2008
    Obituary **2009**:3
Stahl, Lesley 1941- **1997**:1
Stallings, George A., Jr. 1948- **1990**:1
Stallone, Sylvester 1946- **1994**:2
Stamos, John 1963- **2008**:1
Staples, Roebuck Pops 1915-2000
    Obituary **2001**:3
Stapleton, Maureen 1925-2006
    Obituary **2007**:2
Stargell, Willie 1940-2001
    Obituary **2002**:1
Starr, Kenneth 1946- **1998**:3
Steel, Danielle 1947- **1999**:2
Steel, Dawn 1946-1997 **1990**:1
    Obituary **1998**:2
Steele, Michael 1958- **2010**:2
Steele, Shelby 1946- **1991**:2
Stefani, Gwen 1969- **2005**:4
Steger, Will 1945(?)- **1990**:4
Steig, William 1907-2003
    Obituary **2004**:4
Steiger, Rod 1925-2002
    Obituary **2003**:4
Stein, Ben 1944- **2001**:1
Steinberg, Leigh 1949- **1987**:3
Steinbrenner, George 1930- **1991**:1
Steinem, Gloria 1934- **1996**:2
Stella, Frank 1936- **1996**:2
Stempel, Robert 1933- **1991**:3
Stephanopoulos, George 1961- **1994** :3
Sterling, Bruce 1954- **1995**:4
Stern, David 1942- **1991**:4
Stern, Howard 1954- **1988**:2
Stern, Isaac 1920-2001
    Obituary **2002**:4
Stevens, Anne 1949(?)- **2006**:3
Stevens, Eileen 1939- **1987**:3
Stevenson, McLean 1929-1996
    Obituary **1996**:3
Stewart, Dave 1957- **1991**:1
Stewart, Jimmy 1908-1997
    Obituary **1997**:4
Stewart, Jon 1962- **2001**:2
Stewart, Julia 1955- **2008**:3
Stewart, Martha 1942(?)- **1992**:1
Stewart, Payne 1957-1999
    Obituary **2000**:2
Stewart, Potter 1915-1985
    Obituary **1986**:1
Stewart, Tony 1971- **2003**:4
Stiles, Julia 1981- **2002**:3
Stiller, Ben 1965- **1999**:1
Stine, R. L. 1943- **2003**:1
Stockton, John Houston 1962- **1997**:3
Stockton, Shreve 1977- **2009**:4
Stofflet, Ty
    Brief entry **1987**:1
Stokes, Carl 1927-1996
    Obituary **1996**:4
Stone, I.F. 1907-1989
    Obituary **1990**:1
Stone, Irving 1903-1989
    Obituary **1990**:2
Stone, Oliver 1946- **1990**:4
Stone, Sharon 1958- **1993**:4
Stonesifer, Patty 1956- **1997**:1
Storm, Gale 1922-2009

Obituary **2010**:4
Strait, George 1952- **1998**:3
Strange, Curtis 1955- **1988**:4
Strauss, Robert 1918- **1991**:4
Streep, Meryl 1949- **1990**:2
Street, Picabo 1971- **1999**:3
Streisand, Barbra 1942- **1992**:2
Stritch, Elaine 1925- **2002**:4
Stroh, Peter W. 1927- **1985**:2
Stroman, Susan **2000**:4
Strout, Elizabeth 1956- **2009**:1
Strug, Kerri 1977- **1997**:3
Studi, Wes 1944(?)- **1994**:3
Styne, Jule 1905-1994
    Obituary **1995**:1
Styron, William 1925-2006
    Obituary **2008**:1
Suarez, Xavier
    Brief entry **1986**:2
Suckling, Kierán 1964- **2009**:2
Sugarland 1970- **2009**:2
Sui, Anna 1955(?)- **1995**:1
Sullivan, Leon 1922-2001
    Obituary **2002**:2
Sullivan, Louis 1933- **1990**:4
Sulzberger, Arthur O., Jr. 1951- **1998** :3
Summitt, Pat 1952- **2004**:1
Sun Ra 1914(?)-1993
    Obituary **1994**:1
Sununu, John 1939- **1989**:2
Susskind, David 1920-1987
    Obituary **1987**:2
Sutphen, Mona 1967- **2010**:4
Sutton, Percy 1920-2009
    Obituary **2011**:4
Swaggart, Jimmy 1935- **1987**:3
Swank, Hilary 1974- **2000**:3
Swanson, Mary Catherine 1944- **2002**:2
Swayze, John Cameron 1906-1995
    Obituary **1996**:1
Swayze, Patrick 1952-2009
    Obituary **2011**:1
Sweeney, Alison 1976- **2010**:1
Sweeney, John J. 1934- **2000**:3
Swift, Jane 1965(?)- **2002**:1
Swift, Taylor 1989- **2009**:3
Swoopes, Sheryl 1971- **1998**:2
Sykes, Wanda 1964- **2007**:4
System of a Down **2006**:4
Szent-Gyoergyi, Albert 1893-1986
    Obituary **1987**:2
T. I. 1980- **2008**:1
Tafel, Richard 1962- **2000**:4
Tagliabue, Paul 1940- **1990**:2
Tan, Amy 1952- **1998**:3
Tandy, Jessica 1901-1994 **1990**:4
    Obituary **1995**:1
Tannen, Deborah 1945- **1995**:1
Tanny, Vic 1912(?)-1985
    Obituary **1985**:3
Tarantino, Quentin 1963(?)- **1995**:1
Tarkenian, Jerry 1930- **1990**:4
Tartakovsky, Genndy 1970- **2004**:4
Tartikoff, Brandon 1949-1997 **1985**:2
    Obituary **1998**:1
Tartt, Donna 1963- **2004**:3
Tatum, Channing 1980- **2011**:3
Taylor, Jeff 1960- **2001**:3
Taylor, Koko 1928-2009
    Obituary **2010**:3

Taylor, Lawrence 1959- **1987**:3
Taylor, Lili 1967- **2000**:2
Taylor, Maxwell 1901-1987
    Obituary **1987**:3
Taylor, Paul 1930- **1992**:3
Taylor, Susan L. 1946- **1998**:2
Tellem, Nancy 1953(?)- **2004**:4
Tenet, George 1953- **2000**:3
Terkel, Studs 1912-2008
    Obituary **2010**:1
Terry, Randall **1991**:4
Tesh, John 1952- **1996**:3
Testaverde, Vinny 1962- **1987**:2
Teter, Hannah 1987- **2006**:4
Thain, John 1955- **2009**:2
Thalheimer, Richard 1948-
    Brief entry **1988**:3
Tharp, Twyla 1942- **1992**:4
Thiebaud, Wayne 1920- **1991**:1
Third Day 1976- **2011**:2
Thomas, Betty 1948- **2011**:4
Thomas, Clarence 1948- **1992**:2
Thomas, Danny 1914-1991
    Obituary **1991**:3
Thomas, Dave **1986**:2
    Obituary **2003**:1
Thomas, Debi 1967- **1987**:2
Thomas, Derrick 1967-2000
    Obituary **2000**:3
Thomas, Edmond J. 1943(?)- **2005**:1
Thomas, Frank 1968- **1994**:3
Thomas, Helen 1920- **1988**:4
Thomas, Isiah 1961- **1989**:2
Thomas, Michael Tilson 1944- **1990**:3
Thomas, Michel 1911(?)- **1987**:4
Thomas, Thurman 1966- **1993**:1
Thomas-Graham, Pamela 1963- **2007** :1
Thompson, Fred 1942- **1998**:2
Thompson, Hunter S. 1939- **1992**:1
Thompson, John 1941- **1988**:3
Thompson, John W. 1949- **2005**:1
Thompson, Lonnie 1948- **2003**:3
Thompson, Starley
    Brief entry **1987**:3
Thomson, James 1958- **2002**:3
Thornton, Billy Bob 1956(?)- **1997**:4
Thurman, Uma 1970- **1994**:2
Thurmond, Strom 1902-2003
    Obituary **2004**:3
Tiffany 1972- **1989**:1
Tillman, Robert L. 1944(?)- **2004**:1
Tillstrom, Burr 1917-1985
    Obituary **1986**:1
Tilly, Jennifer 1958(?)- **1997**:2
Timbaland 1971- **2007**:4
Timberlake, Justin 1981- **2008**:4
Tisch, Laurence A. 1923- **1988**:2
Tischler, Joyce 1956- **2011**:3
Tisdale, Wayman 1964-2009
    Obituary **2010**:3
Tito, Dennis 1940(?)- **2002**:1
TLC **1996**:1
Toguri, Iva 1916-2006
    Obituary **2007**:4
Tohe, Laura 1953- **2009**:2
Tom and Ray Magliozzi **1991**:4
Tomei, Marisa 1964- **1995**:2
Tompkins, Susie
    Brief entry **1987**:2
Tone-Loc 1966- **1990**:3
Toomer, Ron 1930- **1990**:1

Zemeckis, Robert 1952- **2002**:1
Zerhouni, Elias A. 1951- **2004**:3
Zetcher, Arnold B. 1940- **2002**:1
Zevon, Warren 1947-2003
  Obituary **2004**:4
Ziff, William B., Jr. 1930- **1986**:4
Zigler, Edward 1930- **1994**:1
Zinnemann, Fred 1907-1997
  Obituary **1997**:3
Zinni, Anthony 1943- **2003**:1
Ziskin, Laura 1950- **2008**:2
Zito, Barry 1978- **2003**:3
Zoe, Rachel 1971- **2010**:2
Zucker, Jeff 1965(?)- **1993**:3
Zucker, Jerry 1950- **2002**:2
Zuckerberg, Mark 1984- **2008**:2
Zuckerman, Mortimer 1937- **1986**:3
Zwilich, Ellen 1939- **1990**:1

ANGOLAN
  Savimbi, Jonas 1934- **1986**:2

ARGENTINIAN
  Barenboim, Daniel 1942- **2001**:1
  Bocca, Julio 1967- **1995**:3
  Duhalde, Eduardo 1941- **2003**:3
  Fernández de Kirchner, Cristina
    1953- **2009**:1
  Herrera, Paloma 1975- **1996**:2
  Maradona, Diego 1961(?)- **1991**:3
  Pelli, Cesar 1927(?)- **1991**:4
  Sabatini, Gabriela
    Brief entry **1985**:4
  Sosa, Mercedes 1935-2009
    Obituary **2011**:2
  Timmerman, Jacobo 1923-1999
    Obituary **2000**:3

ARMENIAN
  Sargsyan, Serzh 1954- **2009**:3

AUSTRALIAN
  AC/DC Grammy Awards- **2011**:2
  Allen, Peter 1944-1992
    Obituary **1993**:1
  Allenby, Robert 1971- **2007**:1
  Anderson, Judith 1899(?)-1992
    Obituary **1992**:3
  Baker, Simon 1969- **2009**:4
  Bee Gees, The **1997**:4
  Blackburn, Elizabeth 1948- **2010**:1
  Blanchett, Cate 1969- **1999**:3
  Bloom, Natalie 1971- **2007**:1
  Bond, Alan 1938- **1989**:2
  Bradman, Sir Donald 1908-2001
    Obituary **2002**:1
  Bright, Torah 1986- **2010**:2
  Byrne, Rhonda 1955- **2008**:2
  Clavell, James 1924(?)-1994
    Obituary **1995**:1
  Collette, Toni 1972- **2009**:4
  Freeman, Cathy 1973- **2001**:3
  Gibb, Andy 1958-1988
    Obituary **1988**:3
  Gibson, Mel 1956- **1990**:1
  Gillard, Julia 1961- **2011**:4
  Helfgott, David 1937(?)- **1997**:2
  Hewitt, Lleyton 1981- **2002**:2
  Hughes, Robert 1938- **1996**:4

Humphries, Barry 1934- **1993**:1
Hutchence, Michael 1960-1997
  Obituary **1998**:1
Irwin, Steve 1962- **2001**:2
Jackman, Hugh 1968- **2004**:4
Kidman, Nicole 1967- **1992**:4
Klensch, Elsa **2001**:4
Larbalestier, Justine 1968(?)- **2008**:4
Ledger, Heath 1979- **2006**:3
Luhrmann, Baz 1962- **2002**:3
McMahon, Julian 1968- **2006**:1
Minogue, Kylie 1968- **2003**:4
Mueck, Ron 1958- **2008**:3
Murdoch, Rupert 1931- **1988**:4
Norman, Greg 1955- **1988**:3
Powter, Susan 1957(?)- **1994**:3
Rafter, Patrick 1972- **2001**:1
Rudd, Kevin 1957- **2009**:1
Rush, Geoffrey 1951- **2002**:1
Stone, Curtis 1975- **2011**:3
Summers, Anne 1945- **1990**:2
Travers, P.L. 1899(?)-1996
  Obituary **1996**:4
Tyler, Richard 1948(?)- **1995**:3
Urban, Keith 1967- **2006**:3
Webb, Karrie 1974- **2000**:4

AUSTRIAN
  Brabeck-Letmathe, Peter 1944- **2001**:4
  Brandauer, Klaus Maria 1944- **1987**:3
  Djerassi, Carl 1923- **2000**:4
  Drucker, Peter F. 1909- **1992**:3
  Falco
    Brief entry **1987**:2
  Frankl, Viktor E. 1905-1997
    Obituary **1998**:1
  Hrabal, Bohumil 1914-1997
    Obituary **1997**:3
  Jelinek, Elfriede 1946- **2005**:3
  Lamarr, Hedy 1913-2000
    Obituary **2000**:3
  Lang, Helmut 1956- **1999**:2
  Lorenz, Konrad 1903-1989
    Obituary **1989**:3
  Mateschitz, Dietrich 1944- **2008**:1
  Perutz, Max 1914-2002
    Obituary **2003**:2
  Porsche, Ferdinand 1909-1998
    Obituary **1998**:4
  Pouillon, Nora 1943- **2005**:1
  Puck, Wolfgang 1949- **1990**:1
  Strobl, Fritz 1972- **2003**:3
  von Karajan, Herbert 1908-1989
    Obituary **1989**:4
  von Trapp, Maria 1905-1987
    Obituary **1987**:3
  Waltz, Christoph 1956- **2011**:1
  Wiesenthal, Simon 1908-2005
    Obituary **2006**:4

AZERI
  Aliyev, Ilham 1961- **2010**:2

BANGLADESHI
  Nasrin, Taslima 1962- **1995**:1
  Yunus, Muhammad 1940- **2007**:3

BARBADIAN
  Rihanna 1988- **2008**:4

BELARUSSIAN
  Lukashenko, Alexander 1954- **2006**:4

BELGIAN
  Clijsters, Kim 1983- **2006**:3
  Henin-Hardenne, Justine 1982- **2004**:4
  Hepburn, Audrey 1929-1993
    Obituary **1993**:2
  Verhofstadt, Guy 1953- **2006**:3
  von Furstenberg, Diane 1946- **1994**:2

BENGALI
  Khan, Ali 1922-2009
    Obituary **2010**:3

BOLIVIAN
  Morales, Evo 1959- **2007**:2
  Sanchez de Lozada, Gonzalo 1930- **2004**:3

BOSNIAN
  Izetbegovic, Alija 1925- **1996**:4

BRAZILIAN
  Bundchen, Gisele 1980- **2009**:1
  Cardoso, Fernando Henrique 1931- **1996**:4
  Castaneda, Carlos 1931-1998
    Obituary **1998**:4
  Castroneves, Helio 1975- **2010**:1
  Collor de Mello, Fernando 1949- **1992**:4
  Costa, Francisco 1961- **2010**:2
  Fittipaldi, Emerson 1946- **1994**:2
  Ronaldinho 1980- **2007**:3
  Ronaldo 1976- **1999**:2
  Salgado, Sebastiao 1944- **1994**:2
  Senna, Ayrton 1960(?)-1994 **1991**:4
    Obituary **1994**:4
  Silva, Luiz Inacio Lula da 1945- **2003**:4
  Szot, Paulo 1969- **2009**:3
  Xuxa 1963(?)- **1994**:2

BRITISH
  Adamson, George 1906-1989
    Obituary **1990**:2
  Adele 1988- **2009**:4
  Baddeley, Hermione 1906(?)-1986
    Obituary **1986**:4
  Beck, Jeff 1944- **2011**:4
  Beckett, Wendy (Sister) 1930- **1998**:3
  Boyle, Danny 1956- **2009**:4
  Bradford, Chris 1937- **2011**:1
  Brand, Russell 1975- **2010**:2
  Branson, Richard 1951- **1987**:1
  Butler, Gerard 1969- **2011**:2
  Chatwin, Bruce 1940-1989
    Obituary **1989**:2
  Clarke, Arthur C. 1917-2008
    Obituary **2009**:2
  Cleese, John 1939- **1989**:2
  Cummings, Sam 1927- **1986**:3
  Dalton, Timothy 1946- **1988**:4
  Dancy, Hugh 1975- **2010**:3
  David Neville and Marcus
    Wainwright 1976- **2010**:3
  Davison, Ian Hay 1931- **1986**:1
  Day-Lewis, Daniel 1957- **1989**:4

Dench, Judi 1934- **1999**:4
Depeche Mode 1961- **2010**:3
Egan, John 1939- **1987**:2
Eliasch, Johan 1962- **2011**:3
Emin, Tracey 1963- **2009**:2
Eno, Brian 1948- **1986**:2
Ferguson, Sarah 1959- **1990**:3
Fiennes, Ranulph 1944- **1990**:3
Foster, Norman 1935- **1999**:4
Gaiman, Neil 1960- **2010**:1
Gift, Roland 1960(?)- **1990**:2
Goodall, Jane 1934- **1991**:1
Granger, Clive 1934-2009
    Obituary **2010**:3
Gray, Simon 1936-2008
    Obituary **2009**:4
Gregory, Philippa 1954- **2010**:1
Greiner, Helen 1967- **2010**:2
Griffith, Nicola 1960- **2010**:2
Grylls, Bear 1974- **2010**:2
Hamilton, Hamish 1900-1988
    Obituary **1988**:4
Harrison, Rex 1908-1990
    Obituary **1990**:4
Hawking, Stephen W. 1942- **1990**:1
Hawkins, Sally 1976- **2009**:4
Henderson, Tom **2011**:2
Hockney, David 1937- **1988**:3
Hoskins, Bob 1942- **1989**:1
Hounsfield, Godfrey 1919- **1989**:2
Howard, Trevor 1916-1988
    Obituary **1988**:2
Ireland, Jill 1936-1990
    Obituary **1990**:4
Ive, Jonathan 1967- **2009**:2
Judas Priest 1951- **2011**:3
Knopfler, Mark 1949- **1986**:2
Laing, R.D. 1927-1989
    Obituary **1990**:1
Lawrence, Ruth
    Brief entry **1986**:3
Leach, Robin 1942(?)-
    Brief entry **1985**:4
Lennox, Annie 1954- **1985**:4
Livingstone, Ken 1945- **1988**:3
Lloyd Webber, Andrew 1948- **1989**:1
Lythgoe, Nigel 1949- **2010**:4
Macmillan, Harold 1894-1986
    Obituary **1987**:2
MacMillan, Kenneth 1929-1992
    Obituary **1993**:2
Mantel, Hilary 1952- **2011**:2
Maxwell, Robert 1923- **1990**:1
Michael, George 1963- **1989**:2
Milne, Christopher Robin 1920-1996
    Obituary **1996**:4
Moore, Henry 1898-1986
    Obituary **1986**:4
Murdoch, Iris 1919-1999
    Obituary **1999**:4
Norrington, Roger 1934- **1989**:4
Oldman, Gary 1958- **1998**:1
Olivier, Laurence 1907-1989
    Obituary **1989**:4
Page, Dick 1955- **2010**:1
Pattinson, Robert 1986- **2010**:1
Philby, Kim 1912-1988
    Obituary **1988**:3
Radiohead **2009**:3
Rattle, Simon 1955- **1989**:4
Redgrave, Vanessa 1937- **1989**:2
Rhodes, Zandra 1940- **1986**:2

Richardson, Natasha 1963-2009
    Obituary **2010**:2
Roddick, Anita 1943(?)- **1989**:4
Runcie, Robert 1921-2000 **1989**:4
    Obituary **2001**:1
Rylance, Mark 1960- **2009**:3
Saatchi, Charles 1943- **1987**:3
Scott Thomas, Kristin 1960- **2010**:2
Steptoe, Patrick 1913-1988
    Obituary **1988**:3
Stevens, James
    Brief entry **1988**:1
Thatcher, Margaret 1925- **1989**:2
Tudor, Antony 1908(?)-1987
    Obituary **1987**:4
Ullman, Tracey 1961- **1988**:3
Wilson, Peter C. 1913-1984
    Obituary **1985**:2
Wintour, Anna 1949- **1990**:4
Woodward, Edward 1930-2009
    Obituary **2011**:3
Wright, Richard 1943-2008
    Obituary **2009**:4

BRUNEI
    Bolkiah, Sultan Muda Hassanal
        1946- **1985**:4

BULGARIAN
    Christo 1935- **1992**:3
    Dimitrova, Ghena 1941- **1987**:1

BURMESE
    Suu Kyi, Aung San 1945(?)- **1996**:2

CAMBODIAN
    Lon Nol
        Obituary **1986**:1
    Pol Pot 1928-1998
        Obituary **1998**:4

CAMEROONIAN
    Biya, Paul 1933- **2006**:1

CANADIAN
    Altman, Sidney 1939- **1997**:2
    Arbour, Louise 1947- **2005**:1
    Atwood, Margaret 1939- **2001**:2
    Balsillie, Jim and Mike Lazaridis
        2006:4
    Barenaked Ladies **1997**:2
    Black, Conrad 1944- **1986**:2
    Bouchard, Lucien 1938- **1999**:2
    Bourassa, Robert 1933-1996
        Obituary **1997**:1
    Bourque, Raymond Jean 1960- **1997**
        :3
    Buble, Michael 1975- **2010**:4
    Burr, Raymond 1917-1993
        Obituary **1994**:1
    Campbell, Kim 1947- **1993**:4
    Campbell, Neve 1973- **1998**:2
    Campeau, Robert 1923- **1990**:1
    Candy, John 1950-1994 **1988**:2
        Obituary **1994**:3
    Carrey, Jim 1962- **1995**:1
    Cavanagh, Tom 1968- **2003**:1
    Cerovsek, Corey
        Brief entry **1987**:4
    Charney, Dov 1969- **2008**:2

Cherry, Don 1934- **1993**:4
Chretien, Jean 1934- **1990**:4
Christensen, Hayden 1981- **2003**:3
Coffey, Paul 1961- **1985**:4
Copps, Sheila 1952- **1986**:4
Cronenberg, David 1943- **1992**:3
Cronyn, Hume 1911-2003
    Obituary **2004**:3
Crosby, Sidney 1987- **2006**:3
Dewhurst, Colleen 1924-1991
    Obituary **1992**:2
Dion, Celine 1970(?)- **1995**:3
Doherty, Denny 1940-2007
    Obituary **2008**:2
Eagleson, Alan 1933- **1987**:4
Ebbers, Bernie 1943- **1998**:1
Egoyan, Atom 1960- **2000**:2
Erickson, Arthur 1924- **1989**:3
Fillion, Nathan 1971- **2011**:3
Fonyo, Steve
    Brief entry **1985**:4
Foster, David 1950(?)- **1988**:2
Fox, Michael J. 1961- **1986**:1
Frank, Robert 1924- **1995**:2
Frye, Northrop 1912-1991
    Obituary **1991**:3
Fuhr, Grant 1962- **1997**:3
Furtado, Nelly 1978- **2007**:2
Garneau, Marc 1949- **1985**:1
Gatien, Peter
    Brief entry **1986**:1
Giguere, Jean-Sebastien 1977- **2004**:2
Gilmour, Doug 1963- **1994**:3
Gold, Christina A. 1947- **2008**:1
Gordon, Mary 1947- **2011**:4
Graham, Nicholas 1960(?)- **1991**:4
Granholm, Jennifer 1959- **2003**:3
Green, Tom 1972- **1999**:4
Greene, Graham 1952- **1997**:2
Greene, Lorne 1915-1987
    Obituary **1988**:1
Gretzky, Wayne 1961- **1989**:2
Haggis, Paul 1953- **2006**:4
Haney, Chris
    Brief entry **1985**:1
Harper, Stephen J. 1959- **2007**:3
Harris, Michael Deane 1945- **1997**:2
Hayakawa, Samuel Ichiye 1906-1992
    Obituary **1992**:3
Hennessy, Jill 1969- **2003**:2
Hextall, Ron 1964- **1988**:2
Hill, Graham 1971- **2010**:3
Hull, Brett 1964- **1991**:4
Jennings, Peter Charles 1938- **1997**:2
Johnson, Pierre Marc 1946- **1985**:4
Jones, Jenny 1946- **1998**:2
Juneau, Pierre 1922- **1988**:3
Jung, Andrea **2000**:2
Karsh, Yousuf 1908-2002
    Obituary **2003**:4
Keeler, Ruby 1910-1993
    Obituary **1993**:4
Kent, Arthur 1954- **1991**:4
Kielburger, Craig 1983- **1998**:1
Kilgore, Marcia 1968- **2006**:3
Korchinsky, Mike 1961- **2004**:2
Lalonde, Marc 1929- **1985**:1
Lang, K.D. 1961- **1988**:4
Lanois, Daniel 1951- **1991**:1
Lansens, Lori 1962- **2011**:3
Lavigne, Avril 1984- **2005**:2
Lemieux, Claude 1965- **1996**:1

Kukoc, Toni 1968- **1995**:4
Maxwell, Robert 1923-1991
    Obituary **1992**:2
Porizkova, Paulina
    Brief entry **1986**:4
Reisz, Karel 1926-2002
    Obituary **2004**:1
Serkin, Rudolf 1903-1991
    Obituary **1992**:1
Stoppard, Tom 1937- **1995**:4
Trump, Ivana 1949- **1995**:2
Zatopek, Emil 1922-2000
    Obituary **2001**:3

DANISH
Bohr, Aage 1922-2009
    Obituary **2011**:1
Borge, Victor 1909-2000
    Obituary **2001**:3
Hau, Lene Vestergaard 1959- **2006**:4
Kristiansen, Kjeld Kirk 1948(?)- **1988**
    :3
Lander, Toni 1931-1985
    Obituary **1985**:4
Rasmussen, Anders Fogh 1953- **2006**
    :1

DJIBOUTI
Guelleh, Ismail Omar 1947- **2006**:2

DOMINICAN
Balaguer, Joaquin 1907-2002
    Obituary **2003**:4
de la Renta, Oscar 1932- **2005**:4
Fernández, Leonel 1953- **2009**:2
Pujols, Albert 1980- **2005**:3
Ramirez, Manny 1972- **2005**:4
Soriano, Alfonso 1976- **2008**:1
Sosa, Sammy 1968- **1999**:1

DUTCH
Appel, Karel 1921-2006
    Obituary **2007**:2
de Hoop Scheffer, Jaap 1948- **2005**:1
de Kooning, Willem 1904-1997 **1994**
    :4
    Obituary **1997**:3
Duisenberg, Wim 1935-2005
    Obituary **2006**:4
Heineken, Alfred 1923-2002
    Obituary **2003**:1
Juliana 1909-2004
    Obituary **2005**:3
Koolhaas, Rem 1944- **2001**:1
Matadin, Vinoodh and Inez van
    Lamsweerde **2007**:4
Parker, Colonel Tom 1929-1997
    Obituary **1997**:2

ECUADORAN
Correa, Rafael 1963- **2008**:1

EGYPTIAN
Chahine, Youssef 1926-2008
    Obituary **2009**:3
ElBaradei, Mohamed 1942- **2006**:3
Ghali, Boutros Boutros 1922- **1992**:3
Mahfouz, Naguib 1911-2006

Obituary **2007**:4
Mubarak, Hosni 1928- **1991**:4
Rahman, Sheik Omar Abdel- 1938-
    1993:3

ENGLISH
Adams, Douglas 1952-2001
    Obituary **2002**:2
Ali, Monica 1967- **2007**:4
Altea, Rosemary 1946- **1996**:3
Amanpour, Christiane 1958- **1997**:2
Ambler, Eric 1909-1998
    Obituary **1999**:2
Ames, Roger 1950(?)- **2005**:2
Amis, Kingsley 1922-1995
    Obituary **1996**:2
Amis, Martin 1949- **2008**:3
Andrews, Julie 1935- **1996**:1
Ashcroft, Peggy 1907-1991
    Obituary **1992**:1
Ashwell, Rachel 1960(?)- **2004**:2
Atkinson, Rowan 1955- **2004**:3
Banksy 1975(?)- **2007**:2
Barker, Clive 1952- **2003**:3
Barker, Pat 1943- **2009**:1
Baron Cohen, Sacha 1971- **2007**:3
Barrett, Syd 1946-2006
    Obituary **2007**:3
Bates, Alan 1934-2003
    Obituary **2005**:1
Beckham, David 1975- **2003**:1
Bee Gees, The **1997**:4
Bell, Gabrielle 1975(?)- **2007**:4
Berners-Lee, Tim 1955(?)- **1997**:4
Blair, Tony 1953- **1996**:3
Bloom, Orlando 1977- **2004**:2
Bonham Carter, Helena 1966- **1998**:4
Bowie, David 1947- **1998**:2
Broadbent, Jim 1949- **2008**:4
Brown, Gordon 1951- **2008**:3
Brown, Tina 1953- **1992**:1
Burgess, Anthony 1917-1993
    Obituary **1994**:2
Burnett, Mark 1960- **2003**:1
Bush, Kate 1958- **1994**:3
Caine, Michael 1933- **2000**:4
Campbell, Naomi 1970- **2000**:2
Carey, George 1935- **1992**:3
Charles, Prince of Wales 1948- **1995**
    :3
Child, Lee 1954- **2007**:3
Choo, Jimmy 1957(?)- **2006**:3
Christie, Julie 1941- **2008**:4
Clapton, Eric 1945- **1993**:3
Coldplay **2004**:4
Collins, Jackie 1941- **2004**:4
Comfort, Alex 1920-2000
    Obituary **2000**:4
Cook, Peter 1938-1995
    Obituary **1995**:2
Cooke, Alistair 1908-2004
    Obituary **2005**:3
Costello, Elvis 1954(?)- **1994**:4
Cowell, Simon 1959- **2003**:4
Craig, Daniel 1968- **2008**:1
Crawford, Michael 1942- **1994**:2
Crick, Francis 1916-2004
    Obituary **2005**:4
Crisp, Quentin 1908-1999
    Obituary **2000**:3
Cushing, Peter 1913-1994
    Obituary **1995**:1

Davis, Crispin 1949- **2004**:1
Dee, Janie 1966(?)- **2001**:4
Diana, Princess of Wales 1961-1997
    1993:1
    Obituary **1997**:4
Dido 1971- **2004**:4
Driver, Minnie 1971- **2000**:1
Duran Duran **2005**:3
Dyson, James 1947- **2005**:4
Elliott, Denholm 1922-1992
    Obituary **1993**:2
Entwistle, John 1944-2002
    Obituary **2003**:3
Everett, Rupert 1959- **2003**:1
Everything But The Girl **1996**:4
Faldo, Nick 1957- **1993**:3
Fforde, Jasper 1961- **2006**:3
Fielding, Helen 1959- **2000**:4
Fiennes, Ralph 1962- **1996**:2
Finney, Albert 1936- **2003**:3
Fonteyn, Margot 1919-1991
    Obituary **1991**:3
Freud, Lucian 1922- **2000**:4
Frieda, John 1951- **2004**:1
Fuller, Simon 1960- **2008**:2
Furse, Clara 1957- **2008**:2
Galliano, John 1960- **2005**:2
Gielgud, John 1904-2000
    Obituary **2000**:4
Goldsworthy, Andy 1956- **2007**:2
Gordon, Michael 1951(?)- **2005**:1
Grant, Hugh 1960- **1995**:3
Gray, David 1970- **2001**:4
Green, Philip 1952- **2008**:2
Greene, Graham 1904-1991
    Obituary **1991**:4
Guinness, Alec 1914-2000
    Obituary **2001**:1
Haddon, Mark 1962- **2005**:2
Hadid, Zaha 1950- **2005**:3
Hamilton, Lewis 1985- **2008**:4
Harris, Richard 1930-2002
    Obituary **2004**:1
Harrison, George 1943-2001
    Obituary **2003**:1
Harvey, Polly Jean 1970(?)- **1995**:4
Headroom, Max 1985- **1986**:4
Hebard, Caroline 1944- **1998**:2
Hemming, Nikki 1967- **2009**:1
Hempleman-Adams, David 1956-
    2004:3
Hicks, India 1967- **2008**:2
Hill, Benny 1925-1992
    Obituary **1992**:3
Hindmarch, Anya 1969- **2008**:2
Hollinghurst, Alan 1954- **2006**:1
Hornby, Nick 1957- **2002**:2
Houser, Sam 1972(?)- **2004**:4
Hoyle, Sir Fred 1915-2001
    Obituary **2002**:4
Hughes, Ted 1930-1998
    Obituary **1999**:2
Hume, Basil Cardinal 1923-1999
    Obituary **2000**:1
Humphry, Derek 1931(?)- **1992**:2
Hurley, Elizabeth **1999**:2
Irons, Jeremy 1948- **1991**:4
Izzard, Eddie 1963- **2008**:1
Jacques, Brian 1939- **2002**:2
Jagger, Jade 1971- **2005**:1
John, Elton 1947- **1995**:4
Kerr, Deborah 1921-2007

Dubuffet, Jean 1901-1985
  Obituary **1985**:4
Duras, Marguerite 1914-1996
  Obituary **1996**:3
Fekkai, Frederic 1959(?)- **2003**:2
Gaultier, Jean-Paul 1952- **1998**:1
Ghosn, Carlos 1954- **2008**:3
Godard, Jean-Luc 1930- **1998**:1
Grappelli, Stephane 1908-1997
  Obituary **1998**:1
Guillem, Sylvie 1965(?)- **1988**:2
Indurain, Miguel 1964- **1994**:1
Jarre, Maurice 1924-2009
  Obituary **2010**:2
Klarsfeld, Beate 1939- **1989**:1
Kouchner, Bernard 1939- **2005**:3
Lacroix, Christian 1951- **2005**:2
Lefebvre, Marcel 1905- **1988**:4
Levi-Strauss, Claude 1908-2009
  Obituary **2011**:3
Louboutin, Christian 1963- **2006**:1
Malle, Louis 1932-1995
  Obituary **1996**:2
Marceau, Marcel 1923-2007
  Obituary **2008**:4
Mauresmo, Amelie 1979- **2007**:2
Mercier, Laura 1959(?)- **2002**:2
Millepied, Benjamin 1977(?)- **2006**:4
Mitterrand, Francois 1916-1996
  Obituary **1996**:2
Nars, Francois 1959- **2003**:1
Parker, Tony 1982- **2008**:1
Pépin, Jacques 1935- **2010**:2
Petrossian, Christian
  Brief entry **1985**:3
Phoenix **2011**:1
Picasso, Paloma 1949- **1991**:1
Ponty, Jean-Luc 1942- **1985**:4
Prost, Alain 1955- **1988**:1
Rampal, Jean-Pierre 1922- **1989**:2
Reza, Yasmina 1959(?)- **1999**:2
Ronis, Willy 1910-2009
  Obituary **2011**:1
Rothschild, Philippe de 1902-1988
  Obituary **1988**:2
Rykiel, Sonia 1930- **2000**:3
Saint Laurent, Yves 1936-2008
  Obituary **2009**:3
Sarkozy, Nicolas 1955- **2008**:4
Simone, Nina 1933-2003
  Obituary **2004**:2
Starck, Philippe 1949- **2004**:1
Tautou, Audrey 1978- **2004**:2
Thom, Rene 1923-2002
  Obituary **2004**:1
Thomas, Michel 1911(?)- **1987**:4
Tillion, Germaine 1907-2008
  Obituary **2009**:2
Touitou, Jean 1952(?)- **2008**:4
Ungaro, Emanuel 1933- **2001**:3
Villechaize, Herve 1943(?)-1993
  Obituary **1994**:1
Xenakis, Iannis 1922-2001
  Obituary **2001**:4

GABONESE
  Bozize, Francois 1946- **2006**:3

GEORGIAN
  Saakashvili, Mikhail 1967- **2008**:4

GERMAN
  Barbie, Klaus 1913-1991
    Obituary **1992**:2
  Bausch, Pina 1940-2009
    Obituary **2010**:4
  Becker, Boris
    Brief entry **1985**:3
  Bernhard, Wolfgang 1960- **2007**:1
  Bethe, Hans 1906-2005
    Obituary **2006**:2
  Beuys, Joseph 1921-1986
    Obituary **1986**:3
  Blobel, Gunter 1936- **2000**:4
  Boyle, Gertrude 1924- **1995**:3
  Brandt, Willy 1913-1992
    Obituary **1993**:2
  Breitschwerdt, Werner 1927- **1988**:4
  Casper, Gerhard 1937- **1993**:1
  Dietrich, Marlene 1901-1992
    Obituary **1992**:4
  Etzioni, Amitai 1929- **1994**:3
  Fischer, Joschka 1948- **2005**:2
  Frank, Anthony M. 1931(?)- **1992**:1
  Graf, Steffi 1969- **1987**:4
  Grass, Gunter 1927- **2000**:2
  Gursky, Andreas 1955- **2002**:2
  Hahn, Carl H. 1926- **1986**:4
  Hess, Rudolph 1894-1987
    Obituary **1988**:1
  Honecker, Erich 1912-1994
    Obituary **1994**:4
  Kiefer, Anselm 1945- **1990**:2
  Kinski, Klaus 1926-1991 **1987**:2
    Obituary **1992**:2
  Klarsfeld, Beate 1939- **1989**:1
  Klemperer, Werner 1920-2000
    Obituary **2001**:3
  Klum, Heidi 1973- **2006**:3
  Kohl, Helmut 1930- **1994**:1
  Krogner, Heinz 1941(?)- **2004**:2
  Lagerfeld, Karl 1938- **1999**:4
  Max, Peter 1937- **1993**:2
  Mengele, Josef 1911-1979
    Obituary **1985**:2
  Merkel, Angela 1954- **2010**:2
  Mutter, Anne-Sophie 1963- **1990**:3
  Newton, Helmut 1920- **2002**:1
  Nowitzki, Dirk 1978- **2007**:2
  Nuesslein-Volhard, Christiane 1942- **1998**:1
  Pfeiffer, Eckhard 1941- **1998**:4
  Pilatus, Robert 1966(?)-1998
    Obituary **1998**:3
  Polke, Sigmar 1941- **1999**:4
  Rey, Margret E. 1906-1996
    Obituary **1997**:2
  Richter, Gerhard 1932- **1997**:2
  Sander, Jil 1943- **1995**:2
  Schily, Otto
    Brief entry **1987**:4
  Schrempp, Juergen 1944- **2000**:2
  Schroder, Gerhard 1944- **1999**:1
  Schumacher, Michael 1969- **2005**:2
  Schwarzkopf, Elisabeth 1915-2006
    Obituary **2007**:3
  Sonnenfeldt, Richard 1923-2009
    Obituary **2011**:2
  Tillmans, Wolfgang 1968- **2001**:4

  Von Hellermann, Sophie 1975- **2006**:3
  Werner, Ruth 1907-2000
    Obituary **2001**:1
  Witt, Katarina 1966(?)- **1991**:3
  Zetsche, Dieter 1953- **2002**:3

GHANAIAN
  Annan, Kofi 1938- **1999**:1
  Atta Mills, John 1944- **2010**:3
  Chambas, Mohammed ibn 1950- **2003**:3
  Kufuor, John Agyekum 1938- **2005**:4

GREEK
  George and Lena Korres 1971- **2009**:1
  Huffington, Arianna 1950- **1996**:2
  Karamanlis, Costas 1956- **2009**:1
  Papandreou, Andrea 1919-1996
    Obituary **1997**:1
  Stefanidis, John 1937- **2007**:3

GUATEMALAN
  Berger, Oscar 1946- **2004**:4
  Menchu, Rigoberta 1960(?)- **1993**:2

GUINEA-BISSAUNI
  Makeba, Miriam 1934- **1989**:2
  Ture, Kwame 1941-1998
    Obituary **1999**:2

GUYANESE
  Jagdeo, Bharrat 1964- **2008**:1

HAITIAN
  Aristide, Jean-Bertrand 1953- **1991**:3
  Cedras, Raoul 1950- **1994**:4
  Danticat, Edwidge 1969- **2005**:4
  Preaaval, Reneaa 1943- **1997**:2

HONDURAN
  Lobo, Porfirio 1947- **2011**:3

HONG KONGER
  Chow, Stephen 1962- **2006**:1
  Chow Yun-fat 1955- **1999**:4
  Lee, Martin 1938- **1998**:2

HUNGARIAN
  Dorati, Antal 1906-1988
    Obituary **1989**:2
  Fodor, Eugene 1906(?)-1991
    Obituary **1991**:3
  Gabor, Eva 1921(?)-1995
    Obituary **1996**:1
  Grove, Andrew S. 1936- **1995**:3
  Ligeti, Gyorgy 1923-2006
    Obituary **2007**:3
  Polgar, Judit 1976- **1993**:3
  Solti, Georg 1912-1997
    Obituary **1998**:1

ICELANDIC
  Bjork 1965- **1996**:1
  Finnbogadoaattir, Vigdiaas
    Brief entry **1986**:2

JAPANESE

Akihito, Emperor of Japan 1933-
1990:1
Ando, Tadao 1941- **2005**:4
Aoki, Rocky 1940- **1990**:2
Arakawa, Shizuka 1981- **2006**:4
Doi, Takako
Brief entry **1987**:4
Hirohito, Emperor of Japan
1901-1989
Obituary **1989**:2
Honda, Soichiro 1906-1991
Obituary **1986**:1
Hosokawa, Morihiro 1938- **1994**:1
Isozaki, Arata 1931- **1990**:2
Itami, Juzo 1933-1997 **1998**:2
Katayama, Yutaka 1909- **1987**:1
Koizumi, Junichiro 1942- **2002**:1
Kuma, Kengo 1954- **2009**:1
Kurokawa, Kisho 1934-2007
Obituary **2008**:4
Kurosawa, Akira 1910-1998 **1991**:1
Obituary **1999**:1
Kutaragi, Ken 1950- **2005**:3
Mako 1933-2006
Obituary **2007**:3
Masako, Crown Princess 1963- **1993**
:4
Matsuhisa, Nobuyuki 1949- **2002**:3
Matsui, Hideki 1974- **2007**:4
Mitarai, Fujio 1935- **2002**:4
Miyake, Issey 1939- **1985**:2
Miyazaki, Hayao 1941- **2006**:2
Miyazawa, Kiichi 1919- **1992**:2
Mori, Yoshiro 1937- **2000**:4
Morita, Akio 1921- **1989**:4
Morita, Akio 1921-1999
Obituary **2000**:2
Murakami, Haruki 1949- **2008**:3
Murakami, Takashi 1962- **2004**:2
Nagako, Empress Dowager
1903-2000
Obituary **2001**:1
Nara, Yoshitomo 1959- **2006**:2
Nomo, Hideo 1968- **1996**:2
Obuchi, Keizo 1937- **1999**:2
Obuchi, Keizo 1937-2000
Obituary **2000**:4
Oe, Kenzaburo 1935- **1997**:1
Sasakawa, Ryoichi
Brief entry **1988**:1
Shimomura, Tsutomu 1965- **1996**:1
Suzuki, Ichiro 1973- **2002**:2
Suzuki, Sin'ichi 1898-1998
Obituary **1998**:3
Takada, Kenzo 1938- **2003**:2
Takei, Kei 1946- **1990**:2
Takeshita, Noburu 1924-2000
Obituary **2001**:1
Tanaka, Tomoyuki 1910-1997
Obituary **1997**:3
Tange, Kenzo 1913-2005
Obituary **2006**:2
Taniguchi, Yoshio 1937- **2005**:4
Toyoda, Akio 1956- **2011**:1
Toyoda, Eiji 1913- **1985**:2
Uchida, Mitsuko 1949(?)- **1989**:3
Umeki, Miyoshi 1929-2007
Obituary **2008**:4
Yamamoto, Kenichi 1922- **1989**:1

JORDANIAN

Abdullah II, King 1962- **2002**:4
al-Abdullah, Rania 1970- **2001**:1
Hussein I, King 1935-1999 **1997**:3
Obituary **1999**:3

KAZAKHSTANI

Nazarbayev, Nursultan 1940- **2006**:4

KENYAN

Kibaki, Mwai 1931- **2003**:4
Maathai, Wangari 1940- **2005**:3
Moi, Daniel arap 1924- **1993**:2

KOREAN

Chung Ju Yung 1915-2001
Obituary **2002**:1
Kim Dae Jung 1925- **1998**:3
Kim Il Sung 1912-1994
Obituary **1994**:4
Kim Jong Il 1942- **1995**:2
Lee Jong-Wook 1945- **2005**:1
Lee Myung-bak 1941- **2009**:2
Pak, Se Ri 1977- **1999**:4
Roh Moo-hyun 1946- **2005**:1

KOSOVOAN

Rugova, Ibrahim 1944-2006
Obituary **2007**:1

KYRGYZSTANI

Bakiyev, Kurmanbek 1949- **2007**:1

LATVIAN

Baryshnikov, Mikhail Nikolaevich
1948- **1997**:3

LEBANESE

Berri, Nabih 1939(?)- **1985**:2
Haladjian, Rafi 1962(?)- **2008**:3
Jumblatt, Walid 1949(?)- **1987**:4
Sarkis, Elias 1924-1985
Obituary **1985**:3
Suleiman, Michel 1948- **2010**:1

LIBERIAN

Doe, Samuel 1952-1990
Obituary **1991**:1
Sirleaf, Ellen Johnson 1938- **2007**:3

LIBYAN

Qaddhafi, Muammar 1942- **1998**:3

LITHUANIAN

Landsbergis, Vytautas 1932- **1991**:3

MACEDONIAN

Trajkovski, Boris 1956-2004
Obituary **2005**:2

MADAGASCAN

Ravalomanana, Marc 1950(?)- **2003**:1

MALAWI

Banda, Hastings 1898- **1994**:3

MALAYSIAN

Badawi, Abdullah Ahmad 1939-
2009:3
Choo, Jimmy 1957(?)- **2006**:3
Lum, Olivia 1961- **2009**:1
Ngau, Harrison **1991**:3
Razak, Datuk 1953- **2011**:1
Yeang, Ken 1948- **2008**:3
Yeoh, Michelle 1962- **2003**:2

MEXICAN

Alvarez Bravo, Manuel 1902-2002
Obituary **2004**:1
Catlett, Elizabeth 1915(?)- **1999**:3
Colosio, Luis Donaldo 1950-1994
1994:3
Cuaron, Alfonso 1961- **2008**:2
Del Toro, Guillermo 1964- **2010**:3
Esquivel, Juan 1918- **1996**:2
Felix, Maria 1914-2002
Obituary **2003**:2
Fox, Vicente 1942- **2001**:1
Garcia, Amalia 1951- **2005**:3
Graham, Robert 1938- **1993**:4
Hayek, Salma 1968- **1999**:1
Kahlo, Frida 1907-1954 **1991**:3
Ochoa, Lorena 1981- **2007**:4
Paz, Octavio 1914- **1991**:2
Salinas, Carlos 1948- **1992**:1
Santana, Carlos 1947- **2000**:2
Tamayo, Rufino 1899-1991
Obituary **1992**:1
Zedillo, Ernesto 1951- **1995**:1

MONACO

Albert, Prince of Monaco 1958- **2006**
:2
Rainier III, Prince of Monaco
1923-2005
Obituary **2006**:2

MONGOLIAN

Enkhbayar, Nambaryn 1958- **2007**:1

MOROCCAN

Elbaz, Alber 1961- **2008**:1
King Hassan II 1929-1999
Obituary **2000**:1
Lalami, Laila **2007**:1

MOZAMBICAN

Chissano, Joaquim 1939- **1987**:4
Dhlakama, Afonso 1953- **1993**:3
Guebuza, Armando 1943- **2008**:4
Machel, Samora 1933-1986
Obituary **1987**:1

NAMIBIAN

Nujoma, Sam 1929- **1990**:4

NEPALI

Shah, Gyanendra 1947- **2006**:1

NEW ZEALANDER

Campion, Jane **1991**:4
Castle-Hughes, Keisha 1990- **2004**:4
Crowe, Russell 1964- **2000**:4

Frame, Janet 1924-2004
  Obituary **2005**:2
Hillary, Edmund 1919-2008
  Obituary **2009**:1
Jackson, Peter 1961- **2004**:4
Kleinpaste, Ruud 1952- **2006**:2
Shipley, Jenny 1952- **1998**:3

NICARAGUAN
Astorga, Nora 1949(?)-1988 **1988**:2
Cruz, Arturo 1923- **1985**:1
Obando, Miguel 1926- **1986**:4
Ortega, Daniel 1945- **2008**:2
Robelo, Alfonso 1940(?)- **1988**:1

NIGERIAN
Abacha, Sani 1943- **1996**:3
Babangida, Ibrahim Badamosi 1941-
  1992:4
Obasanjo, Olusegun 1937(?)- **2000**:2
Okoye, Christian 1961- **1990**:2
Olajuwon, Akeem 1963- **1985**:1
Olopade, Olufunmilayo 1957(?)-
  2006:3
Sade 1959- **1993**:2
Saro-Wiwa, Ken 1941-1995
  Obituary **1996**:2
Yar'Adua, Umaru 1951- **2008**:3

NORWEGIAN
Brundtland, Gro Harlem 1939- **2000**
  :1
Cammermeyer, Margarethe 1942-
  1995:2
Carlsen, Magnus 1990- **2011**:3
Olav, King of Norway 1903-1991
  Obituary **1991**:3
Stoltenberg, Jens 1959- **2006**:4
Svindal, Aksel 1982- **2011**:2

PAKISTANI
Bhutto, Benazir 1953- **1989**:4
Zia ul-Haq, Mohammad 1924-1988
  Obituary **1988**:4

PALESTINIAN
Abbas, Mahmoud 1935- **2008**:4
Arafat, Yasser 1929- **1989**:3
Darwish, Mahmud 1942-2008
  Obituary **2009**:4
Freij, Elias 1920- **1986**:4
Habash, George 1925(?)- **1986**:1
Husseini, Faisal 1940- **1998**:4
Nidal, Abu 1937- **1987**:1
Sharon, Ariel 1928- **2001**:4
Terzi, Zehdi Labib 1924- **1985**:3

PANAMANIAN
Blades, Ruben 1948- **1998**:2

PARAGUAYAN
Lugo, Fernando 1951- **2010**:1
Stroessner, Alfredo 1912-2006
  Obituary **2007**:4

PERUVIAN
Fujimori, Alberto 1938- **1992**:4
Garcia, Alan 1949- **2007**:4
Perez de Cuellar, Javier 1920- **1991**:3
Testino, Mario 1954- **2002**:1

POLISH
Begin, Menachem 1913-1992
  Obituary **1992**:3
Eisenstaedt, Alfred 1898-1995
  Obituary **1996**:1
John Paul II, Pope 1920- **1995**:3
Kaczynski, Lech 1949- **2007**:2
Kieslowski, Krzysztof 1941-1996
  Obituary **1996**:3
Kosinski, Jerzy 1933-1991
  Obituary **1991**:4
Masur, Kurt 1927- **1993**:4
Niezabitowska, Malgorzata 1949(?)-
  1991:3
Rosten, Leo 1908-1997
  Obituary **1997**:3
Sabin, Albert 1906-1993
  Obituary **1993**:4
Sendler, Irena 1910-2008
  Obituary **2009**:2
Singer, Isaac Bashevis 1904-1991
  Obituary **1992**:1
Walesa, Lech 1943- **1991**:2

PORTUGUESE
Cavaco Silva, Anibal 1939- **2011**:3
Saramago, Jose 1922- **1999**:1

PUERTO RICAN
Alvarez, Aida **1999**:2
Del Toro, Benicio 1967- **2001**:4
Ferrer, Jose 1912-1992
  Obituary **1992**:3
Julia, Raul 1940-1994
  Obituary **1995**:1
Martin, Ricky 1971- **1999**:4
Novello, Antonia 1944- **1991**:2
Trinidad, Felix 1973- **2000**:4

ROMANIAN
Basescu, Traian 1951- **2006**:2
Ceausescu, Nicolae 1918-1989
  Obituary **1990**:2
Codrescu, Andreaa 1946- **1997**:3

RUSSIAN
Brodsky, Joseph 1940-1996
  Obituary **1996**:3
Ginzburg, Vitaly 1916-2009
  Obituary **2011**:3
Gorbachev, Raisa 1932-1999
  Obituary **2000**:2
Gordeeva, Ekaterina 1972- **1996**:4
Grinkov, Sergei 1967-1995
  Obituary **1996**:2
Kasparov, Garry 1963- **1997**:4
Kasyanov, Mikhail 1957- **2001**:1
Konstantinov, Vladimir 1967- **1997**:4
Kournikova, Anna 1981- **2000**:3
Lapidus, Morris 1902-2001
  Obituary **2001**:4
Lebed, Alexander 1950- **1997**:1
Medvedev, Dmitry 1965- **2009**:4
Moiseyev, Igor 1906-2007
  Obituary **2009**:1
Ovechkin, Alexander 1985- **2009**:2
Primakov, Yevgeny 1929- **1999**:3
Putin, Vladimir 1952- **2000**:3
Rostropovich, Mstislav 1927-2007
  Obituary **2008**:3
Safin, Marat 1980- **2001**:3

Sarraute, Nathalie 1900-1999
  Obituary **2000**:2
Schneerson, Menachem Mendel
  1902-1994 **1992**:4
  Obituary **1994**:4
Sharapova, Maria 1987- **2005**:2
Solzhenitsyn, Aleksandr 1918-2008
  Obituary **2009**:4
Titov, Gherman 1935-2000
  Obituary **2001**:3

RWANDAN
Kagame, Paul 1957- **2001**:4

SALVADORAN
Duarte, Jose Napoleon 1925-1990
  Obituary **1990**:3

SAUDI
Fahd, King of Saudi Arabia
  1923(?)-2005
  Obituary **2006**:4

SCOTTISH
Butler, Gerard 1969- **2011**:2
Coldplay **2004**:4
Connery, Sean 1930- **1990**:4
Ferguson, Craig 1962- **2005**:4
Ferguson, Niall 1964- **2006**:1
Franchitti, Dario 1973- **2008**:1
Macquarrie, John 1919-2007
  Obituary **2008**:3
McGregor, Ewan 1971(?)- **1998**:2
Mina, Denise 1966- **2006**:1
Paolozzi, Eduardo 1924-2005
  Obituary **2006**:3
Ramsay, Mike 1950(?)- **2002**:1
Rankin, Ian 1960- **2010**:3
Rowling, J.K. 1965- **2000**:1

SENEGALESE
Senghor, Leopold 1906-2001
  Obituary **2003**:1

SERBIAN
Djokovic, Novak 1987- **2008**:4
Patriarch Pavle 1914-2009
  Obituary **2011**:3
Tadic, Boris 1958- **2009**:3

SLOVENIAN
Turk, Danilo 1952- **2009**:3

SOMALI
Ahmed, Sharif 1964- **2010**:3
Iman 1955- **2001**:3

SOUTH AFRICAN
Barnard, Christiaan 1922-2001
  Obituary **2002**:4
Blackburn, Molly 1931(?)-1985
  Obituary **1985**:4
Botha, P. W. 1916-2006
  Obituary **2008**:1
Buthelezi, Mangosuthu Gatsha
  1928- **1989**:3
Coetzee, J. M. 1940- **2004**:4
de Klerk, F.W. 1936- **1990**:1
Duncan, Sheena

Brief entry **1987**:1
Fugard, Athol 1932- **1992**:3
Hani, Chris 1942-1993
   Obituary **1993**:4
Horn, Mike 1966- **2009**:3
Makeba, Miriam 1934- **1989**:2
Mandela, Nelson 1918- **1990**:3
Mandela, Winnie 1934- **1989**:3
Matthews, Dave 1967- **1999**:3
Mbeki, Thabo 1942- **1999**:4
Oppenheimer, Harry 1908-2000
   Obituary **2001**:3
Paton, Alan 1903-1988
   Obituary **1988**:3
Ramaphosa, Cyril 1953- **1988**:2
Sisulu, Walter 1912-2003
   Obituary **2004**:2
Slovo, Joe 1926- **1989**:2
Suzman, Helen 1917- **1989**:3
Tambo, Oliver 1917- **1991**:3
Theron, Charlize 1975- **2001**:4
Treurnicht, Andries 1921- **1992**:2
Woods, Donald 1933-2001
   Obituary **2002**:3

SOUTH KOREAN
Ban, Ki-moon 1944- **2011**:2
Kim, Yu-Na 1990- **2011**:2

SOVIET
Asimov, Isaac 1920-1992
   Obituary **1992**:3
Chernenko, Konstantin 1911-1985
   Obituary **1985**:1
Dalai Lama 1935- **1989**:1
Dubinin, Yuri 1930- **1987**:4
Dzhanibekov, Vladimir 1942- **1988**:1
Erte 1892-1990
   Obituary **1990**:4
Federov, Sergei 1969- **1995**:1
Godunov, Alexander 1949-1995
   Obituary **1995**:4
Gorbachev, Mikhail 1931- **1985**:2
Grebenshikov, Boris 1953- **1990**:1
Gromyko, Andrei 1909-1989
   Obituary **1990**:2
Karadzic, Radovan 1945- **1995**:3
Milosevic, Slobodan 1941- **1993**:2
Molotov, Vyacheslav Mikhailovich
   1890-1986
   Obituary **1987**:1
Nureyev, Rudolf 1938-1993
   Obituary **1993**:2
Sakharov, Andrei Dmitrievich
   1921-1989
   Obituary **1990**:2
Smirnoff, Yakov 1951- **1987**:2
Vidov, Oleg 194- **1987**:4
Yeltsin, Boris 1931- **1991**:1
Zhirinovsky, Vladimir 1946- **1994**:2

SPANISH
Almodovar, Pedro 1951- **2000**:3
Ayala, Francisco 1906-2009
   Obituary **2011**:3
Banderas, Antonio 1960- **1996**:2
Bardem, Javier 1969- **2008**:4
Blahnik, Manolo 1942- **2000**:2
Calatrava, Santiago 1951- **2005**:1
Carreras, Jose 1946- **1995**:2
Cela, Camilo Jose 1916-2001

Obituary **2003**:1
Chillida, Eduardo 1924-2002
   Obituary **2003**:4
Cruz, Penelope 1974- **2001**:4
Dali, Salvador 1904-1989
   Obituary **1989**:2
de Larrocha, Alicia 1923-2009
   Obituary **2011**:1
de Pinies, Jamie
   Brief entry **1986**:3
Domingo, Placido 1941- **1993**:2
Juan Carlos I 1938- **1993**:1
Lopez de Arriortua, Jose Ignacio
   1941- **1993**:4
Miro, Joan 1893-1983
   Obituary **1985**:1
Moneo, Jose Rafael 1937- **1996**:4
Montoya, Carlos 1903-1993
   Obituary **1993**:4
Nadal, Rafael 1986- **2009**:1
Samaranch, Juan Antonio 1920- **1986**
   :2
Sanz, Alejandro 1968- **2011**:3
Segovia, Andreaas 1893-1987
   Obituary **1987**:3
Wences, Senor 1896-1999
   Obituary **1999**:4

SRI LANKAN
Bandaranaike, Sirimavo 1916-2000
   Obituary **2001**:2
Ondaatje, Philip Michael 1943- **1997**
   :3
Wickramasinghe, Ranil 1949- **2003**:2

SUDANESE
al-Bashir, Omar 1944- **2009**:1
Turabi, Hassan 1932(?)- **1995**:4

SWEDISH
Bergman, Ingmar 1918- **1999**:4
Cardigans, The **1997**:4
Carlsson, Arvid 1923- **2001**:2
Garbo, Greta 1905-1990
   Obituary **1990**:3
Hallstrom, Lasse 1946- **2002**:3
Lidstrom, Nicklas 1970- **2009**:1
Lindbergh, Pelle 1959-1985
   Obituary **1985**:4
Lindgren, Astrid 1907-2002
   Obituary **2003**:1
Nilsson, Birgit 1918-2005
   Obituary **2007**:1
Olin, Lena 1956- **1991**:2
Palme, Olof 1927-1986
   Obituary **1986**:2
Persson, Stefan 1947- **2004**:1
Renvall, Johan
   Brief entry **1987**:4
Soderstrom, Elisabeth 1927-2009
   Obituary **2011**:3
Sorenstam, Annika 1970- **2001**:1

SWISS
del Ponte, Carla 1947- **2001**:1
Federer, Roger 1981- **2004**:2
Frank, Robert 1924- **1995**:2
Vasella, Daniel 1953- **2005**:3
Vollenweider, Andreas 1953- **1985**:2

SYRIAN
al-Assad, Bashar 1965- **2004**:2
Assad, Hafez 1930-2000
   Obituary **2000**:4
Assad, Hafez al- 1930(?)- **1992**:1
Assad, Rifaat 1937(?)- **1986**:3

TAHITIAN
Brando, Cheyenne 1970-1995
   Obituary **1995**:4

TAIWANESE
Chen Shui-bian 1950(?)- **2001**:2
Ho, David 1952- **1997**:2
Lee Teng-hui 1923- **2000**:1
Ma Ying-jeou 1950- **2009**:4

TANZANIAN
Nyerere, Julius 1922(?)-1999
   Obituary **2000**:2

THAI
Thaksin Shinawatra 1949- **2005**:4

TRINIDADIAN
Headley, Heather 1974- **2011**:1
Ture, Kwame 1941-1998
   Obituary **1999**:2

TUNISIAN
Azria, Max 1949- **2001**:4

TURKISH
Ecevit, Bulent 1925-2006
   Obituary **2008**:1
Gul, Abdullah 1950- **2009**:4
Ocalan, Abdullah 1948(?)- **1999**:4
Pamuk, Orhan 1952- **2007**:3

UGANDAN
Amin, Idi 1925(?)-2003
   Obituary **2004**:4
Museveni, Yoweri 1944- **2002**:1

UKRAINIAN
Baiul, Oksana 1977- **1995**:3
Gelfand, Israel 1913-2009
   Obituary **2011**:2
Tymoshenko, Yulia 1960- **2009**:1
Yanukovych, Viktor 1950- **2011**:4
Yushchenko, Viktor 1954- **2006**:1

URUGUAYAN
Vazquez, Tabare 1940- **2006**:2

UZBEKISTANI
Karimov, Islam 1938- **2006**:3

VENEZUELAN
Caldera, Rafael 1916-2009
   Obituary **2011**:4
Chavez, Hugo 1954- **2010**:4
Hernandez, Felix 1986- **2008**:2
Herrera, Carolina 1939- **1997**:1
Perez, Carlos Andre 1922- **1990**:2
Santana, Johan 1979- **2008**:1

VIETNAMESE
Dong, Pham Van 1906-2000
Obituary **2000**:4
Le Duan 1908(?)-1986
Obituary **1986**:4
Le Duc Tho 1911-1990
Obituary **1991**:1

WELSH
Bale, Christian 1974- **2001**:3
Dahl, Roald 1916-1990
Obituary **1991**:2
Hopkins, Anthony 1937- **1992**:4
Jenkins, Roy Harris 1920-2003

Obituary **2004**:1
Jones, Tom 1940- **1993**:4
Macdonald, Julien 1973(?)- **2005**:3
William, Prince of Wales 1982- **2001**
:3
Zeta-Jones, Catherine 1969- **1999**:4

YEMENI
Saleh, Ali Abdullah 1942- **2001**:3

YUGOSLAVIAN
Filipovic, Zlata 1981(?)- **1994**:4
Kostunica, Vojislav 1944- **2001**:1
Pogorelich, Ivo 1958- **1986**:4

Seles, Monica 1974(?)- **1991**:3

ZAIRAN
Mobutu Sese Seko 1930-1997 **1993**:4
Obituary **1998**:1

ZAMBIAN
Chiluba, Frederick 1943- **1992**:3

ZIMBABWEAN
Mugabe, Robert 1924- **1988**:4
Smith, Ian 1919-2007
Obituary **2009**:1

2011 Occupation Index

This index lists all newsmakers alphabetically by their occupations or fields of primary activity. Indexes in softbound issues allow access to the current year's entries; indexes in annual hardbound volumes are cumulative, covering the entire *Newsmakers* series.

Listee names are followed by a year and issue number; thus **1996**:3 indicates that an entry on that individual appears in both 1996, Issue 3, and the 1996 cumulation. For access to newsmakers appearing earlier than the current softbound issue, see the previous year's cumulation.

ART AND DESIGN

Adams, Scott 1957- **1996**:4
Adams-Geller, Paige 1969(?)- **2006**:4
Addams, Charles 1912-1988
    Obituary **1989**:1
Adler, Jonathan 1966- **2006**:3
Agnes B 1941- **2002**:3
al-Ani, Jananne 1966- **2008**:4
Albou, Sophie 1967- **2007**:2
Allard, Linda 1940- **2003**:2
Alvarez Bravo, Manuel 1902-2002
    Obituary **2004**:1
Anderson, Laurie 1947- **2000**:2
Ando, Tadao 1941- **2005**:4
Appel, Karel 1921-2006
    Obituary **2007**:2
Arman 1928- **1993**:1
Armani, Giorgio 1934(?)- **1991**:2
Ashwell, Rachel 1960(?)- **2004**:2
Aucoin, Kevyn 1962- **2001**:3
Avedon, Richard 1923- **1993**:4
Azria, Max 1949- **2001**:4
Badgley, Mark and James Mischka **2004**:3
Baldessari, John 1931(?)- **1991**:4
Ball, Michael 1964(?)- **2007**:3
Banks, Jeffrey 1953- **1998**:2
Banksy 1975(?)- **2007**:2
Barbera, Joseph 1911- **1988**:2
Barks, Carl 1901-2000
    Obituary **2001**:2
Barnes, Ernie 1938- **1997**:4
Barry, Lynda 1956(?)- **1992**:1
Batali, Mario 1960- **2010**:4
Bean, Alan L. 1932- **1986**:2
Beene, Geoffrey 1927-2004
    Obituary **2005**:4
Bell, Gabrielle 1975(?)- **2007**:4
Bellissimo, Wendy 1967(?)- **2007**:1
Beuys, Joseph 1921-1986
    Obituary **1986**:3
Bird, Brad 1956(?)- **2005**:4
Blahnik, Manolo 1942- **2000**:2
Blass, Bill 1922-2002
    Obituary **2003**:3
Bohbot, Michele 1959(?)- **2004**:2
Bontecou, Lee 1931- **2004**:4

Boone, Mary 1951- **1985**:1
Borofsky, Jonathan 1942- **2006**:4
Botero, Fernando 1932- **1994**:3
Bourgeois, Louise 1911- **1994**:1
Bowie, David 1947- **1998**:2
Boynton, Sandra 1953- **2004**:1
Breathed, Berkeley 1957- **2005**:3
Brown, Bobbi 1957- **2001**:4
Brown, Howard and Karen Stewart **2007**:3
Brown, J. Carter 1934-2002
    Obituary **2003**:3
Buchman, Dana 1951- **2010**:2
Bundchen, Gisele 1980- **2009**:1
Bunshaft, Gordon 1909-1990 **1989**:3
    Obituary **1991**:1
Burch, Tory 1966- **2009**:3
Calatrava, Santiago 1951- **2005**:1
Cameron, David
    Brief entry **1988**:1
Campbell, Ben Nighthorse 1933-**1998**:1
Campbell, Naomi 1970- **2000**:2
Cardin, Pierre 1922- **2003**:3
Cartier-Bresson, Henri 1908-2004
    Obituary **2005**:4
Cassini, Oleg 1913-2006
    Obituary **2007**:2
Castelli, Leo 1907-1999
    Obituary **2000**:1
Catlett, Elizabeth 1915(?)- **1999**:3
Cavalli, Roberto 1940- **2004**:4
Chagall, Marc 1887-1985
    Obituary **1985**:2
Chalayan, Hussein 1970- **2003**:2
Charlesworth, Sarah 1947- **2010**:3
Chast, Roz 1955- **1992**:4
Chatham, Russell 1939- **1990**:1
Chia, Sandro 1946- **1987**:2
Chihuly, Dale 1941- **1995**:2
Chillida, Eduardo 1924-2002
    Obituary **2003**:4
Choo, Jimmy 1957(?)- **2006**:3
Christo 1935- **1992**:3
Chung, Doo-Ri 1973- **2011**:3
Claiborne, Liz 1929- **1986**:3
Clemente, Francesco 1952- **1992**:2

Cole, Anne 1930(?)- **2007**:3
Cole, Kenneth 1954(?)- **2003**:1
Colescott, Robert 1925-2009
    Obituary **2010**:3
Conner, Bruce 1933-2008
    Obituary **2009**:3
Cooper, Alexander 1936- **1988**:4
Costa, Francisco 1961- **2010**:2
Courtney, Erica 1957- **2009**:3
Crumb, R. 1943- **1995**:4
Dali, Salvador 1904-1989
    Obituary **1989**:2
David Neville and Marcus
    Wainwright 1976- **2010**:3
Davis, Paige 1969- **2004**:2
DeCarava, Roy 1919- **1996**:3
de Kooning, Willem 1904-1997 **1994**:4
    Obituary **1997**:3
de la Renta, Oscar 1932- **2005**:4
Diebenkorn, Richard 1922-1993
    Obituary **1993**:4
Diller, Elizabeth and Ricardo
    Scofidio **2004**:3
Dith Pran 1942-2008
    Obituary **2009**:2
Dolce, Domenico and Stefano
    Gabbana **2005**:4
Donghia, Angelo R. 1935-1985
    Obituary **1985**:2
Doubilet, Anne 1948- **2011**:1
Duarte, Henry 1963(?)- **2003**:3
Dubuffet, Jean 1901-1985
    Obituary **1985**:4
Dunham, Carroll 1949- **2003**:4
Ecko, Marc 1972- **2006**:3
Eisenman, Peter 1932- **1992**:4
Eisenstaedt, Alfred 1898-1995
    Obituary **1996**:1
Eisner, Will 1917-2005
    Obituary **2006**:1
Elbaz, Alber 1961- **2008**:1
Ellis, David 1971- **2009**:4
Ellis, Perry 1940-1986
    Obituary **1986**:3
Emin, Tracey 1963- **2009**:2
Engelbreit, Mary 1952(?)- **1994**:3

Erickson, Arthur 1924- **1989**:3
Erte 1892-1990
  Obituary **1990**:4
Eve 1978- **2004**:3
Fekkai, Frederic 1959(?)- **2003**:2
Ferre, Gianfranco 1944-2007
  Obituary **2008**:3
Ferretti, Alberta 1950(?)- **2004**:1
Field, Patricia 1942(?)- **2002**:2
Finley, Karen 1956- **1992**:4
Fisher, Mary 1948- **1994**:3
Flay, Bobby 1964- **2009**:2
Florence, Tyler 1971- **2011**:4
Ford, Tom 1962- **1999**:3
Foster, Norman 1935- **1999**:4
Frank, Robert 1924- **1995**:2
Frankenthaler, Helen 1928- **1990**:1
Freud, Lucian 1922- **2000**:4
Frieda, John 1951- **2004**:1
Gaines, William M. 1922-1992
  Obituary **1993**:1
Galliano, John 1960- **2005**:2
Gaultier, Jean-Paul 1952- **1998**:1
Gehry, Frank O. 1929- **1987**:1
Giannulli, Mossimo 1963- **2002**:3
Gioia, Dana 1950- **2008**:4
Gober, Robert 1954- **1996**:3
Golden, Thelma 1965- **2003**:3
Goldman, Duff 1974- **2010**:1
Goldsworthy, Andy 1956- **2007**:2
Goody, Joan 1935- **1990**:2
Gorder, Genevieve 1974- **2005**:4
Gordon, Michael 1951(?)- **2005**:1
Gottlieb, William 1917-2006
  Obituary **2007**:2
Gould, Chester 1900-1985
  Obituary **1985**:2
Graham, Nicholas 1960(?)- **1991**:4
Graham, Robert 1938- **1993**:4
Graves, Michael 1934- **2000**:1
Graves, Nancy 1940- **1989**:3
Greenberg, Robert 1940(?)- **2003**:2
Gregory, Rogan 1972- **2008**:2
Groening, Matt 1955(?)- **1990**:4
Guccione, Bob 1930- **1986**:1
Gund, Agnes 1938- **1993**:2
Gursky, Andreas 1955- **2002**:2
Hadid, Zaha 1950- **2005**:3
Halston 1932-1990
  Obituary **1990**:3
Handford, Martin **1991**:3
Haring, Keith 1958-1990
  Obituary **1990**:3
Hart, Johnny 1931-2007
  Obituary **2008**:2
Held, Abbe 1966- **2011**:1
Held, Al 1928-2005
  Obituary **2006**:4
Hernandez, Lazaro and Jack
  McCollough **2008**:4
Hershberger, Sally 1961(?)- **2006**:4
Hicks, India 1967- **2008**:2
Hilfiger, Tommy 1952- **1993**:3
Hindmarch, Anya 1969- **2008**:2
Hockney, David 1937- **1988**:3
Hoff, Syd 1912-2004
  Obituary **2005**:3
Holl, Steven 1947- **2003**:1
Hoving, Thomas 1931-2009
  Obituary **2011**:4
Hughes, Robert 1938- **1996**:4
Hutchins, Carleen 1911-2009

  Obituary **2010**:4
Isozaki, Arata 1931- **1990**:2
Jacobs, Marc 1963- **2002**:3
Jagger, Jade 1971- **2005**:1
Jahn, Helmut 1940- **1987**:3
Jeanne-Claude 1935-2009
  Obituary **2011**:3
Johnson, Betsey 1942- **1996**:2
Johnson, Philip 1906- **1989**:2
Jones, E. Fay 1921-2004
  Obituary **2005**:4
Jordan, Charles M. 1927- **1989**:4
Joseph, Wendy Evans 1955(?)- **2006**
  :2
Judge, Mike 1963(?)- **1994**:2
July, Miranda 1974- **2008**:2
Kahlo, Frida 1907-1954 **1991**:3
Kamali, Norma 1945- **1989**:1
Karan, Donna 1948- **1988**:1
Karsh, Yousuf 1908-2002
  Obituary **2003**:4
Kashuk, Sonia 1959(?)- **2002**:4
Kaskey, Ray
  Brief entry **1987**:2
Katz, Alex 1927- **1990**:3
Kelly, Ellsworth 1923- **1992**:1
Kelly, Patrick 1954(?)-1990
  Obituary **1990**:2
Kent, Corita 1918-1986
  Obituary **1987**:1
Keplinger, Dan 1973- **2001**:1
Ketcham, Hank 1920-2001
  Obituary **2002**:2
Kidd, Jemma 1974- **2009**:1
Kiefer, Anselm 1945- **1990**:2
Kiley, Dan 1912-2004
  Obituary **2005**:2
Kim, Eugenia 1974(?)- **2006**:1
Kinney, Jeff 1971- **2009**:3
Kitaj, R. B. 1932-2007
  Obituary **2008**:4
Klein, Calvin 1942- **1996**:2
Koolhaas, Rem 1944- **2001**:1
Koons, Jeff 1955(?)- **1991**:4
Kors, Michael 1959- **2000**:4
Kostabi, Mark 1960- **1989**:4
Kuma, Kengo 1954- **2009**:1
Kurokawa, Kisho 1934-2007
  Obituary **2008**:4
Lacroix, Christian 1951- **2005**:2
Lagerfeld, Karl 1938- **1999**:4
Lam, Derek 1966- **2009**:2
Lang, Helmut 1956- **1999**:2
Lange, Liz 1967(?)- **2003**:4
Lapidus, Morris 1902-2001
  Obituary **2001**:4
Lasdun, Denys 1914-2001
  Obituary **2001**:4
Lauren, Ralph 1939- **1990**:1
Leibovitz, Annie 1949- **1988**:4
Leigh, Dorian 1917-2008
  Obituary **2009**:3
Lepore, Nanette 1964(?)- **2006**:4
Levitt, Helen 1913-2009
  Obituary **2010**:2
LeWitt, Sol 1928- **2001**:2
Lhuillier, Monique 1971(?)- **2007**:4
Libeskind, Daniel 1946- **2004**:1
Lichtenstein, Roy 1923-1997 **1994**:1
  Obituary **1998**:1
Lim, Phillip 1974(?)- **2008**:1
Lin, Maya 1960(?)- **1990**:3

Lobell, Jeanine 1964(?)- **2002**:3
Longo, Robert 1953(?)- **1990**:4
Louboutin, Christian 1963- **2006**:1
Macdonald, Julien 1973(?)- **2005**:3
MacFarlane, Seth 1973- **2006**:1
MacNelly, Jeff 1947-2000
  Obituary **2000**:4
Madden, Chris 1948- **2006**:1
Mann, Sally 1951- **2001**:2
Mansion, Gracie
  Brief entry **1986**:3
Mapplethorpe, Robert 1946-1989
  Obituary **1989**:3
Mardin, Brice 1938- **2007**:4
Mark, Mary Ellen 1940- **2006**:2
Martin, Agnes 1912-2004
  Obituary **2006**:1
Massimo and Lella Vignelli 1931-
  2010:1
Matadin, Vinoodh and Inez van
  Lamsweerde **2007**:4
Mauldin, Bill 1921-2003
  Obituary **2004**:2
Max, Peter 1937- **1993**:2
McCartney, Linda 1942-1998
  Obituary **1998**:4
McCartney, Stella 1971- **2001**:3
McDonnell, Patrick 1956- **2009**:4
McDonough, William 1951- **2003**:1
McFarlane, Todd 1961- **1999**:1
McGinley, Ryan 1977- **2009**:1
McGruder, Aaron 1974- **2005**:4
Meier, Richard 1934- **2001**:4
Meisel, Steven 1954- **2002**:4
Melendez, Bill 1916-2008
  Obituary **2009**:4
Mellinger, Frederick 1924(?)-1990
  Obituary **1990**:4
Mercier, Laura 1959(?)- **2002**:2
Messick, Dale 1906-2005
  Obituary **2006**:2
Miller, Nicole 1951(?)- **1995**:4
Mills, Malia 1966- **2003**:1
Minkoff, Rebecca 1981- **2011**:3
Miro, Joan 1893-1983
  Obituary **1985**:1
Misrach, Richard 1949- **1991**:2
Miyake, Issey 1939- **1985**:2
Miyazaki, Hayao 1941- **2006**:2
Mizrahi, Isaac 1961- **1991**:1
Moneo, Jose Rafael 1937- **1996**:4
Moore, Henry 1898-1986
  Obituary **1986**:4
Morris, Robert 1947- **2010**:3
Motherwell, Robert 1915-1991
  Obituary **1992**:1
Mueck, Ron 1958- **2008**:3
Mumford, Lewis 1895-1990
  Obituary **1990**:2
Murakami, Takashi 1962- **2004**:2
Mydans, Carl 1907-2004
  Obituary **2005**:4
Nara, Yoshitomo 1959- **2006**:2
Nars, Francois 1959- **2003**:1
Natori, Josie 1947- **1994**:3
Nauman, Bruce 1941- **1995**:4
Nechita, Alexandra 1985- **1996**:4
Neiman, LeRoy 1927- **1993**:3
Nevelson, Louise 1900-1988
  Obituary **1988**:3
Newman, Arnold 1918- **1993**:1
Newton, Helmut 1920- **2002**:1

2011 Occupation Index

Nipon, Albert
  Brief entry **1986**:4
Ogilvy, David 1911-1999
  Obituary **2000**:1
Oldham, Todd 1961- **1995**:4
Olsen, Sigrid 1953- **2007**:1
Ono, Yoko 1933- **1989**:2
Page, Bettie 1923-2008
  Obituary **2010**:1
Page, Dick 1955- **2010**:1
Panichgul, Thakoon 1974- **2009**:4
Paolozzi, Eduardo 1924-2005
  Obituary **2006**:3
Parker, Brant 1920-2007
  Obituary **2008**:2
Parker, Suzy 1932-2003
  Obituary **2004**:2
Parks, Gordon 1912-2006
  Obituary **2006**:2
Pépin, Jacques 1935- **2010**:2
Pedersen, William 1938(?)- **1989**:4
Pei, I.M. 1917- **1990**:4
Pelli, Cesar 1927(?)- **1991**:4
Penn, Irving 1917-2009
  Obituary **2011**:2
Penn & Teller **1992**:1
Pennington, Ty 1965- **2005**:4
Peyton, Elizabeth 1965- **2007**:1
Piano, Renzo 1937- **2009**:2
Picasso, Paloma 1949- **1991**:1
Pinto, Maria 1957- **2011**:2
Plater-Zyberk, Elizabeth 1950- **2005**
  :2
Polke, Sigmar 1941- **1999**:4
Portman, John 1924- **1988**:2
Posen, Zac 1980- **2009**:3
Potok, Anna Maximilian
  Brief entry **1985**:2
Pozzi, Lucio 1935- **1990**:2
Prada, Miuccia 1950(?)- **1996**:1
Pratt, Christopher 1935- **1985**:3
Predock, Antoine 1936- **1993**:2
Puryear, Martin 1941- **2002**:4
Queer Eye for the Straight Guy cast
  2004:3
Radocy, Robert
  Brief entry **1986**:3
Raimondi, John
  Brief entry **1987**:4
Raskin, Jef 1943(?)- **1997**:4
Rauschenberg, Robert 1925- **1991**:2
Reese, Tracy 1964- **2010**:1
Rhodes, Zandra 1940- **1986**:2
Richardson, Steve 1939- **2010**:4
Richter, Gerhard 1932- **1997**:2
Ringgold, Faith 1930- **2000**:3
Ritts, Herb 1954(?)- **1992**:4
Roberts, Xavier 1955- **1985**:3
Roche, Kevin 1922- **1985**:1
Rockwell, David 1956- **2003**:3
Rodriguez, Narciso 1961- **2005**:1
Roncal, Mally 1972- **2009**:4
Ronis, Willy 1910-2009
  Obituary **2011**:1
Ronson, Charlotte 1977(?)- **2007**:3
Rose, Lela 1969- **2011**:1
Rosenberg, Evelyn 1942- **1988**:2
Rosenthal, Joseph 1911-2006
  Obituary **2007**:4
Rosenzweig, Ilene 1965(?)- **2004**:1
Rosso, Renzo 1955- **2005**:2
Rothenberg, Susan 1945- **1995**:3

Rouse, James 1914-1996
  Obituary **1996**:4
Rowley, Cynthia 1958- **2002**:1
Rykiel, Sonia 1930- **2000**:3
Saatchi, Charles 1943- **1987**:3
Saint Laurent, Yves 1936-2008
  Obituary **2009**:3
Salgado, Sebastiao 1944- **1994**:2
Scavullo, Francesco 1921-2004
  Obituary **2005**:1
Schnabel, Julian 1951- **1997**:1
Schulz, Charles 1922-2000
  Obituary **2000**:3
Schulz, Charles M. 1922- **1998**:1
Schwartz, Allen 1945(?)- **2008**:2
Scott, Pamella 1975- **2010**:4
Segal, Shelli 1955(?)- **2005**:3
Serra, Richard 1939- **2009**:1
Serrano, Andres 1950- **2000**:4
Shaw, Carol 1958(?)- **2002**:1
Sherman, Cindy 1954- **1992**:3
Shulman, Julius 1910-2009
  Obituary **2010**:4
Simmons, Laurie 1949- **2010**:1
Simpson, Lorna 1960- **2008**:1
Skaist-Levy, Pam and Gela Taylor
  2005:1
Slick, Grace 1939- **2001**:2
Smith, Paul 1946- **2002**:4
Smith, Willi 1948-1987
  Obituary **1987**:3
Som, Peter 1971- **2009**:1
Spade, Kate 1962- **2003**:1
Spiegelman, Art 1948- **1998**:3
Sprouse, Stephen 1953-2004
  Obituary **2005**:2
Starck, Philippe 1949- **2004**:1
Stefani, Gwen 1969- **2005**:4
Stefanidis, John 1937- **2007**:3
Stella, Frank 1936- **1996**:2
Stockton, Shreve 1977- **2009**:4
Stone, Curtis 1975- **2011**:3
Sui, Anna 1955(?)- **1995**:1
Takada, Kenzo 1938- **2003**:2
Tamayo, Rufino 1899-1991
  Obituary **1992**:1
Tange, Kenzo 1913-2005
  Obituary **2006**:2
Taniguchi, Yoshio 1937- **2005**:4
Temperley, Alice 1975- **2008**:2
Testino, Mario 1954- **2002**:1
Thiebaud, Wayne 1920- **1991**:1
Tillmans, Wolfgang 1968- **2001**:4
Tompkins, Susie
  Brief entry **1987**:2
Touitou, Jean 1952(?)- **2008**:4
Trudeau, Garry 1948- **1991**:2
Truitt, Anne 1921- **1993**:1
Tunick, Spencer 1967- **2008**:1
Twombley, Cy 1928(?)- **1995**:1
Tyler, Richard 1948(?)- **1995**:3
Ungaro, Emanuel 1933- **2001**:3
Valastro, Buddy 1977- **2011**:4
Valli, Giambattista 1966- **2008**:3
Valvo, Carmen Marc 1954- **2003**:4
Venturi, Robert 1925- **1994**:4
Versace, Donatella 1955- **1999**:1
Versace, Gianni 1946-1997
  Brief entry **1988**:1
  Obituary **1998**:2
Von D, Kat 1982- **2008**:3

von Furstenberg, Diane 1946- **1994**:2
Von Hellermann, Sophie 1975- **2006**
  :3
Vreeland, Diana 1903(?)-1989
  Obituary **1990**:1
Wagner, Catherine F. 1953- **2002**:3
Walker, Kara 1969- **1999**:2
Wang, Alexander 1984- **2011**:4
Wang, Vera 1949- **1998**:4
Warhol, Andy 1927(?)-1987
  Obituary **1987**:2
Washington, Alonzo 1967- **2000**:1
Waterman, Cathy 1950(?)- **2002**:2
Watterson, Bill 1958(?)- **1990**:3
Wegman, William 1942(?)- **1991**:1
Westwood, Vivienne 1941- **1998**:3
Whitney, Patrick 1952(?)- **2006**:1
Wilson, Peter C. 1913-1984
  Obituary **1985**:2
Winick, Judd 1970- **2005**:3
Wintour, Anna 1949- **1990**:4
Witkin, Joel-Peter 1939- **1996**:1
Wu, Jason 1983- **2010**:3
Wyeth, Andrew 1917-2009
  Obituary **2010**:1
Wyland, Robert 1956- **2009**:3
Yamasaki, Minoru 1912-1986
  Obituary **1986**:2
Yeang, Ken 1948- **2008**:3
Yosca, Gerard **2011**:2

BUSINESS
Abraham, S. Daniel 1924- **2003**:3
Ackerman, Will 1949- **1987**:4
Adams-Geller, Paige 1969(?)- **2006**:4
Adelson, Jay 1970- **2011**:1
Adler, Jonathan 1966- **2006**:3
Agnelli, Giovanni 1921- **1989**:4
Ailes, Roger 1940- **1989**:3
Akers, John F. 1934- **1988**:3
Akin, Phil
  Brief entry **1987**:3
Albou, Sophie 1967- **2007**:2
Albrecht, Chris 1952(?)- **2005**:4
Allaire, Jeremy 1971- **2006**:4
Allaire, Paul 1938- **1995**:1
Allard, Linda 1940- **2003**:2
Allen, Bob 1935- **1992**:4
Allen, John 1930- **1992**:1
Alter, Hobie
  Brief entry **1985**:1
Alvarez, Aida **1999**:2
Ames, Roger 1950(?)- **2005**:2
Amos, Wally 1936- **2000**:1
Ancier, Garth 1957- **1989**:1
Anderson, Brad 1949- **2007**:3
Anderson, Tom and Chris DeWolfe
  2007:2
Andreessen, Marc 1972- **1996**:2
Annenberg, Walter 1908- **1992**:3
Antonini, Joseph 1941- **1991**:2
Aoki, Rocky 1940- **1990**:2
Arad, Avi 1948- **2003**:2
Aretsky, Ken 1941- **1988**:1
Arison, Ted 1924- **1990**:3
Arledge, Roone 1931- **1992**:2
Armstrong, C. Michael 1938- **2002**:1
Arnault, Bernard 1949- **2000**:4
Arrington, Michael 1970- **2011**:4
Ash, Mary Kay 1915(?)- **1996**:1
Ashwell, Rachel 1960(?)- **2004**:2
Aurre, Laura

Brief entry **1986**:3
Ball, Michael 1964(?)- **2007**:3
Ballmer, Steven 1956- **1997**:2
Balsillie, Jim and Mike Lazaridis
 2006:4
Banks, Jeffrey 1953- **1998**:2
Barad, Jill 1951- **1994**:2
Barksdale, James L. 1943- **1998**:2
Barnes, Brenda C. 1955(?)- **2007**:4
Barrett, Craig R. 1939- **1999**:4
Bartlett, Arthur 1933-2009
 Obituary **2011**:4
Bauer, Eddie 1899-1986
 Obituary **1986**:3
Baxter, Pamela 1949- **2009**:4
Beals, Vaughn 1928- **1988**:2
Becker, Brian 1957(?)- **2004**:4
Beene, Geoffrey 1927-2004
 Obituary **2005**:4
Beers, Charlotte 1935- **1999**:3
Beisler, Gary J. 1956- **2010**:3
Bellissimo, Wendy 1967(?)- **2007**:1
Ben & Jerry **1991**:3
Benetton, Luciano 1935- **1988**:1
Berliner, Andy and Rachel **2008**:2
Berlusconi, Silvio 1936(?)- **1994**:4
Berman, Gail 1957(?)- **2006**:1
Bern, Dorrit J. 1950(?)- **2006**:3
Bernhard, Wolfgang 1960- **2007**:1
Besse, Georges 1927-1986
 Obituary **1987**:1
Bezos, Jeff 1964- **1998**:4
Bibliowicz, Jessica 1959- **2009**:3
Bieber, Owen 1929- **1986**:1
Bikoff, J. Darius 1962(?)- **2007**:3
Bikoff, James L.
 Brief entry **1986**:2
Black, Carole 1945- **2003**:1
Black, Cathleen 1944- **1998**:4
Black, Conrad 1944- **1986**:2
Bloch, Henry 1922- **1988**:4
Bloch, Ivan 1940- **1986**:3
Blodgett, Leslie 1963- **2010**:1
Bloom, Natalie 1971- **2007**:1
Bloomberg, Michael 1942- **1997**:1
Bohbot, Michele 1959(?)- **2004**:2
Boiardi, Hector 1897-1985
 Obituary **1985**:3
Bolkiah, Sultan Muda Hassanal
 1946- **1985**:4
Bond, Alan 1938- **1989**:2
Bose, Amar
 Brief entry **1986**:4
Boyer, Herbert Wayne 1936- **1985**:1
Boyle, Gertrude 1924- **1995**:3
Boynton, Sandra 1953- **2004**:1
Brabeck-Letmathe, Peter 1944- **2001**
 :4
Bradford, Chris 1937- **2011**:1
Bradley, Todd 1958- **2003**:3
Branson, Richard 1951- **1987**:1
Bravo, Ellen 1944- **1998**:2
Bravo, Rose Marie 1951(?)- **2005**:3
Breitschwerdt, Werner 1927- **1988**:4
Brennan, Edward A. 1934- **1989**:1
Brennan, Robert E. 1943(?)- **1988**:1
Bronfman, Edgar, Jr. 1955- **1994**:4
Brooks, Diana D. 1950- **1990**:1
Brosius, Christopher **2007**:1
Brown, Howard and Karen Stewart
 2007:3
Brown, John Seely 1940- **2004**:1

Brown, Tina 1953- **1992**:1
Buchman, Dana 1951- **2010**:2
Buffett, Jimmy 1946- **1999**:3
Buffett, Warren 1930- **1995**:2
Burch, Tory 1966- **2009**:3
Burnison, Chantal Simone 1950(?)-
 1988:3
Burns, Robin 1953(?)- **1991**:2
Burr, Donald Calvin 1941- **1985**:3
Burton, Jake 1954- **2007**:1
Busch, August A. III 1937- **1988**:2
Busch, August Anheuser, Jr.
 1899-1989
 Obituary **1990**:2
Bushnell, Nolan 1943- **1985**:1
Buss, Jerry 1933- **1989**:3
Cain, Herman 1945- **1998**:3
Callaway, Ely 1919-2001
 Obituary **2002**:3
Calloway, D. Wayne 1935- **1987**:3
Campeau, Robert 1923- **1990**:1
Canfield, Alan B.
 Brief entry **1986**:3
Carlino, Cristina 1961(?)- **2008**:4
Carter, Billy 1937-1988
 Obituary **1989**:1
Case, Steve 1958- **1995**:4
Cassidy, Mike 1963(?)- **2006**:1
Cassini, Oleg 1913-2006
 Obituary **2007**:2
Centrello, Gina 1959(?)- **2008**:3
Chalayan, Hussein 1970- **2003**:2
Chambers, John 1949- **2010**:2
Chappell, Tom 1943- **2002**:3
Charney, Dov 1969- **2008**:2
Charron, Paul 1942- **2004**:1
Chen, Steve and Chad Hurley **2007**
 :2
Chenault, Kenneth I. 1951- **1999**:3
Chiasson, William 1953- **2011**:4
Chidsey, John 1962- **2010**:4
Chiquet, Maureen 1963- **2010**:1
Chizen, Bruce 1955(?)- **2004**:2
Choo, Jimmy 1957(?)- **2006**:3
Chouinard, Yvon 1938(?)- **2002**:2
Chung, Doo-Ri 1973- **2011**:3
Chung Ju Yung 1915-2001
 Obituary **2002**:1
Cipriano, Salvatore 1941- **2011**:4
Claiborne, Liz 1929- **1986**:3
Clark, Jim 1944- **1997**:1
Clark, Maxine 1949- **2009**:4
Cole, Anne 1930(?)- **2007**:3
Cole, Kenneth 1954(?)- **2003**:1
Coleman, Sheldon, Jr. 1953- **1990**:2
Collier, Sophia 1956(?)- **2001**:2
Combs, Sean Puffy 1970- **1998**:4
Condit, Phil 1941- **2001**:3
Conseil, Dominique Nils 1962(?)-
 2007:2
Cooper, Alexander 1936- **1988**:4
Cooper, Stephen F. 1946- **2005**:4
Coors, William K.
 Brief entry **1985**:1
Copeland, Al 1944(?)- **1988**:3
Cornell, Brian C. 1959- **2009**:2
Costa, Francisco 1961- **2010**:2
Covey, Stephen R. 1932- **1994**:4
Cox, Richard Joseph
 Brief entry **1985**:1
Craig, James 1956- **2001**:1
Craig, Sid and Jenny **1993**:4

Crandall, Robert L. 1935- **1992**:1
Crawford, Cheryl 1902-1986
 Obituary **1987**:1
Cray, Seymour R. 1925-1996
 Brief entry **1986**:3
 Obituary **1997**:2
Crump, Scott 1954(?)- **2008**:1
Cummings, Sam 1927- **1986**:3
D'Alessio, Kitty
 Brief entry **1987**:3
David, George 1942- **2005**:1
David Neville and Marcus
 Wainwright 1976- **2010**:3
Davis, Crispin 1949- **2004**:1
Davis, Todd 1967- **2010**:1
Davison, Ian Hay 1931- **1986**:1
DeBartolo, Edward J., Jr. 1946- **1989**
 :3
de la Renta, Oscar 1932- **2005**:4
Dell, Michael 1965- **1996**:2
DeLuca, Fred 1947- **2003**:3
De Luca, Guerrino 1952- **2007**:1
Deming, W. Edwards 1900-1993
 1992:2
 Obituary **1994**:2
de Passe, Suzanne 1946(?)- **1990**:4
Devine, John M. 1944- **2003**:2
Diemer, Walter E. 1904(?)-1998 **1998**
 :2
DiFranco, Ani 1970(?)- **1997**:1
Diller, Barry 1942- **1991**:1
Dimon, Jamie 1956- **2010**:3
Disney, Lillian 1899-1997
 Obituary **1998**:3
Disney, Roy E. 1930- **1986**:3
Dolby, Ray Milton
 Brief entry **1986**:1
Dolce, Domenico and Stefano
 Gabbana **2005**:4
Donahue, Tim 1950(?)- **2004**:3
Doubleday, Nelson, Jr. 1933- **1987**:1
Downey, Bruce 1947- **2003**:1
Drexler, Millard S. 1944- **1990**:3
Drucker, Peter F. 1909- **1992**:3
Duisenberg, Wim 1935-2005
 Obituary **2006**:4
Dunlap, Albert J. **1997**:2
Dupri, Jermaine 1972- **1999**:1
Dyson, James 1947- **2005**:4
Eagleson, Alan 1933- **1987**:4
Eaton, Robert J. 1940- **1994**:2
Ebbers, Bernie 1943- **1998**:1
Eckert, Robert A. 1955(?)- **2002**:3
Ecko, Marc 1972- **2006**:3
Egan, John 1939- **1987**:2
Eisner, Michael 1942- **1989**:2
Elbaz, Alber 1961- **2008**:1
Eliasch, Johan 1962- **2011**:3
Ellis, Perry 1940-1986
 Obituary **1986**:3
Ellison, Larry 1944- **2004**:2
Ells, Steve 1965- **2010**:1
Engibous, Thomas J. 1953- **2003**:3
Engles, Gregg L. 1957- **2007**:3
Engstrom, Elmer W. 1901-1984
 Obituary **1985**:2
Epstein, Jason 1928- **1991**:1
Ertegun, Ahmet 1923- **1986**:3
Estes, Pete 1916-1988
 Obituary **1988**:3
Evans, Nancy 1950- **2000**:4
Eyler, John. H., Jr. 1948(?)- **2001**:3

Kingsborough, Donald
  Brief entry **1986**:2
Kingsley, Patricia 1932- **1990**:2
Klein, Calvin 1942- **1996**:2
Kloss, Henry E.
  Brief entry **1985**:2
Kluge, John 1914- **1991**:1
Knight, Philip H. 1938- **1994**:1
Koch, Bill 1940- **1992**:3
Koch, Jim 1949- **2004**:3
Kohnstamm, Abby 1954- **2001**:1
Koogle, Tim 1951- **2000**:4
Koplovitz, Kay 1945- **1986**:3
Korchinsky, Mike 1961- **2004**:2
Kordich, Jay 1923- **1993**:2
Kovacevich, Dick 1943- **2004**:3
Kristiansen, Kjeld Kirk 1948(?)- **1988**
  :3
Kroc, Ray 1902-1984
  Obituary **1985**:1
Krogner, Heinz 1941(?)- **2004**:2
Kroll, Alexander S. 1938- **1989**:3
Kullman, Ellen 1956- **2009**:4
Kurzweil, Raymond 1948- **1986**:3
Kutaragi, Ken 1950- **2005**:3
Lacroix, Christian 1951- **2005**:2
Lafley, A. G. 1947- **2003**:4
Laimbeer, Bill 1957- **2004**:3
Lam, Derek 1966- **2009**:2
Lamborghini, Ferrucio 1916-1993
  Obituary **1993**:3
Land, Edwin H. 1909-1991
  Obituary **1991**:3
Lang, Eugene M. 1919- **1990**:3
Lansing, Sherry 1944- **1995**:4
Larian, Isaac 1954- **2008**:1
Lauder, Estee 1908(?)- **1992**:2
Lauren, Dylan 1974- **2010**:3
Lauren, Ralph 1939- **1990**:1
Laybourne, Geraldine 1947- **1997**:1
Lazarus, Charles 1923- **1992**:4
Lazarus, Shelly 1947- **1998**:3
Lear, Frances 1923- **1988**:3
Leigh, Dorian 1917-2008
  Obituary **2009**:3
Lelyveld, Joseph S. 1937- **1994**:4
Lemon, Ted
  Brief entry **1986**:4
Lepore, Nanette 1964(?)- **2006**:4
Lerner, Sandy 1955(?)- **2005**:1
Lester, W. 1935- **2011**:3
Levin, Gerald 1939- **1995**:2
Levinson, Arthur D. 1950- **2008**:3
Lewis, Kenneth D. 1947- **2009**:2
Lewis, Loida Nicolas 1942- **1998**:3
Lewis, Reginald F. 1942-1993 **1988**:4
  Obituary **1993**:3
Lhuillier, Monique 1971(?)- **2007**:4
Liguori, Peter 1960- **2005**:2
Lim, Phillip 1974(?)- **2008**:1
Lines, Ray 1960(?)- **2004**:1
Lopez de Arriortua, Jose Ignacio
  1941- **1993**:4
Louboutin, Christian 1963- **2006**:1
Lowe, Edward 1921- **1990**:2
Lowe, Mitch 1953- **2011**:2
Lowry, Adam and Eric Ryan **2008**:1
Lum, Olivia 1961- **2009**:1
Lutz, Robert A. 1932- **1990**:1
Lyne, Susan 1950- **2005**:4
Ma, Jack 1964- **2007**:1
Ma, Pony 1971(?)- **2006**:3

Macdonald, Julien 1973(?)- **2005**:3
Mack, John J. 1944- **2006**:3
Mackey, John 1953- **2008**:2
Madden, Chris 1948- **2006**:1
Madden, Steve 1958- **2007**:2
Malone, Jo 1964(?)- **2004**:3
Malone, John C. 1941- **1988**:3
Manheimer, Heidi 1963- **2009**:3
Maniscalco, Chuck 1953- **2010**:3
Marchionne, Sergio 1952- **2010**:4
Marcus, Stanley 1905-2002
  Obituary **2003**:1
Margolis, Bobby 1948(?)- **2007**:2
Marineau, Philip 1946- **2002**:4
Markle, C. Wilson 1938- **1988**:1
Marriott, J. Willard 1900-1985
  Obituary **1985**:4
Marriott, J. Willard, Jr. 1932- **1985**:4
Mas Canosa, Jorge 1939-1997 **1998**:2
Mashouf, Manny 1938(?)- **2008**:1
Master P 1970- **1999**:4
Mateschitz, Dietrich 1944- **2008**:1
Matsuhisa, Nobuyuki 1949- **2002**:3
Matthias, Rebecca 1953- **2010**:1
Maxwell, Hamish 1926- **1989**:4
Maxwell, Robert 1923- **1990**:1
Maxwell, Robert 1923-1991
  Obituary **1992**:2
McCauley, Matthew 1973- **2011**:1
McCloy, John J. 1895-1989
  Obituary **1989**:3
McColough, C. Peter 1922- **1990**:2
McDonald, Camille 1953(?)- **2004**:1
McDonnell, Sanford N. 1922- **1988**:4
McDougall, Ron 1942- **2001**:4
McElligott, Thomas J. 1943- **1987**:4
McGowan, William 1927- **1985**:2
McGowan, William G. 1927-1992
  Obituary **1993**:1
McGrath, Judy 1953- **2006**:1
McIntyre, Richard
  Brief entry **1986**:2
McKinnell, Henry 1943(?)- **2002**:3
McLaughlin, Betsy 1962(?)- **2004**:3
McMahon, Vince, Jr. 1945(?)- **1985**:4
McNamara, Robert S. 1916- **1995**:4
McNealy, Scott 1954- **1999**:4
McNerney, W. James 1949- **2006**:3
Mellinger, Frederick 1924(?)-1990
  Obituary **1990**:4
Mello, Dawn 1938(?)- **1992**:2
Melman, Richard
  Brief entry **1986**:1
Mengers, Sue 1938- **1985**:3
Millard, Barbara J.
  Brief entry **1985**:3
Miller, Merton H. 1923-2000
  Obituary **2001**:1
Miller, Rand 1959(?)- **1995**:4
Minkoff, Rebecca 1981- **2011**:3
Mitarai, Fujio 1935- **2002**:4
Mittal, Lakshmi 1950- **2007**:2
Mohajer, Dineh 1972- **1997**:3
Monaghan, Tom 1937- **1985**:1
Mondavi, Robert 1913- **1989**:2
Moody, John 1943- **1985**:3
Moonves, Les 1949- **2004**:2
Moore, Ann 1950- **2009**:1
Moreno, Arturo 1946- **2005**:2
Morgan, Dodge 1932(?)- **1987**:1
Morita, Akio 1921- **1989**:4
Morita, Akio 1921-1999

Obituary **2000**:2
Moritz, Charles 1936- **1989**:3
Morris, Doug 1938- **2005**:1
Morris, Robert 1947- **2010**:3
Mosbacher, Georgette 1947(?)- **1994**
  :2
Mulally, Alan 1945- **2010**:3
Mulcahy, Anne M. 1952- **2003**:2
Murakami, Takashi 1962- **2004**:2
Murdoch, Rupert 1931- **1988**:4
Murphy, Kathleen A. **2009**:2
Murray, Arthur 1895-1991
  Obituary **1991**:3
Musk, Elon 1971- **2011**:2
Nardelli, Robert 1948- **2008**:4
Nars, Francois 1959- **2003**:1
Neeleman, David 1959- **2003**:3
Neuharth, Allen H. 1924- **1986**:1
Newhouse, Samuel I., Jr. 1927- **1997**
  :1
Nick Friedman and Omar Soliman
  1982- **2011**:3
Nipon, Albert
  Brief entry **1986**:4
Nooyi, Indra 1955- **2004**:3
Noyce, Robert N. 1927- **1985**:4
Nussbaum, Karen 1950- **1988**:3
Ollila, Jorma 1950- **2003**:4
Olsen, Kenneth H. 1926- **1986**:4
Olsen, Sigrid 1953- **2007**:1
Oppenheimer, Harry 1908-2000
  Obituary **2001**:3
Orman, Suze 1951(?)- **2003**:1
Ostin, Mo 1927- **1996**:2
Otte, Ruth 1949- **1992**:4
Ovitz, Michael 1946- **1990**:1
Owen-Jones, Lindsay 1946(?)- **2004**:2
Packard, David 1912-1996
  Obituary **1996**:3
Page, Dick 1955- **2010**:1
Palmisano, Samuel J. 1952(?)- **2003**:1
Panichgul, Thakoon 1974- **2009**:4
Parsons, Gary 1950(?)- **2006**:2
Paulucci, Jeno
  Brief entry **1986**:3
Peebles, R. Donahue 1960- **2003**:2
Peller, Clara 1902(?)-1987
  Obituary **1988**:1
Peluso, Michelle 1971(?)- **2007**:4
Penske, Roger 1937- **1988**:3
Perdue, Frank 1920-2005
  Obituary **2006**:2
Perelman, Ronald 1943- **1989**:2
Perot, H. Ross 1930- **1992**:4
Persson, Stefan 1947- **2004**:1
Peters, Tom 1942- **1998**:1
Petersen, Donald Eugene 1926- **1985**
  :1
Petrossian, Christian
  Brief entry **1985**:3
Pfeiffer, Eckhard 1941- **1998**:4
Phelan, John Joseph, Jr. 1931- **1985**:4
Phillips, Sam 1923-2003
  Obituary **2004**:4
Pierce, Frederick S. 1934(?)- **1985**:3
Pincus, Mark 1966- **2011**:1
Pinto, Maria 1957- **2011**:2
Pittman, Robert W. 1953- **1985**:1
Pocklington, Peter H. 1941- **1985**:2
Popcorn, Faith
  Brief entry **1988**:1
Pope, Generoso 1927-1988 **1988**:4

Porizkova, Paulina
  Brief entry **1986**:4
Porsche, Ferdinand 1909-1998
  Obituary **1998**:4
Porter, Sylvia 1913-1991
  Obituary **1991**:4
Portman, John 1924- **1988**:2
Posen, Zac 1980- **2009**:3
Potter, Michael 1960(?)- **2003**:3
Pouillon, Nora 1943- **2005**:1
Prada, Miuccia 1950(?)- **1996**:1
Pratt, Jane 1963(?)- **1999**:1
Presser, Jackie 1926-1988
  Obituary **1988**:4
Pressler, Paul 1956(?)- **2003**:4
Prevor, Barry and Steven Shore **2006**
  :2
Price, Lisa 1962- **2010**:2
Price, Sol 1916-2009
  Obituary **2011**:4
Pritzker, A.N. 1896-1986
  Obituary **1986**:2
Probst, Larry 1951(?)- **2005**:1
Proctor, Barbara Gardner 1933(?)-
  1985:3
Puck, Wolfgang 1949- **1990**:1
Questrom, Allen 1940- **2001**:4
Quinn, Jane Bryant 1939(?)- **1993**:4
Radocy, Robert
  Brief entry **1986**:3
Ramsay, Gordon 1966- **2008**:2
Rand, A. Barry 1944- **2000**:3
Rapp, C.J.
  Brief entry **1987**:3
Rawlings, Mike 1954- **2003**:1
Raymond, Lee R. 1930- **2000**:3
Redenbacher, Orville 1907-1995
  Obituary **1996**:1
Redmond, Tim 1947- **2008**:1
Redstone, Sumner 1923- **1994**:1
Reese, Tracy 1964- **2010**:1
Regan, Judith 1953- **2003**:1
Reynolds, Paula Rosput 1956- **2008**:4
Rhodes, Zandra 1940- **1986**:2
Rice, Peter 1967(?)- **2007**:2
Richardson, Steve 1939- **2010**:4
Riggio, Leonard S. 1941- **1999**:4
Rigopulos, Alex 1970- **2009**:4
Riney, Hal 1932- **1989**:1
Riordan, Richard 1930- **1993**:4
Roberts, Xavier 1955- **1985**:3
Roddick, Anita 1943(?)- **1989**:4
Rodriguez, Narciso 1961- **2005**:1
Roedy, Bill 1949(?)- **2003**:2
Roncal, Mally 1972- **2009**:4
Ronson, Charlotte 1977(?)- **2007**:3
Rooney, Art 1901-1988
  Obituary **1989**:1
Roosevelt, Franklin D., Jr. 1914-1988
  Obituary **1989**:1
Rose, Lela 1969- **2011**:1
Rosenfeld, Irene 1953- **2008**:3
Ross, Percy
  Brief entry **1986**:2
Ross, Steven J. 1927-1992
  Obituary **1993**:3
Rossellini, Isabella 1952- **2001**:4
Rosso, Renzo 1955- **2005**:2
Rothschild, Philippe de 1902-1988
  Obituary **1988**:2
Rothstein, Ruth **1988**:2
Rovinescu, Calin 1955- **2010**:3

Rowe, Jack 1944- **2005**:2
Rowland, Pleasant **1992**:3
Rowley, Coleen 1955(?)- **2004**:2
Russo, Patricia 1952- **2008**:4
Saatchi, Maurice 1946- **1995**:4
Sachs, Jeffrey D. 1954- **2004**:4
Sagansky, Jeff 1952- **1993**:2
Saint Laurent, Yves 1936-2008
  Obituary **2009**:3
Sammons, Mary 1946- **2007**:4
Sams, Craig 1944- **2007**:3
Sander, Jil 1943- **1995**:2
Sanger, Steve 1946- **2002**:3
Sasakawa, Ryoichi
  Brief entry **1988**:1
Scardino, Marjorie 1947- **2002**:1
Schlessinger, David
  Brief entry **1985**:1
Schmelzer, Sheri 1965- **2009**:4
Schoenfeld, Gerald 1924- **1986**:2
Schott, Marge 1928- **1985**:4
Schrempp, Juergen 1944- **2000**:2
Schultz, Howard 1953- **1995**:3
Schwab, Charles 1937(?)- **1989**:3
Schwartz, Allen 1945(?)- **2008**:2
Schwinn, Edward R., Jr.
  Brief entry **1985**:4
Scott, H. Lee, Jr. 1949- **2008**:3
Scott, Pamella 1975- **2010**:4
Sculley, John 1939- **1989**:4
Sedelmaier, Joe 1933- **1985**:3
Segal, Shelli 1955(?)- **2005**:3
Seidenberg, Ivan 1946- **2004**:1
Senk, Glen 1956- **2009**:3
Shaich, Ron 1953- **2004**:4
Siebert, Muriel 1932(?)- **1987**:2
Simmons, Russell and Kimora Lee
  2003:2
Skaist-Levy, Pam and Gela Taylor
  2005:1
Slatkin, Harry 1961(?)- **2006**:2
Smale, John G. 1927- **1987**:3
Smith, Frederick W. 1944- **1985**:4
Smith, Jack 1938- **1994**:3
Smith, Lanty 1942- **2009**:3
Smith, Roger 1925- **1990**:3
Smyth, Russell P. 1958- **2009**:4
Snider, Stacey 1961(?)- **2002**:4
Snyder, Ron 1956(?)- **2007**:4
Som, Peter 1971- **2009**:1
Spade, Kate 1962- **2003**:1
Spector, Phil 1940- **1989**:1
Spitzer, Silda Wall 1957- **2010**:2
Spray, Ed 1941- **2004**:1
Sprouse, Stephen 1953-2004
  Obituary **2005**:2
Starck, Philippe 1949- **2004**:1
Steel, Dawn 1946-1997 **1990**:1
  Obituary **1998**:2
Steinberg, Leigh 1949- **1987**:3
Steinbrenner, George 1930- **1991**:1
Stempel, Robert 1933- **1991**:3
Stephens, Arran and Ratana **2008**:4
Stern, David 1942- **1991**:4
Stevens, Anne 1949(?)- **2006**:3
Stewart, Julia 1955- **2008**:3
Stewart, Martha 1942(?)- **1992**:1
Stonesifer, Patty 1956- **1997**:1
Stroh, Peter W. 1927- **1985**:2
Strong, Maurice 1929- **1993**:1
Sullivan, Andrew 1964(?)- **1996**:1
Summers, Anne 1945- **1990**:2

Tagliabue, Paul 1940- **1990**:2
Takada, Kenzo 1938- **2003**:2
Tanny, Vic 1912(?)-1985
  Obituary **1985**:3
Tartikoff, Brandon 1949-1997 **1985**:2
  Obituary **1998**:1
Tellem, Nancy 1953(?)- **2004**:4
Temperley, Alice 1975- **2008**:2
Thain, John 1955- **2009**:2
Thalheimer, Richard 1948-
  Brief entry **1988**:3
Thomas, Dave **1986**:2
  Obituary **2003**:1
Thomas, Michel 1911(?)- **1987**:4
Thomas-Graham, Pamela 1963- **2007**
  :1
Thompson, John W. 1949- **2005**:1
Tilberis, Elizabeth 1947(?)- **1994**:3
Tillman, Robert L. 1944(?)- **2004**:1
Timberlake, Justin 1981- **2008**:4
Tisch, Laurence A. 1923- **1988**:2
Tompkins, Susie
  Brief entry **1987**:2
Touitou, Jean 1952(?)- **2008**:4
Toyoda, Akio 1956- **2011**:1
Toyoda, Eiji 1913- **1985**:2
Trask, Amy 1961- **2003**:3
Traub, Marvin
  Brief entry **1987**:3
Treybig, James G. 1940- **1988**:3
Trotman, Alex 1933- **1995**:4
Trotter, Charlie 1960- **2000**:4
Troutt, Kenny A. 1948- **1998**:1
Trump, Donald 1946- **1989**:2
Trump, Ivana 1949- **1995**:2
Turlington, Christy 1969(?)- **2001**:4
Turner, Ted 1938- **1989**:1
Tyler, Richard 1948(?)- **1995**:3
Tyson, Don 1930- **1995**:3
Unz, Ron 1962(?)- **1999**:1
Upshaw, Gene 1945- **1988**:1
Vagelos, P. Roy 1929- **1989**:4
Valli, Giambattista 1966- **2008**:3
Van Andel, Jay 1924-2004
  Obituary **2006**:1
Varvatos, John 1956(?)- **2006**:2
Vasella, Daniel 1953- **2005**:3
Veeck, Bill 1914-1986
  Obituary **1986**:1
Versace, Donatella 1955- **1999**:1
Versace, Gianni 1946-1997
  Brief entry **1988**:1
  Obituary **1998**:2
Vigdor, Ron 1970- **2011**:4
Vinton, Will
  Brief entry **1988**:1
Vischer, Phil 1966- **2002**:2
Von D, Kat 1982- **2008**:3
von Furstenberg, Diane 1946- **1994**:2
Wachner, Linda 1946- **1988**:3
Waitt, Ted 1963(?)- **1997**:4
Waldron, Hicks B. 1923- **1987**:3
Walgreen, Charles III
  Brief entry **1987**:4
Walker, Jay 1955- **2004**:2
Walton, Sam 1918-1992 **1986**:2
  Obituary **1993**:1
Wang, Alexander 1984- **2011**:4
Wang, An 1920-1990 **1986**:1
  Obituary **1990**:3
Ware, Lancelot 1915-2000
  Obituary **2001**:1

Waters, Alice 1944- **2006**:3
Watkins, Sherron 1959- **2003**:1
Weill, Sandy 1933- **1990**:4
Weinstein, Bob and Harvey **2000**:4
Weintraub, Jerry 1937- **1986**:1
Welch, Jack 1935- **1993**:3
Weldon, William 1948- **2007**:4
Westwood, Vivienne 1941- **1998**:3
Whiting, Susan 1956- **2007**:4
Whitman, Meg 1957- **2000**:3
Whittle, Christopher 1947- **1989**:3
Williams, Edward Bennett 1920-1988
    Obituary **1988**:4
Williams, Lynn 1924- **1986**:4
Wilson, Jerry
    Brief entry **1986**:2
Wilson, Peter C. 1913-1984
    Obituary **1985**:2
Wintour, Anna 1949- **1990**:4
Woertz, Patricia A. 1953- **2007**:3
Wolf, Stephen M. 1941- **1989**:3
Wong, Andrea 1966- **2009**:1
Woodcock, Leonard 1911-2001
    Obituary **2001**:4
Woodruff, Robert Winship 1889-1985
    Obituary **1985**:1
Wren, John 1952(?)- **2007**:2
Wrigley, William, Jr. 1964(?)- **2002**:2
Wu, Jason 1983- **2010**:3
Wynn, Stephen A. 1942- **1994**:3
Yamamoto, Kenichi 1922- **1989**:1
Yetnikoff, Walter 1933- **1988**:1
Yunus, Muhammad 1940- **2007**:3
Zagat, Tim and Nina **2004**:3
Zamboni, Frank J.
    Brief entry **1986**:4
Zanker, Bill
    Brief entry **1987**:3
Zetcher, Arnold B. 1940- **2002**:1
Zetsche, Dieter 1953- **2002**:3
Ziff, William B., Jr. 1930- **1986**:4
Zoe, Rachel 1971- **2010**:2
Zuckerman, Mortimer 1937- **1986**:3

DANCE

Abdul, Paula 1962- **1990**:3
Acosta, Carlos 1973(?)- **1997**:4
Ailey, Alvin 1931-1989 **1989**:2
    Obituary **1990**:2
Allen, Debbie 1950- **1998**:2
Astaire, Fred 1899-1987
    Obituary **1987**:4
Baryshnikov, Mikhail Nikolaevich
    1948- **1997**:3
Bausch, Pina 1940-2009
    Obituary **2010**:4
Bejart, Maurice 1927-2007
    Obituary **2009**:1
Bennett, Michael 1943-1987
    Obituary **1988**:1
Bissell, Patrick 1958-1987
    Obituary **1988**:2
Bocca, Julio 1967- **1995**:3
Bujones, Fernando 1955-2005
    Obituary **2007**:1
Campbell, Neve 1973- **1998**:2
Charisse, Cyd 1922-2008
    Obituary **2009**:3
Cunningham, Merce 1919- **1998**:1
Davis, Sammy, Jr. 1925-1990
    Obituary **1990**:4
Dean, Laura 1945- **1989**:4

de Mille, Agnes 1905-1993
    Obituary **1994**:2
de Valois, Dame Ninette 1898-2001
    Obituary **2002**:1
Dudley, Jane 1912-2001
    Obituary **2002**:4
Dunham, Katherine 1909-2006
    Obituary **2007**:2
Englund, Richard 1932(?)-1991
    Obituary **1991**:3
Fagan, Garth 1940- **2000**:1
Farrell, Suzanne 1945- **1996**:3
Feld, Eliot 1942- **1996**:1
Fenley, Molissa 1954- **1988**:3
Ferri, Alessandra 1963- **1987**:2
Flatley, Michael 1958- **1997**:3
Fonteyn, Margot 1919-1991
    Obituary **1991**:3
Forsythe, William 1949- **1993**:2
Fosse, Bob 1927-1987
    Obituary **1988**:1
Garr, Teri 1949- **1988**:4
Glover, Savion 1973- **1997**:1
Godunov, Alexander 1949-1995
    Obituary **1995**:4
Graham, Martha 1894-1991
    Obituary **1991**:4
Gregory, Cynthia 1946- **1990**:2
Guillem, Sylvie 1965(?)- **1988**:2
Herrera, Paloma 1975- **1996**:2
Hewitt, Jennifer Love 1979- **1999**:2
Hines, Gregory 1946- **1992**:4
Jackson, Janet 1966(?)- **1990**:4
Jamison, Judith 1944- **1990**:3
Joffrey, Robert 1930-1988
    Obituary **1988**:3
Jones, Bill T. **1991**:4
Kaye, Nora 1920-1987
    Obituary **1987**:4
Keeler, Ruby 1910-1993
    Obituary **1993**:4
Kelly, Gene 1912-1996
    Obituary **1996**:3
Kidd, Michael 1915-2007
    Obituary **2009**:1
Kistler, Darci 1964- **1993**:1
Lander, Toni 1931-1985
    Obituary **1985**:4
Lewitzky, Bella 1916-2004
    Obituary **2005**:3
Lythgoe, Nigel 1949- **2010**:4
MacMillan, Kenneth 1929-1992
    Obituary **1993**:2
Madonna 1958- **1985**:2
Marshall, Susan 1958- **2000**:4
Millepied, Benjamin 1977(?)- **2006**:4
Miller, Ann 1923-2004
    Obituary **2005**:2
Miller, Bebe 1950- **2000**:2
Mitchell, Arthur 1934- **1995**:1
Moiseyev, Igor 1906-2007
    Obituary **2009**:1
Moore, Rachel 1965- **2008**:2
Morris, Mark 1956- **1991**:1
Murray, Arthur 1895-1991
    Obituary **1991**:3
North, Alex 1910- **1986**:3
Nureyev, Rudolf 1938-1993
    Obituary **1993**:2
Parker, Sarah Jessica 1965- **1999**:2
Parsons, David 1959- **1993**:4
Perez, Rosie **1994**:2

Prowse, Juliet 1937-1996
    Obituary **1997**:1
Rauschenberg, Robert 1925- **1991**:2
Renvall, Johan
    Brief entry **1987**:4
Robbins, Jerome 1918-1998
    Obituary **1999**:1
Rogers, Ginger 1911(?)-1995
    Obituary **1995**:4
Stroman, Susan **2000**:4
Swayze, Patrick 1952-2009
    Obituary **2011**:1
Takei, Kei 1946- **1990**:2
Taylor, Paul 1930- **1992**:3
Tharp, Twyla 1942- **1992**:4
Tudor, Antony 1908(?)-1987
    Obituary **1987**:4
Tune, Tommy 1939- **1994**:2
Varone, Doug 1956- **2001**:2
Verdi-Fletcher, Mary 1955- **1998**:2
Verdon, Gwen 1925-2000
    Obituary **2001**:2
Whelan, Wendy 1967(?)- **1999**:3

EDUCATION

Abramson, Lyn 1950- **1986**:3
Alexander, Lamar 1940- **1991**:2
Ayala, Francisco 1906-2009
    Obituary **2011**:3
Bakker, Robert T. 1950(?)- **1991**:3
Bayley, Corrine
    Brief entry **1986**:4
Billington, James 1929- **1990**:3
Bollinger, Lee C. 1946- **2003**:2
Botstein, Leon 1946- **1985**:3
Bush, Millie 1987- **1992**:1
Campbell, Bebe Moore 1950- **1996**:2
Cartwright, Carol Ann 1941- **2009**:4
Casper, Gerhard 1937- **1993**:1
Cavazos, Lauro F. 1927- **1989**:2
Cheek, James Edward
    Brief entry **1987**:1
Cheney, Lynne V. 1941- **1990**:4
Clements, George 1932- **1985**:1
Cole, Johnetta B. 1936- **1994**:3
Coleman, Mary Sue 1943- **2010**:1
Coles, Robert 1929(?)- **1995**:1
Commager, Henry Steele 1902-1998
    Obituary **1998**:3
Cowen, Scott 1946- **2011**:2
Crow, Michael 1956- **2011**:3
Curran, Charles E. 1934- **1989**:2
Davis, Angela 1944- **1998**:3
Delany, Sarah 1889-1999
    Obituary **1999**:3
Deming, W. Edwards 1900-1993
    1992:2
    Obituary **1994**:2
Dershowitz, Alan 1938(?)- **1992**:1
Dove, Rita 1952- **1994**:3
Drucker, Peter F. 1909- **1992**:3
Duncan, Arne 1964- **2011**:3
Eberhart, Richard 1904-2005
    Obituary **2006**:3
Edelman, Marian Wright 1939- **1990**
    :4
Edwards, Harry 1942- **1989**:4
Etzioni, Amitai 1929- **1994**:3
Faust, Drew Gilpin 1947- **2008**:1
Feldman, Sandra 1939- **1987**:3
Ferguson, Niall 1964- **2006**:1
Fernandez, Joseph 1935- **1991**:3

Folkman, Judah 1933- **1999**:1
Fox, Matthew 1940- **1992**:2
Friedman, Milton 1912-2006
  Obituary **2008**:1
Fulbright, J. William 1905-1995
  Obituary **1995**:3
Futrell, Mary Hatwood 1940- **1986**:1
Futter, Ellen V. 1949- **1995**:1
Garcia, Juliet 1949- **2011**:1
Gee, E. 1944- **2011**:3
Ghali, Boutros Boutros 1922- **1992**:3
Giamatti, A. Bartlett 1938-1989 **1988**
  :4
  Obituary **1990**:1
Goldhaber, Fred
  Brief entry **1986**:3
Gordon, Mary 1947- **2011**:4
Gray, Hanna 1930- **1992**:4
Green, Richard R. 1936- **1988**:3
Gregorian, Vartan 1934- **1990**:3
Groves, Robert 1949- **2011**:3
Gund, Agnes 1938- **1993**:2
Gutmann, Amy 1949- **2008**:4
Hackney, Sheldon 1933- **1995**:1
Hair, Jay D. 1945- **1994**:3
Harker, Patrick T. 1958- **2001**:2
Hayakawa, Samuel Ichiye 1906-1992
  Obituary **1992**:3
Healy, Bernadine 1944- **1993**:1
Healy, Timothy S. 1923- **1990**:2
Heaney, Seamus 1939- **1996**:2
Heller, Walter 1915-1987
  Obituary **1987**:4
Hennessy, John L. 1952- **2002**:2
Hill, Anita 1956- **1994**:1
Hill, J. Edward 1938- **2006**:2
Hillegass, Clifton Keith 1918- **1989**:4
Hockfield, Susan 1951- **2009**:2
Horwich, Frances 1908-2001
  Obituary **2002**:3
Hunter, Madeline 1916(?)- **1991**:2
Jablonski, Nina G. 1953- **2009**:3
Janzen, Daniel H. 1939- **1988**:4
Jin, Ha 1956- **2011**:3
Jones, Edward P. 1950- **2005**:1
Jordan, King 1943(?)- **1990**:1
Justiz, Manuel J. 1948- **1986**:4
Kandel, Eric 1929- **2005**:2
Kellerman, Jonathan 1949- **2009**:1
Kemp, Jan 1949- **1987**:2
Kerr, Clark 1911-2003
  Obituary **2005**:1
King, Mary-Claire 1946- **1998**:3
Kopp, Wendy **1993**:3
Kozol, Jonathan 1936- **1992**:1
Lagasse, Emeril 1959- **1998**:3
Lamb, Wally 1950- **1999**:1
Lang, Eugene M. 1919- **1990**:3
Langston, J. William
  Brief entry **1986**:2
Lawrence, Ruth
  Brief entry **1986**:3
Laybourne, Geraldine 1947- **1997**:1
Leach, Penelope 1937- **1992**:4
Lee, Chang-Rae 1965- **2005**:1
Lerner, Michael 1943- **1994**:2
Levine, Arnold 1939- **2002**:3
Liebowitz, Ronald 1957- **2011**:1
MacKinnon, Catharine 1946- **1993**:2
Malloy, Edward Monk 1941- **1989**:4
Manson, JoAnn E. 1953- **2008**:3
Marier, Rebecca 1974- **1995**:4

McAuliffe, Christa 1948-1986
  Obituary **1985**:4
McCall Smith, Alexander 1948- **2005**
  :2
McMillan, Terry 1951- **1993**:2
Melton, Douglas 1954- **2008**:3
Morrison, Toni 1931- **1998**:1
Mumford, Lewis 1895-1990
  Obituary **1990**:2
Murano, Elsa 1959- **2009**:1
Nemerov, Howard 1920-1991
  Obituary **1992**:1
Nocera, Fred 1957- **2010**:3
Nye, Bill 1955- **1997**:2
O'Keefe, Sean 1956- **2005**:2
Owens, Delia and Mark **1993**:3
Padron, Eduardo 1946- **2011**:2
Pagels, Elaine 1943- **1997**:1
Paglia, Camille 1947- **1992**:3
Paige, Rod 1933- **2003**:2
Parizeau, Jacques 1930- **1995**:1
Pausch, Randy 1960-2008
  Obituary **2009**:3
Peter, Valentine J. 1934- **1988**:2
Riley, Richard W. 1933- **1996**:3
Rodin, Judith 1945(?)- **1994**:4
Rosendahl, Bruce R.
  Brief entry **1986**:4
Rowland, Pleasant **1992**:3
Samuelson, Paul 1915-2009
  Obituary **2011**:4
Scheck, Barry 1949- **2000**:4
Schuman, Patricia Glass 1943- **1993**
  :2
Sexton, John 1942- **2011**:4
Shalala, Donna 1941- **1992**:3
Sherman, Russell 1930- **1987**:4
Silber, Joan 1945- **2009**:4
Silber, John 1926- **1990**:1
Simmons, Adele Smith 1941- **1988**:4
Simmons, Ruth 1945- **1995**:2
Simon, Lou Anna K. 1947- **2005**:4
Singer, Margaret Thaler 1921-2003
  Obituary **2005**:1
Sizer, Theodore 1932-2009
  Obituary **2011**:2
Smoot, George F. 1945- **1993**:3
Sowell, Thomas 1930- **1998**:3
Spellings, Margaret 1957- **2005**:4
Spock, Benjamin 1903-1998 **1995**:2
  Obituary **1998**:3
Steele, Shelby 1946- **1991**:2
Strout, Elizabeth 1956- **2009**:1
Swanson, Mary Catherine 1944-
  2002:2
Tannen, Deborah 1945- **1995**:1
Thiebaud, Wayne 1920- **1991**:1
Thomas, Michel 1911(?)- **1987**:4
Tilghman, Shirley M. 1946- **2002**:1
Tohe, Laura 1953- **2009**:2
Tretheway, Natasha 1966- **2008**:3
Tribe, Laurence H. 1941- **1988**:1
Tyson, Laura D'Andrea 1947- **1994**:1
Unz, Ron 1962(?)- **1999**:1
Van Duyn, Mona 1921- **1993**:2
Vickrey, William S. 1914-1996
  Obituary **1997**:2
Warren, Elizabeth 1949- **2010**:2
Warren, Robert Penn 1905-1989
  Obituary **1990**:1
West, Cornel 1953- **1994**:2
Wexler, Nancy S. 1945- **1992**:3

Whitney, Patrick 1952(?)- **2006**:1
Wiesel, Elie 1928- **1998**:1
Wigand, Jeffrey 1943(?)- **2000**:4
Wiles, Andrew 1953(?)- **1994**:1
Wilson, Edward O. 1929- **1994**:4
Wilson, William Julius 1935- **1997**:1
Wolff, Tobias 1945- **2005**:1
Wu, Harry 1937- **1996**:1
Yudof, Mark 1944- **2009**:4
Zanker, Bill
  Brief entry **1987**:3
Zigler, Edward 1930- **1994**:1

FILM

Abbott, George 1887-1995
  Obituary **1995**:3
Abrams, J. J. 1966- **2007**:3
Adams, Amy 1974- **2008**:4
Adjani, Isabelle 1955- **1991**:1
Affleck, Ben 1972- **1999**:1
Aiello, Danny 1933- **1990**:4
Albert, Eddie 1906-2005
  Obituary **2006**:3
Alda, Robert 1914-1986
  Obituary **1986**:3
Alexander, Jane 1939- **1994**:2
Alexander, Jason 1962(?)- **1993**:3
Allen, Debbie 1950- **1998**:2
Allen, Joan 1956- **1998**:1
Allen, Woody 1935- **1994**:1
Alley, Kirstie 1955- **1990**:3
Allyson, June 1917-2006
  Obituary **2007**:3
Almodovar, Pedro 1951- **2000**:3
Altman, Robert 1925- **1993**:2
Ameche, Don 1908-1993
  Obituary **1994**:2
Anderson, Judith 1899(?)-1992
  Obituary **1992**:3
Andrews, Julie 1935- **1996**:1
Aniston, Jennifer 1969- **2000**:3
Apatow, Judd 1967- **2006**:3
Applegate, Christina 1972- **2000**:4
Arad, Avi 1948- **2003**:2
Arden, Eve 1912(?)-1990
  Obituary **1991**:2
Arkin, Alan 1934- **2007**:4
Arkoff, Samuel Z. 1918-2001
  Obituary **2002**:4
Arlen, Harold 1905-1986
  Obituary **1986**:3
Arnaz, Desi 1917-1986
  Obituary **1987**:1
Arnold, Tom 1959- **1993**:2
Arquette, Patricia 1968- **2001**:3
Arquette, Rosanna 1959- **1985**:2
Arthur, Jean 1901(?)-1991
  Obituary **1992**:1
Ashcroft, Peggy 1907-1991
  Obituary **1992**:1
Astaire, Fred 1899-1987
  Obituary **1987**:4
Astin, Sean 1971- **2005**:1
Astor, Mary 1906-1987
  Obituary **1988**:1
Atkinson, Rowan 1955- **2004**:3
Autry, Gene 1907-1998
  Obituary **1999**:1
Aykroyd, Dan 1952- **1989**:3
Bacall, Lauren 1924- **1997**:3
Backus, Jim 1913-1989
  Obituary **1990**:1

Bacon, Kevin 1958- **1995**:3
Baddeley, Hermione 1906(?)-1986
   Obituary **1986**:4
Bailey, Pearl 1918-1990
   Obituary **1991**:1
Bakula, Scott 1954- **2003**:1
Baldwin, Alec 1958- **2002**:2
Bale, Christian 1974- **2001**:3
Ball, Alan 1957- **2005**:1
Ball, Lucille 1911-1989
   Obituary **1989**:3
Bancroft, Anne 1931-2005
   Obituary **2006**:3
Banderas, Antonio 1960- **1996**:2
Banks, Tyra 1973- **1996**:3
Bardem, Javier 1969- **2008**:4
Barker, Clive 1952- **2003**:3
Barkin, Ellen 1955- **1987**:3
Baron Cohen, Sacha 1971- **2007**:3
Barr, Roseanne 1953(?)- **1989**:1
Barry, Gene 1919-2009
   Obituary **2011**:4
Barrymore, Drew 1975- **1995**:3
Baryshnikov, Mikhail Nikolaevich
   1948- **1997**:3
Basinger, Kim 1953- **1987**:2
Bassett, Angela 1959(?)- **1994**:4
Bateman, Jason 1969- **2005**:3
Bateman, Justine 1966- **1988**:4
Bates, Alan 1934-2003
   Obituary **2005**:1
Bates, Kathy 1949(?)- **1991**:4
Baxter, Anne 1923-1985
   Obituary **1986**:1
Beals, Jennifer 1963- **2005**:2
Beatty, Warren 1937- **2000**:1
Belushi, Jim 1954- **1986**:2
Benigni, Roberto 1952- **1999**:2
Bening, Annette 1958(?)- **1992**:1
Bennett, Joan 1910-1990
   Obituary **1991**:2
Bergen, Candice 1946- **1990**:1
Bergeron, Tom 1955- **2010**:1
Bergman, Ingmar 1918- **1999**:4
Berman, Gail 1957(?)- **2006**:1
Bernardi, Herschel 1923-1986
   Obituary **1986**:4
Bernhard, Sandra 1955(?)- **1989**:4
Bernsen, Corbin 1955- **1990**:2
Berry, Halle 1968- **1996**:2
Beyonce 1981- **2009**:3
Bialik, Mayim 1975- **1993**:3
Bigelow, Kathryn 1951- **2011**:1
Bigelow, Kathryn 1952(?)- **1990**:4
Binoche, Juliette 1965- **2001**:3
Birch, Thora 1982- **2002**:4
Bird, Brad 1956(?)- **2005**:4
Bishop, Joey 1918-2007
   Obituary **2008**:4
Black, Jack 1969- **2002**:3
Blades, Ruben 1948- **1998**:2
Blanc, Mel 1908-1989
   Obituary **1989**:4
Blanchett, Cate 1969- **1999**:3
Bloom, Orlando 1977- **2004**:2
Bogosian, Eric 1953- **1990**:4
Bolger, Ray 1904-1987
   Obituary **1987**:2
Bonet, Lisa 1967- **1989**:2
Bonham Carter, Helena 1966- **1998**:4
Booth, Shirley 1898-1992
   Obituary **1993**:2

Bosworth, Kate 1983- **2006**:3
Bowen, Julie 1970- **2007**:1
Bowie, David 1947- **1998**:2
Boyle, Danny 1956- **2009**:4
Boyle, Lara Flynn 1970- **2003**:4
Boyle, Peter 1935- **2002**:3
Braff, Zach 1975- **2005**:2
Branagh, Kenneth 1960- **1992**:2
Brand, Russell 1975- **2010**:2
Brandauer, Klaus Maria 1944- **1987**:3
Brando, Marlon 1924-2004
   Obituary **2005**:3
Bratt, Benjamin 1963- **2009**:3
Bridges, Jeff 1949- **2011**:1
Bridges, Lloyd 1913-1998
   Obituary **1998**:3
Brillstein, Bernie 1931-2008
   Obituary **2009**:4
Broadbent, Jim 1949- **2008**:4
Brody, Adrien 1973- **2006**:3
Bronson, Charles 1921-2003
   Obituary **2004**:4
Brooks, Albert 1948(?)- **1991**:4
Brooks, Mel 1926- **2003**:1
Brosnan, Pierce 1952- **2000**:3
Brown, James 1928(?)- **1991**:4
Brown, Jim 1936- **1993**:2
Brown, Ruth 1928-2006
   Obituary **2008**:1
Bruckheimer, Jerry 1945- **2007**:2
Brynner, Yul 1920(?)-1985
   Obituary **1985**:4
Buckley, Betty 1947- **1996**:2
Bullock, Sandra 1967- **1995**:4
Burnett, Carol 1933- **2000**:3
Burns, Edward 1968- **1997**:1
Burns, George 1896-1996
   Obituary **1996**:3
Burns, Ken 1953- **1995**:2
Burr, Raymond 1917-1993
   Obituary **1994**:1
Burstyn, Ellen 1932- **2001**:4
Burton, Tim 1959- **1993**:1
Burum, Stephen H.
   Brief entry **1987**:2
Buscemi, Steve 1957- **1997**:4
Butler, Gerard 1969- **2011**:2
Buttons, Red 1919-2006
   Obituary **2007**:3
Bynes, Amanda 1986- **2005**:1
Byrne, Gabriel 1950- **1997**:4
Caan, James 1939- **2004**:4
Caesar, Adolph 1934-1986
   Obituary **1986**:3
Cage, Nicolas 1964- **1991**:1
Cagney, James 1899-1986
   Obituary **1986**:2
Caine, Michael 1933- **2000**:4
Calhoun, Rory 1922-1999
   Obituary **1999**:4
Campbell, Naomi 1970- **2000**:2
Campbell, Neve 1973- **1998**:2
Campion, Jane **1991**:4
Candy, John 1950-1994 **1988**:2
   Obituary **1994**:3
Cannon, Nick 1980- **2006**:4
Capra, Frank 1897-1991
   Obituary **1992**:2
Carell, Steve 1963- **2006**:4
Carey, Drew 1958- **1997**:4
Carlin, George 1937- **1996**:3
Carney, Art 1918-2003

   Obituary **2005**:1
Carradine, David 1936-2009
   Obituary **2010**:3
Carradine, John 1906-1988
   Obituary **1989**:2
Carrey, Jim 1962- **1995**:1
Carson, Lisa Nicole 1969- **1999**:3
Caruso, David 1956(?)- **1994**:3
Carvey, Dana 1955- **1994**:1
Cassavetes, John 1929-1989
   Obituary **1989**:2
Castellucci, Cecil 1969- **2008**:3
Castle-Hughes, Keisha 1990- **2004**:4
Cattrall, Kim 1956- **2003**:3
Caulfield, Joan 1922(?)-1991
   Obituary **1992**:1
Cavanagh, Tom 1968- **2003**:1
Caviezel, Jim 1968- **2005**:3
Chahine, Youssef 1926-2008
   Obituary **2009**:3
Chan, Jackie 1954- **1996**:1
Chandler, Kyle 1965- **2010**:4
Channing, Stockard 1946- **1991**:3
Chappelle, Dave 1973- **2005**:3
Charisse, Cyd 1922-2008
   Obituary **2009**:3
Chase, Chevy 1943- **1990**:1
Chase, Debra Martin 1956- **2009**:1
Cheadle, Don 1964- **2002**:1
Chen, Joan 1961- **2000**:2
Cher 1946- **1993**:1
Chiklis, Michael 1963- **2003**:3
Chow, Stephen 1962- **2006**:1
Chow Yun-fat 1955- **1999**:4
Christensen, Hayden 1981- **2003**:3
Christie, Julie 1941- **2008**:4
Clarkson, Patricia 1959- **2005**:3
Clay, Andrew Dice 1958- **1991**:1
Cleese, John 1939- **1989**:2
Close, Glenn 1947- **1988**:3
Coburn, James 1928-2002
   Obituary **2004**:1
Coco, James 1929(?)-1987
   Obituary **1987**:2
Cody, Diablo 1978- **2009**:1
Coen, Joel and Ethan **1992**:1
Colbert, Claudette 1903-1996
   Obituary **1997**:1
Colbert, Stephen 1964- **2007**:4
Coleman, Dabney 1932- **1988**:3
Collette, Toni 1972- **2009**:4
Condon, Bill 1955- **2007**:3
Connelly, Jennifer 1970- **2002**:4
Connery, Sean 1930- **1990**:4
Connick, Harry, Jr. 1967- **1991**:1
Cooper, Chris 1951- **2004**:1
Coppola, Carmine 1910-1991
   Obituary **1991**:4
Coppola, Francis Ford 1939- **1989**:4
Coppola, Sofia 1971- **2004**:3
Corbett, John 1962- **2004**:1
Cosby, Bill 1937- **1999**:2
Cosgrove, Miranda 1993- **2011**:4
Costner, Kevin 1955- **1989**:4
Cotillard, Marion 1975- **2009**:1
Cox, Courteney 1964- **1996**:2
Craig, Daniel 1968- **2008**:1
Cranston, Bryan 1956- **2010**:1
Craven, Wes 1939- **1997**:3
Crawford, Broderick 1911-1986
   Obituary **1986**:3
Crenna, Richard 1926-2003

Obituary **2004**:1
Crichton, Michael 1942- **1995**:3
Cronenberg, David 1943- **1992**:3
Cronyn, Hume 1911-2003
   Obituary **2004**:3
Crothers, Scatman 1910-1986
   Obituary **1987**:1
Crowe, Cameron 1957- **2001**:2
Crowe, Russell 1964- **2000**:4
Cruise, Tom 1962(?)- **1985**:4
Cruz, Penelope 1974- **2001**:4
Cryer, Jon 1965- **2010**:4
Crystal, Billy 1947- **1985**:3
Cuaron, Alfonso 1961- **2008**:2
Culkin, Macaulay 1980(?)- **1991**:3
Curtis, Jamie Lee 1958- **1995**:1
Cusack, John 1966- **1999**:3
Cushing, Peter 1913-1994
   Obituary **1995**:1
Dafoe, Willem 1955- **1988**:1
Dalton, Timothy 1946- **1988**:4
Damon, Matt 1970- **1999**:1
Dancy, Hugh 1975- **2010**:3
Danes, Claire 1979- **1999**:4
Dangerfield, Rodney 1921-2004
   Obituary **2006**:1
Daniels, Jeff 1955- **1989**:4
Danza, Tony 1951- **1989**:1
David, Larry 1948- **2003**:4
Davis, Bette 1908-1989
   Obituary **1990**:1
Davis, Geena 1957- **1992**:1
Davis, Ossie 1917-2005
   Obituary **2006**:1
Davis, Sammy, Jr. 1925-1990
   Obituary **1990**:4
Davis, Viola 1965- **2011**:4
Dawson, Rosario 1979- **2007**:2
Day, Dennis 1917-1988
   Obituary **1988**:4
Day-Lewis, Daniel 1957- **1989**:4
De Cordova, Frederick 1910- **1985**:2
Dee, Sandra 1942-2005
   Obituary **2006**:2
DeGeneres, Ellen **1995**:3
Delany, Dana 1956- **2008**:4
Del Toro, Benicio 1967- **2001**:4
Del Toro, Guillermo 1964- **2010**:3
DeLuise, Dom 1933-2009
   Obituary **2010**:2
De Matteo, Drea 1973- **2005**:2
Demme, Jonathan 1944- **1992**:4
Dempsey, Patrick 1966- **2006**:1
Dench, Judi 1934- **1999**:4
Deneuve, Catherine 1943- **2003**:2
De Niro, Robert 1943- **1999**:1
Dennehy, Brian 1938- **2002**:1
Dennis, Sandy 1937-1992
   Obituary **1992**:4
De Palma, Brian 1940- **2007**:3
Depardieu, Gerard 1948- **1991**:2
Depp, Johnny 1963(?)- **1991**:3
Dern, Laura 1967- **1992**:3
Deschanel, Zooey 1980- **2010**:4
De Vito, Danny 1944- **1987**:1
Diamond, I.A.L. 1920-1988
   Obituary **1988**:3
Diamond, Selma 1921(?)-1985
   Obituary **1985**:2
Diaz, Cameron 1972- **1999**:1
DiCaprio, Leonardo Wilhelm 1974-
   1997:2

Diesel, Vin 1967- **2004**:1
Dietrich, Marlene 1901-1992
   Obituary **1992**:4
Diggs, Taye 1971- **2000**:1
Diller, Barry 1942- **1991**:1
Dillon, Matt 1964- **1992**:2
Disney, Roy E. 1930- **1986**:3
Divine 1946-1988
   Obituary **1988**:3
Doherty, Shannen 1971(?)- **1994**:2
Donahue, Troy 1936-2001
   Obituary **2002**:4
Douglas, Michael 1944- **1986**:2
Downey, Robert, Jr. 1965- **2007**:1
Drescher, Fran 1957(?)- **1995**:3
Dreyfuss, Richard 1947- **1996**:3
Driver, Minnie 1971- **2000**:1
Duchovny, David 1960- **1998**:3
Duff, Hilary 1987- **2004**:4
Duffy, Karen 1962- **1998**:1
Dukakis, Olympia 1931- **1996**:4
Dunagan, Deanna 1940- **2009**:2
Dunst, Kirsten 1982- **2001**:4
Duvall, Robert 1931- **1999**:3
Eastwood, Clint 1930- **1993**:3
Ebersole, Christine 1953- **2007**:2
Ebsen, Buddy 1908-2003
   Obituary **2004**:3
Eckhart, Aaron 1968- **2009**:2
Efron, Zac 1987- **2008**:2
Egoyan, Atom 1960- **2000**:2
Eisner, Michael 1942- **1989**:2
Elliott, Denholm 1922-1992
   Obituary **1993**:2
Engvall, Bill 1957- **2010**:1
Ephron, Henry 1912-1992
   Obituary **1993**:2
Ephron, Nora 1941- **1992**:3
Epps, Omar 1973- **2000**:4
Estevez, Emilio 1962- **1985**:4
Evans, Robert 1930- **2004**:1
Eve 1978- **2004**:3
Everett, Rupert 1959- **2003**:1
Fairbanks, Douglas, Jr. 1909-2000
   Obituary **2000**:4
Falco, Edie 1963- **2010**:2
Fallon, Jimmy 1974- **2003**:1
Fanning, Dakota 1994- **2005**:2
Faris, Anna 1976- **2010**:3
Farley, Chris 1964-1997 **1998**:2
Farrell, Colin 1976- **2004**:1
Farrow, Mia 1945- **1998**:3
Favreau, Jon 1966- **2002**:3
Fawcett, Farrah 1947- **1998**:4
Feldshuh, Tovah 1952- **2005**:3
Felix, Maria 1914-2002
   Obituary **2003**:2
Fell, Norman 1924-1998
   Obituary **1999**:2
Fellini, Federico 1920-1993
   Obituary **1994**:2
Ferguson, Craig 1962- **2005**:4
Ferrell, Will 1968- **2004**:4
Ferrer, Jose 1912-1992
   Obituary **1992**:3
Ferrera, America 1984- **2006**:2
Fetchit, Stepin 1892(?)-1985
   Obituary **1986**:1
Fey, Tina 1970- **2005**:3
Fforde, Jasper 1961- **2006**:3
Field, Sally 1946- **1995**:3
Fiennes, Ralph 1962- **1996**:2

Fierstein, Harvey 1954- **2004**:2
Fillion, Nathan 1971- **2011**:3
Finney, Albert 1936- **2003**:3
Fishburne, Laurence 1961(?)- **1995**:3
Fisher, Carrie 1956- **1991**:1
Flanders, Ed 1934-1995
   Obituary **1995**:3
Fleiss, Mike 1964- **2003**:4
Fleming, Art 1925(?)-1995
   Obituary **1995**:4
Flockhart, Calista 1964- **1998**:4
Fonda, Bridget 1964- **1995**:1
Foote, Horton 1916-2009
   Obituary **2010**:2
Ford, Faith 1964- **2005**:3
Ford, Glenn 1916-2006
   Obituary **2007**:4
Ford, Harrison 1942- **1990**:2
Fosse, Bob 1927-1987
   Obituary **1988**:1
Foster, Jodie 1962- **1989**:2
Fox, Michael J. 1961- **1986**:1
Fox, Vivica 1964- **1999**:1
Franciscus, James 1934-1991
   Obituary **1992**:1
Frank, Robert 1924- **1995**:2
Frankenheimer, John 1930-2002
   Obituary **2003**:4
Franz, Dennis 1944- **1995**:2
Fraser, Brendan 1967- **2000**:1
Freeman, Morgan 1937- **1990**:4
Freleng, Friz 1906(?)-1995
   Obituary **1995**:4
Fugard, Athol 1932- **1992**:3
Gabor, Eva 1921(?)-1995
   Obituary **1996**:1
Gaiman, Neil 1960- **2010**:1
Gallagher, Peter 1955- **2004**:3
Garbo, Greta 1905-1990
   Obituary **1990**:3
Garcia, Andy 1956- **1999**:3
Gardenia, Vincent 1922-1992
   Obituary **1993**:2
Gardner, Ava Lavinia 1922-1990
   Obituary **1990**:2
Garner, Jennifer 1972- **2003**:1
Garofalo, Janeane 1964- **1996**:4
Garr, Teri 1949- **1988**:4
Garson, Greer 1903-1996
   Obituary **1996**:4
Gassman, Vittorio 1922-2000
   Obituary **2001**:1
Geffen, David 1943- **1985**:3
Gelbart, Larry 1928-2009
   Obituary **2011**:1
Gellar, Sarah Michelle 1977- **1999**:3
Gere, Richard 1949- **1994**:3
Getty, Estelle 1923-2008
   Obituary **2009**:3
Giamatti, Paul 1967- **2009**:4
Gibson, Mel 1956- **1990**:1
Gielgud, John 1904-2000
   Obituary **2000**:4
Gift, Roland 1960(?)- **1990**:2
Gilford, Jack 1907-1990
   Obituary **1990**:4
Gish, Lillian 1893-1993
   Obituary **1993**:4
Gleason, Jackie 1916-1987
   Obituary **1987**:4
Gless, Sharon 1944- **1989**:3
Glover, Danny 1947- **1998**:4

Gobel, George 1920(?)-1991
  Obituary **1991**:4
Godard, Jean-Luc 1930- **1998**:1
Godunov, Alexander 1949-1995
  Obituary **1995**:4
Goldberg, Leonard 1934- **1988**:4
Goldberg, Whoopi 1955- **1993**:3
Goldblum, Jeff 1952- **1988**:1
Gong Li 1965- **1998**:4
Gooding, Cuba, Jr. 1968- **1997**:3
Goodman, John 1952- **1990**:3
Gordon, Dexter 1923-1990 **1987**:1
Gordon, Gale 1906-1995
  Obituary **1996**:1
Gossett, Louis, Jr. 1936- **1989**:3
Goulet, Robert 1933-2007
  Obituary **2008**:4
Grace, Topher 1978- **2005**:4
Graham, Heather 1970- **2000**:1
Graham, Lauren 1967- **2003**:4
Grant, Cary 1904-1986
  Obituary **1987**:1
Grant, Hugh 1960- **1995**:3
Grant, Rodney A. **1992**:1
Gray, Spalding 1941-2004
  Obituary **2005**:2
Grazer, Brian 1951- **2006**:4
Green, Seth 1974- **2010**:1
Greene, Graham 1952- **1997**:2
Greene, Lorne 1915-1987
  Obituary **1988**:1
Grier, Pam 1949- **1998**:3
Griffin, Kathy 1961- **2010**:4
Griffith, Melanie 1957- **1989**:2
Grodin, Charles 1935- **1997**:3
Grusin, Dave
  Brief entry **1987**:2
Guest, Christopher 1948- **2004**:2
Guggenheim, Charles 1924-2002
  Obituary **2003**:4
Guinness, Alec 1914-2000
  Obituary **2001**:1
Gyllenhaal, Jake 1980- **2005**:3
Gyllenhaal, Maggie 1977- **2009**:2
Hackett, Buddy 1924-2003
  Obituary **2004**:3
Hackman, Gene 1931- **1989**:3
Hagen, Uta 1919-2004
  Obituary **2005**:2
Haggis, Paul 1953- **2006**:4
Hall, Anthony Michael 1968- **1986**:3
Hall, Arsenio 1955- **1990**:2
Hall, Michael 1971- **2011**:1
Hallstrom, Lasse 1946- **2002**:3
Hamilton, Margaret 1902-1985
  Obituary **1985**:3
Hamm, Jon 1971- **2009**:2
Hammer, Jan 1948- **1987**:3
Hanks, Tom 1956- **1989**:2
Hannah, Daryl 1961- **1987**:4
Hannigan, Alyson 1974- **2007**:3
Harden, Marcia Gay 1959- **2002**:4
Hargitay, Mariska 1964- **2006**:2
Harmon, Mark 1951- **1987**:1
Harrelson, Woody 1961- **2011**:1
Harris, Ed 1950- **2002**:2
Harris, Richard 1930-2002
  Obituary **2004**:1
Harrison, Rex 1908-1990
  Obituary **1990**:4
Harry, Deborah 1945- **1990**:1
Hart, Kitty Carlisle 1910-2007

Obituary **2008**:2
Hartman, Phil 1948-1998 **1996**:2
  Obituary **1998**:4
Harvey, Steve 1956- **2010**:1
Harwell, Ernie 1918- **1997**:3
Hatcher, Teri 1964- **2005**:4
Hathaway, Anne 1982- **2007**:2
Hawke, Ethan 1971(?)- **1995**:4
Hawkins, Sally 1976- **2009**:4
Hawn, Goldie Jeanne 1945- **1997**:2
Hayek, Salma 1968- **1999**:1
Hayes, Helen 1900-1993
  Obituary **1993**:4
Hayes, Isaac 1942- **1998**:4
Haysbert, Dennis 1954- **2007**:1
Hayworth, Rita 1918-1987
  Obituary **1987**:3
Heche, Anne 1969- **1999**:1
Heckerling, Amy 1954- **1987**:2
Heigl, Katharine 1978- **2008**:3
Hemingway, Margaux 1955-1996
  Obituary **1997**:1
Hennessy, Jill 1969- **2003**:2
Henson, Brian 1964(?)- **1992**:1
Henson, Jim 1936-1990 **1989**:1
  Obituary **1990**:4
Hepburn, Audrey 1929-1993
  Obituary **1993**:2
Hepburn, Katharine 1909- **1991**:2
Hershey, Barbara 1948- **1989**:1
Heston, Charlton 1924- **1999**:4
Hewitt, Jennifer Love 1979- **1999**:2
Hill, George Roy 1921-2002
  Obituary **2004**:1
Hill, Lauryn 1975- **1999**:3
Hines, Gregory 1946- **1992**:4
Hoffman, Dustin 1937- **2005**:4
Hoffman, Philip Seymour 1967-
  2006:3
Holmes, John C. 1945-1988
  Obituary **1988**:3
Hope, Bob 1903-2003
  Obituary **2004**:4
Hopkins, Anthony 1937- **1992**:4
Horne, Lena 1917- **1998**:4
Hoskins, Bob 1942- **1989**:1
Hou Hsiao-hsien 1947- **2000**:2
Houseman, John 1902-1988
  Obituary **1989**:1
Howard, Ken 1944- **2010**:4
Howard, Ron **1997**:2
Howard, Trevor 1916-1988
  Obituary **1988**:2
Hudson, Jennifer 1981- **2008**:1
Hudson, Kate 1979- **2001**:2
Hudson, Rock 1925-1985
  Obituary **1985**:4
Huffman, Felicity 1962- **2006**:2
Hughes, John 1950-2009
  Obituary **2010**:4
Humphries, Barry 1934- **1993**:1
Hunt, Helen 1963- **1994**:4
Hunter, Holly 1958- **1989**:4
Hurley, Elizabeth **1999**:2
Hurt, William 1950- **1986**:1
Huston, Anjelica 1952(?)- **1989**:3
Huston, John 1906-1987
  Obituary **1988**:1
Hutton, Timothy 1960- **1986**:3
Ice Cube 1969- **1999**:2
Ice-T **1992**:3
Ireland, Jill 1936-1990

Obituary **1990**:4
Irons, Jeremy 1948- **1991**:4
Irving, John 1942- **2006**:2
Itami, Juzo 1933-1997 **1998**:2
Ives, Burl 1909-1995
  Obituary **1995**:4
Izzard, Eddie 1963- **2008**:1
Jackman, Hugh 1968- **2004**:4
Jackson, Peter 1961- **2004**:4
Jackson, Samuel L. 1949(?)- **1995**:4
Jacobson, Nina 1965- **2009**:2
Jane, Thomas 1969- **2010**:3
Janney, Allison 1959- **2003**:3
Jarmusch, Jim 1953- **1998**:3
Jay, Ricky 1949(?)- **1995**:1
Jillian, Ann 1951- **1986**:4
Johansson, Scarlett 1984- **2005**:4
Johnson, Beverly 1952- **2005**:2
Johnson, Don 1949- **1986**:1
Johnson, Van 1916-2008
  Obituary **2010**:1
Jolie, Angelina 1975- **2000**:2
Jones, Cherry 1956- **1999**:3
Jones, Jennifer 1919-2009
  Obituary **2011**:4
Jones, Tommy Lee 1947(?)- **1994**:2
Jonze, Spike 1961(?)- **2000**:3
Jordan, Neil 1950(?)- **1993**:3
Jovovich, Milla 1975- **2002**:1
Joyce, William 1957- **2006**:1
Judd, Ashley 1968- **1998**:1
Julia, Raul 1940-1994
  Obituary **1995**:1
Kahn, Madeline 1942-1999
  Obituary **2000**:2
Kanakaredes, Melina 1967- **2007**:1
Kasem, Casey 1933(?)- **1987**:1
Katzenberg, Jeffrey 1950- **1995**:3
Kaufman, Charlie 1958- **2005**:1
Kavner, Julie 1951- **1992**:3
Kaye, Danny 1913-1987
  Obituary **1987**:2
Kazan, Elia 1909-2003
  Obituary **2004**:4
Keaton, Diane 1946- **1997**:1
Keaton, Michael 1951- **1989**:4
Keeler, Ruby 1910-1993
  Obituary **1993**:4
Keitel, Harvey 1939- **1994**:3
Keith, Brian 1921-1997
  Obituary **1997**:4
Kelly, Gene 1912-1996
  Obituary **1996**:3
Kendrick, Anna 1985- **2011**:2
Kerr, Deborah 1921-2007
  Obituary **2008**:4
Kidman, Nicole 1967- **1992**:4
Kilmer, Val **1991**:4
Kimmel, Jimmy 1967- **2009**:2
King, Alan 1927-2004
  Obituary **2005**:3
King, Stephen 1947- **1998**:1
Kinski, Klaus 1926-1991 **1987**:2
  Obituary **1992**:2
Kitt, Eartha 1927-2008
  Obituary **2010**:1
Kline, Kevin 1947- **2000**:1
Knight, Wayne 1956- **1997**:1
Knightley, Keira 1985- **2005**:2
Knotts, Don 1924-2006
  Obituary **2007**:1
Kramer, Larry 1935- **1991**:2

Kramer, Stanley 1913-2001
Obituary **2002**:1
Krause, Peter 1965- **2009**:2
Kubrick, Stanley 1928-1999
Obituary **1999**:3
Kulp, Nancy 1921-1991
Obituary **1991**:3
Kurosawa, Akira 1910-1998 **1991**:1
Obituary **1999**:1
Kutcher, Ashton 1978- **2003**:4
LaBeouf, Shia 1986- **2008**:1
Lahti, Christine 1950- **1988**:2
Lake, Ricki 1968(?)- **1994**:4
Lamarr, Hedy 1913-2000
Obituary **2000**:3
Lamour, Dorothy 1914-1996
Obituary **1997**:1
Lancaster, Burt 1913-1994
Obituary **1995**:1
Lane, Diane 1965- **2006**:2
Lane, Nathan 1956- **1996**:4
Lange, Jessica 1949- **1995**:4
Langella, Frank 1940- **2008**:3
Lansbury, Angela 1925- **1993**:1
Lansing, Sherry 1944- **1995**:4
LaPaglia, Anthony 1959- **2004**:4
Lardner Jr., Ring 1915-2000
Obituary **2001**:2
Larroquette, John 1947- **1986**:2
Lasseter, John 1957- **2007**:2
Laurie, Hugh 1959- **2007**:2
Law, Jude 1971- **2000**:3
Lawless, Lucy 1968- **1997**:4
Lawrence, Martin 1966(?)- **1993**:4
Leary, Denis 1958- **1993**:3
LeBlanc, Matt 1967- **2005**:4
Ledger, Heath 1979- **2006**:3
Lee, Ang 1954- **1996**:3
Lee, Brandon 1965(?)-1993
Obituary **1993**:4
Lee, Jason 1970- **2006**:4
Lee, Pamela 1967(?)- **1996**:4
Lee, Spike 1957- **1988**:4
Leguizamo, John 1965- **1999**:1
Leigh, Janet 1927-2004
Obituary **2005**:4
Leigh, Jennifer Jason 1962- **1995**:2
Lemmon, Jack 1925- **1998**:4
Obituary **2002**:3
Leno, Jay 1950- **1987**:1
Leone, Sergio 1929-1989
Obituary **1989**:4
Levi, Zachary 1980- **2009**:4
Levinson, Barry 1932- **1989**:3
Levy, Eugene 1946- **2004**:3
Lewis, Juliette 1973- **1999**:3
Lewis, Richard 1948(?)- **1992**:1
Li, Jet 1963- **2005**:3
Liberace 1919-1987
Obituary **1987**:2
Liman, Doug 1965- **2007**:1
Ling, Bai 1970- **2000**:3
Linklater, Richard 1960- **2007**:2
Linney, Laura 1964- **2009**:4
Lithgow, John 1945- **1985**:2
Little, Cleavon 1939-1992
Obituary **1993**:2
Liu, Lucy 1968- **2000**:4
Lively, Blake 1987- **2009**:1
Livingston, Ron 1968- **2007**:2
LL Cool J 1968- **1998**:2
Lloyd Webber, Andrew 1948- **1989**:1

Locklear, Heather 1961- **1994**:3
Loewe, Frederick 1901-1988
Obituary **1988**:2
Logan, Joshua 1908-1988
Obituary **1988**:4
Lohan, Lindsay 1986- **2005**:3
Long, Nia 1970- **2001**:3
Long, Shelley 1950(?)- **1985**:1
Lopez, Jennifer 1970- **1998**:4
Lord, Jack 1920-1998 **1998**:2
Lords, Traci 1968- **1995**:4
Louis-Dreyfus, Julia 1961(?)- **1994**:1
Lovett, Lyle 1958(?)- **1994**:1
Lowe, Rob 1964(?)- **1990**:4
Loy, Myrna 1905-1993
Obituary **1994**:2
Lucas, George 1944- **1999**:4
Luhrmann, Baz 1962- **2002**:3
Lupino, Ida 1918(?)-1995
Obituary **1996**:1
LuPone, Patti 1949- **2009**:2
Lynch, David 1946- **1990**:4
Lynch, Jane 1960- **2011**:2
Lyne, Adrian 1941- **1997**:2
Mac, Bernie 1957- **2003**:1
MacDonald, Laurie and Walter
Parkes **2004**:1
MacDowell, Andie 1958(?)- **1993**:4
MacMurray, Fred 1908-1991
Obituary **1992**:2
MacRae, Gordon 1921-1986
Obituary **1986**:2
Macy, William H. **1999**:3
Madonna 1958- **1985**:2
Maguire, Tobey 1975- **2002**:2
Maher, Bill 1956- **1996**:2
Mako 1933-2006
Obituary **2007**:3
Malden, Karl 1912-2009
Obituary **2010**:4
Malkovich, John 1953- **1988**:2
Malle, Louis 1932-1995
Obituary **1996**:2
Mamet, David 1947- **1998**:4
Mancini, Henry 1924-1994
Obituary **1994**:4
Mandel, Howie 1955- **1989**:1
Mantegna, Joe 1947- **1992**:1
Marber, Patrick 1964- **2007**:4
Margulies, Julianna 1966- **2011**:1
Marin, Cheech 1946- **2000**:1
Markle, C. Wilson 1938- **1988**:1
Marsalis, Branford 1960- **1988**:3
Marshall, Penny 1942- **1991**:3
Martin, Dean 1917-1995
Obituary **1996**:2
Martin, Dean Paul 1952(?)-1987
Obituary **1987**:3
Martin, Steve 1945- **1992**:2
Marvin, Lee 1924-1987
Obituary **1988**:1
Masina, Giulietta 1920-1994
Obituary **1994**:3
Mastroianni, Marcello 1914-1996
Obituary **1997**:2
Matlin, Marlee 1965- **1992**:2
Matthau, Walter 1920- **2000**:3
Matuszak, John 1951(?)-1989
Obituary **1989**:4
McConaughey, Matthew David
1969- **1997**:1

McCrea, Joel 1905-1990
Obituary **1991**:1
McDonagh, Martin 1970- **2007**:3
McDonnell, Mary 1952- **2008**:2
McDormand, Frances 1957- **1997**:3
McDowall, Roddy 1928-1998
Obituary **1999**:1
McGillis, Kelly 1957- **1989**:3
McGinley, Ted 1958- **2004**:4
McGoohan, Patrick 1928-2009
Obituary **2010**:1
McGregor, Ewan 1971(?)- **1998**:2
McGuire, Dorothy 1918-2001
Obituary **2002**:4
McHale, Joel 1971- **2010**:4
McKee, Lonette 1952(?)- **1996**:1
McKellen, Ian 1939- **1994**:1
McLaren, Norman 1914-1987
Obituary **1987**:2
McMahon, Julian 1968- **2006**:1
Meadows, Audrey 1925-1996
Obituary **1996**:3
Melnick, Daniel 1932-2009
Obituary **2011**:2
Merchant, Ismail 1936-2005
Obituary **2006**:3
Meredith, Burgess 1909-1997
Obituary **1998**:1
Merkerson, S. Epatha 1952- **2006**:4
Messing, Debra 1968- **2004**:4
Meyers, Nancy 1949- **2006**:1
Midler, Bette 1945- **1989**:4
Milano, Alyssa 1972- **2002**:3
Milland, Ray 1908(?)-1986
Obituary **1986**:2
Miller, Ann 1923-2004
Obituary **2005**:2
Miller, Frank 1957- **2008**:2
Milligan, Spike 1918-2002
Obituary **2003**:2
Minghella, Anthony 1954- **2004**:3
Minogue, Kylie 1968- **2003**:4
Mirren, Helen 1945- **2005**:1
Mitchell, Elizabeth 1970- **2011**:4
Mitchum, Robert 1917-1997
Obituary **1997**:4
Miyazaki, Hayao 1941- **2006**:2
Molina, Alfred 1953- **2005**:3
Mo'Nique 1967- **2008**:1
Montalban, Ricardo 1920-2009
Obituary **2010**:1
Montand, Yves 1921-1991
Obituary **1992**:2
Montgomery, Elizabeth 1933-1995
Obituary **1995**:4
Moore, Clayton 1914-1999
Obituary **2000**:3
Moore, Demi 1963(?)- **1991**:4
Moore, Dudley 1935-2002
Obituary **2003**:2
Moore, Julianne 1960- **1998**:1
Moore, Mandy 1984- **2004**:2
Moore, Mary Tyler 1936- **1996**:2
Moore, Michael 1954(?)- **1990**:3
Morgan, Tracy 1968- **2009**:3
Morita, Noriyuki Pat 1932- **1987**:3
Morris, Kathryn 1969- **2006**:4
Morrow, Rob 1962- **2006**:4
Mortensen, Viggo 1958- **2003**:3
Mos Def 1973- **2005**:4
Moss, Carrie-Anne 1967- **2004**:3
Murphy, Brittany 1977- **2005**:1

Murphy, Eddie 1961- **1989**:2
Murray, Bill 1950- **2002**:4
Myers, Mike 1964(?)- **1992**:3
Nair, Mira 1957- **2007**:4
Nance, Jack 1943(?)-1996
   Obituary **1997**:3
Neeson, Liam 1952- **1993**:4
Nelson, Harriet 1909(?)-1994
   Obituary **1995**:1
Nelson, Rick 1940-1985
   Obituary **1986**:1
Nelson, Willie 1933- **1993**:4
Newman, Paul 1925- **1995**:3
Newton-John, Olivia 1948- **1998**:4
Nichols, Mike 1931- **1994**:4
Nicholson, Jack 1937- **1989**:2
Nixon, Bob 1954(?)- **2006**:4
Nolan, Christopher 1970(?)- **2006**:3
Nolan, Lloyd 1902-1985
   Obituary **1985**:4
Nolte, Nick 1941- **1992**:4
North, Alex 1910- **1986**:3
Northam, Jeremy 1961- **2003**:2
Norton, Edward 1969- **2000**:2
O'Connor, Donald 1925-2003
   Obituary **2004**:4
O'Donnell, Chris 1970- **2011**:4
O'Donnell, Rosie 1962- **1994**:3
O'Hara, Catherine 1954- **2007**:4
Oldman, Gary 1958- **1998**:1
Olin, Ken 1955(?)- **1992**:3
Olin, Lena 1956- **1991**:2
Olivier, Laurence 1907-1989
   Obituary **1989**:4
Olmos, Edward James 1947- **1990**:1
O'Neill, Ed 1946- **2010**:4
O'Sullivan, Maureen 1911-1998
   Obituary **1998**:4
Ovitz, Michael 1946- **1990**:1
Owen, Clive 1964- **2006**:2
Paar, Jack 1918-2004
   Obituary **2005**:2
Pacino, Al 1940- **1993**:4
Page, Geraldine 1924-1987
   Obituary **1987**:4
Pakula, Alan 1928-1998
   Obituary **1999**:2
Palance, Jack 1919-2006
   Obituary **2008**:1
Paltrow, Gwyneth 1972- **1997**:1
Panettiere, Hayden 1989- **2008**:4
Pantoliano, Joe 1951- **2002**:3
Paquin, Anna 1982- **2009**:4
Park, Nick 1958- **1997**:3
Parker, Mary-Louise 1964- **2002**:2
Parker, Sarah Jessica 1965- **1999**:2
Parker, Trey and Matt Stone **1998**:2
Parks, Bert 1914-1992
   Obituary **1992**:3
Parks, Gordon 1912-2006
   Obituary **2006**:2
Pascal, Amy 1958- **2003**:3
Patrick, Robert 1959- **2002**:1
Pattinson, Robert 1986- **2010**:1
Paxton, Bill 1955- **1999**:3
Payne, Alexander 1961- **2005**:4
Peck, Gregory 1916-2003
   Obituary **2004**:3
Peete, Holly Robinson 1964- **2005**:2
Pegg, Simon 1970- **2009**:1
Penn, Kal 1977- **2009**:1
Penn, Sean 1960- **1987**:2

Perez, Rosie **1994**:2
Perkins, Anthony 1932-1992
   Obituary **1993**:2
Perry, Luke 1966(?)- **1992**:3
Perry, Matthew 1969- **1997**:2
Perry, Tyler 1969- **2006**:1
Pesci, Joe 1943- **1992**:4
Peters, Bernadette 1948- **2000**:1
Peterson, Cassandra 1951- **1988**:1
Pfeiffer, Michelle 1957- **1990**:2
Phifer, Mekhi 1975- **2004**:1
Phillips, Julia 1944- **1992**:1
Phoenix, Joaquin 1974- **2000**:4
Phoenix, River 1970-1993 **1990**:2
   Obituary **1994**:2
Picasso, Paloma 1949- **1991**:1
Pinchot, Bronson 1959(?)- **1987**:4
Pinkett Smith, Jada 1971- **1998**:3
Pitt, Brad 1964- **1995**:2
Piven, Jeremy 1965- **2007**:3
Pleasence, Donald 1919-1995
   Obituary **1995**:3
Pleshette, Suzanne 1937-2008
   Obituary **2009**:2
Plimpton, George 1927-2003
   Obituary **2004**:4
Poehler, Amy 1971- **2009**:1
Poitier, Sidney 1927- **1990**:3
Pollack, Sydney 1934-2008
   Obituary **2009**:2
Ponti, Carlo 1912-2007
   Obituary **2008**:2
Portman, Natalie 1981- **2000**:3
Potts, Annie 1952- **1994**:1
Preminger, Otto 1906-1986
   Obituary **1986**:3
Presley, Pricilla 1945- **2001**:1
Preston, Robert 1918-1987
   Obituary **1987**:3
Price, Vincent 1911-1993
   Obituary **1994**:2
Prince 1958- **1995**:3
Prinze, Freddie, Jr. 1976- **1999**:3
Probst, Jeff 1962- **2011**:2
Prowse, Juliet 1937-1996
   Obituary **1997**:1
Pryor, Richard **1999**:3
Puzo, Mario 1920-1999
   Obituary **2000**:1
Quaid, Dennis 1954- **1989**:4
Queen Latifah 1970(?)- **1992**:2
Quinn, Anthony 1915-2001
   Obituary **2002**:2
Radcliffe, Daniel 1989- **2007**:4
Radner, Gilda 1946-1989
   Obituary **1989**:4
Raimi, Sam 1959- **1999**:2
Randall, Tony 1920-2004
   Obituary **2005**:3
Raven 1985- **2005**:1
Rawls, Lou 1933-2006
   Obituary **2007**:1
Raye, Martha 1916-1994
   Obituary **1995**:1
Reagan, Ronald 1911-2004
   Obituary **2005**:3
Redford, Robert 1937- **1993**:2
Redgrave, Lynn 1943- **1999**:3
Redgrave, Vanessa 1937- **1989**:2
Reed, Donna 1921-1986
   Obituary **1986**:1
Reese, Della 1931- **1999**:2

Reeve, Christopher 1952- **1997**:2
Reeves, Keanu 1964- **1992**:1
Reeves, Steve 1926-2000
   Obituary **2000**:4
Reilly, John C. 1965- **2003**:4
Reiner, Rob 1947- **1991**:2
Reiser, Paul 1957- **1995**:2
Reisz, Karel 1926-2002
   Obituary **2004**:1
Reitman, Ivan 1946- **1986**:3
Reitman, Jason 1977- **2011**:3
Remick, Lee 1936(?)-1991
   Obituary **1992**:1
Reuben, Gloria 1964- **1999**:4
Reubens, Paul 1952- **1987**:2
Rhone, Trevor 1940-2009
   Obituary **2011**:1
Rhys Meyers, Jonathan 1977- **2007**:1
Ricci, Christina 1980- **1999**:1
Rice, Peter 1967(?)- **2007**:2
Richards, Michael 1949(?)- **1993**:4
Richardson, Natasha 1963-2009
   Obituary **2010**:2
Riddle, Nelson 1921-1985
   Obituary **1985**:4
Ringwald, Molly 1968- **1985**:4
Ritchie, Guy 1968- **2001**:3
Ritter, John 1948- **2003**:4
Robards, Jason 1922-2000
   Obituary **2001**:3
Robbins, Jerome 1918-1998
   Obituary **1999**:1
Robbins, Tim 1959- **1993**:1
Roberts, Doris 1930- **2003**:4
Roberts, Julia 1967- **1991**:3
Rock, Chris 1967(?)- **1998**:1
Rodriguez, Robert 1968- **2005**:1
Rogen, Seth 1982- **2009**:3
Rogers, Ginger 1911(?)-1995
   Obituary **1995**:4
Rogers, Roy 1911-1998
   Obituary **1998**:4
Roker, Roxie 1929(?)-1995
   Obituary **1996**:2
Rolle, Esther 1922-1998
   Obituary **1999**:2
Rollins, Henry 1961- **2007**:3
Rollins, Howard E., Jr. 1950- **1986**:1
Romijn, Rebecca 1972- **2007**:1
Ross, Herbert 1927-2001
   Obituary **2002**:4
Roth, Tim 1961- **1998**:2
Rourke, Mickey 1956- **1988**:4
Rowan, Dan 1922-1987
   Obituary **1988**:1
Rudd, Paul 1969- **2009**:4
Rudner, Rita 1956- **1993**:2
Rudnick, Paul 1957(?)- **1994**:3
Ruehl, Mercedes 1948(?)- **1992**:4
Ruffalo, Mark 1967- **2011**:4
RuPaul 1961(?)- **1996**:1
Rush, Geoffrey 1951- **2002**:1
Russell, Kurt 1951- **2007**:4
Russell, Nipsey 1924-2005
   Obituary **2007**:1
Russo, Rene 1954- **2000**:2
Ryan, Meg 1962(?)- **1994**:1
Ryder, Winona 1971- **1991**:2
Sagal, Katey 1954- **2005**:2
Saldana, Zoe 1978- **2010**:1
Salonga, Lea 1971- **2003**:3
Sandler, Adam 1966- **1999**:2

Sarandon, Susan 1946- **1995**:3
Savage, Fred 1976- **1990**:1
Savalas, Telly 1924-1994
  Obituary **1994**:3
Scheider, Roy 1932-2008
  Obituary **2009**:2
Schlesinger, John 1926-2003
  Obituary **2004**:3
Schneider, Rob 1965- **1997**:4
Schreiber, Liev 1967- **2007**:2
Schroeder, Barbet 1941- **1996**:1
Schumacher, Joel 1929- **2004**:3
Schwarzenegger, Arnold 1947- **1991**
  :1
Schwimmer, David 1966(?)- **1996**:2
Scorsese, Martin 1942- **1989**:1
Scott, George C. 1927-1999
  Obituary **2000**:2
Scott, Jill 1972- **2010**:1
Scott, Randolph 1898(?)-1987
  Obituary **1987**:2
Scott, Ridley 1937- **2001**:1
Scott Thomas, Kristin 1960- **2010**:2
Sedaris, Amy 1961- **2009**:3
Sedgwick, Kyra 1965- **2006**:2
Seidelman, Susan 1953(?)- **1985**:4
Sevigny, Chloe 1974- **2001**:4
Seyfried, Amanda 1985- **2009**:3
Seymour, Jane 1951- **1994**:4
Shaffer, Paul 1949- **1987**:1
Shanley, John Patrick 1950- **2006**:1
Sharkey, Ray 1953-1993
  Obituary **1994**:1
Shawn, Dick 1924(?)-1987
  Obituary **1987**:3
Sheedy, Ally 1962- **1989**:1
Sheen, Martin 1940- **2002**:1
Sheldon, Sidney 1917-2007
  Obituary **2008**:2
Shepard, Sam 1943- **1996**:4
Shields, Brooke 1965- **1996**:3
Shore, Dinah 1917-1994
  Obituary **1994**:3
Short, Martin 1950- **1986**:1
Shue, Andrew 1964- **1994**:4
Shyamalan, M. Night 1970- **2003**:2
Silverman, Jonathan 1966- **1997**:2
Silverman, Sarah 1970- **2008**:1
Silvers, Phil 1912-1985
  Obituary **1985**:4
Silverstone, Alicia 1976- **1997**:4
Sinatra, Frank 1915-1998
  Obituary **1998**:4
Singer, Bryan 1965- **2007**:3
Singleton, John 1968- **1994**:3
Sinise, Gary 1955(?)- **1996**:1
Siskel, Gene 1946-1999
  Obituary **1999**:3
Slater, Christian 1969- **1994**:1
Smirnoff, Yakov 1951- **1987**:2
Smith, Kevin 1970- **2000**:4
Smith, Will 1968- **1997**:2
Smits, Jimmy 1956- **1990**:1
Snipes, Wesley 1962- **1993**:1
Sobieski, Leelee 1982- **2002**:3
Soderbergh, Steven 1963- **2001**:4
Sondheim, Stephen 1930- **1994**:4
Sorkin, Aaron 1961- **2003**:2
Sorvino, Mira 1970(?)- **1996**:3
Sothern, Ann 1909-2001
  Obituary **2002**:1
Southern, Terry 1926-1995

  Obituary **1996**:2
Spacek, Sissy 1949- **2003**:1
Spacey, Kevin 1959- **1996**:4
Spade, David 1965- **1999**:2
Spader, James 1960- **1991**:2
Spelling, Tori 1973- **2008**:3
Spheeris, Penelope 1945(?)- **1989**:2
Spielberg, Steven 1947- **1993**:4
Stack, Robert 1919-2003
  Obituary **2004**:2
Staller, Ilona 1951- **1988**:3
Stallone, Sylvester 1946- **1994**:2
Stamos, John 1963- **2008**:1
Stapleton, Maureen 1925-2006
  Obituary **2007**:2
Steel, Dawn 1946-1997 **1990**:1
  Obituary **1998**:2
Stefani, Gwen 1969- **2005**:4
Steiger, Rod 1925-2002
  Obituary **2003**:4
Stevenson, McLean 1929-1996
  Obituary **1996**:3
Stewart, Jimmy 1908-1997
  Obituary **1997**:4
Stewart, Patrick 1940- **1996**:1
Stiles, Julia 1981- **2002**:3
Stiller, Ben 1965- **1999**:1
Sting 1951- **1991**:4
Stone, Oliver 1946- **1990**:4
Stone, Sharon 1958- **1993**:4
Stoppard, Tom 1937- **1995**:4
Storm, Gale 1922-2009
  Obituary **2010**:4
Streep, Meryl 1949- **1990**:2
Streisand, Barbra 1942- **1992**:2
Strummer, Joe 1952-2002
  Obituary **2004**:1
Studi, Wes 1944(?)- **1994**:3
Styler, Trudie 1954- **2009**:1
Styne, Jule 1905-1994
  Obituary **1995**:1
Susskind, David 1920-1987
  Obituary **1987**:2
Sutherland, Kiefer 1966- **2002**:4
Swank, Hilary 1974- **2000**:3
Swayze, Patrick 1952-2009
  Obituary **2011**:1
Swinton, Tilda 1960- **2008**:4
Sykes, Wanda 1964- **2007**:4
Tanaka, Tomoyuki 1910-1997
  Obituary **1997**:3
Tandy, Jessica 1901-1994 **1990**:4
  Obituary **1995**:1
Tarantino, Quentin 1963(?)- **1995**:1
Tatum, Channing 1980- **2011**:3
Tautou, Audrey 1978- **2004**:2
Taylor, Elizabeth 1932- **1993**:3
Taylor, Lili 1967- **2000**:2
Theron, Charlize 1975- **2001**:4
Thiebaud, Wayne 1920- **1991**:1
Thomas, Betty 1948- **2011**:4
Thompson, Emma 1959- **1993**:2
Thompson, Fred 1942- **1998**:2
Thornton, Billy Bob 1956(?)- **1997**:4
Thurman, Uma 1970- **1994**:2
Tilly, Jennifer 1958(?)- **1997**:2
Timberlake, Justin 1981- **2008**:4
Tomei, Marisa 1964- **1995**:2
Travolta, John 1954- **1995**:2
Tucci, Stanley 1960- **2003**:2
Tucker, Chris 1973(?)- **1999**:1
Tucker, Forrest 1919-1986

  Obituary **1987**:1
Turner, Janine 1962- **1993**:2
Turner, Kathleen 1954(?)- **1985**:3
Turner, Lana 1921-1995
  Obituary **1996**:1
Turturro, John 1957- **2002**:2
Tyler, Liv 1978- **1997**:2
Ullman, Tracey 1961- **1988**:3
Umeki, Miyoshi 1929-2007
  Obituary **2008**:4
Union, Gabrielle 1972- **2004**:2
Urich, Robert 1947- **1988**:1
  Obituary **2003**:3
Usher 1979- **2005**:1
Ustinov, Peter 1921-2004
  Obituary **2005**:3
Valenti, Jack 1921-2007
  Obituary **2008**:3
Vanilla Ice 1967(?)- **1991**:3
Van Sant, Gus 1952- **1992**:2
Vardalos, Nia 1962- **2003**:4
Varney, Jim 1949-2000
  Brief entry **1985**:4
  Obituary **2000**:3
Vaughn, Vince 1970- **1999**:2
Ventura, Jesse 1951- **1999**:2
Vidal, Gore 1925- **1996**:2
Vidov, Oleg 194- **1987**:4
Villechaize, Herve 1943(?)-1993
  Obituary **1994**:1
Vincent, Fay 1938- **1990**:2
Voight, Jon 1938- **2002**:3
Walker, Nancy 1922-1992
  Obituary **1992**:3
Wallis, Hal 1898(?)-1986
  Obituary **1987**:1
Waltz, Christoph 1956- **2011**:1
Warden, Jack 1920-2006
  Obituary **2007**:3
Warhol, Andy 1927(?)-1987
  Obituary **1987**:2
Washington, Denzel 1954- **1993**:2
Wasserman, Lew 1913-2002
  Obituary **2003**:3
Waters, John 1946- **1988**:3
Waterston, Sam 1940- **2006**:1
Watson, Emily 1967- **2001**:1
Watts, Naomi 1968- **2006**:1
Wayans, Damon 1960- **1998**:4
Wayans, Keenen Ivory 1958(?)- **1991**
  :1
Wayne, David 1914-1995
  Obituary **1995**:3
Weaver, Sigourney 1949- **1988**:3
Wegman, William 1942(?)- **1991**:1
Weinstein, Bob and Harvey **2000**:4
Weintraub, Jerry 1937- **1986**:1
Weisz, Rachel 1971- **2006**:4
Whedon, Joss 1964- **2006**:3
Whitaker, Forest 1961- **1996**:2
White, Julie 1961- **2008**:2
Wiest, Dianne 1948- **1995**:2
Wilder, Billy 1906-2002
  Obituary **2003**:2
Wilkinson, Tom 1948- **2003**:2
Williams, Robin 1952- **1988**:4
Williams, Treat 1951- **2004**:3
Williams, Vanessa L. 1963- **1999**:2
Willis, Bruce 1955- **1986**:4
Wilson, Owen 1968- **2002**:3
Winfield, Paul 1941-2004
  Obituary **2005**:2

Winfrey, Oprah 1954- **1986**:4
Winger, Debra 1955- **1994**:3
Winokur, Marissa Jaret 1973- **2005**:1
Winslet, Kate 1975- **2002**:4
Winters, Shelley 1920-2006
  Obituary **2007**:1
Wise, Robert 1914-2005
  Obituary **2006**:4
Wiseman, Len 1973- **2008**:2
Witherspoon, Reese 1976- **2002**:1
Wolfman Jack 1938-1995
  Obituary **1996**:1
Wong, B.D. 1962- **1998**:1
Woo, John 1945(?)- **1994**:2
Wood, Elijah 1981- **2002**:4
Woods, James 1947- **1988**:3
Woodward, Edward 1930-2009
  Obituary **2011**:3
Wright, Joe 1972- **2009**:1
Wright, Robin 1966- **2011**:3
Wyle, Noah 1971- **1997**:3
Wyman, Jane 1917-2007
  Obituary **2008**:4
Wynn, Keenan 1916-1986
  Obituary **1987**:1
Xzibit 1974- **2005**:4
Yeoh, Michelle 1962- **2003**:2
Young, Loretta 1913-2000
  Obituary **2001**:1
Young, Robert 1907-1998
  Obituary **1999**:1
Zanuck, Lili Fini 1954- **1994**:2
Zeffirelli, Franco 1923- **1991**:3
Zellweger, Renee 1969- **2001**:1
Zemeckis, Robert 1952- **2002**:1
Zeta-Jones, Catherine 1969- **1999**:4
Zhang, Ziyi 1979- **2006**:2
Ziskin, Laura 1950- **2008**:2
Zucker, Jerry 1950- **2002**:2

LAW

Abzug, Bella 1920-1998 **1998**:2
Achtenberg, Roberta **1993**:4
Allred, Gloria 1941- **1985**:2
Andrews, Lori B. 1952- **2005**:3
Angelos, Peter 1930- **1995**:4
Archer, Dennis 1942- **1994**:4
Astorga, Nora 1949(?)-1988 **1988**:2
Babbitt, Bruce 1938- **1994**:1
Bailey, F. Lee 1933- **1995**:4
Baker, James A. III 1930- **1991**:2
Bikoff, James L.
  Brief entry **1986**:2
Blackmun, Harry A. 1908-1999
  Obituary **1999**:3
Boies, David 1941- **2002**:1
Bradley, Tom 1917-1998
  Obituary **1999**:1
Brennan, William 1906-1997
  Obituary **1997**:4
Breyer, Stephen Gerald 1938- **1994**:4
Brown, Willie 1934- **1996**:4
Brown, Willie L. 1934- **1985**:2
Burger, Warren E. 1907-1995
  Obituary **1995**:4
Burnison, Chantal Simone 1950(?)-
  1988:3
Campbell, Kim 1947- **1993**:4
Cantrell, Ed
  Brief entry **1985**:3
Carter, Stephen L. **2008**:2
Casey, William 1913-1987

Obituary **1987**:3
Casper, Gerhard 1937- **1993**:1
Chase, Debra Martin 1956- **2009**:1
Clark, Marcia 1954(?)- **1995**:1
Clinton, Bill 1946- **1992**:1
Clinton, Hillary Rodham 1947- **1993**
  :2
Cochran, Johnnie 1937- **1996**:1
Colby, William E. 1920-1996
  Obituary **1996**:4
Counter, Nick 1940-2009
  Obituary **2011**:3
Cuomo, Mario 1932- **1992**:2
Darden, Christopher 1957(?)- **1996**:4
Dees, Morris 1936- **1992**:1
del Ponte, Carla 1947- **2001**:1
Dershowitz, Alan 1938(?)- **1992**:1
Deutch, John 1938- **1996**:4
Dole, Elizabeth Hanford 1936- **1990**
  :1
Dukakis, Michael 1933- **1988**:3
Eagleson, Alan 1933- **1987**:4
Ehrlichman, John 1925-1999
  Obituary **1999**:3
Ervin, Sam 1896-1985
  Obituary **1985**:2
Estrich, Susan 1953- **1989**:1
Fairstein, Linda 1948(?)- **1991**:1
Fehr, Donald 1948- **1987**:2
Fieger, Geoffrey 1950- **2001**:3
Fitzgerald, Patrick 1960- **2006**:4
Florio, James J. 1937- **1991**:2
Foster, Vincent 1945(?)-1993
  Obituary **1994**:1
France, Johnny
  Brief entry **1987**:1
Freeh, Louis J. 1950- **1994**:2
Fulbright, J. William 1905-1995
  Obituary **1995**:3
Furman, Rosemary
  Brief entry **1986**:4
Garrison, Jim 1922-1992
  Obituary **1993**:2
Ginsburg, Ruth Bader 1933- **1993**:4
Giuliani, Rudolph 1944- **1994**:2
Glasser, Ira 1938- **1989**:1
Gore, Albert, Sr. 1907-1998
  Obituary **1999**:2
Grisham, John 1955- **1994**:4
Harvard, Beverly 1950- **1995**:2
Hayes, Robert M. 1952- **1986**:3
Hill, Anita 1956- **1994**:1
Hills, Carla 1934- **1990**:3
Hirschhorn, Joel
  Brief entry **1986**:1
Hoffa, Jim, Jr. 1941- **1999**:2
Hyatt, Joel 1950- **1985**:3
Ireland, Patricia 1946(?)- **1992**:2
Ito, Lance 1950(?)- **1995**:3
Janklow, Morton 1930- **1989**:3
Kennedy, John F., Jr. 1960-1999 **1990**
  :1
  Obituary **1999**:4
Kennedy, Weldon 1938- **1997**:3
Kunstler, William 1919-1995
  Obituary **1996**:1
Kunstler, William 1920(?)- **1992**:3
Kurzban, Ira 1949- **1987**:2
Lee, Henry C. 1938- **1997**:1
Lee, Martin 1938- **1998**:2
Lewis, Loida Nicolas 1942- **1998**:3
Lewis, Reginald F. 1942-1993 **1988**:4

Obituary **1993**:3
Lightner, Candy 1946- **1985**:1
Liman, Arthur 1932- **1989**:4
Lipsig, Harry H. 1901- **1985**:1
Lipton, Martin 1931- **1987**:3
MacKinnon, Catharine 1946- **1993**:2
Marshall, Thurgood 1908-1993
  Obituary **1993**:3
McCloskey, James 1944(?)- **1993**:1
Mitchell, George J. 1933- **1989**:3
Mitchell, John 1913-1988
  Obituary **1989**:2
Mitchelson, Marvin 1928- **1989**:2
Morrison, Trudi
  Brief entry **1986**:2
Nader, Ralph 1934- **1989**:4
Napolitano, Janet 1957- **1997**:1
Neal, James Foster 1929- **1986**:2
O'Connor, Sandra Day 1930- **1991**:1
O'Leary, Hazel 1937- **1993**:4
O'Steen, Van
  Brief entry **1986**:3
Panetta, Leon 1938- **1995**:1
Pirro, Jeanine 1951- **1998**:2
Powell, Lewis F. 1907-1998
  Obituary **1999**:1
Puccio, Thomas P. 1944- **1986**:4
Quayle, Dan 1947- **1989**:2
Raines, Franklin 1949- **1997**:4
Ramaphosa, Cyril 1953- **1988**:2
Ramo, Roberta Cooper 1942- **1996**:1
Rehnquist, William H. 1924- **2001**:2
Reno, Janet 1938- **1993**:3
Rothwax, Harold 1930- **1996**:3
Scalia, Antonin 1936- **1988**:2
Scheck, Barry 1949- **2000**:4
Schily, Otto
  Brief entry **1987**:4
Sheehan, Daniel P. 1945(?)- **1989**:1
Sheindlin, Judith 1942(?)- **1999**:1
Sirica, John 1904-1992
  Obituary **1993**:2
Skinner, Sam 1938- **1992**:3
Slater, Rodney E. 1955- **1997**:4
Slotnick, Barry
  Brief entry **1987**:4
Souter, David 1939- **1991**:3
Spitzer, Eliot 1959- **2007**:2
Spitzer, Silda Wall 1957- **2010**:2
Starr, Kenneth 1946- **1998**:3
Steinberg, Leigh 1949- **1987**:3
Stern, David 1942- **1991**:4
Stewart, Potter 1915-1985
  Obituary **1986**:1
Strauss, Robert 1918- **1991**:4
Tagliabue, Paul 1940- **1990**:2
Thomas, Clarence 1948- **1992**:2
Thompson, Fred 1942- **1998**:2
Tribe, Laurence H. 1941- **1988**:1
Vincent, Fay 1938- **1990**:2
Violet, Arlene 1943- **1985**:3
Wapner, Joseph A. 1919- **1987**:1
Watson, Elizabeth 1949- **1991**:2
White, Byron 1917-2002
  Obituary **2003**:3
Williams, Edward Bennett 1920-1988
  Obituary **1988**:4
Williams, Willie L. 1944(?)- **1993**:1
Wilson, Bertha
  Brief entry **1986**:1
Yudof, Mark 1944- **2009**:4

MUSIC

Aaliyah 1979-2001 **2001**:3
Abdul, Paula 1962- **1990**:3
AC/DC Grammy Awards- **2011**:2
Ackerman, Will 1949- **1987**:4
Acuff, Roy 1903-1992
 Obituary **1993**:2
Adams, Yolanda 1961- **2008**:2
Adele 1988- **2009**:4
AFI **2007**:3
Aguilera, Christina 1980- **2000**:4
Albert, Stephen 1941- **1986**:1
Allen, Peter 1944-1992
 Obituary **1993**:1
Alsop, Marin 1956- **2008**:3
Ames, Roger 1950(?)- **2005**:2
Amos, Tori 1963- **1995**:1
Anderson, Marion 1897-1993
 Obituary **1993**:4
Andrews, Julie 1935- **1996**:1
Andrews, Maxene 1916-1995
 Obituary **1996**:2
Anthony, Marc 1969- **2000**:3
Apple, Fiona 1977- **2006**:3
Arlen, Harold 1905-1986
 Obituary **1986**:3
Arnaz, Desi 1917-1986
 Obituary **1987**:1
Arnold, Eddy 1918-2008
 Obituary **2009**:2
Arrau, Claudio 1903-1991
 Obituary **1992**:1
Arrested Development **1994**:2
Ashanti 1980- **2004**:1
Asheton, Ron 1948-2009
 Obituary **2010**:1
Astaire, Fred 1899-1987
 Obituary **1987**:4
Autry, Gene 1907-1998
 Obituary **1999**:1
Backstreet Boys **2001**:3
Badu, Erykah 1971- **2000**:4
Baez, Joan 1941- **1998**:3
Bailey, Pearl 1918-1990
 Obituary **1991**:1
Baker, Anita 1958- **1987**:4
Barenboim, Daniel 1942- **2001**:1
Barrett, Syd 1946-2006
 Obituary **2007**:3
Bartoli, Cecilia 1966- **1994**:1
Basie, Count 1904(?)-1984
 Obituary **1985**:1
Battle, Kathleen 1948- **1998**:1
Beastie Boys, The **1999**:1
Becaud, Gilbert 1927-2001
 Obituary **2003**:1
Beck 1970- **2000**:2
Beck, Jeff 1944- **2011**:4
Bee Gees, The **1997**:4
Benatar, Pat 1953- **1986**:1
Bennett, Tony 1926- **1994**:4
Bentley, Dierks 1975- **2007**:3
Berio, Luciano 1925-2003
 Obituary **2004**:2
Berlin, Irving 1888-1989
 Obituary **1990**:1
Bernhard, Sandra 1955(?)- **1989**:4
Bernstein, Elmer 1922-2004
 Obituary **2005**:4
Bernstein, Leonard 1918-1990
 Obituary **1991**:1
Berry, Chuck 1926- **2001**:2

Beyonce 1981- **2009**:3
Bjork 1965- **1996**:1
Black Eyed Peas **2006**:2
Blades, Ruben 1948- **1998**:2
Blakey, Art 1919-1990
 Obituary **1991**:1
Blige, Mary J. 1971- **1995**:3
Bogle, Bob 1934-2009
 Obituary **2010**:3
Bolton, Michael 1953(?)- **1993**:2
Bon Jovi, Jon 1962- **1987**:4
Bono 1960- **1988**:4
Bono, Sonny 1935-1998 **1992**:2
 Obituary **1998**:2
Borge, Victor 1909-2000
 Obituary **2001**:3
Botstein, Leon 1946- **1985**:3
Bowie, David 1947- **1998**:2
Bowles, Paul 1910-1999
 Obituary **2000**:3
Boxcar Willie 1931-1999
 Obituary **1999**:4
Boyz II Men **1995**:1
Brandy 1979- **1996**:4
Branson, Richard 1951- **1987**:1
Braxton, Toni 1967- **1994**:3
Brooks, Garth 1962- **1992**:1
Brown, James 1928(?)- **1991**:4
Brown, Les 1912-2001
 Obituary **2001**:3
Brown, Ruth 1928-2006
 Obituary **2008**:1
Bruni, Carla 1967- **2009**:3
Buble, Michael 1975- **2010**:4
Buckley, Jeff 1966-1997
 Obituary **1997**:4
Buffett, Jimmy 1946- **1999**:3
Bush, Kate 1958- **1994**:3
Butterfield, Paul 1942-1987
 Obituary **1987**:3
Cage, John 1912-1992
 Obituary **1993**:1
Calloway, Cab 1908-1994
 Obituary **1995**:2
Cannon, Nick 1980- **2006**:4
Cardigans, The **1997**:4
Carey, Mariah 1970(?)- **1991**:3
Carlisle, Belinda 1958- **1989**:3
Carpenter, Mary-Chapin 1958(?)-
 1994:1
Carreras, Jose 1946- **1995**:2
Carroll, Jim 1949-2009
 Obituary **2011**:1
Carter, Benny 1907-2003
 Obituary **2004**:3
Carter, Nell 1948-2003
 Obituary **2004**:2
Carter, Ron 1937- **1987**:3
Cash, Johnny 1932- **1995**:3
Cash, June Carter 1929-2003
 Obituary **2004**:2
Castellucci, Cecil 1969- **2008**:3
Cerovsek, Corey
 Brief entry **1987**:4
Chapman, Tracy 1964- **1989**:2
Charles, Ray 1930-2004
 Obituary **2005**:3
Cheatham, Adolphus Doc 1905-1997
 Obituary **1997**:4
Chenoweth, Kristin 1968- **2010**:4
Cher 1946- **1993**:1
Chesney, Kenny 1968- **2008**:2

Chesnutt, Vic 1964-2009
 Obituary **2011**:4
Christian Jacobs and Scott Schultz
 1972- **2011**:4
Clapton, Eric 1945- **1993**:3
Clarke, Stanley 1951- **1985**:4
Clarkson, Kelly 1982- **2003**:3
Cleveland, James 1932(?)-1991
 Obituary **1991**:3
Cliburn, Van 1934- **1995**:1
Clooney, Rosemary 1928-2002
 Obituary **2003**:4
Cobain, Kurt 1967-1944
 Obituary **1994**:3
Coldplay **2004**:4
Cole, Natalie 1950- **1992**:4
Collette, Toni 1972- **2009**:4
Collins, Albert 1932-1993
 Obituary **1994**:2
Combs, Sean Puffy 1970- **1998**:4
Como, Perry 1912-2001
 Obituary **2002**:2
Connick, Harry, Jr. 1967- **1991**:1
Coolio 1963- **1996**:4
Copland, Aaron 1900-1990
 Obituary **1991**:2
Coppola, Carmine 1910-1991
 Obituary **1991**:4
Corea, Chick 1941- **1986**:3
Cosgrove, Miranda 1993- **2011**:4
Costello, Elvis 1954(?)- **1994**:4
Cowell, Simon 1959- **2003**:4
Crawford, Michael 1942- **1994**:2
Cray, Robert 1953- **1988**:2
Crosby, David 1941- **2000**:4
Crothers, Scatman 1910-1986
 Obituary **1987**:1
Crow, Sheryl 1964- **1995**:2
Crowe, Russell 1964- **2000**:4
Cruz, Celia 1925-2003
 Obituary **2004**:3
Cugat, Xavier 1900-1990
 Obituary **1991**:2
Cyrus, Billy Ray 1961(?)- **1993**:1
Cyrus, Miley 1992- **2008**:3
Daft Punk 1975- **2009**:4
D'Arby, Terence Trent 1962- **1988**:4
Darling, Erik 1933-2008
 Obituary **2009**:4
Davis, Miles 1926-1991
 Obituary **1992**:2
Davis, Sammy, Jr. 1925-1990
 Obituary **1990**:4
Day, Dennis 1917-1988
 Obituary **1988**:4
Dean, Laura 1945- **1989**:4
Dekker, Desmond 1941-2006
 Obituary **2007**:2
de Larrocha, Alicia 1923-2009
 Obituary **2011**:1
Denver, John 1943-1997
 Obituary **1998**:1
de Passe, Suzanne 1946(?)- **1990**:4
Depeche Mode 1961- **2010**:3
Deschanel, Zooey 1980- **2010**:4
Destiny's Child **2001**:3
Diddley, Bo 1928-2008
 Obituary **2009**:3
Dido 1971- **2004**:4
DiFranco, Ani 1970(?)- **1997**:1
Di Meola, Al 1954- **1986**:4
Dimitrova, Ghena 1941- **1987**:1

Dion, Celine 1970(?)- **1995**:3
Dixie Chicks **2001**:2
Doherty, Denny 1940-2007
  Obituary **2008**:2
Dolenz, Micky 1945- **1986**:4
Domingo, Placido 1941- **1993**:2
Dorati, Antal 1906-1988
  Obituary **1989**:2
Dorsey, Thomas A. 1899-1993
  Obituary **1993**:3
Douglas, Mike 1925-2006
  Obituary **2007**:4
Dr. Demento 1941- **1986**:1
Dr. Dre 1965(?)- **1994**:3
Duff, Hilary 1987- **2004**:4
Duncan, Todd 1903-1998
  Obituary **1998**:3
Dupri, Jermaine 1972- **1999**:1
Duran Duran **2005**:3
Dylan, Bob 1941- **1998**:1
Earle, Steve 1955- **2011**:2
Eazy-E 1963(?)-1995
  Obituary **1995**:3
Eckstine, Billy 1914-1993
  Obituary **1993**:4
Edmonds, Kenneth Babyface
  1958(?)- **1995**:3
Eldridge, Roy 1911-1989
  Obituary **1989**:3
Elliott, Missy 1971- **2003**:4
Eminem 1974- **2001**:2
Eno, Brian 1948- **1986**:2
Entwistle, John 1944-2002
  Obituary **2003**:3
En Vogue **1994**:1
Enya 1962(?)- **1992**:3
Ertegun, Ahmet 1923- **1986**:3
Esquivel, Juan 1918- **1996**:2
Estefan, Gloria **1991**:4
Etheridge, Melissa 1961(?)- **1995**:4
Eve 1978- **2004**:3
Everything But The Girl **1996**:4
Falco
  Brief entry **1987**:2
Farrell, Perry 1960- **1992**:2
Fender, Leo 1909-1991
  Obituary **1992**:1
Fitzgerald, Ella 1917-1996
  Obituary **1996**:4
Flavor Flav 1959- **2007**:3
Fleck, Bela 1958- **2011**:3
Fleming, Renee **2001**:4
Fogelberg, Dan 1951-2007
  Obituary **2009**:1
Foo Fighters **2006**:2
Ford, Tennessee Ernie 1919-1991
  Obituary **1992**:2
Foster, David 1950(?)- **1988**:2
Franklin, Aretha 1942- **1998**:3
Franklin, Kirk 1970- **2010**:2
Franklin, Melvin 1942-1995
  Obituary **1995**:3
Fuller, Simon 1960- **2008**:2
Furtado, Nelly 1978- **2007**:2
Garbage **2002**:3
Garcia, Jerry 1942-1995 **1988**:3
  Obituary **1996**:1
Geffen, David 1943- **1985**:3
Geldof, Bob 1954(?)- **1985**:3
Getz, Stan 1927-1991
  Obituary **1991**:4
Gibb, Andy 1958-1988

  Obituary **1988**:3
Gifford, Kathie Lee 1953- **1992**:2
Gift, Roland 1960(?)- **1990**:2
Gill, Vince 1957- **1995**:2
Gillespie, Dizzy 1917-1993
  Obituary **1993**:2
Glass, Philip 1937- **1991**:4
Gomez, Selena 1992- **2011**:1
Goodman, Benny 1909-1986
  Obituary **1986**:3
Goody, Sam 1904-1991
  Obituary **1992**:1
Gordon, Dexter 1923-1990 **1987**:1
Gore, Tipper 1948- **1985**:4
Goulet, Robert 1933-2007
  Obituary **2008**:4
Graham, Bill 1931-1991 **1986**:4
  Obituary **1992**:2
Grant, Amy 1961(?)- **1985**:4
Grappelli, Stephane 1908-1997
  Obituary **1998**:1
Gray, David 1970- **2001**:4
Gray, Macy 1970(?)- **2002**:1
Grebenshikov, Boris 1953- **1990**:1
Green Day **1995**:4
Greenwald, Julie 1970- **2008**:1
Groban, Josh 1981- **2009**:1
Grusin, Dave
  Brief entry **1987**:2
Guccione, Bob, Jr. 1956- **1991**:4
Guest, Christopher 1948- **2004**:2
Hammer, Jan 1948- **1987**:3
Hammer, M. C. **1991**:2
Hammond, John 1910-1987
  Obituary **1988**:2
Hampton, Lionel 1908-2002
  Obituary **2003**:4
Hancock, Herbie 1940- **1985**:1
Harris, Emmylou 1947- **1991**:3
Harrison, George 1943-2001
  Obituary **2003**:1
Harry, Deborah 1945- **1990**:1
Hart, Mary
  Brief entry **1988**:1
Hart, Mickey 1944(?)- **1991**:2
Harvey, Polly Jean 1970(?)- **1995**:4
Hawkins, Screamin' Jay 1929-1999
  Obituary **2000**:3
Hayes, Isaac 1942- **1998**:4
Headley, Heather 1974- **2011**:1
Heard, J.C. 1917-1988
  Obituary **1989**:1
Heid, Bill
  Brief entry **1987**:2
Heifetz, Jascha 1901-1987
  Obituary **1988**:2
Helfgott, David 1937(?)- **1997**:2
Helms, Bobby 1936-1997
  Obituary **1997**:4
Hewitt, Jennifer Love 1979- **1999**:2
Hill, Andrew 1931-2007
  Obituary **2008**:3
Hill, Faith 1967- **2000**:1
Hill, Lauryn 1975- **1999**:3
Hinton, Milt 1910-2000
  Obituary **2001**:3
Hirt, Al 1922-1999
  Obituary **1999**:4
Ho, Don 1930-2007
  Obituary **2008**:2
Hoffs, Susanna 1962(?)- **1988**:2
Hooker, John Lee 1917- **1998**:1

  Obituary **2002**:3
Hootie and the Blowfish **1995**:4
Horne, Lena 1917- **1998**:4
Hornsby, Bruce 1954(?)- **1989**:3
Horovitz, Adam 1968(?)- **1988**:3
Horowitz, Vladimir 1903-1989
  Obituary **1990**:1
Houston, Cissy 1933- **1999**:3
Houston, Whitney 1963- **1986**:3
Hubbard, Freddie 1938- **1988**:4
Hudson, Jennifer 1981- **2008**:1
Hutchence, Michael 1960-1997
  Obituary **1998**:1
Hynde, Chrissie 1951- **1991**:1
Ice Cube 1969- **1999**:2
Ice-T **1992**:3
Iglesias, Enrique 1975- **2000**:1
Indigo Girls **1994**:4
Interior, Lux 1946-2009
  Obituary **2010**:1
Iovine, Jimmy 1953- **2006**:3
Ives, Burl 1909-1995
  Obituary **1995**:4
Jackson, Alan 1958- **2003**:1
Jackson, Cordell 1923- **1992**:4
Jackson, Janet 1966(?)- **1990**:4
Jackson, Michael 1958- **1996**:2
Jacobs, Christian 1972-. See
  Christian Jacobs and Scott Schultz
James, Etta 1938- **1995**:2
James, Rick 1948-2004
  Obituary **2005**:4
Jarre, Maurice 1924-2009
  Obituary **2010**:2
Jarrett, Keith 1945- **1992**:4
Jay-Z 1970- **2006**:1
Jennings, Waylon 1937-2002
  Obituary **2003**:2
Jewel 1974- **1999**:2
Joel, Billy 1949- **1994**:3
John, Elton 1947- **1995**:4
Johnson, Jack 1975- **2006**:4
Jonas Brothers **2008**:4
Jones, Etta 1928-2001
  Obituary **2002**:4
Jones, Jenny 1946- **1998**:2
Jones, Norah 1979- **2004**:1
Jones, Quincy 1933- **1990**:4
Jones, Tom 1940- **1993**:4
Juanes 1972- **2004**:4
Judas Priest 1951- **2011**:3
Kaye, Sammy 1910-1987
  Obituary **1987**:4
Kelly, R. 1968- **1997**:3
Kendricks, Eddie 1939-1992
  Obituary **1993**:2
Kenny G 1957(?)- **1994**:4
Keys, Alicia 1981- **2006**:1
Khan, Ali 1922-2009
  Obituary **2010**:3
Kid Rock 1972- **2001**:1
Kilmer, Val **1991**:4
King, Coretta Scott 1927- **1999**:3
Kings of Leon 1982- **2010**:3
Kirchner, Leon 1919-2009
  Obituary **2011**:1
Kitt, Eartha 1927-2008
  Obituary **2010**:1
Knopfler, Mark 1949- **1986**:2
Kravitz, Lenny 1964(?)- **1991**:1
Kronos Quartet **1993**:1
Kurzweil, Raymond 1948- **1986**:3

Kyser, Kay 1906(?)-1985
  Obituary **1985**:3
Lachey, Nick and Jessica Simpson
  2004:4
Lady Antebellum 1982- **2011**:2
Lady Gaga **2011**:1
Landon, H. C. Robbins 1926-2009
  Obituary **2011**:3
Lane, Burton 1912-1997
  Obituary **1997**:2
Lane, Ronnie 1946-1997
  Obituary **1997**:4
Lang, K.D. 1961- **1988**:4
Lanois, Daniel 1951- **1991**:1
Larson, Jonathan 1961(?)-1996
  Obituary **1997**:2
Lauper, Cyndi 1953- **1985**:1
Lavigne, Avril 1984- **2005**:2
Lee, Peggy 1920-2002
  Obituary **2003**:1
Legend, John 1978- **2007**:1
Lennox, Annie 1954- **1985**:4
Levine, James 1943- **1992**:3
Lewis, Henry 1932-1996
  Obituary **1996**:3
Lewis, Huey 1951- **1987**:3
Lewis, John 1920-2001
  Obituary **2002**:1
Liberace 1919-1987
  Obituary **1987**:2
Ligeti, Gyorgy 1923-2006
  Obituary **2007**:3
Lil Wayne 1982- **2009**:3
Living Colour **1993**:3
LL Cool J 1968- **1998**:2
Lloyd Webber, Andrew 1948- **1989**:1
Loewe, Frederick 1901-1988
  Obituary **1988**:2
Lohan, Lindsay 1986- **2005**:3
Lopes, Lisa 1971-2002
  Obituary **2003**:3
Lords, Traci 1968- **1995**:4
Lovato, Demi 1992- **2011**:2
Love, Courtney 1964(?)- **1995**:1
Loveless, Patty 1957- **1998**:2
Lovett, Lyle 1958(?)- **1994**:1
Ludacris 1977- **2007**:4
Lynn, Loretta 1935(?)- **2001**:1
Machover, Tod 1953- **2010**:3
MacRae, Gordon 1921-1986
  Obituary **1986**:2
Madonna 1958- **1985**:2
Makeba, Miriam 1934- **1989**:2
Mancini, Henry 1924-1994
  Obituary **1994**:4
Manson, Marilyn 1969- **1999**:4
Marky Mark 1971- **1993**:3
Marley, Ziggy 1968- **1990**:4
Maroon 5 **2008**:1
Marsalis, Branford 1960- **1988**:3
Marsalis, Wynton 1961- **1997**:4
Martin, Dean 1917-1995
  Obituary **1996**:2
Martin, Dean Paul 1952(?)-1987
  Obituary **1987**:3
Martin, Ricky 1971- **1999**:4
Mary Mary 1972- **2009**:4
Master P 1970- **1999**:4
Masur, Kurt 1927- **1993**:4
Matthews, Dave 1967- **1999**:3
Maxwell 1973- **2010**:4
Mayer, John 1977- **2007**:4

McBride, Martina 1966- **2010**:1
McCartney, Linda 1942-1998
  Obituary **1998**:4
McCartney, Paul 1942- **2002**:4
McDuffie, Robert 1958- **1990**:2
McEntire, Reba 1954- **1987**:3
McFerrin, Bobby 1950- **1989**:1
McGraw, Tim 1966- **2000**:3
McLachlan, Sarah 1968- **1998**:4
McMurtry, James 1962- **1990**:2
McRae, Carmen 1920(?)-1994
  Obituary **1995**:2
Mehta, Zubin 1938(?)- **1994**:3
Mendoza, Lydia 1916-2007
  Obituary **2009**:1
Menuhin, Yehudi 1916-1999
  Obituary **1999**:3
Merchant, Natalie 1963- **1996**:3
Mercury, Freddie 1946-1991
  Obituary **1992**:2
Metallica **2004**:2
Michael, George 1963- **1989**:2
Michaels, Bret 1963- **2011**:4
Michelangeli, Arturo Benedetti 1920-
  1988:2
Midler, Bette 1945- **1989**:4
Miller, Roger 1936-1992
  Obituary **1993**:2
Minogue, Kylie 1968- **2003**:4
Mintz, Shlomo 1957- **1986**:2
Mitchell, Joni 1943- **1991**:4
Moby 1965- **2000**:1
Monica 1980- **2004**:2
Monroe, Bill 1911-1996
  Obituary **1997**:1
Montand, Yves 1921-1991
  Obituary **1992**:2
Montoya, Carlos 1903-1993
  Obituary **1993**:4
Moog, Robert 1934-2005
  Obituary **2006**:4
Moore, Dudley 1935-2002
  Obituary **2003**:2
Moore, Mandy 1984- **2004**:2
Morissette, Alanis 1974- **1996**:2
Morris, Doug 1938- **2005**:1
Morrison, Sterling 1942-1995
  Obituary **1996**:1
Morrissey 1959- **2005**:2
Mos Def 1973- **2005**:4
Mottola, Tommy 1949- **2002**:1
Mraz, Jason 1977- **2010**:2
Mutter, Anne-Sophie 1963- **1990**:3
Nas 1973- **2009**:2
Ne-Yo 1982- **2009**:4
Nelson, Rick 1940-1985
  Obituary **1986**:1
Nelson, Willie 1933- **1993**:4
New Kids on the Block **1991**:2
Newton-John, Olivia 1948- **1998**:4
Nickelback **2007**:2
Nilsson, Birgit 1918-2005
  Obituary **2007**:1
Nirvana **1992**:4
No Doubt **1997**:3
Norrington, Roger 1934- **1989**:4
North, Alex 1910- **1986**:3
Notorious B.I.G. 1973(?)-1997
  Obituary **1997**:3
'N Sync **2001**:4
Nyro, Laura 1947-1997
  Obituary **1997**:3

Oasis **1996**:3
O'Connor, Sinead 1967- **1990**:4
O'Day, Anita 1919-2006
  Obituary **2008**:1
Ono, Yoko 1933- **1989**:2
Orbison, Roy 1936-1988
  Obituary **1989**:2
Ormandy, Eugene 1899-1985
  Obituary **1985**:2
Osborne, Joan 1962- **1996**:4
Osbournes, The **2003**:4
Ostin, Mo 1927- **1996**:2
OutKast **2004**:4
Owens, Buck 1929-2006
  Obituary **2007**:2
Paisley, Brad 1972- **2008**:3
Palmer, Keke 1993- **2011**:3
Palmer, Robert 1949-2003
  Obituary **2004**:4
Parker, Colonel Tom 1929-1997
  Obituary **1997**:2
Parton, Dolly 1946- **1999**:4
Pass, Joe 1929-1994
  Obituary **1994**:4
Pastorius, Jaco 1951-1987
  Obituary **1988**:1
Paul, Les 1915-2009
  Obituary **2010**:4
Pavarotti, Luciano 1935- **1997**:4
Payton, Lawrence 1938(?)-1997
  Obituary **1997**:4
Pearl, Minnie 1912-1996
  Obituary **1996**:3
Pearl Jam **1994**:2
Perkins, Carl 1932-1998 **1998**:2
Peterson, Oscar 1925-2007
  Obituary **2009**:1
Petty, Tom 1952- **1988**:1
Phair, Liz 1967- **1995**:3
Phillips, John 1935-2001
  Obituary **2002**:1
Phillips, Sam 1923-2003
  Obituary **2004**:4
Phoenix **2011**:1
Pickett, Wilson 1941-2006
  Obituary **2007**:1
Pilatus, Robert 1966(?)-1998
  Obituary **1998**:3
Pink 1979- **2004**:3
Pittman, Robert W. 1953- **1985**:1
Pogorelich, Ivo 1958- **1986**:4
Ponty, Jean-Luc 1942- **1985**:4
Potts, Paul 1970- **2009**:1
Presley, Lisa Marie 1968- **2004**:3
Preston, Billy 1946-2006
  Obituary **2007**:3
Preston, Robert 1918-1987
  Obituary **1987**:3
Pride, Charley 1938(?)- **1998**:1
Prince 1958- **1995**:3
Public Enemy **1992**:1
Puente, Tito 1923-2000
  Obituary **2000**:4
Queen Latifah 1970(?)- **1992**:2
Quinn, Martha 1959- **1986**:4
Rabbitt, Eddie 1941-1998
  Obituary **1998**:4
Radiohead **2009**:3
Raffi 1948- **1988**:1
Raitt, Bonnie 1949- **1990**:2
Ramone, Joey 1951-2001
  Obituary **2002**:2

Wynette, Tammy 1942-1998
    Obituary **1998**:3
Wynonna 1964- **1993**:3
Xenakis, Iannis 1922-2001
    Obituary **2001**:4
Xzibit 1974- **2005**:4
Yankovic, Frank 1915-1998
    Obituary **1999**:2
Yankovic, Weird Al 1959- **1985**:4
Yearwood, Trisha 1964- **1999**:1
Yoakam, Dwight 1956- **1992**:4
Young, Neil 1945- **1991**:2
Zappa, Frank 1940-1993
    Obituary **1994**:2
Zevon, Warren 1947-2003
    Obituary **2004**:4
Zinnemann, Fred 1907-1997
    Obituary **1997**:3
Zwilich, Ellen 1939- **1990**:1

POLITICS AND GOVERNMENT--FOREIGN

Abacha, Sani 1943- **1996**:3
Abbas, Mahmoud 1935- **2008**:4
Abdullah II, King 1962- **2002**:4
Adams, Gerald 1948- **1994**:1
Afwerki, Isaias 1946- **2010**:1
Ahern, Bertie 1951- **1999**:3
Ahmadinejad, Mahmoud 1956- **2007**
    :1
Ahmed, Sharif 1964- **2010**:3
Akihito, Emperor of Japan 1933-
    1990:1
al-Abdullah, Rania 1970- **2001**:1
al-Assad, Bashar 1965- **2004**:2
al-Bashir, Omar 1944- **2009**:1
Albert, Prince of Monaco 1958- **2006**
    :2
Albright, Madeleine 1937- **1994**:3
Aliyev, Ilham 1961- **2010**:2
Amin, Idi 1925(?)-2003
    Obituary **2004**:4
Annan, Kofi 1938- **1999**:1
Aquino, Corazon 1933- **1986**:2
Aquino III, Benigno 1960- **2011**:4
Arafat, Yasser 1929- **1989**:3
Arens, Moshe 1925- **1985**:1
Arias Sanchez, Oscar 1941- **1989**:3
Aristide, Jean-Bertrand 1953- **1991**:3
Assad, Hafez 1930-2000
    Obituary **2000**:4
Assad, Hafez al- 1930(?)- **1992**:1
Assad, Rifaat 1937(?)- **1986**:3
Astorga, Nora 1949(?)-1988 **1988**:2
Atta Mills, John 1944- **2010**:3
Babangida, Ibrahim Badamosi 1941-
    1992:4
Bachelet, Michelle 1951- **2007**:3
Badawi, Abdullah Ahmad 1939-
    2009:3
Bakiyev, Kurmanbek 1949- **2007**:1
Balaguer, Joaquin 1907-2002
    Obituary **2003**:4
Ban, Ki-moon 1944- **2011**:2
Banda, Hastings 1898- **1994**:3
Bandaranaike, Sirimavo 1916-2000
    Obituary **2001**:2
Barak, Ehud 1942- **1999**:4
Barbie, Klaus 1913-1991
    Obituary **1992**:2
Basescu, Traian 1951- **2006**:2
Begin, Menachem 1913-1992

Obituary **1992**:3
Berger, Oscar 1946- **2004**:4
Berlusconi, Silvio 1936(?)- **1994**:4
Berri, Nabih 1939(?)- **1985**:2
Bhutto, Benazir 1953- **1989**:4
Biya, Paul 1933- **2006**:1
Blair, Tony 1953- **1996**:3
Bolkiah, Sultan Muda Hassanal
    1946- **1985**:4
Botha, P. W. 1916-2006
    Obituary **2008**:1
Bouchard, Lucien 1938- **1999**:2
Bourassa, Robert 1933-1996
    Obituary **1997**:1
Bouteflika, Abdelaziz 1937- **2010**:2
Bozize, Francois 1946- **2006**:3
Brandt, Willy 1913-1992
    Obituary **1993**:2
Brown, Gordon 1951- **2008**:3
Brundtland, Gro Harlem 1939- **2000**
    :1
Buthelezi, Mangosuthu Gatsha
    1928- **1989**:3
Caldera, Rafael 1916-2009
    Obituary **2011**:4
Campbell, Kim 1947- **1993**:4
Cardoso, Fernando Henrique 1931-
    1996:4
Castro, Fidel 1926- **1991**:4
Castro, Raúl 1931- **2010**:2
Cavaco Silva, Anibal 1939- **2011**:3
Ceausescu, Nicolae 1918-1989
    Obituary **1990**:2
Cedras, Raoul 1950- **1994**:4
Chaing Kai-Shek, Madame
    1898-2003
    Obituary **2005**:1
Chambas, Mohammed ibn 1950-
    2003:3
Chavez, Hugo 1954- **2010**:4
Chen Shui-bian 1950(?)- **2001**:2
Chernenko, Konstantin 1911-1985
    Obituary **1985**:1
Chiluba, Frederick 1943- **1992**:3
Chirac, Jacques 1932- **1995**:4
Chissano, Joaquim 1939- **1987**:4
Chretien, Jean 1934- **1990**:4
Ciampi, Carlo Azeglio 1920- **2004**:3
Collor de Mello, Fernando 1949-
    1992:4
Colosio, Luis Donaldo 1950-1994
    1994:3
Copps, Sheila 1952- **1986**:4
Correa, Rafael 1963- **2008**:1
Cresson, Edith 1934- **1992**:1
Cruz, Arturo 1923- **1985**:1
Dalai Lama 1935- **1989**:1
Deby, Idriss 1952- **2002**:2
de Hoop Scheffer, Jaap 1948- **2005**:1
de Klerk, F.W. 1936- **1990**:1
Delors, Jacques 1925- **1990**:2
Deng Xiaoping 1904-1997 **1995**:1
    Obituary **1997**:3
de Pinies, Jamie
    Brief entry **1986**:3
Devi, Phoolan 1955(?)- **1986**:1
    Obituary **2002**:3
Dhlakama, Afonso 1953- **1993**:3
Doe, Samuel 1952-1990
    Obituary **1991**:1
Doi, Takako
    Brief entry **1987**:4

Dong, Pham Van 1906-2000
    Obituary **2000**:4
Duarte, Jose Napoleon 1925-1990
    Obituary **1990**:3
Dubinin, Yuri 1930- **1987**:4
Duhalde, Eduardo 1941- **2003**:3
Ecevit, Bulent 1925-2006
    Obituary **2008**:1
Enkhbayar, Nambaryn 1958- **2007**:1
Fahd, King of Saudi Arabia
    1923(?)-2005
    Obituary **2006**:4
Ferguson, Sarah 1959- **1990**:3
Fernández, Leonel 1953- **2009**:2
Fernández de Kirchner, Cristina
    1953- **2009**:1
Finnbogadoaattir, Vigdiaas
    Brief entry **1986**:2
Fischer, Joschka 1948- **2005**:2
Fox, Vicente 1942- **2001**:1
Freij, Elias 1920- **1986**:4
Fujimori, Alberto 1938- **1992**:4
Galvin, Martin
    Brief entry **1985**:3
Gandhi, Indira 1917-1984
    Obituary **1985**:1
Gandhi, Rajiv 1944-1991
    Obituary **1991**:4
Gandhi, Sonia 1947- **2000**:2
Garcia, Alan 1949- **2007**:4
Garcia, Amalia 1951- **2005**:3
Garneau, Marc 1949- **1985**:1
Gbagbo, Laurent 1945- **2003**:2
Ghali, Boutros Boutros 1922- **1992**:3
Gillard, Julia 1961- **2011**:4
Gorbachev, Mikhail 1931- **1985**:2
Gorbachev, Raisa 1932-1999
    Obituary **2000**:2
Gowda, H. D. Deve 1933- **1997**:1
Gromyko, Andrei 1909-1989
    Obituary **1990**:2
Guebuza, Armando 1943- **2008**:4
Guelleh, Ismail Omar 1947- **2006**:2
Gul, Abdullah 1950- **2009**:4
Habash, George 1925(?)- **1986**:1
Habibie, Bacharuddin Jusuf 1936-
    1999:3
Halonen, Tarja 1943- **2006**:4
Hani, Chris 1942-1993
    Obituary **1993**:4
Harper, Stephen J. 1959- **2007**:3
Harriman, Pamela 1920- **1994**:4
Harris, Michael Deane 1945- **1997**:2
Havel, Vaclav 1936- **1990**:3
Herzog, Chaim 1918-1997
    Obituary **1997**:3
Hess, Rudolph 1894-1987
    Obituary **1988**:1
Hillery, Patrick 1923-2008
    Obituary **2009**:2
Hirohito, Emperor of Japan
    1901-1989
    Obituary **1989**:2
Honecker, Erich 1912-1994
    Obituary **1994**:4
Hosokawa, Morihiro 1938- **1994**:1
Hua Guofeng 1921-2008
    Obituary **2009**:4
Hu Jintao 1942- **2004**:1
Hume, John 1938- **1987**:1
Hussein, Saddam 1937- **1991**:1
Husseini, Faisal 1940- **1998**:4

Hussein I, King 1935-1999 **1997**:3
  Obituary **1999**:3
Hu Yaobang 1915-1989
  Obituary **1989**:4
Ilves, Toomas Hendrik 1953- **2007**:4
Izetbegovic, Alija 1925- **1996**:4
Jagdeo, Bharrat 1964- **2008**:1
Jenkins, Roy Harris 1920-2003
  Obituary **2004**:1
Jiang Quing 1914-1991
  Obituary **1992**:1
Jiang Zemin 1926- **1996**:1
Johnson, Pierre Marc 1946- **1985**:4
Juan Carlos I 1938- **1993**:1
Juliana 1909-2004
  Obituary **2005**:3
Jumblatt, Walid 1949(?)- **1987**:4
Juneau, Pierre 1922- **1988**:3
Kabila, Joseph 1971- **2003**:2
Kabila, Laurent 1939- **1998**:1
  Obituary **2001**:3
Kaczynski, Lech 1949- **2007**:2
Kagame, Paul 1957- **2001**:4
Kamel, Hussein 1954- **1996**:1
Karadzic, Radovan 1945- **1995**:3
Karamanlis, Costas 1956- **2009**:1
Karimov, Islam 1938- **2006**:3
Karzai, Hamid 1955(?)- **2002**:3
Kasyanov, Mikhail 1957- **2001**:1
Kekkonen, Urho 1900-1986
  Obituary **1986**:4
Khatami, Mohammed 1943- **1997**:4
Khomeini, Ayatollah Ruhollah
  1900(?)-1989
  Obituary **1989**:4
Kibaki, Mwai 1931- **2003**:4
Kim Dae Jung 1925- **1998**:3
Kim Il Sung 1912-1994
  Obituary **1994**:4
Kim Jong Il 1942- **1995**:2
King Hassan II 1929-1999
  Obituary **2000**:1
Kohl, Helmut 1930- **1994**:1
Koizumi, Junichiro 1942- **2002**:1
Kostunica, Vojislav 1944- **2001**:1
Kouchner, Bernard 1939- **2005**:3
Kufuor, John Agyekum 1938- **2005**:4
Kyprianou, Spyros 1932-2002
  Obituary **2003**:2
Lagos, Ricardo 1938- **2005**:3
Lalonde, Marc 1929- **1985**:1
Landsbergis, Vytautas 1932- **1991**:3
Lebed, Alexander 1950- **1997**:1
Le Duan 1908(?)-1986
  Obituary **1986**:4
Le Duc Tho 1911-1990
  Obituary **1991**:1
Lee, Martin 1938- **1998**:2
Lee Jong-Wook 1945- **2005**:1
Lee Myung-bak 1941- **2009**:2
Lee Teng-hui 1923- **2000**:1
Leaavesque, Reneaa
  Obituary **1988**:1
Levy, David 1938- **1987**:2
Lewis, Stephen 1937- **1987**:2
Livingstone, Ken 1945- **1988**:3
Lobo, Porfirio 1947- **2011**:3
Lon Nol
  Obituary **1986**:1
Lugo, Fernando 1951- **2010**:1
Lukashenko, Alexander 1954- **2006**:4

Macapagal-Arroyo, Gloria 1947-
  2001:4
Machel, Samora 1933-1986
  Obituary **1987**:1
Macmillan, Harold 1894-1986
  Obituary **1987**:2
Major, John 1943- **1991**:2
Mandela, Nelson 1918- **1990**:3
Mandela, Winnie 1934- **1989**:3
Mara, Ratu Sir Kamisese 1920-2004
  Obituary **2005**:3
Marcos, Ferdinand 1917-1989
  Obituary **1990**:1
Martin, Paul 1938- **2004**:4
Masako, Crown Princess 1963- **1993**
  :4
Mas Canosa, Jorge 1939-1997 **1998**:2
Ma Ying-jeou 1950- **2009**:4
Mbeki, Thabo 1942- **1999**:4
McGuinness, Martin 1950(?)- **1985**:4
McLaughlin, Audrey 1936- **1990**:3
Medvedev, Dmitry 1965- **2009**:4
Megawati Sukarnoputri 1947- **2000**:1
Merkel, Angela 1954- **2010**:2
Mesic, Stipe 1934- **2005**:4
Milosevic, Slobodan 1941- **1993**:2
Mitterrand, Francois 1916-1996
  Obituary **1996**:2
Miyazawa, Kiichi 1919- **1992**:2
Mobutu Sese Seko 1930-1997 **1993**:4
  Obituary **1998**:1
Mobutu Sese Seko 1930-1998
  Obituary **1998**:4
Moi, Daniel arap 1924- **1993**:2
Molotov, Vyacheslav Mikhailovich
  1890-1986
  Obituary **1987**:1
Morales, Evo 1959- **2007**:2
Mori, Yoshiro 1937- **2000**:4
Mubarak, Hosni 1928- **1991**:4
Mugabe, Robert 1924- **1988**:4
Mulroney, Brian 1939- **1989**:2
Museveni, Yoweri 1944- **2002**:1
Musharraf, Pervez 1943- **2000**:2
Nagako, Empress Dowager
  1903-2000
  Obituary **2001**:1
Nazarbayev, Nursultan 1940- **2006**:4
Netanyahu, Benjamin 1949- **1996**:4
Nidal, Abu 1937- **1987**:1
Niezabitowska, Malgorzata 1949(?)-
  1991:3
Nujoma, Sam 1929- **1990**:4
Nyerere, Julius 1922(?)-1999
  Obituary **2000**:2
Obando, Miguel 1926- **1986**:4
Obasanjo, Olusegun 1937(?)- **2000**:2
Obuchi, Keizo 1937- **1999**:2
Obuchi, Keizo 1937-2000
  Obituary **2000**:4
Ocalan, Abdullah 1948(?)- **1999**:4
Olav, King of Norway 1903-1991
  Obituary **1991**:3
Ortega, Daniel 1945- **2008**:2
Palme, Olof 1927-1986
  Obituary **1986**:2
Papandreou, Andrea 1919-1996
  Obituary **1997**:1
Parizeau, Jacques 1930- **1995**:1
Pastrana, Andres 1954- **2002**:1
Paton, Alan 1903-1988
  Obituary **1988**:3

Patten, Christopher 1944- **1993**:3
Paz, Octavio 1914- **1991**:2
Peckford, Brian 1942- **1989**:1
Peres, Shimon 1923- **1996**:3
Perez, Carlos Andre 1922- **1990**:2
Perez de Cuellar, Javier 1920- **1991**:3
Peterson, David 1943- **1987**:1
Philby, Kim 1912-1988
  Obituary **1988**:3
Pinera, Sebastian 1949- **2011**:2
Pinochet, Augusto 1915- **1999**:2
Pol Pot 1928-1998
  Obituary **1998**:4
Preaaval, Reneaa 1943- **1997**:2
Primakov, Yevgeny 1929- **1999**:3
Princess Margaret, Countess of
  Snowdon 1930-2002
  Obituary **2003**:2
Putin, Vladimir 1952- **2000**:3
Qaddhafi, Muammar 1942- **1998**:3
Queen Elizabeth the Queen Mother
  1900-2002
  Obituary **2003**:2
Rabin, Leah 1928-2000
  Obituary **2001**:2
Rabin, Yitzhak 1922-1995 **1993**:1
  Obituary **1996**:2
Rafsanjani, Ali Akbar Hashemi
  1934(?)- **1987**:3
Rahman, Sheik Omar Abdel- 1938-
  1993:3
Rainier III, Prince of Monaco
  1923-2005
  Obituary **2006**:2
Ram, Jagjivan 1908-1986
  Obituary **1986**:4
Ramos, Fidel 1928- **1995**:2
Rao, P. V. Narasimha 1921- **1993**:2
Rasmussen, Anders Fogh 1953- **2006**
  :1
Ravalomanana, Marc 1950(?)- **2003**:1
Razak, Datuk 1953- **2011**:1
Reisman, Simon 1919- **1987**:4
Robelo, Alfonso 1940(?)- **1988**:1
Robinson, Mary 1944- **1993**:1
Roh Moo-hyun 1946- **2005**:1
Rudd, Kevin 1957- **2009**:1
Rugova, Ibrahim 1944-2006
  Obituary **2007**:1
Saakashvili, Mikhail 1967- **2008**:4
Saleh, Ali Abdullah 1942- **2001**:3
Salinas, Carlos 1948- **1992**:1
Sanchez de Lozada, Gonzalo 1930-
  2004:3
Sargsyan, Serzh 1954- **2009**:3
Sarkis, Elias 1924-1985
  Obituary **1985**:3
Sarkozy, Nicolas 1955- **2008**:4
Saro-Wiwa, Ken 1941-1995
  Obituary **1996**:2
Savimbi, Jonas 1934- **1986**:2
Schily, Otto
  Brief entry **1987**:4
Schroder, Gerhard 1944- **1999**:1
Shah, Gyanendra 1947- **2006**:1
Sharon, Ariel 1928- **2001**:4
Shipley, Jenny 1952- **1998**:3
Silva, Luiz Inacio Lula da 1945-
  2003:4
Simpson, Wallis 1896-1986
  Obituary **1986**:3
Sirleaf, Ellen Johnson 1938- **2007**:3

Falkenberg, Nanette 1951- **1985**:2
Farmer, James 1920-1999
  Obituary **2000**:1
Farrakhan, Louis 1933- **1990**:4
Faubus, Orval 1910-1994
  Obituary **1995**:2
Feinstein, Dianne 1933- **1993**:3
Felt, W. Mark 1913-2008
  Obituary **2010**:1
Fenwick, Millicent H.
  Obituary **1993**:2
Ferraro, Geraldine 1935- **1998**:3
Fish, Hamilton 1888-1991
  Obituary **1991**:3
Fitzgerald, A. Ernest 1926- **1986**:2
Fleischer, Ari 1960- **2003**:1
Florio, James J. 1937- **1991**:2
Flynn, Ray 1939- **1989**:1
Foley, Thomas S. 1929- **1990**:1
Forbes, Steve 1947- **1996**:2
Ford, Gerald R. 1913-2007
  Obituary **2008**:2
Foster, Vincent 1945(?)-1993
  Obituary **1994**:1
Frank, Anthony M. 1931(?)- **1992**:1
Frank, Barney 1940- **1989**:2
Franks, Tommy 1945- **2004**:1
Frist, Bill 1952- **2003**:4
Fulbright, J. William 1905-1995
  Obituary **1995**:3
Galvin, John R. 1929- **1990**:1
Garrison, Jim 1922-1992
  Obituary **1993**:2
Gates, Robert M. 1943- **1992**:2
Gebbie, Kristine 1944(?)- **1994**:2
Geithner, Timothy F. 1961- **2009**:4
Gephardt, Richard 1941- **1987**:3
Gergen, David 1942- **1994**:1
Gingrich, Newt 1943- **1991**:1
Giuliani, Rudolph 1944- **1994**:2
Glenn, John 1921- **1998**:3
Goldwater, Barry 1909-1998
  Obituary **1998**:4
Gore, Albert, Jr. 1948(?)- **1993**:2
Gore, Albert, Sr. 1907-1998
  Obituary **1999**:2
Gramm, Phil 1942- **1995**:2
Granholm, Jennifer 1959- **2003**:3
Greenspan, Alan 1926- **1992**:2
Gregoire, Chris 1947- **2010**:2
Griffiths, Martha 1912-2003
  Obituary **2004**:2
Groves, Robert 1949- **2011**:3
Haldeman, H. R. 1926-1993
  Obituary **1994**:2
Hall, Gus 1910-2000
  Obituary **2001**:2
Harriman, Pamela 1920- **1994**:4
Harriman, W. Averell 1891-1986
  Obituary **1986**:4
Harris, Katherine 1957- **2001**:3
Harris, Patricia Roberts 1924-1985
  Obituary **1985**:2
Hastert, Dennis 1942- **1999**:3
Hatch, Orin G. 1934- **2000**:2
Hawkins, Paula 1927-2009
  Obituary **2011**:4
Hayakawa, Samuel Ichiye 1906-1992
  Obituary **1992**:3
Heinz, John 1938-1991
  Obituary **1991**:4
Heller, Walter 1915-1987

Obituary **1987**:4
Helms, Jesse 1921- **1998**:1
Hills, Carla 1934- **1990**:3
Hiss, Alger 1904-1996
  Obituary **1997**:2
Holbrooke, Richard 1941(?)- **1996**:2
Holder, Jr., Eric H. 1951- **2009**:4
Howard, Michelle 1960- **2010**:2
Hughes, Karen 1957- **2001**:2
Hull, Jane Dee 1935- **1999**:2
Hundt, Reed Eric 1948- **1997**:2
Hyde, Henry 1924- **1999**:1
Inman, Bobby Ray 1931- **1985**:1
Jackson, Jesse 1941- **1996**:1
Jackson, Jesse, Jr. 1965- **1998**:3
Jackson, Lisa P. 1962- **2009**:4
Jackson, Thomas Penfield 1937- **2000**
  :2
Jarrett, Valerie 1956- **2010**:4
Jeffords, James 1934- **2002**:2
Jeffrey, Mildred 1910-2004
  Obituary **2005**:2
Jindal, Bobby 1971- **2006**:1
Johnson, Lady Bird 1912-2007
  Obituary **2008**:4
Jordan, Barbara 1936-1996
  Obituary **1996**:3
Kagan, Elena 1960- **2011**:4
Kassebaum, Nancy 1932- **1991**:1
Kemp, Jack 1935- **1990**:4
Kennan, George 1904-2005
  Obituary **2006**:2
Kennedy, Rose 1890-1995
  Obituary **1995**:3
Kennedy, Ted 1932-2009
  Obituary **2011**:1
Kerrey, Bob 1943- **1986**:1
Kerry, John 1943- **2005**:2
Kessler, David 1951- **1992**:1
Keyes, Alan 1950- **1996**:2
Kilpatrick, Kwame 1970- **2009**:2
Kirkpatrick, Jeane 1926-2006
  Obituary **2008**:1
Kissinger, Henry 1923- **1999**:4
Koop, C. Everett 1916- **1989**:3
Kundra, Vivek 1974- **2010**:3
Landon, Alf 1887-1987
  Obituary **1988**:1
Landrieu, Mary L. 1955- **2002**:2
Langevin, James R. 1964- **2001**:2
Lansdale, Edward G. 1908-1987
  Obituary **1987**:2
Lantos, Tom 1928-2008
  Obituary **2009**:2
Levitt, Arthur 1931- **2004**:2
Lieberman, Joseph 1942- **2001**:1
Lilley, James 1928-2009
  Obituary **2011**:3
Liman, Arthur 1932- **1989**:4
Lincoln, Blanche 1960- **2003**:1
Lindsay, John V. 1921-2000
  Obituary **2001**:3
Lodge, Henry Cabot 1902-1985
  Obituary **1985**:1
Lord, Winston
  Brief entry **1987**:4
Lott, Trent 1941- **1998**:1
Luce, Clare Boothe 1903-1987
  Obituary **1988**:1
Lucke, Lewis 1951(?)- **2004**:4
Manchin, Joe 1947- **2006**:4
Mankiller, Wilma P.

Brief entry **1986**:2
Mansfield, Mike 1903-2001
  Obituary **2002**:4
Martin, Lynn 1939- **1991**:4
Martinez, Bob 1934- **1992**:1
Matalin, Mary 1953- **1995**:2
Mathias, Bob 1930-2006
  Obituary **2007**:4
McCain, John S. 1936- **1998**:4
McCarthy, Carolyn 1944- **1998**:4
McChrystal, Stanley 1954- **2011**:3
McCloy, John J. 1895-1989
  Obituary **1989**:3
McDonnell, Bob 1954- **2011**:2
McGreevey, James 1957- **2005**:2
McKinney, Cynthia A. 1955- **1997**:1
McKinney, Stewart B. 1931-1987
  Obituary **1987**:4
McMillen, Tom 1952- **1988**:4
McNamara, Robert S. 1916- **1995**:4
Mfume, Kweisi 1948- **1996**:3
Mikulski, Barbara 1936- **1992**:4
Mills, Wilbur 1909-1992
  Obituary **1992**:4
Minner, Ruth Ann 1935- **2002**:2
Mitchell, George J. 1933- **1989**:3
Mitchell, John 1913-1988
  Obituary **1989**:2
Moakley, Joseph 1927-2001
  Obituary **2002**:2
Molinari, Susan 1958- **1996**:4
Morris, Dick 1948- **1997**:3
Morrison, Trudi
  Brief entry **1986**:2
Mott, William Penn, Jr. 1909- **1986**:1
Moyers, Bill 1934- **1991**:4
Moynihan, Daniel Patrick 1927-2003
  Obituary **2004**:2
Muskie, Edmund S. 1914-1996
  Obituary **1996**:3
Nagin, Ray 1956- **2007**:1
Natsios, Andrew 1949- **2005**:1
Neal, James Foster 1929- **1986**:2
Nelson, Gaylord A. 1914-2005
  Obituary **2006**:3
Newsom, Gavin 1967- **2009**:3
Newton, Huey 1942-1989
  Obituary **1990**:1
Nixon, Pat 1912-1993
  Obituary **1994**:1
Nixon, Richard 1913-1994
  Obituary **1994**:4
Noonan, Peggy 1950- **1990**:3
North, Oliver 1943- **1987**:4
Novello, Antonia 1944- **1991**:2
Nunn, Sam 1938- **1990**:2
Obama, Barack 1961- **2007**:4
O'Leary, Hazel 1937- **1993**:4
Oliver, Daniel 1939- **1988**:2
Onassis, Jacqueline Kennedy
  1929-1994
  Obituary **1994**:4
O'Neill, Paul H. 1935- **2001**:4
O'Neill, Tip 1912-1994
  Obituary **1994**:3
Orr, Kay 1939- **1987**:4
Paige, Emmett, Jr.
  Brief entry **1986**:4
Paige, Rod 1933- **2003**:2
Palin, Sarah 1964- **2009**:1
Panetta, Leon 1938- **1995**:1
Pataki, George 1945- **1995**:2

Pelosi, Nancy 1940- **2004**:2
Pendleton, Clarence M. 1930-1988
  Obituary **1988**:4
Pepper, Claude 1900-1989
  Obituary **1989**:4
Perot, H. Ross 1930- **1992**:4
Perry, Carrie Saxon 1932(?)- **1989**:2
Perry, William 1927- **1994**:4
Peters, Mary E. 1948- **2008**:3
Powell, Colin 1937- **1990**:1
Powell, Lewis F. 1907-1998
  Obituary **1999**:1
Pryce, Deborah 1951- **2006**:3
Quayle, Dan 1947- **1989**:2
Raines, Franklin 1949- **1997**:4
Reagan, Ronald 1911-2004
  Obituary **2005**:3
Reed, Ralph 1961(?)- **1995**:1
Reich, Robert 1946- **1995**:4
Reid, Harry 1939- **2006**:1
Rendell, Ed 1944- **2010**:1
Reno, Janet 1938- **1993**:3
Ribicoff, Abraham 1910-1998
  Obituary **1998**:3
Rice, Condoleezza 1954- **2002**:1
Rice, Susan E. 1964- **2010**:3
Richards, Ann 1933- **1991**:2
Rickover, Hyman 1900-1986
  Obituary **1986**:4
Ridge, Tom 1945- **2002**:2
Riordan, Richard 1930- **1993**:4
Rizzo, Frank 1920-1991
  Obituary **1992**:1
Robb, Charles S. 1939- **1987**:2
Robertson, Pat 1930- **1988**:2
Roemer, Buddy 1943- **1991**:4
Rogers, William P. 1913-2001
  Obituary **2001**:4
Roosevelt, Franklin D., Jr. 1914-1988
  Obituary **1989**:1
Ros-Lehtinen, Ileana 1952- **2000**:2
Roth, William Victor, Jr. 1921-2003
  Obituary **2005**:1
Rove, Karl 1950- **2006**:2
Roybal-Allard, Lucille 1941- **1999**:4
Rumsfeld, Donald 1932- **2004**:1
Rusk, Dean 1909-1994
  Obituary **1995**:2
Salazar, Ken 1955- **2011**:4
Sanchez, Loretta 1960- **2000**:3
Sanders, Bernie 1941(?)- **1991**:4
Satcher, David 1941- **2001**:4
Scalia, Antonin 1936- **1988**:2
Schaefer, William Donald 1921- **1988**
  :1
Schiavo, Mary 1955- **1998**:2
Schwarzenegger, Arnold 1947- **1991**
  :1
Schwarzkopf, Norman 1934- **1991**:3
Sebelius, Kathleen 1948- **2008**:4
Senghor, Leopold 1906-2001
  Obituary **2003**:1
Shalikashvili, John 1936- **1994**:2
Sheehan, Daniel P. 1945(?)- **1989**:1
Sidney, Ivan
  Brief entry **1987**:2
Sigmund, Barbara Boggs 1939-1990
  Obituary **1991**:1
Simon, Paul 1928-2003
  Obituary **2005**:1
Skinner, Sam 1938- **1992**:3
Slater, Rodney E. 1955- **1997**:4

Snow, John W. 1939- **2006**:2
Snow, Tony 1955-2008
  Obituary **2009**:3
Snowe, Olympia 1947- **1995**:3
Solis, Hilda 1957- **2010**:1
Sotomayor, Sonia 1954- **2010**:4
Spellings, Margaret 1957- **2005**:4
Spitzer, Eliot 1959- **2007**:2
Starr, Kenneth 1946- **1998**:3
Steele, Michael 1958- **2010**:2
Stephanopoulos, George 1961- **1994**
  :3
Stewart, Potter 1915-1985
  Obituary **1986**:1
Stokes, Carl 1927-1996
  Obituary **1996**:4
Strauss, Robert 1918- **1991**:4
Suarez, Xavier
  Brief entry **1986**:2
Sullivan, Louis 1933- **1990**:4
Sununu, John 1939- **1989**:2
Sutphen, Mona 1967- **2010**:4
Sutton, Percy 1920-2009
  Obituary **2011**:4
Swift, Jane 1965(?)- **2002**:1
Taylor, Maxwell 1901-1987
  Obituary **1987**:3
Tenet, George 1953- **2000**:3
Thomas, Clarence 1948- **1992**:2
Thomas, Edmond J. 1943(?)- **2005**:1
Thomas, Helen 1920- **1988**:4
Thompson, Fred 1942- **1998**:2
Thurmond, Strom 1902-2003
  Obituary **2004**:3
Tower, John 1926-1991
  Obituary **1991**:4
Townsend, Kathleen Kennedy 1951-
  2001:3
Tsongas, Paul Efthemios 1941-1997
  Obituary **1997**:2
Tutwiler, Margaret 1950- **1992**:4
Tyson, Laura D'Andrea 1947- **1994**:1
Udall, Mo 1922-1998
  Obituary **1999**:2
Ventura, Jesse 1951- **1999**:2
Vilsack, Tom 1950- **2011**:1
Violet, Arlene 1943- **1985**:3
Wallace, George 1919-1998
  Obituary **1999**:1
Washington, Harold 1922-1987
  Obituary **1988**:1
Waters, Maxine 1938- **1998**:4
Watts, J.C. 1957- **1999**:2
Webb, Wellington E. 1941- **2000**:3
Weicker, Lowell P., Jr. 1931- **1993**:1
Weinberger, Caspar 1917-2006
  Obituary **2007**:2
Wellstone, Paul 1944-2002
  Obituary **2004**:1
Westmoreland, William C. 1914-2005
  Obituary **2006**:4
Whitman, Christine Todd 1947(?)-
  1994:3
Whitmire, Kathy 1946- **1988**:2
Wilder, L. Douglas 1931- **1990**:3
Williams, Anthony 1952- **2000**:4
Williams, G. Mennen 1911-1988
  Obituary **1988**:2
Wilson, Pete 1933- **1992**:3
Yard, Molly **1991**:4
Young, Coleman A. 1918-1997
  Obituary **1998**:1

Zech, Lando W.
  Brief entry **1987**:4
Zerhouni, Elias A. 1951- **2004**:3
Zinni, Anthony 1943- **2003**:1

RADIO

Adams, Yolanda 1961- **2008**:2
Albert, Marv 1943- **1994**:3
Albom, Mitch 1958- **1999**:3
Ameche, Don 1908-1993
  Obituary **1994**:2
Autry, Gene 1907-1998
  Obituary **1999**:1
Backus, Jim 1913-1989
  Obituary **1990**:1
Barber, Red 1908-1992
  Obituary **1993**:2
Becker, Brian 1957(?)- **2004**:4
Bell, Art 1945- **2000**:1
Bergeron, Tom 1955- **2010**:1
Blanc, Mel 1908-1989
  Obituary **1989**:4
Campbell, Bebe Moore 1950- **1996**:2
Caray, Harry 1914(?)-1998 **1988**:3
  Obituary **1998**:3
Carson, Johnny 1925-2005
  Obituary **2006**:1
Cherry, Don 1934- **1993**:4
Codrescu, Andreaa 1946- **1997**:3
Cosell, Howard 1918-1995
  Obituary **1995**:4
Costas, Bob 1952- **1986**:4
Crenna, Richard 1926-2003
  Obituary **2004**:1
Day, Dennis 1917-1988
  Obituary **1988**:4
Denver, Bob 1935-2005
  Obituary **2006**:4
Donnellan, Nanci **1995**:2
Douglas, Mike 1925-2006
  Obituary **2007**:4
Dr. Demento 1941- **1986**:1
Durrell, Gerald 1925-1995
  Obituary **1995**:3
Edwards, Bob 1947- **1993**:2
Fleming, Art 1925(?)-1995
  Obituary **1995**:4
Ford, Tennessee Ernie 1919-1991
  Obituary **1992**:2
Glass, Ira 1959- **2008**:2
Gobel, George 1920(?)-1991
  Obituary **1991**:4
Goodman, Benny 1909-1986
  Obituary **1986**:3
Gordon, Gale 1906-1995
  Obituary **1996**:1
Graham, Billy 1918- **1992**:1
Granato, Cammi 1971- **1999**:3
Grange, Red 1903-1991
  Obituary **1991**:3
Greene, Lorne 1915-1987
  Obituary **1988**:1
Griffin, Merv 1925-2008
  Obituary **2008**:4
Gross, Terry 1951- **1998**:3
Harmon, Tom 1919-1990
  Obituary **1990**:3
Harvey, Paul 1918- **1995**:3
Harvey, Steve 1956- **2010**:1
Harwell, Ernie 1918- **1997**:3
Hill, George Roy 1921-2002
  Obituary **2004**:1

Hollander, Joel 1956(?)- **2006**:4
Hope, Bob 1903-2003
   Obituary **2004**:4
Houseman, John 1902-1988
   Obituary **1989**:1
Hughes, Cathy 1947- **1999**:1
Imus, Don 1940- **1997**:1
Ives, Burl 1909-1995
   Obituary **1995**:4
Karmazin, Mel 1943- **2006**:1
Kasem, Casey 1933(?)- **1987**:1
Keillor, Garrison 1942- **2011**:2
Keyes, Alan 1950- **1996**:2
Kimmel, Jimmy 1967- **2009**:2
King, Larry 1933- **1993**:1
Kyser, Kay 1906(?)-1985
   Obituary **1985**:3
Leaavesque, Reneaa
   Obituary **1988**:1
Limbaugh, Rush **1991**:3
Magliozzi, Tom and Ray **1991**:4
Milligan, Spike 1918-2002
   Obituary **2003**:2
Nelson, Harriet 1909(?)-1994
   Obituary **1995**:1
Olbermann, Keith 1959- **2010**:3
Olson, Johnny 1910(?)-1985
   Obituary **1985**:4
Osgood, Charles 1933- **1996**:2
Paar, Jack 1918-2004
   Obituary **2005**:2
Paley, William S. 1901-1990
   Obituary **1991**:2
Parks, Bert 1914-1992
   Obituary **1992**:3
Parsons, Gary 1950(?)- **2006**:2
Porter, Sylvia 1913-1991
   Obituary **1991**:4
Quivers, Robin 1953(?)- **1995**:4
Raphael, Sally Jessy 1943- **1992**:4
Raye, Martha 1916-1994
   Obituary **1995**:1
Reagan, Ronald 1911-2004
   Obituary **2005**:3
Riddle, Nelson 1921-1985
   Obituary **1985**:4
Roberts, Cokie 1943- **1993**:4
Rollins, Henry 1961- **2007**:3
Sales, Soupy 1926-2009
   Obituary **2011**:2
Saralegui, Cristina 1948- **1999**:2
Schlessinger, Laura 1947(?)- **1996**:3
Seacrest, Ryan 1976- **2004**:4
Sedaris, David 1956- **2005**:3
Sevareid, Eric 1912-1992
   Obituary **1993**:1
Shore, Dinah 1917-1994
   Obituary **1994**:3
Smith, Buffalo Bob 1917-1998
   Obituary **1999**:1
Smith, Kate 1907(?)-1986
   Obituary **1986**:3
Stern, Howard 1954- **1988**:2
Swayze, John Cameron 1906-1995
   Obituary **1996**:1
Terkel, Studs 1912-2008
   Obituary **2010**:1
Toguri, Iva 1916-2006
   Obituary **2007**:4
Tom and Ray Magliozzi **1991**:4
Totenberg, Nina 1944- **1992**:2
Wolfman Jack 1938-1995

Obituary **1996**:1
Young, Robert 1907-1998
   Obituary **1999**:1

RELIGION

Abernathy, Ralph 1926-1990
   Obituary **1990**:3
Altea, Rosemary 1946- **1996**:3
Applewhite, Marshall Herff
   1931-1997
   Obituary **1997**:3
Aristide, Jean-Bertrand 1953- **1991**:3
Beckett, Wendy (Sister) 1930- **1998**:3
Benson, Ezra Taft 1899-1994
   Obituary **1994**:4
Bernardin, Cardinal Joseph
   1928-1996 **1997**:2
Berri, Nabih 1939(?)- **1985**:2
Browning, Edmond
   Brief entry **1986**:2
Burns, Charles R.
   Brief entry **1988**:1
Carey, George 1935- **1992**:3
Chavis, Benjamin 1948- **1993**:4
Chittister, Joan D. 1936- **2002**:2
Chopra, Deepak 1947- **1996**:3
Clements, George 1932- **1985**:1
Cleveland, James 1932(?)-1991
   Obituary **1991**:3
Coffin, William Sloane, Jr. 1924- **1990**
   :3
Cunningham, Reverend William
   1930-1997
   Obituary **1997**:4
Curran, Charles E. 1934- **1989**:2
Daily, Bishop Thomas V. 1927- **1990**
   :4
Dalai Lama 1935- **1989**:1
Dearden, John Cardinal 1907-1988
   Obituary **1988**:4
Dorsey, Thomas A. 1899-1993
   Obituary **1993**:3
Eilberg, Amy
   Brief entry **1985**:3
Falwell, Jerry 1933-2007
   Obituary **2008**:3
Farrakhan, Louis 1933- **1990**:4
Fox, Matthew 1940- **1992**:2
Fulghum, Robert 1937- **1996**:1
Gottschalk, Alfred 1930-2009
   Obituary **2011**:1
Graham, Billy 1918- **1992**:1
Grant, Amy 1961(?)- **1985**:4
Hahn, Jessica 1960- **1989**:4
Harris, Barbara **1996**:3
Harris, Barbara 1930- **1989**:3
Healy, Timothy S. 1923- **1990**:2
Henry, Carl F.H. 1913-2003
   Obituary **2005**:1
Huffington, Arianna 1950- **1996**:2
Hume, Basil Cardinal 1923-1999
   Obituary **2000**:1
Hunter, Howard 1907- **1994**:4
Hybels, Bill 1951- **2011**:1
Irwin, James 1930-1991
   Obituary **1992**:1
Jackson, Jesse 1941- **1996**:1
Jefferts Schori, Katharine 1954- **2007**
   :2
John Paul II, Pope 1920- **1995**:3
Jumblatt, Walid 1949(?)- **1987**:4
Kahane, Meir 1932-1990

Obituary **1991**:2
Khomeini, Ayatollah Ruhollah
   1900(?)-1989
   Obituary **1989**:4
Kissling, Frances 1943- **1989**:2
Koresh, David 1960(?)-1993
   Obituary **1993**:4
Krol, John 1910-1996
   Obituary **1996**:3
Lefebvre, Marcel 1905- **1988**:4
Levinger, Moshe 1935- **1992**:1
Macquarrie, John 1919-2007
   Obituary **2008**:3
Mahesh Yogi, Maharishi 1911(?)-
   1991:3
Mahony, Roger M. 1936- **1988**:2
Maida, Adam Cardinal 1930- **1998**:2
Malloy, Edward Monk 1941- **1989**:4
McCloskey, James 1944(?)- **1993**:1
Morris, Henry M. 1918-2006
   Obituary **2007**:2
Mother Teresa 1910-1997 **1993**:1
   Obituary **1998**:1
Muller, Jim 1943- **2011**:3
Obando, Miguel 1926- **1986**:4
O'Connor, Cardinal John 1920- **1990**
   :3
O'Connor, John 1920-2000
   Obituary **2000**:4
Osteen, Joel 1963- **2006**:2
Patriarch Pavle 1914-2009
   Obituary **2011**:3
Perry, Harold A. 1917(?)-1991
   Obituary **1992**:1
Peter, Valentine J. 1934- **1988**:2
Rafsanjani, Ali Akbar Hashemi
   1934(?)- **1987**:3
Rahman, Sheik Omar Abdel- 1938-
   1993:3
Rajneesh, Bhagwan Shree 1931-1990
   Obituary **1990**:2
Reed, Ralph 1961(?)- **1995**:1
Reese, Della 1931- **1999**:2
Reverend Ike 1935-2009
   Obituary **2010**:4
Roberts, Oral 1918-2009
   Obituary **2011**:4
Robertson, Pat 1930- **1988**:2
Robinson, V. Gene 1947- **2004**:4
Rogers, Adrian 1931- **1987**:4
Runcie, Robert 1921-2000 **1989**:4
   Obituary **2001**:1
Schneerson, Menachem Mendel
   1902-1994 **1992**:4
   Obituary **1994**:4
Scott, Gene
   Brief entry **1986**:1
Sentamu, John 1949- **2006**:2
Sharpton, Al 1954- **1991**:2
Shaw, William 1934(?)- **2000**:3
Sin, Jaime 1928-2005
   Obituary **2006**:3
Smith, Jeff 1939(?)- **1991**:4
Spong, John 1931- **1991**:3
Stallings, George A., Jr. 1948- **1990**:1
Swaggart, Jimmy 1935- **1987**:3
Taylor, Graham 1958(?)- **2005**:3
Turabi, Hassan 1932(?)- **1995**:4
Violet, Arlene 1943- **1985**:3
Warren, Rick 1954- **2010**:3
Wildmon, Donald 1938- **1988**:4

Williamson, Marianne 1953(?)- **1991**:4
Youngblood, Johnny Ray 1948- **1994**:1

SCIENCE

Abramson, Lyn 1950- **1986**:3
Adams, Patch 1945(?)- **1999**:2
Adamson, George 1906-1989
  Obituary **1990**:2
Agatston, Arthur 1947- **2005**:1
Allen, John 1930- **1992**:1
Altman, Sidney 1939- **1997**:2
Aronson, Jane 1951- **2009**:3
Atkins, Robert C. 1930-2003
  Obituary **2004**:2
Axelrod, Julius 1912-2004
  Obituary **2006**:1
Bahcall, John N. 1934-2005
  Obituary **2006**:4
Bakker, Robert T. 1950(?)- **1991**:3
Ballard, Robert D. 1942- **1998**:4
Barnard, Christiaan 1922-2001
  Obituary **2002**:4
Baulieu, Étienne-Emile 1926- **1990**:1
Bayley, Corrine
  Brief entry **1986**:4
Bean, Alan L. 1932- **1986**:2
Beattie, Owen
  Brief entry **1985**:2
Benes, Francine 1946- **2008**:2
Berkley, Seth 1956- **2002**:3
Berle, Peter A.A.
  Brief entry **1987**:3
Berman, Jennifer and Laura **2003**:2
Besser, Richard 1959- **2010**:2
Bethe, Hans 1906-2005
  Obituary **2006**:2
Bettelheim, Bruno 1903-1990
  Obituary **1990**:3
Blackburn, Elizabeth 1948- **2010**:1
Blanc, Patrick 1953- **2011**:3
Blobel, Gunter 1936- **2000**:4
Bloch, Erich 1925- **1987**:4
Blumenthal, Susan J. 1951(?)- **2007**:3
Bohr, Aage 1922-2009
  Obituary **2011**:1
Borlaug, Norman 1914-2009
  Obituary **2011**:1
Boyer, Herbert Wayne 1936- **1985**:1
Brinker, Nancy 1946- **2007**:1
Bristow, Lonnie 1930- **1996**:1
Brown, John Seely 1940- **2004**:1
Buck, Linda 1956(?)- **2004**:2
Burnison, Chantal Simone 1950(?)- **1988**:3
Carlsson, Arvid 1923- **2001**:2
Carson, Ben 1951- **1998**:2
Cerf, Vinton G. 1943- **1999**:2
Chaudhari, Praveen 1937- **1989**:4
Chu, Paul C.W. 1941- **1988**:2
Coles, Robert 1929(?)- **1995**:1
Collins, Eileen 1956- **1995**:3
Colwell, Rita Rossi 1934- **1999**:3
Comfort, Alex 1920-2000
  Obituary **2000**:4
Conrad, Pete 1930-1999
  Obituary **2000**:1
Cousteau, Jacques-Yves 1910-1997
  1998:2
Cousteau, Jean-Michel 1938- **1988**:2
Cram, Donald J. 1919-2001

  Obituary **2002**:2
Cray, Seymour R. 1925-1996
  Brief entry **1986**:3
  Obituary **1997**:2
Crewe, Albert 1927-2009
  Obituary **2011**:3
Crick, Francis 1916-2004
  Obituary **2005**:4
Davis, Noel **1990**:3
Davis, Raymond, Jr. 1914-2006
  Obituary **2007**:3
DeBakey, Michael 1908-2008
  Obituary **2009**:3
DeVita, Vincent T., Jr. 1935- **1987**:3
Diemer, Walter E. 1904(?)-1998 **1998**:2
Djerassi, Carl 1923- **2000**:4
Domar, Alice 1958- **2007**:1
Douglas, Marjory Stoneman 1890-1998 **1993**:1
  Obituary **1998**:4
Downey, Bruce 1947- **2003**:1
Duke, Red
  Brief entry **1987**:1
Durrell, Gerald 1925-1995
  Obituary **1995**:3
Earle, Sylvia 1935- **2001**:1
Fang Lizhi 1937- **1988**:1
Fano, Ugo 1912-2001
  Obituary **2001**:4
Fauci, Anthony S. 1940- **2004**:1
Fields, Evelyn J. 1949- **2001**:3
Fiennes, Ranulph 1944- **1990**:3
Fisher, Mel 1922(?)- **1985**:4
Folkman, Judah 1933- **1999**:1
Fossey, Dian 1932-1985
  Obituary **1986**:1
Foster, Tabatha 1985-1988
  Obituary **1988**:3
Fraser, Claire M. 1955- **2005**:2
Friedman, Milton 1912-2006
  Obituary **2008**:1
Friedman, Rose 1910-2009
  Obituary **2010**:4
Furchgott, Robert 1916-2009
  Obituary **2010**:3
Futter, Ellen V. 1949- **1995**:1
Gale, Robert Peter 1945- **1986**:4
Gallo, Robert 1937- **1991**:1
Garneau, Marc 1949- **1985**:1
Gayle, Helene 1955- **2008**:2
Gelfand, Israel 1913-2009
  Obituary **2011**:2
Geller, Margaret Joan 1947- **1998**:2
George and Lena Korres 1971- **2009**:1
Gerba, Charles 1945- **1999**:4
Gerberding, Julie 1955- **2004**:1
Gilbert, Walter 1932- **1988**:3
Gilruth, Robert 1913-2000
  Obituary **2001**:1
Ginzburg, Vitaly 1916-2009
  Obituary **2011**:3
Glenn, John 1921- **1998**:3
Gold, Thomas 1920-2004
  Obituary **2005**:3
Goldman-Rakic, Patricia 1937- **2002**:4
Goodall, Jane 1934- **1991**:1
Gordon, James 1941- **2009**:4
Gould, Gordon 1920- **1987**:1
Gould, Stephen Jay 1941-2002

  Obituary **2003**:3
Grandin, Temple 1947- **2006**:1
Granger, Clive 1934-2009
  Obituary **2010**:3
Greene, Brian 1963- **2003**:4
Gupta, Sanjay 1969- **2009**:4
Hagelstein, Peter
  Brief entry **1986**:3
Hair, Jay D. 1945- **1994**:3
Hale, Alan 1957- **1997**:3
Hale, Victoria 1961(?)- **2008**:4
Hammond, E. Cuyler 1912-1986
  Obituary **1987**:1
Haseltine, William A. 1944- **1999**:2
Hatem, George 1910(?)-1988
  Obituary **1989**:1
Hau, Lene Vestergaard 1959- **2006**:4
Hawking, Stephen W. 1942- **1990**:1
Healy, Bernadine 1944- **1993**:1
Herbert, Don 1917-2007
  Obituary **2008**:3
Herz, Rachel 1963- **2008**:1
Hill, J. Edward 1938- **2006**:2
Ho, David 1952- **1997**:2
Hoagland, Mahlon 1921-2009
  Obituary **2011**:2
Hodges, Carl 1937- **2008**:1
Horner, Jack 1946- **1985**:2
Horowitz, Paul 1942- **1988**:2
Hounsfield, Godfrey 1919- **1989**:2
Hoyle, Sir Fred 1915-2001
  Obituary **2002**:4
Irwin, James 1930-1991
  Obituary **1992**:1
Jablonski, Nina G. 1953- **2009**:3
Jacobs, Joe 1945(?)- **1994**:1
Janzen, Daniel H. 1939- **1988**:4
Jarvik, Robert K. 1946- **1985**:1
Jemison, Mae C. 1956- **1993**:1
Jorgensen, Christine 1926-1989
  Obituary **1989**:4
Kandel, Eric 1929- **2005**:2
Keeling, Charles 1928-2005
  Obituary **2006**:3
Keith, Louis 1935- **1988**:2
Kellerman, Jonathan 1949- **2009**:1
Kessler, David 1951- **1992**:1
Kevorkian, Jack 1928(?)- **1991**:3
King, Mary-Claire 1946- **1998**:3
Klass, Perri 1958- **1993**:2
Kleinpaste, Ruud 1952- **2006**:2
Kolff, Willem 1911-2009
  Obituary **2010**:2
Koop, C. Everett 1916- **1989**:3
Kopits, Steven E.
  Brief entry **1987**:1
Kornberg, Arthur 1918(?)- **1992**:1
Krebs, Edwin 1918-2009
  Obituary **2011**:4
Krim, Mathilde 1926- **1989**:2
Kubler-Ross, Elisabeth 1926-2004
  Obituary **2005**:4
Kwoh, Yik San 1946(?)- **1988**:2
Laing, R.D. 1927-1989
  Obituary **1990**:1
Langer, Robert 1948- **2003**:4
Langston, J. William
  Brief entry **1986**:2
Lanza, Robert 1956- **2004**:3
Leakey, Mary Douglas 1913-1996
  Obituary **1997**:2
Leakey, Richard 1944- **1994**:2

2011 Occupation Index

Berliner, Andy and Rachel **2008**:2
Berresford, Susan V. 1943- **1998**:4
Biehl, Amy 1967(?)-1993
  Obituary **1994**:1
Blackburn, Molly 1931(?)-1985
  Obituary **1985**:4
Block, Herbert 1909-2001
  Obituary **2002**:4
Bly, Robert 1926- **1992**:4
Bradford, Chris 1937- **2011**:1
Bradshaw, John 1933- **1992**:1
Brady, Sarah and James S. **1991**:4
Bravo, Ellen 1944- **1998**:2
Breathed, Berkeley 1957- **2005**:3
Bristow, Lonnie 1930- **1996**:1
Brockovich-Ellis, Erin 1960- **2003**:3
Brooks, Gwendolyn 1917-2000 **1998**:1
  Obituary **2001**:2
Brower, David 1912- **1990**:4
Brown, Howard and Karen Stewart **2007**:3
Brown, Jim 1936- **1993**:2
Brown, Judie 1944- **1986**:2
Brutus, Dennis 1924-2009
  Obituary **2011**:4
Burk, Martha 1941- **2004**:1
Bush, Barbara 1925- **1989**:3
Cammermeyer, Margarethe 1942- **1995**:2
Caplan, Arthur L. 1950- **2000**:2
Caras, Roger 1928-2001
  Obituary **2002**:1
Carter, Amy 1967- **1987**:4
Carter, Rubin 1937- **2000**:3
Chase, Robin 1958- **2010**:4
Chavez, Cesar 1927-1993
  Obituary **1993**:4
Chavez-Thompson, Linda 1944- **1999**:1
Chavis, Benjamin 1948- **1993**:4
Clark, Kenneth B. 1914-2005
  Obituary **2006**:3
Cleaver, Eldridge 1935-1998
  Obituary **1998**:4
Clements, George 1932- **1985**:1
Clinton, Hillary Rodham 1947- **1993**:2
Coffin, William Sloane, Jr. 1924- **1990**:3
Cole, Johnetta B. 1936- **1994**:3
Coles, Robert 1929(?)- **1995**:1
Connerly, Ward 1939- **2000**:2
Conseil, Dominique Nils 1962(?)- **2007**:2
Coors, William K.
  Brief entry **1985**:1
Corwin, Jeff 1967- **2005**:1
Cozza, Stephen 1985- **2001**:1
Crisp, Quentin 1908-1999
  Obituary **2000**:3
Cruzan, Nancy 1957(?)-1990
  Obituary **1991**:3
Davis, Angela 1944- **1998**:3
Dees, Morris 1936- **1992**:1
DeMayo, Neda 1960(?)- **2006**:2
Devi, Phoolan 1955(?)- **1986**:1
  Obituary **2002**:3
Dickinson, Brian 1937- **1998**:2
Dorris, Michael 1945-1997
  Obituary **1997**:3

Douglas, Marjory Stoneman 1890-1998 **1993**:1
  Obituary **1998**:4
Downey, Morton, Jr. 1932- **1988**:4
Duncan, Sheena
  Brief entry **1987**:1
Dworkin, Andrea 1946-2005
  Obituary **2006**:2
Ebadi, Shirin 1947- **2004**:3
Edelman, Marian Wright 1939- **1990**:4
Edwards, Harry 1942- **1989**:4
ElBaradei, Mohamed 1942- **2006**:3
Elders, Joycelyn 1933- **1994**:1
Ellison, Ralph 1914-1994
  Obituary **1994**:4
Ensler, Eve 1954(?)- **2002**:4
Etzioni, Amitai 1929- **1994**:3
Evers-Williams, Myrlie 1933- **1995**:4
Falkenberg, Nanette 1951- **1985**:2
Faludi, Susan 1959- **1992**:4
Farrakhan, Louis 1933- **1990**:4
Fassa, Lynda 1963(?)- **2008**:4
Faubus, Orval 1910-1994
  Obituary **1995**:2
Faulkner, Shannon 1975- **1994**:4
Ferguson, Niall 1964- **2006**:1
Ferrell, Trevor
  Brief entry **1985**:2
Filipovic, Zlata 1981(?)- **1994**:4
Finley, Karen 1956- **1992**:4
Fisher, Mary 1948- **1994**:3
Foer, Jonathan 1977- **2011**:2
Fonyo, Steve
  Brief entry **1985**:4
Foreman, Dave 1947(?)- **1990**:3
Francis, Philip L. 1946- **2007**:4
Friedan, Betty 1921- **1994**:2
Friend, Patricia A. 1946- **2003**:3
Fuller, Millard 1935-2009
  Obituary **2010**:1
Galvin, Martin
  Brief entry **1985**:3
Gandy, Kim 1954(?)- **2002**:2
Garcia, Jerry 1942-1995 **1988**:3
  Obituary **1996**:1
Gates, Melinda 1964- **2010**:4
Gayle, Helene 1955- **2008**:2
Gebbie, Kristine 1944(?)- **1994**:2
Geldof, Bob 1954(?)- **1985**:3
George and Lena Korres 1971- **2009**:1
Gerrity, Sean 1958- **2011**:3
Gertz, Alison 1966(?)-1992
  Obituary **1993**:2
Glaser, Elizabeth 1947-1994
  Obituary **1995**:2
Glasser, Ira 1938- **1989**:1
Goetz, Bernhard Hugo 1947(?)- **1985**:3
Goldhaber, Fred
  Brief entry **1986**:3
Goodall, Jane 1934- **1991**:1
Goodman, Drew and Myra **2007**:4
Gore, Tipper 1948- **1985**:4
Grandin, Temple 1947- **2006**:1
Grant, Charity
  Brief entry **1985**:2
Greenberg, Hank 1911-1986
  Obituary **1986**:4
Gregory, Rogan 1972- **2008**:2
Griffin, Toni 1964- **2011**:3

Guyer, David
  Brief entry **1988**:1
Hackney, Sheldon 1933- **1995**:1
Hahn, Jessica 1960- **1989**:4
Hale, Clara 1905-1992
  Obituary **1993**:3
Harrelson, Woody 1961- **2011**:1
Hayes, Robert M. 1952- **1986**:3
Hayse, Bruce 1949(?)- **2004**:3
Healey, Jack 1938(?)- **1990**:1
Hebard, Caroline 1944- **1998**:2
Hefner, Christie 1952- **1985**:1
Heinricher, Jackie 1961- **2010**:1
Henderson, Tom **2011**:2
Hepburn, Audrey 1929-1993
  Obituary **1993**:2
Hero, Peter 1942- **2001**:2
Hill, Graham 1971- **2010**:3
Hindmarch, Anya 1969- **2008**:2
Hirshberg, Gary 1954(?)- **2007**:2
Hoffman, Abbie 1936-1989
  Obituary **1989**:3
Hudson, Rock 1925-1985
  Obituary **1985**:4
Huerta, Dolores 1930- **1998**:1
Huffington, Arianna 1950- **1996**:2
Hullinger, Charlotte
  Brief entry **1985**:1
Hume, John 1938- **1987**:1
Humphry, Derek 1931(?)- **1992**:2
Ireland, Jill 1936-1990
  Obituary **1990**:4
Ireland, Patricia 1946(?)- **1992**:2
Iyengar, B.K.S. 1918- **2005**:1
Jackson, Jesse 1941- **1996**:1
Jacobs, Joe 1945(?)- **1994**:1
Jeffrey, Mildred 1910-2004
  Obituary **2005**:2
Jennifer Boulden and Heather Stephenson 1973- **2010**:2
Jones, Van 1968- **2010**:3
Jordan, King 1943(?)- **1990**:1
Jordan, Vernon, Jr. 1935- **2002**:3
Jorgensen, Christine 1926-1989
  Obituary **1989**:4
Judkins, Reba
  Brief entry **1987**:3
Kathwari, M. Farooq 1944- **2005**:4
Kennedy, Rose 1890-1995
  Obituary **1995**:3
Kevorkian, Jack 1928(?)- **1991**:3
Kielburger, Craig 1983- **1998**:1
King, Bernice 1963- **2000**:2
King, Coretta Scott 1927- **1999**:3
Kingsolver, Barbara 1955- **2005**:1
Kissling, Frances 1943- **1989**:2
Klarsfeld, Beate 1939- **1989**:1
Korchinsky, Mike 1961- **2004**:2
Kouchner, Bernard 1939- **2005**:3
Kozinski, Alex 1950- **2002**:2
Kozol, Jonathan 1936- **1992**:1
Kramer, Larry 1935- **1991**:2
Krim, Mathilde 1926- **1989**:2
Krupp, Fred 1954- **2008**:3
Kunstler, William 1919-1995
  Obituary **1996**:1
Kurzban, Ira 1949- **1987**:2
LaDuke, Winona 1959- **1995**:2
Lang, Eugene M. 1919- **1990**:3
Leary, Timothy 1920-1996
  Obituary **1996**:4
Lerner, Sandy 1955(?)- **2005**:1

SPORTS

Abbott, Jim 1967- **1988**:3
Abercrombie, Josephine 1925- **1987**:2
Adu, Freddy 1989- **2005**:3
Agassi, Andre 1970- **1990**:2
Agee, Tommie 1942-2001
  Obituary **2001**:4
Aikman, Troy 1966- **1994**:2
Ainge, Danny 1959- **1987**:1
Akers, Michelle 1966- **1996**:1
Albert, Marv 1943- **1994**:3
Albom, Mitch 1958- **1999**:3
Ali, Laila 1977- **2001**:2
Ali, Muhammad 1942- **1997**:2
Allen, Mel 1913-1996
  Obituary **1996**:4
Allen, Ray 1975- **2002**:1
Allenby, Robert 1971- **2007**:1
Allgaier, Justin 1986- **2011**:3
Alter, Hobie
  Brief entry **1985**:1
Andersen, Chris 1978- **2010**:2
Angelos, Peter 1930- **1995**:4
Anthony, Earl 1938-2001
  Obituary **2002**:3
Aoki, Rocky 1940- **1990**:2
Arakawa, Shizuka 1981- **2006**:4
Armstrong, Henry 1912-1988
  Obituary **1989**:1
Armstrong, Lance 1971- **2000**:1
Artest, Ron 1979- **2011**:1
Ashe, Arthur 1943-1993
  Obituary **1993**:3
Auerbach, Red 1911-2006
  Obituary **2008**:1
Austin, Stone Cold Steve 1964- **2001**:3
Axthelm, Pete 1943(?)-1991
  Obituary **1991**:3
Azinger, Paul 1960- **1995**:2
Babilonia, Tai 1959- **1997**:2
Baiul, Oksana 1977- **1995**:3
Baker, Kathy
  Brief entry **1986**:1
Barber, Tiki 1975- **2007**:1
Barkley, Charles 1963- **1988**:2
Barnes, Ernie 1938- **1997**:4
Baumgartner, Bruce
  Brief entry **1987**:3
Becker, Boris
  Brief entry **1985**:3
Beckham, David 1975- **2003**:1
Bell, Ricky 1955-1984
  Obituary **1985**:1
Belle, Albert 1966- **1996**:4
Benoit, Joan 1957- **1986**:3
Best, George 1946-2005
  Obituary **2007**:1
Bias, Len 1964(?)-1986
  Obituary **1986**:3
Bird, Larry 1956- **1990**:3
Blair, Bonnie 1964- **1992**:3
Bledsoe, Drew 1972- **1995**:1
Boggs, Wade 1958- **1989**:3
Boitano, Brian 1963- **1988**:3
Bolt, Usain 1986- **2009**:2
Bonds, Barry 1964- **1993**:3
Bonilla, Bobby 1963- **1992**:2
Borel, Calvin 1966- **2010**:1
Bosworth, Brian 1965- **1989**:1
Boudreau, Louis 1917-2001
  Obituary **2002**:3

Bourque, Raymond Jean 1960- **1997**:3
Bowe, Riddick 1967(?)- **1993**:2
Bowman, Scotty 1933- **1998**:4
Bradman, Sir Donald 1908-2001
  Obituary **2002**:1
Brady, Tom 1977- **2002**:4
Brees, Drew 1979- **2011**:2
Bremen, Barry 1947- **1987**:3
Bright, Torah 1986- **2010**:2
Brown, Jim 1936- **1993**:2
Brown, Paul 1908-1991
  Obituary **1992**:1
Bryant, Kobe 1978- **1998**:3
Burton, Jake 1954- **2007**:1
Busch, August Anheuser, Jr. 1899-1989
  Obituary **1990**:2
Busch, Kurt 1978- **2006**:1
Busch, Kyle 1985- **2011**:4
Buss, Jerry 1933- **1989**:3
Butcher, Susan 1954- **1991**:1
Callaway, Ely 1919-2001
  Obituary **2002**:3
Campanella, Roy 1921-1993
  Obituary **1994**:1
Canseco, Jose 1964- **1990**:2
Capriati, Jennifer 1976- **1991**:1
Caray, Harry 1914(?)-1998 **1988**:3
  Obituary **1998**:3
Carlsen, Magnus 1990- **2011**:3
Carter, Gary 1954- **1987**:1
Carter, Joe 1960- **1994**:2
Carter, Rubin 1937- **2000**:3
Carter, Vince 1977- **2001**:4
Castroneves, Helio 1975- **2010**:1
Chamberlain, Joba 1985- **2008**:3
Chamberlain, Wilt 1936-1999
  Obituary **2000**:2
Chaney, John 1932- **1989**:1
Chastain, Brandi 1968- **2001**:3
Chen, T.C.
  Brief entry **1987**:3
Cherry, Don 1934- **1993**:4
Chyna 1970- **2001**:4
Clemens, Roger 1962- **1991**:4
Clijsters, Kim 1983- **2006**:3
Coffey, Paul 1961- **1985**:4
Collins, Kerry 1972- **2002**:3
Conigliaro, Tony 1945-1990
  Obituary **1990**:3
Conner, Dennis 1943- **1987**:2
Cooper, Cynthia **1999**:1
Copeland, Al 1944(?)- **1988**:3
Cosell, Howard 1918-1995
  Obituary **1995**:4
Costas, Bob 1952- **1986**:4
Couples, Fred 1959- **1994**:4
Courier, Jim 1970- **1993**:2
Creamer, Paula 1986- **2006**:2
Crosby, Sidney 1987- **2006**:3
Cunningham, Randall 1963- **1990**:1
Curren, Tommy
  Brief entry **1987**:4
Curtis, Ben 1977- **2004**:2
Daly, Chuck 1930-2009
  Obituary **2010**:3
Damon, Johnny 1973- **2005**:4
Danza, Tony 1951- **1989**:1
Davenport, Lindsay 1976- **1999**:2
Davis, Eric 1962- **1987**:4
Davis, Terrell 1972- **1998**:2

Day, Pat 1953- **1995**:2
DeBartolo, Edward J., Jr. 1946- **1989**:3
De La Hoya, Oscar 1973- **1998**:2
Desormeaux, Kent 1970- **1990**:2
DiBello, Paul
  Brief entry **1986**:4
DiMaggio, Dom 1917-2009
  Obituary **2010**:2
DiMaggio, Joe 1914-1999
  Obituary **1999**:3
Djokovic, Novak 1987- **2008**:4
Dolan, Tom 1975- **2001**:2
Donnellan, Nanci **1995**:2
Donovan, Landon 1982- **2011**:4
Doubleday, Nelson, Jr. 1933- **1987**:1
Douglas, Buster 1960(?)- **1990**:4
Dravecky, Dave 1956- **1992**:1
Drexler, Clyde 1962- **1992**:4
Drysdale, Don 1936-1993
  Obituary **1994**:1
Duncan, Tim 1976- **2000**:1
Durocher, Leo 1905-1991
  Obituary **1992**:2
Duval, David 1971- **2000**:3
Duvall, Camille
  Brief entry **1988**:1
Dykstra, Lenny 1963- **1993**:4
Eagleson, Alan 1933- **1987**:4
Earnhardt, Dale 1951-2001
  Obituary **2001**:4
Earnhardt, Dale, Jr. 1974- **2004**:4
Ederle, Gertrude 1905-2003
  Obituary **2005**:1
Edwards, Harry 1942- **1989**:4
Elway, John 1960- **1990**:3
Epstein, Theo 1973- **2003**:4
Esiason, Boomer 1961- **1991**:1
Evans, Janet 1971- **1989**:1
Ewing, Patrick 1962- **1985**:3
Fabris, Enrico 1981- **2006**:4
Faldo, Nick 1957- **1993**:3
Favre, Brett Lorenzo 1969- **1997**:2
Federer, Roger 1981- **2004**:2
Federov, Sergei 1969- **1995**:1
Fehr, Donald 1948- **1987**:2
Ferrari, Enzo 1898-1988 **1988**:4
Fidrych, Mark 1954-2009
  Obituary **2010**:2
Fielder, Cecil 1963- **1993**:2
Fiennes, Ranulph 1944- **1990**:3
Firestone, Roy 1953- **1988**:2
Fischer, Bobby 1943-2008
  Obituary **2009**:1
Fittipaldi, Emerson 1946- **1994**:2
Flood, Curt 1938-1997
  Obituary **1997**:2
Flutie, Doug 1962- **1999**:2
Foreman, George 1949- **2004**:2
Foss, Joe 1915- **1990**:3
Fossett, Steve 1944- **2007**:2
Franchitti, Dario 1973- **2008**:1
Freeman, Cathy 1973- **2001**:3
Fuhr, Grant 1962- **1997**:3
Furyk, Jim 1970- **2004**:2
Galindo, Rudy 1969- **2001**:2
Garcia, Joe
  Brief entry **1986**:4
Gardner, Randy 1957- **1997**:2
Garnett, Kevin 1976- **2000**:3
Gathers, Hank 1967(?)-1990
  Obituary **1990**:3

Gault, Willie 1960- **1991**:2

Gerulaitis, Vitas 1954-1994
  Obituary **1995**:1

Giamatti, A. Bartlett 1938-1989 **1988**:4
  Obituary **1990**:1

Gibson, Althea 1927-2003
  Obituary **2004**:4

Gibson, Kirk 1957- **1985**:2

Giguere, Jean-Sebastien 1977- **2004**:2

Gilmour, Doug 1963- **1994**:3

Glaus, Troy 1976- **2003**:3

Gomez, Lefty 1909-1989
  Obituary **1989**:3

Gooden, Dwight 1964- **1985**:2

Gordeeva, Ekaterina 1972- **1996**:4

Gordon, Jeff 1971- **1996**:1

Graf, Steffi 1969- **1987**:4

Granato, Cammi 1971- **1999**:3

Grange, Red 1903-1991
  Obituary **1991**:3

Graziano, Rocky 1922-1990
  Obituary **1990**:4

Greenberg, Hank 1911-1986
  Obituary **1986**:4

Gretzky, Wayne 1961- **1989**:2

Griffey, Ken Jr. 1969- **1994**:1

Grinkov, Sergei 1967-1995
  Obituary **1996**:2

Gruden, Jon 1963- **2003**:4

Gumbel, Greg 1946- **1996**:4

Guo Jingjing 1981- **2009**:2

Gwynn, Tony 1960- **1995**:1

Hagler, Marvelous Marvin 1954-
  1985:2

Hamels, Cole 1983- **2009**:4

Hamilton, Lewis 1985- **2008**:4

Hamilton, Scott 1958- **1998**:2

Hamm, Mia 1972- **2000**:1

Hamm, Paul 1982- **2005**:1

Hanauer, Chip 1954- **1986**:2

Hardaway, Anfernee 1971- **1996**:2

Harkes, John 1967- **1996**:4

Harmon, Tom 1919-1990
  Obituary **1990**:3

Hart, Carey 1975- **2006**:4

Harwell, Ernie 1918- **1997**:3

Hasek, Dominik 1965- **1998**:3

Hawk, Tony 1968- **2001**:4

Hayes, Woody 1913-1987
  Obituary **1987**:2

Helton, Todd 1973- **2001**:1

Hempleman-Adams, David 1956-
  2004:3

Henderson, Rickey 1958- **2002**:3

Henin-Hardenne, Justine 1982- **2004**:4

Henrich, Tommy 1913-2009
  Obituary **2011**:4

Hernandez, Felix 1986- **2008**:2

Hernandez, Willie 1954- **1985**:1

Hershiser, Orel 1958- **1989**:2

Hewitt, Lleyton 1981- **2002**:2

Hextall, Ron 1964- **1988**:2

Hill, Grant 1972- **1995**:3

Hill, Lynn 1961(?)- **1991**:2

Hillary, Edmund 1919-2008
  Obituary **2009**:1

Hingis, Martina 1980- **1999**:1

Hogan, Ben 1912-1997
  Obituary **1997**:4

Hogan, Hulk 1953- **1987**:3

Holcomb, Steven 1980- **2011**:2

Holtz, Lou 1937- **1986**:4

Holyfield, Evander 1962- **1991**:3

Horn, Mike 1966- **2009**:3

Howard, Desmond Kevin 1970-
  1997:2

Howard, Dwight 1985- **2010**:1

Howser, Dick 1936-1987
  Obituary **1987**:4

Hughes, Sarah 1985- **2002**:4

Hull, Brett 1964- **1991**:4

Hunter, Catfish 1946-1999
  Obituary **2000**:1

Indurain, Miguel 1964- **1994**:1

Inkster, Juli 1960- **2000**:2

Irvin, Michael 1966- **1996**:3

Irwin, Hale 1945- **2005**:2

Ivanisevic, Goran 1971- **2002**:1

Iverson, Allen 1975- **2001**:4

Jackson, Bo 1962- **1986**:3

Jackson, Phil 1945- **1996**:3

Jagr, Jaromir 1972- **1995**:4

James, LeBron 1984- **2007**:1

Jenkins, Sally 1960(?)- **1997**:2

Jeter, Derek 1974- **1999**:4

Johnson, Earvin Magic 1959- **1988**:4

Johnson, Jimmie 1975- **2007**:2

Johnson, Jimmy 1943- **1993**:3

Johnson, Kevin 1966(?)- **1991**:1

Johnson, Keyshawn 1972- **2000**:4

Johnson, Larry 1969- **1993**:3

Johnson, Michael **2000**:1

Johnson, Randy 1963- **1996**:2

Johnson, Shawn 1992- **2009**:2

Jones, Jerry 1942- **1994**:4

Jones, Marion 1975- **1998**:4

Jordan, Michael 1963- **1987**:2

Joyner, Florence Griffith 1959-1998
  1989:2
  Obituary **1999**:1

Joyner-Kersee, Jackie 1962- **1993**:1

Kallen, Jackie 1946(?)- **1994**:1

Kane, Patrick 1988- **2011**:4

Kanokogi, Rusty
  Brief entry **1987**:1

Kasparov, Garry 1963- **1997**:4

Kelly, Jim 1960- **1991**:4

Kemp, Jack 1935- **1990**:4

Kemp, Jan 1949- **1987**:2

Kemp, Shawn 1969- **1995**:1

Kerr, Cristie 1977- **2008**:2

Kerrigan, Nancy 1969- **1994**:3

Kidd, Jason 1973- **2003**:2

Kim, Yu-Na 1990- **2011**:2

King, Don 1931- **1989**:1

Kiraly, Karch
  Brief entry **1987**:1

Kite, Tom 1949- **1990**:3

Klima, Petr 1964- **1987**:1

Knievel, Evel 1938-2007
  Obituary **2009**:1

Knievel, Robbie 1963- **1990**:1

Knight, Bobby 1940- **1985**:3

Koch, Bill 1940- **1992**:3

Konstantinov, Vladimir 1967- **1997**:4

Kournikova, Anna 1981- **2000**:3

Kramer, Jack 1921-2009
  Obituary **2011**:1

Kroc, Ray 1902-1984
  Obituary **1985**:1

Krone, Julie 1963(?)- **1989**:2

Kruk, John 1961- **1994**:4

Krzyzewski, Mike 1947- **1993**:2

Kukoc, Toni 1968- **1995**:4

Laettner, Christian 1969- **1993**:1

LaFontaine, Pat 1965- **1985**:1

Laimbeer, Bill 1957- **2004**:3

Lalas, Alexi 1970- **1995**:1

Landry, Tom 1924-2000
  Obituary **2000**:3

Lemieux, Claude 1965- **1996**:1

Lemieux, Mario 1965- **1986**:4

LeMond, Greg 1961- **1986**:4

Leonard, Sugar Ray 1956- **1989**:4

Leslie, Lisa 1972- **1997**:4

Lewis, Lennox 1965- **2000**:2

Lewis, Ray 1975- **2001**:3

Lewis, Reggie 1966(?)-1993
  Obituary **1994**:1

Leyland, Jim 1944- **1998**:2

Lidstrom, Nicklas 1970- **2009**:1

Lindbergh, Pelle 1959-1985
  Obituary **1985**:4

Lindros, Eric 1973- **1992**:1

Lipinski, Tara 1982- **1998**:3

Lofton, Kenny 1967- **1998**:1

Lopez, Nancy 1957- **1989**:3

Louganis, Greg 1960- **1995**:3

Lowell, Mike 1974- **2003**:2

Lukas, D. Wayne 1936(?)- **1986**:2

Lysacek, Evan 1985- **2011**:2

MacArthur, Ellen 1976- **2005**:3

Madden, John 1936- **1995**:1

Maddux, Greg 1966- **1996**:2

Majerle, Dan 1965- **1993**:4

Malone, Karl 1963- **1990**:1

Manning, Eli 1981- **2008**:4

Manning, Peyton 1976- **2007**:4

Mantle, Mickey 1931-1995
  Obituary **1996**:1

Maradona, Diego 1961(?)- **1991**:3

Maravich, Pete 1948-1988
  Obituary **1988**:2

Maris, Roger 1934-1985
  Obituary **1986**:1

Martin, Billy 1928-1989 **1988**:4
  Obituary **1990**:2

Martin, Casey 1972- **2002**:1

Mathias, Bob 1930-2006
  Obituary **2007**:4

Mathis, Clint 1976- **2003**:1

Matsui, Hideki 1974- **2007**:4

Mattingly, Don 1961- **1986**:2

Matuszak, John 1951(?)-1989
  Obituary **1989**:4

Mauresmo, Amelie 1979- **2007**:2

McAfee, George 1918-2009
  Obituary **2010**:2

McCarron, Chris 1955- **1995**:4

McCartney, Bill 1940- **1995**:3

McGraw, Tug 1944-2004
  Obituary **2005**:1

McGwire, Mark 1963- **1999**:1

McMahon, Jim 1959- **1985**:4

McMahon, Vince, Jr. 1945(?)- **1985**:4

Messier, Mark 1961- **1993**:1

Michaels, Jillian 1974- **2011**:4

Mickelson, Phil 1970- **2004**:4

Mikan, George 1924-2005
  Obituary **2006**:3

Milbrett, Tiffeny 1972- **2001**:1

Milburn, Rodney Jr. 1950-1997 **1998**:2

Miller, Andre 1976- **2003**:3

Vitale, Dick 1939- **1988**:4
Vonn, Lindsey 1984- **2011**:2
Waddell, Thomas F. 1937-1987
   Obituary **1988**:2
Wade, Dwyane 1982- **2007**:1
Wallace, Ben 1974- **2004**:3
Walsh, Bill 1931- **1987**:4
Wariner, Jeremy 1984- **2006**:3
Warner, Kurt 1971- **2000**:3
Webb, Karrie 1974- **2000**:4
Webber, Chris 1973- **1994**:1
Weber, Pete 1962- **1986**:3
Weir, Mike 1970- **2004**:1
Welch, Bob 1956- **1991**:3
Wells, David 1963- **1999**:3
Wescott, Seth 1976- **2006**:4
Whaley, Suzy 1966- **2003**:4
White, Bill 1934- **1989**:3
White, Byron 1917-2002
   Obituary **2003**:3
White, Reggie 1961- **1993**:4
White, Shaun 1986- **2011**:2
Wilkens, Lenny 1937- **1995**:2
Williams, Doug 1955- **1988**:2
Williams, Edward Bennett 1920-1988
   Obituary **1988**:4
Williams, Ricky 1977- **2000**:2
Williams, Serena 1981- **1999**:4
Williams, Ted 1918-2002
   Obituary **2003**:4
Williams, Venus 1980- **1998**:2
Witt, Katarina 1966(?)- **1991**:3
Woodard, Lynette 1959(?)- **1986**:2
Woods, Tiger 1975- **1995**:4
Woodson, Ron 1965- **1996**:4
Worthy, James 1961- **1991**:2
Yamaguchi, Kristi 1971- **1992**:3
Yao Ming 1980- **2004**:1
Young, Steve 1961- **1995**:2
Yzerman, Steve 1965- **1991**:2
Zamboni, Frank J.
   Brief entry **1986**:4
Zanardi, Alex 1966- **1998**:2
Zatopek, Emil 1922-2000
   Obituary **2001**:3
Zito, Barry 1978- **2003**:3

TECHNOLOGY
Adair, Red 1915- **1987**:3
Adelson, Jay 1970- **2011**:1
Allaire, Jeremy 1971- **2006**:4
Allaire, Paul 1938- **1995**:1
Anderson, Tom and Chris DeWolfe
   2007:2
Andreessen, Marc 1972- **1996**:2
Arrington, Michael 1970- **2011**:4
Backus, John W. 1924-2007
   Obituary **2008**:2
Balsillie, Jim and Mike Lazaridis
   2006:4
Barbara and Richard Mikkelson
   1959- **2011**:4
Barksdale, James L. 1943- **1998**:2
Beal, Deron 1968(?)- **2005**:3
Belluzzo, Rick 1953- **2001**:3
Berners-Lee, Tim 1955(?)- **1997**:4
Bezos, Jeff 1964- **1998**:4
Bird, Brad 1956(?)- **2005**:4
Bose, Amar
   Brief entry **1986**:4
Boyer, Herbert Wayne 1936- **1985**:1

Bradley, Todd 1958- **2003**:3
Burum, Stephen H.
   Brief entry **1987**:2
Bushnell, Nolan 1943- **1985**:1
Butterfield, Stewart and Caterina
   Fake **2007**:3
Case, Steve 1958- **1995**:4
Cassidy, Mike 1963(?)- **2006**:1
Cerf, Vinton G. 1943- **1999**:2
Chaudhari, Praveen 1937- **1989**:4
Chen, Steve and Chad Hurley **2007**
   :2
Chizen, Bruce 1955(?)- **2004**:2
Clarke, Richard A. 1951(?)- **2002**:2
Cray, Seymour R. 1925-1996
   Brief entry **1986**:3
   Obituary **1997**:2
David, George 1942- **2005**:1
Davis, Noel **1990**:3
Dell, Michael 1965- **1996**:2
De Luca, Guerrino 1952- **2007**:1
Dolby, Ray Milton
   Brief entry **1986**:1
Donahue, Tim 1950(?)- **2004**:3
Dunlap, Albert J. **1997**:2
Dzhanibekov, Vladimir 1942- **1988**:1
Ellison, Larry 1944- **2004**:2
Engibous, Thomas J. 1953- **2003**:3
Engstrom, Elmer W. 1901-1984
   Obituary **1985**:2
Evans, Nancy 1950- **2000**:4
Fanning, Shawn 1980- **2001**:1
Fender, Leo 1909-1991
   Obituary **1992**:1
Filo, David and Jerry Yang **1998**:3
Freiberg, Steven 1957- **2011**:4
Gardner, David and Tom **2001**:4
Garneau, Marc 1949- **1985**:1
Gates, Bill 1955- **1987**:4
Gevinson, Tavi 1996- **2011**:1
Gould, Gordon 1920- **1987**:1
Greiner, Helen 1967- **2010**:2
Hagelstein, Peter
   Brief entry **1986**:3
Haladjian, Rafi 1962(?)- **2008**:3
Han, Jeff 1975- **2011**:2
Hemming, Nikki 1967- **2009**:1
Hewlett, William 1913-2001
   Obituary **2001**:4
Hounsfield, Godfrey 1919- **1989**:2
Housenbold, Jeffrey 1969- **2009**:2
Hurd, Mark 1957- **2010**:4
Inman, Bobby Ray 1931- **1985**:1
Irwin, James 1930-1991
   Obituary **1992**:1
Ive, Jonathan 1967- **2009**:2
Jacuzzi, Candido 1903-1986
   Obituary **1987**:1
Jarvik, Robert K. 1946- **1985**:1
Jemison, Mae C. 1956- **1993**:1
Jennifer Boulden and Heather
   Stephenson 1973- **2010**:2
Kalin, Rob 1980- **2011**:3
Kamen, Dean 1951(?)- **2003**:1
Khosla, Vinod 1955- **2011**:2
Kilar, Jason 1971- **2010**:1
Kilby, Jack 1923- **2002**:2
Kimsey, James V. 1940(?)- **2001**:1
Kloss, Henry E.
   Brief entry **1985**:2
Koch, Bill 1940- **1992**:3
Kolff, Willem 1911-2009

   Obituary **2010**:2
Kundra, Vivek 1974- **2010**:3
Kurzweil, Raymond 1948- **1986**:3
Kutaragi, Ken 1950- **2005**:3
Kwoh, Yik San 1946(?)- **1988**:2
Lalami, Laila **2007**:1
Lamborghini, Ferrucio 1916-1993
   Obituary **1993**:3
Lancaster, Jen 1967- **2010**:2
Land, Edwin H. 1909-1991
   Obituary **1991**:3
Langer, Robert 1948- **2003**:4
Lanier, Jaron 1961(?)- **1993**:4
Ma, Jack 1964- **2007**:1
Ma, Pony 1971(?)- **2006**:3
MacCready, Paul 1925- **1986**:4
Machover, Tod 1953- **2010**:3
Malda, Rob 1976- **2007**:3
McGowan, William 1927- **1985**:2
McLaren, Norman 1914-1987
   Obituary **1987**:2
McNealy, Scott 1954- **2009**:3
Mikkelson, Barbara 1959-. See
   Barbara and Richard Mikkelson
Mikkelson, Richard 1959-. See
   Barbara and Richard Mikkelson
Minsky, Marvin 1927- **1994**:3
Moody, John 1943- **1985**:3
Morita, Akio 1921- **1989**:4
Morita, Akio 1921-1999
   Obituary **2000**:2
Newman, Joseph 1936- **1987**:1
Noyce, Robert N. 1927- **1985**:4
Ollila, Jorma 1950- **2003**:4
Pack, Ellen 1963(?)- **2001**:2
Palmisano, Samuel J. 1952(?)- **2003**:1
Parsons, Richard 1949- **2002**:4
Peluso, Michelle 1971(?)- **2007**:4
Perlman, Steve 1961(?)- **1998**:2
Perry, William 1927- **1994**:4
Pfeiffer, Eckhard 1941- **1998**:4
Pincus, Mark 1966- **2011**:1
Probst, Larry 1951(?)- **2005**:1
Ramsay, Mike 1950(?)- **2002**:1
Raskin, Jef 1943(?)- **1997**:4
Rifkin, Jeremy 1945- **1990**:3
Rigopulos, Alex 1970- **2009**:4
Ritchie, Dennis and Kenneth
   Thompson **2000**:1
Roberts, Brian L. 1959- **2002**:4
Roberts, Steven K. 1952(?)- **1992**:1
Rosedale, Philip 1968- **2011**:3
Rutan, Burt 1943- **1987**:2
Schank, Roger 1946- **1989**:2
Schmidt, Eric 1955- **2002**:4
Scholz, Tom 1949- **1987**:2
Schroeder, William J. 1932-1986
   Obituary **1986**:4
Sculley, John 1939- **1989**:4
Seidenberg, Ivan 1946- **2004**:1
Semel, Terry 1943- **2002**:2
Shirley, Donna 1941- **1999**:1
Sinclair, Mary 1918- **1985**:2
Taylor, Jeff 1960- **2001**:3
Thomas, Edmond J. 1943(?)- **2005**:1
Thompson, John W. 1949- **2005**:1
Tito, Dennis 1940(?)- **2002**:1
Titov, Gherman 1935-2000
   Obituary **2001**:3
Tom and Ray Magliozzi **1991**:4
Toomer, Ron 1930- **1990**:1
Torvalds, Linus 1970(?)- **1999**:3

Treybig, James G. 1940- **1988**:3
Walker, Jay 1955- **2004**:2
Wang, An 1920-1990 **1986**:1
   Obituary **1990**:3
Wright, Will 1960- **2003**:4
Yamamoto, Kenichi 1922- **1989**:1
Zuckerberg, Mark 1984- **2008**:2

TELEVISION
Abrams, J. J. 1966- **2007**:3
Adams, Amy 1974- **2008**:4
Adams, Don 1923-2005
   Obituary **2007**:1
Affleck, Ben 1972- **1999**:1
Alba, Jessica 1981- **2001**:2
Albert, Eddie 1906-2005
   Obituary **2006**:3
Albert, Marv 1943- **1994**:3
Albom, Mitch 1958- **1999**:3
Albrecht, Chris 1952(?)- **2005**:4
Alda, Robert 1914-1986
   Obituary **1986**:3
Alexander, Jane 1939- **1994**:2
Alexander, Jason 1962(?)- **1993**:3
Allen, Debbie 1950- **1998**:2
Allen, Steve 1921-2000
   Obituary **2001**:2
Allen, Tim 1953- **1993**:1
Alley, Kirstie 1955- **1990**:3
Allyson, June 1917-2006
   Obituary **2007**:3
Altman, Robert 1925- **1993**:2
Amanpour, Christiane 1958- **1997**:2
Ameche, Don 1908-1993
   Obituary **1994**:2
Amsterdam, Morey 1912-1996
   Obituary **1997**:1
Ancier, Garth 1957- **1989**:1
Anderson, Gillian 1968- **1997**:1
Anderson, Harry 1951(?)- **1988**:2
Anderson, Judith 1899(?)-1992
   Obituary **1992**:3
Andrews, Julie 1935- **1996**:1
Angelou, Maya 1928- **1993**:4
Aniston, Jennifer 1969- **2000**:3
Apatow, Judd 1967- **2006**:3
Applegate, Christina 1972- **2000**:4
Arden, Eve 1912(?)-1990
   Obituary **1991**:2
Arkin, Alan 1934- **2007**:4
Arledge, Roone 1931- **1992**:2
Arlen, Harold 1905-1986
   Obituary **1986**:3
Arnaz, Desi 1917-1986
   Obituary **1987**:1
Arnold, Tom 1959- **1993**:2
Arquette, Rosanna 1959- **1985**:2
Arthur, Bea 1922-2009
   Obituary **2010**:2
Astin, Sean 1971- **2005**:1
Atkinson, Rowan 1955- **2004**:3
Autry, Gene 1907-1998
   Obituary **1999**:1
Axthelm, Pete 1943(?)-1991
   Obituary **1991**:3
Aykroyd, Dan 1952- **1989**:3
Azaria, Hank 1964- **2001**:3
Bacall, Lauren 1924- **1997**:3
Backus, Jim 1913-1989
   Obituary **1990**:1
Bacon, Kevin 1958- **1995**:3
Baddeley, Hermione 1906(?)-1986

   Obituary **1986**:4
Bailey, Ben 1970- **2011**:4
Bailey, Pearl 1918-1990
   Obituary **1991**:1
Baker, Simon 1969- **2009**:4
Bakula, Scott 1954- **2003**:1
Ball, Alan 1957- **2005**:1
Ball, Lucille 1911-1989
   Obituary **1989**:3
Baranski, Christine 1952- **2001**:2
Barbera, Joseph 1911- **1988**:2
Bardem, Javier 1969- **2008**:4
Barkin, Ellen 1955- **1987**:3
Barney **1993**:4
Baron Cohen, Sacha 1971- **2007**:3
Barr, Roseanne 1953(?)- **1989**:1
Barry, Gene 1919-2009
   Obituary **2011**:4
Barrymore, Drew 1975- **1995**:3
Basinger, Kim 1953- **1987**:2
Bassett, Angela 1959(?)- **1994**:4
Batali, Mario 1960- **2010**:4
Bateman, Jason 1969- **2005**:3
Bateman, Justine 1966- **1988**:4
Baxter, Anne 1923-1985
   Obituary **1986**:1
Beals, Jennifer 1963- **2005**:2
Beatty, Warren 1937- **2000**:1
Belushi, Jim 1954- **1986**:2
Belzer, Richard 1944- **1985**:3
Bergen, Candice 1946- **1990**:1
Bergeron, Tom 1955- **2010**:1
Berle, Milton 1908-2002
   Obituary **2003**:2
Berman, Gail 1957(?)- **2006**:1
Bernardi, Herschel 1923-1986
   Obituary **1986**:4
Bernsen, Corbin 1955- **1990**:2
Bernstein, Leonard 1918-1990
   Obituary **1991**:1
Berry, Halle 1968- **1996**:2
Bialik, Mayim 1975- **1993**:3
Bigelow, Kathryn 1951- **2011**:1
Bird, Brad 1956(?)- **2005**:4
Bishop, Joey 1918-2007
   Obituary **2008**:4
Bixby, Bill 1934-1993
   Obituary **1994**:2
Black, Carole 1945- **2003**:1
Blades, Ruben 1948- **1998**:2
Blaine, David 1973- **2003**:3
Blanc, Mel 1908-1989
   Obituary **1989**:4
Blanchett, Cate 1969- **1999**:3
Bloodworth-Thomason, Linda 1947-
   1994:1
Bloom, Orlando 1977- **2004**:2
Bochco, Steven 1943- **1989**:1
Bolger, Ray 1904-1987
   Obituary **1987**:2
Bonet, Lisa 1967- **1989**:2
Bono, Sonny 1935-1998 **1992**:2
   Obituary **1998**:2
Booth, Shirley 1898-1992
   Obituary **1993**:2
Bourdain, Anthony 1956- **2008**:3
Bowen, Julie 1970- **2007**:1
Boyle, Lara Flynn 1970- **2003**:4
Boyle, Peter 1935- **2002**:3
Bradley, Ed 1941-2006
   Obituary **2008**:1
Bradshaw, John 1933- **1992**:1

Brady, Wayne 1972- **2008**:3
Braff, Zach 1975- **2005**:2
Brand, Russell 1975- **2010**:2
Brandy 1979- **1996**:4
Bratt, Benjamin 1963- **2009**:3
Brenneman, Amy 1964- **2002**:1
Bridges, Jeff 1949- **2011**:1
Bridges, Lloyd 1913-1998
   Obituary **1998**:3
Brinkley, David 1920-2003
   Obituary **2004**:3
Broadbent, Jim 1949- **2008**:4
Brokaw, Tom 1940- **2000**:3
Bronson, Charles 1921-2003
   Obituary **2004**:4
Brooks, Mel 1926- **2003**:1
Brosnan, Pierce 1952- **2000**:3
Brown, Alton 1962- **2011**:1
Brown, Les 1945- **1994**:3
Brown, Ruth 1928-2006
   Obituary **2008**:1
Brown, Samantha 1969- **2011**:3
Bruckheimer, Jerry 1945- **2007**:2
Buckley, Betty 1947- **1996**:2
Bullock, Sandra 1967- **1995**:4
Burnett, Carol 1933- **2000**:3
Burnett, Mark 1960- **2003**:1
Burns, George 1896-1996
   Obituary **1996**:3
Burns, Ken 1953- **1995**:2
Burr, Raymond 1917-1993
   Obituary **1994**:1
Burrows, James 1940- **2005**:3
Butler, Brett 1958(?)- **1995**:1
Butler, Gerard 1969- **2011**:2
Buttons, Red 1919-2006
   Obituary **2007**:3
Bynes, Amanda 1986- **2005**:1
Byrne, Rhonda 1955- **2008**:2
Caan, James 1939- **2004**:4
Caine, Michael 1933- **2000**:4
Calhoun, Rory 1922-1999
   Obituary **1999**:4
Campbell, Neve 1973- **1998**:2
Campion, Jane **1991**:4
Candy, John 1950-1994 **1988**:2
   Obituary **1994**:3
Cannon, Nick 1980- **2006**:4
Carell, Steve 1963- **2006**:4
Carey, Drew 1958- **1997**:4
Carlin, George 1937- **1996**:3
Carney, Art 1918-2003
   Obituary **2005**:1
Carradine, David 1936-2009
   Obituary **2010**:3
Carrey, Jim 1962- **1995**:1
Carson, Johnny 1925-2005
   Obituary **2006**:1
Carson, Lisa Nicole 1969- **1999**:3
Carter, Chris 1956- **2000**:1
Carter, Nell 1948-2003
   Obituary **2004**:2
Caruso, David 1956(?)- **1994**:3
Carvey, Dana 1955- **1994**:1
Cassavetes, John 1929-1989
   Obituary **1989**:2
Cattrall, Kim 1956- **2003**:3
Caulfield, Joan 1922(?)-1991
   Obituary **1992**:1
Cavanagh, Tom 1968- **2003**:1
Caviezel, Jim 1968- **2005**:3
Chancellor, John

Obituary **1997**:1
Chandler, Kyle 1965- **2010**:4
Channing, Stockard 1946- **1991**:3
Chappelle, Dave 1973- **2005**:3
Chase, Chevy 1943- **1990**:1
Chase, Debra Martin 1956- **2009**:1
Chavez, Linda 1947- **1999**:3
Chenoweth, Kristin 1968- **2010**:4
Cher 1946- **1993**:1
Cherry, Don 1934- **1993**:4
Chiklis, Michael 1963- **2003**:3
Child, Julia 1912- **1999**:4
Cho, Margaret 1970- **1995**:2
Chow Yun-fat 1955- **1999**:4
Christensen, Hayden 1981- **2003**:3
Christian Jacobs and Scott Schultz
  1972- **2011**:4
Chung, Connie 1946- **1988**:4
Clarkson, Kelly 1982- **2003**:3
Clarkson, Patricia 1959- **2005**:3
Clay, Andrew Dice 1958- **1991**:1
Cleese, John 1939- **1989**:2
Clooney, George 1961- **1996**:4
Close, Glenn 1947- **1988**:3
Coca, Imogene 1908-2001
  Obituary **2002**:2
Coco, James 1929(?)-1987
  Obituary **1987**:2
Colasanto, Nicholas 1923(?)-1985
  Obituary **1985**:2
Colbert, Stephen 1964- **2007**:4
Coleman, Dabney 1932- **1988**:3
Collette, Toni 1972- **2009**:4
Condon, Bill 1955- **2007**:3
Connery, Sean 1930- **1990**:4
Convy, Bert 1934(?)-1991
  Obituary **1992**:1
Cook, Peter 1938-1995
  Obituary **1995**:2
Cooke, Alistair 1908-2004
  Obituary **2005**:3
Cooper, Anderson 1967- **2006**:1
Cooper, Chris 1951- **2004**:1
Copperfield, David 1957- **1986**:3
Coppola, Francis Ford 1939- **1989**:4
Corbett, John 1962- **2004**:1
Corwin, Jeff 1967- **2005**:1
Cosby, Bill 1937- **1999**:2
Cosell, Howard 1918-1995
  Obituary **1995**:4
Cosgrove, Miranda 1993- **2011**:4
Costas, Bob 1952- **1986**:4
Couric, Katherine 1957- **1991**:4
Cousteau, Jacques-Yves 1910-1997
  1998:2
Cowell, Simon 1959- **2003**:4
Cox, Courteney 1964- **1996**:2
Cox, Richard Joseph
  Brief entry **1985**:1
Craig, Daniel 1968- **2008**:1
Crais, Robert 1954(?)- **2007**:4
Cranston, Bryan 1956- **2010**:1
Crawford, Broderick 1911-1986
  Obituary **1986**:3
Crawford, Cindy 1966- **1993**:3
Crawford, Michael 1942- **1994**:2
Crenna, Richard 1926-2003
  Obituary **2004**:1
Crichton, Michael 1942- **1995**:3
Cronkite, Walter Leland 1916- **1997**:3
Crothers, Scatman 1910-1986
  Obituary **1987**:1

Cryer, Jon 1965- **2010**:4
Crystal, Billy 1947- **1985**:3
Curry, Ann 1956- **2001**:1
Curtis, Jamie Lee 1958- **1995**:1
Cushing, Peter 1913-1994
  Obituary **1995**:1
Cyrus, Miley 1992- **2008**:3
Dalton, Timothy 1946- **1988**:4
Daly, Carson 1973- **2002**:4
Damon, Matt 1970- **1999**:1
Dancy, Hugh 1975- **2010**:3
Danes, Claire 1979- **1999**:4
Dangerfield, Rodney 1921-2004
  Obituary **2006**:1
Daniels, Faith 1958- **1993**:3
Daniels, Jeff 1955- **1989**:4
Danza, Tony 1951- **1989**:1
David, Larry 1948- **2003**:4
Davis, Bette 1908-1989
  Obituary **1990**:1
Davis, Geena 1957- **1992**:1
Davis, Paige 1969- **2004**:2
Davis, Sammy, Jr. 1925-1990
  Obituary **1990**:4
Davis, Viola 1965- **2011**:4
Day, Dennis 1917-1988
  Obituary **1988**:4
De Cordova, Frederick 1910- **1985**:2
Deen, Paula 1947- **2008**:3
DeGeneres, Ellen **1995**:3
Delany, Dana 1956- **2008**:4
De Laurentiis, Giada 1970- **2011**:1
DeLuise, Dom 1933-2009
  Obituary **2010**:2
De Matteo, Drea 1973- **2005**:2
Dempsey, Patrick 1966- **2006**:1
Denver, Bob 1935-2005
  Obituary **2006**:4
Depardieu, Gerard 1948- **1991**:2
Depp, Johnny 1963(?)- **1991**:3
Deschanel, Zooey 1980- **2010**:4
De Vito, Danny 1944- **1987**:1
Dewhurst, Colleen 1924-1991
  Obituary **1992**:2
Diamond, Selma 1921(?)-1985
  Obituary **1985**:2
DiCaprio, Leonardo Wilhelm 1974-
  1997:2
Dickerson, Nancy H. 1927-1997 **1998**
  :2
Dickinson, Janice 1953- **2005**:2
Diller, Barry 1942- **1991**:1
Disney, Roy E. 1930- **1986**:3
Doherty, Shannen 1971(?)- **1994**:2
Dolenz, Micky 1945- **1986**:4
Douglas, Michael 1944- **1986**:2
Douglas, Mike 1925-2006
  Obituary **2007**:4
Downey, Morton, Jr. 1932- **1988**:4
Downey, Robert, Jr. 1965- **2007**:1
Drescher, Fran 1957(?)- **1995**:3
Duchovny, David 1960- **1998**:3
Duff, Hilary 1987- **2004**:4
Duffy, Karen 1962- **1998**:1
Dukakis, Olympia 1931- **1996**:4
Duke, Red
  Brief entry **1987**:1
Dunagan, Deanna 1940- **2009**:2
Durrell, Gerald 1925-1995
  Obituary **1995**:3
Duvall, Robert 1931- **1999**:3
Eastwood, Clint 1930- **1993**:3

Ebersole, Christine 1953- **2007**:2
Ebert, Roger 1942- **1998**:3
Ebsen, Buddy 1908-2003
  Obituary **2004**:3
Eckhart, Aaron 1968- **2009**:2
Efron, Zac 1987- **2008**:2
Eisner, Michael 1942- **1989**:2
Elfman, Jenna 1971- **1999**:4
Ellerbee, Linda 1944- **1993**:3
Elliott, Denholm 1922-1992
  Obituary **1993**:2
Engstrom, Elmer W. 1901-1984
  Obituary **1985**:2
Engvall, Bill 1957- **2010**:1
Evans, Dale 1912-2001
  Obituary **2001**:3
Eve 1978- **2004**:3
Falco, Edie 1963- **2010**:2
Fallon, Jimmy 1974- **2003**:1
Fanning, Dakota 1994- **2005**:2
Faris, Anna 1976- **2010**:3
Farley, Chris 1964-1997 **1998**:2
Fawcett, Farrah 1947- **1998**:4
Feldshuh, Tovah 1952- **2005**:3
Fell, Norman 1924-1998
  Obituary **1999**:2
Ferguson, Craig 1962- **2005**:4
Ferrell, Will 1968- **2004**:4
Ferrer, Jose 1912-1992
  Obituary **1992**:3
Ferrera, America 1984- **2006**:2
Fey, Tina 1970- **2005**:3
Field, Sally 1946- **1995**:3
Fieri, Guy 1968- **2010**:3
Fillion, Nathan 1971- **2011**:3
Finney, Albert 1936- **2003**:3
Firestone, Roy 1953- **1988**:2
Fishburne, Laurence 1961(?)- **1995**:3
Fisher, Carrie 1956- **1991**:1
Flanders, Ed 1934-1995
  Obituary **1995**:3
Flavor Flav 1959- **2007**:3
Flay, Bobby 1964- **2009**:2
Fleiss, Mike 1964- **2003**:4
Fleming, Art 1925(?)-1995
  Obituary **1995**:4
Flockhart, Calista 1964- **1998**:4
Florence, Tyler 1971- **2011**:4
Fonda, Bridget 1964- **1995**:1
Ford, Faith 1964- **2005**:3
Ford, Glenn 1916-2006
  Obituary **2007**:4
Ford, Tennessee Ernie 1919-1991
  Obituary **1992**:2
Fosse, Bob 1927-1987
  Obituary **1988**:1
Foster, Jodie 1962- **1989**:2
Foster, Phil 1914-1985
  Obituary **1985**:3
Fox, Matthew 1966- **2006**:1
Fox, Michael J. 1961- **1986**:1
Fox, Vivica 1964- **1999**:1
Foxworthy, Jeff 1958- **1996**:1
Foxx, Jamie 1967- **2001**:1
Foxx, Redd 1922-1991
  Obituary **1992**:2
Franciscus, James 1934-1991
  Obituary **1992**:1
Frankenheimer, John 1930-2002
  Obituary **2003**:4
Franz, Dennis 1944- **1995**:2
Freeman, Morgan 1937- **1990**:4

Sagansky, Jeff 1952- **1993**:2
Sajak, Pat
  Brief entry **1985**:4
Saldana, Zoe 1978- **2010**:1
Sales, Soupy 1926-2009
  Obituary **2011**:2
Sandler, Adam 1966- **1999**:2
Saralegui, Cristina 1948- **1999**:2
Sarandon, Susan 1946- **1995**:3
Savage, Fred 1976- **1990**:1
Savalas, Telly 1924-1994
  Obituary **1994**:3
Sawyer, Diane 1945- **1994**:4
Schaap, Dick 1934-2001
  Obituary **2003**:1
Schneider, Rob 1965- **1997**:4
Schreiber, Liev 1967- **2007**:2
Schultz, Scott 1972-. See Christian
  Jacobs and Scott Schultz
Schwimmer, David 1966(?)- **1996**:2
Scott, Gene
  Brief entry **1986**:1
Scott, Jill 1972- **2010**:1
Scott Thomas, Kristin 1960- **2010**:2
Seacrest, Ryan 1976- **2004**:4
Sedaris, Amy 1961- **2009**:3
Sedelmaier, Joe 1933- **1985**:3
Sedgwick, Kyra 1965- **2006**:2
Seinfeld, Jerry 1954- **1992**:4
Sethi, Simran 1971(?)- **2008**:1
Sevareid, Eric 1912-1992
  Obituary **1993**:1
Seyfried, Amanda 1985- **2009**:3
Seymour, Jane 1951- **1994**:4
Shaffer, Paul 1949- **1987**:1
Shandling, Garry 1949- **1995**:1
Sharkey, Ray 1953-1993
  Obituary **1994**:1
Shawn, Dick 1924(?)-1987
  Obituary **1987**:3
Sheedy, Ally 1962- **1989**:1
Sheen, Charlie 1965- **2001**:2
Sheindlin, Judith 1942(?)- **1999**:1
Sheldon, Sidney 1917-2007
  Obituary **2008**:2
Shepherd, Cybill 1950- **1996**:3
Shields, Brooke 1965- **1996**:3
Shore, Dinah 1917-1994
  Obituary **1994**:3
Short, Martin 1950- **1986**:1
Shriver, Maria
  Brief entry **1986**:2
Shue, Andrew 1964- **1994**:4
Silverman, Jonathan 1966- **1997**:2
Silverman, Sarah 1970- **2008**:1
Silvers, Phil 1912-1985
  Obituary **1985**:4
Silverstone, Alicia 1976- **1997**:4
Simpson-Wentz, Ashlee 1984- **2009**:1
Singer, Bryan 1965- **2007**:3
Sinise, Gary 1955(?)- **1996**:1
Siskel, Gene 1946-1999
  Obituary **1999**:3
Skelton, Red 1913-1997
  Obituary **1998**:1
Slater, Christian 1969- **1994**:1
Smigel, Robert 1959(?)- **2001**:3
Smiley, Tavis 1964- **2010**:3
Smirnoff, Yakov 1951- **1987**:2
Smith, Anna Nicole 1967-2007
  Obituary **2008**:2
Smith, Buffalo Bob 1917-1998

  Obituary **1999**:1
Smith, Howard K. 1914-2002
  Obituary **2003**:2
Smith, Jeff 1939(?)- **1991**:4
Smith, Kate 1907(?)-1986
  Obituary **1986**:3
Smits, Jimmy 1956- **1990**:1
Snipes, Wesley 1962- **1993**:1
Somers, Suzanne 1946- **2000**:1
Sondheim, Stephen 1930- **1994**:4
Sorkin, Aaron 1961- **2003**:2
Southern, Terry 1926-1995
  Obituary **1996**:2
Spade, David 1965- **1999**:2
Spelling, Aaron 1923-2006
  Obituary **2007**:3
Spelling, Tori 1973- **2008**:3
Spheeris, Penelope 1945(?)- **1989**:2
Spielberg, Steven 1947- **1993**:4
Spray, Ed 1941- **2004**:1
Springer, Jerry 1944- **1998**:4
Stack, Robert 1919-2003
  Obituary **2004**:2
Stamos, John 1963- **2008**:1
Stapleton, Maureen 1925-2006
  Obituary **2007**:2
Stein, Ben 1944- **2001**:1
Stern, Howard 1954- **1988**:2
Stevenson, McLean 1929-1996
  Obituary **1996**:3
Stewart, Jon 1962- **2001**:2
Stewart, Martha 1942(?)- **1992**:1
Stewart, Patrick 1940- **1996**:1
Stiller, Ben 1965- **1999**:1
Stone, Sharon 1958- **1993**:4
Stoppard, Tom 1937- **1995**:4
Storm, Gale 1922-2009
  Obituary **2010**:4
Streisand, Barbra 1942- **1992**:2
Studi, Wes 1944(?)- **1994**:3
Susskind, David 1920-1987
  Obituary **1987**:2
Sutherland, Kiefer 1966- **2002**:4
Swaggart, Jimmy 1935- **1987**:3
Swayze, John Cameron 1906-1995
  Obituary **1996**:1
Swayze, Patrick 1952-2009
  Obituary **2011**:1
Sweeney, Alison 1976- **2010**:1
Swinton, Tilda 1960- **2008**:4
Sykes, Wanda 1964- **2007**:4
Tandy, Jessica 1901-1994 **1990**:4
  Obituary **1995**:1
Tartakovsky, Genndy 1970- **2004**:4
Tartikoff, Brandon 1949-1997 **1985**:2
  Obituary **1998**:1
Tautou, Audrey 1978- **2004**:2
Taylor, Elizabeth 1932- **1993**:3
Tellem, Nancy 1953(?)- **2004**:4
Terkel, Studs 1912-2008
  Obituary **2010**:1
Tesh, John 1952- **1996**:3
Thomas, Betty 1948- **2011**:4
Thomas, Danny 1914-1991
  Obituary **1991**:3
Thompson, Emma 1959- **1993**:2
Thornton, Billy Bob 1956(?)- **1997**:4
Tillstrom, Burr 1917-1985
  Obituary **1986**:1
Tilly, Jennifer 1958(?)- **1997**:2
Timberlake, Justin 1981- **2008**:4
Tisch, Laurence A. 1923- **1988**:2

Tomei, Marisa 1964- **1995**:2
Totenberg, Nina 1944- **1992**:2
Travolta, John 1954- **1995**:2
Trebek, Alex 1940- **2010**:4
Trotter, Charlie 1960- **2000**:4
Trudeau, Garry 1948- **1991**:2
Tucci, Stanley 1960- **2003**:2
Tucker, Chris 1973(?)- **1999**:1
Tucker, Forrest 1919-1986
  Obituary **1987**:1
Turner, Janine 1962- **1993**:2
Turner, Lana 1921-1995
  Obituary **1996**:1
Turner, Ted 1938- **1989**:1
Ullman, Tracey 1961- **1988**:3
Umeki, Miyoshi 1929-2007
  Obituary **2008**:4
Underwood, Carrie 1983- **2008**:1
Urich, Robert 1947- **1988**:1
  Obituary **2003**:3
Usher 1979- **2005**:1
Ustinov, Peter 1921-2004
  Obituary **2005**:3
Valastro, Buddy 1977- **2011**:4
Vanilla Ice 1967(?)- **1991**:3
Vardalos, Nia 1962- **2003**:4
Varney, Jim 1949-2000
  Brief entry **1985**:4
  Obituary **2000**:3
Vaughn, Vince 1970- **1999**:2
Ventura, Jesse 1951- **1999**:2
Vidal, Gore 1925- **1996**:2
Vieira, Meredith 1953- **2001**:3
Villechaize, Herve 1943(?)-1993
  Obituary **1994**:1
Vitale, Dick 1939- **1988**:4
Von D, Kat 1982- **2008**:3
Wagoner, Porter 1927-2007
  Obituary **2008**:4
Walker, Nancy 1922-1992
  Obituary **1992**:3
Walters, Barbara 1931- **1998**:3
Waltz, Christoph 1956- **2011**:1
Wapner, Joseph A. 1919- **1987**:1
Ward, Sela 1956- **2001**:3
Warden, Jack 1920-2006
  Obituary **2007**:3
Washington, Denzel 1954- **1993**:2
Wasserman, Lew 1913-2002
  Obituary **2003**:3
Waterston, Sam 1940- **2006**:1
Wayans, Damon 1960- **1998**:4
Wayans, Keenen Ivory 1958(?)- **1991**
  :1
Wayne, David 1914-1995
  Obituary **1995**:3
Weisz, Rachel 1971- **2006**:4
Weitz, Bruce 1943- **1985**:4
Whedon, Joss 1964- **2006**:3
Whitaker, Forest 1961- **1996**:2
White, Jaleel 1976- **1992**:3
White, Julie 1961- **2008**:2
Whiting, Susan 1956- **2007**:4
Whitmore, James 1921-2009
  Obituary **2010**:1
Whittle, Christopher 1947- **1989**:3
Wilkinson, Tom 1948- **2003**:2
Williams, Brian 1959- **2009**:4
Williams, Robin 1952- **1988**:4
Williams, Treat 1951- **2004**:3
Williams, Vanessa L. 1963- **1999**:2
Willis, Bruce 1955- **1986**:4

Wilson, Flip 1933-1998
  Obituary **1999**:2
Winfield, Paul 1941-2004
  Obituary **2005**:2
Winfrey, Oprah 1954- **1986**:4
Winger, Debra 1955- **1994**:3
Winokur, Marissa Jaret 1973- **2005**:1
Wolfman Jack 1938-1995
  Obituary **1996**:1
Wong, Andrea 1966- **2009**:1
Wong, B.D. 1962- **1998**:1
Woods, James 1947- **1988**:3
Woodward, Edward 1930-2009
  Obituary **2011**:3
Wright, Steven 1955- **1986**:3
Wyatt, Jane 1910-2006
  Obituary **2008**:1
Wyle, Noah 1971- **1997**:3
Wyman, Jane 1917-2007
  Obituary **2008**:4
Wynn, Keenan 1916-1986
  Obituary **1987**:1
Xuxa 1963(?)- **1994**:2
Xzibit 1974- **2005**:4
Yetnikoff, Walter 1933- **1988**:1
York, Dick 1923-1992
  Obituary **1992**:4
Young, Robert 1907-1998
  Obituary **1999**:1
Youngman, Henny 1906(?)-1998
  Obituary **1998**:3
Zahn, Paula 1956(?)- **1992**:3
Zamora, Pedro 1972-1994
  Obituary **1995**:2
Zeta-Jones, Catherine 1969- **1999**:4
Zoe, Rachel 1971- **2010**:2
Zucker, Jeff 1965(?)- **1993**:3

THEATER
Abbott, George 1887-1995
  Obituary **1995**:3
Adjani, Isabelle 1955- **1991**:1
Albee, Edward 1928- **1997**:1
Albert, Eddie 1906-2005
  Obituary **2006**:3
Alda, Robert 1914-1986
  Obituary **1986**:3
Alexander, Jane 1939- **1994**:2
Alexander, Jason 1962(?)- **1993**:3
Allen, Joan 1956- **1998**:1
Allen, Peter 1944-1992
  Obituary **1993**:1
Ameche, Don 1908-1993
  Obituary **1994**:2
Andrews, Julie 1935- **1996**:1
Angelou, Maya 1928- **1993**:4
Arden, Eve 1912(?)-1990
  Obituary **1991**:2
Arkin, Alan 1934- **2007**:4
Arthur, Bea 1922-2009
  Obituary **2010**:2
Ashcroft, Peggy 1907-1991
  Obituary **1992**:1
Atkinson, Rowan 1955- **2004**:3
Aykroyd, Dan 1952- **1989**:3
Bacall, Lauren 1924- **1997**:3
Bacon, Kevin 1958- **1995**:3
Baddeley, Hermione 1906(?)-1986
  Obituary **1986**:4
Bailey, Pearl 1918-1990
  Obituary **1991**:1
Ball, Alan 1957- **2005**:1

Bancroft, Anne 1931-2005
  Obituary **2006**:3
Barkin, Ellen 1955- **1987**:3
Barry, Gene 1919-2009
  Obituary **2011**:4
Barry, Lynda 1956(?)- **1992**:1
Bassett, Angela 1959(?)- **1994**:4
Bates, Alan 1934-2003
  Obituary **2005**:1
Bates, Kathy 1949(?)- **1991**:4
Becker, Brian 1957(?)- **2004**:4
Beckett, Samuel Barclay 1906-1989
  Obituary **1990**:2
Belushi, Jim 1954- **1986**:2
Bening, Annette 1958(?)- **1992**:1
Bennett, Joan 1910-1990
  Obituary **1991**:2
Bennett, Michael 1943-1987
  Obituary **1988**:1
Bernardi, Herschel 1923-1986
  Obituary **1986**:4
Bernhard, Sandra 1955(?)- **1989**:4
Bernstein, Leonard 1918-1990
  Obituary **1991**:1
Bishop, Andre 1948- **2000**:1
Bishop, Joey 1918-2007
  Obituary **2008**:4
Blackstone, Harry Jr. 1934-1997
  Obituary **1997**:4
Blanchett, Cate 1969- **1999**:3
Bloch, Ivan 1940- **1986**:3
Bloom, Orlando 1977- **2004**:2
Bogosian, Eric 1953- **1990**:4
Bolger, Ray 1904-1987
  Obituary **1987**:2
Bonham Carter, Helena 1966- **1998**:4
Booth, Shirley 1898-1992
  Obituary **1993**:2
Bowen, Julie 1970- **2007**:1
Bowie, David 1947- **1998**:2
Brady, Wayne 1972- **2008**:3
Branagh, Kenneth 1960- **1992**:2
Brandauer, Klaus Maria 1944- **1987**:3
Brando, Marlon 1924-2004
  Obituary **2005**:3
Broadbent, Jim 1949- **2008**:4
Brooks, Mel 1926- **2003**:1
Brown, Ruth 1928-2006
  Obituary **2008**:1
Brynner, Yul 1920(?)-1985
  Obituary **1985**:4
Buckley, Betty 1947- **1996**:2
Bullock, Sandra 1967- **1995**:4
Burck, Wade
  Brief entry **1986**:1
Burr, Raymond 1917-1993
  Obituary **1994**:1
Busch, Charles 1954- **1998**:3
Butler, Gerard 1969- **2011**:2
Byrne, Gabriel 1950- **1997**:4
Caan, James 1939- **2004**:4
Caesar, Adolph 1934-1986
  Obituary **1986**:3
Cagney, James 1899-1986
  Obituary **1986**:2
Caine, Michael 1933- **2000**:4
Candy, John 1950-1994 **1988**:2
  Obituary **1994**:3
Carney, Art 1918-2003
  Obituary **2005**:1
Carradine, David 1936-2009
  Obituary **2010**:3

Carrey, Jim 1962- **1995**:1
Carson, Lisa Nicole 1969- **1999**:3
Carter, Nell 1948-2003
  Obituary **2004**:2
Cassavetes, John 1929-1989
  Obituary **1989**:2
Caulfield, Joan 1922(?)-1991
  Obituary **1992**:1
Cavanagh, Tom 1968- **2003**:1
Caviezel, Jim 1968- **2005**:3
Channing, Stockard 1946- **1991**:3
Chenoweth, Kristin 1968- **2010**:4
Christie, Julie 1941- **2008**:4
Clarkson, Patricia 1959- **2005**:3
Close, Glenn 1947- **1988**:3
Coco, James 1929(?)-1987
  Obituary **1987**:2
Collette, Toni 1972- **2009**:4
Connery, Sean 1930- **1990**:4
Convy, Bert 1934(?)-1991
  Obituary **1992**:1
Cook, Peter 1938-1995
  Obituary **1995**:2
Cooper, Chris 1951- **2004**:1
Coppola, Carmine 1910-1991
  Obituary **1991**:4
Costner, Kevin 1955- **1989**:4
Craig, Daniel 1968- **2008**:1
Crawford, Broderick 1911-1986
  Obituary **1986**:3
Crawford, Cheryl 1902-1986
  Obituary **1987**:1
Crawford, Michael 1942- **1994**:2
Crisp, Quentin 1908-1999
  Obituary **2000**:3
Cronyn, Hume 1911-2003
  Obituary **2004**:3
Cruz, Nilo 1961(?)- **2004**:4
Cryer, Jon 1965- **2010**:4
Culkin, Macaulay 1980(?)- **1991**:3
Cusack, John 1966- **1999**:3
Cushing, Peter 1913-1994
  Obituary **1995**:1
Dafoe, Willem 1955- **1988**:1
Dalton, Timothy 1946- **1988**:4
Dancy, Hugh 1975- **2010**:3
Daniels, Jeff 1955- **1989**:4
Davis, Ossie 1917-2005
  Obituary **2006**:1
Davis, Paige 1969- **2004**:2
Davis, Viola 1965- **2011**:4
Dawson, Rosario 1979- **2007**:2
Day-Lewis, Daniel 1957- **1989**:4
Dee, Janie 1966(?)- **2001**:4
Delany, Dana 1956- **2008**:4
DeLuise, Dom 1933-2009
  Obituary **2010**:2
Dench, Judi 1934- **1999**:4
De Niro, Robert 1943- **1999**:1
Dennis, Sandy 1937-1992
  Obituary **1992**:4
Denver, Bob 1935-2005
  Obituary **2006**:4
Depardieu, Gerard 1948- **1991**:2
Dern, Laura 1967- **1992**:3
De Vito, Danny 1944- **1987**:1
Dewhurst, Colleen 1924-1991
  Obituary **1992**:2
Diggs, Taye 1971- **2000**:1
Douglas, Michael 1944- **1986**:2
Dukakis, Olympia 1931- **1996**:4
Dunagan, Deanna 1940- **2009**:2

Duncan, Todd 1903-1998
  Obituary **1998**:3
Duvall, Robert 1931- **1999**:3
Ebersole, Christine 1953- **2007**:2
Ebsen, Buddy 1908-2003
  Obituary **2004**:3
Eckhart, Aaron 1968- **2009**:2
Efron, Zac 1987- **2008**:2
Elliott, Denholm 1922-1992
  Obituary **1993**:2
Ephron, Henry 1912-1992
  Obituary **1993**:2
Falco, Edie 1963- **2010**:2
Faris, Anna 1976- **2010**:3
Fawcett, Farrah 1947- **1998**:4
Feld, Kenneth 1948- **1988**:2
Feldshuh, Tovah 1952- **2005**:3
Ferguson, Craig 1962- **2005**:4
Ferrer, Jose 1912-1992
  Obituary **1992**:3
Fiennes, Ralph 1962- **1996**:2
Fierstein, Harvey 1954- **2004**:2
Finney, Albert 1936- **2003**:3
Fishburne, Laurence 1961(?)- **1995**:3
Fisher, Carrie 1956- **1991**:1
Flanders, Ed 1934-1995
  Obituary **1995**:3
Flockhart, Calista 1964- **1998**:4
Fo, Dario 1926- **1998**:1
Foote, Horton 1916-2009
  Obituary **2010**:2
Ford, Faith 1964- **2005**:3
Fosse, Bob 1927-1987
  Obituary **1988**:1
Foster, Sutton 1975- **2003**:2
Freeman, Morgan 1937- **1990**:4
Fugard, Athol 1932- **1992**:3
Gabor, Eva 1921(?)-1995
  Obituary **1996**:1
Gallagher, Peter 1955- **2004**:3
Gardenia, Vincent 1922-1992
  Obituary **1993**:2
Garr, Teri 1949- **1988**:4
Geffen, David 1943- **1985**:3
Gelbart, Larry 1928-2009
  Obituary **2011**:1
Gere, Richard 1949- **1994**:3
Gielgud, John 1904-2000
  Obituary **2000**:4
Gilford, Jack 1907-1990
  Obituary **1990**:4
Gleason, Jackie 1916-1987
  Obituary **1987**:4
Glover, Danny 1947- **1998**:4
Glover, Savion 1973- **1997**:1
Gobel, George 1920(?)-1991
  Obituary **1991**:4
Goldberg, Whoopi 1955- **1993**:3
Goldblum, Jeff 1952- **1988**:1
Gossett, Louis, Jr. 1936- **1989**:3
Goulet, Robert 1933-2007
  Obituary **2008**:4
Grammer, Kelsey 1955(?)- **1995**:1
Grant, Cary 1904-1986
  Obituary **1987**:1
Grant, Hugh 1960- **1995**:3
Gray, Simon 1936-2008
  Obituary **2009**:4
Gray, Spalding 1941-2004
  Obituary **2005**:2
Greene, Graham 1952- **1997**:2
Gregory, Dick 1932- **1990**:3

Gyllenhaal, Jake 1980- **2005**:3
Gyllenhaal, Maggie 1977- **2009**:2
Hagen, Uta 1919-2004
  Obituary **2005**:2
Hall, Anthony Michael 1968- **1986**:3
Hall, Michael 1971- **2011**:1
Hamilton, Margaret 1902-1985
  Obituary **1985**:3
Harrelson, Woody 1961- **2011**:1
Harris, Richard 1930-2002
  Obituary **2004**:1
Harrison, Rex 1908-1990
  Obituary **1990**:4
Hart, Kitty Carlisle 1910-2007
  Obituary **2008**:2
Hathaway, Anne 1982- **2007**:2
Havel, Vaclav 1936- **1990**:3
Hawke, Ethan 1971(?)- **1995**:4
Hayes, Helen 1900-1993
  Obituary **1993**:4
Headley, Heather 1974- **2011**:1
Hennessy, Jill 1969- **2003**:2
Henning, Doug 1947-1999
  Obituary **2000**:3
Hepburn, Katharine 1909- **1991**:2
Hill, George Roy 1921-2002
  Obituary **2004**:1
Hines, Gregory 1946- **1992**:4
Hoffman, Dustin 1937- **2005**:4
Hoffman, Philip Seymour 1967-
  2006:3
Hopkins, Anthony 1937- **1992**:4
Horne, Lena 1917- **1998**:4
Hoskins, Bob 1942- **1989**:1
Houseman, John 1902-1988
  Obituary **1989**:1
Houston, Cissy 1933- **1999**:3
Howard, Ken 1944- **2010**:4
Huffman, Felicity 1962- **2006**:2
Humphries, Barry 1934- **1993**:1
Hunt, Helen 1963- **1994**:4
Hunter, Holly 1958- **1989**:4
Hurt, William 1950- **1986**:1
Hwang, David Henry 1957- **1999**:1
Irons, Jeremy 1948- **1991**:4
Irwin, Bill **1988**:3
Itami, Juzo 1933-1997 **1998**:2
Ives, Burl 1909-1995
  Obituary **1995**:4
Izzard, Eddie 1963- **2008**:1
Jackman, Hugh 1968- **2004**:4
Jackson, Samuel L. 1949(?)- **1995**:4
Jane, Thomas 1969- **2010**:3
Janney, Allison 1959- **2003**:3
Jay, Ricky 1949(?)- **1995**:1
Jillian, Ann 1951- **1986**:4
Johansson, Scarlett 1984- **2005**:4
Johnson, Van 1916-2008
  Obituary **2010**:1
Jones, Cherry 1956- **1999**:3
Jones, Sarah 1974(?)- **2005**:2
Jones, Tommy Lee 1947(?)- **1994**:2
Julia, Raul 1940-1994
  Obituary **1995**:1
Kahn, Madeline 1942-1999
  Obituary **2000**:2
Kanakaredes, Melina 1967- **2007**:1
Kavner, Julie 1951- **1992**:3
Kaye, Danny 1913-1987
  Obituary **1987**:2
Kaye, Nora 1920-1987
  Obituary **1987**:4

Kazan, Elia 1909-2003
  Obituary **2004**:4
Keeler, Ruby 1910-1993
  Obituary **1993**:4
Keitel, Harvey 1939- **1994**:3
Kendrick, Anna 1985- **2011**:2
Kerr, Deborah 1921-2007
  Obituary **2008**:4
Kerr, Jean 1922-2003
  Obituary **2004**:1
Kilmer, Val **1991**:4
King, Alan 1927-2004
  Obituary **2005**:3
Kinski, Klaus 1926-1991 **1987**:2
  Obituary **1992**:2
Kitt, Eartha 1927-2008
  Obituary **2010**:1
Kline, Kevin 1947- **2000**:1
Kramer, Larry 1935- **1991**:2
Krause, Peter 1965- **2009**:2
Kushner, Tony 1956- **1995**:2
Lahti, Christine 1950- **1988**:2
Lane, Burton 1912-1997
  Obituary **1997**:2
Lane, Nathan 1956- **1996**:4
Lange, Jessica 1949- **1995**:4
Langella, Frank 1940- **2008**:3
Lansbury, Angela 1925- **1993**:1
Larson, Jonathan 1961(?)-1996
  Obituary **1997**:2
Lawless, Lucy 1968- **1997**:4
Leary, Denis 1958- **1993**:3
Leigh, Jennifer Jason 1962- **1995**:2
Lithgow, John 1945- **1985**:2
Little, Cleavon 1939-1992
  Obituary **1993**:2
Lloyd Webber, Andrew 1948- **1989**:1
Loewe, Frederick 1901-1988
  Obituary **1988**:2
Logan, Joshua 1908-1988
  Obituary **1988**:4
Lord, Jack 1920-1998 **1998**:2
LuPone, Patti 1949- **2009**:2
Lynch, Jane 1960- **2011**:2
MacRae, Gordon 1921-1986
  Obituary **1986**:2
Macy, William H. **1999**:3
Maher, Bill 1956- **1996**:2
Malden, Karl 1912-2009
  Obituary **2010**:4
Malkovich, John 1953- **1988**:2
Maltby, Richard, Jr. 1937- **1996**:3
Mamet, David 1947- **1998**:4
Mantegna, Joe 1947- **1992**:1
Marber, Patrick 1964- **2007**:4
Marceau, Marcel 1923-2007
  Obituary **2008**:4
Margulies, Julianna 1966- **2011**:1
Marshall, Penny 1942- **1991**:3
Martin, Mary 1913-1990
  Obituary **1991**:2
McDonagh, Martin 1970- **2007**:3
McDonnell, Mary 1952- **2008**:2
McDormand, Frances 1957- **1997**:3
McDowall, Roddy 1928-1998
  Obituary **1999**:1
McGillis, Kelly 1957- **1989**:3
McGregor, Ewan 1971(?)- **1998**:2
McKee, Lonette 1952(?)- **1996**:1
McKellen, Ian 1939- **1994**:1
McMahon, Julian 1968- **2006**:1
Merkerson, S. Epatha 1952- **2006**:4

Merrick, David 1912-2000
  Obituary **2000**:4
Messing, Debra 1968- **2004**:4
Midler, Bette 1945- **1989**:4
Minghella, Anthony 1954- **2004**:3
Mirren, Helen 1945- **2005**:1
Molina, Alfred 1953- **2005**:3
Montalban, Ricardo 1920-2009
  Obituary **2010**:1
Montand, Yves 1921-1991
  Obituary **1992**:2
Montgomery, Elizabeth 1933-1995
  Obituary **1995**:4
Moore, Dudley 1935-2002
  Obituary **2003**:2
Moore, Mary Tyler 1936- **1996**:2
Morrow, Rob 1962- **2006**:4
Mos Def 1973- **2005**:4
Moss, Carrie-Anne 1967- **2004**:3
Neeson, Liam 1952- **1993**:4
Newman, Paul 1925- **1995**:3
Nichols, Mike 1931- **1994**:4
Nolan, Lloyd 1902-1985
  Obituary **1985**:4
Nolte, Nick 1941- **1992**:4
North, Alex 1910- **1986**:3
Northam, Jeremy 1961- **2003**:2
Nottage, Lynn 1964- **2010**:1
Nunn, Trevor 1940- **2000**:2
O'Donnell, Rosie 1962- **1994**:3
Oldman, Gary 1958- **1998**:1
Olin, Ken 1955(?)- **1992**:3
Olin, Lena 1956- **1991**:2
Olivier, Laurence 1907-1989
  Obituary **1989**:4
O'Neill, Ed 1946- **2010**:4
Orbach, Jerry 1935-2004
  Obituary **2006**:1
Osborne, John 1929-1994
  Obituary **1995**:2
O'Sullivan, Maureen 1911-1998
  Obituary **1998**:4
Owen, Clive 1964- **2006**:2
Pacino, Al 1940- **1993**:4
Page, Geraldine 1924-1987
  Obituary **1987**:4
Papp, Joseph 1921-1991
  Obituary **1992**:2
Parks, Suzan-Lori 1964- **2003**:2
Paulsen, Pat 1927-1997
  Obituary **1997**:4
Peck, Gregory 1916-2003
  Obituary **2004**:3
Penn, Sean 1960- **1987**:2
Penn & Teller **1992**:1
Perkins, Anthony 1932-1992
  Obituary **1993**:2
Perry, Tyler 1969- **2006**:1
Peters, Bernadette 1948- **2000**:1
Pfeiffer, Michelle 1957- **1990**:2
Picasso, Paloma 1949- **1991**:1
Pinchot, Bronson 1959(?)- **1987**:4
Piven, Jeremy 1965- **2007**:3
Pleasence, Donald 1919-1995
  Obituary **1995**:3
Poitier, Sidney 1927- **1990**:3
Poston, Tom 1921-2007
  Obituary **2008**:3
Preminger, Otto 1906-1986
  Obituary **1986**:3
Preston, Robert 1918-1987
  Obituary **1987**:3

Price, Vincent 1911-1993
  Obituary **1994**:2
Prince, Faith 1959(?)- **1993**:2
Quaid, Dennis 1954- **1989**:4
Radcliffe, Daniel 1989- **2007**:4
Radner, Gilda 1946-1989
  Obituary **1989**:4
Raitt, John 1917-2005
  Obituary **2006**:2
Randall, Tony 1920-2004
  Obituary **2005**:3
Rashad, Phylicia 1948- **1987**:3
Raye, Martha 1916-1994
  Obituary **1995**:1
Redford, Robert 1937- **1993**:2
Redgrave, Lynn 1943- **1999**:3
Redgrave, Vanessa 1937- **1989**:2
Reeves, Keanu 1964- **1992**:1
Reilly, Charles Nelson
  Obituary **2008**:3
Reilly, John C. 1965- **2003**:4
Reitman, Ivan 1946- **1986**:3
Reza, Yasmina 1959(?)- **1999**:2
Rhone, Trevor 1940-2009
  Obituary **2011**:1
Richards, Lloyd 1919-2006
  Obituary **2007**:3
Richards, Michael 1949(?)- **1993**:4
Richardson, Natasha 1963-2009
  Obituary **2010**:2
Ritter, John 1948- **2003**:4
Robbins, Jerome 1918-1998
  Obituary **1999**:1
Roberts, Doris 1930- **2003**:4
Roker, Roxie 1929(?)-1995
  Obituary **1996**:2
Rolle, Esther 1922-1998
  Obituary **1999**:2
Rowe, Mike 1962- **2010**:2
Rudd, Paul 1969- **2009**:4
Rudner, Rita 1956- **1993**:2
Rudnick, Paul 1957(?)- **1994**:3
Ruehl, Mercedes 1948(?)- **1992**:4
Ruffalo, Mark 1967- **2011**:4
Rylance, Mark 1960- **2009**:3
Salonga, Lea 1971- **2003**:3
Sarandon, Susan 1946- **1995**:3
Schoenfeld, Gerald 1924- **1986**:2
Schreiber, Liev 1967- **2007**:2
Schwimmer, David 1966(?)- **1996**:2
Scott, George C. 1927-1999
  Obituary **2000**:2
Scott Thomas, Kristin 1960- **2010**:2
Seymour, Jane 1951- **1994**:4
Shaffer, Paul 1949- **1987**:1
Shanley, John Patrick 1950- **2006**:1
Shawn, Dick 1924(?)-1987
  Obituary **1987**:3
Sheldon, Sidney 1917-2007
  Obituary **2008**:2
Shepard, Sam 1943- **1996**:4
Short, Martin 1950- **1986**:1
Silvers, Phil 1912-1985
  Obituary **1985**:4
Sinise, Gary 1955(?)- **1996**:1
Slater, Christian 1969- **1994**:1
Smith, Anna Deavere 1950- **2002**:2
Snipes, Wesley 1962- **1993**:1
Sondheim, Stephen 1930- **1994**:4
Spacey, Kevin 1959- **1996**:4
Stamos, John 1963- **2008**:1
Stapleton, Maureen 1925-2006

  Obituary **2007**:2
Steiger, Rod 1925-2002
  Obituary **2003**:4
Stewart, Jimmy 1908-1997
  Obituary **1997**:4
Stewart, Patrick 1940- **1996**:1
Stiller, Ben 1965- **1999**:1
Sting 1951- **1991**:4
Stoppard, Tom 1937- **1995**:4
Streep, Meryl 1949- **1990**:2
Streisand, Barbra 1942- **1992**:2
Stritch, Elaine 1925- **2002**:4
Styne, Jule 1905-1994
  Obituary **1995**:1
Susskind, David 1920-1987
  Obituary **1987**:2
Swinton, Tilda 1960- **2008**:4
Szot, Paulo 1969- **2009**:3
Tandy, Jessica 1901-1994 **1990**:4
  Obituary **1995**:1
Taylor, Elizabeth 1932- **1993**:3
Taylor, Lili 1967- **2000**:2
Thompson, Emma 1959- **1993**:2
Tomei, Marisa 1964- **1995**:2
Tucci, Stanley 1960- **2003**:2
Tune, Tommy 1939- **1994**:2
Ullman, Tracey 1961- **1988**:3
Umeki, Miyoshi 1929-2007
  Obituary **2008**:4
Urich, Robert 1947- **1988**:1
  Obituary **2003**:3
Ustinov, Peter 1921-2004
  Obituary **2005**:3
Vardalos, Nia 1962- **2003**:4
Vogel, Paula 1951- **1999**:2
Walker, Nancy 1922-1992
  Obituary **1992**:3
Washington, Denzel 1954- **1993**:2
Wasserstein, Wendy 1950- **1991**:3
Waterston, Sam 1940- **2006**:1
Watts, Naomi 1968- **2006**:1
Wayne, David 1914-1995
  Obituary **1995**:3
Weaver, Sigourney 1949- **1988**:3
Weisz, Rachel 1971- **2006**:4
Weitz, Bruce 1943- **1985**:4
Wences, Senor 1896-1999
  Obituary **1999**:4
Whitaker, Forest 1961- **1996**:2
White, Julie 1961- **2008**:2
Whitehead, Robert 1916-2002
  Obituary **2003**:3
Whitmore, James 1921-2009
  Obituary **2010**:1
Wiest, Dianne 1948- **1995**:2
Wilkinson, Tom 1948- **2003**:2
Williams, Treat 1951- **2004**:3
Willis, Bruce 1955- **1986**:4
Winfield, Paul 1941-2004
  Obituary **2005**:2
Winokur, Marissa Jaret 1973- **2005**:1
Wong, B.D. 1962- **1998**:1
Woods, James 1947- **1988**:3
Worth, Irene 1916-2002
  Obituary **2003**:2
Wyatt, Jane 1910-2006
  Obituary **2008**:1
Wyle, Noah 1971- **1997**:3
Youngman, Henny 1906(?)-1998
  Obituary **1998**:3
Zeffirelli, Franco 1923- **1991**:3

WRITING

Adams, Douglas 1952-2001
  Obituary **2002**:2
Adams, Scott 1957- **1996**:4
Adiga, Aravind 1974- **2010**:3
Ahern, Cecelia 1981- **2008**:4
Albom, Mitch 1958- **1999**:3
Alexie, Sherman 1966- **1998**:4
Ali, Monica 1967- **2007**:4
Amanpour, Christiane 1958- **1997**:2
Ambler, Eric 1909-1998
  Obituary **1999**:2
Ambrose, Stephen 1936- **2002**:3
Amis, Kingsley 1922-1995
  Obituary **1996**:2
Amis, Martin 1949- **2008**:3
Amory, Cleveland 1917-1998
  Obituary **1999**:2
Anderson, Poul 1926-2001
  Obituary **2002**:3
Angelou, Maya 1928- **1993**:4
Angier, Natalie 1958- **2000**:3
Asimov, Isaac 1920-1992
  Obituary **1992**:3
Atkins, Robert C. 1930-2003
  Obituary **2004**:2
Atwood, Margaret 1939- **2001**:2
Axthelm, Pete 1943(?)-1991
  Obituary **1991**:3
Ayala, Francisco 1906-2009
  Obituary **2011**:3
Bacall, Lauren 1924- **1997**:3
Bakker, Robert T. 1950(?)- **1991**:3
Baldwin, James 1924-1987
  Obituary **1988**:2
Ball, Edward 1959- **1999**:2
Banks, Russell 1940- **2009**:2
Baraka, Amiri 1934- **2000**:3
Barber, Red 1908-1992
  Obituary **1993**:2
Barker, Clive 1952- **2003**:3
Barker, Pat 1943- **2009**:1
Barry, Dave 1947(?)- **1991**:2
Barry, Lynda 1956(?)- **1992**:1
Batali, Mario 1960- **2010**:4
Bechdel, Alison 1960- **2007**:3
Beckett, Samuel Barclay 1906-1989
  Obituary **1990**:2
Bedford, Deborah 1958- **2006**:3
Bell, Gabrielle 1975(?)- **2007**:4
Bellow, Saul 1915-2005
  Obituary **2006**:2
Benchley, Peter 1940-2006
  Obituary **2007**:1
Binchy, Maeve 1940- **2010**:2
Bloodworth-Thomason, Linda 1947-
  1994:1
Bloom, Amy 1953- **2011**:3
Blume, Judy 1936- **1998**:4
Bly, Robert 1926- **1992**:4
Blyth, Myrna 1939- **2002**:4
Bombeck, Erma 1927-1996
  Obituary **1996**:4
Bourdain, Anthony 1956- **2008**:3
Bowles, Paul 1910-1999
  Obituary **2000**:3
Boyle, T. C. 1948- **2007**:2
Boynton, Sandra 1953- **2004**:1
Bradford, Barbara Taylor 1933- **2002**
  :4
Bradshaw, John 1933- **1992**:1
Branagh, Kenneth 1960- **1992**:2

Bray, Libba 1964- **2011**:1
Breathed, Berkeley 1957- **2005**:3
Brite, Poppy Z. 1967- **2005**:1
Brodsky, Joseph 1940-1996
  Obituary **1996**:3
Brokaw, Tom 1940- **2000**:3
Brooks, Gwendolyn 1917-2000 **1998**
  :1
  Obituary **2001**:2
Brown, Alton 1962- **2011**:1
Brown, Dan 1964- **2004**:4
Brown, Dee 1908-2002
  Obituary **2004**:1
Brown, Tina 1953- **1992**:1
Brutus, Dennis 1924-2009
  Obituary **2011**:4
Buchwald, Art 1925-2007
  Obituary **2008**:2
Buffett, Jimmy 1946- **1999**:3
Burgess, Anthony 1917-1993
  Obituary **1994**:2
Burroughs, William S. 1914- **1994**:2
Burroughs, William S. 1914-1997
  Obituary **1997**:4
Buscaglia, Leo 1924-1998
  Obituary **1998**:4
Busch, Charles 1954- **1998**:3
Bush, Millie 1987- **1992**:1
Bushnell, Candace 1959(?)- **2004**:2
Butler, Octavia E. 1947- **1999**:3
Byrne, Gabriel 1950- **1997**:4
Byrne, Rhonda 1955- **2008**:2
Cabot, Meg 1967- **2008**:4
Caen, Herb 1916-1997
  Obituary **1997**:4
Campbell, Bebe Moore 1950- **1996**:2
Caplan, Arthur L. 1950- **2000**:2
Carcaterra, Lorenzo 1954- **1996**:1
Carey, George 1935- **1992**:3
Carlson, Richard 1961- **2002**:1
Carroll, Jim 1949-2009
  Obituary **2011**:1
Carter, Stephen L. **2008**:2
Carver, Raymond 1938-1988
  Obituary **1989**:1
Castaneda, Carlos 1931-1998
  Obituary **1998**:4
Castellucci, Cecil 1969- **2008**:3
Castillo, Ana 1953- **2000**:4
Cela, Camilo Jose 1916-2001
  Obituary **2003**:1
Chabon, Michael 1963- **2002**:1
Chatwin, Bruce 1940-1989
  Obituary **1989**:2
Chavez, Linda 1947- **1999**:3
Cheney, Lynne V. 1941- **1990**:4
Chenoweth, Kristin 1968- **2010**:4
Child, Julia 1912- **1999**:4
Child, Lee 1954- **2007**:3
Chopra, Deepak 1947- **1996**:3
Christensen, Kate 1962- **2009**:4
Clancy, Tom 1947- **1998**:4
Clark, Mary Higgins 1929- **2000**:4
Clarke, Arthur C. 1917-2008
  Obituary **2009**:2
Clavell, James 1924(?)-1994
  Obituary **1995**:1
Cleaver, Eldridge 1935-1998
  Obituary **1998**:4
Clowes, Daniel 1961- **2007**:1
Codrescu, Andreaa 1946- **1997**:3
Cody, Diablo 1978- **2009**:1

Coetzee, J. M. 1940- **2004**:4
Cohen, Arianne 1981- **2011**:2
Colbert, Stephen 1964- **2007**:4
Cole, Johnetta B. 1936- **1994**:3
Coles, Robert 1929(?)- **1995**:1
Collins, Billy 1941- **2002**:2
Collins, Jackie 1941- **2004**:4
Comfort, Alex 1920-2000
  Obituary **2000**:4
Condon, Richard 1915-1996
  Obituary **1996**:4
Connelly, Michael 1956- **2007**:1
Cook, Robin 1940- **1996**:3
Cornwell, Patricia 1956- **2003**:1
Cosby, Bill 1937- **1999**:2
Covey, Stephen R. 1932- **1994**:4
Cowley, Malcolm 1898-1989
  Obituary **1989**:3
Crais, Robert 1954(?)- **2007**:4
Crichton, Michael 1942- **1995**:3
Cronenberg, David 1943- **1992**:3
Crosley, Sloane 1978- **2011**:4
Cruz, Nilo 1961(?)- **2004**:4
Cunningham, Michael 1952- **2003**:4
Dahl, Roald 1916-1990
  Obituary **1991**:2
Dangerfield, Rodney 1921-2004
  Obituary **2006**:1
Danticat, Edwidge 1969- **2005**:4
Darden, Christopher 1957(?)- **1996**:4
Darwish, Mahmud 1942-2008
  Obituary **2009**:4
David, Larry 1948- **2003**:4
Davis, Patti 1952- **1995**:1
Deen, Paula 1947- **2008**:3
Delany, Sarah 1889-1999
  Obituary **1999**:3
Del Toro, Guillermo 1964- **2010**:3
Derrida, Jacques 1930-2005
  Obituary **2006**:1
Dershowitz, Alan 1938(?)- **1992**:1
Diamond, I.A.L. 1920-1988
  Obituary **1988**:3
Diamond, Selma 1921(?)-1985
  Obituary **1985**:2
Dickey, James 1923-1997 **1998**:2
Dickinson, Brian 1937- **1998**:2
Dickinson, Janice 1953- **2005**:2
Djerassi, Carl 1923- **2000**:4
Doctorow, E. L. 1931- **2007**:1
Dorris, Michael 1945-1997
  Obituary **1997**:3
Douglas, Marjory Stoneman
  1890-1998 **1993**:1
  Obituary **1998**:4
Dove, Rita 1952- **1994**:3
Dowd, Maureen Brigid 1952- **1997**:1
Doyle, Roddy 1958- **2008**:1
Drucker, Peter F. 1909- **1992**:3
Dunn, Jancee 1966- **2010**:1
Dunne, Dominick 1925- **1997**:1
Duras, Marguerite 1914-1996
  Obituary **1996**:3
Durrell, Gerald 1925-1995
  Obituary **1995**:3
Dworkin, Andrea 1946-2005
  Obituary **2006**:2
Dyer, Wayne 1940- **2010**:4
Eberhart, Richard 1904-2005
  Obituary **2006**:3
Ebert, Roger 1942- **1998**:3
Edwards, Bob 1947- **1993**:2

Eggers, Dave 1970- **2001**:3
Eisner, Will 1917-2005
 Obituary **2006**:1
Elliott, Missy 1971- **2003**:4
Ellison, Ralph 1914-1994
 Obituary **1994**:4
Ellroy, James 1948- **2003**:4
Elon, Amos 1926-2009
 Obituary **2010**:3
Ephron, Nora 1941- **1992**:3
Epstein, Jason 1928- **1991**:1
Erdrich, Louise 1954- **2005**:3
Etzioni, Amitai 1929- **1994**:3
Evanovich, Janet 1943- **2005**:2
Evans, Joni 1942- **1991**:4
Evans, Robert 1930- **2004**:1
Fabio 1961(?)- **1993**:4
Falconer, Ian 1960(?)- **2003**:1
Faludi, Susan 1959- **1992**:4
Farmer, Philip José 1918-2009
 Obituary **2010**:2
Fast, Howard 1914-2003
 Obituary **2004**:2
Ferguson, Niall 1964- **2006**:1
Fforde, Jasper 1961- **2006**:3
Fielding, Helen 1959- **2000**:4
Filipovic, Zlata 1981(?)- **1994**:4
Finnamore, Suzanne 1959- **2009**:1
Fish, Hamilton 1888-1991
 Obituary **1991**:3
Fisher, Carrie 1956- **1991**:1
Flay, Bobby 1964- **2009**:2
Flynt, Larry 1942- **1997**:3
Fo, Dario 1926- **1998**:1
Fodor, Eugene 1906(?)-1991
 Obituary **1991**:3
Foer, Jonathan 1977- **2011**:2
Foote, Horton 1916-2009
 Obituary **2010**:2
Foote, Shelby 1916- **1991**:2
Forbes, Steve 1947- **1996**:2
Foxworthy, Jeff 1958- **1996**:1
Frame, Janet 1924-2004
 Obituary **2005**:2
Franken, Al 1952(?)- **1996**:3
Frankl, Viktor E. 1905-1997
 Obituary **1998**:1
Franzen, Jonathan 1959- **2002**:3
Frazier, Charles 1950- **2003**:2
Freeman, Jr., Castle 1944- **2010**:2
French, Marilyn 1929-2009
 Obituary **2010**:2
French, Tana 1973- **2009**:3
Freston, Kathy 1965- **2009**:3
Friedan, Betty 1921- **1994**:2
Frye, Northrop 1912-1991
 Obituary **1991**:3
Fugard, Athol 1932- **1992**.3
Fulbright, J. William 1905-1995
 Obituary **1995**:3
Fulghum, Robert 1937- **1996**:1
Gaiman, Neil 1960- **2010**:1
Gaines, William M. 1922-1992
 Obituary **1993**:1
Gao Xingjian 1940- **2001**:2
Garcia, Cristina 1958- **1997**:4
Garcia Marquez, Gabriel 1928- **2005**:2
Geisel, Theodor 1904-1991
 Obituary **1992**:2
George, Elizabeth 1949- **2003**:3

Gibson, William Ford, III 1948- **1997**:2
Gilbert, Elizabeth 1969- **2011**:1
Gillespie, Marcia 1944- **1999**:4
Ginsberg, Allen 1926-1997
 Obituary **1997**:3
Gladwell, Malcolm 1963- **2010**:3
Goldman, William 1931- **2001**:1
Gore, Albert, Jr. 1948(?)- **1993**:2
Goren, Charles H. 1901-1991
 Obituary **1991**:4
Gottlieb, William 1917-2006
 Obituary **2007**:2
Grafton, Sue 1940- **2000**:2
Graham, Billy 1918- **1992**:1
Graham, Katharine Meyer 1917-**1997**:3
 Obituary **2002**:3
Grandin, Temple 1947- **2006**:1
Grass, Gunter 1927- **2000**:2
Gray, John 1952(?)- **1995**:3
Gray, Simon 1936-2008
 Obituary **2009**:4
Gray, Spalding 1941-2004
 Obituary **2005**:2
Greene, Graham 1904-1991
 Obituary **1991**:4
Gregory, David 1970- **2010**:2
Gregory, Philippa 1954- **2010**:1
Griffith, Nicola 1960- **2010**:2
Grisham, John 1955- **1994**:4
Grodin, Charles 1935- **1997**:3
Grylls, Bear 1974- **2010**:2
Guccione, Bob, Jr. 1956- **1991**:4
Gupta, Sanjay 1969- **2009**:4
Haddon, Mark 1962- **2005**:2
Ha Jin 1956- **2000**:3
Halberstam, David 1934-2007
 Obituary **2008**:3
Haley, Alex 1924-1992
 Obituary **1992**:3
Hamilton, Laurell K. 1963- **2008**:2
Hand, Elizabeth 1957- **2007**:2
Handford, Martin **1991**:3
Handler, Chelsea 1975- **2009**:3
Handler, Daniel 1970- **2003**:3
Harris, E. Lynn 1955- **2004**:2
Harris, Thomas 1940(?)- **2001**:1
Hart, Johnny 1931-2007
 Obituary **2008**:2
Hart, Mickey 1944(?)- **1991**:2
Hautzig, Esther 1930-2009
 Obituary **2011**:3
Havel, Vaclav 1936- **1990**:3
Hayakawa, Samuel Ichiye 1906-1992
 Obituary **1992**:3
Heaney, Seamus 1939- **1996**:2
Heat-Moon, William Least 1939-**2000**.2
Heller, Joseph 1923-1999
 Obituary **2000**:2
Heloise 1951- **2001**:4
Henry, Carl F.H. 1913-2003
 Obituary **2005**:1
Herzog, Chaim 1918-1997
 Obituary **1997**:3
Hiaasen, Carl 1953- **2007**:2
Hicks, India 1967- **2008**:2
Highsmith, Patricia 1921-1995
 Obituary **1995**:3
Hills, L. Rust 1924-2008
 Obituary **2009**:4

Hilton, Perez 1978- **2010**:3
Hoff, Syd 1912-2004
 Obituary **2005**:3
Hollinghurst, Alan 1954- **2006**:1
hooks, bell 1952- **2000**:2
Horn, Mike 1966- **2009**:3
Hornby, Nick 1957- **2002**:2
Hosseini, Khaled 1965- **2008**:3
Hrabal, Bohumil 1914-1997
 Obituary **1997**:3
Hughes, Robert 1938- **1996**:4
Hughes, Ted 1930-1998
 Obituary **1999**:2
Humphries, Barry 1934- **1993**:1
Humphry, Derek 1931(?)- **1992**:2
Hunter, Evan 1926-2005
 Obituary **2006**:4
Hwang, David Henry 1957- **1999**:1
Hybels, Bill 1951- **2011**:1
Ice-T **1992**:3
Irving, John 1942- **2006**:2
Ivins, Molly 1942(?)- **1993**:4
Jablonski, Nina G. 1953- **2009**:3
Jacques, Brian 1939- **2002**:2
Jay, Ricky 1949(?)- **1995**:1
Jelinek, Elfriede 1946- **2005**:3
Jen, Gish 1955- **2000**:1
Jenkins, Sally 1960(?)- **1997**:2
Jennings, Peter Charles 1938- **1997**:2
Jewel 1974- **1999**:2
Jin, Ha 1956- **2011**:3
Johnson, Beverly 1952- **2005**:2
Johnson, Diane 1934- **2004**:3
Jones, Edward P. 1950- **2005**:1
Jones, Gayl 1949- **1999**:4
Jones, Jenny 1946- **1998**:2
Jong, Erica 1942- **1998**:3
Jordan, Neil 1950(?)- **1993**:3
Joyce, William 1957- **2006**:1
Julavits, Heidi 1968- **2007**:4
July, Miranda 1974- **2008**:2
Jurgensen, Karen 1949(?)- **2004**:3
Kael, Pauline 1919-2001 **2000**:4
 Obituary **2002**:4
Kahane, Meir 1932-1990
 Obituary **1991**:2
Karr, Mary 1955- **2011**:2
Kasparov, Garry 1963- **1997**:4
Kazan, Elia 1909-2003
 Obituary **2004**:4
Keillor, Garrison 1942- **2011**:2
Kellerman, Jonathan 1949- **2009**:1
Kennedy, John F., Jr. 1960-1999 **1990**:1
 Obituary **1999**:4
Kent, Arthur 1954- **1991**:4
Kerr, Jean 1922-2003
 Obituary **2004**:1
Kerr, Walter 1913-1996
 Obituary **1997**:1
Kesey, Ken 1935-2001
 Obituary **2003**:1
Keyes, Marian 1963- **2006**:2
Kieslowski, Krzysztof 1941-1996
 Obituary **1996**:3
Kim Barnouin and Rory Freedman 1971- **2009**:4
King, Alan 1927-2004
 Obituary **2005**:3
King, Coretta Scott 1927- **1999**:3
King, Larry 1933- **1993**:1
King, Stephen 1947- **1998**:1

Kingsolver, Barbara 1955- **2005**:1
Kinney, Jeff 1971- **2009**:3
Kinsella, Sophie 1969- **2005**:2
Kirk, David 1956(?)- **2004**:1
Klass, Perri 1958- **1993**:2
Kleinpaste, Ruud 1952- **2006**:2
Knowles, John 1926-2001
    Obituary **2003**:1
Koontz, Dean 1945- **1999**:3
Kordich, Jay 1923- **1993**:2
Kosinski, Jerzy 1933-1991
    Obituary **1991**:4
Kostova, Elizabeth 1964- **2006**:2
Kozol, Jonathan 1936- **1992**:1
Kramer, Larry 1935- **1991**:2
Krantz, Judith 1928- **2003**:1
Kunitz, Stanley J. 1905- **2001**:2
Lahiri, Jhumpa 1967- **2001**:3
Laird, Nick 1975- **2010**:4
Lalami, Laila **2007**:1
Lamb, Wally 1950- **1999**:1
L'Amour, Louis 1908-1988
    Obituary **1988**:4
Lancaster, Jen 1967- **2010**:2
Landers, Ann 1918-2002
    Obituary **2003**:3
Landsbergis, Vytautas 1932- **1991**:3
Lansens, Lori 1962- **2011**:3
Larbalestier, Justine 1968(?)- **2008**:4
Lawson, Nigella 1960- **2003**:2
Leach, Penelope 1937- **1992**:4
le Carre, John 1931- **2000**:1
Lee, Chang-Rae 1965- **2005**:1
Lee, Sandra 1966- **2008**:3
Lehane, Dennis 1965- **2001**:4
Lelyveld, Joseph S. 1937- **1994**:4
L'Engle, Madeleine 1918-2007
    Obituary **2008**:4
Leonard, Elmore 1925- **1998**:4
Lerner, Michael 1943- **1994**:2
Lessing, Doris 1919- **2008**:4
Levin, Ira 1929-2007
    Obituary **2009**:1
Levy, Eugene 1946- **2004**:3
Lewis, Edward T. 1940- **1999**:4
Lindbergh, Anne Morrow 1906-2001
    Obituary **2001**:4
Lindgren, Astrid 1907-2002
    Obituary **2003**:1
Lindsay-Abaire, David 1970(?)- **2008**
    :2
Lippman, Laura 1959- **2010**:2
Lisick, Beth 1969(?)- **2006**:2
Little, Benilde 1959(?)- **2006**:2
Litzenburger, Liesel 1967(?)- **2008**:1
Lively, Penelope 1933- **2007**:4
Logan, Joshua 1908-1988
    Obituary **1988**:4
Lord, Bette Bao 1938- **1994**:1
Louv, Richard 1949- **2006**:2
Ludlum, Robert 1927-2001
    Obituary **2002**:1
Lupino, Ida 1918(?)-1995
    Obituary **1996**:1
Madden, Chris 1948- **2006**:1
Maddow, Rachel 1973- **2010**:2
Mahfouz, Naguib 1911-2006
    Obituary **2007**:4
Mailer, Norman 1923- **1998**:1
Mamet, David 1947- **1998**:4
Mantel, Hilary 1952- **2011**:2

Marchetto, Marisa Acocella 1962(?)-
    2007:3
Martin, Judith 1938- **2000**:3
Mayes, Frances 1940(?)- **2004**:3
Maynard, Joyce 1953- **1999**:4
McCall, Nathan 1955- **1994**:4
McCall Smith, Alexander 1948- **2005**
    :2
McCarthy, Cormac 1933- **2008**:1
McCourt, Frank 1930- **1997**:4
McDermott, Alice 1953- **1999**:2
McDonell, Nick 1984- **2011**:2
McDonnell, Patrick 1956- **2009**:4
McEwan, Ian 1948- **2004**:2
McGahern, John 1934-2006
    Obituary **2007**:2
McGraw, Phil 1950- **2005**:2
McKenna, Terence **1993**:3
McMillan, Terry 1951- **1993**:2
McMurtry, Larry 1936- **2006**:4
McNamara, Robert S. 1916- **1995**:4
Melendez, Bill 1916-2008
    Obituary **2009**:4
Meltzer, Brad 1970- **2005**:4
Menchu, Rigoberta 1960(?)- **1993**:2
Menninger, Karl 1893-1990
    Obituary **1991**:1
Merrill, James 1926-1995
    Obituary **1995**:3
Meyer, Stephenie 1973- **2009**:1
Michener, James A. 1907-1997
    Obituary **1998**:1
Millan, Cesar 1969- **2007**:4
Miller, Arthur 1915- **1999**:4
Miller, Frank 1957- **2008**:2
Miller, Sue 1943- **1999**:3
Milne, Christopher Robin 1920-1996
    Obituary **1996**:4
Milosz, Czeslaw 1911-2004
    Obituary **2005**:4
Mina, Denise 1966- **2006**:1
Mitchard, Jacquelyn 1956- **2010**:4
Mo'Nique 1967- **2008**:1
Montagu, Ashley 1905-1999
    Obituary **2000**:2
Moody, Rick 1961- **2002**:2
Moore, Michael 1954(?)- **1990**:3
Morgan, Robin 1941- **1991**:1
Morris, Henry M. 1918-2006
    Obituary **2007**:2
Morrison, Toni 1931- **1998**:1
Mortensen, Viggo 1958- **2003**:3
Mortenson, Greg 1957- **2011**:1
Mosley, Walter 1952- **2003**:4
Moyers, Bill 1934- **1991**:4
Munro, Alice 1931- **1997**:1
Murakami, Haruki 1949- **2008**:3
Murdoch, Iris 1919-1999
    Obituary **1999**:4
Murkoff, Heidi 1958- **2009**:3
Narayan, R.K. 1906-2001
    Obituary **2002**:2
Nasrin, Taslima 1962- **1995**:1
Nelson, Jack 1929-2009
    Obituary **2011**:2
Nemerov, Howard 1920-1991
    Obituary **1992**:1
Newkirk, Ingrid 1949- **1992**:3
Niezabitowska, Malgorzata 1949(?)-
    1991:3
Nissel, Angela 1974- **2006**:4
Noonan, Peggy 1950- **1990**:3

Northrop, Peggy 1954- **2009**:2
Norton, Andre 1912-2005
    Obituary **2006**:2
Nottage, Lynn 1964- **2010**:1
Novak, Robert 1931-2009
    Obituary **2010**:4
Oates, Joyce Carol 1938- **2000**:1
Obama, Barack 1961- **2007**:4
O'Brien, Conan 1963(?)- **1994**:1
Oe, Kenzaburo 1935- **1997**:1
Onassis, Jacqueline Kennedy
    1929-1994
    Obituary **1994**:4
Ondaatje, Philip Michael 1943- **1997**
    :3
Ornish, Dean 1953- **2004**:2
Osborne, John 1929-1994
    Obituary **1995**:2
Osteen, Joel 1963- **2006**:2
Owens, Delia and Mark **1993**:3
Oz, Mehmet 1960- **2007**:2
Pagels, Elaine 1943- **1997**:1
Paglia, Camille 1947- **1992**:3
Palahniuk, Chuck 1962- **2004**:1
Pamuk, Orhan 1952- **2007**:3
Paretsky, Sara 1947- **2002**:4
Parker, Brant 1920-2007
    Obituary **2008**:2
Parks, Suzan-Lori 1964- **2003**:2
Patchett, Ann 1963- **2003**:2
Patterson, Richard North 1947- **2001**
    :4
Paz, Octavio 1914- **1991**:2
Penny, Louise 1958- **2011**:1
Percy, Walker 1916-1990
    Obituary **1990**:4
Peters, Tom 1942- **1998**:1
Phillips, Julia 1944- **1992**:1
Picoult, Jodi 1966- **2008**:1
Pilkey, Dav 1966- **2001**:1
Pipher, Mary 1948(?)- **1996**:4
Plimpton, George 1927-2003
    Obituary **2004**:4
Politkovskaya, Anna 1958-2006
    Obituary **2007**:4
Pollan, Michael 1955- **2011**:3
Porter, Sylvia 1913-1991
    Obituary **1991**:4
Post, Peggy 1940(?)- **2001**:4
Potok, Chaim 1929-2002
    Obituary **2003**:4
Pouillon, Nora 1943- **2005**:1
Powter, Susan 1957(?)- **1994**:3
Pratt, Jane 1963(?)- **1999**:1
Proulx, E. Annie 1935- **1996**:1
Pullman, Philip 1946- **2003**:2
Pynchon, Thomas 1937- **1997**:4
Quindlen, Anna 1952- **1993**:1
Quinn, Jane Bryant 1939(?)- **1993**:4
Ramsay, Gordon 1966- **2008**:2
Rankin, Ian 1960- **2010**:3
Redfield, James 1952- **1995**:2
Reichs, Kathleen J. 1948- **2007**:3
Rendell, Ruth 1930- **2007**:2
Rey, Margret E. 1906-1996
    Obituary **1997**:2
Reza, Yasmina 1959(?)- **1999**:2
Rhone, Trevor 1940-2009
    Obituary **2011**:1
Rice, Anne 1941- **1995**:1
Ringgold, Faith 1930- **2000**:3
Robbins, Harold 1916-1997

2011 Subject Index

This index lists all newsmakers by subjects, company names, products, organizations, issues, awards, and professional specialties. Indexes in softbound issues allow access to the current year's entries; indexes in annual hardbound volumes are cumulative, covering the entire *Newsmakers* series.

Listee names are followed by a year and issue number; thus **1996**:3 indicates that an entry on that individual appears in both 1996, Issue 3, and the 1996 cumulation. For access to newsmakers appearing earlier than the current softbound issue, see the previous year's cumulation.

ABC Television
Arledge, Roone 1931- **1992**:2
Diller, Barry 1942- **1991**:1
Funt, Allen 1914-1999
　Obituary **2000**:1
Philbin, Regis 1933- **2000**:2
Pierce, Frederick S. 1934(?)- **1985**:3

Abortion
Allred, Gloria 1941- **1985**:2
Baird, Bill
　Brief entry **1987**:2
Baulieu, Etienne-Emile 1926- **1990**:1
Brown, Judie 1944- **1986**:2
Falkenberg, Nanette 1951- **1985**:2
Kissling, Frances 1943- **1989**:2
Morgentaler, Henry 1923- **1986**:3
Terry, Randall **1991**:4
Wattleton, Faye 1943- **1989**:1
Yard, Molly **1991**:4

Abscam
Neal, James Foster 1929- **1986**:2
Puccio, Thomas P. 1944- **1986**:4

Academy Awards
Affleck, Ben 1972- **1999**:1
Allen, Woody 1935- **1994**:1
Almodovar, Pedro 1951- **2000**:3
Ameche, Don 1908-1993
　Obituary **1994**:2
Andrews, Julie 1935- **1996**:1
Arkin, Alan 1934- **2007**:4
Arlen, Harold 1905-1986
　Obituary **1986**:3
Arthur, Jean 1901(?)-1991
　Obituary **1992**:1
Ashcroft, Peggy 1907-1991
　Obituary **1992**:1
Astor, Mary 1906-1987
　Obituary **1988**:1
Ball, Alan 1957- **2005**:1
Bancroft, Anne 1931-2005
　Obituary **2006**:3
Barbera, Joseph 1911- **1988**:2
Bardem, Javier 1969- **2008**:4

Baryshnikov, Mikhail Nikolaevich 1948- **1997**:3
Bates, Kathy 1949(?)- **1991**:4
Baxter, Anne 1923-1985
　Obituary **1986**:1
Beatty, Warren 1937- **2000**:1
Benigni, Roberto 1952- **1999**:2
Bergman, Ingmar 1918- **1999**:4
Berlin, Irving 1888-1989
　Obituary **1990**:1
Bernstein, Elmer 1922-2004
　Obituary **2005**:4
Bigelow, Kathryn 1951- **2011**:1
Binoche, Juliette 1965- **2001**:3
Bird, Brad 1956(?)- **2005**:4
Booth, Shirley 1898-1992
　Obituary **1993**:2
Boyle, Danny 1956- **2009**:4
Brando, Marlon 1924-2004
　Obituary **2005**:3
Bridges, Jeff 1949- **2011**:1
Broadbent, Jim 1949- **2008**:4
Brody, Adrien 1973- **2006**:3
Brooks, Mel 1926- **2003**:1
Brynner, Yul 1920(?)-1985
　Obituary **1985**:4
Burstyn, Ellen 1932- **2001**:4
Buttons, Red 1919-2006
　Obituary **2007**:3
Cagney, James 1899-1986
　Obituary **1986**:2
Caine, Michael 1933- **2000**:4
Capra, Frank 1897-1991
　Obituary **1992**:2
Carney, Art 1918-2003
　Obituary **2005**:1
Cassavetes, John 1929-1989
　Obituary **1989**:2
Cher 1946- **1993**:1
Christie, Julie 1941- **2008**:4
Coburn, James 1928-2002
　Obituary **2004**:1
Condon, Bill 1955- **2007**:3
Connelly, Jennifer 1970- **2002**:4
Connery, Sean 1930- **1990**:4
Cooper, Chris 1951- **2004**:1
Copland, Aaron 1900-1990

Obituary **1991**:2
Coppola, Carmine 1910-1991
　Obituary **1991**:4
Coppola, Francis Ford 1939- **1989**:4
Coppola, Sofia 1971- **2004**:3
Crawford, Broderick 1911-1986
　Obituary **1986**:3
Damon, Matt 1970- **1999**:1
Davis, Bette 1908-1989
　Obituary **1990**:1
Davis, Geena 1957- **1992**:1
Del Toro, Benicio 1967- **2001**:4
Demme, Jonathan 1944- **1992**:4
Dench, Judi 1934- **1999**:4
De Niro, Robert 1943- **1999**:1
Dennis, Sandy 1937-1992
　Obituary **1992**:4
Diamond, I.A.L. 1920-1988
　Obituary **1988**:3
Douglas, Michael 1944- **1986**:2
Duvall, Robert 1931- **1999**:3
Eastwood, Clint 1930- **1993**:3
Elliott, Denholm 1922-1992
　Obituary **1993**:2
Fellini, Federico 1920-1993
　Obituary **1994**:2
Ferrer, Jose 1912-1992
　Obituary **1992**:3
Field, Sally 1946- **1995**:3
Foote, Horton 1916-2009
　Obituary **2010**:2
Fosse, Bob 1927-1987
　Obituary **1988**:1
Gielgud, John 1904-2000
　Obituary **2000**:4
Gish, Lillian 1893-1993
　Obituary **1993**:4
Goldberg, Whoopi 1955- **1993**:3
Goldman, William 1931- **2001**:1
Gooding, Cuba, Jr. 1968- **1997**:3
Gossett, Louis, Jr. 1936- **1989**:3
Grant, Cary 1904-1986
　Obituary **1987**:1
Grazer, Brian 1951- **2006**:4
Guggenheim, Charles 1924-2002
　Obituary **2003**:4
Hackman, Gene 1931- **1989**:3

Haggis, Paul 1953- **2006**:4
Hanks, Tom 1956- **1989**:2
Harden, Marcia Gay 1959- **2002**:4
Hawn, Goldie Jeanne 1945- **1997**:2
Hayes, Helen 1900-1993
    Obituary **1993**:4
Hayes, Isaac 1942- **1998**:4
Hepburn, Audrey 1929-1993
    Obituary **1993**:2
Hepburn, Katharine 1909- **1991**:2
Heston, Charlton 1924- **1999**:4
Hill, George Roy 1921-2002
    Obituary **2004**:1
Hoffman, Dustin 1937- **2005**:4
Hoffman, Philip Seymour 1967-
    2006:3
Hope, Bob 1903-2003
    Obituary **2004**:4
Hopkins, Anthony 1937- **1992**:4
Houseman, John 1902-1988
    Obituary **1989**:1
Hudson, Jennifer 1981- **2008**:1
Hurt, William 1950- **1986**:1
Huston, Anjelica 1952(?)- **1989**:3
Huston, John 1906-1987
    Obituary **1988**:1
Hutton, Timothy 1960- **1986**:3
Irons, Jeremy 1948- **1991**:4
Irving, John 1942- **2006**:2
Ives, Burl 1909-1995
    Obituary **1995**:4
Jackson, Peter 1961- **2004**:4
Jarre, Maurice 1924-2009
    Obituary **2010**:2
Jones, Chuck 1912- **2001**:2
Jones, Jennifer 1919-2009
    Obituary **2011**:4
Jones, Tommy Lee 1947(?)- **1994**:2
Jordan, Neil 1950(?)- **1993**:3
Kaye, Danny 1913-1987
    Obituary **1987**:2
Kazan, Elia 1909-2003
    Obituary **2004**:4
Keaton, Diane 1946- **1997**:1
Kline, Kevin 1947- **2000**:1
Kubrick, Stanley 1928-1999
    Obituary **1999**:3
Kurosawa, Akira 1910-1998 **1991**:1
    Obituary **1999**:1
Lange, Jessica 1949- **1995**:4
Lardner Jr., Ring 1915-2000
    Obituary **2001**:2
Lasseter, John 1957- **2007**:2
Lemmon, Jack 1925- **1998**:4
    Obituary **2002**:3
Levinson, Barry 1932- **1989**:3
Lithgow, John 1945- **1985**:2
Loy, Myrna 1905-1993
    Obituary **1994**:2
Lucas, George 1944- **1999**:4
Malden, Karl 1912-2009
    Obituary **2010**:4
Malle, Louis 1932-1995
    Obituary **1996**:2
Mancini, Henry 1924-1994
    Obituary **1994**:4
Marvin, Lee 1924-1987
    Obituary **1988**:1
Matlin, Marlee 1965- **1992**:2
Matthau, Walter 1920- **2000**:3
McCartney, Paul 1942- **2002**:4
McDonagh, Martin 1970- **2007**:3

McDormand, Frances 1957- **1997**:3
McDowall, Roddy 1928-1998
    Obituary **1999**:1
McLaren, Norman 1914-1987
    Obituary **1987**:2
McMurtry, Larry 1936- **2006**:4
Milland, Ray 1908(?)-1986
    Obituary **1986**:2
Minghella, Anthony 1954- **2004**:3
Miyazaki, Hayao 1941- **2006**:2
Newman, Paul 1925- **1995**:3
Nichols, Mike 1931- **1994**:4
Nicholson, Jack 1937- **1989**:2
North, Alex 1910- **1986**:3
Pacino, Al 1940- **1993**:4
Page, Geraldine 1924-1987
    Obituary **1987**:4
Pakula, Alan 1928-1998
    Obituary **1999**:2
Palance, Jack 1919-2006
    Obituary **2008**:1
Paquin, Anna 1982- **2009**:4
Park, Nick 1958- **1997**:3
Payne, Alexander 1961- **2005**:4
Peck, Gregory 1916-2003
    Obituary **2004**:3
Pesci, Joe 1943- **1992**:4
Phillips, Julia 1944- **1992**:1
Poitier, Sidney 1927- **1990**:3
Pollack, Sydney 1934-2008
    Obituary **2009**:2
Prince 1958- **1995**:3
Puzo, Mario 1920-1999
    Obituary **2000**:1
Quinn, Anthony 1915-2001
    Obituary **2002**:2
Redford, Robert 1937- **1993**:2
Redgrave, Vanessa 1937- **1989**:2
Reed, Donna 1921-1986
    Obituary **1986**:1
Riddle, Nelson 1921-1985
    Obituary **1985**:4
Robards, Jason 1922-2000
    Obituary **2001**:3
Robbins, Jerome 1918-1998
    Obituary **1999**:1
Rogers, Ginger 1911(?)-1995
    Obituary **1995**:4
Rollins, Howard E., Jr. 1950- **1986**:1
Ruehl, Mercedes 1948(?)- **1992**:4
Rush, Geoffrey 1951- **2002**:1
Sainte-Marie, Buffy 1941- **2000**:1
Schlesinger, John 1926-2003
    Obituary **2004**:3
Schulberg, Budd 1914-2009
    Obituary **2010**:4
Scott, George C. 1927-1999
    Obituary **2000**:2
Shanley, John Patrick 1950- **2006**:1
Sheldon, Sidney 1917-2007
    Obituary **2008**:2
Sinatra, Frank 1915-1998
    Obituary **1998**:4
Soderbergh, Steven 1963- **2001**:4
Sorvino, Mira 1970(?)- **1996**:3
Spacek, Sissy 1949- **2003**:1
Spacey, Kevin 1959- **1996**:4
Springsteen, Bruce 1949- **2011**:1
Stallone, Sylvester 1946- **1994**:2
Stapleton, Maureen 1925-2006
    Obituary **2007**:2
Steiger, Rod 1925-2002

    Obituary **2003**:4
Streep, Meryl 1949- **1990**:2
Streisand, Barbra 1942- **1992**:2
Styne, Jule 1905-1994
    Obituary **1995**:1
Swank, Hilary 1974- **2000**:3
Swinton, Tilda 1960- **2008**:4
Tan Dun 1957- **2002**:1
Tandy, Jessica 1901-1994 **1990**:4
    Obituary **1995**:1
Taylor, Elizabeth 1932- **1993**:3
Thompson, Emma 1959- **1993**:2
Tomei, Marisa 1964- **1995**:2
Trudeau, Garry 1948- **1991**:2
Umeki, Miyoshi 1929-2007
    Obituary **2008**:4
Ustinov, Peter 1921-2004
    Obituary **2005**:3
Vinton, Will
    Brief entry **1988**:1
Voight, Jon 1938- **2002**:3
Wallis, Hal 1898(?)-1986
    Obituary **1987**:1
Waltz, Christoph 1956- **2011**:1
Washington, Denzel 1954- **1993**:2
Weisz, Rachel 1971- **2006**:4
Wiest, Dianne 1948- **1995**:2
Wilder, Billy 1906-2002
    Obituary **2003**:2
Winters, Shelley 1920-2006
    Obituary **2007**:1
Wise, Robert 1914-2005
    Obituary **2006**:4
Wyman, Jane 1917-2007
    Obituary **2008**:4
Zanuck, Lili Fini 1954- **1994**:2
Zemeckis, Robert 1952- **2002**:1

Acoustics
    Kloss, Henry E.
        Brief entry **1985**:2

**Acquired Immune Deficiency Syndrome
[AIDS]**
    Ashe, Arthur 1943-1993
        Obituary **1993**:3
    Bennett, Michael 1943-1987
        Obituary **1988**:1
    Bergalis, Kimberly 1968(?)-1991
        Obituary **1992**:3
    Berkley, Seth 1956- **2002**:3
    Dolan, Terry 1950-1986 **1985**:2
    Eazy-E 1963(?)-1995
        Obituary **1995**:3
    Fisher, Mary 1948- **1994**:3
    Gallo, Robert 1937- **1991**:1
    Gebbie, Kristine 1944(?)- **1994**:2
    Gertz, Alison 1966(?)-1992
        Obituary **1993**:2
    Glaser, Elizabeth 1947-1994
        Obituary **1995**:2
    Halston 1932-1990
        Obituary **1990**:3
    Haring, Keith 1958-1990
        Obituary **1990**:3
    Ho, David 1952- **1997**:2
    Holmes, John C. 1945-1988
        Obituary **1988**:3
    Hudson, Rock 1925-1985
        Obituary **1985**:4
    Kramer, Larry 1935- **1991**:2
    Krim, Mathilde 1926- **1989**:2

Obituary **2000**:1
Dzhanibekov, Vladimir 1942- **1988**:1
Garneau, Marc 1949- **1985**:1
Glenn, John 1921- **1998**:3
Lucid, Shannon 1943- **1997**:1
McAuliffe, Christa 1948-1986
Obituary **1985**:4
Whitson, Peggy 1960- **2003**:3

Astronomy
Bahcall, John N. 1934-2005
Obituary **2006**:4
Bopp, Thomas 1949- **1997**:3
Geller, Margaret Joan 1947- **1998**:2
Hale, Alan 1957- **1997**:3
Hawking, Stephen W. 1942- **1990**:1
Hoyle, Sir Fred 1915-2001
Obituary **2002**:4
Marsden, Brian 1937- **2004**:4
Smoot, George F. 1945- **1993**:3

AT&T
Allen, Bob 1935- **1992**:4
Armstrong, C. Michael 1938- **2002**:1

Atari
Bushnell, Nolan 1943- **1985**:1
Kingsborough, Donald
Brief entry **1986**:2
Perlman, Steve 1961(?)- **1998**:2

Atlanta Braves baseball team
Lofton, Kenny 1967- **1998**:1
Maddux, Greg 1966- **1996**:2
Sanders, Deion 1967- **1992**:4
Smoltz, John 1967- **2010**:3
Spahn, Warren 1921-2003
Obituary **2005**:1
Turner, Ted 1938- **1989**:1

Atlanta Falcons football team
Sanders, Deion 1967- **1992**:4

Atlanta Hawks basketball team
Maravich, Pete 1948-1988
Obituary **1988**:2
McMillen, Tom 1952- **1988**:4
Turner, Ted 1938- **1989**:1
Wilkens, Lenny 1937- **1995**:2

Atlantic Records
Ertegun, Ahmet 1923- **1986**:3
Greenwald, Julie 1970- **2008**:1

Automobile racing
Allgaier, Justin 1986- **2011**:3
Busch, Kurt 1978- **2006**:1
Busch, Kyle 1985- **2011**:4
Castroneves, Helio 1975- **2010**:1
Earnhardt, Dale, Jr. 1974- **2004**:4
Ferrari, Enzo 1898-1988 **1988**:4
Fittipaldi, Emerson 1946- **1994**:2
Franchitti, Dario 1973- **2008**:1
Gordon, Jeff 1971- **1996**:1
Johnson, Jimmie 1975- **2007**:2
Muldowney, Shirley 1940- **1986**:1
Munter, Leilani 1976- **2010**:4
Newman, Paul 1925- **1995**:3
Newman, Ryan 1977- **2005**:1
Penske, Roger 1937- **1988**:3

Porsche, Ferdinand 1909-1998
Obituary **1998**:4
Prost, Alain 1955- **1988**:1
Schumacher, Michael 1969- **2005**:2
Senna, Ayrton 1960(?)-1994 **1991**:4
Obituary **1994**:4
St. James, Lyn 1947- **1993**:2
Villeneuve, Jacques 1971- **1997**:1
Zanardi, Alex 1966- **1998**:2

Aviation
Burr, Donald Calvin 1941- **1985**:3
Dubrof, Jessica 1989-1996
Obituary **1996**:4
Fossett, Steve 1944- **2007**:2
Lindbergh, Anne Morrow 1906-2001
Obituary **2001**:4
MacCready, Paul 1925- **1986**:4
Martin, Dean Paul 1952(?)-1987
Obituary **1987**:3
Moody, John 1943- **1985**:3
Rutan, Burt 1943- **1987**:2
Schiavo, Mary 1955- **1998**:2
Wolf, Stephen M. 1941- **1989**:3
Yeager, Chuck 1923- **1998**:1

Avis Rent A Car
Rand, A. Barry 1944- **2000**:3

Avon Products, Inc.
Gold, Christina A. 1947- **2008**:1
Jung, Andrea 2000:2
Waldron, Hicks B. 1923- **1987**:3

Bad Boy Records
Combs, Sean Puffy 1970- **1998**:4

Ballet West
Lander, Toni 1931-1985
Obituary **1985**:4

Ballooning
Aoki, Rocky 1940- **1990**:2

Baltimore, Md., city government
Schaefer, William Donald 1921- **1988**:1

Baltimore Orioles baseball team
Angelos, Peter 1930- **1995**:4
Palmeiro, Rafael 1964- **2005**:1
Palmer, Jim 1945- **1991**:2
Ripken, Cal, Jr. 1960- **1986**:2
Ripken, Cal, Sr. 1936(?)-1999
Obituary **1999**:4
Robinson, Frank 1935- **1990**:2
Williams, Edward Bennett 1920-1988
Obituary **1988**:4

Band Aid
Geldof, Bob 1954(?)- **1985**:3

Bard College
Botstein, Leon 1946- **1985**:3

Barnes & Noble, Inc.
Riggio, Leonard S. 1941- **1999**:4

Baseball
Abbott, Jim 1967- **1988**:3
Ainge, Danny 1959- **1987**:1
Barber, Red 1908-1992

Obituary **1993**:2
Boggs, Wade 1958- **1989**:3
Bonds, Barry 1964- **1993**:3
Campanella, Roy 1921-1993
Obituary **1994**:1
Canseco, Jose 1964- **1990**:2
Caray, Harry 1914(?)-1998 **1988**:3
Obituary **1998**:3
Carter, Gary 1954- **1987**:1
Carter, Joe 1960- **1994**:2
Chamberlain, Joba 1985- **2008**:3
Clemens, Roger 1962- **1991**:4
Damon, Johnny 1973- **2005**:4
Davis, Eric 1962- **1987**:4
DiMaggio, Dom 1917-2009
Obituary **2010**:2
DiMaggio, Joe 1914-1999
Obituary **1999**:3
Doubleday, Nelson, Jr. 1933- **1987**:1
Dravecky, Dave 1956- **1992**:1
Drysdale, Don 1936-1993
Obituary **1994**:1
Durocher, Leo 1905-1991
Obituary **1992**:2
Dykstra, Lenny 1963- **1993**:4
Edwards, Harry 1942- **1989**:4
Fehr, Donald 1948- **1987**:2
Fidrych, Mark 1954-2009
Obituary **2010**:2
Fielder, Cecil 1963- **1993**:2
Giamatti, A. Bartlett 1938-1989 **1988**:4
Obituary **1990**:1
Gibson, Kirk 1957- **1985**:2
Glaus, Troy 1976- **2003**:3
Gomez, Lefty 1909-1989
Obituary **1989**:3
Gooden, Dwight 1964- **1985**:2
Greenberg, Hank 1911-1986
Obituary **1986**:4
Griffey, Ken Jr. 1969- **1994**:1
Gwynn, Tony 1960- **1995**:1
Hamels, Cole 1983- **2009**:4
Helton, Todd 1973- **2001**:1
Henrich, Tommy 1913-2009
Obituary **2011**:4
Hernandez, Felix 1986- **2008**:2
Hernandez, Willie 1954- **1985**:1
Howser, Dick 1936-1987
Obituary **1987**:4
Hunter, Catfish 1946-1999
Obituary **2000**:1
Jackson, Bo 1962- **1986**:3
Johnson, Randy 1963- **1996**:2
Kroc, Ray 1902-1984
Obituary **1985**:1
Kruk, John 1961- **1994**:4
Leyland, Jim 1944- **1998**:2
Lofton, Kenny 1967- **1998**:1
Lowell, Mike 1974- **2003**:2
Maddux, Greg 1966- **1996**:2
Mantle, Mickey 1931-1995
Obituary **1996**:1
Maris, Roger 1934-1985
Obituary **1986**:1
Martin, Billy 1928-1989 **1988**:4
Obituary **1990**:2
Matsui, Hideki 1974- **2007**:4
Mattingly, Don 1961- **1986**:2
McGraw, Tug 1944-2004
Obituary **2005**:1
McGwire, Mark 1963- **1999**:1

Monaghan, Tom 1937- **1985**:1
Moreno, Arturo 1946- **2005**:2
Nomo, Hideo 1968- **1996**:2
O'Neil, Buck 1911-2006
  Obituary **2007**:4
Palmeiro, Rafael 1964- **2005**:1
Palmer, Jim 1945- **1991**:2
Piazza, Mike 1968- **1998**:4
Puckett, Kirby 1960-2006
  Obituary **2007**:2
Pujols, Albert 1980- **2005**:3
Ramirez, Manny 1972- **2005**:4
Rhodes, Dusty 1927-2009
  Obituary **2010**:3
Ripken, Cal, Jr. 1960- **1986**:2
Robinson, Frank 1935- **1990**:2
Rose, Pete 1941- **1991**:1
Ryan, Nolan 1947- **1989**:4
Saberhagen, Bret 1964- **1986**:1
Sanders, Deion 1967- **1992**:4
Santana, Johan 1979- **2008**:1
Schembechler, Bo 1929(?)- **1990**:3
Schilling, Curt 1966- **2002**:3
Schmidt, Mike 1949- **1988**:3
Schott, Marge 1928- **1985**:4
Selig, Bud 1934- **1995**:2
Sheffield, Gary 1968- **1998**:1
Smoltz, John 1967- **2010**:3
Soriano, Alfonso 1976- **2008**:1
Sosa, Sammy 1968- **1999**:1
Spahn, Warren 1921-2003
  Obituary **2005**:1
Steinbrenner, George 1930- **1991**:1
Stewart, Dave 1957- **1991**:1
Thomas, Frank 1968- **1994**:3
Utley, Chase 1978- **2010**:4
Van Slyke, Andy 1960- **1992**:4
Vaughn, Mo 1967- **1999**:2
Veeck, Bill 1914-1986
  Obituary **1986**:1
Vincent, Fay 1938- **1990**:2
Welch, Bob 1956- **1991**:3
Wells, David 1963- **1999**:3
White, Bill 1934- **1989**:3
Williams, Ted 1918-2002
  Obituary **2003**:4
Zito, Barry 1978- **2003**:3

Basketball
Ainge, Danny 1959- **1987**:1
Allen, Ray 1975- **2002**:1
Andersen, Chris 1978- **2010**:2
Artest, Ron 1979- **2011**:1
Auerbach, Red 1911-2006
  Obituary **2008**:1
Barkley, Charles 1963- **1988**:2
Bias, Len 1964(?)-1986
  Obituary **1986**:3
Bird, Larry 1956- **1990**:3
Carter, Vince 1977- **2001**:4
Chaney, John 1932- **1989**:1
Cooper, Cynthia **1999**:1
Daly, Chuck 1930-2009
  Obituary **2010**:3
Drexler, Clyde 1962- **1992**:4
Ewing, Patrick 1962- **1985**:3
Gathers, Hank 1967(?)-1990
  Obituary **1990**:3
Hardaway, Anfernee 1971- **1996**:2
Howard, Dwight 1985- **2010**:1
Jackson, Phil 1945- **1996**:3
James, LeBron 1984- **2007**:3
Johnson, Earvin Magic 1959- **1988**:4

Johnson, Kevin 1966(?)- **1991**:1
Johnson, Larry 1969- **1993**:3
Jordan, Michael 1963- **1987**:2
Kemp, Shawn 1969- **1995**:1
Kidd, Jason 1973- **2003**:2
Knight, Bobby 1940- **1985**:3
Krzyzewski, Mike 1947- **1993**:2
Kukoc, Toni 1968- **1995**:4
Laettner, Christian 1969- **1993**:1
Laimbeer, Bill 1957- **2004**:3
Leslie, Lisa 1972- **1997**:4
Lewis, Reggie 1966(?)-1993
  Obituary **1994**:1
Majerle, Dan 1965- **1993**:4
Malone, Karl 1963- **1990**:1
Maravich, Pete 1948-1988
  Obituary **1988**:2
McMillen, Tom 1952- **1988**:4
Mikan, George 1924-2005
  Obituary **2006**:3
Miller, Andre 1976- **2003**:3
Miller, Reggie 1965- **1994**:4
Mourning, Alonzo 1970- **1994**:2
Mulkey-Robertson, Kim 1962- **2006**:1
Nowitzki, Dirk 1978- **2007**:2
Olajuwon, Akeem 1963- **1985**:1
O'Malley, Susan 1962(?)- **1995**:2
O'Neal, Shaquille 1972- **1992**:1
Palmer, Violet 1964(?)- **2005**:2
Parker, Tony 1982- **2008**:1
Pierce, Paul 1977- **2009**:2
Riley, Pat 1945- **1994**:3
Robinson, David 1965- **1990**:4
Rodman, Dennis 1961- **1991**:3
Stern, David 1942- **1991**:4
Stockton, John Houston 1962- **1997**:3
Summitt, Pat 1952- **2004**:1
Swoopes, Sheryl 1971- **1998**:2
Tarkenian, Jerry 1930- **1990**:4
Thomas, Isiah 1961- **1989**:2
Thompson, John 1941- **1988**:3
Tisdale, Wayman 1964-2009
  Obituary **2010**:3
Vitale, Dick 1939- **1988**:4
Wade, Dwyane 1982- **2007**:1
Wallace, Ben 1974- **2004**:3
Webber, Chris 1973- **1994**:1
Wilkens, Lenny 1937- **1995**:2
Woodard, Lynette 1959(?)- **1986**:2
Worthy, James 1961- **1991**:2
Yao Ming 1980- **2004**:1

Beatrice International
Lewis, Reginald F. 1942-1993 **1988**:4
  Obituary **1993**:3

Benetton Group
Benetton, Luciano 1935- **1988**:1

Benihana of Tokyo, Inc.
Aoki, Rocky 1940- **1990**:2

Berkshire Hathaway, Inc.
Buffett, Warren 1930- **1995**:2

Bethlehem, Jordan, city government
Freij, Elias 1920- **1986**:4

Bicycling
Armstrong, Lance 1971- **2000**:1
Indurain, Miguel 1964- **1994**:1
LeMond, Greg 1961- **1986**:4

Roberts, Steven K. 1952(?)- **1992**:1

Billiards
Minnesota Fats 1900(?)-1996
  Obituary **1996**:3

Bill T. Jones/Arnie Zane & Company
Jones, Bill T. **1991**:4

Biodiversity
Wilson, Edward O. 1929- **1994**:4

Bioethics
Andrews, Lori B. 1952- **2005**:3
Bayley, Corrine
  Brief entry **1986**:4
Caplan, Arthur L. 1950- **2000**:2

Biogen, Inc.
Gilbert, Walter 1932- **1988**:3

Biosphere 2
Allen, John 1930- **1992**:1

Biotechnology
Gilbert, Walter 1932- **1988**:3
Haseltine, William A. 1944- **1999**:2

Birds
Berle, Peter A.A.
  Brief entry **1987**:3
Pough, Richard Hooper 1904- **1989**:1
Redig, Patrick 1948- **1985**:3
Toone, Bill
  Brief entry **1987**:2

Birth control
Baird, Bill
  Brief entry **1987**:2
Baulieu, Etienne-Emile 1926- **1990**:1
Djerassi, Carl 1923- **2000**:4
Falkenberg, Nanette 1951- **1985**:2
Morgentaler, Henry 1923- **1986**:3
Rock, John
  Obituary **1985**:1
Wattleton, Faye 1943- **1989**:1

Black Panther Party
Cleaver, Eldridge 1935-1998
  Obituary **1998**:4
Newton, Huey 1942-1989
  Obituary **1990**:1
Ture, Kwame 1941-1998
  Obituary **1999**:2

Black Sash
Duncan, Sheena
  Brief entry **1987**:1

Blockbuster Video
Huizenga, Wayne 1938(?)- **1992**:1
Keyes, James 1955- **2011**:3

Bloomingdale's
Campeau, Robert 1923- **1990**:1
Traub, Marvin
  Brief entry **1987**:3

Obituary **1998**:1
Totenberg, Nina 1944- **1992**:2
Turner, Ted 1938- **1989**:1
Vitale, Dick 1939- **1988**:4
Walters, Barbara 1931- **1998**:3
Zahn, Paula 1956(?)- **1992**:3
Zucker, Jeff 1965(?)- **1993**:3

Brokerage
Brennan, Robert E. 1943(?)- **1988**:1
Fomon, Robert M. 1925- **1985**:3
Phelan, John Joseph, Jr. 1931- **1985**:4
Schwab, Charles 1937(?)- **1989**:3
Siebert, Muriel 1932(?)- **1987**:2

Brooklyn Dodgers baseball team
Campanella, Roy 1921-1993
Obituary **1994**:1
Drysdale, Don 1936-1993
Obituary **1994**:1

Brown University
Gregorian, Vartan 1934- **1990**:3

Buddhism
Dalai Lama 1935- **1989**:1

Buffalo Bills football team
Flutie, Doug 1962- **1999**:2
Kelly, Jim 1960- **1991**:4
Thomas, Thurman 1966- **1993**:1

Buffalo Sabres
Hasek, Dominik 1965- **1998**:3

Cabbage Patch Kids
Roberts, Xavier 1955- **1985**:3

Cable Ace Awards
Blades, Ruben 1948- **1998**:2
Carey, Drew 1958- **1997**:4
Cuaron, Alfonso 1961- **2008**:2
Fierstein, Harvey 1954- **2004**:2
Graden, Brian 1963- **2004**:2
Maher, Bill 1956- **1996**:2
Olbermann, Keith 1959- **2010**:3
Rock, Chris 1967(?)- **1998**:1

Cable News Network (CNN)
Amanpour, Christiane 1958- **1997**:2
Cooper, Anderson 1967- **2006**:1
Gupta, Sanjay 1969- **2009**:4
Isaacson, Walter 1952- **2003**:2
Novak, Robert 1931-2009
Obituary **2010**:4

Cable television
Albrecht, Chris 1952(?)- **2005**:4
Cox, Richard Joseph
Brief entry **1985**:1
Firestone, Roy 1953- **1988**:2
Hammer, Bonnie 1950- **2011**:4
Harbert, Ted 1955- **2007**:2
Headroom, Max 1985- **1986**:4
Hefner, Christie 1952- **1985**:1
Johnson, Robert L. 1946- **2000**:4
Koplovitz, Kay 1945- **1986**:3
Malone, John C. 1941- **1988**:3
Murdoch, Rupert 1931- **1988**:4

Otte, Ruth 1949- **1992**:4
Pittman, Robert W. 1953- **1985**:1
Quinn, Martha 1959- **1986**:4
Roberts, Brian L. 1959- **2002**:4
Robertson, Pat 1930- **1988**:2
Vitale, Dick 1939- **1988**:4

Caldecott Book Awards
Falconer, Ian 1960(?)- **2003**:1
Pilkey, Dav 1966- **2001**:1
Ringgold, Faith 1930- **2000**:3
Steig, William 1907-2003
Obituary **2004**:4

California Angels baseball team
Abbott, Jim 1967- **1988**:3
Autry, Gene 1907-1998
Obituary **1999**:1
Conigliaro, Tony 1945-1990
Obituary **1990**:3
Ryan, Nolan 1947- **1989**:4

California state government
Brown, Edmund G., Sr. 1905-1996
Obituary **1996**:3
Brown, Jerry 1938- **1992**:4
Brown, Willie L. 1934- **1985**:2
Roybal-Allard, Lucille 1941- **1999**:4
Wilson, Pete 1933- **1992**:3

Camping equipment
Bauer, Eddie 1899-1986
Obituary **1986**:3
Coleman, Sheldon, Jr. 1953- **1990**:2

Canadian Broadcasting Corp. [CBC]
Juneau, Pierre 1922- **1988**:3

Cancer research
DeVita, Vincent T., Jr. 1935- **1987**:3
Folkman, Judah 1933- **1999**:1
Fonyo, Steve
Brief entry **1985**:4
Gale, Robert Peter 1945- **1986**:4
Hammond, E. Cuyler 1912-1986
Obituary **1987**:1
King, Mary-Claire 1946- **1998**:3
Krim, Mathilde 1926- **1989**:2
Love, Susan 1948- **1995**:2
Rosenberg, Steven 1940- **1989**:1
Szent-Gyoergyi, Albert 1893-1986
Obituary **1987**:2
Wigler, Michael
Brief entry **1985**:1

Cannes Film Festival
Brando, Marlon 1924-2004
Obituary **2005**:3
Egoyan, Atom 1960- **2000**:2
Hou Hsiao-hsien 1947- **2000**:2
July, Miranda 1974- **2008**:2
Mirren, Helen 1945- **2005**:1
Nair, Mira 1957- **2007**:4
Smith, Kevin 1970- **2000**:4
Waltz, Christoph 1956- **2011**:1

Carnival Cruise Lines
Arison, Ted 1924- **1990**:3

Car repair
Magliozzi, Tom and Ray **1991**:4

Cartoons
Addams, Charles 1912-1988
Obituary **1989**:1
Barbera, Joseph 1911- **1988**:2
Barry, Lynda 1956(?)- **1992**:1
Bechdel, Alison 1960- **2007**:3
Blanc, Mel 1908-1989
Obituary **1989**:4
Chast, Roz 1955- **1992**:4
Disney, Roy E. 1930- **1986**:3
Freleng, Friz 1906(?)-1995
Obituary **1995**:4
Gaines, William M. 1922-1992
Obituary **1993**:1
Gould, Chester 1900-1985
Obituary **1985**:2
Groening, Matt 1955(?)- **1990**:4
Hart, Johnny 1931-2007
Obituary **2008**:2
Judge, Mike 1963(?)- **1994**:2
Kinney, Jeff 1971- **2009**:3
MacFarlane, Seth 1973- **2006**:1
MacNelly, Jeff 1947-2000
Obituary **2000**:4
Marchetto, Marisa Acocella 1962(?)-
2007:3
Mauldin, Bill 1921-2003
Obituary **2004**:2
McDonnell, Patrick 1956- **2009**:4
Melendez, Bill 1916-2008
Obituary **2009**:4
Messick, Dale 1906-2005
Obituary **2006**:2
Parker, Brant 1920-2007
Obituary **2008**:2
Parker, Trey and Matt Stone **1998**:2
Schulz, Charles 1922-2000
Obituary **2000**:3
Schulz, Charles M. 1922- **1998**:1
Spiegelman, Art 1948- **1998**:3
Tartakovsky, Genndy 1970- **2004**:4
Trudeau, Garry 1948- **1991**:2
Watterson, Bill 1958(?)- **1990**:3

Catholic Church
Beckett, Wendy (Sister) 1930- **1998**:3
Bernardin, Cardinal Joseph
1928-1996 **1997**:2
Burns, Charles R.
Brief entry **1988**:1
Clements, George 1932- **1985**:1
Cunningham, Reverend William
1930-1997
Obituary **1997**:4
Curran, Charles E. 1934- **1989**:2
Daily, Bishop Thomas V. 1927- **1990**
:4
Dearden, John Cardinal 1907-1988
Obituary **1988**:4
Fox, Matthew 1940- **1992**:2
Healy, Timothy S. 1923- **1990**:2
Hume, Basil Cardinal 1923-1999
Obituary **2000**:1
John Paul II, Pope 1920- **1995**:3
Kissling, Frances 1943- **1989**:2
Krol, John 1910-1996
Obituary **1996**:3
Lefebvre, Marcel 1905- **1988**:4
Mahony, Roger M. 1936- **1988**:2
Maida, Adam Cardinal 1930- **1998**:2
Obando, Miguel 1926- **1986**:4
O'Connor, Cardinal John 1920- **1990**
:3

O'Connor, John 1920-2000
  Obituary **2000**:4
Peter, Valentine J. 1934- **1988**:2
Rock, John
  Obituary **1985**:1
Sin, Jaime 1928-2005
  Obituary **2006**:3
Stallings, George A., Jr. 1948- **1990**:1

CAT Scanner
  Hounsfield, Godfrey 1919- **1989**:2

Cattle rustling
  Cantrell, Ed
    Brief entry **1985**:3

Caviar
  Petrossian, Christian
    Brief entry **1985**:3

CBS, Inc.
  Bradley, Ed 1941-2006
    Obituary **2008**:1
  Buttons, Red 1919-2006
    Obituary **2007**:3
  Cox, Richard Joseph
    Brief entry **1985**:1
  Cronkite, Walter Leland 1916- **1997**:3
  Moonves, Les 1949- **2004**:2
  Paley, William S. 1901-1990
    Obituary **1991**:2
  Reasoner, Harry 1923-1991
    Obituary **1992**:1
  Sagansky, Jeff 1952- **1993**:2
  Tellem, Nancy 1953(?)- **2004**:4
  Tisch, Laurence A. 1923- **1988**:2
  Yetnikoff, Walter 1933- **1988**:1

Center for Equal Opportunity
  Chavez, Linda 1947- **1999**:3

Centers for Living
  Williamson, Marianne 1953(?)- **1991**
    :4

Central America
  Astorga, Nora 1949(?)-1988 **1988**:2
  Cruz, Arturo 1923- **1985**:1
  Obando, Miguel 1926- **1986**:4
  Robelo, Alfonso 1940(?)- **1988**:1

Central Intelligence Agency [CIA]
  Carter, Amy 1967- **1987**:4
  Casey, William 1913-1987
    Obituary **1987**:3
  Colby, William E. 1920-1996
    Obituary **1996**:4
  Deutch, John 1938- **1996**:4
  Gates, Robert M. 1943- **1992**:2
  Inman, Bobby Ray 1931- **1985**:1
  Tenet, George 1953- **2000**:3

Centurion Ministries
  McCloskey, James 1944(?)- **1993**:1

Cesar Awards
  Adjani, Isabelle 1955- **1991**:1
  Deneuve, Catherine 1943- **2003**:2
  Depardieu, Gerard 1948- **1991**:2

Tautou, Audrey 1978- **2004**:2

Chanel, Inc.
  Chiquet, Maureen 1963- **2010**:1
  D'Alessio, Kitty
    Brief entry **1987**:3
  Lagerfeld, Karl 1938- **1999**:4

Chantal Pharmacentical Corp.
  Burnison, Chantal Simone 1950(?)-
    1988:3

Charlotte Hornets basketball team
  Bryant, Kobe 1978- **1998**:3
  Johnson, Larry 1969- **1993**:3
  Mourning, Alonzo 1970- **1994**:2

Chef Boy-ar-dee
  Boiardi, Hector 1897-1985
    Obituary **1985**:3

Chess
  Carlsen, Magnus 1990- **2011**:3
  Kasparov, Garry 1963- **1997**:4
  Polgar, Judit 1976- **1993**:3

Chicago, Ill., city government
  Washington, Harold 1922-1987
    Obituary **1988**:1

Chicago Bears football team
  McAfee, George 1918-2009
    Obituary **2010**:2
  McMahon, Jim 1959- **1985**:4
  Payton, Walter 1954-1999
    Obituary **2000**:2

Chicago Blackhawks
  Hasek, Dominik 1965- **1998**:3
  Kane, Patrick 1988- **2011**:4

Chicago Bulls basketball team
  Artest, Ron 1979- **2011**:1
  Jackson, Phil 1945- **1996**:3
  Jordan, Michael 1963- **1987**:2
  Kukoc, Toni 1968- **1995**:4
  Pippen, Scottie 1965- **1992**:2

Chicago Cubs baseball team
  Caray, Harry 1914(?)-1998 **1988**:3
    Obituary **1998**:3
  Soriano, Alfonso 1976- **2008**:1
  Sosa, Sammy 1968- **1999**:1

Chicago White Sox baseball team
  Caray, Harry 1914(?)-1998 **1988**:3
    Obituary **1998**:3
  Leyland, Jim 1944- **1998**:2
  Thomas, Frank 1968- **1994**:3
  Veeck, Bill 1914-1986
    Obituary **1986**:1

Child care
  Hale, Clara 1905-1992
    Obituary **1993**:3
  Leach, Penelope 1937- **1992**:4
  Spock, Benjamin 1903-1998 **1995**:2
    Obituary **1998**:3

Children's Defense Fund [CDF]
  Clinton, Hillary Rodham 1947- **1993**
    :2
  Edelman, Marian Wright 1939- **1990**
    :4

Chimpanzees
  Goodall, Jane 1934- **1991**:1

Choreography
  Abdul, Paula 1962- **1990**:3
  Ailey, Alvin 1931-1989 **1989**:2
    Obituary **1990**:2
  Astaire, Fred 1899-1987
    Obituary **1987**:4
  Bausch, Pina 1940-2009
    Obituary **2010**:4
  Bennett, Michael 1943-1987
    Obituary **1988**:1
  Cunningham, Merce 1919- **1998**:1
  Dean, Laura 1945- **1989**:4
  de Mille, Agnes 1905-1993
    Obituary **1994**:2
  Feld, Eliot 1942- **1996**:1
  Fenley, Molissa 1954- **1988**:3
  Forsythe, William 1949- **1993**:2
  Fosse, Bob 1927-1987
    Obituary **1988**:1
  Glover, Savion 1973- **1997**:1
  Graham, Martha 1894-1991
    Obituary **1991**:4
  Jamison, Judith 1944- **1990**:3
  Joffrey, Robert 1930-1988
    Obituary **1988**:3
  Jones, Bill T. **1991**:4
  Lewitzky, Bella 1916-2004
    Obituary **2005**:3
  Lythgoe, Nigel 1949- **2010**:4
  MacMillan, Kenneth 1929-1992
    Obituary **1993**:2
  Mitchell, Arthur 1934- **1995**:1
  Morris, Mark 1956- **1991**:1
  Nureyev, Rudolf 1938-1993
    Obituary **1993**:2
  Parsons, David 1959- **1993**:4
  Ross, Herbert 1927-2001
    Obituary **2002**:4
  Takei, Kei 1946- **1990**:2
  Taylor, Paul 1930- **1992**:3
  Tharp, Twyla 1942- **1992**:4
  Tudor, Antony 1908(?)-1987
    Obituary **1987**:4
  Tune, Tommy 1939- **1994**:2
  Varone, Doug 1956- **2001**:2

Christian Coalition
  Reed, Ralph 1961(?)- **1995**:1

Christic Institute
  Sheehan, Daniel P. 1945(?)- **1989**:1

Chrysler Motor Corp.
  Eaton, Robert J. 1940- **1994**:2
  Iacocca, Lee 1924- **1993**:1
  Lutz, Robert A. 1932- **1990**:1
  Marchionne, Sergio 1952- **2010**:4
  Nardelli, Robert 1948- **2008**:4

Church of England
  Carey, George 1935- **1992**:3
  Runcie, Robert 1921-2000 **1989**:4
    Obituary **2001**:1

Cincinatti Bengals football team
Esiason, Boomer 1961- **1991**:1

Cincinnati Reds baseball team
Davis, Eric 1962- **1987**:4
Rose, Pete 1941- **1991**:1
Schott, Marge 1928- **1985**:4

Cinematography
Burum, Stephen H.
Brief entry **1987**:2
Markle, C. Wilson 1938- **1988**:1
McLaren, Norman 1914-1987
Obituary **1987**:2

Civil rights
Abernathy, Ralph 1926-1990
Obituary **1990**:3
Abzug, Bella 1920-1998 **1998**:2
Allen Jr., Ivan 1911-2003
Obituary **2004**:3
Allred, Gloria 1941- **1985**:2
Aquino, Corazon 1933- **1986**:2
Baldwin, James 1924-1987
Obituary **1988**:2
Banks, Dennis J. 193- **1986**:4
Blackburn, Molly 1931(?)-1985
Obituary **1985**:4
Buthelezi, Mangosuthu Gatsha
1928- **1989**:3
Chavez, Linda 1947- **1999**:3
Chavis, Benjamin 1948- **1993**:4
Clements, George 1932- **1985**:1
Connerly, Ward 1939- **2000**:2
Davis, Angela 1944- **1998**:3
Dees, Morris 1936- **1992**:1
Delany, Sarah 1889-1999
Obituary **1999**:3
Duncan, Sheena
Brief entry **1987**:1
Farmer, James 1920-1999
Obituary **2000**:1
Faubus, Orval 1910-1994
Obituary **1995**:2
Glasser, Ira 1938- **1989**:1
Griffiths, Martha 1912-2003
Obituary **2004**:2
Harris, Barbara 1930- **1989**:3
Healey, Jack 1938(?)- **1990**:1
Hoffman, Abbie 1936-1989
Obituary **1989**:3
Hume, John 1938- **1987**:1
Jordan, Vernon, Jr. 1935- **2002**:3
King, Bernice 1963- **2000**:2
King, Coretta Scott 1927- **1999**:3
Kunstler, William 1920(?)- **1992**:3
Makeba, Miriam 1934- **1989**:2
Mandela, Winnie 1934- **1989**:3
Marshall, Thurgood 1908-1993
Obituary **1993**:3
McGuinness, Martin 1950(?)- **1985**:4
Parks, Rosa 1913-2005
Obituary **2007**:1
Pendleton, Clarence M. 1930-1988
Obituary **1988**:4
Ram, Jagjivan 1908-1986
Obituary **1986**:4
Shabazz, Betty 1936-1997
Obituary **1997**:4
Sharpton, Al 1954- **1991**:2
Shcharansky, Anatoly 1948- **1986**:2
Simone, Nina 1933-2003

Obituary **2004**:2
Slovo, Joe 1926- **1989**:2
Stallings, George A., Jr. 1948- **1990**:1
Steele, Shelby 1946- **1991**:2
Sullivan, Leon 1922-2001
Obituary **2002**:2
Suzman, Helen 1917- **1989**:3
Travers, Mary 1936-2009
Obituary **2011**:1
Ture, Kwame 1941-1998
Obituary **1999**:2
Washington, Harold 1922-1987
Obituary **1988**:1
West, Cornel 1953- **1994**:2
Williams, G. Mennen 1911-1988
Obituary **1988**:2
Williams, Hosea 1926-2000
Obituary **2001**:2
Wu, Harry 1937- **1996**:1

Civil War
Foote, Shelby 1916- **1991**:2

Claymation
Park, Nick 1958- **1997**:3
Vinton, Will
Brief entry **1988**:1

Cleveland Ballet Dancing Wheels
Verdi-Fletcher, Mary 1955- **1998**:2

Cleveland Browns football team
Brown, Jim 1936- **1993**:2

Cleveland Cavaliers basketball team
James, LeBron 1984- **2007**:3
Wilkens, Lenny 1937- **1995**:2

Cleveland city government
Stokes, Carl 1927-1996
Obituary **1996**:4

Cleveland Indians baseball team
Belle, Albert 1966- **1996**:4
Boudreau, Louis 1917-2001
Obituary **2002**:3
Greenberg, Hank 1911-1986
Obituary **1986**:4
Lofton, Kenny 1967- **1998**:1
Veeck, Bill 1914-1986
Obituary **1986**:1

Cliff's Notes
Hillegass, Clifton Keith 1918- **1989**:4

Climatology
Thompson, Starley
Brief entry **1987**:3

Clio Awards
Proctor, Barbara Gardner 1933(?)-
1985:3
Riney, Hal 1932- **1989**:1
Rivers, Joan 1933- **2005**:3
Sedelmaier, Joe 1933- **1985**:3

Cloning
Lanza, Robert 1956- **2004**:3
Wilmut, Ian 1944- **1997**:3

Coaching
Bowman, Scotty 1933- **1998**:4
Brown, Paul 1908-1991
Obituary **1992**:1
Chaney, John 1932- **1989**:1
Hayes, Woody 1913-1987
Obituary **1987**:2
Holtz, Lou 1937- **1986**:4
Howser, Dick 1936-1987
Obituary **1987**:4
Jackson, Phil 1945- **1996**:3
Johnson, Jimmy 1943- **1993**:3
Knight, Bobby 1940- **1985**:3
Leyland, Jim 1944- **1998**:2
Lukas, D. Wayne 1936(?)- **1986**:2
Martin, Billy 1928-1989 **1988**:4
Obituary **1990**:2
McCartney, Bill 1940- **1995**:3
Paterno, Joe 1926- **1995**:4
Schembechler, Bo 1929(?)- **1990**:3
Shula, Don 1930- **1992**:2
Tarkenian, Jerry 1930- **1990**:4
Walsh, Bill 1931- **1987**:4

Coca-Cola Co.
Goizueta, Roberto 1931-1997 **1996**:1
Obituary **1998**:1
Keough, Donald Raymond 1926-
1986:1
Woodruff, Robert Winship 1889-1985
Obituary **1985**:1

Coleman Co.
Coleman, Sheldon, Jr. 1953- **1990**:2

Colorado Avalanche hockey team
Lemieux, Claude 1965- **1996**:1

Colorization
Markle, C. Wilson 1938- **1988**:1

Columbia Pictures
Melnick, Daniel 1932-2009
Obituary **2011**:2
Pascal, Amy 1958- **2003**:3
Steel, Dawn 1946-1997 **1990**:1
Obituary **1998**:2
Vincent, Fay 1938- **1990**:2

Columbia Sportswear
Boyle, Gertrude 1924- **1995**:3

Comedy
Adams, Don 1923-2005
Obituary **2007**:1
Alexander, Jason 1962(?)- **1993**:3
Allen, Steve 1921-2000
Obituary **2001**:2
Allen, Tim 1953- **1993**:1
Allen, Woody 1935- **1994**:1
Anderson, Harry 1951(?)- **1988**:2
Arnold, Tom 1959- **1993**:2
Arthur, Bea 1922-2009
Obituary **2010**:2
Atkinson, Rowan 1955- **2004**:3
Bailey, Ben 1970- **2011**:4
Baron Cohen, Sacha 1971- **2007**:3
Barr, Roseanne 1953(?)- **1989**:1
Bateman, Jason 1969- **2005**:3
Belushi, Jim 1954- **1986**:2

Dell, Michael 1965- **1996**:2
De Luca, Guerrino 1952- **2007**:1
Gates, Bill 1955- **1987**:4
Grove, Andrew S. 1936- **1995**:3
Hawkins, Jeff and Donna Dubinsky
    2000:2
Headroom, Max 1985- **1986**:4
Hounsfield, Godfrey 1919- **1989**:2
Inatome, Rick 1953- **1985**:4
Inman, Bobby Ray 1931- **1985**:1
Isaacson, Portia
    Brief entry **1986**:1
Kapor, Mitch 1950- **1990**:3
Kurzweil, Raymond 1948- **1986**:3
Lanier, Jaron 1961(?)- **1993**:4
McNealy, Scott 1954- **1999**:4
Millard, Barbara J.
    Brief entry **1985**:3
Miller, Rand 1959(?)- **1995**:4
Noyce, Robert N. 1927- **1985**:4
Olsen, Kenneth H. 1926- **1986**:4
Packard, David 1912-1996
    Obituary **1996**:3
Raskin, Jef 1943(?)- **1997**:4
Ritchie, Dennis and Kenneth
    Thompson **2000**:1
Roberts, Steven K. 1952(?)- **1992**:1
Schank, Roger 1946- **1989**:2
Sculley, John 1939- **1989**:4
Shimomura, Tsutomu 1965- **1996**:1
Sterling, Bruce 1954- **1995**:4
Torvalds, Linus 1970(?)- **1999**:3
Treybig, James G. 1940- **1988**:3
Wang, An 1920-1990 **1986**:1
    Obituary **1990**:3

Conducting (musical)
Alsop, Marin 1956- **2008**:3
Bernstein, Leonard 1918-1990
    Obituary **1991**:1
Dorati, Antal 1906-1988
    Obituary **1989**:2
Goodman, Benny 1909-1986
    Obituary **1986**:3
Levine, James 1943- **1992**:3
Lewis, Henry 1932-1996
    Obituary **1996**:3
Mehta, Zubin 1938(?)- **1994**:3
Menuhin, Yehudi 1916-1999
    Obituary **1999**:3
Norrington, Roger 1934- **1989**:4
Ormandy, Eugene 1899-1985
    Obituary **1985**:2
Rattle, Simon 1955- **1989**:4
Riddle, Nelson 1921-1985
    Obituary **1985**:4
Rostropovich, Mstislav 1927-2007
    Obituary **2008**:3
Solti, Georg 1912-1997
    Obituary **1998**:1
Thomas, Michael Tilson 1944- **1990**:3
von Karajan, Herbert 1908-1989
    Obituary **1989**:4

Congressional Medal of Honor
Hope, Bob 1903-2003
    Obituary **2004**:4
Kerrey, Bob 1943- **1986**:1
Parks, Rosa 1913-2005
    Obituary **2007**:1
Shepard, Alan 1923-1998
    Obituary **1999**:1

Connecticut state government
Lieberman, Joseph 1942- **2001**:1
Perry, Carrie Saxon 1932(?)- **1989**:2
Ribicoff, Abraham 1910-1998
    Obituary **1998**:3
Weicker, Lowell P., Jr. 1931- **1993**:1

Conseco, Inc.
Hilbert, Stephen C. 1946- **1997**:4

Conservation (wildlife)
Adamson, George 1906-1989
    Obituary **1990**:2
Babbitt, Bruce 1938- **1994**:1
Brower, David 1912- **1990**:4
Corwin, Jeff 1967- **2005**:1
Douglas, Marjory Stoneman
    1890-1998 **1993**:1
    Obituary **1998**:4
Durrell, Gerald 1925-1995
    Obituary **1995**:3
Eliasch, Johan 1962- **2011**:3
Foreman, Dave 1947(?)- **1990**:3
Gerrity, Sean 1958- **2011**:3
Goodall, Jane 1934- **1991**:1
Hair, Jay D. 1945- **1994**:3
Hayse, Bruce 1949(?)- **2004**:3
Moss, Cynthia 1940- **1995**:2
Owens, Delia and Mark **1993**:3
Wilson, Edward O. 1929- **1994**:4

Conservative Judaism
Eilberg, Amy
    Brief entry **1985**:3

Conservative Party (Great Britain)
Major, John 1943- **1991**:2
Thatcher, Margaret 1925- **1989**:2

Consumer protection
Nader, Ralph 1934- **1989**:4

Cooking
Batali, Mario 1960- **2010**:4
Bourdain, Anthony 1956- **2008**:3
Brown, Alton 1962- **2011**:1
Deen, Paula 1947- **2008**:3
De Laurentiis, Giada 1970- **2011**:1
Fieri, Guy 1968- **2010**:3
Flay, Bobby 1964- **2009**:2
Florence, Tyler 1971- **2011**:4
Ford, Faith 1964- **2005**:3
Lawson, Nigella 1960- **2003**:2
Lee, Sandra 1966- **2008**:3
Matsuhisa, Nobuyuki 1949- **2002**:3
Oliver, Jamie 1975- **2002**:3
Pépin, Jacques 1935- **2010**:2
Pouillon, Nora 1943- **2005**:1
Ramsay, Gordon 1966- **2008**:2
Ray, Rachael 1968- **2007**:1
Stone, Curtis 1975- **2011**:3
Trotter, Charlie 1960- **2000**:4
Valastro, Buddy 1977- **2011**:4
Waters, Alice 1944- **2006**:3

Cosmetics
Ash, Mary Kay 1915(?)- **1996**:1
Aucoin, Kevyn 1962- **2001**:3
Baxter, Pamela 1949- **2009**:4
Blodgett, Leslie 1963- **2010**:1

Bloom, Natalie 1971- **2007**:1
Carlino, Cristina 1961(?)- **2008**:4
Iman 1955- **2001**:3
Kashuk, Sonia 1959(?)- **2002**:4
Kelly, Maureen 1972(?)- **2007**:3
Lerner, Sandy 1955(?)- **2005**:1
Lobell, Jeanine 1964(?)- **2002**:3
Manheimer, Heidi 1963- **2009**:3
Mercier, Laura 1959(?)- **2002**:2
Mohajer, Dineh 1972- **1997**:3
Nars, Francois 1959- **2003**:1
Owen-Jones, Lindsay 1946(?)- **2004**:2
Page, Dick 1955- **2010**:1
Roncal, Mally 1972- **2009**:4
Shaw, Carol 1958(?)- **2002**:1

Coty Awards
Beene, Geoffrey 1927-2004
    Obituary **2005**:4
Blass, Bill 1922-2002
    Obituary **2003**:3
de la Renta, Oscar 1932- **2005**:4
Ellis, Perry 1940-1986
    Obituary **1986**:3
Halston 1932-1990
    Obituary **1990**:3
Johnson, Betsey 1942- **1996**:2
Kamali, Norma 1945- **1989**:1
Karan, Donna 1948- **1988**:1
Klein, Calvin 1942- **1996**:2
Lauren, Ralph 1939- **1990**:1
Morris, Robert 1947- **2010**:3
Smith, Willi 1948-1987
    Obituary **1987**:3

Council of Economic Advisers
Tyson, Laura D'Andrea 1947- **1994**:1

Counseling
Bradshaw, John 1933- **1992**:1
Gray, John 1952(?)- **1995**:3

Counterfeiting
Bikoff, James L.
    Brief entry **1986**:2

Country Music Awards
Bentley, Dierks 1975- **2007**:3
Brooks, Garth 1962- **1992**:1
Carpenter, Mary-Chapin 1958(?)-
    1994:1
Chesney, Kenny 1968- **2008**:2
Harris, Emmylou 1947- **1991**:3
Hill, Faith 1967- **2000**:1
Jackson, Alan 1958- **2003**:1
Lady Antebellum 1982- **2011**:2
Loveless, Patty 1957- **1998**:2
McBride, Martina 1966- **2010**:1
McEntire, Reba 1954- **1987**:3
McGraw, Tim 1966- **2000**:3
Nelson, Willie 1933- **1993**:4
Newton-John, Olivia 1948- **1998**:4
Paisley, Brad 1972- **2008**:3
Parton, Dolly 1946- **1999**:4
Pride, Charley 1938(?)- **1998**:1
Rascal Flatts **2007**:1
Spacek, Sissy 1949- **2003**:1
Strait, George 1952- **1998**:3
Sugarland 1970- **2009**:2
Travis, Randy 1959- **1988**:4
Twitty, Conway 1933-1993

Obituary **1994**:1
Underwood, Carrie 1983- **2008**:1
Urban, Keith 1967- **2006**:3
Wagoner, Porter 1927-2007
  Obituary **2008**:4
Wilson, Gretchen 1970- **2006**:3
Womack, Lee Ann 1966- **2002**:1
Wynette, Tammy 1942-1998
  Obituary **1998**:3
Wynonna 1964- **1993**:3
Yearwood, Trisha 1964- **1999**:1

Creation Spirituality
Altea, Rosemary 1946- **1996**:3
Fox, Matthew 1940- **1992**:2

Creative Artists Agency
Ovitz, Michael 1946- **1990**:1

Cy Young Award
Clemens, Roger 1962- **1991**:4
Hernandez, Willie 1954- **1985**:1
Hershiser, Orel 1958- **1989**:2
Johnson, Randy 1963- **1996**:2
Maddux, Greg 1966- **1996**:2
Palmer, Jim 1945- **1991**:2
Saberhagen, Bret 1964- **1986**:1
Santana, Johan 1979- **2008**:1
Smoltz, John 1967- **2010**:3

Daimler-Benz AG [Mercedes-Benz]
Breitschwerdt, Werner 1927- **1988**:4

DaimlerChrysler Corp.
Schrempp, Juergen 1944- **2000**:2
Zetsche, Dieter 1953- **2002**:3

Dallas Cowboys football team
Aikman, Troy 1966- **1994**:2
Irvin, Michael 1966- **1996**:3
Johnson, Jimmy 1943- **1993**:3
Jones, Jerry 1942- **1994**:4
Landry, Tom 1924-2000
  Obituary **2000**:3
Romo, Tony 1980- **2008**:3
Smith, Emmitt **1994**:1

Dance Theatre of Harlem
Fagan, Garth 1940- **2000**:1
Mitchell, Arthur 1934- **1995**:1

Dell Computer Corp.
Dell, Michael 1965- **1996**:2

Democratic National Committee [DNC]
Brown, Ron 1941- **1990**:3
Brown, Ron 1941-1996
  Obituary **1996**.4
Dean, Howard 1948- **2005**:4
Waters, Maxine 1938- **1998**:4

Denver Broncos football team
Barnes, Ernie 1938- **1997**:4
Davis, Terrell 1972- **1998**:2
Elway, John 1960- **1990**:3

Department of Commerce
Baldrige, Malcolm 1922-1987
  Obituary **1988**:1
Brown, Ron 1941-1996

Obituary **1996**:4

Department of Defense
Cohen, William S. 1940- **1998**:1
Perry, William 1927- **1994**:4

Department of Education
Cavazos, Lauro F. 1927- **1989**:2
Riley, Richard W. 1933- **1996**:3

Department of Energy
O'Leary, Hazel 1937- **1993**:4

Department of Health, Education, and Welfare [HEW]
Harris, Patricia Roberts 1924-1985
  Obituary **1985**:2
Ribicoff, Abraham 1910-1998
  Obituary **1998**:3

Department of Health and Human Services [HHR]
Kessler, David 1951- **1992**:1
Sullivan, Louis 1933- **1990**:4

Department of Housing and Urban Development [HUD]
Achtenberg, Roberta **1993**:4
Donovan, Shaun 1966- **2010**:4
Harris, Patricia Roberts 1924-1985
  Obituary **1985**:2
Kemp, Jack 1935- **1990**:4
Morrison, Trudi
  Brief entry **1986**:2

Department of Labor
Dole, Elizabeth Hanford 1936- **1990**:1
Martin, Lynn 1939- **1991**:4

Department of State
Christopher, Warren 1925- **1996**:3
Muskie, Edmund S. 1914-1996
  Obituary **1996**:3

Department of the Interior
Babbitt, Bruce 1938- **1994**:1

Department of Transportation
Dole, Elizabeth Hanford 1936- **1990**:1
Schiavo, Mary 1955- **1998**:2

Depression
Abramson, Lyn 1950- **1986**:3

Desilu Productions
Arnaz, Desi 1917-1986
  Obituary **1987**:1
Ball, Lucille 1911-1989
  Obituary **1989**:3

Detroit city government
Archer, Dennis 1942- **1994**:4
Maida, Adam Cardinal 1930- **1998**:2
Young, Coleman A. 1918-1997
  Obituary **1998**:1

Detroit Lions football team
Ford, William Clay, Jr. 1957- **1999**:1
Sanders, Barry 1968- **1992**:1
White, Byron 1917-2002
  Obituary **2003**:3

Detroit Pistons basketball team
Daly, Chuck 1930-2009
  Obituary **2010**:3
Hill, Grant 1972- **1995**:3
Laimbeer, Bill 1957- **2004**:3
Rodman, Dennis 1961- **1991**:3
Thomas, Isiah 1961- **1989**:2
Vitale, Dick 1939- **1988**:4
Wallace, Ben 1974- **2004**:3

Detroit Red Wings hockey team
Bowman, Scotty 1933- **1998**:4
Federov, Sergei 1969- **1995**:1
Ilitch, Mike 1929- **1993**:4
Klima, Petr 1964- **1987**:1
Konstantinov, Vladimir 1967- **1997**:4
Osgood, Chris 1972- **2010**:1
Yzerman, Steve 1965- **1991**:2

Detroit Tigers baseball team
Fidrych, Mark 1954-2009
  Obituary **2010**:2
Fielder, Cecil 1963- **1993**:2
Gibson, Kirk 1957- **1985**:2
Greenberg, Hank 1911-1986
  Obituary **1986**:4
Harwell, Ernie 1918- **1997**:3
Hernandez, Willie 1954- **1985**:1
Ilitch, Mike 1929- **1993**:4
Monaghan, Tom 1937- **1985**:1
Schembechler, Bo 1929(?)- **1990**:3

Diets
Agatston, Arthur 1947- **2005**:1
Atkins, Robert C. 1930-2003
  Obituary **2004**:2
Gregory, Dick 1932- **1990**:3
Ornish, Dean 1953- **2004**:2
Powter, Susan 1957(?)- **1994**:3
Sears, Barry 1947- **2004**:2

Digital Equipment Corp. [DEC]
Olsen, Kenneth H. 1926- **1986**:4

Dilbert cartoon
Adams, Scott 1957- **1996**:4

Dinosaurs
Bakker, Robert T. 1950(?)- **1991**:3
Barney **1993**:4
Crichton, Michael 1942- **1995**:3
Henson, Brian 1964(?)- **1992**:1

Diplomacy
Abrams, Elliott 1948- **1987**:1
Albright, Madeleine 1937- **1994**:3
Astorga, Nora 1949(?)-1988 **1988**:2
Baker, James A. III 1930- **1991**:2
Begin, Menachem 1913-1992
  Obituary **1992**:3
Berri, Nabih 1939(?)- **1985**:2
Carter, Jimmy 1924- **1995**:1
de Pinies, Jamie
  Brief entry **1986**:3

Emmy Awards

Abrams, J. J. 1966- **2007**:3
Adams, Don 1923-2005
    Obituary **2007**:1
Albert, Marv 1943- **1994**:3
Alexander, Jane 1939- **1994**:2
Alexander, Jason 1962(?)- **1993**:3
Allen, Debbie 1950- **1998**:2
Anderson, Judith 1899(?)-1992
    Obituary **1992**:3
Apatow, Judd 1967- **2006**:3
Arledge, Roone 1931- **1992**:2
Arthur, Bea 1922-2009
    Obituary **2010**:2
Aykroyd, Dan 1952- **1989**:3
Azaria, Hank 1964- **2001**:3
Bailey, Ben 1970- **2011**:4
Ball, Lucille 1911-1989
    Obituary **1989**:3
Bancroft, Anne 1931-2005
    Obituary **2006**:3
Baranski, Christine 1952- **2001**:2
Barbera, Joseph 1911- **1988**:2
Bergeron, Tom 1955- **2010**:1
Berle, Milton 1908-2002
    Obituary **2003**:2
Bernstein, Elmer 1922-2004
    Obituary **2005**:4
Bochco, Steven 1943- **1989**:1
Boyle, Peter 1935- **2002**:3
Bradley, Ed 1941-2006
    Obituary **2008**:1
Brady, Wayne 1972- **2008**:3
Burnett, Carol 1933- **2000**:3
Burnett, Mark 1960- **2003**:1
Burrows, James 1940- **2005**:3
Carney, Art 1918-2003
    Obituary **2005**:1
Carter, Chris 1956- **2000**:1
Carter, Nell 1948-2003
    Obituary **2004**:2
Chase, Chevy 1943- **1990**:1
Chenoweth, Kristin 1968- **2010**:4
Chiklis, Michael 1963- **2003**:3
Child, Julia 1912- **1999**:4
Clarkson, Patricia 1959- **2005**:3
Coca, Imogene 1908-2001
    Obituary **2002**:2
Coco, James 1929(?)-1987
    Obituary **1987**:2
Colbert, Stephen 1964- **2007**:4
Collette, Toni 1972- **2009**:4
Cooke, Alistair 1908-2004
    Obituary **2005**:3
Copperfield, David 1957- **1986**:3
Corwin, Jeff 1967- **2005**:1
Cosby, Bill 1937- **1999**:2
Cranston, Bryan 1956- **2010**:1
Cronkite, Walter Leland 1916- **1997**:3
Cryer, Jon 1965- **2010**:4
Davis, Bette 1908-1989
    Obituary **1990**:1
De Cordova, Frederick 1910- **1985**:2
Delany, Dana 1956- **2008**:4
De Laurentiis, Giada 1970- **2011**:1
De Matteo, Drea 1973- **2005**:2
De Vito, Danny 1944- **1987**:1
Dewhurst, Colleen 1924-1991
    Obituary **1992**:2
Douglas, Mike 1925-2006
    Obituary **2007**:4
Falco, Edie 1963- **2010**:2

Fey, Tina 1970- **2005**:3
Field, Patricia 1942(?)- **2002**:2
Field, Sally 1946- **1995**:3
Finney, Albert 1936- **2003**:3
Flanders, Ed 1934-1995
    Obituary **1995**:3
Flay, Bobby 1964- **2009**:2
Fosse, Bob 1927-1987
    Obituary **1988**:1
Foster, Jodie 1962- **1989**:2
Frankenheimer, John 1930-2002
    Obituary **2003**:4
Franz, Dennis 1944- **1995**:2
Freleng, Friz 1906(?)-1995
    Obituary **1995**:4
Gandolfini, James 1961- **2001**:3
Gelbart, Larry 1928-2009
    Obituary **2011**:1
Gellar, Sarah Michelle 1977- **1999**:3
Getty, Estelle 1923-2008
    Obituary **2009**:3
Giamatti, Paul 1967- **2009**:4
Gless, Sharon 1944- **1989**:3
Gobel, George 1920(?)-1991
    Obituary **1991**:4
Goldberg, Gary David 1944- **1989**:4
Goldberg, Leonard 1934- **1988**:4
Gossett, Louis, Jr. 1936- **1989**:3
Goulet, Robert 1933-2007
    Obituary **2008**:4
Grammer, Kelsey 1955(?)- **1995**:1
Griffin, Kathy 1961- **2010**:4
Griffin, Merv 1925-2008
    Obituary **2008**:4
Grodin, Charles 1935- **1997**:3
Guest, Christopher 1948- **2004**:2
Gupta, Sanjay 1969- **2009**:4
Haggis, Paul 1953- **2006**:4
Hanks, Tom 1956- **1989**:2
Harrelson, Woody 1961- **2011**:1
Hartman, Phil 1948-1998 **1996**:2
    Obituary **1998**:4
Heaton, Patricia 1958- **2010**:4
Heche, Anne 1969- **1999**:1
Heigl, Katharine 1978- **2008**:3
Helgenberger, Marg 1958- **2002**:2
Henning, Doug 1947-1999
    Obituary **2000**:3
Hopkins, Anthony 1937- **1992**:4
Howard, Ken 1944- **2010**:4
Howard, Trevor 1916-1988
    Obituary **1988**:2
Huffman, Felicity 1962- **2006**:2
Izzard, Eddie 1963- **2008**:1
Janney, Allison 1959- **2003**:3
Jennings, Peter Charles 1938- **1997**:2
Johnson, Don 1949- **1986**:1
Jones, Tommy Lee 1947(?)- **1994**:2
Joyce, William 1957- **2006**:1
Kavner, Julie 1951- **1992**:3
Kaye, Danny 1913-1987
    Obituary **1987**:2
Keeshan, Bob 1927-2004
    Obituary **2005**:2
Kimmel, Jimmy 1967- **2009**:2
Knight, Ted 1923-1986
    Obituary **1986**:4
Knotts, Don 1924-2006
    Obituary **2007**:1
Koppel, Ted 1940- **1989**:1
Kuralt, Charles 1934-1997
    Obituary **1998**:3

LaBeouf, Shia 1986- **2008**:1
LaPaglia, Anthony 1959- **2004**:4
Larroquette, John 1947- **1986**:2
Lemmon, Jack 1925- **1998**:4
    Obituary **2002**:3
Letterman, David 1947- **1989**:3
Levinson, Barry 1932- **1989**:3
Levy, Eugene 1946- **2004**:3
Lewis, Shari 1934-1998 **1993**:1
    Obituary **1999**:1
Liberace 1919-1987
    Obituary **1987**:2
Linney, Laura 1964- **2009**:4
Lucci, Susan 1946(?)- **1999**:4
MacFarlane, Seth 1973- **2006**:1
Malkovich, John 1953- **1988**:2
Mantegna, Joe 1947- **1992**:1
Margulies, Julianna 1966- **2011**:1
McFarlane, Todd 1961- **1999**:1
McGoohan, Patrick 1928-2009
    Obituary **2010**:1
Melendez, Bill 1916-2008
    Obituary **2009**:4
Melnick, Daniel 1932-2009
    Obituary **2011**:2
Meredith, Burgess 1909-1997
    Obituary **1998**:1
Merkerson, S. Epatha 1952- **2006**:4
Messing, Debra 1968- **2004**:4
Midler, Bette 1945- **1989**:4
Miller, Arthur 1915- **1999**:4
Mirren, Helen 1945- **2005**:1
Moore, Julianne 1960- **1998**:1
Moore, Mary Tyler 1936- **1996**:2
Murray, Bill 1950- **2002**:4
Myers, Mike 1964(?)- **1992**:3
North, Alex 1910- **1986**:3
O'Brien, Conan 1963(?)- **1994**:1
O'Connor, Carroll 1924-2001
    Obituary **2002**:3
O'Connor, Donald 1925-2003
    Obituary **2004**:4
Olmos, Edward James 1947- **1990**:1
Olson, Johnny 1910(?)-1985
    Obituary **1985**:4
Page, Geraldine 1924-1987
    Obituary **1987**:4
Palance, Jack 1919-2006
    Obituary **2008**:1
Paulsen, Pat 1927-1997
    Obituary **1997**:4
Piven, Jeremy 1965- **2007**:3
Poston, Tom 1921-2007
    Obituary **2008**:3
Probst, Jeff 1962- **2011**:2
Pryor, Richard **1999**:3
Randall, Tony 1920-2004
    Obituary **2005**:3
Ray, Rachael 1968- **2007**:1
Redgrave, Vanessa 1937- **1989**:2
Ritter, John 1948- **2003**:4
Rivera, Geraldo 1943- **1989**:1
Rivers, Joan 1933- **2005**:3
Roberts, Doris 1930- **2003**:4
Rock, Chris 1967(?)- **1998**:1
Rolle, Esther 1922-1998
    Obituary **1999**:2
Rollins, Howard E., Jr. 1950- **1986**:1
Romano, Ray 1957- **2001**:4
Rose, Charlie 1943- **1994**:2
Saralegui, Cristina 1948- **1999**:2
Schulz, Charles M. 1922- **1998**:1

Seo, Danny 1977- **2008**:3
Sethi, Simran 1971(?)- **2008**:1
Stephens, Arran and Ratana **2008**:4
Strong, Maurice 1929- **1993**:1
Strummer, Joe 1952-2002
    Obituary **2004**:1
Styler, Trudie 1954- **2009**:1
Suckling, Kierán 1964- **2009**:2
Vitousek, Peter 1949- **2003**:1
Whelan, Tensie 1960- **2007**:1
Yeang, Ken 1948- **2008**:3

Environmental Protection Agency [EPA]
    Browner, Carol M. 1955- **1994**:1
    Jackson, Lisa P. 1962- **2009**:4

Episcopal Church
    Browning, Edmond
        Brief entry **1986**:2
    Harris, Barbara **1996**:3
    Harris, Barbara 1930- **1989**:3
    Jefferts Schori, Katharine 1954- **2007**
        :2
    Spong, John 1931- **1991**:3

Espionage
    Philby, Kim 1912-1988
        Obituary **1988**:3

Esprit clothing
    Krogner, Heinz 1941(?)- **2004**:2
    Tompkins, Susie
        Brief entry **1987**:2

Essence magazine
    Gillespie, Marcia 1944- **1999**:4
    Lewis, Edward T. 1940- **1999**:4
    Taylor, Susan L. 1946- **1998**:2

Estee Lauder
    Baxter, Pamela 1949- **2009**:4
    Burns, Robin 1953(?)- **1991**:2
    Lauder, Estee 1908(?)- **1992**:2

Ethnobotany
    Plotkin, Mark 1955(?)- **1994**:3

European Commission
    Delors, Jacques 1925- **1990**:2

Euthanasia
    Cruzan, Nancy 1957(?)-1990
        Obituary **1991**:3
    Humphry, Derek 1931(?)- **1992**:2
    Kevorkian, Jack 1928(?)- **1991**:3

Excel Communications
    Troutt, Kenny A. 1948- **1998**:1

Exploration
    Ballard, Robert D. 1942- **1998**:4
    Fiennes, Ranulph 1944- **1990**:3
    Hempleman-Adams, David 1956-
        2004:3
    Horn, Mike 1966- **2009**:3
    Steger, Will 1945(?)- **1990**:4

ExxonMobil Oil
    Raymond, Lee R. 1930- **2000**:3

**Fabbrica Italiana Automobili Torino
SpA [Fiat]**
    Agnelli, Giovanni 1921- **1989**:4

Faith Center Church
    Scott, Gene
        Brief entry **1986**:1

Fallon McElligott
    McElligott, Thomas J. 1943- **1987**:4

Famous Amos Chocolate Chip Cookies
    Amos, Wally 1936- **2000**:1

Fashion
    Adams-Geller, Paige 1969(?)- **2006**:4
    Agnes B 1941- **2002**:3
    Albou, Sophie 1967- **2007**:2
    Allard, Linda 1940- **2003**:2
    Armani, Giorgio 1934(?)- **1991**:2
    Avedon, Richard 1923- **1993**:4
    Bacall, Lauren 1924- **1997**:3
    Badgley, Mark and James Mischka
        2004:3
    Ball, Michael 1964(?)- **2007**:3
    Banks, Jeffrey 1953- **1998**:2
    Beene, Geoffrey 1927-2004
        Obituary **2005**:4
    Benetton, Luciano 1935- **1988**:1
    Blahnik, Manolo 1942- **2000**:2
    Blass, Bill 1922-2002
        Obituary **2003**:3
    Bohbot, Michele 1959(?)- **2004**:2
    Bravo, Rose Marie 1951(?)- **2005**:3
    Brown, Howard and Karen Stewart
        2007:3
    Bruni, Carla 1967- **2009**:3
    Buchman, Dana 1951- **2010**:2
    Burch, Tory 1966- **2009**:3
    Cameron, David
        Brief entry **1988**:1
    Cardin, Pierre 1922- **2003**:3
    Cassini, Oleg 1913-2006
        Obituary **2007**:2
    Cavalli, Roberto 1940- **2004**:4
    Chalayan, Hussein 1970- **2003**:2
    Charney, Dov 1969- **2008**:2
    Charron, Paul 1942- **2004**:1
    Choo, Jimmy 1957(?)- **2006**:3
    Chung, Doo-Ri 1973- **2011**:3
    Claiborne, Liz 1929- **1986**:3
    Cole, Anne 1930(?)- **2007**:3
    Cole, Kenneth 1954(?)- **2003**:1
    Costa, Francisco 1961- **2010**:2
    Crawford, Cindy 1966- **1993**:3
    D'Alessio, Kitty
        Brief entry **1987**:3
    David Neville and Marcus
        Wainwright 1976- **2010**:3
    de la Renta, Oscar 1932- **2005**:4
    Dickinson, Janice 1953- **2005**:2
    Dolce, Domenico and Stefano
        Gabbana **2005**:4
    Duarte, Henry 1963(?)- **2003**:3
    Ecko, Marc 1972- **2006**:3
    Elbaz, Alber 1961- **2008**:1
    Ellis, Perry 1940-1986
        Obituary **1986**:3
    Erte 1892-1990
        Obituary **1990**:4
    Eve 1978- **2004**:3

Ferre, Gianfranco 1944-2007
    Obituary **2008**:3
Ferretti, Alberta 1950(?)- **2004**:1
Ford, Tom 1962- **1999**:3
Frankfort, Lew 1946- **2008**:2
Galliano, John 1960- **2005**:2
Gaultier, Jean-Paul 1952- **1998**:1
Giannulli, Mossimo 1963- **2002**:3
Green, Philip 1952- **2008**:2
Gregory, Rogan 1972- **2008**:2
Gucci, Maurizio
    Brief entry **1985**:4
Haas, Robert D. 1942- **1986**:4
Halston 1932-1990
    Obituary **1990**:3
Held, Abbe 1966- **2011**:1
Hernandez, Lazaro and Jack
    McCollough **2008**:4
Herrera, Carolina 1939- **1997**:1
Hilfiger, Tommy 1952- **1993**:3
Hindmarch, Anya 1969- **2008**:2
Jacobs, Marc 1963- **2002**:3
Johnson, Betsey 1942- **1996**:2
Johnson, Beverly 1952- **2005**:2
Kamali, Norma 1945- **1989**:1
Karan, Donna 1948- **1988**:1
Kelly, Patrick 1954(?)-1990
    Obituary **1990**:2
Kim, Eugenia 1974(?)- **2006**:1
Klein, Calvin 1942- **1996**:2
Klensch, Elsa **2001**:4
Korchinsky, Mike 1961- **2004**:2
Kors, Michael 1959- **2000**:4
Krogner, Heinz 1941(?)- **2004**:2
Lacroix, Christian 1951- **2005**:2
Lagerfeld, Karl 1938- **1999**:4
Lam, Derek 1966- **2009**:2
Lang, Helmut 1956- **1999**:2
Lange, Liz 1967(?)- **2003**:4
Lauren, Ralph 1939- **1990**:1
Leigh, Dorian 1917-2008
    Obituary **2009**:3
Lepore, Nanette 1964(?)- **2006**:4
Lhuillier, Monique 1971(?)- **2007**:4
Lim, Phillip 1974(?)- **2008**:1
Louboutin, Christian 1963- **2006**:1
Macdonald, Julien 1973(?)- **2005**:3
Madden, Steve 1958- **2007**:2
Margolis, Bobby 1948(?)- **2007**:2
Mashouf, Manny 1938(?)- **2008**:1
Matadin, Vinoodh and Inez van
    Lamsweerde **2007**:4
Matthias, Rebecca 1953- **2010**:1
McCauley, Matthew 1973- **2011**:1
McLaughlin, Betsy 1962(?)- **2004**:3
Mellinger, Frederick 1924(?)-1990
    Obituary **1990**:4
Mello, Dawn 1938(?)- **1992**:2
Miller, Nicole 1951(?)- **1995**:4
Mills, Malia 1966- **2003**:1
Minkoff, Rebecca 1981- **2011**:3
Miyake, Issey 1939- **1985**:2
Mizrahi, Isaac 1961- **1991**:1
Murakami, Takashi 1962- **2004**:2
Natori, Josie 1947- **1994**:3
Nipon, Albert
    Brief entry **1986**:4
Oldham, Todd 1961- **1995**:4
Olsen, Sigrid 1953- **2007**:1
Panichgul, Thakoon 1974- **2009**:4
Parker, Suzy 1932-2003
    Obituary **2004**:2

Ritter, John 1948- **2003**:4
Roberts, Julia 1967- **1991**:3
Russell, Keri 1976- **2000**:1
Sheen, Martin 1940- **2002**:1
Spacek, Sissy 1949- **2003**:1
Springsteen, Bruce 1949- **2011**:1
Streisand, Barbra 1942- **1992**:2
Sutherland, Kiefer 1966- **2002**:4
Swank, Hilary 1974- **2000**:3
Taylor, Lili 1967- **2000**:2
Thompson, Emma 1959- **1993**:2
Ullman, Tracey 1961- **1988**:3
Waltz, Christoph 1956- **2011**:1
Washington, Denzel 1954- **1993**:2
Waterston, Sam 1940- **2006**:1
Weisz, Rachel 1971- **2006**:4
Woodward, Edward 1930-2009
  Obituary **2011**:3

Golden State Warriors basketball team
Sprewell, Latrell 1970- **1999**:4
Webber, Chris 1973- **1994**:1

Golf
Allenby, Robert 1971- **2007**:1
Azinger, Paul 1960- **1995**:2
Baker, Kathy
  Brief entry **1986**:1
Callaway, Ely 1919-2001
  Obituary **2002**:3
Chen, T.C.
  Brief entry **1987**:3
Couples, Fred 1959- **1994**:4
Creamer, Paula 1986- **2006**:2
Curtis, Ben 1977- **2004**:2
Duval, David 1971- **2000**:3
Faldo, Nick 1957- **1993**:3
Furyk, Jim 1970- **2004**:2
Hogan, Ben 1912-1997
  Obituary **1997**:4
Irwin, Hale 1945- **2005**:2
Kerr, Cristie 1977- **2008**:2
Kite, Tom 1949- **1990**:3
Lopez, Nancy 1957- **1989**:3
Martin, Casey 1972- **2002**:1
Mickelson, Phil 1970- **2004**:4
Nelson, Byron 1912-2006
  Obituary **2007**:4
Norman, Greg 1955- **1988**:3
Ochoa, Lorena 1981- **2007**:4
Pak, Se Ri 1977- **1999**:4
Pavin, Corey 1959- **1996**:4
Peete, Calvin 1943- **1985**:4
Sarazen, Gene 1902-1999
  Obituary **1999**:4
Singh, Vijay 1963- **2000**:4
Snead, Sam 1912-2002
  Obituary **2003**:3
Strange, Curtis 1955- **1988**:4
Webb, Karrie 1974- **2000**:4
Weir, Mike 1970- **2004**:1
Whaley, Suzy 1966- **2003**:4
Woods, Tiger 1975- **1995**:4

Gorillas
Fossey, Dian 1932-1985
  Obituary **1986**:1

Gospel music
Adams, Yolanda 1961- **2008**:2
Dorsey, Thomas A. 1899-1993
  Obituary **1993**:3

Franklin, Aretha 1942- **1998**:3
Franklin, Kirk 1970- **2010**:2
Houston, Cissy 1933- **1999**:3
Reese, Della 1931- **1999**:2
Staples, Roebuck Pops 1915-2000
  Obituary **2001**:3

Grammy Awards
Adams, Yolanda 1961- **2008**:2
Adele 1988- **2009**:4
Aguilera, Christina 1980- **2000**:4
Anderson, Marion 1897-1993
  Obituary **1993**:4
Anthony, Marc 1969- **2000**:3
Apple, Fiona 1977- **2006**:3
Arrested Development **1994**:2
Ashanti 1980- **2004**:1
Badu, Erykah 1971- **2000**:4
Baker, Anita 1958- **1987**:4
Battle, Kathleen 1948- **1998**:1
Beck 1970- **2000**:2
Beck, Jeff 1944- **2011**:4
Bee Gees, The **1997**:4
Benatar, Pat 1953- **1986**:1
Bennett, Tony 1926- **1994**:4
Berry, Chuck 1926- **2001**:2
Beyonce 1981- **2009**:3
Blades, Ruben 1948- **1998**:2
Bolton, Michael 1953(?)- **1993**:2
Bono 1960- **1988**:4
Boyz II Men **1995**:1
Brandy 1979- **1996**:4
Braxton, Toni 1967- **1994**:3
Brown, James 1928(?)- **1991**:4
Brown, Ruth 1928-2006
  Obituary **2008**:1
Buble, Michael 1975- **2010**:4
Carey, Mariah 1970(?)- **1991**:3
Carpenter, Mary-Chapin 1958(?)-
  1994:1
Carter, Benny 1907-2003
  Obituary **2004**:3
Cash, Johnny 1932- **1995**:3
Cash, June Carter 1929-2003
  Obituary **2004**:2
Chapman, Tracy 1964- **1989**:2
Charles, Ray 1930-2004
  Obituary **2005**:3
Clapton, Eric 1945- **1993**:3
Cleveland, James 1932(?)-1991
  Obituary **1991**:3
Coldplay **2004**:4
Cole, Natalie 1950- **1992**:4
Collins, Albert 1932-1993
  Obituary **1994**:2
Corea, Chick 1941- **1986**:3
Cosby, Bill 1937- **1999**:2
Cray, Robert 1953- **1988**:2
Crosby, David 1941- **2000**:4
Crow, Sheryl 1964- **1995**:2
Cruz, Celia 1925-2003
  Obituary **2004**:3
Daft Punk 1975- **2009**:4
Dangerfield, Rodney 1921-2004
  Obituary **2006**:1
de Larrocha, Alicia 1923-2009
  Obituary **2011**:1
Destiny's Child **2001**:3
Diddley, Bo 1928-2008
  Obituary **2009**:3
Di Meola, Al 1954- **1986**:4
Dion, Celine 1970(?)- **1995**:3
Dixie Chicks **2001**:2

Duran Duran **2005**:3
Dylan, Bob 1941- **1998**:1
Earle, Steve 1955- **2011**:2
Edmonds, Kenneth Babyface
  1958(?)- **1995**:3
Elliott, Missy 1971- **2003**:4
Eminem 1974- **2001**:2
Ertegun, Ahmet 1923- **1986**:3
Etheridge, Melissa 1961(?)- **1995**:4
Eve 1978- **2004**:3
Farrell, Perry 1960- **1992**:2
Fleck, Bela 1958- **2011**:3
Foo Fighters **2006**:2
Ford, Tennessee Ernie 1919-1991
  Obituary **1992**:2
Foster, David 1950(?)- **1988**:2
Franklin, Aretha 1942- **1998**:3
Franklin, Kirk 1970- **2010**:2
Franklin, Melvin 1942-1995
  Obituary **1995**:3
Furtado, Nelly 1978- **2007**:2
Getz, Stan 1927-1991
  Obituary **1991**:4
Gill, Vince 1957- **1995**:2
Goldberg, Whoopi 1955- **1993**:3
Goodman, Benny 1909-1986
  Obituary **1986**:3
Goulet, Robert 1933-2007
  Obituary **2008**:4
Grant, Amy 1961(?)- **1985**:4
Gray, Macy 1970(?)- **2002**:1
Green Day **1995**:4
Hammer, Jan 1948- **1987**:3
Hammer, M. C. **1991**:2
Hancock, Herbie 1940- **1985**:1
Harris, Emmylou 1947- **1991**:3
Harrison, George 1943-2001
  Obituary **2003**:1
Hayes, Isaac 1942- **1998**:4
Headley, Heather 1974- **2011**:1
Hill, Lauryn 1975- **1999**:3
Hirt, Al 1922-1999
  Obituary **1999**:4
Hooker, John Lee 1917- **1998**:1
  Obituary **2002**:3
Horne, Lena 1917- **1998**:4
Hornsby, Bruce 1954(?)- **1989**:3
Houston, Cissy 1933- **1999**:3
Houston, Whitney 1963- **1986**:3
Hubbard, Freddie 1938- **1988**:4
Iglesias, Enrique 1975- **2000**:1
Indigo Girls **1994**:4
Jackson, Michael 1958- **1996**:2
James, Rick 1948-2004
  Obituary **2005**:4
Jarre, Maurice 1924-2009
  Obituary **2010**:2
Jay-Z 1970- **2006**:1
Jennings, Waylon 1937-2002
  Obituary **2003**:2
Joel, Billy 1949- **1994**:3
John, Elton 1947- **1995**:4
Jones, Norah 1979- **2004**:1
Judas Priest 1951- **2011**:3
Keillor, Garrison 1942- **2011**:2
Kenny G 1957(?)- **1994**:4
Keys, Alicia 1981- **2006**:1
Kings of Leon 1982- **2010**:3
Knopfler, Mark 1949- **1986**:2
Kronos Quartet **1993**:1
Lady Antebellum 1982- **2011**:2
Lady Gaga **2011**:1

Harley-Davidson Motor Co., Inc.
Beals, Vaughn 1928- **1988**:2

Hartford, Conn., city government
Perry, Carrie Saxon 1932(?)- **1989**:2

Hasbro, Inc.
Hassenfeld, Stephen 1942- **1987**:4

Hasidism
Schneerson, Menachem Mendel
1902-1994 **1992**:4
Obituary **1994**:4

Hasty Pudding Theatricals
Beatty, Warren 1937- **2000**:1
Burnett, Carol 1933- **2000**:3
Hanks, Tom 1956- **1989**:2
Peters, Bernadette 1948- **2000**:1

Hearst Magazines
Black, Cathleen 1944- **1998**:4
Ganzi, Victor 1947- **2003**:3

Heisman Trophy
Flutie, Doug 1962- **1999**:2
Howard, Desmond Kevin 1970- **1997**:2
Jackson, Bo 1962- **1986**:3
Testaverde, Vinny 1962- **1987**:2
Williams, Ricky 1977- **2000**:2

Helmsley Hotels, Inc.
Helmsley, Leona 1920- **1988**:1

Hemlock Society
Humphry, Derek 1931(?)- **1992**:2

Herbalife International
Hughes, Mark 1956- **1985**:3

Hereditary Disease Foundation
Wexler, Nancy S. 1945- **1992**:3

Herut Party (Israel)
Levy, David 1938- **1987**:2

Hewlett-Packard
Fiorina, Carleton S. 1954- **2000**:1
Hewlett, William 1913-2001
Obituary **2001**:4
Hurd, Mark 1957- **2010**:4
Packard, David 1912-1996
Obituary **1996**:3

High Flight Foundation
Irwin, James 1930-1991
Obituary **1992**:1

Hitchhiking
Heid, Bill
Brief entry **1987**:2

Hobie Cat
Alter, Hobie
Brief entry **1985**:1

Hockey
Bourque, Raymond Jean 1960- **1997**:3
Cherry, Don 1934- **1993**:4
Coffey, Paul 1961- **1985**:4
Crosby, Sidney 1987- **2006**:3
Eagleson, Alan 1933- **1987**:4
Federov, Sergei 1969- **1995**:1
Fuhr, Grant 1962- **1997**:3
Giguere, Jean-Sebastien 1977- **2004**:2
Gilmour, Doug 1963- **1994**:3
Granato, Cammi 1971- **1999**:3
Gretzky, Wayne 1961- **1989**:2
Hextall, Ron 1964- **1988**:2
Hull, Brett 1964- **1991**:4
Jagr, Jaromir 1972- **1995**:4
Kane, Patrick 1988- **2011**:4
Klima, Petr 1964- **1987**:1
Konstantinov, Vladimir 1967- **1997**:4
LaFontaine, Pat 1965- **1985**:1
Lemieux, Claude 1965- **1996**:1
Lemieux, Mario 1965- **1986**:4
Lindbergh, Pelle 1959-1985
Obituary **1985**:4
Lindros, Eric 1973- **1992**:1
Messier, Mark 1961- **1993**:1
Modano, Mike 1970- **2008**:2
Osgood, Chris 1972- **2010**:1
Ovechkin, Alexander 1985- **2009**:2
Pocklington, Peter H. 1941- **1985**:2
Richard, Maurice 1921-2000
Obituary **2000**:4
Roy, Patrick 1965- **1994**:2
Sakic, Joe 1969- **2002**:1
Yzerman, Steve 1965- **1991**:2
Zamboni, Frank J.
Brief entry **1986**:4

Honda Motor Co.
Honda, Soichiro 1906-1991
Obituary **1986**:1

Hong Kong government
Lee, Martin 1938- **1998**:2
Patten, Christopher 1944- **1993**:3

Horror fiction
Barker, Clive 1952- **2003**:3
Brite, Poppy Z. 1967- **2005**:1
Harris, Thomas 1940(?)- **2001**:1
King, Stephen 1947- **1998**:1
Koontz, Dean 1945- **1999**:3
Stine, R. L. 1943- **2003**:1

Horse racing
Borel, Calvin 1966- **2010**:1
Day, Pat 1953- **1995**:2
Desormeaux, Kent 1970- **1990**:2
Krone, Julie 1963(?)- **1989**:2
Lukas, D. Wayne 1936(?)- **1986**:2
McCarron, Chris 1955- **1995**:4
Mellon, Paul 1907-1999
Obituary **1999**:3
O'Donnell, Bill
Brief entry **1987**:4
Pincay, Laffit, Jr. 1946- **1986**:3
Secretariat 1970-1989
Obituary **1990**:1
Shoemaker, Bill 1931-2003
Obituary **2004**:4

Houston, Tex., city government
Watson, Elizabeth 1949- **1991**:2
Whitmire, Kathy 1946- **1988**:2

Houston Astros baseball team
Lofton, Kenny 1967- **1998**:1
Ryan, Nolan 1947- **1989**:4

Houston Oilers football team
Moon, Warren 1956- **1991**:3

Houston Rockets basketball team
Artest, Ron 1979- **2011**:1
Olajuwon, Akeem 1963- **1985**:1
Yao Ming 1980- **2004**:1

Hugo Awards
Asimov, Isaac 1920-1992
Obituary **1992**:3
Farmer, Philip José 1918-2009
Obituary **2010**:2

Human Genome Sciences, Inc. [HGS]
Haseltine, William A. 1944- **1999**:2

Huntington's disease
Wexler, Nancy S. 1945- **1992**:3

Hustler Magazine
Flynt, Larry 1942- **1997**:3

Hyatt Legal Services
Bloch, Henry 1922- **1988**:4
Hyatt, Joel 1950- **1985**:3

Hydroponics
Davis, Noel **1990**:3

Ice cream
Ben & Jerry **1991**:3

Ice skating
Arakawa, Shizuka 1981- **2006**:4
Baiul, Oksana 1977- **1995**:3
Gordeeva, Ekaterina 1972- **1996**:4
Grinkov, Sergei 1967-1995
Obituary **1996**:2
Hamilton, Scott 1958- **1998**:2
Hughes, Sarah 1985- **2002**:4
Kerrigan, Nancy 1969- **1994**:3
Lipinski, Tara 1982- **1998**:3
Thomas, Debi 1967- **1987**:2
Witt, Katarina 1966(?)- **1991**:3
Yamaguchi, Kristi 1971- **1992**:3
Zamboni, Frank J.
Brief entry **1986**:4

Imani Temple
Stallings, George A., Jr. 1948- **1990**:1

Immigration
Brewer, Jan 1944- **2011**:4
Kurzban, Ira 1949- **1987**:2
Lewis, Loida Nicolas 1942- **1998**:3
Mahony, Roger M. 1936- **1988**:2

Imposters
Bremen, Barry 1947- **1987**:3

Inacomp Computer Centers, Inc.
Inatome, Rick 1953- **1985**:4

Hasek, Dominik 1965- **1998**:3

Indiana Pacers basketball team
Artest, Ron 1979- **2011**:1
Miller, Reggie 1965- **1994**:4
Tisdale, Wayman 1964-2009
Obituary **2010**:3

Indiana University basketball team
Knight, Bobby 1940- **1985**:3

Indonesia
Wahid, Abdurrahman 1940- **2000**:3

Insurance
Davison, Ian Hay 1931- **1986**:1
Hilbert, Stephen C. 1946- **1997**:4

Integrated circuit
Noyce, Robert N. 1927- **1985**:4

Intel Corp.
Barrett, Craig R. 1939- **1999**:4
Grove, Andrew S. 1936- **1995**:3
Noyce, Robert N. 1927- **1985**:4

Interarms Corp.
Cummings, Sam 1927- **1986**:3

International Anticounterfeiting Coalition [IACC]
Bikoff, James L.
Brief entry **1986**:2

International Brotherhood of Teamsters
Carey, Ron 1936- **1993**:3
Hoffa, Jim, Jr. 1941- **1999**:2
Presser, Jackie 1926-1988
Obituary **1988**:4
Saporta, Vicki
Brief entry **1987**:3

International Business Machines Corp. [IBM Corp.]
Akers, John F. 1934- **1988**:3
Chaudhari, Praveen 1937- **1989**:4
Gerstner, Lou 1942- **1993**:4
Kohnstamm, Abby 1954- **2001**:1
Palmisano, Samuel J. 1952(?)- **2003**:1

International Creative Management Associates
Mengers, Sue 1938- **1985**:3

International Olympic Committee [IOC]
Eagleson, Alan 1933- **1987**:4
Samaranch, Juan Antonio 1920- **1986**:2

Internet
Adelson, Jay 1970- **2011**:1
Allaire, Jeremy 1971- **2006**:4
Anderson, Tom and Chris DeWolfe **2007**:2
Arrington, Michael 1970- **2011**:4
Barbara and Richard Mikkelson 1959- **2011**:4
Beal, Deron 1968(?)- **2005**:3
Berners-Lee, Tim 1955(?)- **1997**:4
Butterfield, Stewart and Caterina Fake **2007**:3
Chen, Steve and Chad Hurley **2007**:2
Clark, Jim 1944- **1997**:1
Ebbers, Bernie 1943- **1998**:1
Evans, Nancy 1950- **2000**:4
Fanning, Shawn 1980- **2001**:1
Filo, David and Jerry Yang **1998**:3
Gardner, David and Tom **2001**:4
Haladjian, Rafi 1962(?)- **2008**:3
Hill, Graham 1971- **2010**:3
Hilton, Perez 1978- **2010**:3
Housenbold, Jeffrey 1969- **2009**:2
Jennifer Boulden and Heather Stephenson 1973- **2010**:2
Kalin, Rob 1980- **2011**:3
Kilar, Jason 1971- **2010**:1
Koogle, Tim 1951- **2000**:4
Kundra, Vivek 1974- **2010**:3
Lancaster, Jen 1967- **2010**:2
Ma, Jack 1964- **2007**:1
Malda, Rob 1976- **2007**:3
Mikkelson, Barbara 1959- (
See Barbara and Richard Mikkelson)
Mikkelson, Richard 1959- (
See Barbara and Richard Mikkelson)
Nissel, Angela 1974- **2006**:4
Pack, Ellen 1963(?)- **2001**:2
Peluso, Michelle 1971(?)- **2007**:4
Pincus, Mark 1966- **2011**:1
Pirro, Jeanine 1951- **1998**:2
Rosedale, Philip 1968- **2011**:3
Schmidt, Eric 1955- **2002**:4
Stockton, Shreve 1977- **2009**:4
Taylor, Jeff 1960- **2001**:3
Zuckerberg, Mark 1984- **2008**:2

Investment banking
Fomon, Robert M. 1925- **1985**:3

Irish Northern Aid Committee [NORAID]
Galvin, Martin
Brief entry **1985**:3

Irish Republican Army [IRA]
Adams, Gerald 1948- **1994**:1
Galvin, Martin
Brief entry **1985**:3
McGuinness, Martin 1950(?)- **1985**:4

Jacuzzi Bros., Inc.
Jacuzzi, Candido 1903-1986
Obituary **1987**:1

Jaguar Cars PLC
Egan, John 1939- **1987**:2

Jane magazine
Pratt, Jane 1963(?) **1999**:1

Jewish Defense League
Kahane, Meir 1932-1990
Obituary **1991**:2

Joe Boxer Corp.
Graham, Nicholas 1960(?)- **1991**:4

Joffrey Ballet
Joffrey, Robert 1930-1988
Obituary **1988**:3

Jolt Cola
Rapp, C.J.
Brief entry **1987**:3

Judo
Kanokogi, Rusty
Brief entry **1987**:1

Juno Awards
Buble, Michael 1975- **2010**:4
Furtado, Nelly 1978- **2007**:2
Lavigne, Avril 1984- **2005**:2
McLachlan, Sarah 1968- **1998**:4
Nickelback **2007**:2
Sainte-Marie, Buffy 1941- **2000**:1
Timbaland 1971- **2007**:4

Justin Industries
Justin, John Jr. 1917- **1992**:2

Kansas City Chiefs football team
Okoye, Christian 1961- **1990**:2
Thomas, Derrick 1967-2000
Obituary **2000**:3

Kansas City Royals baseball team
Howser, Dick 1936-1987
Obituary **1987**:4
Jackson, Bo 1962- **1986**:3
Saberhagen, Bret 1964- **1986**:1

Kelly Services
Kelly, William R. 1905-1998 **1998**:2

Khmer Rouge
Lon Nol
Obituary **1986**:1

Kitty Litter
Lowe, Edward 1921- **1990**:2

Kloss Video Corp.
Kloss, Henry E.
Brief entry **1985**:2

K Mart Corp.
Antonini, Joseph 1941- **1991**:2
Stewart, Martha 1942(?)- **1992**:1

Kraft General Foods
Fudge, Ann 1951- **2000**:3
Holden, Betsy 1955- **2003**:2
Rosenfeld, Irene 1953- **2008**:3

Ku Klux Klan
Duke, David 1951(?)- **1990**:2

Labor
Bieber, Owen 1929- **1986**:1
Carey, Ron 1936- **1993**:3
Eagleson, Alan 1933- **1987**:4
Fehr, Donald 1948- **1987**:2
Feldman, Sandra 1939- **1987**:3
Hoffa, Jim, Jr. 1941- **1999**:2
Huerta, Dolores 1930- **1998**:1
Kielburger, Craig 1983- **1998**:1
Martin, Lynn 1939- **1991**:4
Nussbaum, Karen 1950- **1988**:3

Presser, Jackie 1926-1988
Obituary **1988**:4
Ramaphosa, Cyril 1953- **1988**:2
Rothstein, Ruth **1988**:2
Saporta, Vicki
Brief entry **1987**:3
Steinberg, Leigh 1949- **1987**:3
Upshaw, Gene 1945- **1988**:1
Williams, Lynn 1924- **1986**:4

Labour Party (Great Britain)
Blair, Tony 1953- **1996**:3
Jenkins, Roy Harris 1920-2003
Obituary **2004**:1
Livingstone, Ken 1945- **1988**:3
Maxwell, Robert 1923- **1990**:1

Ladies Professional Golf Association [LPGA]
Baker, Kathy
Brief entry **1986**:1
Creamer, Paula 1986- **2006**:2
Inkster, Juli 1960- **2000**:2
Kerr, Cristie 1977- **2008**:2
Lopez, Nancy 1957- **1989**:3
Ochoa, Lorena 1981- **2007**:4
Pak, Se Ri 1977- **1999**:4
Sorenstam, Annika 1970- **2001**:1
Webb, Karrie 1974- **2000**:4
Whaley, Suzy 1966- **2003**:4

Language instruction
Thomas, Michel 1911(?)- **1987**:4

Lasers
Gould, Gordon 1920- **1987**:1
Hagelstein, Peter
Brief entry **1986**:3
Maiman, Theodore 1927-2007
Obituary **2008**:3

Law enforcement
Cantrell, Ed
Brief entry **1985**:3
France, Johnny
Brief entry **1987**:1
Harvard, Beverly 1950- **1995**:2
Rizzo, Frank 1920-1991
Obituary **1992**:1
Watson, Elizabeth 1949- **1991**:2
Williams, Willie L. 1944(?)- **1993**:1

Learning Annex
Zanker, Bill
Brief entry **1987**:3

Lear's magazine
Lear, Frances 1923- **1988**:3

Lego toy system
Kristiansen, Kjeld Kirk 1948(?)- **1988**:3

Lenin Peace Prize
Kekkonen, Urho 1900-1986
Obituary **1986**:4

Lettuce Entertain You Enterprises, Inc.
Melman, Richard
Brief entry **1986**:1

Leukemia research
Gale, Robert Peter 1945- **1986**:4

Levi Strauss & Co.
Haas, Robert D. 1942- **1986**:4
Marineau, Philip 1946- **2002**:4

Liberal Democratic Party (Japan)
Miyazawa, Kiichi 1919- **1992**:2

Liberal Party (Canada)
Chretien, Jean 1934- **1990**:4
Peterson, David 1943- **1987**:1

Liberal Party (South Africa)
Paton, Alan 1903-1988
Obituary **1988**:3

Library of Congress
Billington, James 1929- **1990**:3
Dickey, James 1923-1997 **1998**:2
Van Duyn, Mona 1921- **1993**:2

Likud Party (Israel)
Netanyahu, Benjamin 1949- **1996**:4

Lillian Vernon Corp.
Katz, Lillian 1927- **1987**:4

Limelight clubs
Gatien, Peter
Brief entry **1986**:1

Lincoln Savings and Loan
Keating, Charles H., Jr. 1923- **1990**:4

Linguistics
Tannen, Deborah 1945- **1995**:1

Literacy
Bush, Millie 1987- **1992**:1
Kozol, Jonathan 1936- **1992**:1

Little Caesars pizza restaurants
Ilitch, Mike 1929- **1993**:4

Little People's Research Fund
Kopits, Steven E.
Brief entry **1987**:1

Live Aid
Bono 1960- **1988**:4
Dylan, Bob 1941- **1998**:1
Geldof, Bob 1954(?)- **1985**:3
Graham, Bill 1931-1991 **1986**:4
Obituary **1992**:2

L.L. Bean Co.
Gorman, Leon
Brief entry **1987**:1

Lloyd's of London
Davison, Ian Hay 1931- **1986**:1

Loews Corp.
Tisch, Laurence A. 1923- **1988**:2

Log Cabin Republicans
Tafel, Richard 1962- **2000**:4

Lone Ranger
Moore, Clayton 1914-1999
Obituary **2000**:3

Los Angeles city government
Bradley, Tom 1917-1998
Obituary **1999**:1
Riordan, Richard 1930- **1993**:4

Los Angeles Dodgers baseball team
Hershiser, Orel 1958- **1989**:2
Nomo, Hideo 1968- **1996**:2
Welch, Bob 1956- **1991**:3

Los Angeles Express football team
Young, Steve 1961- **1995**:2

Los Angeles Kings hockey team
Gretzky, Wayne 1961- **1989**:2

Los Angeles Lakers basketball team
Artest, Ron 1979- **2011**:1
Bryant, Kobe 1978- **1998**:3
Buss, Jerry 1933- **1989**:3
Chamberlain, Wilt 1936-1999
Obituary **2000**:2
Johnson, Earvin Magic 1959- **1988**:4
Riley, Pat 1945- **1994**:3
Worthy, James 1961- **1991**:2

Los Angeles Museum of Contemporary Art
Isozaki, Arata 1931- **1990**:2

Los Angeles Raiders football team
Gault, Willie 1960- **1991**:2
Upshaw, Gene 1945- **1988**:1

Los Angeles Sparks basketball team
Leslie, Lisa 1972- **1997**:4

Louisiana Legislature
Duke, David 1951(?)- **1990**:2

Louisiana state government
Roemer, Buddy 1943- **1991**:4

Luis Vuitton
Arnault, Bernard 1949- **2000**:4

Magic
Anderson, Harry 1951(?)- **1988**:2
Blackstone, Harry Jr. 1934-1997
Obituary **1997**:4
Blaine, David 1973- **2003**:3
Copperfield, David 1957- **1986**:3
Henning, Doug 1947-1999
Obituary **2000**:3
Jay, Ricky 1949(?)- **1995**:1

Maine State Government
Muskie, Edmund S. 1914-1996
Obituary **1996**:3

Major League Baseball Players Association
Fehr, Donald 1948- **1987**:2
Selig, Bud 1934- **1995**:2

National Academy of Science
Djerassi, Carl 1923- **2000**:4
Van Allen, James 1914-2006
Obituary **2007**:4

National Aeronautics and Space Administration [NASA]
Bean, Alan L. 1932- **1986**:2
Collins, Eileen 1956- **1995**:3
Conrad, Pete 1930-1999
Obituary **2000**:1
Garneau, Marc 1949- **1985**:1
Glenn, John 1921- **1998**:3
Jemison, Mae C. 1956- **1993**:1
Lucid, Shannon 1943- **1997**:1
McAuliffe, Christa 1948-1986
Obituary **1985**:4
O'Keefe, Sean 1956- **2005**:2
Schirra, Wally 1923-2007
Obituary **2008**:3
Shepard, Alan 1923-1998
Obituary **1999**:1

National Association for the Advancement of Colored People [NAACP]
Adams, Yolanda 1961- **2008**:2
Chavis, Benjamin 1948- **1993**:4
Evers-Williams, Myrlie 1933- **1995**:4
Johnson, Robert L. 1946- **2000**:4
LL Cool J 1968- **1998**:2
Mfume, Kweisi 1948- **1996**:3
Parks, Rosa 1913-2005
Obituary **2007**:1

National Audubon Society
Berle, Peter A.A.
Brief entry **1987**:3

National Baptist Convention
Shaw, William 1934(?)- **2000**:3

National Basketball Association [NBA]
Auerbach, Red 1911-2006
Obituary **2008**:1
Bryant, Kobe 1978- **1998**:3
Duncan, Tim 1976- **2000**:1
Garnett, Kevin 1976- **2000**:3
Laimbeer, Bill 1957- **2004**:3
Malone, Karl 1963- **1990**:1
Mikan, George 1924-2005
Obituary **2006**:3
O'Malley, Susan 1962(?)- **1995**:2
Parker, Tony 1982- **2008**:1
Stockton, John Houston 1962- **1997**:3
Wallace, Ben 1974- **2004**:3
Yao Ming 1980- **2004**:1

National Cancer Institute
DeVita, Vincent T., Jr. 1935- **1987**:3
King, Mary-Claire 1946- **1998**:3
Rosenberg, Steven 1940- **1989**:1

National Center for Atmospheric Research
Thompson, Starley
Brief entry **1987**:3

National Coalition for the Homeless
Hayes, Robert M. 1952- **1986**:3

National Coalition on Television Violence [NCTV]
Radecki, Thomas
Brief entry **1986**:2

National Commission on Excellence
Justiz, Manuel J. 1948- **1986**:4

National Conservative Political Action Committee [NCPAC]
Dolan, Terry 1950-1986 **1985**:2

National Education Association [NEA]
Chavez, Linda 1947- **1999**:3
Futrell, Mary Hatwood 1940- **1986**:1

National Endowment for the Arts
Alexander, Jane 1939- **1994**:2
Alexie, Sherman 1966- **1998**:4
Anderson, Laurie 1947- **2000**:2
Bishop, Andre 1948- **2000**:1
Brooks, Gwendolyn 1917-2000 **1998**:1
Obituary **2001**:2
Castillo, Ana 1953- **2000**:4
Charlesworth, Sarah 1947- **2010**:3
Cruz, Nilo 1961(?)- **2004**:4
Erdrich, Louise 1954- **2005**:3
Fagan, Garth 1940- **2000**:1
Gioia, Dana 1950- **2008**:4
Jones, Gayl 1949- **1999**:4
Karr, Mary 1955- **2011**:2
Khan, Ali 1922-2009
Obituary **2010**:3
Lewitzky, Bella 1916-2004
Obituary **2005**:3
Marshall, Susan 1958- **2000**:4
Miller, Bebe 1950- **2000**:2
Oates, Joyce Carol 1938- **2000**:1
Parks, Suzan-Lori 1964- **2003**:2
Reeve, Christopher 1952- **1997**:2
Ringgold, Faith 1930- **2000**:3
Serrano, Andres 1950- **2000**:4
Simmons, Laurie 1949- **2010**:1
Wagner, Catherine F. 1953- **2002**:3
Wolff, Tobias 1945- **2005**:1

National Endowment for the Humanities [NEH]
Cheney, Lynne V. 1941- **1990**:4
Hackney, Sheldon 1933- **1995**:1

National Federation for Decency
Wildmon, Donald 1938- **1988**:4

National Football League [NFL]
Favre, Brett Lorenzo 1969- **1997**:2
Flutie, Doug 1962- **1999**:2
Howard, Desmond Kevin 1970- **1997**:2
Moss, Randy 1977- **1999**:3
Shula, Don 1930- **1992**:2
Tagliabue, Paul 1940- **1990**:2

National Football League Players Association
Upshaw, Gene 1945- **1988**:1

National Hockey League Players Association [NHLPA]
Bourque, Raymond Jean 1960- **1997**:3
Eagleson, Alan 1933- **1987**:4

Fuhr, Grant 1962- **1997**:3

National Hot Rod Association [NHRA]
Muldowney, Shirley 1940- **1986**:1

National Institute of Education
Justiz, Manuel J. 1948- **1986**:4

National Institutes of Health [NIH]
Healy, Bernadine 1944- **1993**:1
Jacobs, Joe 1945(?)- **1994**:1
Zerhouni, Elias A. 1951- **2004**:3

National Organization for Women [NOW]
Abzug, Bella 1920-1998 **1998**:2
Friedan, Betty 1921- **1994**:2
Gandy, Kim 1954(?)- **2002**:2
Ireland, Patricia 1946(?)- **1992**:2
Yard, Molly **1991**:4

National Park Service
Mott, William Penn, Jr. 1909- **1986**:1

National Public Radio [NPR]
Codrescu, Andreaa 1946- **1997**:3
Edwards, Bob 1947- **1993**:2
Gross, Terry 1951- **1998**:3
Magliozzi, Tom and Ray **1991**:4
Maynard, Joyce 1953- **1999**:4
Roberts, Cokie 1943- **1993**:4
Tom and Ray Magliozzi **1991**:4
Totenberg, Nina 1944- **1992**:2

National Restaurant Association
Cain, Herman 1945- **1998**:3

National Rifle Association [NRA]
Foss, Joe 1915- **1990**:3
Helms, Jesse 1921- **1998**:1
Heston, Charlton 1924- **1999**:4

National Science Foundation [NSF]
Bloch, Erich 1925- **1987**:4
Colwell, Rita Rossi 1934- **1999**:3
Geller, Margaret Joan 1947- **1998**:2

National Security Agency
Inman, Bobby Ray 1931- **1985**:1

National Union for the Total Independence of Angola [UNITA]
Savimbi, Jonas 1934- **1986**:2

National Union of Mineworkers [NUM]
Ramaphosa, Cyril 1953- **1988**:2

National Wildlife Federation [NWF]
Hair, Jay D. 1945- **1994**:3

Nation of Islam
Cleaver, Eldridge 1935-1998
Obituary **1998**:4
Farrakhan, Louis 1933- **1990**:4
Shabazz, Betty 1936-1997
Obituary **1997**:4

Native American issues
Banks, Dennis J. 1932(?)- **1986**:4
Begaye, Kelsey 1950(?)- **1999**:3
Brown, Dee 1908-2002

Wyeth, Andrew 1917-2009
Obituary **2010**:1
Wyland, Robert 1956- **2009**:3

Pakistan People's Party
Bhutto, Benazir 1953- **1989**:4

Paleontology
Bakker, Robert T. 1950(?)- **1991**:3
Gould, Stephen Jay 1941-2002
Obituary **2003**:3
Horner, Jack 1946- **1985**:2

Palestine Liberation Organization [PLO]
Abbas, Mahmoud 1935- **2008**:4
Arafat, Yasser 1929- **1989**:3
Darwish, Mahmud 1942-2008
Obituary **2009**:4
Habash, George 1925(?)- **1986**:1
Husseini, Faisal 1940- **1998**:4
Hussein I, King 1935-1999 **1997**:3
Obituary **1999**:3
Redgrave, Vanessa 1937- **1989**:2
Terzi, Zehdi Labib 1924- **1985**:3

Palimony
Marvin, Lee 1924-1987
Obituary **1988**:1
Mitchelson, Marvin 1928- **1989**:2

Palm Computing
Hawkins, Jeff and Donna Dubinsky
2000:2

Paralegals
Furman, Rosemary
Brief entry **1986**:4

Paramount Pictures
Diller, Barry 1942- **1991**:1
Lansing, Sherry 1944- **1995**:4
Steel, Dawn 1946-1997 **1990**:1
Obituary **1998**:2

Parents' Music Resource Center [PMRC]
Gore, Tipper 1948- **1985**:4
Snider, Dee 1955- **1986**:1

Parents of Murdered Children
Hullinger, Charlotte
Brief entry **1985**:1

Paris Opera Ballet Company
Guillem, Sylvie 1965(?)- **1988**:2

Parkinson's disease
Ali, Muhammad 1942- **1997**:2
Langston, J. William
Brief entry **1986**:2

Parks
Mott, William Penn, Jr. 1909- **1986**:1

Parsons Dance Company
Parsons, David 1959- **1993**:4

Parti Quebecois
Johnson, Pierre Marc 1946- **1985**:4
Leaavesque, Reneaa
Obituary **1988**:1

Parizeau, Jacques 1930- **1995**:1

Paul Taylor Dance Company
Taylor, Paul 1930- **1992**:3

Peabody Awards
Child, Julia 1912- **1999**:4
Duncan, Todd 1903-1998
Obituary **1998**:3
Gross, Terry 1951- **1998**:3
Herbert, Don 1917-2007
Obituary **2008**:3
Keeshan, Bob 1927-2004
Obituary **2005**:2
Kuralt, Charles 1934-1997
Obituary **1998**:3
Melendez, Bill 1916-2008
Obituary **2009**:4
Miller, Arthur 1915- **1999**:4
O'Connor, Donald 1925-2003
Obituary **2004**:4
Osgood, Charles 1933- **1996**:2
Schulz, Charles M. 1922- **1998**:1
Terkel, Studs 1912-2008
Obituary **2010**:1

Peace Corps
Ruppe, Loret Miller 1936- **1986**:2

Pennsylvania State University
Paterno, Joe 1926- **1995**:4

Penthouse International Ltd.
Guccione, Bob 1930- **1986**:1

People Express Airlines
Burr, Donald Calvin 1941- **1985**:3

People for the Ethical Treatment of Animals [PETA]
Mathews, Dan 1965- **1998**:3
McCartney, Linda 1942-1998
Obituary **1998**:4
Newkirk, Ingrid 1949- **1992**:3

People Organized and Working for Economic Rebirth [POWER]
Farrakhan, Louis 1933- **1990**:4

People's Choice Awards
Almodovar, Pedro 1951- **2000**:3
Applegate, Christina 1972- **2000**:4
Burnett, Carol 1933- **2000**:3
Rihanna 1988- **2008**:4
Somers, Suzanne 1946- **2000**:1
Timberlake, Justin 1981- **2008**:4

Pepsico, Inc.
Calloway, D. Wayne 1935- **1987**:3
Chidsey, John 1962- **2010**:4
Nooyi, Indra 1955- **2004**:3
Sculley, John 1939- **1989**:4

Performance art
Beuys, Joseph 1921-1986
Obituary **1986**:3
Bogosian, Eric 1953- **1990**:4
Ellis, David 1971- **2009**:4

Finley, Karen 1956- **1992**:4
Irwin, Bill **1988**:3
Ono, Yoko 1933- **1989**:2
Penn & Teller **1992**:1
Pozzi, Lucio 1935- **1990**:2

Perry Ellis Award
Cameron, David
Brief entry **1988**:1
Chung, Doo-Ri 1973- **2011**:3
Hernandez, Lazaro and Jack McCollough **2008**:4
Kim, Eugenia 1974(?)- **2006**:1
Lam, Derek 1966- **2009**:2
Posen, Zac 1980- **2009**:3
Rowley, Cynthia 1958- **2002**:1
Spade, Kate 1962- **2003**:1
Varvatos, John 1956(?)- **2006**:2

Persian Gulf War
Amanpour, Christiane 1958- **1997**:2
Hussein I, King 1935-1999 **1997**:3
Obituary **1999**:3
Kent, Arthur 1954- **1991**:4
Powell, Colin 1937- **1990**:1
Schwarzkopf, Norman 1934- **1991**:3

Philadelphia Eagles football team
Cunningham, Randall 1963- **1990**:1

Philadelphia 76ers basketball team
Barkley, Charles 1963- **1988**:2
Chamberlain, Wilt 1936-1999
Obituary **2000**:2
Iverson, Allen 1975- **2001**:4

Philadelphia Flyers hockey team
Hextall, Ron 1964- **1988**:2
Lindbergh, Pelle 1959-1985
Obituary **1985**:4

Philadelphia Phillies baseball team
Dykstra, Lenny 1963- **1993**:4
Hamels, Cole 1983- **2009**:4
Kruk, John 1961- **1994**:4
McGraw, Tug 1944-2004
Obituary **2005**:1
Schmidt, Mike 1949- **1988**:3
Utley, Chase 1978- **2010**:4
Williams, Ricky 1977- **2000**:2

Philanthropy
Annenberg, Walter 1908- **1992**:3
Astor, Brooke 1902-2007
Obituary **2008**:4
Bolkiah, Sultan Muda Hassanal 1946- **1985**:4
Duke, Doris 1912-1993
Obituary **1994**:2
Ferrell, Trevor
Brief entry **1985**:2
Gates, Melinda 1964- **2010**:4
Haas, Robert D. 1942- **1986**:4
Hammer, Armand 1898-1990
Obituary **1991**:3
Heinz, H.J. 1908-1987
Obituary **1987**:2
Hero, Peter 1942- **2001**:2
Judkins, Reba
Brief entry **1987**:3

Dickey, James 1923-1997 **1998**:2
Dove, Rita 1952- **1994**:3
Dylan, Bob 1941- **1998**:1
Eberhart, Richard 1904-2005
    Obituary **2006**:3
Ginsberg, Allen 1926-1997
    Obituary **1997**:3
Gioia, Dana 1950- **2008**:4
Heaney, Seamus 1939- **1996**:2
Hughes, Ted 1930-1998
    Obituary **1999**:2
Jewel 1974- **1999**:2
Jones, Sarah 1974(?)- **2005**:2
Karr, Mary 1955- **2011**:2
Kunitz, Stanley J. 1905- **2001**:2
Milligan, Spike 1918-2002
    Obituary **2003**:2
Milosz, Czeslaw 1911-2004
    Obituary **2005**:4
Mortensen, Viggo 1958- **2003**:3
Nemerov, Howard 1920-1991
    Obituary **1992**:1
Paz, Octavio 1914- **1991**:2
Sapphire 1951(?)- **1996**:4
Senghor, Leopold 1906-2001
    Obituary **2003**:1
Tohe, Laura 1953- **2009**:2
Tretheway, Natasha 1966- **2008**:3
Van Duyn, Mona 1921- **1993**:2
Walker, Alice 1944- **1999**:1

Polaroid Corp.
    Land, Edwin H. 1909-1991
        Obituary **1991**:3

Pole vaulting
    Olson, Billy 1958- **1986**:3

Pop art
    Castelli, Leo 1907-1999
        Obituary **2000**:1
    Lichtenstein, Roy 1923-1997 **1994**:1
        Obituary **1998**:1
    Paolozzi, Eduardo 1924-2005
        Obituary **2006**:3
    Richter, Gerhard 1932- **1997**:2
    Warhol, Andy 1927(?)-1987
        Obituary **1987**:2

**Popular Front for the Liberation of
Palestine [PFLP]**
    Habash, George 1925(?)- **1986**:1

Pornography
    Dworkin, Andrea 1946-2005
        Obituary **2006**:2
    Flynt, Larry 1942- **1997**:3

Portland, Ore., city government
    Clark, J. E.
        Brief entry **1986**:1

Portland Trail Blazers basketball team
    Drexler, Clyde 1962- **1992**:4
    Wilkens, Lenny 1937- **1995**:2

Presidential Medal of Freedom
    Annenberg, Walter 1908- **1992**:3
    Borlaug, Norman 1914-2009
        Obituary **2011**:1

Cagney, James 1899-1986
    Obituary **1986**:2
Cheek, James Edward
    Brief entry **1987**:1
Copland, Aaron 1900-1990
    Obituary **1991**:2
Cronkite, Walter Leland 1916- **1997**:3
DeBakey, Michael 1908-2008
    Obituary **2009**:3
Ellison, Ralph 1914-1994
    Obituary **1994**:4
Ford, Gerald R. 1913-2007
    Obituary **2008**:2
Fulbright, J. William 1905-1995
    Obituary **1995**:3
Kissinger, Henry 1923- **1999**:4
Luce, Clare Boothe 1903-1987
    Obituary **1988**:1
Ormandy, Eugene 1899-1985
    Obituary **1985**:2
Parks, Rosa 1913-2005
    Obituary **2007**:1
Rickover, Hyman 1900-1986
    Obituary **1986**:4
Rumsfeld, Donald 1932- **2004**:1
Salk, Jonas 1914-1995 **1994**:4
    Obituary **1995**:4
Sinatra, Frank 1915-1998
    Obituary **1998**:4
Smith, Kate 1907(?)-1986
    Obituary **1986**:3
Strauss, Robert 1918- **1991**:4
Wasserman, Lew 1913-2002
    Obituary **2003**:3
Wiesenthal, Simon 1908-2005
    Obituary **2006**:4

President's Council for Physical Fitness
    Schwarzenegger, Arnold 1947- **1991**
    :1

Primerica
    Weill, Sandy 1933- **1990**:4

Princeton, N.J., city government
    Sigmund, Barbara Boggs 1939-1990
        Obituary **1991**:1

Pritzker Prize
    Ando, Tadao 1941- **2005**:4
    Bunshaft, Gordon 1909-1990 **1989**:3
        Obituary **1991**:1
    Foster, Norman 1935- **1999**:4
    Hadid, Zaha 1950- **2005**:3
    Johnson, Philip 1906- **1989**:2
    Koolhaas, Rem 1944- **2001**:1
    Piano, Renzo 1937- **2009**:2
    Pritzker, A.N. 1896-1986
        Obituary **1986**:2
    Roche, Kevin 1922- **1985**:1
    Tange, Kenzo 1913-2005
        Obituary **2006**:2
    Venturi, Robert 1925- **1994**:4

Procter & Gamble Co.
    Lafley, A. G. 1947- **2003**:4
    Smale, John G. 1927- **1987**:3

Proctor & Gardner Advertising, Inc.
    Proctor, Barbara Gardner 1933(?)-
    1985:3

Professional Bowlers Association [PBA]
    Weber, Pete 1962- **1986**:3

Professional Flair
    Verdi-Fletcher, Mary 1955- **1998**:2

Professional Golfers Association [PGA]
    Azinger, Paul 1960- **1995**:2
    Chen, T.C.
        Brief entry **1987**:3
    Couples, Fred 1959- **1994**:4
    Curtis, Ben 1977- **2004**:2
    Furyk, Jim 1970- **2004**:2
    Irwin, Hale 1945- **2005**:2
    Nelson, Byron 1912-2006
        Obituary **2007**:4
    Norman, Greg 1955- **1988**:3
    Peete, Calvin 1943- **1985**:4
    Sarazen, Gene 1902-1999
        Obituary **1999**:4
    Singh, Vijay 1963- **2000**:4
    Stewart, Payne 1957-1999
        Obituary **2000**:2
    Strange, Curtis 1955- **1988**:4
    Weir, Mike 1970- **2004**:1

Progress and Freedom Foundation
    Huffington, Arianna 1950- **1996**:2

Project Head Start
    Zigler, Edward 1930- **1994**:1

Promise Keepers
    McCartney, Bill 1940- **1995**:3

Psychedelic drugs
    Castaneda, Carlos 1931-1998
        Obituary **1998**:4
    Leary, Timothy 1920-1996
        Obituary **1996**:4
    McKenna, Terence **1993**:3

Psychiatry
    Bettelheim, Bruno 1903-1990
        Obituary **1990**:3
    Coles, Robert 1929(?)- **1995**:1
    Frankl, Viktor E. 1905-1997
        Obituary **1998**:1
    Gordon, James 1941- **2009**:4
    Laing, R.D. 1927-1989
        Obituary **1990**:1
    Menninger, Karl 1893-1990
        Obituary **1991**:1

Psychology
    Clark, Kenneth B. 1914-2005
        Obituary **2006**:3
    Herz, Rachel 1963- **2008**:1
    Mindell, Jodi 1962- **2010**:4
    Pinker, Steven A. 1954- **2000**:1

Public Broadcasting Service [PBS]
    Barney **1993**:4
    Cooke, Alistair 1908-2004
        Obituary **2005**:3
    Gunn, Hartford N., Jr. 1926-1986
        Obituary **1986**:2
    Kerger, Paula A. 1957- **2007**:2
    Lewis, Shari 1934-1998 **1993**:1

Unitas, Johnny 1933-2002
  Obituary **2003**:4

San Diego Padres baseball team
  Dravecky, Dave 1956- **1992**:1
  Gwynn, Tony 1960- **1995**:1
  Kroc, Ray 1902-1984
    Obituary **1985**:1
  Sheffield, Gary 1968- **1998**:1

SANE/FREEZE
  Coffin, William Sloane, Jr. 1924- **1990**
    :3

San Francisco city government
  Alioto, Joseph L. 1916-1998
    Obituary **1998**:3
  Brown, Willie 1934- **1996**:4

San Francisco 49ers football team
  DeBartolo, Edward J., Jr. 1946- **1989**
    :3
  Montana, Joe 1956- **1989**:2
  Rice, Jerry 1962- **1990**:4
  Walsh, Bill 1931- **1987**:4
  Young, Steve 1961- **1995**:2

San Francisco Giants baseball team
  Bonds, Barry 1964- **1993**:3
  Dravecky, Dave 1956- **1992**:1

Save the Children Federation
  Guyer, David
    Brief entry **1988**:1

Schottco Corp.
  Schott, Marge 1928- **1985**:4

Schwinn Bicycle Co.
  Schwinn, Edward R., Jr.
    Brief entry **1985**:4

Science fiction
  Anderson, Poul 1926-2001
    Obituary **2002**:3
  Asimov, Isaac 1920-1992
    Obituary **1992**:3
  Butler, Octavia E. 1947- **1999**:3
  Clarke, Arthur C. 1917-2008
    Obituary **2009**:2
  Farmer, Philip José 1918-2009
    Obituary **2010**:2
  Hand, Elizabeth 1957- **2007**:2
  Kelley, DeForest 1929-1999
    Obituary **2000**:1
  Lucas, George 1944- **1999**:4
  Norton, Andre 1912-2005
    Obituary **2006**:2
  Sterling, Bruce 1954- **1995**:4

Sculpture
  Appel, Karel 1921-2006
    Obituary **2007**:2
  Beuys, Joseph 1921-1986
    Obituary **1986**:3
  Bontecou, Lee 1931- **2004**:4
  Borofsky, Jonathan 1942- **2006**:4
  Botero, Fernando 1932- **1994**:3
  Bourgeois, Louise 1911- **1994**:1

Chia, Sandro 1946- **1987**:2
Chillida, Eduardo 1924-2002
  Obituary **2003**:4
Christo 1935- **1992**:3
Conner, Bruce 1933-2008
  Obituary **2009**:3
Dubuffet, Jean 1901-1985
  Obituary **1985**:4
Dunham, Carroll 1949- **2003**:4
Ellis, David 1971- **2009**:4
Gober, Robert 1954- **1996**:3
Goldsworthy, Andy 1956- **2007**:2
Graham, Robert 1938- **1993**:4
Graves, Nancy 1940- **1989**:3
Kaskey, Ray
  Brief entry **1987**:2
Kelly, Ellsworth 1923- **1992**:1
Kiefer, Anselm 1945- **1990**:2
Lin, Maya 1960(?)- **1990**:3
Moore, Henry 1898-1986
  Obituary **1986**:4
Mueck, Ron 1958- **2008**:3
Murakami, Takashi 1962- **2004**:2
Nevelson, Louise 1900-1988
  Obituary **1988**:3
Ono, Yoko 1933- **1989**:2
Paolozzi, Eduardo 1924-2005
  Obituary **2006**:3
Puryear, Martin 1941- **2002**:4
Raimondi, John
  Brief entry **1987**:4
Rauschenberg, Robert 1925- **1991**:2
Rosenberg, Evelyn 1942- **1988**:2
Serra, Richard 1939- **2009**:1
Tamayo, Rufino 1899-1991
  Obituary **1992**:1
Truitt, Anne 1921- **1993**:1

Seagram Co.
  Bronfman, Edgar, Jr. 1955- **1994**:4

Sears, Roebuck & Co.
  Brennan, Edward A. 1934- **1989**:1

Seattle Mariners baseball team
  Griffey, Ken Jr. 1969- **1994**:1
  Hernandez, Felix 1986- **2008**:2
  Johnson, Randy 1963- **1996**:2
  Suzuki, Ichiro 1973- **2002**:2

Seattle Seahawks football team
  Bosworth, Brian 1965- **1989**:1

Seattle Supersonics basketball team
  Kemp, Shawn 1969- **1995**:1
  Wilkens, Lenny 1937- **1995**:2

Second City comedy troupe
  Aykroyd, Dan 1952- **1989**:3
  Belushi, Jim 1954- **1986**:2
  Candy, John 1950-1994 **1988**:2
    Obituary **1994**:3
  Fey, Tina 1970- **2005**:3
  Levy, Eugene 1946- **2004**:3
  Radner, Gilda 1946-1989
    Obituary **1989**:4
  Short, Martin 1950- **1986**:1

Sedelmaier Film Productions
  Sedelmaier, Joe 1933- **1985**:3

Seismology
  Richter, Charles Francis 1900-1985
    Obituary **1985**:4

Senate Armed Services Committee
  Cohen, William S. 1940- **1998**:1
  Goldwater, Barry 1909-1998
    Obituary **1998**:4
  McCain, John S. 1936- **1998**:4
  Nunn, Sam 1938- **1990**:2
  Tower, John 1926-1991
    Obituary **1991**:4

Sharper Image, The
  Thalheimer, Richard 1948-
    Brief entry **1988**:3

Shiites
  Berri, Nabih 1939(?)- **1985**:2
  Khomeini, Ayatollah Ruhollah
    1900(?)-1989
    Obituary **1989**:4
  Rafsanjani, Ali Akbar Hashemi
    1934(?)- **1987**:3

ShoWest Awards
  Cuaron, Alfonso 1961- **2008**:2
  Driver, Minnie 1971- **2000**:1
  LaBeouf, Shia 1986- **2008**:1
  Lane, Diane 1965- **2006**:2
  Ledger, Heath 1979- **2006**:3
  Meyers, Nancy 1949- **2006**:1
  Rogen, Seth 1982- **2009**:3
  Swank, Hilary 1974- **2000**:3
  Yeoh, Michelle 1962- **2003**:2

Shubert Organization
  Schoenfeld, Gerald 1924- **1986**:2

Sierra Club
  McCloskey, J. Michael 1934- **1988**:2

Sinn Fein
  Adams, Gerald 1948- **1994**:1
  McGuinness, Martin 1950(?)- **1985**:4

Skiing
  DiBello, Paul
    Brief entry **1986**:4
  Miller, Bode 1977- **2002**:4
  Street, Picabo 1971- **1999**:3
  Strobl, Fritz 1972- **2003**:3
  Svindal, Aksel 1982- **2011**:2
  Tomba, Alberto 1966- **1992**:3
  Vonn, Lindsey 1984- **2011**:2

Sled dog racing
  Butcher, Susan 1954- **1991**:1

Small Business Administration [SBA]
  Alvarez, Aida **1999**:2

Smith College
  Simmons, Ruth 1945- **1995**:2

Smoking
  Horrigan, Edward, Jr. 1929- **1989**:1
  Maxwell, Hamish 1926- **1989**:4

Televangelism
Graham, Billy 1918- **1992**:1
Hahn, Jessica 1960- **1989**:4
Roberts, Oral 1918-2009
Obituary **2011**:4
Robertson, Pat 1930- **1988**:2
Rogers, Adrian 1931- **1987**:4
Swaggart, Jimmy 1935- **1987**:3

Temple University basketball team
Chaney, John 1932- **1989**:1

Tennis
Agassi, Andre 1970- **1990**:2
Ashe, Arthur 1943-1993
Obituary **1993**:3
Becker, Boris
Brief entry **1985**:3
Capriati, Jennifer 1976- **1991**:1
Clijsters, Kim 1983- **2006**:3
Courier, Jim 1970- **1993**:2
Davenport, Lindsay 1976- **1999**:2
Djokovic, Novak 1987- **2008**:4
Federer, Roger 1981- **2004**:2
Gerulaitis, Vitas 1954-1994
Obituary **1995**:1
Gibson, Althea 1927-2003
Obituary **2004**:4
Graf, Steffi 1969- **1987**:4
Henin-Hardenne, Justine 1982- **2004**:4
Hewitt, Lleyton 1981- **2002**:2
Hingis, Martina 1980- **1999**:1
Ivanisevic, Goran 1971- **2002**:1
Kournikova, Anna 1981- **2000**:3
Kramer, Jack 1921-2009
Obituary **2011**:1
Mauresmo, Amelie 1979- **2007**:2
Navratilova, Martina 1956- **1989**:1
Pierce, Mary 1975- **1994**:4
Querrey, Sam 1987- **2010**:3
Riggs, Bobby 1918-1995
Obituary **1996**:2
Roddick, Andy 1982- **2004**:3
Sabatini, Gabriela
Brief entry **1985**:4
Safin, Marat 1980- **2001**:3
Sampras, Pete 1971- **1994**:1
Seles, Monica 1974(?)- **1991**:3
Sharapova, Maria 1987- **2005**:2
Williams, Serena 1981- **1999**:4
Williams, Venus 1980- **1998**:2

Test tube babies
Steptoe, Patrick 1913-1988
Obituary **1988**:3

Texas Rangers baseball team
Rodriguez, Alex 1975- **2001**:2
Ryan, Nolan 1947- **1989**:4

Texas State Government
Bush, George W., Jr. 1946- **1996**:4
Richards, Ann 1933- **1991**:2

Therapeutic Recreation Systems
Radocy, Robert
Brief entry **1986**:3

Timberline Reclamations
McIntyre, Richard
Brief entry **1986**:2

Time Warner Inc.
Ho, David 1952- **1997**:2
Levin, Gerald 1939- **1995**:2
Ross, Steven J. 1927-1992
Obituary **1993**:3

TLC Beatrice International
Lewis, Loida Nicolas 1942- **1998**:3

TLC Group L.P.
Lewis, Reginald F. 1942-1993 **1988**:4
Obituary **1993**:3

9 to 5
Bravo, Ellen 1944- **1998**:2
Nussbaum, Karen 1950- **1988**:3

Today Show
Couric, Katherine 1957- **1991**:4
Gumbel, Bryant 1948- **1990**:2
Norville, Deborah 1958- **1990**:3

Tony Awards
Abbott, George 1887-1995
Obituary **1995**:3
Alda, Robert 1914-1986
Obituary **1986**:3
Alexander, Jane 1939- **1994**:2
Alexander, Jason 1962(?)- **1993**:3
Allen, Debbie 1950- **1998**:2
Allen, Joan 1956- **1998**:1
Arkin, Alan 1934- **2007**:4
Arthur, Bea 1922-2009
Obituary **2010**:2
Bacall, Lauren 1924- **1997**:3
Bailey, Pearl 1918-1990
Obituary **1991**:1
Bancroft, Anne 1931-2005
Obituary **2006**:3
Bates, Alan 1934-2003
Obituary **2005**:1
Bennett, Michael 1943-1987
Obituary **1988**:1
Bloch, Ivan 1940- **1986**:3
Booth, Shirley 1898-1992
Obituary **1993**:2
Brooks, Mel 1926- **2003**:1
Brown, Ruth 1928-2006
Obituary **2008**:1
Brynner, Yul 1920(?)-1985
Obituary **1985**:4
Buckley, Betty 1947- **1996**:2
Burnett, Carol 1933- **2000**:3
Carter, Nell 1948-2003
Obituary **2004**:2
Channing, Stockard 1946- **1991**:3
Chenoweth, Kristin 1968- **2010**:4
Close, Glenn 1947- **1988**:3
Crawford, Cheryl 1902-1986
Obituary **1987**:1
Crawford, Michael 1942- **1994**:2
Cronyn, Hume 1911-2003
Obituary **2004**:3
Davis, Viola 1965- **2011**:4
Dench, Judi 1934- **1999**:4
Dennis, Sandy 1937-1992
Obituary **1992**:4
Dewhurst, Colleen 1924-1991
Obituary **1992**:2
Dunagan, Deanna 1940- **2009**:2
Ebersole, Christine 1953- **2007**:2

Fagan, Garth 1940- **2000**:1
Ferrer, Jose 1912-1992
Obituary **1992**:3
Fiennes, Ralph 1962- **1996**:2
Fierstein, Harvey 1954- **2004**:2
Fishburne, Laurence 1961(?)- **1995**:3
Flanders, Ed 1934-1995
Obituary **1995**:3
Fosse, Bob 1927-1987
Obituary **1988**:1
Foster, Sutton 1975- **2003**:2
Gelbart, Larry 1928-2009
Obituary **2011**:1
Gleason, Jackie 1916-1987
Obituary **1987**:4
Glover, Savion 1973- **1997**:1
Goulet, Robert 1933-2007
Obituary **2008**:4
Hagen, Uta 1919-2004
Obituary **2005**:2
Harrison, Rex 1908-1990
Obituary **1990**:4
Headley, Heather 1974- **2011**:1
Hepburn, Katharine 1909- **1991**:2
Hines, Gregory 1946- **1992**:4
Hoffman, Dustin 1937- **2005**:4
Howard, Ken 1944- **2010**:4
Hwang, David Henry 1957- **1999**:1
Irons, Jeremy 1948- **1991**:4
Jackman, Hugh 1968- **2004**:4
Kahn, Madeline 1942-1999
Obituary **2000**:2
Keaton, Diane 1946- **1997**:1
Kline, Kevin 1947- **2000**:1
Kushner, Tony 1956- **1995**:2
Lane, Nathan 1956- **1996**:4
Langella, Frank 1940- **2008**:3
Lansbury, Angela 1925- **1993**:1
LaPaglia, Anthony 1959- **2004**:4
Lithgow, John 1945- **1985**:2
LuPone, Patti 1949- **2009**:2
Mantegna, Joe 1947- **1992**:1
Matthau, Walter 1920- **2000**:3
McKellen, Ian 1939- **1994**:1
Merrick, David 1912-2000
Obituary **2000**:4
Midler, Bette 1945- **1989**:4
Miller, Arthur 1915- **1999**:4
Moore, Dudley 1935-2002
Obituary **2003**:2
Nichols, Mike 1931- **1994**:4
Nunn, Trevor 1940- **2000**:2
Orbach, Jerry 1935-2004
Obituary **2006**:1
Pacino, Al 1940- **1993**:4
Papp, Joseph 1921-1991
Obituary **1992**:2
Parker, Mary-Louise 1964- **2002**:2
Peters, Bernadette 1948- **2000**:1
Preston, Robert 1918-1987
Obituary **1987**:3
Prince, Faith 1959(?)- **1993**:2
Reilly, Charles Nelson
Obituary **2008**:3
Reza, Yasmina 1959(?)- **1999**:2
Richards, Lloyd 1919-2006
Obituary **2007**:3
Richardson, Natasha 1963-2009
Obituary **2010**:2
Robbins, Jerome 1918-1998
Obituary **1999**:1
Ruehl, Mercedes 1948(?)- **1992**:4

Rylance, Mark 1960- **2009**:3
Salonga, Lea 1971- **2003**:3
Schreiber, Liev 1967- **2007**:2
Shanley, John Patrick 1950- **2006**:1
Sheldon, Sidney 1917-2007
  Obituary **2008**:2
Sondheim, Stephen 1930- **1994**:4
Spacey, Kevin 1959- **1996**:4
Stapleton, Maureen 1925-2006
  Obituary **2007**:2
Stoppard, Tom 1937- **1995**:4
Stritch, Elaine 1925- **2002**:4
Stroman, Susan **2000**:4
Styne, Jule 1905-1994
  Obituary **1995**:1
Szot, Paulo 1969- **2009**:3
Tune, Tommy 1939- **1994**:2
Verdon, Gwen 1925-2000
  Obituary **2001**:2
Wasserstein, Wendy 1950- **1991**:3
Wayne, David 1914-1995
  Obituary **1995**:3
White, Julie 1961- **2008**:2
Whitehead, Robert 1916-2002
  Obituary **2003**:3
Whitmore, James 1921-2009
  Obituary **2010**:1
Winokur, Marissa Jaret 1973- **2005**:1
Wong, B.D. 1962- **1998**:1
Worth, Irene 1916-2002
  Obituary **2003**:2

Toronto Blue Jays baseball team
  Ainge, Danny 1959- **1987**:1
  Carter, Joe 1960- **1994**:2
  Wells, David 1963- **1999**:3

Toronto Maple Leafs hockey team
  Gilmour, Doug 1963- **1994**:3

Tour de France
  Armstrong, Lance 1971- **2000**:1
  Indurain, Miguel 1964- **1994**:1
  LeMond, Greg 1961- **1986**:4

Toyota Motor Corp.
  Toyoda, Akio 1956- **2011**:1
  Toyoda, Eiji 1913- **1985**:2

Toys and games
  Barad, Jill 1951- **1994**:2
  Bushnell, Nolan 1943- **1985**:1
  Hakuta, Ken
    Brief entry **1986**:1
  Haney, Chris
    Brief entry **1985**:1
  Hassenfeld, Stephen 1942- **1987**:4
  Kingsborough, Donald
    Brief entry **1986**:2
  Kristiansen, Kjeld Kirk 1948(?)- **1988**
    :3
  Lazarus, Charles 1923- **1992**:4
  Roberts, Xavier 1955- **1985**:3
  Rowland, Pleasant **1992**:3

Toys R Us
  Eyler, John. H., Jr. 1948(?)- **2001**:3
  Lazarus, Charles 1923- **1992**:4

Track and field
  Bolt, Usain 1986- **2009**:2
  Johnson, Michael **2000**:1
  Jones, Marion 1975- **1998**:4

Joyner, Florence Griffith 1959-1998
  1989:2
  Obituary **1999**:1
Wariner, Jeremy 1984- **2006**:3

Trade negotiation
  Hills, Carla 1934- **1990**:3
  Reisman, Simon 1919- **1987**:4

Tradex
  Hakuta, Ken
    Brief entry **1986**:1

Travel
  Arison, Ted 1924- **1990**:3
  Brown, Samantha 1969- **2011**:3
  Fodor, Eugene 1906(?)-1991
    Obituary **1991**:3
  Steger, Will 1945(?)- **1990**:4

Treasure Salvors, Inc.
  Fisher, Mel 1922(?)- **1985**:4

TreePeople
  Lipkis, Andy
    Brief entry **1985**:3

Trevor's Campaign
  Ferrell, Trevor
    Brief entry **1985**:2

Trivial Pursuit
  Haney, Chris
    Brief entry **1985**:1

Twentieth Century-Fox Film Corp.
  Diller, Barry 1942- **1991**:1
  Goldberg, Leonard 1934- **1988**:4

U2
  Bono 1960- **1988**:4
  U2 **2002**:4

UFW
  Chavez, Cesar 1927-1993
    Obituary **1993**:4

Ultralight aircraft
  MacCready, Paul 1925- **1986**:4
  Moody, John 1943- **1985**:3

Uncle Noname (cookie company)
  Amos, Wally 1936- **2000**:1

UNICEF
  Bellamy, Carol 1942- **2001**:2
  Hepburn, Audrey 1929-1993
    Obituary **1993**:2
  Styler, Trudie 1954- **2009**:1
  Ustinov, Peter 1921-2004
    Obituary **2005**:3

Union Pacific Railroad
  Harriman, W. Averell 1891-1986
    Obituary **1986**:4

United Airlines
  Friend, Patricia A. 1946- **2003**:3
  Wolf, Stephen M. 1941- **1989**:3

United Auto Workers [UAW]
  Bieber, Owen 1929- **1986**:1
  Woodcock, Leonard 1911-2001
    Obituary **2001**:4
  Yokich, Stephen P. 1935- **1995**:4

United Farm Workers [UFW]
  Chavez, Cesar 1927-1993
    Obituary **1993**:4
  Huerta, Dolores 1930- **1998**:1

United Federation of Teachers
  Feldman, Sandra 1939- **1987**:3

United Nations
  Ban, Ki-moon 1944- **2011**:2
  Rice, Susan E. 1964- **2010**:3

United Nations [UN]
  Albright, Madeleine 1937- **1994**:3
  Annan, Kofi 1938- **1999**:1
  Arbour, Louise 1947- **2005**:1
  Astorga, Nora 1949(?)-1988 **1988**:2
  Bailey, Pearl 1918-1990
    Obituary **1991**:1
  de Pinies, Jamie
    Brief entry **1986**:3
  Fulbright, J. William 1905-1995
    Obituary **1995**:3
  Ghali, Boutros Boutros 1922- **1992**:3
  Gromyko, Andrei 1909-1989
    Obituary **1990**:2
  Kirkpatrick, Jeane 1926-2006
    Obituary **2008**:1
  Kouchner, Bernard 1939- **2005**:3
  Lewis, Stephen 1937- **1987**:2
  Lodge, Henry Cabot 1902-1985
    Obituary **1985**:1
  Perez de Cuellar, Javier 1920- **1991**:3
  Terzi, Zehdi Labib 1924- **1985**:3

United Petroleum Corp.
  Aurre, Laura
    Brief entry **1986**:3

United Press International [UPI]
  Thomas, Helen 1920- **1988**:4

United Steelworkers of America [USW]
  Williams, Lynn 1924- **1986**:4

University Network
  Scott, Gene
    Brief entry **1986**:1

University of Chicago
  Friedman, Milton 1912-2006
    Obituary **2008**:1
  Gray, Hanna 1930- **1992**:4

University of Colorado football team
  McCartney, Bill 1940- **1995**:3

University of Las Vegas at Nevada basketball team
  Tarkenian, Jerry 1930- **1990**:4

University of Michigan football team
  Harmon, Tom 1919-1990
    Obituary **1990**:3
  McCartney, Bill 1940- **1995**:3

Schembechler, Bo 1929(?)- **1990**:3

University of Notre Dame
Holtz, Lou 1937- **1986**:4
Malloy, Edward Monk 1941- **1989**:4

University of Pennsylvania
Gutmann, Amy 1949- **2008**:4
Rodin, Judith 1945(?)- **1994**:4

University of Tennessee
Alexander, Lamar 1940- **1991**:2

University of Wisconsin
Shalala, Donna 1941- **1992**:3

UNIX
Ritchie, Dennis and Kenneth
Thompson **2000**:1

Untouchables
Ram, Jagjivan 1908-1986
Obituary **1986**:4

Urban design
Cooper, Alexander 1936- **1988**:4

U.S. Civil Rights Commission
Pendleton, Clarence M. 1930-1988
Obituary **1988**:4

U.S. Department of Transportation
Peters, Mary E. 1948- **2008**:3
Slater, Rodney E. 1955- **1997**:4

U.S. House of Representatives
Abzug, Bella 1920-1998 **1998**:2
Aspin, Les 1938-1995
Obituary **1996**:1
Bono, Sonny 1935-1998 **1992**:2
Obituary **1998**:2
Clyburn, James 1940- **1999**:4
Collins, Cardiss 1931- **1995**:3
Conyers, John, Jr. 1929- **1999**:1
DeLay, Tom 1947- **2000**:1
Fenwick, Millicent H.
Obituary **1993**:2
Ferraro, Geraldine 1935- **1998**:3
Foley, Thomas S. 1929- **1990**:1
Frank, Barney 1940- **1989**:2
Fulbright, J. William 1905-1995
Obituary **1995**:3
Gephardt, Richard 1941- **1987**:3
Gingrich, Newt 1943- **1991**:1
Gore, Albert, Sr. 1907-1998
Obituary **1999**:2
Hastert, Dennis 1942- **1999**:3
Hyde, Henry 1924- **1999**:1
Jackson, Jesse, Jr. 1965- **1998**:3
Jordan, Barbara 1936-1996
Obituary **1996**:3
Langevin, James R. 1964- **2001**:2
McCarthy, Carolyn 1944- **1998**:4
McKinney, Cynthia A. 1955- **1997**:1
McKinney, Stewart B. 1931-1987
Obituary **1987**:4
McMillen, Tom 1952- **1988**:4
Mfume, Kweisi 1948- **1996**:3
Mills, Wilbur 1909-1992

Obituary **1992**:4
O'Neill, Tip 1912-1994
Obituary **1994**:3
Pelosi, Nancy 1940- **2004**:2
Pepper, Claude 1900-1989
Obituary **1989**:4
Quayle, Dan 1947- **1989**:2
Ros-Lehtinen, Ileana 1952- **2000**:2
Roybal-Allard, Lucille 1941- **1999**:4
Sanchez, Loretta 1960- **2000**:3
Sanders, Bernie 1941(?)- **1991**:4
Udall, Mo 1922-1998
Obituary **1999**:2
Waters, Maxine 1938- **1998**:4
Watts, J.C. 1957- **1999**:2

U.S. National Security Adviser
Berger, Sandy 1945- **2000**:1

U.S. Office of Management and Budget
Raines, Franklin 1949- **1997**:4

U.S. Postal Service
Frank, Anthony M. 1931(?)- **1992**:1

U.S. Public Health Service
Koop, C. Everett 1916- **1989**:3
Novello, Antonia 1944- **1991**:2
Sullivan, Louis 1933- **1990**:4

U.S. Senate
Abrams, Elliott 1948- **1987**:1
Biden, Joe 1942- **1986**:3
Boxer, Barbara 1940- **1995**:1
Bradley, Bill 1943- **2000**:2
Braun, Carol Moseley 1947- **1993**:1
Campbell, Ben Nighthorse 1933-
1998:1
Cohen, William S. 1940- **1998**:1
D'Amato, Al 1937- **1996**:1
Dole, Bob 1923- **1994**:2
Ervin, Sam 1896-1985
Obituary **1985**:2
Feinstein, Dianne 1933- **1993**:3
Fulbright, J. William 1905-1995
Obituary **1995**:3
Glenn, John 1921- **1998**:3
Goldwater, Barry 1909-1998
Obituary **1998**:4
Hatch, Orin G. 1934- **2000**:2
Heinz, John 1938-1991
Obituary **1991**:4
Helms, Jesse 1921- **1998**:1
Jackson, Jesse 1941- **1996**:1
Kassebaum, Nancy 1932- **1991**:1
Kemp, Jack 1935- **1990**:4
Lott, Trent 1941- **1998**:1
McCain, John S. 1936- **1998**:4
Mikulski, Barbara 1936- **1992**:4
Mitchell, George J. 1933- **1989**:3
Morrison, Trudi
Brief entry **1986**:2
Muskie, Edmund S. 1914-1996
Obituary **1996**:3
Nunn, Sam 1938- **1990**:2
Pepper, Claude 1900-1989
Obituary **1989**:4
Quayle, Dan 1947- **1989**:2
Ribicoff, Abraham 1910-1998
Obituary **1998**:3
Snowe, Olympia 1947- **1995**:3

Thompson, Fred 1942- **1998**:2
Tower, John 1926-1991
Obituary **1991**:4

U.S. Supreme Court
Blackmun, Harry A. 1908-1999
Obituary **1999**:3
Brennan, William 1906-1997
Obituary **1997**:4
Breyer, Stephen Gerald 1938- **1994**:4
Burger, Warren E. 1907-1995
Obituary **1995**:4
Flynt, Larry 1942- **1997**:3
Ginsburg, Ruth Bader 1933- **1993**:4
Kagan, Elena 1960- **2011**:4
Marshall, Thurgood 1908-1993
Obituary **1993**:3
O'Connor, Sandra Day 1930- **1991**:1
Powell, Lewis F. 1907-1998
Obituary **1999**:1
Rehnquist, William H. 1924- **2001**:2
Scalia, Antonin 1936- **1988**:2
Sotomayor, Sonia 1954- **2010**:4
Souter, David 1939- **1991**:3
Stewart, Potter 1915-1985
Obituary **1986**:1
Thomas, Clarence 1948- **1992**:2

U.S. Trade Representative
Barshefsky, Charlene 1951(?)- **2000**:4

U.S. Treasury
Bentsen, Lloyd 1921- **1993**:3

USA Network
Herzog, Doug 1960(?)- **2002**:4
Koplovitz, Kay 1945- **1986**:3

Utah Jazz basketball team
Malone, Karl 1963- **1990**:1
Maravich, Pete 1948-1988
Obituary **1988**:2
Stockton, John Houston 1962- **1997**:3

Vampires
Kostova, Elizabeth 1964- **2006**:2
Pattinson, Robert 1986- **2010**:1
Rice, Anne 1941- **1995**:1

Vanity Fair magazine
Brown, Tina 1953- **1992**:1

Venezuela
Perez, Carlos Andre 1922- **1990**:2

Veterinary medicine
Redig, Patrick 1948- **1985**:3

Viacom, Inc.
Karmazin, Mel 1943- **2006**:1
Redstone, Sumner 1923- **1994**:1

Vietnam War
Dong, Pham Van 1906-2000
Obituary **2000**:4

Vigilantism
Goetz, Bernhard Hugo 1947(?)- **1985**
:3

Cumulative Newsmakers Index

This index lists all newsmakers included in the entire *Newsmakers* series.

Listee names are followed by a year and issue number; thus **1996**:3 indicates that an entry on that individual appears in both 1996, Issue 3, and the 1996 cumulation.

Gould, Gordon 1920- **1987**:1
Gould, Stephen Jay 1941-2002
   Obituary **2003**:3
Goulet, Robert 1933-2007
   Obituary **2008**:4
Gowda, H. D. Deve 1933- **1997**:1
Grace, J. Peter 1913- **1990**:2
Grace, Topher 1978- **2005**:4
Graden, Brian 1963- **2004**:2
Graf, Steffi 1969- **1987**:4
Grafton, Sue 1940- **2000**:2
Graham, Bill 1931-1991 .... **1986**:4
   Obituary **1992**:2
Graham, Billy 1918- **1992**:1
Graham, Donald 1945- **1985**:4
Graham, Heather 1970- **2000**:1
Graham, Katharine Meyer 1917- .. **1997**:3
   Obituary **2002**:3
Graham, Lauren 1967- **2003**:4
Graham, Martha 1894-1991
   Obituary **1991**:4
Graham, Nicholas 1960(?)- **1991**:4
Graham, Robert 1938- **1993**:4
Grajonca, Wolfgang
   See Graham, Bill
Gramm, Phil 1942- **1995**:2
Grammer, Kelsey 1955(?)- **1995**:1
Granato, Cammi 1971- **1999**:3
Grandin, Temple 1947- **2006**:1
Grange, Harold
   See Grange, Red
Grange, Red 1903-1991
   Obituary **1991**:3
Granger, Clive 1934-2009
   Obituary **2010**:3
Granholm, Jennifer 1959- **2003**:3
Grant, Amy 1961(?)- **1985**:4
Grant, Cary 1904-1986
   Obituary **1987**:1
Grant, Charity
   Brief entry **1985**:2
Grant, Hugh 1960- **1995**:3
Grant, Rodney A. **1992**:1
Grappelli, Stephane 1908-1997
   Obituary **1998**:1
Grass, Gunter 1927- **2000**:2
Graves, Michael 1934- **2000**:1
Graves, Nancy 1940- **1989**:3
Graves, Ron 1967- **2009**:3
Gray, David 1970- **2001**:4
Gray, Frizzell
   See Mfume, Kweisi
Gray, Hanna 1930- **1992**:4
Gray, John 1952(?)- **1995**:3
Gray, Macy 1970(?)- **2002**:1
Gray, Simon 1936-2008
   Obituary **2009**:4
Gray, Spalding 1941-2004
   Obituary **2005**:2
Grazer, Brian 1951- **2006**:4
Graziano, Rocky 1922-1990
   Obituary **1990**:4
Graziano, Thomas Rocco
   See Graziano, Rocky
Grebenshikov, Boris 1953- **1990**:1
Green, Philip 1952- **2008**:2
Green, Richard R. 1936- **1988**:3
Green, Seth 1974- **2010**:1
Green, Tom 1972- **1999**:4
Greenberg, Hank 1911-1986
   Obituary **1986**:4

Greenberg, Henry Benjamin
   See Greenberg, Hank
Greenberg, Robert 1940(?)- **2003**:2
Green Day **1995**:4
Greene, Brian 1963- **2003**:4
Greene, Graham 1904-1991
   Obituary **1991**:4
Greene, Graham 1952- **1997**:2
Greene, Lorne 1915-1987
   Obituary **1988**:1
Greenfield, Jerry
   See Ben & Jerry
Greenspan, Alan 1926- **1992**:2
Greenwald, Julie 1970- **2008**:1
Gregoire, Chris 1947- **2010**:2
Gregorian, Vartan 1934- **1990**:3
Gregory, Cynthia 1946- **1990**:2
Gregory, David 1970- **2010**:2
Gregory, Dick 1932- **1990**:3
Gregory, Philippa 1954- **2010**:1
Gregory, Rogan 1972- **2008**:2
Greiner, Helen 1967- **2010**:2
Gretzky, Wayne 1961- **1989**:2
Grier, Pam 1949- **1998**:3
Griff, Professor
   See Public Enemy
Griffey, Ken Jr. 1969- **1994**:1
Griffin, Kathy 1961- **2010**:4
Griffin, Merv 1925-2008
   Obituary **2008**:4
Griffin, Richard
   See Public Enemy
Griffin, Toni 1964- **2011**:3
Griffith, Melanie 1957- **1989**:2
Griffith, Nicola 1960- **2010**:2
Griffiths, Martha 1912-2003
   Obituary **2004**:2
Grinkov, Sergei 1967-1995
   Obituary **1996**:2
Grisham, John 1955- **1994**:4
Groban, Josh 1981- **2009**:1
Grodin, Charles 1935- **1997**:3
Groening, Matt 1955(?)- **1990**:4
Grohl, Dave
   See Nirvana
Gromyko, Andrei 1909-1989
   Obituary **1990**:2
Gross, Terry 1951- **1998**:3
Grove, Andrew S. 1936- **1995**:3
Groves, Robert 1949- **2011**:3
Grucci, Felix 1905- **1987**:1
Gruden, Jon 1963- **2003**:4
Grusin, Dave
   Brief entry **1987**:2
Grylls, Bear 1974- **2010**:2
Gucci, Maurizio
   Brief entry **1985**:4
Guccione, Bob 1930- **1986**:1
Guccione, Bob, Jr. 1956- **1991**:4
Gudmundsdottir, Bjork
   See Bjork
Guebuza, Armando 1943- **2008**:4
Guelleh, Ismail Omar 1947- **2006**:2
Guest, Christopher 1948- **2004**:2
Guggenheim, Charles 1924-2002
   Obituary **2003**:4
Guillem, Sylvie 1965(?)- **1988**:2
Guinness, Alec 1914-2000
   Obituary **2001**:1
Gul, Abdullah 1950- **2009**:4
Gumbel, Bryant 1948- **1990**:2
Gumbel, Greg 1946- **1996**:4

Gund, Agnes 1938- **1993**:2
Gunn, Hartford N., Jr. 1926-1986
   Obituary **1986**:2
Guo Jingjing 1981- **2009**:2
Gupta, Sanjay 1969- **2009**:4
Gursky, Andreas 1955- **2002**:2
Gustafsson, Greta Lovisa
   See Garbo, Greta
Gutierrez, Carlos M. 1953- **2001**:4
Gutmann, Amy 1949- **2008**:4
Guyer, David
   Brief entry **1988**:1
Gwynn, Tony 1960- **1995**:1
Gyllenhaal, Jake 1980- **2005**:3
Gyllenhaal, Maggie 1977- **2009**:2
Haas, Robert D. 1942- **1986**:4
Habash, George 1925(?)- **1986**:1
Habibie, Bacharuddin
   Jusuf 1936- **1999**:3
Hackett, Buddy 1924-2003
   Obituary **2004**:3
Hackman, Gene 1931- **1989**:3
Hackney, Sheldon 1933- **1995**:1
Haddon, Mark 1962- **2005**:2
Hadid, Zaha 1950- **2005**:3
Hagelstein, Peter
   Brief entry **1986**:3
Hagen, Uta 1919-2004
   Obituary **2005**:2
Haggis, Paul 1953- **2006**:4
Hagler, Marvelous Marvin 1954- .. **1985**:2
Hagler, Marvin Nathaniel
   See Hagler, Marvelous Marvin
Hahn, Carl H. 1926- **1986**:4
Hahn, Jessica 1960- **1989**:4
Hair, Jay D. 1945- **1994**:3
Ha Jin 1956- **2000**:3
Hakuta, Ken
   Brief entry **1986**:1
Haladjian, Rafi 1962(?)- **2008**:3
Halberstam, David 1934-2007
   Obituary **2008**:3
Haldeman, H. R. 1926-1993
   Obituary **1994**:2
Hale, Alan 1957- **1997**:3
Hale, Clara
   See Hale, Clara
Hale, Clara 1905-1992
   Obituary **1993**:3
Hale, Victoria 1961(?)- **2008**:4
Haley, Alex 1924-1992
   Obituary **1992**:3
Hall, Anthony Michael 1968- **1986**:3
Hall, Arsenio 1955- **1990**:2
Hall, Gus 1910-2000
   Obituary **2001**:2
Hall, Michael 1971- **2011**:1
Hall, Michael Anthony Thomas Charles
   See Hall, Anthony Michael
Hallstrom, Lasse 1946- **2002**:3
Halonen, Tarja 1943- **2006**:4
Halston 1932-1990
   Obituary **1990**:3
Hamels, Cole 1983- **2009**:4
Hamilton, Hamish 1900-1988
   Obituary **1988**:4
Hamilton, Laurell K. 1963- **2008**:2
Hamilton, Lewis 1985- **2008**:4
Hamilton, Margaret 1902-1985
   Obituary **1985**:3
Hamilton, Scott 1958- **1998**:2
Hamm, Jon 1971- **2009**:2

Perez, Carlos Andre 1922- **1990**:2
Perez, Rosie **1994**:2
Perez de Cuellar, Javier 1920- **1991**:3
Perkins, Anthony 1932-1992
   Obituary **1993**:2
Perkins, Carl 1932-1998 .... **1998**:2
Perlman, Steve 1961(?)- **1998**:2
Perot, H. Ross 1930- **1992**:4
Perry, Carrie Saxon 1932(?)- **1989**:2
Perry, Harold A. 1917(?)-1991
   Obituary **1992**:1
Perry, Lincoln Theodore Monroe Andrew
   See Fetchit, Stepin
Perry, Luke 1966(?)- **1992**:3
Perry, Matthew 1969- **1997**:2
Perry, Tyler 1969- **2006**:1
Perry, William 1927- **1994**:4
Perske, Betty Joan
   See Bacall, Lauren
Persson, Nina
   See Cardigans, The
Persson, Stefan 1947- **2004**:1
Perutz, Max 1914-2002
   Obituary **2003**:2
Pesci, Joe 1943- **1992**:4
Peter, Valentine J. 1934- **1988**:2
Peters, Bernadette 1948- **2000**:1
Peters, Mary E. 1948- **2008**:3
Peters, Tom 1942- **1998**:1
Petersen, Donald Eugene 1926- **1985**:1
Peterson, Cassandra
   See Peterson, Cassandra
Peterson, Cassandra 1951- **1988**:1
Peterson, David 1943- **1987**:1
Peterson, Oscar 1925-2007
   Obituary **2009**:1
Peterson, Roger Tory 1908-1996
   Obituary **1997**:1
Peterson, Toni Pihl
   See Lander, Toni
Petrossian, Christian
   Brief entry **1985**:3
Petty, Tom 1952- **1988**:1
Peyton, Elizabeth 1965- **2007**:1
Pfeiffer, Eckhard 1941- **1998**:4
Pfeiffer, Michelle 1957- **1990**:2
Phair, Liz 1967- **1995**:3
Phelan, John Joseph, Jr. 1931- **1985**:4
Phelps, Michael 1985- **2009**:2
Phifer, Mekhi 1975- **2004**:1
Philbin, Regis 1933- **2000**:2
Philby, Harold Adrian Russell
   See Philby, Kim
Philby, Kim 1912-1988
   Obituary **1988**:3
Phillips, John 1935-2001
   Obituary **2002**:1
Phillips, Julia 1944- **1992**:1
Phillips, Sam 1923-2003
   Obituary **2004**:4
Phoenix **2011**:1
Phoenix, Joaquin 1974- **2000**:4
Phoenix, River 1970-1993 .... **1990**:2
   Obituary **1994**:2
Piano, Renzo 1937- **2009**:2
Piazza, Mike 1968- **1998**:4
Picasso, Paloma 1949- **1991**:1
Pickett, Wilson 1941-2006
   Obituary **2007**:1
Picoult, Jodi 1966- **2008**:1
Pierce, David Hyde 1959- **1996**:3
Pierce, Frederick S. 1934(?)- **1985**:3

Pierce, Mary 1975- **1994**:4
Pierce, Paul 1977- **2009**:2
Pilatus, Robert 1966(?)-1998
   Obituary **1998**:3
Pilkey, Dav 1966- **2001**:1
Pincay, Laffit, Jr. 1946- **1986**:3
Pinchot, Bronson 1959(?)- **1987**:4
Pincus, Mark 1966- **2011**:1
Pinera, Sebastian 1949- **2011**:2
Pink 1979- **2004**:3
Pinker, Steven A. 1954- **2000**:1
Pinkett Smith, Jada 1971- **1998**:3
Pinochet, Augusto 1915- **1999**:2
Pinto, Maria 1957- **2011**:2
Pipher, Mary 1948(?)- **1996**:4
Pippen, Scottie 1965- **1992**:2
Pirro, Jeanine 1951- **1998**:2
Pitt, Brad 1964- **1995**:2
Pittman, Robert W. 1953- **1985**:1
Piven, Jeremy 1965- **2007**:3
Plater-Zyberk, Elizabeth 1950- **2005**:2
Plato, Dana 1964-1999
   Obituary **1999**:4
Pleasence, Donald 1919-1995
   Obituary **1995**:3
Pleshette, Suzanne 1937-2008
   Obituary **2009**:2
Plimpton, George 1927-2003
   Obituary **2004**:4
Plotkin, Mark 1955(?)- **1994**:3
Pocklington, Peter H. 1941- **1985**:2
Poehler, Amy 1971- **2009**:1
Pogorelich, Ivo 1958- **1986**:4
Poitier, Sidney 1927- **1990**:3
Polgar, Judit 1976- **1993**:3
Politkovskaya, Anna 1958-2006
   Obituary **2007**:4
Polke, Sigmar 1941- **1999**:4
Pollack, Sydney 1934-2008
   Obituary **2009**:2
Pollan, Michael 1955- **2011**:3
Pol Pot 1928-1998
   Obituary **1998**:4
Ponce de Leon, Ernesto Zedillo
   See Zedillo, Ernesto
Ponti, Carlo 1912-2007
   Obituary **2008**:2
Ponty, Jean-Luc 1942- **1985**:4
Popcorn, Faith
   Brief entry **1988**:1
Pope, Generoso 1927-1988 .... **1988**:4
Pople, John 1925-2004
   Obituary **2005**:2
Porco, Carolyn 1953- **2005**:4
Porizkova, Paulina
   Brief entry **1986**:4
Porras, Arturo Jose Cruz
   See Cruz, Arturo
Porsche, Ferdinand 1909-1998
   Obituary **1998**:4
Porter, George 1920-2002
   Obituary **2003**:4
Porter, Sylvia 1913-1991
   Obituary **1991**:4
Portman, John 1924- **1988**:2
Portman, Natalie 1981- **2000**:3
Posen, Zac 1980- **2009**:3
Post, Peggy 1940(?)- **2001**:4
Poston, Tom 1921-2007
   Obituary **2008**:3
Potok, Anna Maximilian
   Brief entry **1985**:2

Potok, Chaim 1929-2002
   Obituary **2003**:4
Potter, Michael 1960(?)- **2003**:3
Potts, Annie 1952- **1994**:1
Potts, Paul 1970- **2009**:1
Pough, Richard Hooper 1904- **1989**:1
Pouillon, Nora 1943- **2005**:1
Povich, Maury 1939(?)- **1994**:3
Powell, Colin 1937- **1990**:1
Powell, Lewis F. 1907-1998
   Obituary **1999**:1
Power, Samantha 1970- **2005**:4
Powter, Susan 1957(?)- **1994**:3
Pozzi, Lucio 1935- **1990**:2
Prada, Miuccia 1950(?)- **1996**:1
Pratt, Christopher 1935- **1985**:3
Pratt, Jane 1963(?)- **1999**:1
Predock, Antoine 1936- **1993**:2
Preminger, Otto 1906-1986
   Obituary **1986**:3
Presley, Lisa Marie 1968- **2004**:3
Presley, Pricilla 1945- **2001**:1
Presser, Jackie 1926-1988
   Obituary **1988**:4
Pressler, Paul 1956(?)- **2003**:4
Preston, Billy 1946-2006
   Obituary **2007**:3
Preston, Robert 1918-1987
   Obituary **1987**:3
Preaaval, Reneaa 1943- **1997**:2
Prevor, Barry and Steven Shore **2006**:2
Price, Lisa 1962- **2010**:2
Price, Sol 1916-2009
   Obituary **2011**:4
Price, Vincent 1911-1993
   Obituary **1994**:2
Pride, Charley 1938(?)- **1998**:1
Priestly, Jason 1970(?)- **1993**:2
Primakov, Yevgeny 1929- **1999**:3
Prince 1958- **1995**:3
Prince, Faith 1959(?)- **1993**:2
Princess Margaret, Countess of Snowdon
   1930-2002
   Obituary **2003**:2
Prinze, Freddie, Jr. 1976- **1999**:3
Pritzker, Abram Nicholas
   See Pritzker, A.N.
Pritzker, A.N. 1896-1986
   Obituary **1986**:2
Probst, Jeff 1962- **2011**:2
Probst, Larry 1951(?)- **2005**:1
Proctor, Barbara Gardner
   1933(?)- **1985**:3
Profet, Margie 1958- **1994**:4
Prost, Alain 1955- **1988**:1
Proulx, E. Annie 1935- **1996**:1
Prowse, Juliet 1937-1996
   Obituary **1997**:1
Prusincr, Stanley 1942- **1998**:2
Pryce, Deborah 1951- **2006**:3
Pryor, Richard **1999**:3
Public Enemy **1992**:1
Puccio, Thomas P. 1944- **1986**:4
Puck, Theodore 1916-2005
   Obituary **2007**:1
Puck, Wolfgang 1949- **1990**:1
Puckett, Kirby 1960-2006
   Obituary **2007**:2
Puente, Tito 1923-2000
   Obituary **2000**:4
Pujols, Albert 1980- **2005**:3

Sedelmaier, John Josef
See Sedelmaier, Joe
Sedgwick, Kyra 1965- **2006**:2
See, Lisa 1955- **2010**:4
Segal, Shelden 1926-2009
Obituary **2011**:2
Segal, Shelli 1955(?)- **2005**:3
Seger, Bob 1945- **1987**:1
Seger, Robert Clark
See Seger, Bob
Segovia, Andreaas 1893-1987
Obituary **1987**:3
Seidelman, Susan 1953(?)- **1985**:4
Seidenberg, Ivan 1946- **2004**:1
Seinfeld, Jerry 1954- **1992**:4
Selena 1971-1995
Obituary **1995**:4
Seles, Monica 1974(?)- **1991**:3
Selig, Bud 1934- **1995**:2
Semel, Terry 1943- **2002**:2
Sendler, Irena 1910-2008
Obituary **2009**:2
Senghor, Leopold 1906-2001
Obituary **2003**:1
Senk, Glen 1956- **2009**:3
Senna, Ayrton 1960(?)-1994 .... **1991**:4
Obituary **1994**:4
Sentamu, John 1949- **2006**:2
Seo, Danny 1977- **2008**:3
Serkin, Rudolf 1903-1991
Obituary **1992**:1
Serra, Richard 1939- **2009**:1
Serrano, Andres 1950- **2000**:4
Serros, Michele 1967(?)- **2008**:2
Sethi, Simran 1971(?)- **2008**:1
Seuss, Dr.
See Geisel, Theodor
Sevareid, Eric 1912-1992
Obituary **1993**:1
Sevigny, Chloe 1974- **2001**:4
Sexton, John 1942- **2011**:4
Seyfried, Amanda 1985- **2009**:3
Seymour, Jane 1951- **1994**:4
Shabazz, Betty 1936-1997
Obituary **1997**:4
Shaffer, Paul 1949- **1987**:1
Shah, Gyanendra 1947- **2006**:1
Shaich, Ron 1953- **2004**:4
Shakira 1977- **2002**:3
Shakur, Tupac 1971-1996
Obituary **1997**:1
Shalala, Donna 1941- **1992**:3
Shalikashvili, John 1936- **1994**:2
Shandling, Garry 1949- **1995**:1
Shanley, John Patrick 1950- **2006**:1
Sharapova, Maria 1987- **2005**:2
Sharkey, Ray 1953-1993
Obituary **1994**:1
Sharma, Nisha 1982(?)- **2004**:2
Sharon, Ariel 1928- **2001**:4
Sharpe, Sterling 1965- **1994**:3
Sharpton, Al 1954- **1991**:2
Shaw, Artie 1910-2004
Obituary **2006**:1
Shaw, Carol 1958(?)- **2002**:1
Shaw, William 1934(?)- **2000**:3
Shawn, Dick 1924(?)-1987
Obituary **1987**:3
Shawn, William 1907-1992
Obituary **1993**:3
Shcharansky, Anatoly 1948- **1986**:2
Shea, Jim, Jr. 1968- **2002**:4

Sheedy, Alexandra Elizabeth
See Sheedy, Ally
Sheedy, Ally 1962- **1989**:1
Sheehan, Daniel P. 1945(?)- **1989**:1
Sheen, Charlie 1965- **2001**:2
Sheen, Martin 1940- **2002**:1
Sheffield, Gary 1968- **1998**:1
Sheindlin, Judith
See Sheindlin, Judith
Sheindlin, Judith 1942(?)- **1999**:1
Sheldon, Sidney 1917-2007
Obituary **2008**:2
Shepard, Alan 1923-1998
Obituary **1999**:1
Shepard, Sam 1943- **1996**:4
Shepherd, Cybill 1950- **1996**:3
Sherba, John
See Kronos Quartet
Sherman, Cindy 1954- **1992**:3
Sherman, Jack
See Red Hot Chili Peppers
Sherman, Russell 1930- **1987**:4
Shields, Brooke 1965- **1996**:3
Shields, Carol 1935-2003
Obituary **2004**:3
Shilts, Randy 1951-1994 .... **1993**:4
Obituary **1994**:3
Shimomura, Tsutomu 1965- **1996**:1
Shipley, Jenny 1952- **1998**:3
Shirley, Donna 1941- **1999**:1
Shocked, Michelle 1963(?)- **1989**:4
Shocklee, Hank
See Public Enemy
Shocklee, Keith
See Public Enemy
Shoemaker, Bill 1931-2003
Obituary **2004**:4
Shore, Dinah 1917-1994
Obituary **1994**:3
Short, Martin 1950- **1986**:1
Shreve, Anita 1946(?)- **2003**:4
Shriver, Eunice 1921-2009
Obituary **2011**:1
Shriver, Lionel 1957- **2008**:4
Shriver, Maria
Brief entry **1986**:2
Shue, Andrew 1964- **1994**:4
Shula, Don 1930- **1992**:2
Shulman, Julius 1910-2009
Obituary **2010**:4
Shyamalan, M. Night 1970- **2003**:2
Sidney, Ivan
Brief entry **1987**:2
Sidransky, David 1960- **2002**:4
Siebert, Muriel 1932(?)- **1987**:2
Sigmund, Barbara Boggs 1939-1990
Obituary **1991**:1
Silber, Joan 1945- **2009**:4
Silber, John 1926- **1990**:1
Silva, Daniel 1960- **2010**:1
Silva, Luiz Inacio Lula da 1945- ... **2003**:4
Silverman, Jonathan 1966- **1997**:2
Silverman, Sarah 1970- **2008**:1
Silvers, Phil 1912-1985
Obituary **1985**:4
Silversmith, Philip
See Silvers, Phil
Silverstein, Shel 1932-1999
Obituary **1999**:4
Silverstone, Alicia 1976- **1997**:4
Simmons, Adele Smith 1941- **1988**:4
Simmons, Laurie 1949- **2010**:1

Simmons, Russell and Kimora
Lee **2003**:2
Simmons, Ruth 1945- **1995**:2
Simon, Lou Anna K. 1947- **2005**:4
Simon, Paul 1928-2003
Obituary **2005**:1
Simon, Paul 1942(?)- **1992**:2
Simone, Nina 1933-2003
Obituary **2004**:2
Simpson, Lorna 1960- **2008**:1
Simpson, Wallis 1896-1986
Obituary **1986**:3
Simpson-Wentz, Ashlee 1984- **2009**:1
Sin, Jaime 1928-2005
Obituary **2006**:3
Sinatra, Frank 1915-1998
Obituary **1998**:4
Sinclair, Mary 1918- **1985**:2
Singer, Bryan 1965- **2007**:3
Singer, Isaac Bashevis 1904-1991
Obituary **1992**:1
Singer, Margaret Thaler 1921-2003
Obituary **2005**:1
Singh, Vijay 1963- **2000**:4
Singleton, John 1968- **1994**:3
Sinise, Gary 1955(?)- **1996**:1
Sinopoli, Giuseppe 1946- **1988**:1
Sirica, John 1904-1992
Obituary **1993**:2
Sirleaf, Ellen Johnson 1938- **2007**:3
Siskel, Gene 1946-1999
Obituary **1999**:3
Sisulu, Walter 1912-2003
Obituary **2004**:2
Sizer, Theodore 1932-2009
Obituary **2011**:2
Skaist-Levy, Pam and Gela
Taylor **2005**:1
Skelton, Red 1913-1997
Obituary **1998**:1
Skillings, Muzz
See Living Colour
Skinner, B.F. 1904-1990
Obituary **1991**:1
Skinner, Burrhus Frederic
See Skinner, B.F.
Skinner, Sam 1938- **1992**:3
Slater, Christian 1969- **1994**:1
Slater, Rodney E. 1955- **1997**:4
Slatkin, Harry 1961(?)- **2006**:2
Slaton, Mary Leta Dorothy
See Lamour, Dorothy
Slaughter, Karin 1971- **2010**:3
Slick, Grace 1939- **2001**:2
Slotnick, Barry
Brief entry **1987**:4
Slovo, Joe 1926- **1989**:2
Smale, John G. 1927- **1987**:3
Smigel, Robert 1959(?)- **2001**:3
Smiley, Jane 1949- **1995**:4
Smiley, Tavis 1964- **2010**:3
Smirnoff, Yakov 1951- **1987**:2
Smith, Anna Deavere 1950- **2002**:2
Smith, Anna Nicole 1967-2007
Obituary **2008**:2
Smith, Anthony Terrell
See Tone-Loc
Smith, Buffalo Bob 1917-1998
Obituary **1999**:1
Smith, Chad
See Red Hot Chili Peppers
Smith, Emmitt **1994**:1

Vidal, Gore 1925- **1996**:2
Vidov, Oleg 194- **1987**:4
Vieira, Meredith 1953- **2001**:3
Vigdor, Ron 1970- **2011**:4
Villechaize, Herve 1943(?)-1993
    Obituary **1994**:1
Villeneuve, Jacques 1971- **1997**:1
Vilsack, Tom 1950- **2011**:1
Vincent, Fay 1938- **1990**:2
Vincent, Francis Thomas, Jr.
    See Vincent, Fay
Vinton, Will
    Brief entry **1988**:1
Violet, Arlene 1943- **1985**:3
Vischer, Phil 1966- **2002**:2
Vitale, Dick 1939- **1988**:4
Vitetta, Ellen S. 1942(?)- **2005**:4
Vitousek, Peter 1949- **2003**:1
Vogel, Paula 1951- **1999**:2
Voight, Jon 1938- **2002**:3
Volkow, Nora 1956- **2009**:1
Vollenweider, Andreas 1953- **1985**:2
Von D, Kat 1982- **2008**:3
von Furstenberg, Diane 1946- **1994**:2
Von Hellermann, Sophie 1975- **2006**:3
von Karajan, Herbert 1908-1989
    Obituary **1989**:4
Vonn, Lindsey 1984- **2011**:2
Vonnegut, Kurt 1922- **1998**:4
von Trapp, Maria 1905-1987
    Obituary **1987**:3
vos Savant, Marilyn 1946- **1988**:2
Vreeland, Diana 1903(?)-1989
    Obituary **1990**:1
Wachner, Linda 1946- **1988**:3
Wadd, Johnny
    See Holmes, John C.
Waddell, Thomas F. 1937-1987
    Obituary **1988**:2
Wade, Dwyane 1982- **2007**:1
Wagner, Catherine F. 1953- **2002**:3
Wagoner, Porter 1927-2007
    Obituary **2008**:4
Wahid, Abdurrahman 1940- **2000**:3
Wahlberg, Donnie
    See New Kids on the Block
Wahlberg, Mark
    See Marky Mark
Waitt, Ted 1963(?)- **1997**:4
Waldron, Hicks B. 1923- **1987**:3
Walesa, Lech 1943- **1991**:2
Walgreen, Charles III
    Brief entry **1987**:4
Walker, Alice 1944- **1999**:1
Walker, Jay 1955- **2004**:2
Walker, Junior 1942(?)-1995
    Obituary **1996**:2
Walker, Kara 1969- **1999**:2
Walker, Nancy 1922-1992
    Obituary **1992**:3
Wallace, Ben 1974- **2004**:3
Wallace, Christopher G.
    See Notorious B.I.G.
Wallace, George 1919-1998
    Obituary **1999**:1
Wallace, Irving 1916-1990
    Obituary **1991**:1
Wallis, Hal 1898(?)-1986
    Obituary **1987**:1
Wallis, Harold Brent
    See Wallis, Hal
Walls, Jeannette 1960(?)- **2006**:3

Walsh, Bill 1931- **1987**:4
Walsh, William
    See Walsh, Bill
Walters, Barbara 1931- **1998**:3
Walton, Sam 1918-1992 .... **1986**:2
    Obituary **1993**:1
Waltz, Christoph 1956- **2011**:1
Wanderone, Rudolf Walter, Jr.
    See Minnesota Fats
Wang, Alexander 1984- **2011**:4
Wang, An 1920-1990 .... **1986**:1
    Obituary **1990**:3
Wang, Vera 1949- **1998**:4
Wapner, Joseph A. 1919- **1987**:1
Ward, Sela 1956- **2001**:3
Warden, Jack 1920-2006
    Obituary **2007**:3
Ware, Lancelot 1915-2000
    Obituary **2001**:1
Warhol, Andy 1927(?)-1987
    Obituary **1987**:2
Warhola, Andrew
    See Warhol, Andy
Wariner, Jeremy 1984- **2006**:3
Warner, Kurt 1971- **2000**:3
Warren, Christopher Minor
    See Christopher, Warren
Warren, Elizabeth 1949- **2010**:2
Warren, Rick 1954- **2010**:3
Warren, Robert Penn 1905-1989
    Obituary **1990**:1
Washington, Alonzo 1967- **2000**:1
Washington, Denzel 1954- **1993**:2
Washington, Grover, Jr. 1943- **1989**:1
Washington, Harold 1922-1987
    Obituary **1988**:1
Wasserman, Lew 1913-2002
    Obituary **2003**:3
Wasserstein, Wendy 1950- **1991**:3
Waterman, Cathy 1950(?)- **2002**:2
Waters, Alice 1944- **2006**:3
Waters, John 1946- **1988**:3
Waters, Maxine 1938- **1998**:4
Waterston, Sam 1940- **2006**:1
Watkins, Sherron 1959- **2003**:1
Watkins, Tionne T-Boz
    See TLC
Watson, Elizabeth 1949- **1991**:2
Watson, Emily 1967- **2001**:1
Watt, Ben 1962-
    See Everything But The Girl
Watterson, Bill 1958(?)- **1990**:3
Watterson, William B., II
    See Watterson, Bill
Wattleton, Alyce Faye
    See Wattleton, Faye
Wattleton, Faye 1943- **1989**:1
Watts, J.C. 1957- **1999**:2
Watts, Naomi 1968- **2006**:1
Wayans, Damon 1960- **1998**:4
Wayans, Keenen Ivory 1958(?)- **1991**:1
Wayne, David 1914-1995
    Obituary **1995**:3
Wayne, Don
    See Johnson, Don
Weaver, Sigourney 1949- **1988**:3
Webb, Karrie 1974- **2000**:4
Webb, Wellington E. 1941- **2000**:3
Webber, Andrew Lloyd
    See Lloyd Webber, Andrew
Webber, Chris 1973- **1994**:1

Webber, Mayce Edward Christopher
    See Webber, Chris
Weber, Pete 1962- **1986**:3
Wegman, William 1942(?)- **1991**:1
Weicker, Lowell P., Jr. 1931- **1993**:1
Weihui, Zhou 1973- **2001**:1
Wei Jingsheng 1950- **1998**:2
Weil, Andrew 1942- **1997**:4
Weill, Sandy 1933- **1990**:4
Weill, Sanford
    See Weill, Sandy
Weinberger, Caspar 1917-2006
    Obituary **2007**:2
Weiner, Jennifer 1970- **2006**:3
Weinstein, Bob
    See Weinstein, Bob and Harvey
Weinstein, Bob and Harvey **2000**:4
Weinstein, Harvey
    See Weinstein, Bob and Harvey
Weintraub, Jerry 1937- **1986**:1
Weir, Mike 1970- **2004**:1
Weisz, Rachel 1971- **2006**:4
Weitz, Bruce 1943- **1985**:4
Weizman, Ezer 1924-2005
    Obituary **2006**:3
Welch, Bob 1956- **1991**:3
Welch, Jack 1935- **1993**:3
Weldon, William 1948- **2007**:4
Wells, David 1963- **1999**:3
Wells, Linda 1958- **2002**:3
Wells, Mary 1943-1992
    Obituary **1993**:1
Wells, Sharlene
    Brief entry **1985**:1
Wellstone, Paul 1944-2002
    Obituary **2004**:1
Welty, Eudora 1909-2001
    Obituary **2002**:3
Wences, Senor 1896-1999
    Obituary **1999**:4
Wenner, Jann 1946- **1993**:1
Werner, Ruth 1907-2000
    Obituary **2001**:1
Wescott, Seth 1976- **2006**:4
West, Cornel 1953- **1994**:2
West, Dorothy 1907- **1996**:1
West, Dottie 1932-1991
    Obituary **1992**:2
West, Kanye 1977- **2006**:1
West, Michael Lee 1953- **2009**:2
Westmoreland, William C. 1914-2005
    Obituary **2006**:4
Westwood, Vivienne 1941- **1998**:3
Wexler, Jerry 1917-2008
    Obituary **2009**:4
Wexler, Nancy S. 1945- **1992**:3
Whaley, Suzy 1966- **2003**:4
Whedon, Joss 1964- **2006**:3
Whelan, Tensie 1960- **2007**:1
Whelan, Wendy 1967(?)- **1999**:3
Whipple, Fred L. 1906-2004
    Obituary **2005**:4
Whitaker, Forest 1961- **1996**:2
Whitcomb, Richard 1921-2009
    Obituary **2011**:2
White, Alan
    See Oasis
White, Barry 1944-2003
    Obituary **2004**:3
White, Bill 1934- **1989**:3
White, Byron 1917-2002
    Obituary **2003**:3

Young, Coleman A. 1918-1997
  Obituary **1998**:1
Young, Loretta 1913-2000
  Obituary **2001**:1
Young, Neil 1945- **1991**:2
Young, Robert 1907-1998
  Obituary **1999**:1
Young, Steve 1961- **1995**:2
Youngblood, Johnny Ray 1948- **1994**:1
Youngman, Henny 1906(?)-1998
  Obituary **1998**:3
Yudhoyono, Susilo 1949- **2009**:4
Yudof, Mark 1944- **2009**:4
Yunus, Muhammad 1940- **2007**:3
Yushchenko, Viktor 1954- **2006**:1
Yzerman, Steve 1965- **1991**:2
Zagat, Tim and Nina **2004**:3
Zahn, Paula 1956(?)- **1992**:3
Zamboni, Frank J.
  Brief entry **1986**:4
Zamora, Pedro 1972-1994
  Obituary **1995**:2
Zanardi, Alex 1966- **1998**:2

Zanker, Bill
  Brief entry **1987**:3
Zanker, William I.
  See Zanker, Bill
Zanuck, Lili Fini 1954- **1994**:2
Zappa, Frank 1940-1993
  Obituary **1994**:2
Zarnocay, Samuel
  See Kaye, Sammy
Zatopek, Emil 1922-2000
  Obituary **2001**:3
Zech, Lando W.
  Brief entry **1987**:4
Zedillo, Ernesto 1951- **1995**:1
Zeffirelli, Franco 1923- **1991**:3
Zellweger, Renee 1969- **2001**:1
Zemeckis, Robert 1952- **2002**:1
Zerhouni, Elias A. 1951- **2004**:3
Zeroual, Liamine 1951- **1996**:2
Zeta-Jones, Catherine 1969- **1999**:4
Zetcher, Arnold B. 1940- **2002**:1
Zetsche, Dieter 1953- **2002**:3

Zevon, Warren 1947-2003
  Obituary **2004**:4
Zhang, Ziyi 1979- **2006**:2
Zhao Ziyang 1919- **1989**:1
Zhirinovsky, Vladimir 1946- **1994**:2
Zia ul-Haq, Mohammad 1924-1988
  Obituary **1988**:4
Ziff, William B., Jr. 1930- **1986**:4
Zigler, Edward 1930- **1994**:1
Zinnemann, Fred 1907-1997
  Obituary **1997**:3
Zinni, Anthony 1943- **2003**:1
Ziskin, Laura 1950- **2008**:2
Zito, Barry 1978- **2003**:3
Zoe, Rachel 1971- **2010**:2
Zucker, Jeff 1965(?)- **1993**:3
Zucker, Jerry 1950- **2002**:2
Zuckerberg, Mark 1984- **2008**:2
Zuckerman, Mortimer 1937- **1986**:3
Zwilich, Ellen 1939- **1990**:1
Zylberberg, Joel
  See Hyatt, Joel